JOHN ASARO

ARTRA

Artra Publishing, Inc.
P.O. Box 575
Encinitas, CA 92024
© Artra Publishing, Inc. 1991
ISBN 0-936725-06-0
Library of Congress Catalogue Number 91-076535

JOHN ASARO

Painting with Light

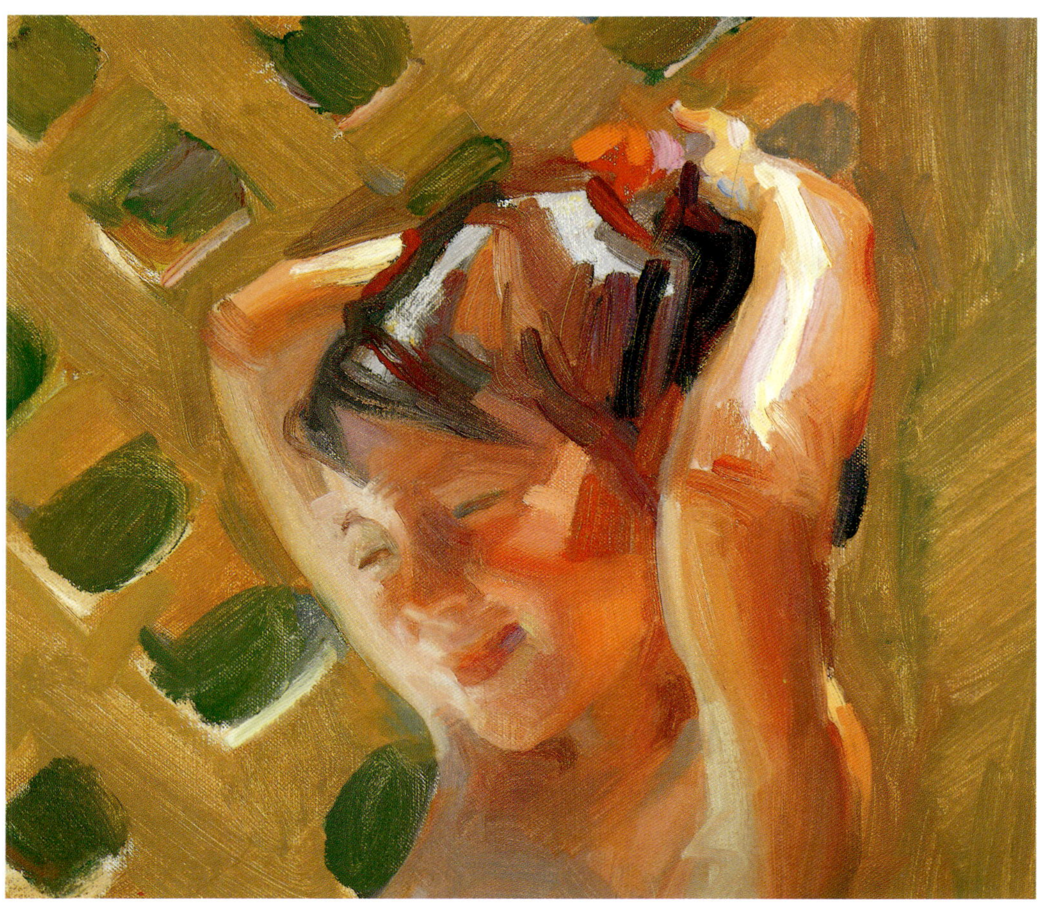

Detail, *The Spa*

ARTRA Publishing, Inc.
Encinitas, California, 1991

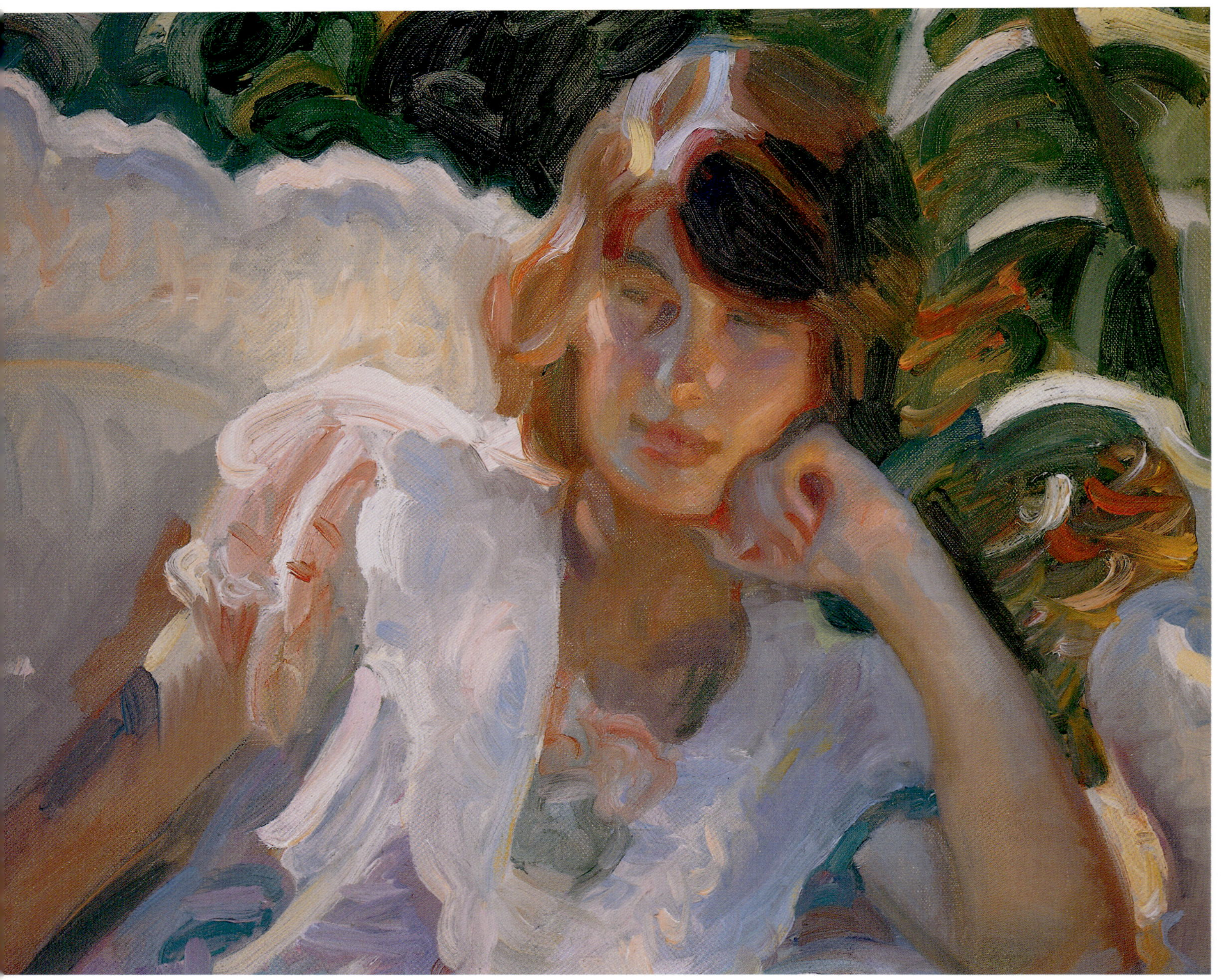

Detail, *Porcelain Ginger*

CONTENTS

FOREWORD

John Asaro bathes his images in sparkling California sunlight. His whites, never simply white, are tinged with pink and golden hues. This tonal warmth imbues his portrayals of family life with positive values. Parent and child share quiet, contemplative moments. Children explore with incorrigible curiosity a world in which much is new and wondrous. Asaro's perceptive use of color — unexpected touches of blue or mauve, shadows that are never simply a darker hue — imparts a cheerful energy to his paintings. Vibrant forms — women in flowing dresses, children frolicking in the surf, gold and blue bird-of-paradise blossoms — dissolve into splashes of paint when viewed up close.

This methodology is the legacy of the Impressionists. Previously, painters had defined volume with gradual modulations in color and tone. The Impressionists used small brushstrokes of pure color, leaving the mixing to the eye. When viewing such work, we see the juxtaposed dabs of color as fused and, at the same time, remain aware of the individual colors. This oscillation between two perceptual modes produces the characteristically Impressionist sensations of moving skies, rippling waters, and vibrant light.

However, philosophically and practically Asaro is closer to the tradition of Joaquin Sorolla y Bastida, sometimes called a Spanish Impressionist, than to that of the French Impressionists. Not unlike our own society, in which artists and writers are our social critics, Sorolla's contemporaries were asking anxious questions about their country and its future role. Sorolla, however, saw something "very different from the dismalness that has invaded our art and out literature." [1] With his images of women, children, and fishermen on the Valencia seashore, he chose to offer a sunny, Mediterranean view of Spain. Asaro, likewise, presents an optimistic look at life in sunlit Southern California. His subjects are in harmony with nature, at the sea or surrounded by lush vegetation with colorful blossoms.

Both artists also share a relation to classicism. The white, flowing dresses that Asaro's and Sorolla's women wear are reminiscent of garments of young Greek goddesses, just risen from the waves. And, there is a hint of the spirit of Hellenistic paganism in the two painters' representation of sunlight, the sea, and the human body as elements essentially connected.

Asaro's figures have not always been so cheery, nor have his paintings always been so luminous. In the 1970s, living in Los Angeles and teaching at Art Center, he used a darker palette, dominated by reds and greens. In a 1974 image of a female sunbather, we *understand* that light is shin-

1. Carmen Garcia, "Sorollism: a Unique Adventure," *The Painter: Joaquin Sorolla y Bastida*, Edmund Peel, Philip Wilson Publishers Ltd., 1989, p.42

ing on the subject, but we do not *feel* the light, as we do with his later work. What is evident here is Asaro's interest in defining shapes with planes, and how the different planes reflect light — a concern that runs as a continuous thread throughout Asaro's oeuvre.

The principle is similar to a mathematical exercise in which we construct a circle out of straight lines. Beginning with a square, we gradually increase the number of lines and decrease their length until the shape becomes rounded. At some point we are comfortable calling it a circle, even though it is still composed of a series of straight lines. Another painting of Asaro's from that period, a landscape, is a three dimensional application of this principle. Intersecting planes form undulating hills. Since each plane faces a different direction, it reflects light differently and is, consequently, a different color from those adjacent to it.

Seeing form in terms of planes is, in part, attributable to an early influence. San Diego sculptor Donal Hord took an interest in the young Asaro, providing encouragement and advice to the teenager. Later, in 1967, when Asaro returned to San Diego after a long stint as an illustrator in Detroit and New York, he used Hord's studio, as the sculptor had died the previous year. "All around me I could see that shapes — the head, legs, back — all had planes," Asaro commented in an interview with Susan Vreeland. "It's a way of seeing shape." [2] Asaro successfully incorporated this sculptural perception into his painting.

In his mature work, Asaro combines this methodology with a fervid interest in light. His palette is lighter — soft pastels dominate — and his brushwork has attained a gay confidence. Fabric, tablecloths, and white stucco walls are infused with the hues of all that is reflected in them and on them.

The gestation of Asaro's artistic personality, from talented youngster to mature artist, has been a long and laborious process, and is still ongoing. "Banana Trees," a newly completed portrait of his daughter, shows signs of further refinements. Still in evidence in the painting are the quintessential Asaro features — the luminosity and the definition of form with colored planes — but there is something more here. A less romanticised rendering of the trees and the figure creates a new harmony between subject and background. If this is, indeed, an indication of a new direction for Asaro's future work, it is one that those who know and appreciate his work will welcome.

— Judith Christensen, Art Critic,
*(San Diego Union, Artweek, Visions,
High Performance,* and *Sculpture Magazine.)*

2. From "John Asaro: In Pursuit of Light," by Susan Vreeland in *Southwest Art* July 1982.

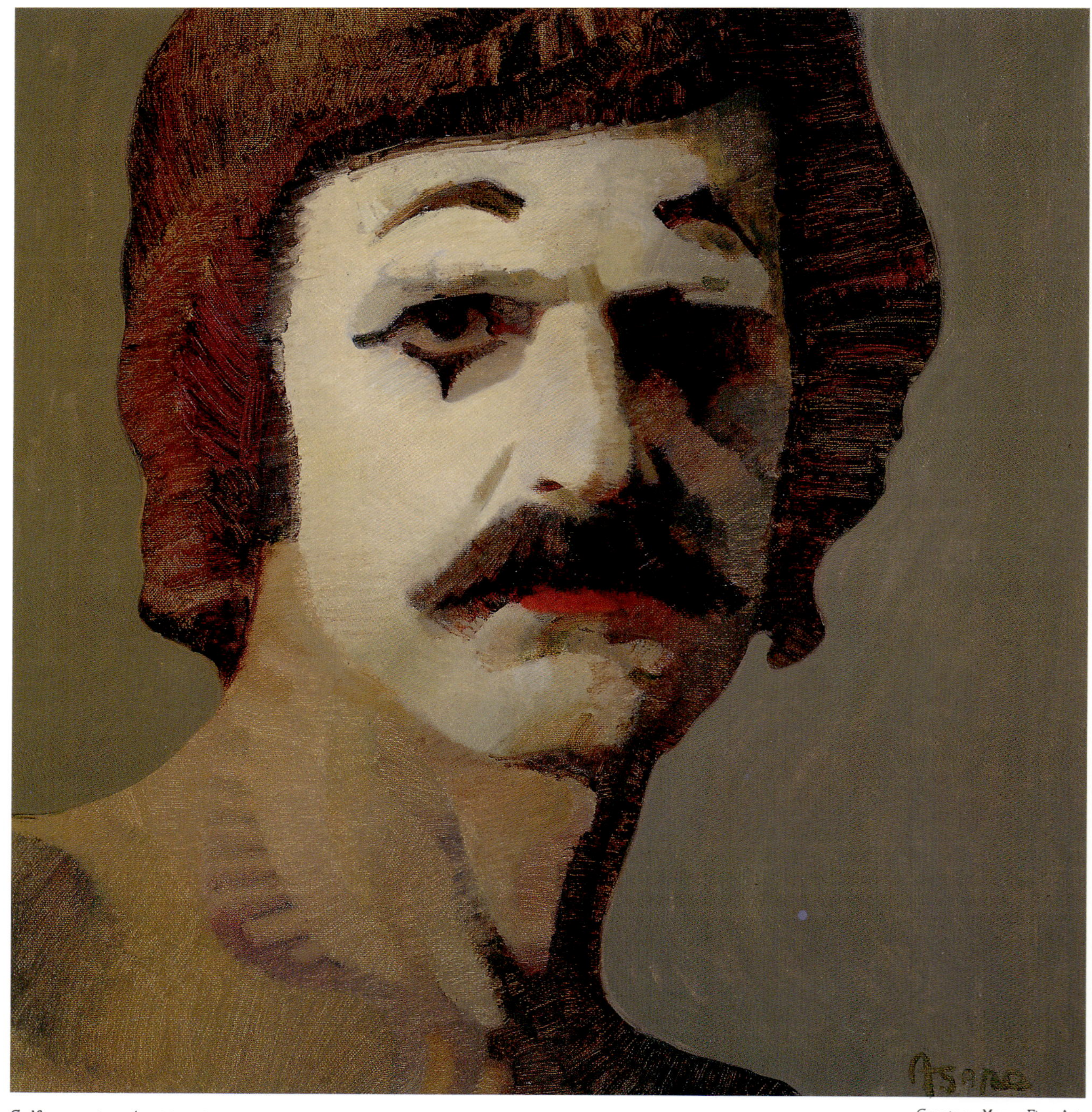

Self-portrait, o/c, 20×20, 1966

INTRODUCTION

If John Robert Asaro had his way, the 1990s would experience a resurgence of romanticism in painting and he would surely be up front, clearing the path. In an historical context Asaro's work could be seen as a bit tardy, an apparent echo of such romantic impressionists as Joaquin Sorolla, Gustav Klimpt, and John Singer Sargent. At least on the surface.

But Asaro's California-born sensibilities and his bumpy trip over the Southland's art training grounds have made him a kind of behind-the-scenes, late-blooming rebel. In the mid to late 1950s, at Art Center School in Los Angeles, where John was a student, the pressures to "make a living" with one's craft were the normal outgrowth of curricula which stressed drawing and design as fundamental to all art enterprise, whether a student's objective was defined as fine art or "commercial" art.

Painting teacher Stanley Reckless had just died when Asaro began classes in 1955, just two weeks before his high school graduation. Reckless had left a legacy, as had Rico Lebrun at Chouinard and Jepson Art institutes in the 1940s, and Joe Mugnaini at Otis during the 1950s. Two decades of students from these four schools had already been indoctrinated and were at least tentative believers in a persistent, centuries-old dogma: for the genuine artist, drawing is sacrosanct. Painting and sculpture were simply considered advanced forms of drawing, the final ingredients necessary for artisthood, a full complement of creative weapons — drawing, composition, color theory, and design.

Reckless's fellow instructor Harry Carmean carried on at Art Center and Asaro fell under his influence. By the end of his third semester, Asaro had received the Stanley Reckless Memorial Scholarship. But since the school leaned heavily toward the applied arts, many of its graduates were encouraged to become illustrators, industrial designers, fashion artists, etc. Consequently, Asaro felt

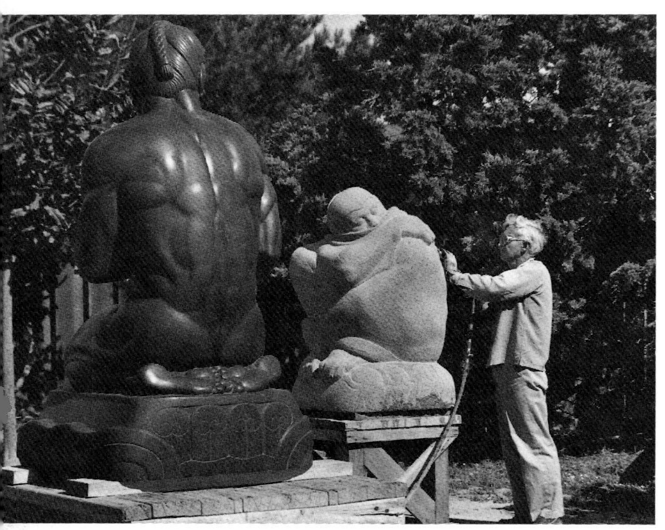

Donal Hord works on *Spring Stirring*, 1948. *El Colorado*, 1945, is on the left.

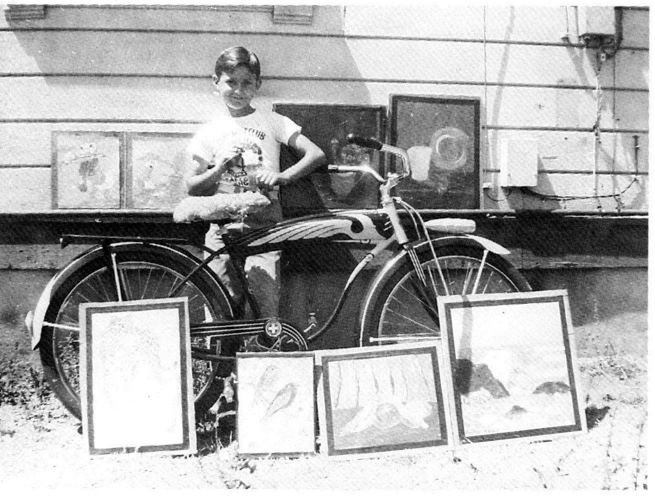

The young artist poses with his oeuvre and his Schwinn, July 1947.

pressure to make a career as an illustrator. Of his teachers, Reynold Brown was the only one urging him to risk a trip to Europe to explore serious painting.

But Asaro was young and confused by the profusion of knowing, adult voices. Like most art students, when they start school, he was shocked – and briefly disillusioned – at no longer being the best artist in his peer group. In San Diego, where he had grown up, he had twice won the Optimist Prize at the San Diego County Fair (1947 and 1948) as a junior high school student. For these consecutive achievements he proudly took home two deluxe Schwinn bikes, back to back. Even before, when Asaro was eleven, his barber father had enrolled in a local adult art class whose students worked from the live model. Frank Asaro, bent on encouraging his son's talent, quickly stepped aside so the boy could take on the challenges of canvas, paint, and the living model.

If being a child prodigy was tantamount to a successful career, Asaro was off and running: supportive family, natural ability, public exposure, and sound apprenticeships. Meeting mentor Milford Ellison had been relatively easy; he was Asaro's watercolor teacher at Point Loma High School. But finding sculptor Donal Hord (1907-1966), San Diego's contribution to national status in the 1930s and 1940s, was serendipitous. At fifteen Asaro had gone to work as an office boy for the architectural firm of Johnson, Hatch, and Wolf. Recognizing John's talent, Johnson introduced him to Hord. Hord showed an immediate interest in a clay figure Asaro was building and continued giving him critiques and technical input during the teenager's high school years. Ellison also knew talent when he saw it and encouraged John to enter Art Center in Los Angeles.

Today when Asaro looks back at these early experiences, he wonders if everyone's expectations of him were too high. Were these pressures to be successful ultimately destructive?

"At Art Center I became a little fish in a big pond," he says, "whereas in San Diego I was the big fish." This, of course, is enough to give any sensitive young artist pause as he looks around the classroom at the awesome force combined talent conjures. Besides being intimidated, Asaro also grew restless. After seeing a memorial show of Nicolai Fechin's work at the Biltmore Hotel, he wondered why such a master as Fechin had not taught at an L.A. art school. He learned that Fechin, like Hord, was committed to small, private classes, reinforcing the then-prevalent idea that drawing and painting, blood brothers in the arts, are best taught over a long period with patience and concentrated, individual attention.

Asaro's study at Art Center continued, but even winning that scholarship did not prevent him from feeling edgy and dissatisfied. He finally yielded to his own pressures, believing that the best training was in New York. Against the wishes of his parents, he enrolled at the Art Students' League (1958), choosing Frank Reilly as mentor. Reilly's famous "paint by the numbers" palette was intriguing enough, and certainly practically instructive, so Asaro set about absorbing all he could from the man whose students "really worshipped him" and who was a "genuine ham" in the classroom.

Early in this one year New York stint, the incomparable portrait painter Pietro Annigoni (1902-1984) came to town and Hord, who had already touted Asaro to the Italian, encouraged John to phone the master, to investigate the possibilities of studying with Annigoni in Florence. Again Asaro felt the expectations, the pressures to succeed on a grand scale. Out of apprehension and fear, he never made the phone call; today, forty years later, he still expresses regret over this lost opportunity.

Awash in the multi-directional currents of Manhattan, Asaro was plagued by loneliness and returned to Art Center school in 1959. There he quickly gained a new appreciation for the quality of instruc-

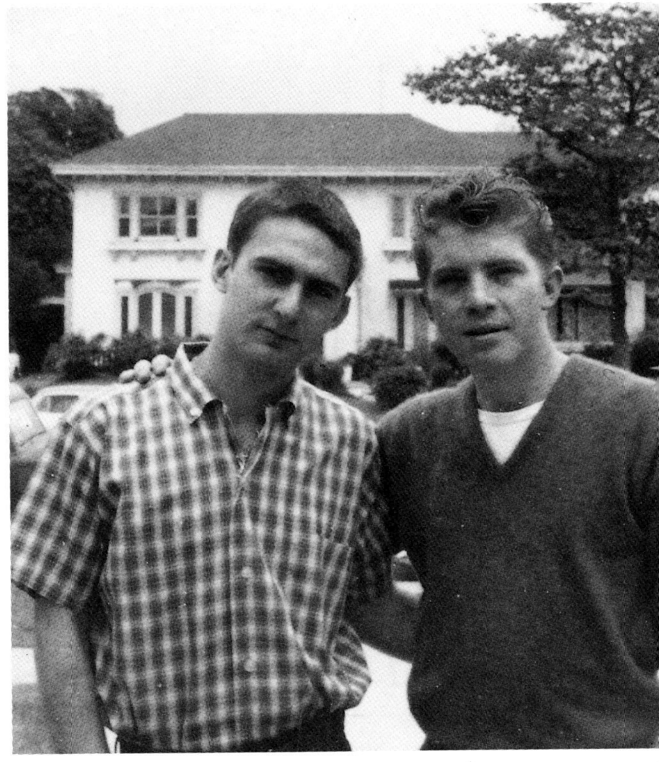

Asaro and fellow Art Center student, Gene Ware, 1956.

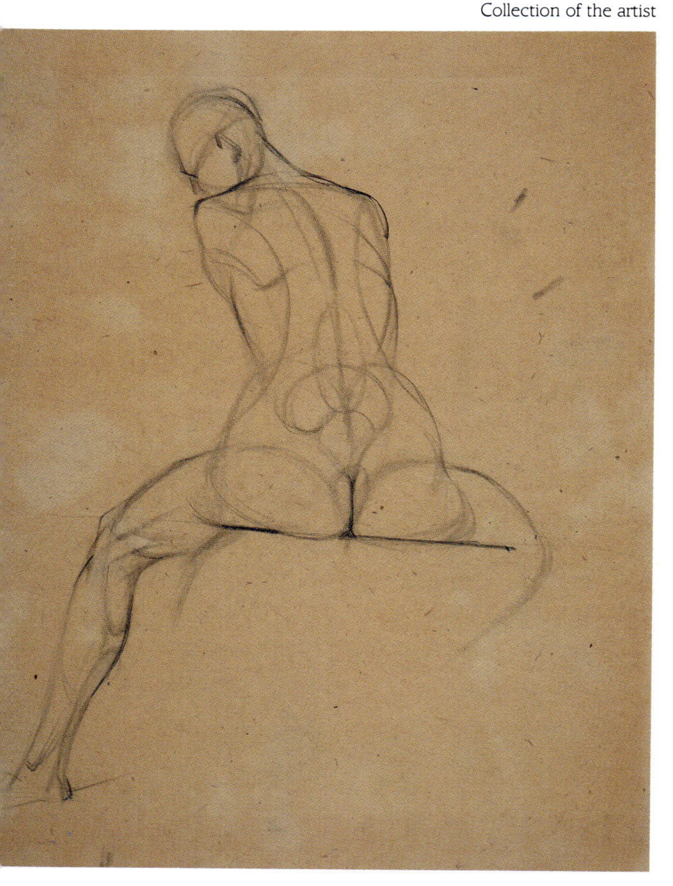

Charcoal drawing from Frank Reilly's class, 1957

tion, especially in design. He was relieved to be home again. But the commercial orientation of the school gradually wooed him back into the illustration mode, the logical, practical end to his specialized training. After three years it was "time to graduate" and his peers urged him to storm the Big Apple once more. Against his better judgement, he returned to the East.

Job hunting in Manhattan in 1960, he looked in vain. Detroit was the place to be, his illustrator friends told him. Eventually, he was offered a slot at the prestigious New Center Studios in Detroit doing "that car stuff," which meant painting in backgrounds and figures on slick automobile renderings. Illustrators, by and large, had dominated magazine and book pages for seventy years, were the heroes of advertising. Though by the 1960s there were indications that photography was supplanting illustration in the minds and tastes of New York's vanguard art directors, Asaro kept at it, bouncing back and forth from Detroit to New York to Los Angeles, investing a dozen years in a profession that was destined to sour him, to thwart his deep ambitions to be a serious painter.

While one might argue that illustration in most aspects is painting, John Asaro had strong ideas about the attitudinal differences, as did John Altoon and Ed Ruscha, former Chouinard students who suffered brief careers in New York as illustrators. Unlike the pragmatic and realistic Norman Rockwell who had asserted "you can tell I'm an illustrator and not a painter because I wear this bow tie," Asaro continued drowning in his own ambivalence. While he was producing highly competent illustrations for numerous pocket books, record album covers, and magazines such as *Cosmopolitan, Good Housekeeping*, and *Argosy*, the independent inner voice continued straining to be heard. Perhaps this voice was reinforced by the New York museums he relished visiting, being especially stimulated by turn-of-the-century paintings. "If the artists at the turn of the century were old-fashioned," he says now, "well, what they did was far more exciting to me than what I was seeing in illustration. They were enough to make me decide I didn't want to be an illustrator any more." On an impulse he suspects was subconsciously driven by Robert Kennedy's assassination in Los Angeles, Asaro decided to cast off his burden, no matter the financial risk.

Back in sunny San Diego, he visited Florence Hord. Donal had died the year before (1966) and his widow invited John to move into his mentor's studio. Here he went into seclusion and began his painting career in earnest; by 1970 he mounted the first of three one-person shows at the Paideia Gallery in Los Angeles (1970, 1973, 1974). Wrote William Wilson in the *Los Angeles Times:*

"Local John Asaro likes to paint old buildings and young women reclining. He often applies pigment thinly in broad strokes, creating a tapestrylike effect that nonetheless carves big volumes of form and space. His color tends to get unpleasantly gaseous. The paintings are like classroom exercises with excellent patches in such examples as 'Santa Monica Pier,' 'Sunday in Griffith Park,' and 'Nude in bathtub.' "[1]

If Wilson's term "unpleasantly gaseous" means expansive and overblown, then Asaro might say that he was simply painting passionately, was in love with the lusciousness of color. The label "classroom exercises" was hardly surprising to him; he had just spent his first year teaching at Art Center and was in the classroom mode. "Excellent patches" refers to the exciting sections on a canvas where an artist has painted beyond himself or has intuitively caught that elusive quality that connects artist to viewer. "Carving big volumes of form and space," of course, is a major objective in the pursuit of impressionistic realism. Though Asaro considered Wilson's short review favorable, the critic had typically balanced his reactions to

(1) William Wilson, Art Walk, *Los Angeles Times,* 3 November 1974.

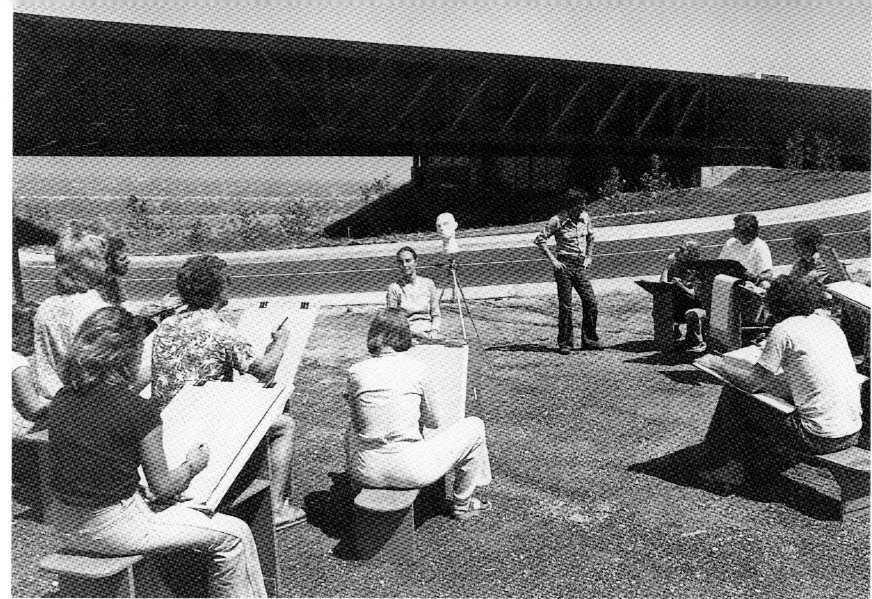

Asaro's drawing class assembles outdoors at the Art Center College of Design, 1976.

read both pro and con.

In Hord's Mission Bay studio, Asaro continued painting, working long hours, taking his time. While Donal Hord and his assistant, Homer Dana, had taken an average of two years to chisel out a black diorite figure, Asaro was taking roughly a month on his oils, not inordinately long as paintings go, but a time frame which he felt, and still feels, is comfortable for working out a specific problem. Today he says, "I can do these smaller ones in a couple of hours, but the bigger figure paintings sometimes take me a month or two." Then he adds: "Painting is nothing more than problem solving, you know. You solve one, no matter how long it takes, then go on to the next."

Of course Asaro, in keeping with his turn-of-the-century mind set, has never been in a hurry, nor has his self-effacing nature allowed lengthy strategies for self promotion. His fourth one-person show was not until 1978 at the Moody Gallery in Pasadena, five years after he began driving to Art Center to teach two days a week (1973-1981). At the intimidating new "Le Corbusier-like" Pasadena facility, he taught head drawing, perspective, life drawing, and life painting, his favorite. During these eight years he renewed his acquaintance with Harry Carmean and Reynold Brown and continued to exhibit. (See "Selected Exhibitions" in biography on page 111).

As a part of this transition from illustration to fine art he enrolled for three semesters of architecture at the Southern California Institute of Architecture in Santa Monica. To these activities Asaro added his fascination with the planes of the head and how these planes reflect light. As an adjunct to his teaching, he spent several years sculpting a thirteen-inch, lifesize model of the human head, defining its planes much as an architect might do. When this model became useful in his drawing classes, he made a mold from which uniform copies were cast, to be used by other artists and teachers. These ceramic heads, plus a definitive booklet entitled "Planes of the Head," are still in use in art classrooms.

In June of 1980, at forty-two, Asaro took another milestone leap forward: *marriage*. To say that his relationship with Janet Close lifted his spirits when he was in doubt – and thus radically changed his life – is a major understatement, as is evidenced by the images at the heart of this book. Janet and daughters Amber and Devon have literally dominated his subject matter in recent years; he is a consumate, appreciative family man. The last decade of Asaro's career has been extremely productive, attributed to these new family relationships, intense but happy, demanding but free. Commenting on recent periods of growth he says, "I am not the same person I was a month ago. To me painting is like walking on a new trail; I look forward to seeing something different on each path I take. Paintings are very sensitive, delicate objects." Of his approach to painting he says: "I almost feel I'm on a stage …. I'm performing almost. It's *not* relaxing; I get nervous before I start a painting. Every little thing is important."

John Asaro has, at last, become a fine artist in the truest sense. The fear and uncertainty of the San Diego kid on his Schwinn bike or the conflicted young illustrator riding the New York subway have been replaced by a mature, dedicated painter "loosening up" his current painting with a palette knife, letting the canvas "work with [him]." Gently invading the atmosphere of his Carlsbad studio are the strains of Puccini and Verdi, the voices of Luciano Pavarotti and Leontyne Price, and, most recently, the haunting minor harmonies of Gregorian chants. Whether conscious or not, Asaro gives us undisputable evidence of his transcendent committment to the restoration of true romanticism in painting. To be "different" has never been an issue in this artist's mind. For him, to be good is different enough.

– *Robert Perine*

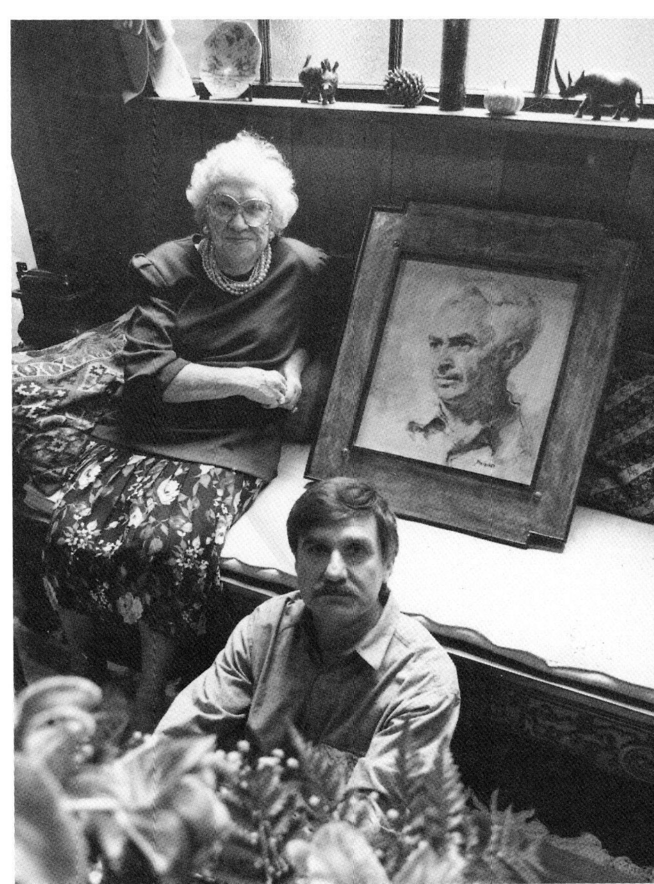

Florence Hord poses with Asaro in April 1991. His portrait of Donal Hord, which hangs in Hord's old studio-home, is dated 1970.

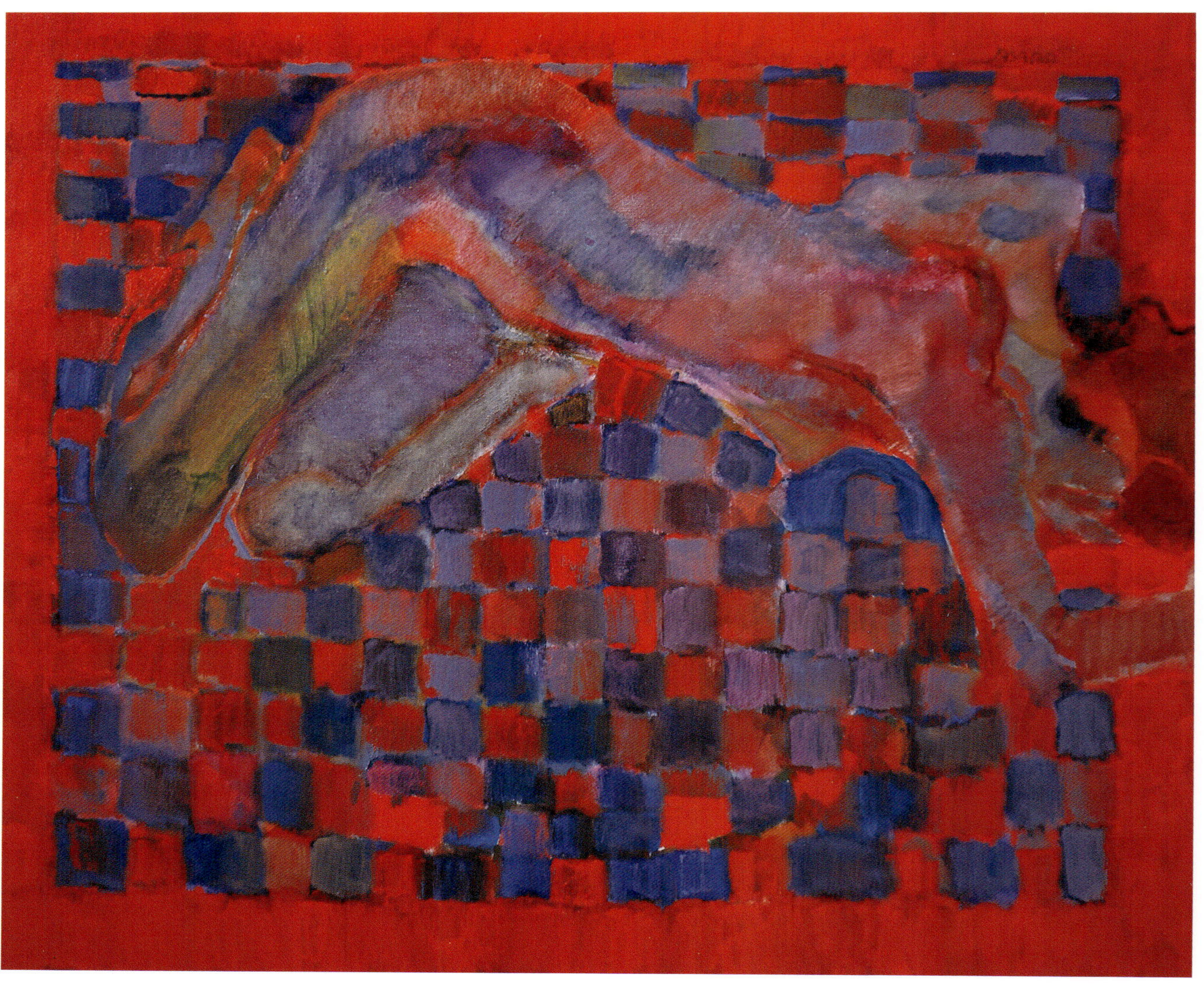

THE ARTIST AS ILLUSTRATOR (1960-1972)

Asaro's expected, though hesitant, entrance into
the commercial world of illustration saw him
involving himself in certain painterly experimen-
tations, as was common among many Art Center
graduates who marched off to New York. Story
subjects demanded a freshness of approach and
a sensitivity to staging that is fundamental to,
and extractable from, narrative. Editors sought
eye-catching techniques to adorn magazine arti-

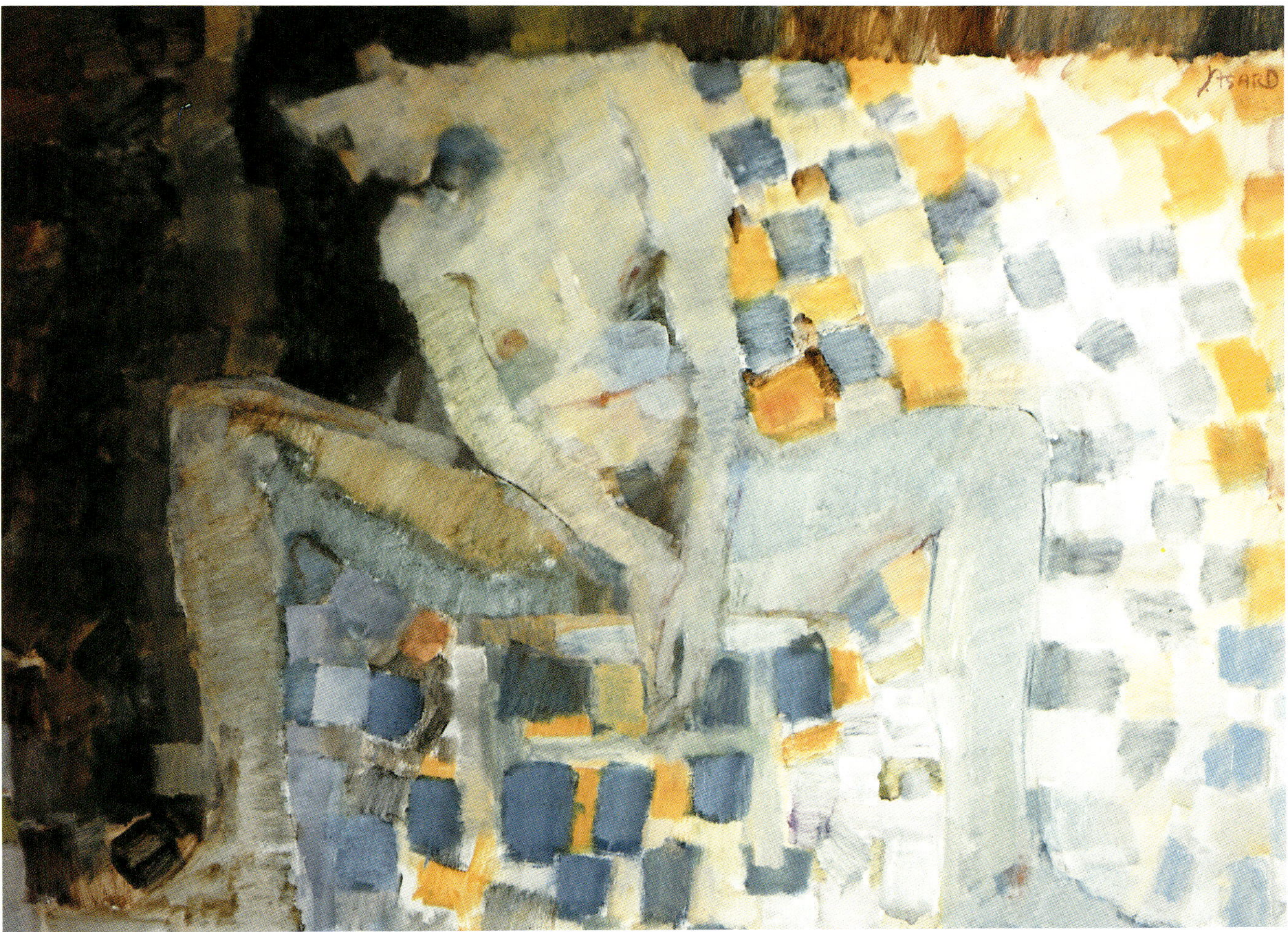

cles, to infuse book covers with sensuality, and to weight posters with colorful, block-buster graphics. Spurred by earlier innovators such as Ben Shahn, Al Parker, David Stone Martin, and Robert Riggs, subsequent generations of New York illustrators would take clues from a rainbow of fine art "isms" and photographic references, turning these idioms into stylistic devices for enhancing specific assignments, heightening their emotional impact.

Working from both the model and the urban landscape, Asaro did his own brand of searching during the unsteady seventies. The examples here grew out of a decade of struggle for identity and a persistent concern with light and its hypnotic,

magical embrace of form. These works display his enormous facility for solving each self-assigned, visual problem. Though he was involved daily with the demands of art directors and clients in Detroit and New York, his desire for a personal statement underlies the bulk of this work, despite disenchantment with the commercial world. Already the emergence of a new purity and a growing obsession to maximize solid form and substance, while minimizing topic or theme, are manifesting themselves during this period. Using the classic nude as subject matter – which appears and reappears in these years – Asaro continued creating new challenges for himself.

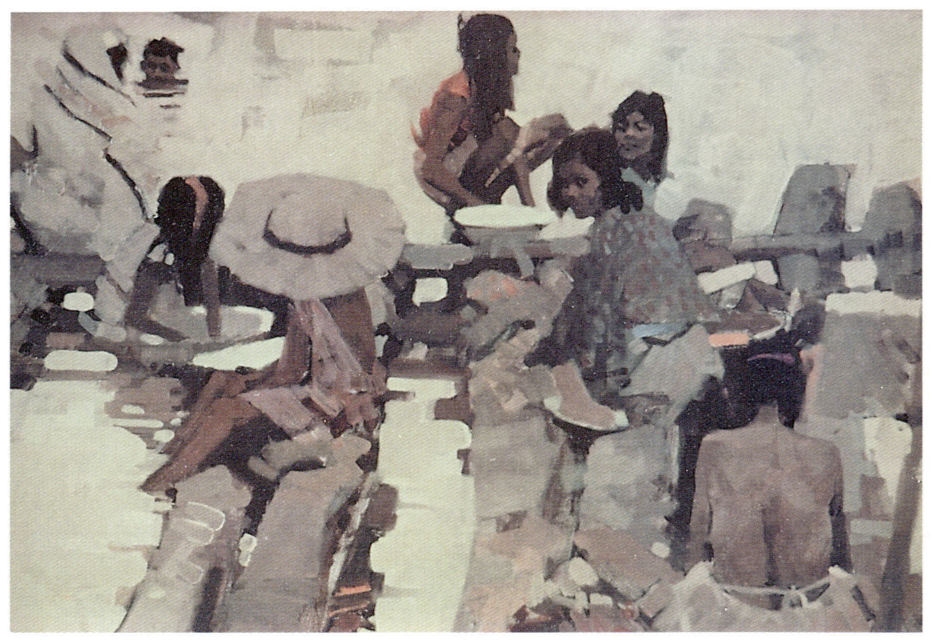

Equitos, Peru, o/c, 24×32, 1967

Courtesy Garrett Corporation

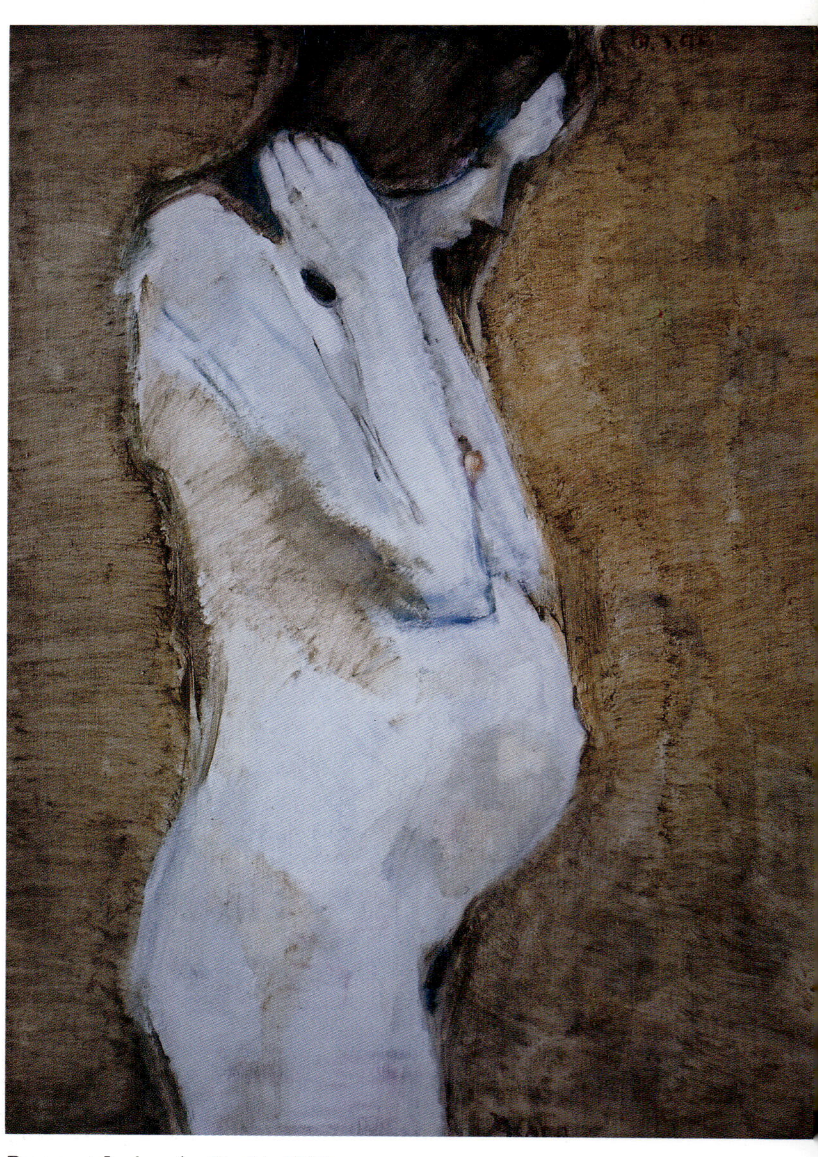

Pregnant Lady, o/c, 36×26, 1969

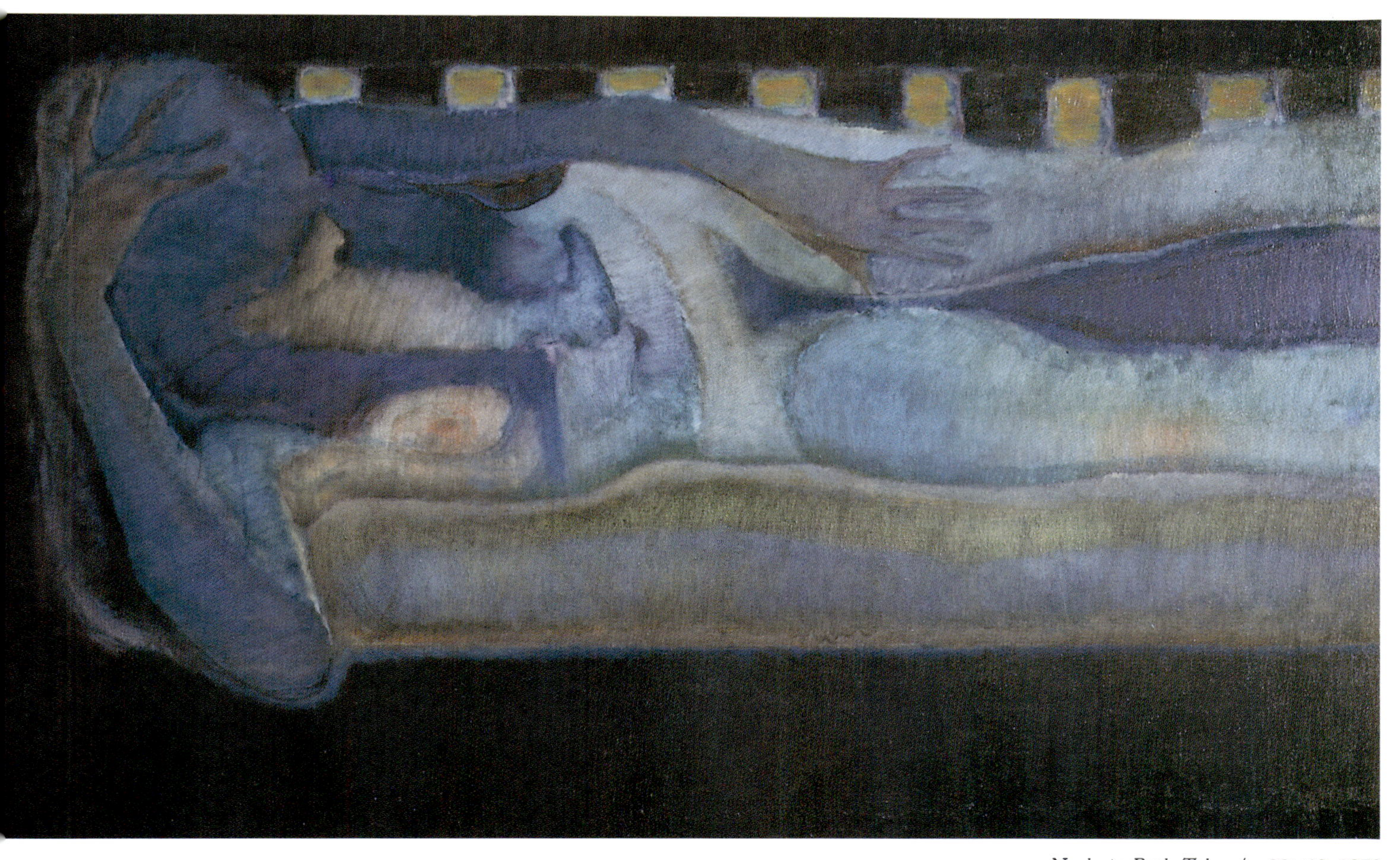

Nude in Bath Tub, o/c, 28×40, 1970

"*Underneath every great realistic painting is an equally great abstract painting.*"

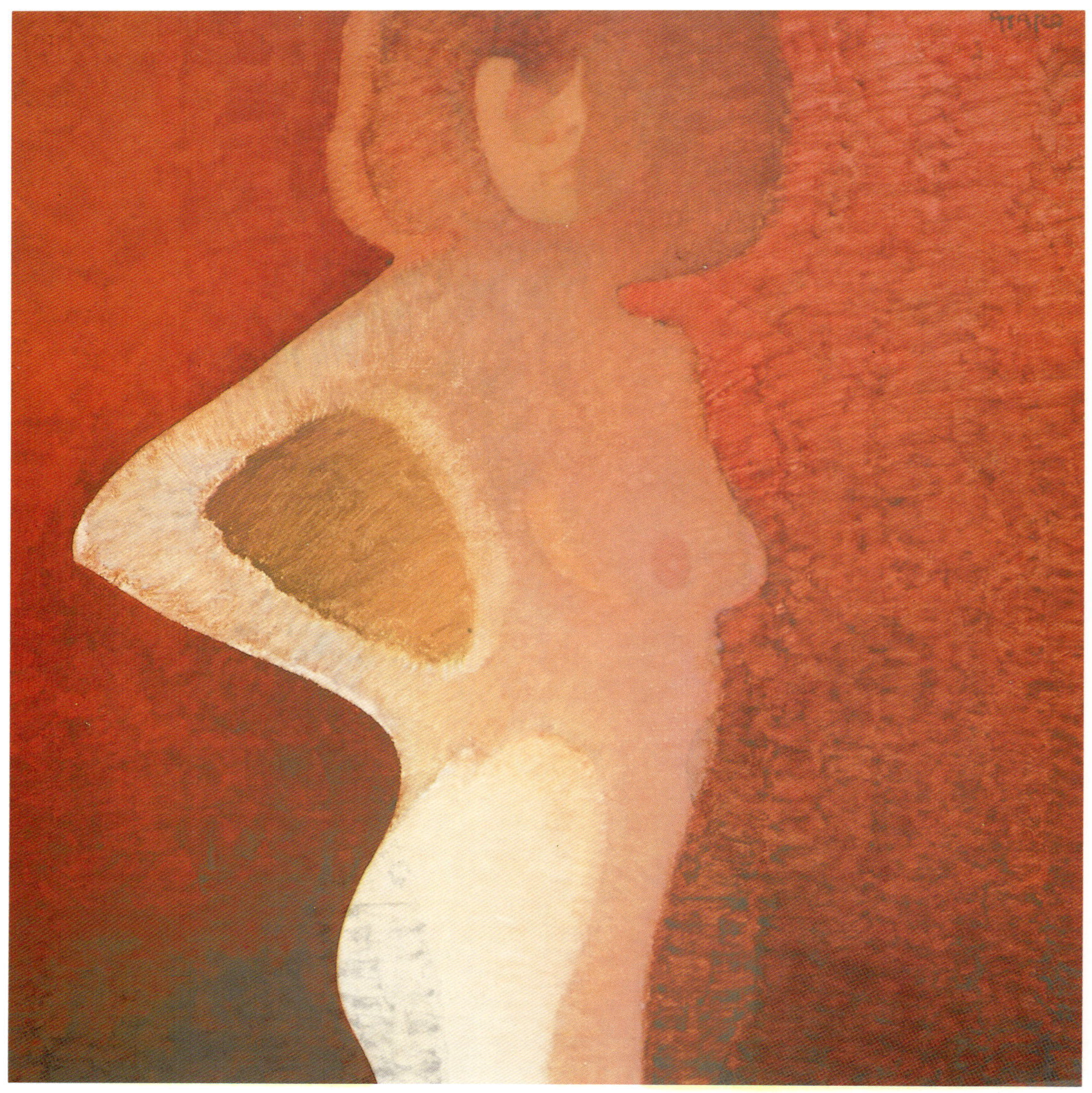

Allison, o/c, 32×30, 1974

THE ARTIST AS TEACHER (1972-1980)

Back in Los Angeles to paint seriously and to teach, Asaro was re-confronted by the classroom and its inherent agonies. To be reimmersed in, but not ensnared by, the student struggle at Art Center was also to reexamine basics and to refuel his growing conviction that he must refine the processes that produced outstanding paintings. He continued to be intrigued by the phenomenon of light playing on the figure, especially what was happening in the shadows. While as a student he had gained some understanding of reflected light,

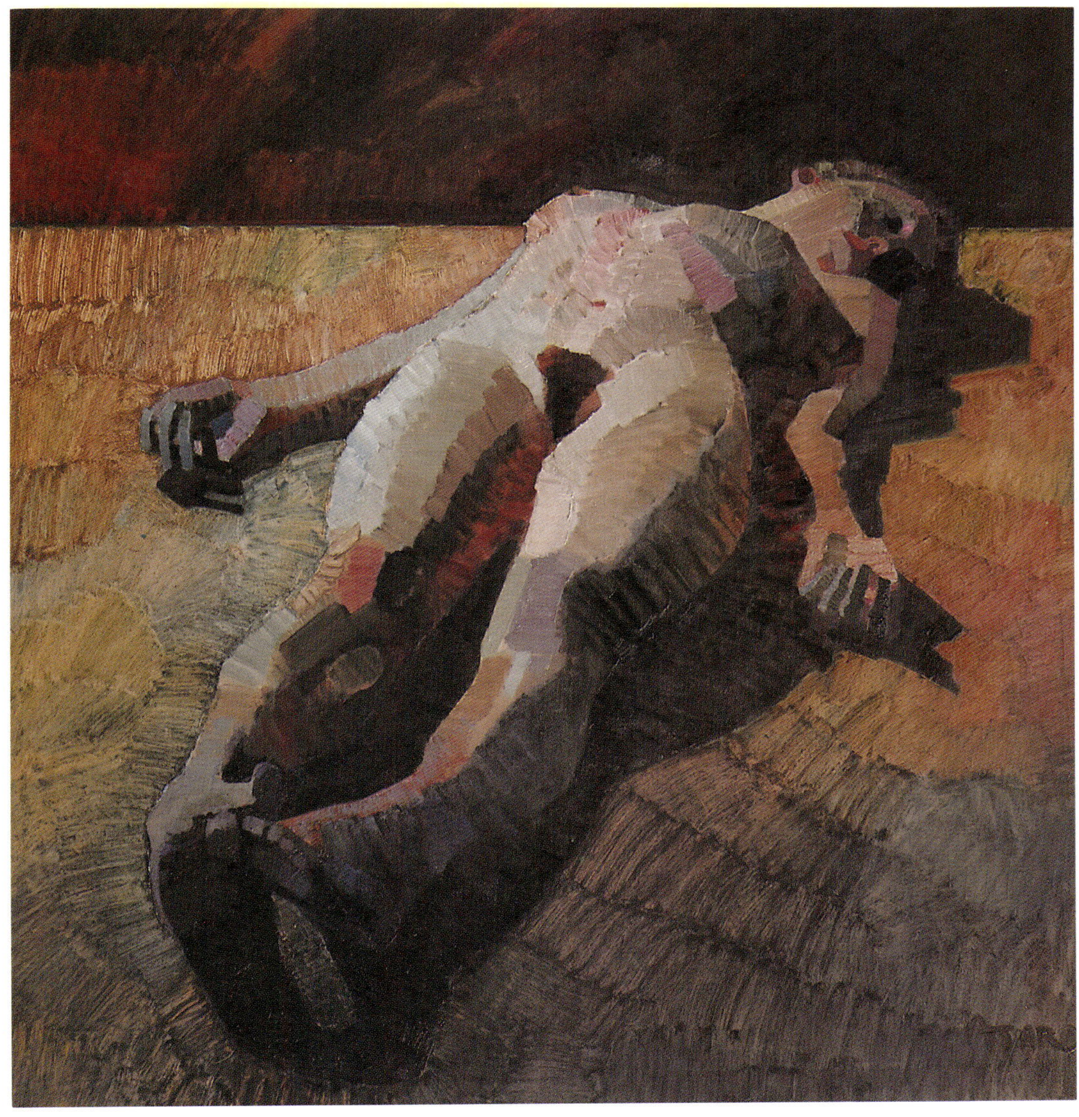

Reclining Nude I, o/c, 38×40, 1975

it wasn't until his return to teaching that he real-
ized that several levels of understanding were
required of a painter. Setting up models to enable
his students to see this phenomenon clearly, "I
began to realize the true ramifications of reflected
light as *apart from* direct light. Simply stated it is
this: The sides or planes of an object will be seen
in varied colors because the reflected light striking
these planes have their own color sources apart
from the object. Therefore, each plane of a given
object or space may reflect a different color."
These classroom exercises confirmed for Asaro
what the Plein Air painters had observed and
rediscovered in the works of such masters as

Rubens.

The selections in this section could all have
been painted in such a classroom, a place where
the female figure and its softened, rounded planes
has intrigued painters for centuries. If these works
look fundamentally familiar – the artist-and-model-
formula – they also possess a dramatic impact that
few contemporary artists pursue these days. Obviously, this interest in drama is an essential ingre-
dient in Asaro's romantic vision, his painful journey
toward emotional freedom. This duality – romantic
vision and emotional depth – are imperative to his
wooing of an empathetic audience, viewers who
dance to his sensuous, inner rhythms.

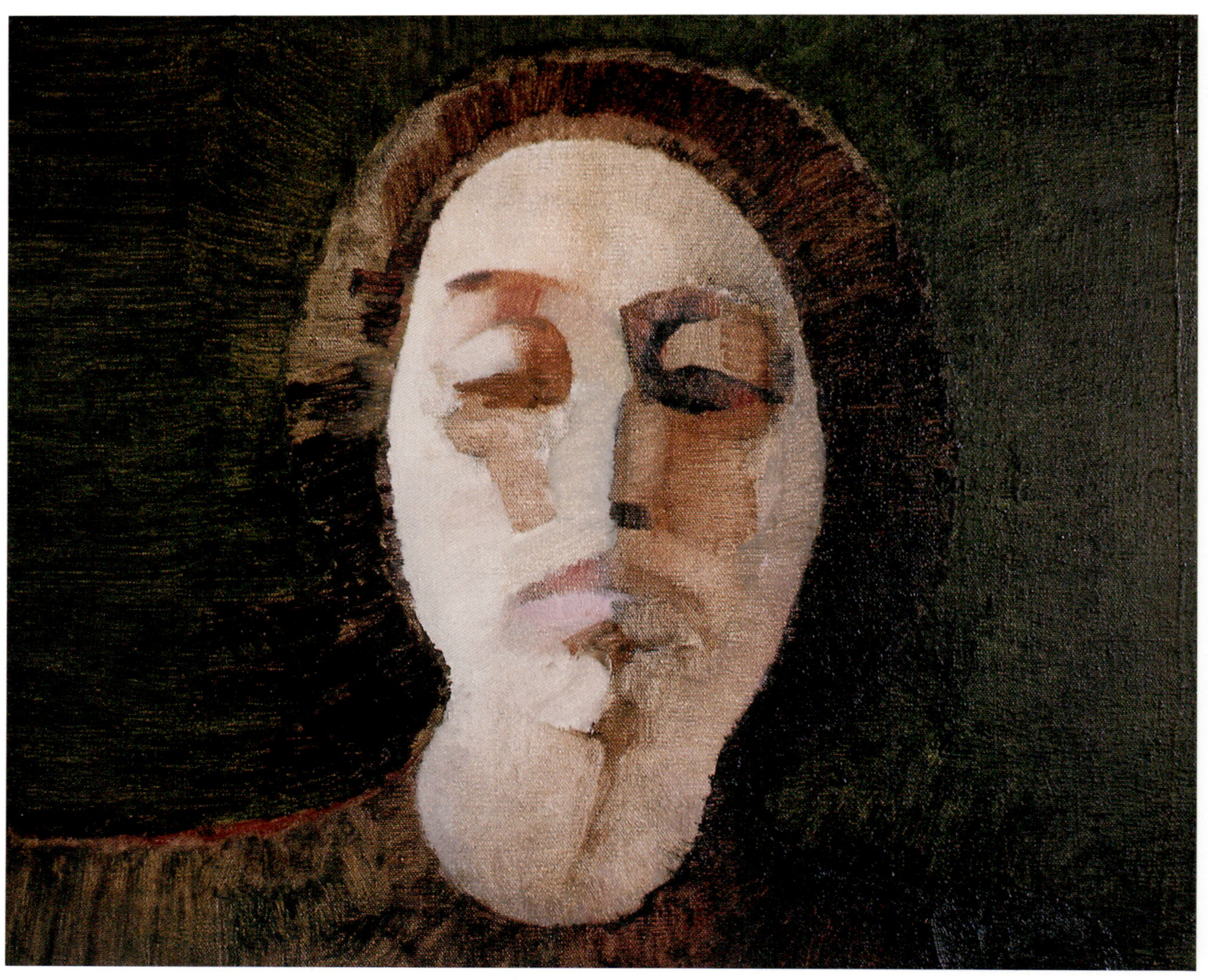

Untitled, o/c, 16×20, 1976

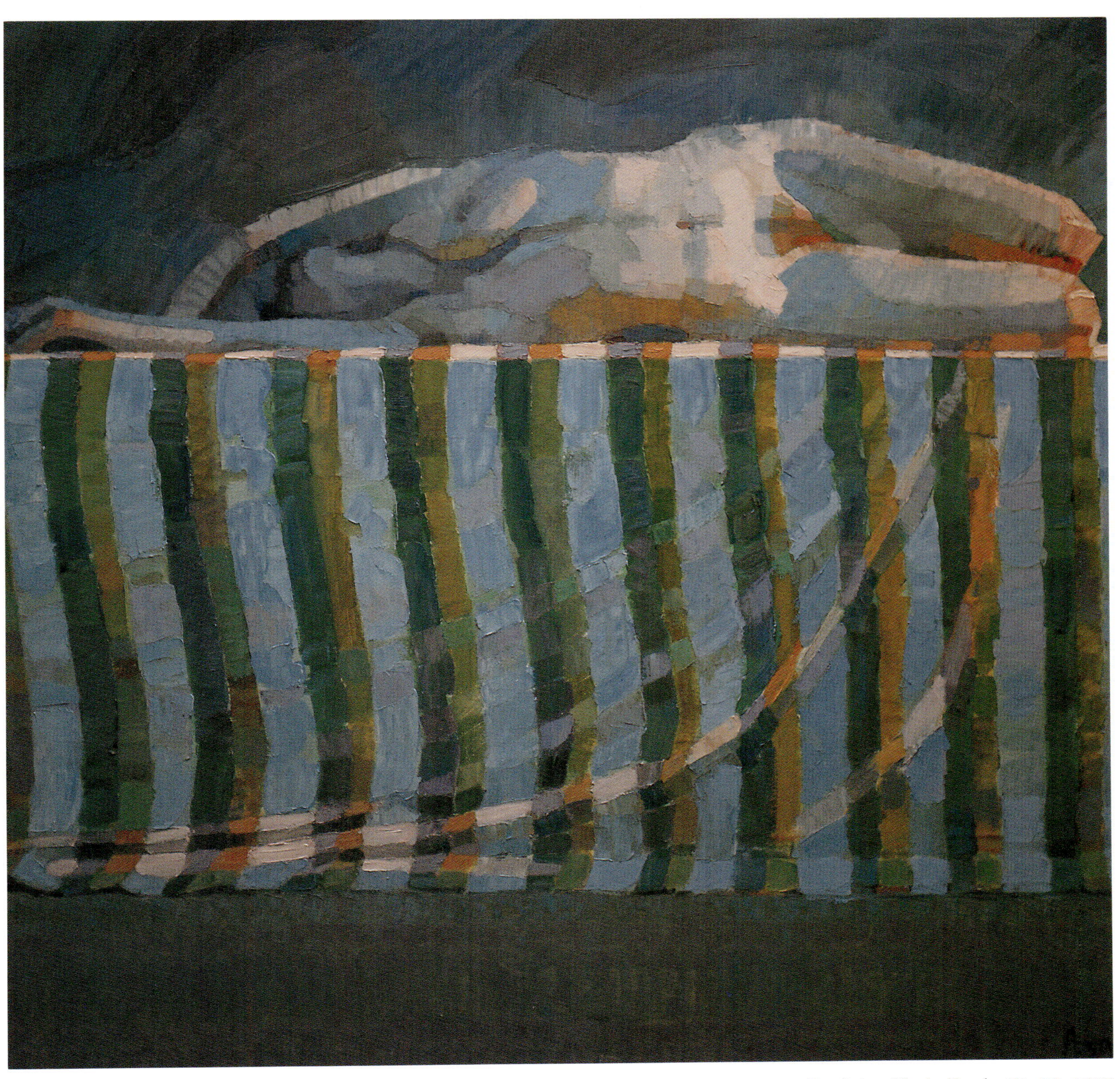

Reclining Nude II, o/c, 36×38, 1977

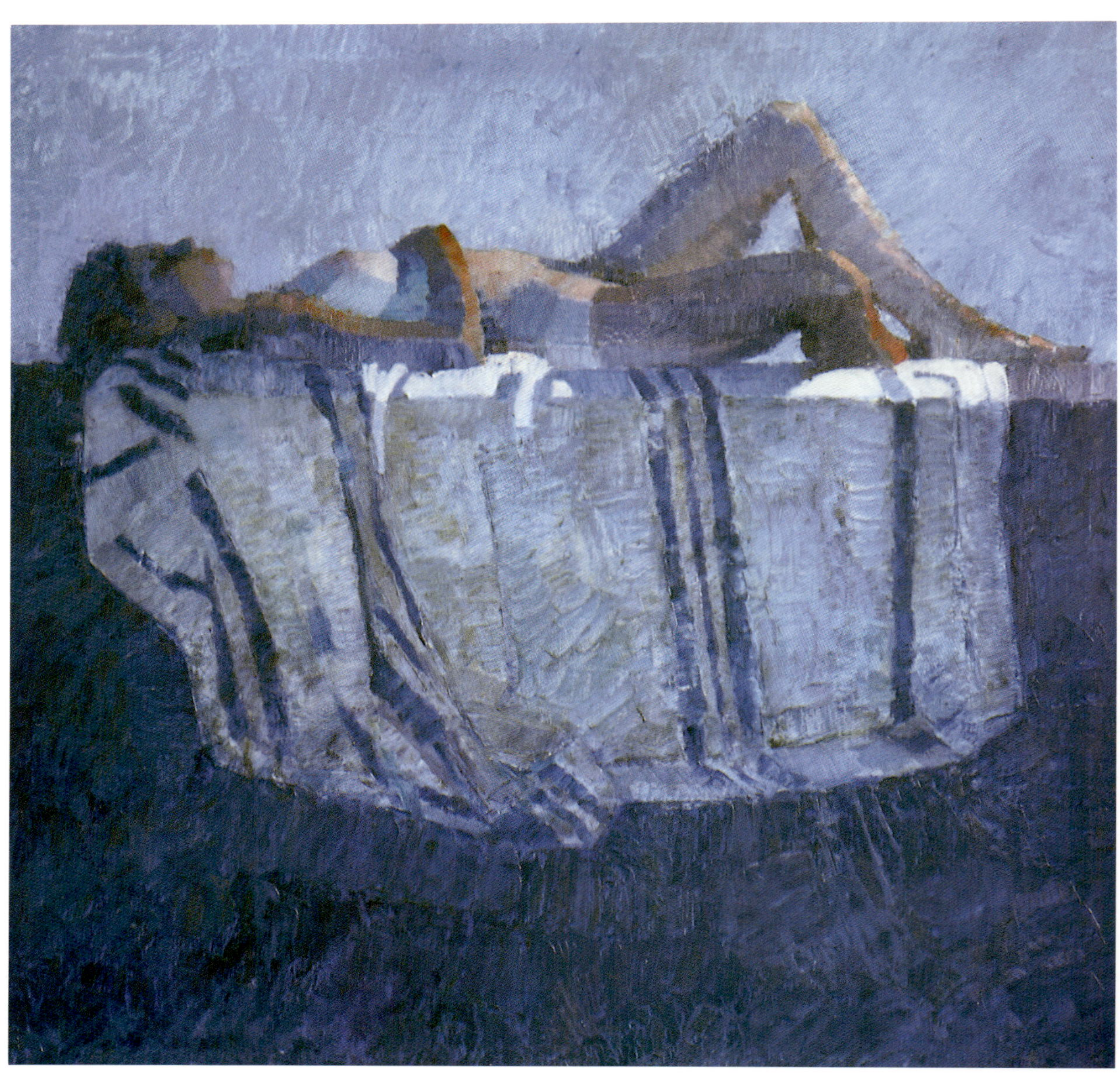

Reclining Nude III, o/c, 36×38, 1979

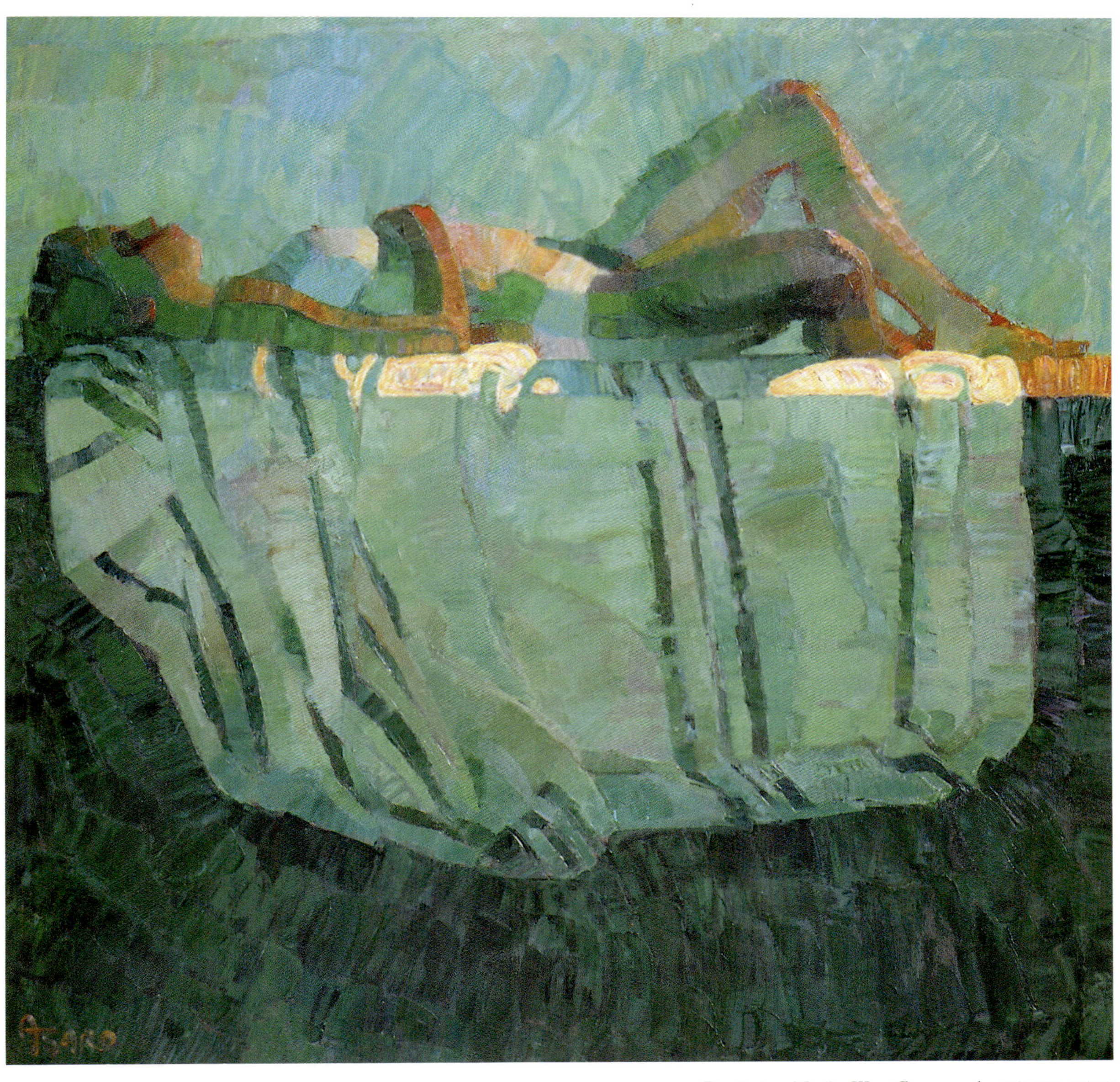

Reclining Nude III – Green, o/c, 36×38, 1979

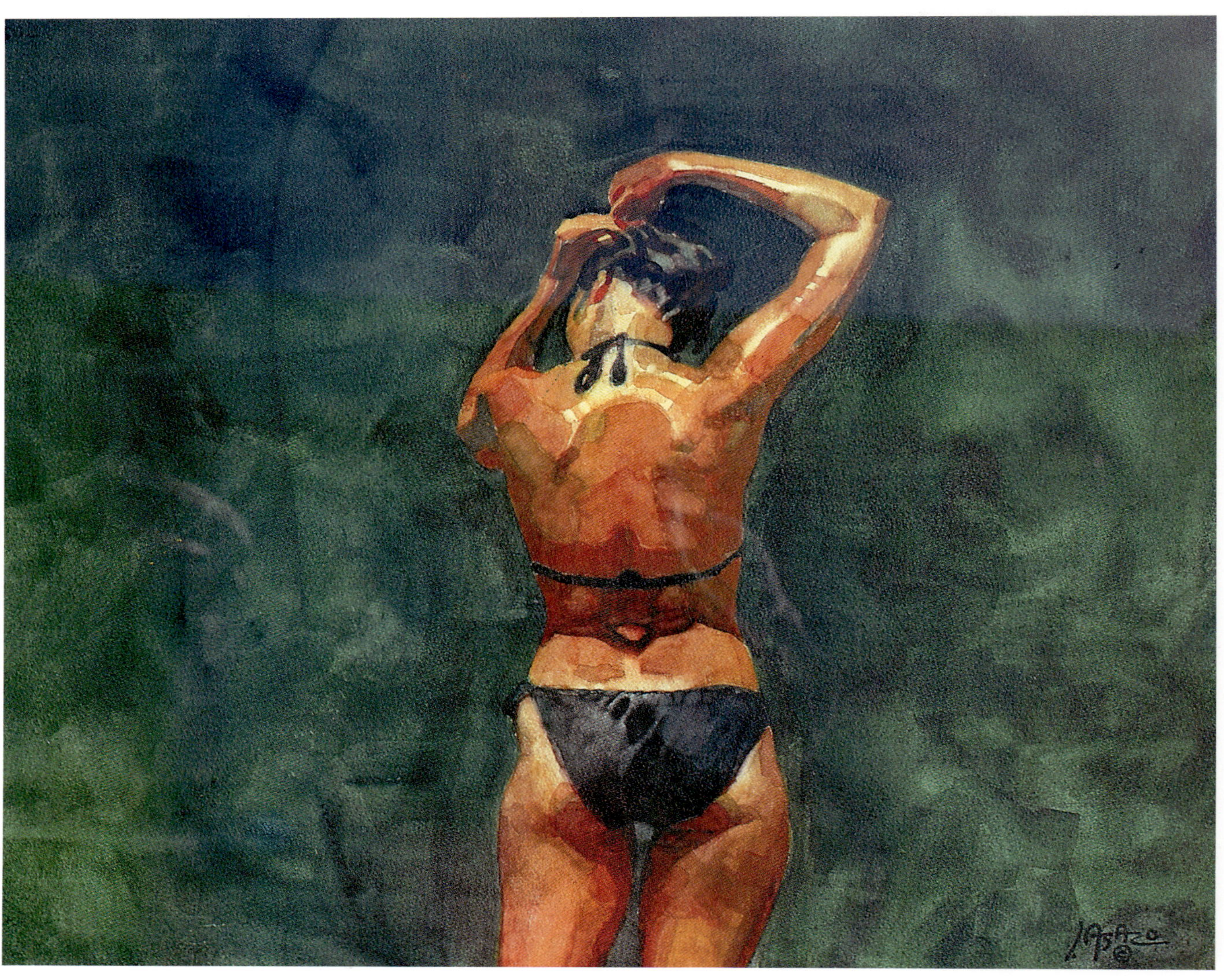

Bather, w/c, 22×28, 1979

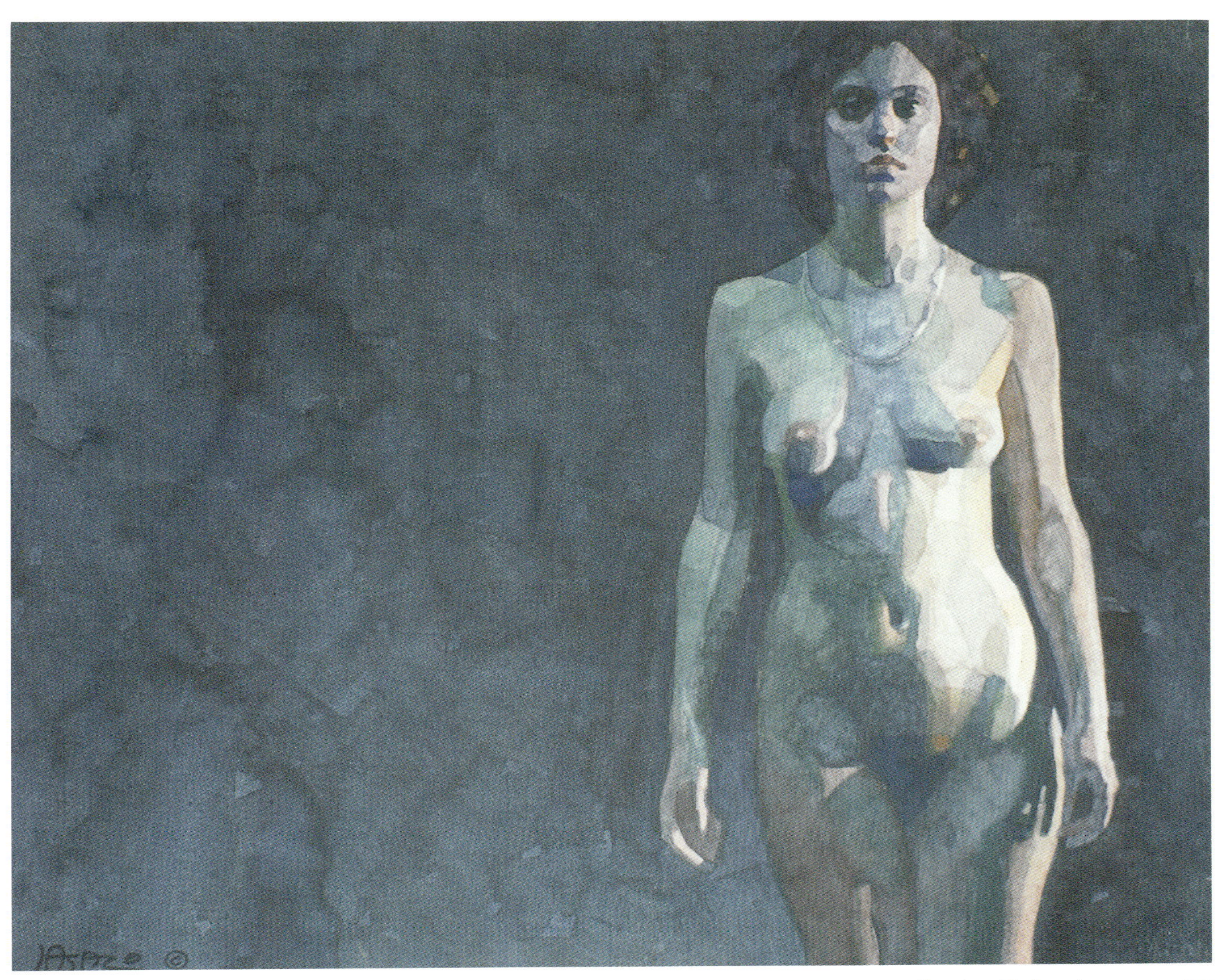

Standing Nude, w/c, 22×28, 1979

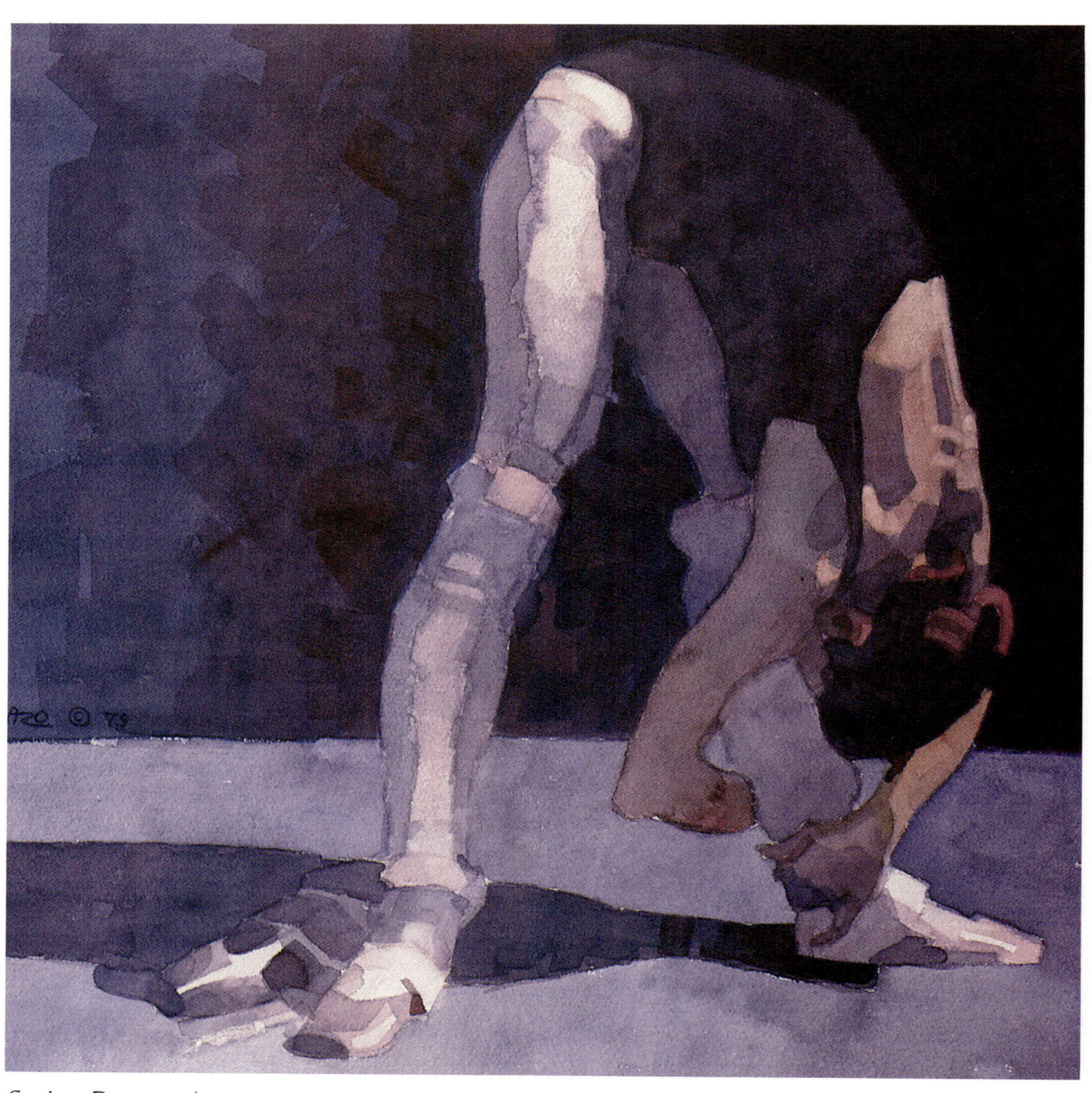

Student Dancer, w/c, 21×22, 1979

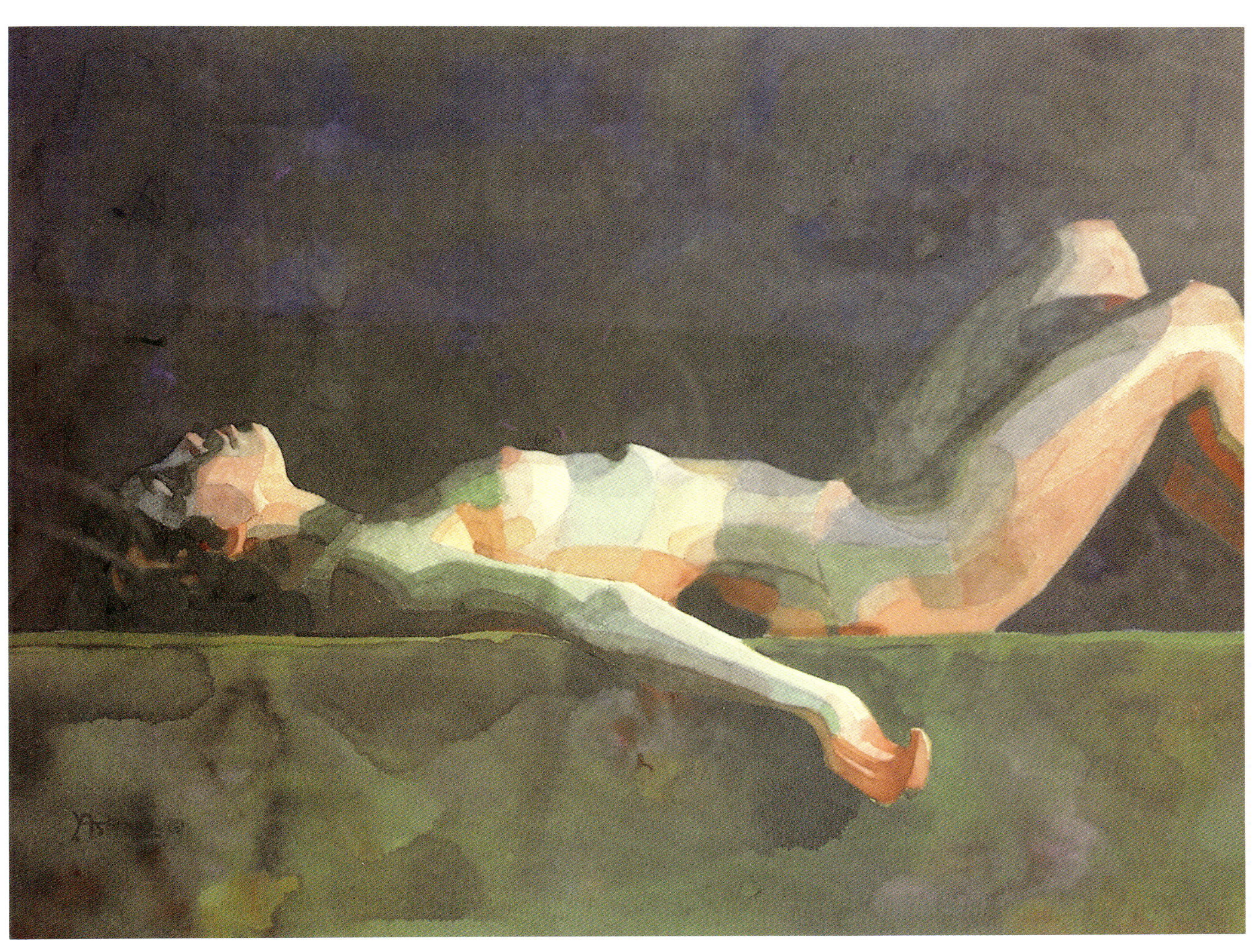

Reclining Nude IV, w/c, 22×30. 1979

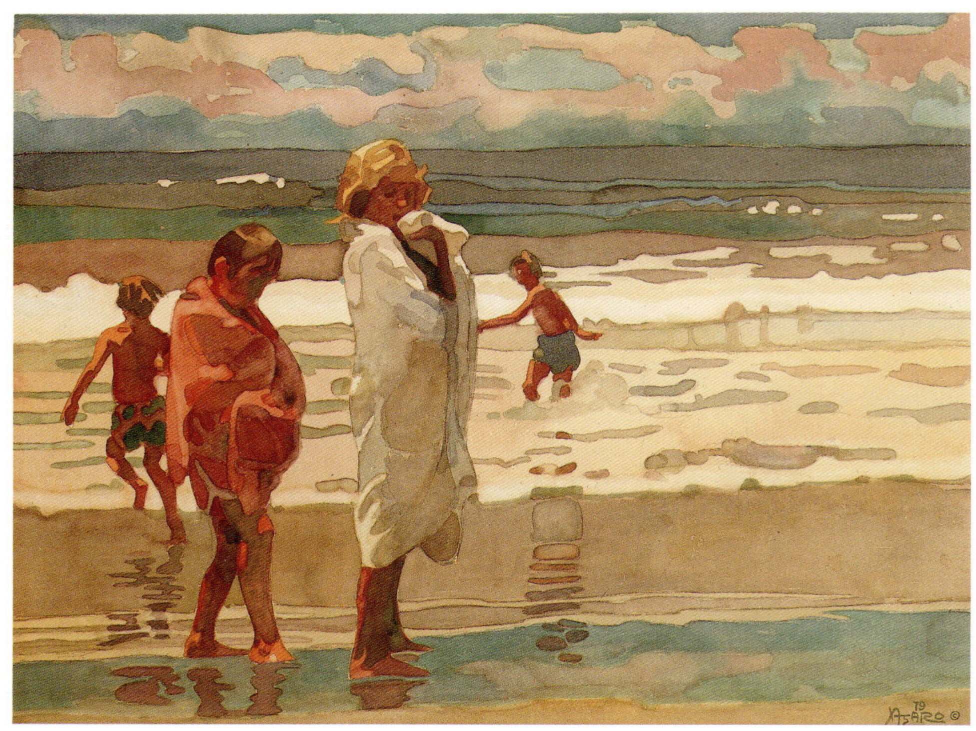

Four Boys, w/c, 22×30, 1979

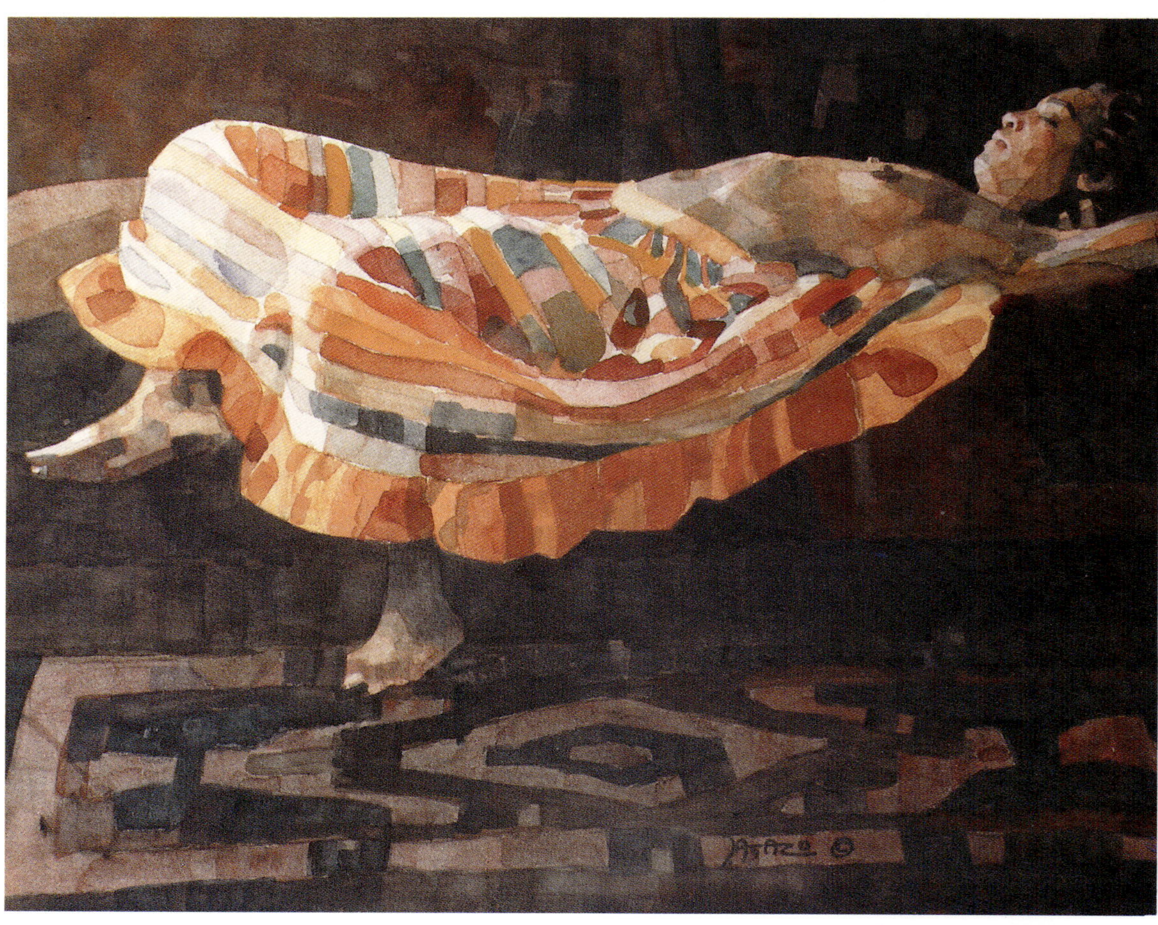

Caribbean Costume, w/c, 21×28, 1979

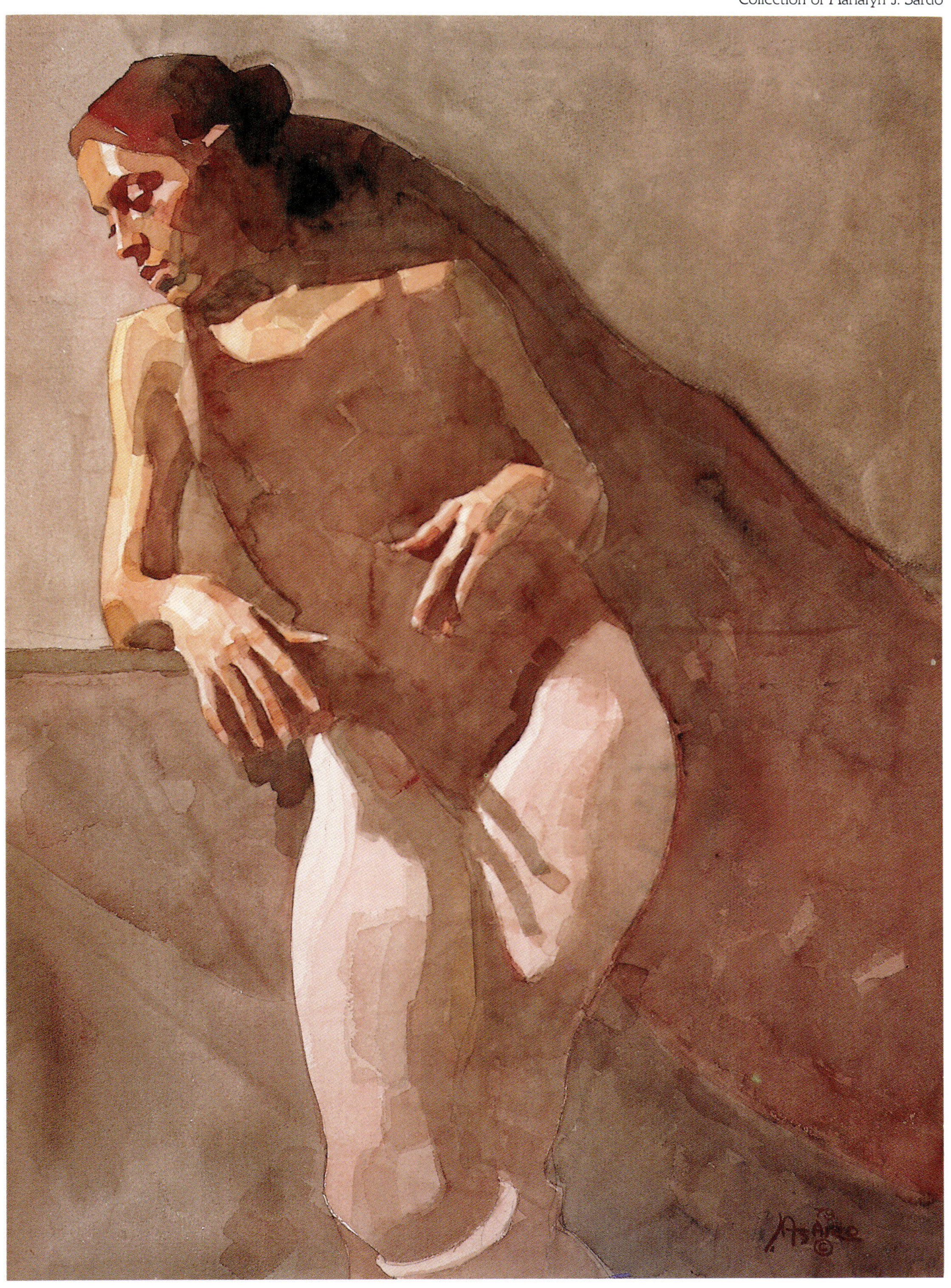

Dancer at Rest, w/c, 30×22, 1979

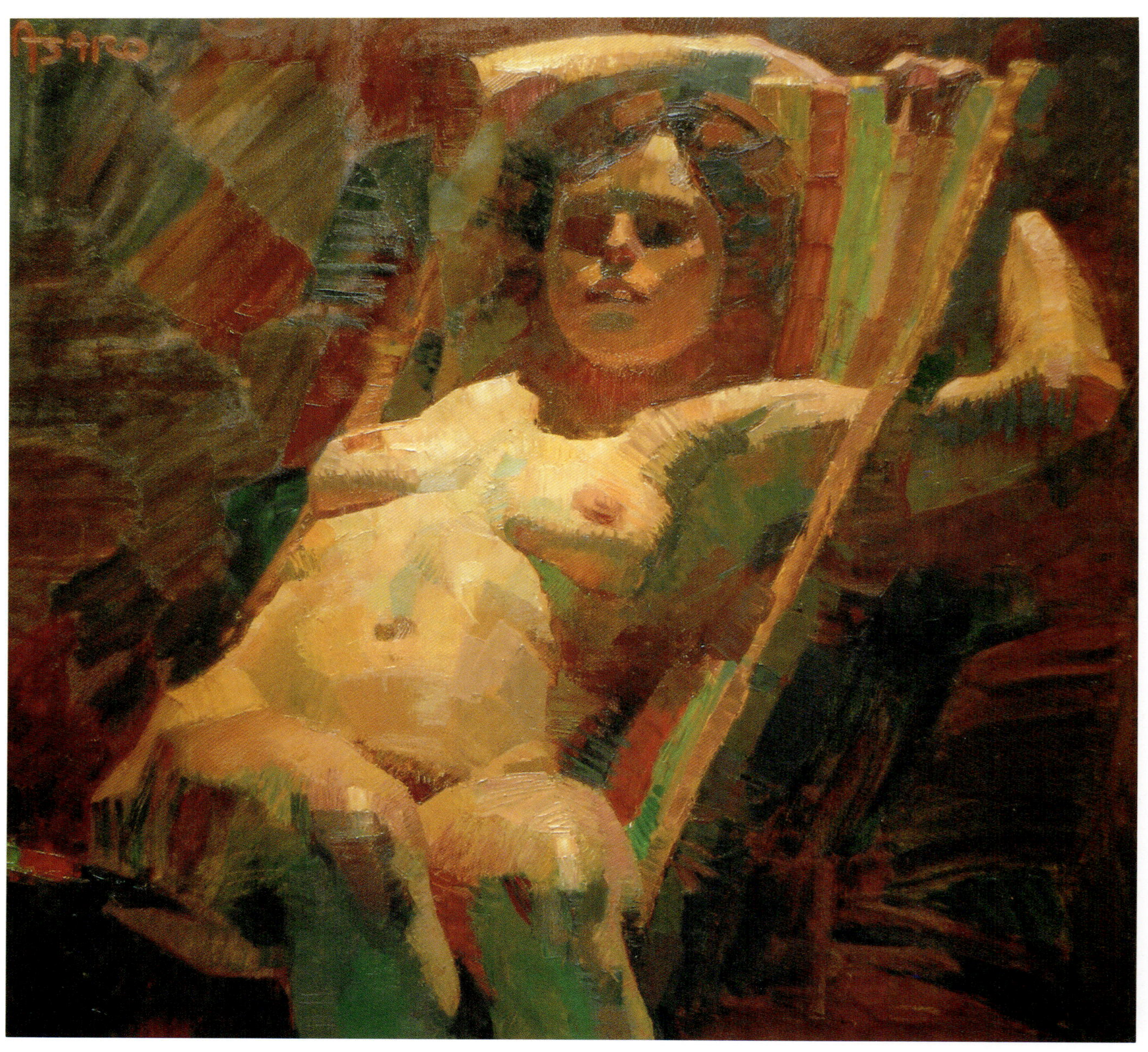

Nude in Burgundy, o/c, 38×42, 1979

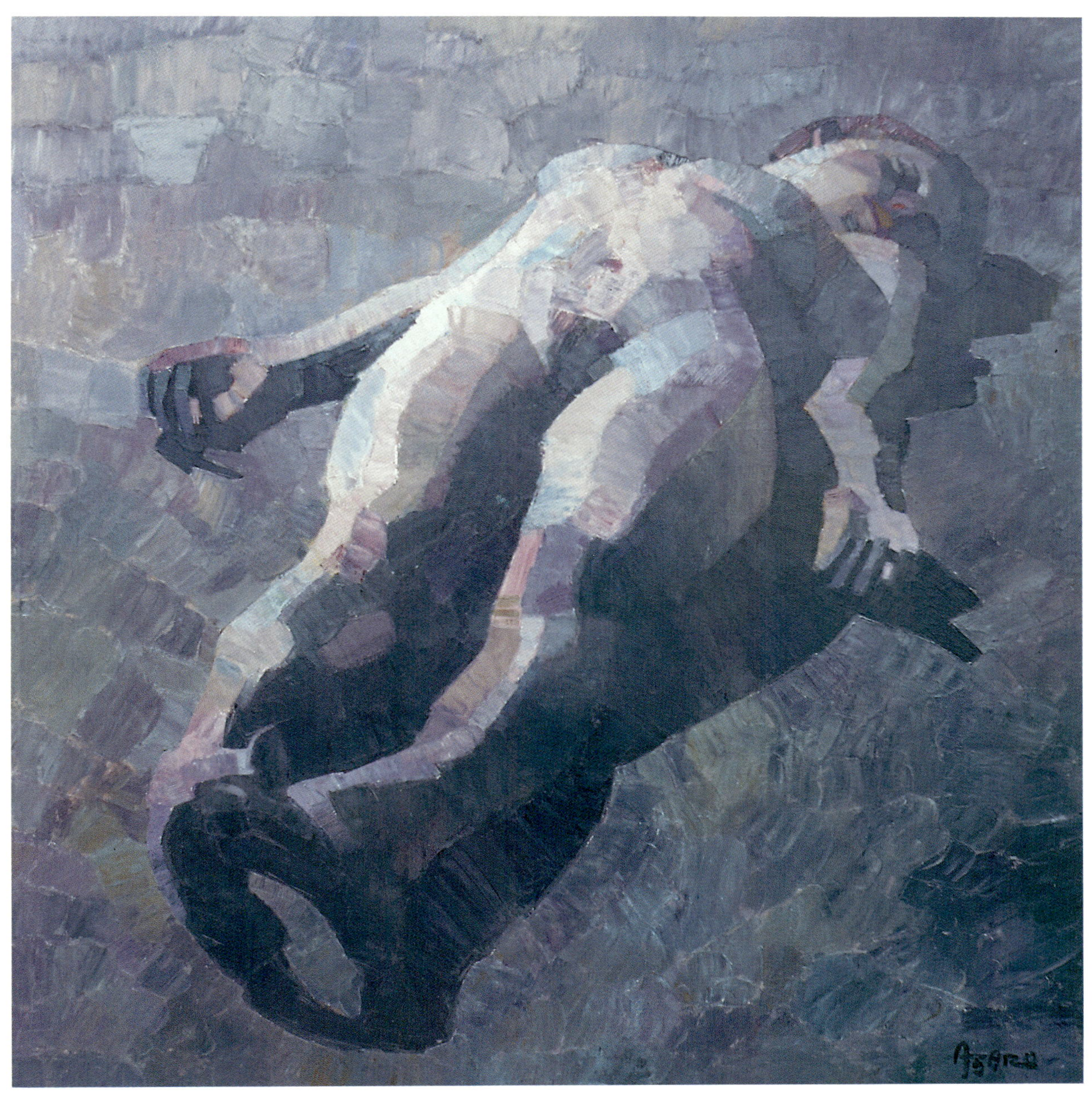

Reclining Nude V, o/c, 40×40, 1979

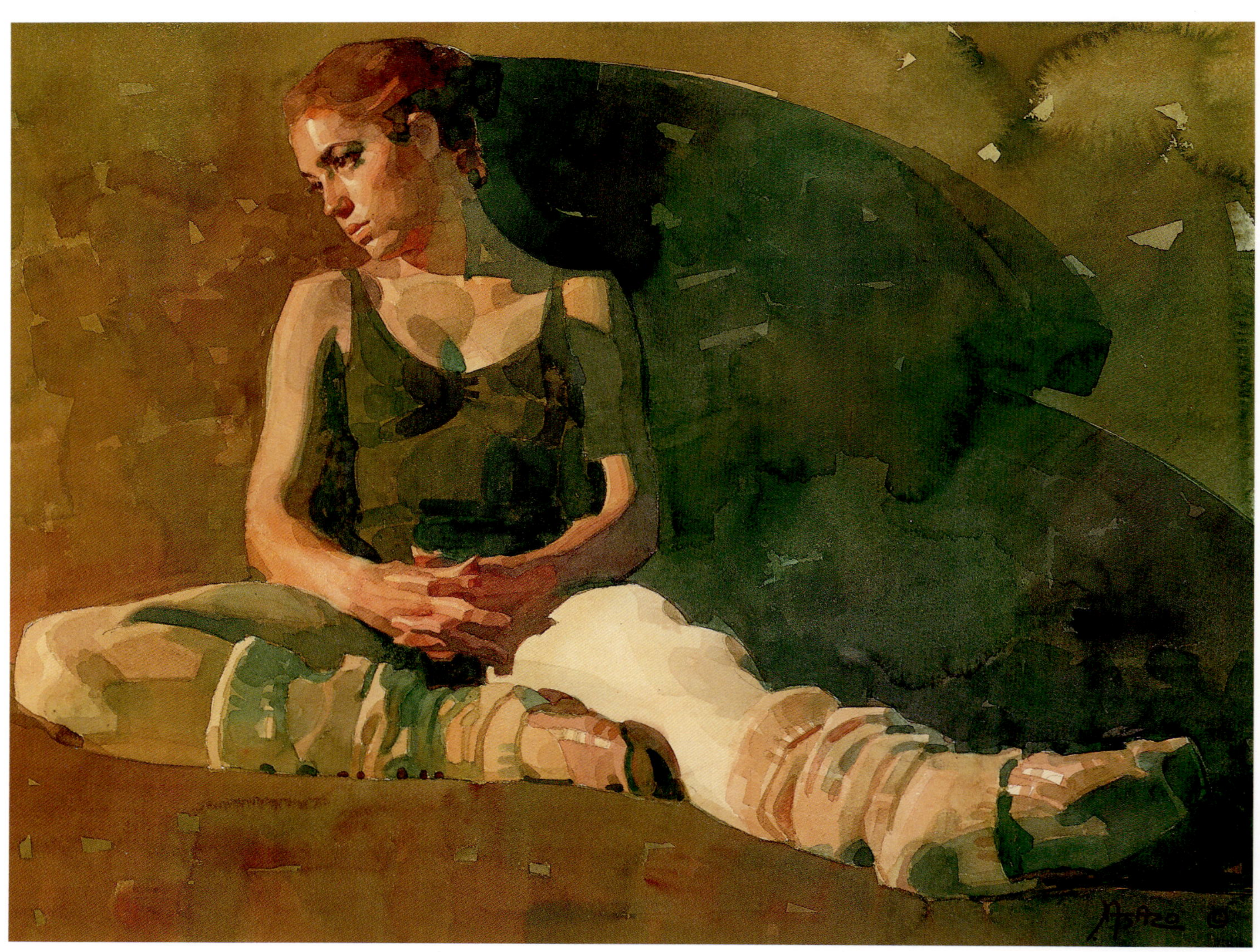

Dolly, w/c, 22×30, 1982

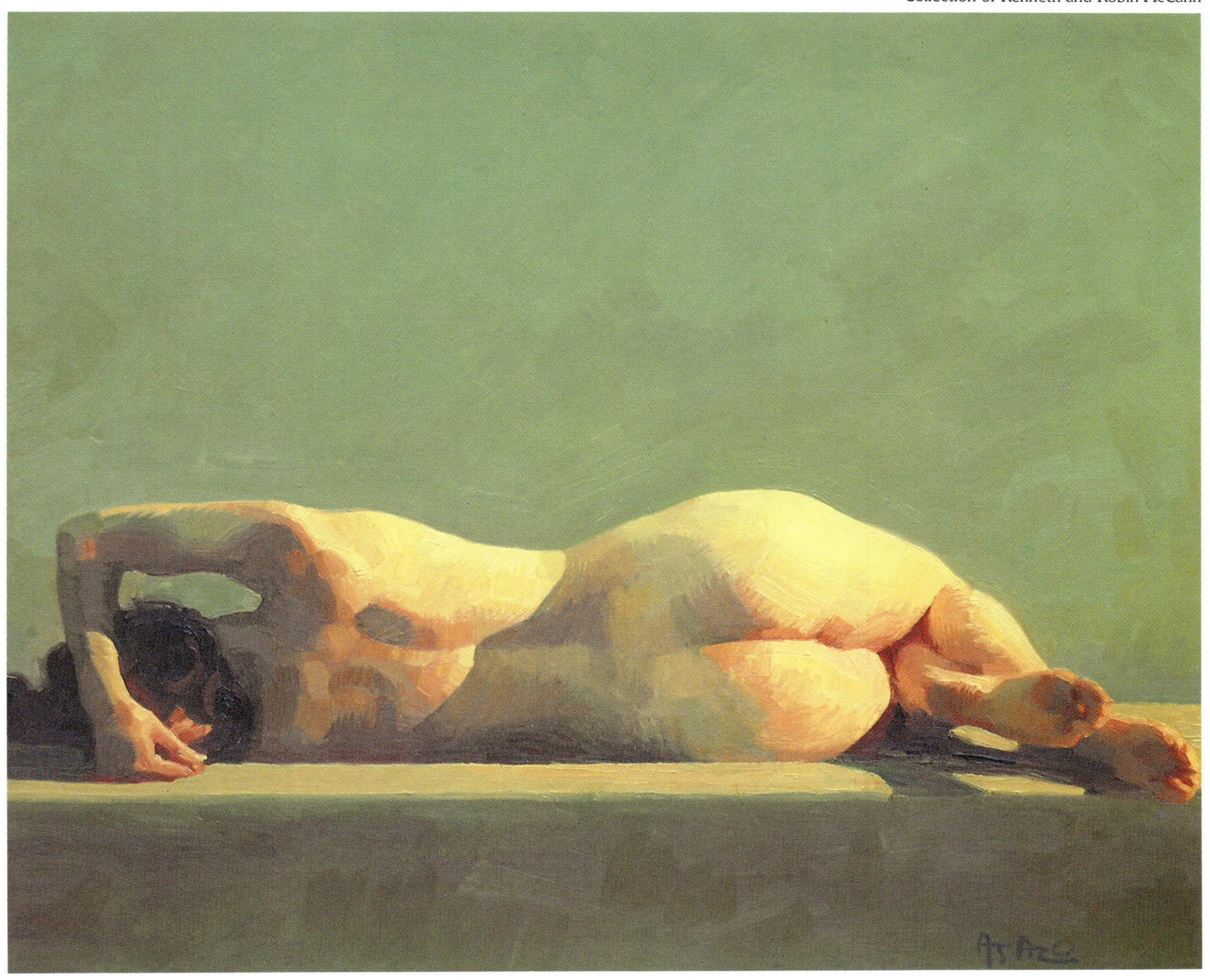

Reclining Nude VI, o/c, 34×42, 1980

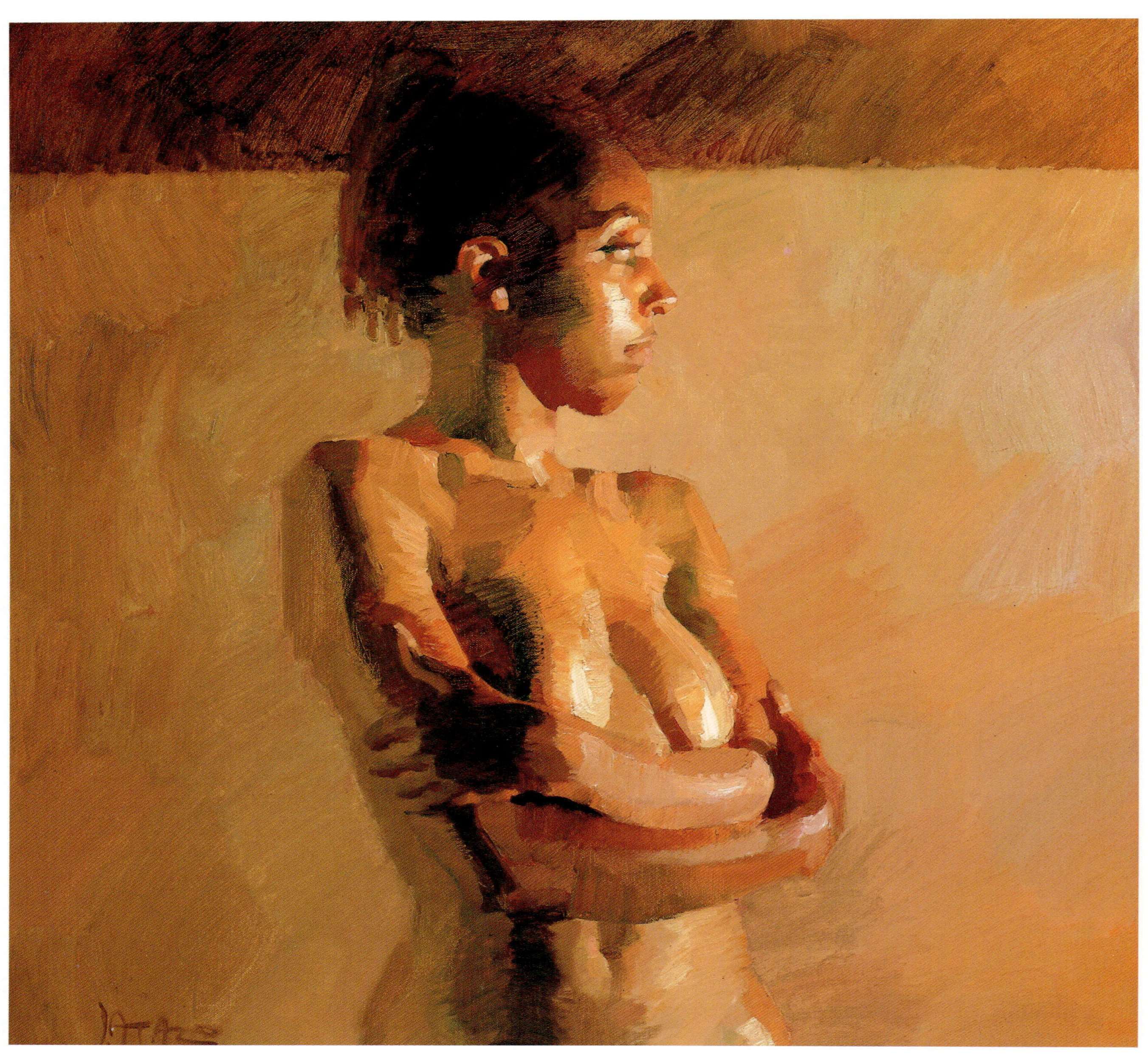

Corn Rows, o/c, 24×28, 1981

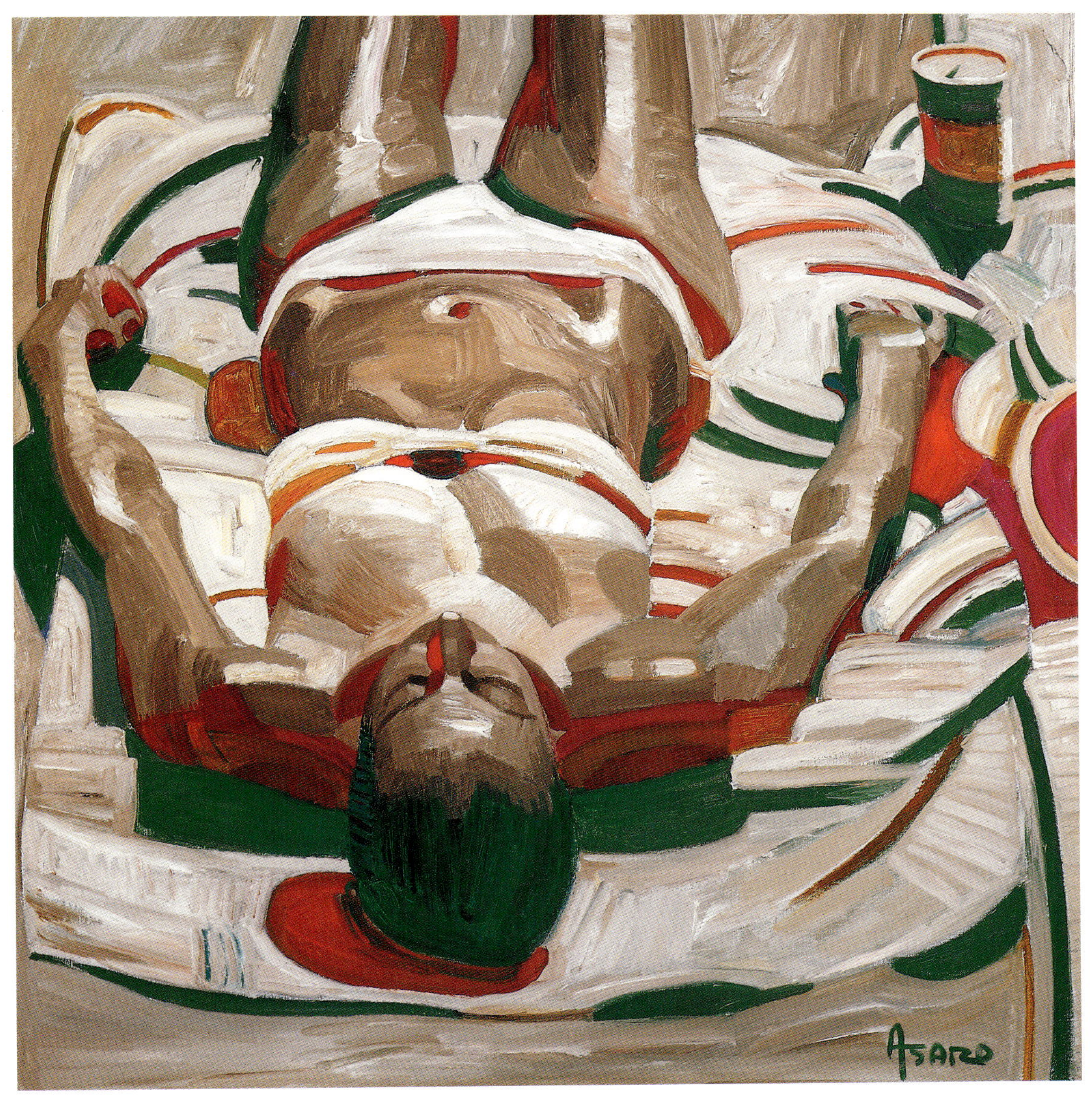

Santana, o/c, 30×30, 1979

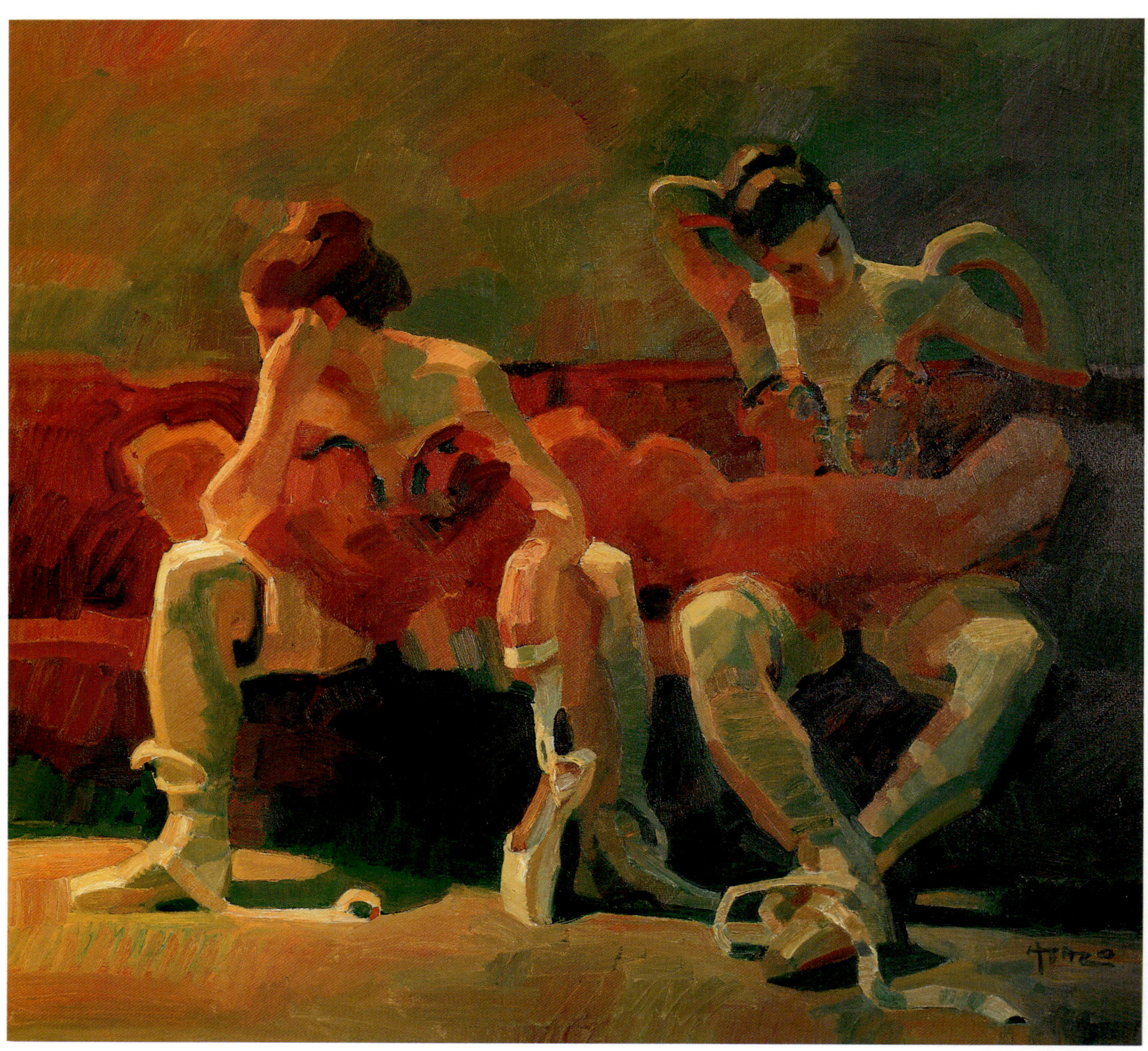

Two Dancers, o/c, 36×40, 1982

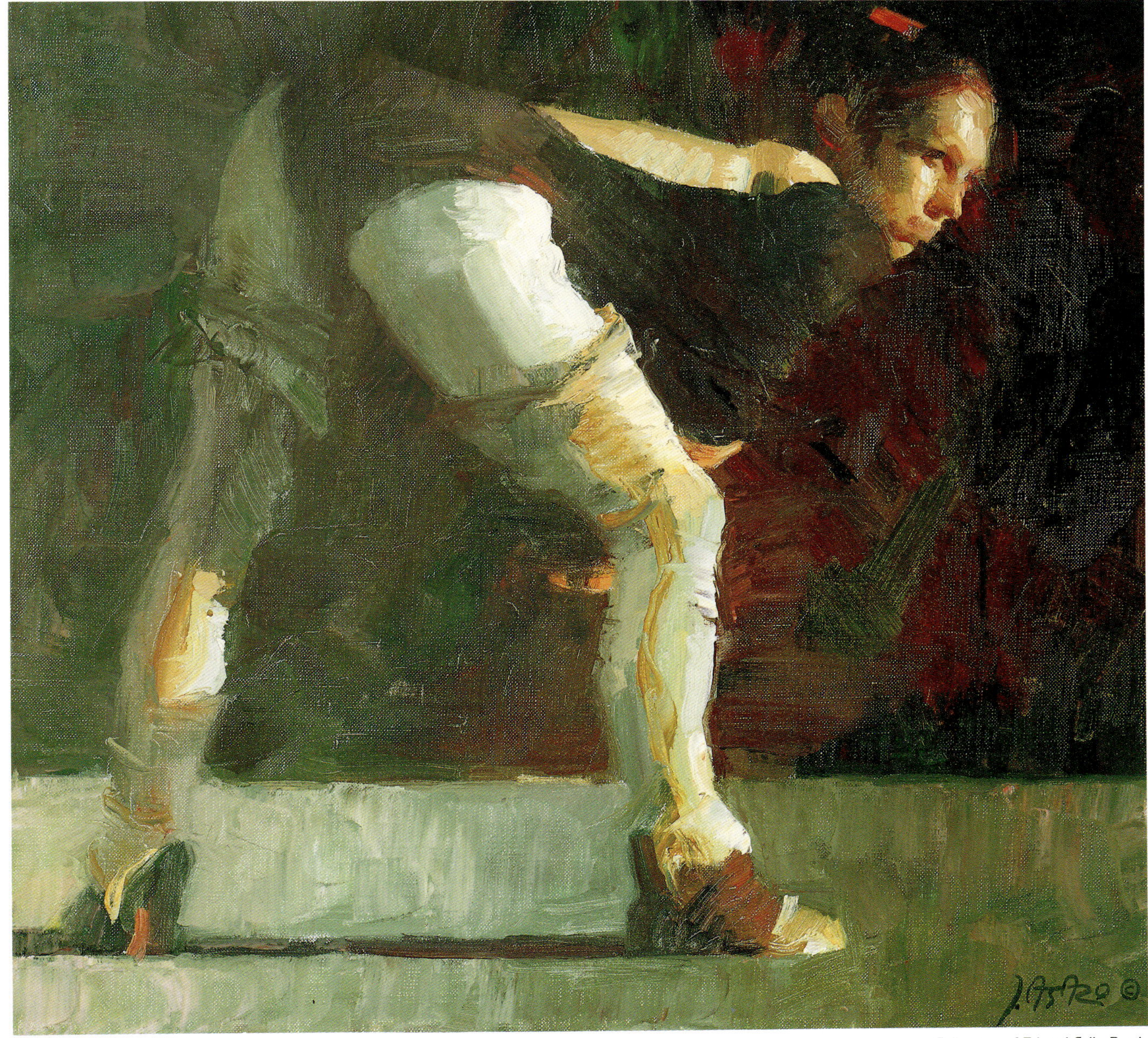

Dancer in Green, o/c, 16×18, 1982

Collection of Ed and Sally Rawls

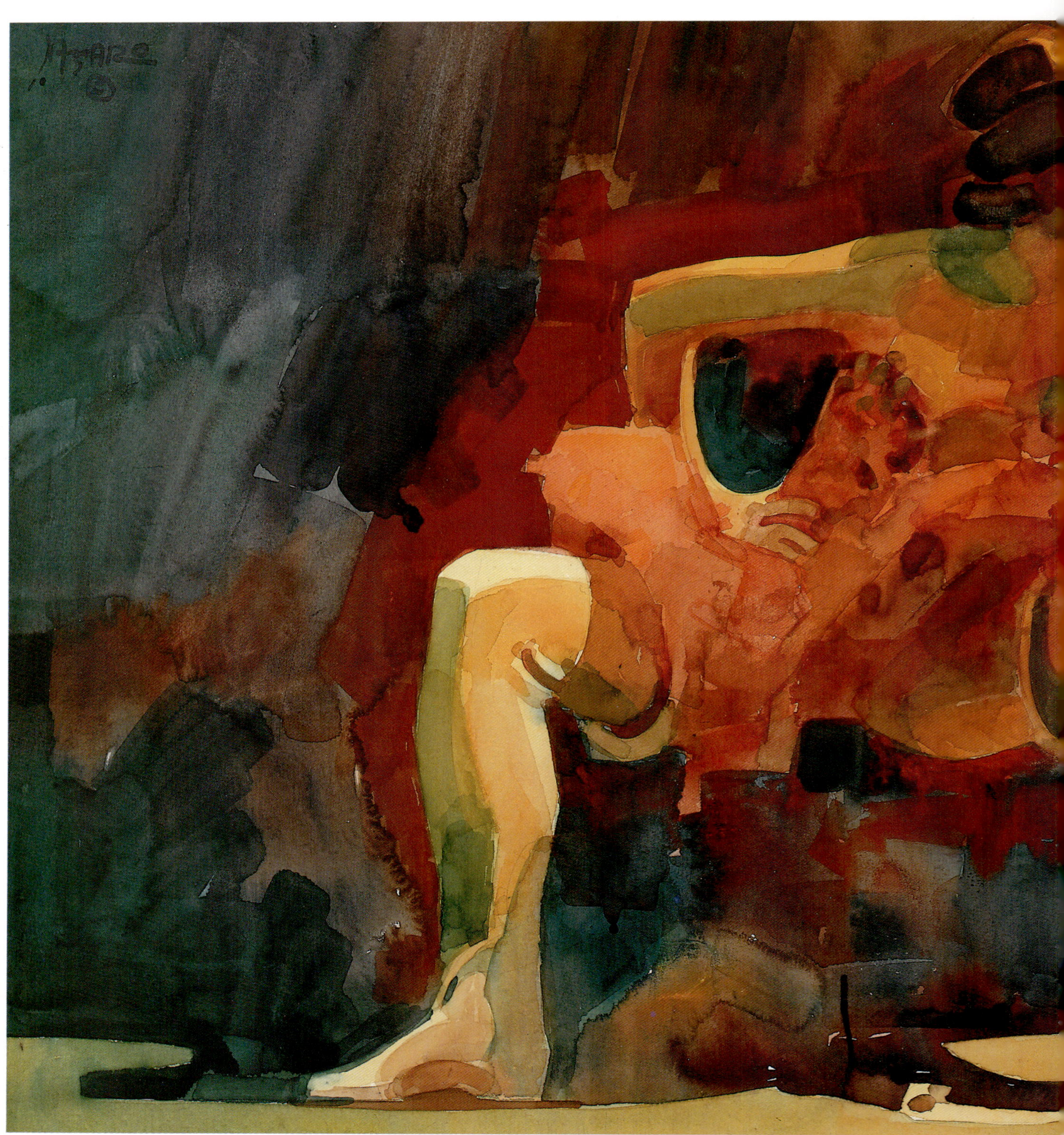

Dress Rehearsal, w/c, 22×30, 1980

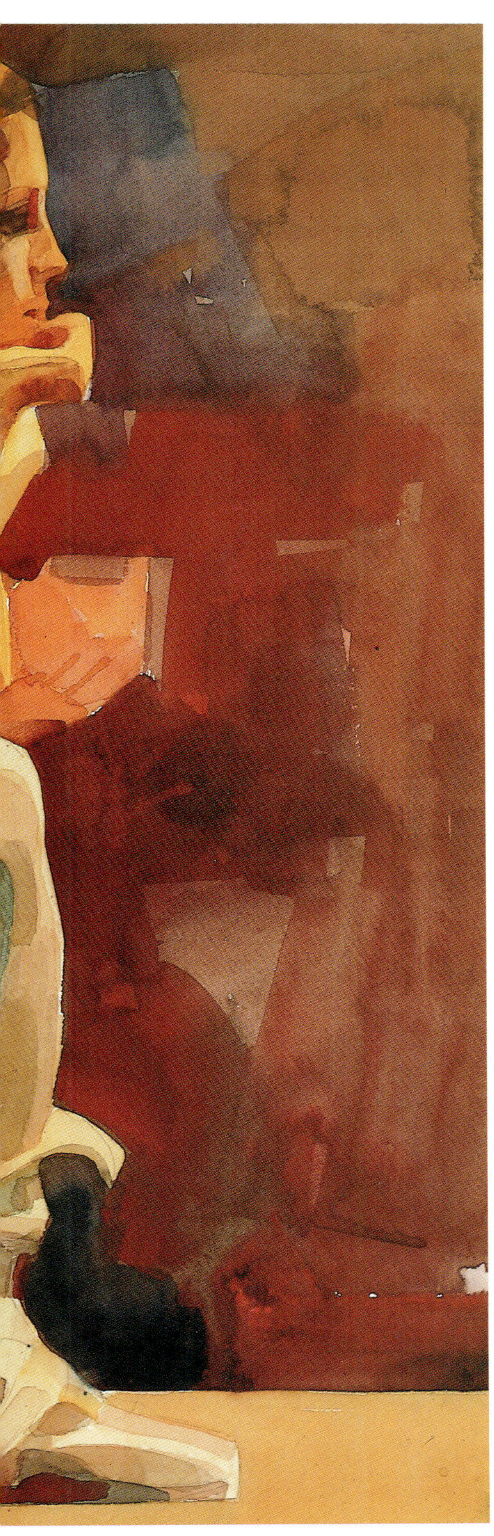

"To follow the path that feels good and right for oneself, one must experiment in style, subject matter, and media, being unafraid to let one's true feelings out…which results in one's personal style."

Drawing in charcoal pencil on newsprint, 24×18, 1985

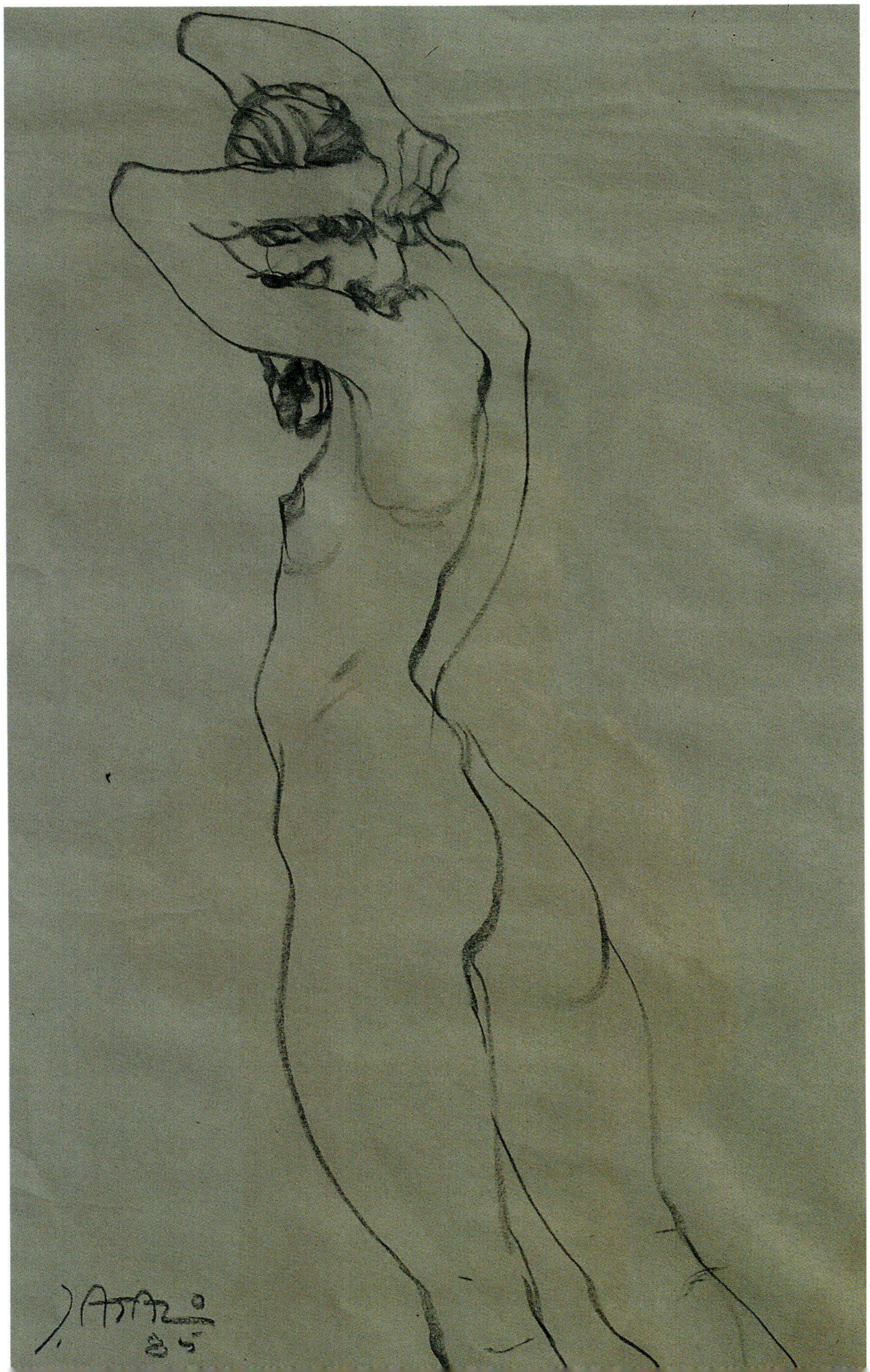

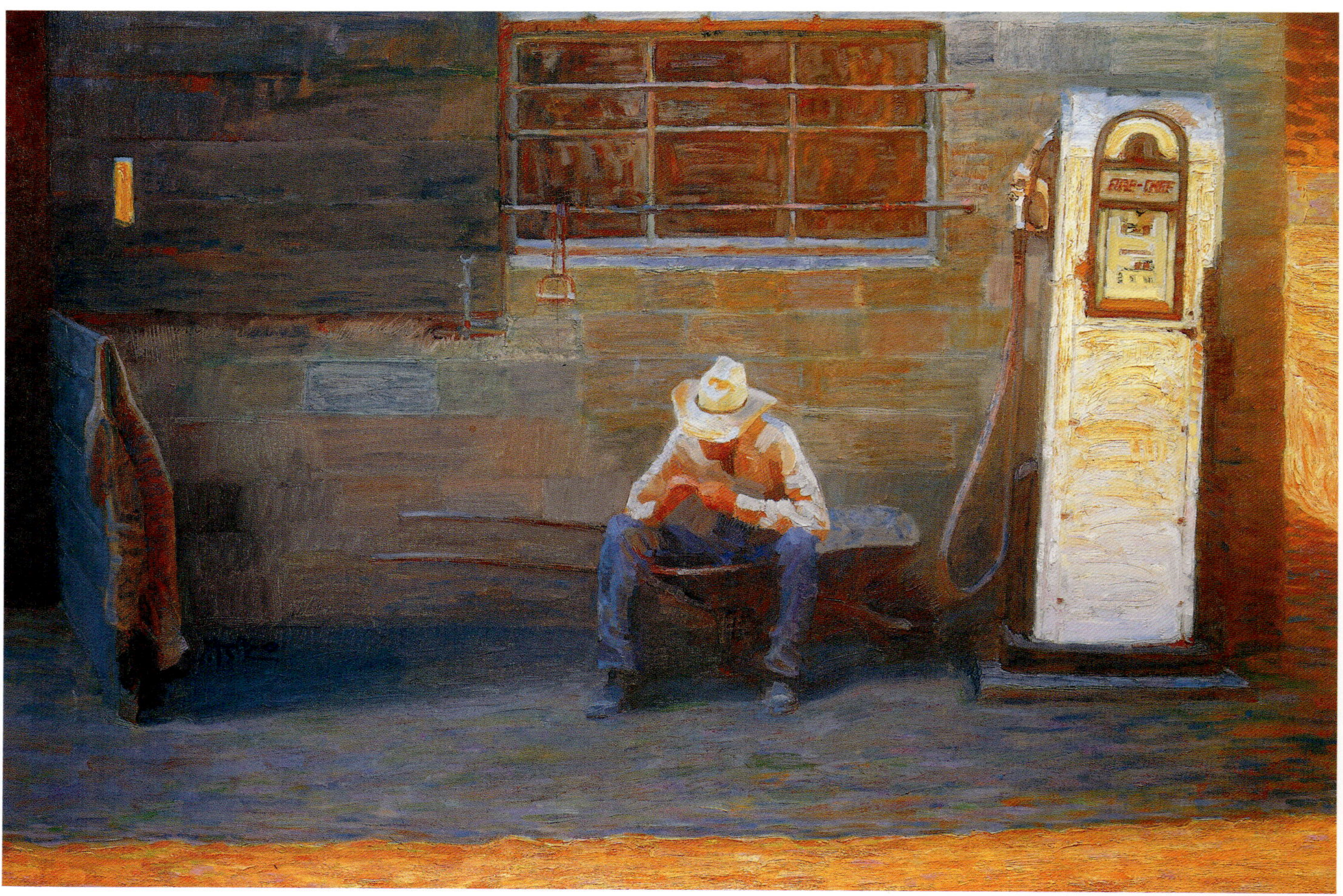

Fire Chief, o/c, 28×44, 1981

THE ARTIST AS WESTERNER (1981 – 1982)

Cowboys and truckers, horses and bulls hardly seem relevent to a sensibility entranced by the female figure. Yet a trip to a San Diego ranch overseen by his brother's law firm introduced Asaro to new possibilities. The arid West, which extends across Southern California to the Pacific, offered Asaro immediate diversionary subject matter and,

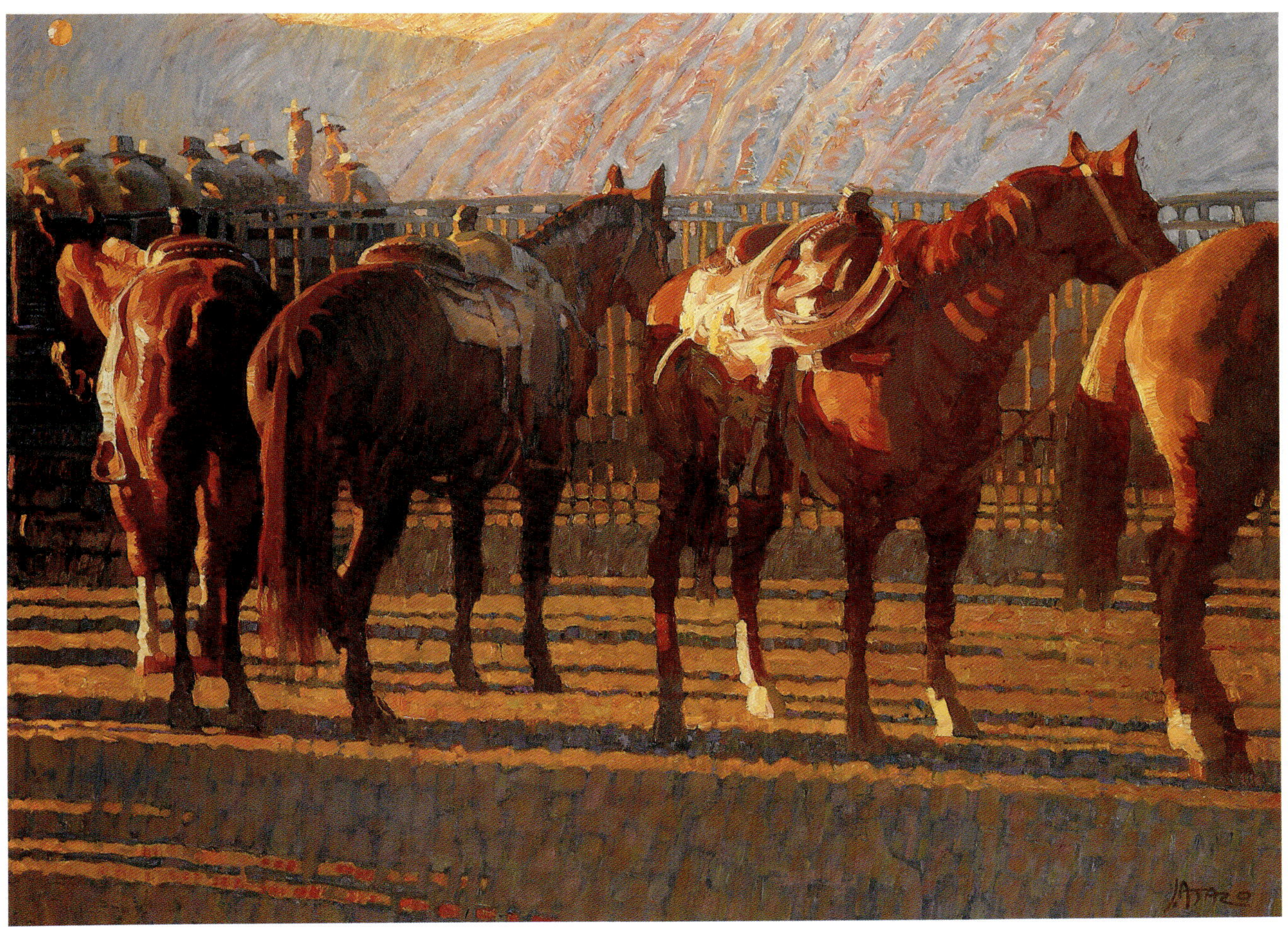

The Last Event, o/c, 34×48, 1982

as an adjunct to his figure studies, he found himself working for two years on a series of paintings,
some of them shown here. Exhibiting these works
at the Western Heritage Shows in Houston and
Denver and at the "Artists of America Art Exhibition" in Denver and having several profiles appear
in *Southwest Art Magazine*, identified Asaro with
"painters of the Southwest," bringing him additional
press. His illustrative skills shine in these paintings,
though he denies any permanent connection to a
particular "school" of cowboy landscape.

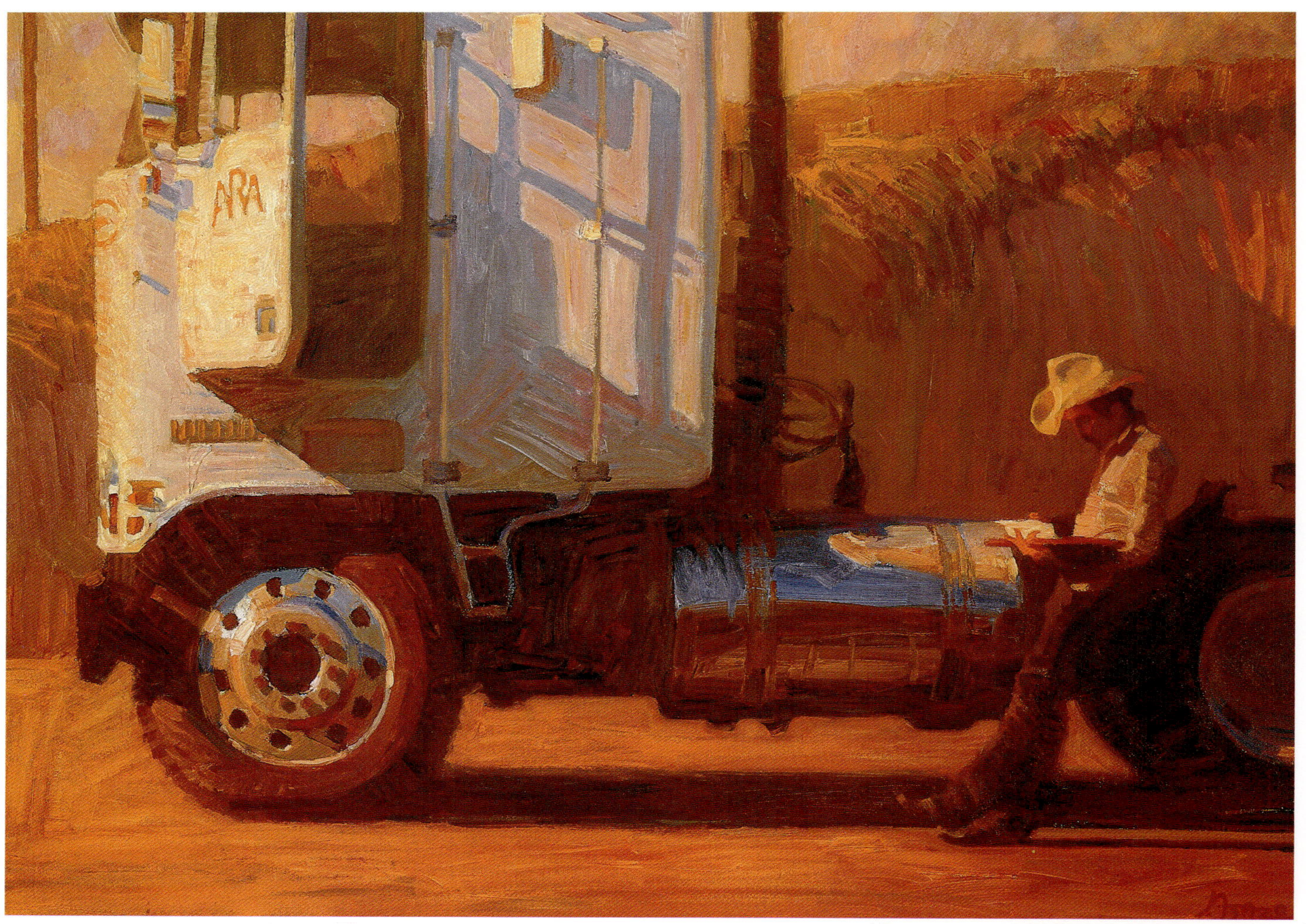

Cowboy, o/c, 28×40, 1983

Collection of Peter and DeAnna Tomaryn

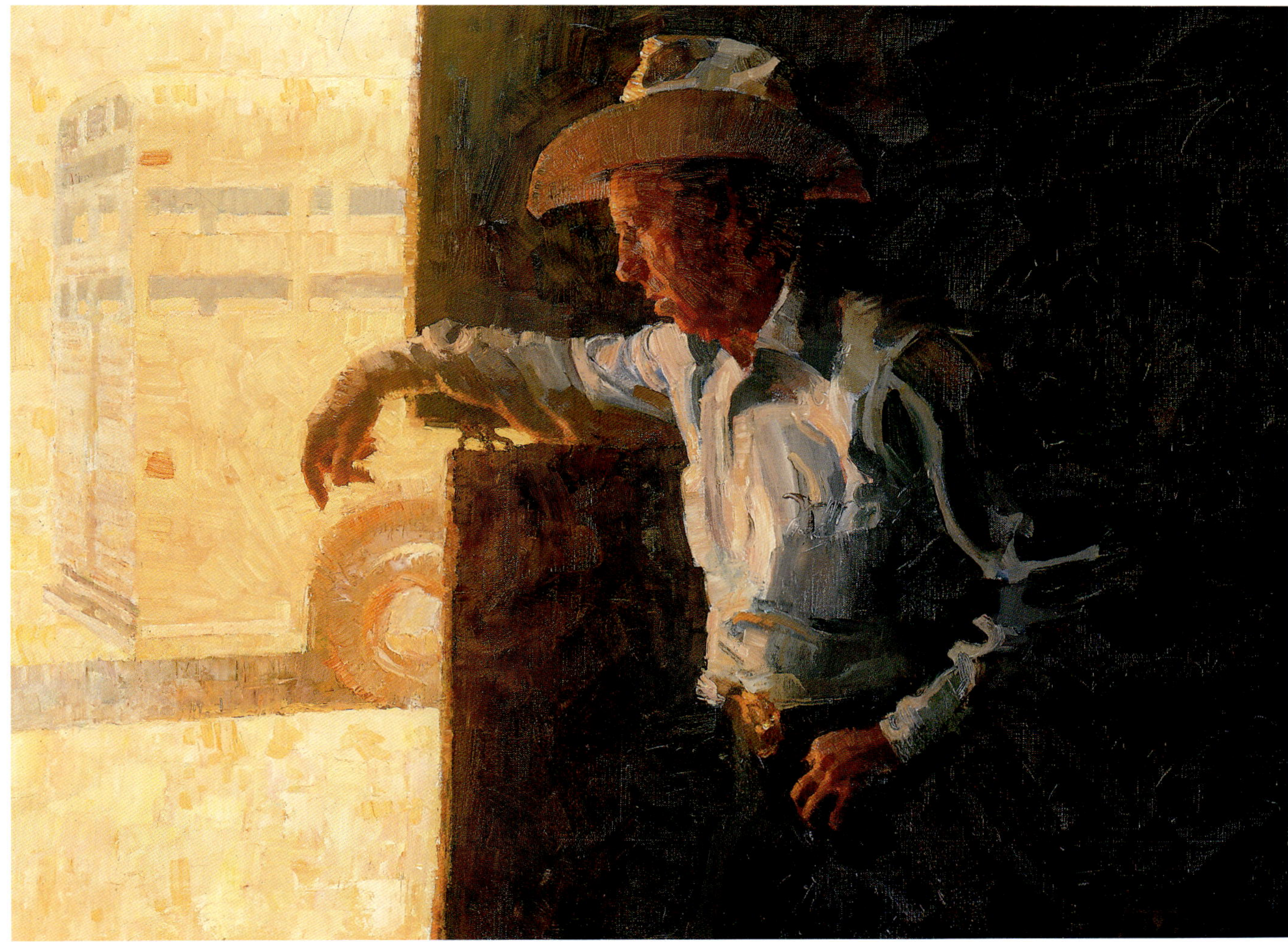

Cotton Grey, o/c, 24×30, 1982

Collection of Mr. and Mrs. Cotton Grey

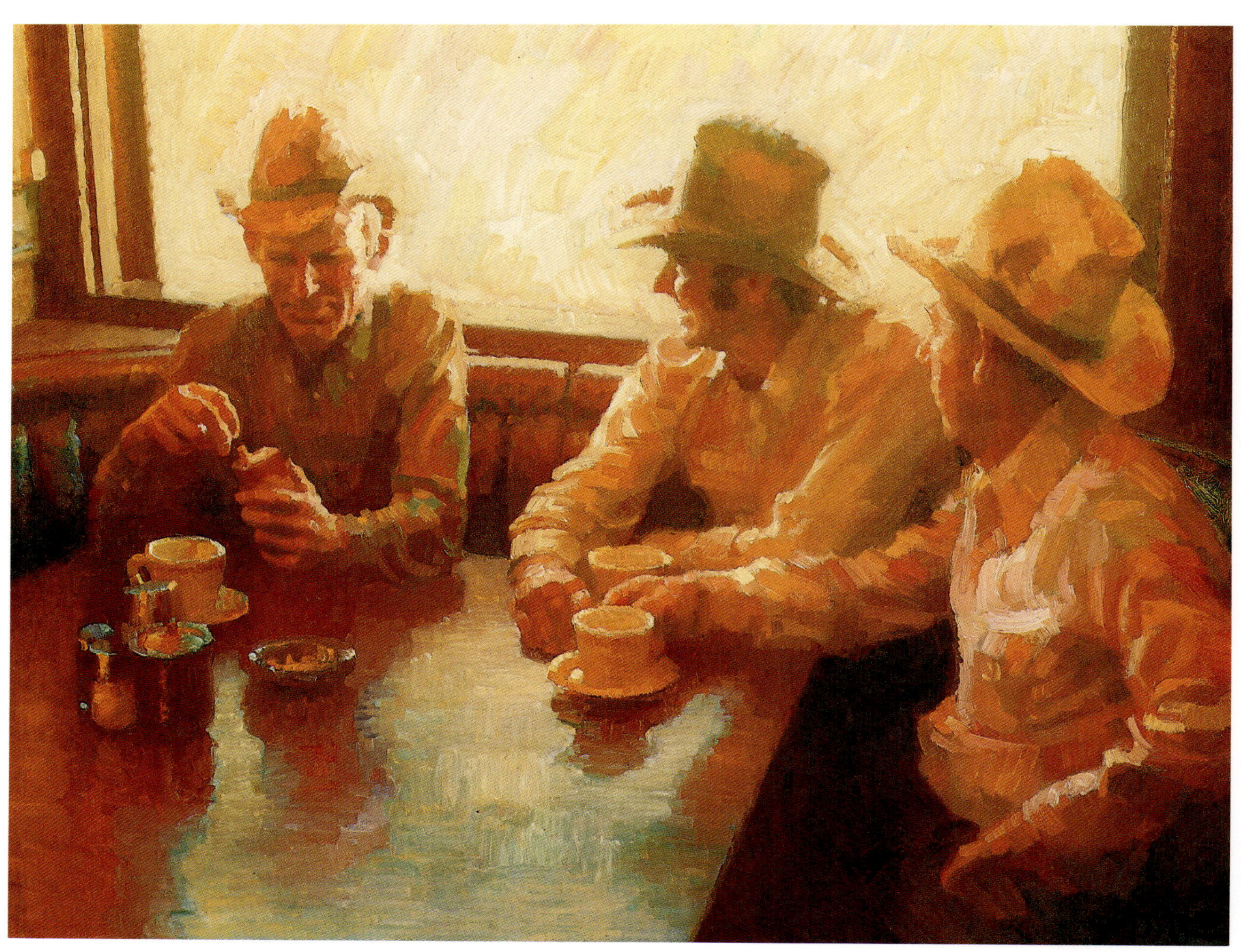

Caffeine, Nicotine, and Cowboys, w/c, 24×30, 1982

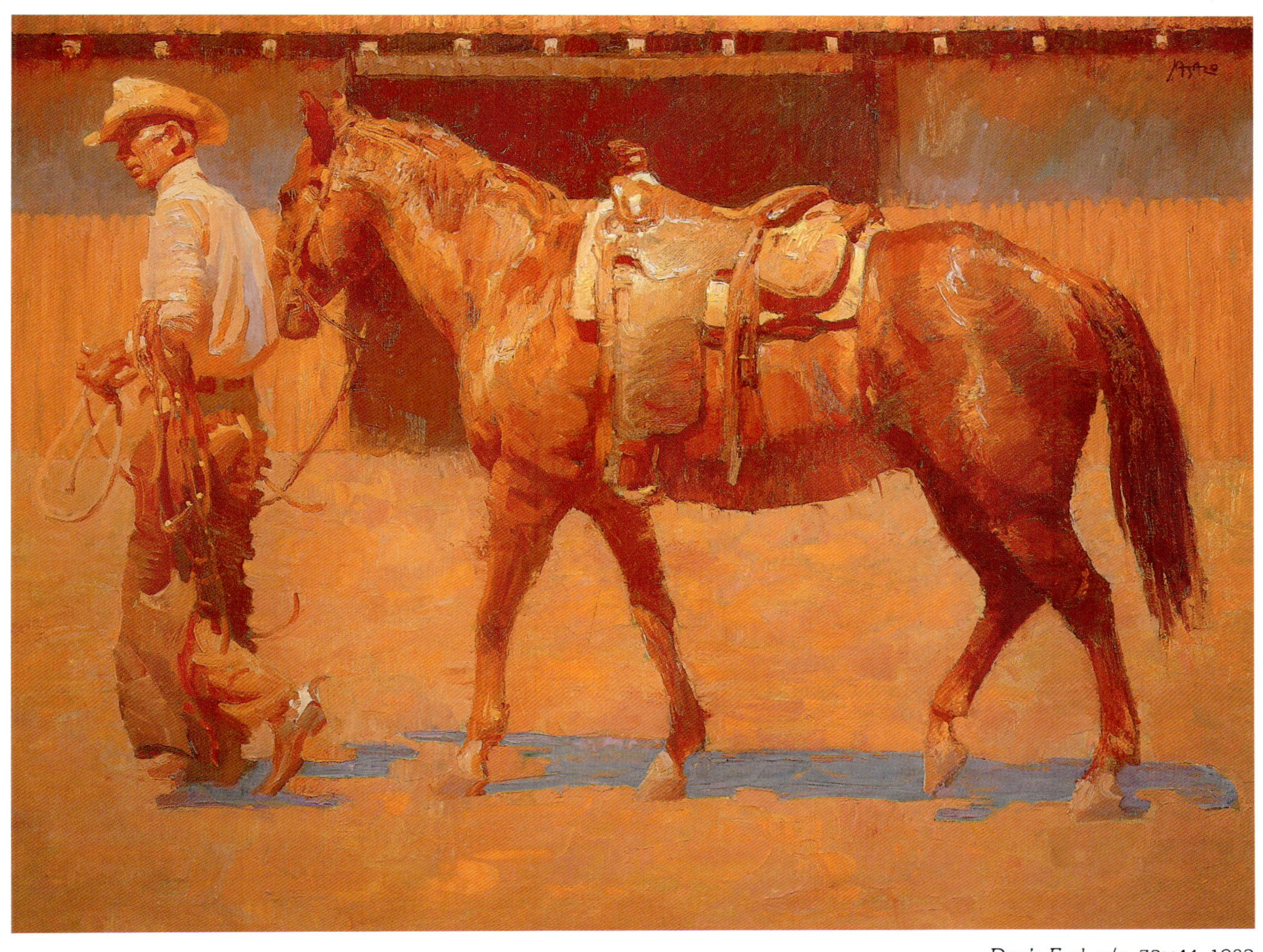

Day's End, o/c, 32×44, 1982

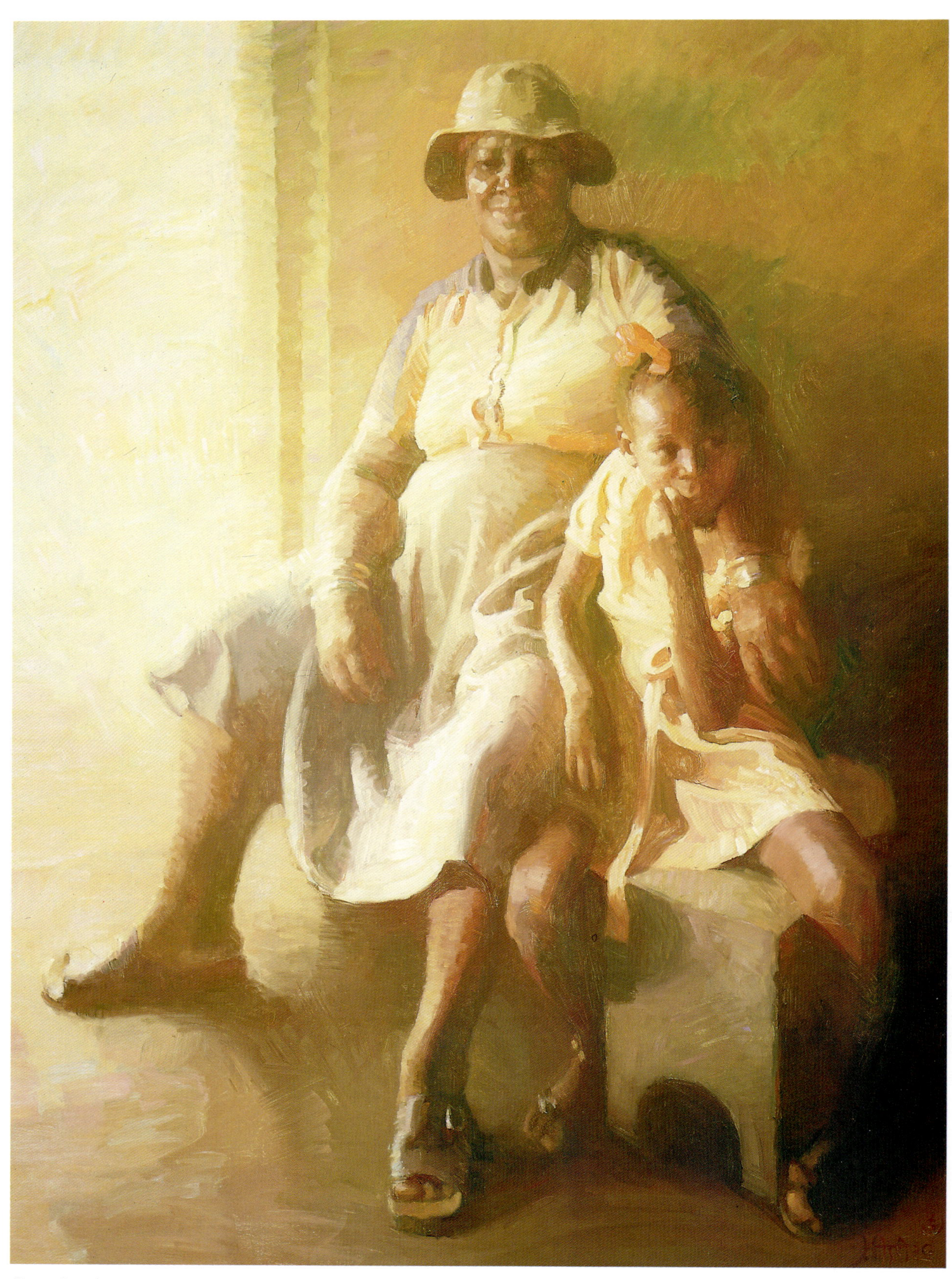

Grenada, o/c, 44×34, 1983

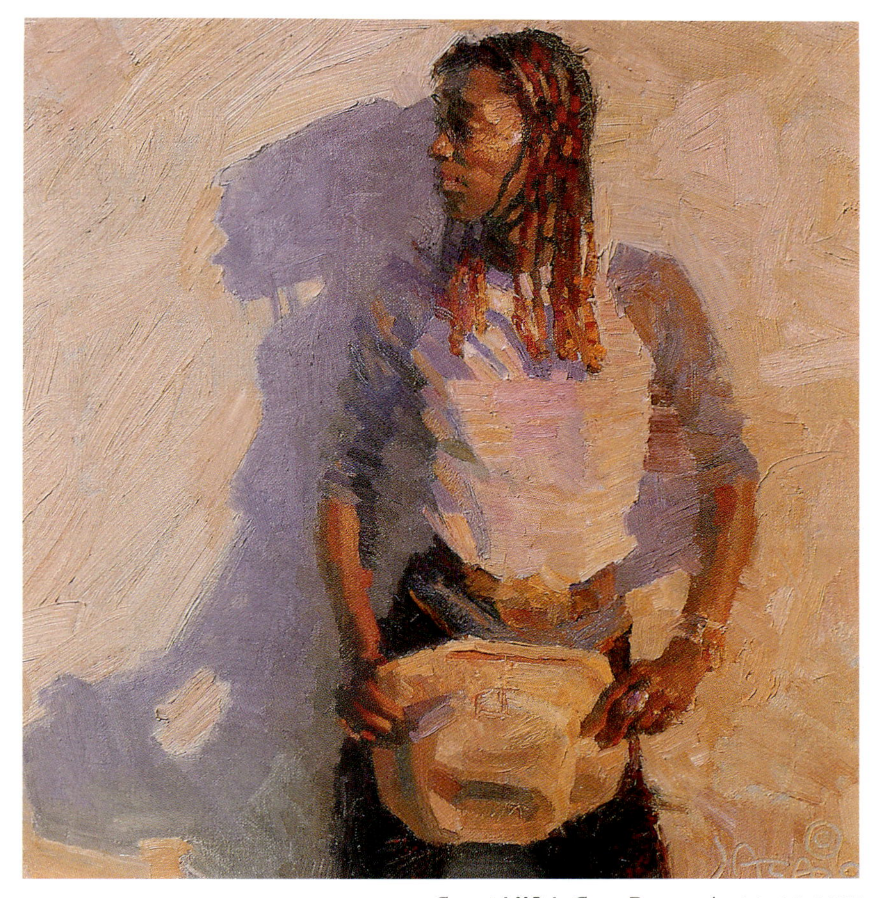

Cowgirl With Corn Rows, o/c, 14×14, 1983

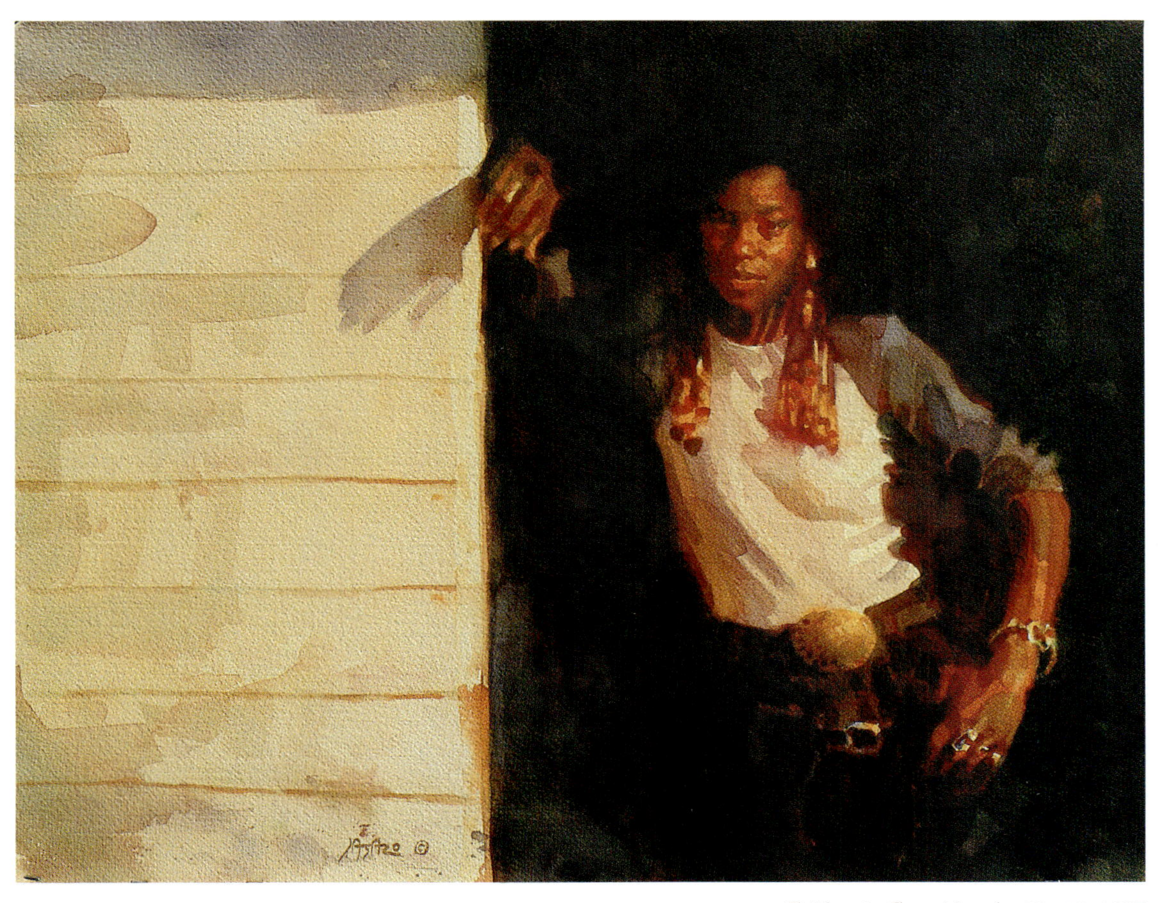

California Cowgirl, w/c, 20×26, 1983

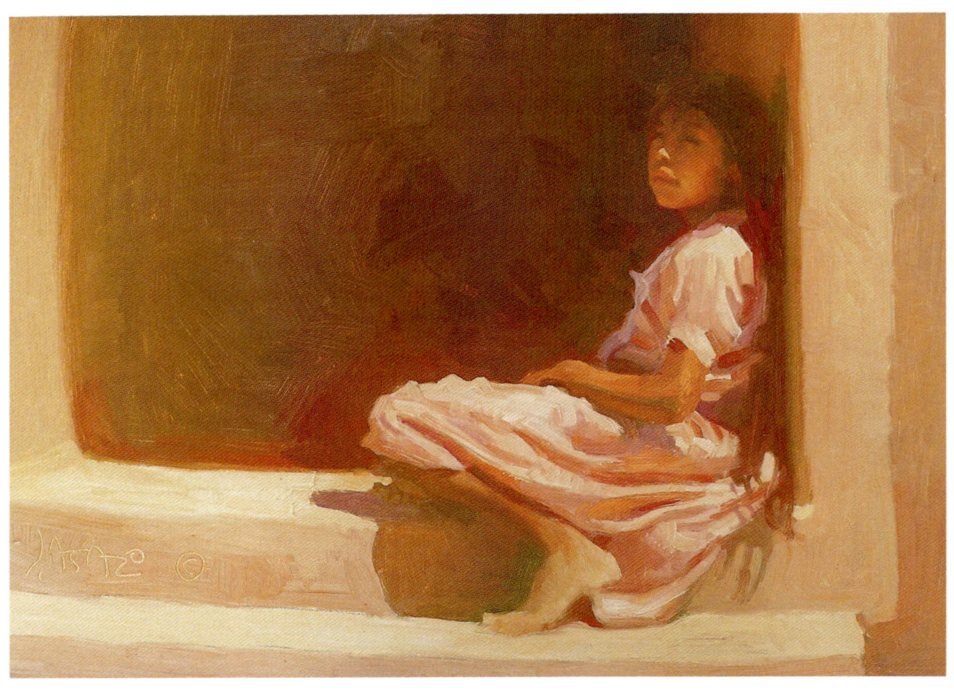

Oaxaca Girl, o/c, 12×14, 1984

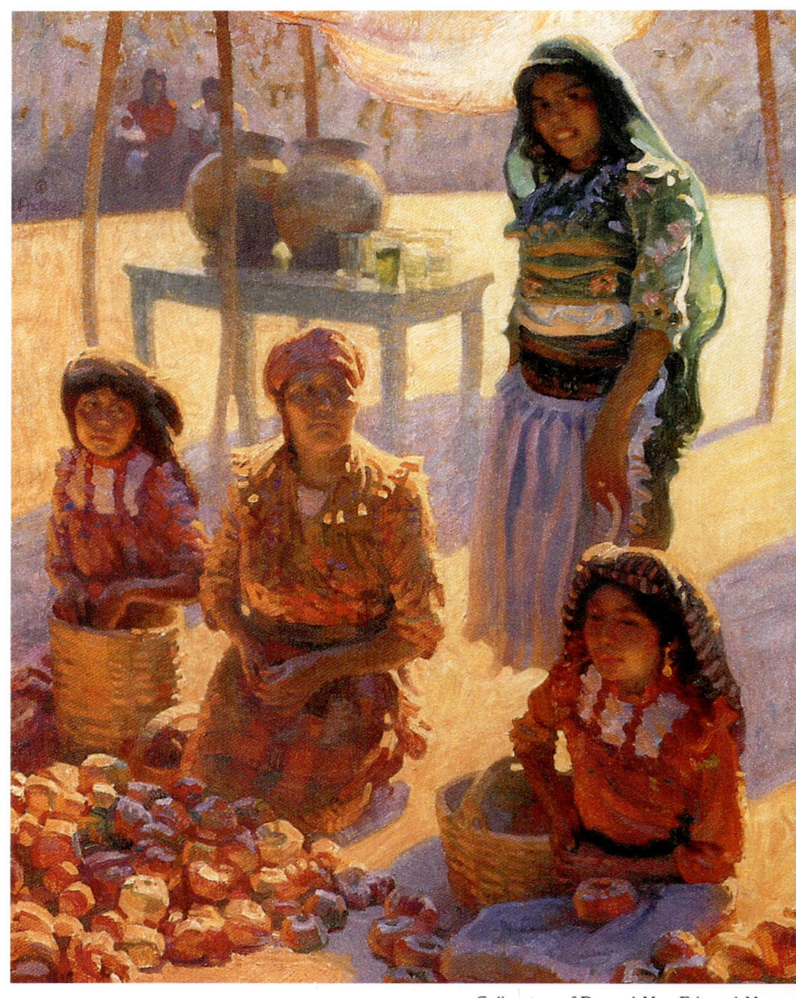

Women of Tlacolula, o/c, 44×36, 1983   Collection of Dr. and Mrs. Edward Marron

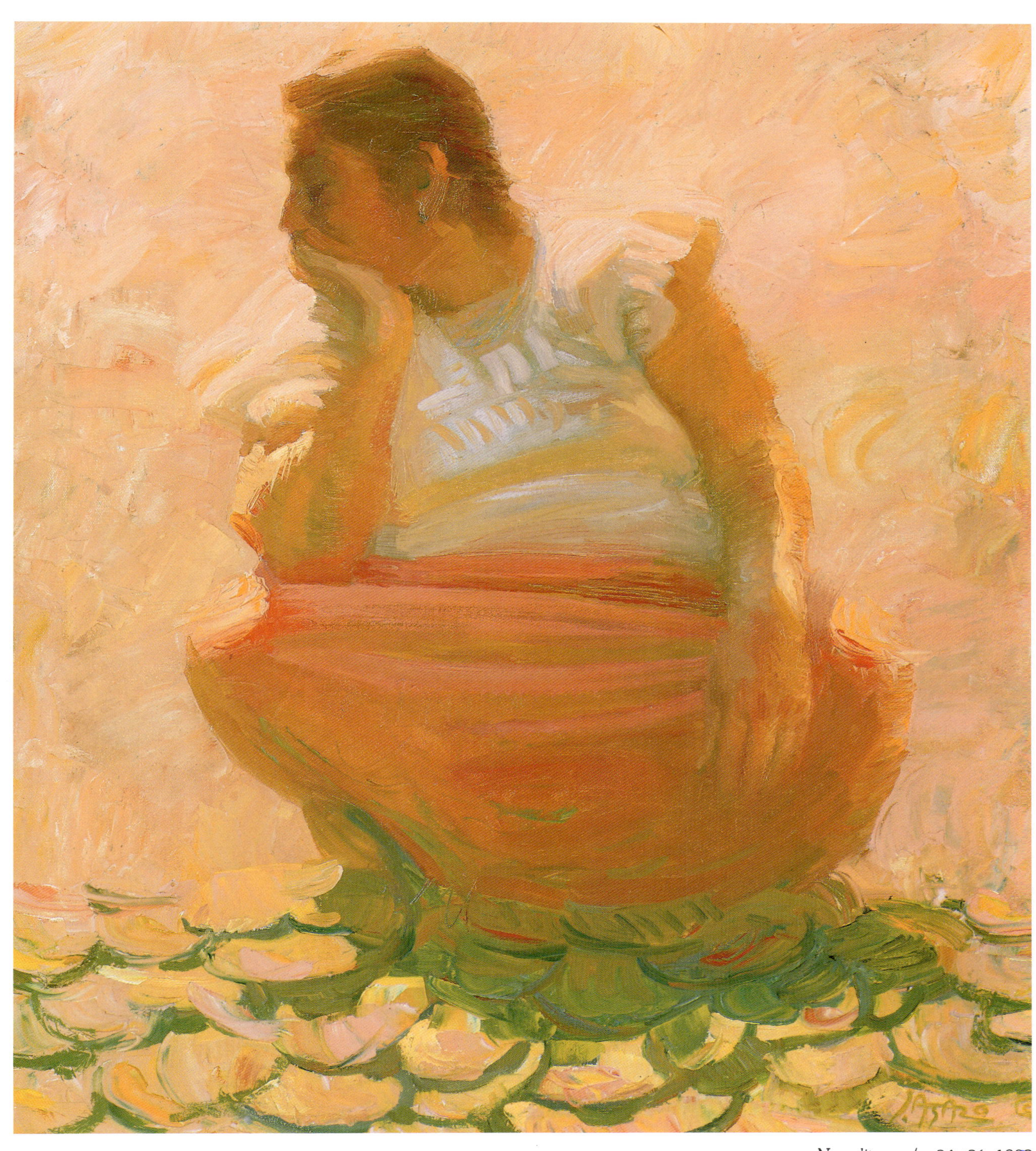

Nopalitos, o/c, 24×26, 1982

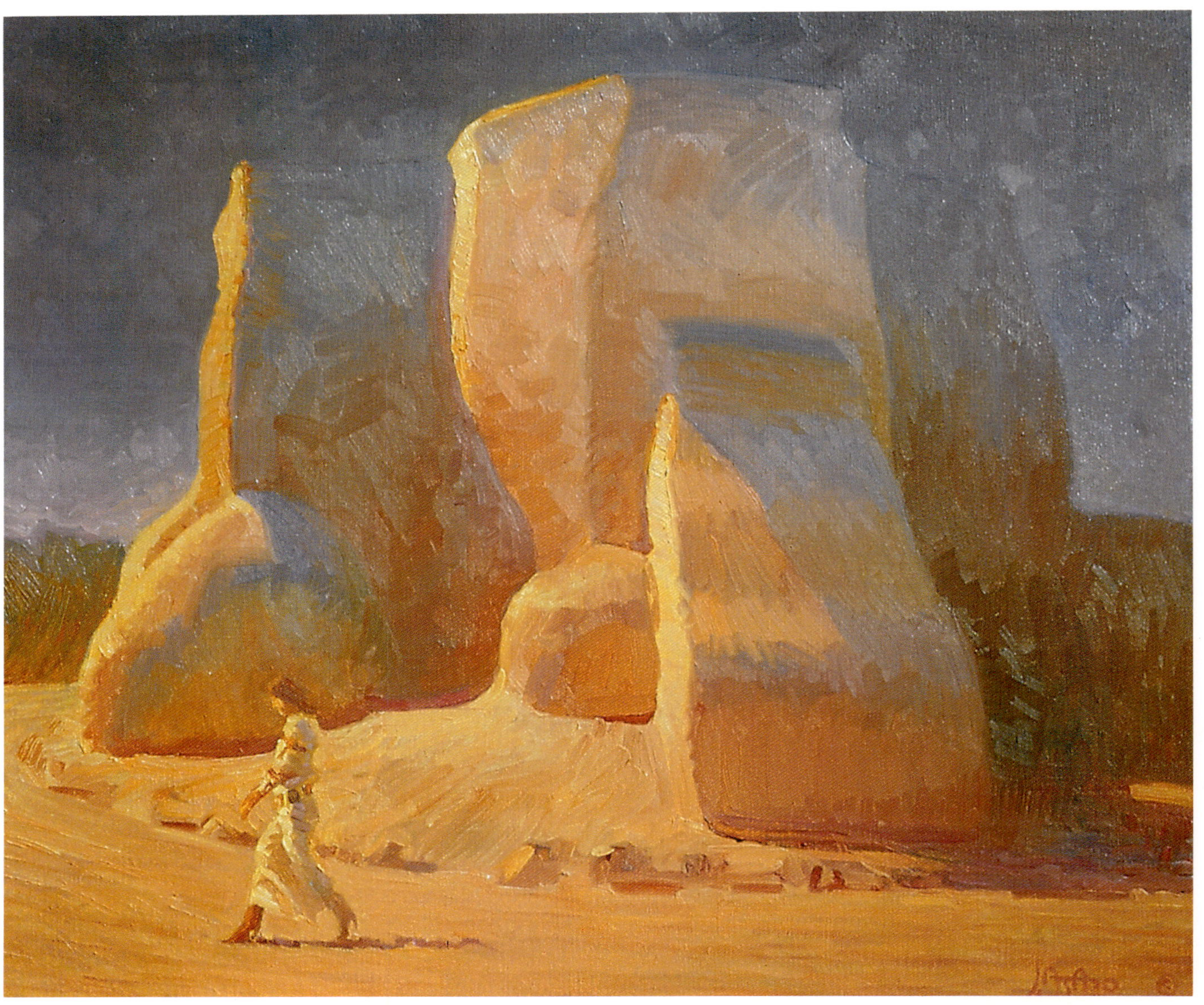

Ranchos Church, o/c, 22×26, 1983

Collection of Ronald and Judy Yordi

52

John Asaro

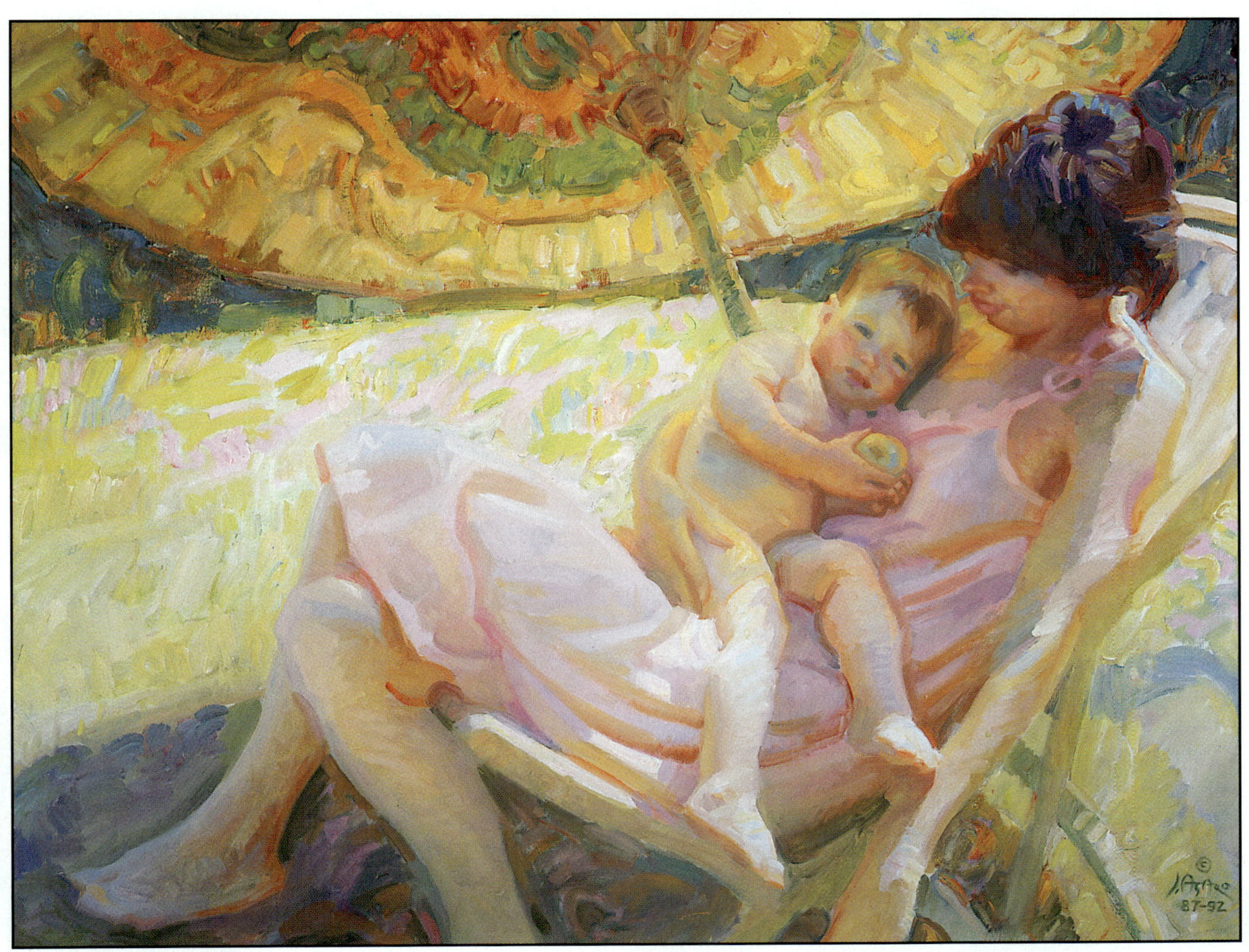

"Chinese Umbrella"

Original Limited Edition Serigraph. Signed and numbered by Master Impressionist John Asaro.
Image Size: 35" X 26" Edition: 1/195

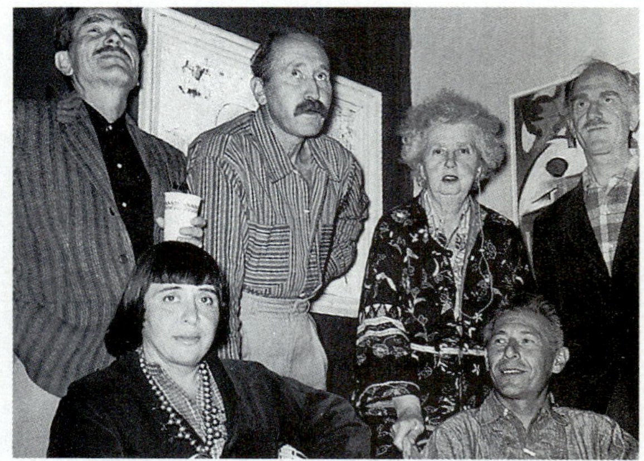

Louis Ribak, Beatrice Mandelman, Alfred Rogoway, Dorothy Brett, Ted Egri & Clay Spohn

important volume covering a significant chapter in American art history.

California Collects

The Pacific Ocean might have first commanded the attention of visitors to Laguna Beach, CA, but eventually the town turned into a mecca for art. In the exhibition *75 Works, 75 Years* the Laguna Art Museum celebrates the city's colorful history since its inception in 1918.

Numerous artists were drawn to the coastal village of Laguna Beach in the early 20th century, among them Edgar Payne. In the early summer of 1918 Payne promoted the idea of converting the old Laguna Beach town hall into an art gallery. The first exhibition there drew 2,000 visitors in the first three weeks, a response so overwhelming that the organizing artists created the Laguna Beach Art Association, making the gallery an institution. With 150 charter members, the LBAA became the social center for the town as it featured changing

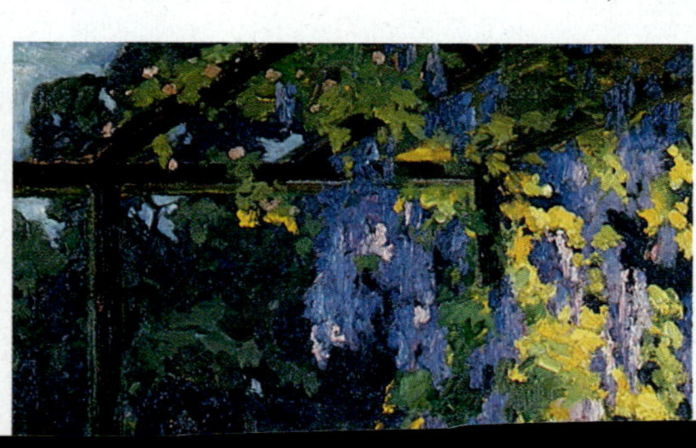

of collecting and exhibiting American art, with an emphasis on California art. On display April 2-June 16, *75 Works, 75 Years* highlights the museum's California collection and includes OUR WYSTERIA by **Jean Mannheim**. The exhibition is accompanied by a catalog.

From The Folk

Whereas we might carry a two-liter plastic jug of soda home to assuage our thirst, people in Latin American villages might tote drinking water in an earthenware jug shaped like a goat. Such decorative items whose scope exceeds function are the mark of the folk artist. Folk art is a vital expression of artists living all over Latin America, and in the exhibition *Visiones del Pueblo: The Folk Art of Latin America*, some 250 examples from 17 countries give testament to this vitality.

The exhibition was curated by Marion Oettinger of the exhibiting San Antonio Museum of Art, TX, and features a selection of objects made for ceremo-

their own communities. *Visiones del Pueblo* chronicles the Latin American folk-art expression from the 16th century to the present.

The exhibition, organized by the Museum of American Folk Art, New York, NY, is on view at SAMA through May 2. ❏

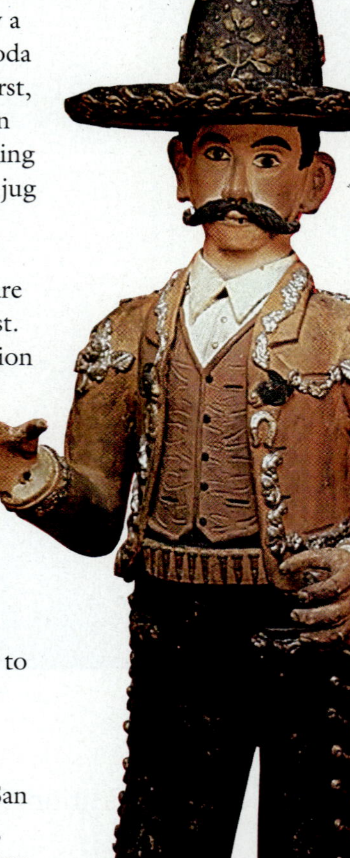

EMILIANO ZAPATA BY EULOGIO ALONZO

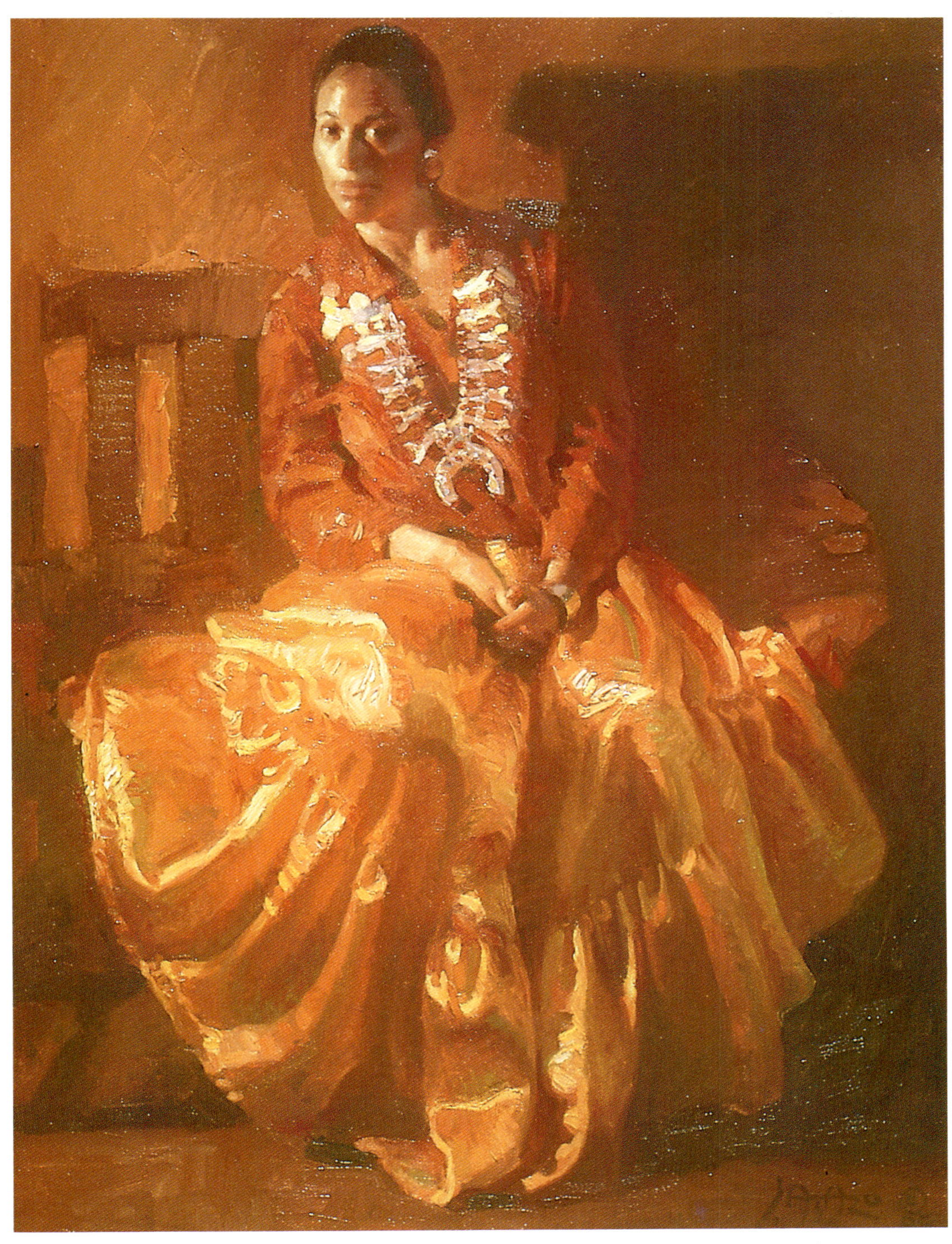

Navaho Portrait, o/c, 42×32, 1985

Dancer in Veridian, o/c, 16×18, 1982

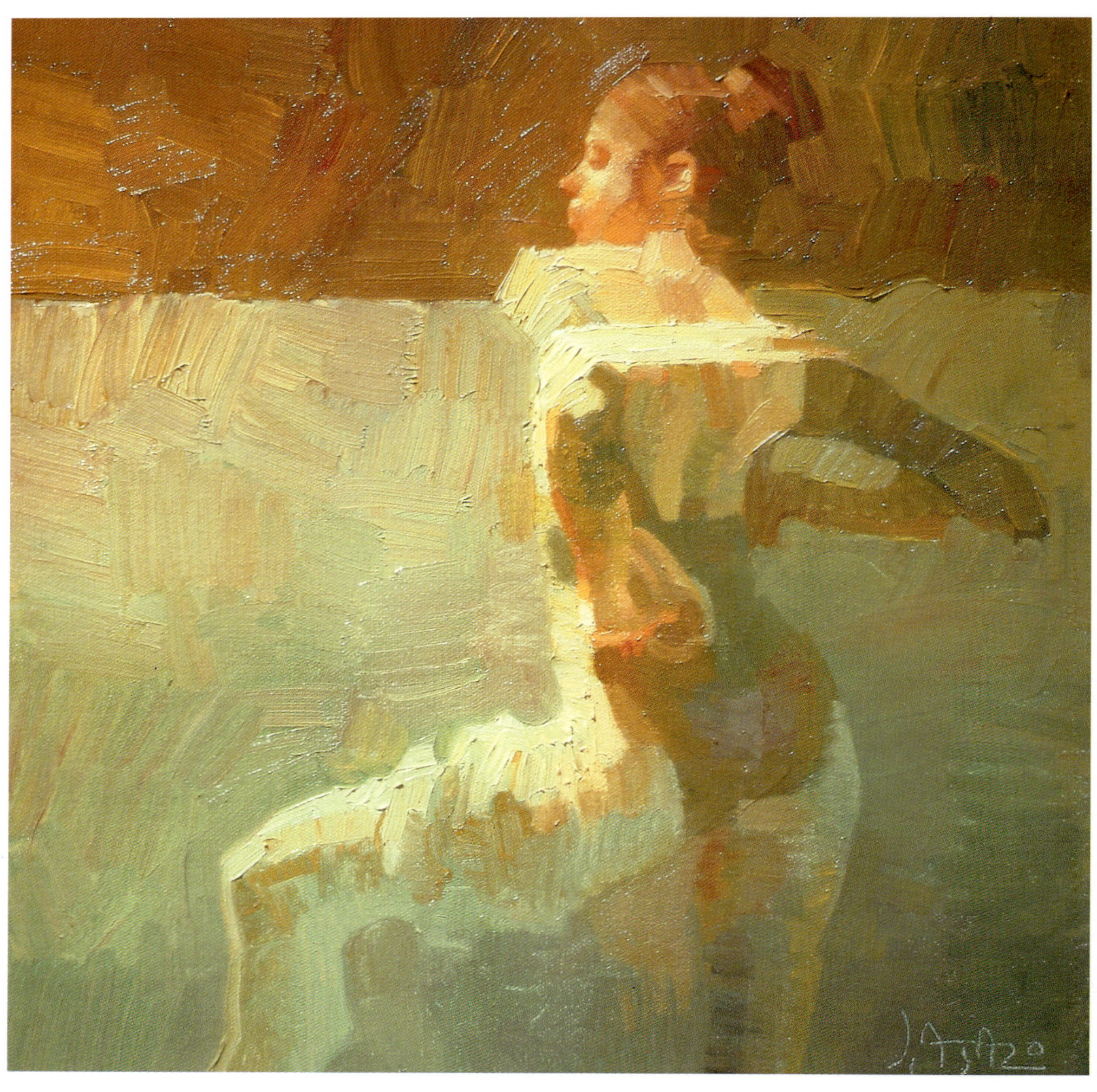

Warming Up, o/c, 24×28, 1983

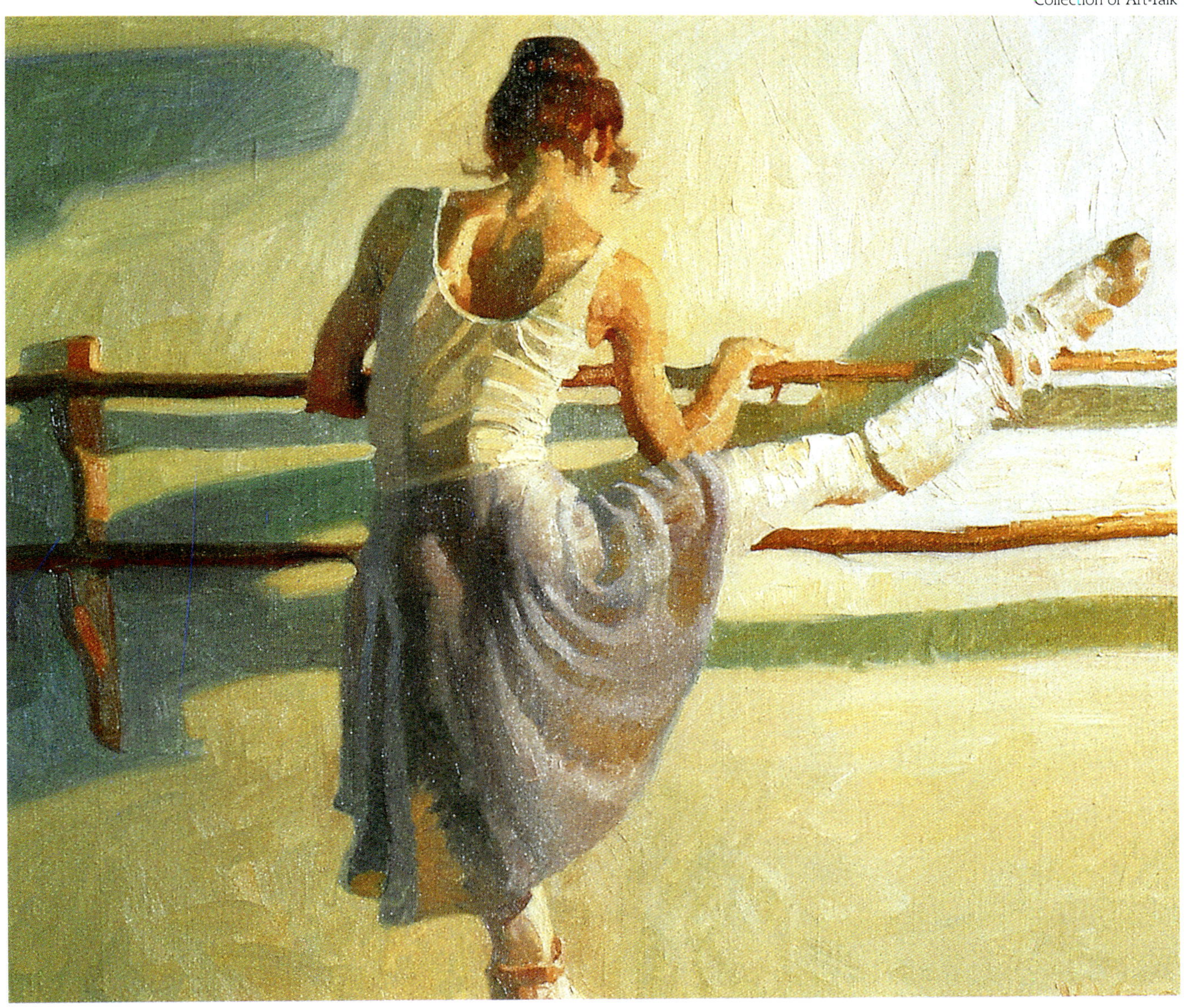

Collection of Art-Talk

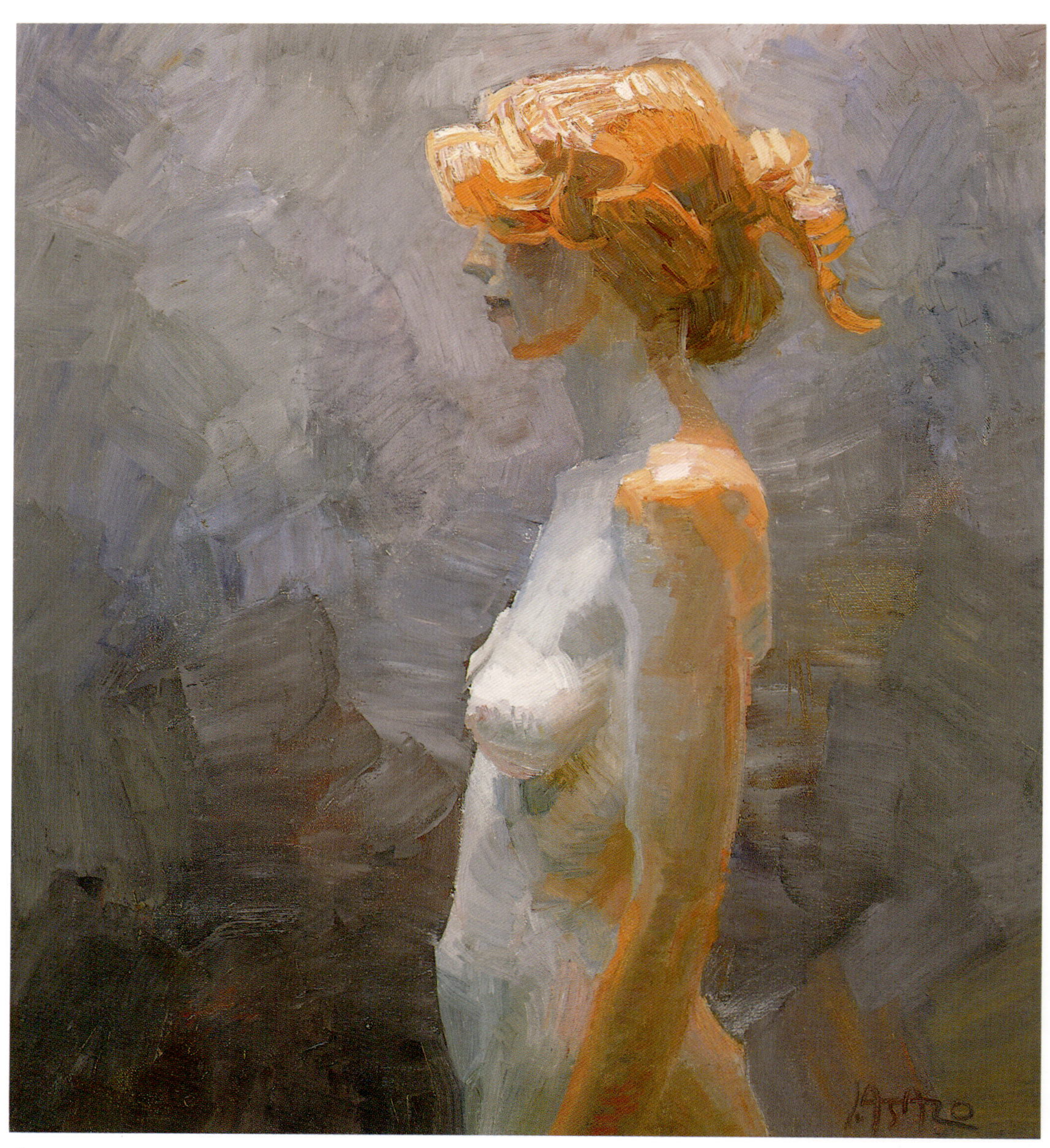

Standing Nude, o/c, 30×26, 1982

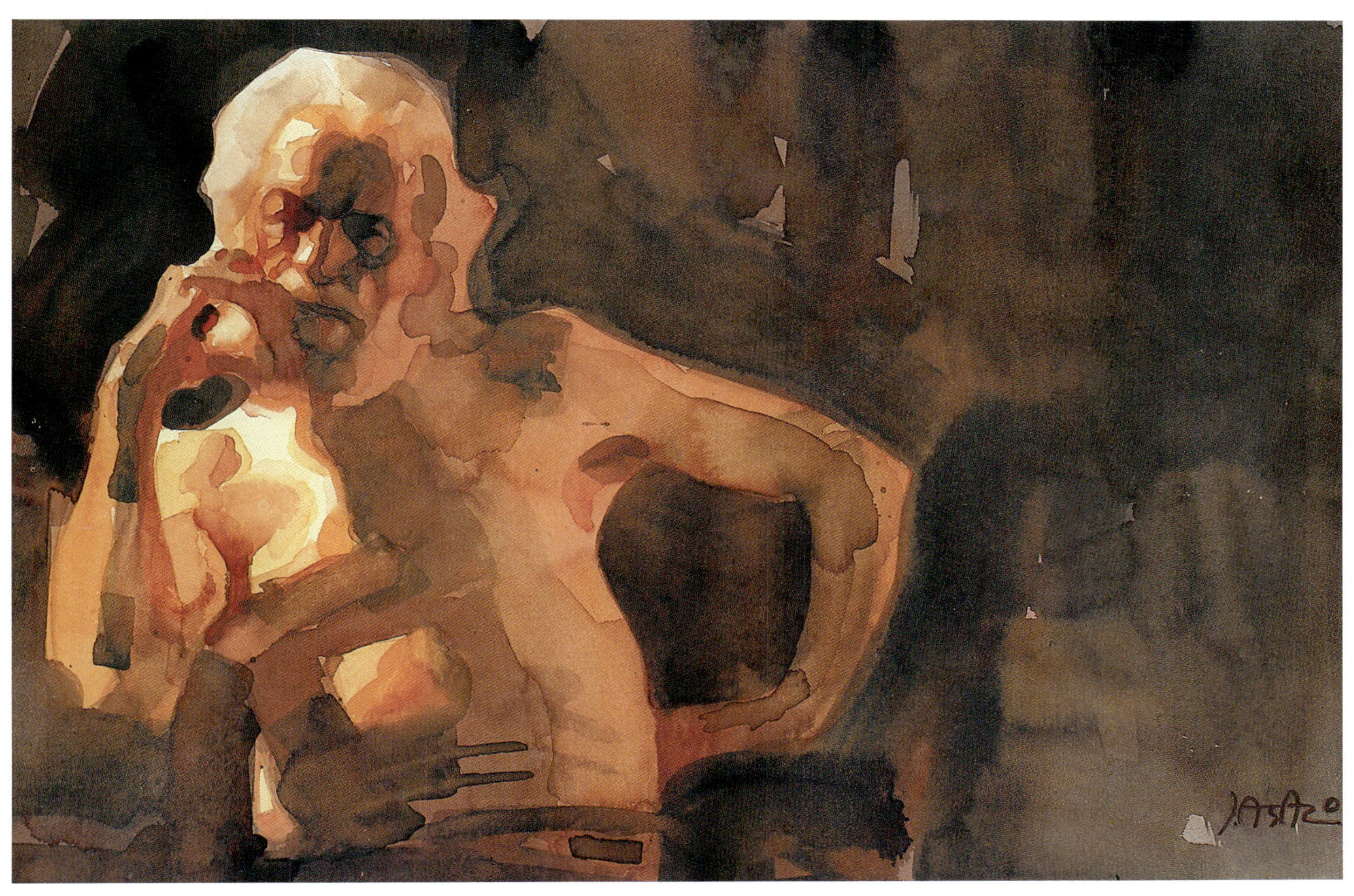

Padilla, w/c, 15×18, 1983

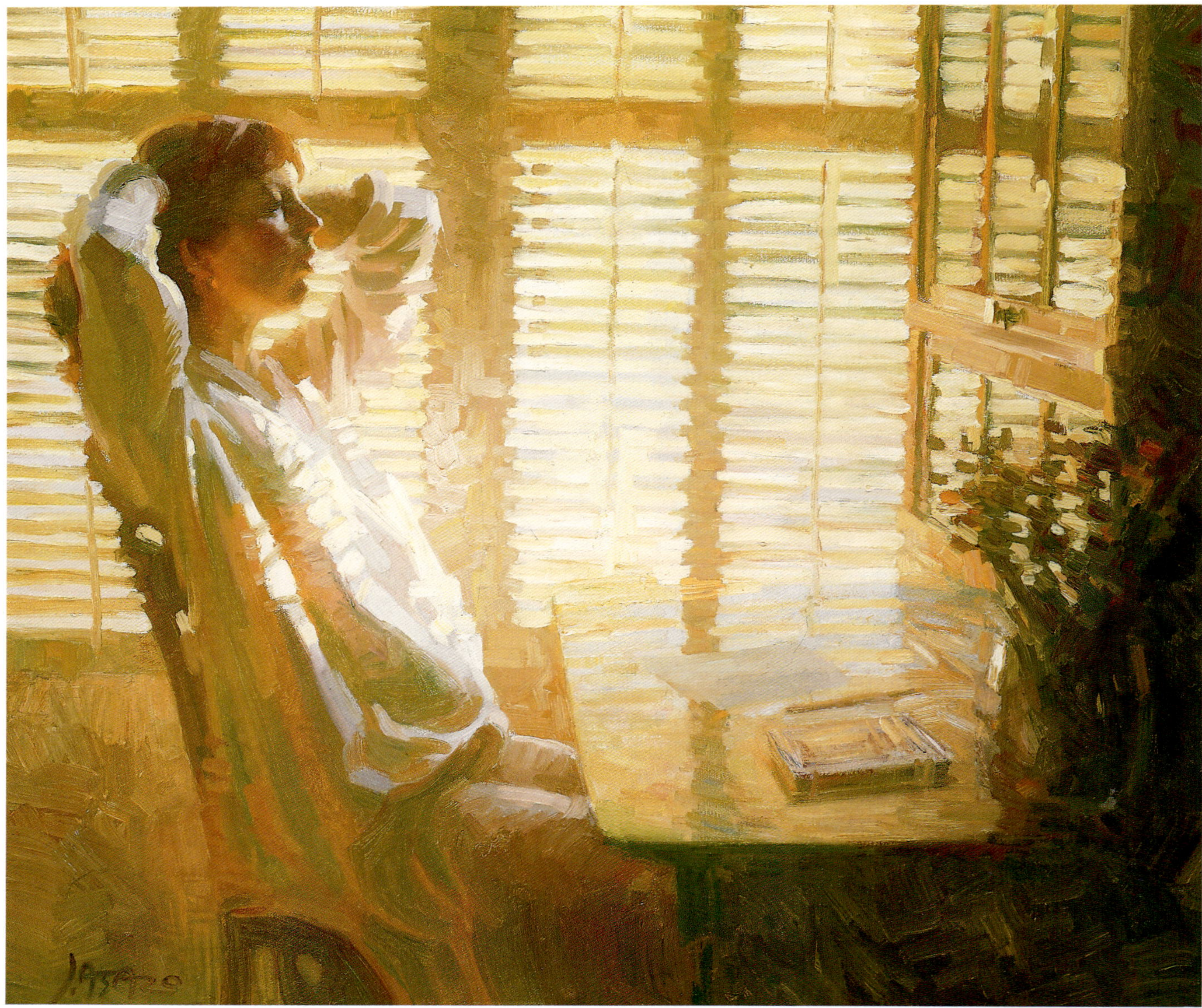

A Summer Birth, o/c, 22×26, 1982

Collection of Albert and Alice Wadle

THE ARTIST AS FAMILY MAN (1982-present)

Marriage has given John Asaro a boost he might not have expected, marking a milestone and a metomorphosis in his thinking as an artist. He characterizes this phase of his life as "happy, peaceful, even languid," and he compares himself now to Velasquez who is often portrayed as the antithesis of the neurotic, starving, self-flagelating artist. Painters assuredly have highs and lows, but Asaro – like Velasquez – may have reached a cer-

tain serenity, at least for the present. This condition, obviously, is subject to both envy and criticism. Time will be the ultimate judge.

Asaro's wife and daughters, central to his life, have hardly been ignored as subjects. Janet, Amber, and Devon are the keystones of his new, more relaxed life-style. The cherubic and voluptuous configurations of babies fascinate viewers as they do the painter. Dipped in the ocean they glitter

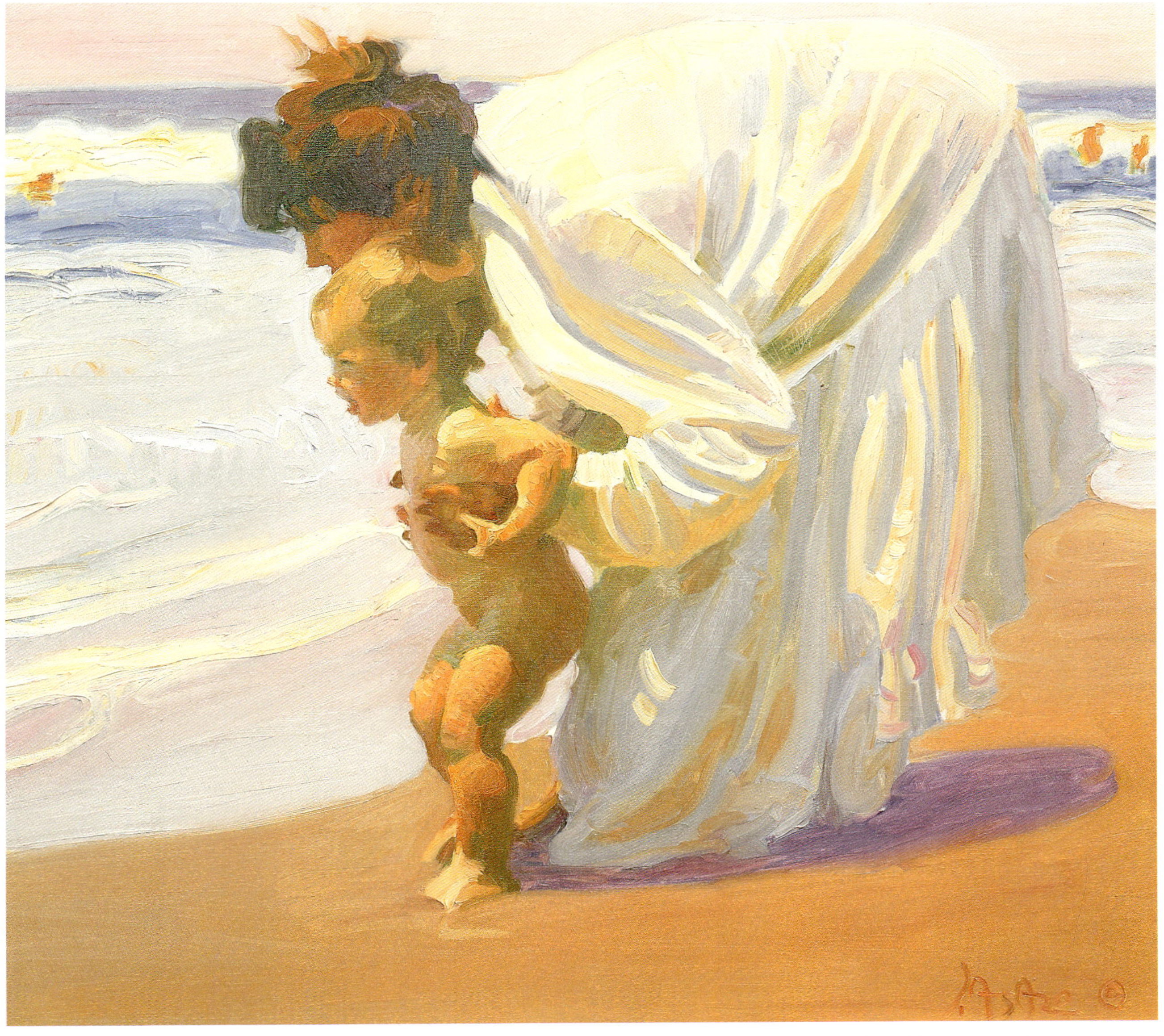

First Encounter, o/c, 30×34, 1983

like playful sea otters. As Janet holds onto her hat and watches her white gauze skirt flap with the westerly, we can almost smell the salty-sweet aroma of summer at Point Loma. In the yard they lounge peacefully among flowers and fruit, warming their bare feet on the hot sidewalk or freshly cut lawn. We might see here hints of the sentient worlds of Renoir, Monet, or even Whistler.

Who will declare that the romantic is sappy or simplistically sentimental? Perhaps only those who have never held a child or reexperienced the wonders of the world through a child's eyes. In a sense, Asaro is reaching back through the art continuum, rebelling in his own way against the relentless proliferation of eclectic modernism. His paintings can also be read as a reaction against a narcissistic, money-oriented world, a place that has become less human, less loving, lost in its complexities. As we approach another "turn-of-the-century" it may not be rash to predict a genuine revival of the figurative in painting.

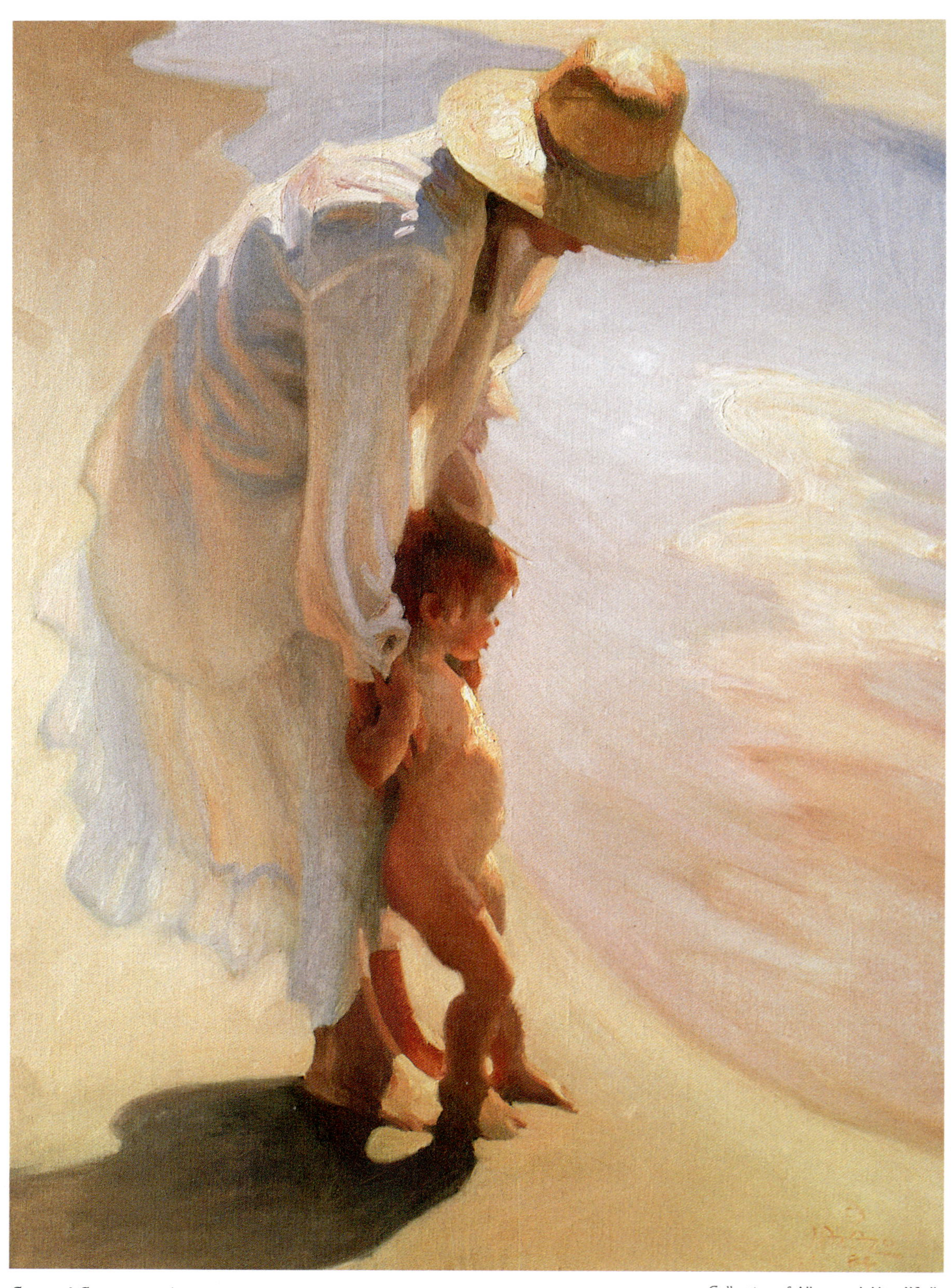

Second Summer, o/c, 48×36, 1984

Collection of Albert and Alice Wadle

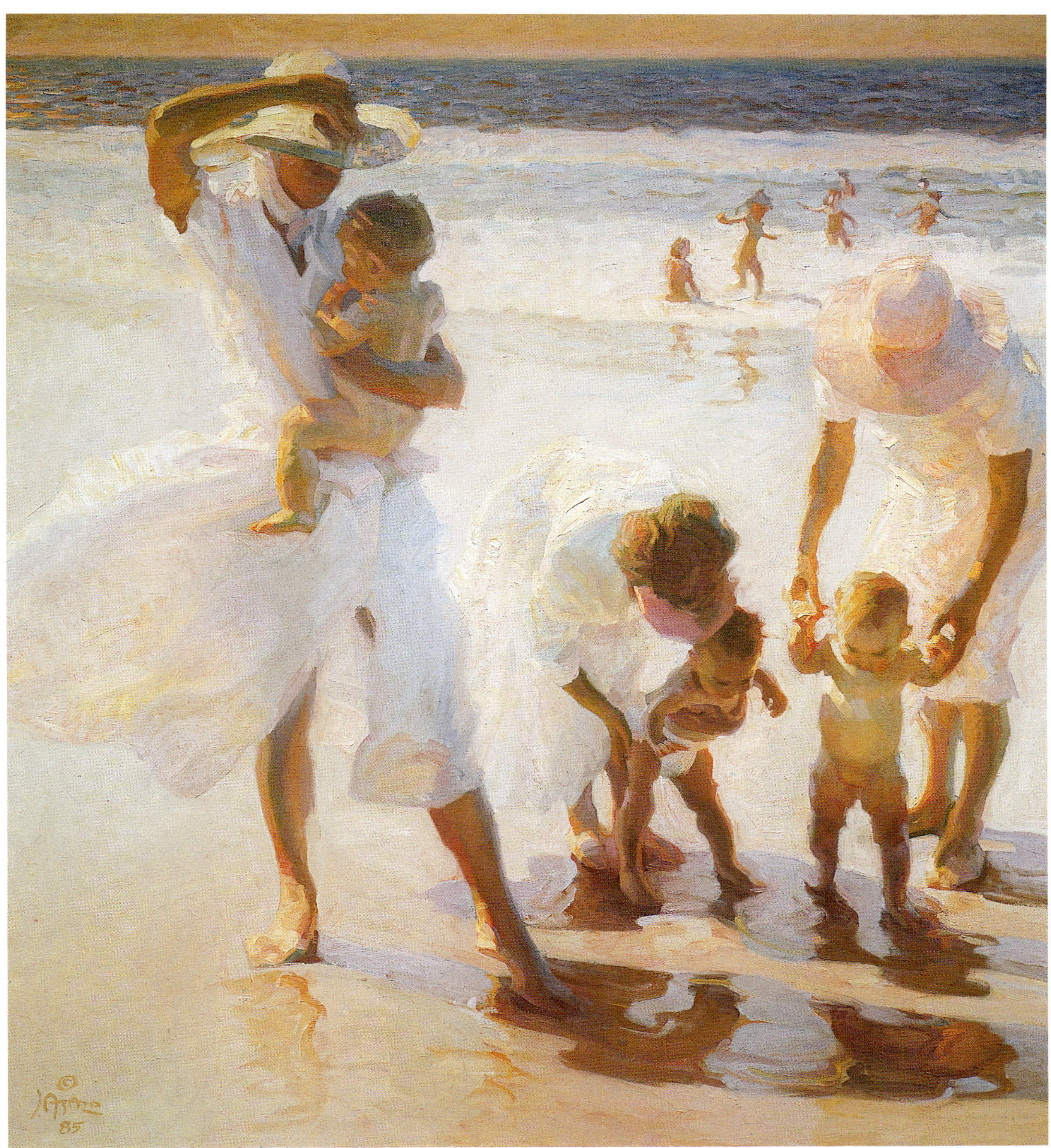

Harmony in White, o/c, 52×48, 1985

Collection of Raymond and Vicki Riley

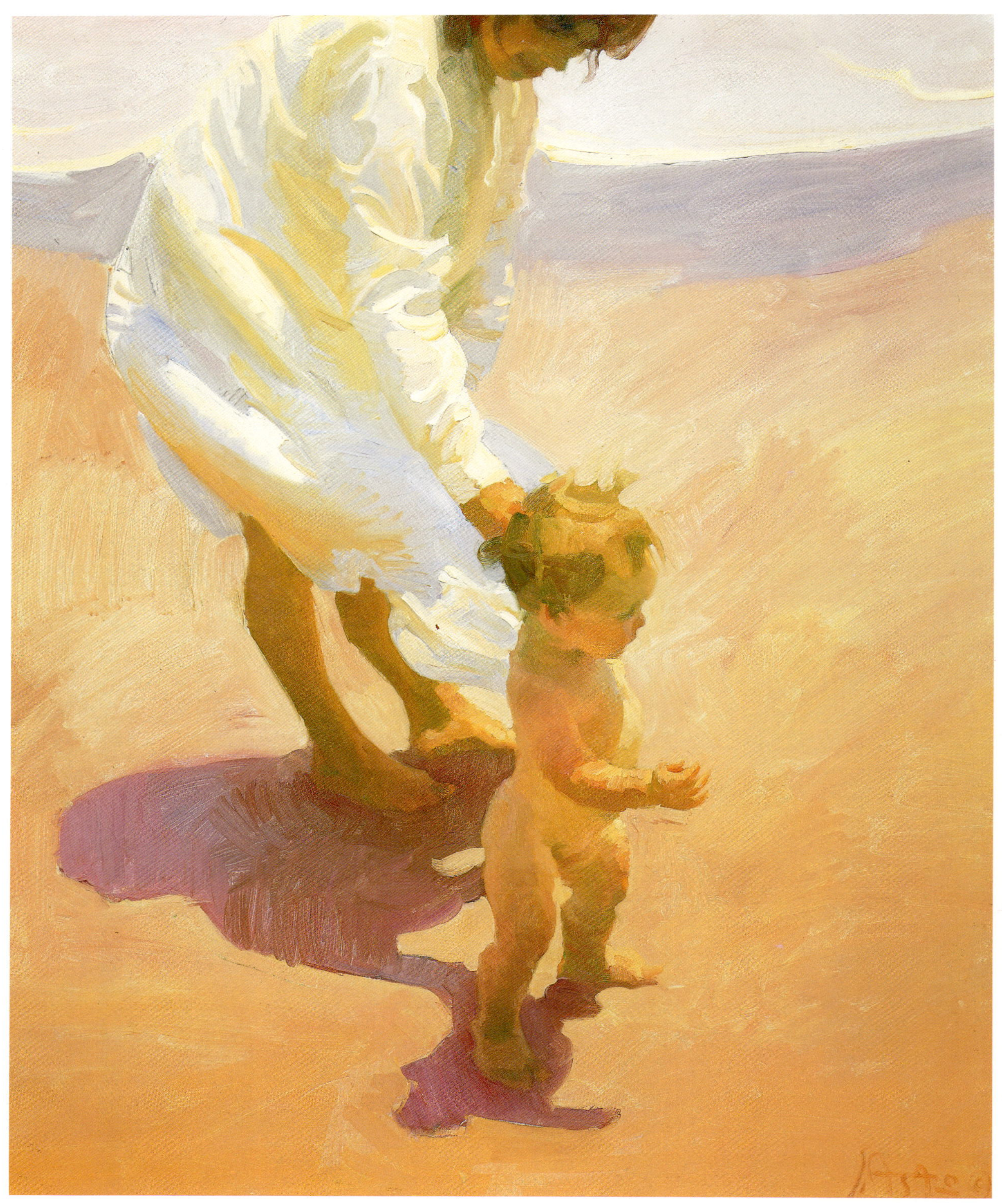

Ocean Breeze, o/c, 36×30, 1983

Collection of Jeff and Cecile Cowans

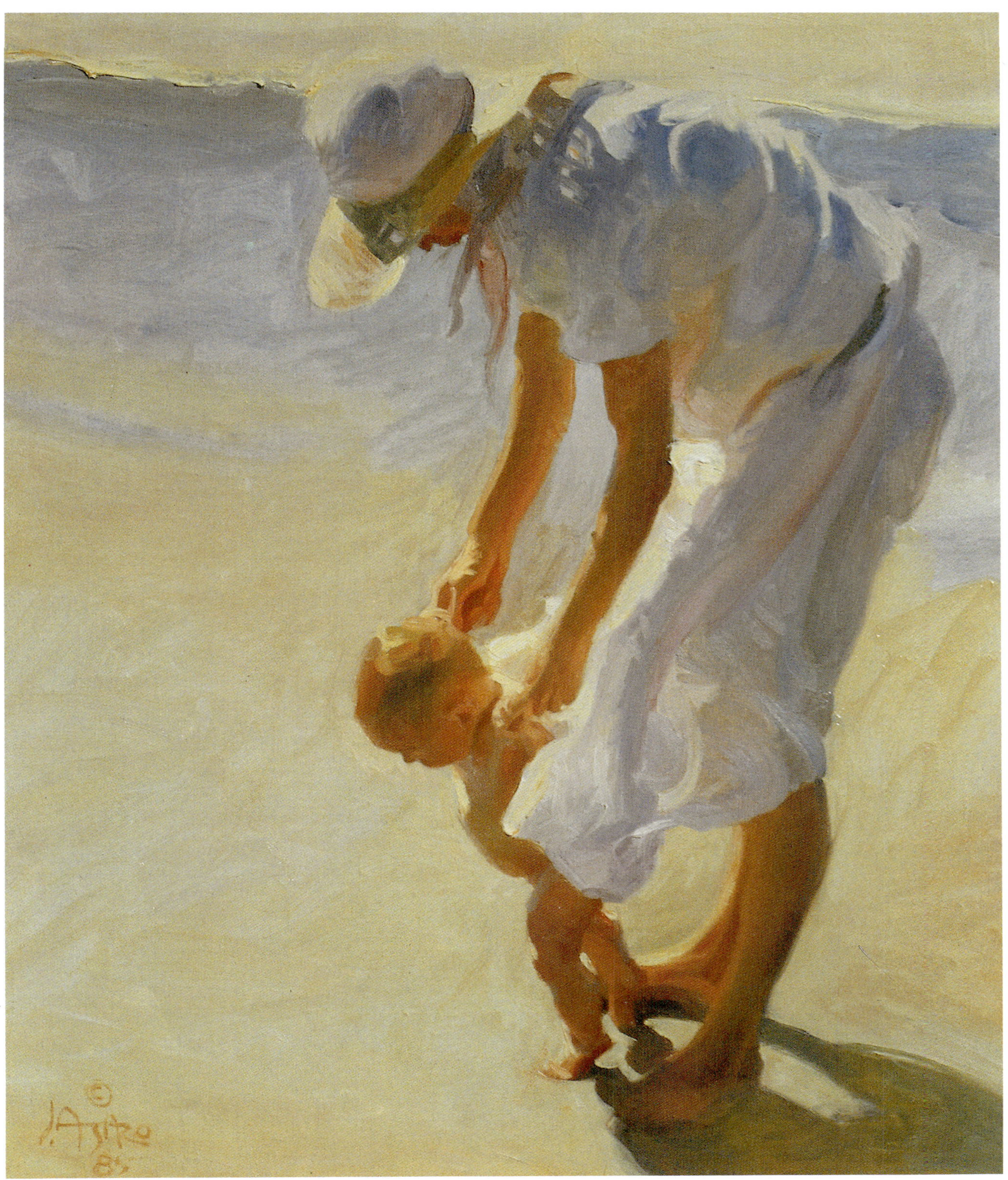

Morning Sun, o/c, 32×28, 1985

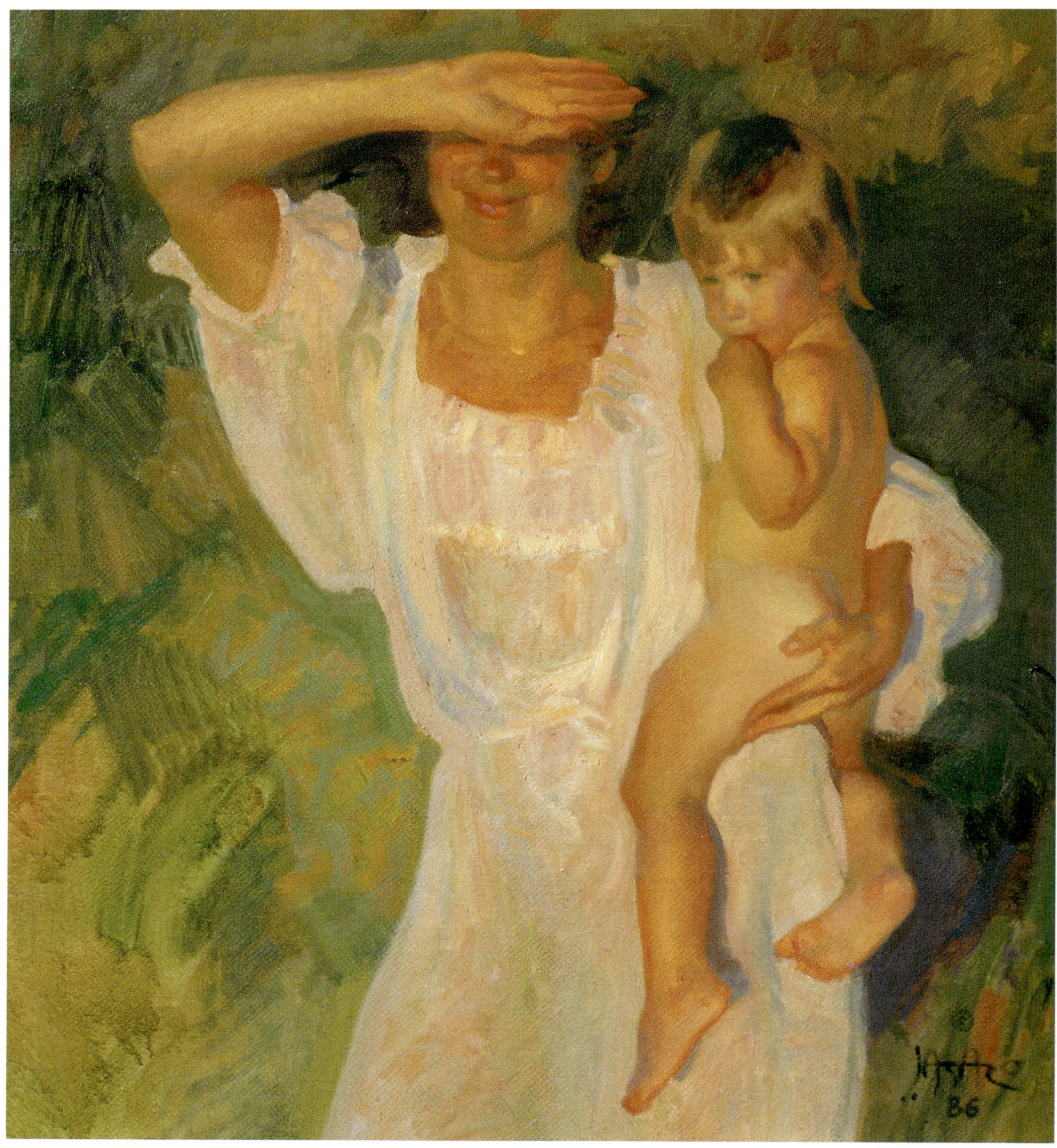

Sunset, o/c, 32×30, 1986

Collection of Warren Ross Jr. and Carole Whitney

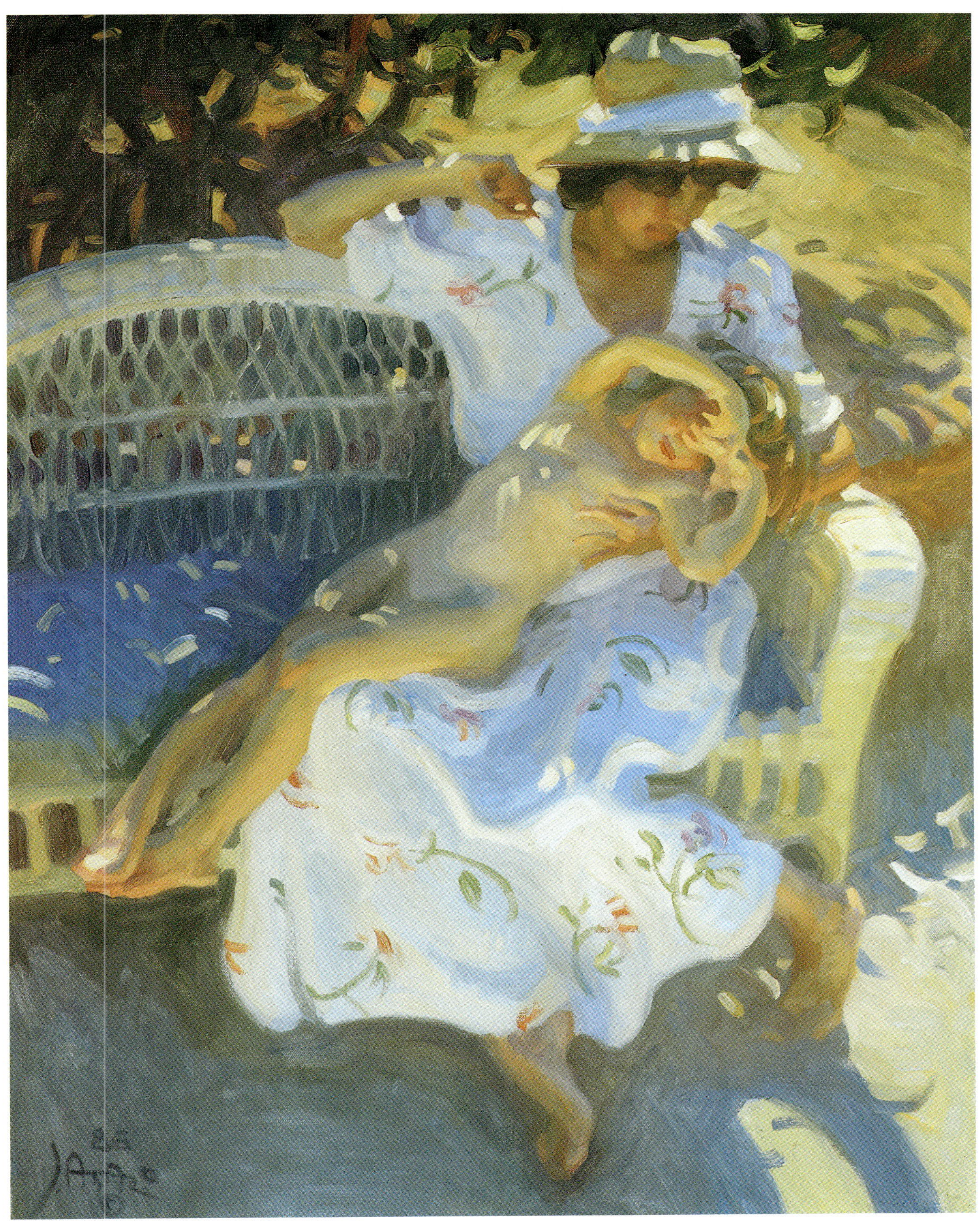

Mother's Carress, o/c, 30×24, 1986

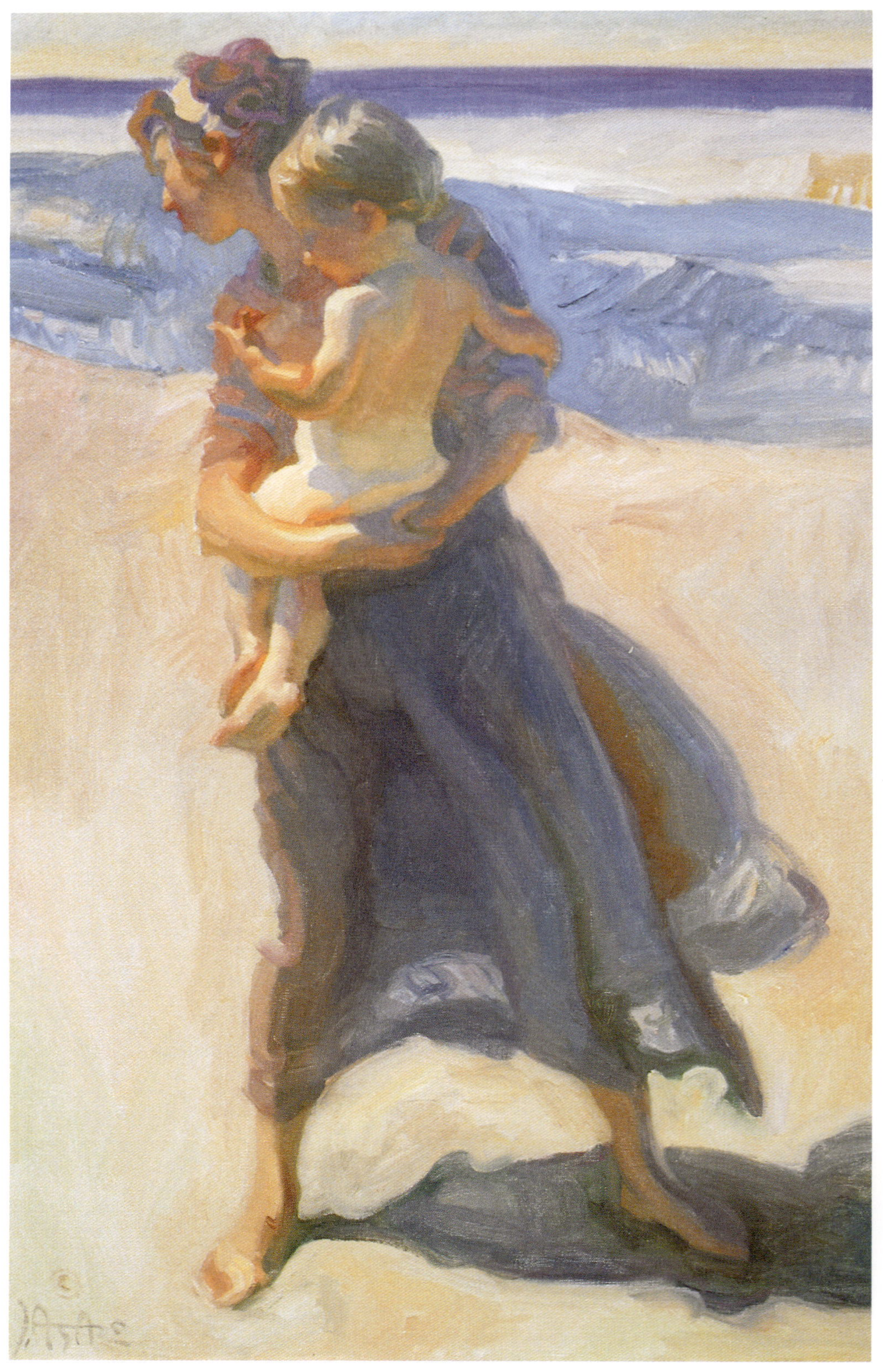

Beach at La Costa, o/c, 34×22, 1987

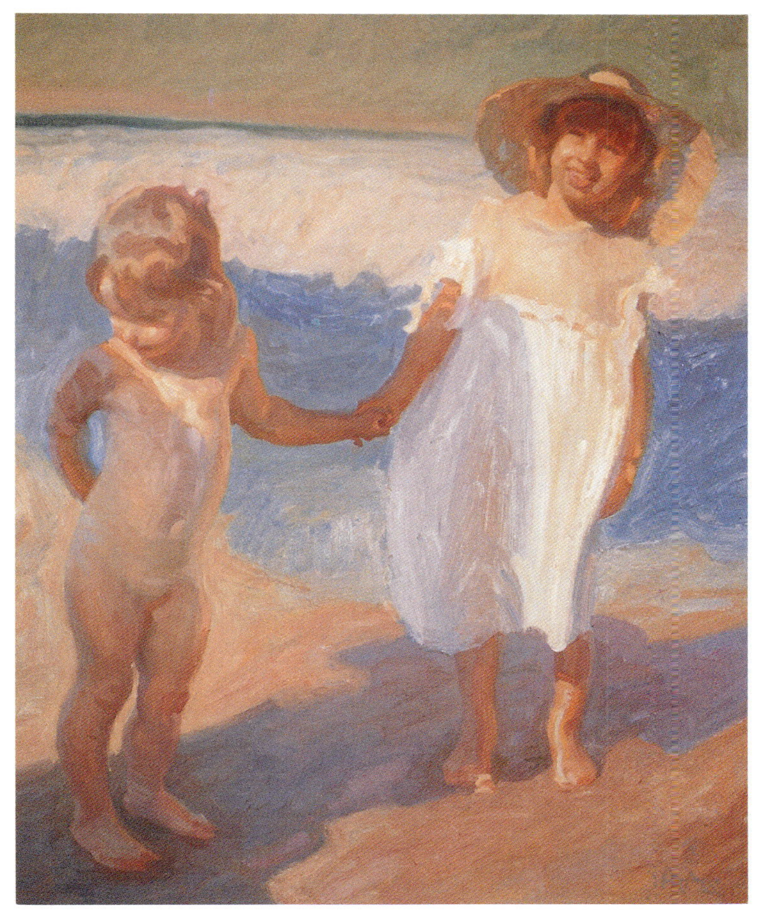

My Sister, o/c, 30×24, 1987

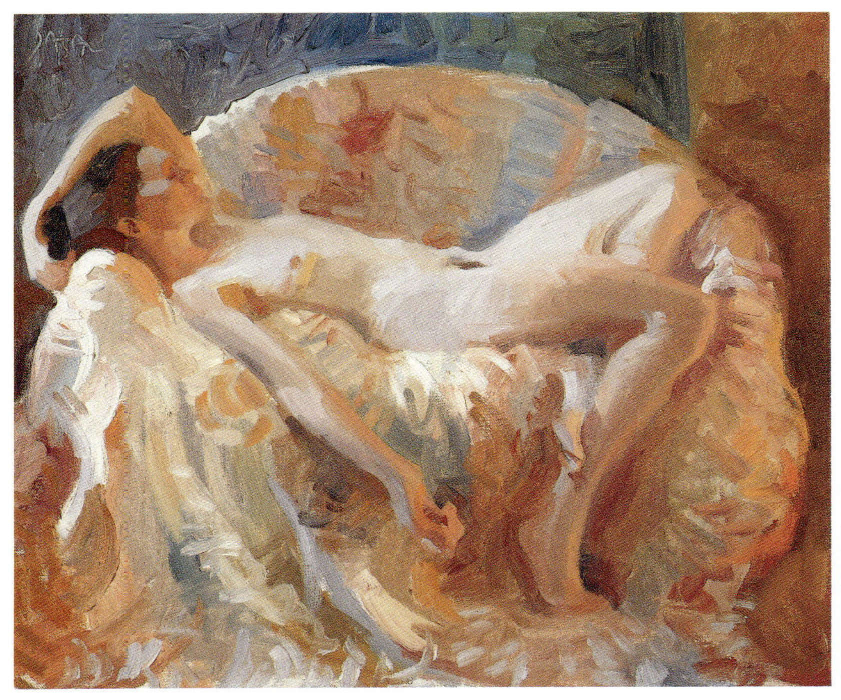

Reclining Nude VII, o/c, 16×20, 1988

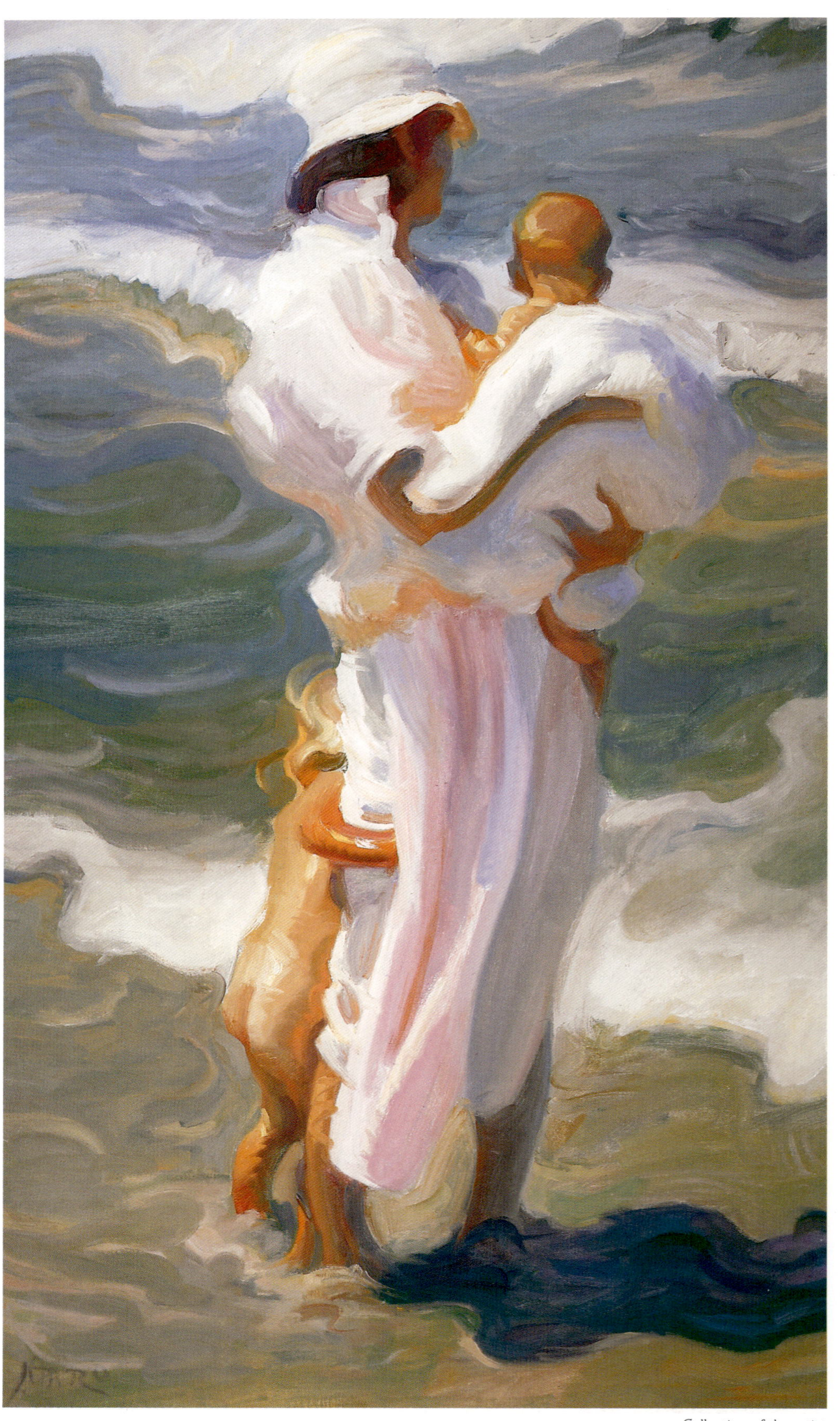

Warm Embrace, o/c, 60×36, 1988

Collection of the artist

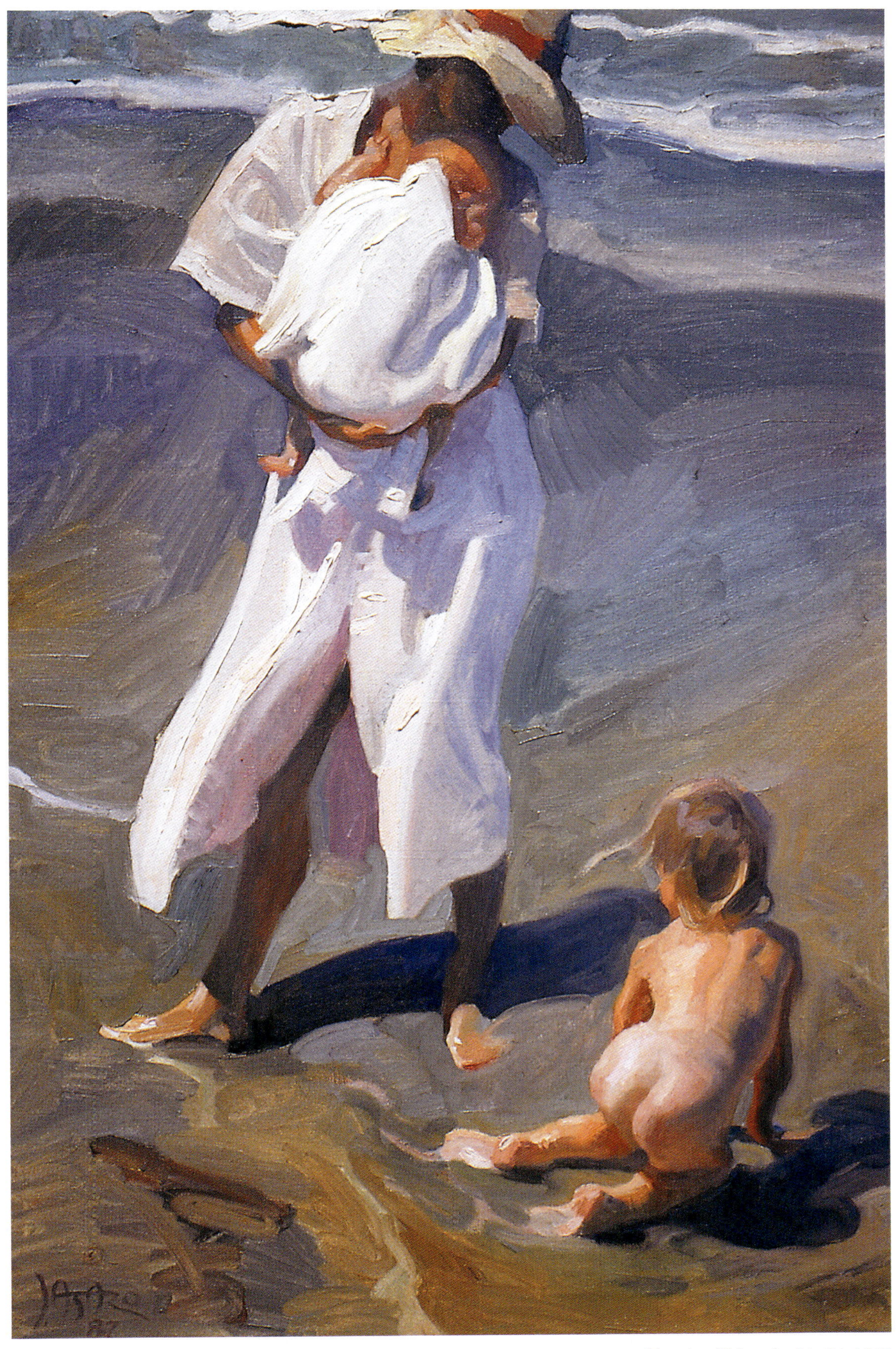

Morning Tide, o/c, 36×24, 1987

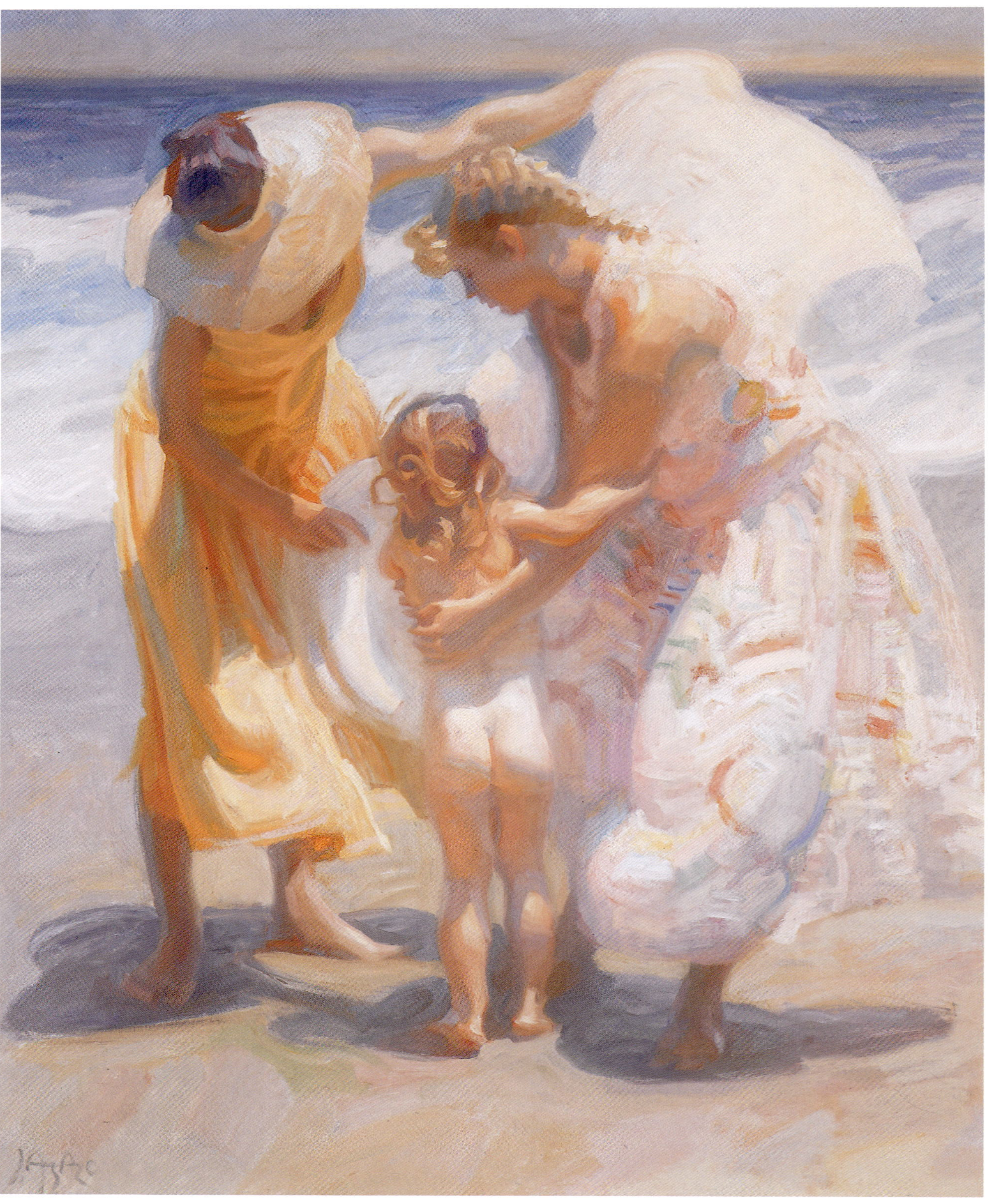

The Bather, o/c, 48×40, 1988.

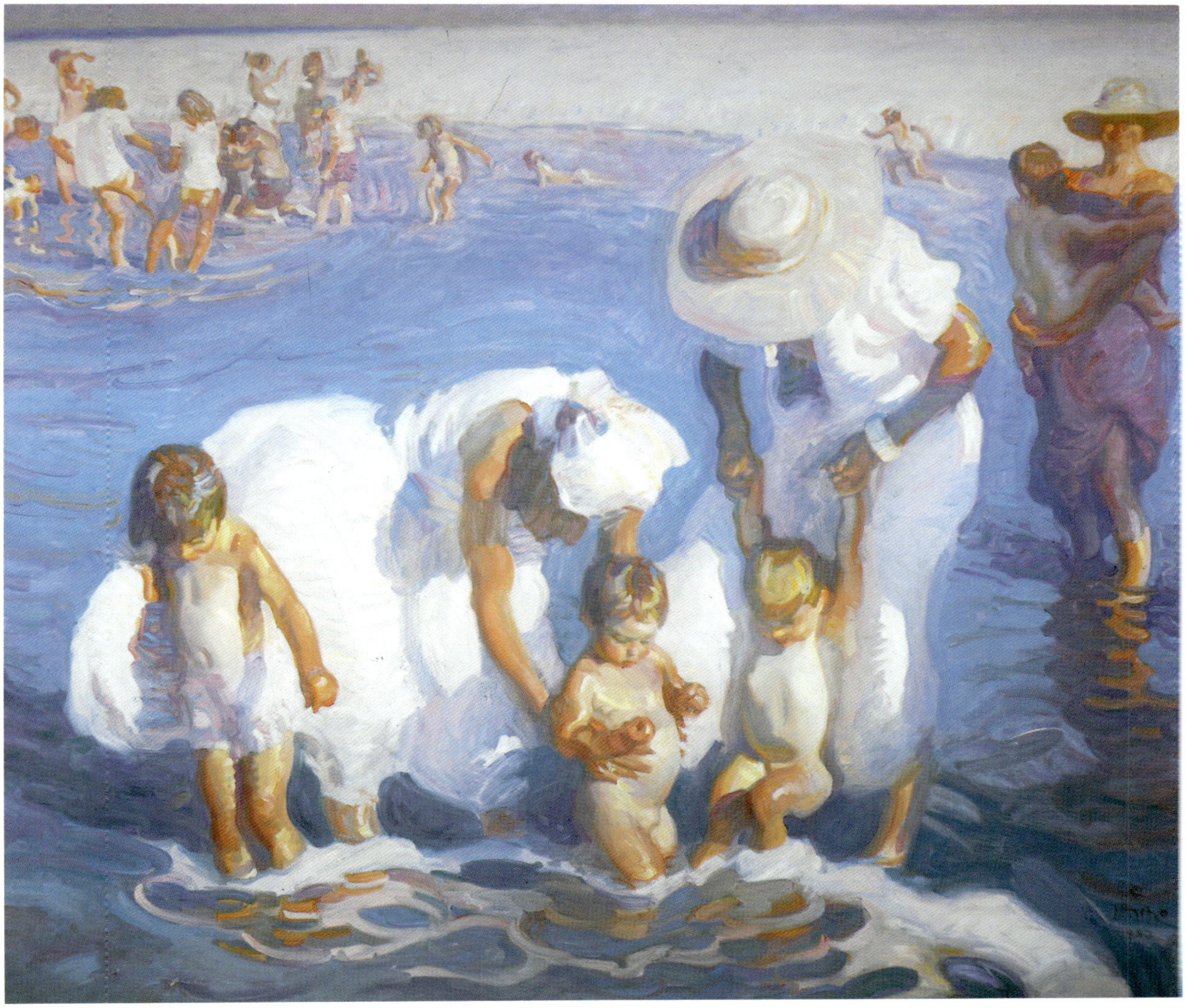

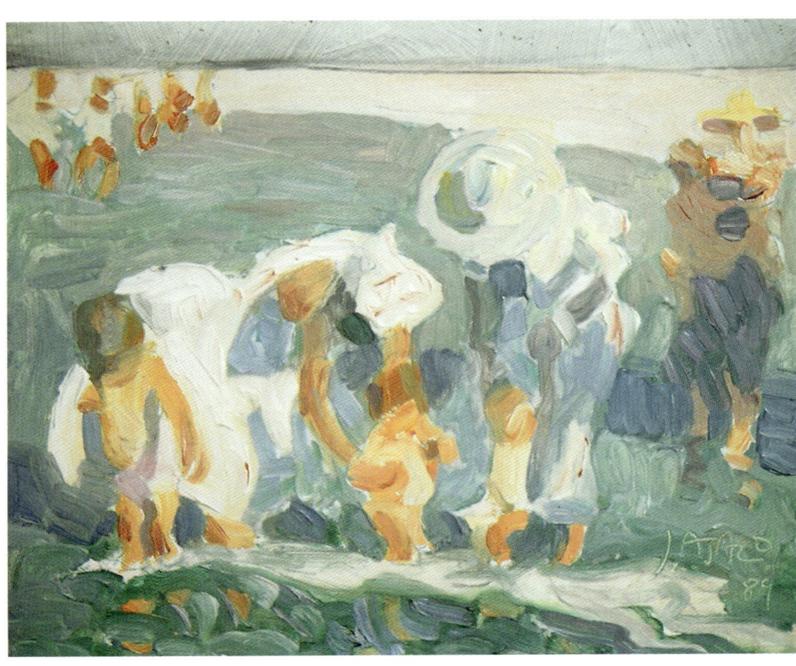

Beach at Del Mar, o/c, 50×60, 1989

Preliminary sketch for *Beach at Del Mar.*

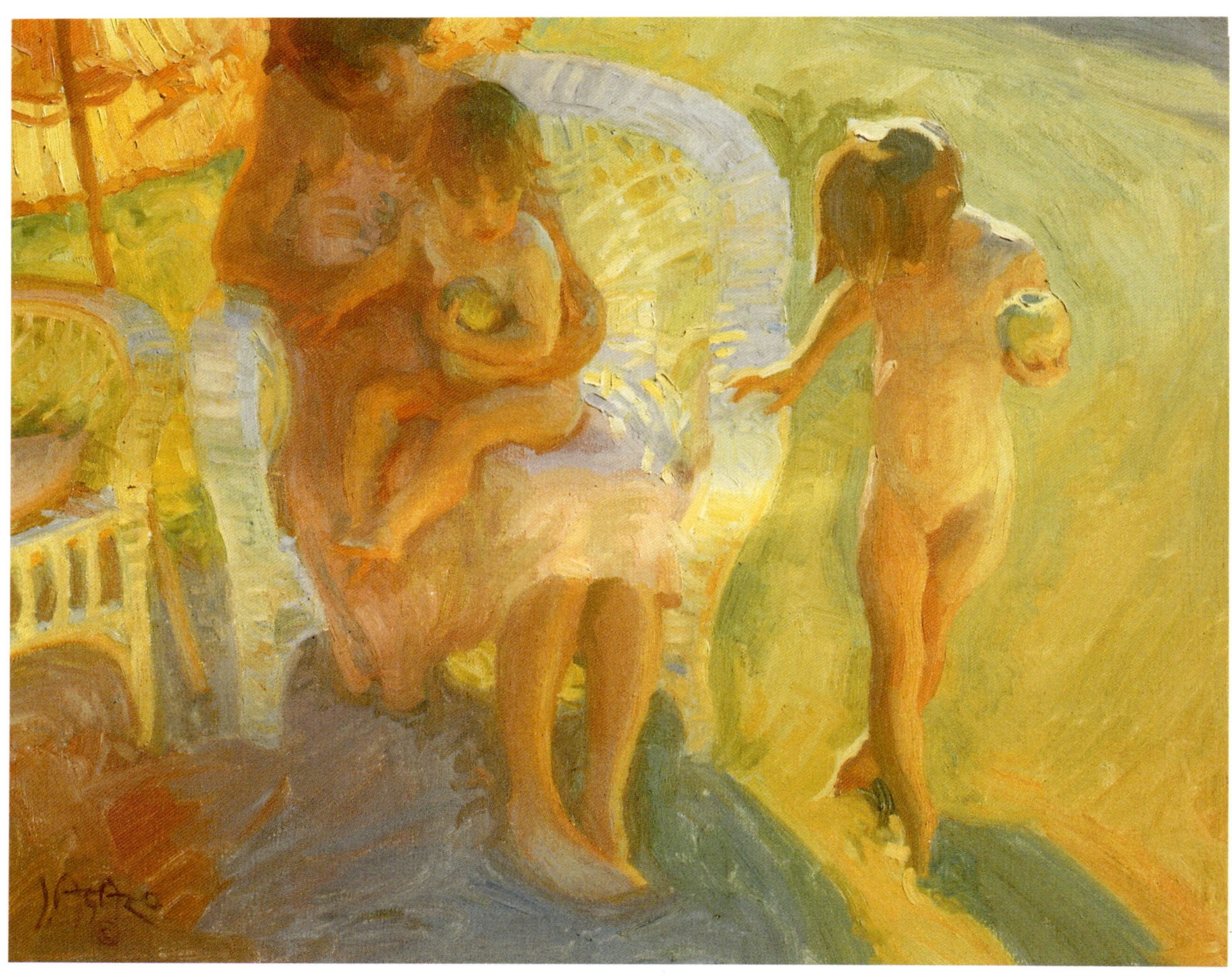

Garden Light, o/c, 20×26, 1987

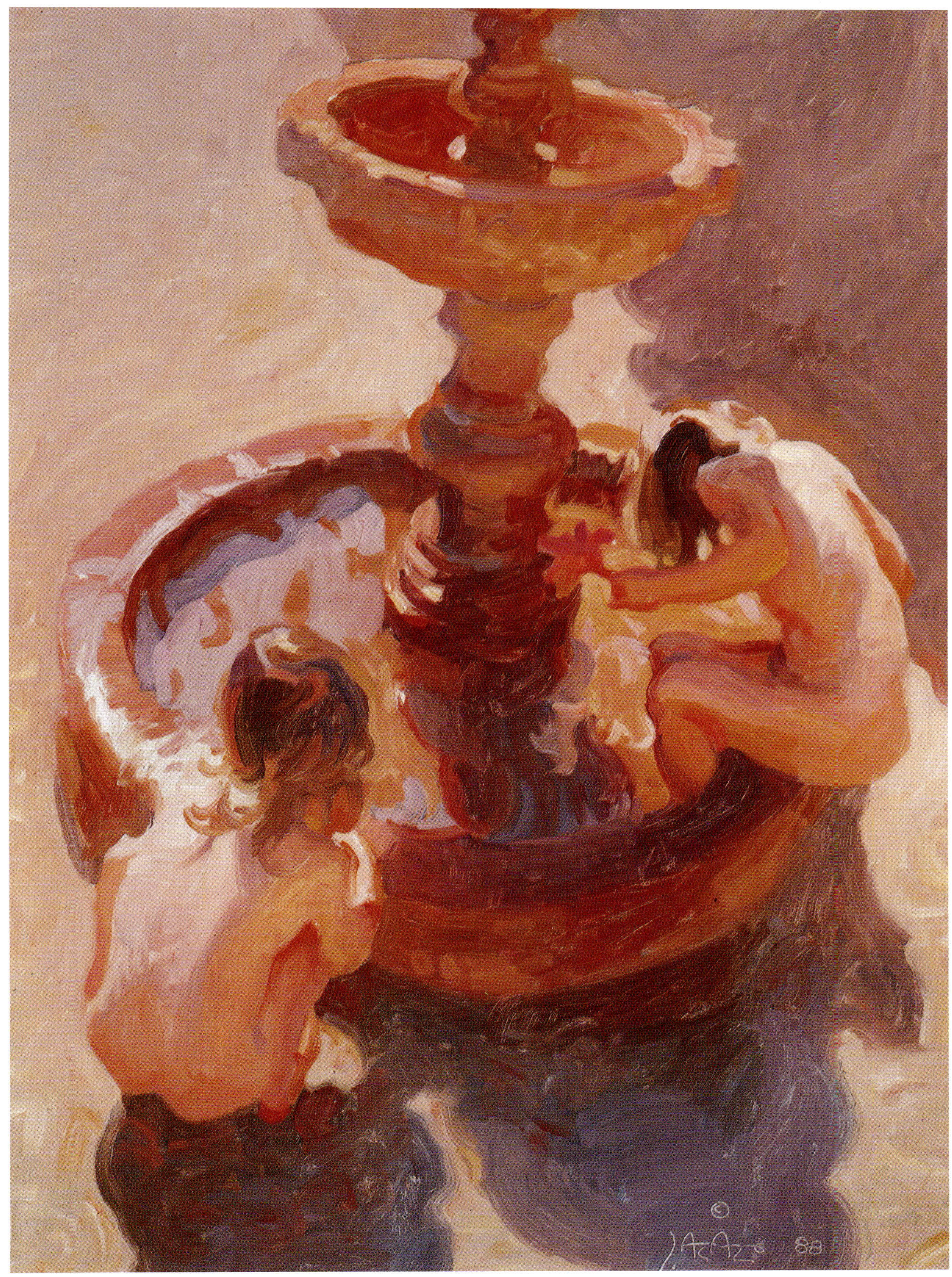

Moorish Fountain, o/c, 24×18, 1988

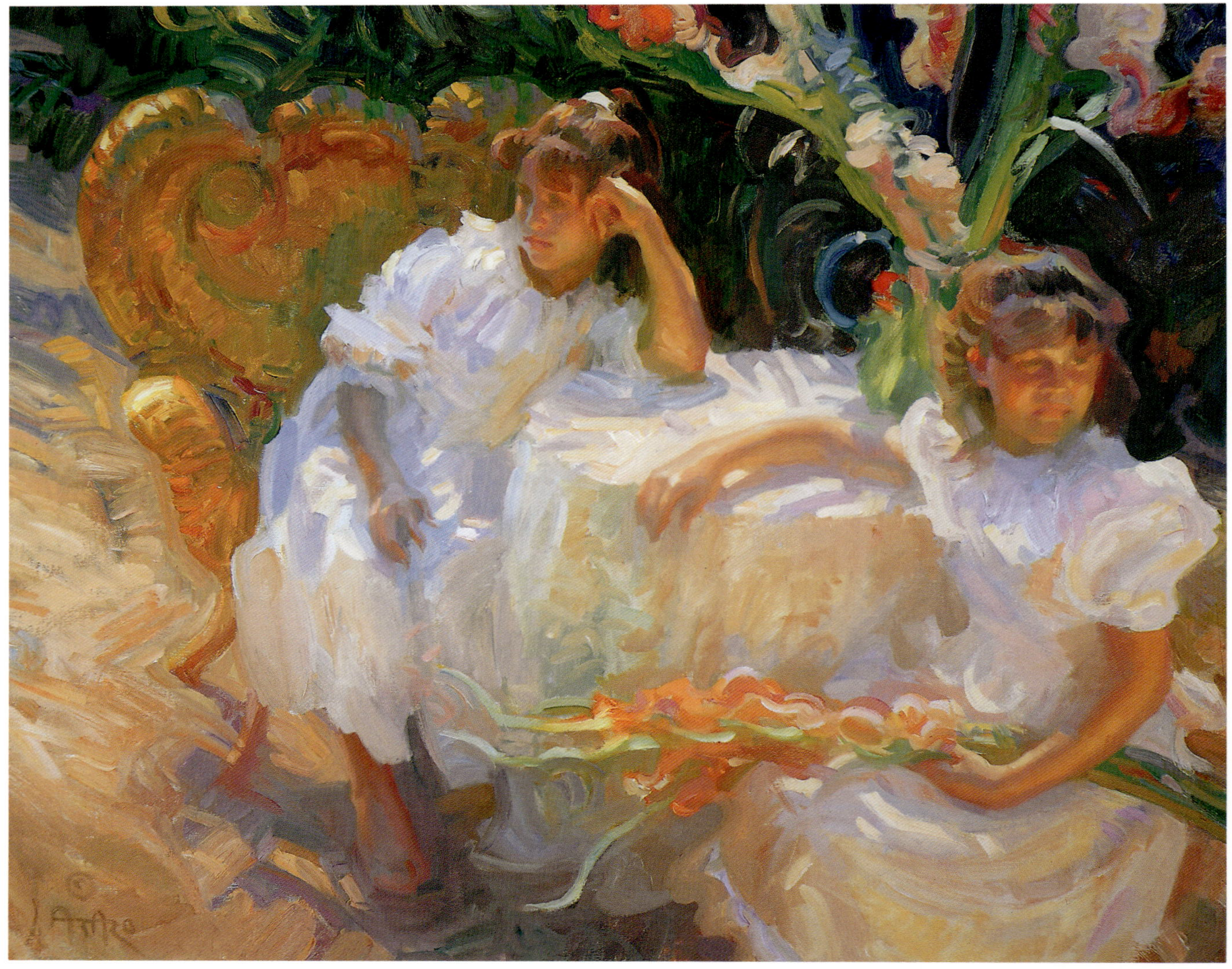

Floral Arrangement, o/c, 30×38, 1988

Collection of Raymond and Vicki Riley

"The process of painting leads me to seek a truer contact with myself, and thus will produce good art…which gets the attention of mutually empathetic people who share these feelings and will reflect and confirm one another's existence. This helps us feel secure and not alone in this world."

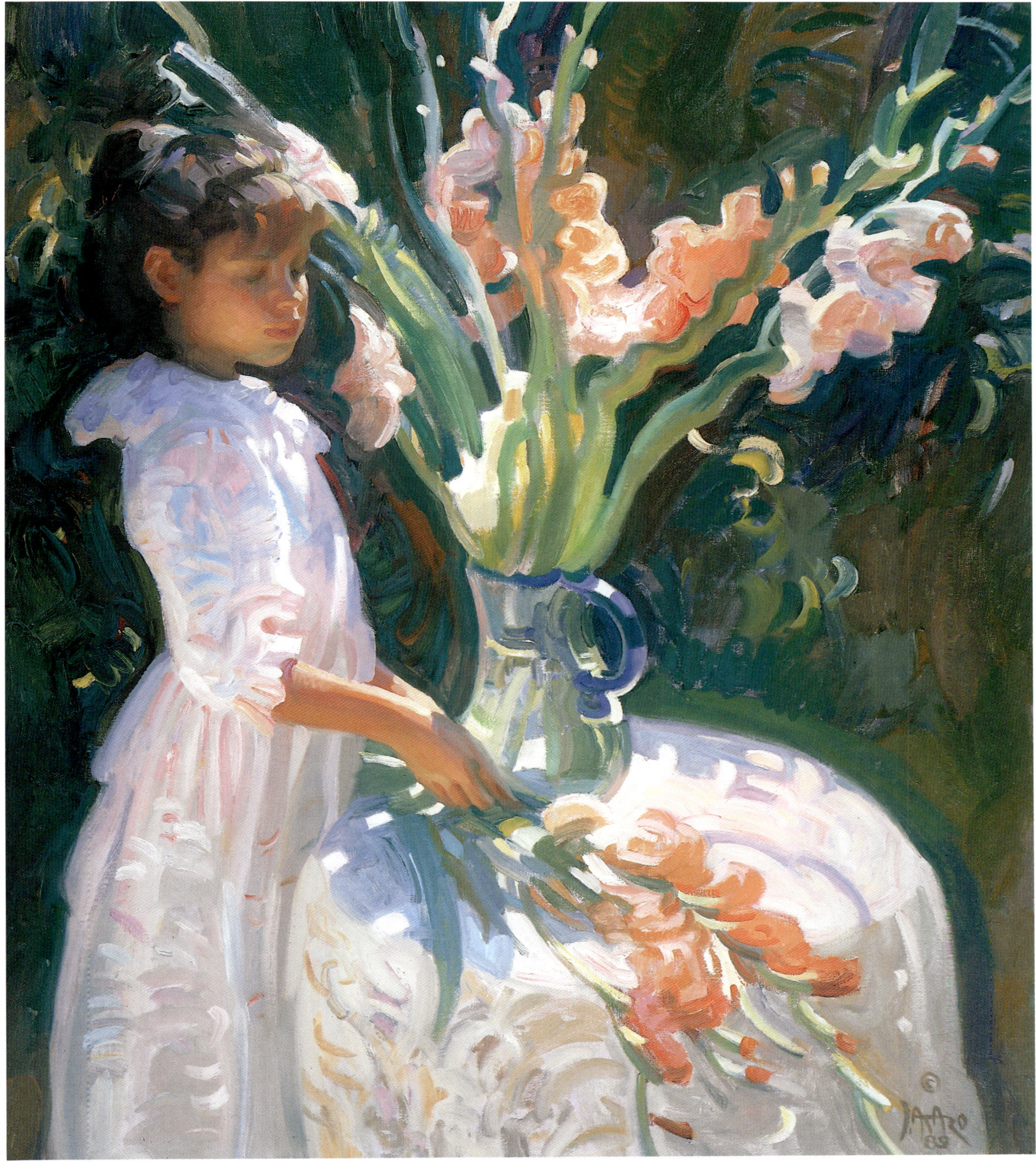

Gladiolas, o/c, 36×32, 1989

Collection of Jennifer and Curtis Cohen

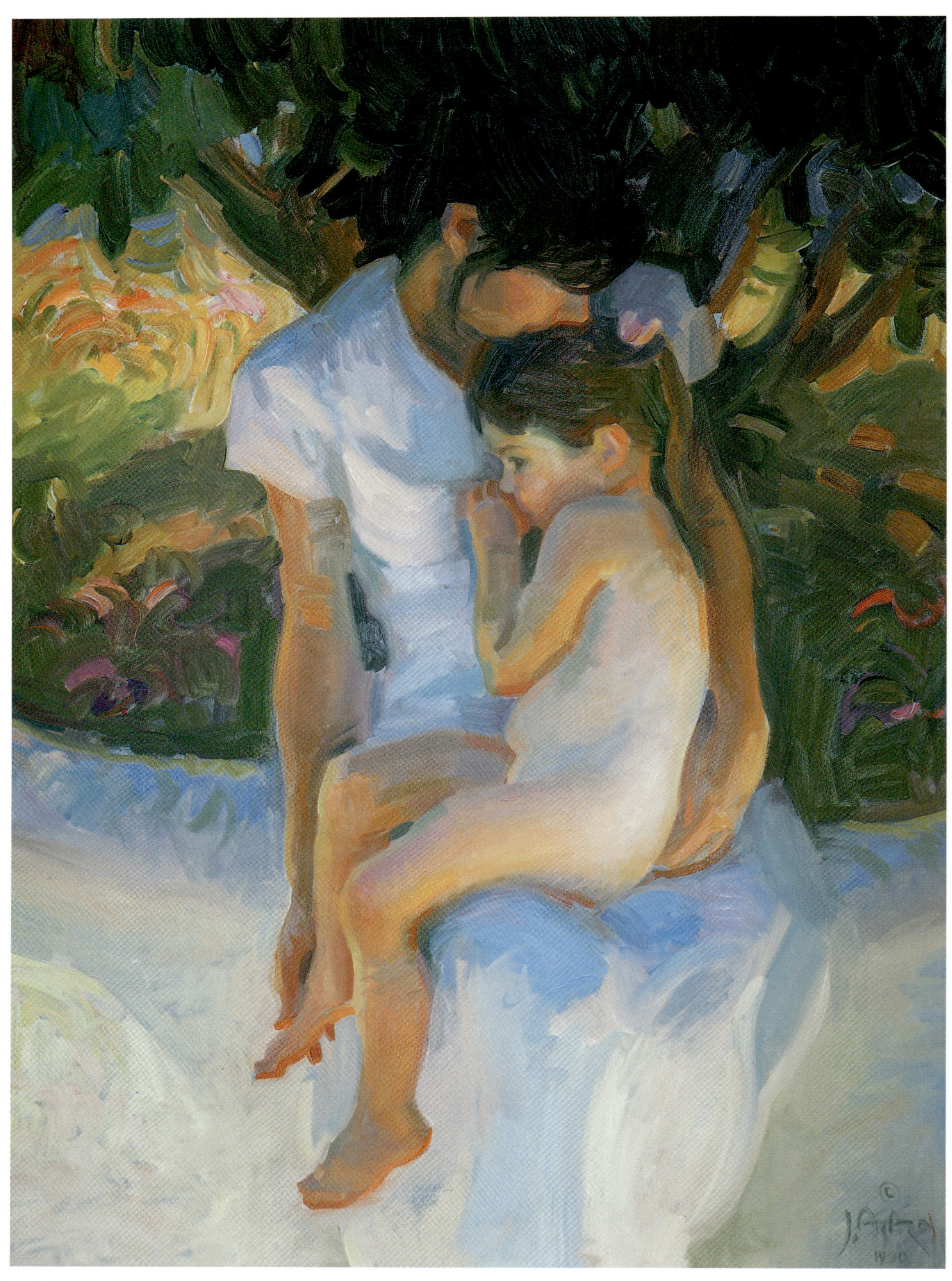

Mother's Love, o/c, 40×30, 1990

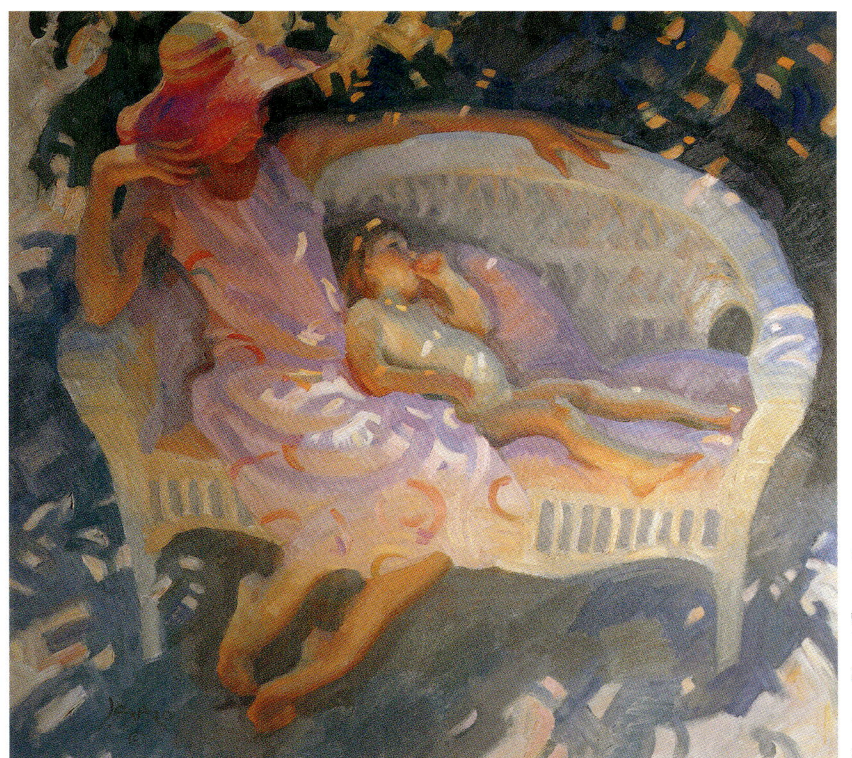

Garden Rose, o/c, 31×34, 1988

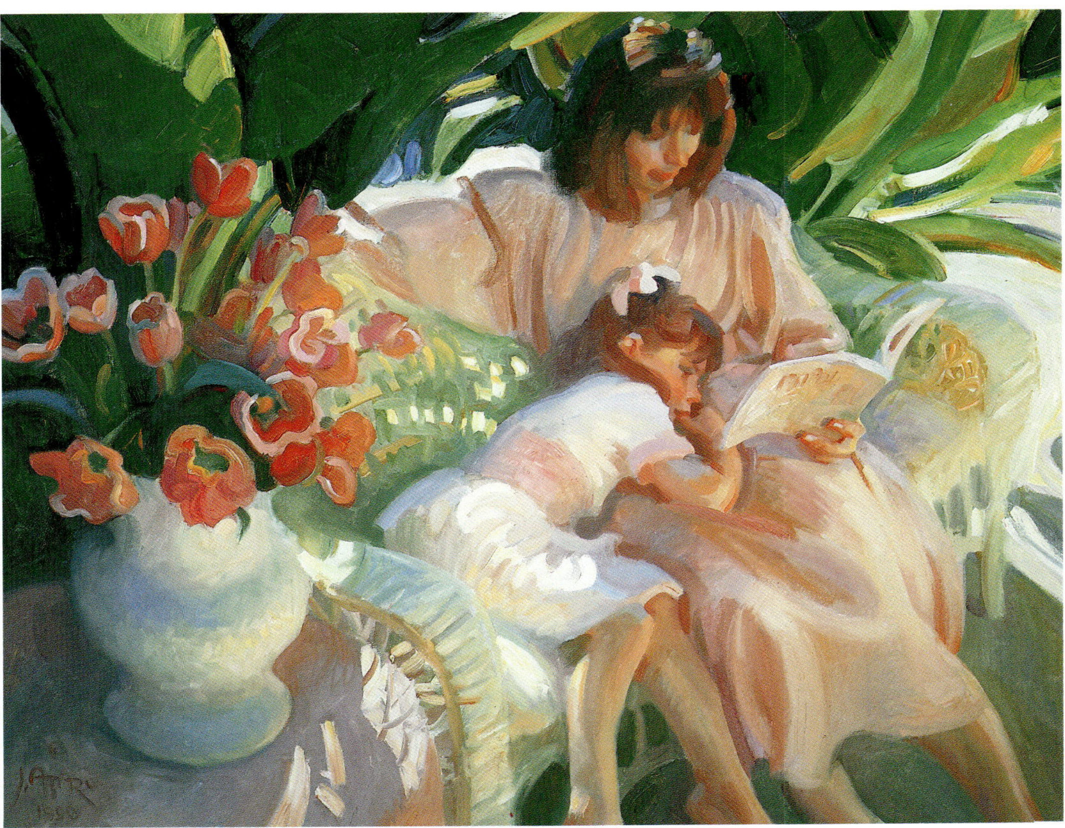

Story Time, o/c, 30×40, 1990

Collection of Jennifer and Curtis Cohen

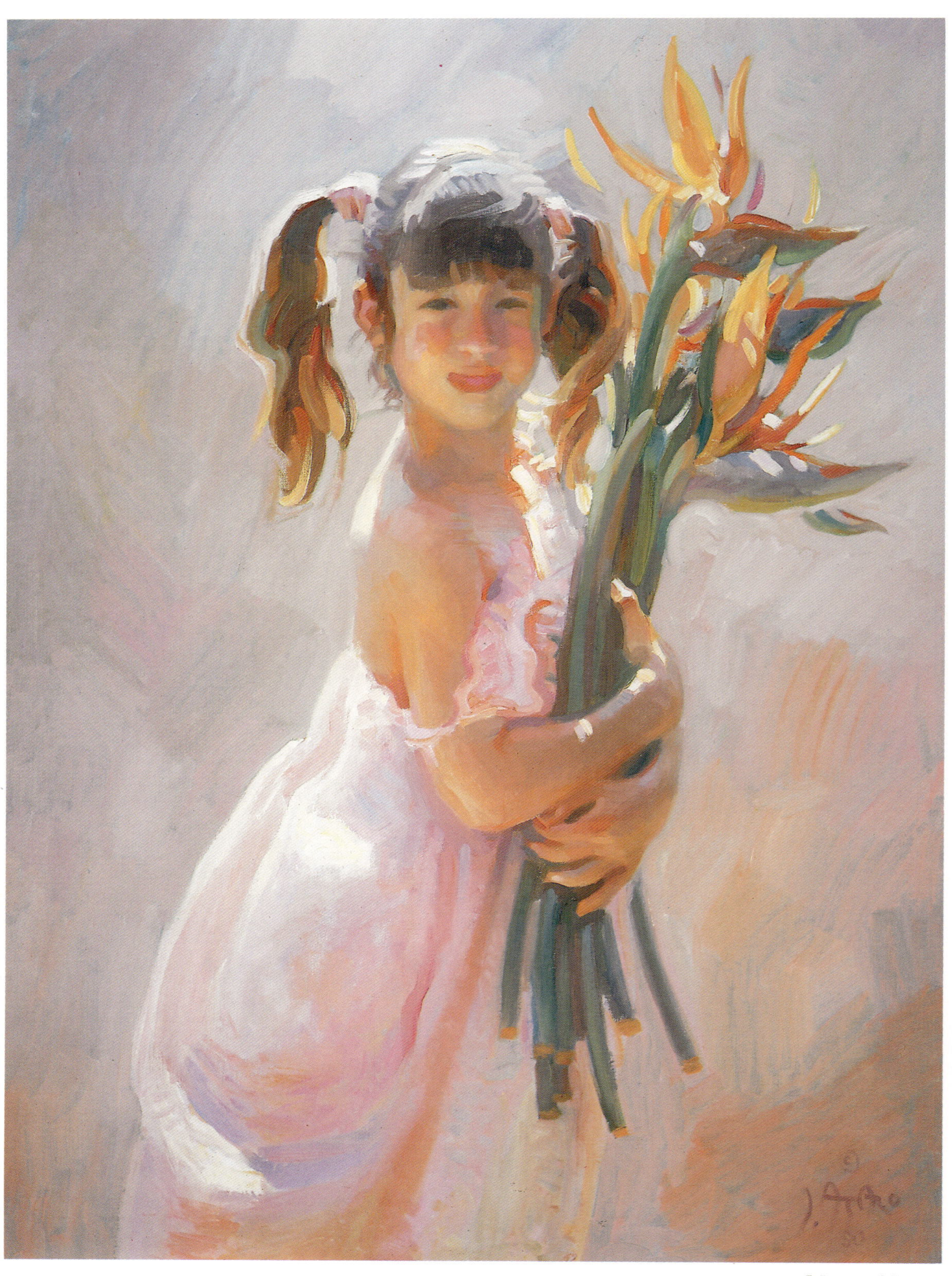

Portrait of Amber, o/c, 40×30, 1990

Collection of the artist

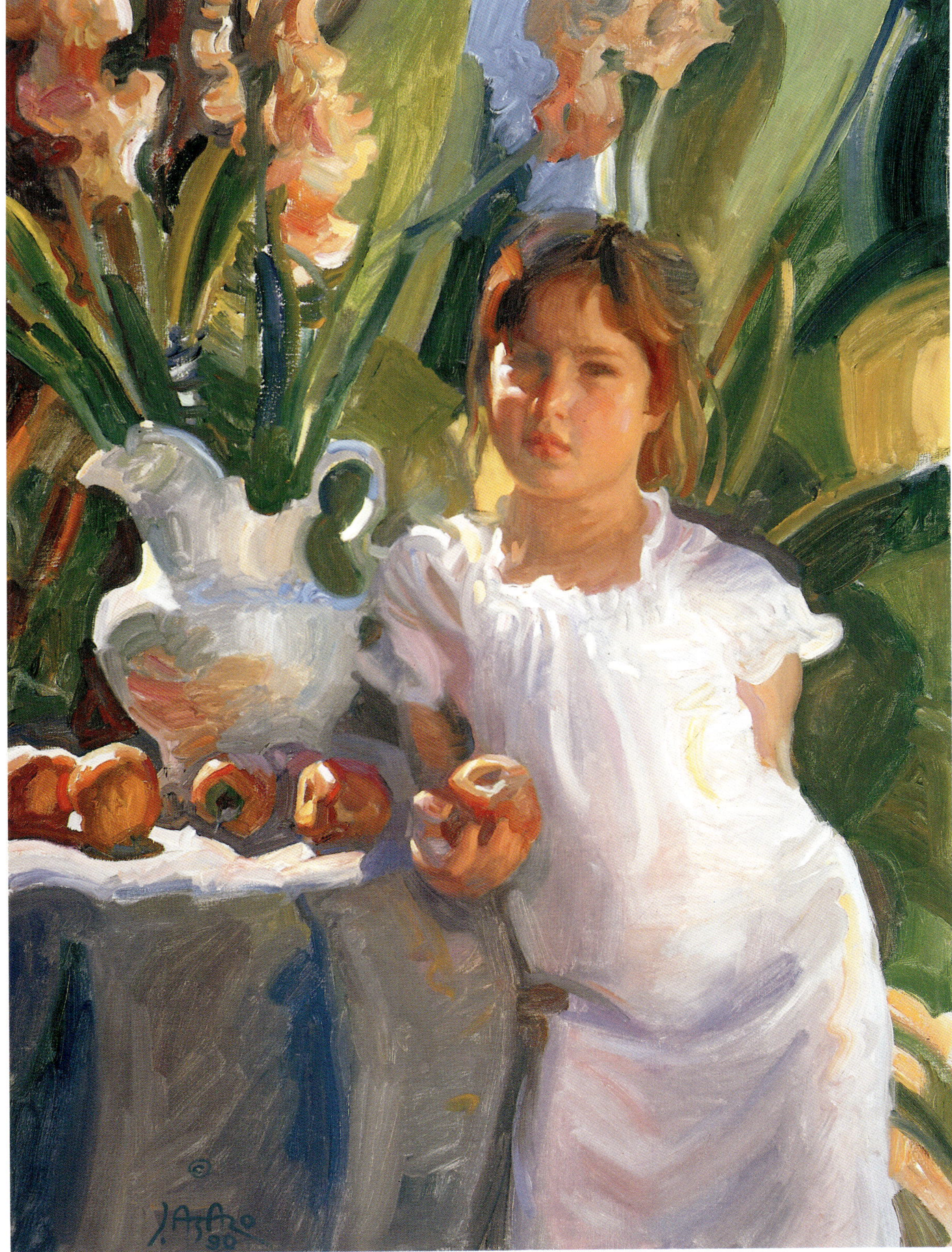

Collection of the artist

Portrait of Devon, o/c, 40×30, 1990

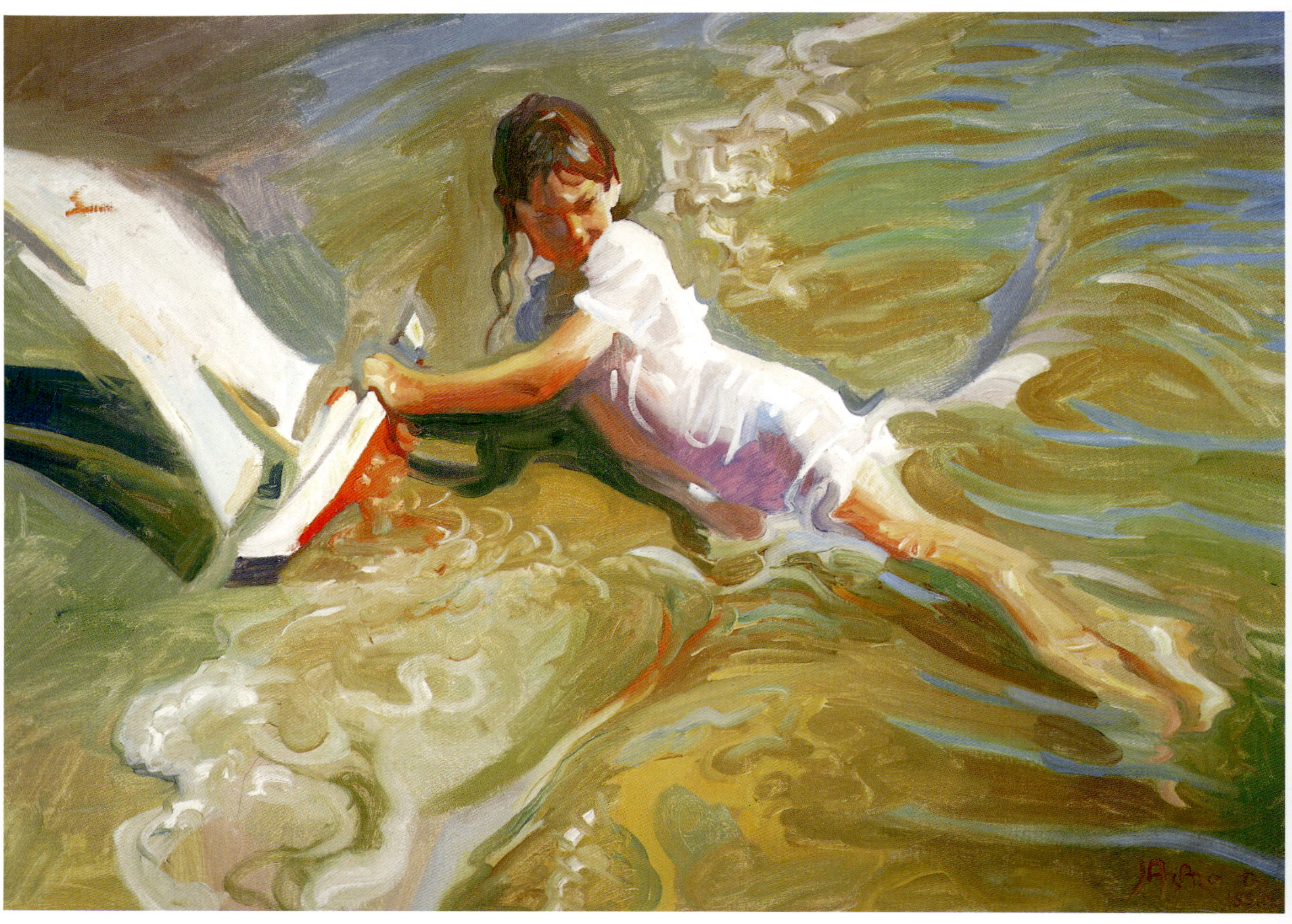

Amber, o/c, 35×50, 1990

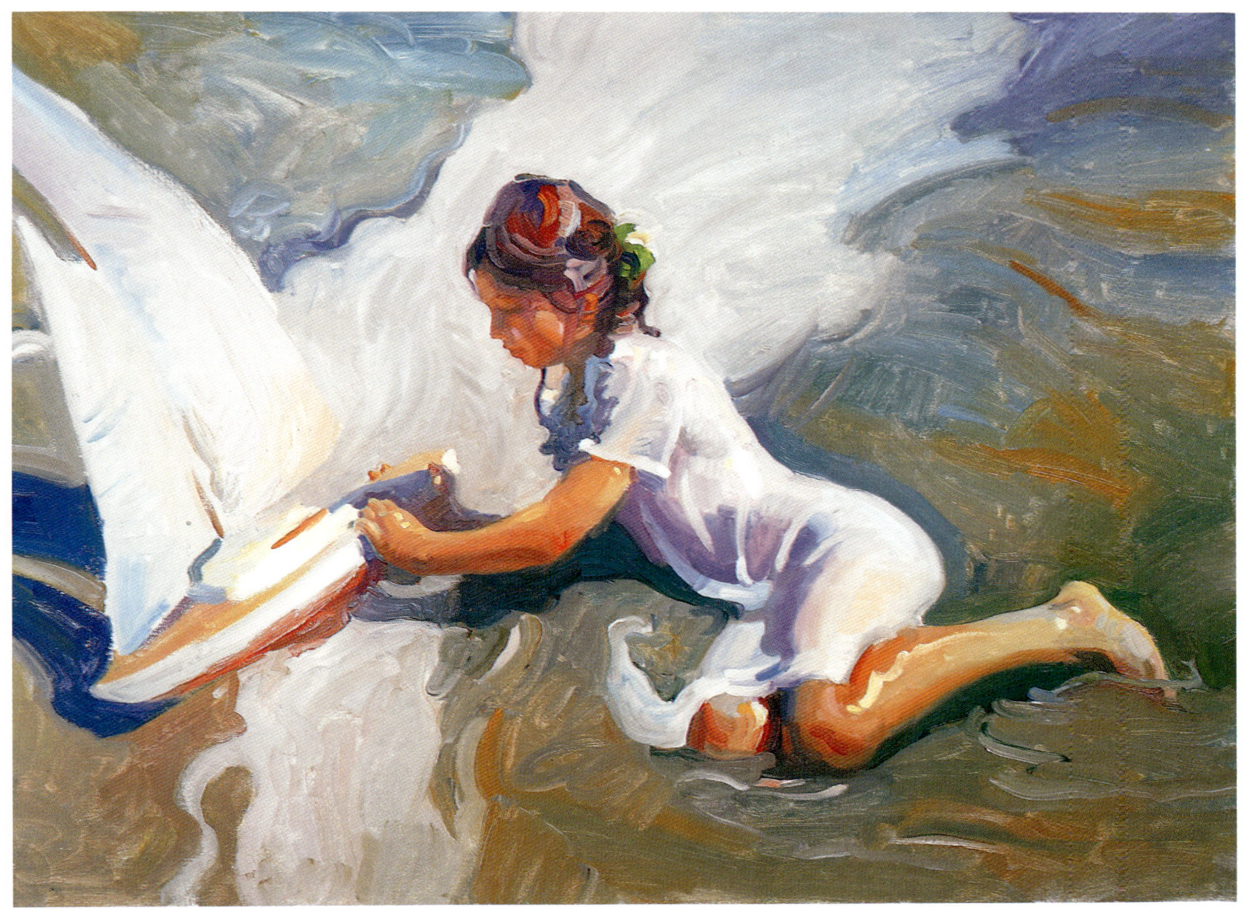

Morning Hues, o/c, 26×36, 1990

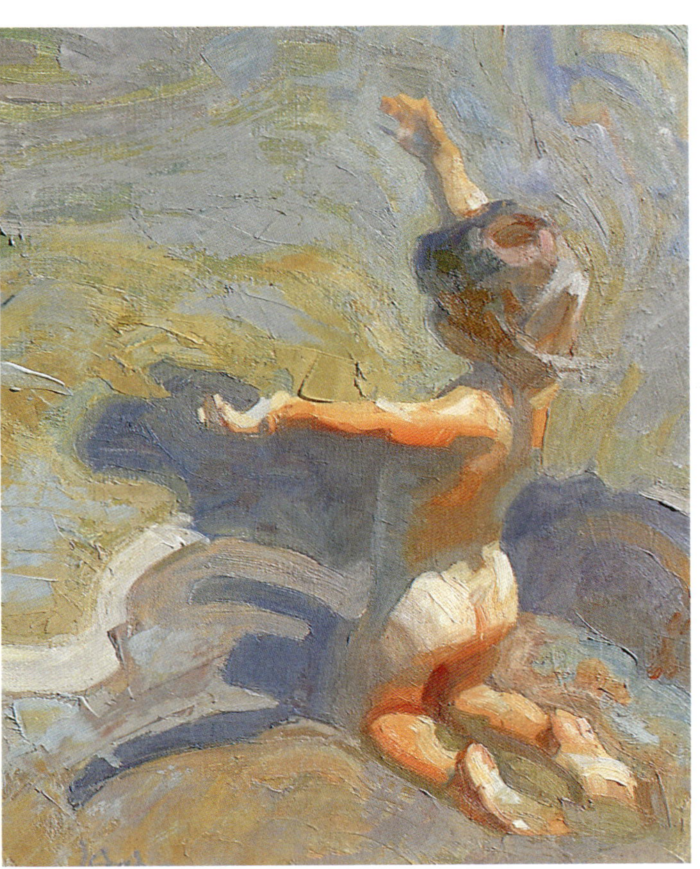

Summer Evening, o/c, 24×20, 1990

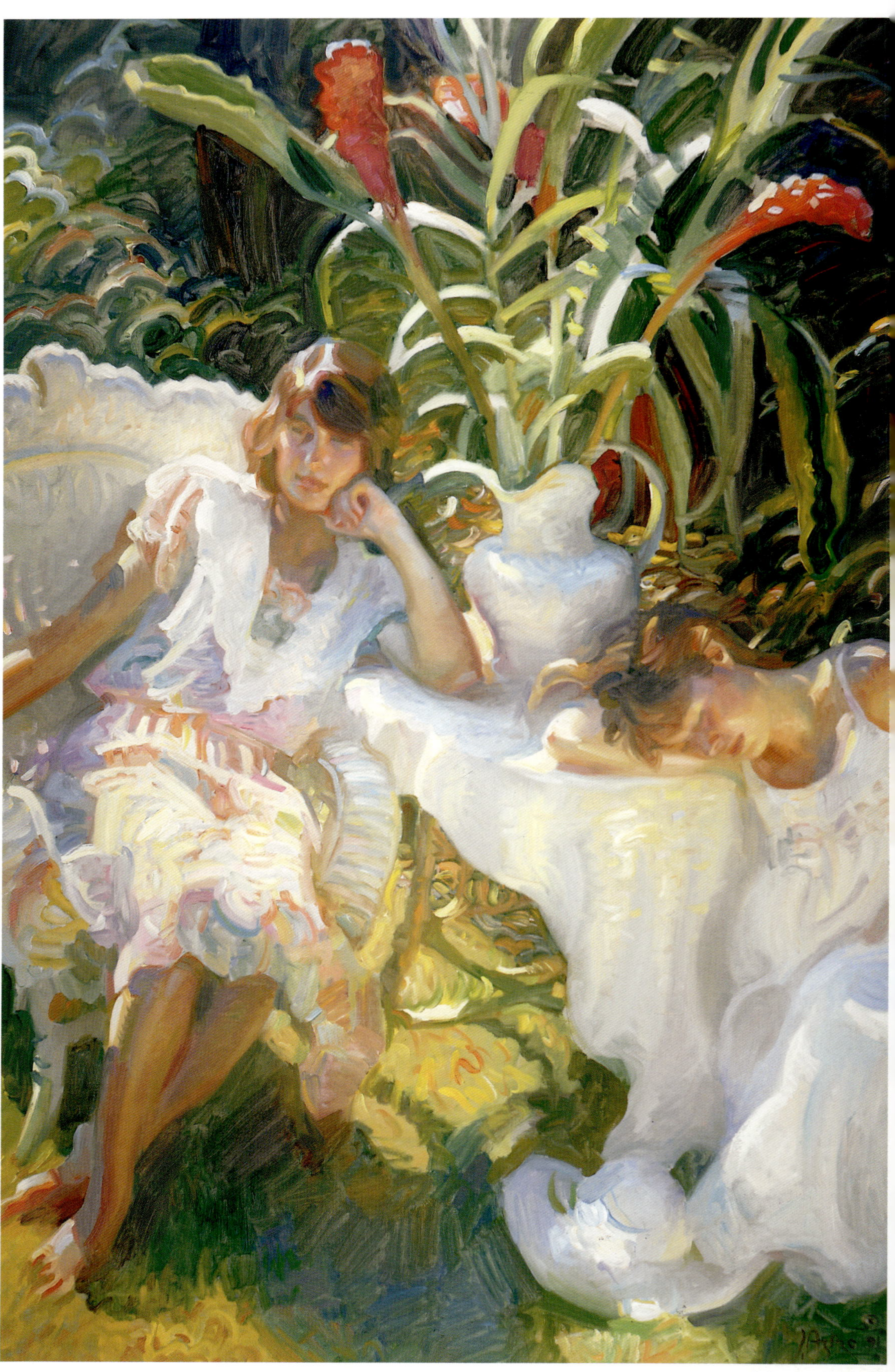

Porcelain Ginger, o/c, 60×40, 1991

Collection of the artist

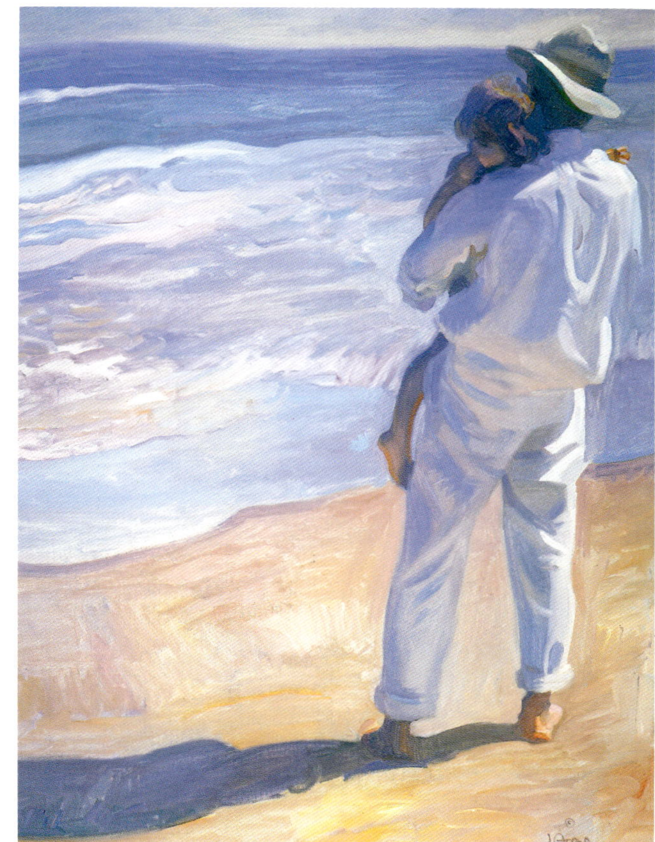

A Special Love, o/c, 48×36, 1991

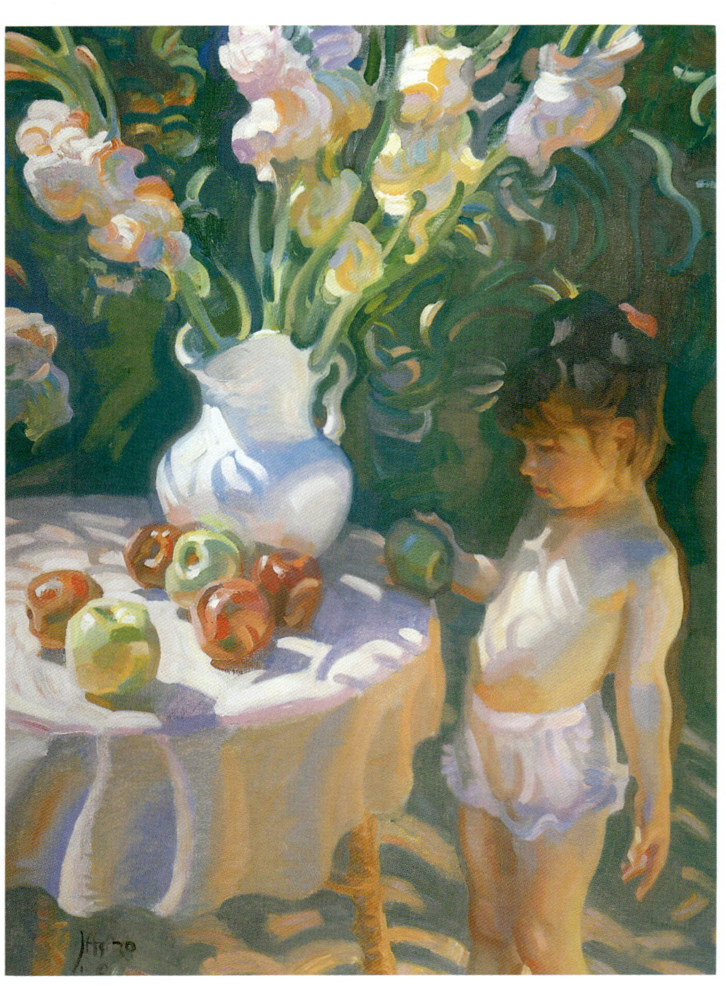

Still Life With Child, o/c, 40×30, 1989

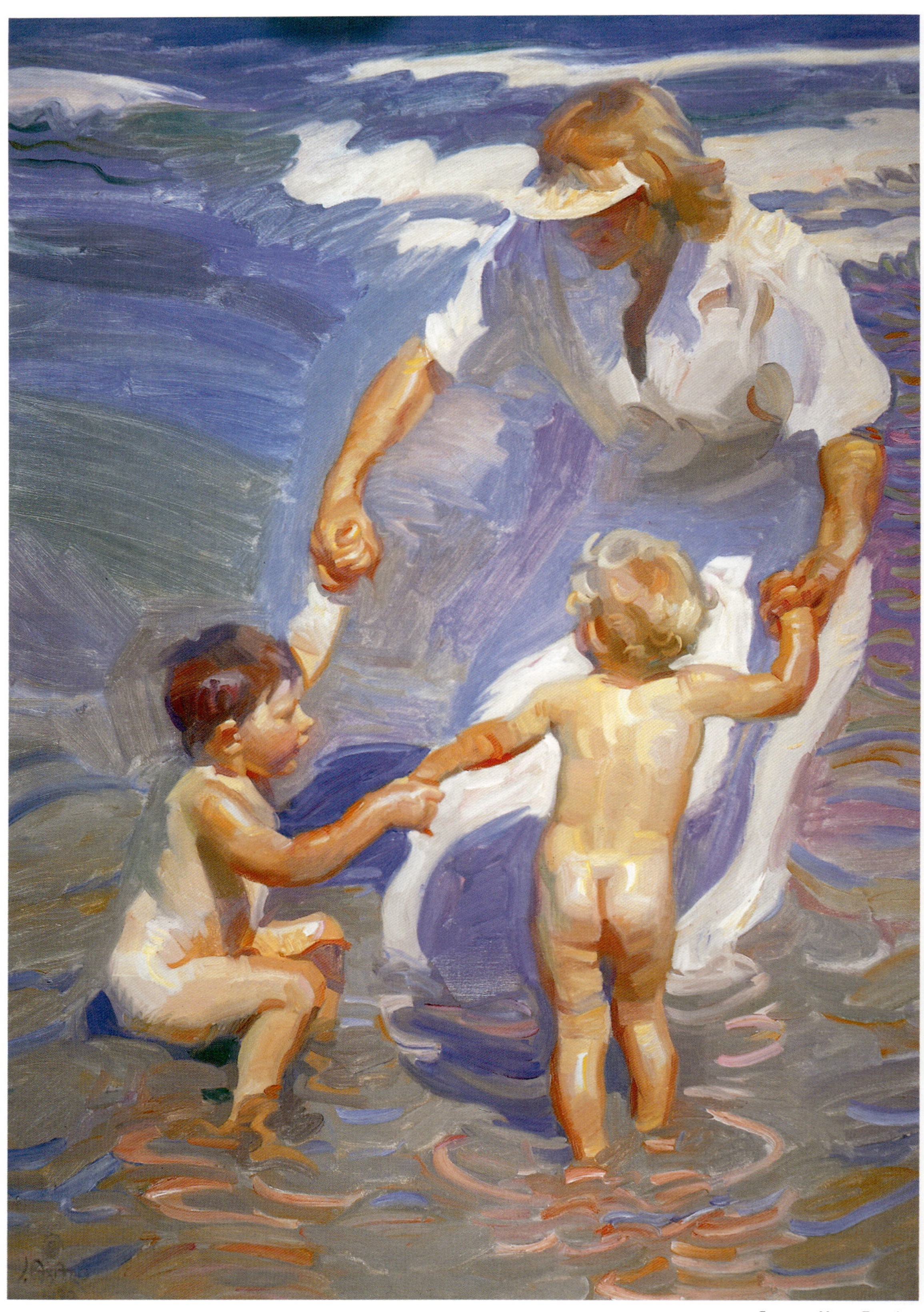

The Bathers, o/c, 50×36, 1991

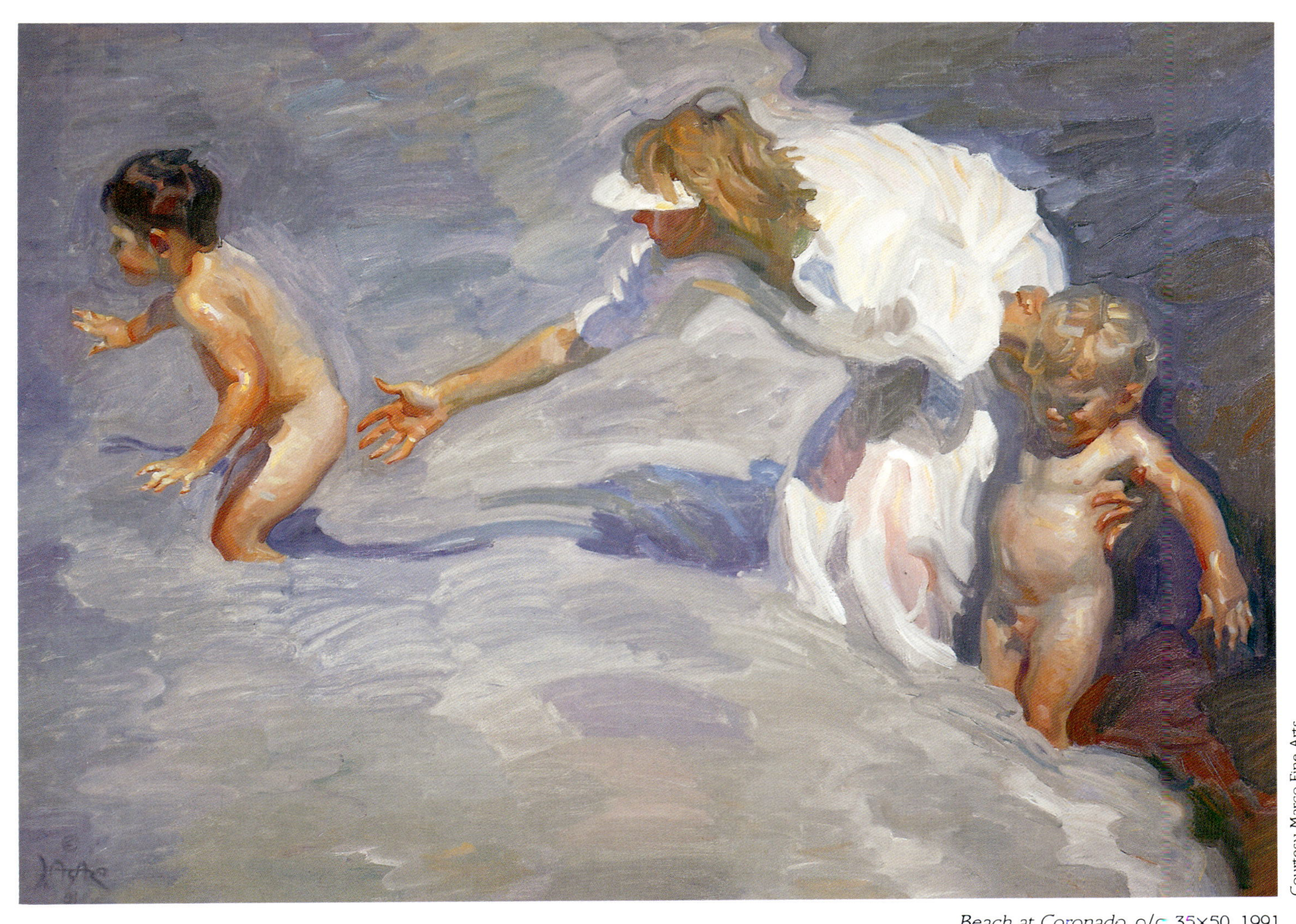

Beach at Coronado, o/c 35×50, 1991

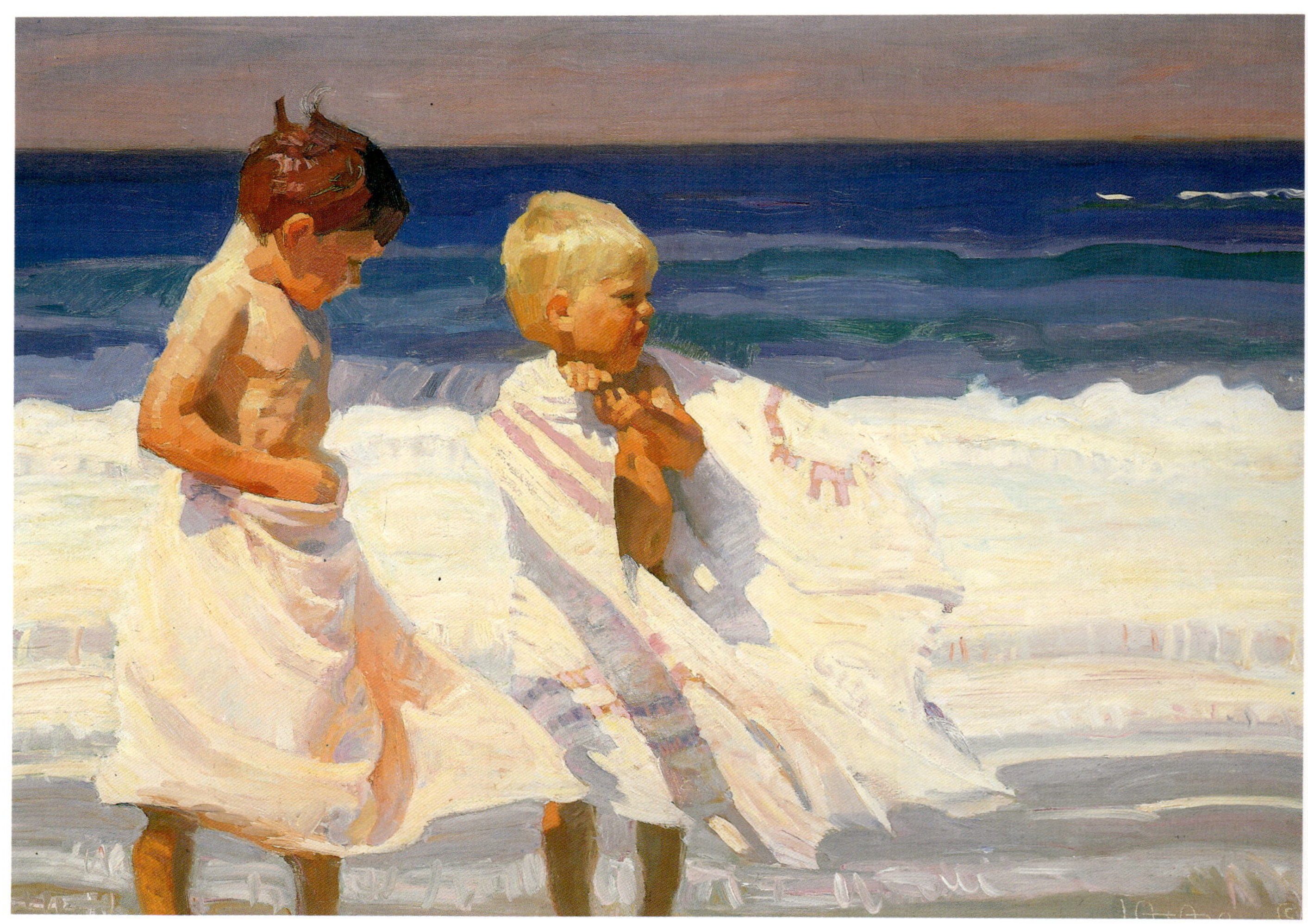

Ocean Breeze, o/c, 28×40, 1986

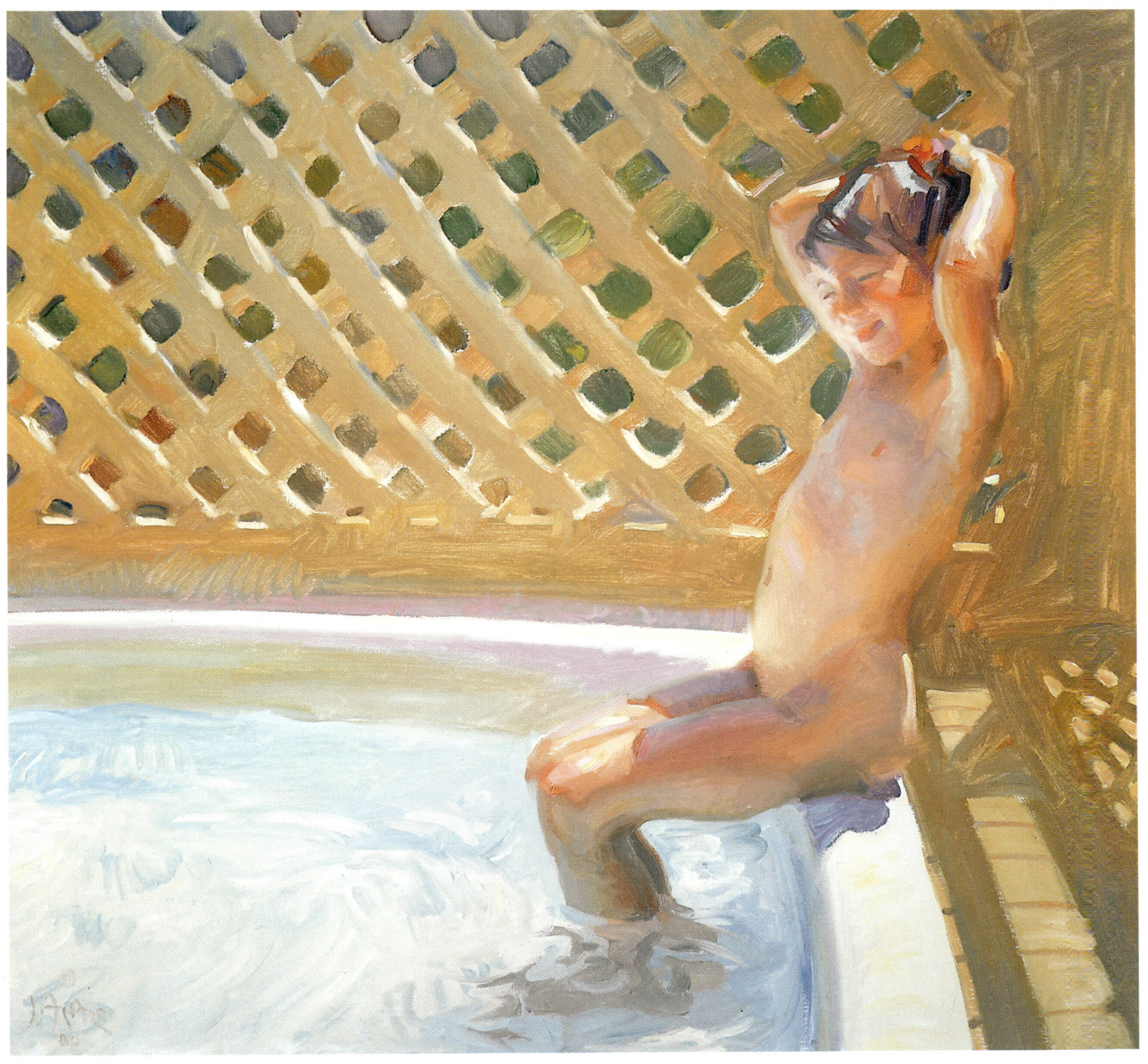

The Spa, o/c, 40×4., 1990

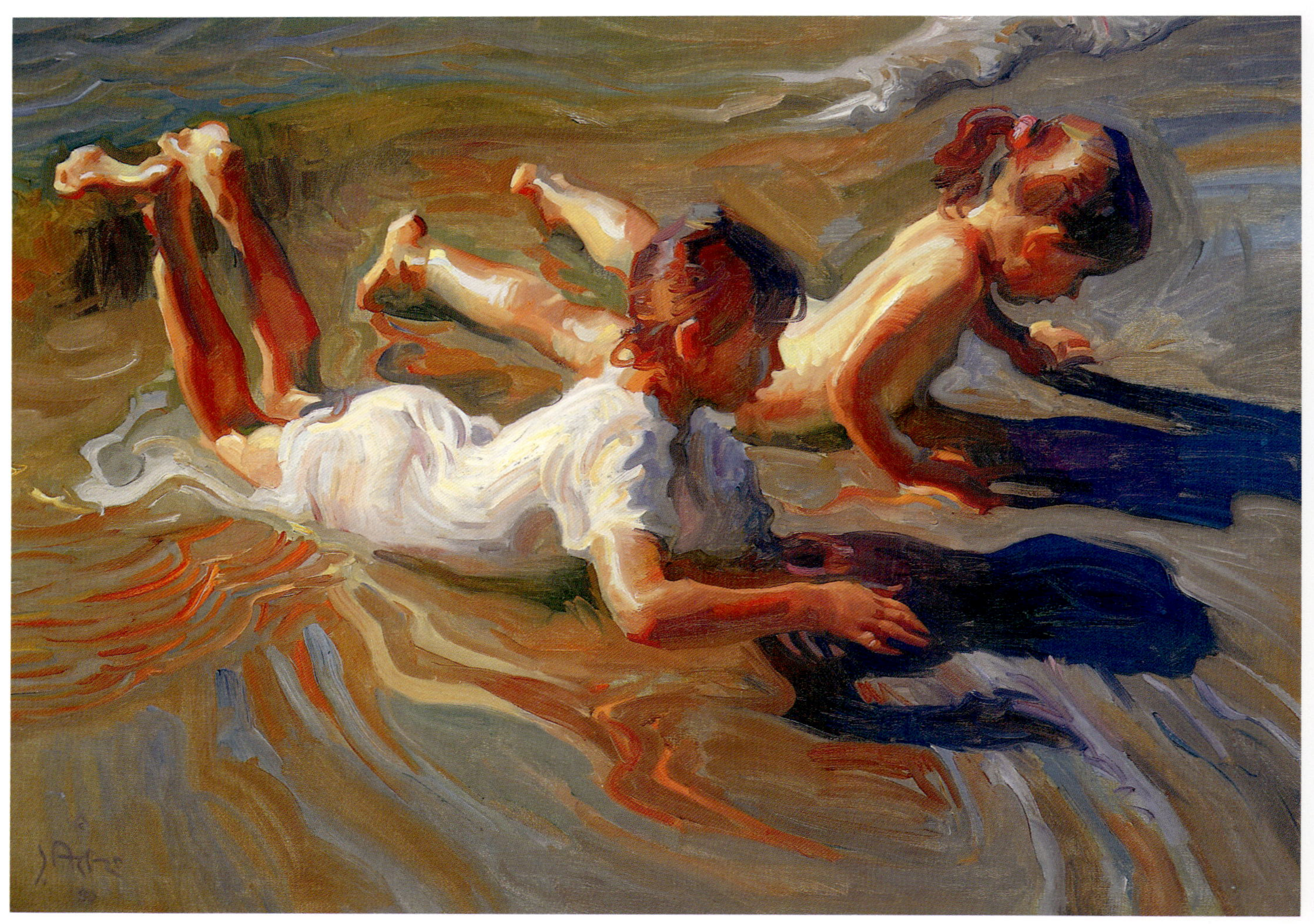

Sisters II. (cover), o/c, 35×50, 1991

Collection of the artist

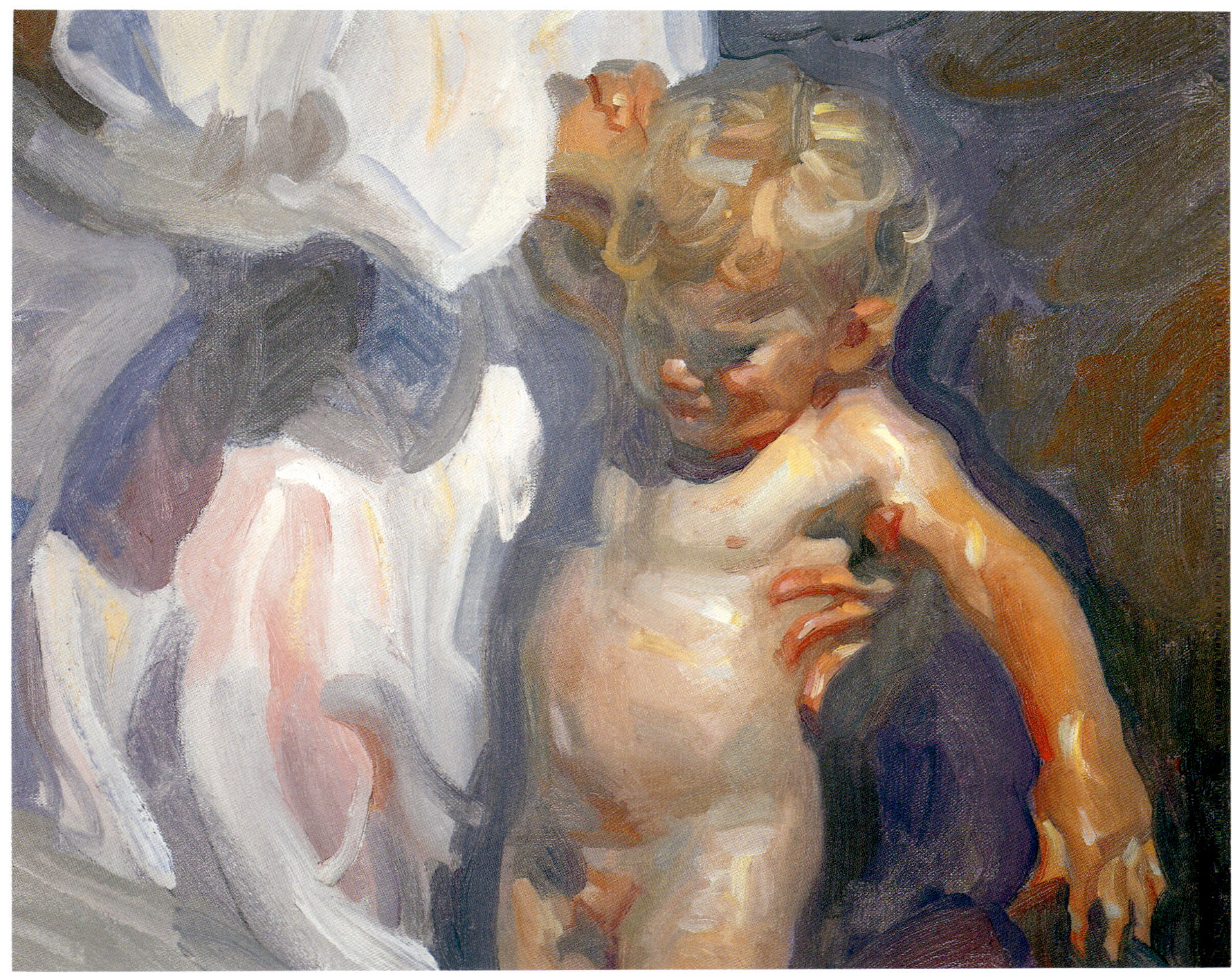

Detail, *Beach at Coronado.*

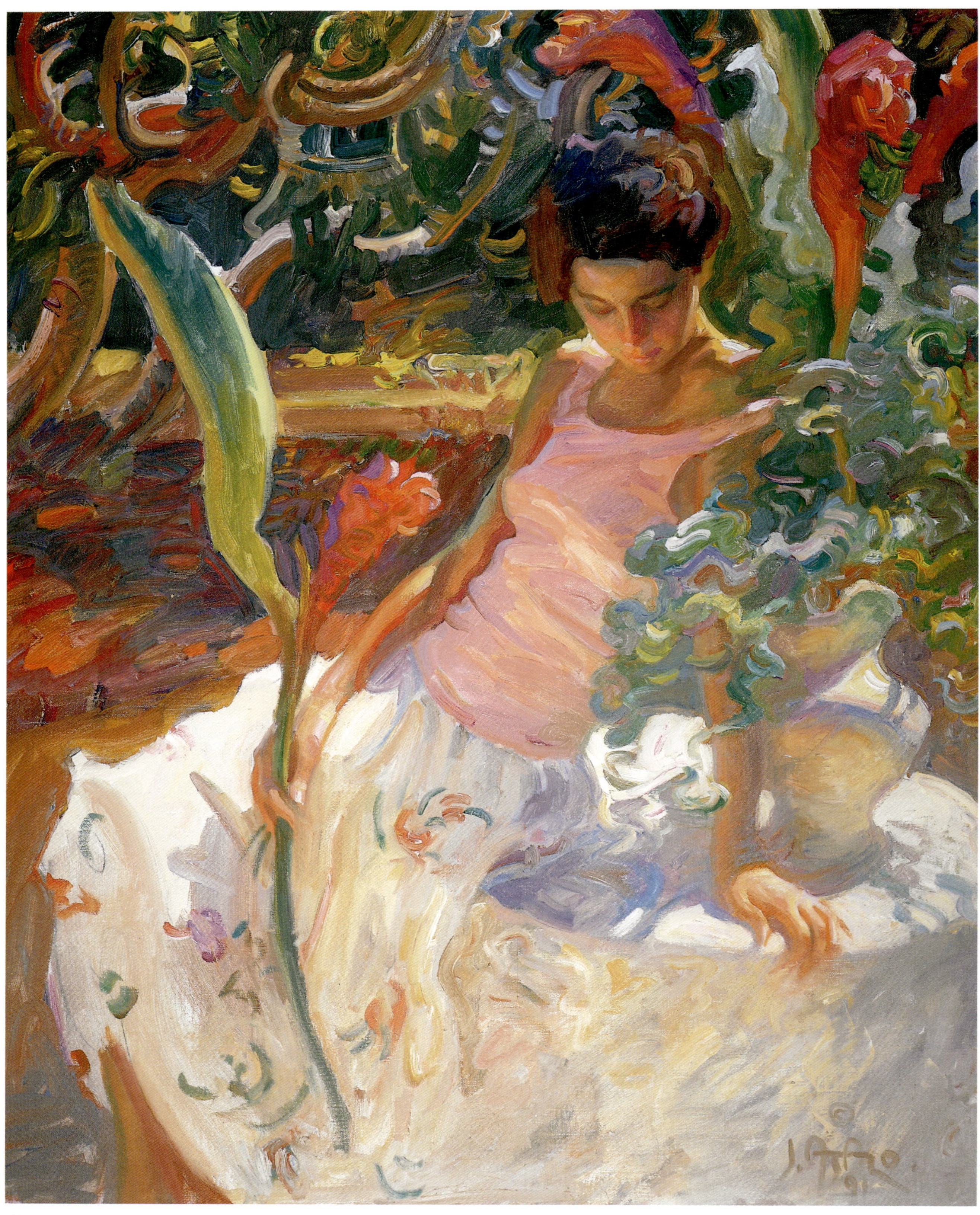

Hawaiian Ginger, o/c, 39×32, 1991

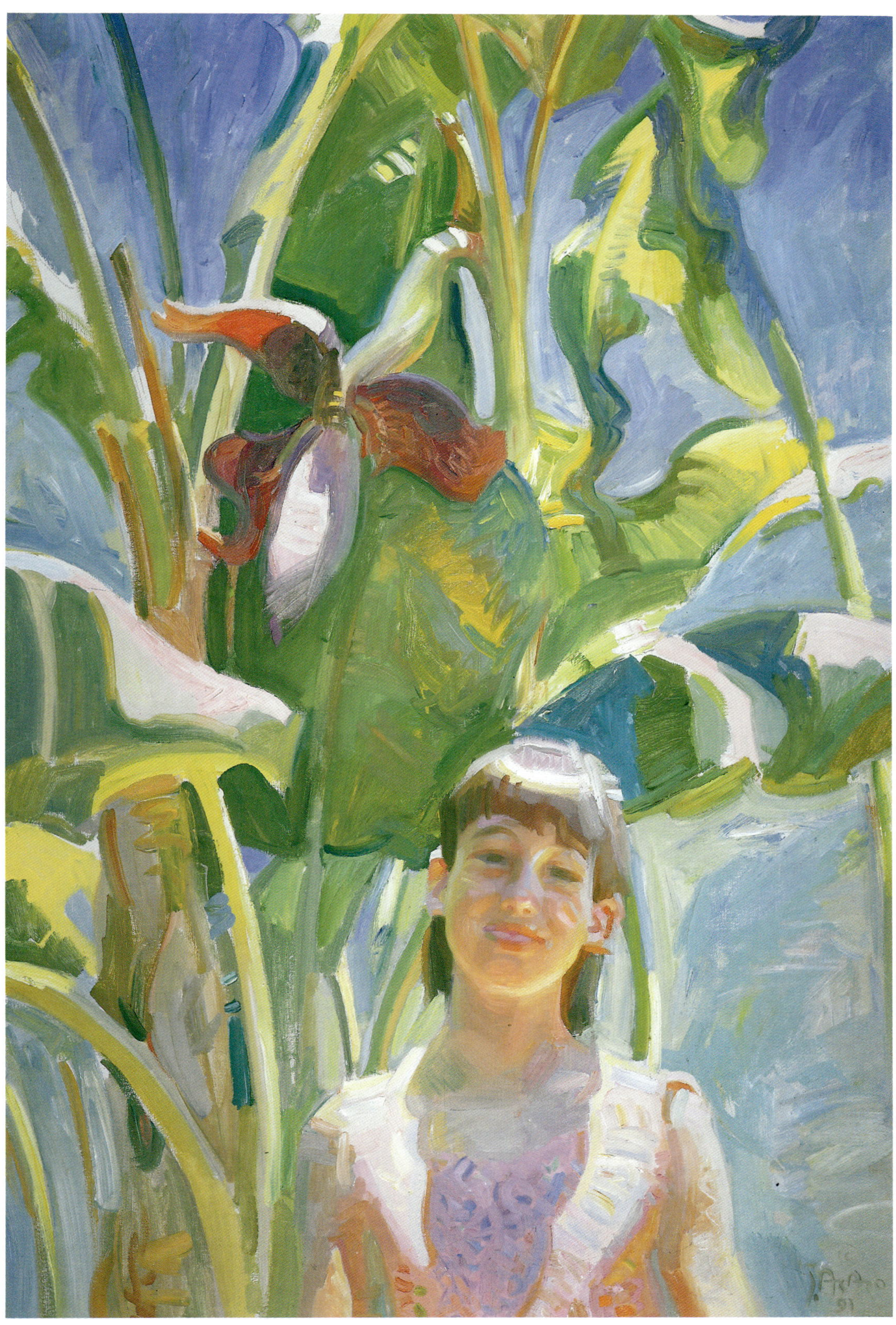

Banana Trees, o/c, 50×34, 1991

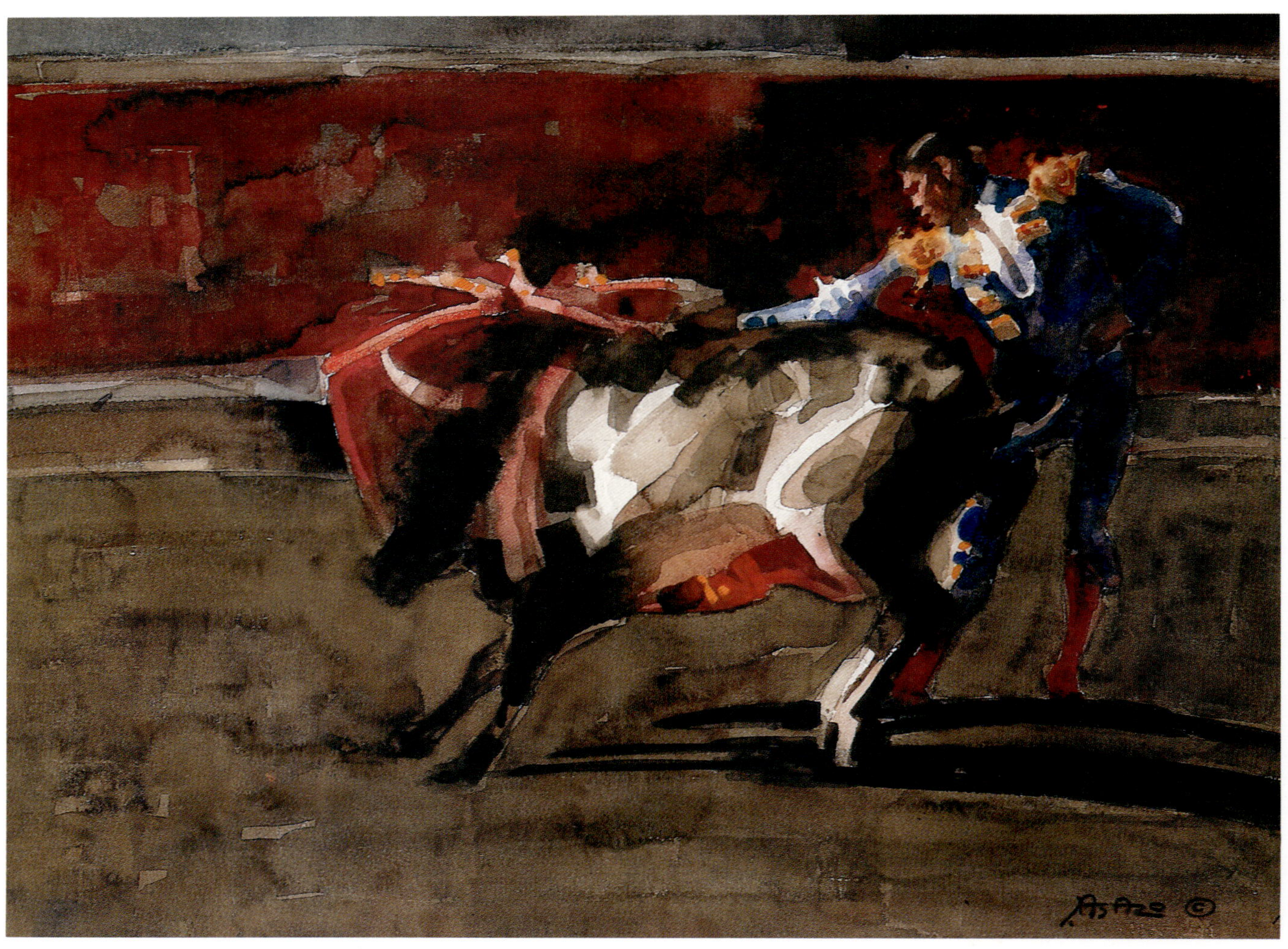

Sunday Afternoon, w/c, 22×30, 1979

THE ARTIST AS TRAVELER

Several trips to Europe (1984, 1985, 1988) gave Asaro a chance to experience Italy and Sicily, the island of his parents' roots. There he photographed and painted energetically (*Ca'D'Oro* is a good example of that energy) while visiting aunts and uncles. The architecture and atmosphere of Venice especially captivated him (see *Venetian Doorway*). To examine the resulting paintings is to realize that Asaro's one-generation removal from Greco-Roman lands has not stopped him from being inexplicably drawn to the solid traditions of his ancestors.

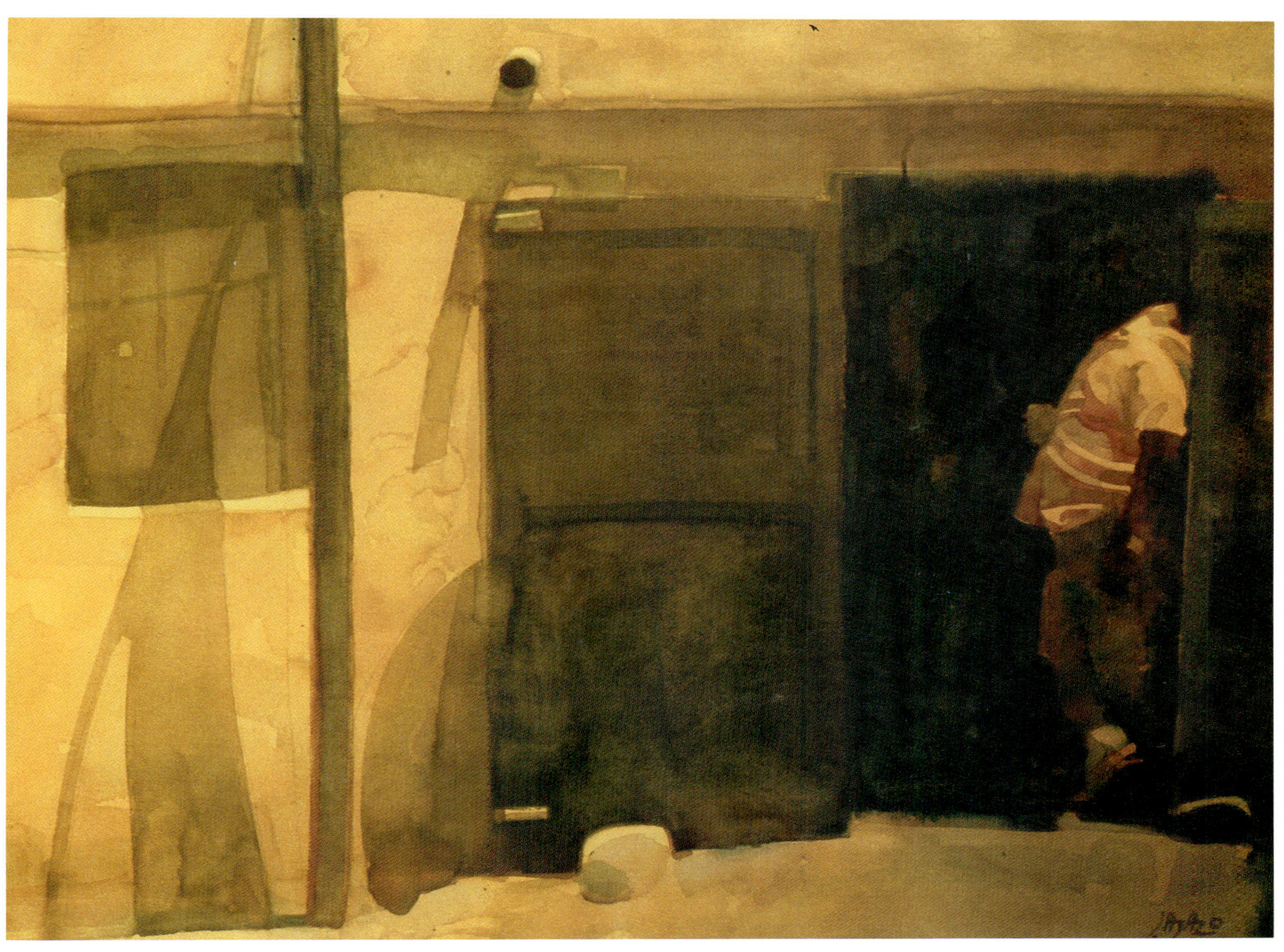

Curacao, w/c, 22×30, 1981

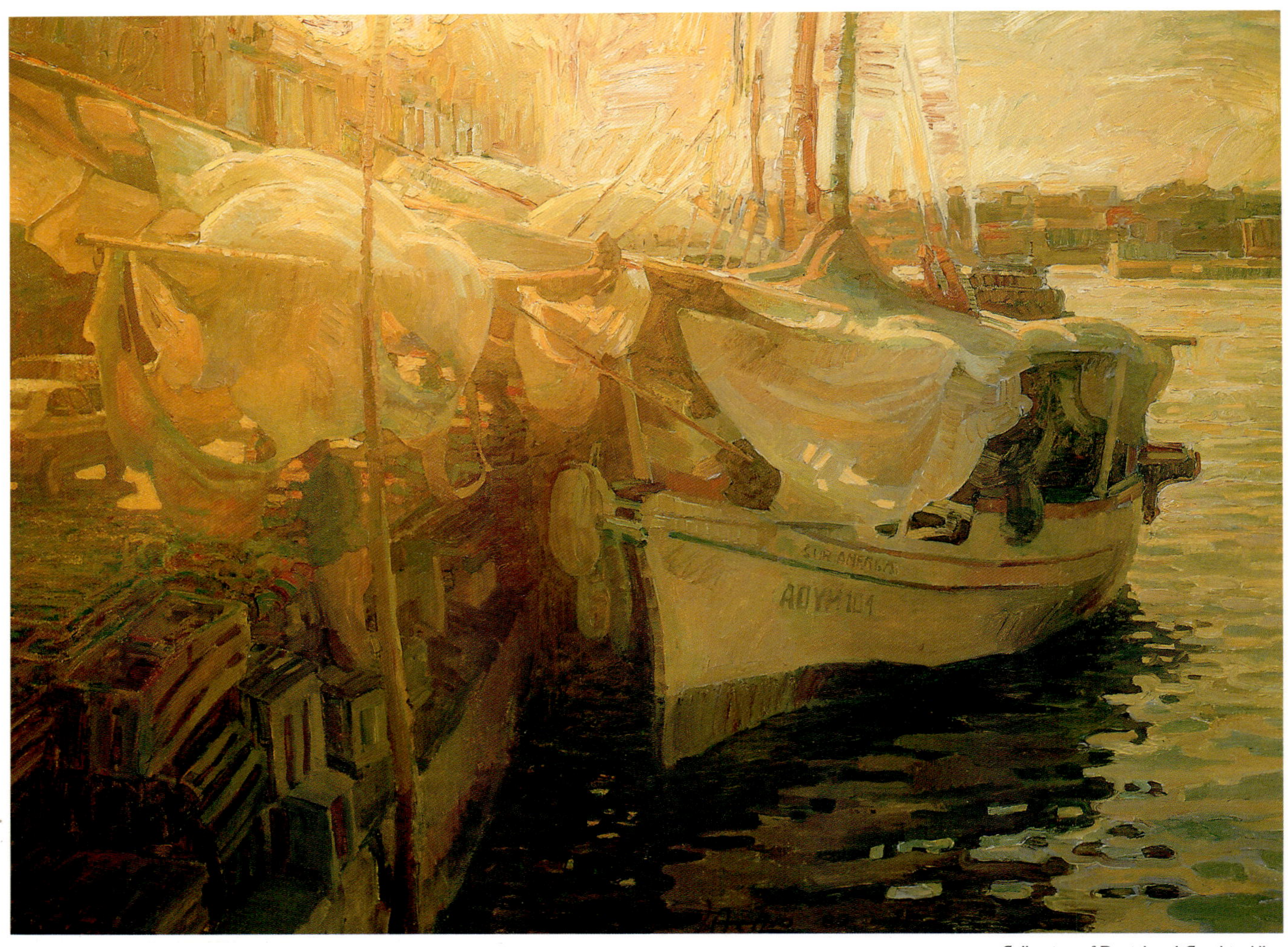

Curacao Floating Market, o/c, 36×50, 1980   Collection of Daniel and Cynthia Allan

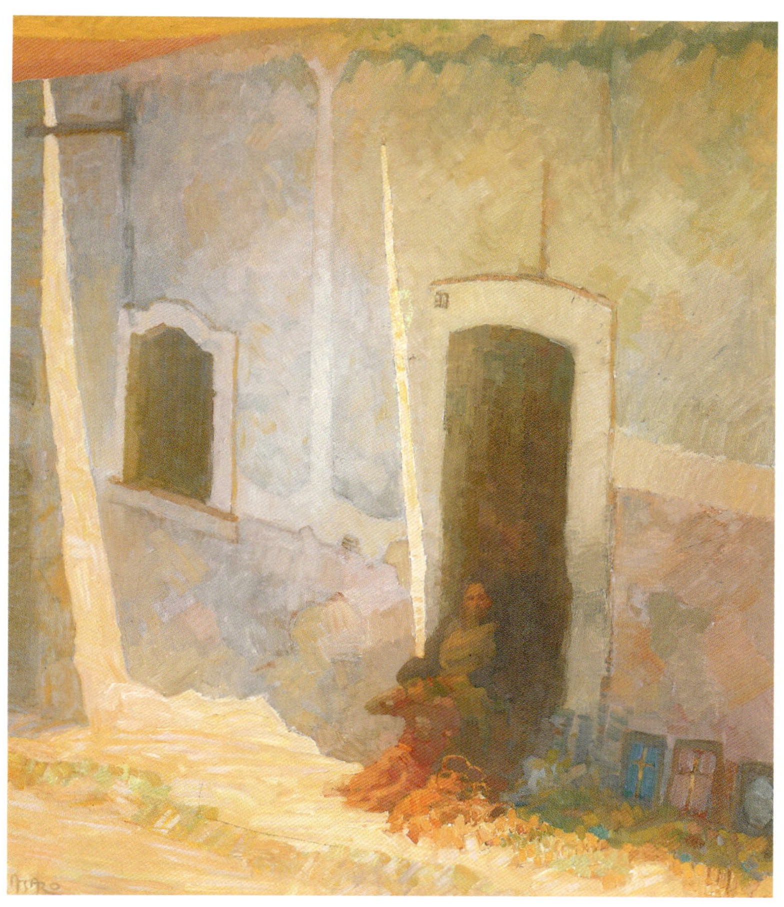

Sunday Afternoon, o/c, 32×28, 1982

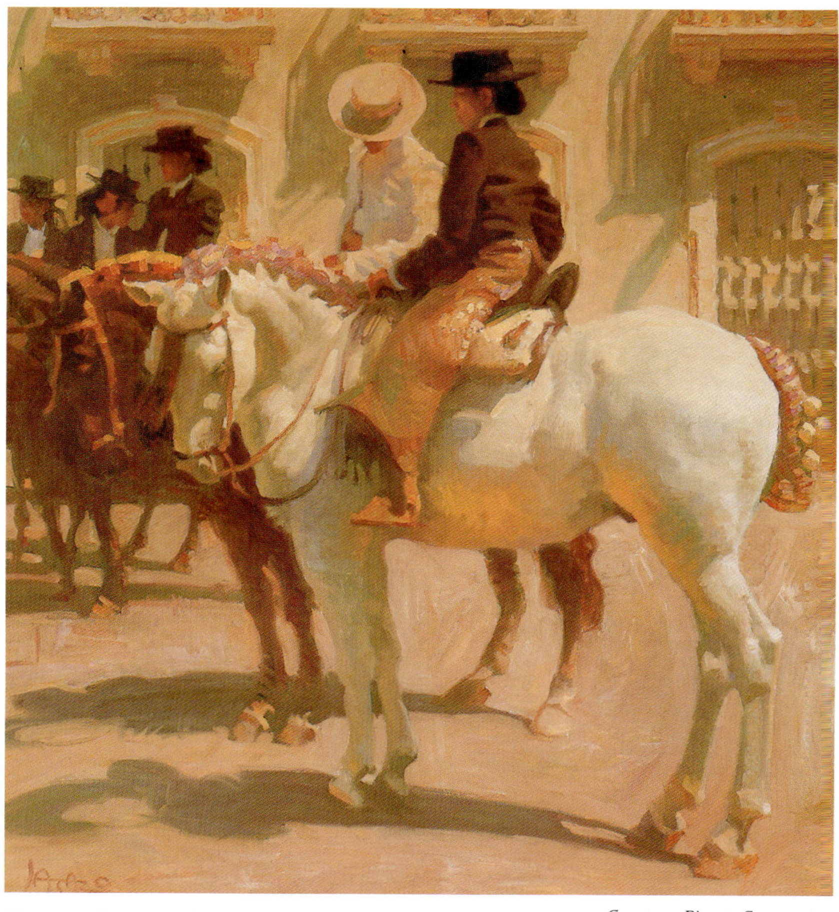

Fiesta at Ronda, o/c, 34×32, 1985

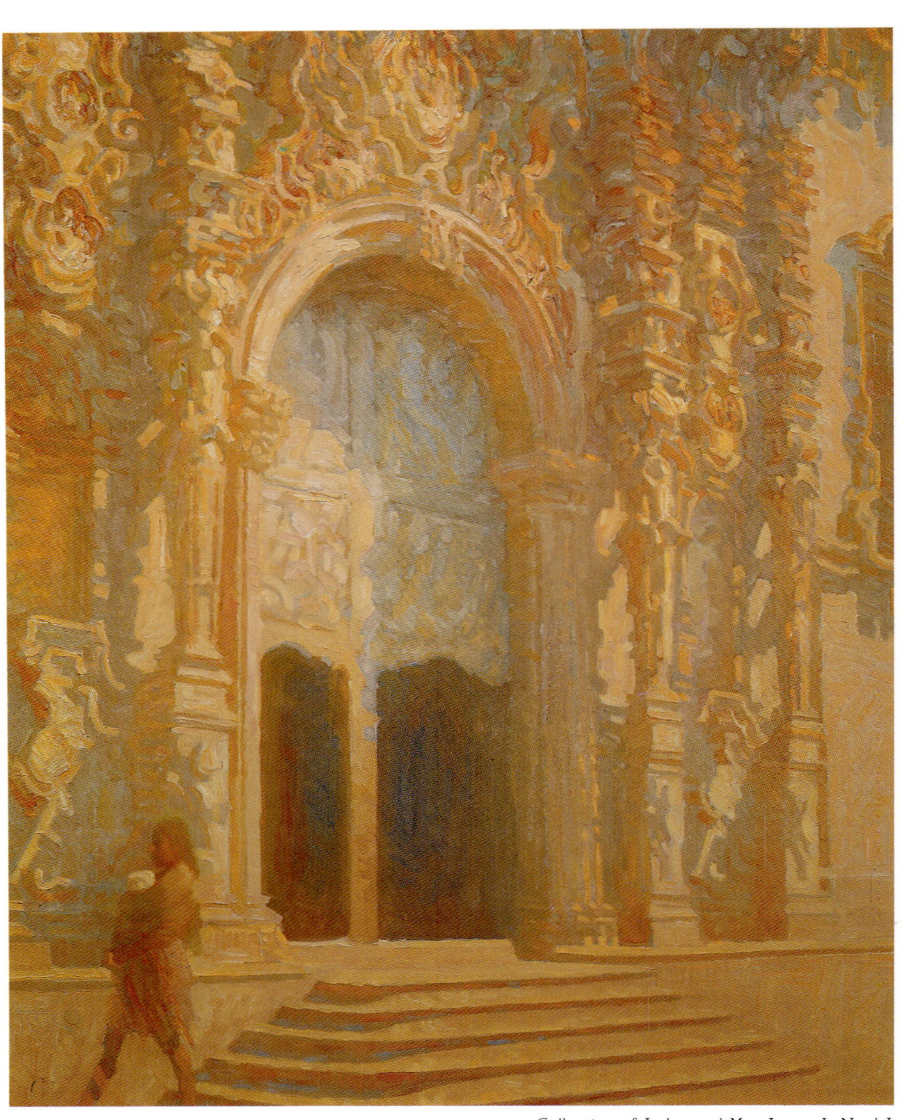

Guanajuato, o/c, 30×26, 1981

Collection of Judge and Mrs. James L. Noel Jr.

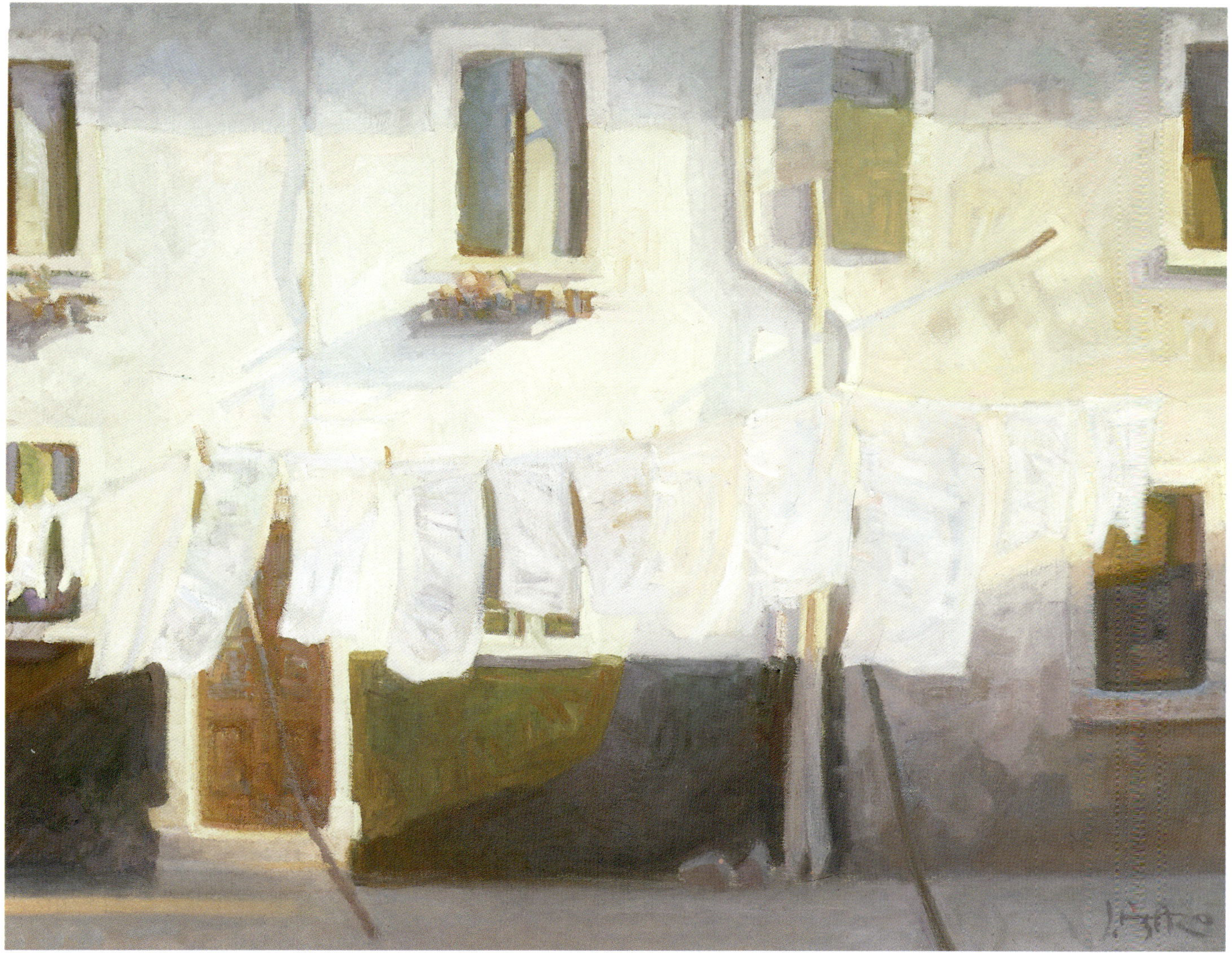

Venetian Doorway, o/c, 26×34, 1986

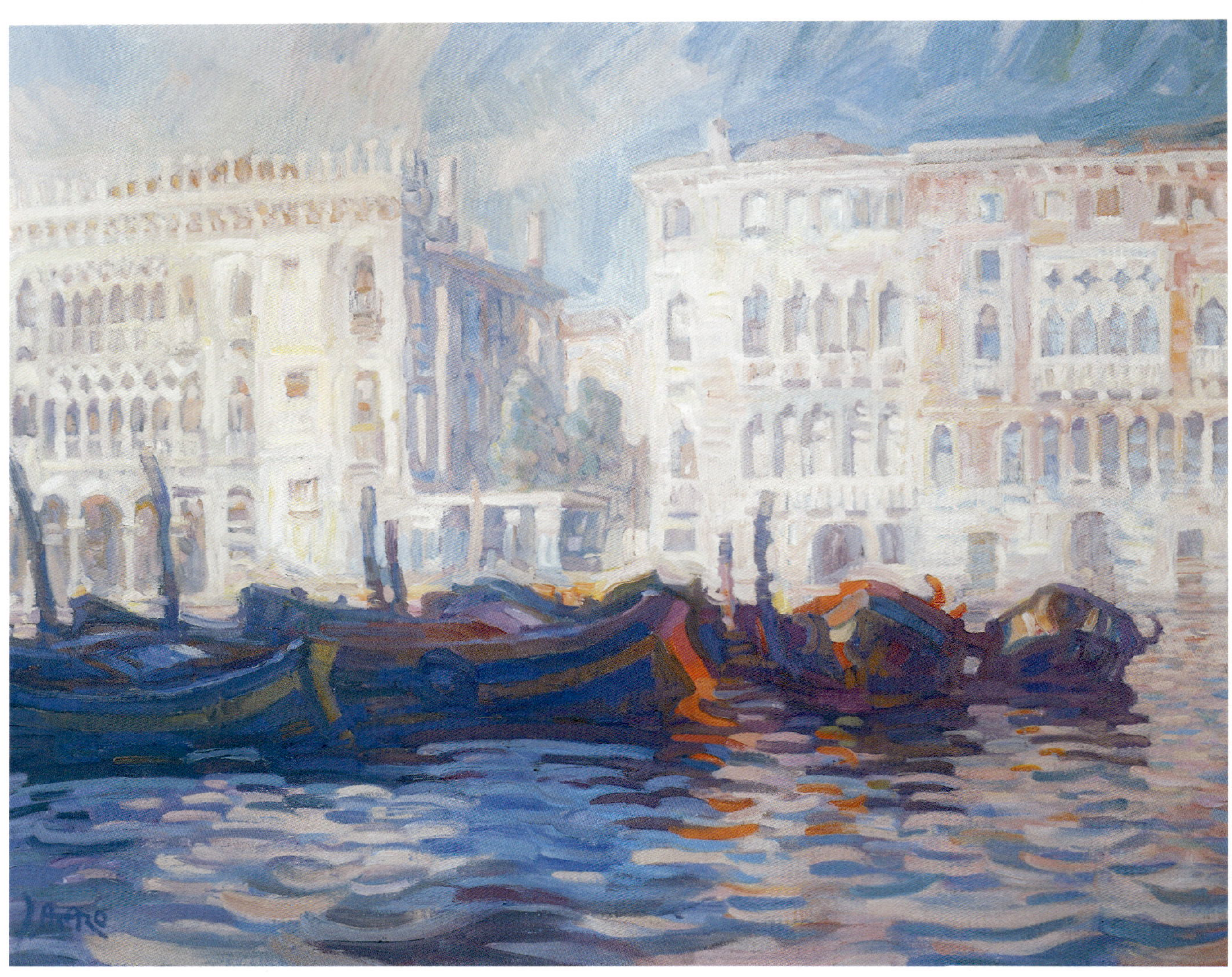
Ca'D'Oro, o/c, 24×32, 1989

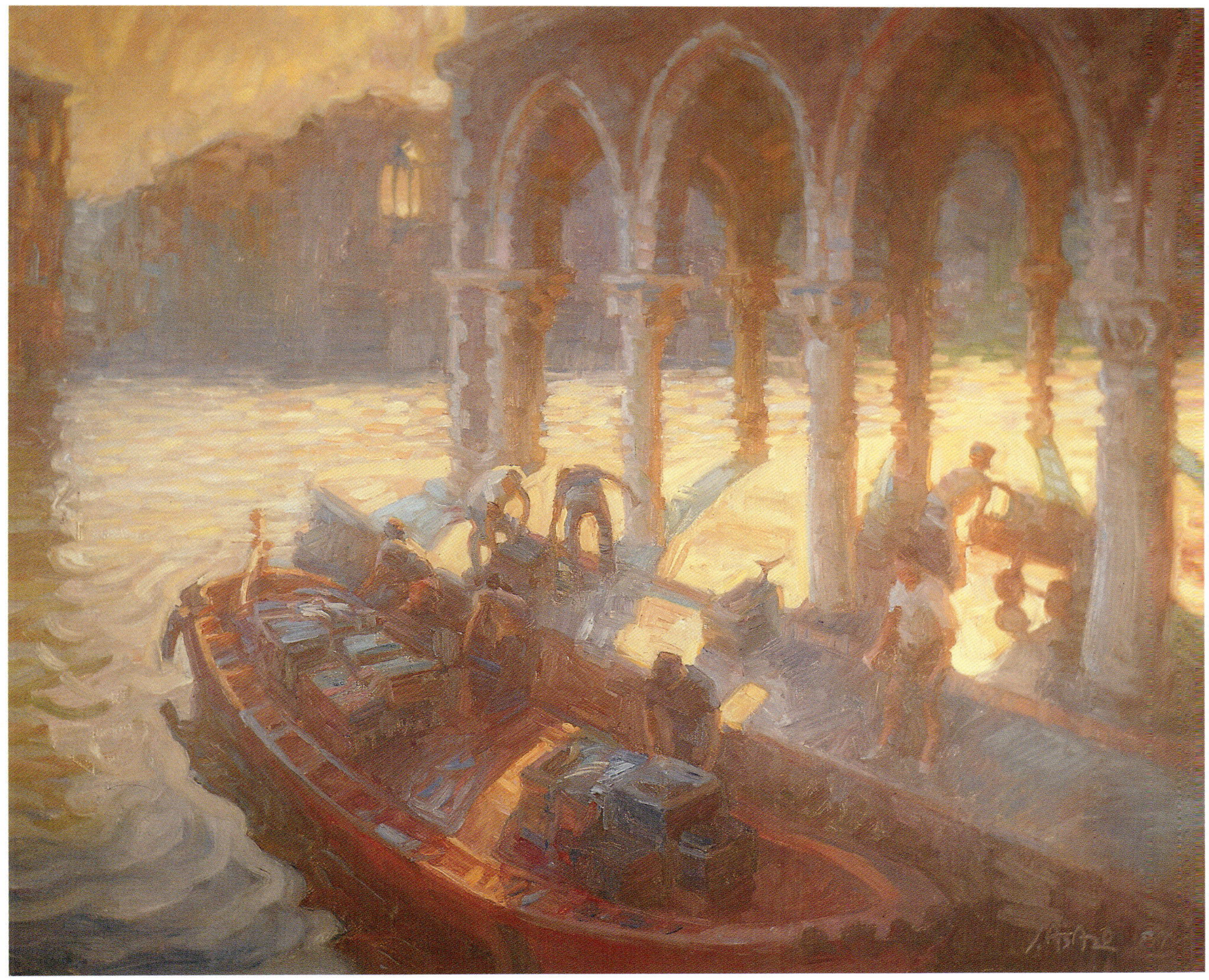

Mercato Pesce Di Venezia, o/c, 24×30, 1987

Collection of Neal and Jean Rains

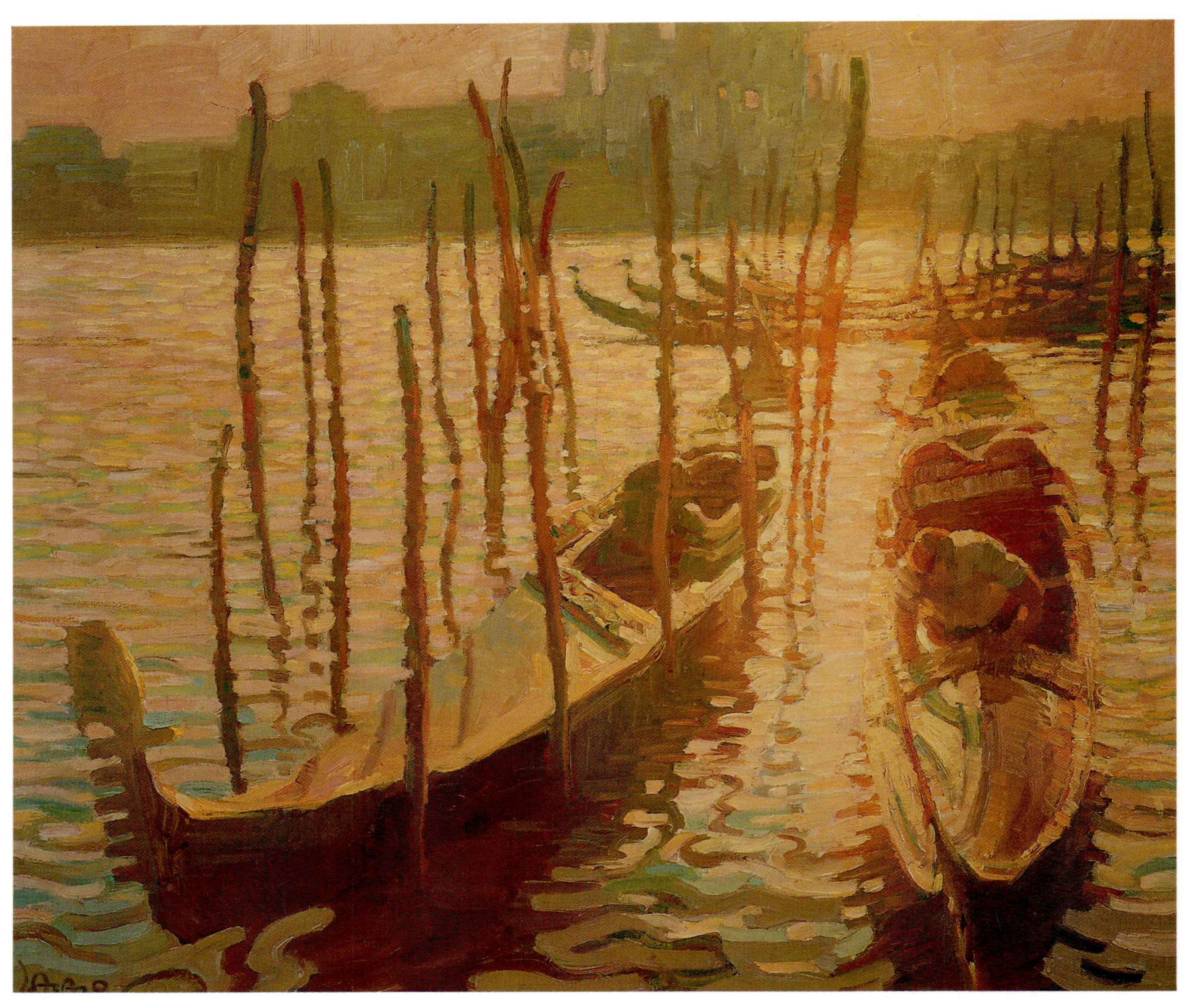

The Grand Canal, o/c, 24×28, 1983

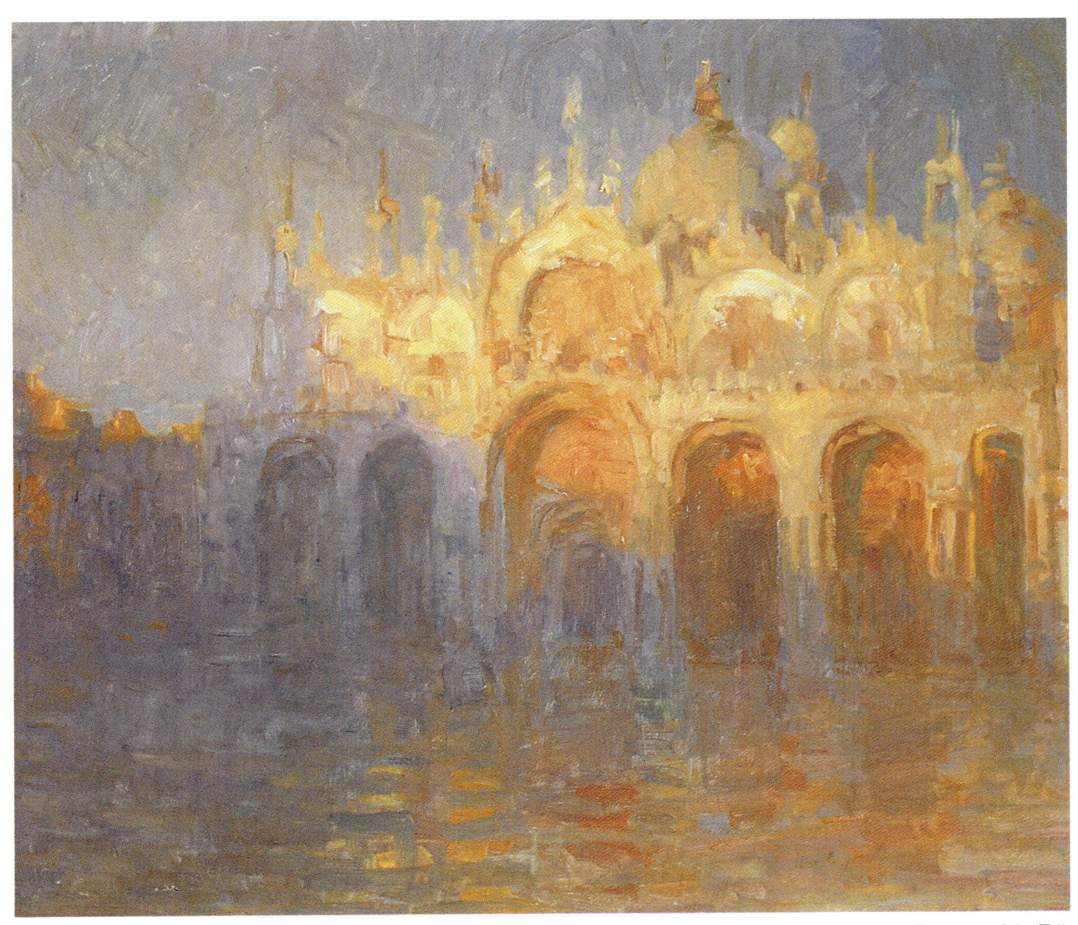

Study for Piazza San Marco, o/c, 14×17, 1987

Courtesy of Art-Talk

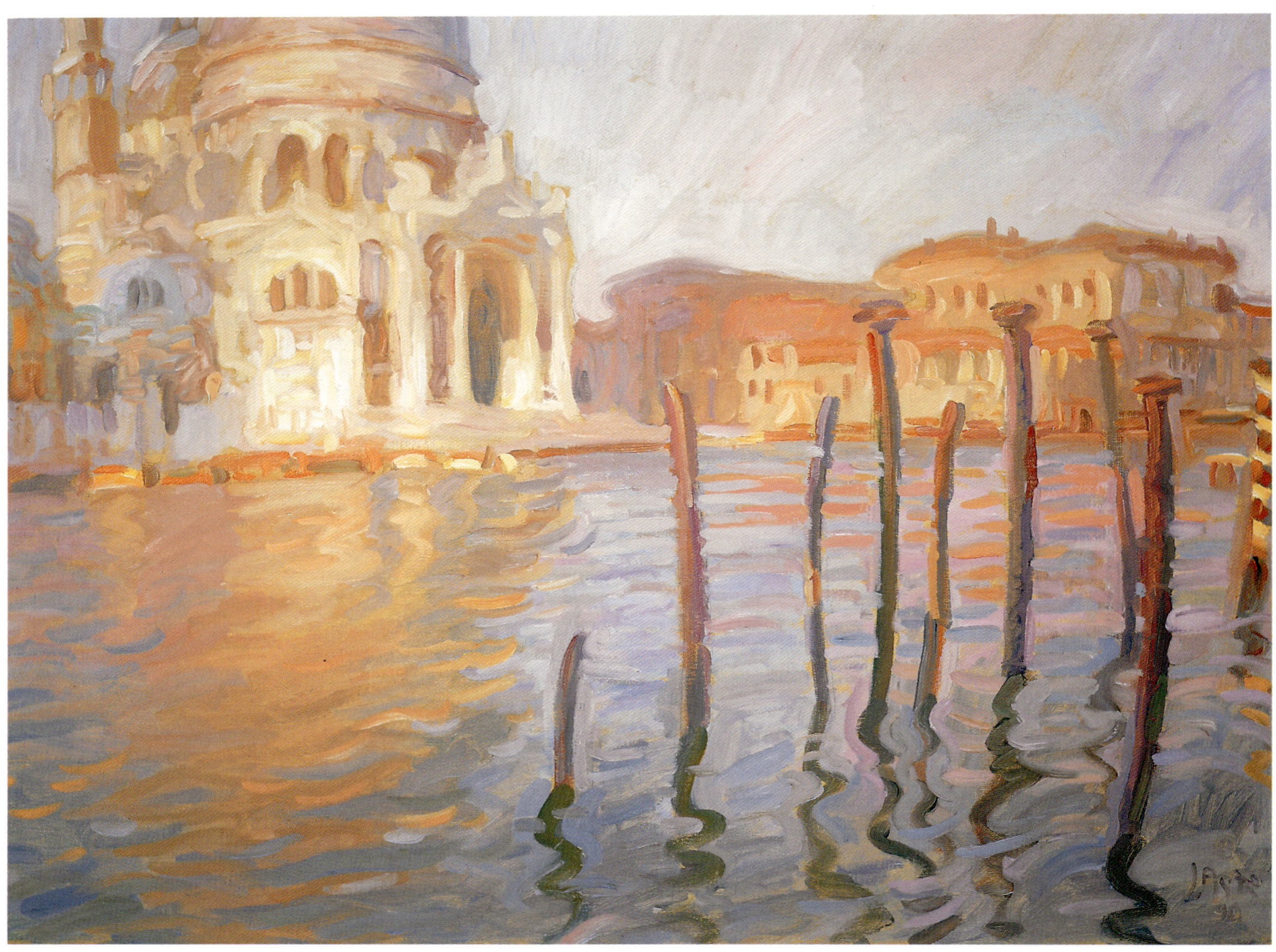

Santa Maria Della Salute, Sunrise, o/c, 26×36, 1990

Collection of Peter and DeAnna Tomaryn

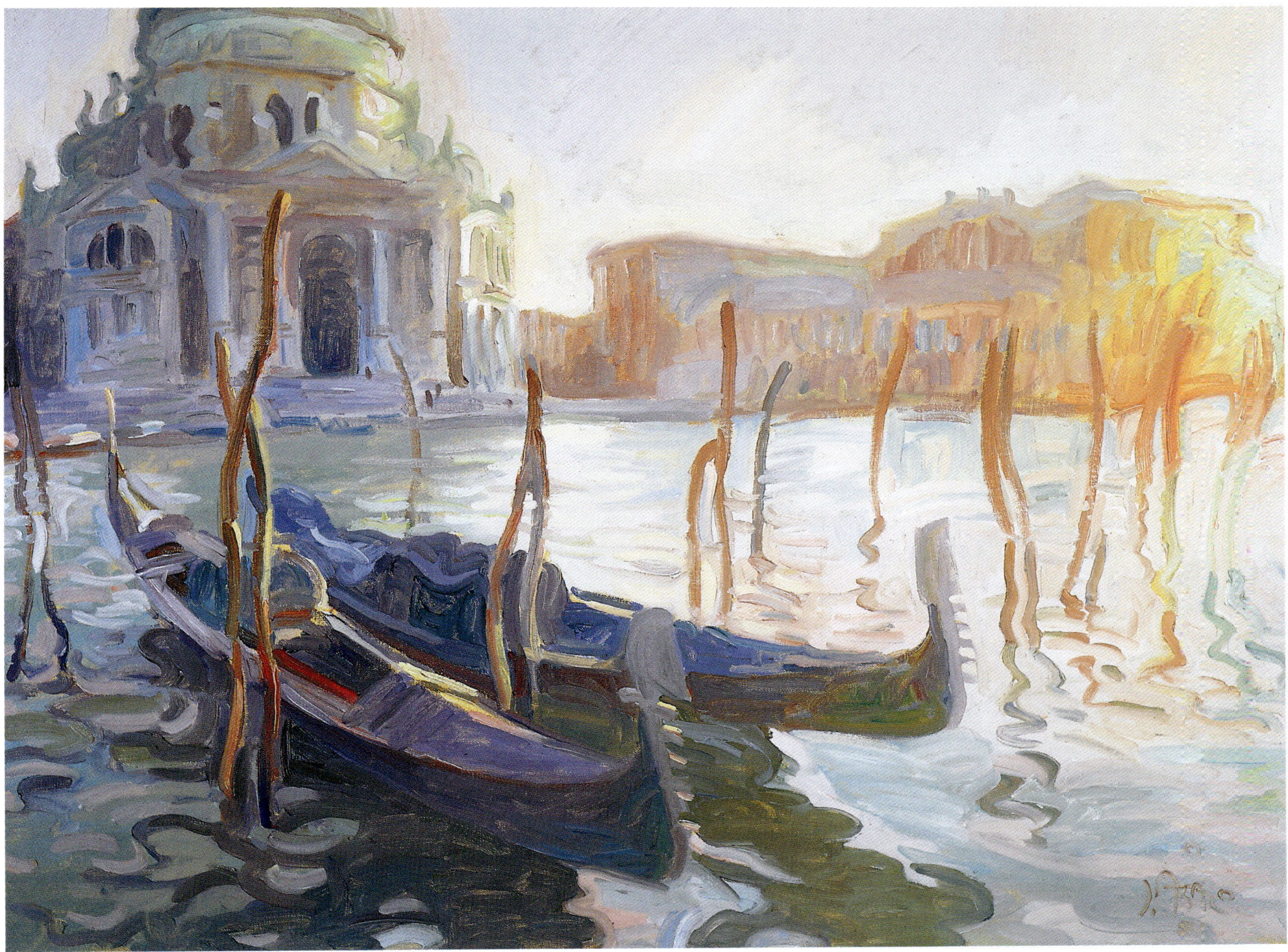

Santa Maria Della Salute, Sunset, o/c, 26×36, 1990

Collection of Peter and DeAnna Tomaryn

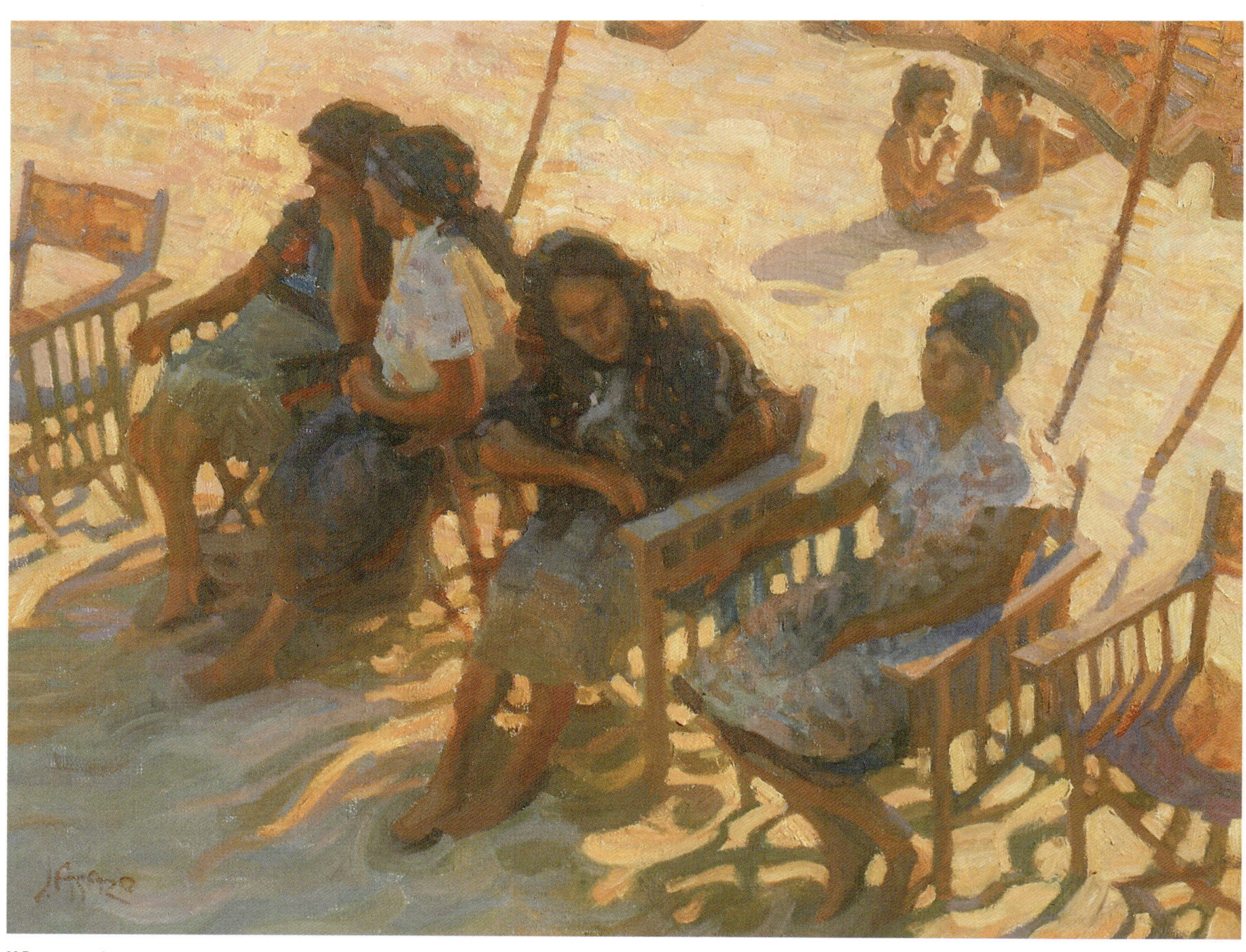

Women of Nazare, o/c, 24×32, 1986

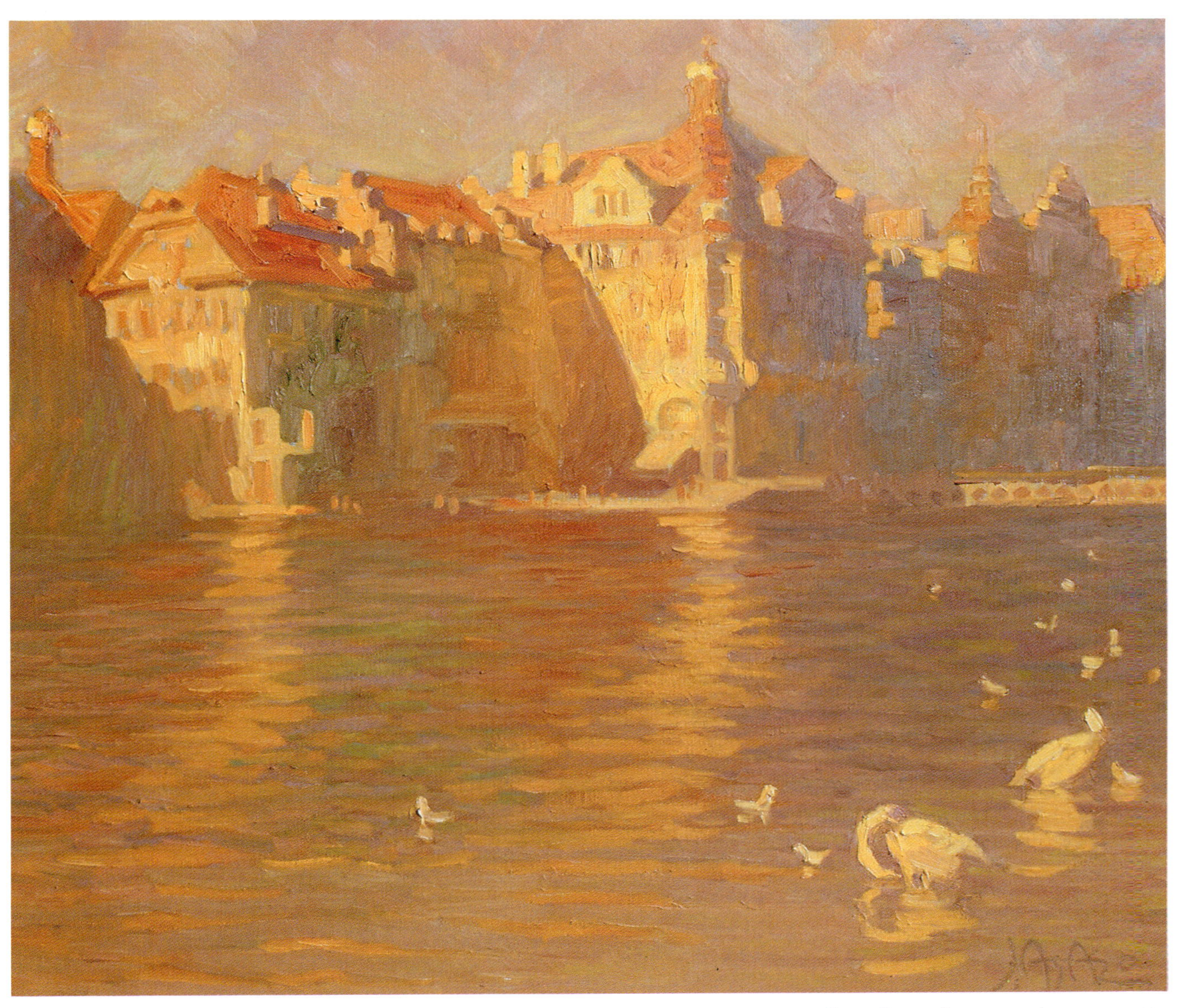

River Reuss, Lucerne, o/c, 18×22, 1984

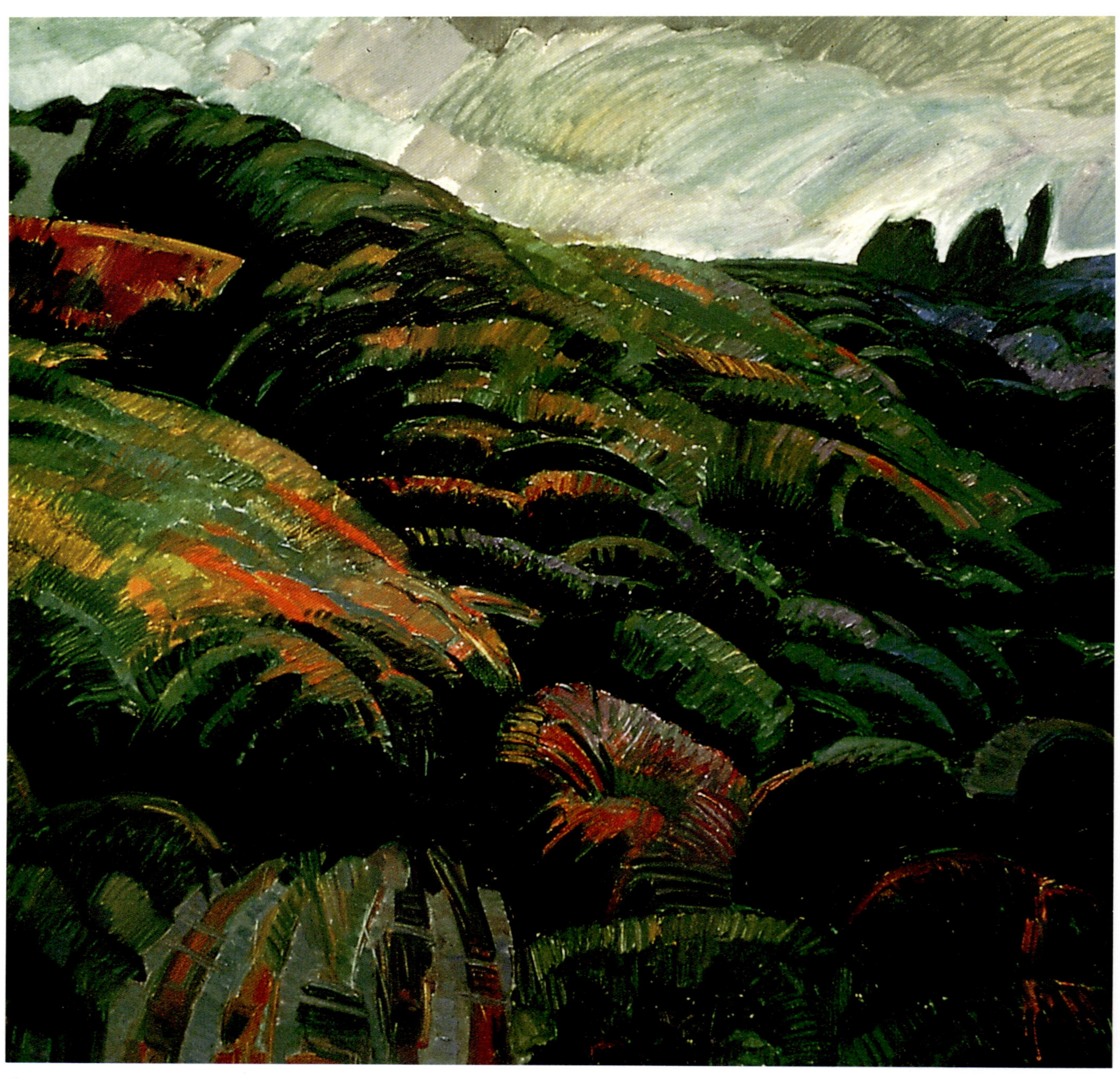

Santa Marguerita, o/c, 36×38, 1978

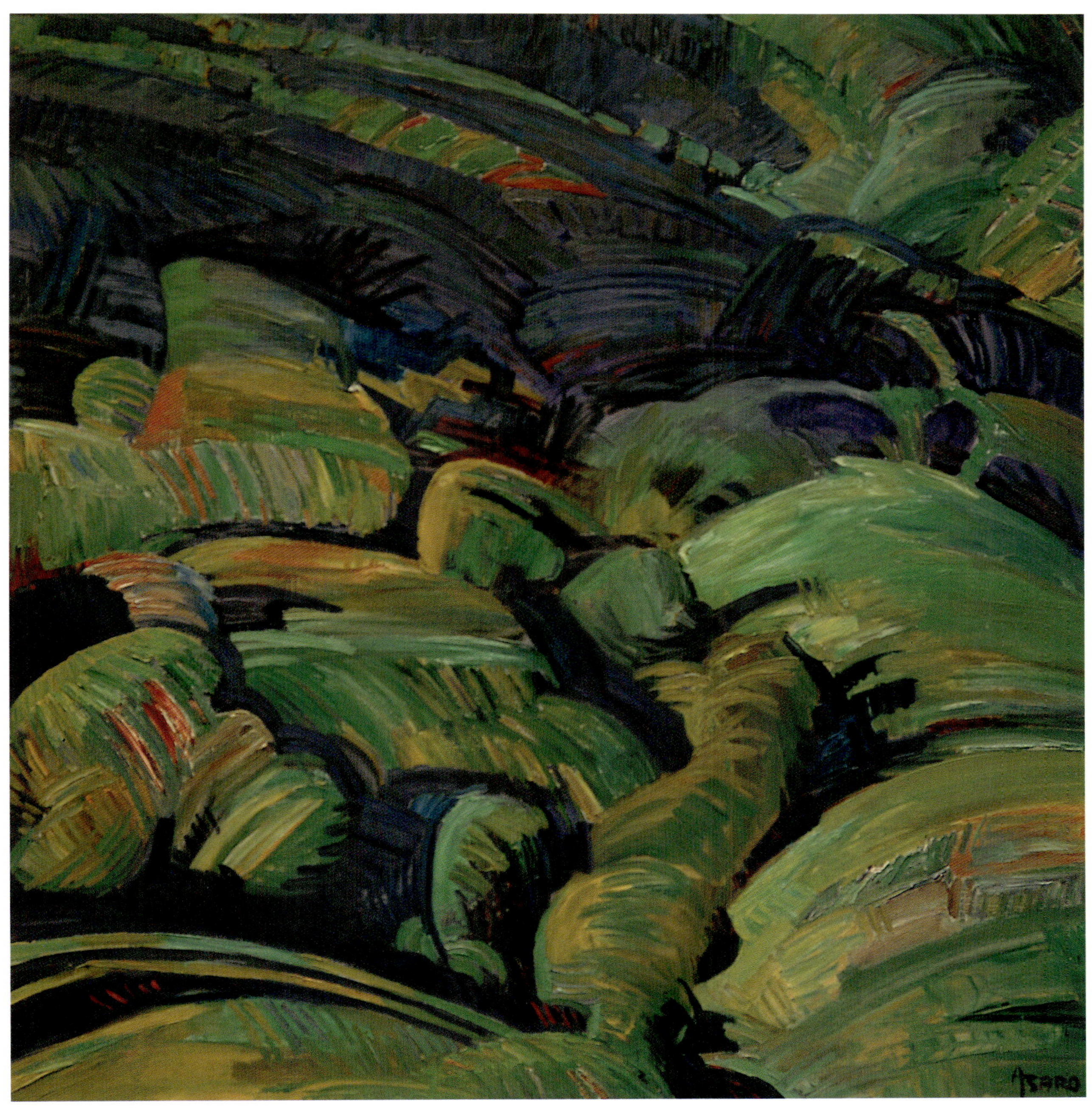

Santa Marguerita II, o/c, 40×40, 1978

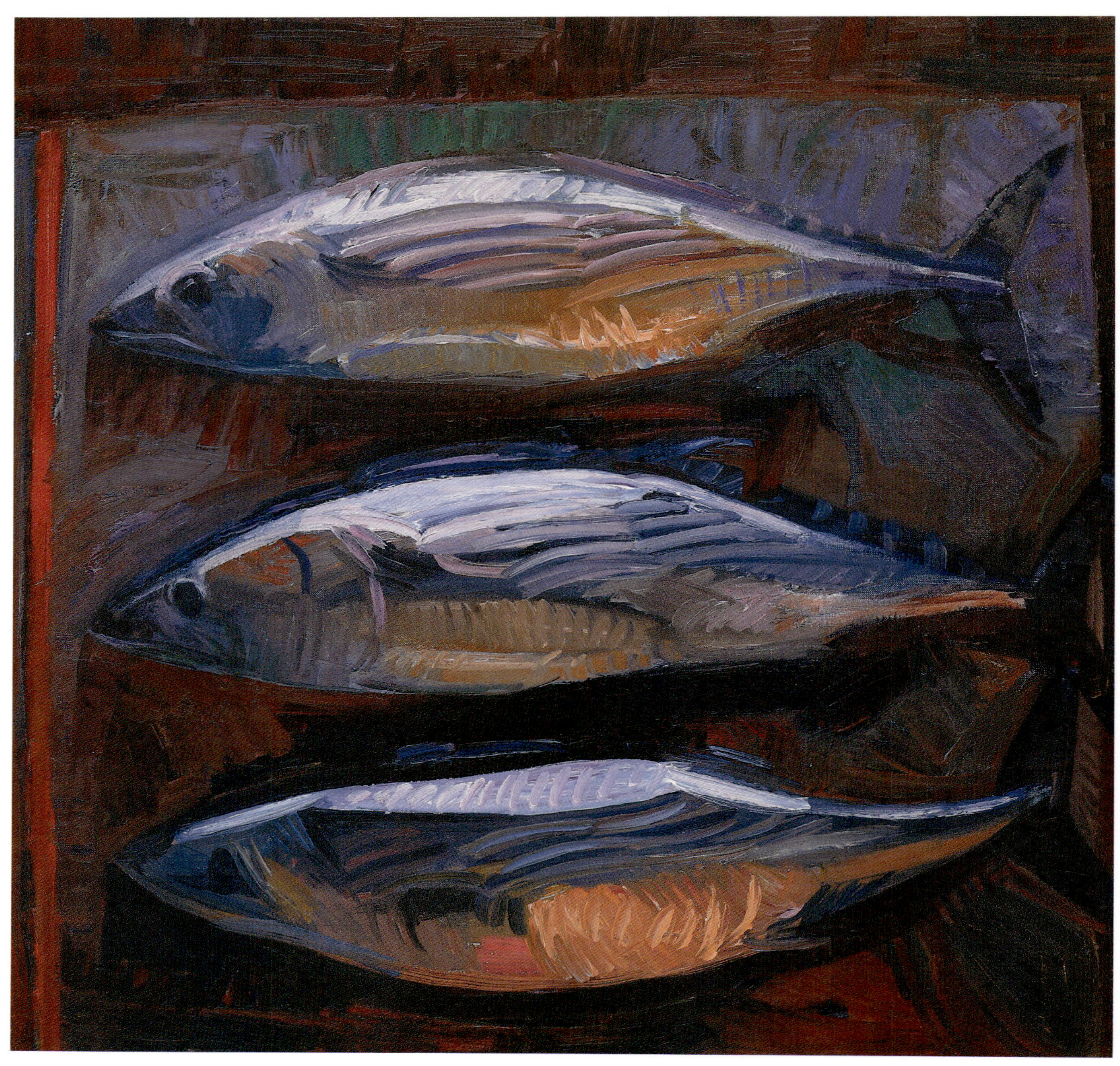

Three Bonita, o/c, 26×28, 1979

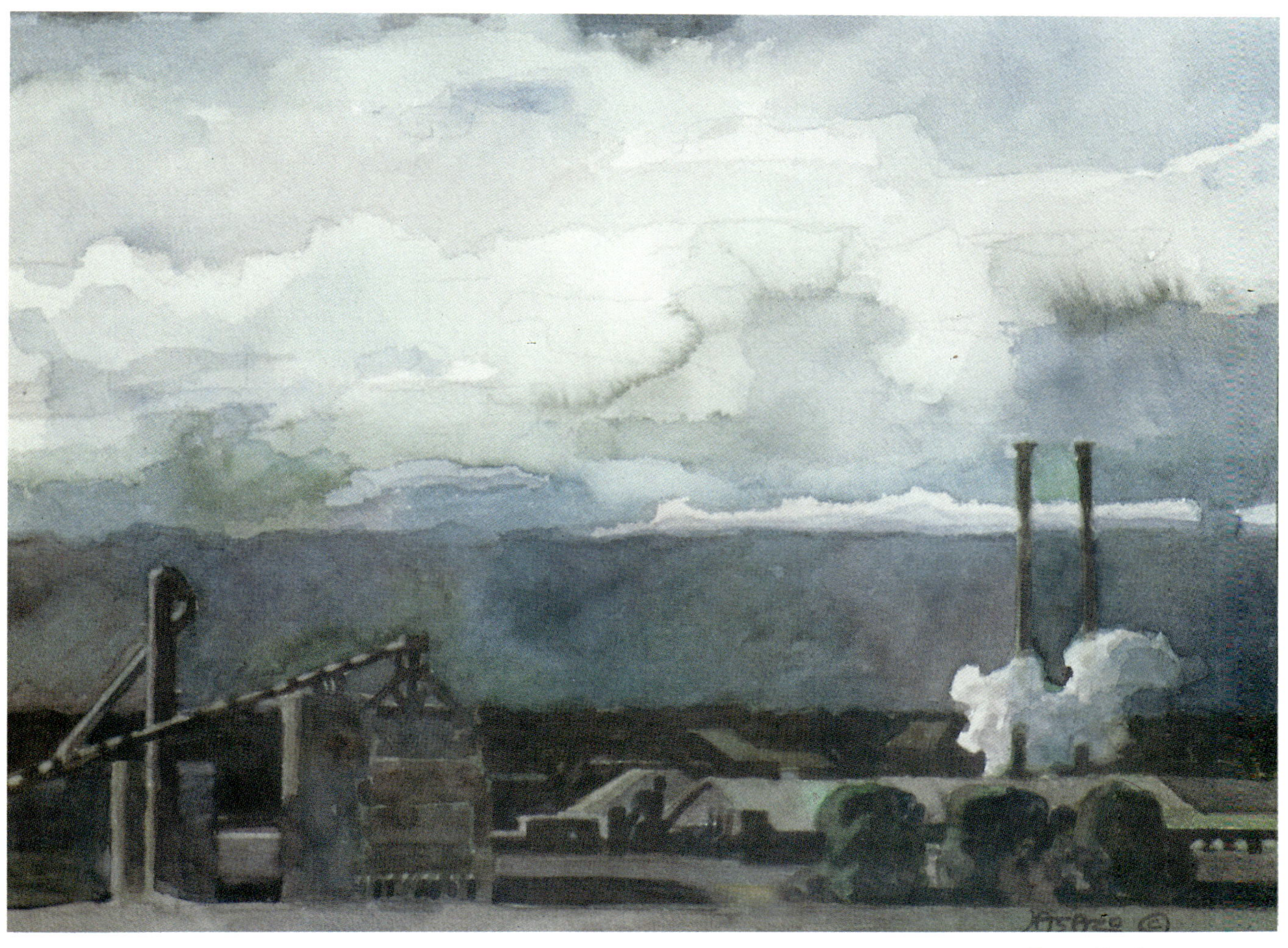

Flagstaff, w/c, 22×30, 1979

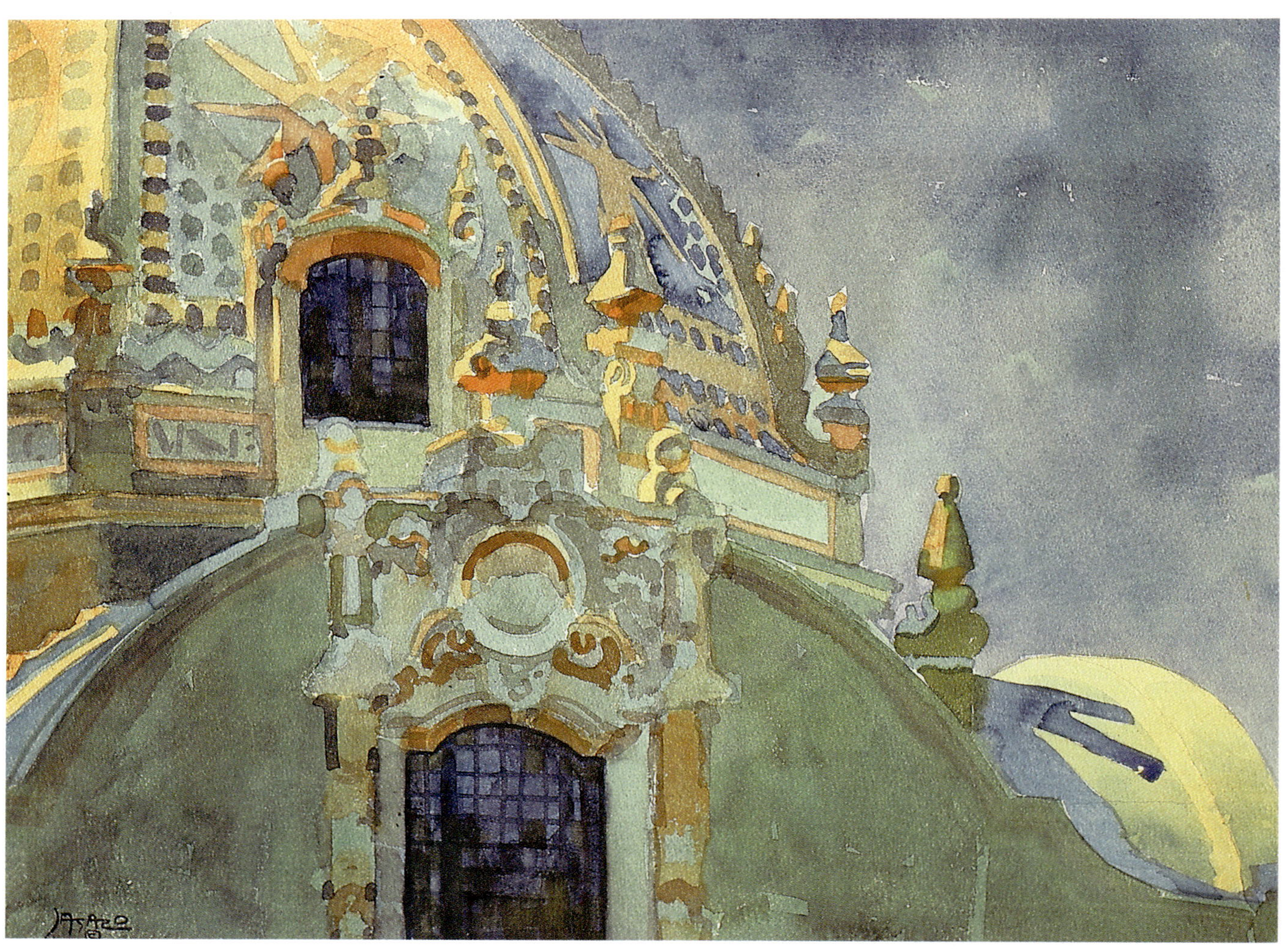

Balboa Park, w/c, 22×30, 1979

BIOGRAPHY

Born San Diego, February 28, 1937
Studied with Donal Hord, San Diego, 1952-1955.
Art Center College of Design, Pasadena, 1955-1959
Art Student's League, New York City, 1957
Illustrator, New Center Studios, Detroit, 1960-1965
Freelance Illustrator, New York City, 1965-1968
Freelance Illustrator, Los Angeles, 1968-1970
Los Angeles Institute of Architecture, 1979

TEACHING

Art Center College of Design, Pasadena, 1974-1981
Laguna Beach School of Art and Design, 1982
Palomar College, San Marcos, California, 1982-1985

SELECTED EXHIBITIONS

1964 – New York Illustrators Club
1965 – New York Illustrators Club
1967 – New York Illustrators Club
       U.S. Air Force Documentary Program, Washington DC
1968 – New York Illustrators Club
       Award of Excellence, New York Art Directors Club
       U.S. Air Force Documentary Program, Washington DC
1969 – U.S. Air Force Documentary Program, Washington DC
1970 – One man show, Paideia Gallery, Los Amgeles
1973 – One man show, Paideia Gallery, Los Angeles
1974 – One man show, Paideia Gallery, Los Angeles
1976 – Group show, Moody Gallery, Pasadena
1977 – Group show, Moody Gallery, Pasadena
1978 – One man show, Moody Gallery, Pasadena
1979 – Group show, Challis Gallery, Laguna Beach, California
       One man show, Challis Gallery, Laguna Beach, California
1980 – Pasadena Fifth Annual Art Exhibition, Pasadena
       Pepper Tree Ranch Invitational, Calabasas, California
       Watercolor West Exhibition, Riverside, California
       Two man show, Innerscape Gallery, Colorado Springs
       Two man show, Varient Gallery, Taos, New Mexico
       Taos Art and Music Festival, Taos, New Mexico
       67th Allied Artists of America, New York City
1981 – *Award*, Watercolor West, Riverside, California
       68th Allied Artists of America, New York City
1983 – American Watercolor Society Annual, New York City
1984 – American Watercolor Society Annual, New York City
1985 – *Cash award*, American Watercolor Society Annual, New York City
       Western Heritage Show, Houston, Texas
1986 – Western Heritage Show, Houston, Texas
       Artist of America Show, Denver, Colorado
1987 – Artist of America Show, Denver, Colorado
1990 – One man show, Upstairs Gallery, Beverly Hills, California
1991 – Cowboy Hall of Fame, NAWA

BIBLIOGRAPHY

Susan Vreeland, "John Asaro, in Pursuit of Light," *Southwest Art Magazine*, July 1982.
Dan Cotterman, "Sage Brush Artist," *Horse and Rider Magazine*, September 1982.
Susan Vreeland, "Southwest Art Lifestyles and Elements," *Rancho Bernardo Magazine*, February 1983.
Anna Katherine, "John Asaro, Artist," *The Santa Fean*, April 1987.
Nancy D'Ambrosio, "Santa Fe – Taos, Visions of Magic," *Horizon Magazine*, October, 1987
Suzanne Deats, "Celebration of Life," cover story, *Focus/Santa Fe Magazine*, Fall 1988.
Richard W. Walker, "The Art of Investment," *Private Club*, March-April, 1989
Franz Brown, "John Asaro," cover story, *Southwest Art Magazine*, May 1990.
J. Matthew Fabris, "Innocent Light," *Stepping Out Arts Magazine*, Issue 29, November 1990.
Lexus TV Commercial, *Southwest Art Magazine*, October 1990.
Robert Perine, *Asaro, A New Romanticism*, Artra Publishing, December 1991.

Book Design: Robert Perine
Production art: Barry Age
Typography: Headline Graphics, Encinitas
Printed and bound in Bangkok, Thailand by Frye & Smith Eastern.

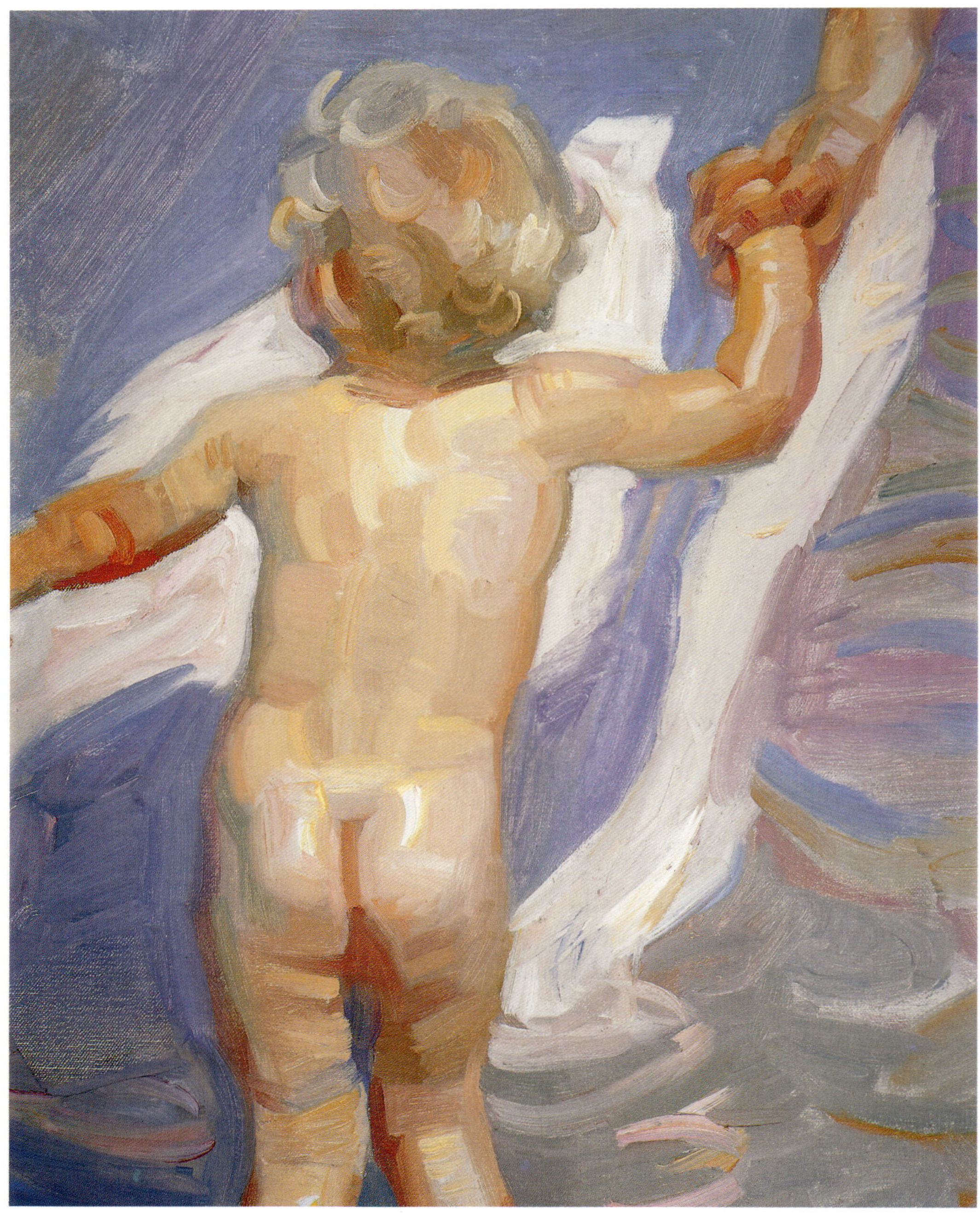

Detail, *The Bathers*, 1991.

112

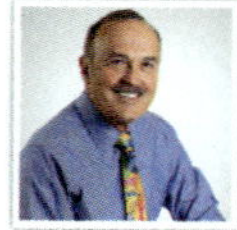

Mike Holt's Illustrated Guide to

UNDERSTANDING NEC® REQUIREMENTS FOR

SOLAR PHOTOVOLTAIC AND ENERGY STORAGE SYSTEMS

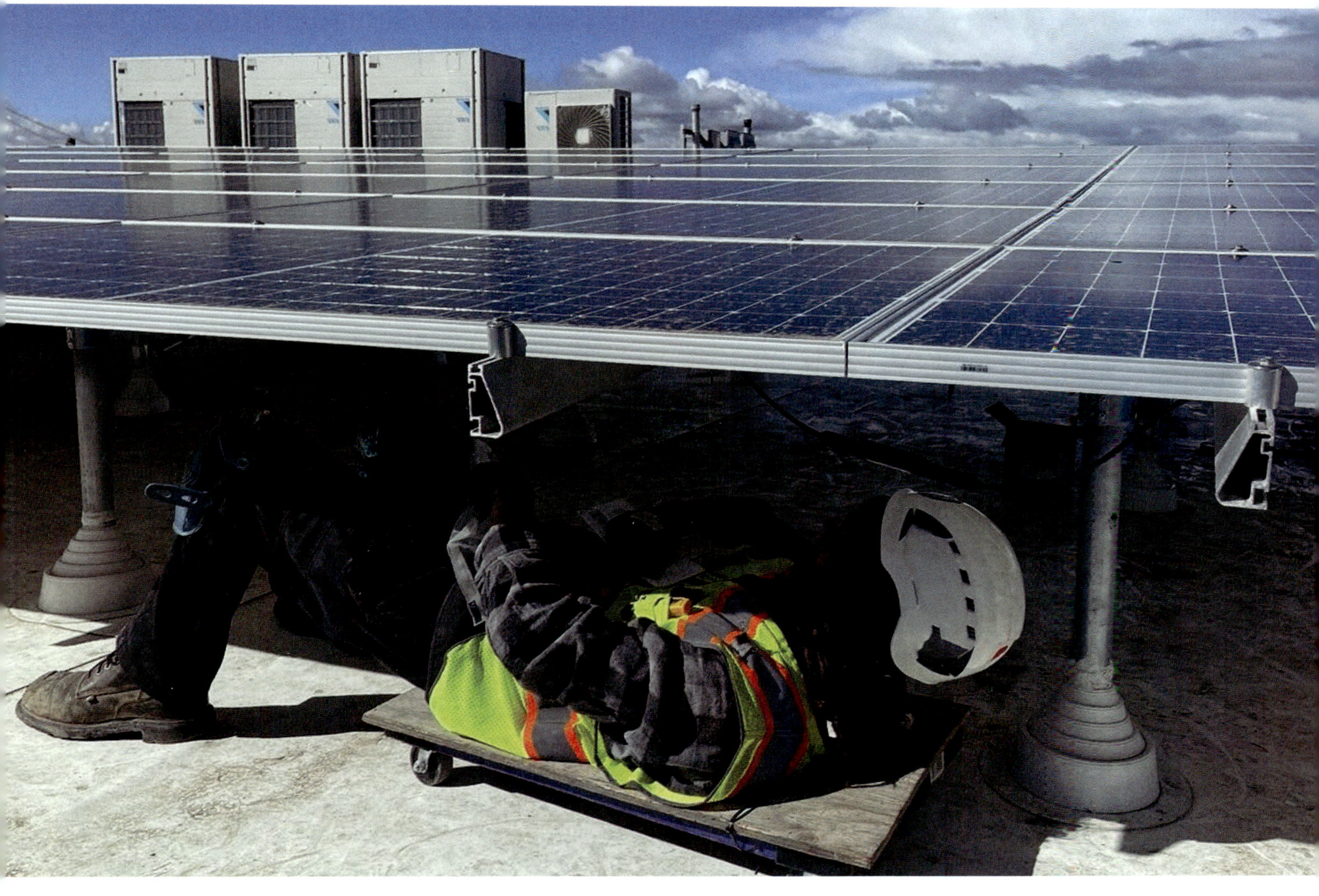

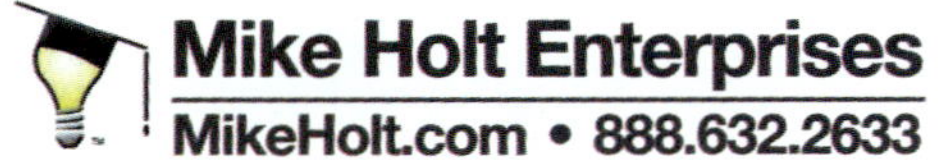
Mike Holt Enterprises
MikeHolt.com • 888.632.2633

BASED ON THE
2023 NEC®

NOTICE TO THE READER

Mike Holt's Illustrated Guide to Understanding NEC® Requirements for Solar Photovoltaic and Energy Storage Systems, based on the 2023 NEC®

First Printing: March 2023
Author: Mike Holt
Technical Illustrator: Mike Culbreath
Cover Design: Bryan Burch
Cover Photo Credit: Joseph Gemma Montiel,
  President & Director of Field Operations,
  Bay-Tech Electric Inc., San Francisco, California
Layout Design and Typesetting: Cathleen Kwas
COPYRIGHT © 2023 Charles Michael Holt
ISBN 978-1-950431-75-5

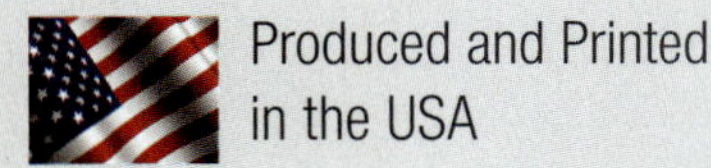

Produced and Printed
in the USA

This logo is a registered trademark of Mike Holt Enterprises, Inc.

NEC®, NFPA 70®, NFPA 70E® and *National Electrical Code*® are registered trademarks of the National Fire Protection Association.

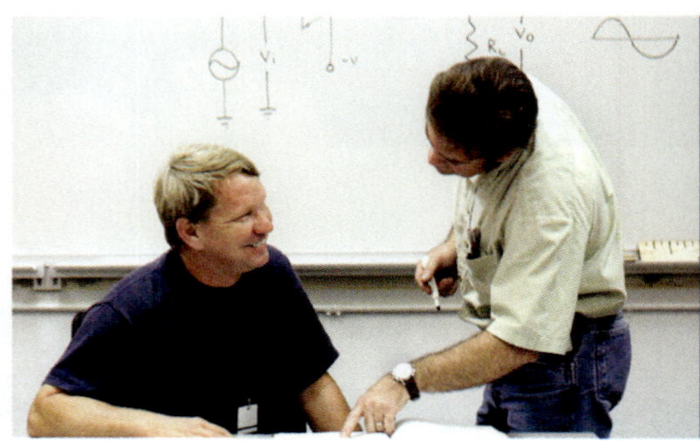

Are you an Instructor?

You can request a review copy of this or other Mike Holt Publications:

888.632.2633 • Training@MikeHolt.com

Download a sample PDF of all our publications by visiting MikeHolt.com/Instructors

I dedicate this book to the

Lord Jesus Christ, *my mentor and teacher.*

Proverbs 16:3

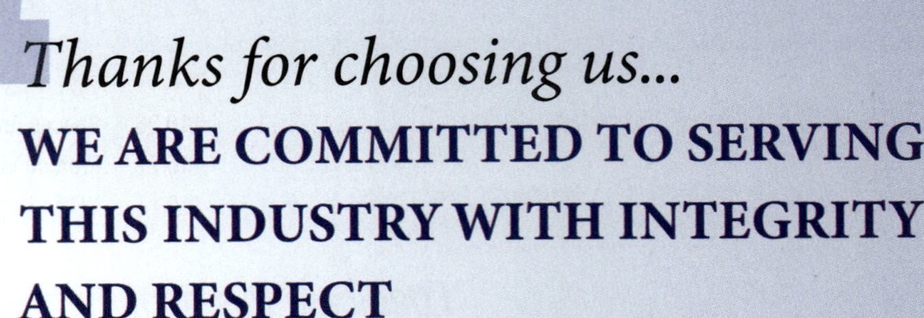

> *Thanks for choosing us...*
> ## WE ARE COMMITTED TO SERVING THIS INDUSTRY WITH INTEGRITY AND RESPECT

Since 1975, we have worked hard to develop products that get results, and to help individuals in their pursuit of success in this exciting industry.

From the very beginning we have been committed to the idea that customers come first. Everyone on my team will do everything they possibly can to help you succeed. I want you to know that we value you and are honored that you have chosen us to be your partner in training.

You are the future of this industry and we know that it is you who will make the difference in the years to come. My goal is to share with you everything that I know and to encourage you to pursue your education on a continuous basis. I hope that not only will you learn theory, *Code*, calculations, or how to pass an exam, but that in the process, you will become the expert in the field and the person others know to trust.

To put it simply, we genuinely care about your success and will do everything that we can to help you take your skills to the next level!

We are happy to partner with you on your educational journey.

God bless and much success,

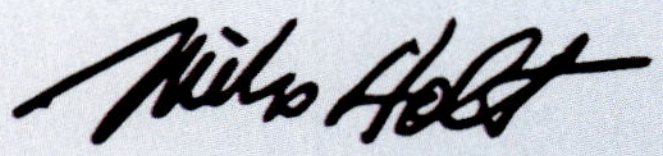

TABLE OF CONTENTS

ABOUT THIS TEXTBOOK

Mike Holt's Illustrated Guide to Understanding NEC Requirements for Solar Photovoltaic and Energy Storage Systems, based on the 2023 NEC

This textbook covers the *National Electrical Code®* requirements as they relate to Solar Photovoltaic (PV) systems. While some may think that only Articles 690 and 691 relate to Solar PV installations, the reality is that almost every chapter in the *NEC®* pertains to some part of a PV installation or to a location where PV may be installed. This text covers not only the conductors and equipment that are directly responsible for the production of power, but it also covers the rules that apply to conversion and delivery of this power to the end user and the utility. The *NEC* rules that govern PV systems are very complex and as a result, could easily be misinterpreted. The intent of this textbook is to help you narrow down which rules relate to a PV installation and to better understand how and when they should be applied. Changes to these *NEC* rules for 2023, are indicated by underlining.

Mike's writing style is informative, practical, easy to understand, and applicable for today's electrical professional. As with all of Mike Holt's textbooks, this one is built around hundreds of full-color illustrations and photographs that show the requirements of the *National Electrical Code* in a practical setting. The images provide a visual representation of the information being discussed, helping you to better understand how the *Code* rules are applied.

This material also explains frequently misinterpreted *NEC* requirements, tips on proper electrical installations, and the hazards related to improper installations. Sometimes a rule seems confusing or it may be difficult to understand its actual application. Where this is the case, you will find additional content and videos that further explain how to apply the *NEC*. Our intention is to help the industry better understand the *NEC* and encourage all *Code* users to be a part of the change process that helps create a better *NEC* for the future.

This textbook is supported by in-depth videos that will take your understanding of PV systems to another level. The guest panel that was assembled for the making of this video was selected from the top experts in the PV industry and they bring a unique perspective to this discussion of *NEC* requirements for solar installations. As the installations of PV systems become more prevalent, the chances that you'll need to work on them will greatly increase. If you haven't participated in any additional training for PV systems, you could create a hazard for both yourself and the end user by working on the system.

Keeping up with the current requirements of the *NEC* should be the goal of everyone involved in the electrical industry, whether you are an installer, contractor, inspector, engineer or instructor, and this textbook is designed to help you do so.

The Scope of This Textbook

This textbook focuses on the *NEC* rules that apply to Solar PV systems. The scope of the textbook covers the general requirements contained in Articles 90 through 480, that every solar installer should know, as well as the rules specific to these systems found in Articles 690, 691, 705, 706, and 710 and is based on the following conditions:

1. Power Systems and Voltage. All power-supply systems are assumed to be one of the following nominal voltages or "voltage class", unless identified otherwise:

- ▸ 2-wire, single-phase, 120V
- ▸ 3-wire, single-phase, 120/240V
- ▸ 4-wire, three-phase, 120/240V Delta High-Leg
- ▸ 4-wire, three-phase, 208Y/120V or 480Y/277V Wye

2. Electrical Calculations. Unless the question or example specifies three-phase, they're based on a single-phase power supply. In addition, all amperage calculations are rounded to the nearest whole number in accordance with Section 220.5(B).

3. Conductor Material/Insulation. The conductor material and insulation are copper THWN-2, unless otherwise indicated.

4. Conductor Sizing.

Circuits Rated 100A or Less. Conductors are sized to the 60°C column of Table 310.16 [110.14(C)(1)(a)(2)]. Where equipment is listed and identified for use with conductors having at least a 75°C temperature rating, the conductors can be sized to the 75°C column of Table 310.16 [110.14(C)(1)(a)(3)].

Circuits Rated Over 100A. Conductors are sized to the 75°C column of Table 310.16 [110.14(C)(1)(b)(2)].

---

5. Overcurrent Protective Device. The term "overcurrent protective device" refers to a molded-case circuit breaker, unless specified otherwise. Where a fuse is specified, it's a single-element type fuse, also known as a "onetime fuse," unless the text specifies otherwise.

How to Use This Textbook

This textbook is intended to help you interpret the *NEC* and is not a replacement for it, so be sure to have a copy of the 2023 *National Electrical Code* handy. You will notice that we have paraphrased a great deal of the wording, and some of the article and section titles appear different than those in the actual *Code* book. We believe doing so makes it easier to understand the content of the rule, so keep that in mind when comparing this textbook to the *NEC*.

Always compare what is being explained in this textbook to what the *Code* book says and underline or highlight pertinent rules. Get with others who are knowledgeable about the *NEC* to discuss any topics you find difficult to understand or join our free Code Forum at www.MikeHolt.com/Forum to post your question.

NEC Content. This textbook follows the *Code* format, but it does not cover every requirement. For example, it does not include every article, section, subsection, exception, or Informational Note. So, do not be concerned if you see that the textbook contains Exception 1 and Exception 3, but not Exception 2.

Cross-References. Many *NEC* rules refer to requirements located in other sections of the *Code*. This textbook does the same with the intention of helping you develop a better understanding of how the *NEC* rules relate to one another. These cross-references are indicated by *Code* section numbers in brackets, an example of which is "[90.4]."

Informational Notes. Informational Notes contained in the *NEC* will be identified in this textbook as "Note."

Exceptions. Where shown in this textbook, Exceptions to *NEC* rules will be identified as simply "Ex" and not spelled out.

As you read through this textbook, allow yourself enough time to review the text using the graphics and follow the step-by-step examples meant to assist you in a more in-depth understanding of the *Code*.

Answer Keys

Digital answer keys are provided for all your purchases of Mike Holt textbooks, and can be found in your online account at Mike Holt Enterprises. Go to MikeHolt.com/MyAccount and log in to your account, or create one if you haven't already. If you are not currently a Mike Holt customer, you can access your answer key at MikeHolt.com/MyAK23SOL.

Watch the Videos That Accompany This Textbook

Mike, along with an expert panel, recorded videos to accompany this textbook. Watching these videos will complete your learning experience. The videos contain explanations and additional commentary that expand on the topics covered in the text. Mike and the panel discuss the nuances behind the rules, and cover their practical application in the field, in a way that is different from what can be conveyed in written format.

To watch a few video clips, scan this QR Code with a smartphone app or visit MikeHolt.com/23SOLvideos for a sample selection. To get the complete video library  that accompanies this book, call 888.632.2633 and let them know you want to add the videos, or visit MikeHolt.com/upgrade23SOL.

Technical Questions

As you progress through this textbook, you might find that you don't understand every explanation, example, calculation, or comment. If you find some topics difficult to understand, they are discussed in detail in the videos that correlate to this book. You may also find it helpful to discuss your questions with instructors, co-workers, other students, or your supervisor—they might have a perspective that will help you understand more clearly. Don't become frustrated, and don't get down on yourself.

 If you have additional questions that aren't covered in this material, visit MikeHolt.com/Forum, and post your question on the Code Forum for help.

Textbook Errors and Corrections

We're committed to providing you the finest product with the fewest errors and take great care to ensure our textbooks are correct. But we're realistic and know that errors might be found after printing. If you believe that there's an error of any kind (typographical, grammatical, technical, etc.) in this textbook or in the Answer Key, please visit MikeHolt.com/Corrections and complete the online Textbook Correction Form.

Textbook Format

The layout and design of this textbook incorporate special features and symbols that were designed for Mike Holt textbooks to help you easily navigate through the material, and to enhance your understanding of the content.

Formulas

$$P = I \times E$$

Formulas are easily identifiable in green text on a gray bar.

Modular Color-Coded Page Layout

Chapters are color-coded and modular to make it easy to navigate through each section of the textbook.

According to Article 100

Throughout the textbook, Mike references definitions that are easily identified by colored text "**According to Article 100,**" at the start of the paragraph.

Additional Background Information Boxes

Where the author believes that information unrelated to the specific rule will help you understand the concept being taught, he includes these topics, easily identified in boxes that are shaded gray.

Dangers of Objectionable Current

Objectionable neutral current on metal parts can cause electric shock, fires, and the improper operation of electronic equipment and overcurrent protective devices such as GFPEs, GFCIs, SPGFCIs, and AFCIs.

Caution, Danger, and Warning Icons

These icons highlight areas of concern.

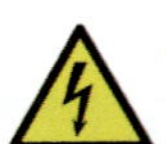

Caution

CAUTION: An explanation of possible damage to property or equipment.

Danger

DANGER: An explanation of possible severe injury or death.

Warning

WARNING: An explanation of possible severe property damage or personal injury.

Key Features

Underlined text denotes changes to the *Code* for the 2023 *NEC*.

Examples and practical application questions and answers are contained in yellow boxes.

Each first level subsection of each *Code* rule is highlighted in yellow to help you navigate through the text.

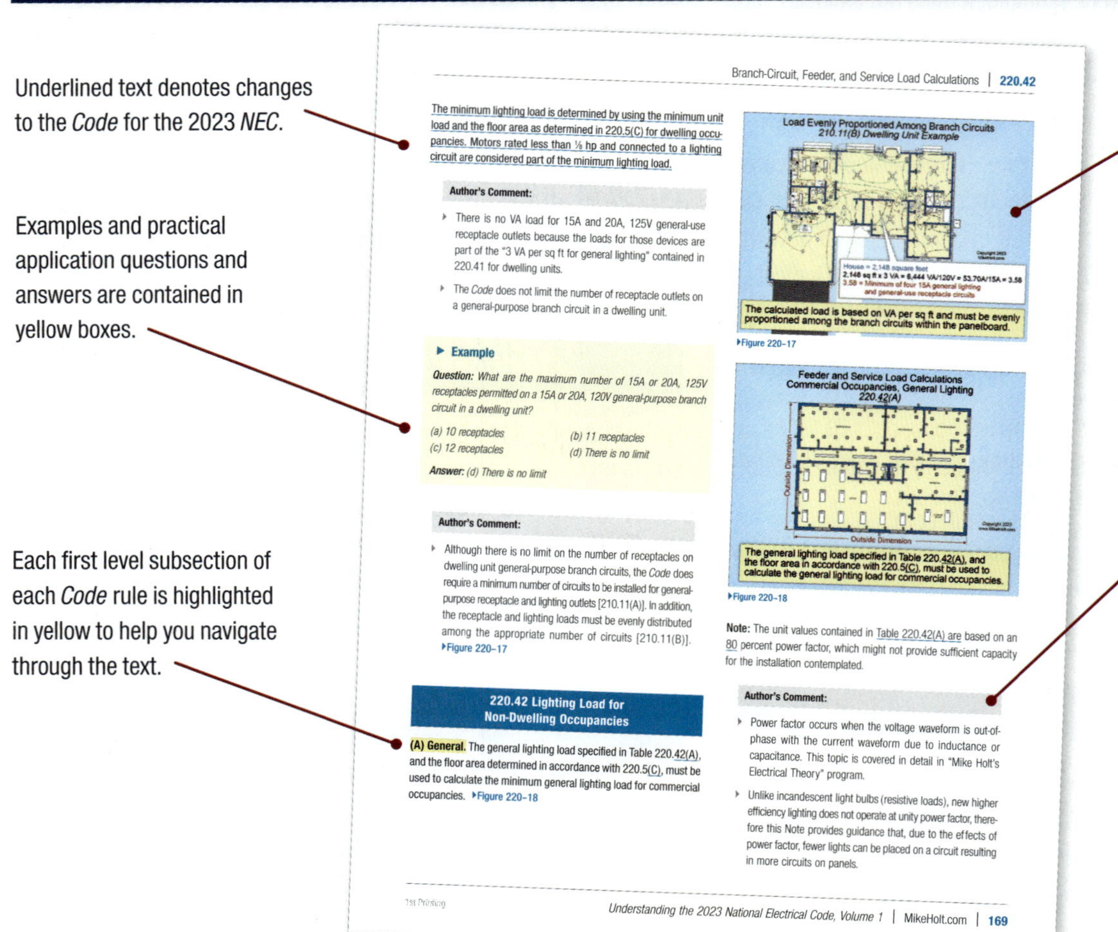

Detailed full-color educational graphics illustrate the rule in a real-world application.

Author's Comments provide additional information to help you understand the context.

If you see an ellipsis (● ● ●) at the bottom right corner of a page or example box, it is continued on the following page.

ADDITIONAL PRODUCTS TO HELP YOU LEARN

Upgrade Your Textbook with the Solar Photovoltaic and Energy Storage Systems Videos, based on the 2023 *NEC*

One of the best ways to get the most out of this textbook is to use it in conjunction with the corresponding videos. These videos showcase dynamic discussions as Mike and his video team of industry experts deep-dive into the 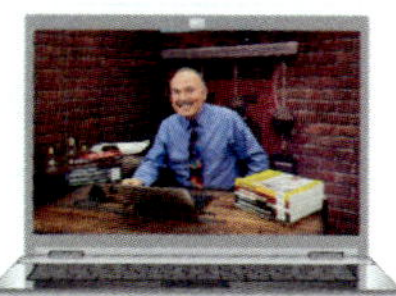 topics in this book. They analyze each rule, its purpose, and its application in the field.

Whether you're a visual or an auditory learner, watching the videos as you work through the textbook will enhance your knowledge and provide additional in-depth insight into each topic. Upgrade your program today, and you will broaden your understanding of the rules and their impact on your work. All upgrade purchases include the corresponding videos plus a digital copy of the textbook.

UPGRADE PACKAGE INCLUDES:

▸ *2023 Solar PV and Energy Storage Systems videos*

Digital answer key

Plus! A digital version of the textbook

 **Ready to get started?** To add the videos that accompany this textbook, scan the QR code, call our office at 888.632.2633, or visit MikeHolt.com/upgrade23SOL.

Have questions? You can e-mail info@MikeHolt.com.

Product Code: [23SOLUPGRADEVI]

Understanding the *NEC* Complete Video Library

Do you want a comprehensive understanding of the *Code*? Then you need Mike's best-selling Understanding the *NEC* Complete Video Library. This program has helped thousands of electricians learn the *Code* because of its easy-to-use format. Mike guides students through the most utilized 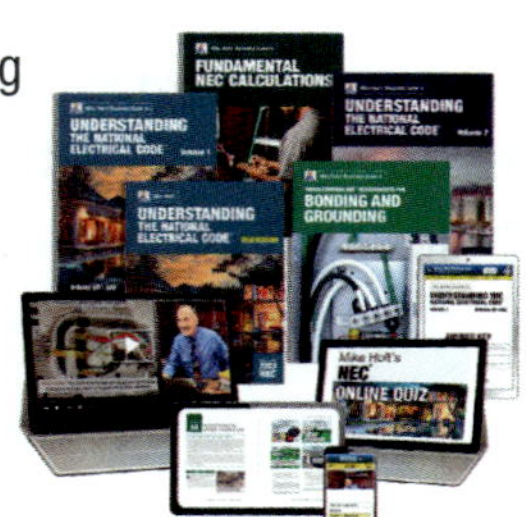 rules and breaks them down in a complete and thorough way. The full-color instructional graphics in the textbooks help students visualize and understand the concepts being taught; the videos provide additional reinforcement with Mike and the panel discussing each article, its meaning and its application in the real world. When you need to know the *Code*, this program is the best tool you can use to start building your knowledge—there's no other product quite like it.

THIS PROGRAM INCLUDES:

Understanding the *National Electrical Code*, Volume 1 Textbook
▸ *Understanding the National Electrical Code Volume 1 videos*

Understanding the *National Electrical Code*, Volume 2 Textbook
▸ *Understanding the National Electrical Code Volume 2 videos*

Bonding and Grounding Textbook
▸ *Bonding and Grounding videos*

Fundamental *NEC* Calculations Textbook
▸ *Fundamental NEC Calculations videos*

Understanding the *National Electrical Code* Workbook (Articles 90-480)

Digital answer keys

Plus! A digital version of each textbook

Product Code: [23UNDLIBMM]

To order visit MikeHolt.com/Code, or call 888.632.2633.

Mike Holt's Business Success Program

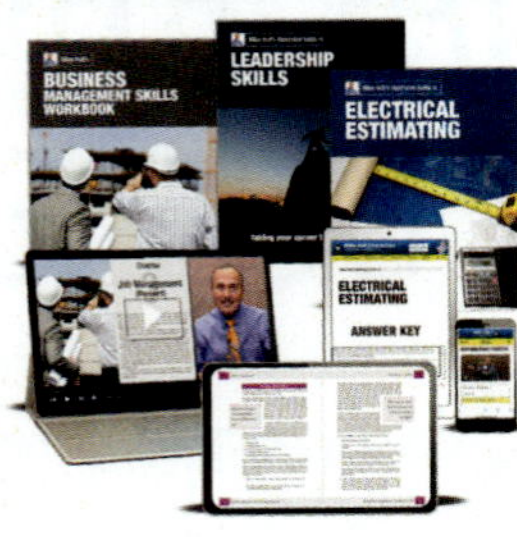

It's time to take your business skills to the next level. Whether you have recently passed an exam, recently opened a business or are just looking to understand the electrical business from a different vantage point, Mike's Business Success Program can help you in the following areas:

Estimating. You will understand estimating and make sure that all your jobs are profitable, with this step-by-step estimating training program.

Business Management. Part motivation, part business wisdom, this module will help you get where you want to go faster.

Leadership. This program distills Mike's knowledge on running a successful business for almost 50 years into the primary building blocks of being a leader.

THIS PROGRAM INCLUDES:

Leadership Skills Textbook

Business Management Workbook
- *Business Management videos*

Electrical Estimating Textbook
- *Electrical Estimating videos*

Digital answer keys

Plus! A digital version of each book

Product Code: [SUCCESSMM]

Mike Holt's Life Skills Program

This program explores the core skills of success. It's a step-by-step training to help you create a program to improve your ability to reach your goals in your professional and personal life.

Learn with Mike as he shares his ups and downs and the skills and wisdom that have made him successful in business for almost 50 years.

THIS PROGRAM INCLUDES:

Life Skills Textbook
- *Life Skills videos*

Plus! A digital version of the book

Product Code: [LIFMM]

To order visit MikeHolt.com/Life, or call 888.632.2633.

HOW TO USE THE *NATIONAL ELECTRICAL CODE*

The original *NEC* document was developed in 1897 as a result of the united efforts of various insurance, electrical, architectural, and other cooperative interests. The National Fire Protection Association (NFPA) has sponsored the *National Electrical Code* since 1911.

The purpose of the *Code* is the practical safeguarding of persons and property from hazards arising from the use of electricity. It isn't intended as a design specification or an instruction manual for untrained persons. It is, in fact, a standard that contains the minimum requirements for an electrical installation that's essentially free from hazard. Learning to understand and use the *Code* is critical to you working safely; whether you're training to become an electrician, or are already an electrician, electrical contractor, inspector, engineer, designer, or instructor.

The *NEC* was written for qualified persons; those who understand electrical terms, theory, safety procedures, and electrical trade practices. Learning to use the *Code* is a lengthy process and can be frustrating if you don't approach it the right way. First, you'll need to understand electrical theory and if you don't have theory as a background when you get into the *NEC*, you're going to struggle. Take one step back if necessary and learn electrical theory. You must also understand the concepts and terms in the *Code* and know grammar and punctuation in order to understand the complex structure of the rules and their intended purpose(s). The *NEC* is written in a formal outline which many of us haven't seen or used since high school or college so it's important for you to pay particular attention to this format. Our goal for the next few pages is to give you some guidelines and suggestions on using your *Code* book to help you understand that standard, and assist you in what you're trying to accomplish and, ultimately, your personal success as an electrical professional!

Language Considerations for the *NEC*

Terms and Concepts

The *NEC* contains many technical terms, and it's crucial for *Code* users to understand their meanings and applications. If you don't understand a term used in a rule, it will be impossible to properly apply the *NEC* requirement. Article 100 defines those that are used generally in two or more articles throughout the *Code*; for example, the term "Dwelling Unit" is found in many articles. If you don't know the *NEC* definition for a "dwelling unit" you can't properly identify its *Code* requirements. Another example worth mentioning is the term "Outlet." For many people it has always meant a receptacle—not so in the *NEC*!

Article 100 contains the definitions of terms used throughout the *Code*. Where a definition is unique to a specific article, the article number is indicated at the end of the definition in parenthesis (xxx). For example, the definition of "Pool" is specific to Article 680 and ends with (680) because it applies ONLY to that article. Definitions of standard terms, such as volt, voltage drop, ampere, impedance, and resistance are not contained in Article 100. If the *NEC* does not define a term, then a dictionary or building code acceptable to the authority having jurisdiction should be consulted.

Small Words, Grammar, and Punctuation

Technical words aren't the only ones that require close attention. Even simple words can make a big difference to the application of a rule. Is there a comma? Does it use "or," "and," "other than," "greater than," or "smaller than"? The word "or" can imply alternate choices for wiring methods. A word like "or" gives us choices while the word "and" can mean an additional requirement must be met.

An example of the important role small words play in the *NEC* is found in 110.26(C)(2), where it says equipment containing overcurrent, switching, "or" control devices that are 1,200A or more "and" over 6 ft wide require a means of egress at each end of the working space. In this section, the word "or" clarifies that equipment containing any of the three types of devices listed must follow this rule. The word "and" clarifies that 110.26(C)(2) only applies if the equipment is both 1,200A or more and over 6 ft wide.

Grammar and punctuation play an important role in establishing the meaning of a rule. The location of a comma can dramatically change the requirement of a rule such as in 250.28(A), where it says a main bonding jumper shall be a wire, bus, screw, or similar suitable conductor. If the comma between "bus" and "screw" was removed, only a "bus screw" could be used. That comma makes a big change in the requirements of the rule.

Slang Terms or Technical Jargon

Trade-related professionals in different areas of the country often use local "slang" terms that aren't shared by all. This can make it difficult to communicate if it isn't clear what the meaning of those slang terms are. Use the proper terms by finding out what their definitions and applications are before you use them. For example, the term "pigtail" is often used to describe the short piece of conductor used to connect a device to a splice, but a "pigtail" is also used for a rubberized light socket with pre-terminated conductors. Although the term is the same, the meaning is very different and could cause confusion. The words "splice" and "tap" are examples of terms often interchanged in the field but are two entirely different things! The uniformity and consistency of the terminology used in the *Code*, makes it so everyone says and means the same thing regardless of geographical location.

NEC Style and Layout

It's important to understand the structure and writing style of the *Code* if you want to use it effectively. The *National Electrical Code* is organized using twelve major components.

1. Table of Contents
2. Chapters—Chapters 1 through 9 (major categories)
3. Articles—Chapter subdivisions that cover specific subjects
4. Parts—Divisions used to organize article subject matter
5. Sections—Divisions used to further organize article subject matter
6. Tables and Figures—Represent the mandatory requirements of a rule
7. Exceptions—Alternatives to the main *Code* rule
8. Informational Notes—Explanatory material for a specific rule (not a requirement)
9. Tables—Applicable as referenced in the *NEC*
10. Annexes—Additional explanatory information such as tables and references (not a requirement)
11. Index
12. Changes to the *Code* from the previous edition

1. Table of Contents. The Table of Contents displays the layout of the chapters, articles, and parts as well as the page numbers. It's an excellent resource and should be referred to periodically to observe the interrelationship of the various *NEC* components. When attempting to locate the rules for a specific situation, knowledgeable *Code* users often go first to the Table of Contents to quickly find the specific *NEC* rule that applies.

2. Chapters. There are nine chapters, each of which is divided into articles. The articles fall into one of four groupings: General Requirements (Chapters 1 through 4), Specific Requirements (Chapters 5 through 7), Communications Systems (Chapter 8), and Tables (Chapter 9).

> Chapter 1—General
> Chapter 2—Wiring and Protection
> Chapter 3—Wiring Methods and Materials
> Chapter 4—Equipment for General Use
> Chapter 5—Special Occupancies
> Chapter 6—Special Equipment
> Chapter 7—Special Conditions
> Chapter 8—Communications Systems (Telephone, Data, Satellite, Cable TV, and Broadband)
> Chapter 9—Tables–Conductor and Raceway Specifications

3. Articles. The *NEC* contains approximately 160 articles, each of which covers a specific subject. It begins with Article 90, the introduction to the *Code* which contains the purpose of the *NEC*, what is covered and isn't covered, along with how the *Code* is arranged. It also gives information on enforcement, how mandatory and permissive rules are written, and how explanatory material is included. Article 90 also includes information on formal interpretations, examination of equipment for safety, wiring planning, and information about formatting units of measurement. Here are some other examples of articles you'll find in the *NEC*:

> Article 110—General Requirements for Electrical Installations
> Article 250—Grounding and Bonding
> Article 300—General Requirements for Wiring Methods and Materials
> Article 430—Motors, Motor Circuits, and Motor Controllers
> Article 500—Hazardous (Classified) Locations
> Article 680—Swimming Pools, Fountains, and Similar Installations
> Article 725—Class 2 and Class 3 Power-Limited Circuits
> Article 800—General Requirements for Communications Systems

4. Parts. Larger articles are subdivided into parts. Because the parts of a *Code* article aren't included in the section numbers, we tend to forget to what "part" an *NEC* rule is relating. For example, Table 110.34(A) contains working space clearances for electrical equipment. If we aren't careful, we might think this table applies to all electrical installations, but Table 110.34(A) is in Part III, which only contains requirements for "Over 1,000 Volts, Nominal" installations. The rules for working clearances for electrical equipment for systems 1,000V, nominal, or less are contained in Table 110.26(A)(1), which is in Part II—1,000 Volts, Nominal, or Less.

5. Sections. Each *NEC* rule is called a "*Code* Section." A *Code* section may be broken down into subdivisions; first level subdivision will be in parentheses like (A), (B),…, the next will be second level subdivisions in parentheses like (1), (2),…, and third level subdivisions in lowercase letters such as (a), (b), and so on.

For example, the rule requiring all receptacles in a dwelling unit bathroom to be GFCI protected is contained in Section 210.8(A)(1) which is in Chapter 2, Article 210, Section 8, first level subdivision (A), and second level subdivision (1).

Note: According to the *NEC Style Manual*, first and second level subdivisions are required to have titles. A title for a third level subdivision is permitted but not required.

Many in the industry incorrectly use the term "Article" when referring to a *Code* section. For example, they say "Article 210.8," when they should say "Section 210.8." Section numbers in this textbook are shown without the word "Section," unless they're at the beginning of a sentence. For example, Section 210.8(A) is shown as simply 210.8(A).

6. Tables and Figures. Many *NEC* requirements are contained within tables, which are lists of *Code* rules placed in a systematic arrangement. The titles of the tables are extremely important; you must read them carefully in order to understand the contents, applications, and limitations of each one. Notes are often provided in or below a table; be sure to read them as well since they're also part of the requirement. For example, Note 1 for Table 300.5(A) explains how to measure the cover when burying cables and raceways and Note 5 explains what to do if solid rock is encountered.

7. Exceptions. Exceptions are *NEC* requirements or permissions that provide an alternative method to a specific rule. There are two types of exceptions—mandatory and permissive. When a rule has several exceptions, those exceptions with mandatory requirements are listed before the permissive exceptions.

Mandatory Exceptions. A mandatory exception uses the words "shall" or "shall not." The word "shall" in an exception means that if you're using the exception, you're required to do it in a specific way. The phrase "shall not" means it isn't permitted.

Permissive Exceptions. A permissive exception uses words such as "shall be permitted," which means it's acceptable (but not mandatory) to do it in this way.

8. Informational Notes. An Informational Note contains explanatory material intended to clarify a rule or give assistance, but it isn't a *Code* requirement.

9. Tables. Chapter 9 consists of tables applicable as referenced in the *NEC*. They're used to calculate raceway sizing, conductor fill, the radius of raceway bends, and conductor voltage drop.

10. Informative Annexes. Annexes aren't a part of the *Code* requirements and are included for informational purposes only.

Annex A. Product Safety Standards
Annex B. Application Information for Ampacity Calculation
Annex C. Conduit, Tubing, and Cable Tray Fill Tables for Conductors and Fixture Wires of the Same Size
Annex D. Examples
Annex E. Types of Construction
Annex F. Availability and Reliability for Critical Operations Power Systems (COPS), and Development and Implementation of Functional Performance Tests (FPTs) for Critical Operations Power Systems
Annex G. Supervisory Control and Data Acquisition (SCADA)
Annex H. Administration and Enforcement
Annex I. Recommended Tightening Torque Tables from UL Standard 486A-486B
Annex J. ADA Standards for Accessible Design
Annex K. Use of Medical Electrical Equipment in Dwellings and Residential Board-and-Care Occupancies

11. Index. The Index at the back of the *NEC* is helpful in locating a specific rule using pertinent keywords to assist in your search.

12. Changes to the *Code*. Changes in the *NEC* are indicated as follows:

▸ Rules that were changed since the previous edition are identified by shading the revised text.

▸ New rules aren't shaded like a change, instead they have a shaded "N" in the margin to the left of the section number.

▸ Relocated rules are treated like new rules with a shaded "N" in the left margin by the section number.

- ▶ Deleted rules are indicated by a bullet symbol " • " located in the left margin where the rule was in the previous edition. Unlike older editions the bullet symbol is only used where one or more complete paragraphs have been deleted.

- ▶ A "Δ" represents partial text deletions and or figure/table revisions somewhere in the text. There's no specific indication of which word, group of words, or a sentence was deleted.

How to Locate a Specific Requirement

How to go about finding what you're looking for in the *Code* book depends, to some degree, on your experience with the *NEC*. Experts typically know the requirements so well that they just go to the correct rule. Very experienced people might only need the Table of Contents to locate the requirement for which they're looking. On the other hand, average users should use all the tools at their disposal, including the Table of Contents, the Index, and the search feature on electronic versions of the *Code* book.

Let's work through a simple example: What *NEC* rule specifies the maximum number of disconnects permitted for a service?

Using the Table of Contents. If you're an experienced *Code* user, you might use the Table of Contents. You'll know Article 230 applies to "Services," and because this article is so large, it's divided up into multiple parts (eight parts to be exact). With this knowledge, you can quickly go to the Table of Contents and see it lists the Service Equipment Disconnecting Means requirements in Part VI.

Author's Comment:

- ▶ The number "70" precedes all page numbers in this standard because the *NEC* is NFPA Standard Number 70.

Using the Index. If you use the Index (which lists subjects in alphabetical order) to look up the term "service disconnect," you'll see there's no listing. If you try "disconnecting means," then "services," you'll find that the Index indicates the rule is in Article 230, Part VI. Because the *NEC* doesn't give a page number in the Index, you'll need to use the Table of Contents to find it, or flip through the *Code* book to Article 230, then continue to flip through pages until you find Part VI.

Many people complain that the *NEC* only confuses them by taking them in circles. Once you gain experience in using the *Code* and deepen your understanding of words, terms, principles, and practices, you'll find it much easier to understand and use than you originally thought.

With enough exposure in the use of the *NEC*, you'll discover that some words and terms are often specific to certain articles. The word "solar" for example will immediately send experienced *Code* book users to Article 690—Solar Photovoltaic (PV) Systems. The word "marina" suggests what you seek might be in Article 555. There are times when a main article will send you to a specific requirement in another one in which compliance is required in which case it will say (for example), "in accordance with 230.xx." Don't think of these situations as a "circle," but rather a map directing you to exactly where you need to be.

Customizing Your *Code* Book

One way to increase your comfort level with your *Code* book is to customize it to meet your needs. You can do this by highlighting and underlining important *NEC* requirements. Preprinted adhesive tabs are also an excellent aid to quickly find important articles and sections that are regularly referenced. However, understand that if you're using your *Code* book to prepare to take an exam, some exam centers don't allow markings of any type. For more information about tabs for your *Code* book, visit MikeHolt.com/Tabs.

Highlighting. As you read through or find answers to your questions, be sure you highlight those requirements in the *NEC* that are the most important or relevant to you. Use one color, like yellow, for general interest and a different one for important requirements you want to find quickly. Be sure to highlight terms in the Index and the Table of Contents as you use them.

Underlining. Underline or circle key words and phrases in the *Code* with a red or blue pen (not a lead pencil) using a short ruler or other straightedge to keep lines straight and neat. This is a very handy way to make important requirements stand out. A short ruler or other straightedge also comes in handy for locating the correct information in a table.

Interpretations

Industry professionals often enjoy the challenge of discussing, and at times debating, the *Code* requirements. These types of discussions are important to the process of better understanding the *NEC* requirements and applications. However, if you decide you're going to participate in one of these discussions, don't spout out what you think without having the actual *Code* book in your hand. The professional way of discussing a requirement is by referring to a specific section rather than talking in vague generalities. This will help everyone involved clearly understand the point and become better educated. In fact, you may become so well educated about the *NEC* that you might even decide to participate in the change process and help to make it even better!

Become Involved in the *NEC* Process

The actual process of changing the *Code* takes about two years and involves hundreds of individuals trying to make the *NEC* as current and accurate as possible. As you advance in your studies and understanding of the *Code*, you might begin to find it very interesting, enjoy it more, and realize that you can also be a part of the process. Rather than sitting back and allowing others to take the lead, you can participate by making proposals and being a part of its development. For the 2023 cycle, there were over 4,000 Public Inputs and 1,956 Public Comments. This resulted in several new articles and a wide array of revised rules to keep the *NEC* up to date with new technologies and pave the way to a safer and more efficient electrical future.

Here's how the process works:

STEP 1—Public Input Stage

Public Input. The revision cycle begins with the acceptance of Public Input (PI) which is the public notice asking for anyone interested to submit input on an existing standard or a committee-approved new draft standard. Following the closing date, the committee conducts a First Draft Meeting to respond to all Public Inputs.

First Draft Meeting. At the First Draft (FD) Meeting, the Technical Committee considers and provides a response to all Public Input. The Technical Committee may use the input to develop First Revisions to the standard. The First Draft documents consist of the initial meeting consensus of the committee by simple majority. However, the final position of the Technical Committee must be established by a ballot which follows.

Committee Ballot on First Draft. The First Draft developed at the First Draft Meeting is balloted. In order to appear in the First Draft, a revision must be approved by at least two-thirds of the Technical Committee.

First Draft Report Posted. First revisions which pass ballot are ultimately compiled and published as the First Draft Report on the document's NFPA web page. This report serves as documentation for the Input Stage and is published for review and comment. The public may review the First Draft Report to determine whether to submit Public Comments on the First Draft.

STEP 2—Public Comment Stage

Public Comment. Once the First Draft Report becomes available, there's a Public Comment period during which anyone can submit a Public Comment on the First Draft. After the Public Comment closing date, the Technical Committee conducts/holds their Second Draft Meeting.

Second Draft Meeting. After the Public Comment closing date, if Public Comments are received or the committee has additional proposed revisions, a Second Draft Meeting is held. At the Second Draft Meeting, the Technical Committee reviews the First Draft and may make additional revisions to the draft Standard. All Public Comments are considered, and the Technical Committee provides an action and response to each Public Comment. These actions result in the Second Draft.

Committee Ballot on Second Draft. The Second Revisions developed at the Second Draft Meeting are balloted. To appear in the Second Draft, a revision must be approved by at least two-thirds of the Technical Committee.

Second Draft Report Posted. Second Revisions which pass ballot are ultimately compiled and published as the Second Draft Report on the document's NFPA website. This report serves as documentation of the Comment Stage and is published for public review.

Once published, the public can review the Second Draft Report to decide whether to submit a Notice of Intent to Make a Motion (NITMAM) for further consideration.

STEP 3—NFPA Technical Meeting (Tech Session)

Following completion of the Public Input and Public Comment stages, there's further opportunity for debate and discussion of issues through the NFPA Technical Meeting that takes place at the NFPA Conference & Expo®. These motions are attempts to change the resulting final Standard from the committee's recommendations published as the Second Draft.

STEP 4—Council Appeals and Issuance of Standard

Issuance of Standards. When the Standards Council convenes to issue an NFPA standard, it also hears any related appeals. Appeals are an important part of assuring that all NFPA rules have been followed and that due process and fairness have continued throughout the standards development process. The Standards Council considers appeals based on the written record and by conducting live hearings during which all interested parties can participate. Appeals are decided on the entire record of the process, as well as all submissions and statements presented.

After deciding all appeals related to a standard, the Standards Council, if appropriate, proceeds to issue the Standard as an official NFPA Standard. The decision of the Standards Council is final subject only to limited review by the NFPA Board of Directors. The new NFPA standard becomes effective twenty days following the Standards Council's action of issuance.

Temporary Interim Amendment—(TIA)

Sometimes, a change to the *NEC* is of an emergency nature. Perhaps an editing mistake was made that can affect an electrical installation to the extent it may create a hazard. Maybe an occurrence in the field created a condition that needs to be addressed immediately and can't wait for the normal *Code* cycle and next edition of the standard. When these circumstances warrant it, a TIA or "Temporary Interim Amendment" can be submitted for consideration.

The NFPA defines a TIA as, "tentative because it has not been processed through the entire standards-making procedures. It is interim because it is effective only between editions of the standard. A TIA automatically becomes a Public Input of the proponent for the next edition of the standard; as such, it then is subject to all of the procedures of the standards-making process."

Author's Comment:

▸ Proposals, comments, and TIAs can be submitted for consideration online at the NFPA website, www.nfpa.org. From the homepage, look for "Codes & Standards," then find "Standards Development," and click on "How the Process Works." If you'd like to see something changed in the *Code*, you're encouraged to participate in the process.

INTRODUCTION TO THE *NATIONAL ELECTRICAL CODE*

Introduction to Article 90—Introduction to the *National Electrical Code*

Article 90 describes the purpose of the *NEC*, when it applies, when it does not, who enforces the *Code*, and the arrangement of the different chapters. Although the information is valuable, this article contains no actual requirements. It only serves to provide the reader with the scope of the *National Electrical Code*.

This article stands alone outside of the chapter structure of the rest of the *Code* and has no parts because it contains no requirements. Take the time to become familiar with all nine sections of Article 90 before you begin your journey through the *NEC*. Doing so will help you better understand when and how to apply the *Code*.

90.1 Scope

Article 90 covers the use, application, arrangement, and enforcement of this *Code*. It also covers how mandatory, permissive, and nonmandatory text is expressed and provides guidance on the examination of equipment, planning wiring, and specifies the use and expression of measurements.

90.2 Use and Application of the *NEC*

(A) Purpose of the *NEC*.

Protect People and Property. The purpose of the *National Electrical Code* is to ensure electrical systems are installed in a manner that protects people and property by minimizing the risks associated with the use of electricity. ▶Figure 90–1

NEC Not a Specification or Instruction Manual. The *NEC* is not a design specification standard, nor is it an instruction manual for the untrained. ▶Figure 90–2

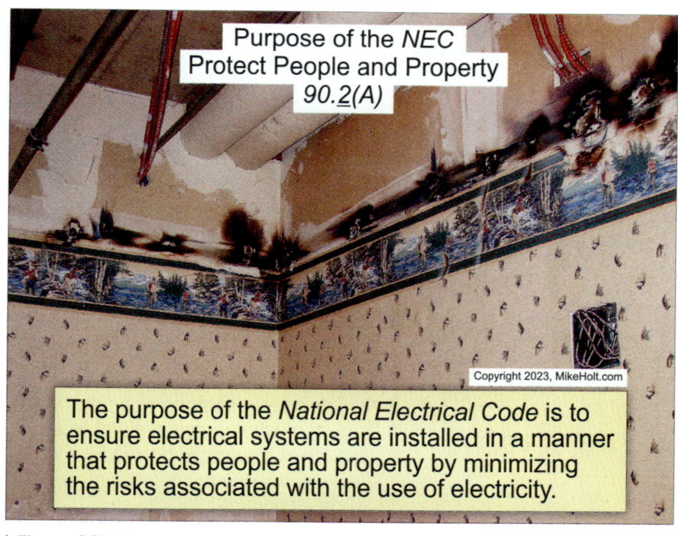

▶Figure 90–1

Author's Comment:

▶ The *Code* is intended to be used by those who are skilled and knowledgeable in electrical theory, electrical systems, building and electrical construction, and the installation and operation of electrical equipment.

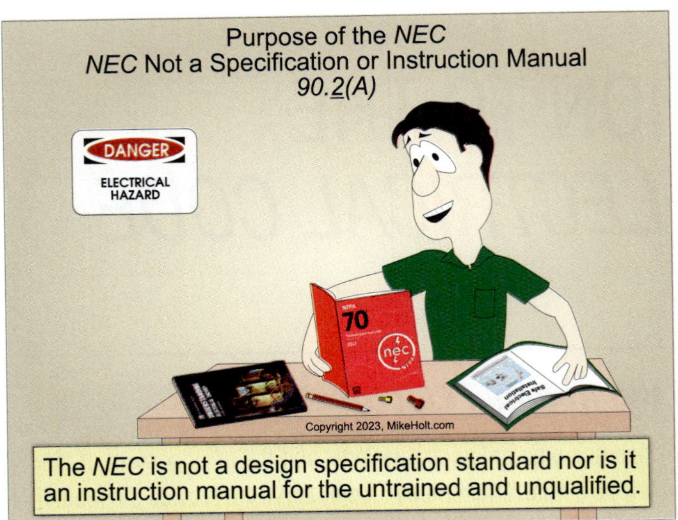

▶Figure 90–2

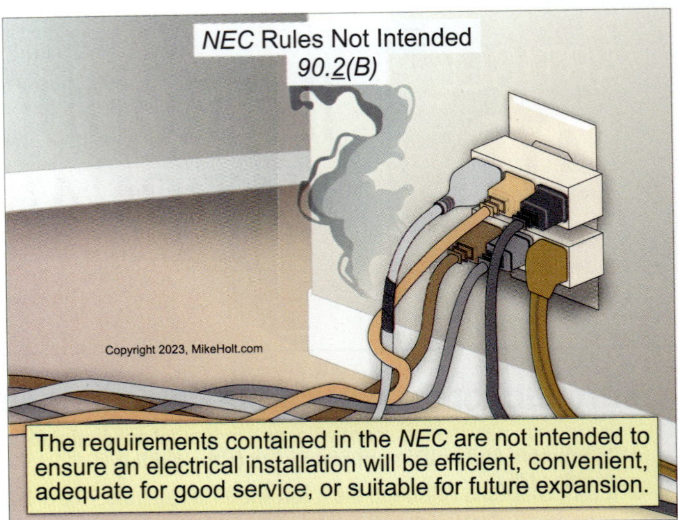

▶Figure 90–4

(B) Essentially Safe Installation.

Considered Safe. The *NEC* contains the requirements considered necessary for safety.

Essentially Free from Hazards. Installations complying with the *Code* and properly maintained are considered essentially free from electrical hazards. ▶**Figure 90–3**

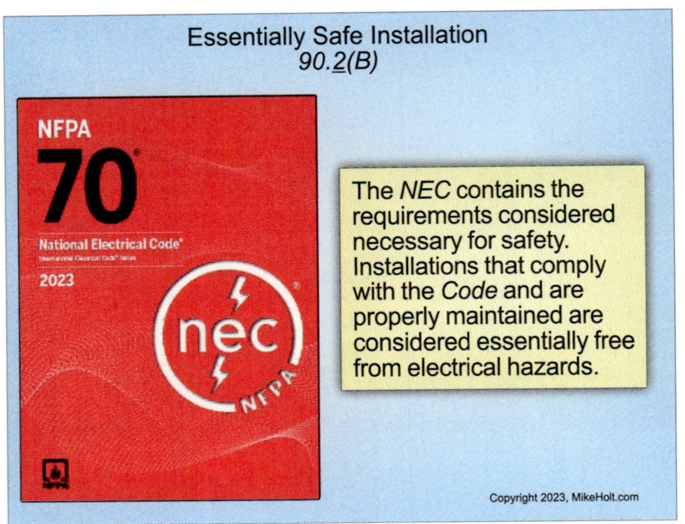

▶Figure 90–3

NEC Rules not Intended. The requirements contained in the *NEC* are not intended to ensure an electrical installation will be efficient, convenient, adequate for good service, or suitable for future expansion. ▶**Figure 90–4**

Note: Hazards often occur because the initial wiring did not provide for increases in the use of electricity resulting in wiring systems becoming overloaded. ▶**Figure 90–5**

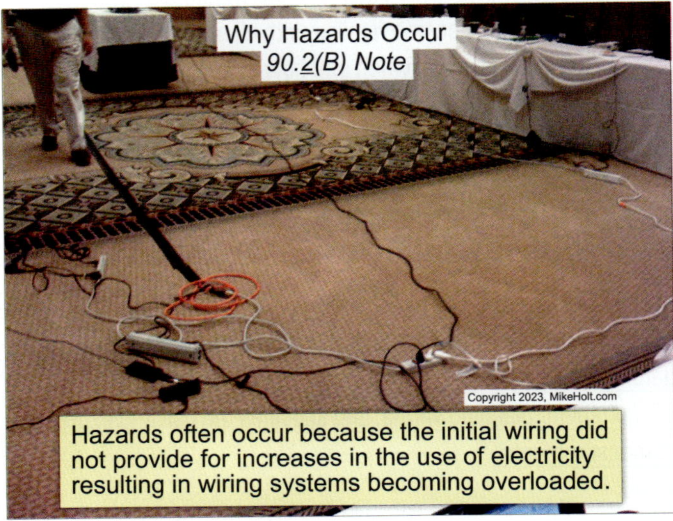

▶Figure 90–5

Author's Comment:

▶ The *NEC* does not require electrical systems to be designed or installed to accommodate future loads. However, consideration should be given not only to ensuring electrical safety (*Code* compliance), but also that the electrical system meets the customers' needs—both for today and in the coming years.

(C) Installations Covered by the NEC. The *Code* covers the installation and removal of electrical conductors, equipment, and raceways. It also covers limited-energy and communications conductors, equipment, and raceways, plus optical fiber cables for the following: ▶**Figure 90–6**

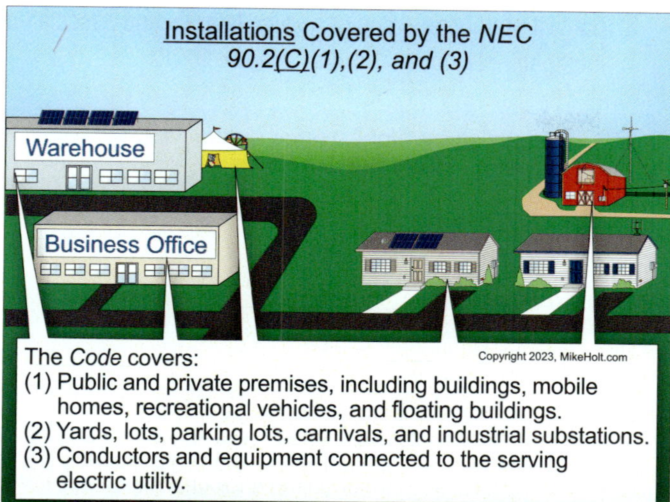

▶Figure 90–6

(1) Public and private premises including buildings, mobile homes, recreational vehicles, and floating buildings.

(2) Yards, lots, parking lots, carnivals, and industrial substations.

(3) Conductors and equipment connected to the serving electric utility.

(4) Installations used by a serving electric utility such as office buildings, warehouses, garages, machine shops, recreational buildings, and other electric utility buildings that are not an integral part of a utility's generating plant, substation, or control center. ▶Figure 90–7

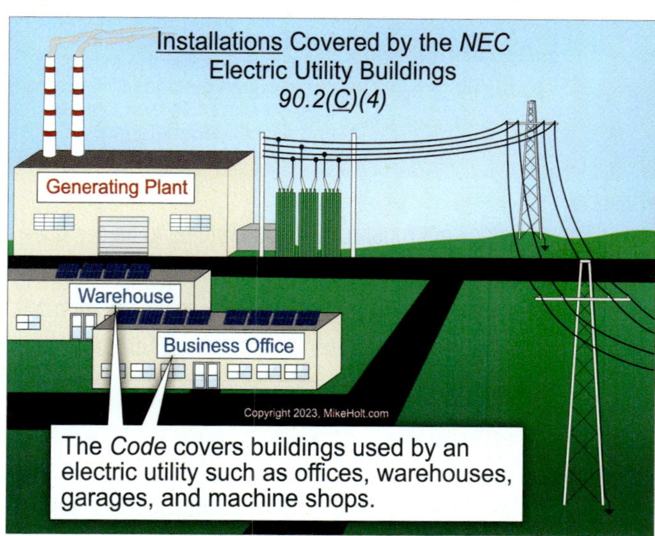

▶Figure 90–7

(5) Installations supplying shore power to ships and watercraft in marinas and boatyards, including monitoring of leakage current. ▶Figure 90–8

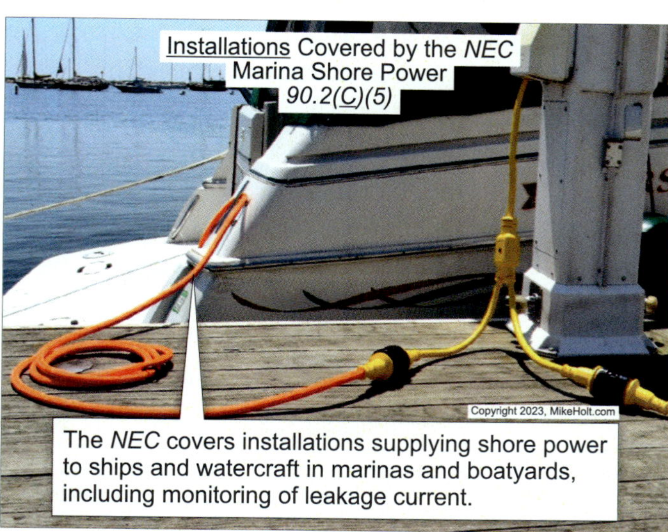

▶Figure 90–8

Author's Comment:

▶ The text in 555.35(B) requires leakage detection equipment to detect leakage current from boats and applies to the load side of the supplying receptacle.

(6) Installations used to export power from vehicles to premises wiring or for bidirectional current flow. ▶Figure 90–9

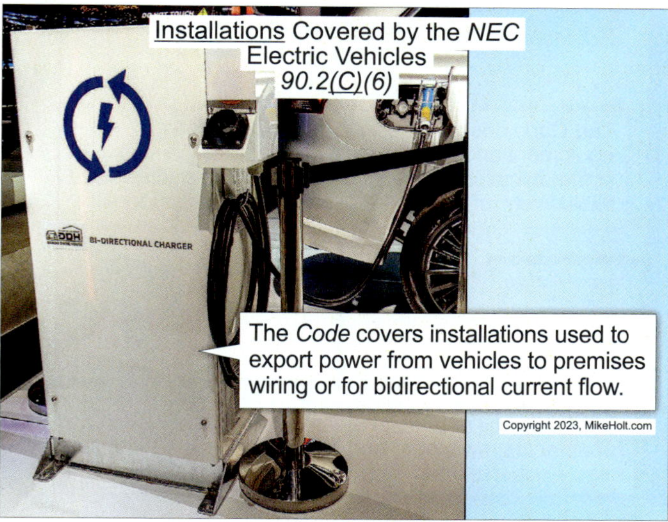

▶Figure 90–9

Author's Comment:

▶ The battery power supply of an electric vehicle can be used "bidirectionally" which means it can be used as a backup or alternate power source to supply premises wiring circuits in the event of a power failure. The rules for this application can be found in Article 625.

(D) Installations Not Covered by the *NEC*. The *Code* does not cover installations of electrical or communications systems for:

(1) Transportation Vehicles. The *NEC* does not cover installations in ships, watercraft (other than floating buildings), aircraft, or automotive vehicles (other than mobile homes and recreational vehicles).

Author's Comment:

▸ An automotive vehicle is any vehicle that may be transported upon a public highway. The wiring of food trucks is not required to comply with the *NEC*, since they are considered automotive vehicles.

(2) Mining Equipment. The *Code* does not cover installations in underground mines or self-propelled mobile surface mining machinery and its attendant electrical trailing cables.

(3) Railways. The *NEC* does not cover installations for railway power, energy storage, and communications wiring.

(4) Communications Utilities. The *Code* does not cover installations of communications equipment under the exclusive control of the communications utility located outdoors or in building spaces used exclusively for these purposes. ▸Figure 90–10

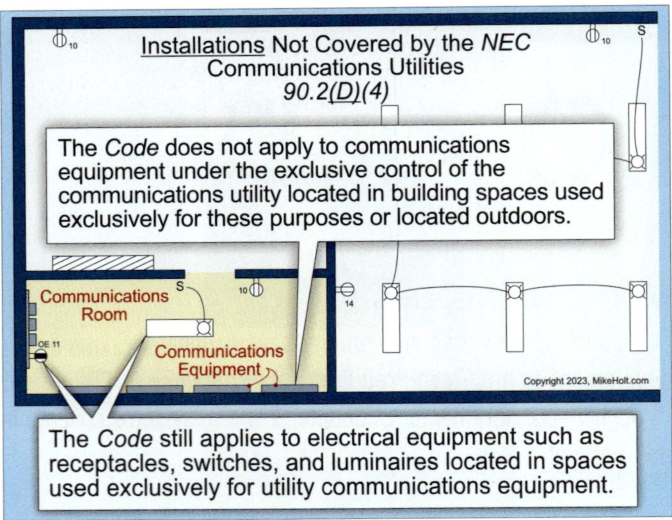

▸Figure 90–10

Author's Comment:

▸ The *Code* still applies to electrical equipment such as receptacles, switches, and luminaires located in spaces used exclusively for utility communications equipment.

(5) Electric Utilities. The *NEC* does not cover installations under the exclusive control of a serving electric utility where such installations:

a. Consist of service drops or service laterals and associated metering. ▸Figure 90–11 and ▸Figure 90–12

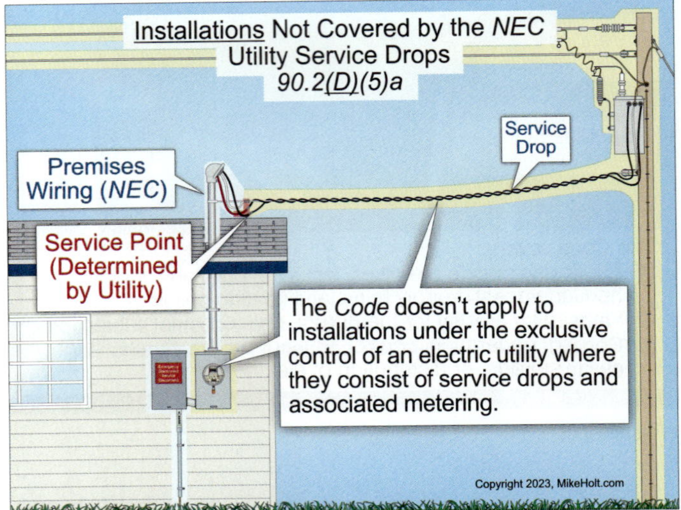

▸Figure 90–11

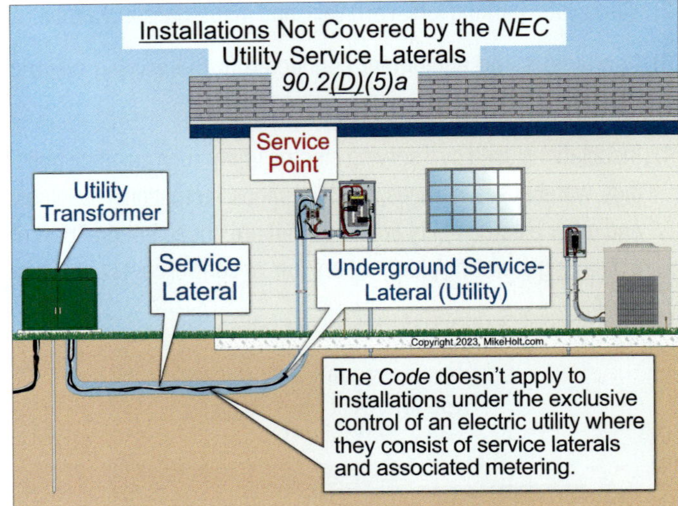

▸Figure 90–12

b. Are on property owned or leased by the utility for the purpose of communications, metering, generation, control, transformation, transmission, energy storage, or distribution of electrical energy. ▸Figure 90–13

c. Are in legally established easements or rights-of-way. ▸Figure 90–14

(E) Relation to International Standards. The requirements of the *NEC* address the fundamental safety principles contained in the International Electrotechnical Commission (IEC) Standard IEC 60364-1, *Low-Voltage Electrical Installations—Part 1: Fundamental Principles, Assessment of General Characteristics, Definitions.*

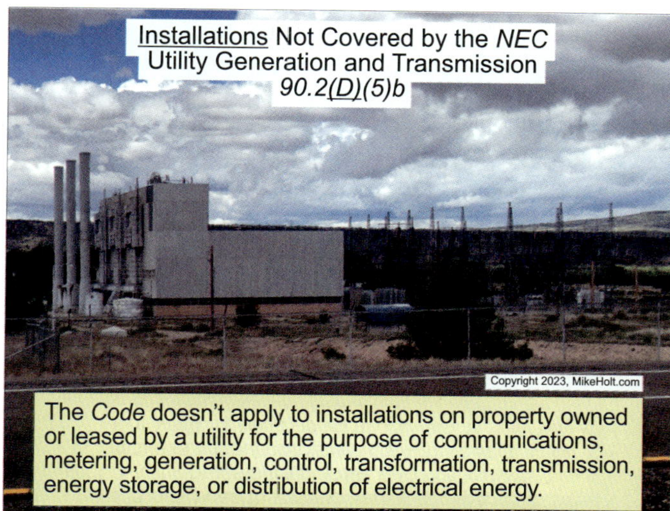

▶Figure 90–13

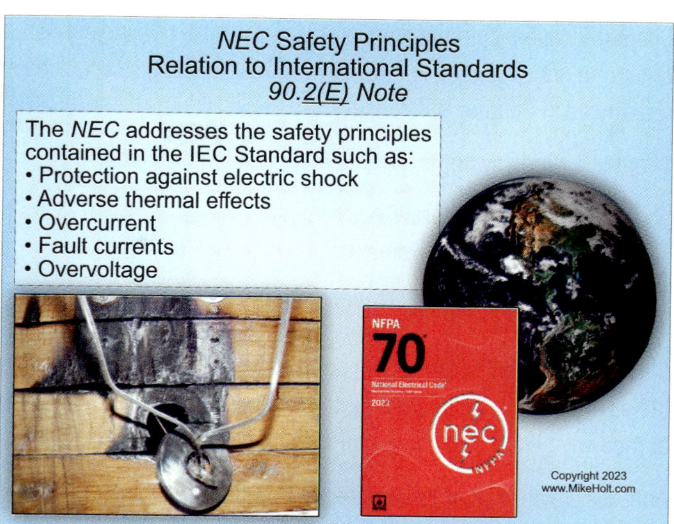

▶Figure 90–15

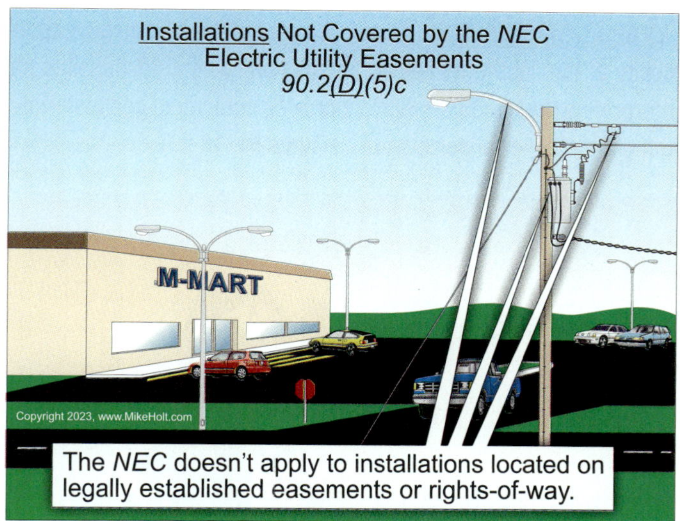

▶Figure 90–14

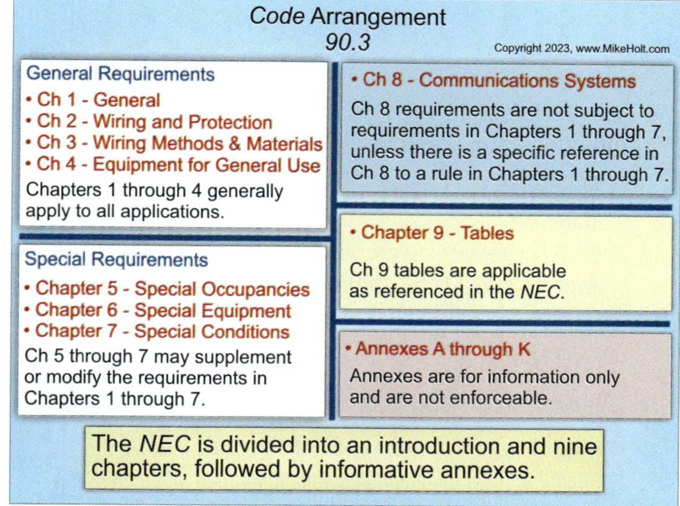

▶Figure 90–16

Note: IEC 60364-1, *Low-Voltage Electrical Installations—Part 1: Fundamental Principles, Assessment of General Characteristics, Definitions, Section 131*, contains fundamental principles of protection for safety that encompass protection against electric shock, thermal effects, overcurrent, fault currents, and overvoltage. All these potential hazards are addressed by the requirements in this *Code*. ▶**Figure 90–15**

90.3 *Code* Arrangement

General Requirements. The *NEC* consists of an introduction and nine chapters followed by informative annexes. The requirements contained in Chapters 1, 2, 3, and 4 apply generally to all electrical installations. ▶**Figure 90–16**

The requirements contained in Chapters 5, 6, and 7 apply to special occupancies, special equipment, or special conditions, which may supplement or modify the requirements contained in Chapters 1 through 7—but not Chapter 8. Chapter 7 wiring systems covered in this material include:

▸ Article 722—Cables for Power-Limited Circuits and Optical Fiber

▸ Article 724—Class 1 Power-Limited Circuits

▸ Article 725—Class 2 Power-Limited Circuits

▸ Article 760—Fire Alarm Circuits

▸ Article 770—Optical Fiber Circuits

Chapter 8 covers communications systems and is not subject to the requirements contained in Chapters 1 through 7, unless specifically referenced in Chapter 8.

Chapter 8 wiring systems covered in this material include:

▸ Article 800—General Requirements for Communications Systems

▸ Article 810—Radio and Television Antennas

Chapter 9 consists of tables that apply as referenced in the *NEC*. The tables are used to calculate raceway sizing, conductor fill, the radius of raceway bends, and conductor voltage drop.

Annexes are not part of the requirements of the *Code,* but are included for informational purposes only. There are eleven annexes:

▸ Annex A. Product Safety Standards

▸ Annex B. Application Information for Ampacity Calculation

▸ Annex C. Conduit, Tubing, and Cable Tray Fill Tables for Conductors and Fixture Wires of the Same Size

▸ Annex D. Examples

▸ Annex E. Types of Construction

▸ Annex F. Availability and Reliability for Critical Operations Power Systems (COPS), and Development and Implementation of Functional Performance Tests (FPTs) for Critical Operations Power Systems

▸ Annex G. Supervisory Control and Data Acquisition (SCADA)

▸ Annex H. Administration and Enforcement

▸ Annex I. Recommended Tightening Torque Tables from UL Standard 486A-486B

▸ Annex J. ADA Standards for Accessible Design

▸ Annex K. Use of Medical Electrical Equipment in Dwellings and Residential Board-and-Care Occupancies

90.4 *NEC* Enforcement

(A) Suitable for Adoption. The *NEC* is intended to be adopted for mandatory application by governmental bodies that exercise legal jurisdiction over electrical installations. ▸Figure 90–17

Author's Comment:

▸ Once adopted (in part, wholly, or amended), the *National Electrical Code* becomes statutory law for the adopting jurisdiction and is thereby considered a legal document.

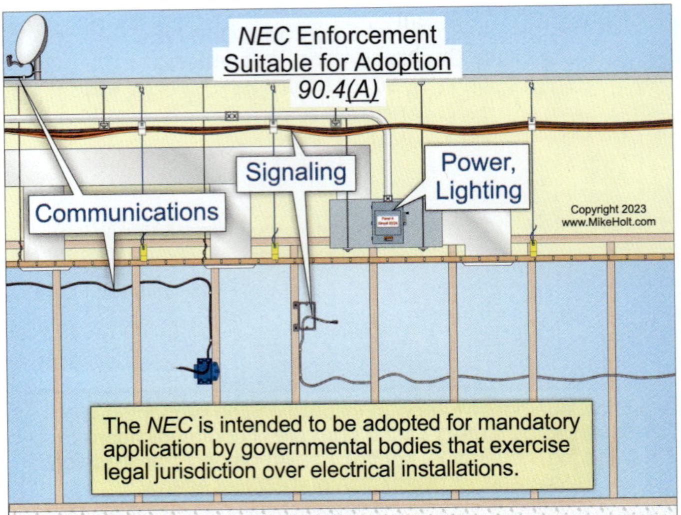

▸Figure 90–17

(B) AHJ Responsibility. The enforcement of the *NEC* is the responsibility of the "authority having jurisdiction" who is responsible for interpreting *Code* requirements, approving equipment and materials, and granting special permission. ▸Figure 90–18

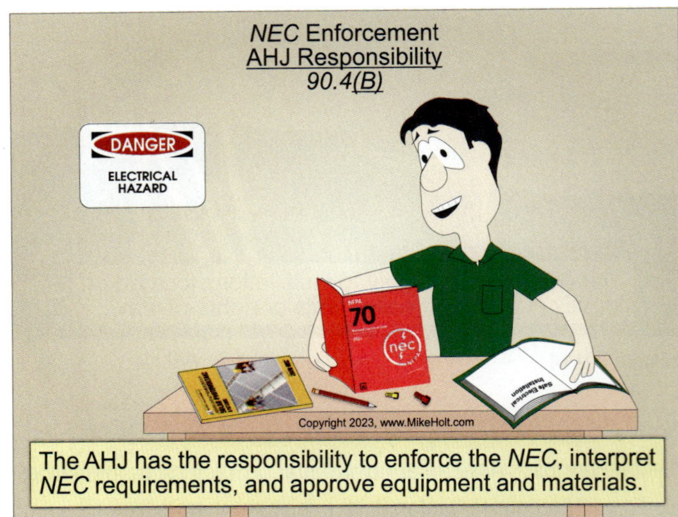

▸Figure 90–18

According to Article 100, "Authority Having Jurisdiction" is defined as the organization, office, or individual responsible for approving equipment, materials, an installation, or a procedure. See 90.4 and 90.7 for more information.

"Approved" is acceptable to the authority having jurisdiction, usually the electrical inspector.

(C) Waiving Requirements and Alternate Methods. By special permission, the authority having jurisdiction may waive *NEC* requirements or approve alternate methods where equivalent safety can be achieved and maintained. ▶Figure 90–19

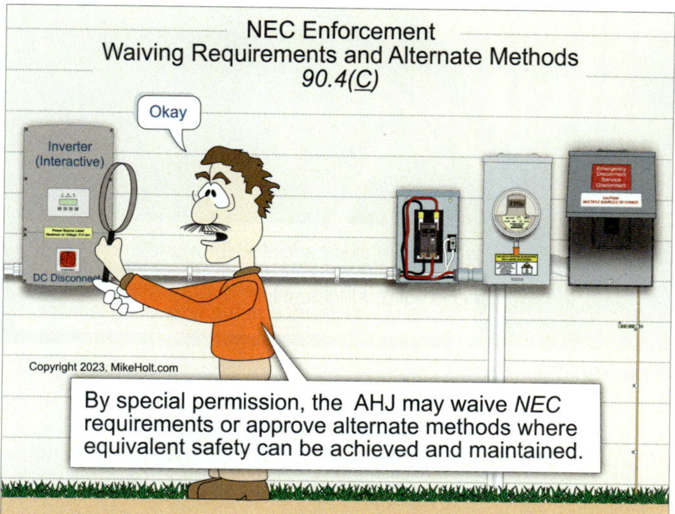

▶Figure 90–19

According to Article 100, "Special Permission" is defined as the written consent of the AHJ.

Author's Comment:

▸ According to 90.4(B), the authority having jurisdiction determines the approval of equipment. This means he/she can reject an installation of listed equipment and approve the use of unlisted equipment. Given our highly litigious society, approval of unlisted equipment is becoming increasingly difficult to obtain.

(D) Waiver of Product Requirements. If the *Code* requires products, constructions, or materials that are not yet available at the time the *NEC* is adopted, the authority having jurisdiction can allow products that were acceptable in the previous *Code* that was adopted in the jurisdiction to continue to be used.

Author's Comment:

▸ Typically, the AHJ will approve equipment listed by a product testing organization such as Underwriters Laboratories, Inc. (UL). The *NEC* does not require all equipment to be listed, but many state and local authorities having jurisdictions do. See 90.7, 110.2, and 110.3 and the definitions for "Approved," "Identified," "Labeled," and "Listed" in Article 100.

▸ Sometimes it takes years for testing laboratories to establish product standards for new *NEC* product requirements. It takes time before manufacturers can design, manufacture, and distribute those products to the marketplace.

90.5 Mandatory Requirements and Explanatory Material

(A) Mandatory Requirements. The words "shall" or "shall not" indicate a mandatory requirement.

Author's Comment:

▸ For greater ease in reading this material, we will use the word "must" instead of "shall," and "must not" will be used instead of "shall not."

(B) Permissive Requirements. The phrases "shall be permitted" or "shall not be required" indicate the action is permitted, but not required, or there are other options or alternatives permitted.

Author's Comment:

▸ For greater ease in reading, the phrase "shall be permitted" (as used in the *NEC*) has been replaced in this material with "is permitted" or "are permitted."

(C) Explanatory Material. Explanatory material referencing other standards, referencing related sections to an *NEC* rule, or just providing information related to a rule, is included in this *Code* in the form of informational notes or informative annexes. These are not enforceable as *NEC* requirements, unless the standard reference includes a date, the reference is to be considered as the latest edition of the standard.

Author's Comment:

▸ For convenience and ease in reading this material, "Informational Notes" will simply be identified as "Note."

▸ A Note, while not enforceable itself, may reference an enforceable *Code* rule elsewhere in the *NEC*.

> **Caution**
>
> **CAUTION:** Informational Notes are not enforceable, but notes to tables are. Within this material, we will call notes contained in a table a "Table Note."

(D) Informative Annexes. Nonmandatory information relative to the use of the *Code* is provided in informative annexes. These annexes are not enforceable as requirements of the *NEC, but* are included for informational purposes only.

90.7 Examination of Equipment for Safety

Product evaluation for *Code* compliance, approval, and safety is typically performed by a qualified electrical testing laboratory (QETL) in accordance with the listing standards.

Except to detect alterations or damage, listed factory-installed internal wiring of equipment does not need to be inspected for *NEC* compliance at the time of installation. ▶Figure 90–20

Note 1: The requirements contained in Article 300 do not apply to the integral parts of electrical equipment [300.1(B)]. See 110.3 for guidance on safety examinations.

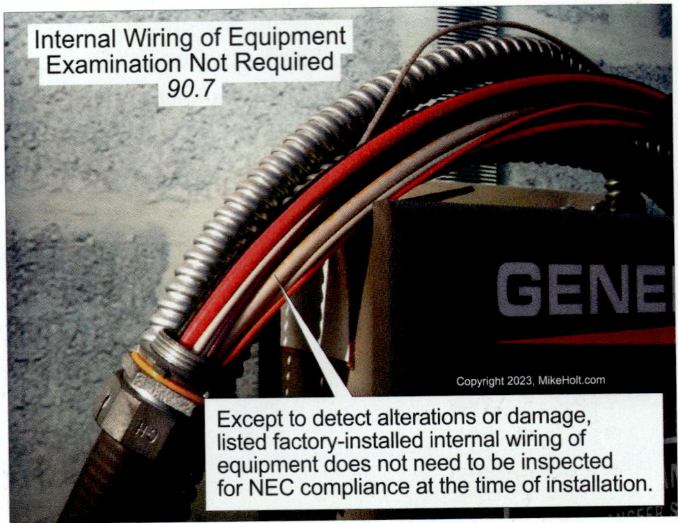

▶Figure 90–20

According to Article 100, "Listed" equipment or materials included in a list published by an organization acceptable to the authority having jurisdiction. The listing organization must periodically inspect the production of listed equipment or material to ensure it meets appropriate designated standards and suitable for a specified purpose.

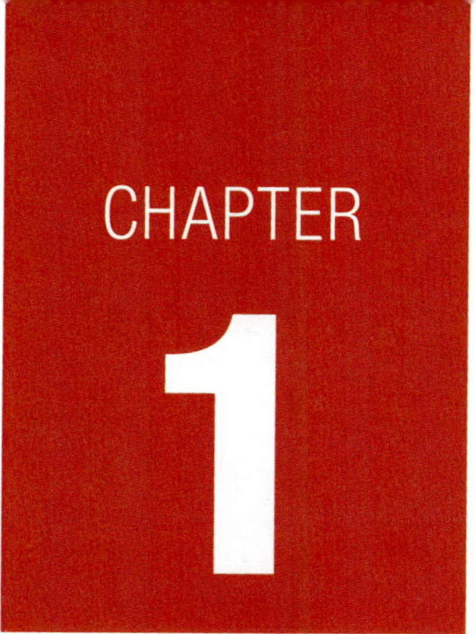

CHAPTER 1

GENERAL RULES

Introduction to Chapter 1—General Rules

The *National Electrical Code* (*NEC*) is a set of standards that are used to ensure the safe installation and operation of electrical systems in the United States. The *NEC* is published by the National Fire Protection Association (NFPA) and is updated every three years. The *NEC* is not a law, but it is widely adopted by local and state governments as a regulatory standard for electrical installations in the United States. The *NEC* is also recognized as a standard for electrical installations in other countries. The value of the *NEC* lies in its role as a set of guidelines for the safe installation and operation of electrical systems, which helps to protect people and property from the dangers of electrical fires and shocks.

Chapter 1 of the *NEC* is divided into two articles. The first contains the definitions of important terms used throughout the *Code*, and the second provides the general requirements for all electrical installations. The definitions and rules in this chapter apply to all electrical installations covered by the *NEC*.

Chapter 1 is often overlooked because the rules are very broad and do not clearly apply to specific situations. Be sure you understand the rules, concepts, definitions, and requirements in Chapter 1 as doing so will make a difficult rule(s) much easier to apply. Chapter 1 articles covered by this material are:

▶ **Article 100—Definitions.** Article 100 contains the definitions essential to the application of this Code. Where terms are not defined in Article 100, the NEC Style Manual directs us to use Webster's Collegiate Dictionary, or to consult with the authority having jurisdiction.

▶ **Article 110—General Requirements for Electrical Installations.** This article covers the general requirements for the examination and approval, installation and use, and access to spaces around electrical equipment.

DEFINITIONS

Introduction to Article 100—Definitions

Have you ever had a conversation with someone only to discover that what you meant and what they understood were completely different? This often happens when people have different interpretations of the words being used, and that is why the definitions of key *NEC* terms are located at the beginning of the *Code*. Definitions used out of context are a leading cause of misinterpretations of rules by people such as electricians, engineers, and inspectors. Because the *NEC* exists to protect people and property, it is important to be able to convey and comprehend the language used. Review and reference Article 100 whenever there is a possibility of an inaccurate (or incorrect) definition of a term being used in a rule.

100 Definitions

Scope. This article contains definitions essential to the application of this *Code.* Definitions of standard terms, such as volt, voltage drop, ampere, impedance, and resistance are not contained in Article 100. If the *NEC* does not define a term, then a dictionary or building code acceptable to the authority having jurisdiction should be consulted.

The *Code* does not include general or technical terms from other codes and standards. An article number in parentheses following the definition indicates that the definition only applies to that article.

Author's Comment:

▶ In this material, the Article 100 definitions that only apply to a specific article can also be found in that specific article.

Accessible, Readily (Readily Accessible). Capable of being reached quickly for operation, renewal, or inspection without requiring those to whom ready access is necessary to use tools (other than keys), climb over or under obstructions, remove obstacles, resort to using portable ladders, and so forth. ▶Figure 100–1

Note: The use of keys for locks on electrical equipment and locked doors to electrical equipment rooms and vaults is a common practice. They are permitted by the *NEC* as this is still considered as readily accessible. ▶Figure 100–2

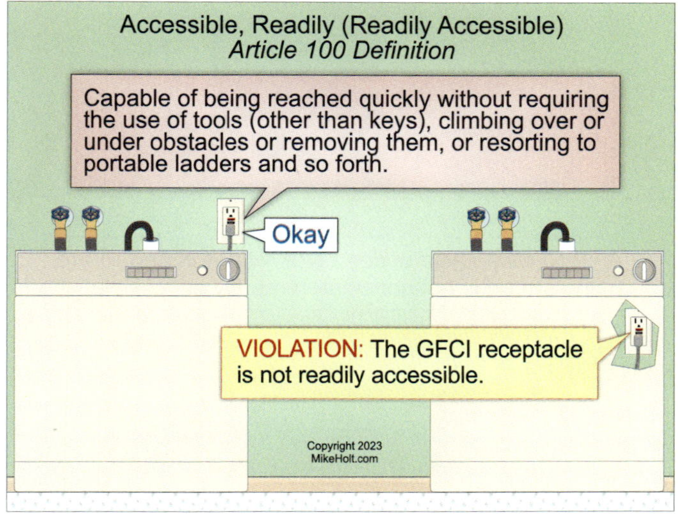

▶Figure 100–1

Author's Comment:

▶ A GFCI receptacle located in a cabinet under a sink is not readily accessible because it is not capable of being reached quickly without having to remove obstacles. ▶Figure 100–3

Ampacity. The maximum current, in amperes, a conductor can carry continuously under its conditions of use—without exceeding its temperature rating. ▶Figure 100–4

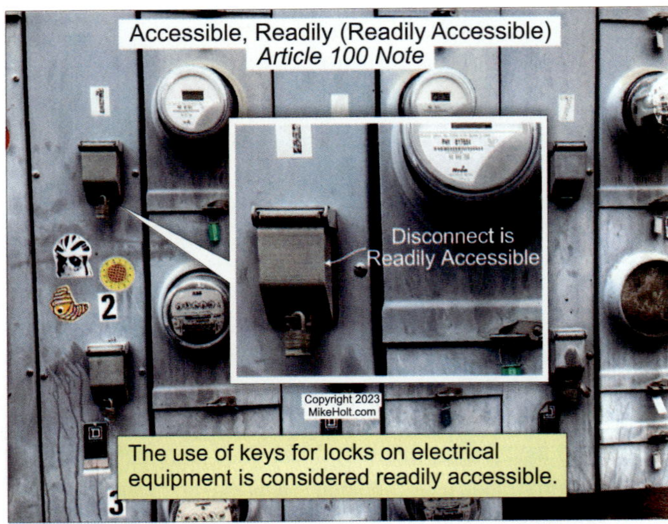

▶Figure 100–2

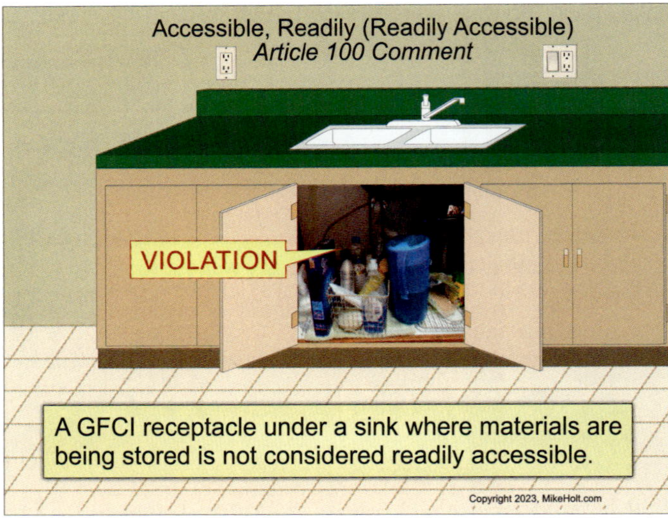

▶Figure 100–3

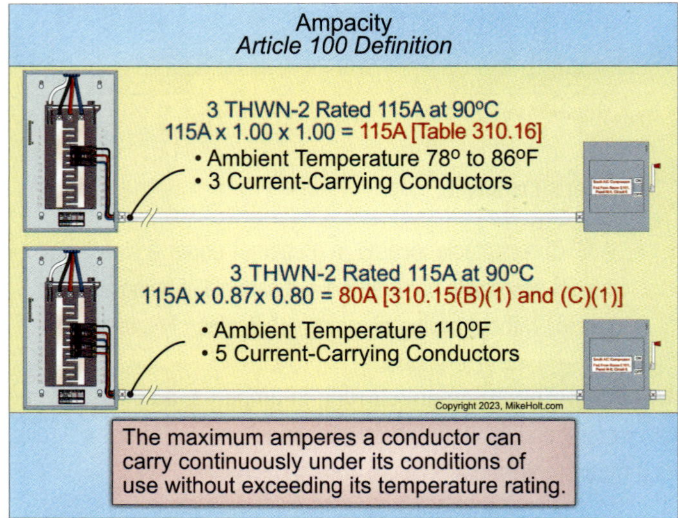

▶Figure 100–4

▶ See 310.14 and 310.15 for details and examples of types of conductors and cables suitable for the conditions of use, their respective temperature ratings, and the ampacity corrections and adjustments depending on the condition of use of those conductors and cables.

Approved. Acceptable to the authority having jurisdiction (AHJ), usually the electrical inspector. ▶Figure 100–5

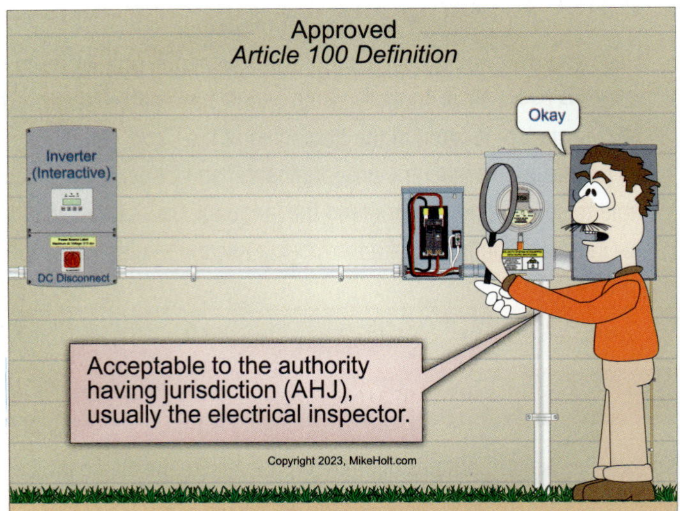

▶Figure 100–5

▶ Product listing does not mean the product is approved, but it can be a basis for approval. See 90.4, 90.7, and 110.2 and the definitions in this article for "Authority Having Jurisdiction," "Identified," "Labeled," and "Listed."

Attachment Plug (Plug Cap). A wiring device at the end of a flexible cord intended to be inserted into a receptacle to make an electrical connection. ▶Figure 100–6

Authority Having Jurisdiction (AHJ). The organization, office, or individual responsible for approving equipment, materials, or installation. See 90.4 and 90.7 for more information. ▶Figure 100–7

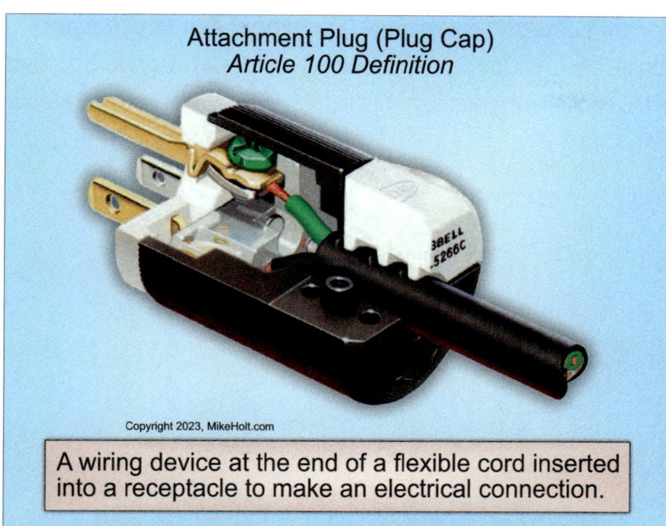

A wiring device at the end of a flexible cord inserted into a receptacle to make an electrical connection.

▶Figure 100–6

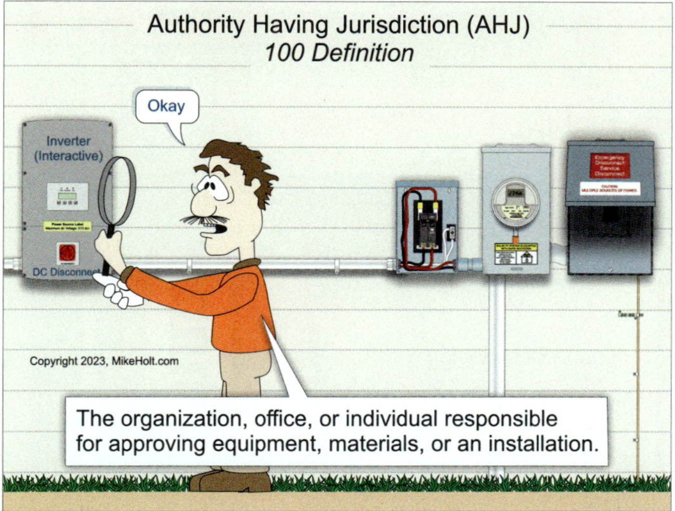

The organization, office, or individual responsible for approving equipment, materials, or an installation.

▶Figure 100–7

Note: The authority having jurisdiction (AHJ) may be a federal, state, or local government department or individual such as a fire chief, fire marshal, chief of a fire prevention bureau, labor or health department, a building official, electrical inspector, or others having statutory authority. The utility company can also be an AHJ. In some circumstances, the property owner or his/her agent assumes the role, and at government installations, the commanding officer, or departmental official may be the AHJ.

Author's Comment:

▸ The AHJ is typically the electrical inspector who has legal statutory authority. In the absence of federal, state, or local regulations, the operator of the facility or his/her agent (such as an architect or engineer of the facility) can assume the role.

▸ Most expect the AHJ to have at least some prior experience in the electrical field, such as having studied electrical engineering or having obtained an electrical contractor's license. In a few states this is a legal requirement. Memberships, certifications, and active participation in electrical organizations such as the International Association of Electrical Inspectors (IAEI) speak to an individual's qualifications. Visit www.IAEI.org for more information about that organization.

Bathroom. An area including a sink as well as one or more toilet, urinal, tub, shower, bidet, or similar plumbing fixture. ▶Figure 100–8

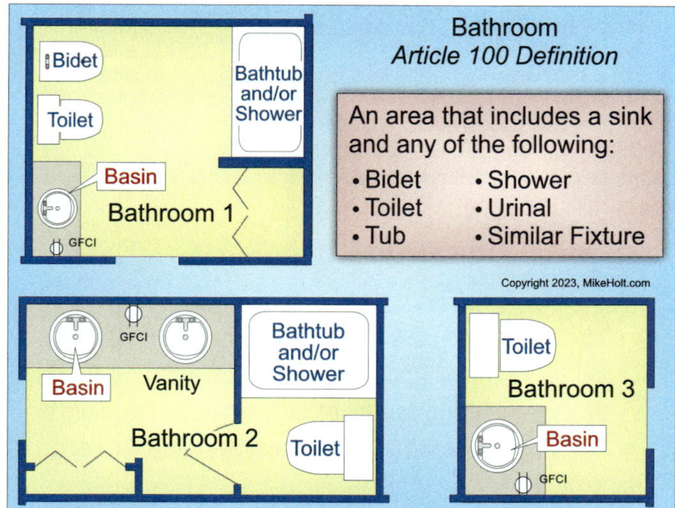

▶Figure 100–8

Battery. A single cell or a group of cells connected together electrically in series, in parallel—or a combination of both. ▶Figure 100–9

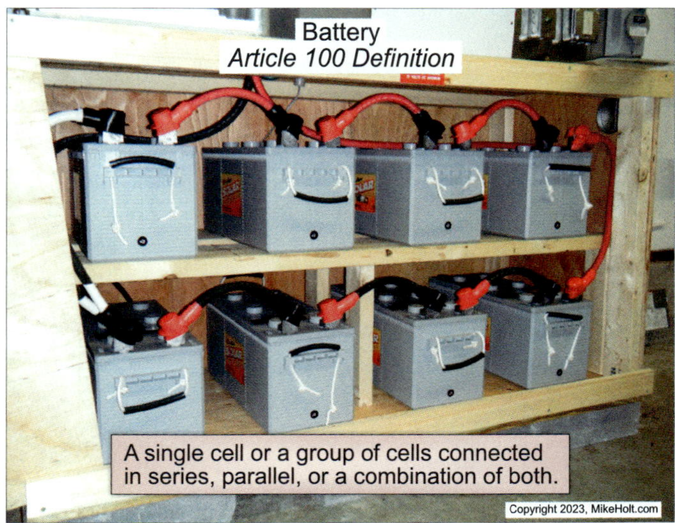

A single cell or a group of cells connected in series, parallel, or a combination of both.

▶Figure 100–9

Bonded (Bonding). Connected to establish electrical continuity and conductivity. ▶Figure 100–10

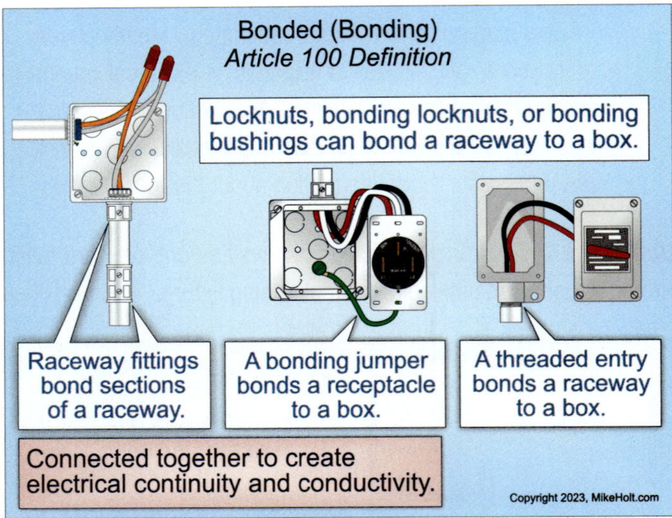

▶Figure 100–10

Author's Comment:

▶ Bonding electrical equipment in accordance with 250.4(A)(3) and bonding metal parts in accordance with 250.4(A)(4) creates an effective path for ground-fault current to return to the supply source and open the overcurrent protective device.

Bonding Conductor (Bonding Jumper). A conductor that ensures electrical conductivity by connecting metal parts of equipment together. ▶Figure 100–11

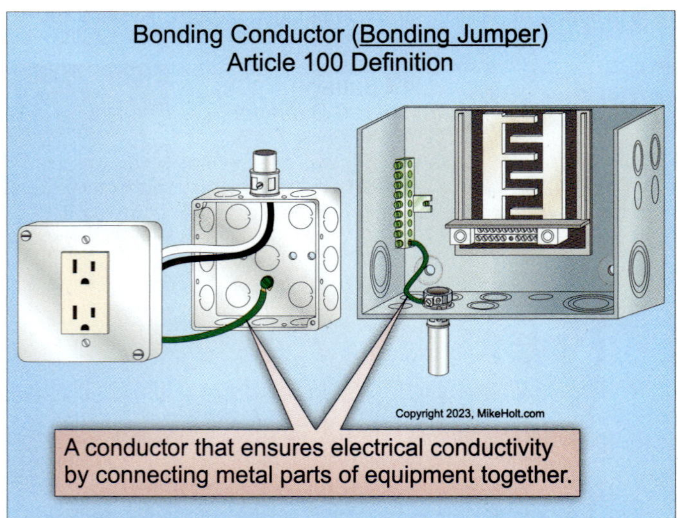

▶Figure 100–11

Bonding Jumper, Equipment (Equipment Bonding Jumper). A connection to ensure electrical continuity between two or more portions of the equipment grounding conductor. ▶Figure 100–12 and ▶Figure 100–13

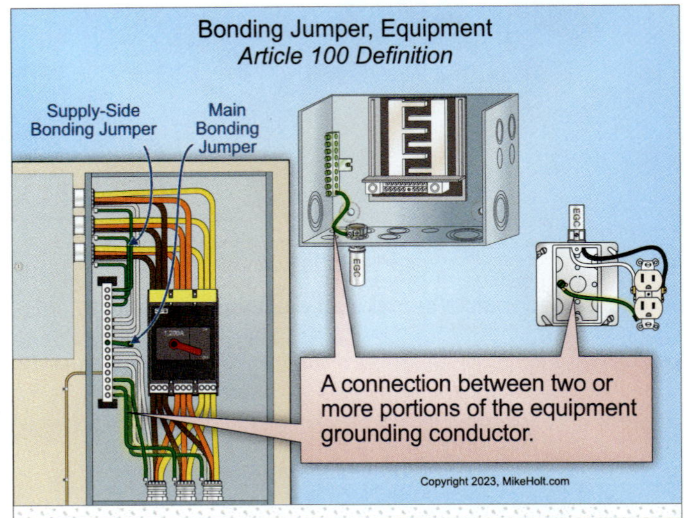

▶Figure 100–12

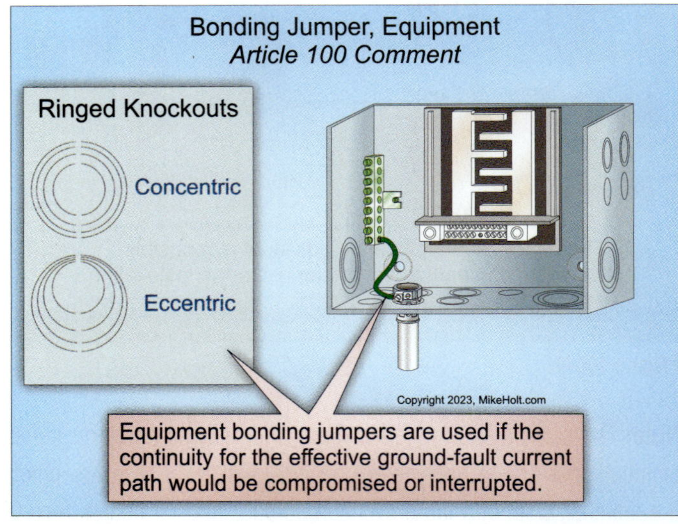

▶Figure 100–13

Bonding Jumper, Main (Main Bonding Jumper). A wire, screw, or busbar used to connect the service neutral conductor to the equipment grounding conductor at the service disconnect enclosure. ▶Figure 100–14, ▶Figure 100–15, and ▶Figure 100–16

Author's Comment:

▶ The main bonding jumper can be a wire, busbar, or screw [250.28(A)]. Connection to the service equipment enclosure must be in accordance with 250.8(A) and 250.24(C).

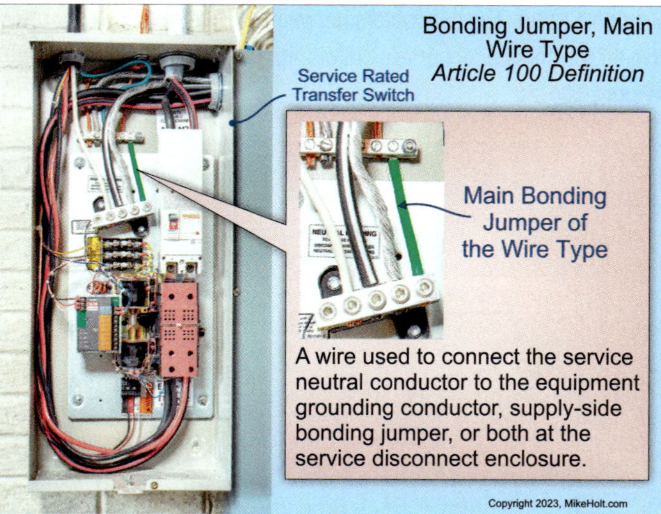

▶Figure 100–14

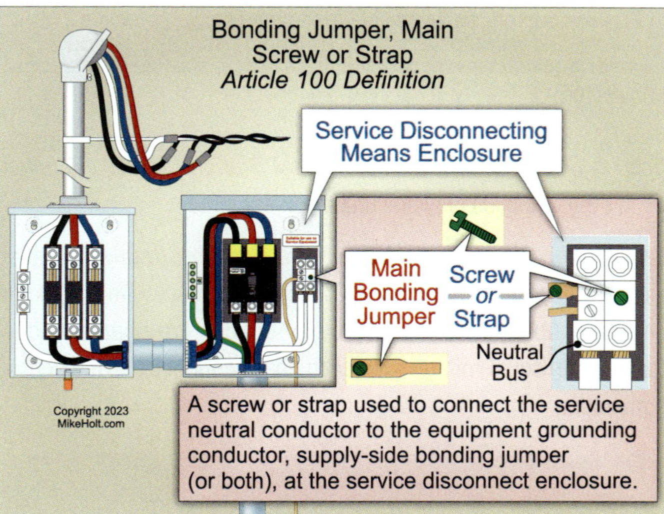

▶Figure 100–15

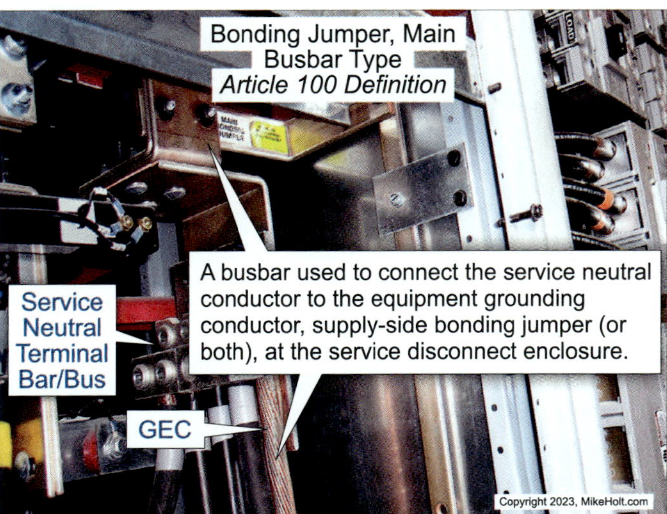

▶Figure 100–16

Bonding Jumper, Supply-Side (Supply-Side Bonding Jumper). The conductor installed on the supply side of a service, within the service equipment, or separately derived system that ensures conductivity between metal parts required to be electrically connected. ▶Figure 100–17, ▶Figure 100–18, and ▶Figure 100–19

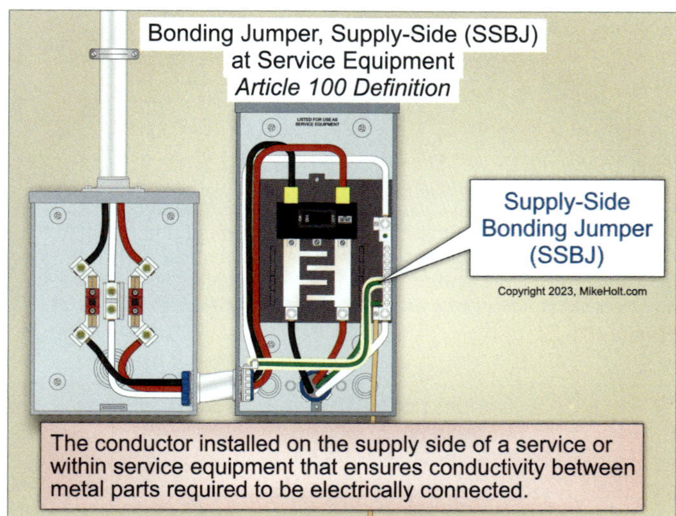

▶Figure 100–17

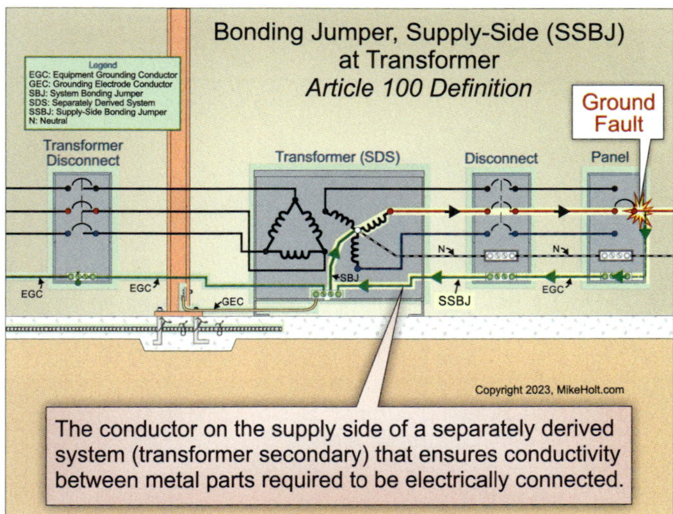

▶Figure 100–18

Bonding Jumper, System (System Bonding Jumper). The connection between the neutral conductor or grounded-phase conductor and the equipment grounding conductor, supply-side bonding jumper, or both at a separately derived system, such as a transformer or generator. ▶Figure 100–20 and ▶Figure 100–21

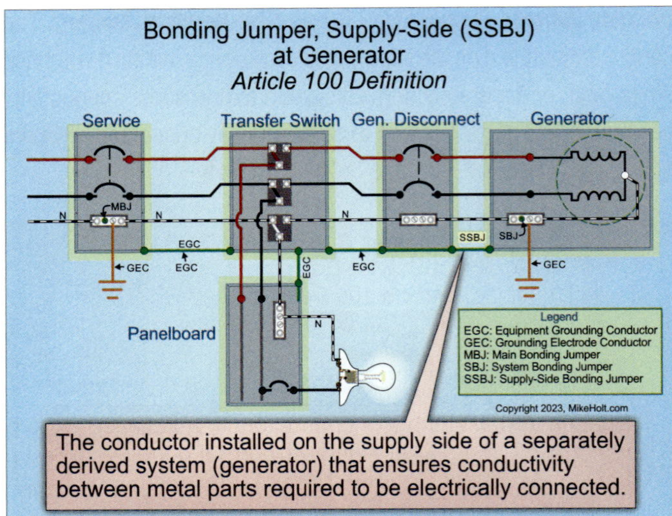

▶Figure 100–19

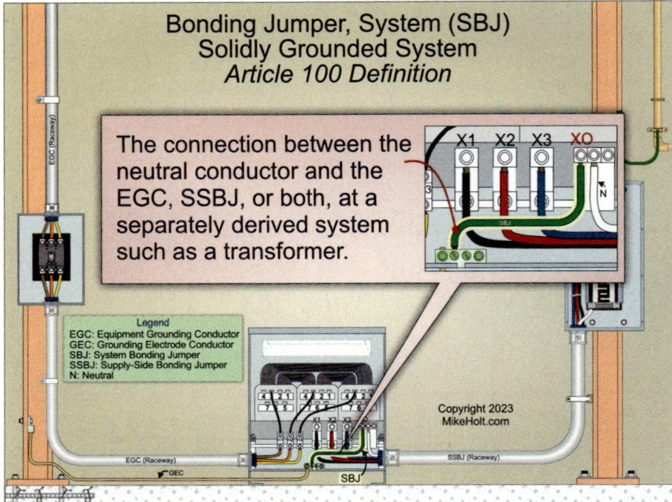

▶Figure 100–20

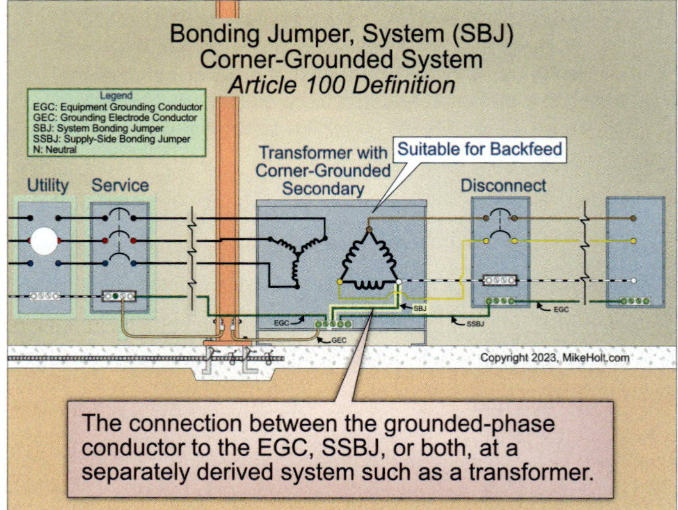

▶Figure 100–21

Branch Circuit. The conductors between the final overcurrent protective device and the receptacle outlets, lighting outlets, or other outlets. ▶Figure 100–22

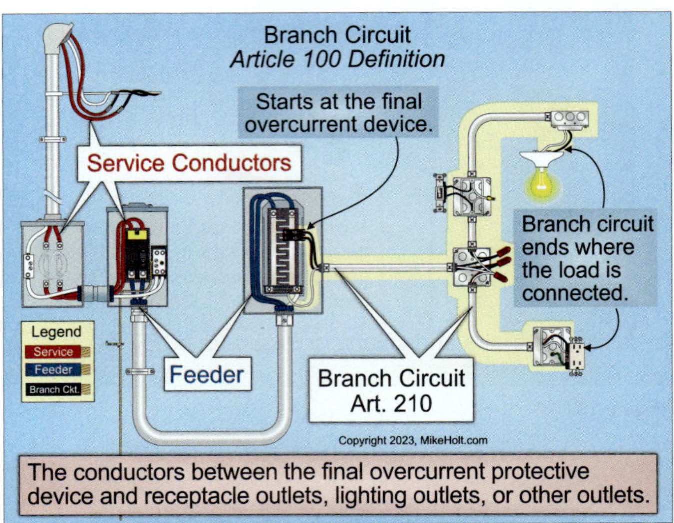

▶Figure 100–22

Branch Circuit, Individual (Individual Branch Circuit). A branch circuit that supplies only one utilization equipment.

Branch Circuit, Multiwire (Multiwire Branch Circuit). A branch circuit consisting of two or more phase conductors with a common neutral conductor having a voltage between the phase conductors, and an equal voltage from each phase conductor to the neutral conductor. ▶Figure 100–23

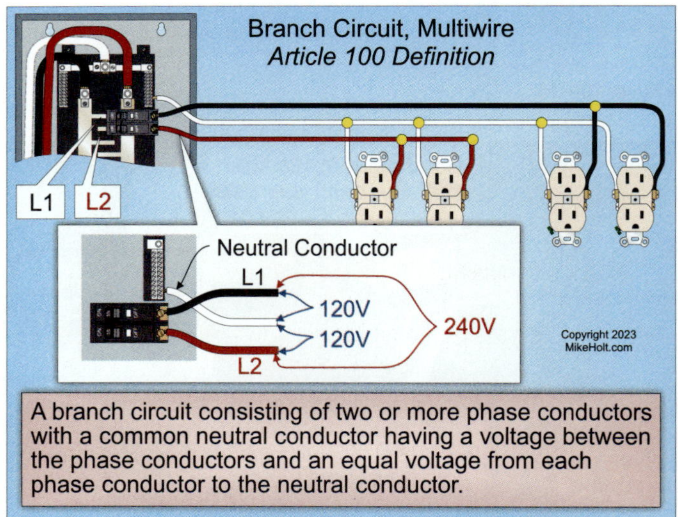

▶Figure 100–23

Building. A structure that stands alone or is separated from adjoining structures by fire walls. ▶Figure 100–24

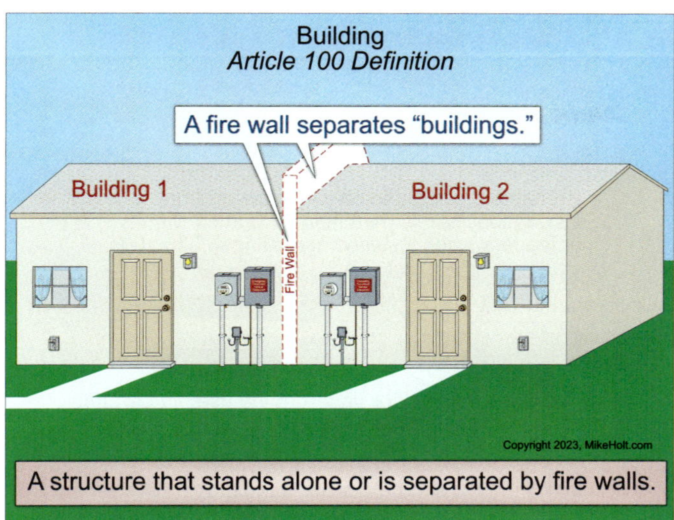

▶Figure 100–24

Cabinet. A surface- or flush-mounted enclosure provided with a frame in which a door can be hung. ▶Figure 100–25

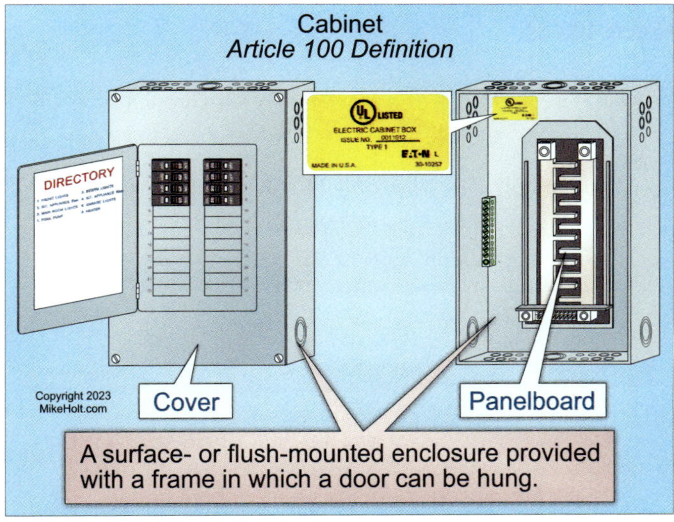

▶Figure 100–25

▶ Cabinets are used to enclose panelboards. See the definition of "Panelboard" in this article.

Cable, Armored (Type AC). A fabricated assembly of conductors in a flexible interlocked metallic armor with an internal bonding strip in intimate contact with the armor for its entire length. ▶Figure 100–26

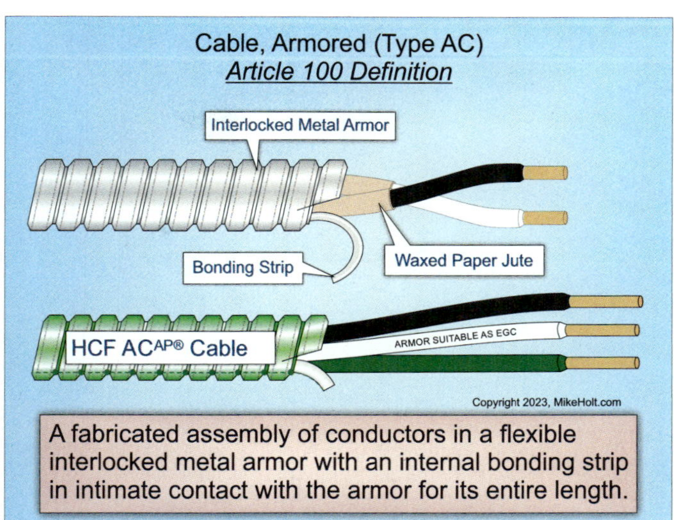

▶Figure 100–26

Cable, Metal-Clad (Type MC). A factory assembly of one or more insulated circuit conductors (with or without optical fiber members) enclosed in an armor of interlocking metal tape, or a smooth or corrugated metallic sheath. ▶Figure 100–27

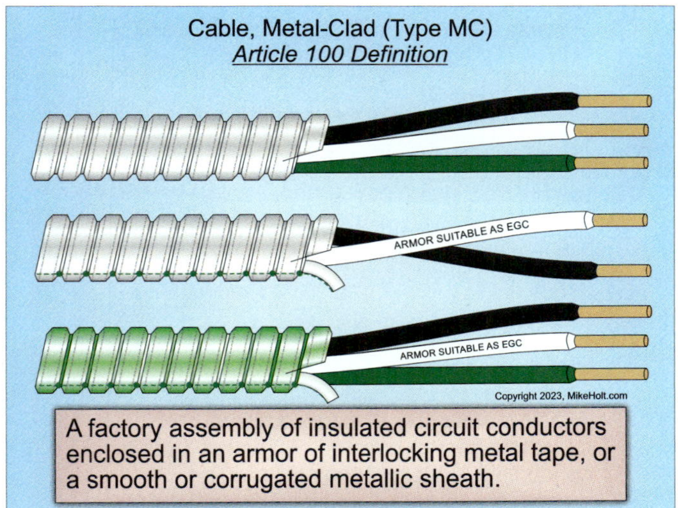

▶Figure 100–27

Cable, Nonmetallic-Sheathed (Type NM). A wiring method that encloses two or more insulated conductors within an outer nonmetallic jacket. ▶Figure 100–28

▶ It is the generally accepted practice in the electrical industry to call Type NM cable "Romex®," a registered trademark of the Southwire Company.

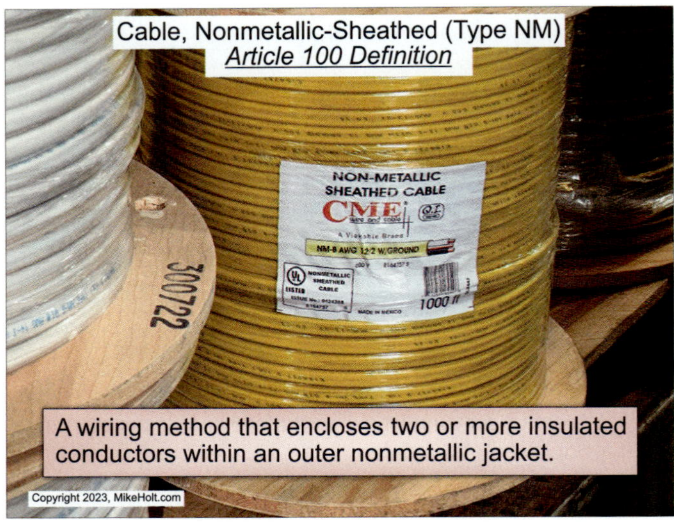

▶Figure 100–28

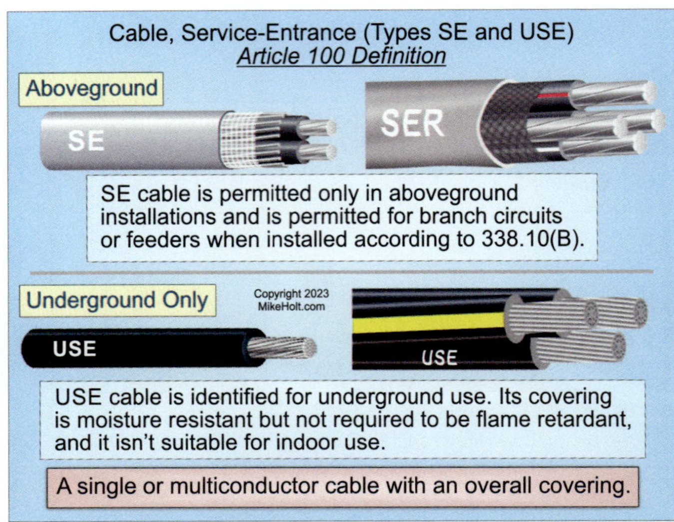

▶Figure 100–30

Cable, Power and Control Tray (Type TC). A factory assembly of two or more insulated conductors (with or without associated bare or covered equipment grounding conductors) under a nonmetallic jacket. ▶Figure 100–29

Cable, Underground Feeder and Branch-Circuit (Type UF). A factory assembly of insulated conductors with an integral or overall covering of nonmetallic material suitable for direct burial in the Earth. ▶Figure 100–31

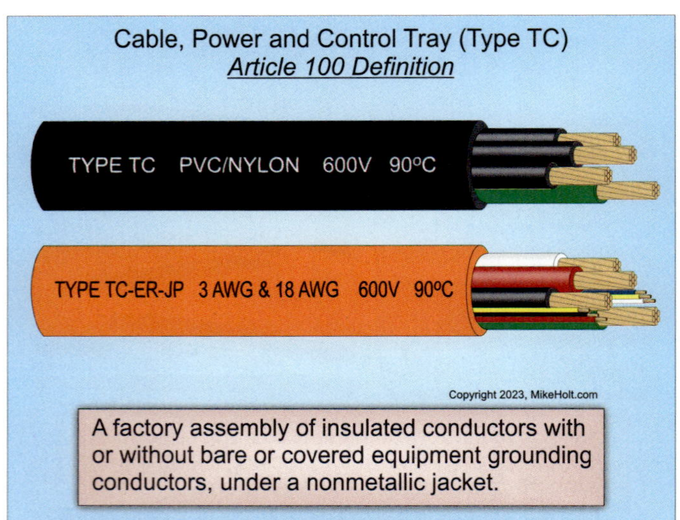

▶Figure 100–29

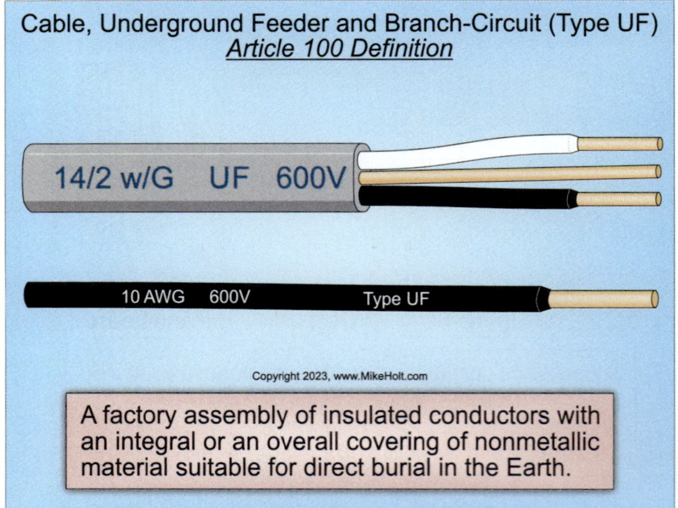

▶Figure 100–31

Cable, Service-Entrance (Types SE and USE). Service-entrance cable is a single or multiconductor cable with an overall covering. ▶Figure 100–30

Type SE. Type SE cables have a flame-retardant, moisture-resistant covering for aboveground installations. These cables are permitted for branch circuits or feeders when installed in accordance with 338.10(B).

Type USE. USE cable is identified as a wiring method permitted for underground use. Its covering is moisture resistant, but not flame retardant.

Cable Tray System. A unit or assembly of units or sections with associated fittings forming a rigid structural system used to securely fasten or support cables and raceways. ▶Figure 100–32

Circuit Breaker. A device designed to be opened and closed manually, but opens automatically during an overcurrent event without damage to itself. ▶Figure 100–33

Circuit Breaker, Adjustable (Adjustable Circuit Breaker). Adjustable circuit breakers can be set to trip at various values of current, time (or both), within a predetermined range. ▶Figure 100–34

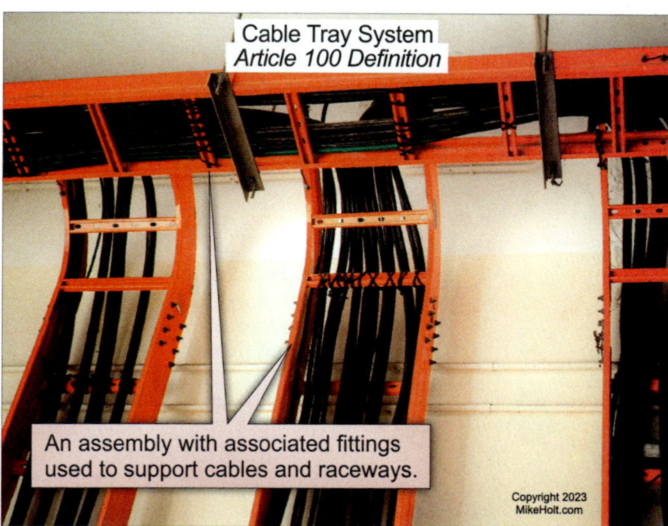

▶Figure 100–32

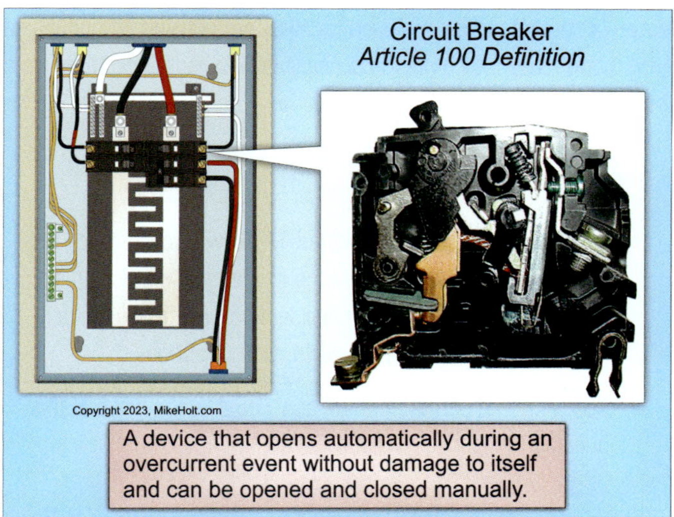

▶Figure 100–33

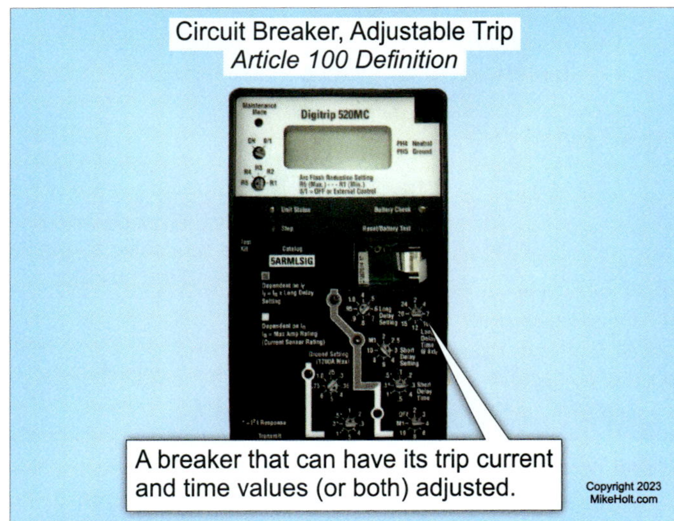

▶Figure 100–34

Circuit Breaker, Inverse Time (Inverse Time Circuit Breaker). This type of circuit breaker is purposely designed to delay its tripping action during an overcurrent condition. The intent is to compensate for the inrush of current during the normal start-up of equipment.

Author's Comment:

▸ Inverse time breakers operate on the principle that as the current increases, the time it takes for the devices to open decreases. They provide ordinary overcurrent protection during overload, short-circuit, or ground-fault conditions. This is the most common type of circuit breaker purchased over the counter. ▶Figure 100–35

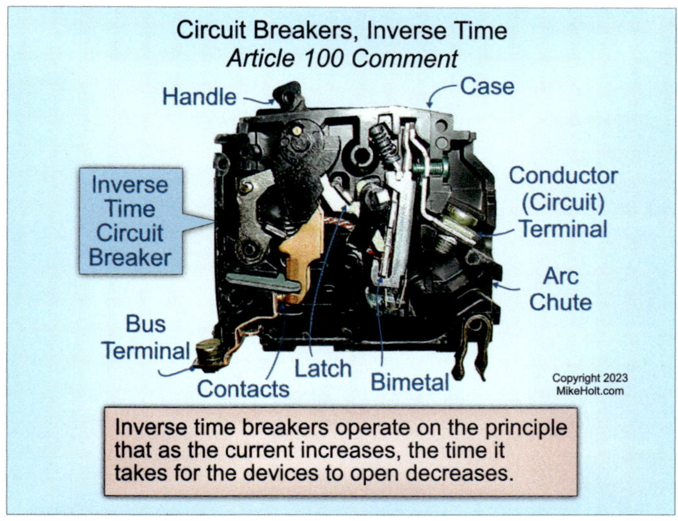

▶Figure 100–35

▸ Most inverse time breakers are "thermal magnetic," with the thermal element providing the inverse time function for clearing overloads, and the magnetic element providing a much quicker clearing of short circuits and ground faults. The magnetic function is also known as the "instantaneous" function.

Clothes Closet Storage Space. The area within a clothes closet in which combustible materials can be kept (Article 410). ▶Figure 100–36

Combiner, DC (DC Combiner). An enclosure that includes devices for the parallel connection of two or more PV system dc circuits (Article 690). ▶Figure 100–37

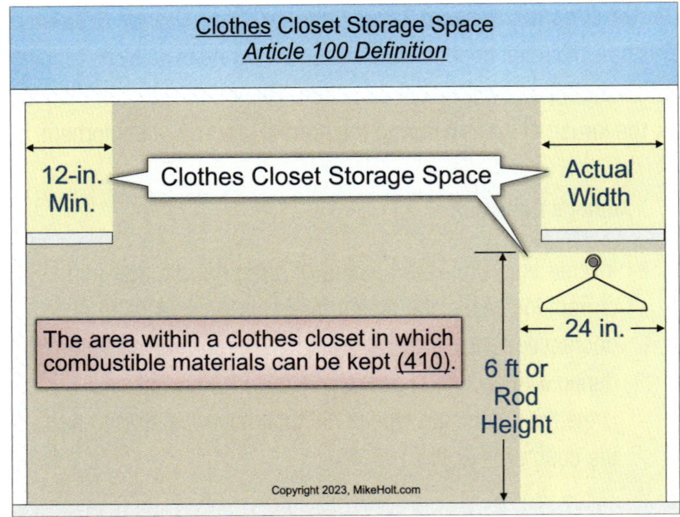

▶Figure 100–36

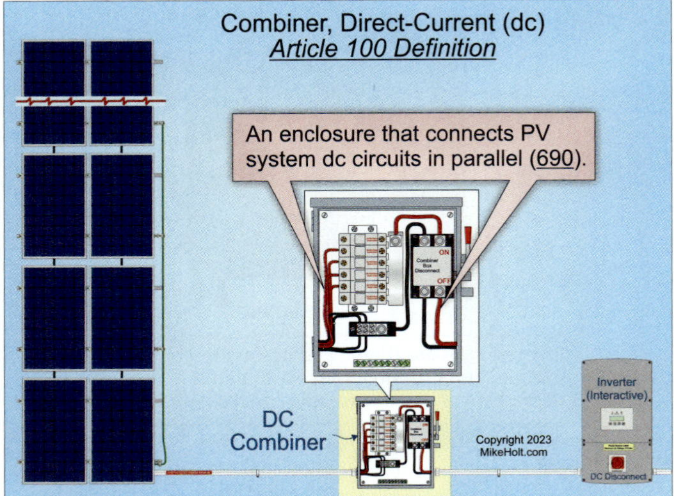

▶Figure 100–37

Commissioning. The process, procedures, and testing used to set up and verify the initial performance, operational controls, safety systems, and sequence of operation of electrical devices and equipment prior to them being placed into active service.

▶ This term is used in Emergency Standby Power Systems 700.3, Legally Required Standby Power Systems 701.3, and Energy Storage Systems 706.7(A).

Concealed. Rendered inaccessible by the structure or finish of the building. ▶Figure 100–38

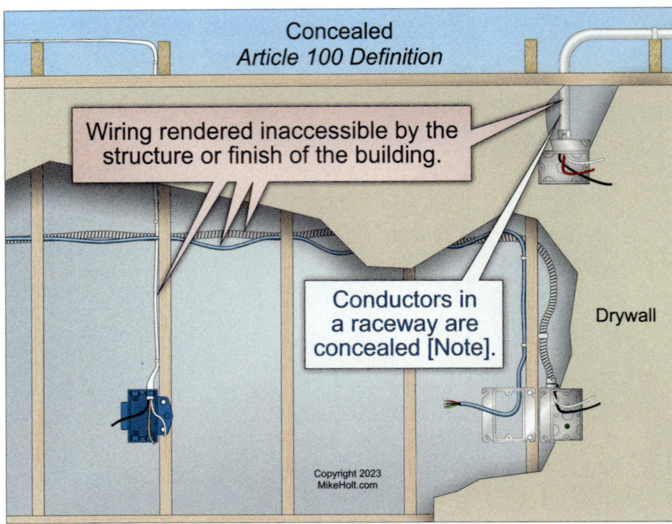

▶Figure 100–38

Note: Conductors in a concealed raceway are considered concealed even though they may be made accessible by withdrawing them from the raceway.

▶ Wiring behind panels designed to allow access, such as removable ceiling tile and wiring in accessible attics, is not considered concealed—it is considered exposed. See the definition of "Exposed (as applied to wiring methods)."

▶ Boxes are not permitted to be concealed by the finish of the building. ▶Figure 100–39

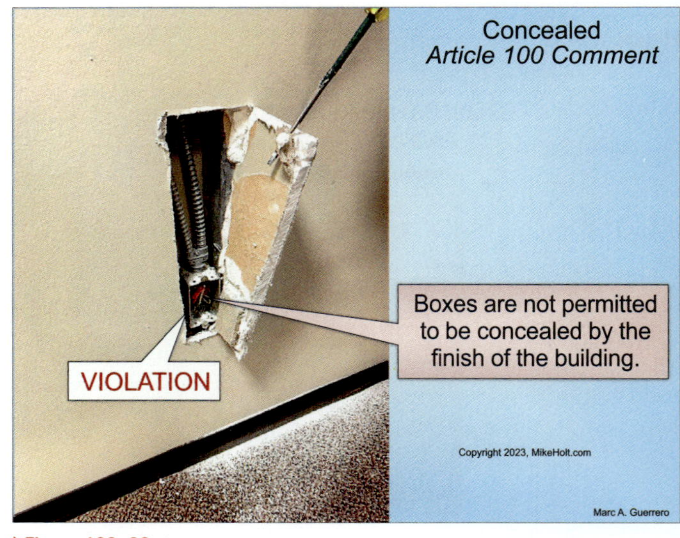

▶Figure 100–39

Conductor, Copper-Clad Aluminum (Copper-Clad Aluminum Conductor). Conductors drawn from a copper-clad aluminum rod, with the copper metallurgically bonded to an aluminum core. ▶Figure 100–40

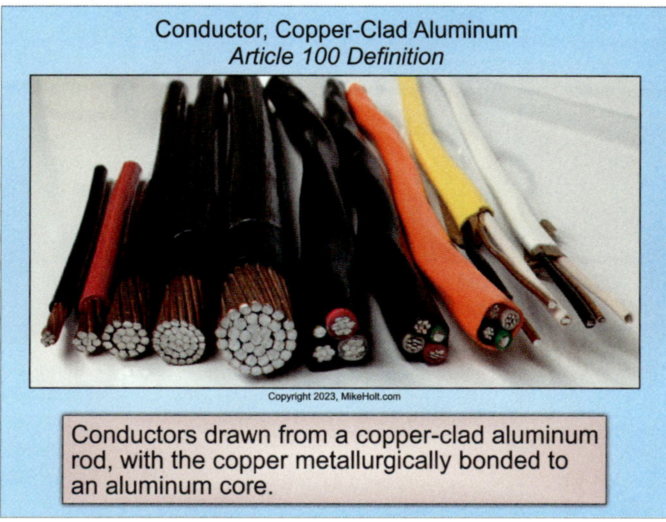

▶Figure 100–40

Conduit, Flexible Metal (FMC). A raceway of circular cross section made of a helically wound, formed, interlocked metal strip, and listed for the installation of electrical conductors. ▶Figure 100–41

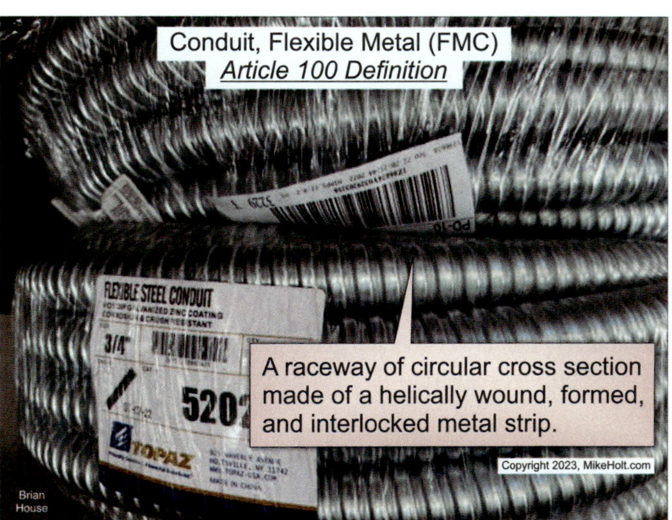

▶Figure 100–41

Conduit, Intermediate Metal (IMC). A steel raceway of circular cross section that can be threaded with integral or associated couplings, and listed for the installation of electrical conductors. ▶Figure 100–42

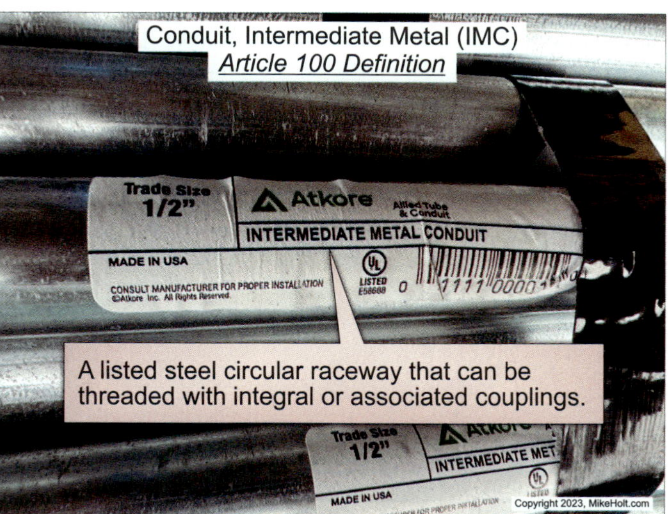

▶Figure 100–42

Conduit, Liquidtight Flexible Metal (LFMC). A raceway of circular cross section (having an outer liquidtight, nonmetallic, sunlight-resistant jacket over an inner flexible metal core) with associated connectors and fittings listed for the installation of electrical conductors. ▶Figure 100–43

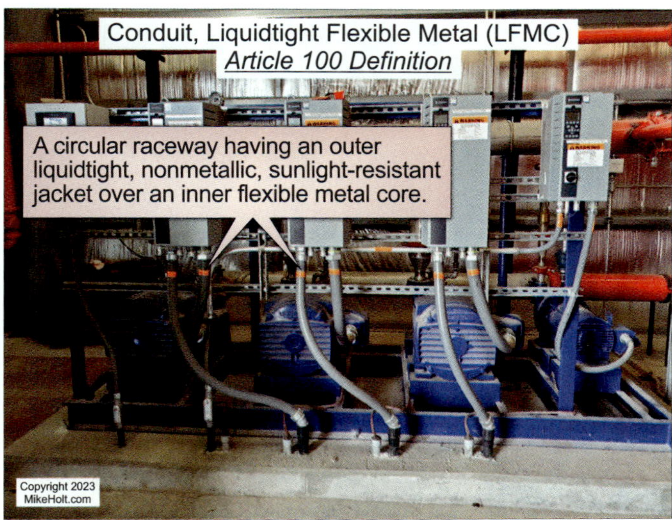

▶Figure 100–43

Conduit, Liquidtight Flexible Nonmetallic (LFNC). A raceway of circular cross section (with an outer liquidtight, nonmetallic, sunlight-resistant jacket over a flexible inner core) with associated couplings, connectors, and fittings listed for the installation of electrical conductors. ▶Figure 100–44

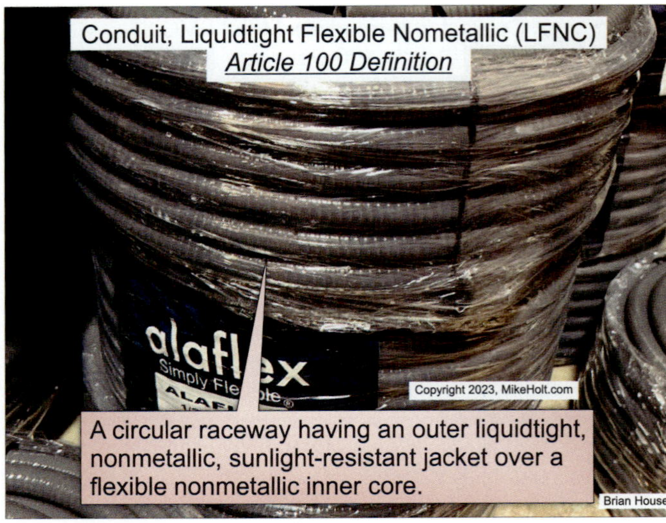

▶Figure 100–44

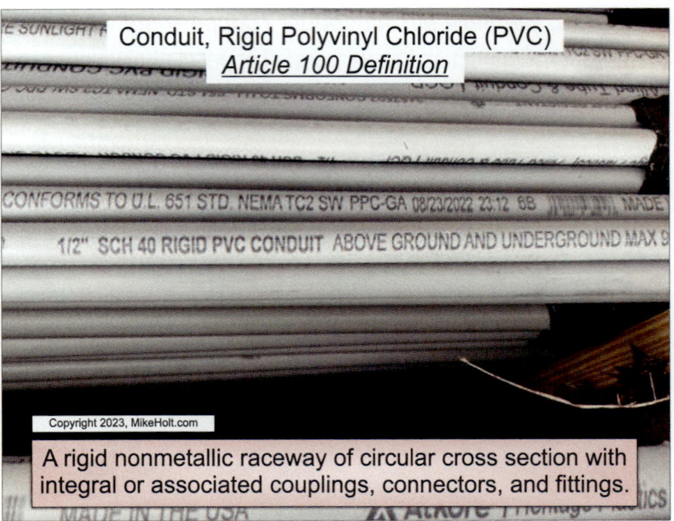

▶Figure 100–46

Conduit, Rigid Metal (RMC). A listed metal raceway of circular cross section with integral or associated couplings listed for the installation of electrical conductors. ▶Figure 100–45

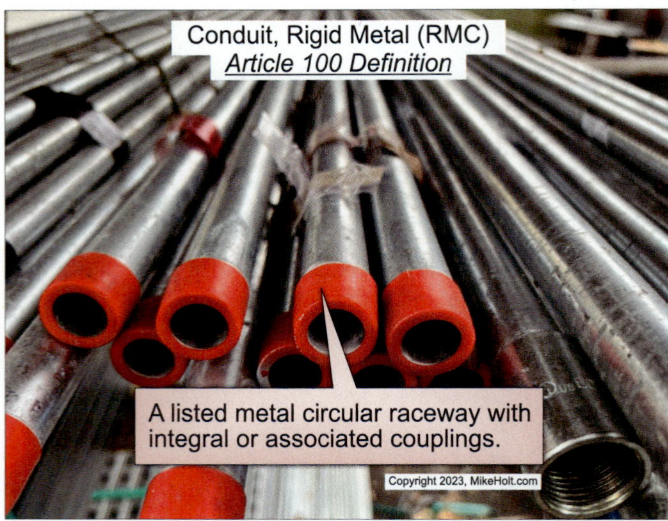

▶Figure 100–45

Conduit, Rigid Polyvinyl Chloride (PVC). A rigid nonmetallic raceway of circular cross section with integral or associated couplings, connectors, and fittings listed for the installation of electrical conductors. ▶Figure 100–46

Conduit Body. A fitting installed on a raceway that provides access to conductors through a removable cover. ▶Figure 100–47

Continuous Load. A load where the maximum current is expected for three hours or more continuously.

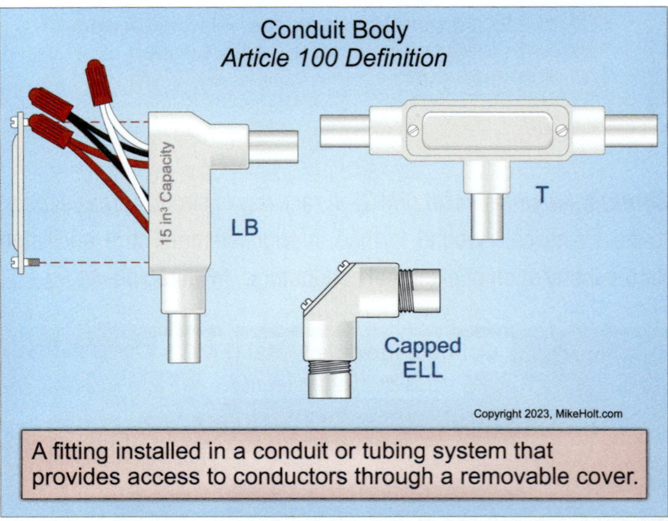

▶Figure 100–47

Converter Circuit, DC-to-DC (DC-to-DC Converter Circuit). The dc circuit conductors connected to the output of dc-to-dc converters (Article 690). ▶Figure 100–48

Author's Comment:

▶ A dc-to-dc converter (optimizer)l enables the inverter to receive the circuit voltage that is maximized for direct-current and/or alternating-current power production by the inverter—regardless of the circuit length, individual module performance, or variance in light exposure between modules.

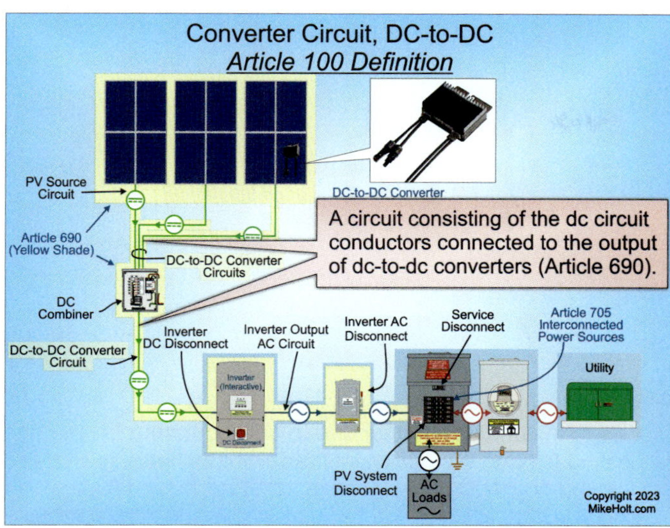

▶Figure 100–48

- A dc combiner connects multiple PV source circuits and dc-to-dc converter source circuits in parallel with each other to create a PV output or dc-to-dc converter output circuit. Direct-current combiners can also recombine multiple PV output circuits and dc-to-dc converter output circuits with a larger 2-wire PV output or dc-to-dc converter output circuit.

Converter, DC-to-DC (DC-to-DC Converter). A electronic device that can provide an output dc voltage and current at a higher or lower value than the input dc voltage and current. ▶Figure 100–49

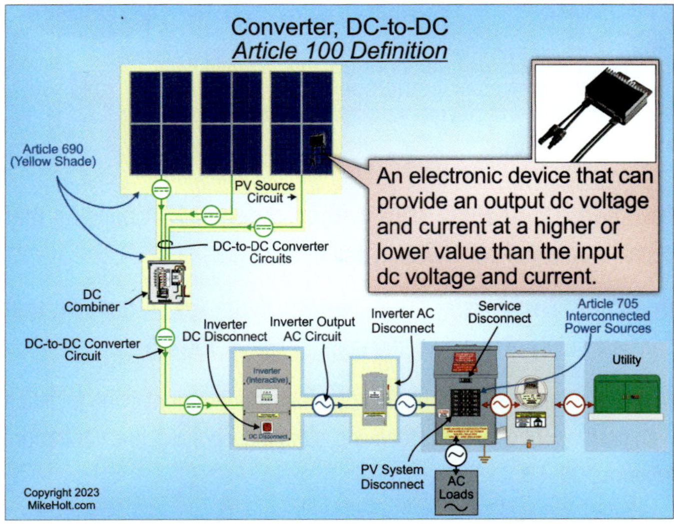

▶Figure 100–49

Author's Comment:

- The dc-to-dc converters are intended to maximize the output of independent PV modules and reduce losses due to variances between modules' outputs. They are directly wired to each module and are bolted to the module frame or the PV rack.

- A dc-to-dc converter (optimizer)l enables a PV inverter to automatically maintain a fixed circuit voltage, at the optimal point for dc/ac conversion by the inverter, regardless of circuit length and individual module performance.

Cord, Flexible (Flexible Cord). Two or more insulated conductors enclosed in a flexible covering. ▶Figure 100–50

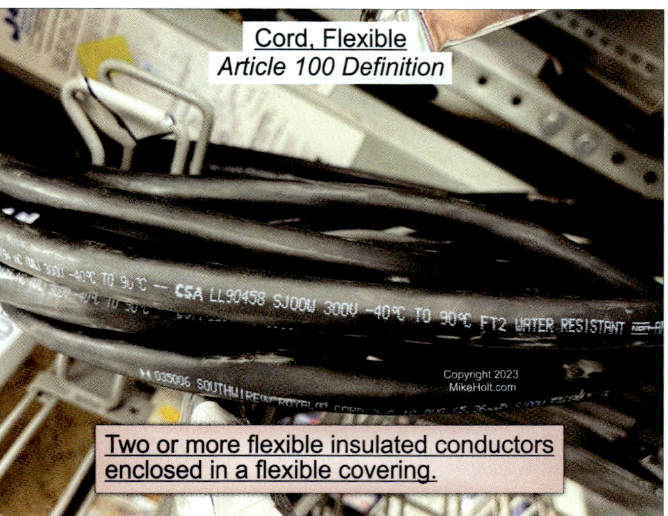

▶Figure 100–50

Author's Comment:

- Article 400 contains the primary requirements for flexible cords.

Cord Connector. A contact device terminated to a flexible cord that accepts an attachment plug or other insertion.

Cord Set. A length of flexible cord having an attachment plug at one end and a cord connector at the other end. ▶Figure 100–51

Author's Comment:

- Article 400 contains the primary requirements for cord sets.

Cutout Box. An enclosure designed for surface mounting that has swinging doors or covers secured directly to and telescoping with the walls of the enclosure. ▶Figure 100–52

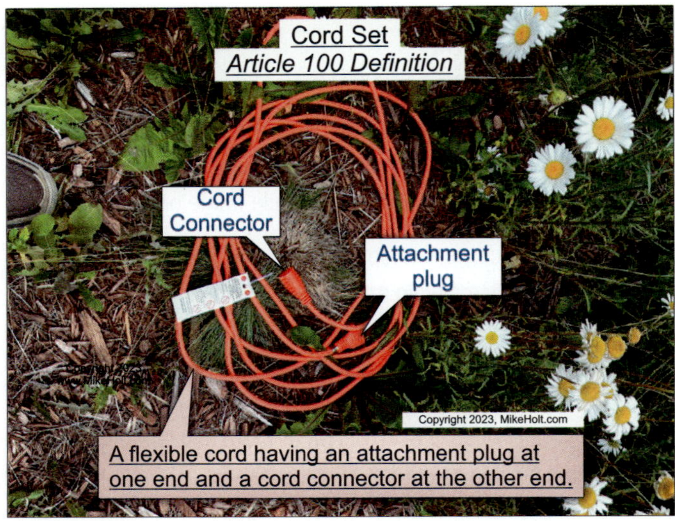

▶Figure 100–51

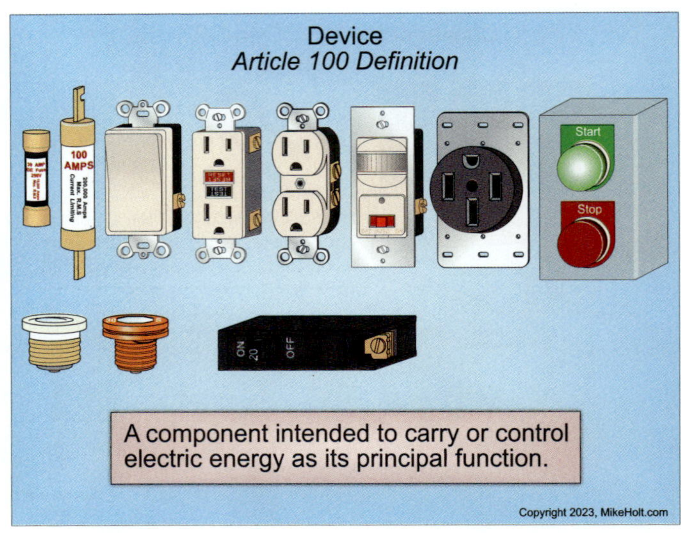

▶Figure 100–53

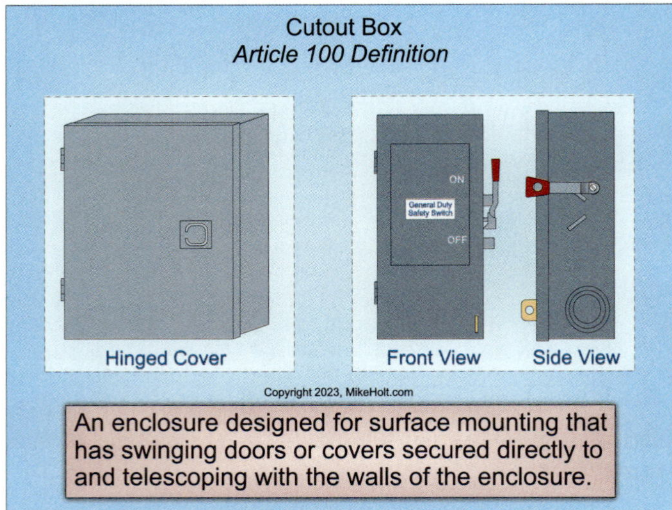

▶Figure 100–52

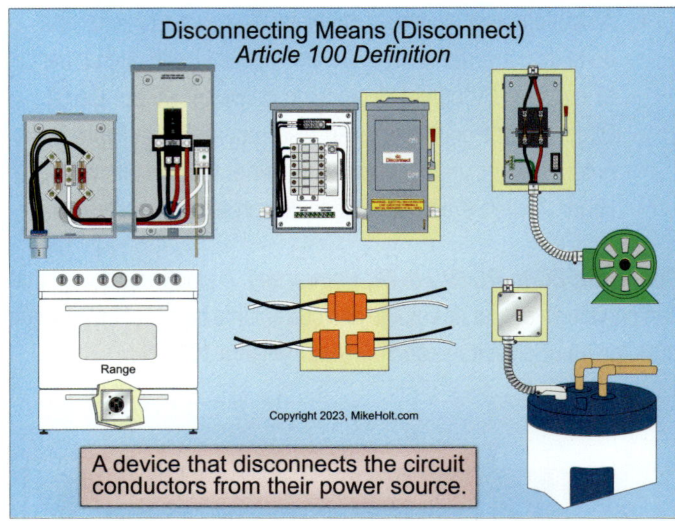

▶Figure 100–54

Device. A component of an electrical installation, other than a conductor, intended to carry or control electric energy as its principal function. ▶Figure 100–53

> **Author's Comment:**
>
> ▶ Devices generally do not consume electric energy and include receptacles, switches, illuminated switches, circuit breakers, fuses, time clocks, controllers, attachment plugs, and so forth. Some (such as illuminated switches, contactors, or relays) consume very small amounts of energy and are still classified as a device based on their primary function.

Disconnecting Means (Disconnect). A device that disconnects the circuit conductors from their power source. ▶Figure 100–54

Dwelling, One-Family (One-Family Dwelling). A building that consists solely of one dwelling unit.

Dwelling, Two-Family (Two-Family Dwelling). A building that consists solely of two dwelling units. ▶Figure 100–55

Dwelling Unit. A single unit that provides independent living facilities with permanent provisions for living, sleeping, cooking, and sanitation. ▶Figure 100–56

Electric Vehicle. An on-road use automobile, bus, truck, van, neighborhood electric vehicle, or motorcycle primarily powered by an electric motor. ▶Figure 100–57

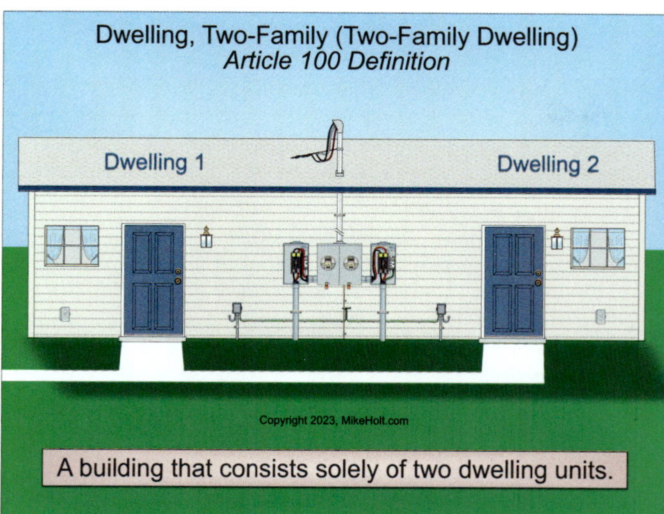

▶Figure 100–55

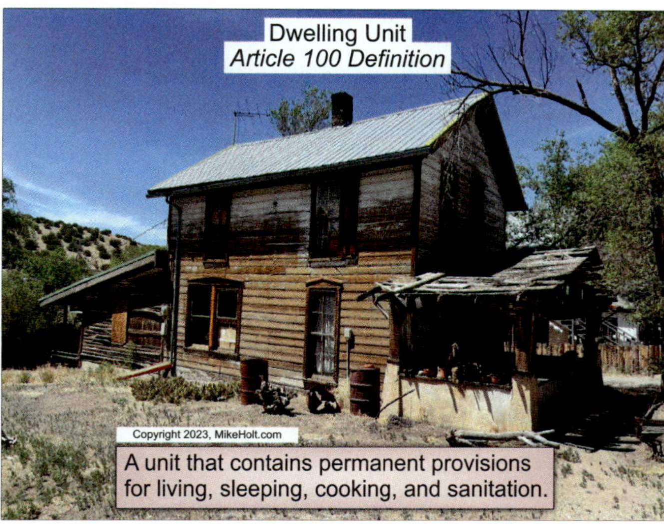

▶Figure 100–56

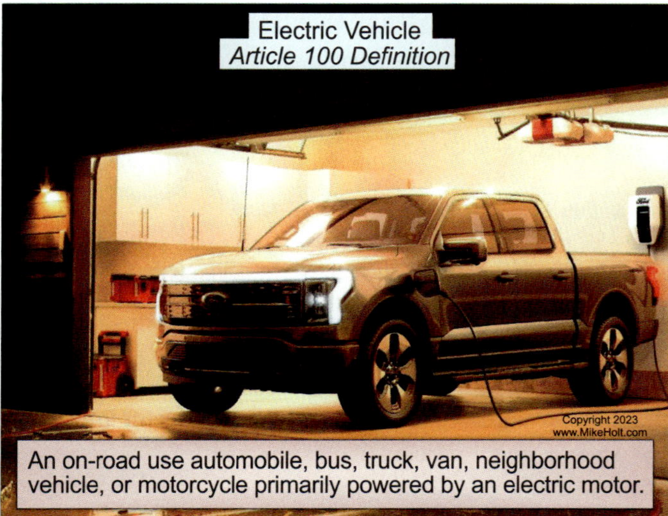

▶Figure 100–57

Note: Off-road, self-propelled electric industrial trucks, hoists, lifts, transports, golf carts, airline ground support equipment, tractors, and boats are not electric vehicles for the purposes of the *NEC*. ▶Figure 100–58

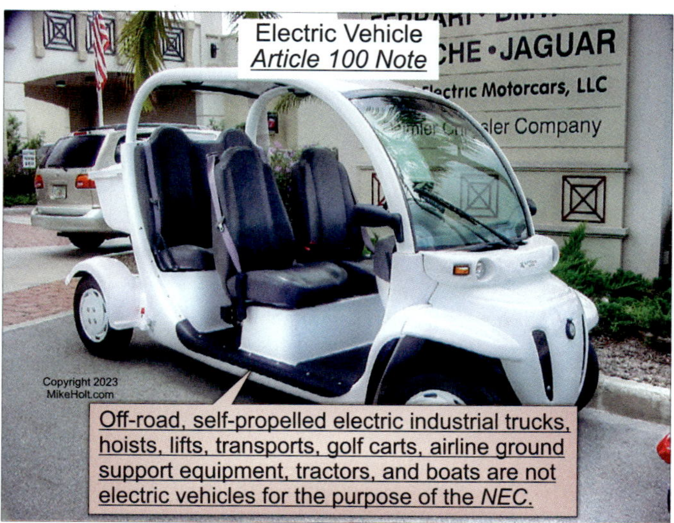

▶Figure 100–58

Author's Comment:

▸ The portion of plug-in vehicles containing both an electric motor and a combustion engine that pertains to re-charging the electric motor is covered by Article 625.

Electric Vehicle Supply Equipment (EVSE). Connectors, attachment plugs, personnel protection systems, devices, and power outlets installed for the purpose of transferring energy between the premises wiring and an electric vehicle (Article 625). ▶Figure 100–59

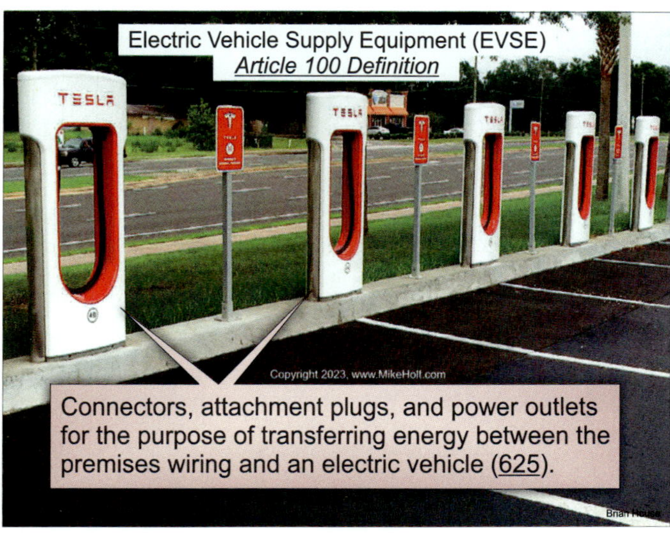

▶Figure 100–59

Electronic Power Converter. A device that uses power electronics to convert one form of electrical power into another form of electrical power. ▶Figure 100–60

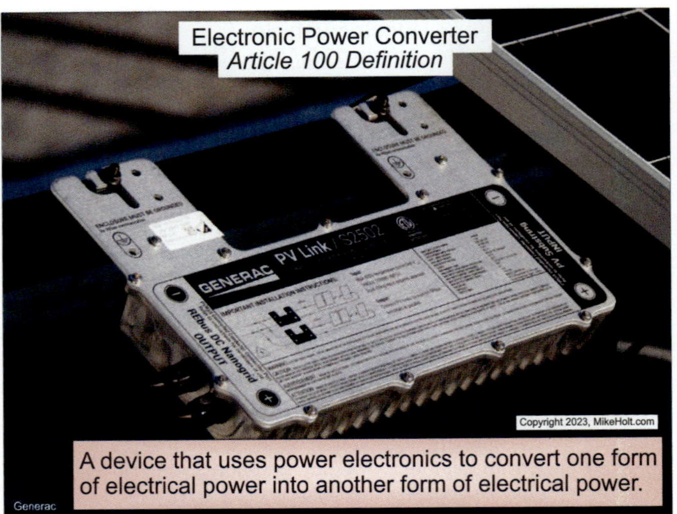

▶Figure 100–60

Note: Examples of electronic power converters include, but are not limited to, inverters and dc-to-dc converters. These devices have limited current capabilities based on the device ratings at continuous rated power.

Energized. Electrically connected to a source of voltage. ▶Figure 100–61

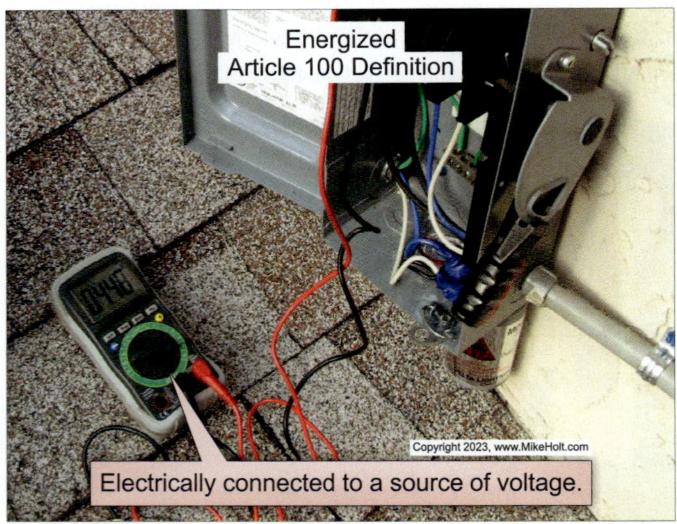

▶Figure 100–61

Energized, Likely to Become (Likely to Become Energized). Conductive material that could become energized because of the failure of electrical insulation or electrical spacing. ▶Figure 100–62

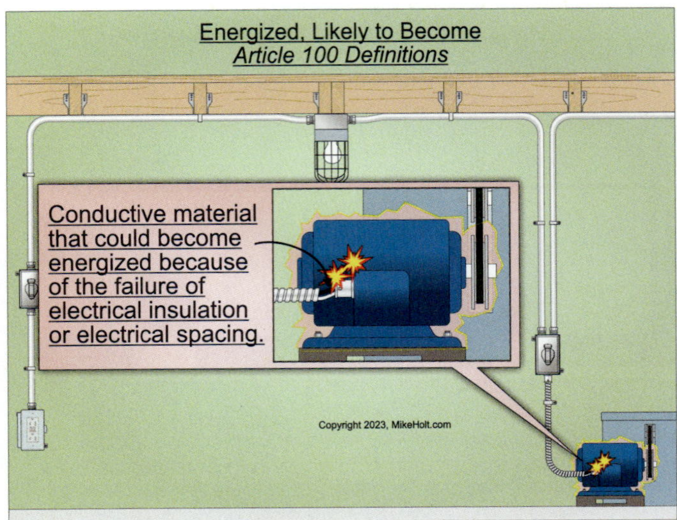

▶Figure 100–62

Energy Management System. A system consisting of monitor(s), communications equipment, controller(s), timer(s), or other device(s) that monitors and/or controls an electrical load or a power production or storage source. ▶Figure 100–63 and ▶Figure 100–64

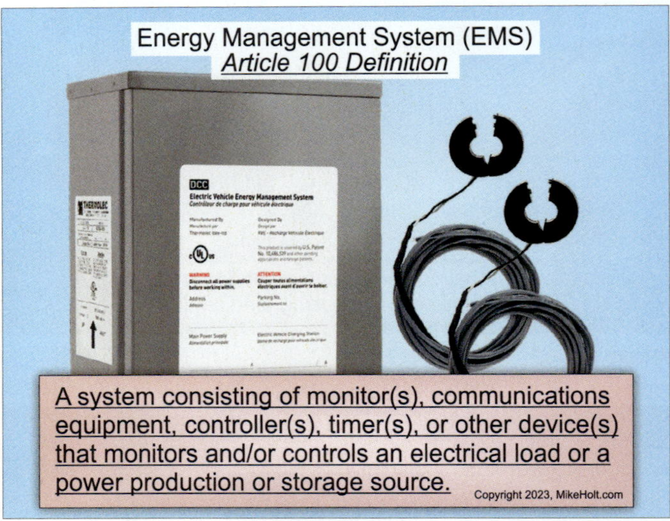

▶Figure 100–63

Author's Comment:

▸ Article 750 contains the primary requirements for energy management systems.

Energy Storage System. One or more devices installed as a system capable of storing energy and providing electrical energy to the premises wiring system. ▶Figure 100–65

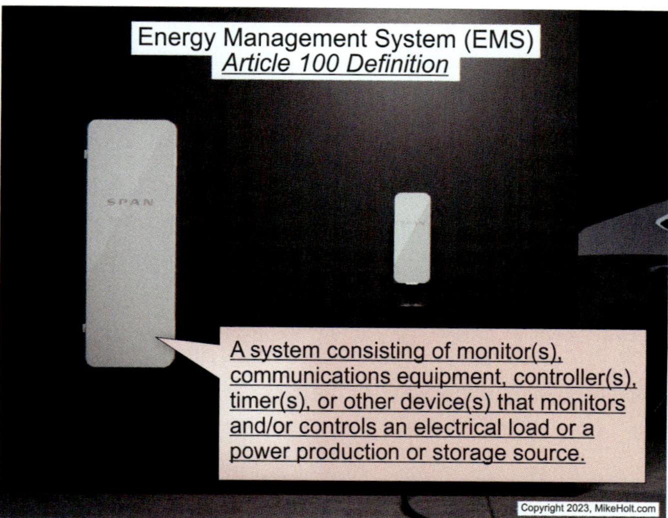

▶Figure 100–64

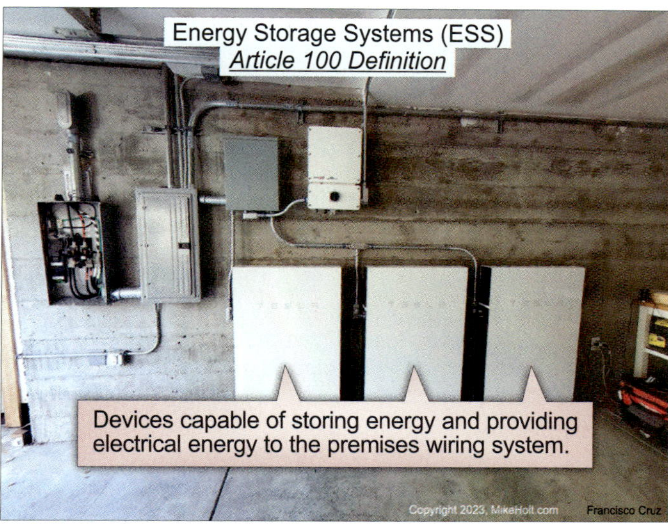

▶Figure 100–65

Note 1: Energy storage systems can include batteries, capacitors, and kinetic energy devices such as flywheels and compressed air. Energy storage systems can include inverters or converters to change voltage levels or to make a change between an alternating-current or a direct-current system.

Author's Comment:

▶ Article 706 contains the primary requirements for energy storage systems.

Exposed (as applied to live parts). Capable of being inadvertently touched or approached nearer than a safe distance by a person.

Note: This term applies to parts that are not suitably guarded, isolated, or insulated.

Exposed (as applied to wiring methods). On or attached to the surface of a building, or behind panels designed to allow access. ▶Figure 100–66

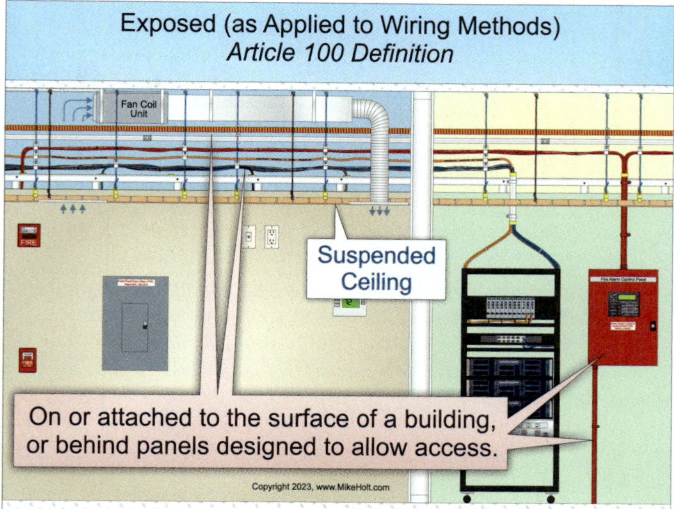

▶Figure 100–66

Fault Current, Available (Available Fault Current). The largest amount of current capable of being delivered at a point on the electrical system during a short-circuit condition. ▶Figure 100–67

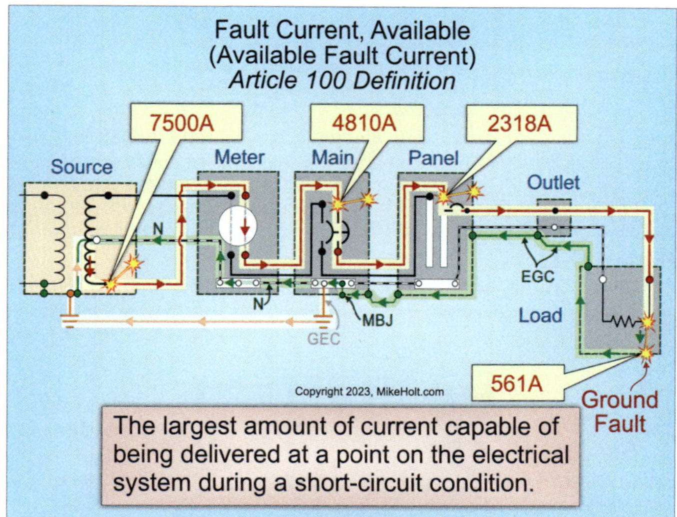

▶Figure 100–67

Feeder. The conductors between a service disconnect, transformer, generator, PV system output circuit, or other power-supply source and the branch-circuit overcurrent protective device. ▶Figure 100–68, ▶Figure 100–69, and ▶Figure 100–70

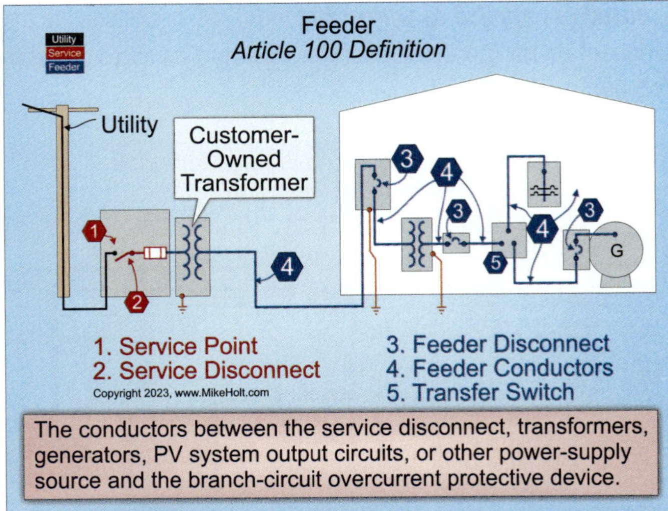

▶Figure 100–68

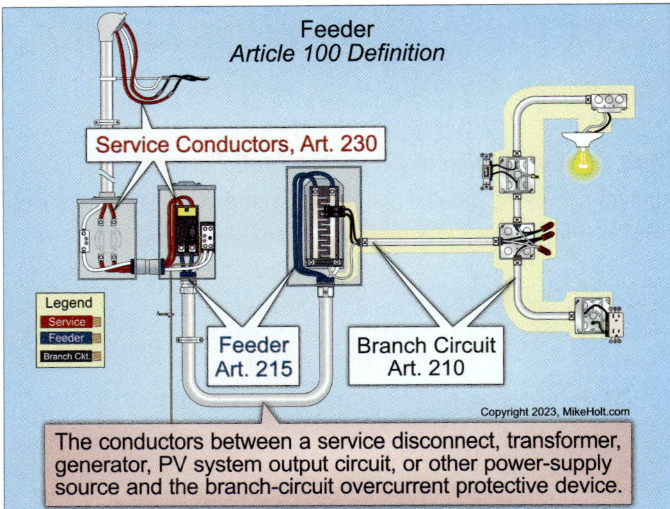

▶Figure 100–69

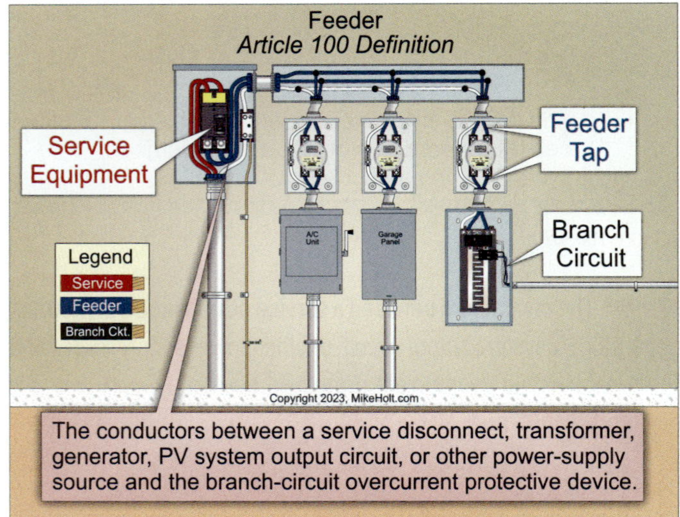

▶Figure 100–70

Field Evaluation Body (FEB). An organization (or part of an organization) that performs field evaluations of electrical equipment and materials.

Field Labeled (as applied to evaluated products). Equipment or materials which have a label, symbol, or other identifying mark of a field evaluation body (FEB) indicating the equipment or materials were evaluated and found to comply with the requirements described in the accompanying field evaluation report.

Fuse. An overcurrent protective device with a circuit-opening fusible part that is heated and severed by the passage of overcurrent. ▶Figure 100–71

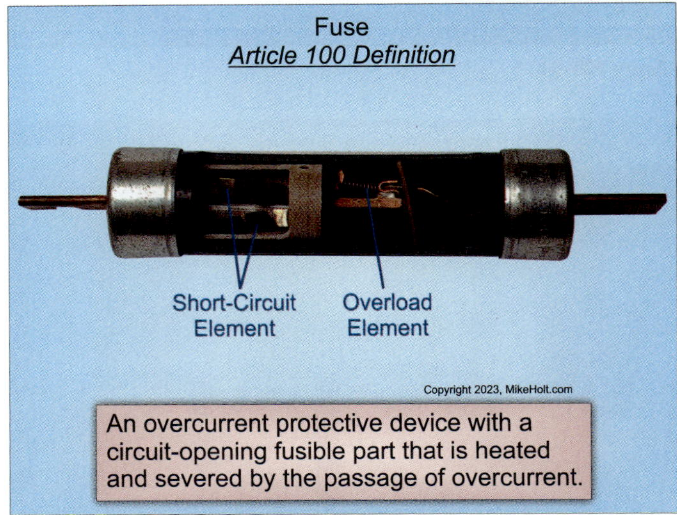

▶Figure 100–71

Generating Capacity, Inverter (Inverter Generating Capacity). The sum of parallel-connected inverter maximum continuous output power at 40°C in watts, kilowatts, volt-amperes, or kilovolt-amperes.

Generator. A machine that converts mechanical energy into electrical energy by means of a prime mover or inverter. ▶Figure 100–72

Ground. The Earth. ▶Figure 100–73

Ground Fault. An unintentional electrical connection between a phase conductor and equipment grounding conductors, metal parts of enclosures, metal raceways, or metal equipment. ▶Figure 100–74

Ground-Fault Current Path, Effective (Effective Ground-Fault Current Path). An intentionally constructed low-impedance conductive path designed to carry ground-fault current during a ground-fault event to the power source. The purpose of the effective ground-fault current path is to assist in opening the circuit overcurrent protective device in the event of a ground fault. ▶Figure 100–75

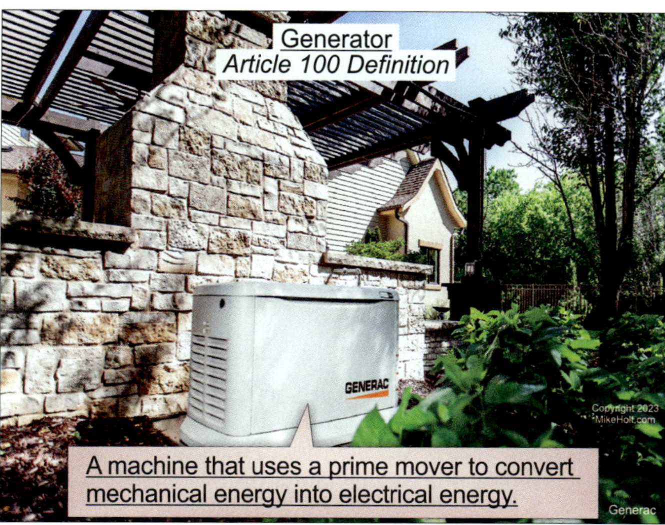

▶Figure 100–72

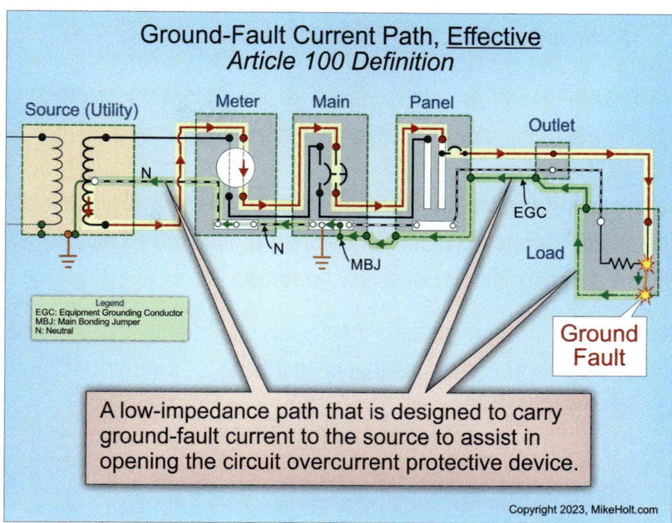

▶Figure 100–75

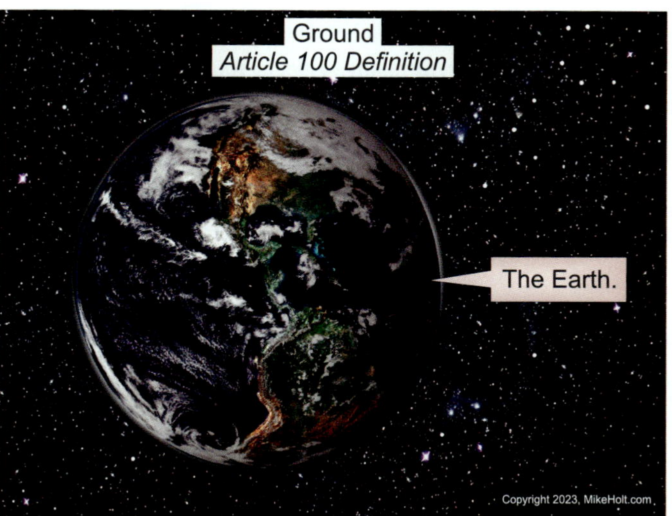

▶Figure 100–73

Author's Comment:

▶ The effective ground-fault current path is intended to help remove dangerous voltage from a ground fault by opening the circuit overcurrent protective device.

Ground-Fault Detector-Interrupter, dc (GFDI). A device that provides protection for PV system dc circuits by detecting a ground fault and could interrupt the fault path in the dc circuit (690).

Ground-Fault Protection of Equipment (GFPE). A system or protective device intended to provide protection of equipment from damaging ground faults. ▶Figure 100–76

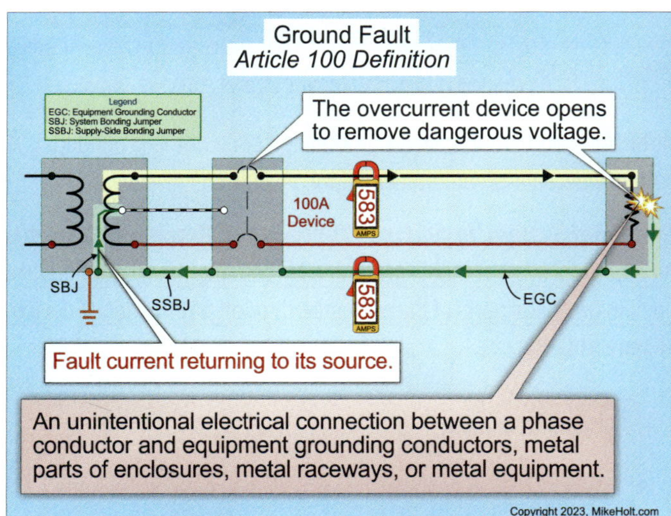

▶Figure 100–74

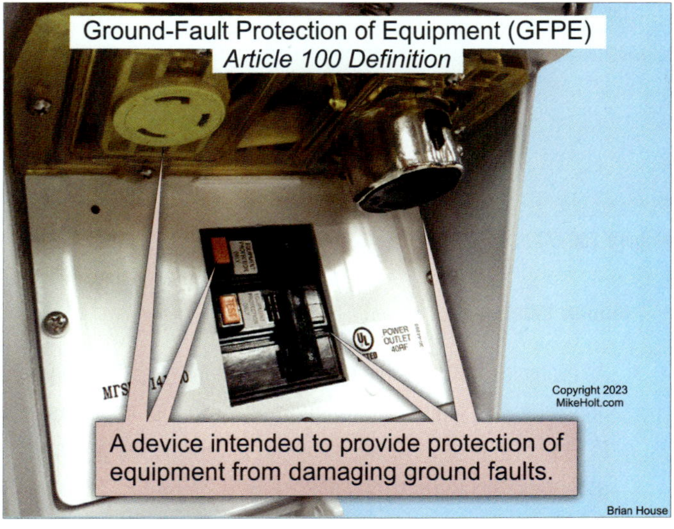

▶Figure 100–76

▸ This type of protective device is not intended to protect persons because its opening ground-fault trip setting is 30 mA.

Grounded, Functionally (Functionally Grounded). A functionally grounded PV system that has an electrical ground reference for operational purposes that is not solidly grounded.

Note: A functionally grounded PV system is often connected to ground through an electronic means that is internal to an inverter or charge controller which provides ground-fault protection.

▸ Most PV arrays are functionally grounded, the exception is usually going to be a very small, stand-alone (off-grid) PV system.

Grounded (Grounding). Connected to the Earth (ground) or to a conductive body that extends the Earth connection. ▸Figure 100–77

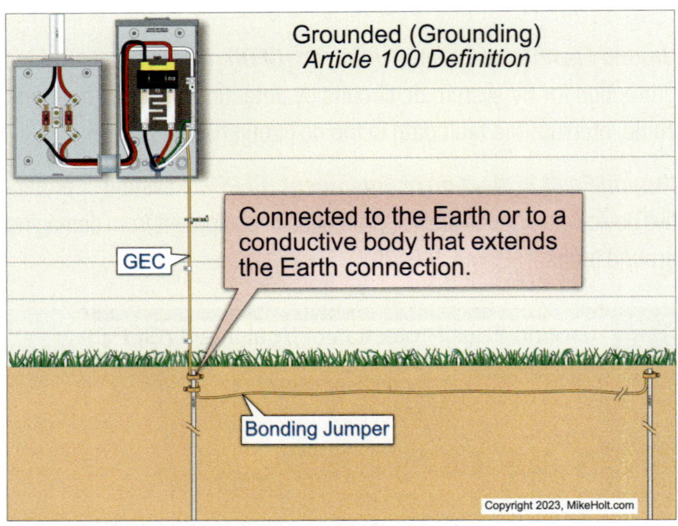

▸Figure 100–77

▸ An example of a "body that extends the ground (Earth) connection" is a termination to structural steel that is connected to the Earth either directly or by the termination to another grounding electrode in accordance with 250.52.

Grounded, Solidly (Solidly Grounded). Connected to ground (Earth) without inserting any resistor or impedance device. ▸Figure 100–78

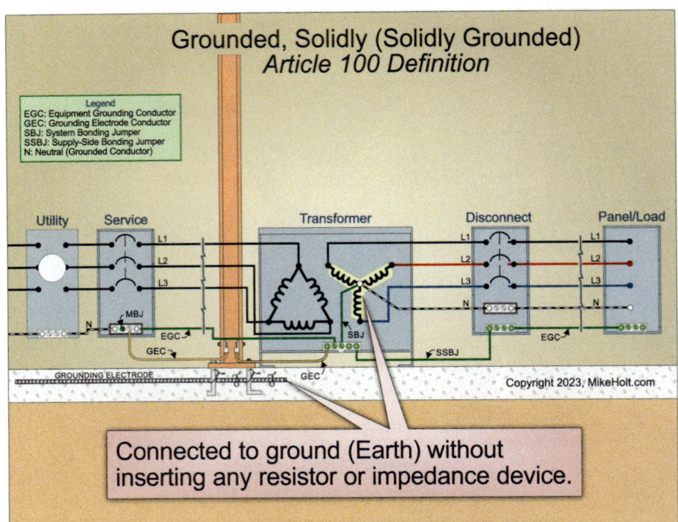

▸Figure 100–78

Grounded Conductor. The system or circuit conductor intentionally connected to the Earth (ground). ▸Figure 100–79

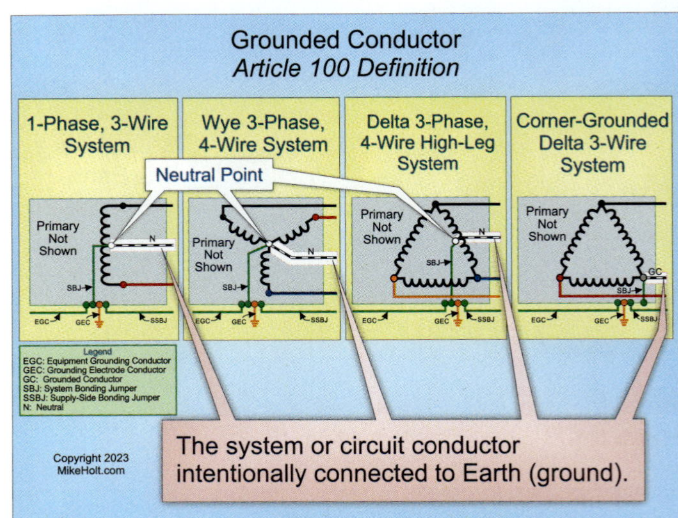

▸Figure 100–79

Note: Although an equipment grounding conductor is grounded, it is not considered a grounded conductor.

Grounded System, Impedance (Impedance Grounded System). An electrical system that is grounded by bonding the system neutral point to the metal parts of the enclosure through an impedance device. ▸Figure 100–80

▸ Section 250.36 contains the primary requirements for impedance grounded systems.

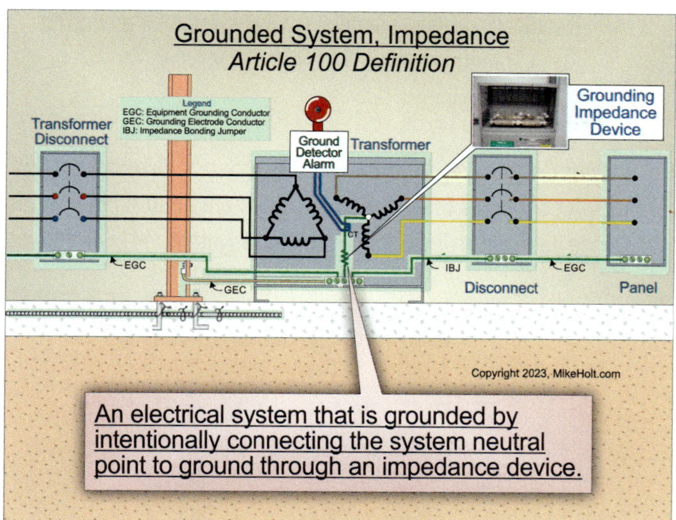

▶Figure 100–80

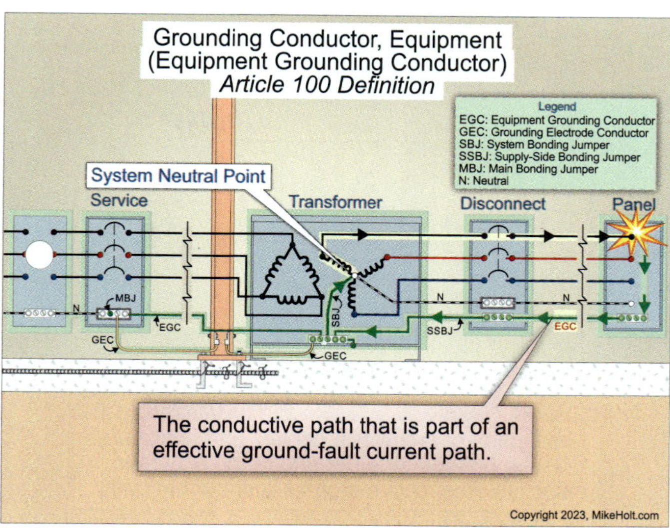

▶Figure 100–82

Grounding Conductor, Equipment (Equipment Grounding Conductor). The conductive path(s) that is part of an effective ground-fault current path. ▶Figure 100–81 and ▶Figure 100–82

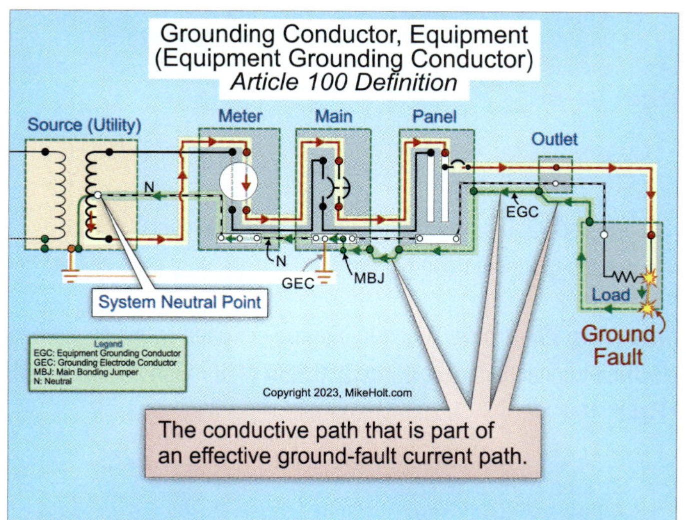

▶Figure 100–81

Author's Comment:

▶ Metal enclosures can be part of the effective ground-fault current path. They are used to connect bonding jumpers and equipment grounding conductors, but are not actually an equipment grounding conductor [250.109]. ▶Figure 100–83

Note 1: The circuit equipment grounding conductor also performs bonding.

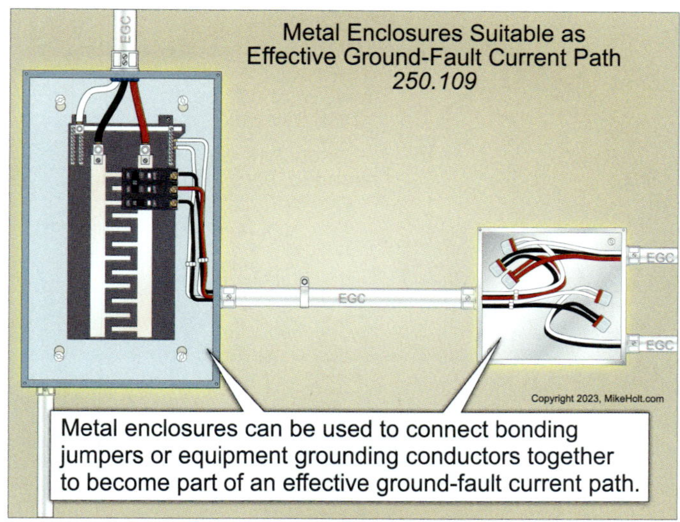

▶Figure 100–83

Author's Comment:

▶ To quickly remove dangerous touch voltage on metal parts from a ground fault, the equipment grounding conductor (EGC) must be connected to the system neutral conductor at the source and have sufficiently low impedance (Z), in accordance with 250.4(A). This permits the ground-fault current to quickly rise to a level that will open the circuit's overcurrent protective device [250.4(A)(3)]. ▶Figure 100–84

Note 2: An equipment grounding conductor can be any one or a combination of the types listed in 250.118(A). ▶Figure 100–85

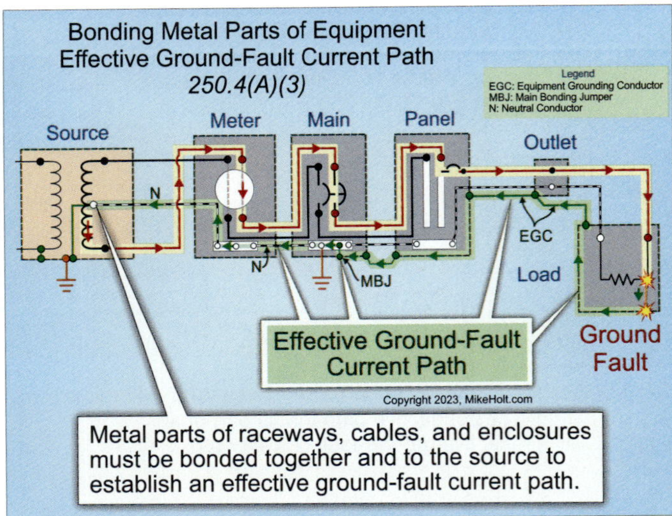

▶Figure 100–84

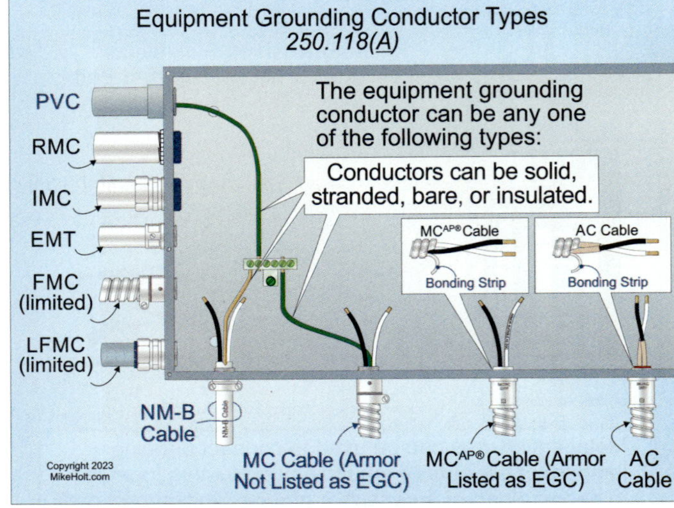

▶Figure 100–85

▸ Equipment grounding conductors include:

  ▸ Bare or insulated conductor
  ▸ Rigid metal conduit
  ▸ Intermediate metal conduit
  ▸ Electrical metallic tubing
  ▸ Listed flexible metal conduit as limited by 250.118(A)(5)
  ▸ Listed liquidtight flexible metal conduit as limited by 250.118(A)(6)
  ▸ Armored cable
  ▸ Copper metal sheath of mineral-insulated cable
  ▸ Metal-clad cable as limited by 250.118(A)(10)
  ▸ Metal cable trays as limited by 250.118(A)(11) and 392.60

▸ Electrically continuous metal raceways listed for grounding
▸ Surface metal raceways listed for grounding
▸ Metal enclosures

Grounding Conductor, Impedance (Impedance Grounding Conductor). A conductor that connects the system neutral point to the impedance device in an impedance grounded system. ▶Figure 100–86

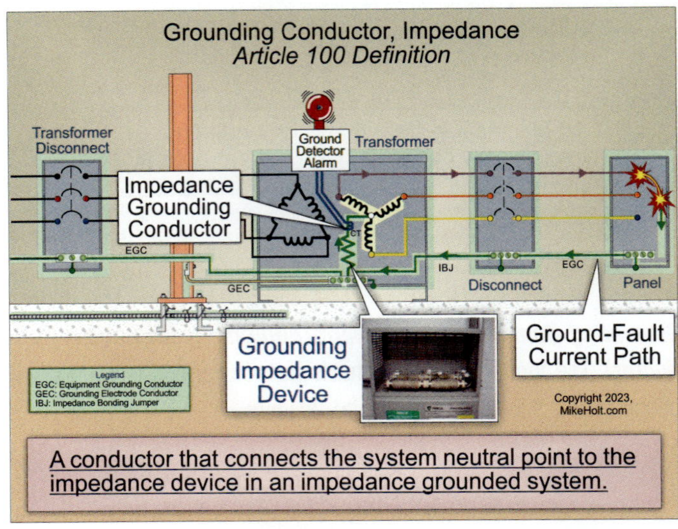

▶Figure 100–86

▸ Section 250.36 contains the primary requirements for impedance grounding conductors.

Grounding Electrode. A conducting object used to make a direct electrical connection to the Earth [250.52(A)(1) through 250.52(A)(8)]. ▶Figure 100–87

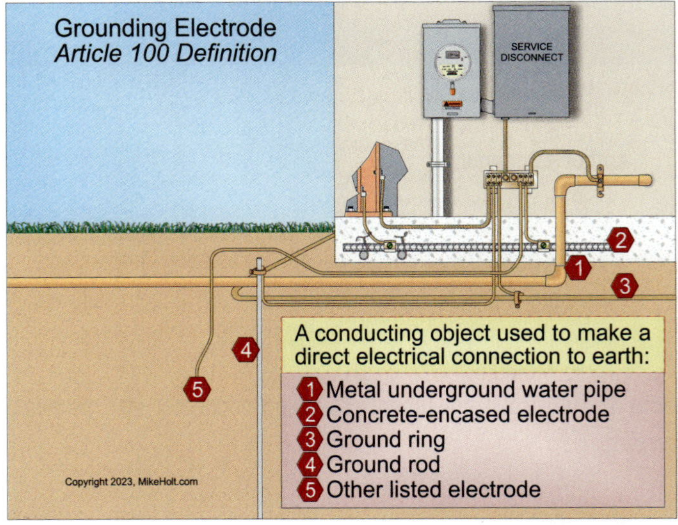

▶Figure 100–87

Grounding Electrode Conductor (GEC). The conductor used to connect the system neutral conductor, grounded-phase conductor, or the equipment to the grounding electrode system. ▶Figure 100–88

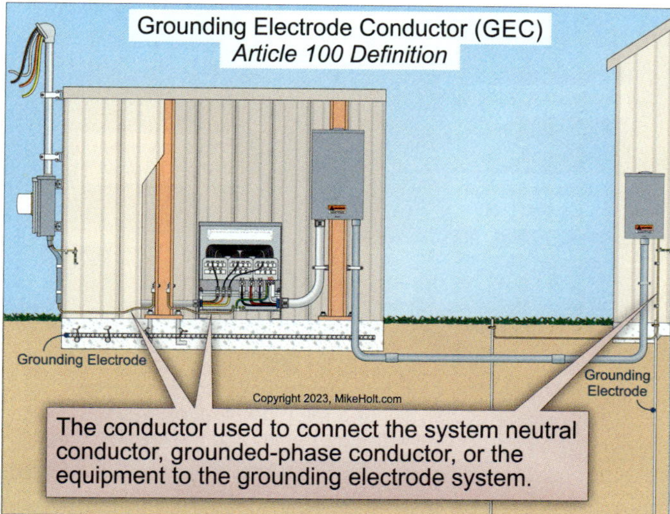

▶Figure 100–88

Habitable Room. A room for living, sleeping, eating, or cooking, excluding bathrooms, toilet rooms, closets, hallways, storage or utility spaces, and similar areas. ▶Figure 100–89

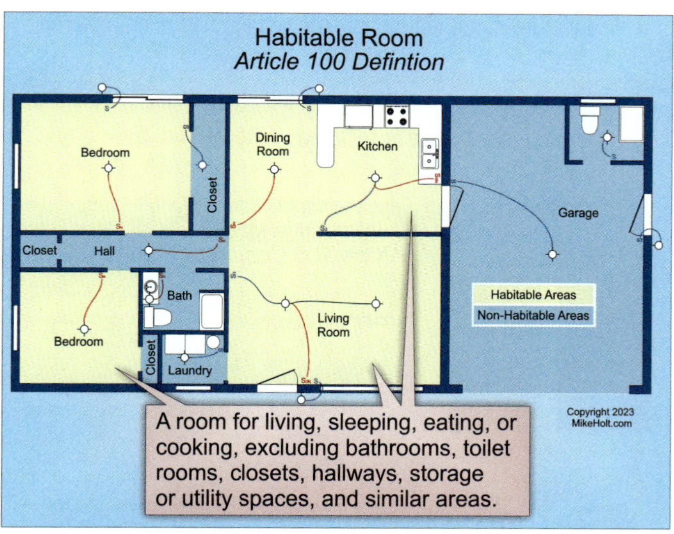

▶Figure 100–89

Handhole Enclosure. An underground enclosure with an open or closed bottom that is sized to allow personnel to reach into but not enter the enclosure. ▶Figure 100–90

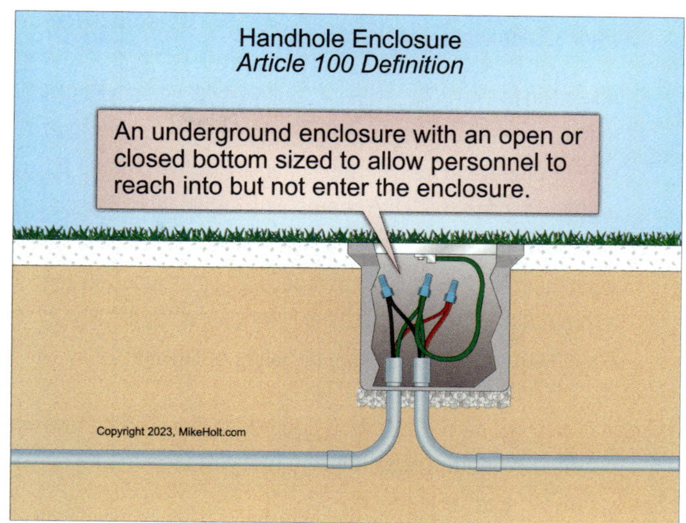

▶Figure 100–90

▶ For the installation requirements for handhole enclosures, see 314.30.

Identified (as applied to equipment). Recognized as suitable for a specific purpose, function, use, environment, or application. ▶Figure 100–91

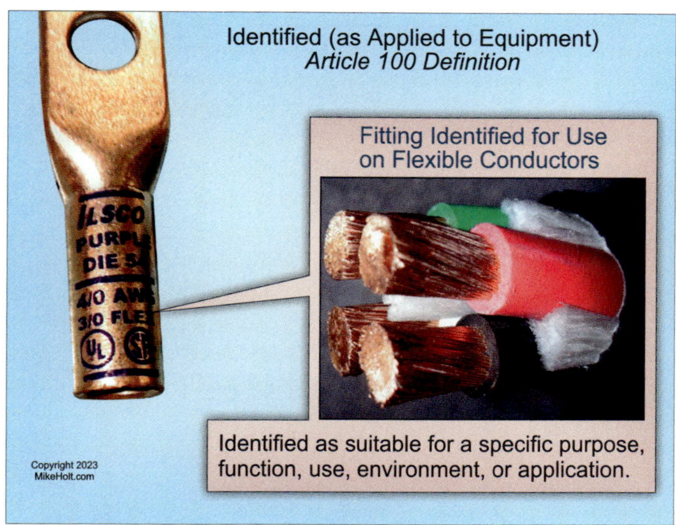

▶Figure 100–91

Author's Comment:

▸ According to 110.3(A)(1) Note 2, "Suitability of equipment use may be identified by a description marked on, or provided with, a product to identify the suitability of the product for a specific purpose, environment, or application. Special conditions of use or other limitations may be marked on the equipment, in the product instructions, or included in the appropriate listing and labeling information. Suitability of equipment may be evidenced by listing or labeling."

In Sight From (Within Sight From). Equipment that is visible and not more than 50 ft away from other equipment is considered within sight. ▸Figure 100–92 and ▸Figure 100–93

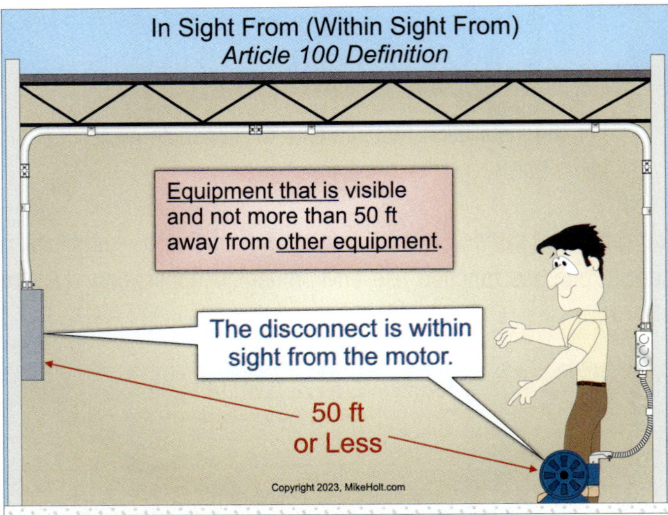

▸Figure 100–92

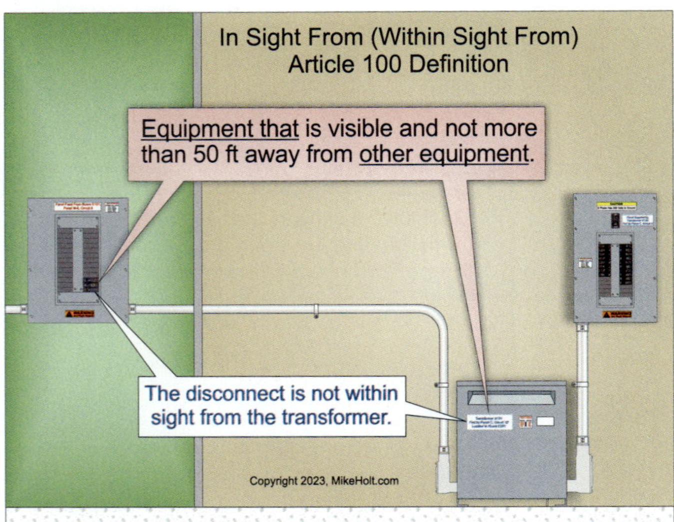

▸Figure 100–93

Interactive Mode. The operating mode for power production equipment or a microgrid that operate in parallel with each other and the electric utility. ▸Figure 100–94

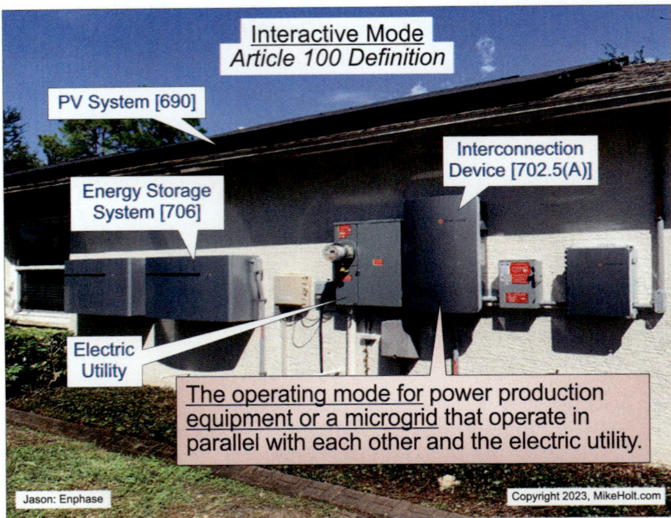

▸Figure 100–94

Author's Comment:

▸ A listed interactive (grid tied) inverter automatically stops exporting power upon loss of electric utility voltage and cannot be reconnected until the voltage has been restored. Interactive (grid tied) inverters can automatically or manually resume exporting power to the electric utility once the electric utility source is restored. ▸Figure 100–95

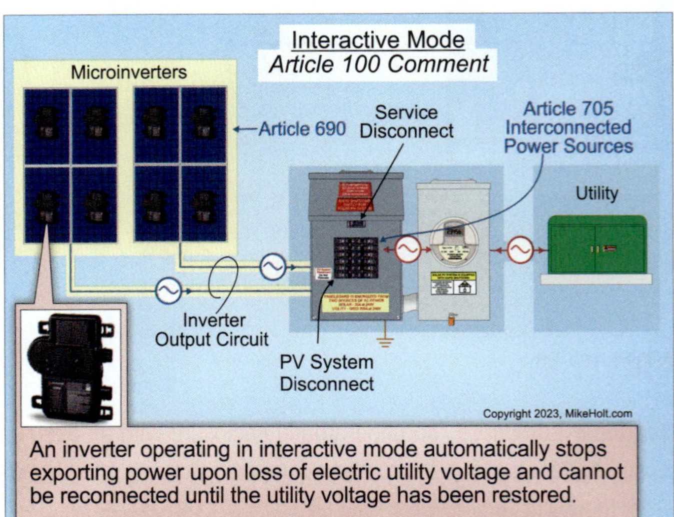

▸Figure 100–95

Interrupting Rating. The highest fault current at rated voltage the device is identified to safely interrupt under standard test conditions.

Intersystem Bonding Termination. A device that provides a means to connect intersystem bonding conductors for communications systems to the grounding electrode system in accordance with 250.94. ▶Figure 100–96

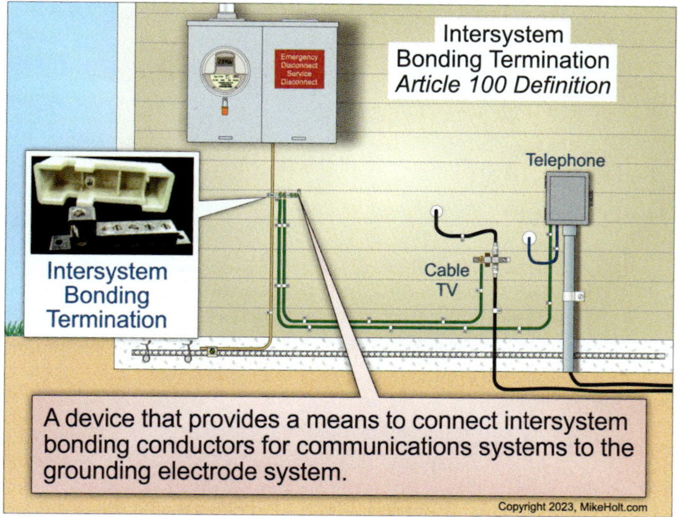

▶Figure 100–96

Inverter. Equipment that changes direct current to alternating current. ▶Figure 100–97

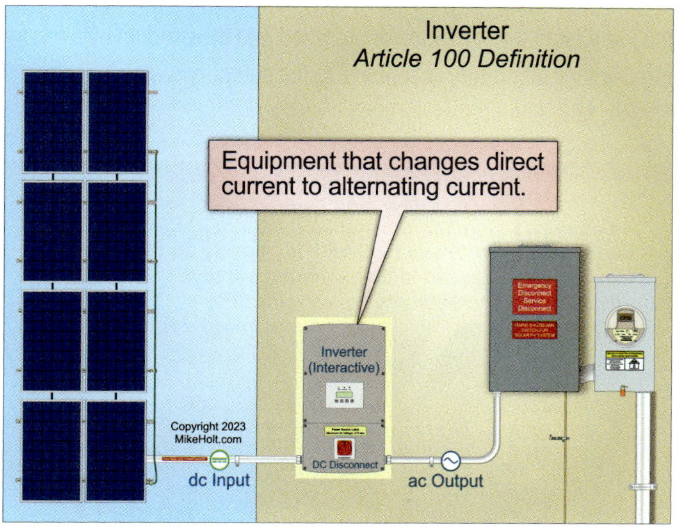

▶Figure 100–97

Inverter, Multimode (Multimode Inverter). Multimode inverters are listed to operate in both interactive (grid tied) and island mode (off-grid). ▶Figure 100–98

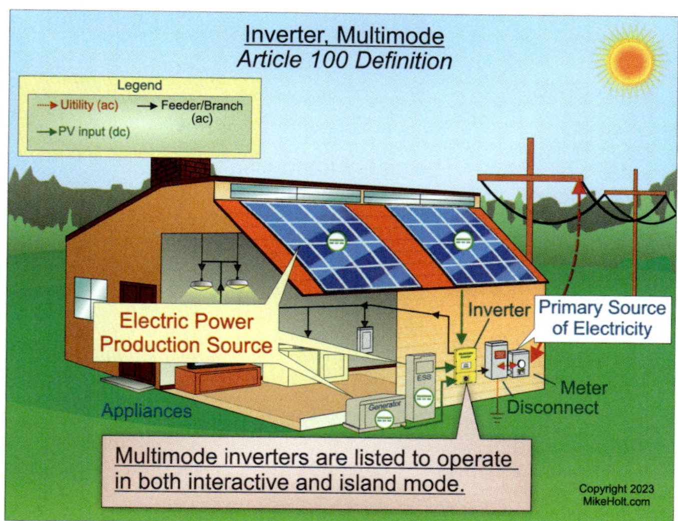

▶Figure 100–98

Inverter, Stand-Alone (Stand-Alone Inverter). Inverter equipment having the capabilities to operate only in island mode.

Inverter Input Circuit. Conductors connected to the dc input of an inverter. ▶Figure 100–99

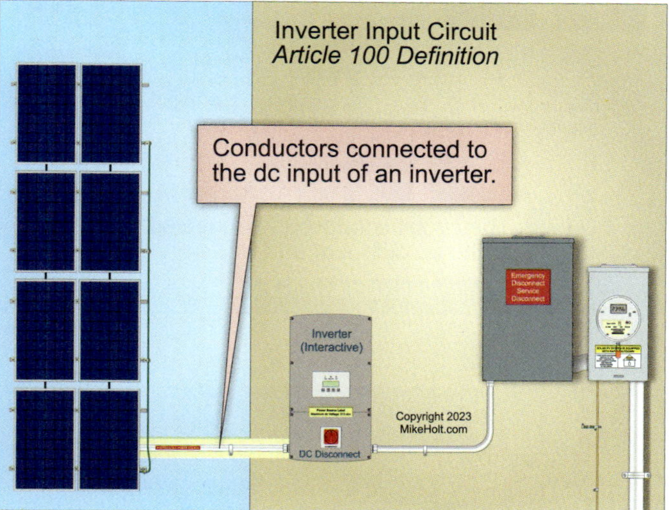

▶Figure 100–99

Inverter Output Circuit. The circuit conductors connected to the ac output of an inverter. ▶Figure 100–100 and ▶Figure 100–101

Island Mode. The operating mode for power production equipment or a microgrid that is disconnected from an electric utility or other primary power source. ▶Figure 100–102

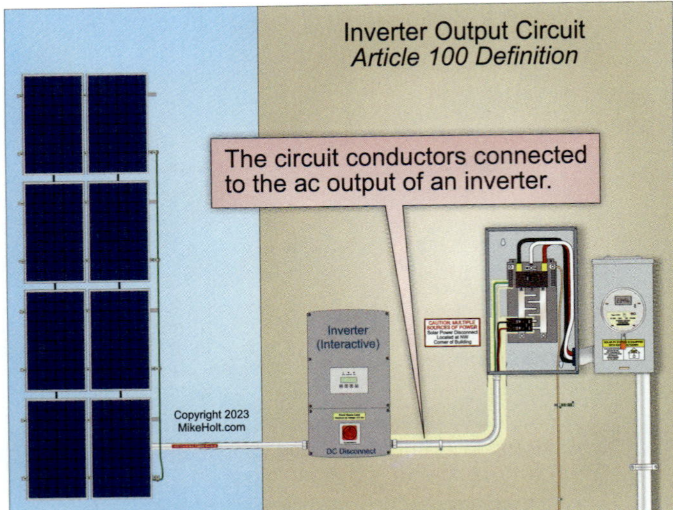

▶Figure 100–100

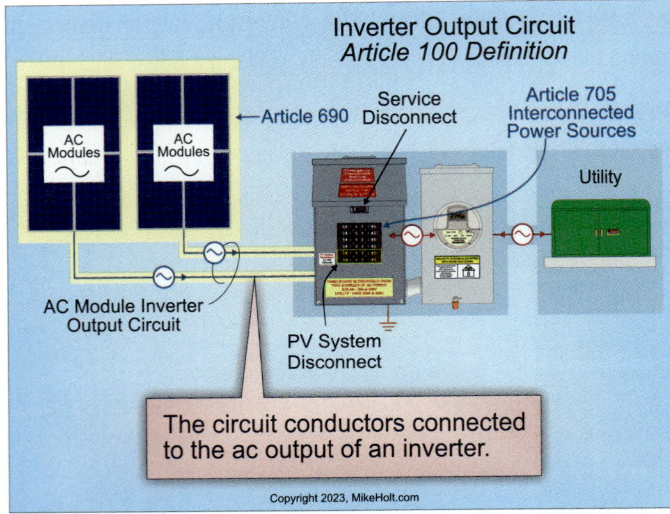

▶Figure 100–101

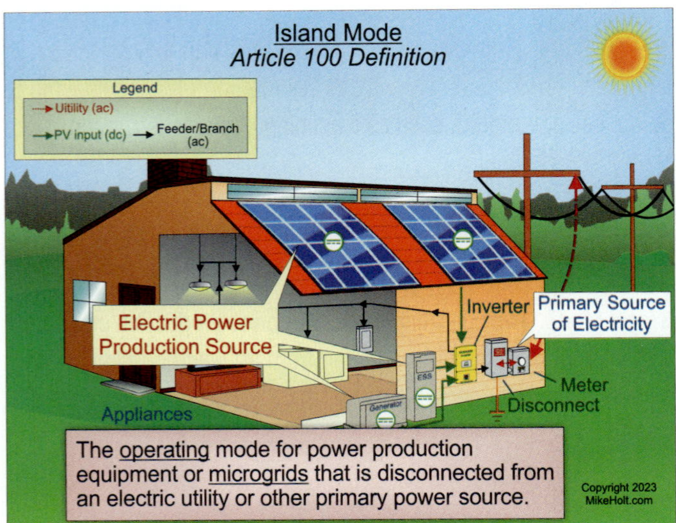

▶Figure 100–102

Kitchen. An area with a sink and permanent provisions for food preparation and cooking. ▶Figure 100–103

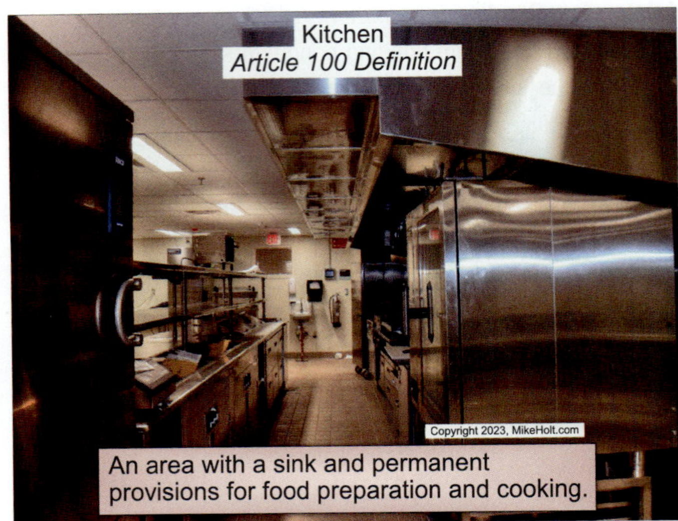

▶Figure 100–103

Author's Comment:

▶ An area like an employee break room with a sink and cord-and-plug-connected cooking appliance such as a microwave oven is not considered a kitchen.

Labeled. Equipment or materials that have a label, symbol, or other identifying mark in the form of a sticker, decal, printed label, or with the identifying mark molded or stamped into the product by a recognized testing laboratory acceptable to the authority having jurisdiction. ▶Figure 100–104

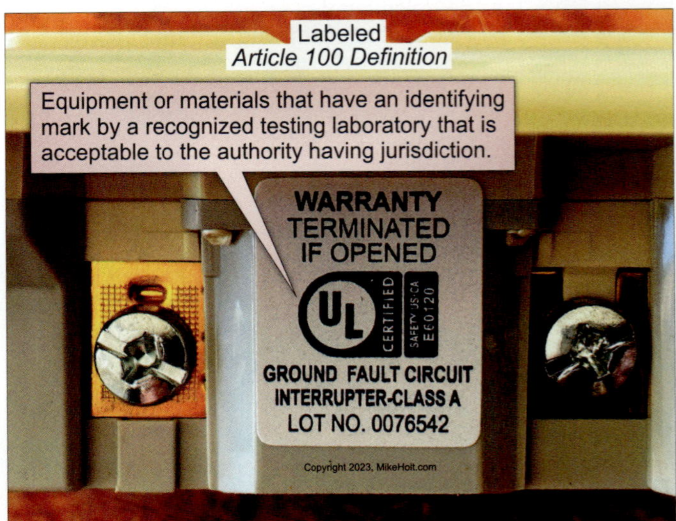

▶Figure 100–104

Note: When a listed product is of such a size, shape, material, or surface texture that it is not possible to legibly apply the complete label to the product, it may appear on the smallest unit container in which the product is packaged.

Author's Comment:

▶ Labeling and listing of equipment typically provide the basis for equipment approval by the authority having jurisdiction [90.4(B), 90.7, 110.2, and 110.3].

Laundry Area. An area containing (or designed to contain) a clothes washer, or clothes dryer. ▶Figure 100–105

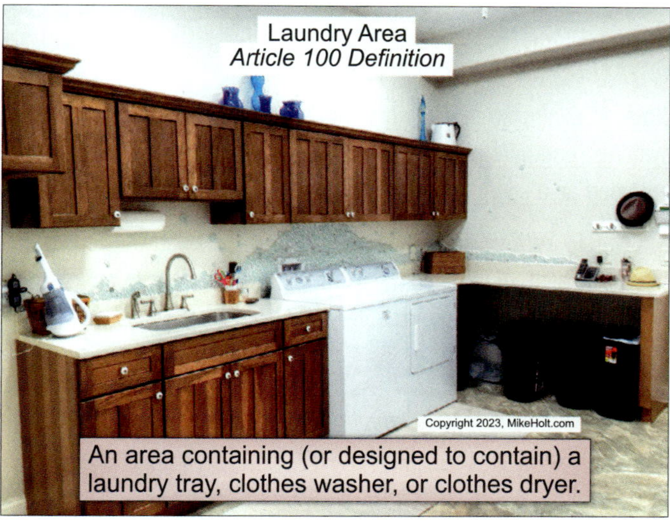

▶Figure 100–105

Listed. Equipment or materials included in a list published by a recognized testing laboratory acceptable to the authority having jurisdiction. The listing organization must periodically inspect the production of listed equipment or material to ensure they meet appropriate designated standards and suitable for a specified purpose.

Author's Comment:

▶ The *NEC* does not require all electrical equipment to be listed, but some *Code* requirements do specifically call for product listing. Organizations such as OSHA are increasingly requiring listed equipment to be used when such equipment is available [90.7, 110.2, and 110.3].

Live Parts. Energized conductive components.

Location, Damp (Damp Location). Locations protected from weather and not subject to saturation with water or other liquids, but subject to moderate degrees of moisture. ▶Figure 100–106

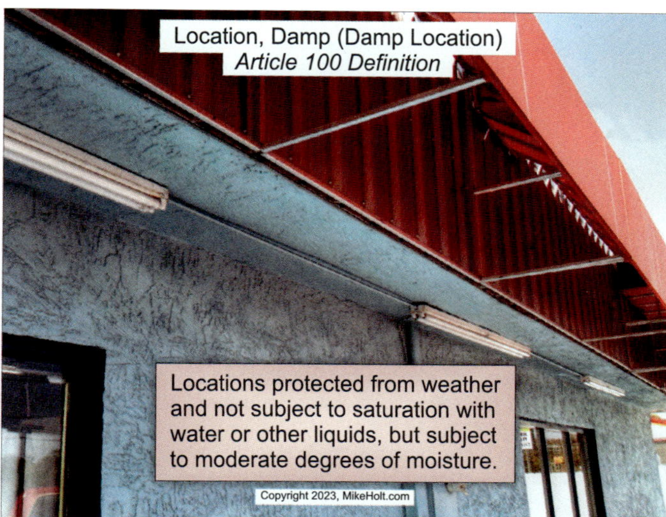

▶Figure 100–106

Note: This includes locations partially protected under canopies, marquees, roofed open porches, and interior locations subject to moderate degrees of moisture such as some basements, barns, and cold-storage warehouses.

Author's Comment:

▶ The key to understanding a damp location is to know that the definition of the term "moisture" is a liquid diffused or condensed in relatively small quantities. According to Webster's Dictionary (www.merriam-webster.com), "liquid diffused or condensed in relatively small quantity."

Location, Dry (Dry Location). An area not normally subjected to dampness or wetness, but which may temporarily be subjected to dampness or wetness, such as a building under construction.

Author's Comment:

▶ Wiring methods and equipment that are listed for dry location use only are permitted to be installed in a building under construction even if the building is subject to temporary dampness or wetness, as it is still considered a dry location. However, the equipment must be protected from damage in accordance with 110.11.

Location, Wet (Wet Location). A location that is one or more of the following: ▶Figure 100–107 and ▶Figure 100–108

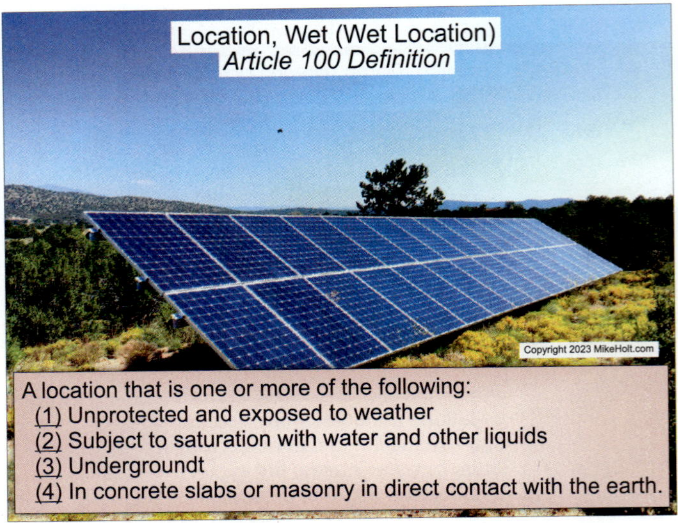

▶Figure 100–107

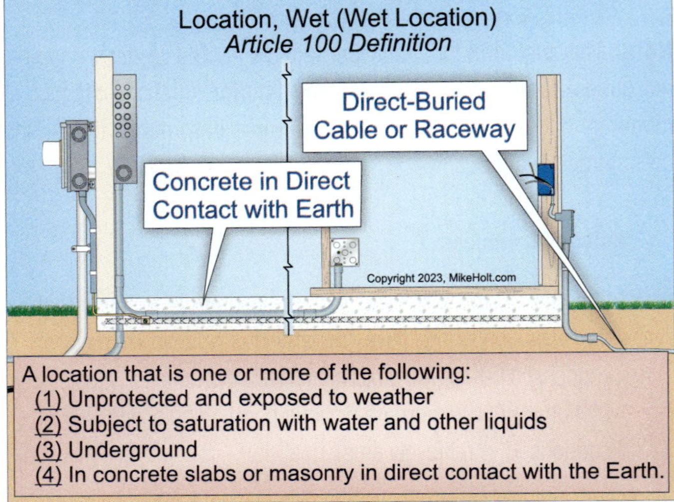

▶Figure 100–108

(1) Unprotected and exposed to weather

(2) Subject to saturation with water and other liquids

(3) Underground

(4) In concrete slabs or masonry in direct contact with the Earth

Note: A vehicle washing area is an example of a wet location saturated with water or other liquids.

Microgrid. An electric power source system capable of operating in island (off-grid) or interactive (grid tied) mode with the electric utility. ▶Figure 100–109

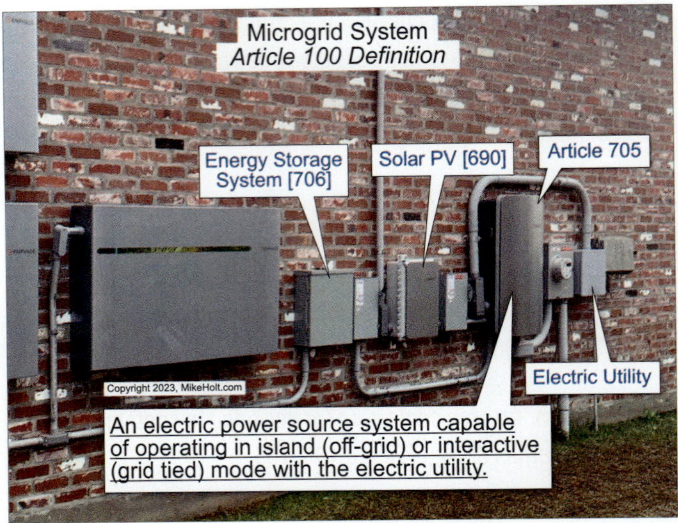

▶Figure 100–109

Note 2: Examples of microgrid power sources include photovoltaic systems, energy storage systems, generators, electric vehicles that are used as a source of supply.

Microgrid Interconnect Device (MID). A device that enables a microgrid system to disconnect from and reconnect to an interconnected primary power source. ▶Figure 100–110

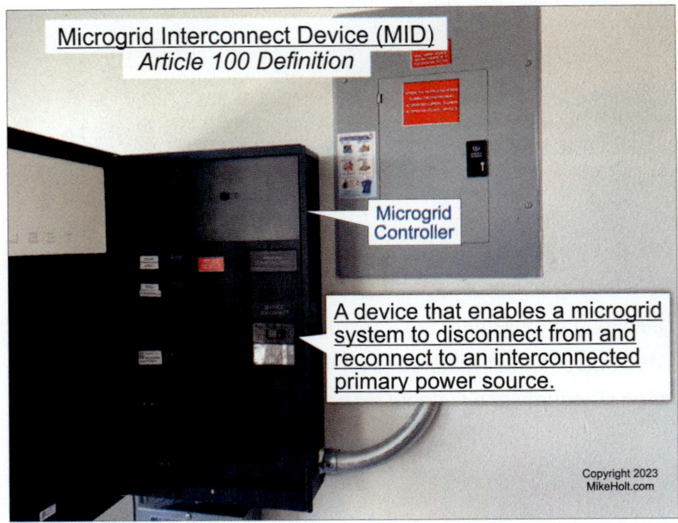

▶Figure 100–110

Module, Alternating-Current (Alternating-Current Module). A module consisting of solar cells, inverter, and other components designed to produce alternating-current power (Article 690). ▶Figure 100–111

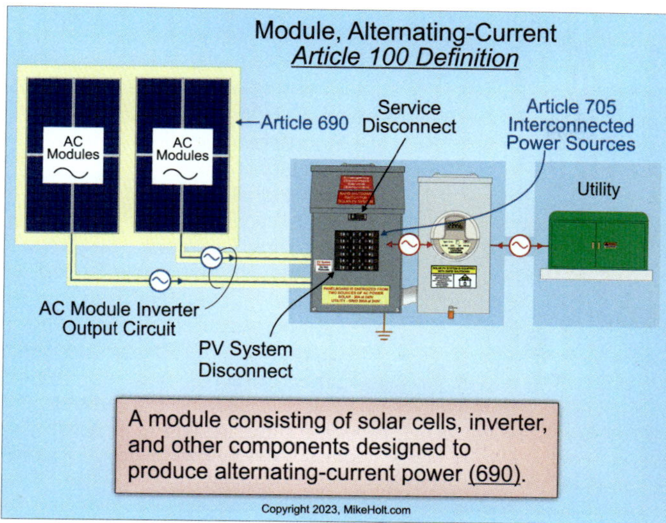

▶Figure 100–111

Author's Comment:

▸ Alternating-current modules are connected in parallel with each other and in parallel with the electric utility in an interactive (grid tied) mode. These modules operate interactively with the electric utility, meaning the ac output current from the ac module will cease exporting power upon sensing the loss of voltage from the electric utility.

▸ Manufacturer's instructions for ac modules will specify the size of the dedicated branch circuit on which they are to be connected and the maximum number of ac modules permitted on the branch circuit.

Multioutlet Assembly. A surface, flush, or freestanding <u>assembly</u> <u>containing receptacles</u>. ▶Figure 100–112

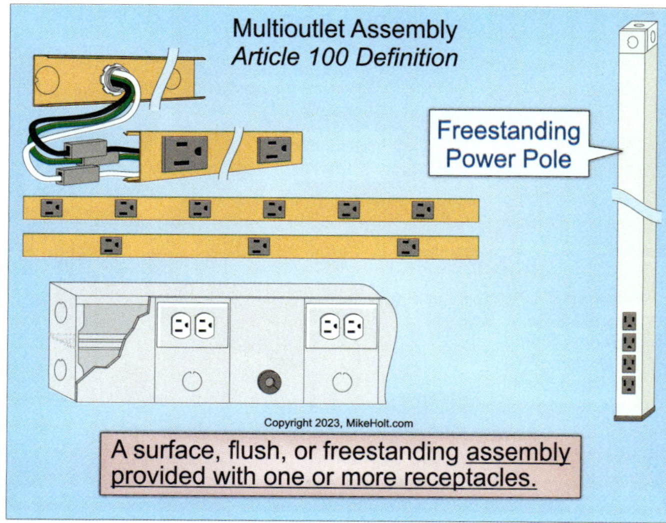

▶Figure 100–112

Author's Comment:

▸ Portable assemblies such as power strips are relocatable power taps, not multioutlet assemblies. ▶Figure 100–113

▸ Article 380 contains the primary requirements for multioutlet assemblies.

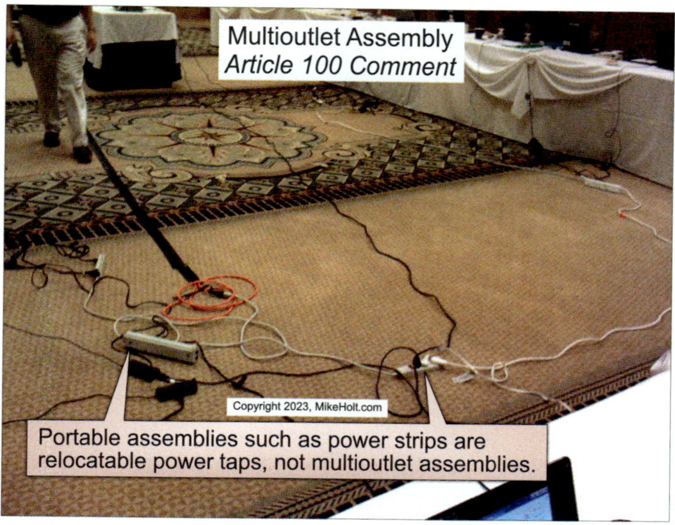

▶Figure 100–113

Neutral Conductor. The conductor connected to the neutral point of a system that is intended to carry current under normal conditions. ▶Figure 100–114

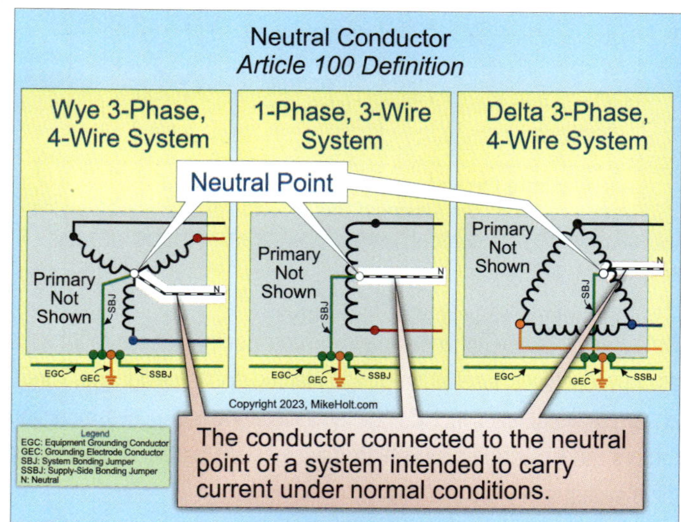

▶Figure 100–114

Neutral Point. The common point of a 4-wire, three-phase, wye-connected system; the midpoint of a 3-wire, single-phase system; or the midpoint of the single-phase portion of a three-phase, delta-connected system. ▶Figure 100–115

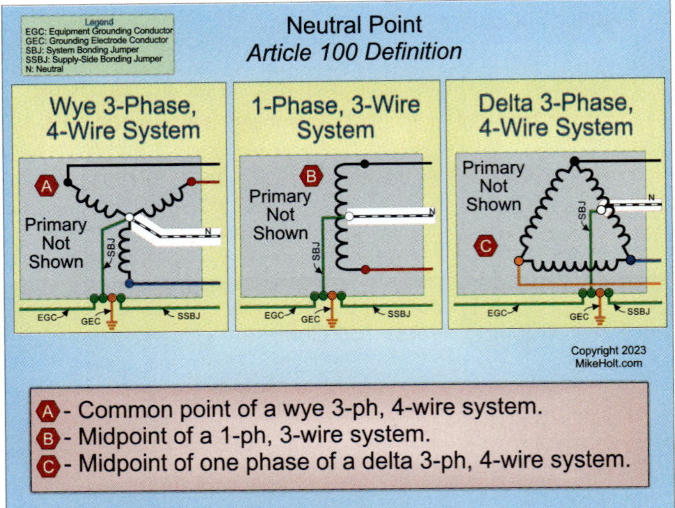

▶Figure 100–115

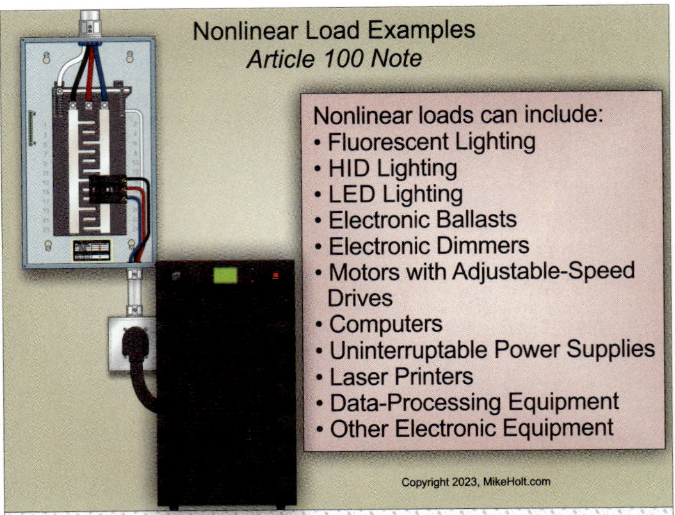

▶Figure 100–117

Nonlinear Load. A load where the shape of the current waveform does not follow the shape of the applied voltage waveform. ▶**Figure 100–116**

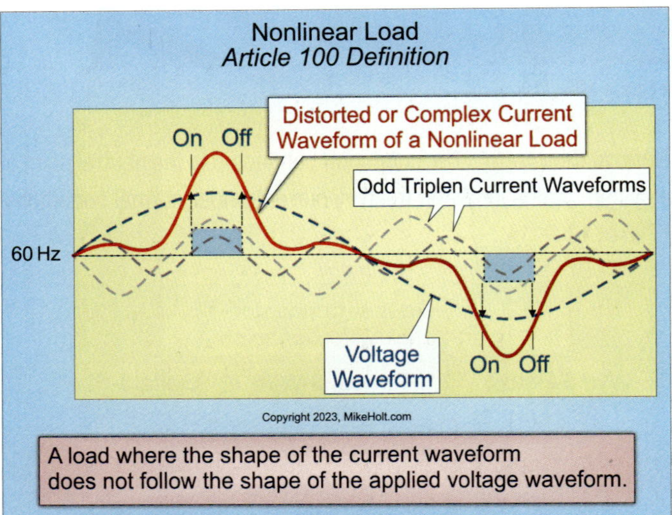

▶Figure 100–116

Note: Single-phase nonlinear loads include electronic equipment such as copy machines, laser printers, and electric-discharge lighting. Three-phase nonlinear loads include uninterruptible power supplies, induction motors, and electronic switching devices such as adjustable-speed drive systems. ▶**Figure 100–117**

Optional Standby Systems. A system intended to supply power where life safety does not depend on the performance of the system. ▶**Figure 100–118** and ▶**Figure 100–119**

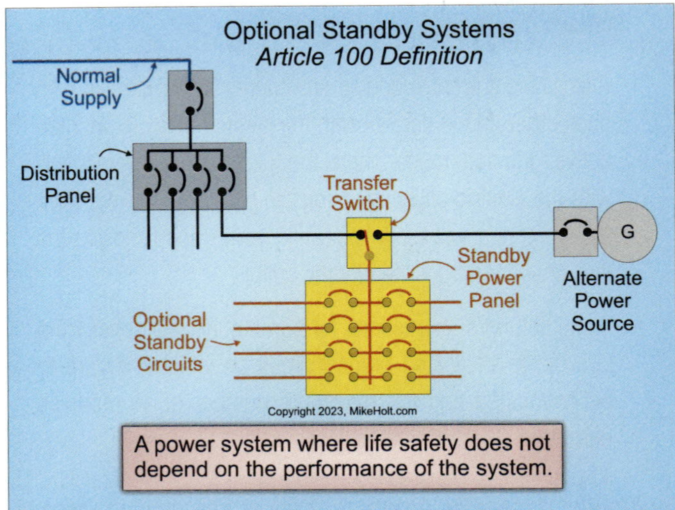

▶Figure 100–118

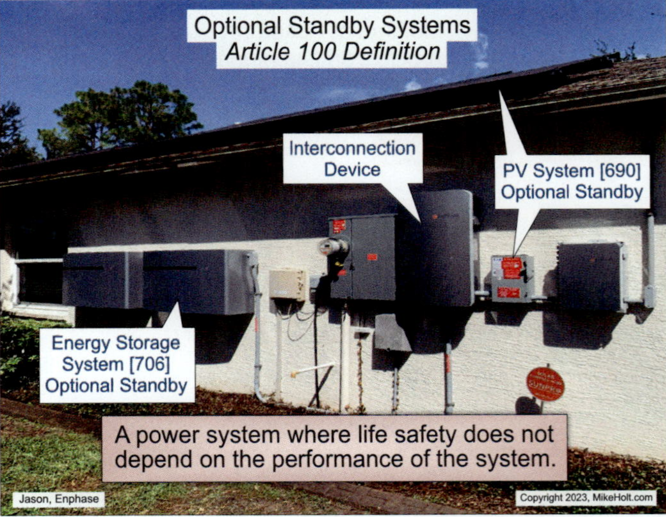

▶Figure 100–119

▶ Optional standby systems are typically installed to provide an alternate source of electric power for such facilities as industrial/commercial buildings, farms, and residences. It serves loads such as heating and refrigeration systems, data processing, and industrial processes that when stopped during any power outage can cause discomfort, economic loss, serious interruption of the process, damage to the product or process, or the like.

Outlet. A point on the wiring system at which current is taken to supply utilization equipment. ▶Figure 100–120

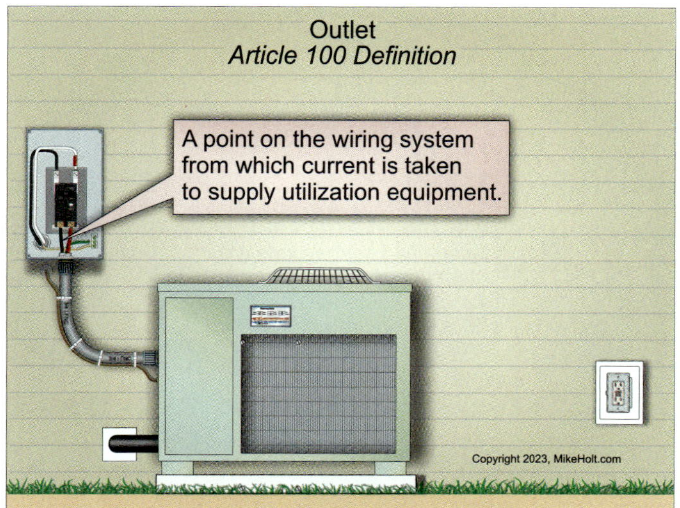

▶Figure 100–120

▶ This includes receptacle outlets, hardwire appliance outlets, and lighting outlets, as well as those for ceiling paddle fans and smoke alarms. ▶Figure 100–121

Overcurrent. Current in excess of the equipment's current rating or a conductor's ampacity caused by an overload, short circuit, or ground fault. ▶Figure 100–122

Overcurrent Protective Device, Branch-Circuit (Branch-Circuit Overcurrent Protective Device). A device capable of providing protection from an overload, short circuit, or ground fault for service, feeder, and branch circuits.

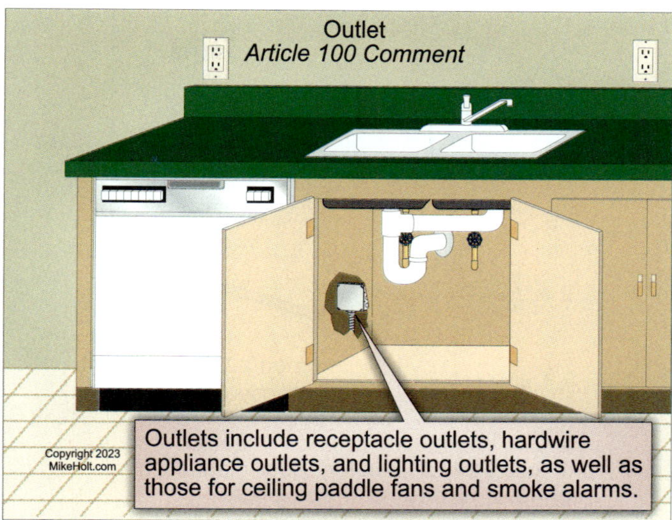

▶Figure 100–121

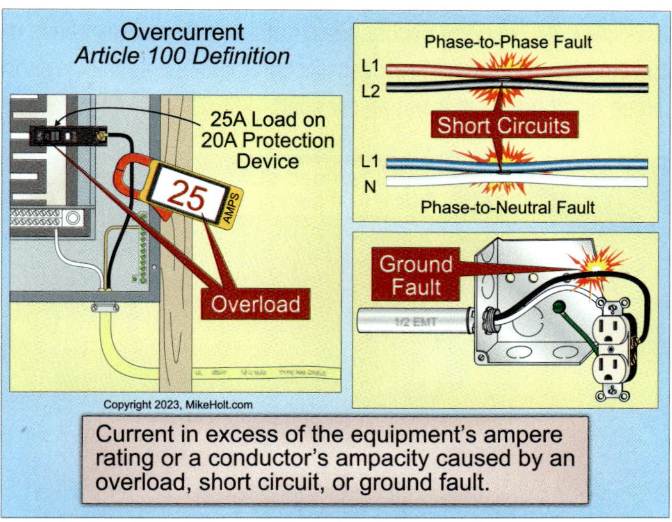

▶Figure 100–122

Overcurrent Protective Device, Supplementary (Supplementary Overcurrent Protective Device). A device intended to provide limited overcurrent protection for specific applications and utilization equipment, such as luminaires and appliances. This limited protection is in addition to the protection required and provided by the branch-circuit overcurrent protective device. ▶Figure 100–123

▶ These supplementary protective devices are sometimes used to prevent a local fault from causing the branch-circuit protective device from opening. An example is parking lot lighting with a single branch circuit serving several poles. Each pole will have a supplementary protective device that will open if a fault occurs at a pole, limiting the outage to the single pole.

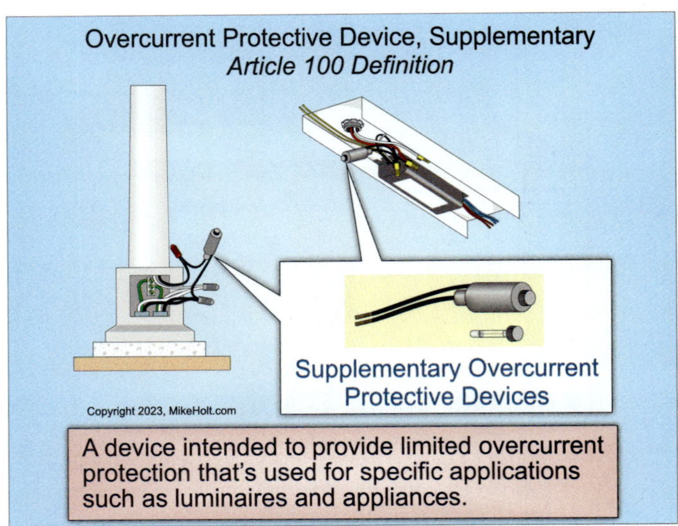

▶Figure 100–123

Overload. An overload occurs when equipment operates above its current rating or current in excess of a conductor's ampacity. A short circuit or ground fault is not an overload. ▶Figure 100–124

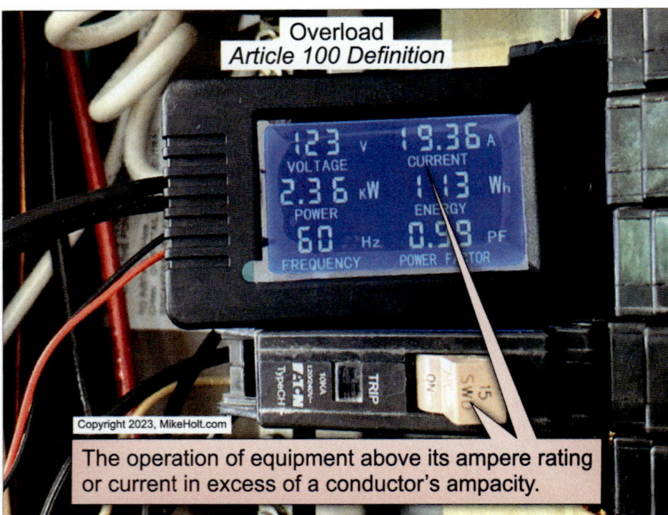

▶Figure 100–124

Panelboard. An assembly with buses and overcurrent protective devices designed to be placed in a cabinet or enclosure. ▶Figure 100–125

Author's Comment:

▶ The slang term in the electrical field for a panelboard is "the guts." The requirements for panelboards are contained in Article 408.

Panelboard, Enclosed (Enclosed Panelboard). Buses and connections with overcurrent protective devices in a cabinet or enclosure suitable for a panelboard application. ▶Figure 100–126

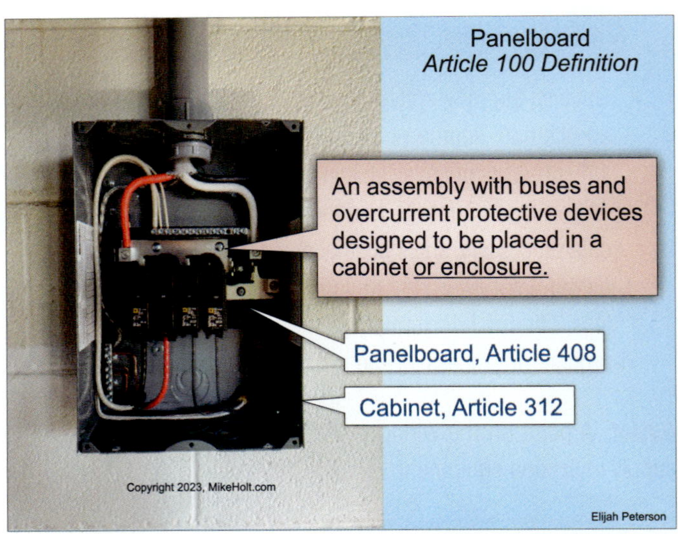

▶Figure 100–125

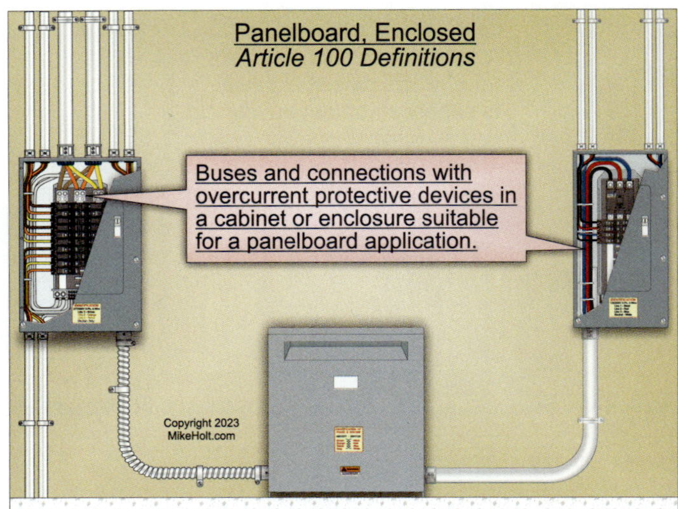

▶Figure 100–126

Author's Comment:

▶ For the purposes of this material, we will use the term "Panelboard" instead of "Enclosed Panelboard."

Power Production Equipment. Electrical generating equipment up to the power production system disconnect supplied by a power source other than the electric utility. ▶Figure 100–127

Note: Examples of power production equipment include generators, solar photovoltaic systems, and energy storage and fuel cell systems. ▶Figure 100–128

Power Source Output Conductors. The conductors from power production equipment to service equipment or premises wiring. ▶Figure 100–129 and ▶Figure 100–130

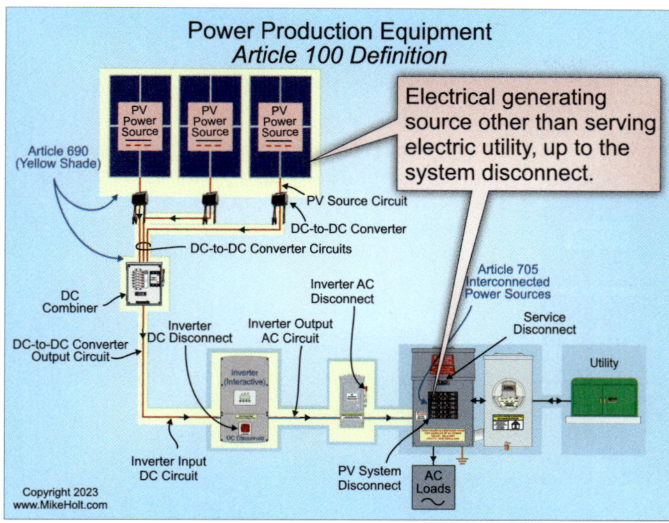

▶Figure 100–127

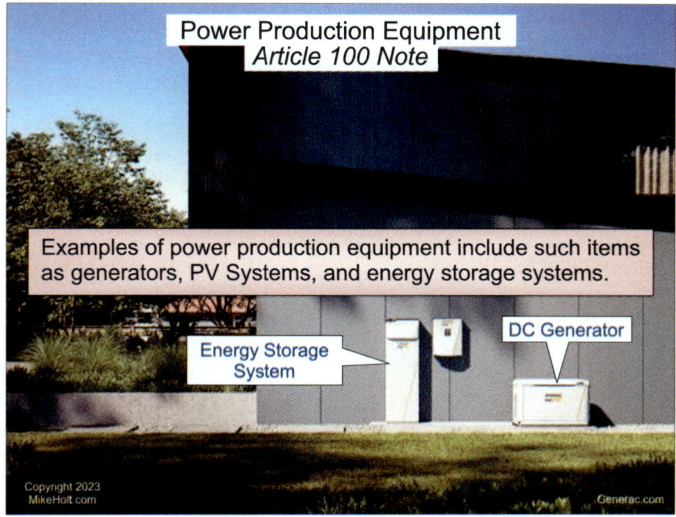

▶Figure 100–128

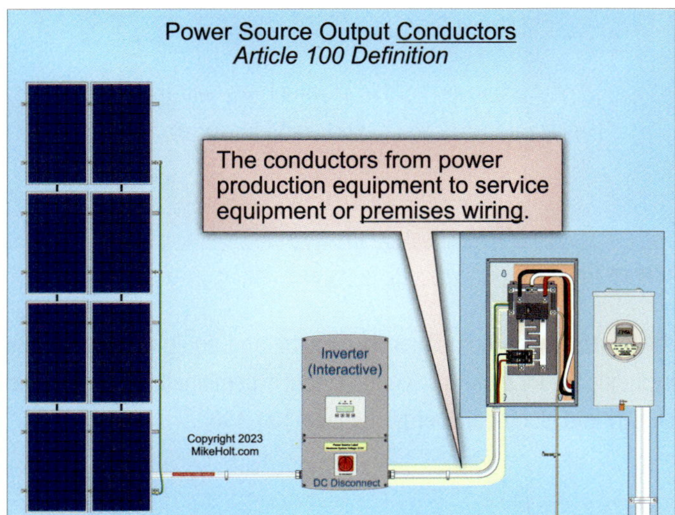

▶Figure 100–129

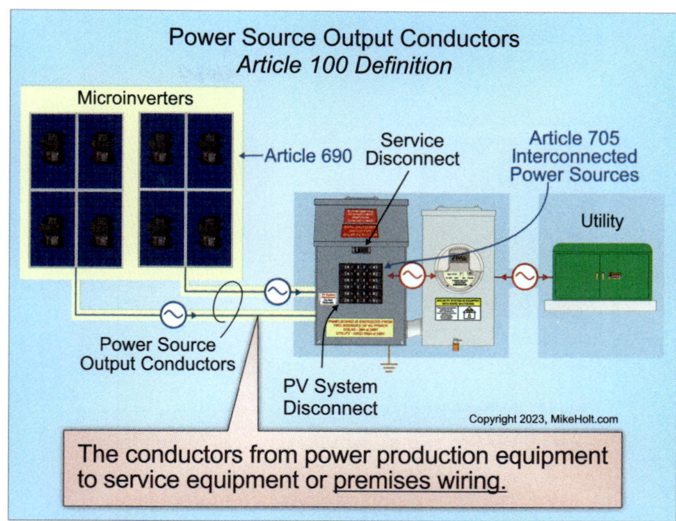

▶Figure 100–130

Power-Supply Cord. An assembly consisting of an attachment plug and a length of flexible cord connected to utilization equipment.

> **Author's Comment:**
>
> ▸ Article 400 contains information on the use of power-supply cords.

Primary Source of Power. The main source of power in an electric power system.

Prime Mover. The machine that supplies mechanical horsepower to a generator. ▶Figure 100–131

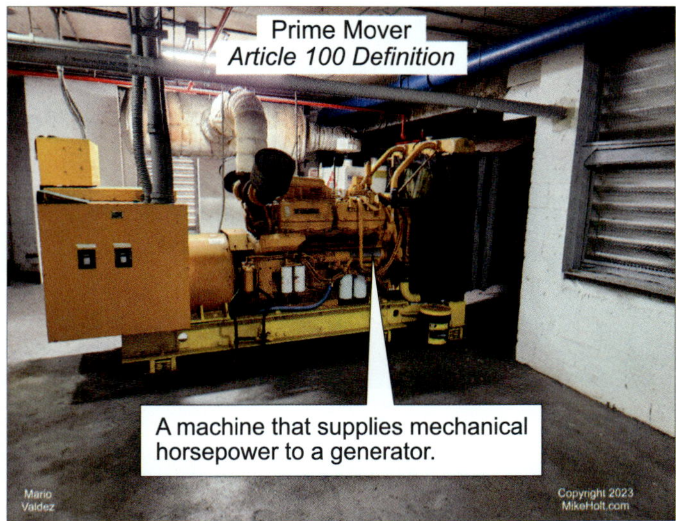

▶Figure 100–131

PV Module. A PV module is a unit of environmentally protected solar cells and components designed to produce dc power. ▶Figure 100–132

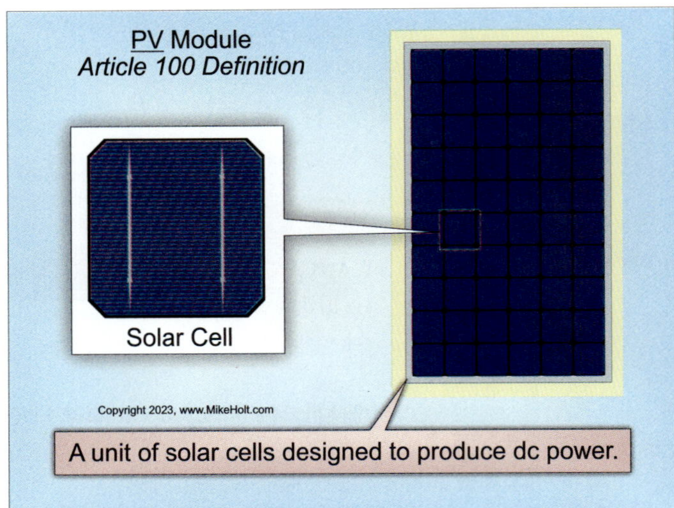

▶Figure 100–132

Author's Comment:

▶ PV modules use sunlight to generate dc electricity by using light (photons) to move electrons in a semiconductor. This is known as the "photovoltaic effect."

PV System DC Circuit. Any dc conductor in PV source circuits, PV string circuits, and PV dc-to-dc converter circuits (Article 690). ▶Figure 100–133

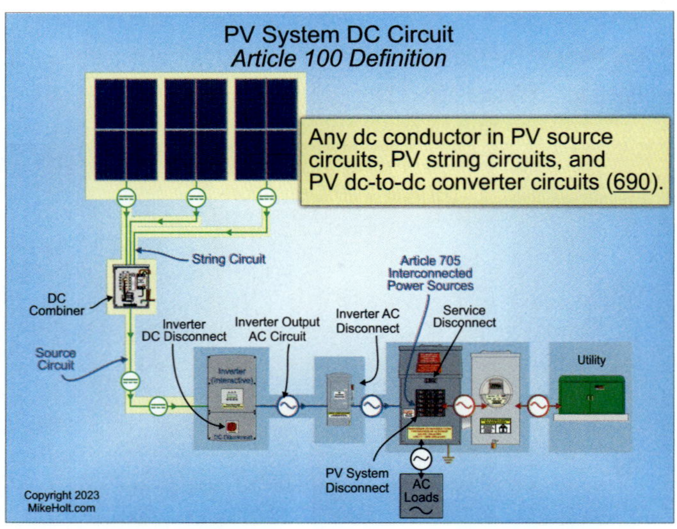

▶Figure 100–133

PV Source Circuit. The PV source circuit consists of the dc circuit conductors between modules in a PV string and from PV string circuits to dc combiners, electronic power converters, or the PV system dc disconnect (Article 690). ▶Figure 100–134

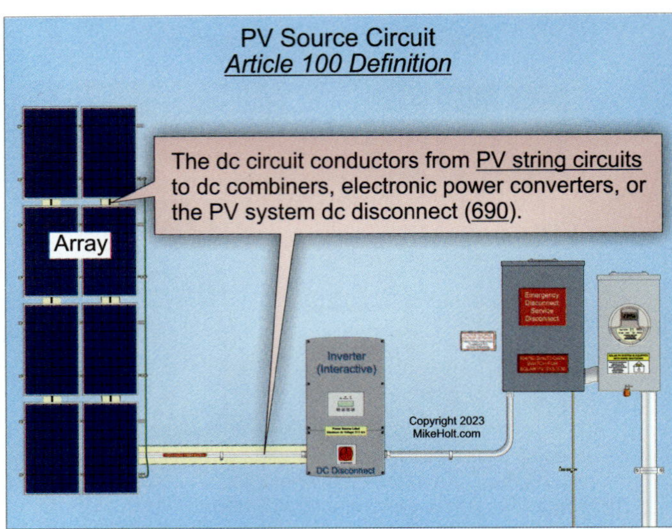

▶Figure 100–134

Author's Comment:

▶ The term "PV String" is the International Electrotechnical Commission term for what the *NEC* identifies as a PV Source Circuit.

PV String Circuit. The PV source circuit conductors of one or more series-connected PV modules (Article 690). ▶Figure 100–135

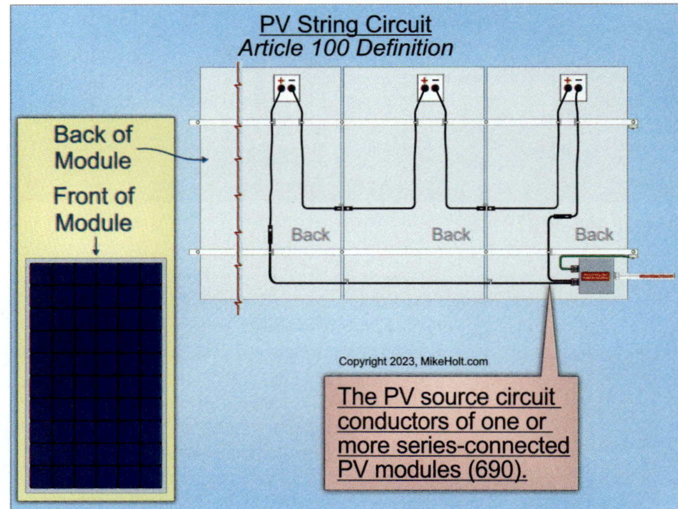

▶Figure 100–135

PV System. The components, circuits, and equipment up to and including the PV system disconnect, that in combination convert solar energy into electrical energy. ▶Figure 100–136

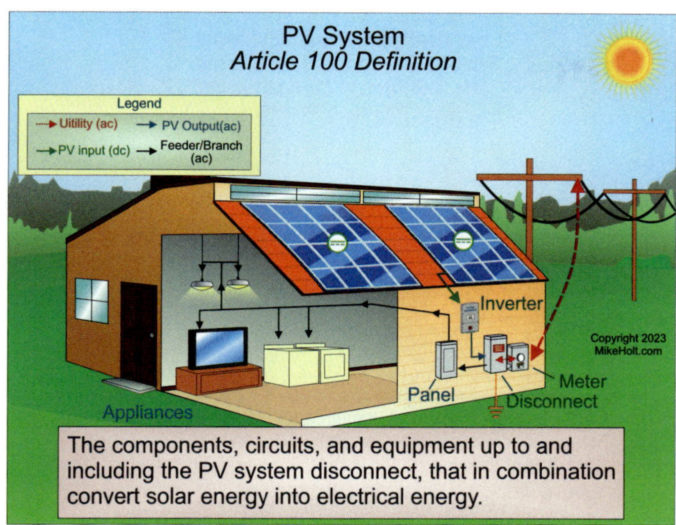

▶Figure 100–136

Qualified Person. A person with skills and knowledge related to the construction and operation of electrical equipment and installations. This person must have received safety training to recognize and avoid the hazards involved with electrical systems. ▶**Figure 100–137**

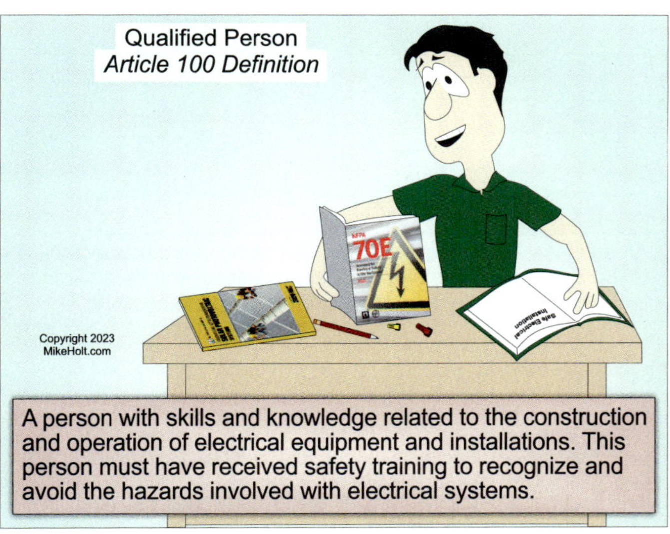

▶Figure 100–137

Note: NFPA 70E, *Standard for Electrical Safety in the Workplace,* provides information on the safety training requirements expected of a "qualified person."

Raceway. An enclosed channel designed for the installation of conductors, cables, or busbars.

Raceway, Surface Metal (Surface Metal Raceway). A metal raceway with associated fittings in which conductors are placed after the raceway has been installed as a complete system. ▶**Figure 100–138**

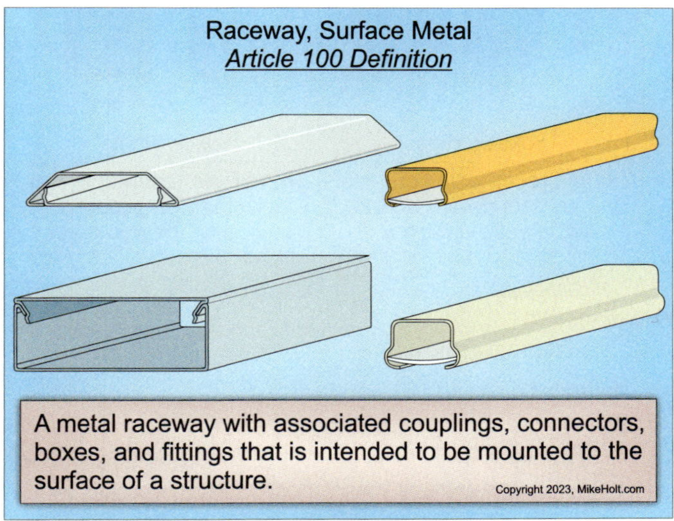

▶Figure 100–138

Receptacle. A contact device installed at an outlet for the connection of an attachment plug, or for the connection of equipment designed to mate with the contact device. ▶**Figure 100–139**

A single receptacle contains one contact device on the same a yoke or strap. A multiple receptacle has more than one contact device on the same yoke or strap. ▶**Figure 100–140**

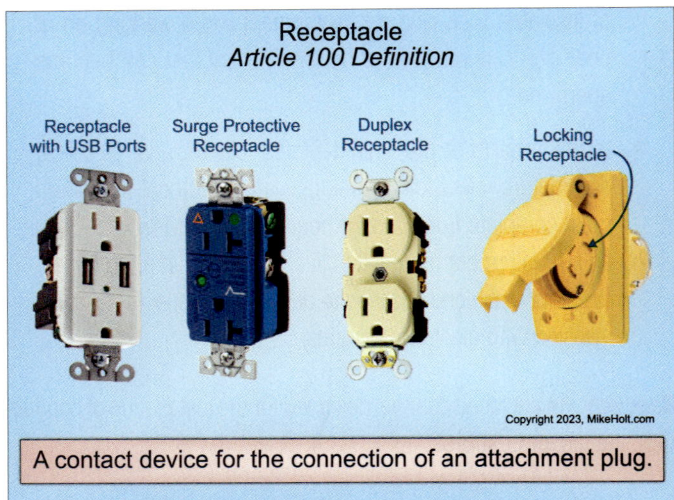

Receptacle
Article 100 Definition

▶Figure 100–139

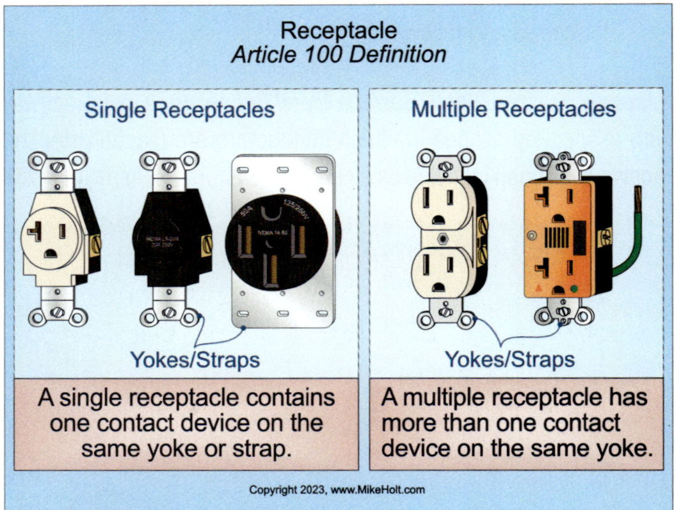

Receptacle
Article 100 Definition

▶Figure 100–140

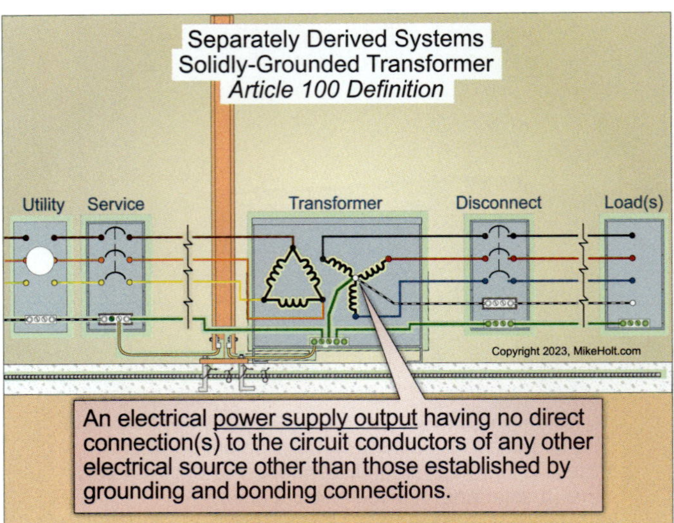

▶Figure 100–141

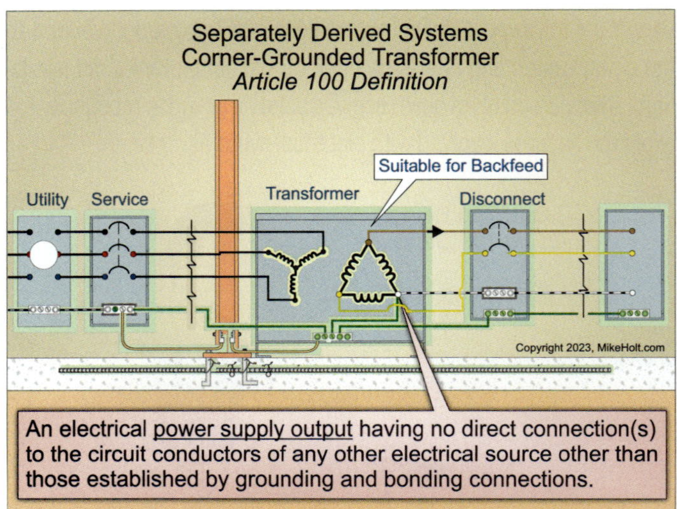

▶Figure 100–142

Author's Comment:

▶ A yoke (also called a "strap") is the metal mounting structure for such items as receptacles, switches, switches with pilot lights, and switch/receptacles to name a few.

Note: A duplex receptacle is an example of a multiple receptacle with two receptacles on the same yoke or strap.

Separately Derived System. An electrical power supply output having no direct connection(s) to the circuit conductors of any other electrical source other than those established by grounding and bonding connections. ▶Figure 100–141 and ▶Figure 100–142

Author's Comment:

▶ A generator with a transfer switch that does not open the neutral conductor is not a separately derived system because the neutral from the generator has a direct electrical connection to the service neutral conductor that is grounded. ▶Figure 100–143 and ▶Figure 100–144

▶ Section 250.30 contains important information on the use of the term "Separately Derived System."

Service. The conductors and equipment connecting the serving electric utility to the premises wiring system. ▶Figure 100–145

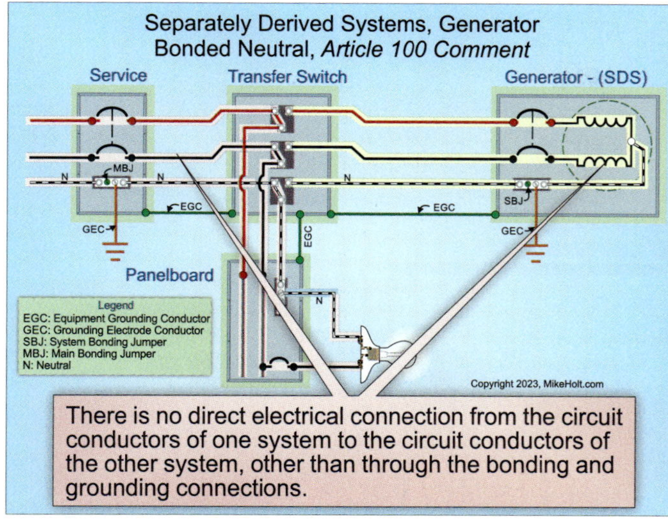

▶Figure 100–143

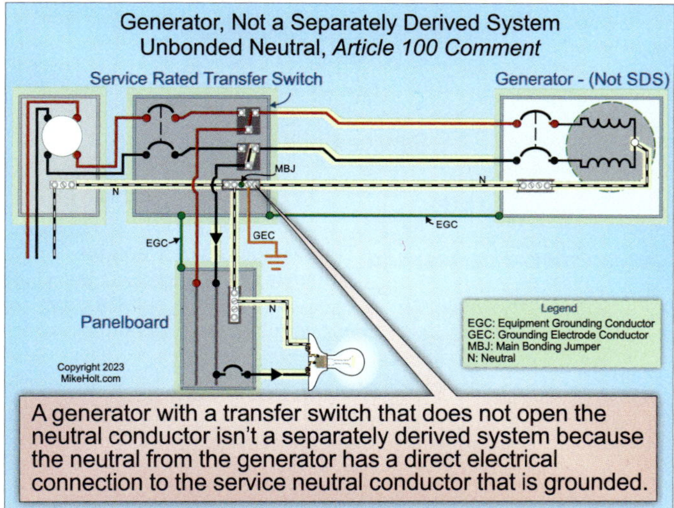

▶Figure 100–144

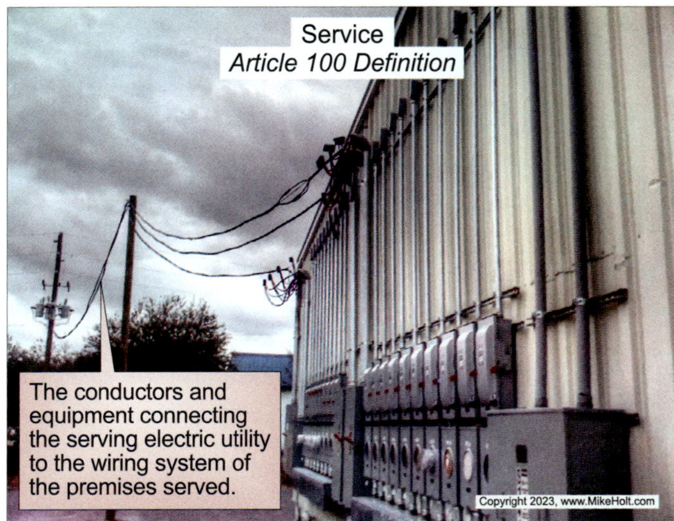

▶Figure 100–145

Service Conductors. The conductors from the serving electric utility service point to the service disconnect. ▶Figure 100–146

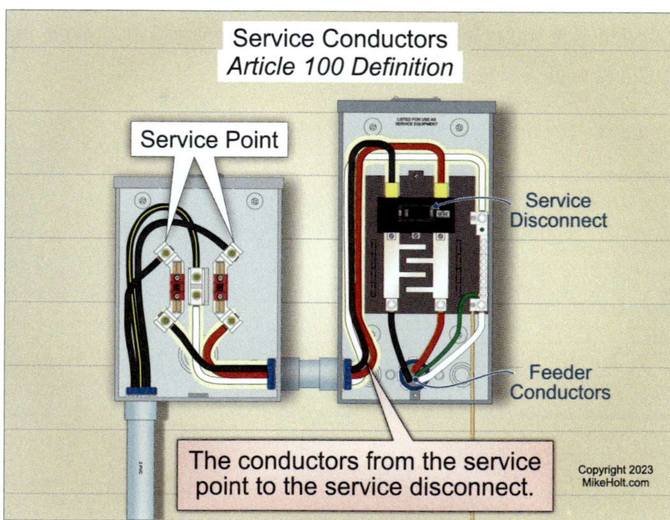

▶Figure 100–146

Author's Comment:

▶ Service conductors can include overhead service conductors, overhead service-entrance conductors, and underground service conductors. These conductors are not under the exclusive control of the serving electric utility, which means they are owned by the customer and are covered by the requirements in Article 230.

Service Conductors, Overhead (Overhead Service Conductors). Overhead conductors between the serving electric utility service point and the first point of connection to the service-entrance conductors at the building. ▶Figure 100–147

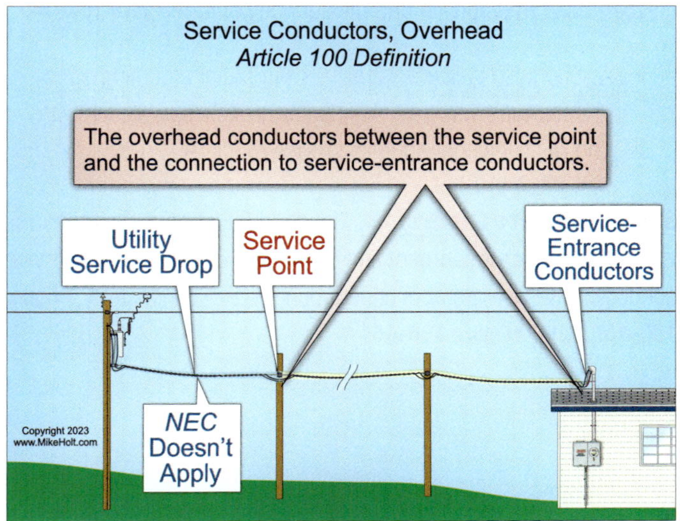

▶Figure 100–147

Service Conductors, Underground (Underground Service Conductors). Underground conductors between the service point and the first point of connection to the service-entrance conductors in a terminal box, meter, or other enclosure whether inside or outside the building wall. ▶Figure 100–148

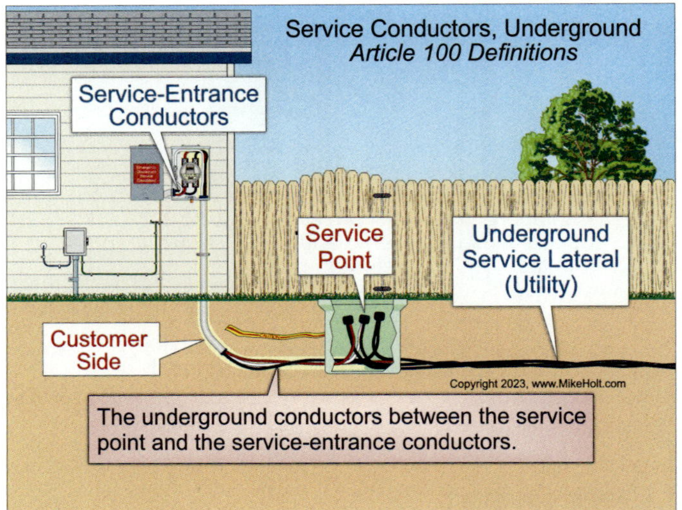

▶Figure 100–148

Author's Comment:

▸ Service conductors fall within the requirements of Article 230 since they are not under the exclusive control of the serving electric utility.

Note: Where there is no terminal box, meter, or other enclosure, the point of connection is the point of entrance of the service conductors into the building.

Service Drop. Utility-owned overhead conductors between the serving electric utility transformer and the service point. ▶Figure 100–149

Author's Comment:

▸ The *NEC* does not apply to service drops [90.2(D)(5)].

Service-Entrance Conductors. The conductors between the terminals of the service equipment and the service drop, overhead service conductors, service lateral, or underground service conductors. ▶Figure 100–150 and ▶Figure 100–151

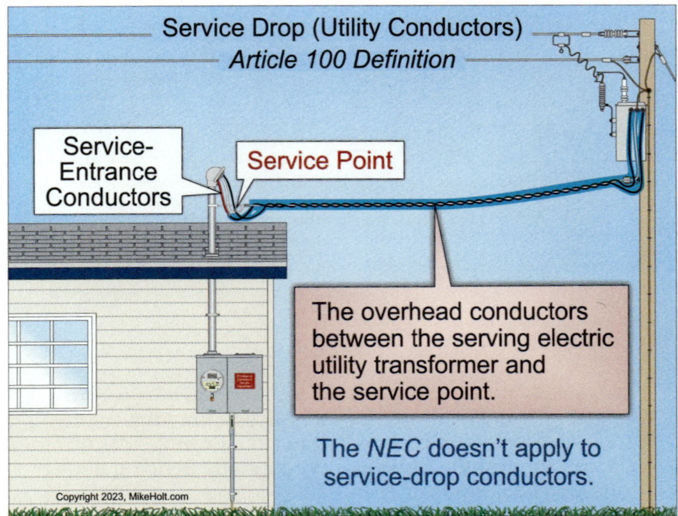

▶Figure 100–149

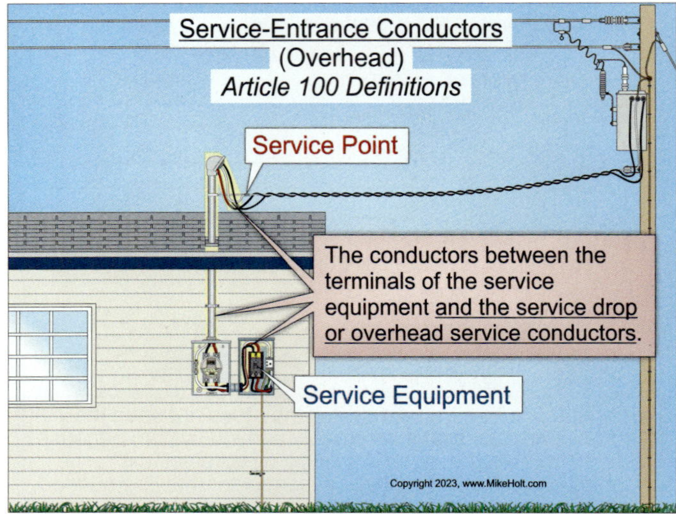

▶Figure 100–150

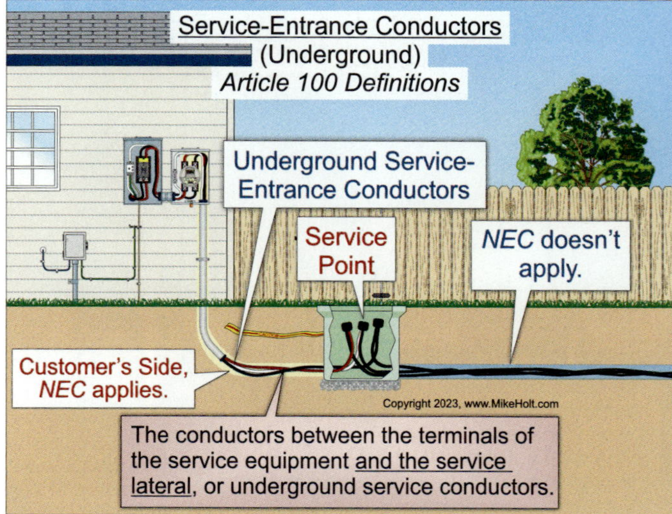

▶Figure 100–151

Service Equipment (Service Disconnect). Equipment such as circuit breakers or switches connected to the serving electric utility and intended to disconnect the power from the serving electric utility. ▶Figure 100–152 and ▶Figure 100–153

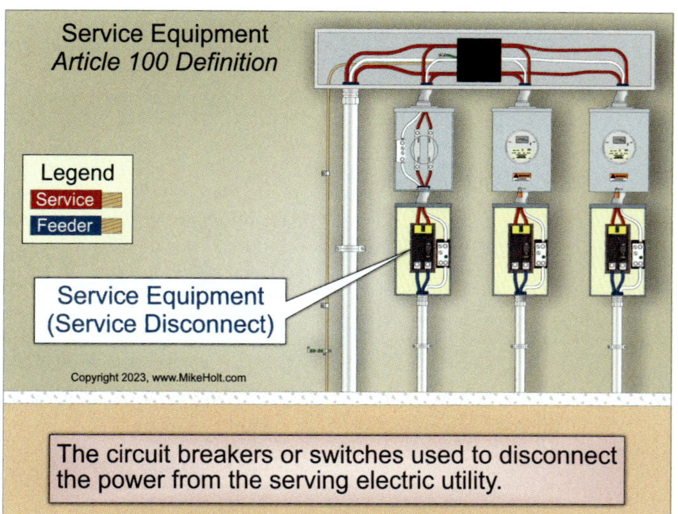

▶Figure 100–152

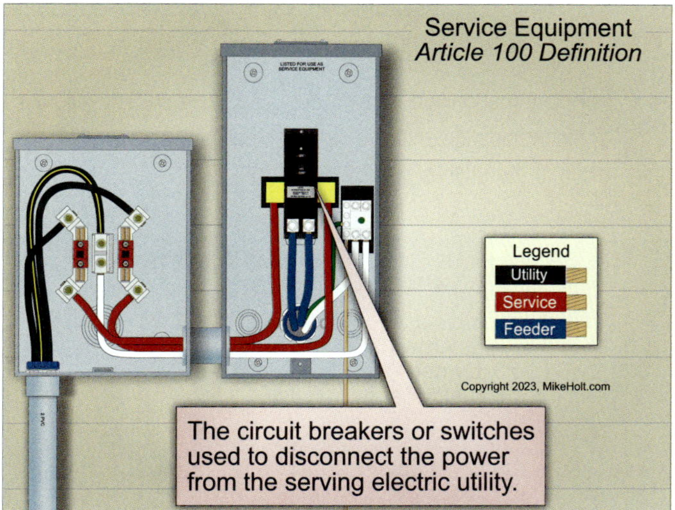

▶Figure 100–153

Author's Comment:

▶ Service equipment is often referred to as the "service disconnect" or "service main."

▶ Meter socket enclosures are not considered service equipment [230.66(B)].

▶ It is important to know where a service begins and where it ends to properly apply the *Code* requirements. The service can begin either before or after the metering equipment. ▶Figure 100–154

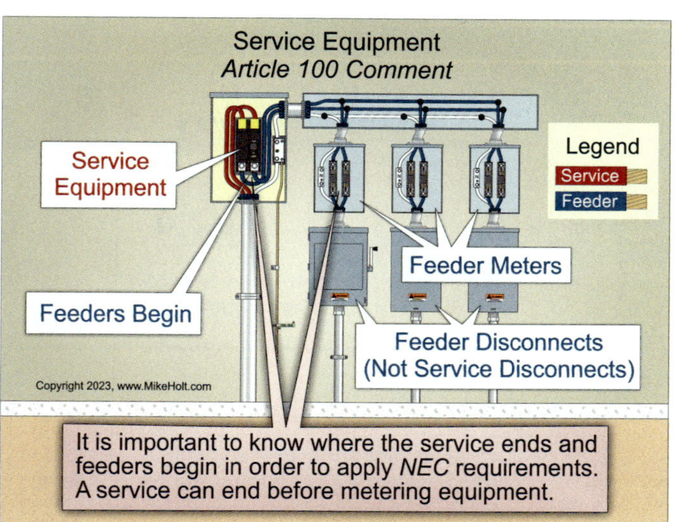

▶Figure 100–154

Service Lateral. Utility-owned underground conductors between the serving electric utility transformer and the service point. ▶Figure 100–155 and ▶Figure 100–156

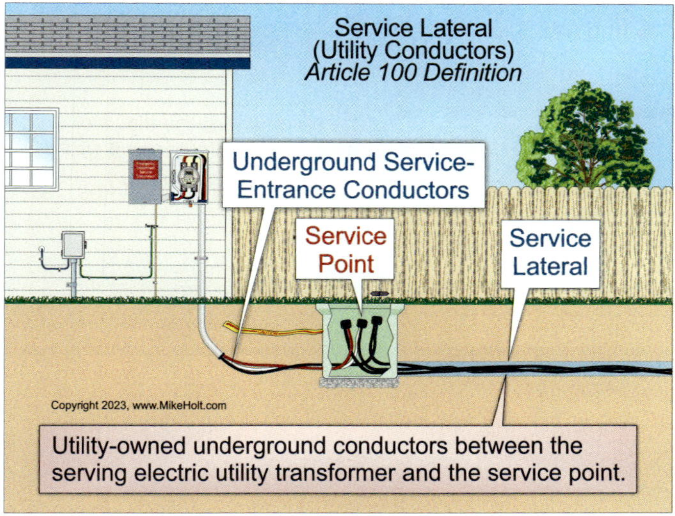

▶Figure 100–155

Service Point. The point where the serving electric utility conductors connect to customer-owned premises wiring. ▶Figure 100–157 and ▶Figure 100–158

Note: The service point is typically determined by the serving electric utility and may vary with different utilities and different types of occupancies.

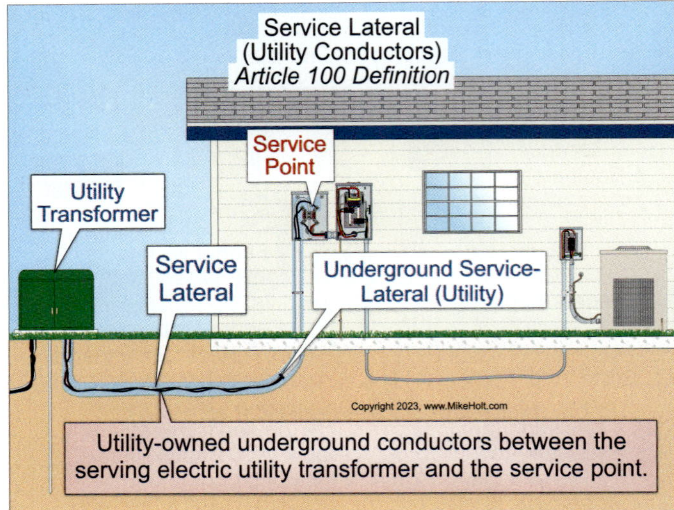

▶Figure 100–156

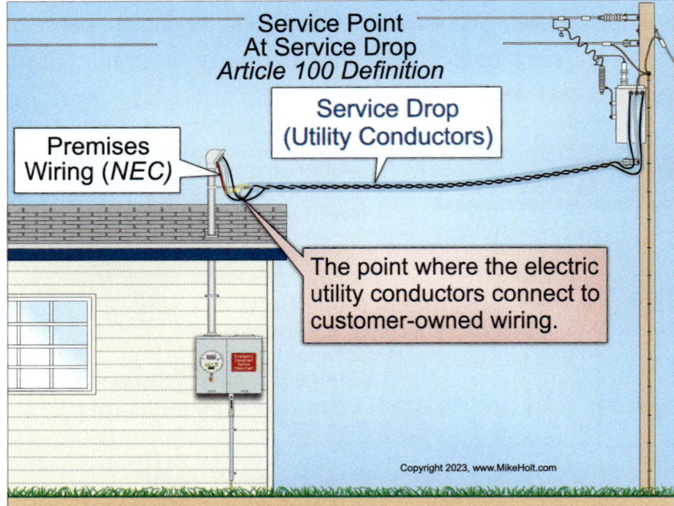

▶Figure 100–157

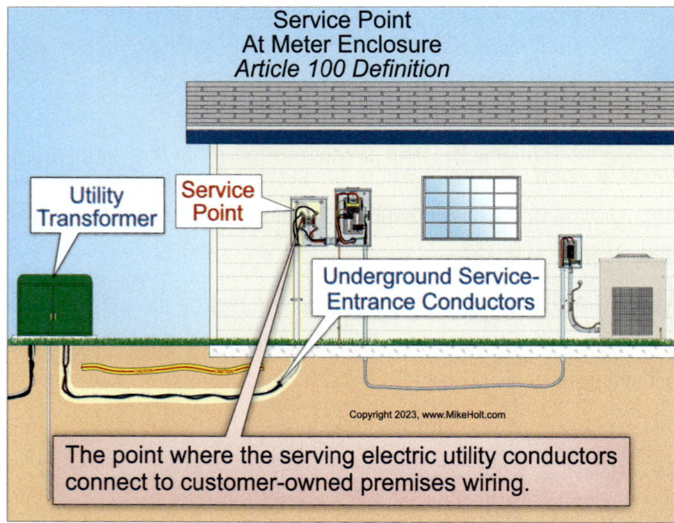

▶Figure 100–158

Author's Comment:

▸ For utility-owned transformers, the service point can be at the serving electric utility's transformer secondary terminals, at the service drop, or at the meter socket enclosure depending on where their conductors terminate. ▶Figure 100–159

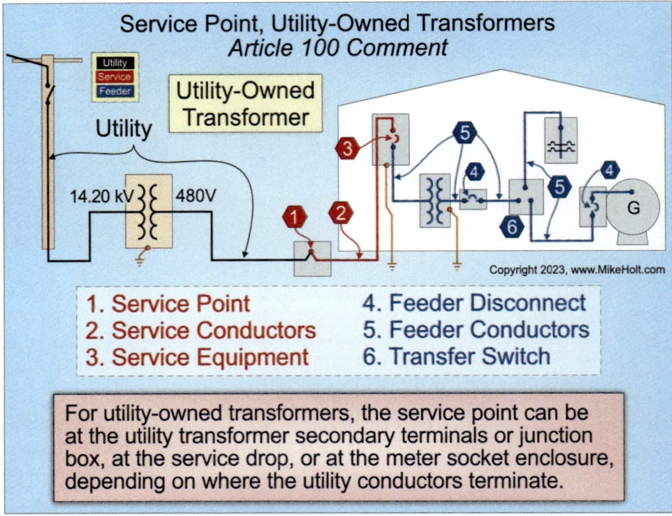

▶Figure 100–159

▸ For customer-owned transformers, the service point will be at the termination of the serving electric utility's conductors—often at the utility's pole. ▶Figure 100–160

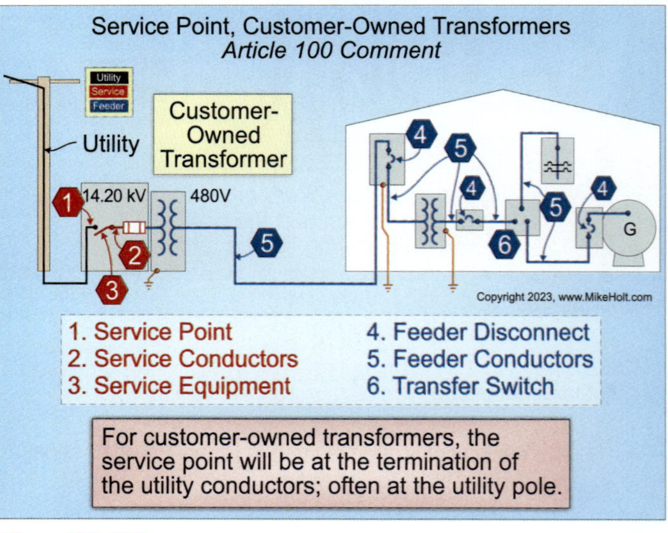

▶Figure 100–160

Servicing. The process of following a manufacturer's instructions or industry standards to analyze, adjust, or perform maintenance and repair of equipment. ▶Figure 100–161

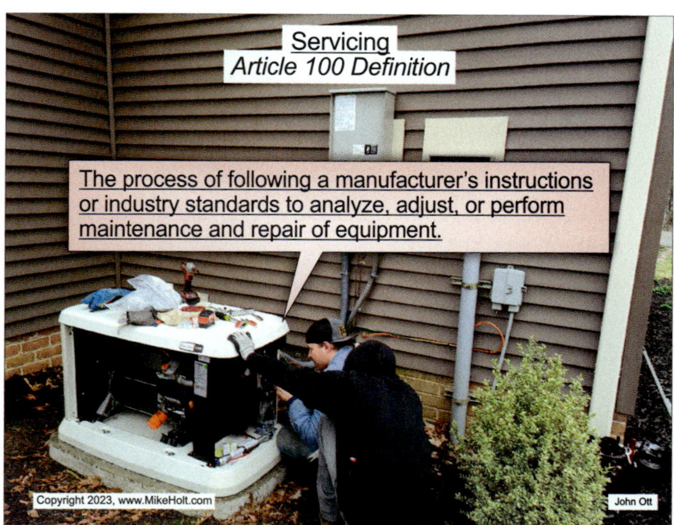

▶Figure 100–161

Note: Servicing often encompasses maintenance and repair activities.

Author's Comment:

▸ See 110.17 on the use of the term "Servicing."

Short Circuit. An abnormal connection of relatively low impedance, whether made accidentally or intentionally, between two or more points of different potential. ▶Figure 100–162

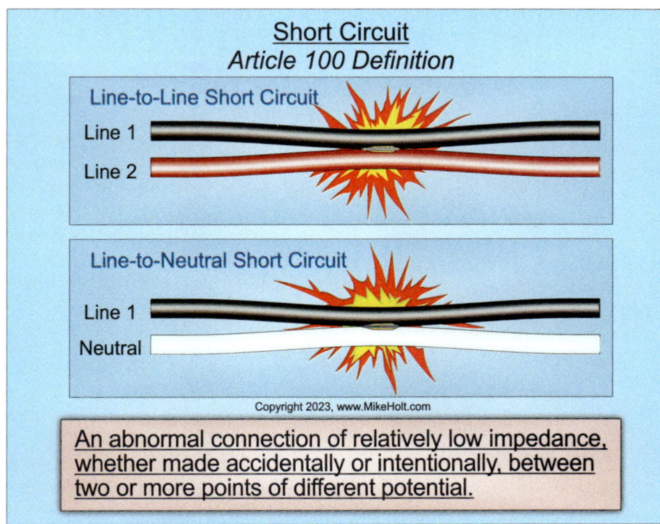

▶Figure 100–162

Author's Comment:

▸ A short circuit occurs when there is an unintentional electrical connection between two phase conductors, or a phase conductor and neutral conductor.

Short-Circuit Current Rating. The prospective symmetrical fault current at a nominal voltage to which electrical equipment can be connected without sustaining damage exceeding defined acceptance criteria.

Special Permission. The written consent of the authority having jurisdiction.

Splash Pad. A fountain intended for recreational use by pedestrians with a water depth of 1 in. or less (Article 680). ▶Figure 100–163

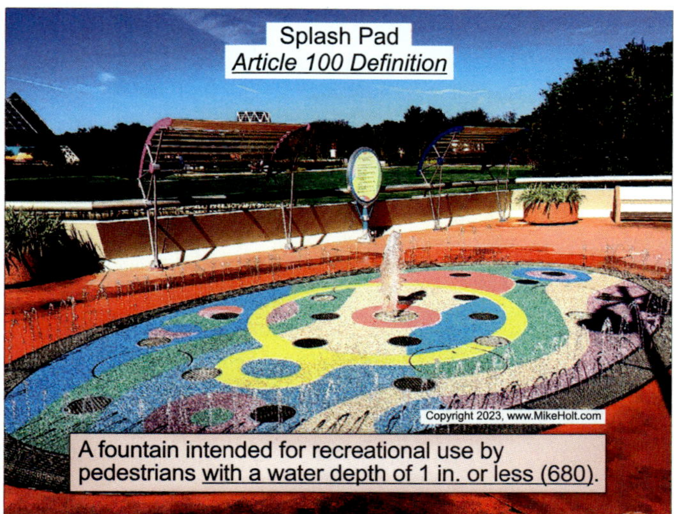

▶Figure 100–163

Stand-Alone System. An electrical power system that is not interconnected to the electric utility.

Author's Comment:

▸ Although stand-alone (off-grid) systems can operate independently of the electric utility, they may include a connection to the electric utility for use when not operating in stand-alone (off-grid) mode ("island mode").

Structure. That which is built or constructed, other than equipment. ▶Figure 100–164

Surge-Protective Device (SPD). A protective device intended to limit transient voltages by diverting or limiting surge current and preventing its continued flow while remaining capable of repeating these functions. ▶Figure 100–165 and ▶Figure 100–166

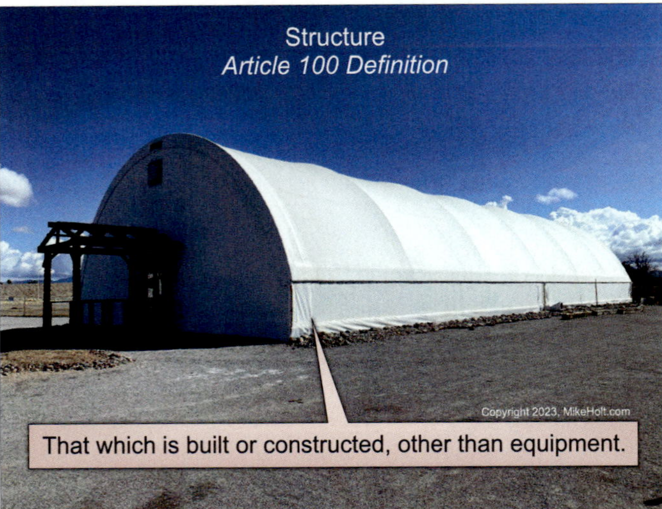

▶Figure 100–164

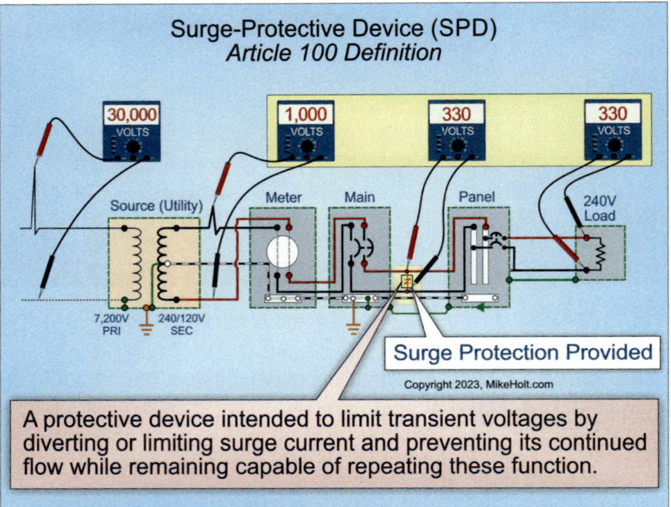

▶Figure 100–165

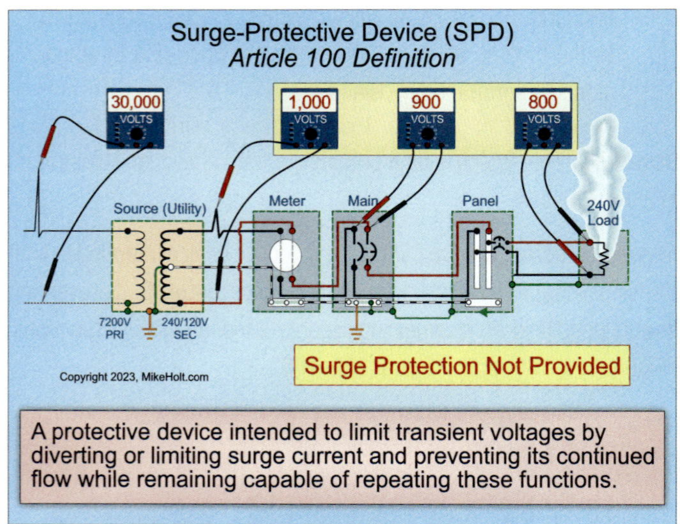

▶Figure 100–166

Author's Comment:

▸ Surge-protective devices are designed to shunt transient voltages away from the load to protect equipment and are arranged so that the voltage to the load does not exceed the equipment's maximum voltage rating as designed by the manufacturer. ▶Figure 100–167

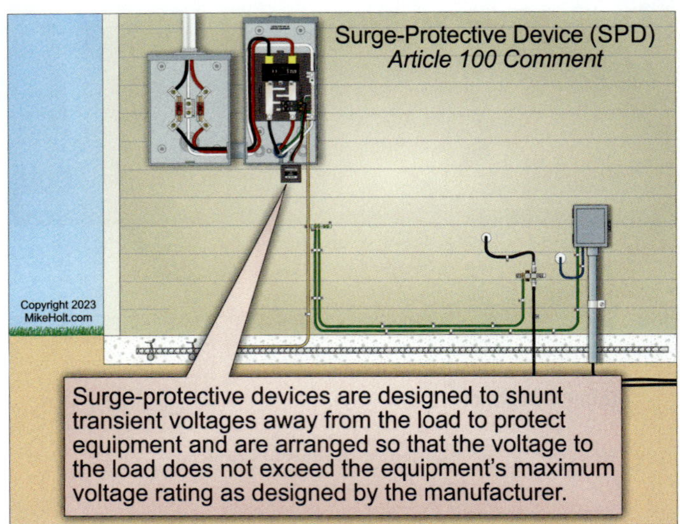

▶Figure 100–167

SPD, Type 1 (Type 1 SPD). A Type 1 surge-protective device is listed for the installation at or ahead of the service disconnect. ▶Figure 100–168

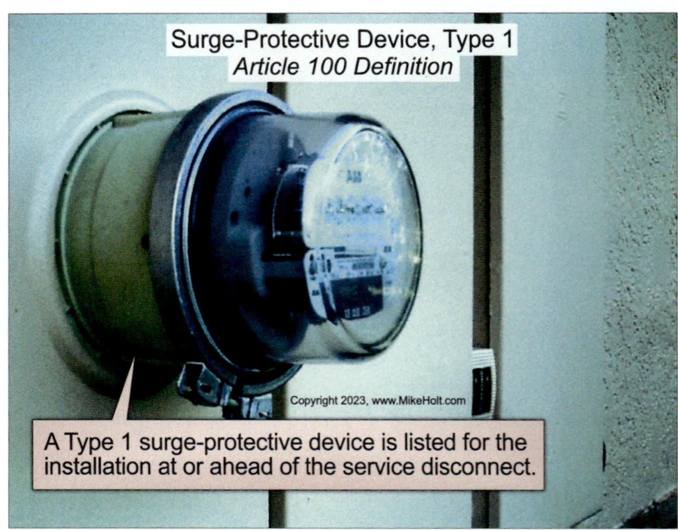

▶Figure 100–168

SPD, Type 2 (Type 2 SPD). A Type 2 surge-protective device is listed for the installation on the load side of the service disconnect. ▶Figure 100–169

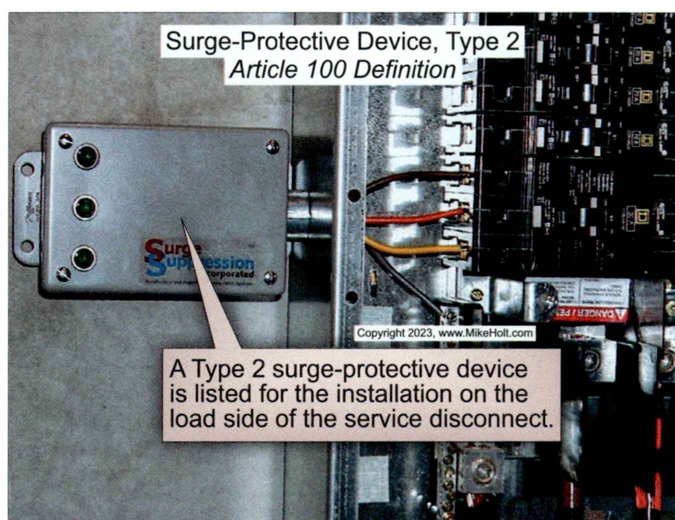

▶Figure 100–169

Note: For further information, see UL 1449, *Standard for Surge-Protective Devices.*

Switch, General-Use Snap (General-Use Snap Switch). A switch constructed to be installed in a device box or a box cover.

Transfer Switch. An automatic or nonautomatic device used for transferring loads from one power source to another. ▶Figure 100–170

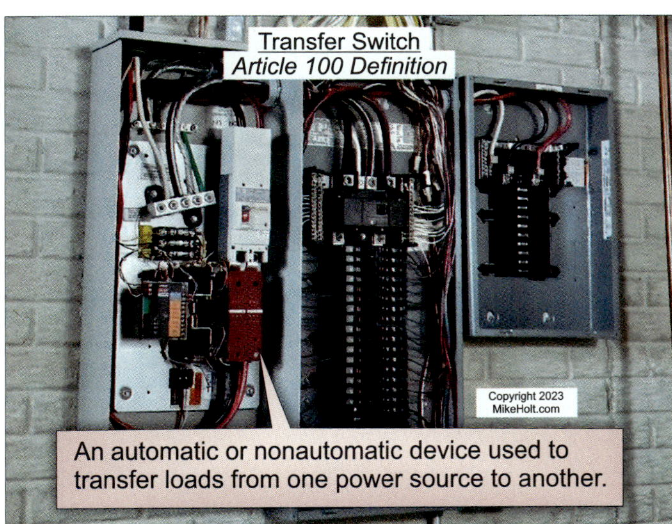

▶Figure 100–170

Transformer. Equipment, either single-phase or three-phase, that uses electromagnetic induction to convert current and voltage in a primary circuit into current and voltage in a secondary circuit. ▶Figure 100–171

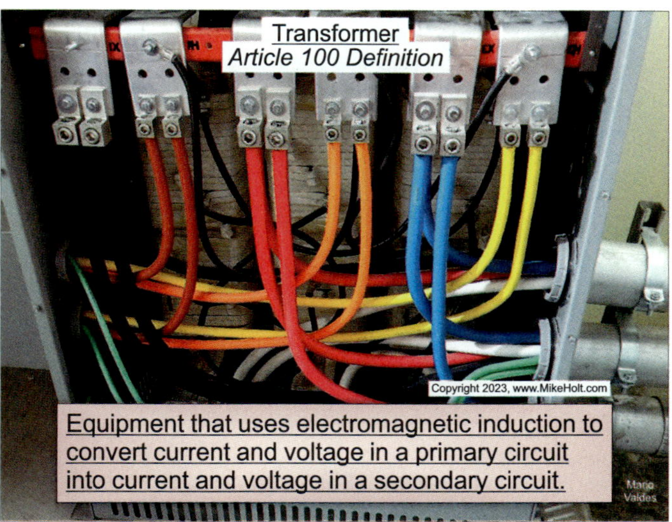

▶Figure 100–171

▶ Article 450 contains the primary requirements for transformers.

Tap Conductors. A conductor, other than a service conductor, with overcurrent protection rated more than the ampacity of the conductor. ▶Figure 100–172

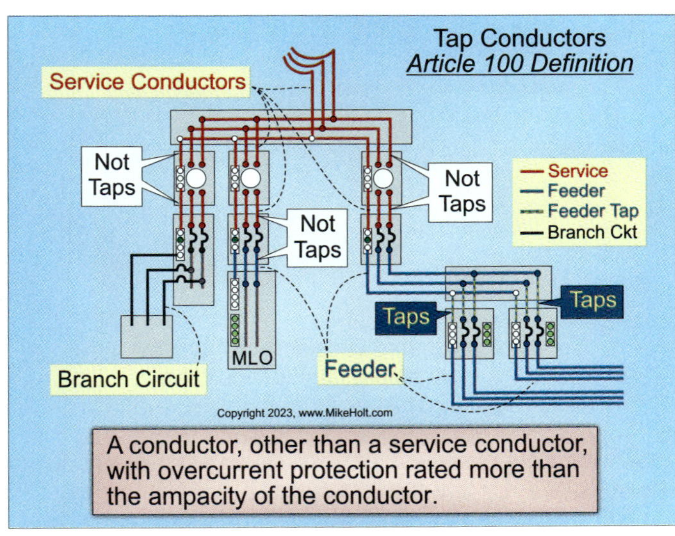

▶Figure 100–172

Tubing, Electrical Metallic (EMT). An unthreaded thinwall circular metallic raceway used for the installation of electrical conductors. When joined together with listed fittings and enclosures as a complete system, it is a reliable wiring method providing both physical protection for conductors as well an effective ground-fault current path. ▶Figure 100–173

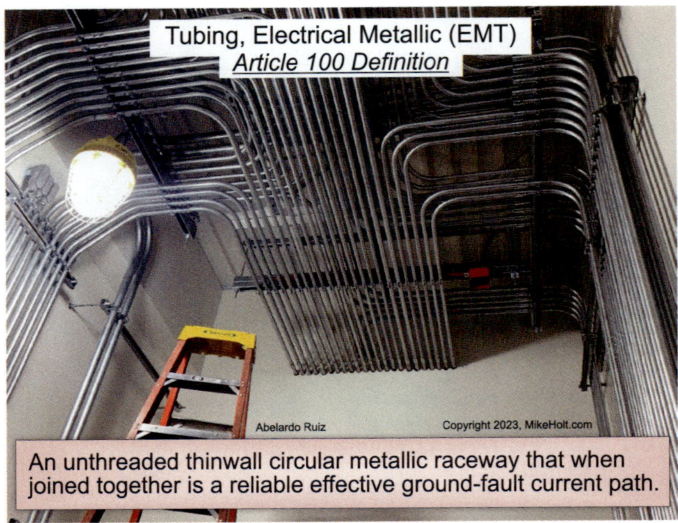

▶Figure 100–173

Tubing, Electrical Nonmetallic (ENT). A pliable corrugated circular raceway of circular cross section with integral or associated couplings, connectors, and fittings that are listed for the installation of electrical conductors. It is composed of a material that is resistant to moisture and chemical atmospheres and is flame retardant. ▶Figure 100–174

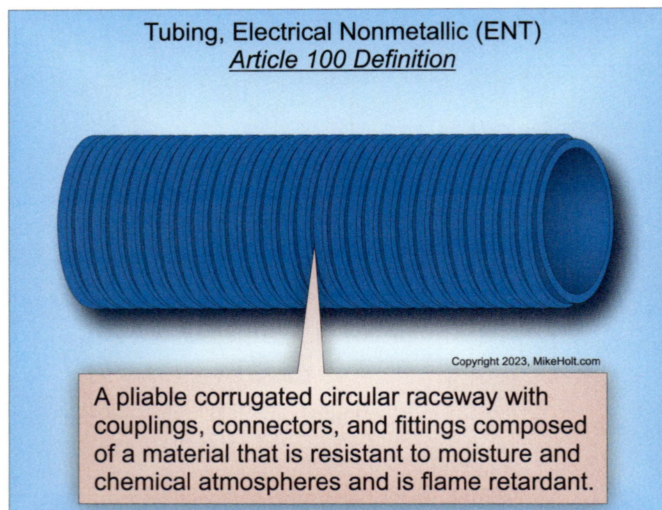

▶Figure 100–174

Author's Comment:

▶ Electrical nonmetallic tubing can be bent by hand with reasonable force and without other assistance.

Voltage, Nominal (Nominal Voltage). A value assigned for conveniently designating voltage classes. Examples include 120/240V, 120/208V, and 277/480V. ▶Figure 100–175

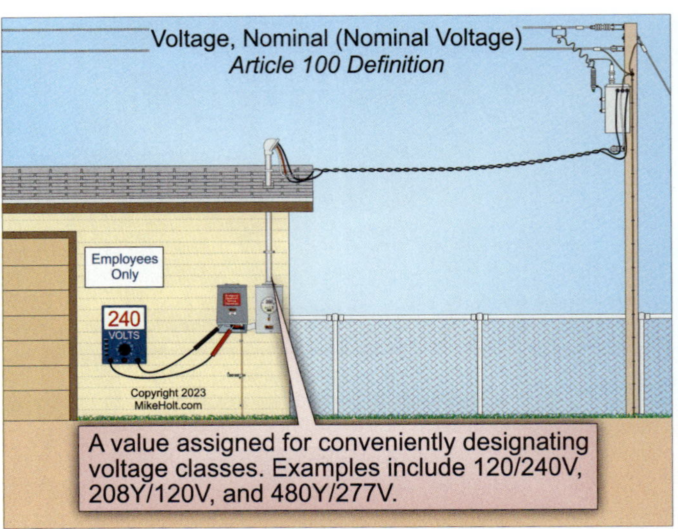

▶Figure 100–175

Note 1: The actual voltage at which a circuit operates can vary from the nominal within a range that permits satisfactory operation of equipment. ▶Figure 100–176

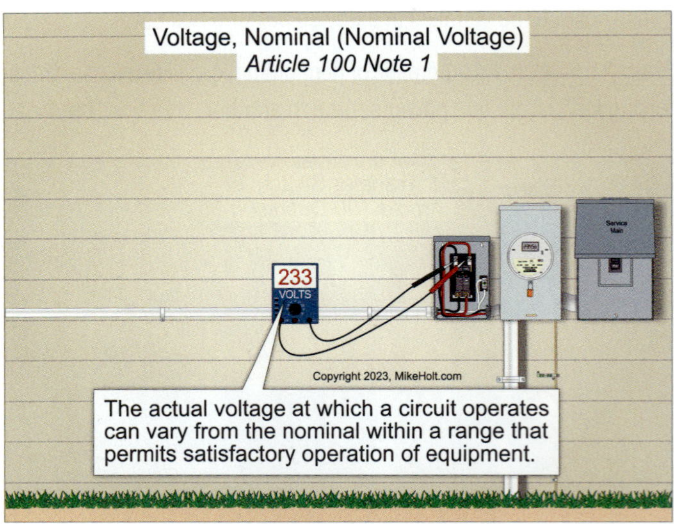

▶Figure 100–176

Voltage-to-Ground, Grounded Systems. For grounded systems, the voltage-to-ground is the voltage between any phase and neutral conductor. ▶Figure 100–177

Weatherproof. Constructed or protected so exposure to the weather will not interfere with successful operation.

Wireless Power Transfer Equipment (WPTE). Equipment for the purpose of transferring energy between premises wiring and an electric vehicle without physical electrical contact (Article 625). ▶Figure 100–178

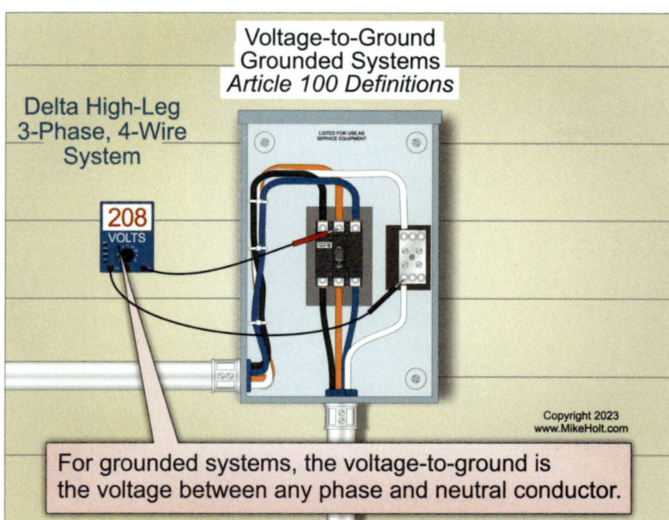

▶Figure 100–177

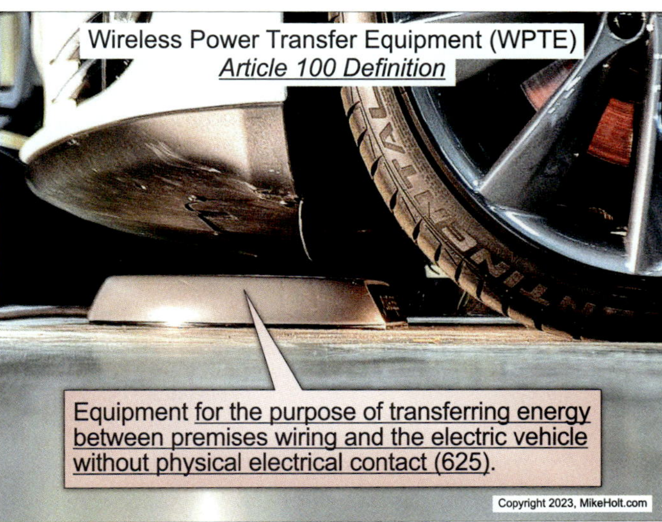

▶Figure 100–178

Wireway, Metal (Metal Wireway). A sheet metal trough with hinged or removable covers for housing and protecting electrical conductors and cable, and in which conductors are placed after the raceway has been installed. ▶Figure 100–179

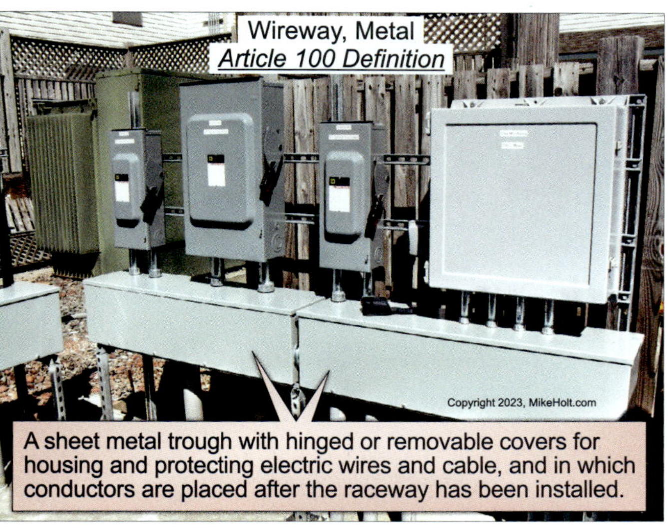

▶Figure 100–179

GENERAL REQUIREMENTS FOR ELECTRICAL INSTALLATIONS

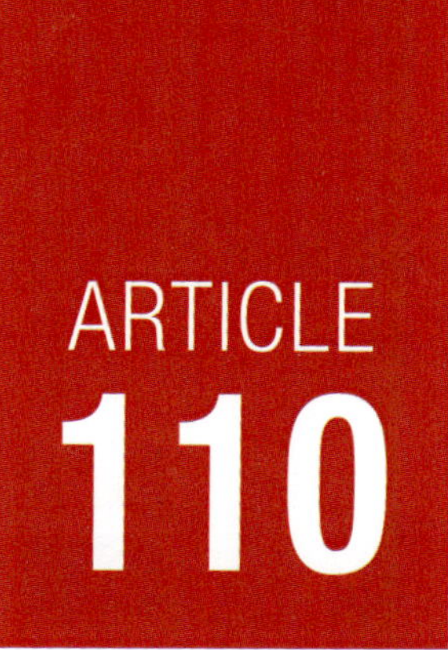

Introduction to Article 110—<u>General</u> Requirements for Electrical Installations

Article 110 is the first article in the *NEC* that contains requirements as opposed to overall scope information or definitions. It contains the general rules that apply to all installations and, as such, is the foundation of the *Code*. Topics covered in our material for Article 110 include:

- ▶ How equipment is approved
- ▶ How to determine when or where equipment can be used
- ▶ How to arrange equipment so it is safe to operate and maintain for the end user
- ▶ How to identify the characteristics of the systems being installed so future alterations, service, or maintenance can be completed safely

This article is divided into five parts. The first two cover systems under 1000V, nominal and are the only parts of this article covered in this material. As you begin your journey to understanding the *NEC*, remember that many other *Code* rules were written with the understanding that you will come to Article 100 to determine the general requirements. Set yourself up for success by taking the time to read and understand each of these rules.

Part I. General Requirements

110.1 Scope

Article 110 covers the general requirements for the examination, approval, installation, use, and access to spaces around electrical equipment. ▶Figure 110–1

Author's Comment:

- ▶ Requirements for people with disabilities include things like mounting heights for switches, receptacles and the requirements for the distance that objects (such as wall sconces) protrude from a wall.

Note: For information regarding ADA accessibility design, see Annex J.

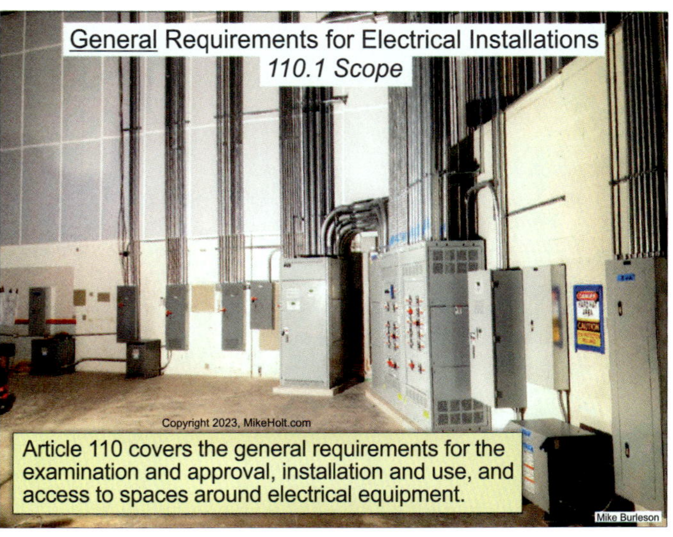

▶Figure 110–1

110.2 Approval of Conductors and Equipment

The authority having jurisdiction must approve all electrical conductors and equipment. ▶Figure 110–2

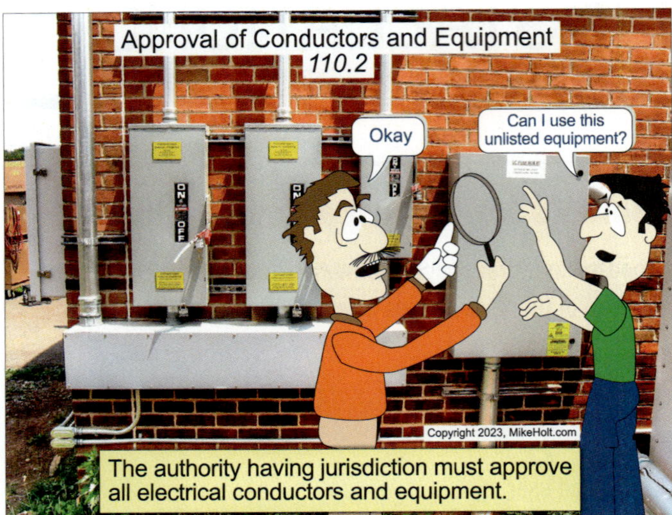

▶Figure 110–2

According to Article 100, "Approved" means acceptable to the authority having jurisdiction (AHJ), usually the electrical inspector. Product listing does not mean the product is approved, but it can be a basis for approval. ▶Figure 110–3

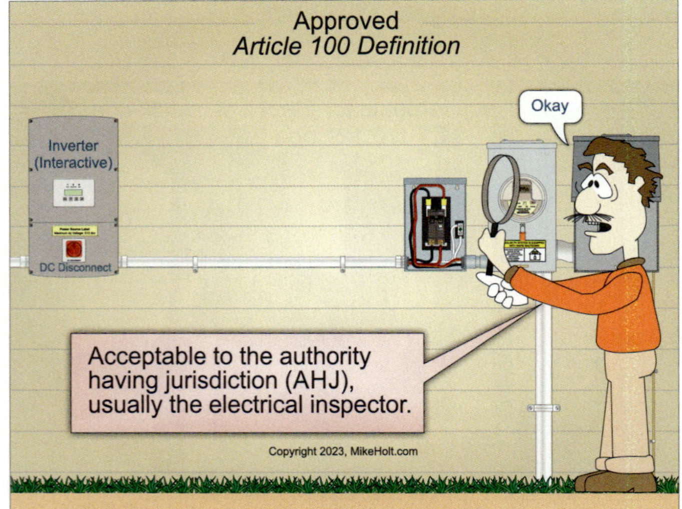

▶Figure 110–3

According to Article 100, "Authority Having Jurisdiction (AHJ)" refers the organization, office, or individual responsible for approving equipment, materials, or an installation. See 90.4 and 90.7 for more information. ▶Figure 110–4

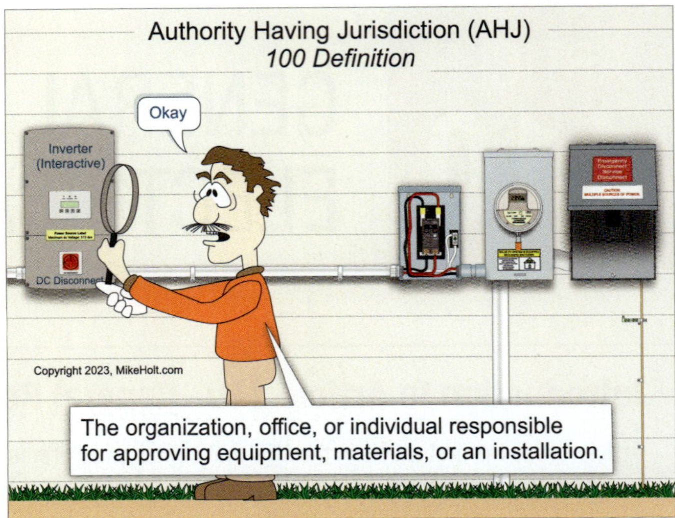

▶Figure 110–4

110.3 Use of Equipment

(A) Guidelines for Approval. The authority having jurisdiction must approve equipment. In doing so, consideration must be given to the following:

(1) Suitability for installation and use in accordance with the *NEC*

Note 1: Equipment may be new, reconditioned, refurbished, or remanufactured.

Note 2: Suitability of equipment use may be identified by a description marked on (or provided with) a product to identify the suitability of the product for a specific purpose, environment, or application. Special conditions of use or other limitations may be marked on the equipment, in the product instructions, or included in the appropriate listing and labeling information. Suitability of equipment may be evidenced by listing or labeling.

According to Article 100, "Identified (as Applied to Equipment)" means that it is recognized as suitable for a specific purpose, function, use, environment, or application. ▶Figure 110–5

(2) Mechanical strength and durability

(3) Wire-bending and connection space

(4) Electrical insulation

(5) Heating effects under all conditions of use

(6) Arcing effects

(7) Classification by type, size, voltage, current capacity, and specific use

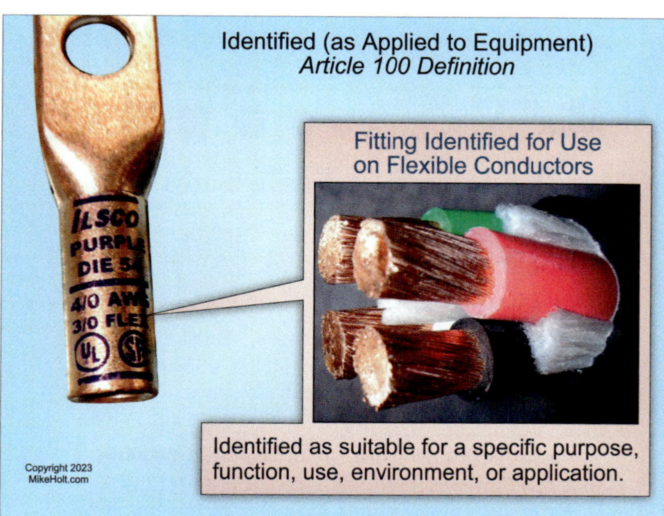

▶Figure 110–5

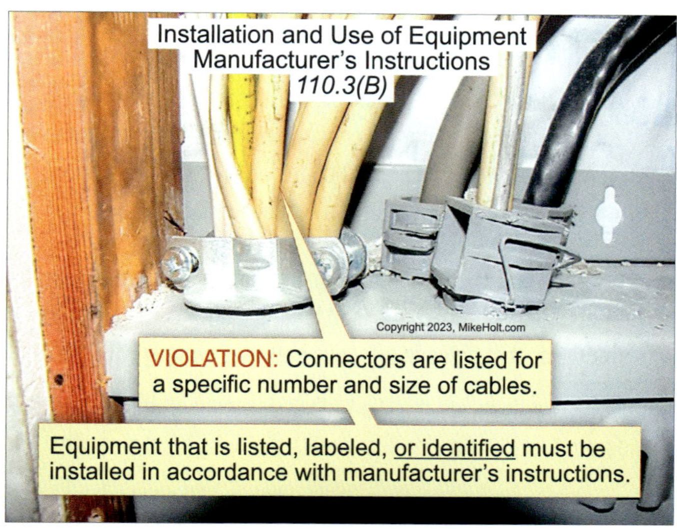

▶Figure 110–6

(8) Cybersecurity for network-connected life safety equipment to address its ability to withstand unauthorized updates and malicious attacks while continuing to perform its intended life safety functionality

Note 3: See the IEC 62443 series of standards for industrial automation and control systems, the UL 2900 series of standards for software cybersecurity for network connectible products, and UL 5500, *Standard for Remote Software Updates*, which are standards that provide frameworks to mitigate current and future security cybersecurity vulnerabilities and address software integrity in systems of electrical equipment.

(9) Other factors contributing to the practical safeguarding of persons using or in contact with the equipment

(B) Installation and Use. Equipment that is listed, labeled, or identified must be installed in accordance with manufacturer's instructions.
▶Figure 110–6

According to Article 100, "Labeled" mean equipment or materials that have a label, symbol, or other identifying mark in the form of a sticker, decal, printed label, or with the identifying mark molded or stamped into the product by a recognized testing laboratory acceptable to the authority having jurisdiction. ▶Figure 110–7

Note: The installation instructions can be provided in the form of printed material, quick response (QR) code, or the address on the Internet where users can download the required instructions. ▶Figure 110–8

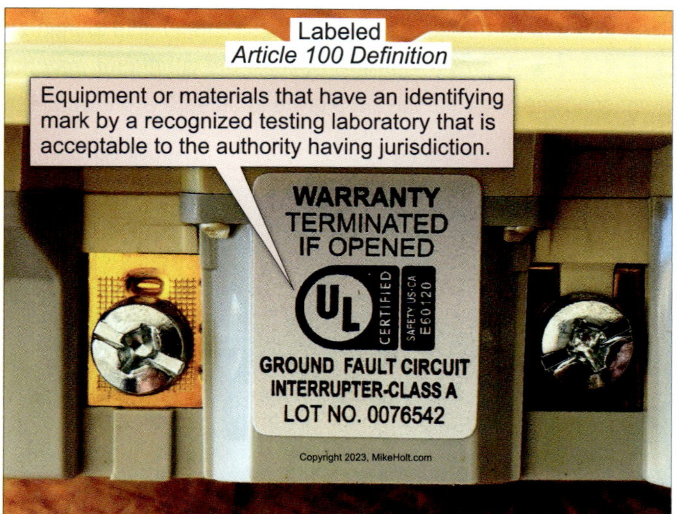

▶Figure 110–7

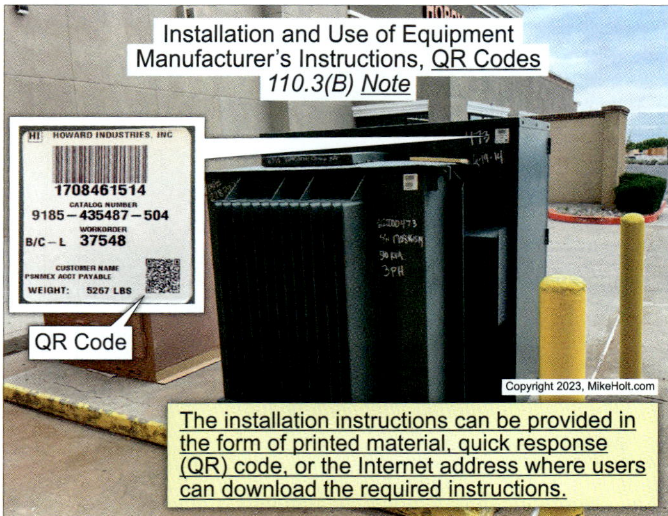

▶Figure 110–8

▸ Many electricians simply throw away installation instructions, but that excuse is now becoming less valid since manufacturers are starting to use QR codes on electrical equipment, so the instructions are always readily available.

(C) Product Listing. Product testing, evaluation, and listing must be performed by a recognized qualified testing laboratory in accordance with standards that achieve effective safety to comply with the *NEC*.

Note: OSHA recognizes qualified electrical testing laboratories that provide product certification that meets their electrical standards.

110.5 Conductor Material

Conductors must be copper, aluminum, or copper-clad aluminum unless otherwise provided in this *Code*. If the conductor material is not specified in a rule, the sizes given in the *NEC* are based on a copper conductor. ▸Figure 110–9

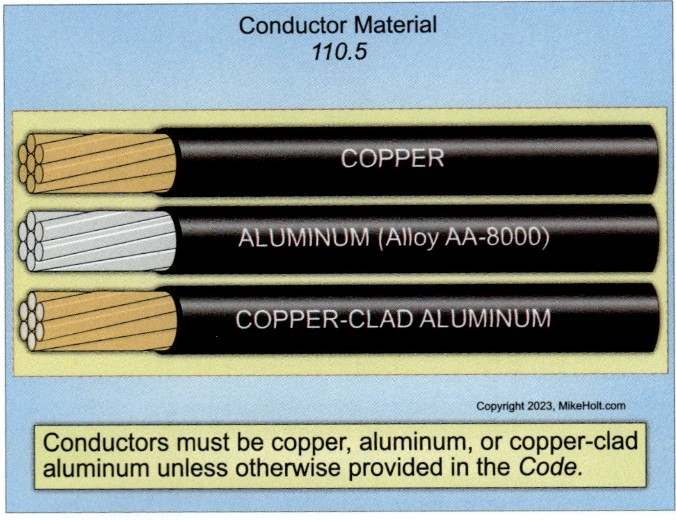

▸Figure 110–9

110.6 Conductor Sizes

Conductor sizes are expressed in American Wire Gauge (AWG) or circular mils (cmil). ▸Figure 110–10

▸ Chapter 9, Table 8 gives the circular mil area of AWG conductors.

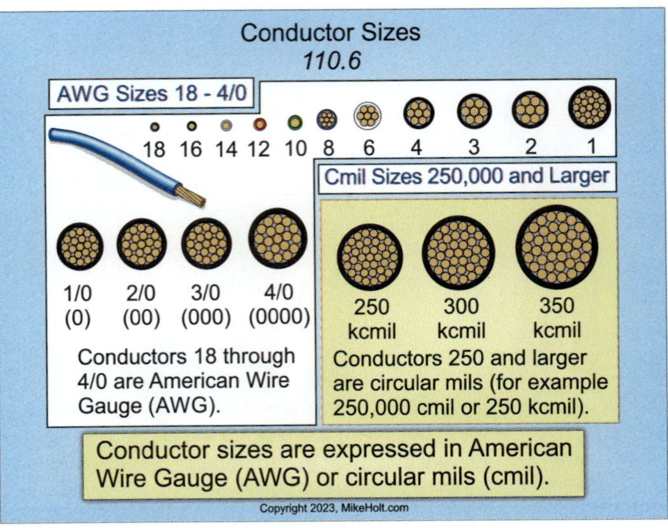

▸Figure 110–10

110.7 Wiring Integrity

Electrical installations must be free from short circuits, ground faults, or neutral to ground connections unless required or permitted by the *Code*. ▸Figure 110–11, ▸Figure 110–12, and ▸Figure 110–13

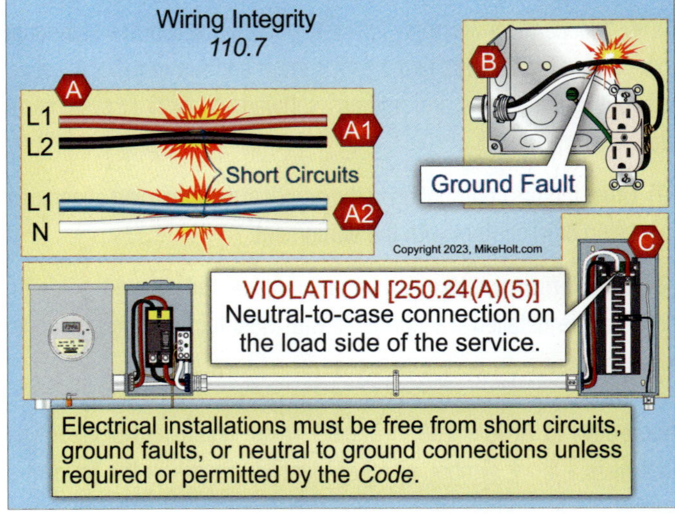

▸Figure 110–11

110.8 Suitable Wiring Methods

The only wiring methods permitted to be installed in buildings, occupancies, or premises are those recognized by the *NEC*. ▸Figure 110–14

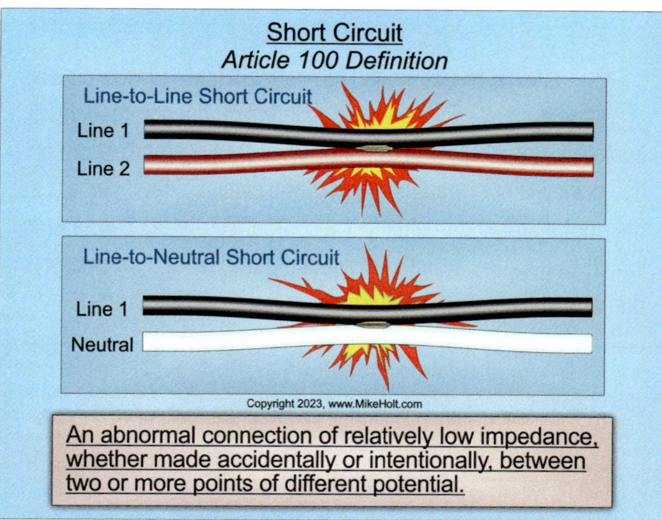

▶Figure 110–12

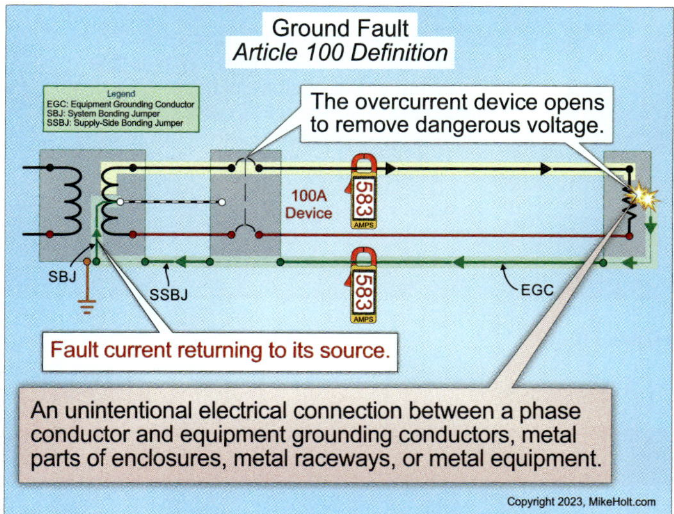

▶Figure 110–13

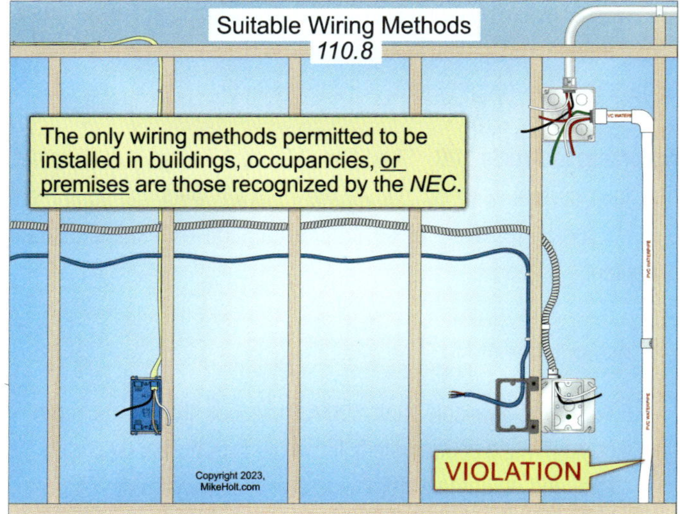

▶Figure 110–14

110.9 Interrupting Rating of Overcurrent Protective Devices

Circuit breakers and fuses must have an interrupting rating equal to or greater than the available fault current at the line terminals of the equipment. ▶Figure 110–15

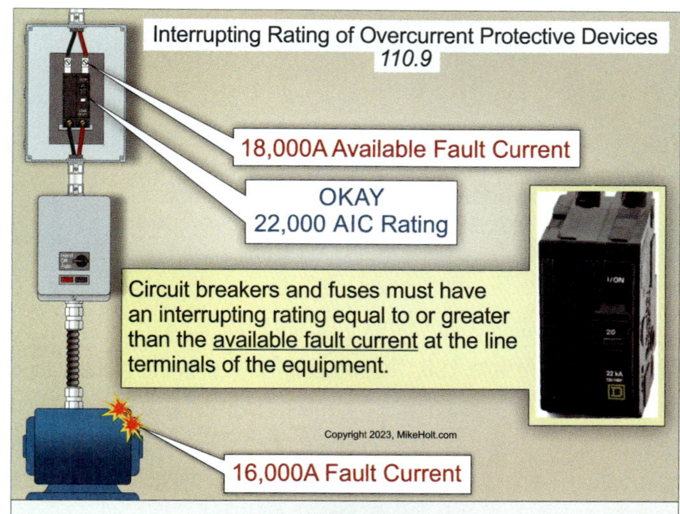

▶Figure 110–15

According to Article 100, "Circuit Breaker" is a device designed to be opened and closed manually, and opens automatically during an overcurrent event without damage to itself. ▶Figure 110–16

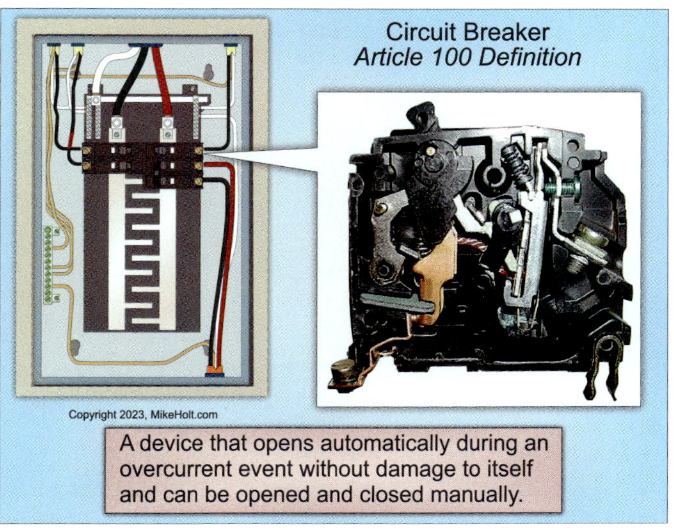

▶Figure 110–16

According to Article 100, "Fuse" is an overcurrent protective device with a circuit-opening fusible part that is heated and severed by the passage of overcurrent. ▶Figure 110–17

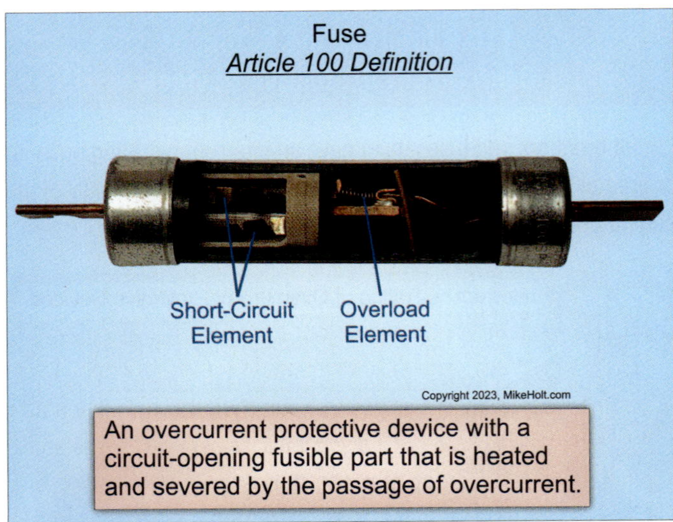

▶Figure 110–17

According to Article 100, "Interrupting Rating" is the highest fault current at rated voltage a device is identified to interrupt under standard test conditions. Interrupting ratings are often referred to as "Ampere Interrupting Rating" (AIR) or "Ampere Interrupting Capacity" (AIC). Both terms/acronyms are about the amount of current a device can safely handle while clearing a fault.

"Available Fault Current" is the largest amount of current capable of being delivered at a point on the electrical system during a short-circuit condition. ▶Figure 110–18

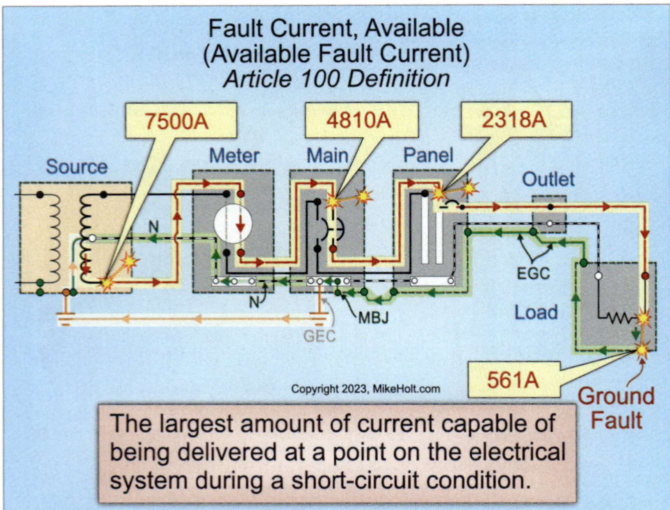

▶Figure 110–18

CAUTION: Extremely high values of fault currents caused by short circuits or ground faults produce tremendously destructive thermal and magnetic forces. If an overcurrent protective device is not rated to interrupt the available fault current at the equipment, it can explode and vaporize metal components which can cause serious injury or death, as well as property damage and electrical system down time. ▶Figure 110–19

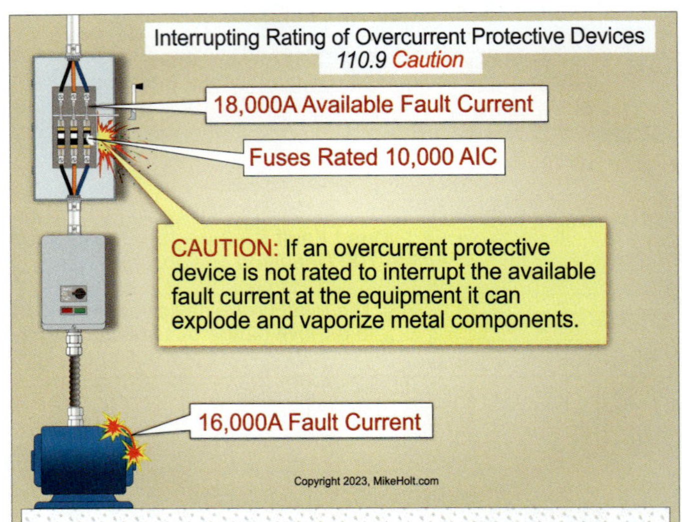

▶Figure 110–19

110.10 Equipment Short-Circuit Current Rating

Electrical equipment must have a short-circuit current rating that permits the circuit protective device to clear a short circuit or ground fault without extensive damage to the electrical equipment of the circuit. Listed equipment applied in accordance with its listing is considered to have met this requirement. ▶Figure 110–20

According to Article 100, "Short-Circuit Current Rating" is the symmetrical fault current at a nominal voltage to which electrical equipment can be connected without sustaining damage exceeding defined acceptance criteria.

Author's Comment:

▶ When the available fault current exceeds the short-circuit current rating of equipment, it can damage busbars, conductors, and equipment from excessive electromagnetic forces and heat.

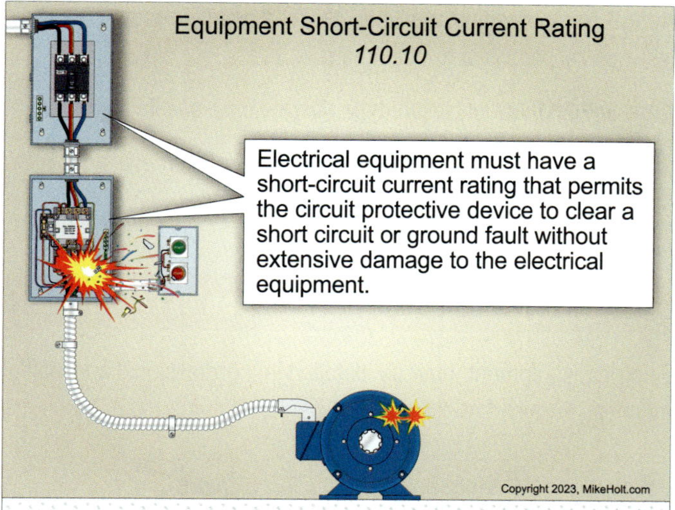

▶Figure 110–20

Danger

DANGER: Equipment can explode if the available fault current exceeds the equipment short-circuit current rating, endangering persons and property. ▶Figure 110–21

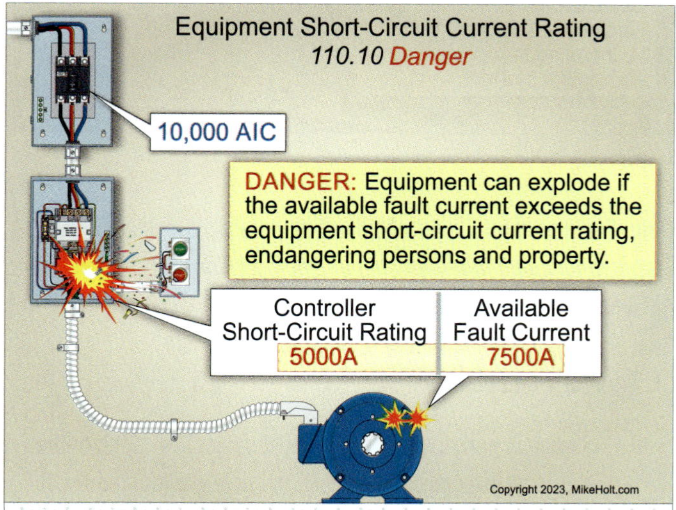

▶Figure 110–21

Available Fault Current

Sections 110.9 and 110.10 use similar sounding terms making it a bit challenging to understand the differences. Be careful not to confuse the term "interrupting rating" with "short-circuit rating."

Available fault current is the largest amount of short-circuit or ground-fault current, in amperes, available at a given point in the electrical system. It is first determined at the secondary terminals of the serving electric utility transformer, as given by the serving electric utility's engineer. After that, it is calculated at the terminals of the service disconnect, then panelboards and other equipment as various connections are made downstream from the main service. Beginning at the serving electric utility transformer, the available fault current decreases at each downstream connection point of the electrical system.

The available fault current at any point depends on the impedance of the circuit. As the circuit impedance increases, the available fault current decreases. ▶Figure 110–22

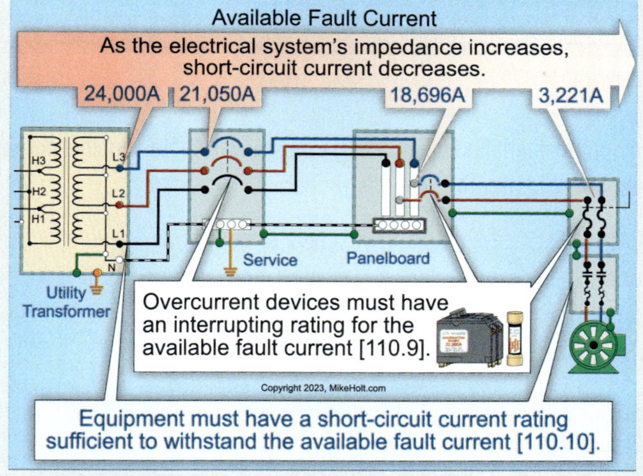

▶Figure 110–22

Factors that affect the available fault current at the serving electric utility transformers are the system voltage, transformer kVA rating, and impedance. Properties that have an impact on the impedance of the circuit include the conductor material (copper versus aluminum), conductor size, conductor length, raceway type (metallic versus nonmetallic), ambient temperature, and motor loads.

110.11 Deteriorating Agents

Electrical equipment and conductors must be suitable for the environment and the conditions for which they will be used. Consideration must also be given to the presence of corrosive gases, fumes, vapors, liquids, or other substances that can have a deteriorating effect on conductors and equipment. ▶Figure 110–23

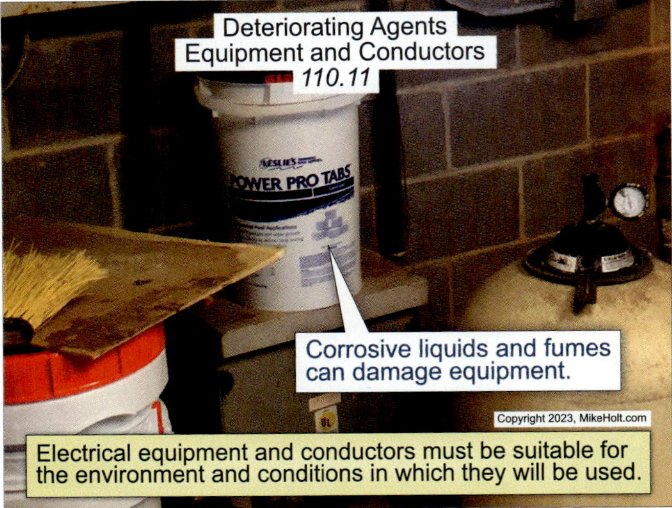

▶Figure 110–23

Equipment identified for indoor use must be protected against damage from the weather during construction.

Note 1: Raceways, cable trays, cable armor, boxes, cable sheathing, cabinets, enclosures, elbows, couplings, fittings, supports, and support hardware must be suitable for the environment. See 300.6. ▶Figure 110–24

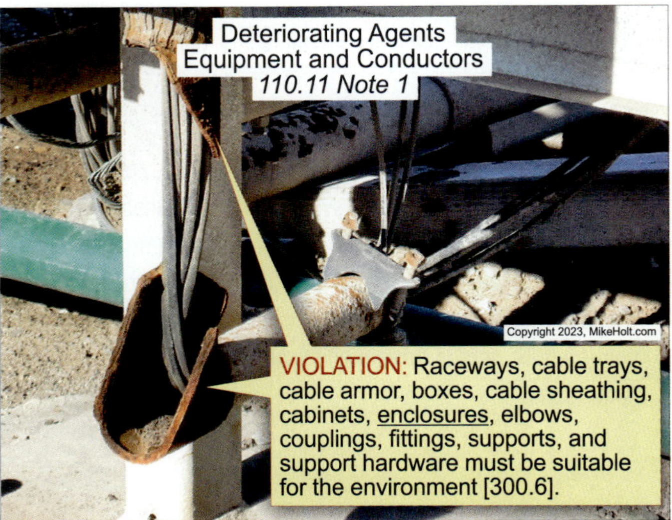

▶Figure 110–24

Note 2: Some cleaning and lubricating compounds contain chemicals that can cause plastic to deteriorate.

Note 3: For NEMA enclosure-type designations, see Table 110.28.

Note 4: For minimum flood provisions, see the *International Building Code* (IBC) and the *International Residential Code* (IRC).

110.12 Mechanical Execution of Work

Electrical equipment must be installed in a professional and skillful manner. ▶Figure 110–25

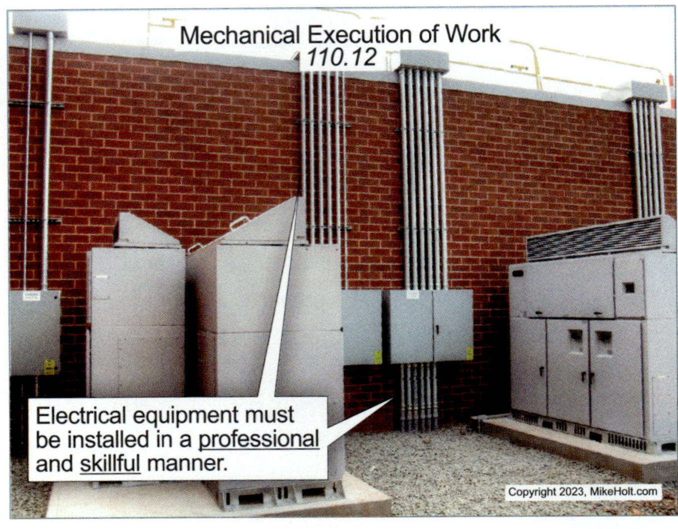

▶Figure 110–25

Note: For information on accepted industry practices, see ANSI/NECA 1, *Standard for Good Workmanship in Electrical Construction*, and other ANSI-approved installation standards. ▶Figure 110–26

Author's Comment:

▶ This rule is perhaps one of the most subjective of the entire *Code,* and its application is still ultimately a judgment call made by the authority having jurisdiction.

(A) Unused Openings. Unused openings (other than those used for mounting equipment or the operation of equipment), must be closed by fittings that provide protection substantially equivalent to the wall of the equipment. Unused openings that are intended for mounting the equipment are not required to be closed. ▶Figure 110–27

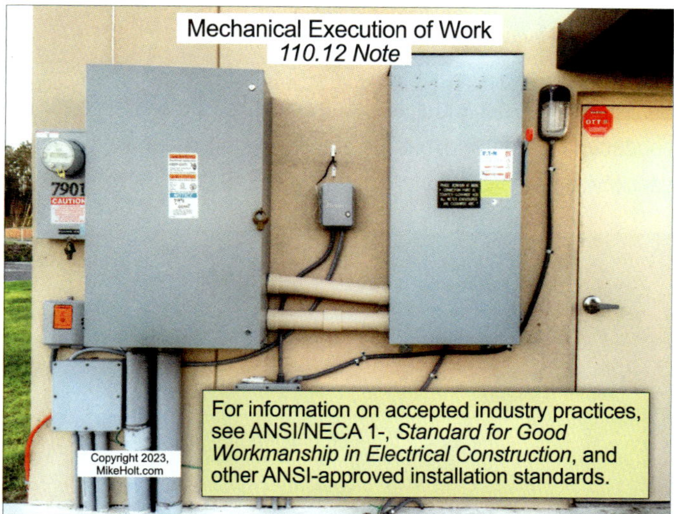

▶Figure 110–26

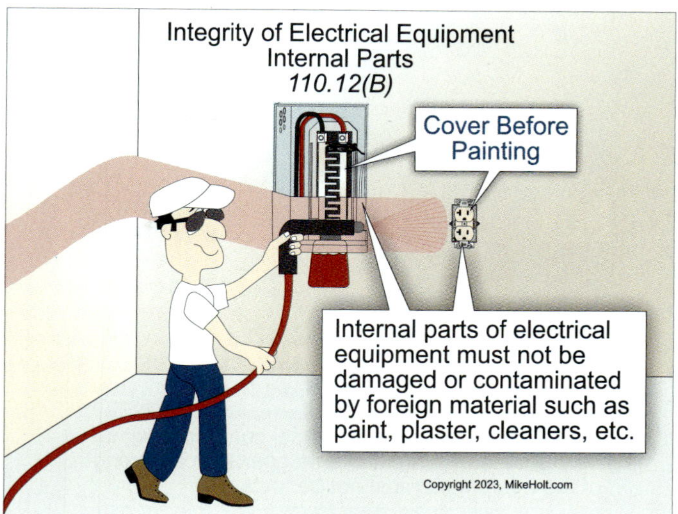

▶Figure 110–28

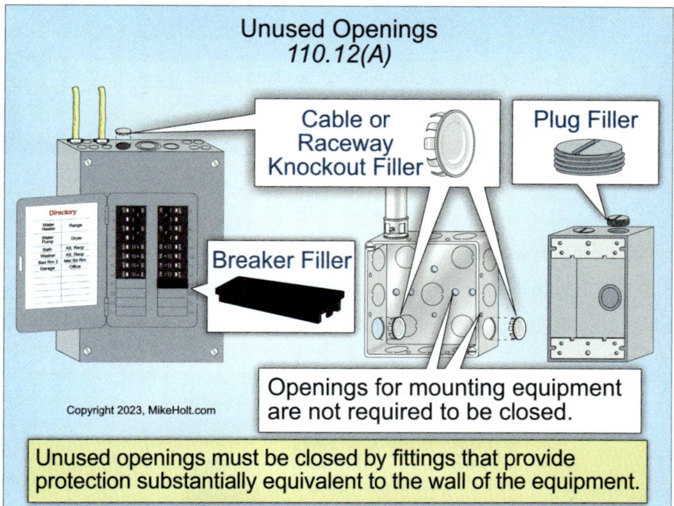

▶Figure 110–27

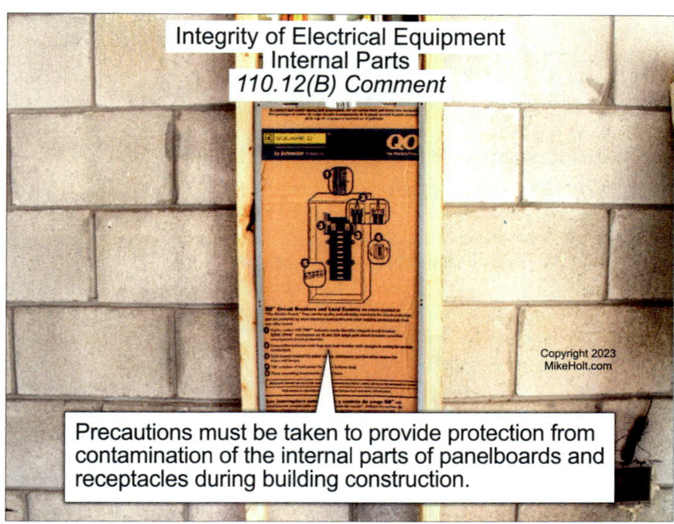

▶Figure 110–29

(B) Integrity of Electrical Equipment. Internal parts of electrical equipment must not be damaged or contaminated by foreign material such as paint, plaster, cleaners, and so forth. ▶Figure 110–28

Author's Comment:

▶ Precautions must be taken to provide protection from the contamination of internal parts of panelboards and receptacles during building construction. Be sure the electrical equipment is properly masked and protected before drywall, painting, or other phases of the project that can contaminate or cause damage begins. ▶Figure 110–29

Electrical equipment containing damaged parts (such as items broken, bent, or cut), or those that have been deteriorated by corrosion, chemical action, or overheating are not permitted to be installed. ▶Figure 110–30

Author's Comment:

▶ Damaged parts include cracked insulators, arc shields not in place, overheated fuse clips, and damaged or missing switch handles or circuit-breaker handles.

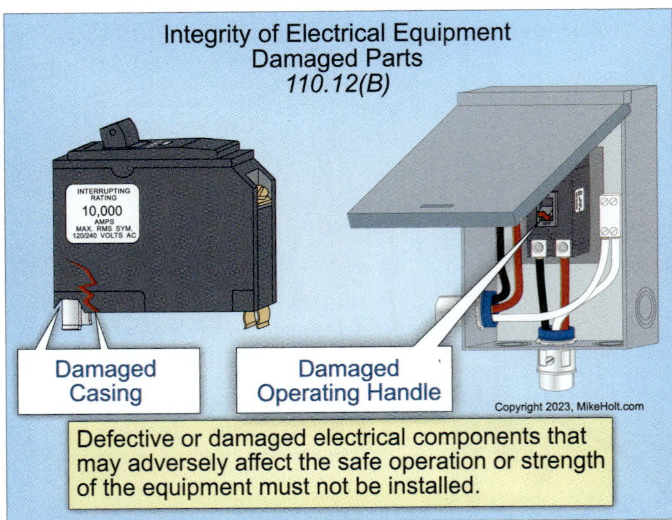

▶Figure 110–30

110.13 Mounting and Cooling of Equipment

(A) Mounting. Electrical equipment must be firmly secured to the surface on which it is mounted. ▶Figure 110–31

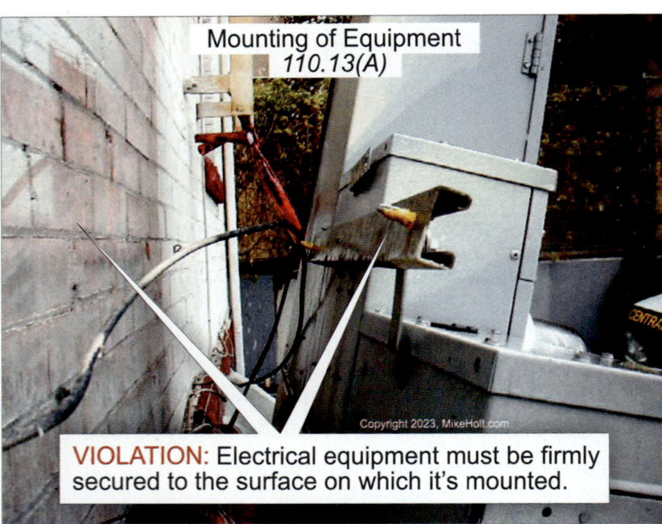

▶Figure 110–31

(B) Cooling. Electrical equipment that depends on heat dissipation must be installed in air-conditioned spaces, or if equipped with a ventilating opening, must maintain proper clearance to dissipate rising warm air.

110.14 Conductor Termination and Splicing

Conductor terminal and splicing devices must be identified for the conductor material and must be properly installed and used in accordance with the manufacturer's instructions [110.3(B)]. ▶Figure 110–32

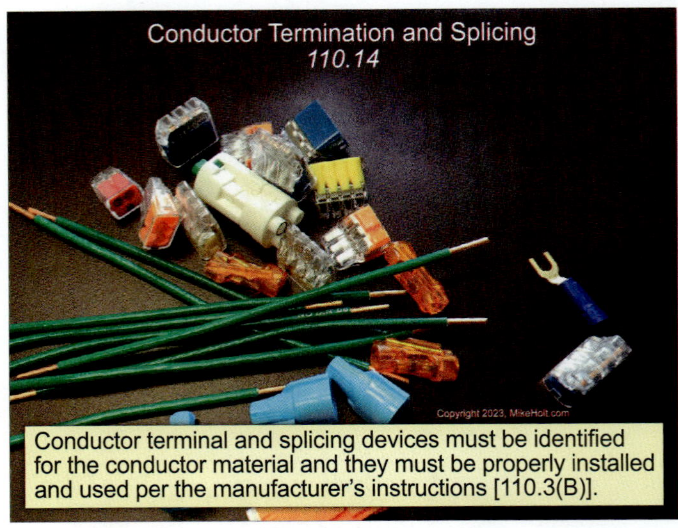

▶Figure 110–32

Conductors of dissimilar materials are not permitted in a terminal or splicing device where contact occurs between dissimilar conductors—unless identified for the purpose and conditions of use. ▶Figure 110–33

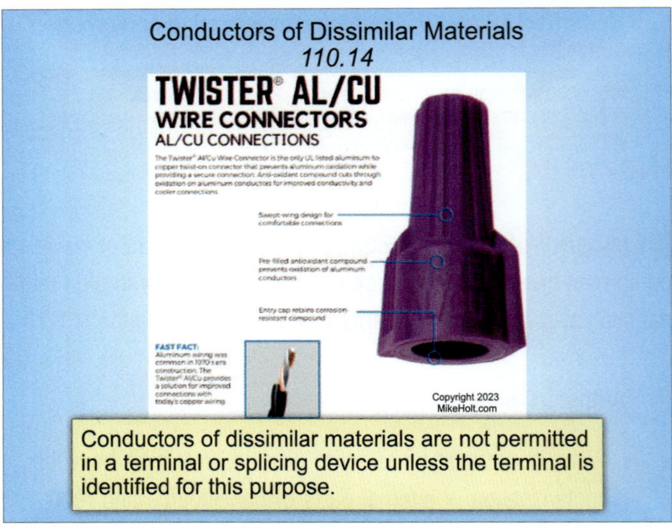

▶Figure 110–33

According to Article 100, "Identified" means recognized as suitable for a specific purpose, function, use, environment, or application. ▶Figure 110–34

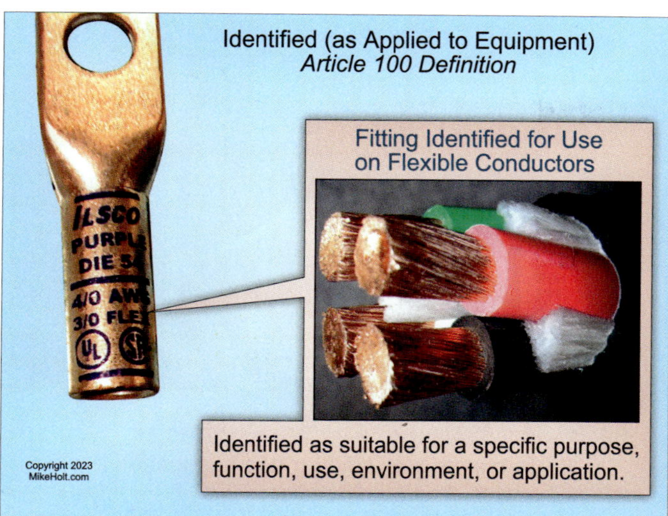

▶Figure 110–34

Author's Comment:

▶ Conductor terminals suitable for aluminum wire only will be marked "AL." Those acceptable for copper wire will be marked "CU." Terminals suitable for copper, copper-clad-aluminum, and aluminum conductors will be marked "CU-AL" or "AL-CU." For 6 AWG and smaller, the markings can be printed on the container or on an information sheet inside the container. A "7" or "75" indicates a 75°C rated terminal, and a "9" or "90" indicates a 90°C rated terminal. If a terminal bears no marking, it can be used only with copper conductors.
▶Figure 110–35

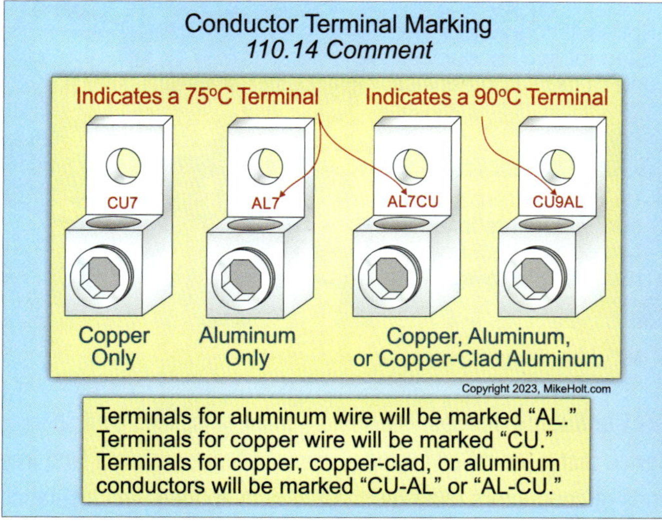

▶Figure 110–35

▶ Aluminum wire that was installed prior to the 1972 was the same wire used for utility power transmission lines. This aluminum wire had a major problem with oxidation at terminations and it required an antioxidant at terminations. When the antioxidant was not properly applied to the wire termination, fires were common at the termination. Since 1983, the *National Electrical Code* [310.3(B)] has required aluminum wire to be made from an aluminum alloy (AA-8000). This conductor does not require an antioxidant at terminations.
▶Figure 110–36

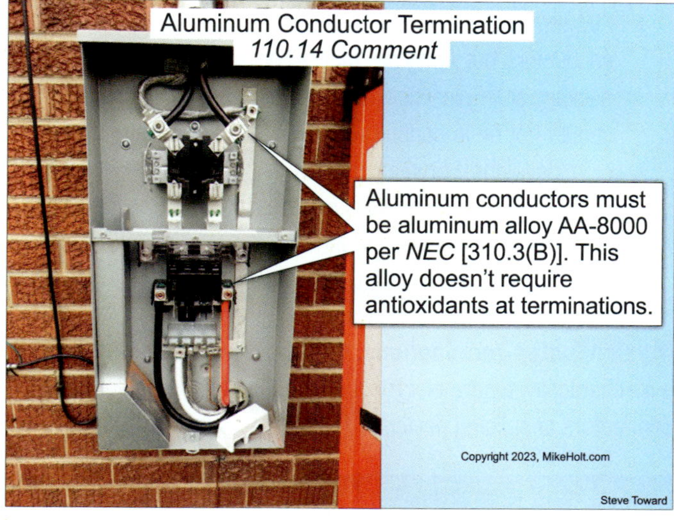

▶Figure 110–36

Connectors and terminals for conductors more finely stranded than Class B and Class C must be identified for the use of finely stranded conductors. ▶Figure 110–37

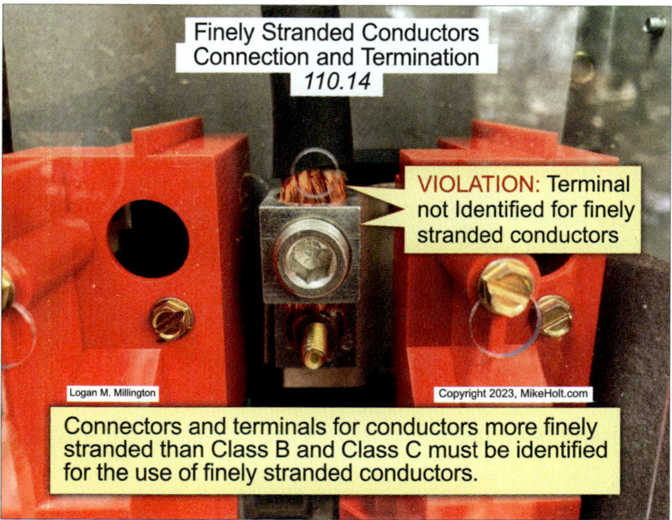

▶Figure 110–37

Author's Comment:

▸ Conductor terminations must comply with the manufacturer's instructions as required by 110.3(B). For example, if the instructions for the device are written, "Suitable for 18–12 AWG Stranded," then only stranded conductors can be used with the terminating device. If they are written, "Suitable for 18–12 AWG Solid," then only solid conductors are permitted, and if the instructions are written, "Suitable for 18–12 AWG," then either solid or stranded conductors can be used with the terminating device.

▸ Few terminations are listed for mixing aluminum and copper conductors, but if they are, that will be marked on the product package or terminal device. The reason copper and aluminum should not be in contact with each other is because corrosion develops between the two different metals due to galvanic action. This results in increased contact resistance at the splicing device, and increased resistance can cause the splice to overheat and result in a fire.

(A) Conductor Terminations. Conductor terminals must ensure a mechanically secure electrical connection by the use of pressure connectors or splicing devices. ▸Figure 110–38

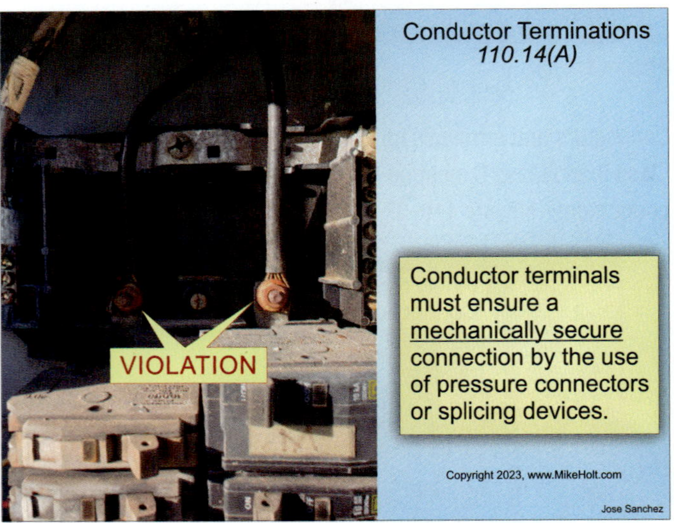

▸Figure 110–38

Terminals are only listed for one conductor, unless marked otherwise. Terminals for more than one conductor must be identified for this purpose, either within the equipment instructions or on the terminal itself. ▸Figure 110–39

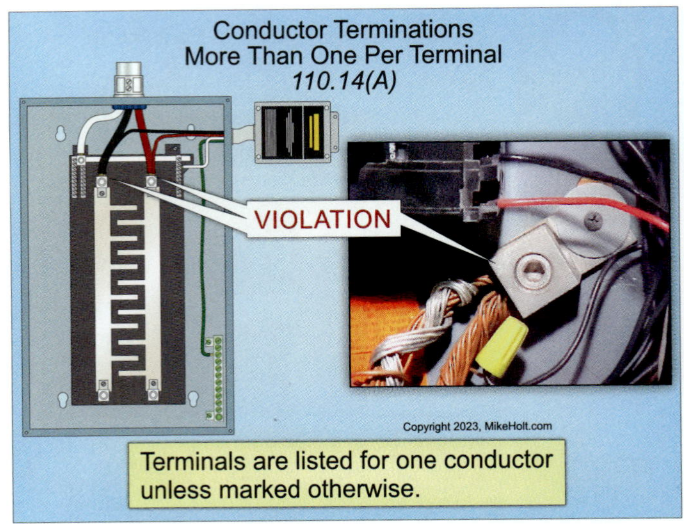

▸Figure 110–39

Author's Comment:

▸ Split-bolt connectors are commonly listed for only two conductors, although some are listed for three. However, it is a common industry practice to terminate as many conductors as possible within a split-bolt connector, even though this violates the *NEC*. ▸Figure 110–40

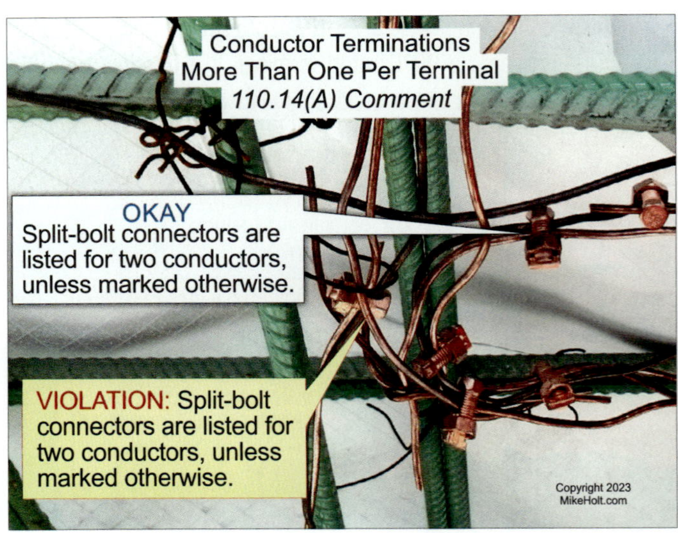

▸Figure 110–40

(B) Conductor Splices. Conductors must be spliced by a splicing device that is identified for the purpose. All splices, joints, and free ends of conductors must be covered with an identified insulating device. ▸Figure 110–41

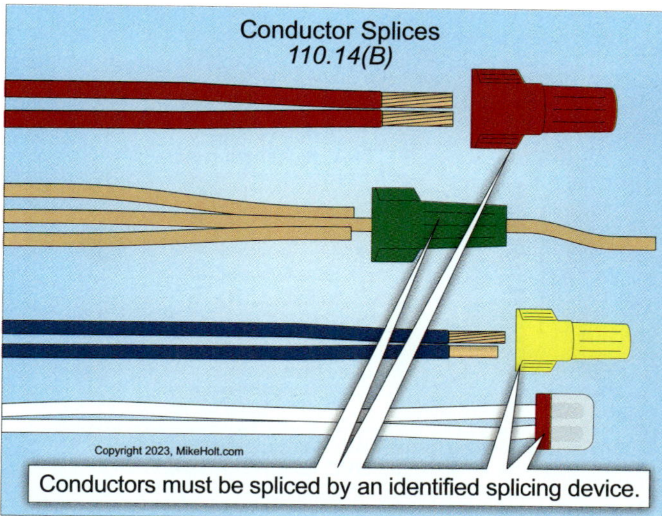

▶Figure 110–41

Author's Comment:

▶ To prevent an electrical hazard, the free ends of conductors must be insulated to prevent the exposed end(s) from touching energized parts. This requirement can be met by using an insulated twist-on or push-on wire connector. ▶**Figure 110–42**

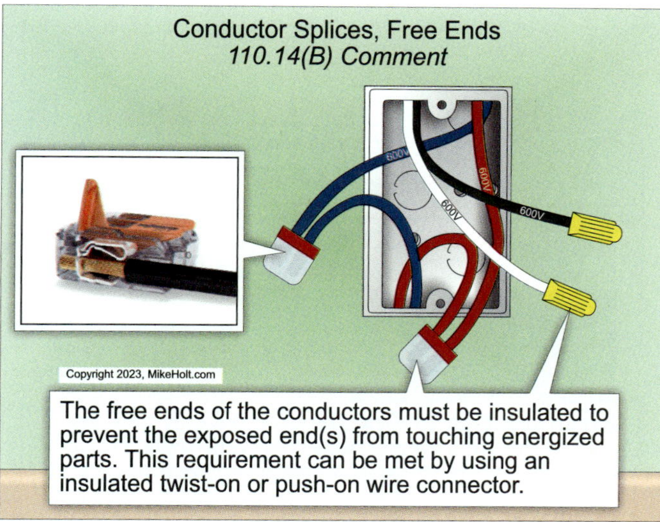

▶Figure 110–42

▶ Pre-twisting conductors before applying twist-on wire connectors has been a very common practice in the field for years. The question (and subsequent debate) has always been, "Is pre-twisting required?" The *NEC* does not require that practice and, in fact, Ideal® made a statement about their Wing-Nut® twist-on connectors which said, "Pre-twisting is acceptable, but not required." Always follow the manufacturer's instructions and there will be no question [110.3(B)]. ▶**Figure 110–43**

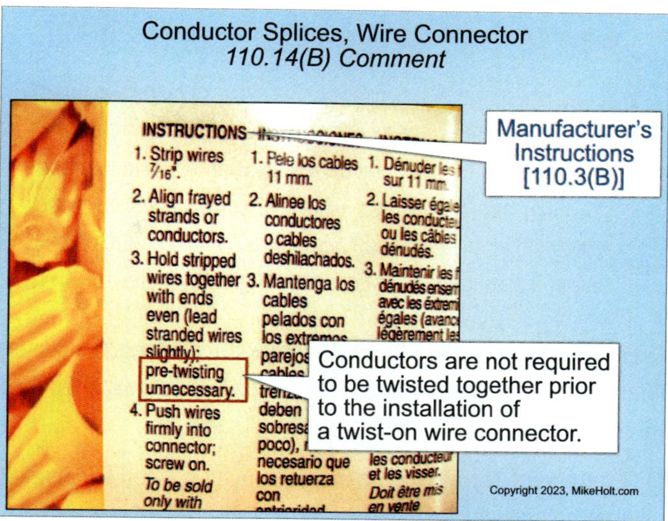

▶Figure 110–43

Single direct burial types UF or USE conductors can be spliced underground with a device listed for direct burial [300.5(E) and 300.15(G)]. ▶Figure 110–44

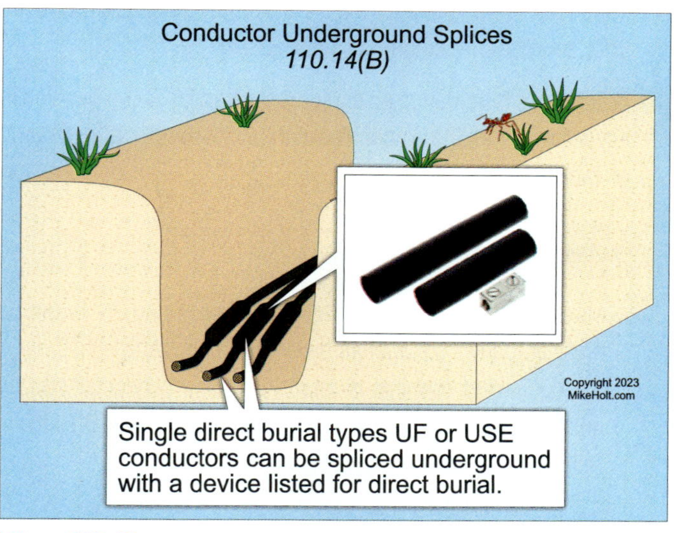

▶Figure 110–44

The individual conductors of multiconductor UF or USE cable can be spliced underground with an underground listed splice kit that encapsulates the conductors and cable jacket.

(C) Conductor Sized to Terminal Temperature Rating. Conductors terminating on equipment must be sized to the lowest terminal temperature rating in accordance with 110.14(C)(1) and (2).

(1) Equipment Terminals. Unless equipment is listed and marked otherwise, conductors are sized based on Table 310.16 in accordance with (a) or (b) as follows:

(a) Equipment Rated 100A or Less. Conductors terminating on equipment for circuits rated 100A or less, or conductors smaller than 1 AWG, must be sized as follows:

(2) Conductors rated 90°C can be used but they must be sized to the 60°C temperature column of Table 310.16.

(3) Conductors terminating on equipment rated 75°C can be sized in accordance with the ampacities in the 75°C temperature column of Table 310.16.

▶ **Example 1**

Question: *According to Table 310.16, what size THWN-2 conductor is required for a 50A circuit where the equipment is rated for 75°C conductors?* ▶Figure 110–45

(a) 10 AWG   (b) 8 AWG   (c) 6 AWG   (d) 4 AWG

Answer: *(b) 8 AWG rated 50A at 75°C [110.14(C)(1)(a)(3) and Table 310.16]*

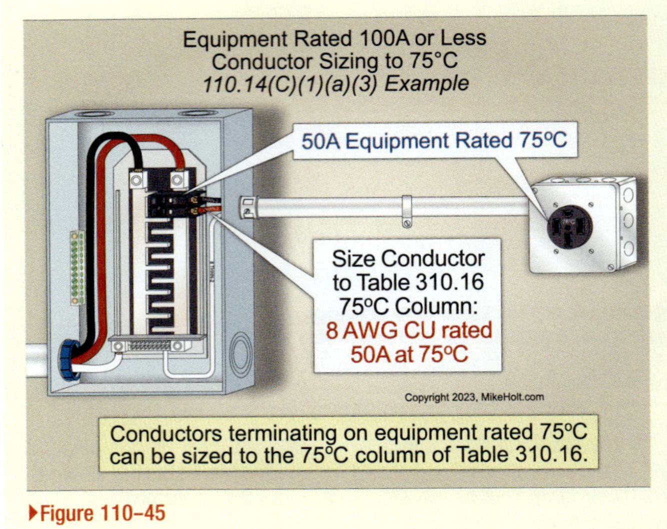

▶Figure 110–45

(b) Equipment Rated Over 100A. Conductors terminating on equipment for circuits rated over 100A, or conductors larger than 1 AWG, must be sized as follows:

(2) Conductors rated 90°C can be used but they must be sized to the 75°C temperature column of Table 310.16. ▶Figure 110–46

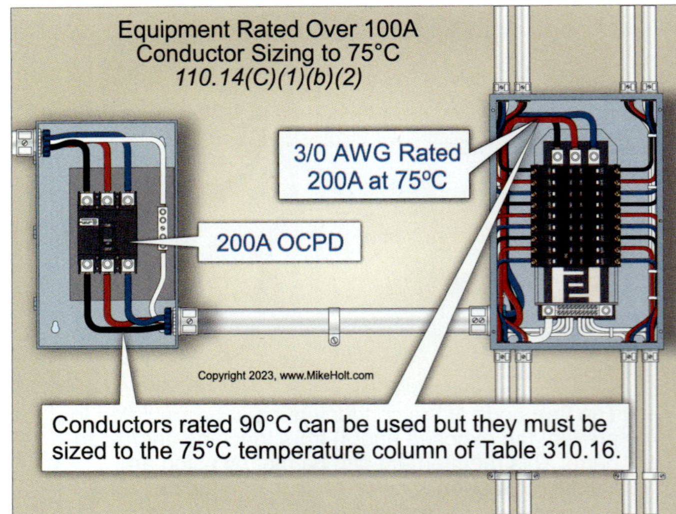

▶Figure 110–46

▶ Example 2

Question: *According to Table 310.16, what size aluminum conductor is required to supply a 200A feeder?* ▶**Figure 110–47**

(a) 2/0 AWG   (b) 3/0 AWG   (c) 4/0 AWG   (d) 250 kcmil

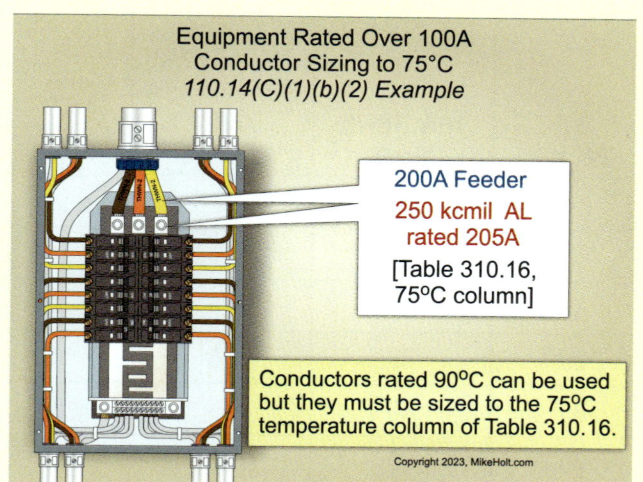

▶Figure 110–47

Answer: *(d) 250 kcmil rated 205A at 75°C [110.14(C)(1)(b)(2) and Table 310.16]*

(2) Separate Connector. Separately installed pressure connectors rated 90°C or more and not connected to electrical equipment, can have the conductors sized in accordance with the 90°C temperature column ampacities of Table 310.16. ▶**Figure 110–48**

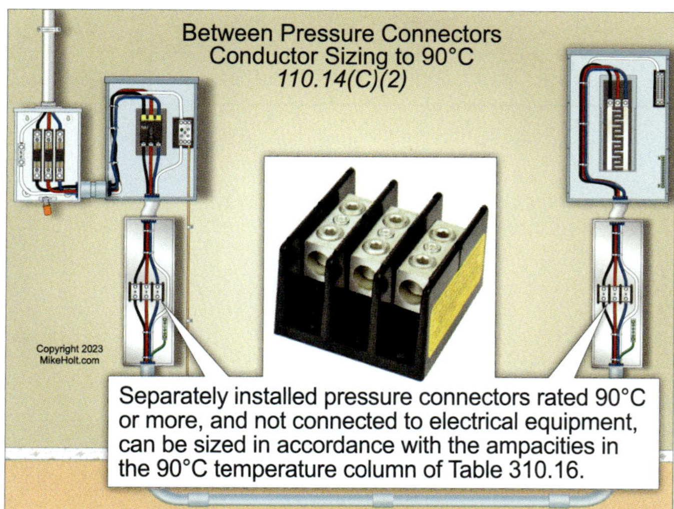

▶Figure 110–48

▶ Example 3

Question: *According to Table 310.16, what size aluminum conductor can be used to interconnect busbars protected by a 200A overcurrent protective device where the equipment is rated for 90°C conductors?*

(a) 1/0 AWG   (b) 2/0 AWG   (c) 3/0 AWG   (d) 4/0 AWG

Answer: *(d) 4/0 AWG aluminum rated 205A at 90°C [110.14(C)(2) and Table 310.16]*

(D) Torquing of Terminal Connections. Tightening torque values for terminal connections must be as indicated on equipment or instructions. The tool or device used to achieve torque values must be approved by the authority having jurisdiction. ▶Figure 110–49

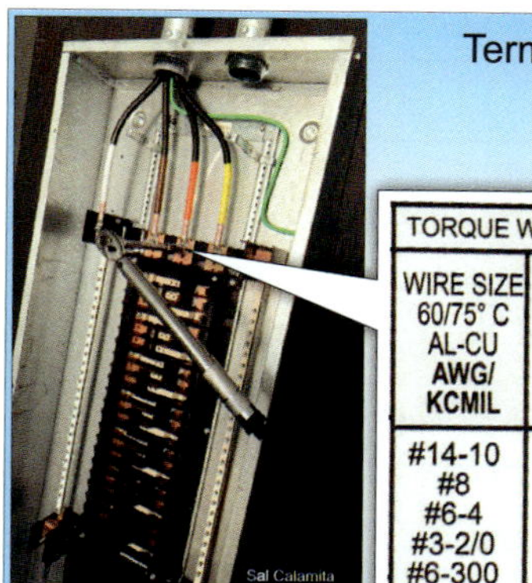

Terminal Connection Torque
110.14(D)

Copyright 2023, MikeHolt.com

TORQUE WIRE PRESSURE SCREW(S) AS FOLLOWS:			
WIRE SIZE 60/75° C AL-CU AWG/ KCMIL	NEUTRAL & GROUND BAR	GROUND LUG (G1) & NEUTRAL LUG (N2)	PANEL LUGS (A & B) & MAIN NEUTRAL (N1)
	LB-IN	LB-IN	LB-IN
#14-10	20	-	-
#8	25	-	-
#6-4	35	60	60
#3-2/0	-	60	60
#6-300	-	-	-

Tightening torque values for terminal connections must be as indicated on equipment or installation instructions. An approved means must be used to achieve the indicated torque value.

▶Figure 110–49

Author's Comment:

▶ Conductors must terminate on device and equipment terminals that have been properly tightened in accordance with the manufacturer's torque specifications included with equipment instructions. Failure to torque terminals properly can result in excessive heating of terminals or splicing devices due to a loose connection. A loose connection can also lead to a glowing arc which increases the heating of the terminal and may ultimately cause a short circuit or ground fault. Any of these can result in a fire or other failure, including an arc flash event. ▶Figure 110–50 and ▶Figure 110–51

Size	60°C (140°F)	75°C (167°F)	90°C (194°F)	60°C (140°F)	75°C (167°F)	90°C (194°F)	Size
	TW, UF	RHW, THHW THW, THWN XHHW, USE	RHH, RHW-2 THHN, THHW THW-2, THWN-2 USE-2, XHHW XHHW-2	TW, UF	THW, THWN XHHW	THHN, THW-2 THWN-2, THHW XHHW, XHHW-2	
AWG kcmil	Copper			Aluminum/Copper-Clad Aluminum			**AWG kcmil**
14	15	20	25				14
12	20	25	30	15	20	25	12
10	30	35	40	25	30	35	10
8	40	50	55	35	40	45	8
6	55	65	75	40	50	55	6
4	70	85	95	55	65	75	4
3	85	100	115	65	75	85	3
2	95	115	130	75	90	100	2
1	110	130	145	85	100	115	1
1/0	125	150	170	100	120	135	1/0
2/0	145	175	195	115	135	150	2/0
3/0	165	200	225	130	155	175	3/0
4/0	195	230	260	150	180	205	4/0
250	215	255	290	170	205	230	250

Table 310.16 Ampacities of Insulated Conductors Based on Not More Than Three Current-Carrying Conductors and Ambient Temperature of 30°C (86°F)

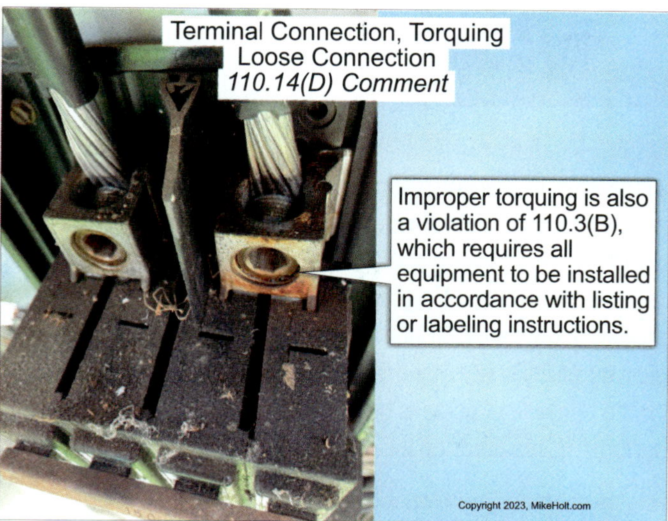

▶Figure 110–50

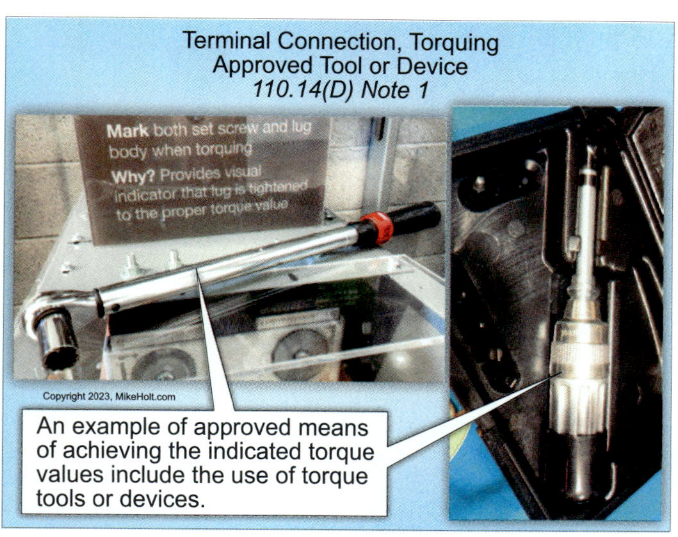

▶Figure 110–52

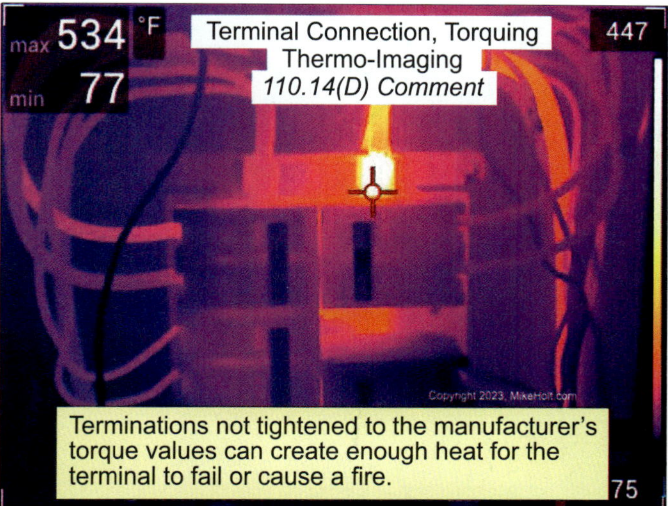

▶Figure 110–51

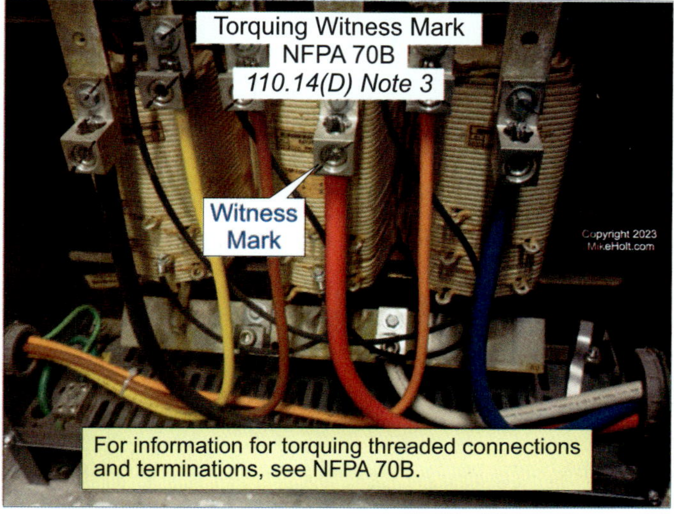

▶Figure 110–53

Note 1: Examples of approved means of achieving the indicated torque values include the use of torque tools or devices (such as shear bolts or breakaway-style devices) with visual indicators that demonstrate the proper torque has been applied. ▶Figure 110–52

Note 2: In the absence of manufacturer's torque requirements, see Annex I or UL Standard 486A-486B, *Standard for Safety-Wire Connectors,* for torque values. The equipment manufacturer can be contacted if numeric torque values are not indicated on the equipment or the instructions are not available.

Note 3: For information for torquing threaded connections and terminations, see NFPA 70B, *Recommended Practice for Electrical Equipment Maintenance*, Section 8.11. ▶Figure 110–53

110.15 High-Leg Conductor Identification

On a 4-wire, delta-connected, three-phase system (where the midpoint of one phase winding of the secondary is grounded) the conductor with the resulting 208V to ground (high-leg) must be durably and permanently marked by an outer finish (insulation) that is orange in color or other effective means. Such identification must be placed at each point where a connection is made if the neutral conductor is present. ▶Figure 110–54 and ▶Figure 110–55

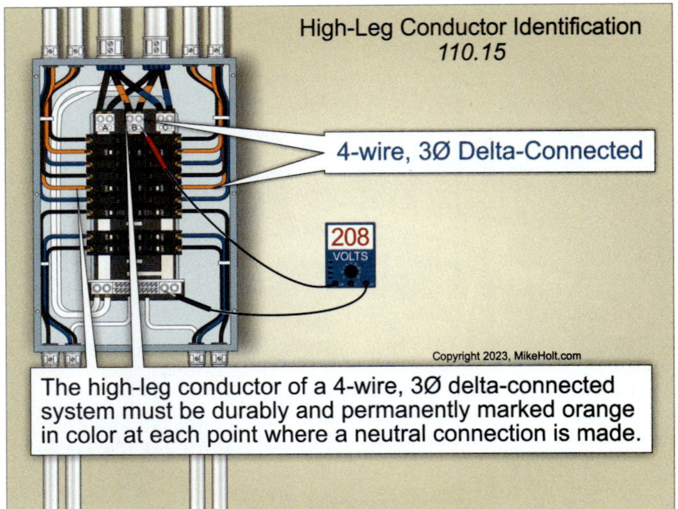

▶Figure 110–54

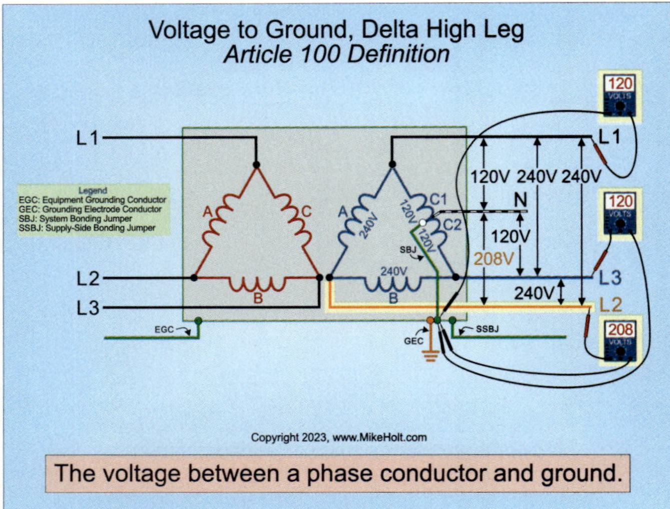

▶Figure 110–55

Author's Comment:

▸ The high-leg conductor is also called the "wild leg" or "stinger leg." In panelboards, the B phase busbar must be the high-leg [408.3(E)(1)], and the panelboard itself must be identified "Caution B Phase has 208V-to-Ground" [408.3(F)(1)].

110.16 Arc-Flash Hazard Warning Label, Other Than Dwelling Units

(A) Arc-Flash Hazard Warning Label. In other than dwelling units, a label must be placed on switchboards, switchgear, enclosed panelboards, industrial control panels, meter socket enclosures, and motor control centers to warn qualified persons of the danger associated with an arc flash resulting from a short circuit or ground fault. The arc-flash hazard warning label must be permanently affixed, have sufficient durability to withstand the environment [110.21(B)], and clearly visible to qualified persons before they examine, adjust, service, or perform maintenance on the equipment. ▶Figure 110–56

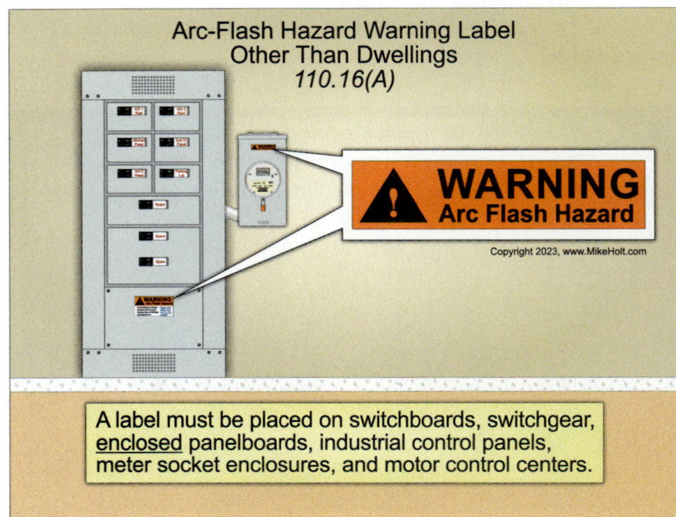

▶Figure 110–56

According to Article 100, "Qualified Person" is one who has the skill and knowledge related to the construction and operation of electrical equipment and its installation. This person must have received safety training to recognize and avoid the hazards involved with electrical systems. ▶Figure 110–57

Author's Comment:

▸ NFPA 70E, *Standard for Electrical Safety in the Workplace*, provides information on the safety training requirements expected of a "qualified person." Examples of this safety training include training in the use of special precautionary techniques, personal protective equipment (PPE), insulating and shielding materials, and insulated tools and test equipment when working on or near exposed conductors or circuit parts that can become energized. ▶Figure 110–58

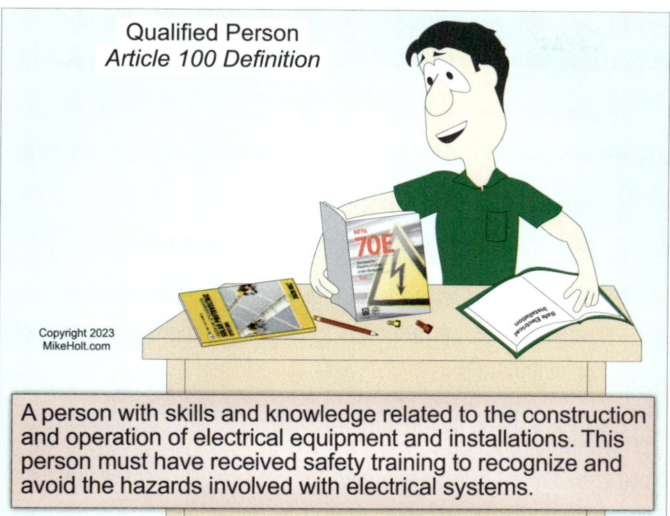

▶Figure 110–57

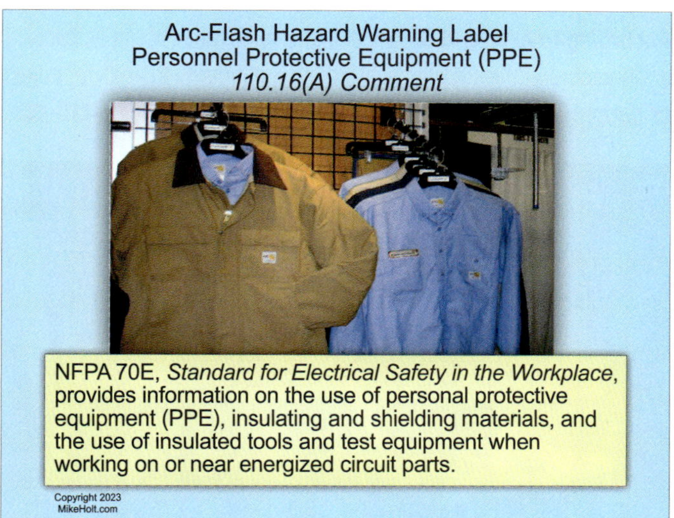

▶Figure 110–58

▸ In many parts of the United States, electricians, electrical contractors, electrical inspectors, and electrical engineers must complete from 6 to 24 hours of *NEC* review each year as a requirement to maintain licensing. This does not necessarily make one qualified to deal with the specific hazards involved with electrical systems.

(B) Service and Feeder Equipment. In other than dwelling units, service and feeder equipment rated 1000A or more must have an arc-flash label in accordance with applicable industry practices that includes the date the label was applied and have sufficient durability to withstand the environment. ▶Figure 110–59

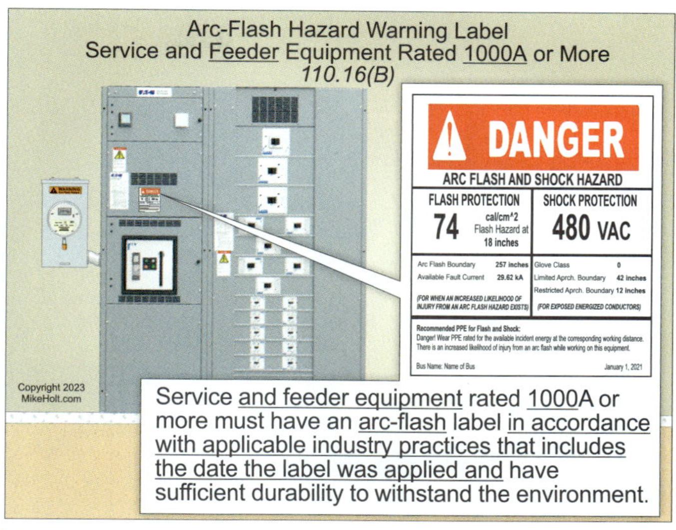

▶Figure 110–59

Author's Comment:

▸ Determining the available fault current on the line side of service or feeder equipment terminals requires you to know the available fault current at the secondary of the utility transformer (provided by the electric utility), conductor material, length of the conductors, and wiring method used to install conductors. With this information, you can use an app or computer software to determine the available fault current at the line terminals of service or feeder equipment.

▸ An arc-flash event can reach temperatures of 35,000°F, which turns metal from a solid to gas vapors, and releases molten shrapnel that pierces the skin causing severe burns—and even death. The reason the arc-flash label is not required in dwelling units is the nominal voltage will be single-phase, 120V line-to-ground (240V line-to-line), so the arc fault will self-extinguish with every zero crossing of the sinusoidal waveform. A three-phase arc fault is sustainable in accordance with IEEE-1584.

Note 2: NFPA 70E, *Standard for Electrical Safety in the Workplace*, provides applicable industry practices for developing arc-flash labels that include nominal system voltage, incident energy levels, arc-flash boundaries, and selecting personal protective equipment. ▶Figure 110–60

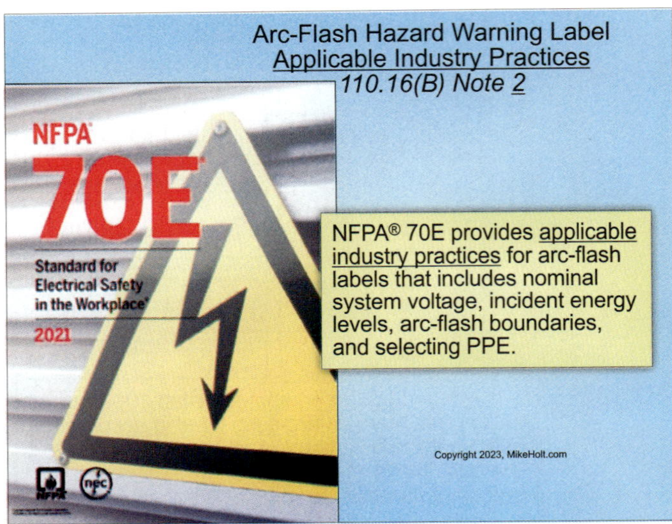

▶Figure 110–60

Author's Comment:

▸ The information required by 110.16(B) is necessary to determine the incident energy and arc-flash boundary distance by using an app or computer software to ensure the label complies with NFPA 70E, *Standard for Electrical Safety in the Workplace*, to increase safety during future work on service and feeder equipment.

110.17 Servicing and Maintenance of Equipment

Equipment servicing and maintenance is required to be performed by a qualified person trained in the servicing and maintenance of equipment and comply with the following: ▶Figure 110–61

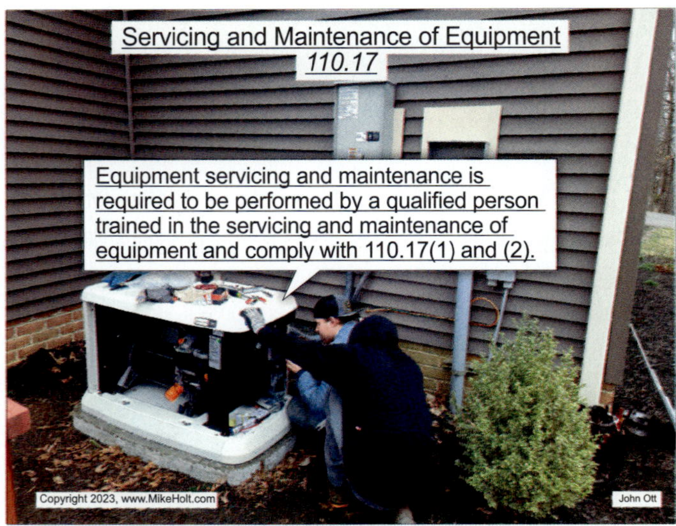

▶Figure 110–61

(1) Standards. Servicing and maintenance must be performed in accordance with the equipment manufacturer's instructions, applicable industry standards, or as approved by the authority having jurisdiction.

(2) Replacement Parts. Servicing and maintenance replacement parts must:

a. Be provided by the original equipment manufacturer.

b. Be designed by an engineer experienced in the design of replacement parts for the type of equipment being serviced or maintained.

c. Be approved by the authority having jurisdiction.

Note 2: See NFPA 70B, *Recommended Practice for Electrical Equipment Maintenance*, for information related to preventive maintenance for electrical equipment.

According to Article 100, "Servicing" means the process of following a manufacturer's instructions or industry standards to analyze, adjust, or perform maintenance and repair of equipment. ▶Figure 110–62

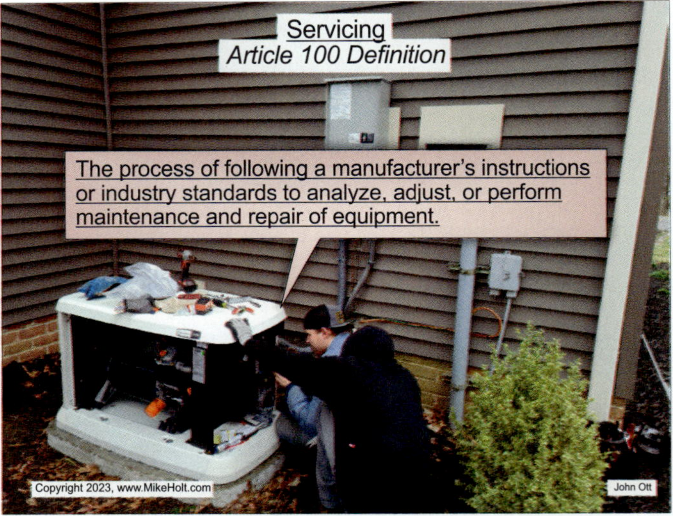

▶Figure 110–62

110.20 Reconditioned Equipment

Equipment that is restored to operating condition must be reconditioned with identified replacement parts and verified under applicable standards. These parts are either provided by the original equipment manufacturer or are designed by an engineer experienced in the design of replacement parts for the type of equipment being reconditioned.

(A) Equipment Required to Be Listed. Equipment that is reconditioned and required by this *Code* to be listed, must be listed or field labeled as "reconditioned" using available instructions from the original equipment manufacturer.

(B) Equipment Not Required to Be Listed. Equipment that is reconditioned and not required by this *Code* to be listed, must comply with one of the following:

(1) Be listed or field labeled as "reconditioned."

(2) Have the reconditioning performed in accordance with the original equipment manufacturer's instructions.

(C) Approved Equipment. If the options specified in 110.20(A) or (B) are not available, the authority having jurisdiction can approve reconditioned equipment. The reconditioner must provide the authority having jurisdiction with documentation of the changes to the product.

110.21 Hazard Markings

(B) Field-Applied Hazard Markings. Where caution, warning, or danger hazard markings are required, the markings must meet the following requirements:

(1) Field-applied hazard markings must be of sufficient durability to withstand the environment and warn of the hazards using effective words, colors, symbols, or a combination of the three. ▶Figure 110–63

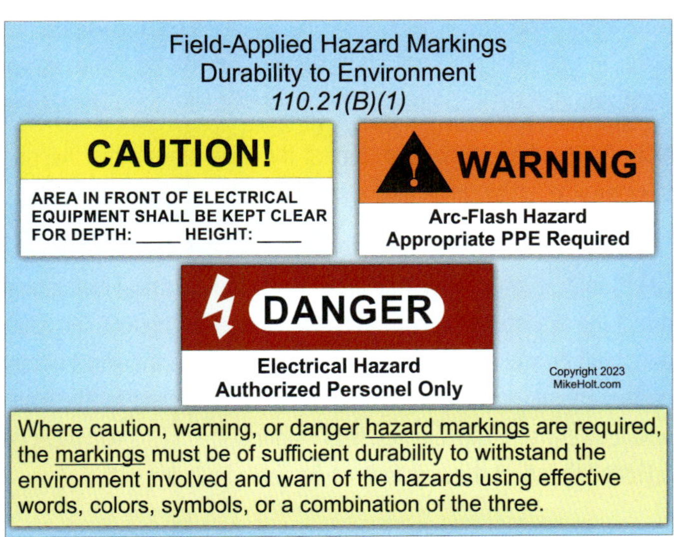

▶Figure 110–63

Note: ANSI Z535.4, *Product Safety Signs and Labels,* provides guidelines for the design and durability of signs and labels.

(2) Field-applied hazard markings cannot be handwritten and must be permanently affixed to the equipment. ▶Figure 110–64

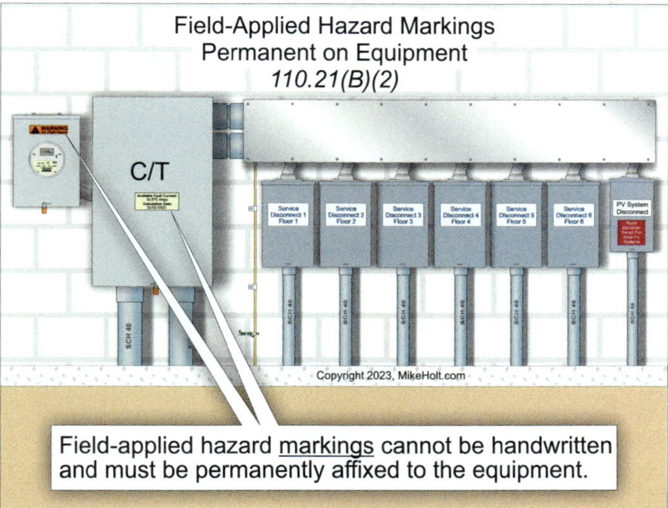

▶Figure 110–64

Ex: Markings containing information that is likely to change can be handwritten, if it is legible.

110.22 Identification of Disconnecting Means

(A) General. Each disconnect must be legibly marked to indicate its purpose unless located and arranged so the purpose is evident.

In other than one- or two-family dwelling units, the disconnect marking must include the identification and location of the circuit source that supplies the disconnect unless located and arranged so the identification and location of the circuit source is evident. The marking must be of sufficient durability to withstand the environment. ▶Figure 110–65

According to Article 100, "Disconnect" is a device that disconnects the circuit conductors from their power source. ▶Figure 110–66

Author's Comment:

▶ See 408.4 for additional requirements for identification markings on circuit directories for switchboards and panelboards.

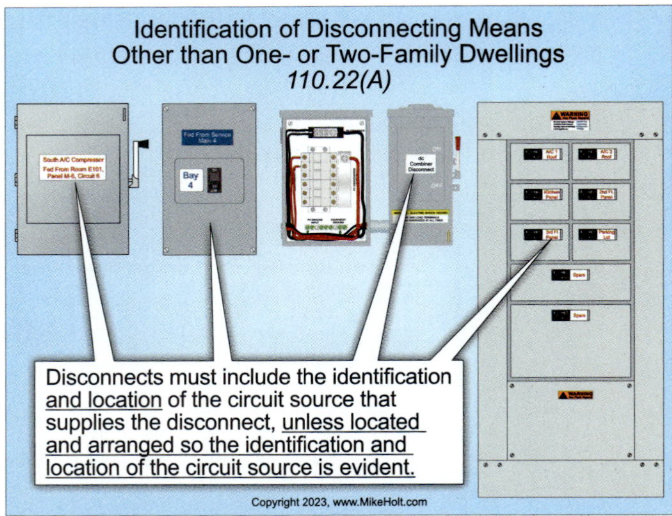

▶Figure 110–65

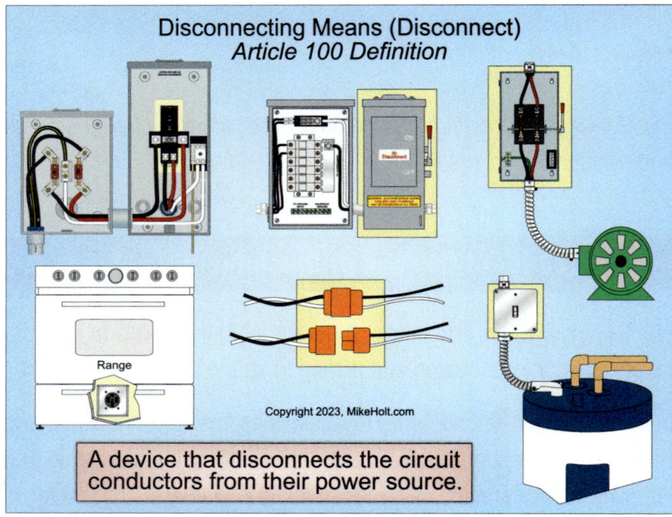

▶Figure 110–66

(C) Tested Series Combination Systems. Tested series-rated installations must be legibly field marked to indicate the equipment has been applied with a series combination rating in accordance with 240.86(B). The marking must be permanently affixed, have sufficient durability to withstand the environment in accordance with 110.21(B), and state:

CAUTION—SERIES COMBINATION SYSTEM RATED _____ AMPERES. IDENTIFIED REPLACEMENT COMPONENTS REQUIRED

(A) Field Marking. In other than dwelling units, service disconnects must be field marked with the available fault current on the line side of the service disconnect, the date the fault current calculation was performed, and must be of sufficient durability to withstand the environment. ▶Figure 110–67

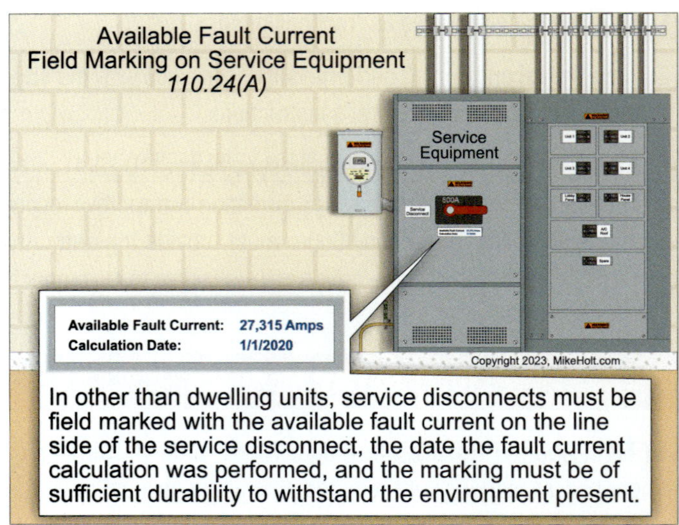

▶Figure 110–67

The available fault current calculation must be documented and available to those who are authorized to design, install, inspect, maintain, or operate the system.

Note 1: For assistance in determining the severity of potential exposures, planning safe work practices, and selecting personal protective equipment, see NFPA 70E, *Standard for Electrical Safety in the Workplace*.

Note 2: The available fault current at the utility transformer needed to determine the available fault current at service equipment must be acquired from the electric utility. ▶Figure 110–68

(B) Modifications. When modifications to the electrical installation affect the available fault current at the service disconnect, the available fault current must be recalculated to ensure the short-circuit current ratings at the service disconnect are sufficient for the available fault current. The required field marking(s) in 110.24(A) must be adjusted to reflect the new level of available fault current.

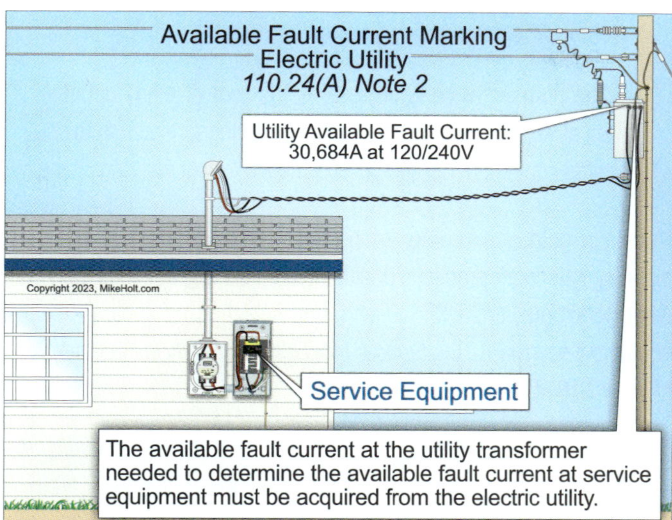

▶Figure 110–68

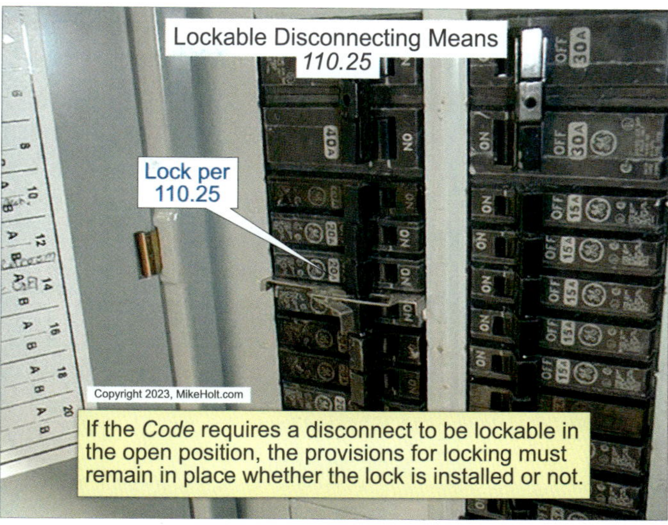

▶Figure 110–69

Author's Comment:

▶ It is common for electrical systems to be modified to accommodate growth. When the capacity of the system increases, either equipment is installed to increase efficiency or alternative energy systems are added. These factors can influence the available fault current if the utility transformer is changed. This increase in available fault current could end up exceeding the short-circuit current ratings of equipment in violation of 110.9 and 110.10.

110.25 Lockable Disconnecting Means

If the *Code* requires a disconnect to be lockable in the open position, the provisions for locking must remain in place whether the lock is installed or not. ▶Figure 110–69 and ▶Figure 110–70

Part II. 1000V, Nominal, or Less

110.26 Spaces Around Electrical Equipment

Working space, access to and egress from working space, must be provided and maintained around equipment to permit safe operation and maintenance of equipment. ▶Figure 110–71

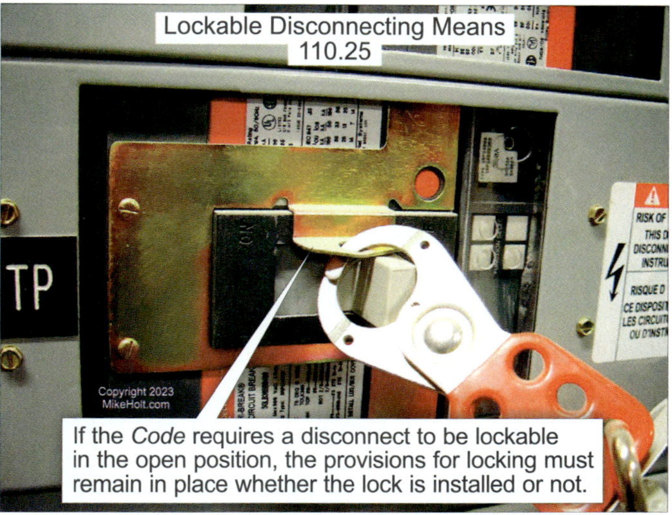

▶Figure 110–70

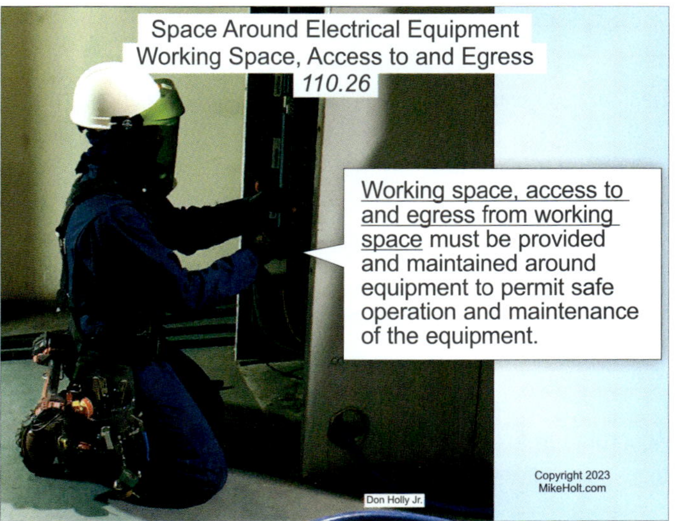

▶Figure 110–71

Open equipment doors must not impede access to and egress from the working space. Access or egress to working space is considered impeded if one or more simultaneously opened equipment doors restrict working space access to less than 24 in. wide and 6½ ft high.
▶Figure 110–72

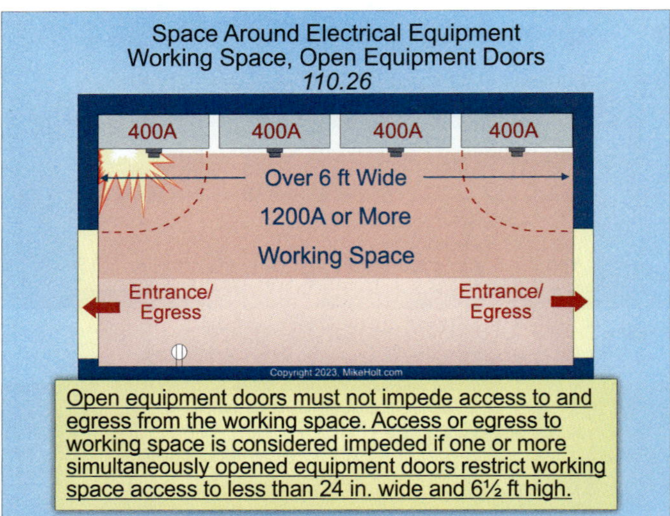

Open equipment doors must not impede access to and egress from the working space. Access or egress to working space is considered impeded if one or more simultaneously opened equipment doors restrict working space access to less than 24 in. wide and 6½ ft high.

▶Figure 110–72

(A) Working Space. Equipment that is likely to need examination, adjustment, servicing, or maintenance while energized must have working space provided in accordance with 110.26(A)(1), (2), (3), and (4):
▶Figure 110–73

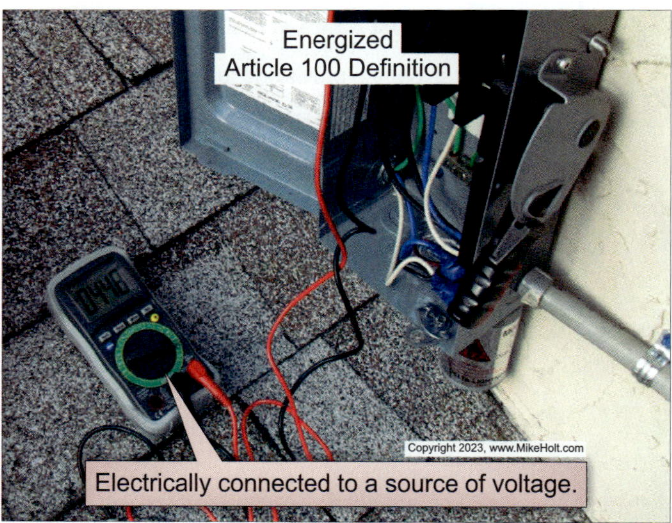

▶Figure 110–73

According to Article 100, "Energized" means electrically connected to a source of voltage.

▶ The phrase "while energized" is the root of many debates. As always, check with the authority having jurisdiction to see what equipment he/she believes needs a clear working space.

Note: For guidance in determining the severity of potential exposure, planning safe work practices (including establishing an electrically safe work condition), arc-flash labeling, and selecting personal protective equipment see NFPA 70E, *Standard for Electrical Safety in the Workplace*.
▶Figure 110–74

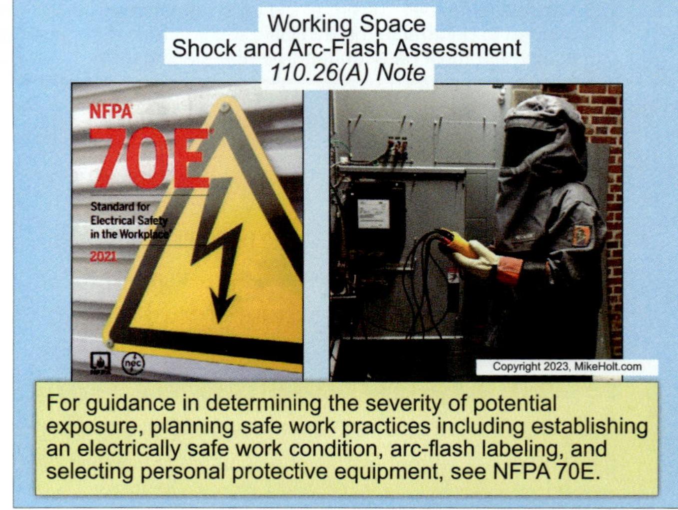

▶Figure 110–74

(1) Depth of Working Space. The depth of working space, which is measured from the enclosure front, cannot be less than the distances contained in Table 110.26(A)(1). These depths are dependent on the voltage-to-ground and three different conditions. ▶Figure 110–75

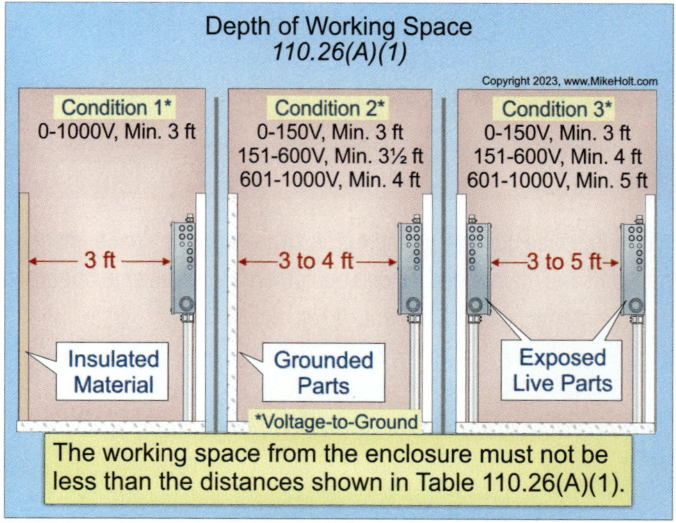

▶Figure 110–75

According to Article 100, "Voltage-to-Ground, Grounded Systems" is the voltage between any phase and neutral conductor. ▶Figure 110–76

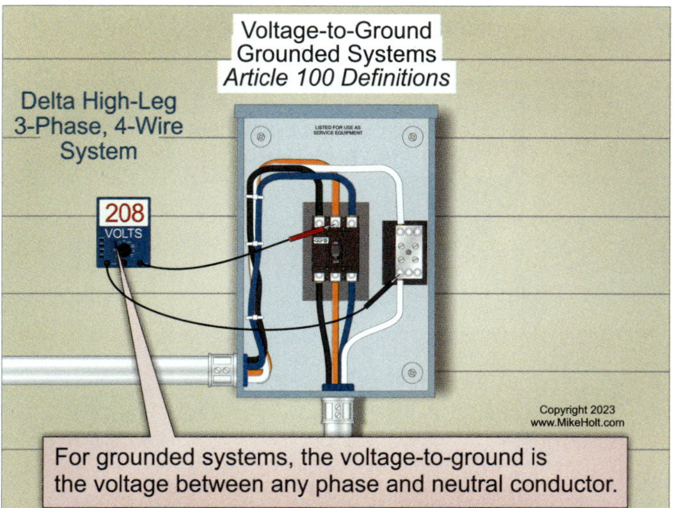

▶Figure 110–76

According to Article 100, "Voltage-to-Ground, Ungrounded Systems" is the voltage between any two phase conductors. ▶Figure 110–77

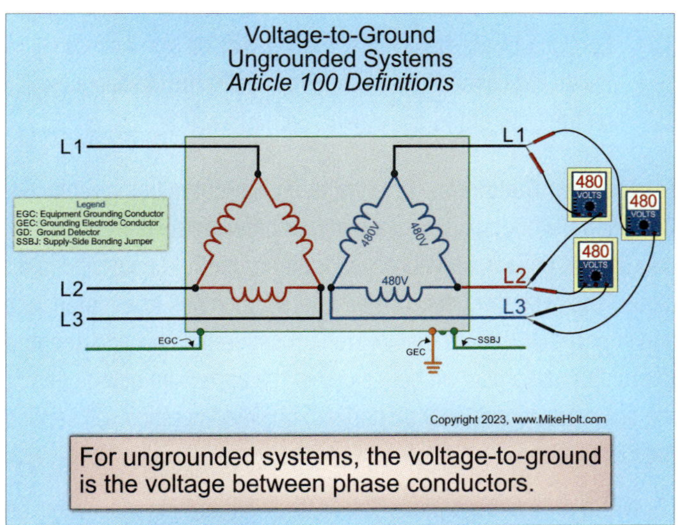

▶Figure 110–77

Depth of working space must be measured from the enclosure front, not the live parts. ▶Figure 110–78

According to Article 100, "Live Parts" means energized conductive components.

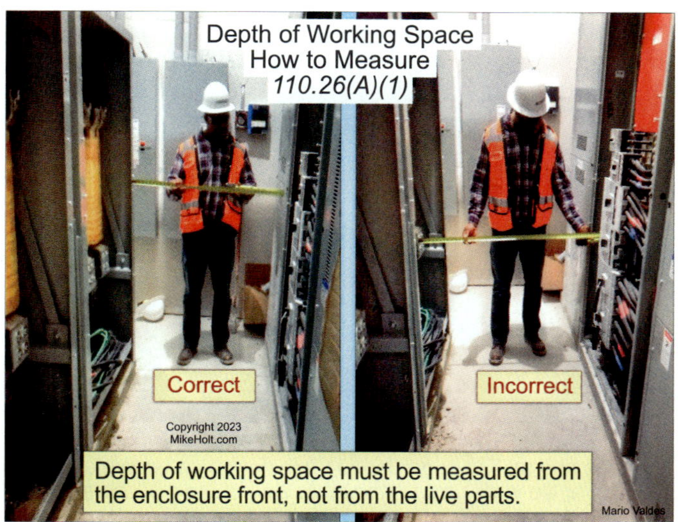

▶Figure 110–78

Table 110.26(A)(1) Working Space			
Voltage-to-Ground	Condition 1	Condition 2	Condition 3
0–150V	3 ft	3 ft	3 ft
151–600V	3 ft	3½ft	4 ft
601–1000V	3 ft	4 ft	5 ft

▶Figure 110–79, ▶Figure 110–80, and ▶Figure 110–81

Table Note:

Condition 1: Exposed live parts on one side of the working space and no live or grounded parts (including concrete, brick, or tile walls) on the other side of the working space.

Condition 2: Exposed live parts on one side of the working space and grounded parts on the other. Concrete, brick, tile, and similar surfaces are considered grounded.

Condition 3: Exposed live parts on both sides of the working space.

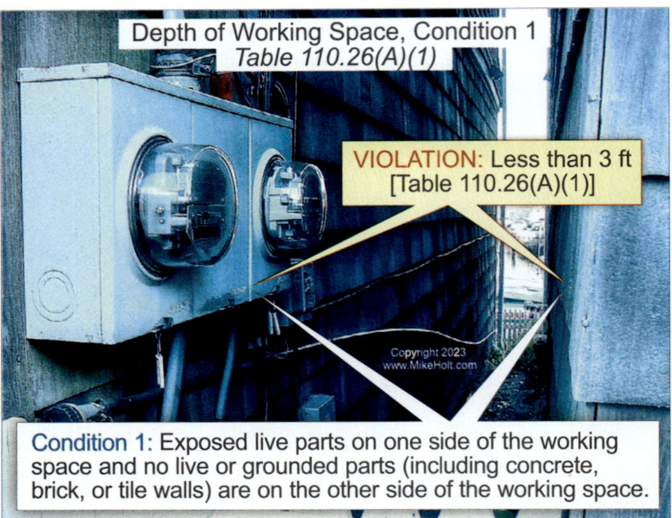

Condition 1: Exposed live parts on one side of the working space and no live or grounded parts (including concrete, brick, or tile walls) are on the other side of the working space.

▶Figure 110–79

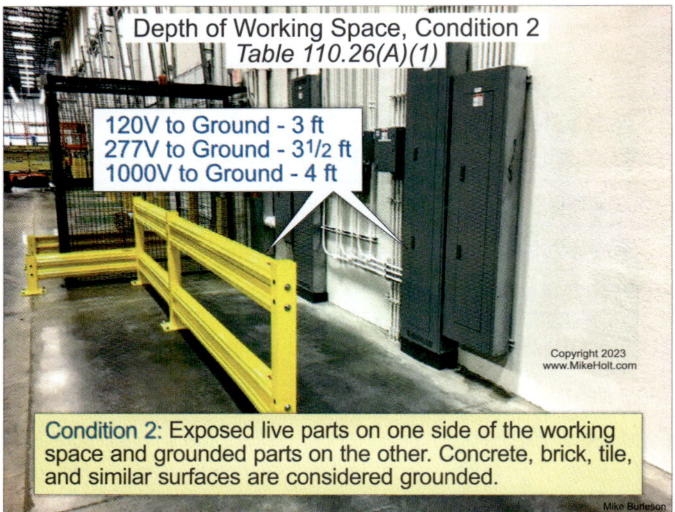

Condition 2: Exposed live parts on one side of the working space and grounded parts on the other. Concrete, brick, tile, and similar surfaces are considered grounded.

▶Figure 110–80

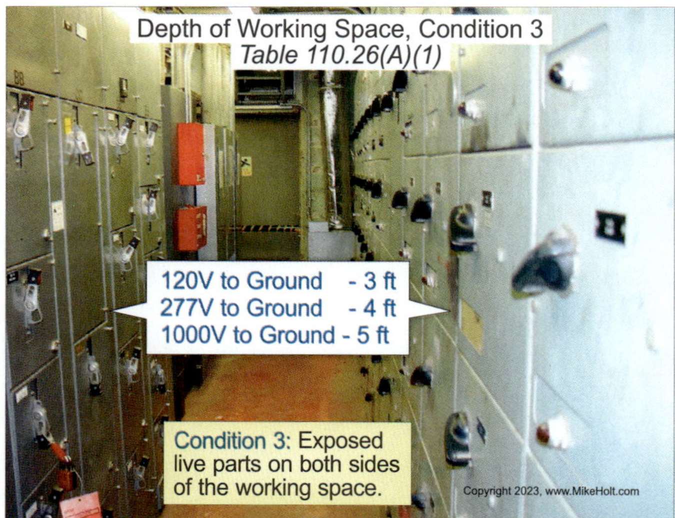

▶Figure 110–81

(a) Rear and Sides of Dead-Front Equipment. Working space is not required at the back or sides of equipment where all connections and renewable, adjustable, or serviceable parts are accessible from the front. ▶Figure 110–82

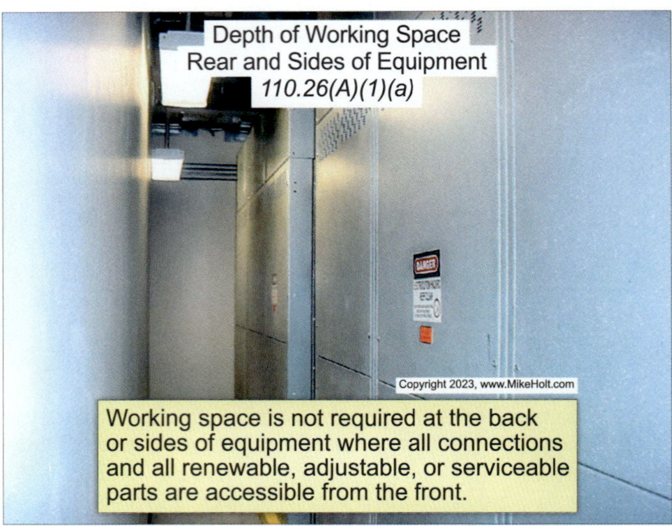

▶Figure 110–82

> **Author's Comment:**

> ▶ Sections of equipment that require rear or side access to make field connections must be marked by the manufacturer on the front of the equipment. See 408.18(C).

(c) Existing Buildings. If electrical equipment is being replaced, Condition 2 working space is permitted between dead-front switchboards, switchgear, panelboards, or motor control centers (located across the aisle from each other where conditions of maintenance and supervision ensure that written procedures have been adopted to prohibit equipment on both sides of the aisle from being open at the same time), and only authorized, qualified persons will service the installation.

(2) Width of Working Space. The width of the working space must be a minimum of 30 in., but in no case less than the width of the equipment. ▶Figure 110–83

> **Author's Comment:**

> ▶ The width of the working space can be measured from left-to-right, from right-to-left, or simply centered on the equipment. It can overlap the working space for other electrical equipment. ▶Figure 110–84 and ▶Figure 110–85

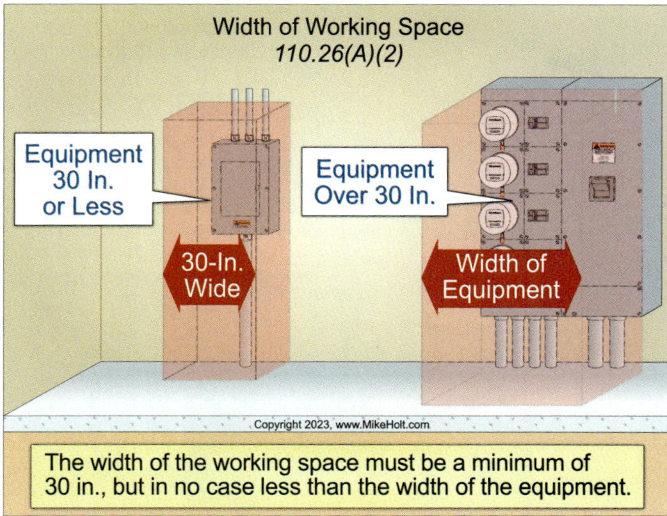

▶Figure 110–83

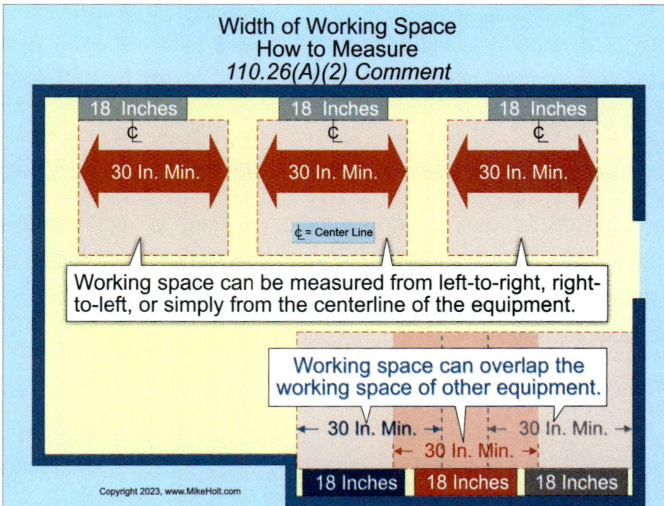

▶Figure 110–84

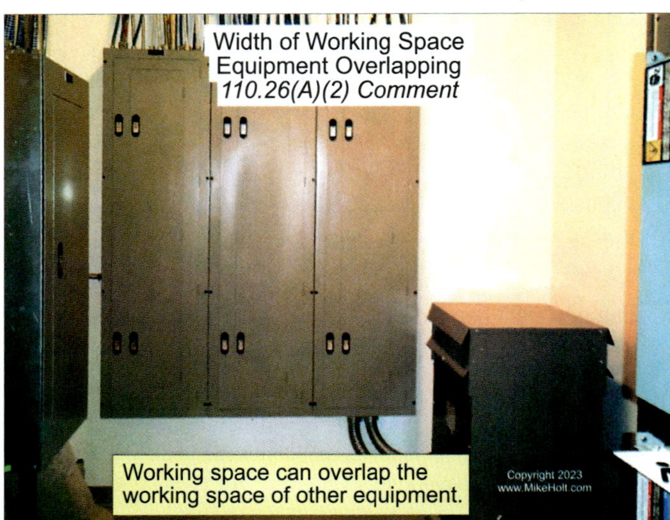

▶Figure 110–85

The working space must be of sufficient width, depth, and height to permit equipment doors to open at least 90 degrees. ▶Figure 110–86

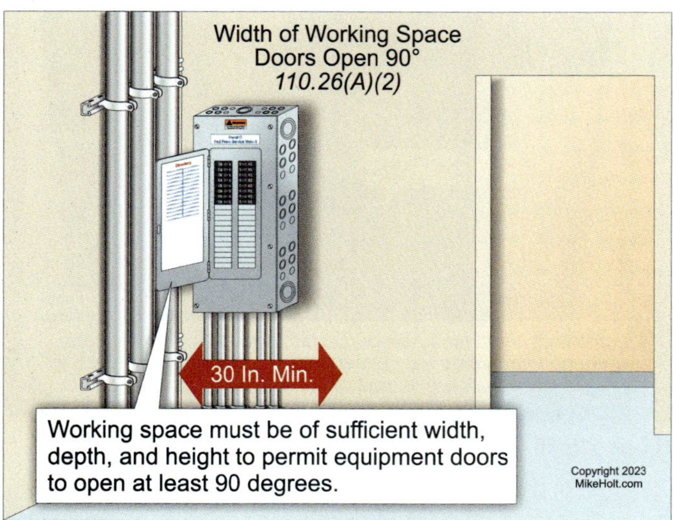

▶Figure 110–86

(3) Height of Working Space. The height of the working space must be clear and extend from the grade, floor, or platform to a height of 6½ ft or the height of the equipment, whichever is greater. ▶Figure 110–87

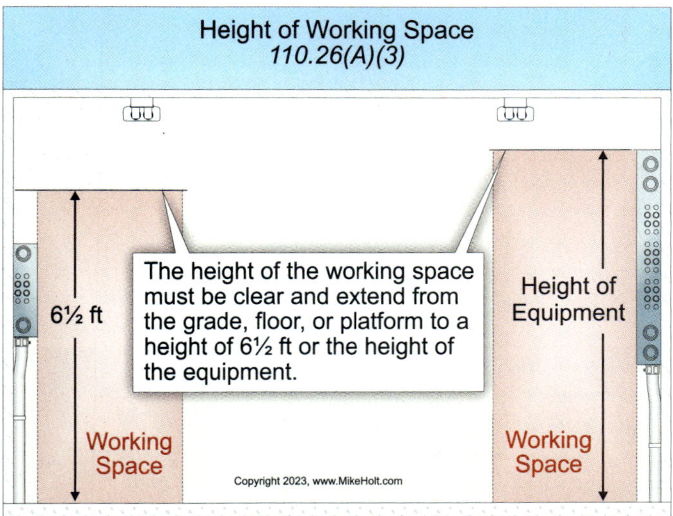

▶Figure 110–87

Other equipment such as raceways, cables, wireways, transformers, or support structures (such as concrete pads) are not permitted to extend more than 6 in. into the working space in front of the electrical equipment. ▶Figure 110–88, ▶Figure 110–89, ▶Figure 110–90, and ▶Figure 110–91

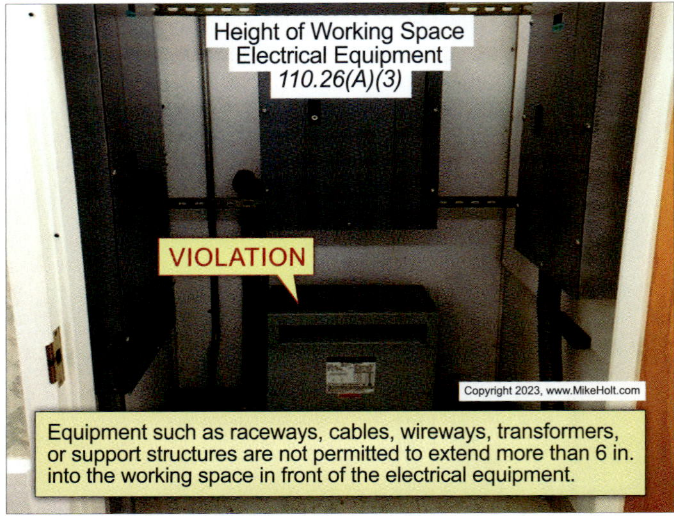

▶Figure 110–88

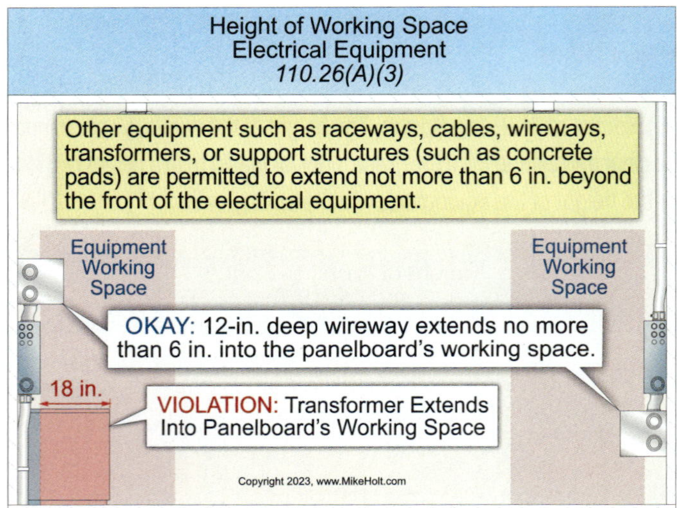

▶Figure 110–89

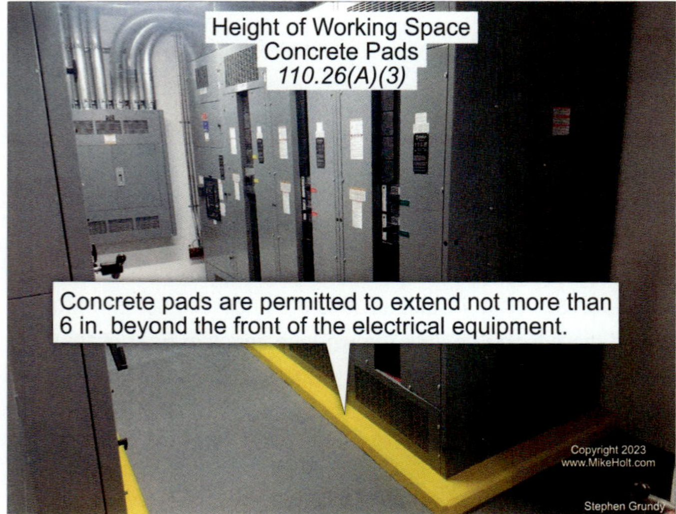

▶Figure 110–90

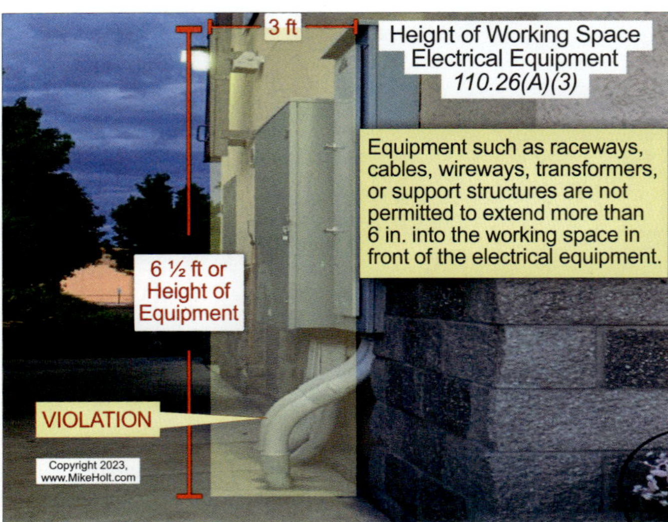

▶Figure 110–91

Ex 2: The minimum height of working space does not apply to a service disconnect or panelboards rated 200A or less located in an existing dwelling unit.

Ex 3: Meters are permitted to be installed in the required working space.

(4) Limited Access. Where equipment is likely to require examination, adjustment, servicing, or maintenance while energized is located above a suspended ceiling or crawl space, all the following conditions apply:

(1) Equipment installed above a suspended ceiling must have an access opening not smaller than 22 in. × 22 in., and equipment installed in a crawl space must have an accessible opening not smaller than 22 in. × 30 in.

(2) The width of the working space must be a minimum of 30 in., but in no case less than the width of the equipment.

(3) The working space must permit equipment doors to open 90 degrees.

(4) The working space in front of equipment must comply with the depth requirements of Table 110.26(A)(1) and be unobstructed to the floor by fixed cabinets, walls, or partitions. Horizontal ceiling structural members are permitted in this space provided the location of weight-bearing structural members does not result in a side reach of more than 6 in. to work within the enclosure.

(6) Grade, Floor, or Working Platform. The grade, floor, or platform for working space must be as level and flat as practical for the required depth and width of the working space. ▶Figure 110–92 and ▶Figure 110–93

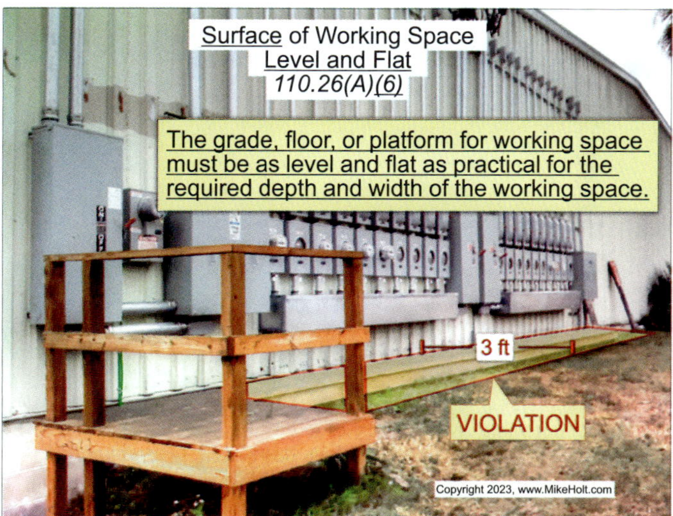

▶Figure 110–92

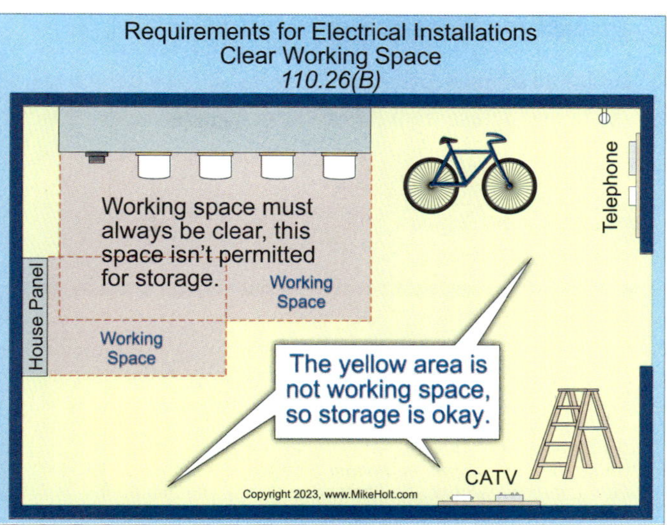

▶Figure 110–94

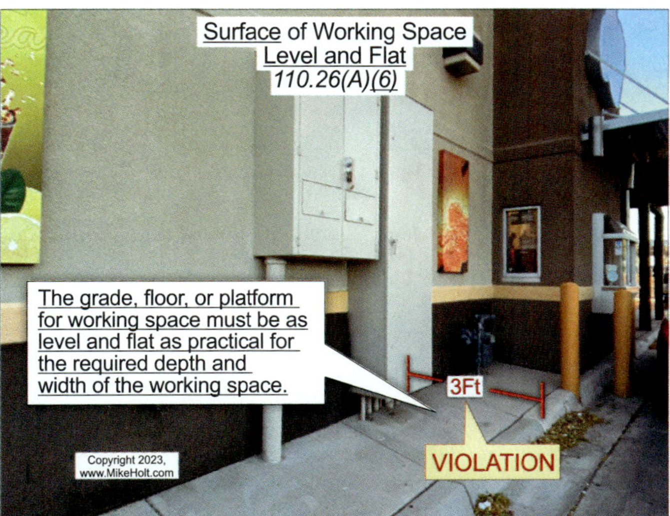

▶Figure 110–93

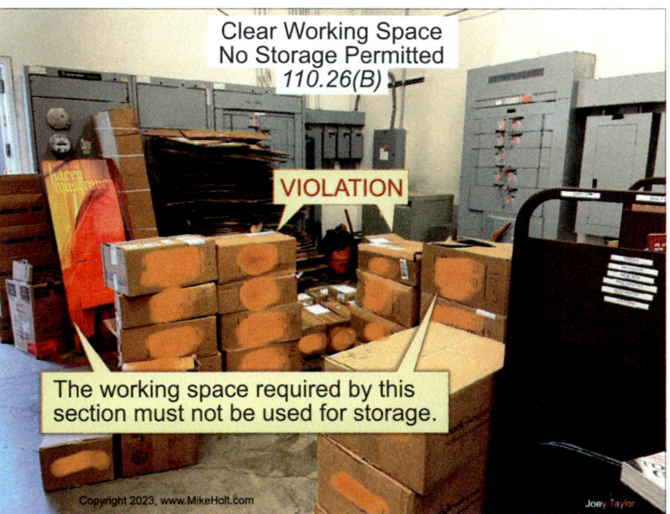

▶Figure 110–95

(B) Clear Working Space. The working space is not permitted to be used for storage. ▶Figure 110–94 and ▶Figure 110–95

> **Caution**
>
> **CAUTION:** It is very dangerous to service energized parts in the first place, and unacceptable to be subjected to additional dangers by working around bicycles, boxes, crates, appliances, and other impediments.

When live parts are exposed for inspection or servicing, the working space, if in a passageway or open space, must be suitably guarded.

According to Article 100, "Exposed (to live parts)" means capable of being inadvertently touched or approached nearer than a safe distance by a person. This term applies to parts that are not suitably guarded, isolated, or insulated.

Author's Comment:

▸ When working in a passageway and live parts are exposed for inspection or servicing, the working space should be guarded from use by occupants. In addition, one must be mindful of a fire alarm. If one occurs, many people will need to be evacuated and might congregate while moving through the area.

(C) Entrance to and Egress from Working Space.

(1) Minimum Required. At least one entrance large enough to give access to and egress from the working space must be provided.
▶Figure 110–96

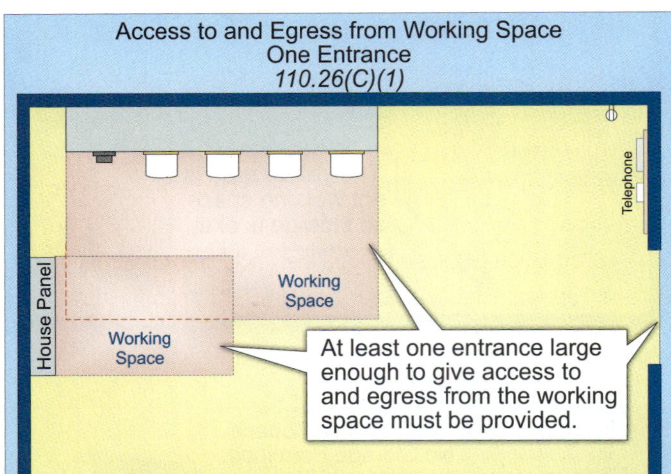

▶Figure 110–96

Author's Comment:

▶ Check to see what the authority having jurisdiction considers "large enough." Building codes contain minimum dimensions for doors and openings for personnel travel.

(2) Large Equipment. For large equipment containing overcurrent, switching, or control devices, an entrance to and egress from the required working space must not be less than 24 in. wide and 6½ ft high at each end of the working space. This requirement applies for either of the following conditions:

(1) Where feeder equipment is rated 1200A or more and over 6 ft wide.
▶Figure 110–97

(2) Where the service disconnects installed in accordance with 230.71(B) have a combined rating of 1200A or more, and where the combined width is over 6 ft. ▶Figure 110–98

A single entrance for access to and egress from the required working space is permitted where either of the following conditions are met:

(a) Unobstructed Egress. Where the location permits a continuous and unobstructed way of egress travel. ▶Figure 110–99

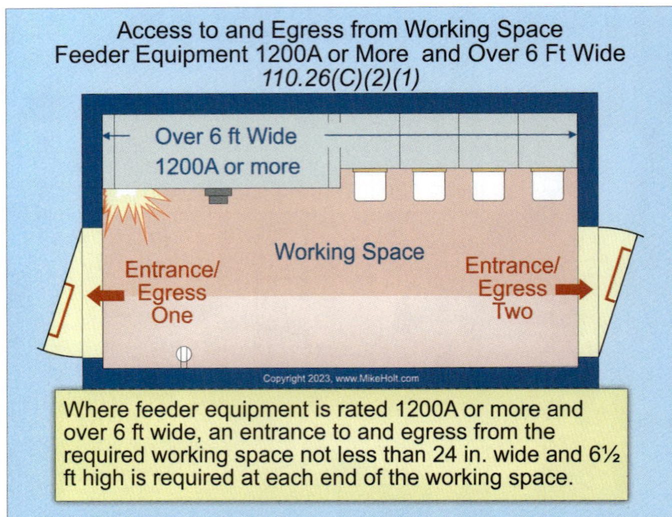

Where feeder equipment is rated 1200A or more and over 6 ft wide, an entrance to and egress from the required working space not less than 24 in. wide and 6½ ft high is required at each end of the working space.

▶Figure 110–97

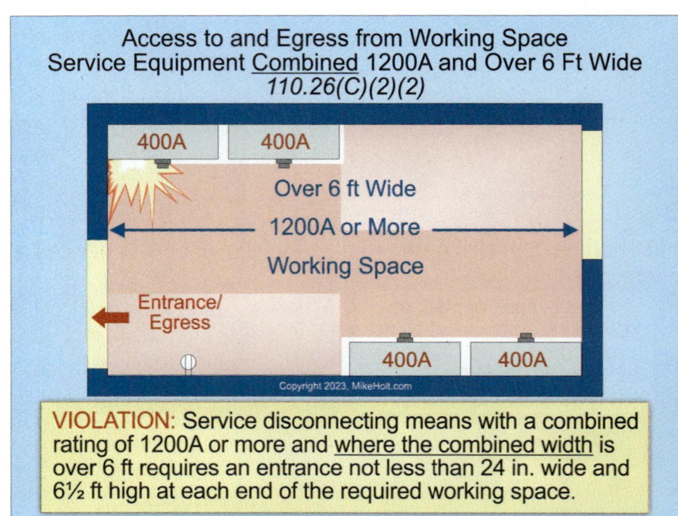

VIOLATION: Service disconnecting means with a combined rating of 1200A or more and where the combined width is over 6 ft requires an entrance not less than 24 in. wide and 6½ ft high at each end of the required working space.

▶Figure 110–98

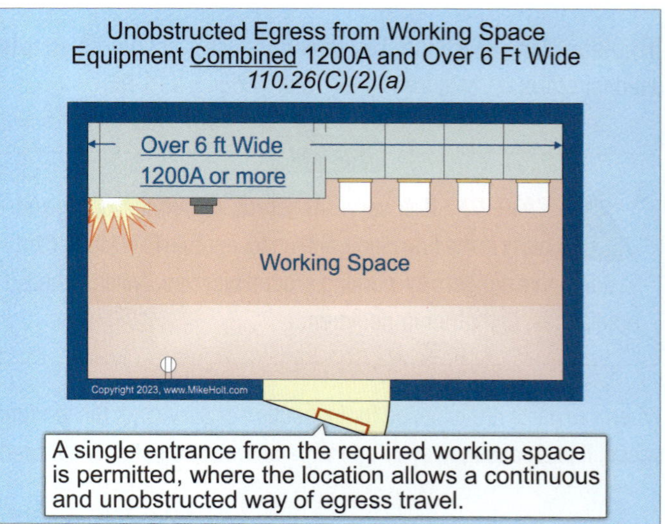

A single entrance from the required working space is permitted, where the location allows a continuous and unobstructed way of egress travel.

▶Figure 110–99

(b) Double Working Space. Where the required working space depth is doubled, and the equipment is located so the edge of the entrance is no closer than the required working space distance required by 110.26(A)(1). ▶Figure 110–100

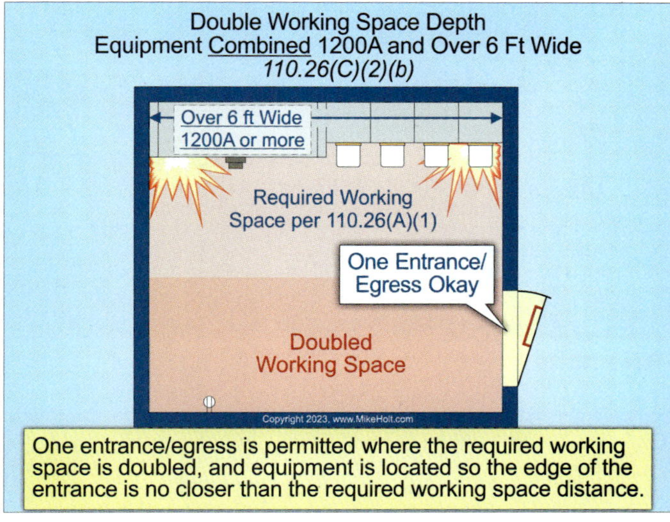

One entrance/egress is permitted where the required working space is doubled, and equipment is located so the edge of the entrance is no closer than the required working space distance.

▶Figure 110–100

(3) Fire Exit Hardware on Personnel Doors. Where equipment rated 800A or more contains overcurrent, switching, or control devices is installed, and there is a personnel door(s) intended for entrance to and egress from the working space less than 25 ft from the nearest edge of the working space, the door(s) are required to open at least 90 degrees in the direction of egress and equipped with listed panic or listed fire exit hardware. ▶Figure 110–101

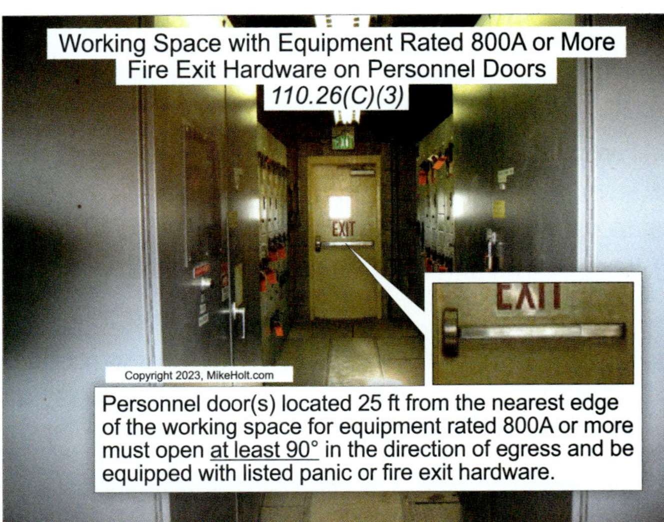

Personnel door(s) located 25 ft from the nearest edge of the working space for equipment rated 800A or more must open at least 90° in the direction of egress and be equipped with listed panic or fire exit hardware.

▶Figure 110–101

▶ History has shown that electricians who suffer burns on their hands in electrical arc flash or arc blast events often cannot open doors equipped with knobs that must be turned or doors that must be pulled open.

▶ Since this requirement is in the *NEC*, electrical contractors are responsible for ensuring panic hardware is installed where required. Some are offended at being held liable for nonelectrical responsibilities, but this rule is designed to save the lives of electricians. For this and other reasons, many construction professionals routinely hold "pre-construction" or "pre-con" meetings to review potential opportunities for miscommunication—before the work begins.

(D) Illumination for Working Space.

Working Space Indoors. Illumination is required for working spaces about service equipment, switchboards, switchgear, enclosed panelboards, or motor control centers installed indoors.

Automatic Means. Illumination for indoor working spaces around service equipment, switchboards, switchgear, enclosed panelboards, or motor control centers cannot be control by automatic means. ▶Figure 110–102

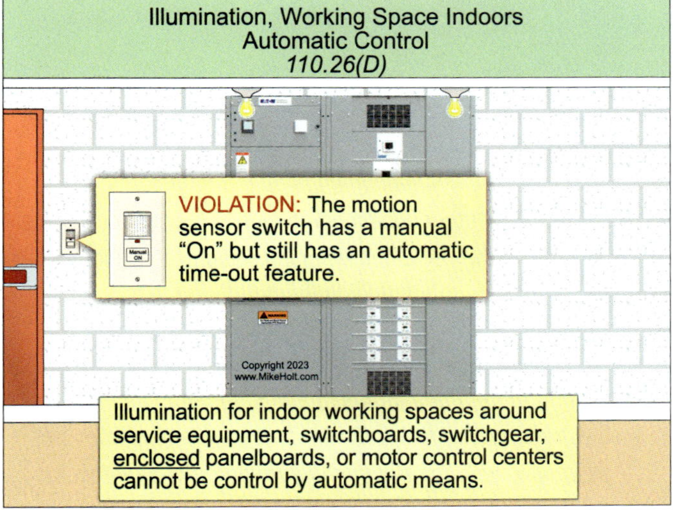

Illumination for indoor working spaces around service equipment, switchboards, switchgear, enclosed panelboards, or motor control centers cannot be control by automatic means.

▶Figure 110–102

▶ The *Code* does not identify the minimum foot-candles required to provide proper illumination even though it is essential in electrical equipment rooms for the safety of those qualified to work on such equipment.

(E) Dedicated Electrical Equipment Space. Service equipment, switchboards, panelboards, and motor control centers must have dedicated electrical equipment space and be protected from damage that could result from condensation, leaks, breaks in the foreign systems, or vehicular traffic as follows:

(1) Indoors. Service equipment, switchboards, panelboard enclosures, and motor control centers installed indoors must comply with the following:

(a) Equipment Space. The footprint space (width and depth of the equipment) of the dedicated electrical space extending from the floor to a height of 6 ft above the equipment or to the structural ceiling, whichever is lower, must be dedicated for the electrical installation. ▶Figure 110–103

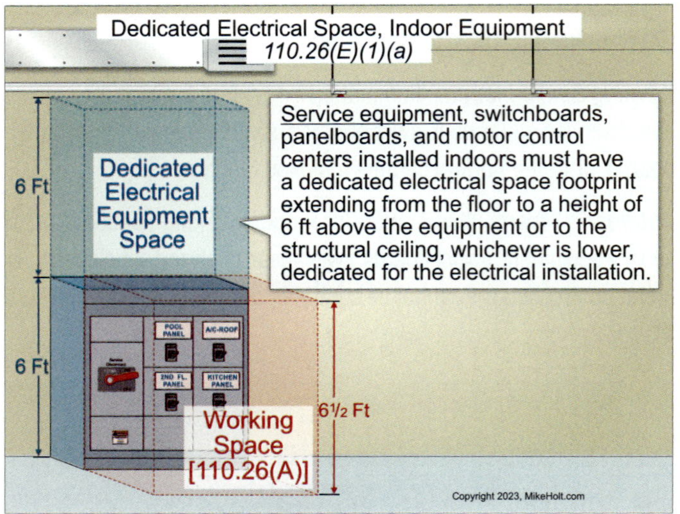

▶Figure 110–103

No piping, ducts, or other equipment foreign to the electrical system can be installed in this dedicated electrical equipment space. ▶Figure 110–104

Author's Comment:

▶ Electrical equipment such as raceways and cables not associated with the electrical installation can be within the dedicated electrical space. ▶Figure 110–105

Ex: Suspended ceilings with removable panels can be within the dedicated space (6-ft zone).

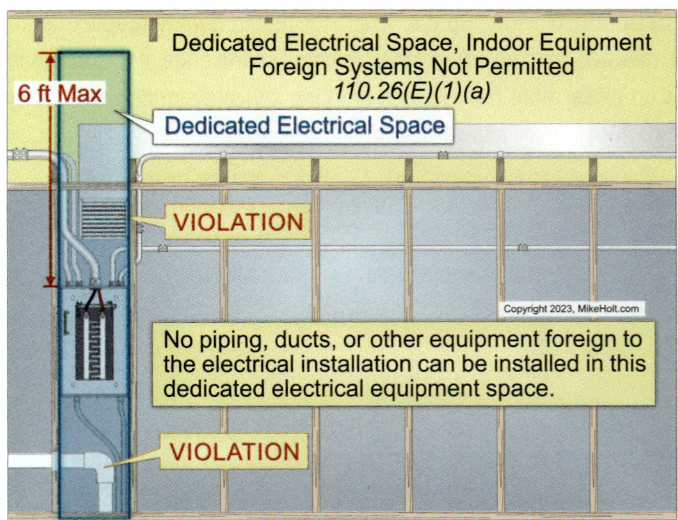

▶Figure 110–104

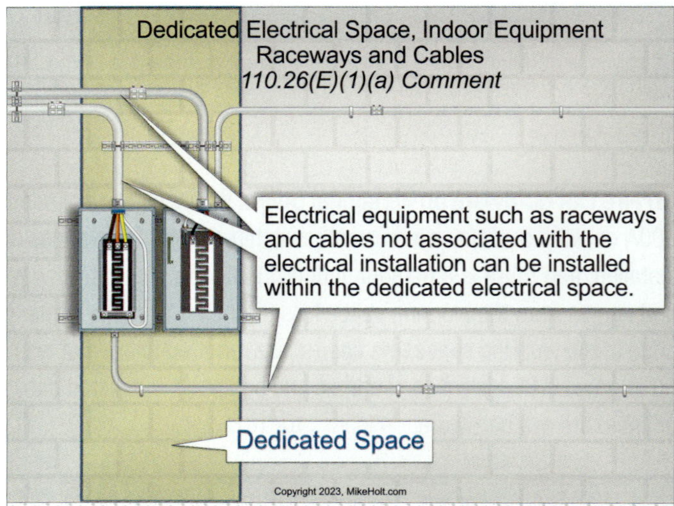

▶Figure 110–105

(b) Foreign Systems. Foreign systems can be located above the dedicated electrical space if protection is installed to prevent damage to the electrical equipment from condensation, leaks, or breaks in the foreign systems. Such protection can be as simple as a drip-pan. ▶Figure 110–106

(c) Sprinkler Protection. Sprinkler protection piping is not permitted in the dedicated space, but the *NEC* does not prohibit sprinklers from spraying water on electrical equipment.

(d) Suspended Ceilings. A dropped, suspended, or similar ceiling is not considered a structural ceiling. ▶Figure 110–107

(2) Outdoor. Outdoor installations for service equipment, switchboards, panelboards, and motor control centers must comply with the following:

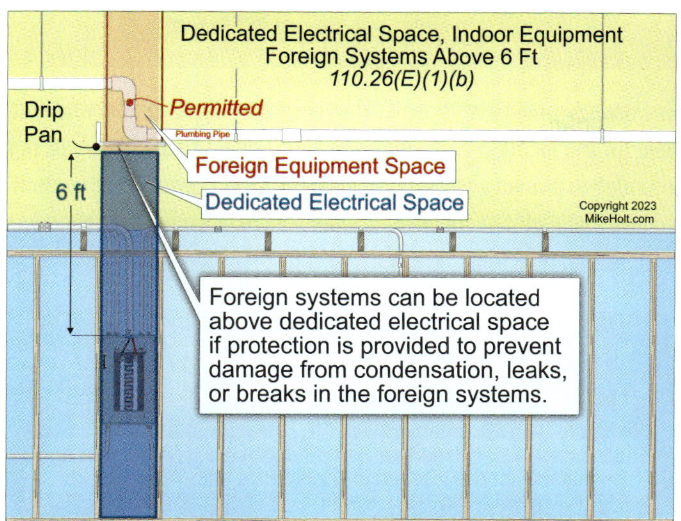

▶Figure 110–106

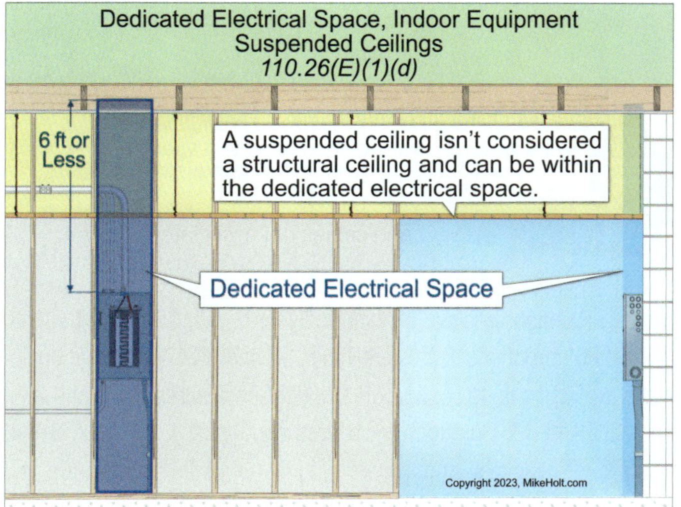

▶Figure 110–107

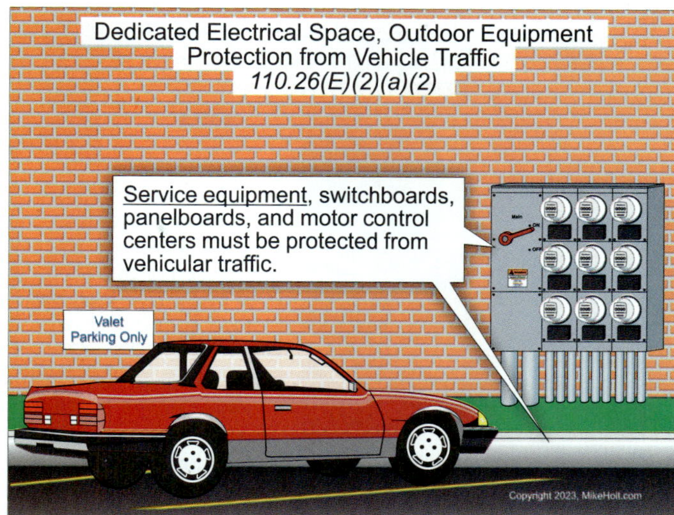

▶Figure 110–108

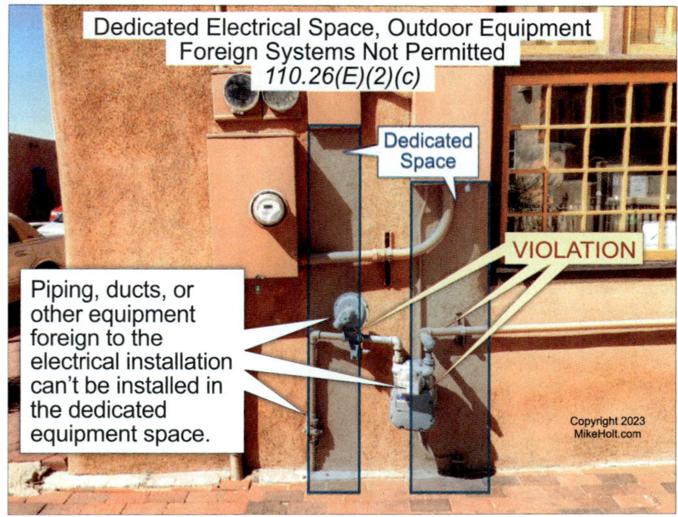

▶Figure 110–109

(a) Installation Requirements.

(1) Installed in identified enclosures.

(2) Protected from vehicular traffic. ▶Figure 110–108

(3) Protected from accidental spillage or leakage from piping systems.

(b) Working Space. The working clearance space includes the zone described in 110.26(A). Architectural appurtenances (attachments) or other equipment are not permitted within this zone.

(c) Dedicated Equipment Space Outdoors. The footprint space (width and depth of the equipment) of the outdoor dedicated space extending from grade to a height of 6 ft above the equipment must be dedicated for electrical installations. No piping, ducts, or other equipment foreign to the electrical installation can be installed in this dedicated space. ▶Figure 110–109

Ex: Structural overhangs and roof extensions are permitted in this zone.

110.27 Protection Against Physical Damage

(B) Physical Damage. In locations where electrical equipment is likely to be exposed to physical damage, enclosures or guards must be arranged and of such strength as to prevent such damage. ▶Figure 110–110

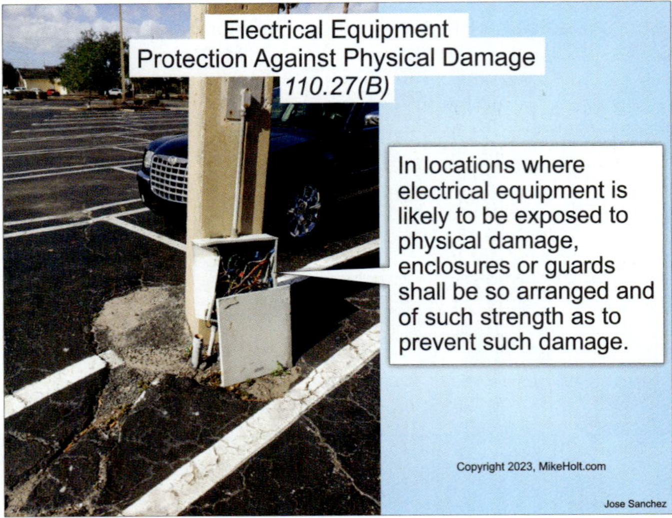

▶Figure 110–110

According to Article 100, "Exposed (as applied to wiring methods)" means on or attached to the surface of a building, or behind panels designed to allow access. ▶Figure 110–111

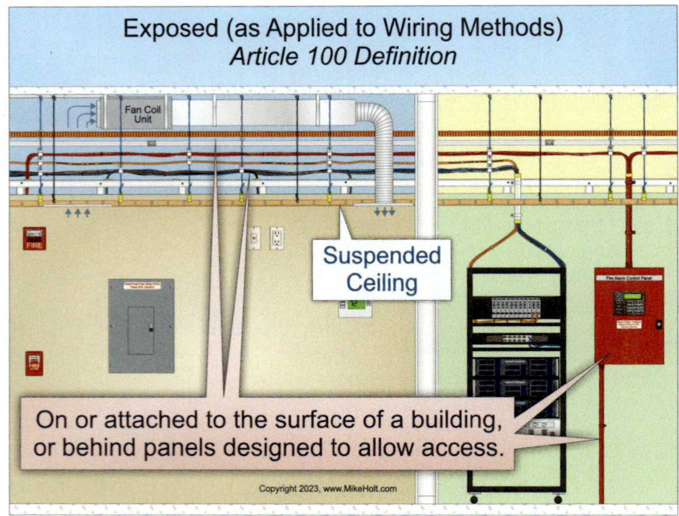

▶Figure 110–111

(C) Warning Signs. Electrical rooms must contain warning signs complying with 110.21(B) forbidding unqualified persons to enter.

110.28 NEMA Enclosure Types

Enclosures must be marked with an enclosure-type number and suitable for the location in accordance with Table 110.28. They are not intended to protect against condensation, icing, corrosion, or contamination that might occur within the enclosure or enters via a raceway or unsealed openings. ▶Figure 110–112

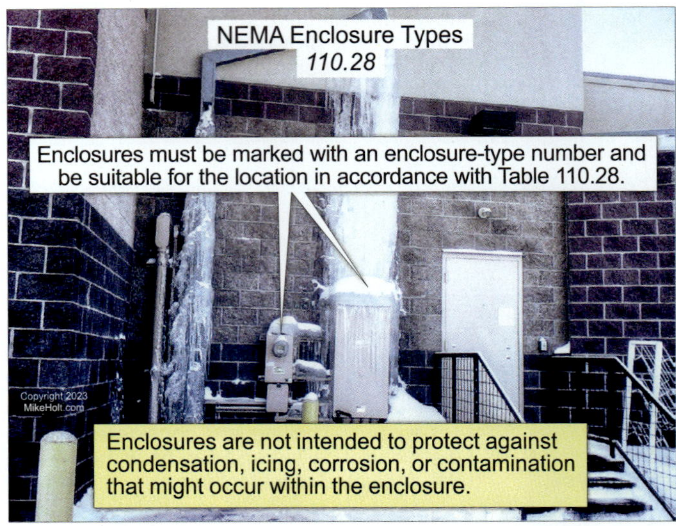

▶Figure 110–112

Note 1: Raintight enclosures include Types 3, 3S, 3SX, 3X, 4, 4X, 6, and 6P. Rainproof enclosures are Types 3R and 3RX. Watertight enclosures are Types 4, 4X, 6, and 6P. Driptight enclosures are Types 2, 5, 12, 12K, and 13. Dusttight enclosures are Types 3, 3S, 3SX, 3X, 4, 4X, 5, 6, 6P, 12, 12K, and 13.

Note 3: Dusttight enclosures are suitable for use in hazardous (classified) locations in accordance with 502.10(B)(4), 503.10(A)(2), and 506.15(C)(9).

Note 4: Dusttight enclosures are suitable for use in unclassified locations and in Class II, Division 2; Class III; and Zone 22 hazardous (classified) locations.

Note 5: Some type 4X enclosures may be marked "indoor only."

WIRING AND PROTECTION

Introduction to Chapter 2—Wiring and Protection

Chapter 2 of the *Code* is divided into eleven articles containing the general rules for wiring and sizing circuits, overcurrent protection of conductors, overvoltage protection of equipment, and bonding and grounding. The rules in this chapter apply to all electrical installations covered by the *NEC*—except as modified in Chapters 5, 6, 7, or specifically referenced in Chapter 8 [90.3].

This chapter can be thought of as the preconstruction phase of a job because it is primarily focused on layout, sizing, and the protection of circuits. Every article in this chapter deals with a different aspect of designing safe wiring for an electrical system. The Chapter 2 articles covered by this material are:

▶ **Article 200—Use and Identification of Neutral and Grounded-Phase Conductors.** This article has one part containing the requirements for the use and identification of the grounded conductor—which in most cases is the neutral conductor.

▶ **Article 210—Branch Circuits.** Article 210 is comprised of three parts which contain requirements for the installation, sizing, and protection of branch circuits. General rules are found in Part I and include topics such as conductor sizing, identification, and AFCI and GFCI protection. Parts II and III contain the requirements for branch circuits and required outlets.

▶ **Article 215—Feeders.** This article covers the requirements for the installation, sizing, and protection of feeders.

▶ **Article 220—Branch-Circuit, Feeder, and Service Calculations.** Article 220 is comprised seven parts. It provides the requirements for calculating branch-circuit, feeder, and service loads. This article also contains the rules for the number of required branch circuits and the number of receptacles on each.

▶ **Article 225—Outside Feeders.** This article covers the requirements for outside wiring methods (both overhead and underground). It includes feeders that run on or between buildings, poles, and other structures which may be present on the premises and used to feed equipment.

▶ **Article 230—Services.** Article 230 covers the installation requirements for service conductors and equipment. It is very important to know where the service begins and ends when applying this article.

▶ **Article 240—Overcurrent Protection.** This article provides the requirements for overcurrent protection and overcurrent protective devices.

▶ **Article 242—Overvoltage Protection.** Part I of Article 242 covers the general installation and connection requirements for surge-protective devices (SPDs) permanently installed on both the line side and load sides of service disconnects. Part II covers SPDs permanently installed on wiring systems 1000V and less.

▶ **Article 250—Bonding and Grounding.** Article 250 covers the grounding requirements for providing a path to the Earth to reduce overvoltage from lightning, and the bonding requirements for the low-impedance fault current path necessary to facilitate the operation of overcurrent protective devices in the event of a ground fault.

USE AND IDENTIFICATION OF GROUNDED CONDUCTORS

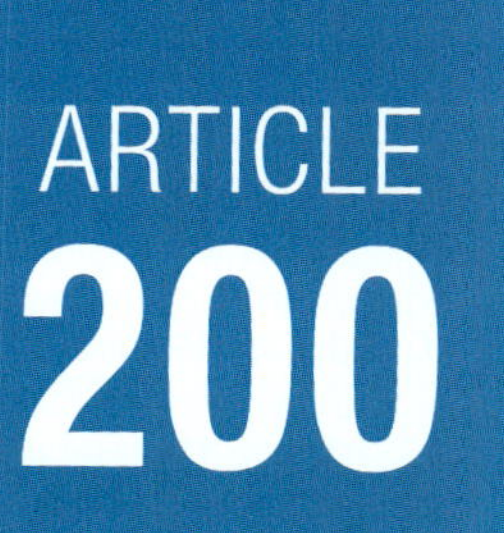

Introduction to Article 200—Use and Identification of Grounded Conductors

Article 200 contains the requirements for the use and identification of grounded conductors and their terminals. This article has eleven sections covering the requirements for neutral conductors and grounded-phase conductors. Take some time to review electrical theory before you try to attack this article, you must understand how current flow is essential for these rules to make sense. Some topics covered in this material for Article 200 include:

▸ Grounded System Connections

▸ Conductor Identification

▸ Equipment Terminal Identification

According to Article 100, "Grounded Conductor" is the circuit conductor that is intentionally connected to the Earth (ground). ▸Figure 200–1

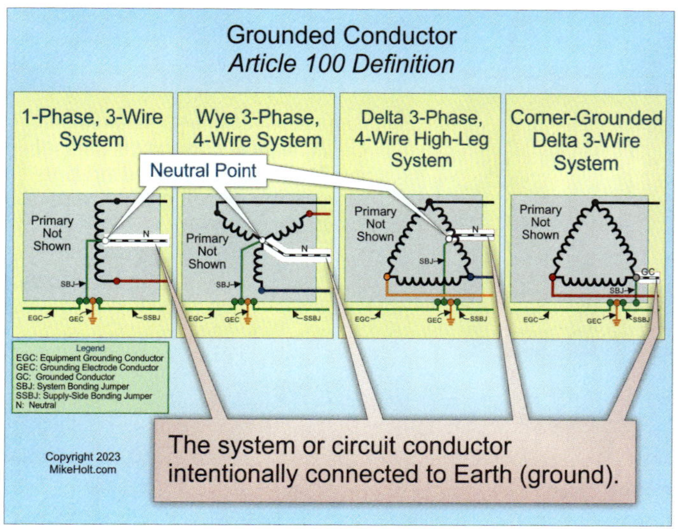

▸Figure 200–1

According to Article 100, "Neutral Conductor" is the conductor connected to the neutral point of a system that is intended to carry current under normal conditions. ▸Figure 200–2

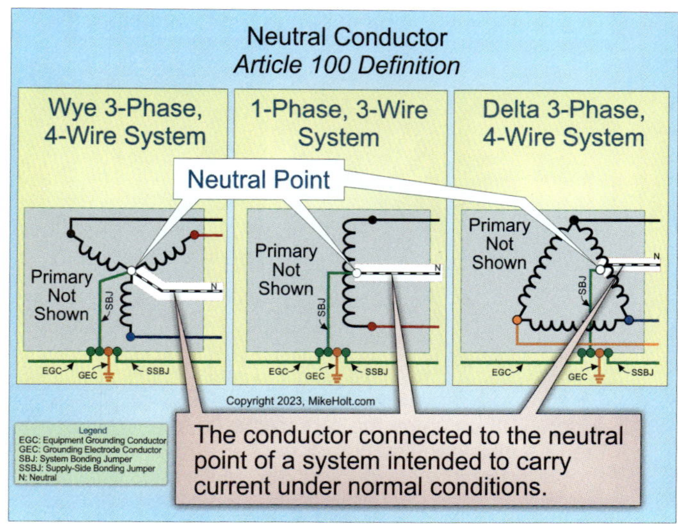

▸Figure 200–2

According to Article 100, "Neutral Point" is the common point of a 4-wire, three-phase, wye-connected system; the midpoint of a 3-wire, single-phase system; or the midpoint of the single-phase portion of a three-phase, delta-connected system. ▸Figure 200–3

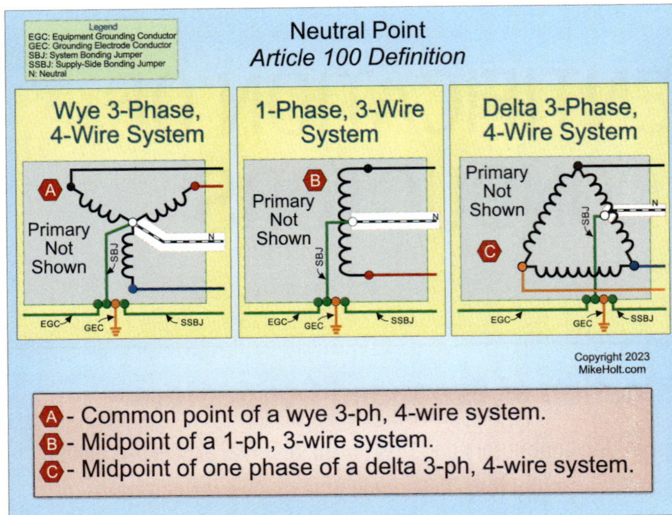

▶Figure 200–3

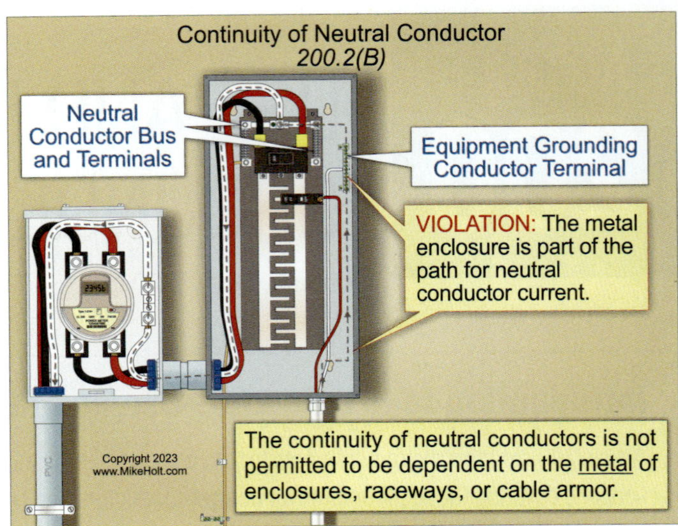

▶Figure 200–5

200.1 Scope

Article 200 contains the requirements for the use and identification of neutral and grounded-phase conductors and terminals. ▶Figure 200–4

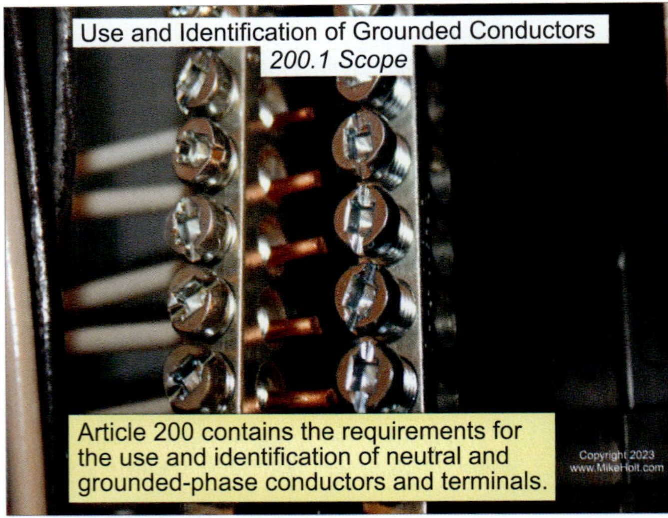

▶Figure 200–4

200.2 General

(B) Continuity. The continuity of neutral and grounded-phase conductors is not permitted to be dependent on the metal of enclosures, raceways, or cable armor. ▶Figure 200–5

200.4 Neutral Conductor

Neutral conductors must comply with 200.4(A) and (B).

(A) Installation. A neutral conductor cannot be used for more than one branch circuit or multiwire branch circuit. ▶Figure 200–6

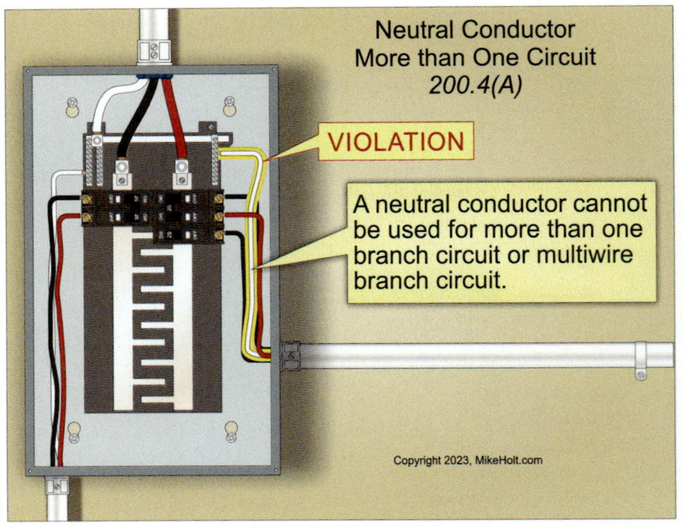

▶Figure 200–6

(B) Multiple Circuits. Where more than one neutral conductor is in an enclosure, the neutral conductors must be identified or grouped to correspond with the phase conductor(s) by wire markers, cable ties, or similar means in at least one location within the enclosure. ▶Figure 200–7 and ▶Figure 200–8

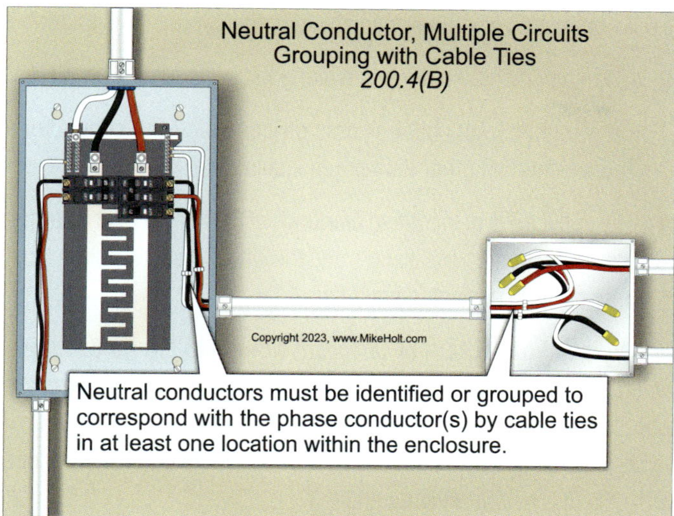

▶Figure 200–7

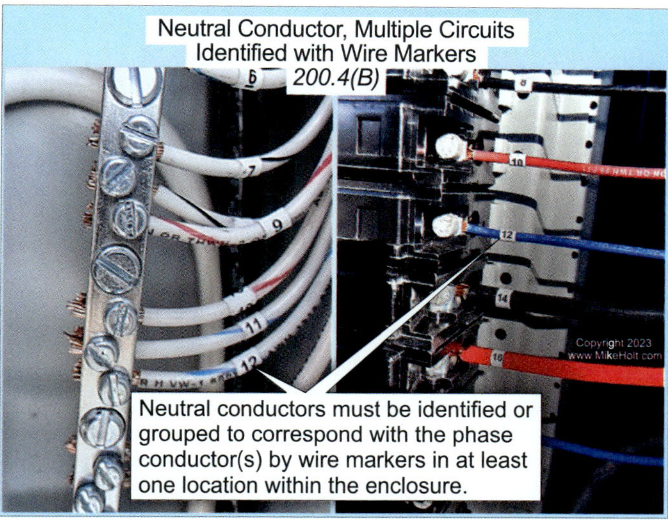

▶Figure 200–8

Ex 1: Grouping is not required where the circuit conductors are contained in a single raceway or cable unique to that circuit making the grouping obvious.

Ex 2: Grouping is not required if the conductors pass through a box or conduit body without any splices or terminations.

Author's Comment:

▶ Grouping all associated conductors by cable ties or other means within the point of origination makes it easier to visually identify conductors of individual branch circuits. Grouping assists in ensuring the correct neutral conductor is paired with the intended phase conductors at junction and splice points, particularly when connecting multiwire branch-circuit conductors to circuit breakers [210.4(D)].

200.6 Identification of Neutral and Grounded Conductors

(A) 6 AWG or Smaller. The insulation of neutral and grounded-phase conductors 6 AWG and smaller must be identified by any of the following means: ▶Figure 200–9

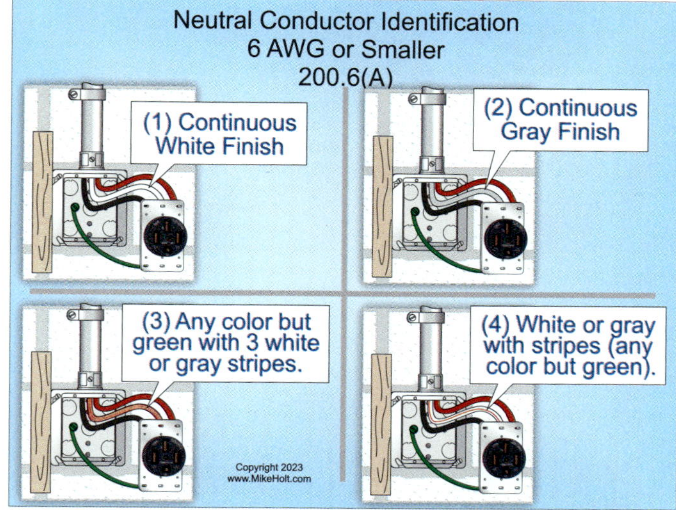

▶Figure 200–9

(1) A continuous white outer finish

(2) A continuous gray outer finish

(3) Three continuous white or gray stripes along their entire length on other than green insulated conductor

(4) An outer covering of a white or gray color with colored tracer threads in the braid identifying the source of manufacture

Author's Comment:

▶ The use of white tape, paint, or other methods of identification are not permitted for the insulation of neutral and grounded-phase conductors 6 AWG and smaller. ▶Figure 200–10

(B) 4 AWG or Larger. Insulated neutral and grounded-phase conductors 4 AWG or larger must be identified by any of the following means: ▶Figure 200–11 and ▶Figure 200–12

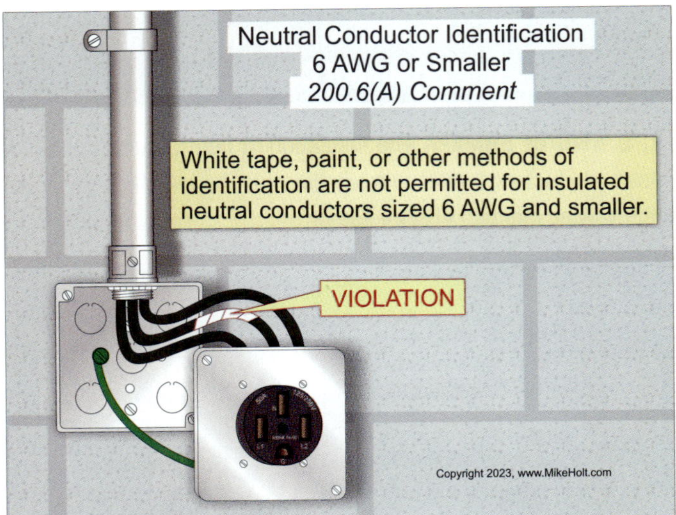

▶Figure 200–10

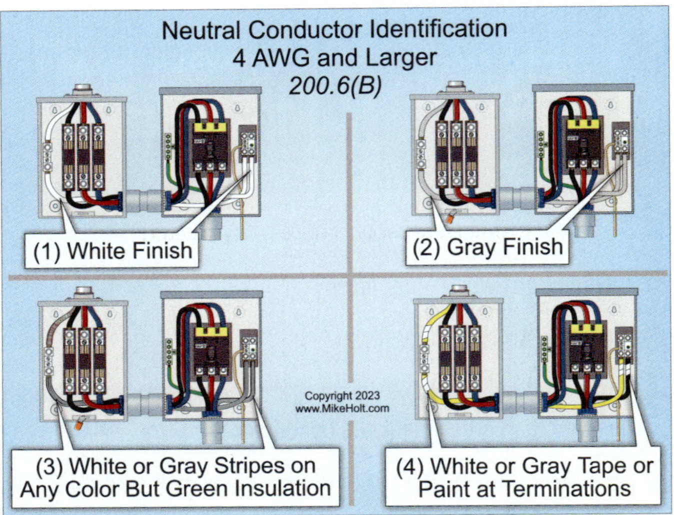

▶Figure 200–11

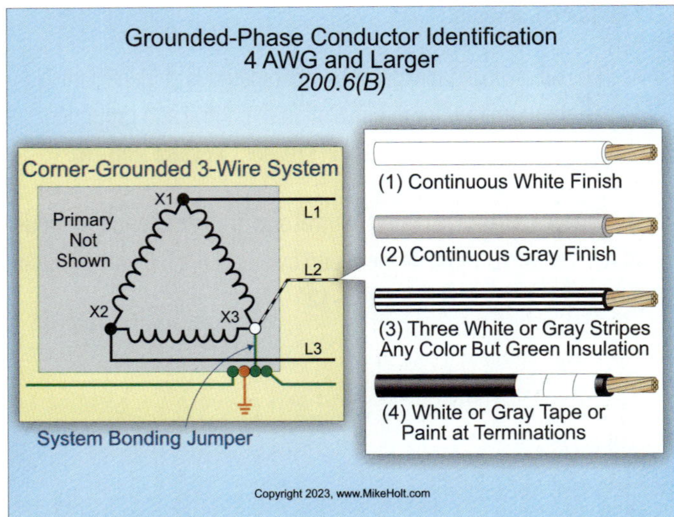

▶Figure 200–12

(1) A continuous white outer finish along the conductor's length

(2) A continuous gray outer finish along the conductor's length

(3) Three continuous white or gray stripes along the conductor's entire length on other than green insulation

(4) The application of identified markings of white or gray at its terminals at the time of installation, and the white or gray marking must encircle the conductor insulation

(D) Neutral Conductors of Different Nominal Voltage Systems.
When neutral conductors of different nominal voltage systems are installed in the same raceway, cable, or enclosure, each nominal voltage system neutral conductor must be identified in accordance with 200.6(1) or (2): ▶Figure 200–13

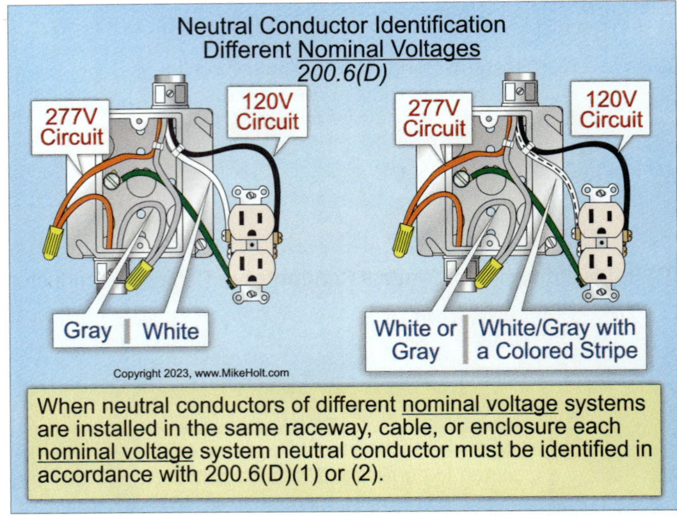

▶Figure 200–13

(1) One neutral conductor of a nominal voltage system installed in the same raceway, cable, or enclosure must have a continuous white or gray outer finish along its entire length in accordance with 200.6(A) and 200.6(B).

(2) The neutral conductor of the other nominal voltage systems installed in the same raceway, cable, or enclosure must have an outer covering of white or gray along its entire length in accordance with 200.6(A) and 200.6(B) or have an outer covering of white or gray with a readily distinguishable color stripe (other than green) along its entire length.

(3) Other identification allowed by 200.6(A) or (B) that will distinguish each nominal voltage system neutral conductor.

(E) Neutral Conductors in Multiconductor Cables.

Ex 1: Neutral conductors within multiconductor cables are permitted to be reidentified at their terminations during installation by a distinctive white or gray marking.

200.7 Use of White or Gray Color

(A) General. The following insulated conductors can only be used for the neutral or grounded-phase conductor except as permitted in 200.7(C):

(1) A conductor with a continuous white or gray covering

(2) A conductor with three continuous white or gray stripes

(3) A marking of a white or gray color at the termination

(C) Reidentification of Neutral Conductor in Cables. A conductor with white or gray insulation used as a phase conductor is permitted in the following:

(1) Cable Assembly. The white or gray conductor within a cable can be used for the phase conductor if the white conductor is permanently reidentified as a phase conductor by marking tape, painting, or other effective means where the conductor is visible. Identification must encircle the insulation and must be a color other than white, gray, or green. ▸Figure 200–14

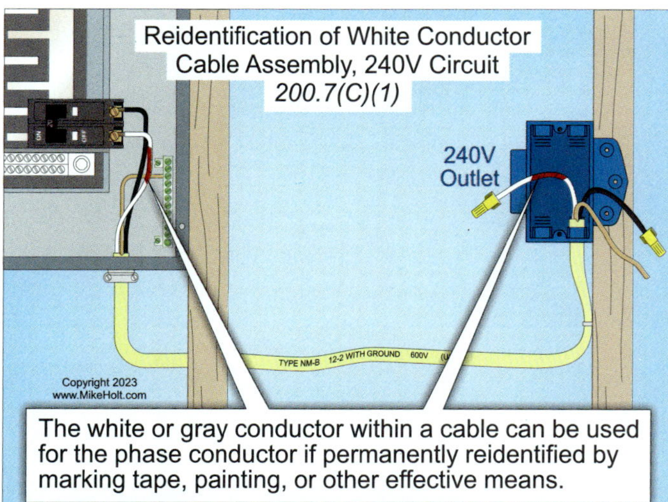

▸Figure 200–14

The white or gray conductor within a cable can be used to supply power to switches if the conductor is reidentified as a phase conductor by marking tape, painting, or other effective means where the conductor is visible. ▸Figure 200–15 and ▸Figure 200–16

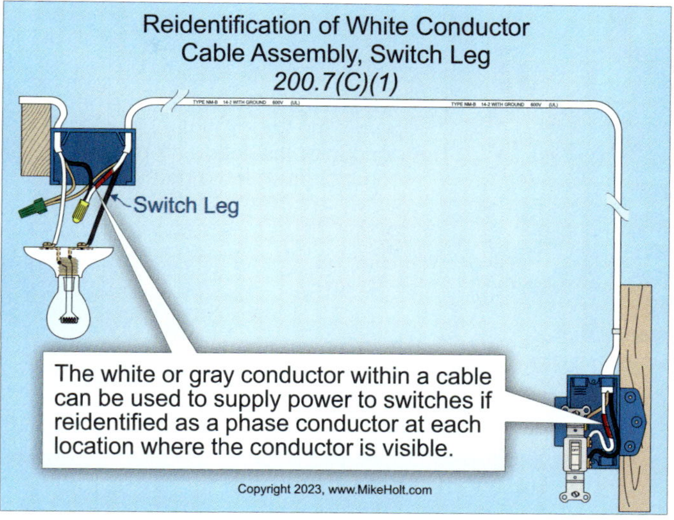

▸Figure 200–15

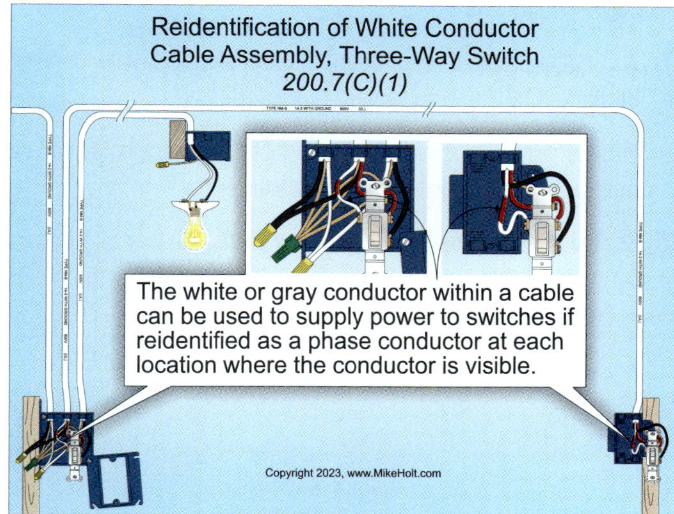

▸Figure 200–16

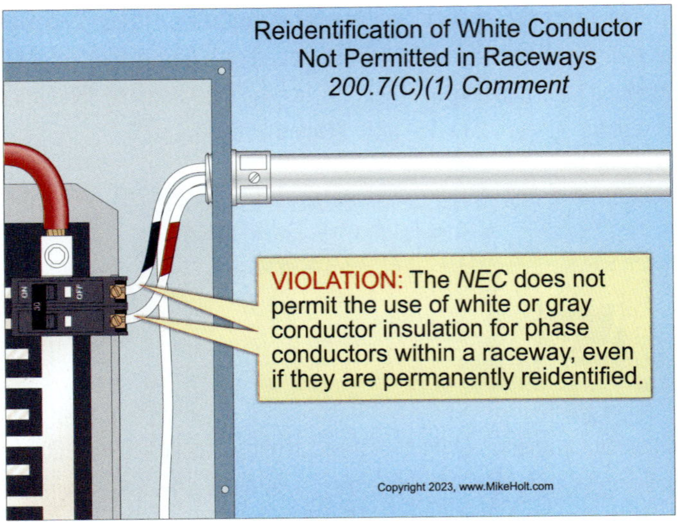

▶Figure 200–17

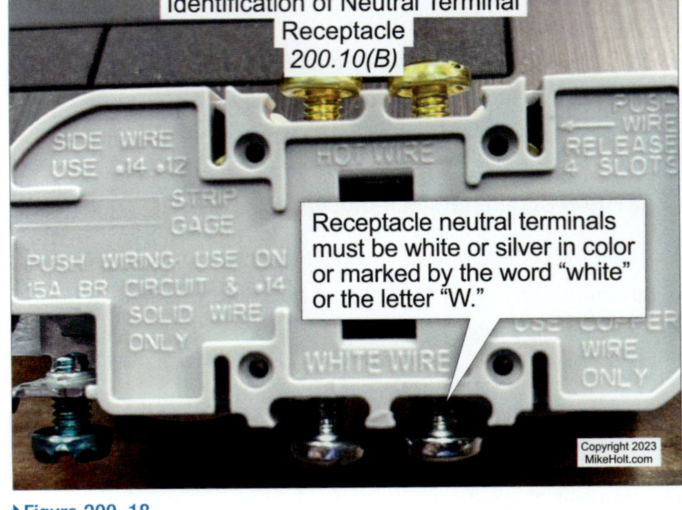

▶Figure 200–18

200.10 Receptacle and Screw Shell Terminal

(B) Receptacles. Receptacles must have the neutral terminal identified by: ▶Figure 200–18

(1) A metal terminal or metal coating terminal that is white or silver or marked by the word "white" or the letter "W."

(2) If the terminal is not visible, the conductor entrance hole must be marked with the word "white" or the letter "W."

(C) Screw Shell. For devices with screw shells, the neutral terminal for the neutral conductor must be the one connected to the screw shell [410.90]. ▶Figure 200–19

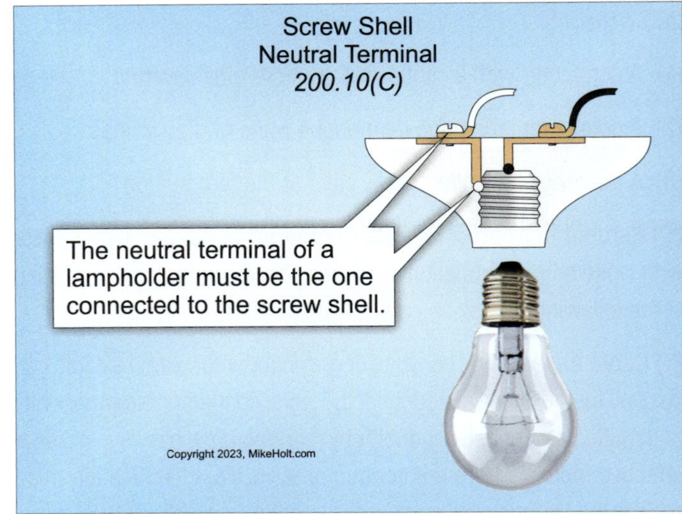

▶Figure 200–19

Introduction to Article 210—Branch Circuits

This article contains the general requirements for branch circuits which extend from the last point of overcurrent protection to the utilization equipment. Branch circuits account for most circuits run in any electrical installation, so you must be sure you are familiar with these rules. Some topics covered in this material for Article 210 include:

- ▸ Identification of Branch Circuits
- ▸ Multi-Wire Branch Circuits
- ▸ Voltage Limitations
- ▸ Required Branch Circuits
- ▸ GFCI and AFCI Requirements
- ▸ Branch-Circuit Ratings
- ▸ Permitted Loads
- ▸ Receptacle and Lighting Outlet Requirements

This article consists of three parts:

- ▸ Part I. General Provisions
- ▸ Part II. Branch-Circuit Ratings
- ▸ Part III. Required Outlets

Part I. General Provisions

210.1 Scope

Article 210 provides the general requirements for branch circuits not over 1000V ac or 1500V dc, such as conductor sizing, overcurrent protection, identification, GFCI and AFCI protection, as well as receptacle outlet and lighting outlet requirements. ▸Figure 210–1

According to Article 100, "Branch Circuit" consists of the conductors between the final overcurrent protective device and the receptacle outlets, lighting outlets, or other outlets. ▸Figure 210–2

210.3 Other Articles

Table 210.3 lists references for specific equipment provisions for branch circuits that amend or supplement those given in Article 210.

210.4 Multiwire Branch Circuits

(A) General. Except as permitted in 300.3(B)(4), all conductors of a multiwire branch circuit must originate from the same equipment containing the branch-circuit overcurrent protective devices. ▸Figure 210–3

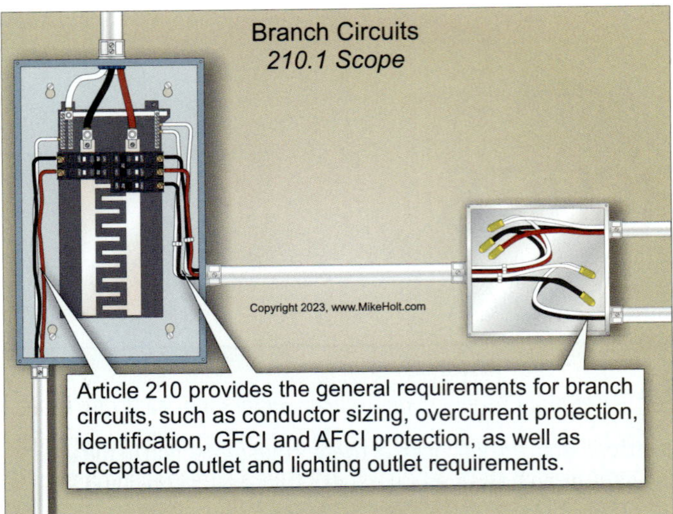

▶Figure 210–1

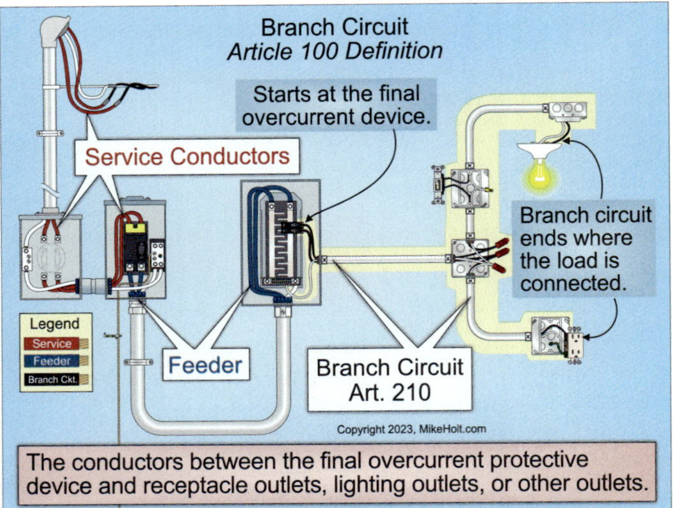

▶Figure 210–2

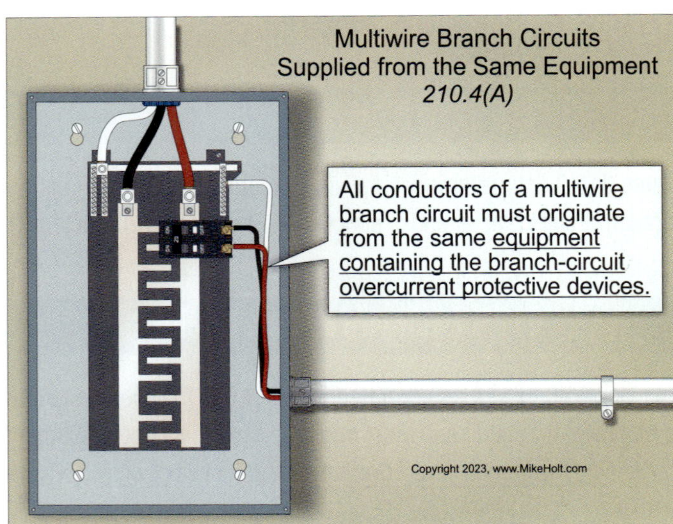

▶Figure 210–3

All conductors of a circuit (including the neutral and equipment grounding conductors) must be installed together in the same raceway, cable, trench, cord, or cable tray [300.3(B)], except as permitted by 300.3(B)(1) through (4).

Note 2: For the requirements relating to the continuity of the neutral conductor on multiwire branch circuits, see 300.13(B). ▶Figure 210–4

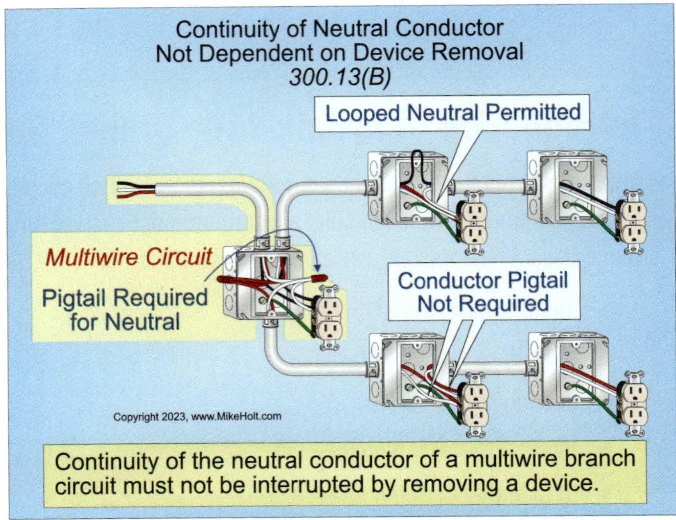

▶Figure 210–4

According to Article 100, "Multiwire Branch Circuit" consists of two or more circuit phase conductors with a common neutral conductor. This type of circuit has a voltage between the phase conductors and an equal difference of voltage from each phase conductor to the common neutral conductor. ▶Figure 210–5

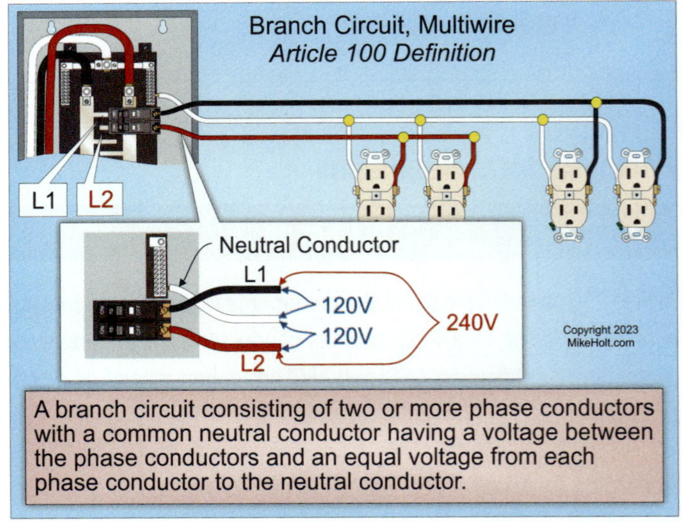

▶Figure 210–5

(B) Disconnecting Means. Each multiwire branch circuit must have a means to simultaneously disconnect phase conductors at the point where the circuit originates. ▶Figure 210–6

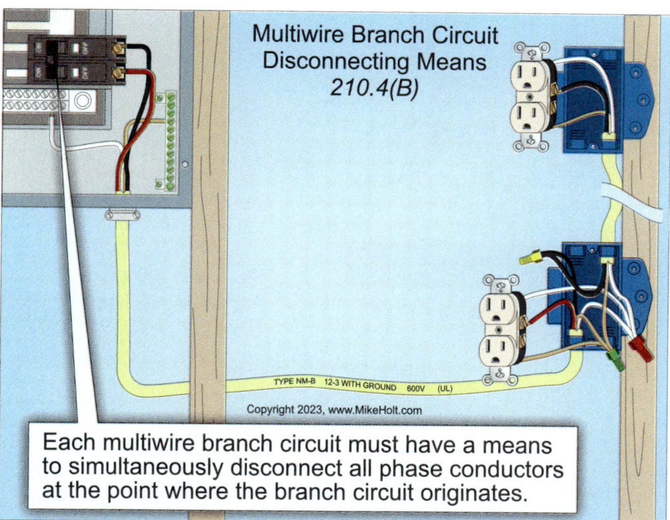

▶Figure 210–6

Note: Individual single-pole circuit breakers with handle ties identified for the purposes or a circuit breaker with a common internal trip, can be used for this application [240.15(B)(1)]. ▶Figure 210–7

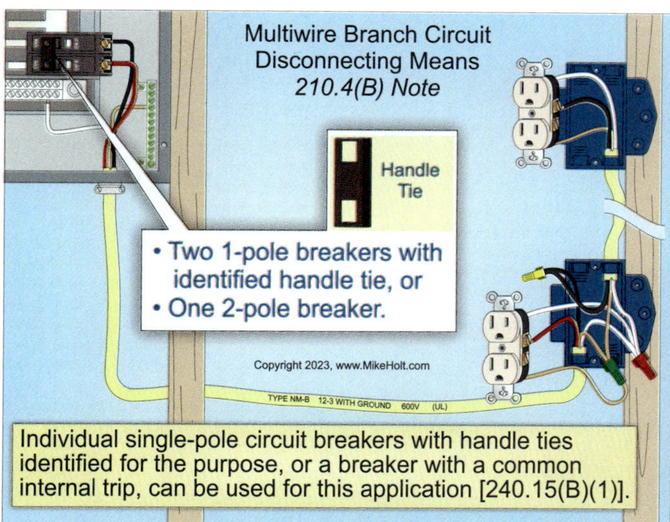

▶Figure 210–7

> **Caution**
>
> ⚠ **CAUTION:** This rule is intended to prevent people from working on energized circuits they thought were disconnected.

(C) Line-to-Neutral Loads. Multiwire branch circuits must supply only line-to-neutral loads.

Ex 1: A multiwire branch circuit can supply an individual utilization equipment with line-to-line and line-to-neutral loads for such equipment as a range or dryer.

Ex 2: A multiwire branch circuit can supply both line-to-line and line-to-neutral loads if the circuit is protected by a circuit breaker with a common internal trip that opens all phase conductors of the multiwire branch circuit simultaneously under a fault condition.

(D) Grouping. Phase and neutral conductors of a multiwire branch circuit must be grouped together by wire markers, cable ties, or similar means in at least one location within the enclosure in accordance with 200.4(B). ▶Figure 210–8 and ▶Figure 210–9

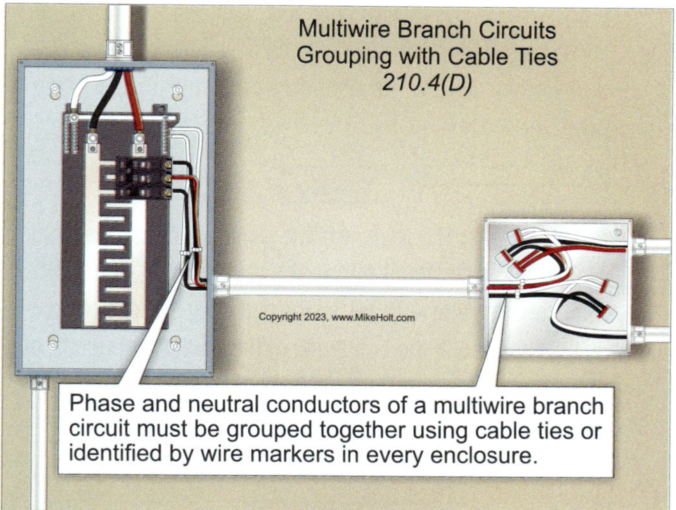

▶Figure 210–8

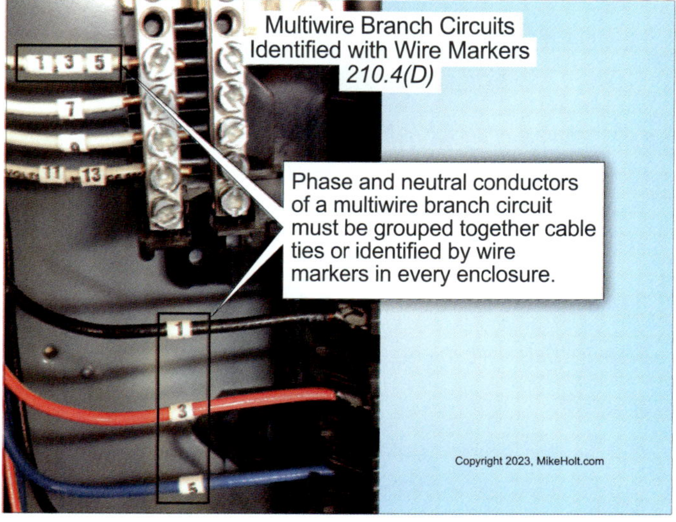

▶Figure 210–9

Author's Comment:

▶ Grouping is not required where the circuit conductors are contained in a single raceway or cable unique to that circuit which makes the grouping obvious [200.4(B) Ex 1].

▶ If the conductors pass through a box or conduit body without any splices or terminations, then grouping is not required [200.4(B) Ex 2].

▶ Grouping associated conductors of a multiwire branch circuit together by cable ties or other means at the point of origin makes it easier to visually identify the conductors of each multiwire branch circuit. The grouping assists in ensuring the correct neutral is paired with the intended circuit conductors at junction points and in correctly connecting multiwire branch-circuit conductors to circuit breakers. If proper care is not exercised when making these connections, two circuit conductors can be accidentally connected to the same phase or line.

Caution

CAUTION: The opening of the phase or neutral conductor of a 2-wire circuit during the replacement of a device does not cause a safety hazard, so the pigtailing of these conductors is not required. If the continuity of the neutral conductor of a multiwire circuit is interrupted (opened), there could be a fire and/or destruction of electrical equipment resulting from overvoltage or undervoltage.

▶ Hazard of an Open Neutral Example

Example: A 3-wire, single-phase, 120/240V multiwire circuit supplies a 1,200W, 120V hair dryer and a 600W, 120V television. ▶Figure 210–10

If the neutral conductor of the multiwire circuit is interrupted, it will cause the 120V television to operate at 160V and consume 1,067W of power (instead of 600W) for only a few seconds before it burns up. ▶Figure 210–11

Solution:

Step 1: Determine the resistance of each appliance.

$R = E^2/P$

R of the Hair Dryer = 120V²/1,200W

R of the Hair Dryer = 12Ω

R of the Television = 120V²/600W

R of the Television = 24Ω

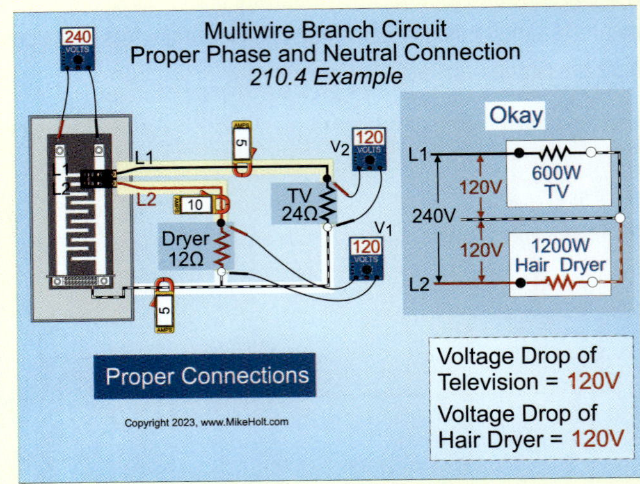

▶Figure 210–10

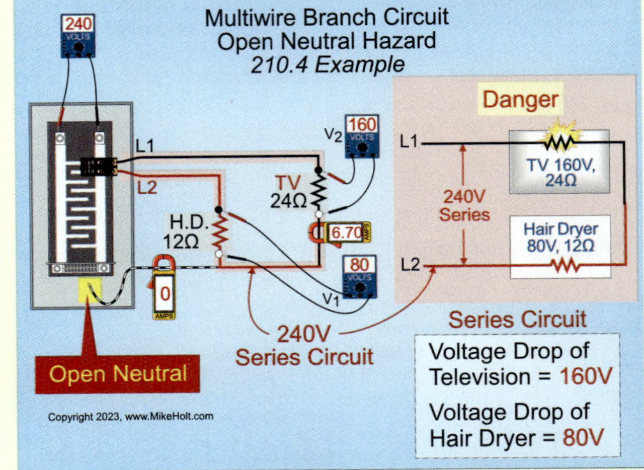

▶Figure 210–11

Step 2: Determine the current of the circuit.

I = Volts/Resistance

Volts = 240V

R = 36Ω (12Ω + 24Ω)

I = 240V/36Ω

I = 6.70A

Step 3: Determine the operating voltage for each appliance.

Volts = I × R

I = 6.70A

R = 12Ω for hair dryer and 24Ω for TV

Voltage of Hair Dryer = 6.70A × 12Ω

Voltage of Hair Dryer = 80V

Voltage of Television = 6.70A × 24Ω

Voltage of Television = 160V

WARNING: Failure to terminate the phase conductors to separate phases can cause the neutral conductor to become overloaded because the current from the phase conductors is additive and the insulation can be damaged or destroyed by excessive heat. Conductor overheating is known to decrease the service life of insulation, which creates the potential for arcing faults and can ultimately lead to fires. It is not known just how long conductor insulation lasts, but heat does decrease its life span. ▶Figure 210–12

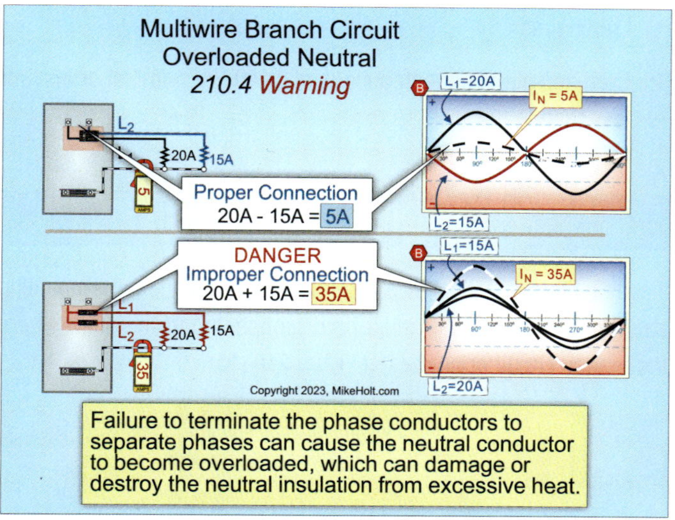

▶Figure 210–12

210.5 Conductor Identification

(A) Neutral Conductor. The branch-circuit neutral conductor must be identified in accordance with 200.6.

(B) Equipment Grounding Conductor. Equipment grounding conductors of the wire type can be bare, covered, or insulated. Insulated equipment grounding conductors 6 AWG and smaller must have a continuous outer finish either green or green with one or more yellow stripes [250.119(A)].

Insulated equipment grounding conductors 4 AWG and larger can be permanently reidentified with green marking at the time of installation where accessible [250.119(B)].

(C) Identification of Phase Conductors. Circuit phase conductors must be identified as follows:

(1) More Than One Nominal Voltage System. Where premises wiring is supplied from more than one nominal voltage system, the phase conductors of branch circuits must be identified by phase or line and by nominal voltage system at termination, connection, and splice points in accordance with 210.5(C)(1)(a) and (b). Different systems within the premises with the same nominal voltage can use the same method of identification.

(a) Means of Identification. Identification of the branch-circuit phase conductors from more than one nominal voltage system can be by color coding, marking tape, tagging, or other means approved by the authority having jurisdiction. ▶Figure 210–13

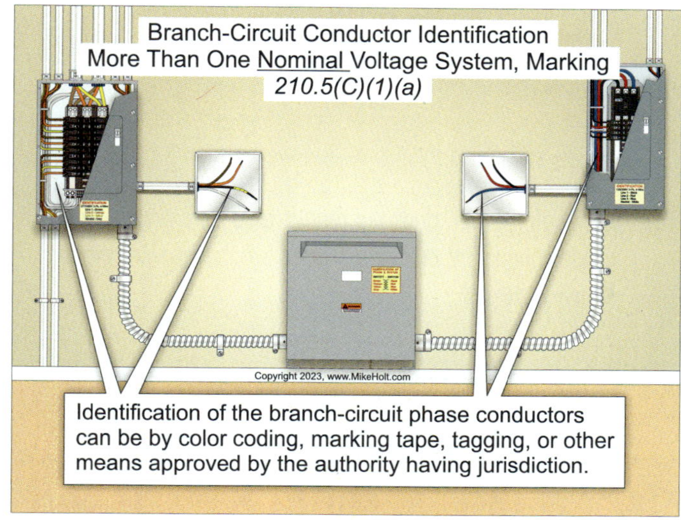

▶Figure 210–13

(b) Posting of Identification. Branch-circuit phase conductor identification must be readily available or posted at panelboard. It is not handwritten and must be sufficiently durable to withstand the environment involved. ▶Figure 210–14

Ex: Where a different voltage system is added to an existing installation, branch-circuit identification is only required for the new one. Each nominal voltage system distribution equipment must have a label with the words "other unidentified systems exist on the premises."

Author's Comment:

▶ When a premises has more than one voltage system supplying branch circuits, the phase conductors must be identified by phase and system. This can be done by permanently posting an identification legend that describes the method used, such as color-coded marking tape or color-coded insulation.

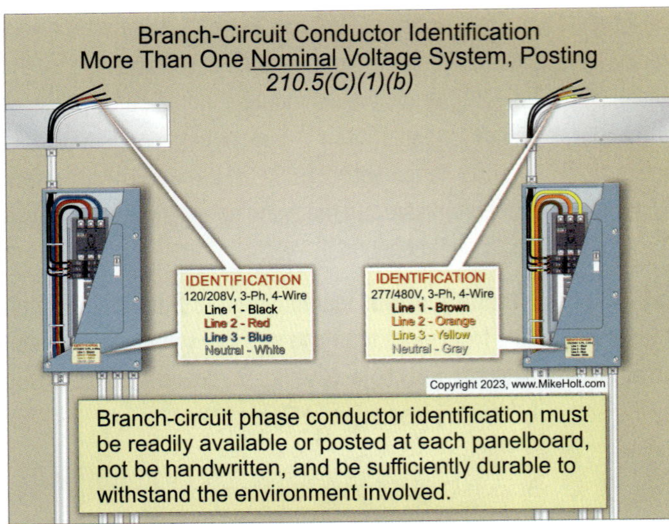

▸Figure 210–14

Author's Comment:

▸ Although the *NEC* does not require a specific color code for
phase conductors, electricians often use the following system:
▸Figure 210–15

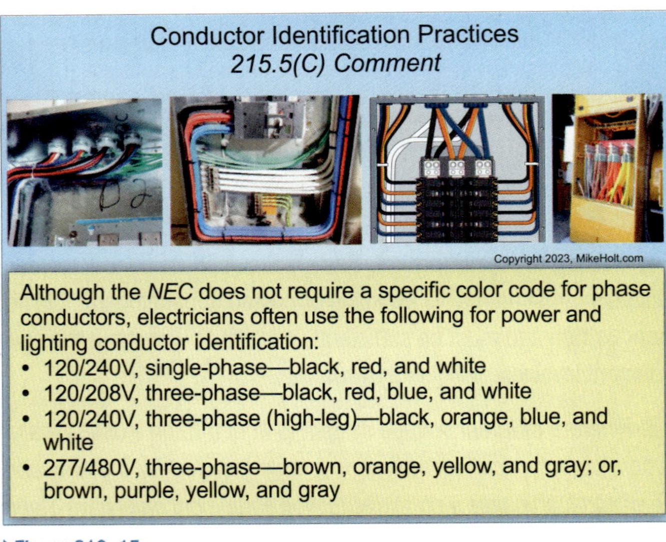

▸Figure 210–15

▸ 120/240V, single-phase–black, red, and white

▸ 120/208V, three-phase–black, red, blue, and white

▸ 120/240V, three-phase (high-leg)–black, orange, blue,
and white

▸ 277/480V, three-phase–brown, orange, yellow, and gray;
or, brown, purple, yellow, and gray

▸ Whichever color scheme is used, it is important for it to
remain consistent wherever phase conductors are terminated or accessible throughout the entire premises. This is
especially important when identifying different system voltages and neutrals.

210.6 Branch-Circuit Voltage

(A) Voltage Limitations. In dwelling units and guest rooms or guest
suites of hotels, motels, and similar occupancies, the voltage between
conductors is not permitted to exceed 120V for:

(1) Luminaires

(2) Cord-and-plug-connected loads of 1440 VA, nominal or less, or
less than ¼ hp

210.7 Multiple Branch Circuits

If two circuits supplying devices or equipment are on the same mounting
strap, phase conductors must be disconnected at the point where
the branch circuit originates. ▸Figure 210–16

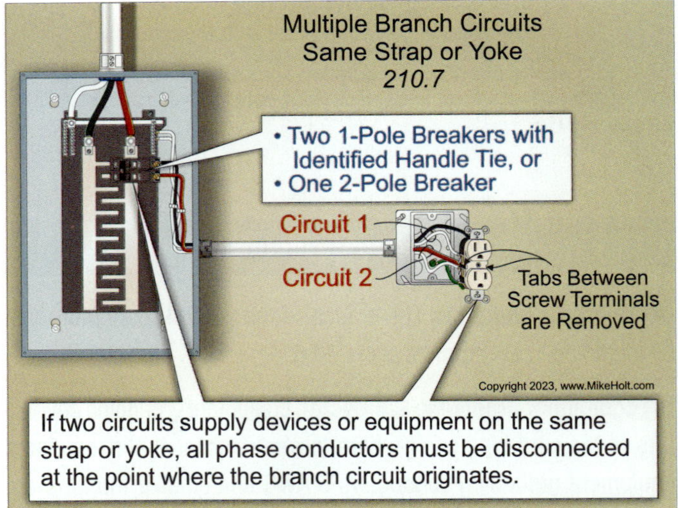

▸Figure 210–16

Author's Comment:

▸ Individual single-pole circuit breakers with handle ties identified for the purpose or a circuit breaker with a common
internal trip can be used for this application [240.15(B)(1)].

210.17 Guest Rooms and Guest Suites

Guest rooms and guest suites with permanent provisions for cooking located in the following locations must have branch circuits installed to meet the rules for dwelling units:

(1) Hotels

(2) Motels

(3) Assisted-living facilities

Note 2: For the definition of assisted-living facilities, see NFPA 101, *Life Safety Code*.

Author's Comment:

▸ In accordance with NFPA 101, *Life Safety Code*, section 3.3.198.12(5), an assisted-living facility is defined as an occupancy used for the lodging and boarding of four or more residents for the purposes of providing personal care services.

Part II. Branch-Circuit Ratings

210.19 Conductor Sizing

Branch Circuits. Branch circuits must be sized to have an ampacity in accordance with 210.19(A) through (D).

Note: The *NEC* recommends that branch-circuit conductors be sized to prevent a voltage drop of not more than 3 percent. In addition, it recommends that the total voltage drop on both feeders and branch circuits should not exceed 5 percent. ▸Figure 210–17

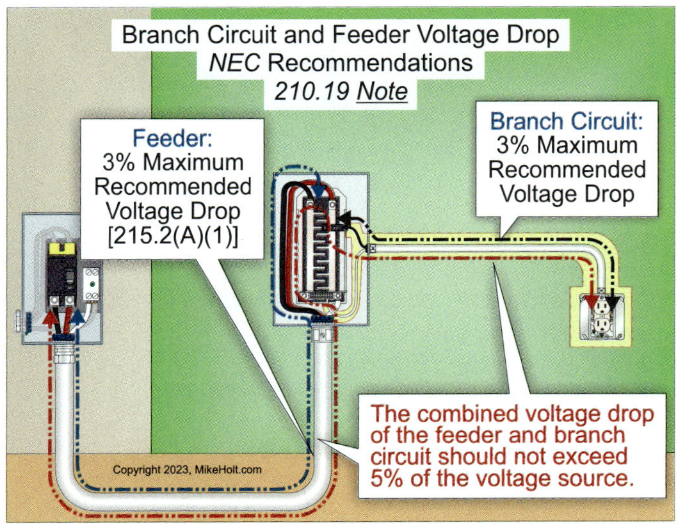

▸Figure 210–17

Author's Comment:

▸ Sizing conductors to accommodate the voltage drop percentages indicated in the *NEC*'s Informational Note is not a *Code* requirement because Informational Notes contain information only and are not enforceable [90.5(C)]. ▸Figure 210–18

▸ See 695.7 for fire pump controller voltage-drop requirements.

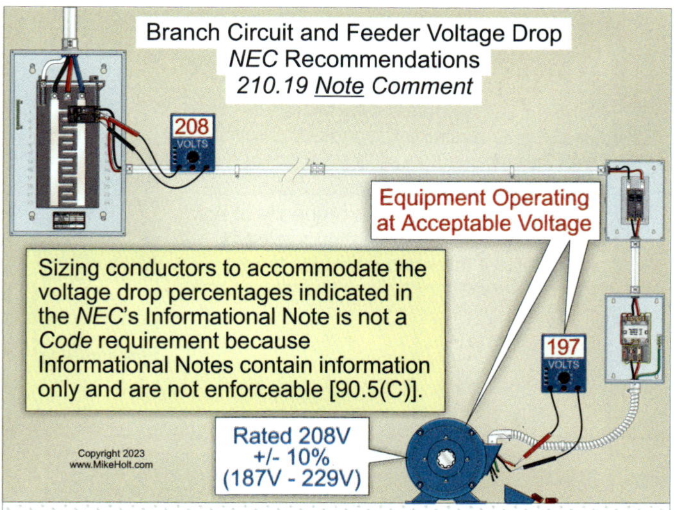

▸Figure 210–18

(A) General. Branch-circuit conductors must be sized to have an ampacity of not less than the largest of 210.19(A)(1) or (2): ▸Figure 210–19

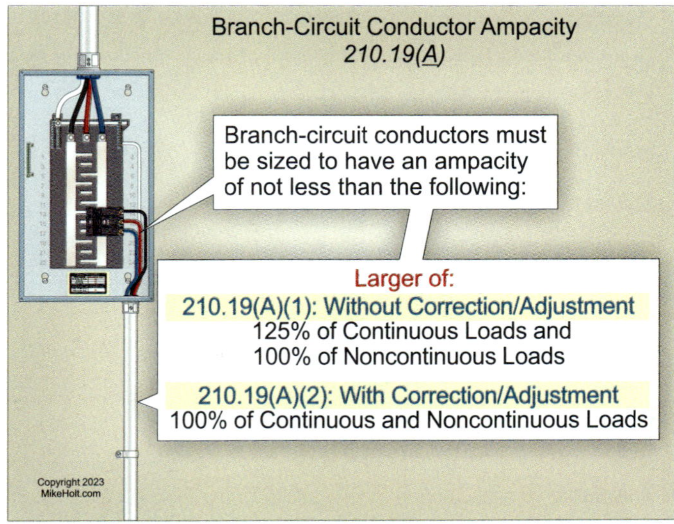

▸Figure 210–19

(1) Without Conductor Ampacity Correction/Adjustment. Branch circuit conductors must be sized to have an ampacity of not less than 125 percent of the continuous loads, plus 100 percent of the noncontinuous loads, based on the temperature rating of equipment in accordance with 110.14(C)(1) and Table 310.16, prior to conductor ampacity correction and/or adjustment. ▶Figure 210–20

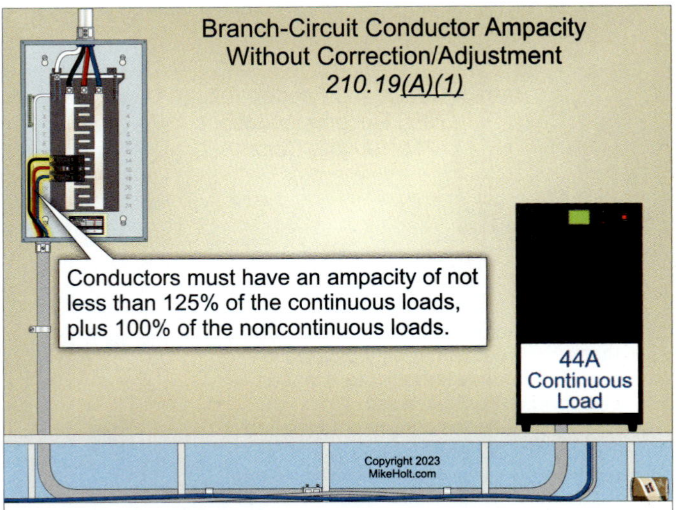

▶Figure 210–20

According to Article 100, "Continuous Load" is expected for three hours or more continuously.

▶ Example 1

Question: What size conductors rated 90°C are required for a circuit supplying a 44A continuous load where the equipment is rated for 75°C conductors? ▶Figure 210–21

(a) 8 AWG   (b) 6 AWG   (c) 4 AWG   (d) 3 AWG

Solution:

Step 1: Conductor Ampacity. The conductor must have an ampacity of not less than 55A (44A × 125%).

Step 2: Size conductors in accordance with 110.14(C)(1)(a)(3) and Table 310.16.

6 AWG rated 65A at 75°C is suitable [Table 310.16].

Answer: (b) 6 AWG

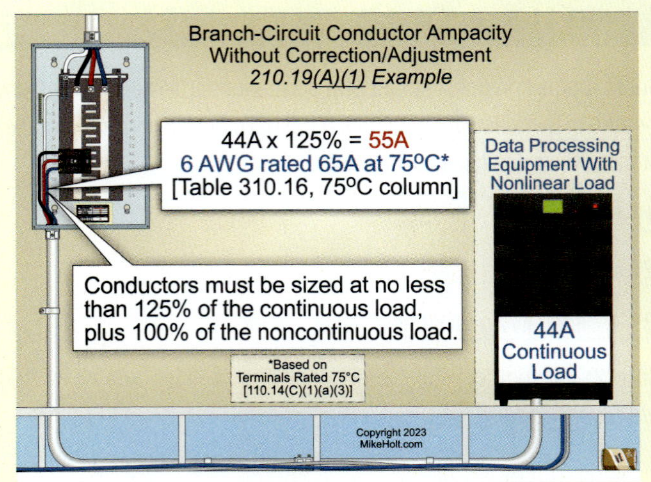

▶Figure 210–21

▶ EV Charger Example

Question: What size conductor is required for EV charger rated 40A continuous where the equipment is rated for 75°C conductors? ▶Figure 210–22

(a) 8 AWG   (b) 6 AWG   (c) 4 AWG   (d) 3 AWG

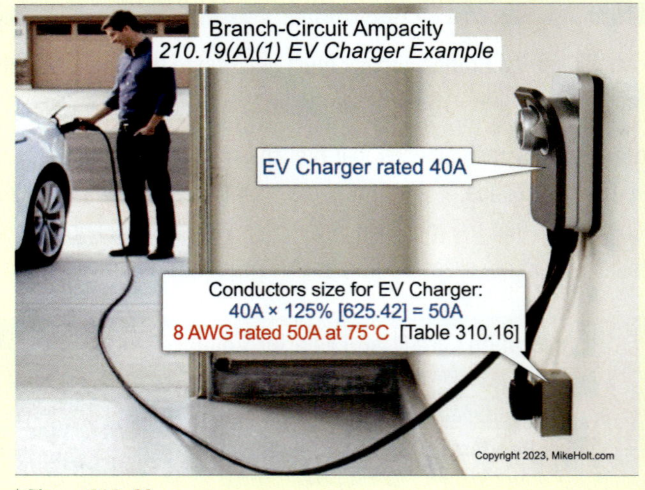

▶Figure 210–22

Solution:

The conductors must have an ampacity of not less than 60A (40A × 125%) [625.42].

8 AWG rated 50A at 75°C is suitable [Table 310.16].

Answer: (a) 8 AWG

▶ EV Charger NM Cable Example

Question: What size Type NM cable is required for an EV charger rated 40A continuous, where the cable is rated 60°C [334.80]? ▶Figure 210–23

(a) 10 AWG   (b) 8 AWG   (c) 6 AWG   (d) 4 AWG

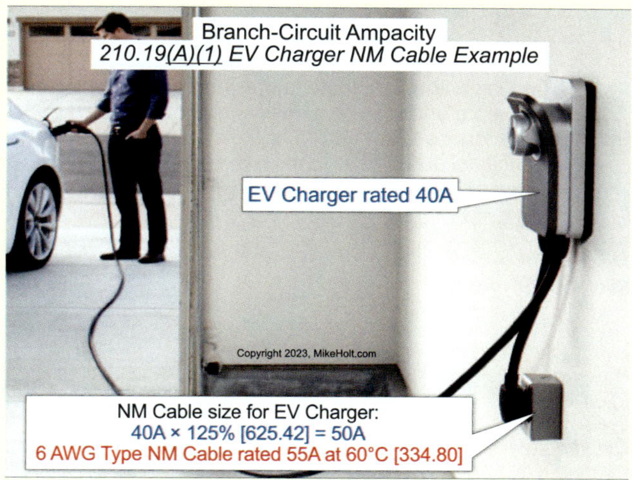

▶Figure 210–23

Solution:

Step 1: *According to 334.80, Type NM Cable must be sized to the 60°C column of Table 310.16.*

Step 2: *Type NM cable conductors must have an ampacity of not less than 50A (40A × 125% [625.42]).*

Step 3: *6 AWG Type NM Cable is rated 55A at 60°C [Table 310.16].*

Answer: *(c) 6 AWG Type NM Cable*

Ex: If the assembly, including the overcurrent devices protecting the branch circuits, is listed for operation at 100 percent of its rating, the ampacity of the branch-circuit conductors can be sized at 100 percent of the continuous load plus the noncontinuous load.

(2) With Conductor Ampacity Correction/Adjustment. Conductors must be sized to have an ampacity of not less than 100 percent of the total load after conductor ampacity correction and/or adjustment in accordance with Table 310.15(B)(1)(1) and Table 310.15(C)(1).
▶Figure 210–24

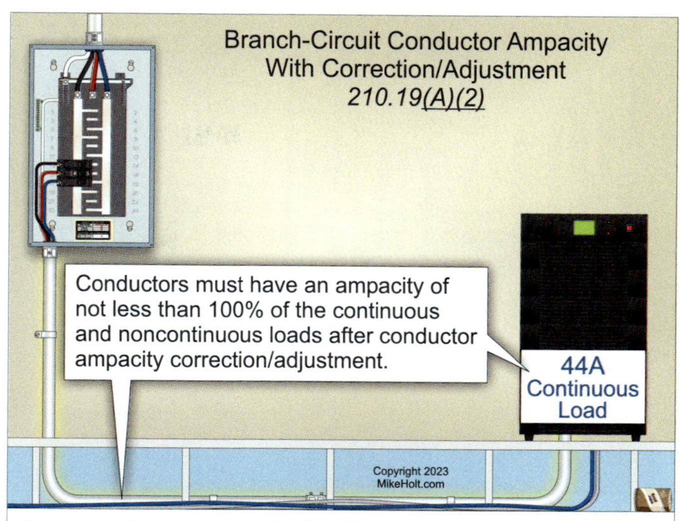

▶Figure 210–24

Author's Comment:

▶ The temperature ampacity correction of 310.15(B)(1)(1) and adjustment ampacity factors of 310.15(C)(1) are applied to the ampacities listed in Table 310.16, based on the conductor insulation temperature rating [310.15(A)].

▶ Example 2

Question: What size conductors rated 90°C are required for a circuit containing four current-carrying conductors supplying a 44A continuous load where the equipment is rated for 75°C conductor?

(a) 10 AWG   (b) 8 AWG   (c) 6 AWG   (d) 4 AWG

Solution:

Step 1: *The circuit conductors must have an ampacity of 44A after conductor ampacity adjustment [Table 310.15(C)(1)], based on the conductor insulation rating of 90°C [110.14(C)(1)(a)(3)].*

Conductor Ampacity at 90°C = Actual Load/Adjustment

Actual Load = 44A

Adjustment [Table 310.15(C)(1)] = 80% (four current-carrying conductors)

Conductor Ampacity at 90°C Column = 44A/80%

Conductor Ampacity at 90°C Column = 55A

Step 2: *Select the conductors from the 90°C column of Table 310.16.*
▶Figure 210–25

• • •

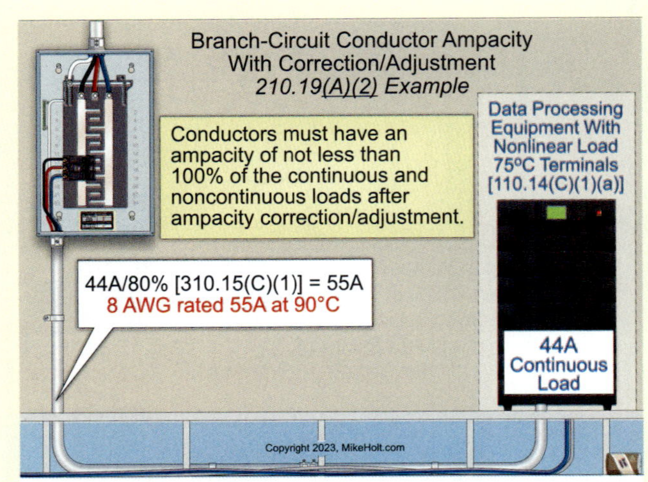

▶Figure 210–25

8 AWG is rated 55A at 90°C before any correction and adjustment.

Note: Branch-circuit conductors must be sized to have an ampacity of not less than the largest of 210.19(A)(1) or (A)(2). In this case, based on the conditions specified in this example, 6 AWG is the minimum permitted size in accordance with 210.19(A)(1). ▶**Figure 210–26**

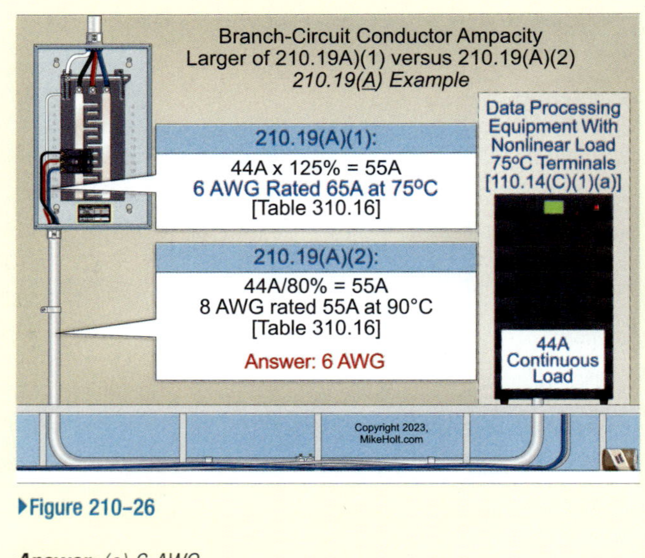

▶Figure 210–26

Answer: *(c) 6 AWG*

Ex to (1) and (2): Conductors that terminate to pressure connectors in separate enclosures or wireways at both ends in accordance with 110.14(C)(2) can have an ampacity of 100 percent of all loads based on the 90°C column of Table 310.16. ▶Figure 210–27

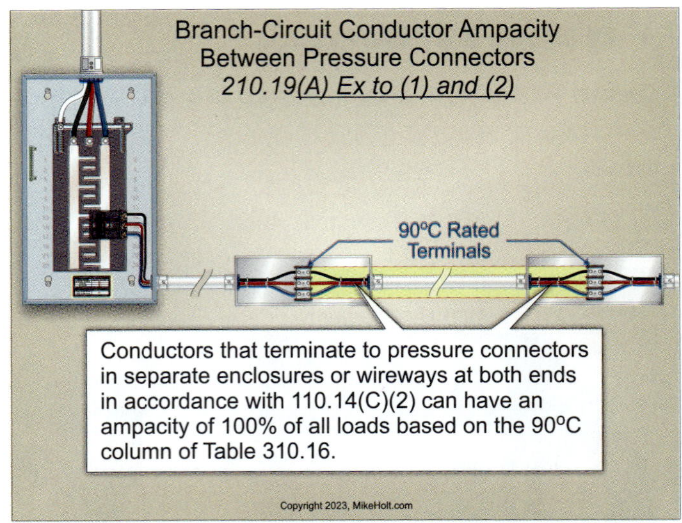

▶Figure 210–27

▶ Example 3

Question: What size branch-circuit conductors rated 90°C are required between terminals rated 90°C for a circuit supplying a 44A continuous load where the conductors are protected by a 60A breaker? ▶**Figure 210–28**

(a) 10 AWG   *(b) 8 AWG*   *(c) 6 AWG*   *(d) 4 AWG*

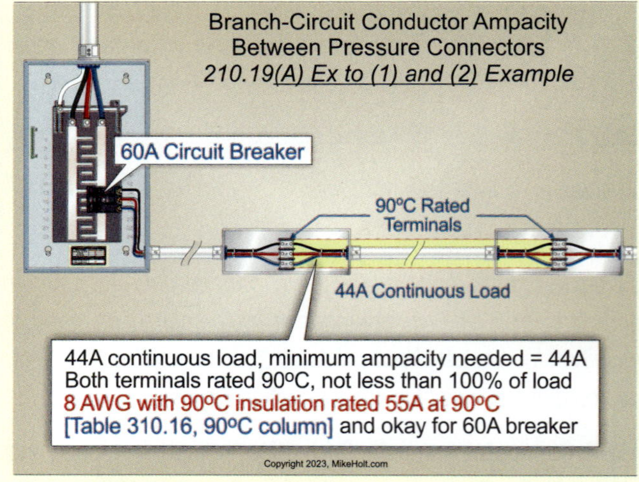

▶Figure 210–28

Solution:

Size conductors in accordance with 110.14(C)(2) and Table 310.16: When terminals at each end of a conductor have different terminal temperature ratings, use the lower temperature rating when sizing conductors from Table 310.16.

In this case, the terminals are both rated 90°C, so the conductors are selected in accordance with the 90°C column of Table 310.16.

Based on the 44A load at 100 percent, 8 AWG is rated 55A at 90°C, and is permitted to be protected by a 60A overcurrent protective device [240.4(B)].

Answer: (b) 8 AWG

210.20 Overcurrent Protection

Branch-circuit conductors and equipment must be protected by overcurrent protective devices with a rating or setting that complies with 210.20(A) through (D).

(A) Continuous and Noncontinuous Loads. Branch-circuit overcurrent protective devices must have an ampere rating of not less than 125 percent of the continuous loads, plus 100 percent of the noncontinuous loads. ▶Figure 210–29

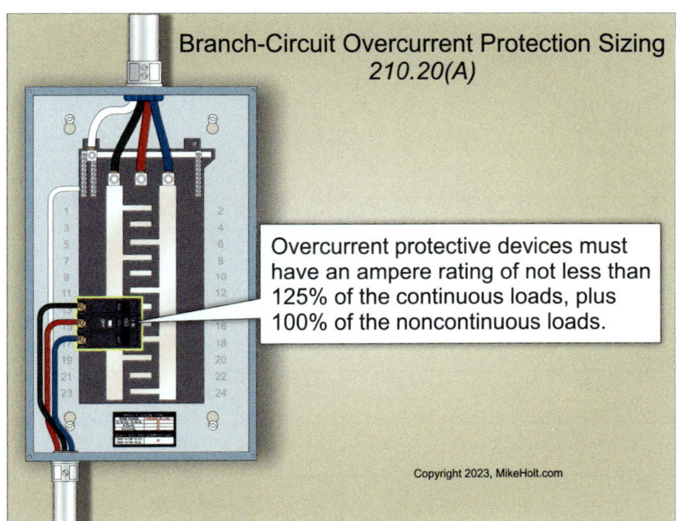

▶Figure 210–29

▶ **Example**

Question: What size circuit breaker is required for a branch circuit that has a 44A continuous load? ▶Figure 210–30

(a) 20A   (b) 30A   (c) 50A   (d) 60A

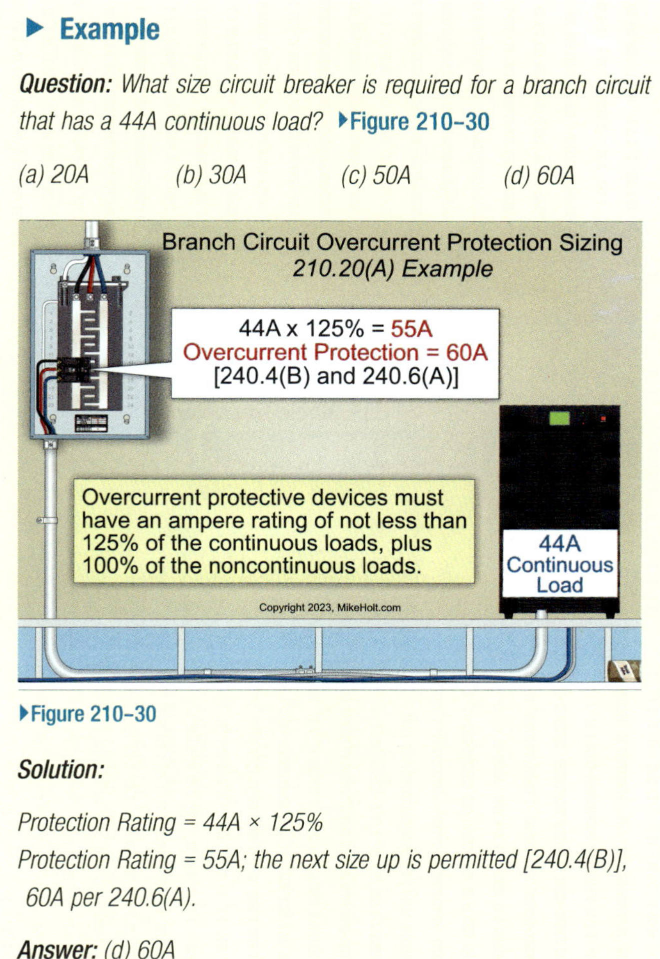

▶Figure 210–30

Solution:

Protection Rating = 44A × 125%
Protection Rating = 55A; the next size up is permitted [240.4(B)], 60A per 240.6(A).

Answer: (d) 60A

Ex: Where the overcurrent protective device is listed for operation at 100 percent of its rating, the ampere rating of the overcurrent protective device must not be less than 100 percent of the sum of the continuous and noncontinuous loads.

(B) Conductor Protection. Conductors must be protected in accordance with 240.4 and flexible cords and fixture wires must be protected in accordance with 240.5.

(C) Equipment. The overcurrent protective device is not permitted to exceed that specified in the applicable articles referenced in Table 240.3 for equipment.

(D) Outlet Devices. The overcurrent protective device is not permitted to exceed that specified in 210.21 for outlet devices.

210.21 Receptacle Rating

(B) Receptacles—Rating and Load Capacity.

(1) Single Receptacle. A single receptacle must have an ampere rating no less than the rating of the circuit overcurrent protective device. ▶Figure 210–31

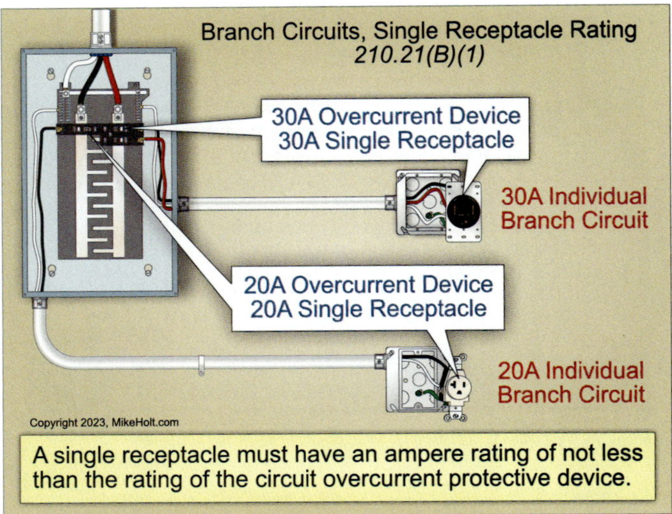

▶Figure 210–31

Note: A single receptacle has only one contact device on its yoke. A duplex receptacle is not a single receptacle since it has two receptacles on the yoke of a receptacle.

According to Article 100, a "Receptacle" is a contact device installed at an outlet for the connection of an attachment plug, or for the connection of equipment designed to mate with the contact device.

(2) Total Cord-and-Plug-Connected Load. Where connected to a branch circuit supplying two or more receptacles or outlets, a receptacle is not permitted to supply a total cord-and-plug-connected load in excess of the maximum specified in Table 210.21(B)(2).

Table 210.21(B)(2) Maximum Cord-and-Plug-Connected Load to Receptacle

Circuit Rating (Amperes)	Receptacle Rating (Amperes)	Maximum Load (Amperes)
15 or 20	15	12
20	20	16
30	30	24

(3) Multiple Receptacles. Where multiple receptacles are connected to a branch circuit, their ampere ratings must be in accordance with Table 210.21(B)(3).

> **Author's Comment:**
>
> ▸ Table 210.21(B)(3) permits both 15A and 20A receptacles on a 20A multioutlet circuit. ▶Figure 210–32

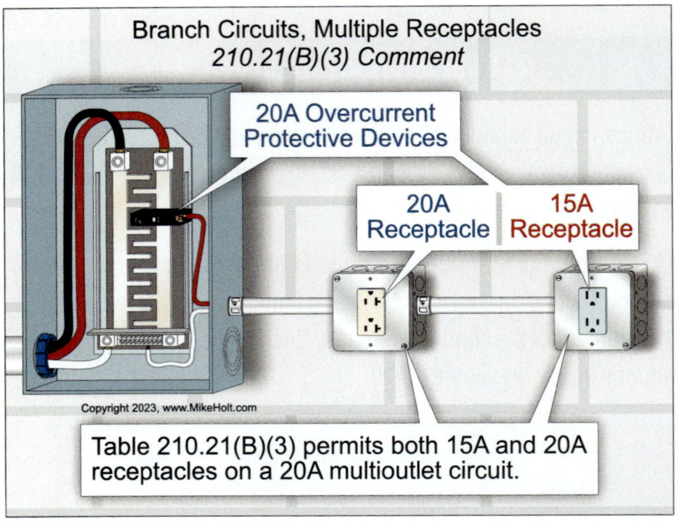

▶Figure 210–32

Table 210.21(B)(3) Receptacle Ratings

Circuit Rating	Receptacle Rating
15A	15A
20A	15A or 20A
30A	30A
40A	50A
50A	50A

210.23 Multiple-Outlet Branch Circuits

(B) 15A and 20A Branch Circuits. A 15A or 20A branch circuit can supply lighting, equipment, or any combination in accordance with 210.23(B)(1) and (B)(2). ▶Figure 210–33

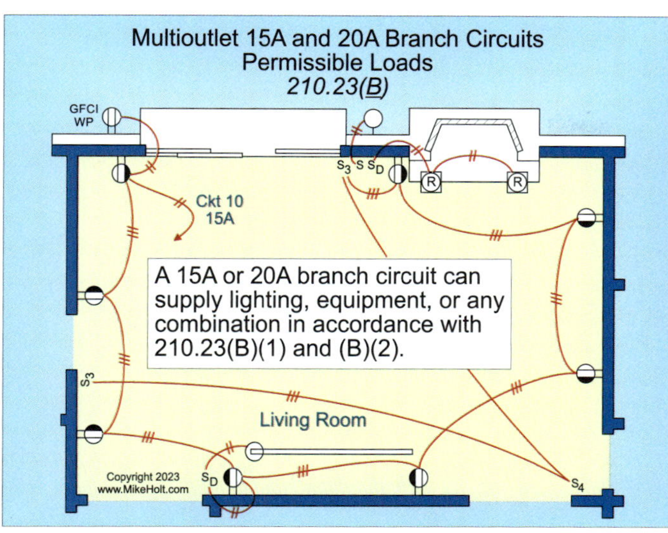

▶Figure 210–33

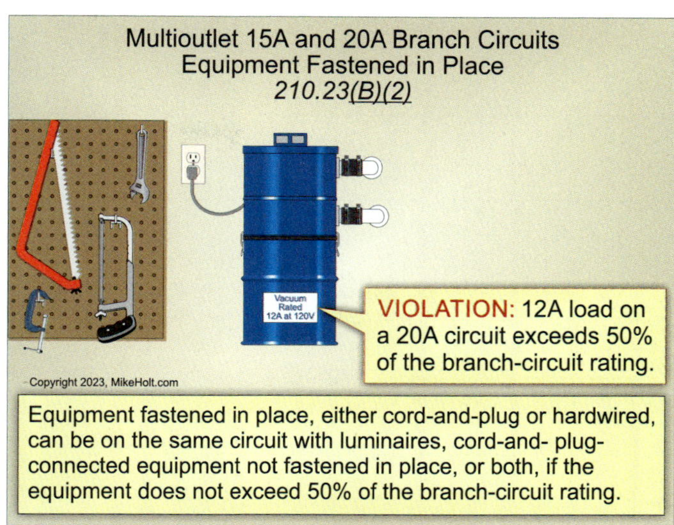

▶Figure 210–34

(2) Equipment Fastened in Place. Equipment fastened in place, either cord-and-plug or hardwired, can be on the same circuit with luminaires, cord-and-plug-connected equipment not fastened in place, (or both) if the equipment does not exceed 50 percent of the branch-circuit rating. ▶Figure 210–34

FEEDERS

Introduction to Article 215—Feeders

Article 215 contains the general requirements for feeder conductors which extend between a service disconnect, transformer, generator, PV system output circuit, or other power-supply source and the branch-circuit overcurrent protective device. Feeders have specific requirement permissions that differ from branch circuits making the proper identification of feeders critical. Some topics covered in this material for Article 215 include:

▸ Feeder Rating and Size

▸ Overcurrent Protection

▸ Feeder GFPE

▸ Identification

▸ Barrier Requirements

▸ Surge-Protective Requirements

215.1 Scope

Article 215 covers the installation, conductor sizing, and overcurrent protection requirements for feeder conductors not over 1000V ac or 1500V dc. ▸Figure 215–1

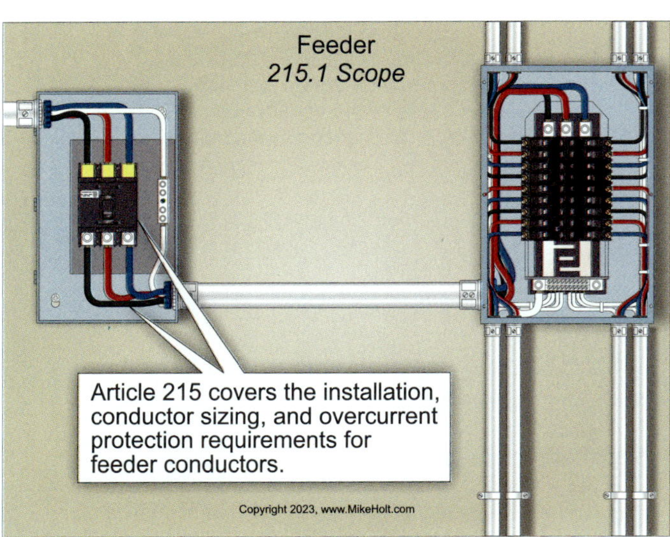

▸Figure 215–1

According to Article 100, "Feeders" are the conductors between the service disconnect, a separately derived system, or other power supply, and the final branch-circuit overcurrent protective device. ▸Figure 215–2 and ▸Figure 215–3

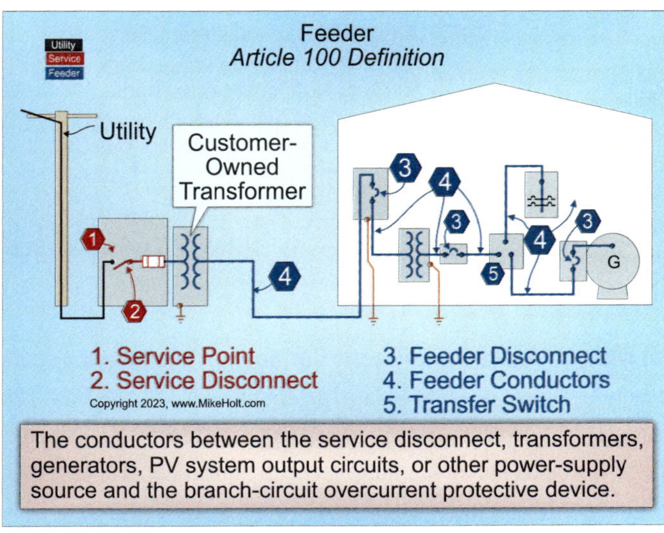

▸Figure 215–2

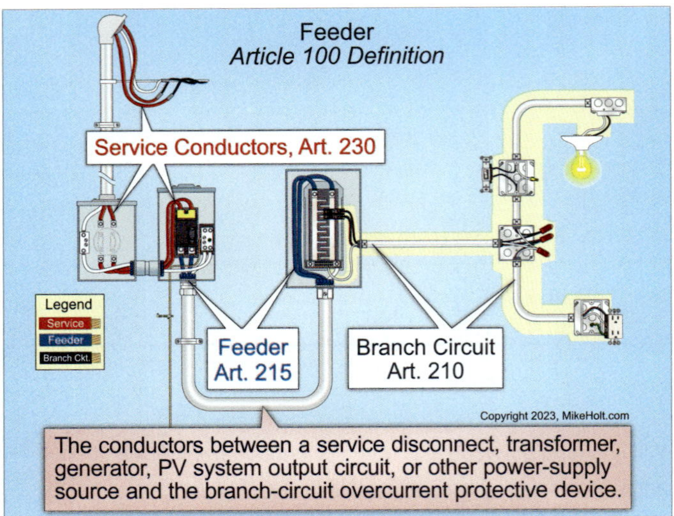

▶Figure 215–3

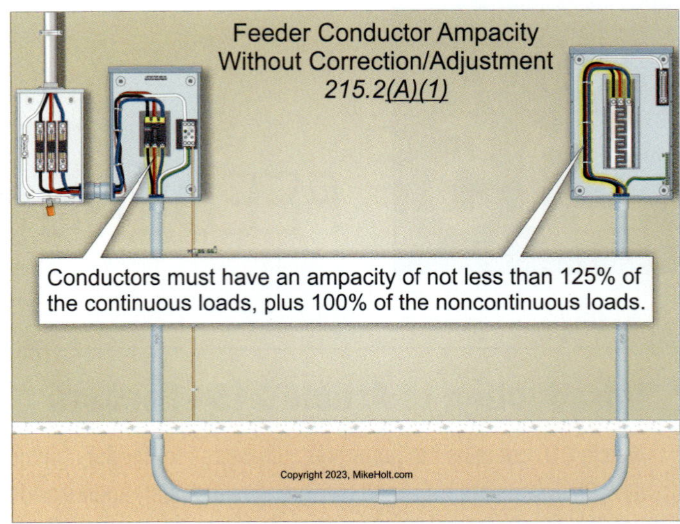

▶Figure 215–5

215.2 Conductor Sizing

(A) General. Feeder conductors must be sized to have an ampacity not less than the largest of the calculations contained in 215.2(1) or (2).
▶Figure 215–4

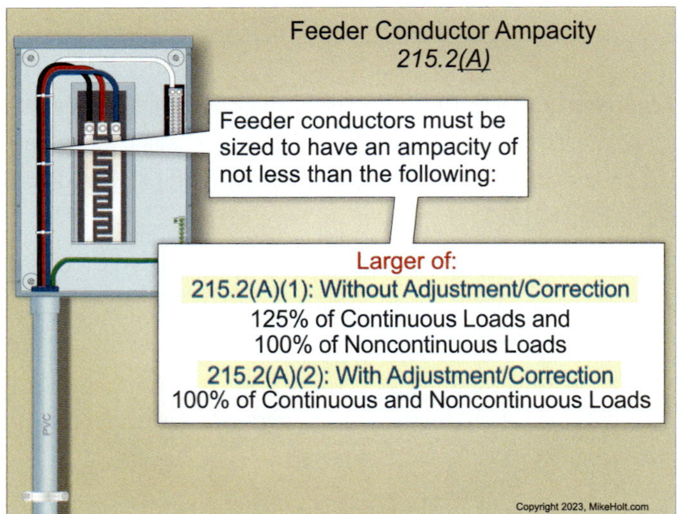

▶Figure 215–4

(1) Without Conductor Ampacity Correction/Adjustment. Feeder conductors must be sized to have an ampacity of not less than 125 percent of the continuous loads, plus 100 percent of the noncontinuous loads, based on the temperature rating of equipment in accordance with 110.14(C)(1) and Table 310.16, prior to conductor ampacity correction and/or adjustment. ▶Figure 215–5

▶ Example 1

Question: What size conductors are required for a 100A continuous load and 100A noncontinuous load where the equipment is rated for 75°C conductor? ▶Figure 215–6

(a) 1/0 AWG   *(b) 2/0 AWG*   *(c) 3/0 AWG*   *(d) 4/0 AWG*

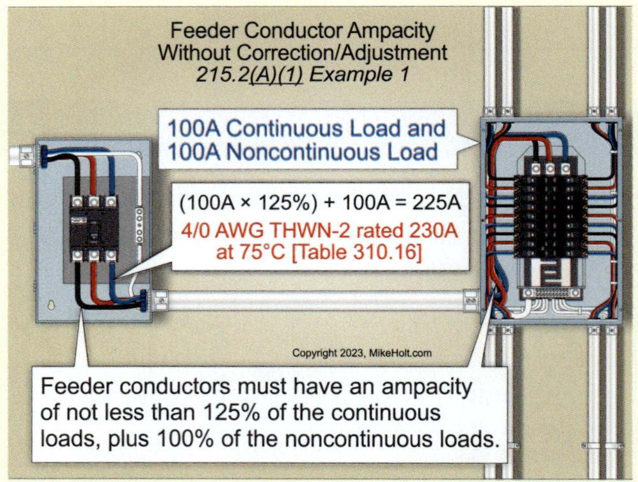

▶Figure 215–6

Solution:

Step 1: Determine the minimum conductor ampacity.

Minimum Conductor Ampacity = (100A × 125%) x 100A
Minimum Conductor Ampacity = 225A

Step 2: Determine the conductor size.

4/0 AWG THWN-2, rated 230A [Table 310.16, 75°C column].

Answer: (d) 4/0 AWG

▶ Example 2

Question: *What size conductors are required for a 180A continuous load where the equipment is rated for 75°C conductor?* ▶Figure 215–7

(a) 1/0 AWG   (b) 2/0 AWG   (c) 3/0 AWG   (d) 4/0 AWG

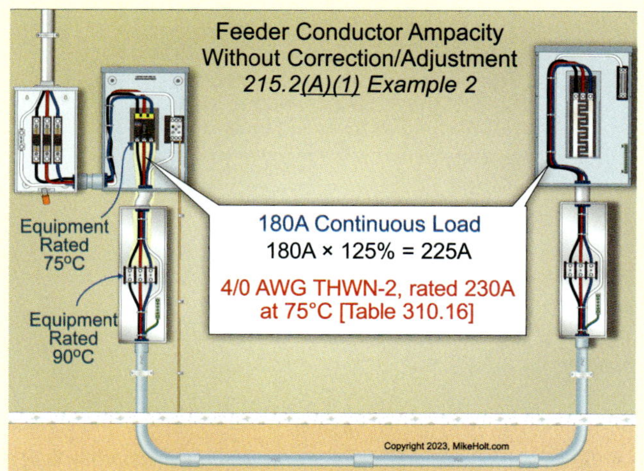

▶Figure 215–7

Solution:

Step 1: *Determine the minimum conductor ampacity.*

Minimum Conductor Ampacity = 180A × 125%
Minimum Conductor Ampacity = 225A

Step 2: *Determine the conductor size.*

4/0 AWG THWN-2, rated 230A [Table 310.16, 75°C column].

Answer: *(d) 4/0 AWG*

Ex 2: Conductors that terminate to pressure connectors in separate enclosures or wireways at both ends in accordance with 110.14(C)(2) can have an ampacity of 100 percent of all loads based on the 90°C column of Table 310.16. ▶Figure 215–8

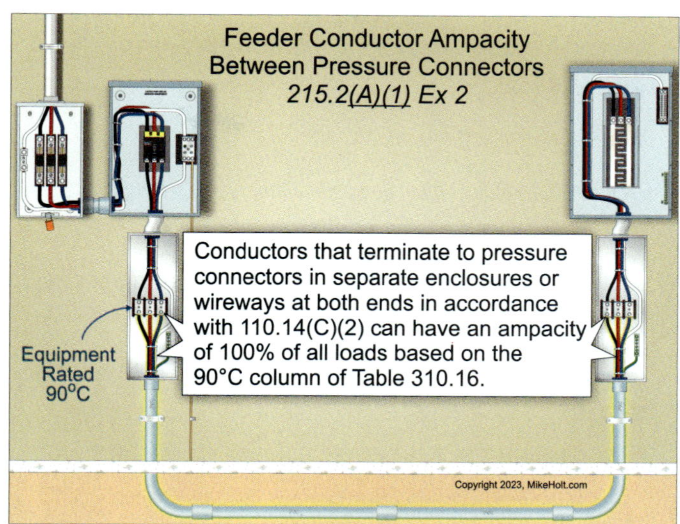

▶Figure 215–8

▶ Example 3

Question: *What size AWG, THWN-2 feeder conductors rated 90°C are required between power distribution blocks rated 90°C for a circuit supplying a 180A continuous load where the circuit overcurrent protection is 400A?* ▶Figure 215–9

(a) 1/0 AWG   (b) 2/0 AWG   (c) 3/0 AWG   (d) 4/0 AWG

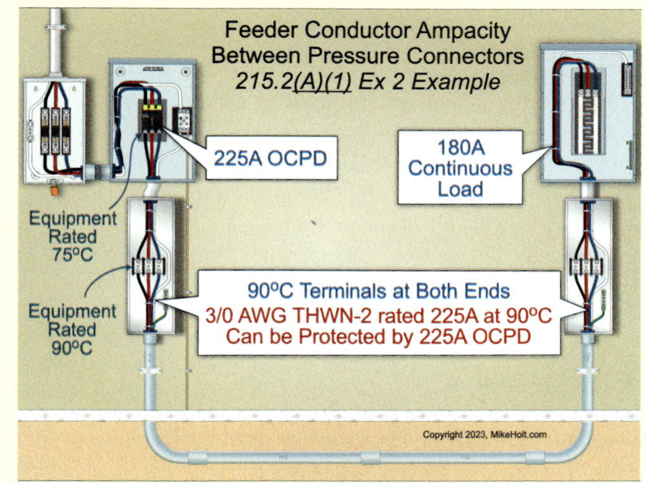

▶Figure 215–9

Solution:

Step 1: *Determine the minimum conductor ampacity.*

When terminals of separately installed connectors at each end of a conductor are rated at least 90°C, the feeder conductor between the 90°C rated connectors can be sized to no less than 100 percent of the 180A continuous load based on the 90°C column of Table 310.16 [215.2(A)(1) Ex 2].

• • •

Minimum Conductor Ampacity = 2/0 AWG THWN-2, rated 195A at 90°C

Step 2: *Determine the conductor size.*

The feeder conductors must be sized so they are protected by a 225A circuit breaker in accordance with 240.4.

2/0 AWG THWN-2 rated 195A at 90°C is not permitted to be protected by a 225A circuit breaker.

3/0 AWG THWN-2 rated 225A at 90°C is permitted to be protected by a 225A circuit breaker.

Answer: *(c) 3/0 AWG*

Ex 3: Neutral conductors are permitted to have an ampacity of 100 percent of the continuous and noncontinuous loads. ▶**Figure 215–10**

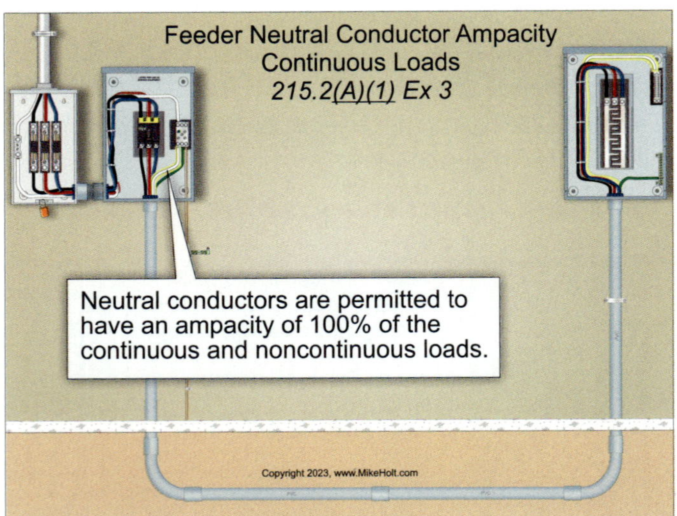

▶Figure 215–10

▶ Example 4

Question: *What size neutral conductor rated 90°C is required for a 125A continuous neutral load where the equipment is rated for 75°C conductor?* ▶**Figure 215–11**

(a) 1 AWG   (b) 2 AWG   (c) 3 AWG   (d) 4 AWG

Solution:

Step 1: *The neutral conductor is sized to the 125A continuous load at 100 percent [215.2(A)(1) Ex 3].*

Step 2: *Size the conductors in accordance with 110.14(C)(1)(b)(2) and Table 310.16.*

1 AWG has an ampacity of 130A [Table 310.16, 75°C column].

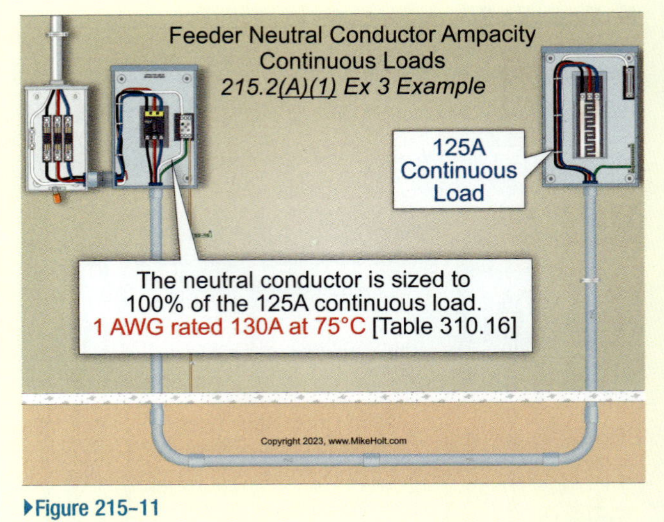

▶Figure 215–11

Answer: *(a) 1 AWG*

Ex: If the assembly, including the overcurrent devices protecting the feeder, is listed for operation at 100 percent of its rating, the ampacity of the conductors can be sized at 100 percent of the continuous load plus the noncontinuous load.

(2) With Conductor Ampacity Correction/Adjustment. Conductors must be sized to have an ampacity of not less than 100 percent of the total load after conductor ampacity correction and/or adjustment in accordance with Table 310.15(B)(1)(1) and Table 310.15(C)(1). ▶**Figure 215–12**

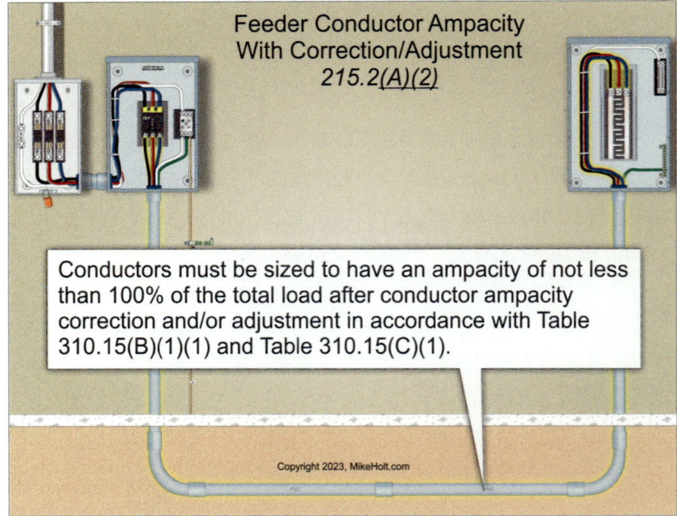

▶Figure 215–12

▶ Example 5

Question: *What size conductors rated 90°C are required for four current-carrying conductors supplying a 180A continuous load in an ambient temperature of 100°F where the equipment is rated for 75°C conductor?*

(a) 4/0 AWG   (b) 300 kcmil   (c) 500 kcmil   (d) 600 kcmil

Note: *According to 215.2(A), the feeder conductor size is determined by the larger of 215.2(A)(1) or (2).*

Solution:

Step 1: *The circuit conductors must have an ampacity of 180A after conductor ampacity temperature correction [Table 310.15(B)(1)(1)] and adjustment [Table 310.15(C)(1)], based on the conductor's insulation rating of 90°C. One way to find the conductor size is to determine the conductor ampacity required to supply a 180A continuous load at 100 percent after correction and adjustment.*

Conductor Ampacity at 90°C = Continuous Load at 100%/ (Correction × Adjustment)

Continuous Load = 180A

Correction [Table 310.15(B)(1)(1)] = 91% (100°F ambient temperature with 90°C Conductor)

Adjustment [Table 310.15(C)(1)] = 80% (four current-carrying conductors)

Conductor Ampacity at 90°C Column = 180A/(91% × 80%)
Conductor Ampacity at 90°C Column = 180A/73%
Conductor Ampacity at 90°C Column = 247A

Step 2: *Select the conductors from the 90°C column of Table 310.16 [110.14(C)(1)(b)(2)].* ▶**Figure 215–13**
4/0 AWG THWN-2 is suitable because it has an ampacity of 260A at 90°C before any correction and adjustment.

Note: *According to 215.2(A), the feeder conductor size is determined by the larger of 215.2(A)(1) or (2). In this case, based on the conditions specified in this example, 4/0 AWG is the minimum size.* ▶**Figure 215–14**

Answer: *(a) 4/0 AWG*

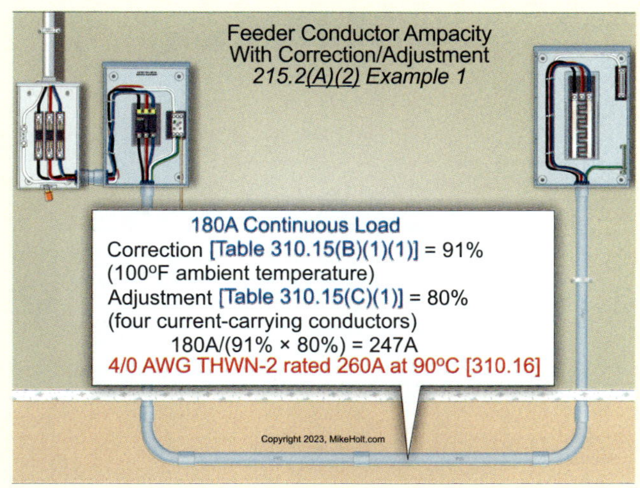

▶Figure 215–13

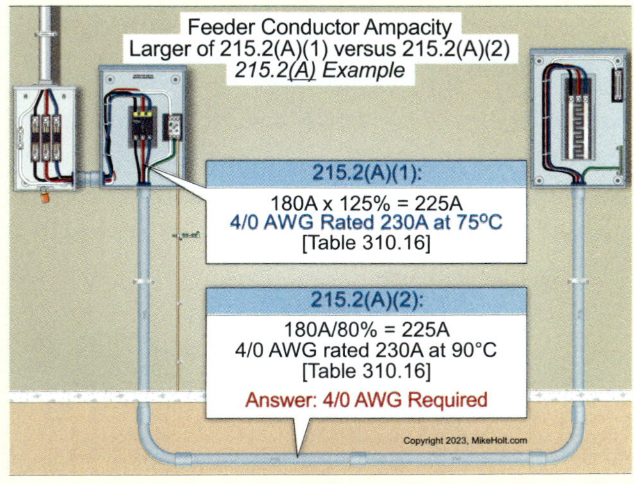

▶Figure 215–14

Note 2: The *NEC* recommends that feeder conductors be sized to prevent a voltage drop of not more than 3 percent. In addition, it recommends that the total voltage drop on both feeders and branch circuits should not exceed 5 percent.

(B) Neutral Conductor Size. The neutral conductor must be sized to carry the maximum unbalanced load in accordance with 220.61, but must not be smaller than the equipment grounding conductor in accordance with 250.122. ▶Figure 215–15

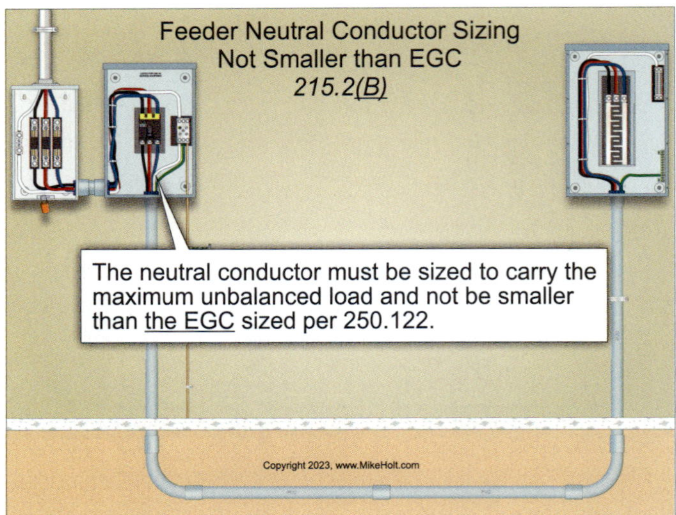

▶Figure 215–15

▶ Example 6

Question: *What size neutral conductor is required for a feeder consisting of 3/0 AWG phase conductors and one neutral conductor protected by a 200A overcurrent protective device when the unbalanced load is 30A and the equipment is rated for 75°C conductor?* ▶Figure 215–16

(a) 3 AWG   (b) 4 AWG   (c) 6 AWG   (d) 8 AWG

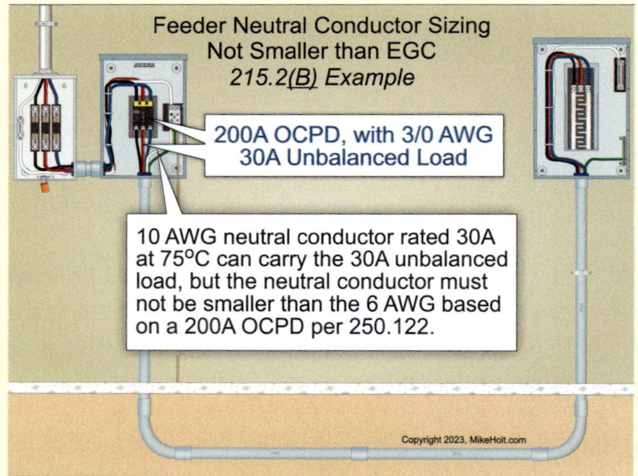

▶Figure 215–16

Solution:

Section 220.61 and Table 310.16 permits 10 AWG neutral conductor rated 30A at 75°C [110.14(C)(1) and Table 310.16] to carry the 30A unbalanced load, but must not be smaller than the 6 AWG equipment grounding conductor in accordance with 250.122.

Answer: *(c) 6 AWG*

215.3 Overcurrent Protection Sizing

Feeder overcurrent protective devices must have an ampere rating of not less than 125 percent of the continuous loads, plus 100 percent of the noncontinuous loads. ▶Figure 215–17

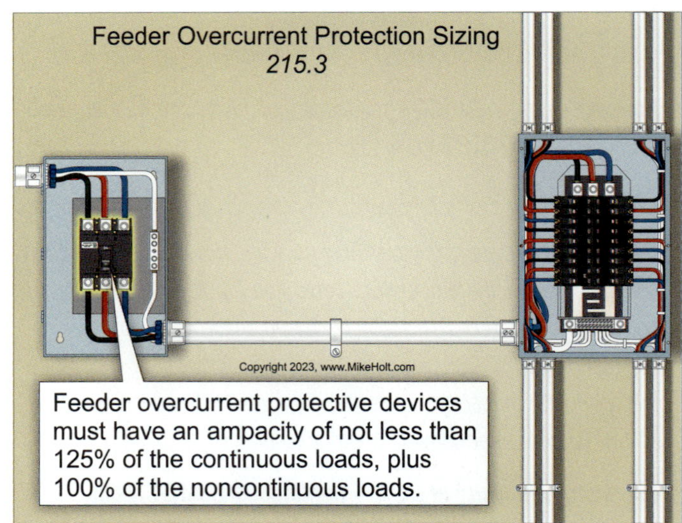

▶Figure 215–17

▶ Example

Question: *What size feeder overcurrent protection is required for a 100A continuous load and a 100A noncontinuous load?* ▶Figure 215–18

(a) 200A   (b) 225A   (c) 250A   (d) 300A

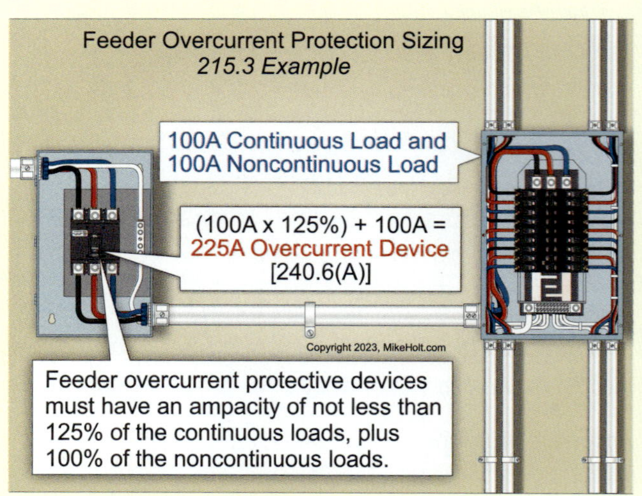

▶Figure 215–18

Solution:

100A Continuous Load × 125 percent continuous load + 100A noncontinuous load = 225A [240.6(A)]

Answer: *(b) 225A*

Ex 1: Where the assembly, including the overcurrent protective devices protecting the feeder(s) is listed for operation at 100 percent of its rating, the ampere rating of the overcurrent protective device can be sized at 100 percent of the continuous and noncontinuous loads.
▶Figure 215–19

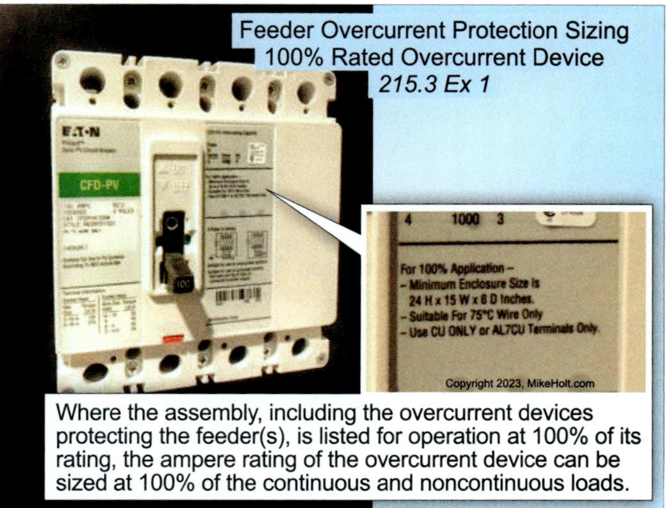

▶Figure 215–19

215.6 Feeder Equipment Grounding Conductor

A feeder must have an equipment grounding conductor. ▶Figure 215–20

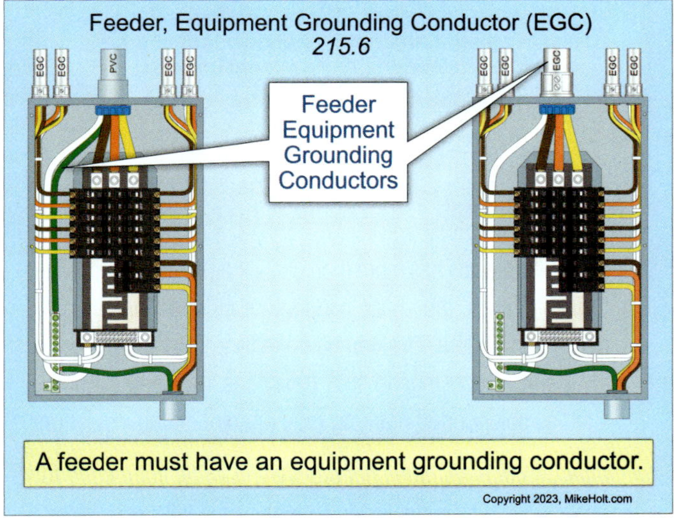

▶Figure 215–20

215.10 Ground-Fault Protection of Equipment

Each feeder disconnect rated 1000A or more supplied by a 4-wire, three-phase, 277/480V wye-connected system must be provided with ground-fault protection of equipment in accordance with 230.95 and 240.13.

Ex 2: This section does not apply if GFPE (ground fault protection of equipment) is provided on the service in accordance with 230.95.

215.12 Conductor Identification

(A) Neutral Conductor. The feeder neutral conductor must be identified in accordance with 200.6.

(B) Equipment Grounding Conductor. Equipment grounding conductors can be bare, covered, or insulated. Insulated equipment grounding conductors 6 AWG and smaller must have a continuous outer finish, either green or green with one or more yellow stripes [250.119(A)]. ▶Figure 215–21

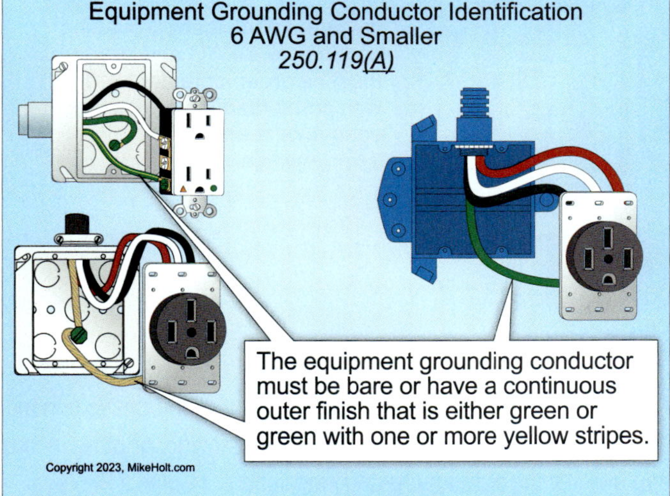

▶Figure 215–21

Insulated equipment grounding conductors 4 AWG and larger can be permanently reidentified with green marking at the time of installation where accessible [250.119(B)]. ▶Figure 215–22

(C) Identification of Phase Conductors. Circuit phase conductors must be identified as follows:

(1) More Than One Nominal Voltage System. Where premises wiring is supplied from more than one nominal voltage system, phase conductors must be identified by phase or line, and by system at termination, connection, and splice points as follows: ▶Figure 215–23

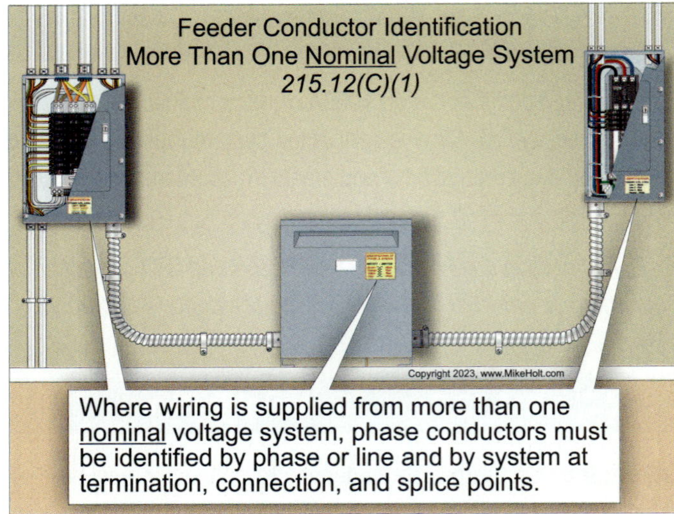

▶Figure 215–22

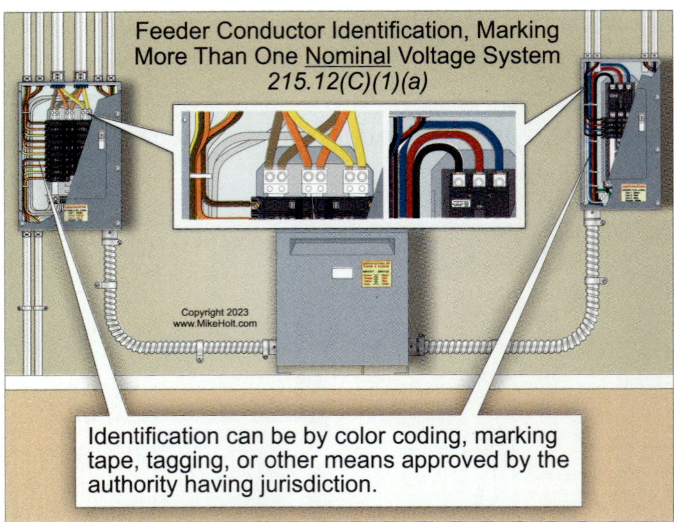

▶Figure 215–24

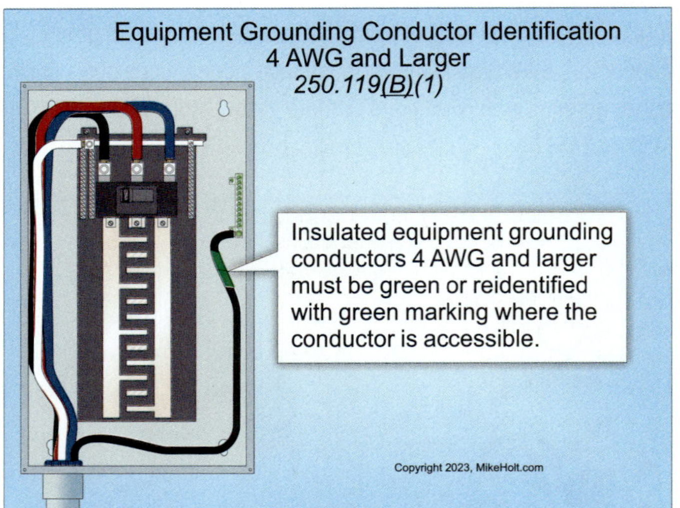

▶Figure 215–23

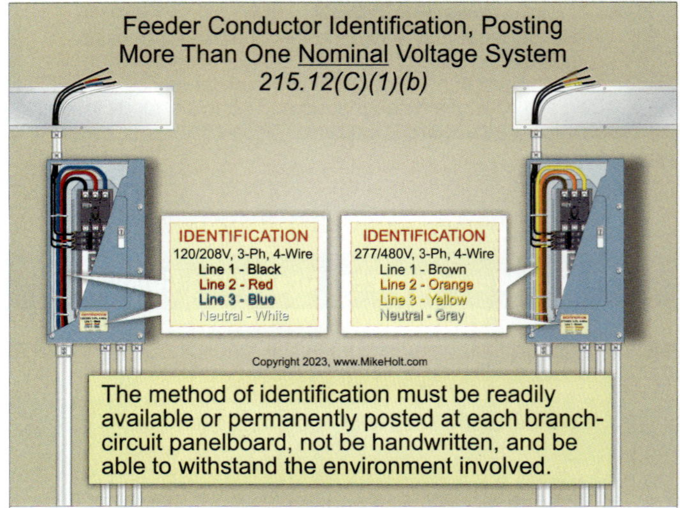

▶Figure 215–25

(a) Means of Identification. Identification of the phase conductors can be by color coding, marking tape, tagging, or other means approved by the authority having jurisdiction. ▶Figure 215–24

(b) Posting of Identification. The method of identification must be readily available or permanently posted at each branch-circuit panelboard. It must not be handwritten and sufficiently durable to withstand the environment involved. ▶Figure 215–25

Author's Comment:

▶ When a premises has more than one voltage system supplying branch circuits, the phase conductors must be identified by phase and system. This can be done by permanently posting an identification legend that describes the method used, such as color-coded marking tape or color-coded insulation.

▶ Although the *NEC* does not require a specific color code for phase conductors, electricians often use the following system: ▶Figure 215–26

  ▶ 120/240V, single-phase—black, red, and white
  ▶ 120/208V, three-phase—black, red, blue, and white
  ▶ 120/240V, three-phase (high-leg)—black, orange, blue, and white

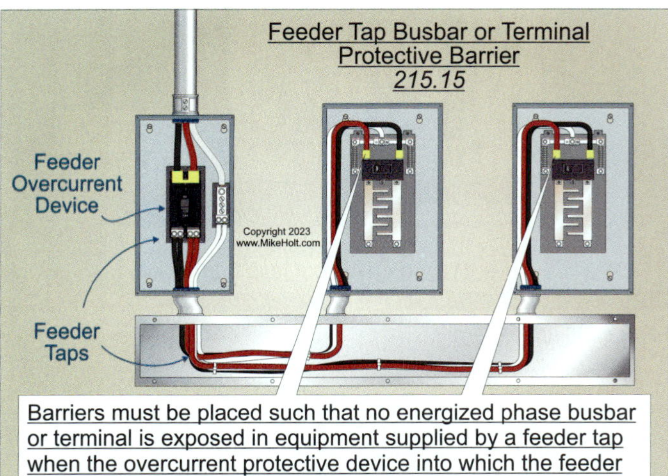

Conductor Identification Practices
215.12(C) Comment

Copyright 2023, www.MikeHolt.com

Although the *NEC* does not require a specific color code for phase conductors, electricians often use the following for power and lighting conductor identification:
- 120/240V, single-phase—black, red, and white
- 120/208V, three-phase—black, red, blue, and white
- 120/240V, three-phase (high-leg)—black, orange, blue, and white
- 277/480V, three-phase—brown, orange, yellow, and gray; or, brown, purple, yellow, and gray

▶Figure 215–26

> ▸ 277/480V, three-phase—brown, orange, yellow, and gray; or, brown, purple, yellow, and gray

> ▶ Whichever color scheme is used, it is important for it to remain consistent wherever phase conductors are terminated or accessible throughout the entire premises. This is especially important when identifying different system voltages and neutrals.

215.15 Barriers

Feeder Taps. Barriers must be placed such that no energized phase busbar or terminal is exposed in equipment supplied by a feeder tap [240.21(B)] when the overcurrent protective device into which the feeder taps terminate is in the open position. ▶Figure 215–27

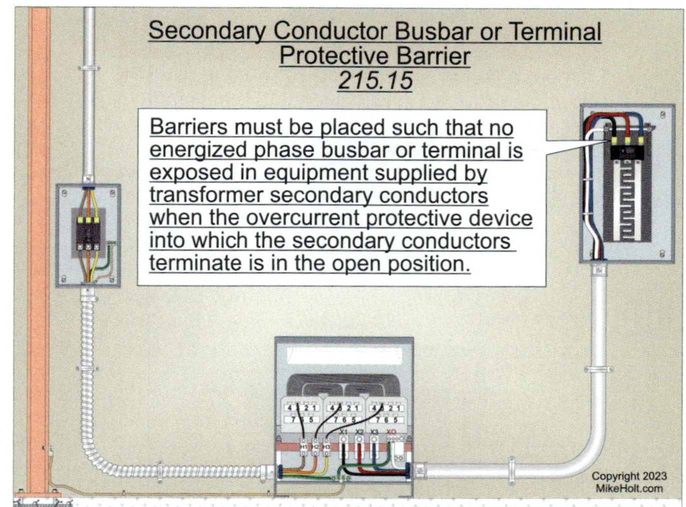

▶Figure 215–27

According to Article 100, "Exposed (as applied to live parts)" means capable of being inadvertently touched or approached nearer than a safe distance by a person.

Secondary Conductors. Barriers must be placed such that no energized phase busbar or terminal is exposed in equipment supplied by transformer secondary conductors [240.21(C)] when the overcurrent protective device into which the secondary conductors terminate is in the open position. ▶Figure 215–28

▶Figure 215–28

Author's Comment:

> ▶ During maintenance and servicing, it is very likely an electrical worker can be exposed to inadvertent contact with energized parts on the line side of a feeder tap or secondary conductor disconnect, even if the disconnect is in the open position. Barriers on feeder tap and transformer secondary conductor disconnects reduce the hazards that exist and create an electrically safe work condition.

215.18 Surge Protection

(A) Surge-Protective Device (SPD). Where a feeder supplies any of the following occupancies, a surge-protective device must be provided:

(1) Dwelling units ▶Figure 215–29 and ▶Figure 215–30

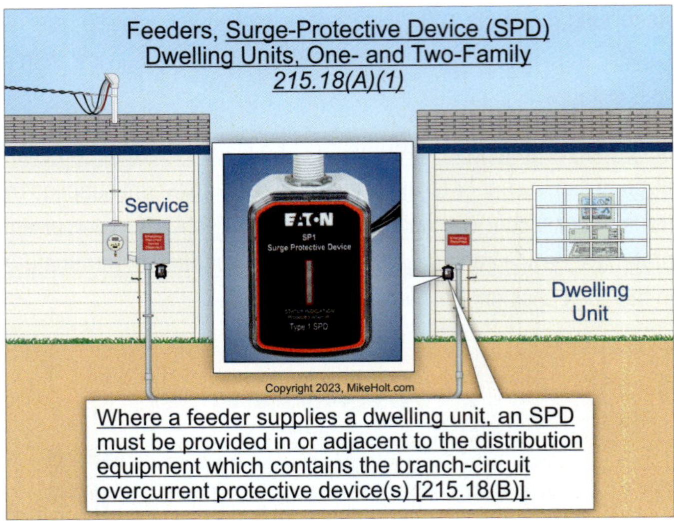

▶Figure 215–29

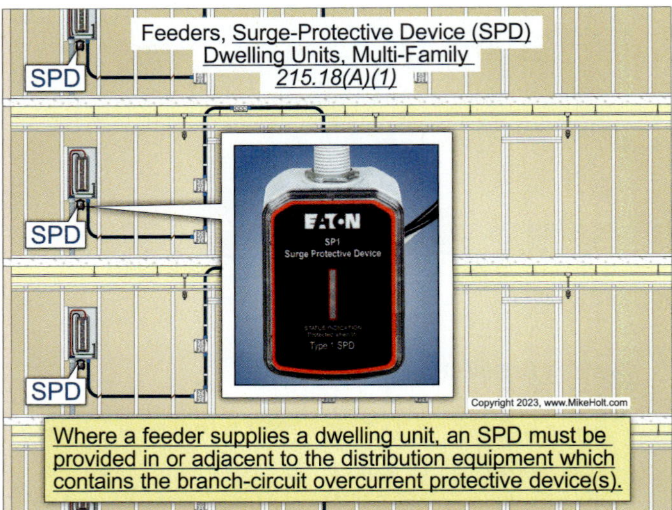

▶Figure 215–30

(2) Dormitory units

(3) Guest rooms and guest suites of hotels and motels

(4) Areas of nursing homes and limited care facilities used exclusively as patient sleeping rooms

(B) Location. The SPD must be installed in or adjacent to distribution equipment which contains the branch-circuit overcurrent protective device(s). ▶Figure 215–31

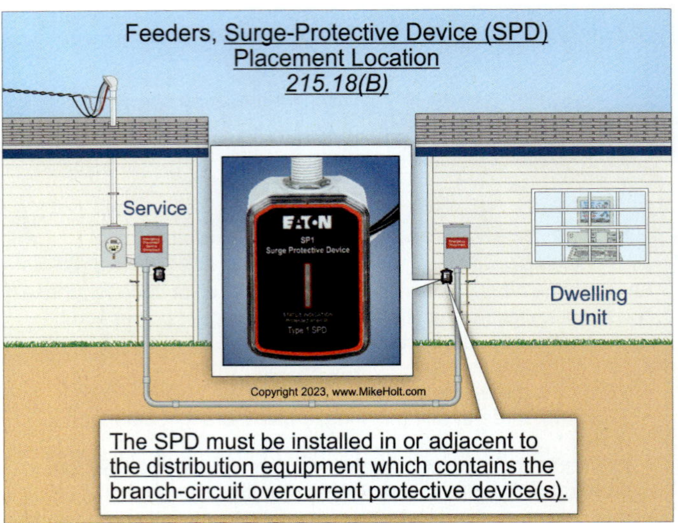

▶Figure 215–31

Note: Surge protection is most effective when closest to the branch circuit. Surges can be generated from multiple sources including, but not limited to, lightning, the electric utility, or utilization equipment.

(C) Type. The SPD must be either Type 1 or Type 2.

(D) Replacement. Where the distribution equipment supplied by the feeder is replaced, all the requirements of this section apply.

(E) Ratings. SPDs must have a nominal discharge current rating (In) of not less than 10kA. ▶Figure 215–32

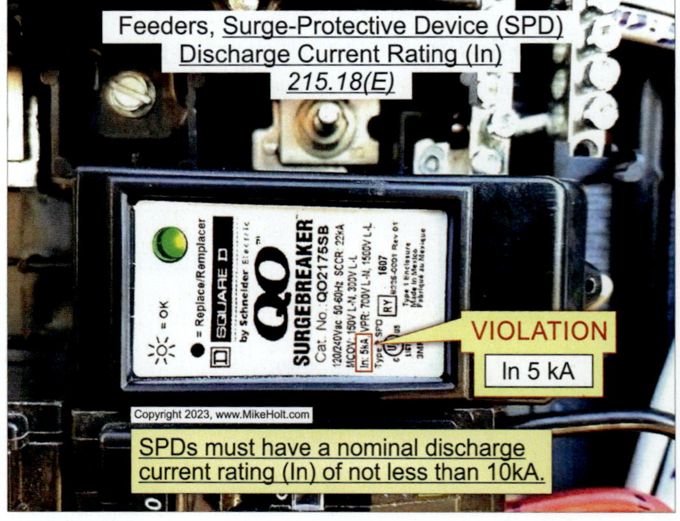

▶Figure 215–32

OUTSIDE BRANCH CIRCUITS AND FEEDERS

Introduction to Article 225—Outside Branch Circuits and Feeders

Article 225 contains the installation requirements for outside branch circuits and feeders not over 1000V ac or 1500V dc, installed on or between buildings, structures, or poles. Conductors installed outdoors can serve many purposes such as area lighting, power for outdoor equipment, or to provide power to separate buildings or structures. Some topics covered in our material for this article include:

- Conductor Support and Attachment
- Clearance for Overhead Conductors and Cables
- Raceways on Exterior Surfaces of Buildings or Other Structures
- Raceway Seals
- Grouping And Identification of Disconnects
- Emergency Disconnects
- Surge Protection

Article 225 consists of two parts:

- Part I—General Requirements
- Part II—Buildings or Other Structures Supplied by a Feeder(s) or Branch Circuit(s)

Part I. General

225.1 Scope

Article 225 contains the installation requirements for outside branch circuits and feeders not over 1000V ac or 1500V dc, installed on or between buildings, structures, or poles. ▶Figure 225–1

225.6 Minimum Conductor Size and Support

(A) Overhead Spans.

(1) Conductor Size. Conductors 10 AWG and larger are permitted for overhead spans up to 50 ft long. For spans over 50 ft, the minimum size conductor is 8 AWG, unless supported by a messenger wire. ▶Figure 225–2

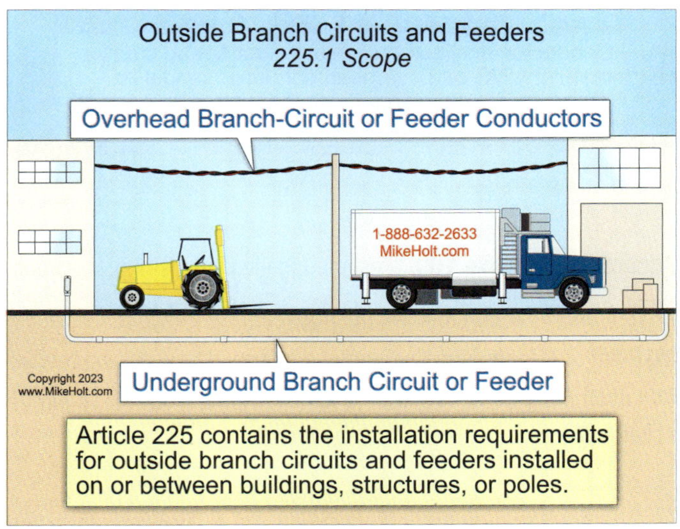

▶Figure 225–1

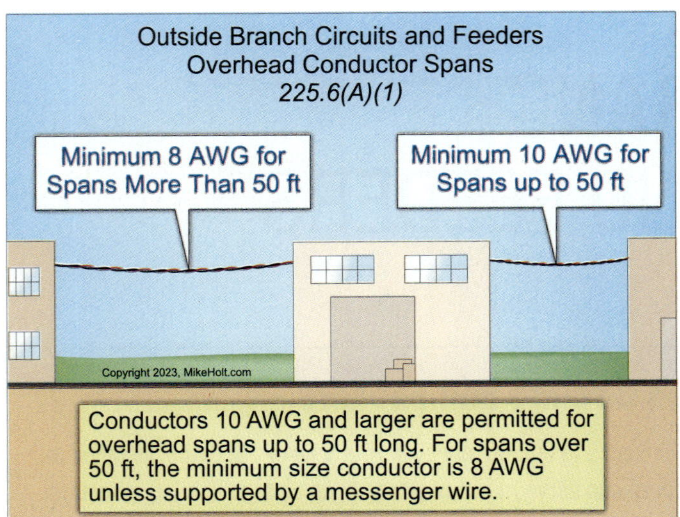

▶Figure 225–2

(B) Festoon Lighting. Overhead conductors for festoon lighting are not permitted to be smaller than 12 AWG and must be supported by messenger wire (with strain insulators) whenever the spans exceed 40 ft in length. ▶Figure 225–3

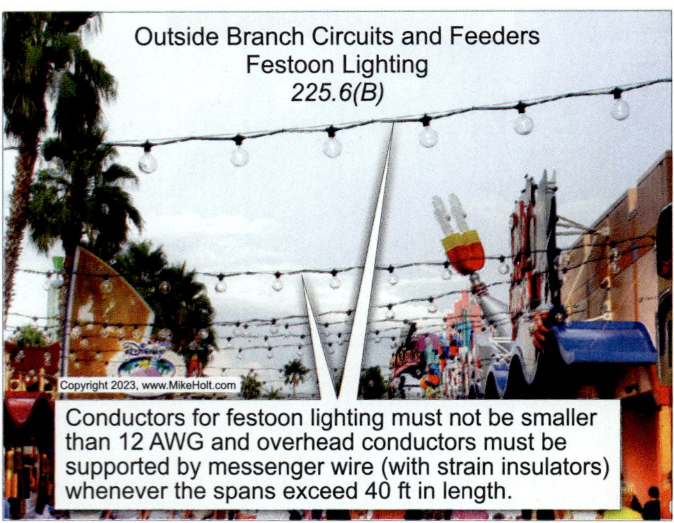

▶Figure 225–3

According to Article 100, "Festoon Lighting" is a string of outdoor lights suspended between two points. ▶Figure 225–4

(A) Point of Attachment. The point of attachment for overhead conductors must not be less than 10 ft above the finished grade [230.26]. ▶Figure 225–5

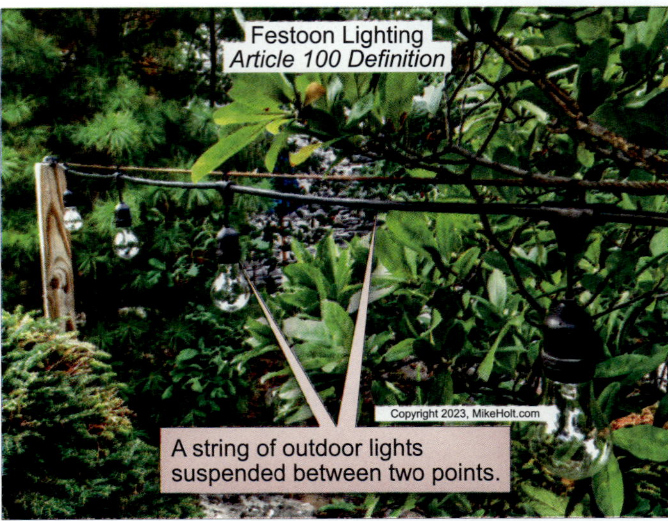

▶Figure 225–4

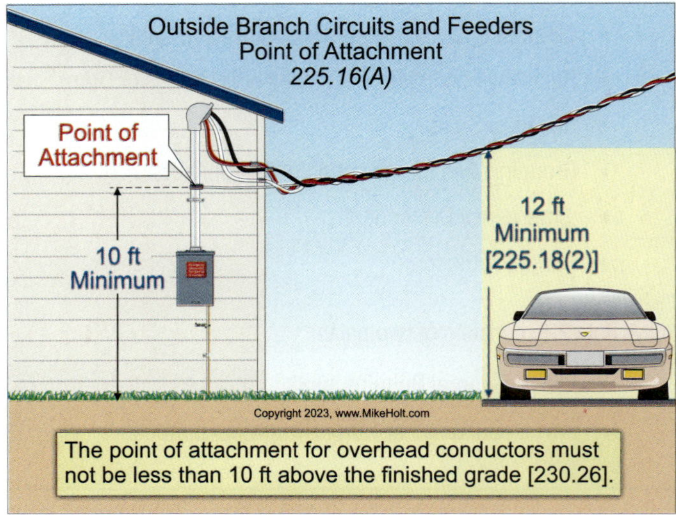

▶Figure 225–5

> **Caution**
>
> **CAUTION:** Conductors might need to have the point of attachment raised so the overhead conductors will comply with the clearances from building openings and other building areas required by 225.19.

(B) Means of Attachment to Buildings. Open conductors must be attached to fittings identified for use with conductors or to noncombustible, nonabsorbent insulators securely attached to the building [230.27].

225.17 Masts as Supports

Masts for the support of overhead conductors must be installed as follows:

(A) Strength. The mast must have adequate mechanical strength, braces, or guy wires to safely withstand the strain caused by the conductors. ▶Figure 225–6

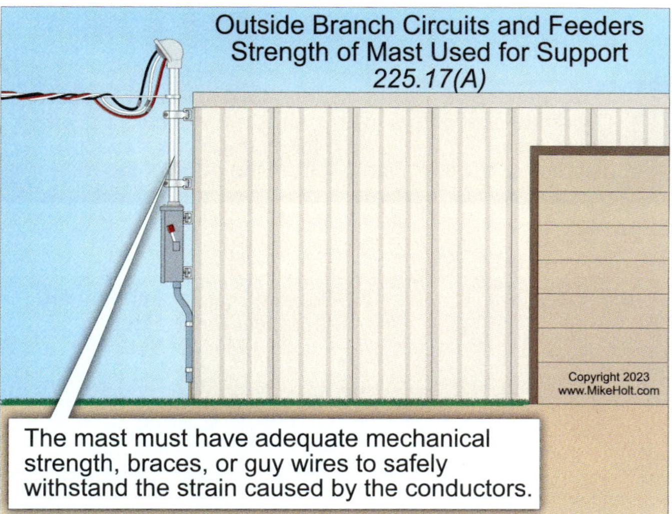

▶Figure 225–6

(B) Attachment. Overhead conductors cannot be attached to a mast where the conductor attachment is between a weatherhead and a coupling above the last point of securement to the building, or where the coupling is above the roof. ▶Figure 225–7

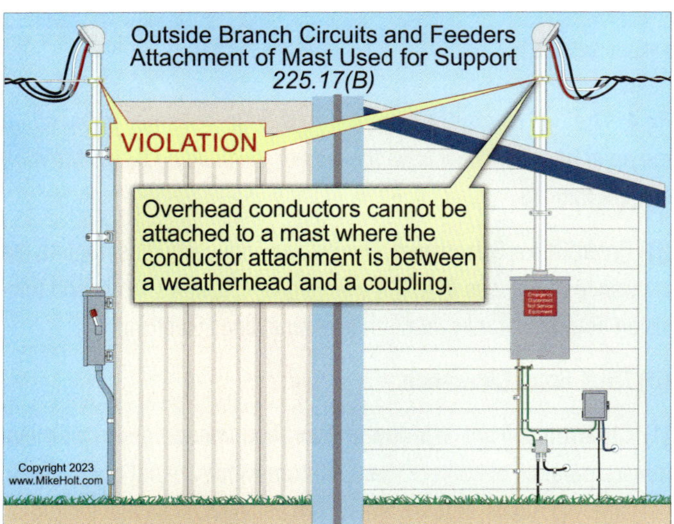

▶Figure 225–7

225.18 Clearance for Overhead Conductors

Overhead conductor spans must maintain vertical clearances of:

(1) 10 ft above finished grade, sidewalks, platforms, or projections that permit personal contact for circuits supplied by 120/208V or 120/240V. ▶Figure 225–8

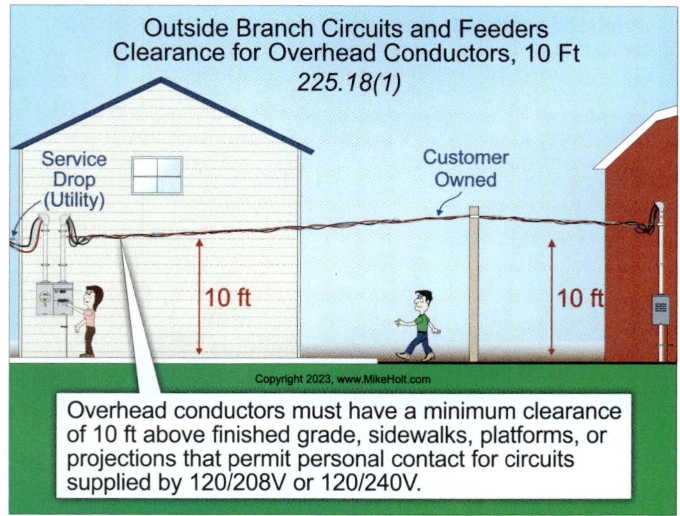

▶Figure 225–8

(2) 12 ft above residential property and driveways, and commercial areas not subject to truck traffic for circuits supplied by 120/208V, 120/240V, or 277V/480V. ▶Figure 225–9

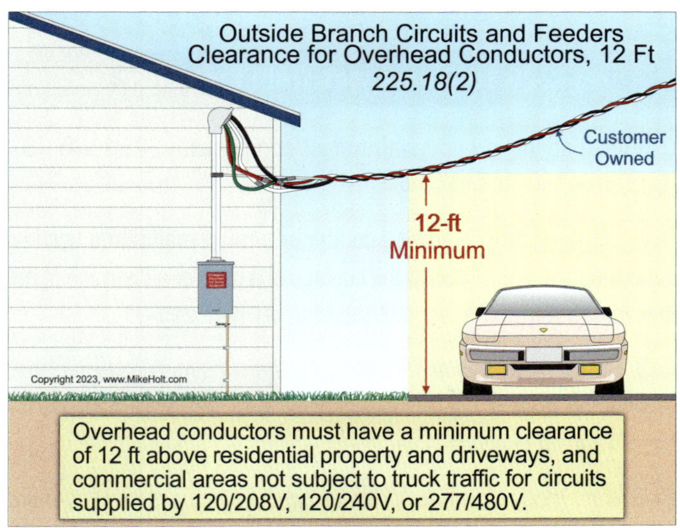

▶Figure 225–9

(3) 15 ft above residential property and driveways, and commercial areas not subject to truck traffic for circuits supplied by a system having a voltage exceeding 300V to ground.

(4) 18 ft over public streets, alleys, roads, parking areas subject to truck traffic, driveways on other than residential property, and other areas traversed by vehicles such as those used for cultivation, grazing, forestry, and orchards. ▶Figure 225–10

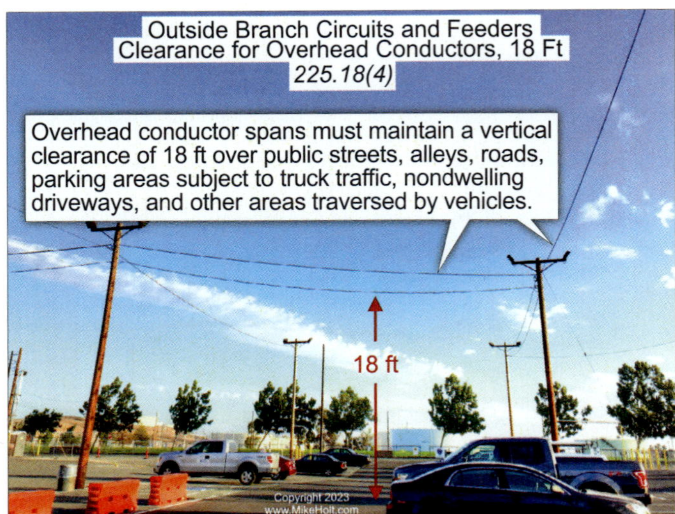

▶Figure 225–10

Author's Comment:

▶ Overhead conductors above pools, outdoor spas, outdoor hot tubs, diving structures, observation stands, towers, or platforms must be installed in accordance with the clearance requirements in 680.9.

225.19 Clearances from Buildings

Overhead spans of conductors must comply with 225.19(A), (B), (C), and (D).

(A) Above Roofs. Overhead conductors must maintain a vertical clearance of 8 ft 6 in. above the surface of a roof for a distance of not less than 3 ft from the edge of the roof. ▶Figure 225–11

Ex 2: The overhead conductor clearances from the roof can be reduced to 3 ft if the slope of the roof meets or exceeds 4 in. of vertical rise for every 12 in. of horizontal run.

Ex 3: If no more than 6 ft of feeder conductors pass over no more than 4 ft of roof overhang, 120/208V or 120/240V overhead service conductor clearances over the roof overhang can be reduced to 18 in. ▶Figure 225–12

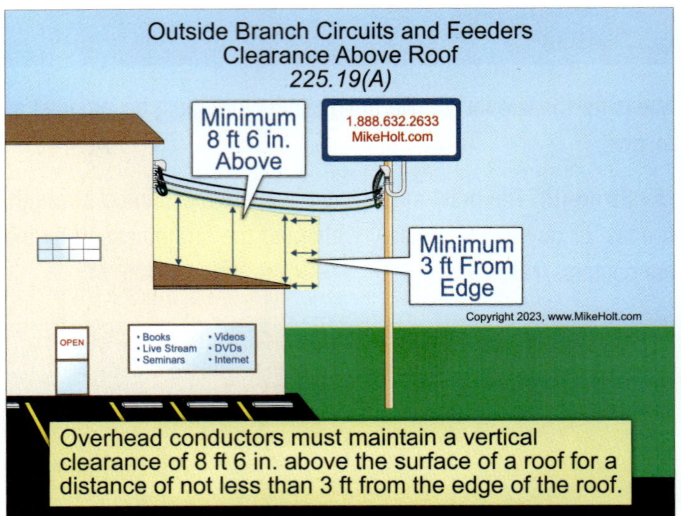

▶Figure 225–11

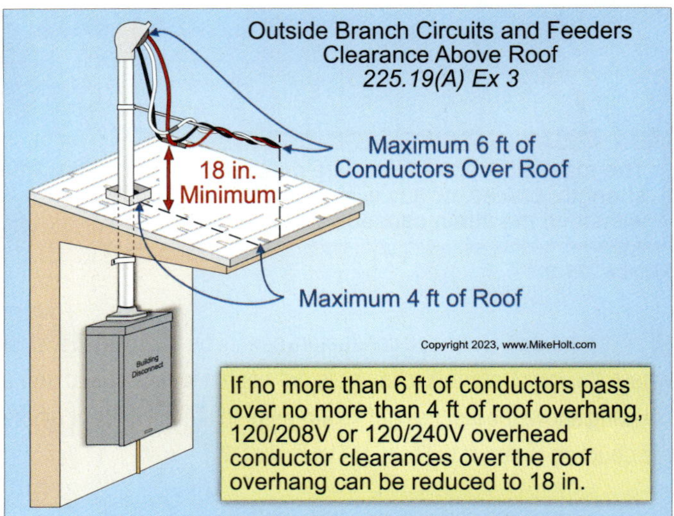

▶Figure 225–12

Ex 4: The 3-ft clearance from the roof edge does not apply when the point of attachment is on the side of the building below the roof. ▶Figure 225–13

(B) From Other Structures. Overhead conductors must maintain a clearance of not less than 3 ft from signs, chimneys, radio and television antennas, tanks, and other nonbuilding structures.

(D) Final Span Clearance.

(1) Clearance from Windows. Overhead conductors must maintain a clearance of not less than 3 ft from windows that open, doors, porches, balconies, ladders, stairs, fire escapes, or similar locations. ▶Figure 225–14

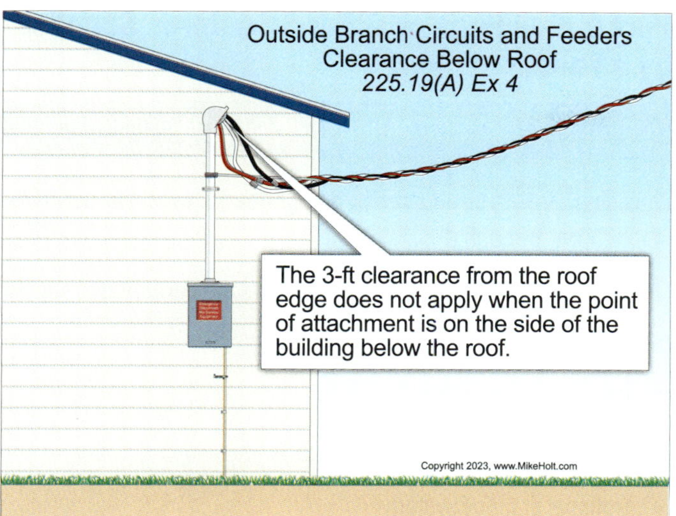

▶Figure 225–13

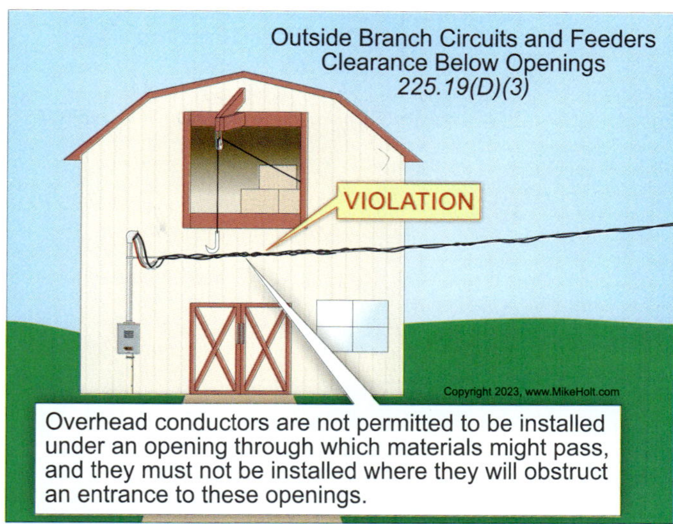

▶Figure 225–15

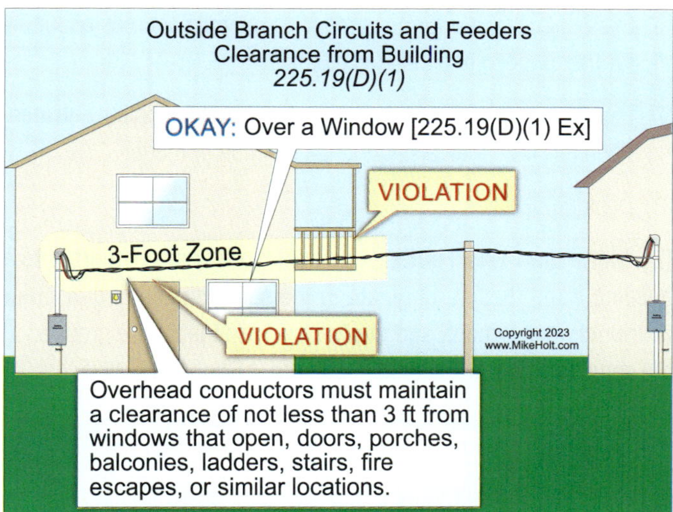

▶Figure 225–14

Ex: Overhead conductors installed above a window are not required to maintain the 3-ft distance from the window.

(2) Vertical Clearance. Overhead conductors must maintain a vertical clearance of not less than 10 ft above platforms, projections, or surfaces that permit personal contact in accordance with 225.18. This vertical clearance must be maintained for 3 ft measured horizontally from the platforms, projections, or surfaces from which they might be reached.

(3) Below Openings. Overhead conductors are not permitted to be installed under an opening through which materials might pass, or where they will obstruct an entrance to these openings. ▶Figure 225–15

225.22 Raceways on Exterior Surfaces of Buildings

Raceways on exteriors of buildings must be arranged to drain and be listed or approved for use in wet locations. ▶Figure 225–16

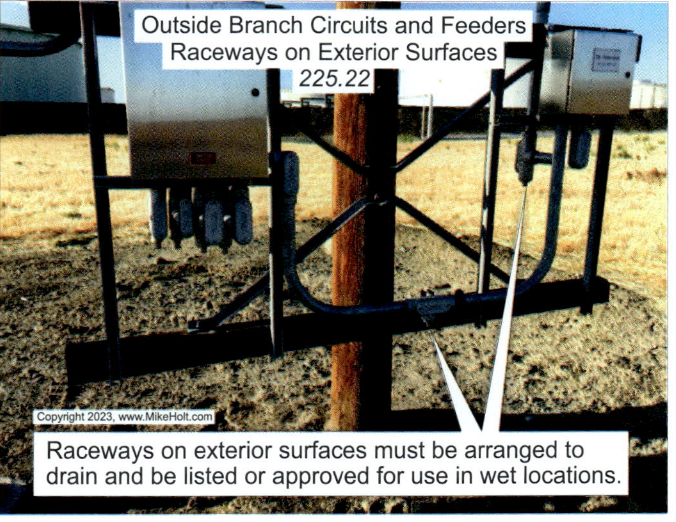

▶Figure 225–16

225.26 Trees for Conductor Support

Trees and other vegetation are not permitted to be used for the support of overhead conductor spans. ▶Figure 225–17

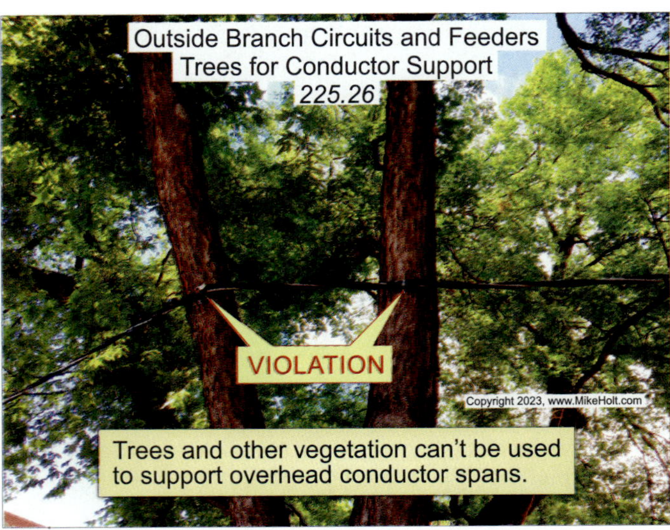

▶Figure 225–17

Author's Comment:

▸ Overhead conductor spans for services [230.10] and temporary wiring [590.4(J)] are not permitted to be supported by vegetation.

225.27 Raceway Seals

Where a raceway enters a building or structure from outside, it must be sealed in accordance with 300.5(G) and 300.7(A). Sealants must be identified for use with cable insulation, conductor insulation, bare conductor, shield, or other components. ▶Figure 225–18

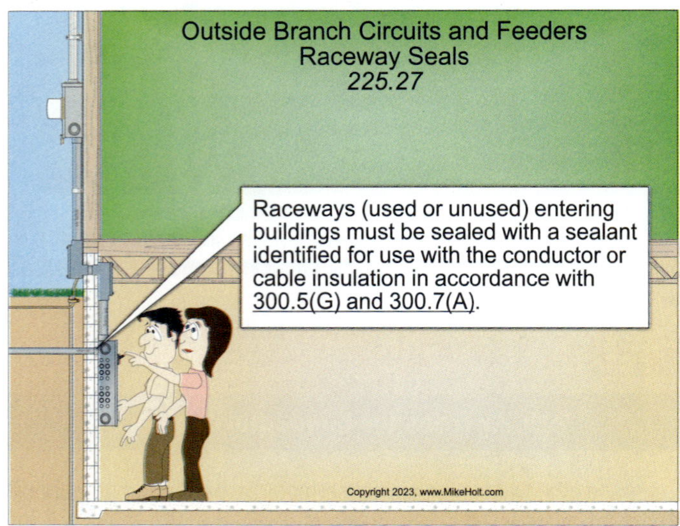

▶Figure 225–18

Part II. Buildings or Other Structures Supplied by a Feeder

225.30 Number of Supplies

A building can only be supplied by a single feeder, except as permitted in 225.30(A) through (F).

(A) Special Conditions. Additional feeders are permitted to supply:

(1) Fire pumps

(2) Emergency systems

(3) Legally required standby systems

(4) Optional standby systems

(5) Parallel power production sources

(6) Systems designed for connection to multiple sources of supply for the purpose of enhanced reliability

(7) Electric vehicle power transfer systems listed, labeled, and identified for more than a single branch circuit or feeder

(8) Docking facilities

(B) More than One Feeder. Up to six feeders are permitted to a building if the feeders originate in the same panelboard or other distribution equipment, and the feeder disconnects are grouped in the same location. ▶Figure 225–19 and ▶Figure 225–20

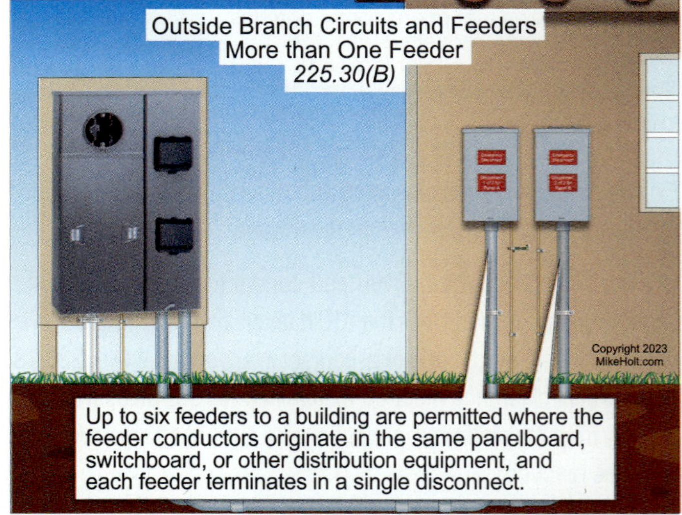

▶Figure 225–19

(C) Special Occupancies. By special permission, additional feeders are permitted for:

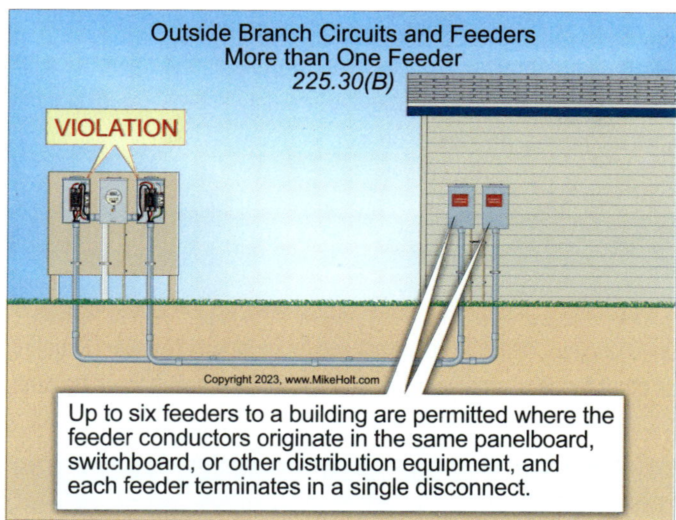

Up to six feeders to a building are permitted where the feeder conductors originate in the same panelboard, switchboard, or other distribution equipment, and each feeder terminates in a single disconnect.

▶Figure 225–20

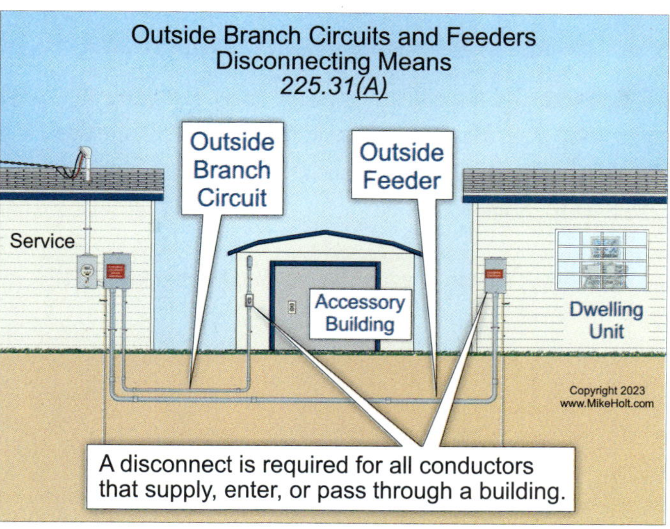

A disconnect is required for all conductors that supply, enter, or pass through a building.

▶Figure 225–21

(1) Multiple-occupancy buildings where there is no available space for supply equipment accessible to all occupants, or

(2) A building so large that two or more supplies are necessary.

(D) Capacity Requirements. Additional feeders are permitted for a building where the capacity requirements exceed 2000A.

(E) Different Characteristics. Additional feeders are permitted for different voltages, frequencies, or uses such as controlling outside lighting from multiple locations.

(F) Documented Switching Procedures. Additional feeders are permitted where documented safe switching procedures are established and maintained.

225.31 Disconnecting Means

(A) General. A disconnect is required for all feeder conductors that supply, enter, or pass through a building. ▶Figure 225–21

(B) Location. The building disconnect must be at a readily accessible location either outside or inside the building nearest the point of entrance of the conductors. ▶Figure 225–22

Feeder conductors are considered outside a building or structure where they are installed under not less than 2 in. of concrete or brick [230.6(1)] or encased in not less than 2 in. of concrete [230.6(2)].

For dirt floor buildings, the raceway must be installed not less than 18 in. below the finished surface [230.6(4)]. ▶Figure 225–23

Ex 3: A disconnect is not required for poles that support luminaires.

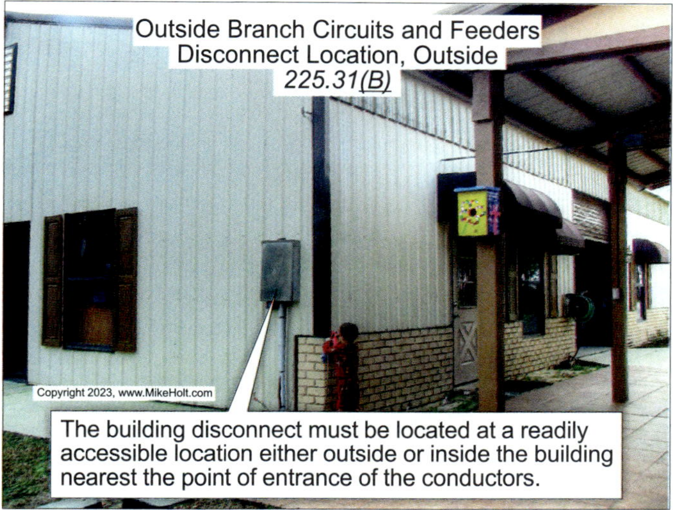

The building disconnect must be located at a readily accessible location either outside or inside the building nearest the point of entrance of the conductors.

▶Figure 225–22

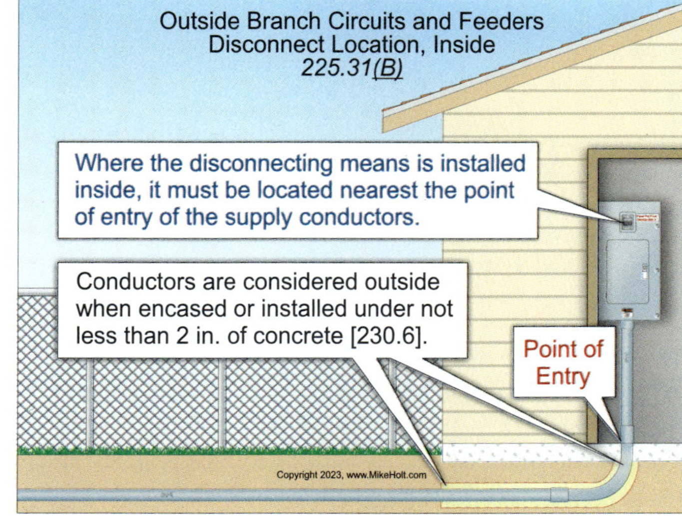

▶Figure 225–23

225.33 Maximum Number of Disconnects

(A) General. The disconnect for each supply permitted by 225.30 can consist of no more than six switches or six circuit breakers in a single enclosure or in separate enclosures grouped in one location [225.34(A)]. ▶Figure 225–24

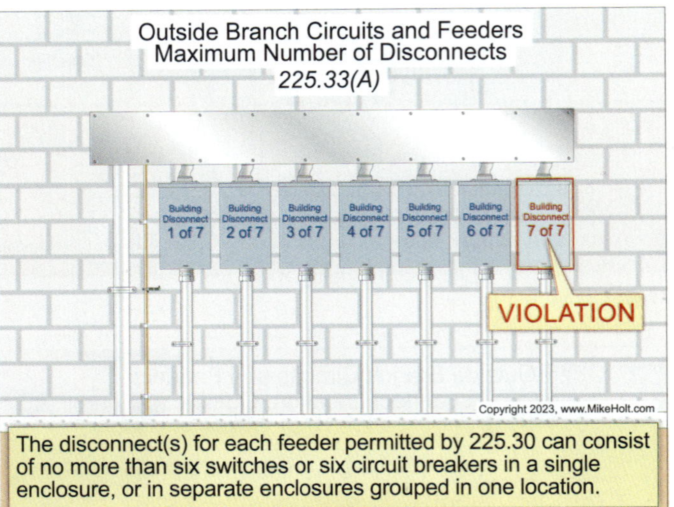

▶Figure 225–24

225.34 Grouping of Disconnects

(A) General. If a building has more than one feeder supplied disconnect as permitted by 225.33, the disconnects must be grouped in one location and marked to indicate the loads they serve [110.22(A)]. ▶Figure 225–25

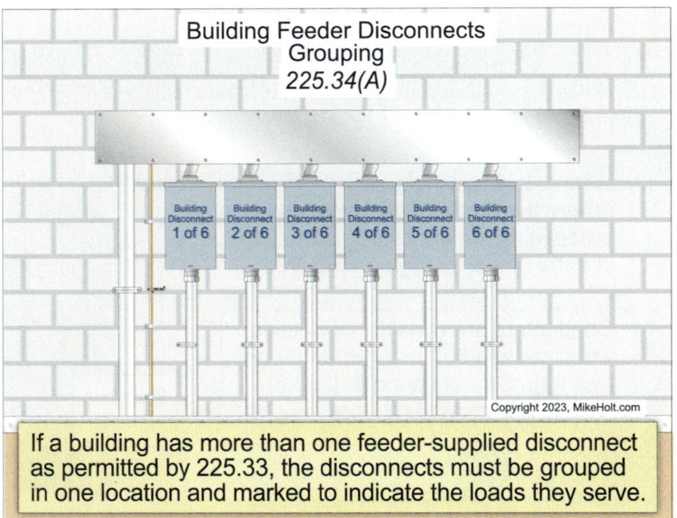

▶Figure 225–25

(B) Additional Disconnects. To minimize the possibility of accidental interruption of critical power systems, the feeder disconnect for a fire pump, emergency power, or standby power must be installed remotely from the normal power disconnect.

225.37 Identification of Multiple Supplies

If a building is fed by more than one supply, a permanent plaque or directory must be installed at each feeder disconnect location denoting all other feeders supplying that building and the area served by each.

225.39 Rating of Disconnecting Means

A single disconnect for a building must have an ampere rating of not less than the calculated load as determined by Article 220. If the disconnect consists of more than one switch or circuit breaker, the combined ratings of the circuit breakers are not permitted to be less than the calculated load as determined by Article 220. In addition, the disconnect is not permitted to be rated less than:

(A) One-Circuit Installation. For installations to supply only a single branch circuit, the disconnect must have an ampere rating of not less than 15A.

(B) Two-Circuit Installation. For installations consisting of two 2-wire branch circuits, the feeder disconnect must have an ampere rating of not less than 30A.

(C) One-Family Dwelling. For a one-family dwelling, the feeder disconnect must have an ampere rating of not less than 100A.

(D) Other Installations. For other installations, the feeder disconnect must have an ampere rating of not less than 60A.

225.41 Emergency (Shutoff) Disconnects

For one- and two-family dwelling units, an emergency disconnect must be installed for first responders and others.

(A) General.

(1) Location. The emergency disconnect must be installed in a readily accessible outdoor location on or within sight of the dwelling unit. ▶Figure 225–26

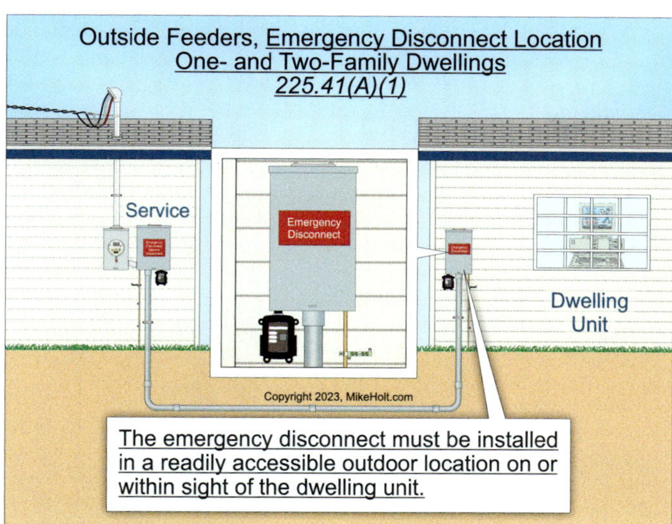

▶Figure 225–26

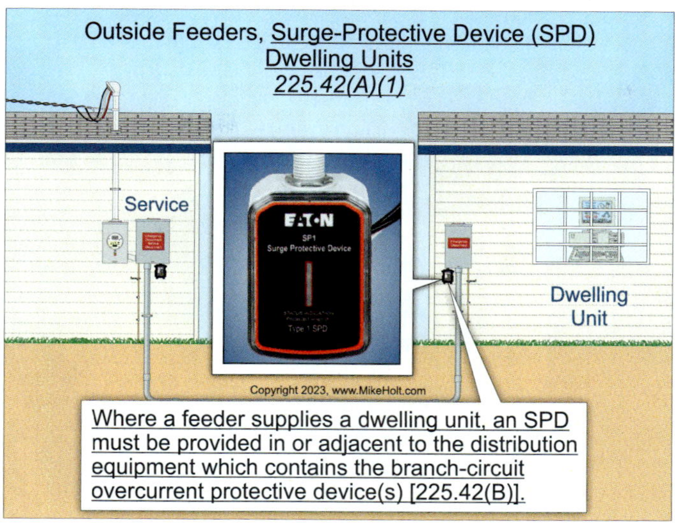

▶Figure 225–27

(2) Rating. The emergency disconnect must have a short-circuit current rating equal to or greater than the available fault current.

(3) Grouping. If more than one emergency disconnect is provided, they must be grouped.

(B) Identification of Other Disconnects. Where disconnects for other energy source systems are not adjacent to the emergency disconnect, a plaque or directory identifying the location of other energy source disconnects must be adjacent to the emergency disconnect.

Note: See 445.18, 480.7, 705.20, and 706.15 for examples of other energy source system isolation means.

(C) Marking. The emergency disconnect must be marked "EMERGENCY DISCONNECT."

Markings must be permanently affixed and be sufficiently durable to withstand the environment involved in accordance with 110.21(B) and comply with following:

(1) The emergency disconnect marking or label must be on the outside front of the disconnect with a red background and white text.

(2) The letters must be at least ½ in. high.

225.42 Surge Protection

(A) Surge-Protective Device (SPD). Where a feeder supplies any of the following occupancies, a SPD must be provided: ▶Figure 225–27

(1) Dwelling units

(2) Dormitory units

(3) Guest rooms and guest suites of hotels and motels

(4) Areas of nursing homes and limited-care facilities used exclusively as patient sleeping rooms

(B) Location. The SPD must be installed in or adjacent to distribution equipment connected to the load side of the feeder, which contains the branch-circuit overcurrent protective device(s).

Note: Surge protection is most effective when closest to the branch circuit. Surges can be generated from multiple sources including, but not limited to, lightning, the electric utility, or utilization equipment.

(C) Type. The SPD must be either Type 1 or Type 2.

(D) Replacement. Where the distribution equipment supplied by the feeder is replaced, an SPD must be installed in or adjacent to the distribution equipment.

(E) Ratings. SPDs must have a nominal discharge current rating (In) of not less than 10 kA. ▶Figure 225–28

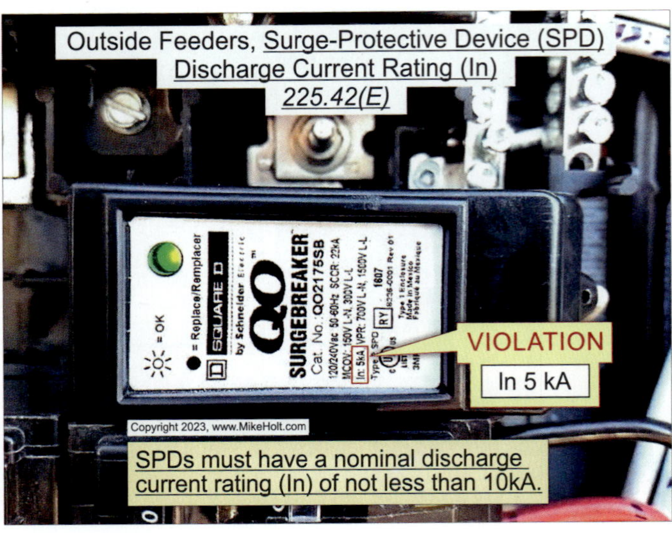

▶Figure 225–28

Note: Lead lengths of conductors to the SPD should be kept as short as possible to reduce let-through voltages.

Introduction to Article 230—Services

Article 230 covers the installation requirements for service conductors and service disconnects. It is crucial to understand what a service is, where it starts, and where it ends to properly apply many of these rules. Some topics covered by our material in this article include:

- Number of Services
- Raceway Sealing
- Clearances on Buildings
- Support and Attachment
- Conductor Size and Ampacity
- Service Equipment Marking and Protection
- Emergency Disconnects

This article consists of seven parts:

- Part I. General
- Part II. Overhead Service Conductors
- Part III. Underground Service Conductors
- Part IV. Service-Entrance Conductors
- Part V. Service Equipment—General
- Part VI. Disconnecting Means
- Part VII. Overcurrent Protection

The *National Electrical Code* does not cover installations under the exclusive control of a serving electric utility where such installations [90.2(D)(5)]:

a. Consist of service drops or service laterals and associated metering, or ▸Figure 230–1 and ▸Figure 230–2

b. Are on property owned or leased by the utility for the purpose of communications, metering, generation, control, transformation, transmission, energy storage, or distribution of electrical energy, or ▸Figure 230–3

c. Are in legally established easements or rights-of-way. ▸Figure 230–4

230.1 Scope

Article 230 covers the installation requirements for service conductors and service equipment. ▸Figure 230–5

According to Article 100, "Service" is the conductors and equipment connecting the serving electric utility to the premises wiring system. ▸Figure 230–6

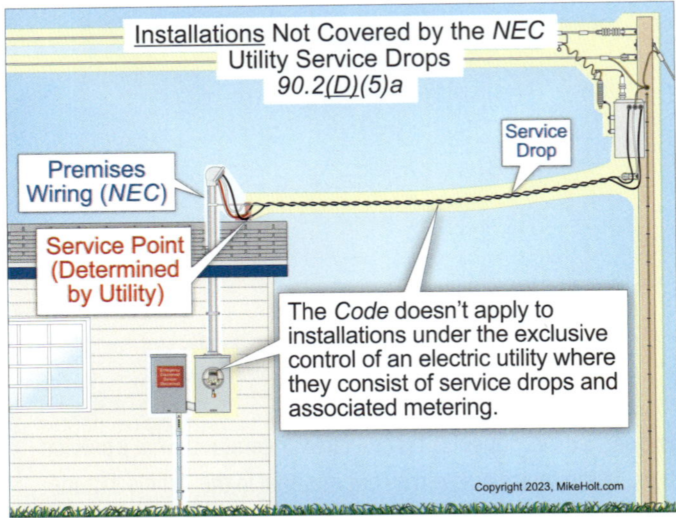

▶Figure 230–1

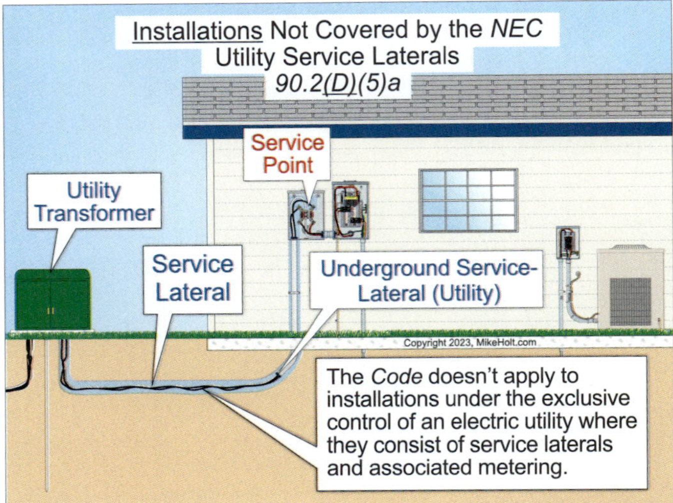

▶Figure 230–2

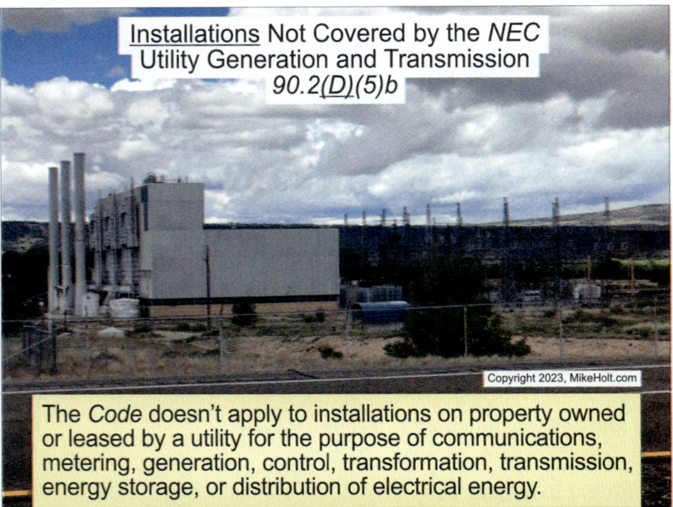

▶Figure 230–3

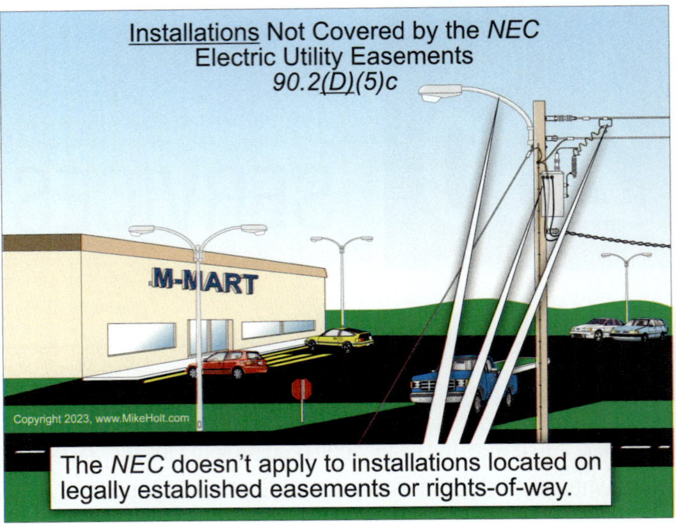

▶Figure 230–4

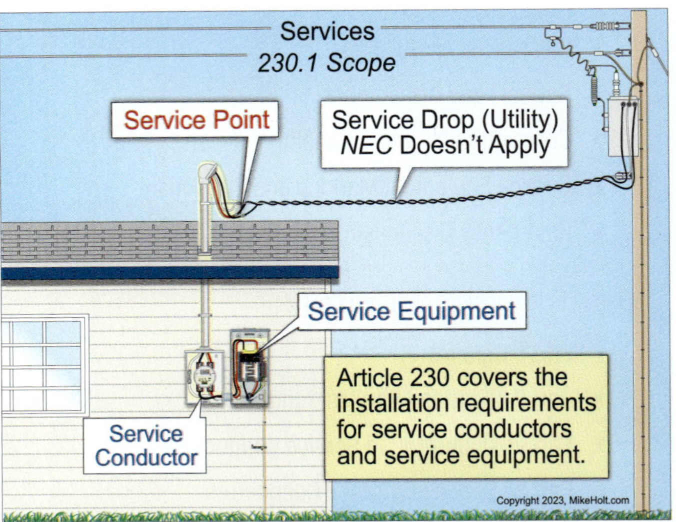

▶Figure 230–5

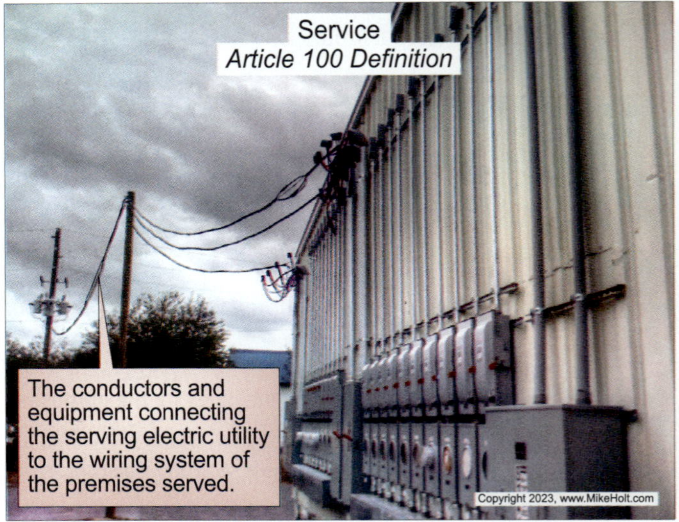

▶Figure 230–6

Part I. General

230.2 Number of Services

A building can only be served by one service except as permitted by (A) through (D). ▶Figure 230–7 and ▶Figure 230–8

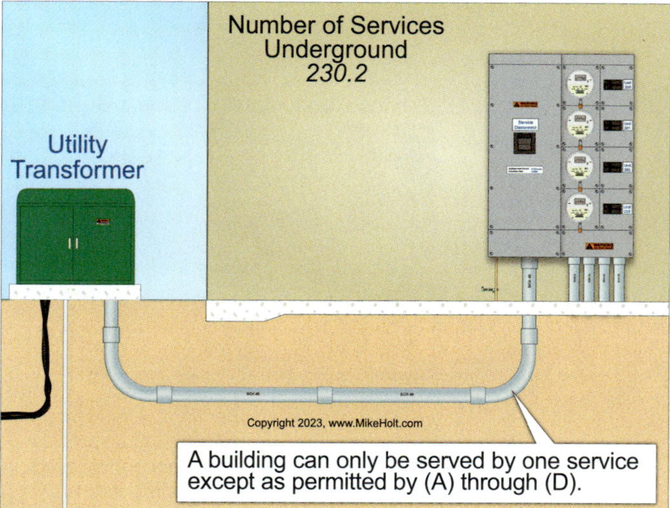

▶Figure 230–7

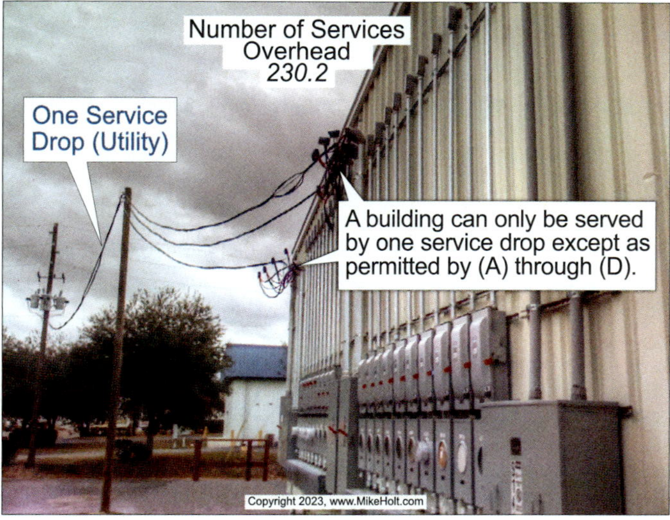

▶Figure 230–8

For the purposes of 230.40 Ex 2, underground sets of conductors 1/0 AWG and larger running to the same location and connected to each other at their supply end (but not connected together at their load end) are considered to be supplying one service. ▶Figure 230–9

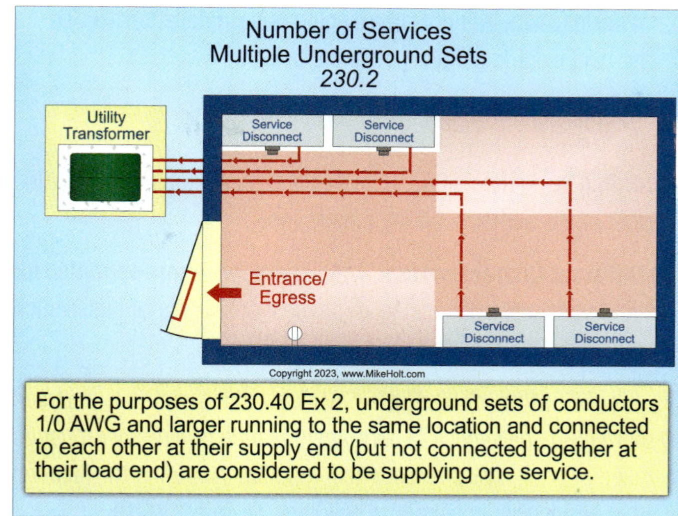

For the purposes of 230.40 Ex 2, underground sets of conductors 1/0 AWG and larger running to the same location and connected to each other at their supply end (but not connected together at their load end) are considered to be supplying one service.

▶Figure 230–9

Author's Comment:

▶ There are many possible combinations of what is considered one service drop or one service lateral. When required, one service drop (or lateral) can typically be split and connected to multiple service disconnects.

(A) Special Conditions. Additional services are permitted for the following:

(1) Fire pumps

(2) Emergency systems

(3) Legally required standby systems

(4) Optional standby power

(5) Interconnected electric power production sources

(6) Systems designed for connection to multiple sources of supply to enhance reliability

(B) Special Occupancies. By special permission, additional services are permitted for:

(1) Multiple-occupancy buildings where there is no available space for supply equipment accessible to all occupants, or

(2) A building so large that two or more services are necessary.

(C) Capacity Requirements. Additional services are permitted as follows:

(1) Buildings with capacity requirements that exceed 2000A, or

(2) If the load requirements of a single-phase installation exceed the serving electric utility's power capacity, or

(3) By special permission.

According to Article 100, "Special Permission" means the written consent of the authority having jurisdiction.

(D) Different Characteristics. Additional services are permitted for different voltages, frequencies, or phases, or for different uses such as varying electricity rate schedules.

(E) Identification of Multiple Services. If a building is supplied by more than one service, a permanent plaque or directory must be installed at each service disconnect location indicating the location of other services supplying that building. ▶Figure 230–10

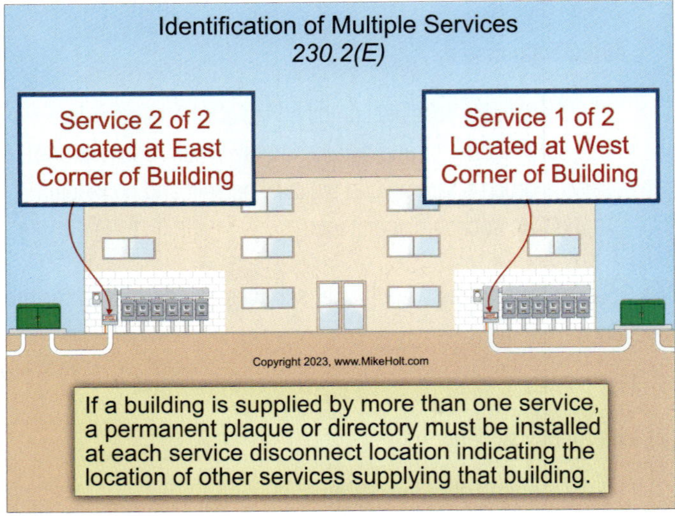

▶Figure 230–10

Author's Comment:

▸ This information is critically important to first responders who need to disconnect power to the building in case of an emergency, such as a flood or fire.

230.3 Not to Pass Through a Building

Service conductors must not pass through the interior of a building to supply another building.

230.6 Conductors Considered Outside a Building or Structure

Conductors are considered outside a building or structure when they are installed:

(1) Under not less than 2 in. of concrete beneath a building ▶Figure 230–11

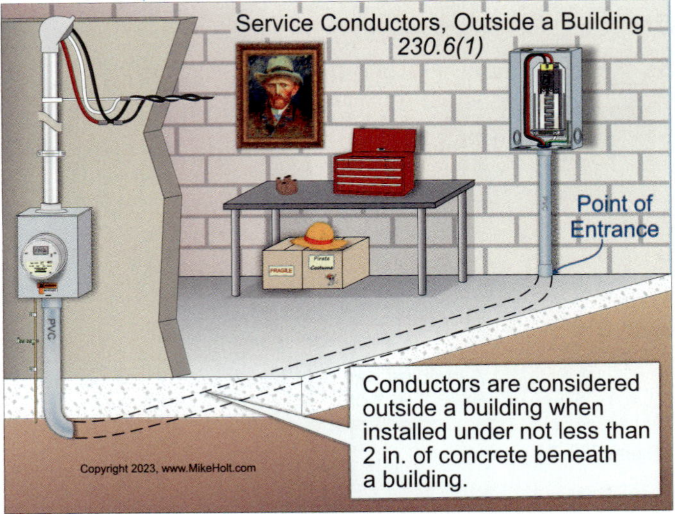

▶Figure 230–11

(2) Within a building or structure in a raceway encased in not less than 2 in. of concrete or brick

(3) In transformer vaults

(4) In dirt floor buildings, with the raceway installed not less than 18 in. below the finished surface

230.7 Service Conductors Separate from Other Conductors

Feeder and branch-circuit conductors are not permitted to be installed in the same raceway, cable, handhole enclosure, or underground box with service conductors. ▶Figure 230–12

Warning

WARNING: If service, feeder, and/or branch-circuit conductors are installed in the same raceway and a short circuit occurs between the service and feeder or branch-circuit conductors, the feeder or branch-circuit overcurrent protection will be bypassed.

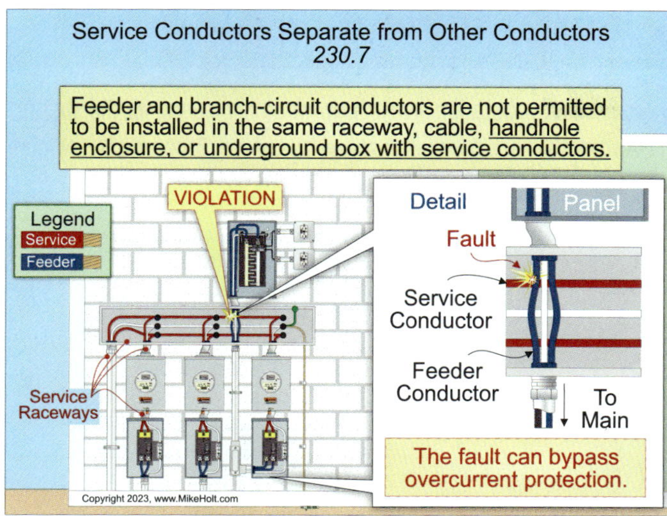

▶Figure 230–12

Author's Comment:

▶ Service, feeder, and branch-circuit conductors are permitted in the service disconnect enclosure.

▶ Feeders and branch-circuit conductors can be in the same raceway or enclosure. ▶Figure 230–13

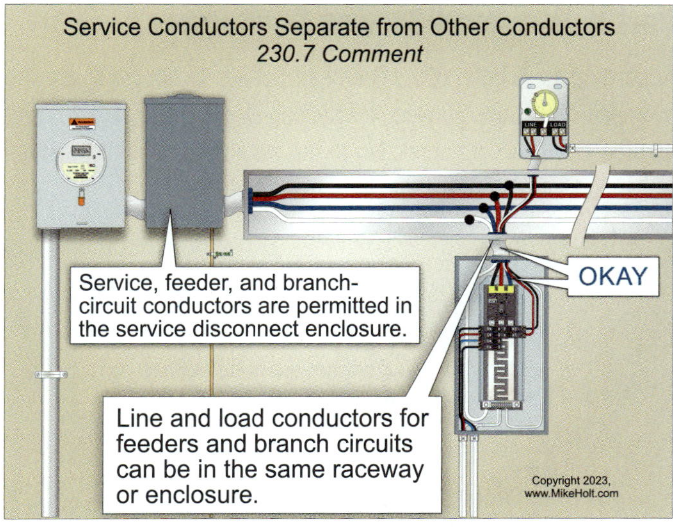

▶Figure 230–13

230.8 Raceway Seals

Where a service raceway enters a building or structure from outside, it must be sealed in accordance with 300.5(G) and 300.7(A). Sealants must be identified for use with cable insulation, conductor insulation, bare conductor, shield, or other components. ▶Figure 230–14 and ▶Figure 230–15

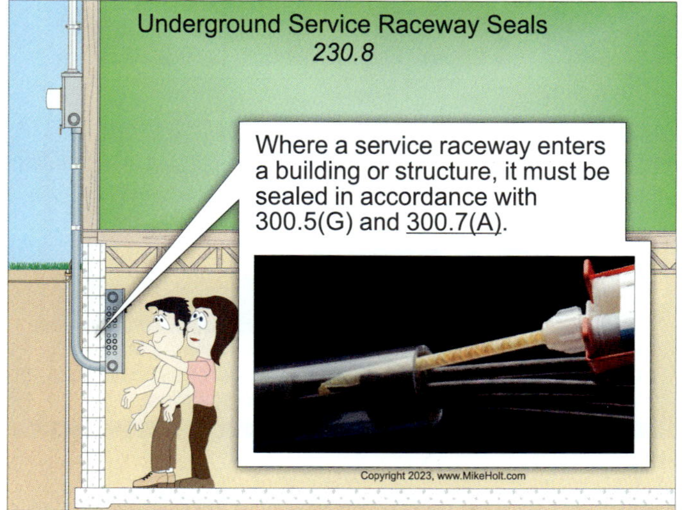

▶Figure 230–14

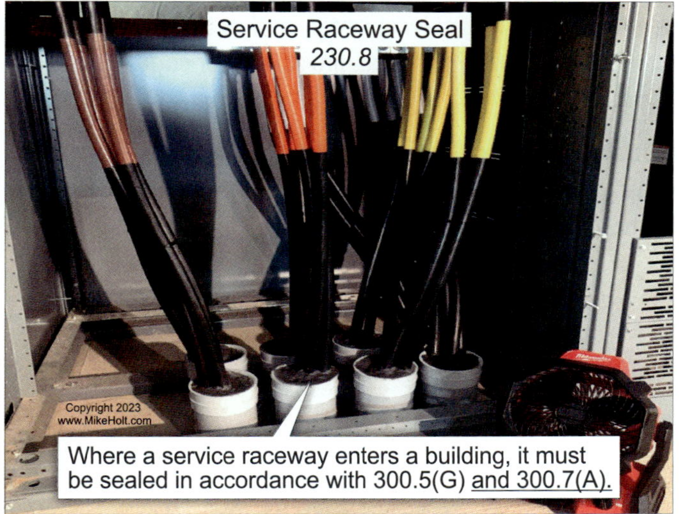

▶Figure 230–15

230.9 Clearances on Buildings

(A) Clearance. Overhead service conductors must maintain a clearance of 3 ft from windows that open, doors, porches, balconies, ladders, stairs, fire escapes, or similar locations. ▶Figure 230–16

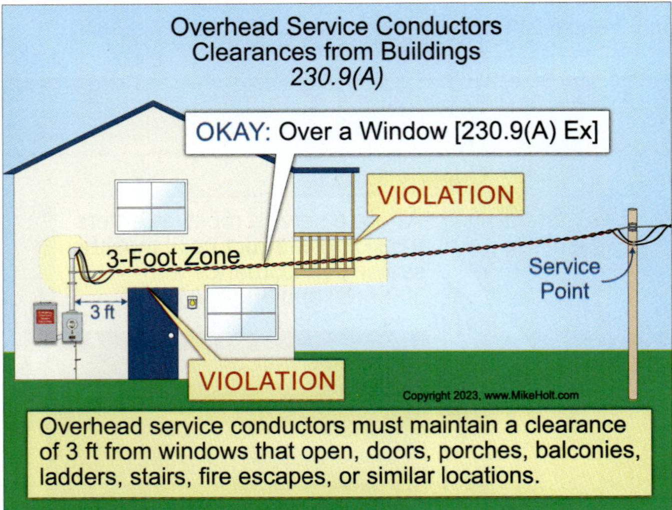

▶Figure 230–16

(B) Vertical Clearance. Overhead service conductors within 3 ft measured horizontally of platforms, projections, or surfaces that will permit personal contact must have a vertical clearance of not less than 10 ft above the platforms, projections, or surfaces in accordance with 230.24(B).

(C) Below Openings. Overhead service conductors cannot be installed under an opening through which materials might pass and where they will obstruct entrance to building openings. ▶Figure 230–17

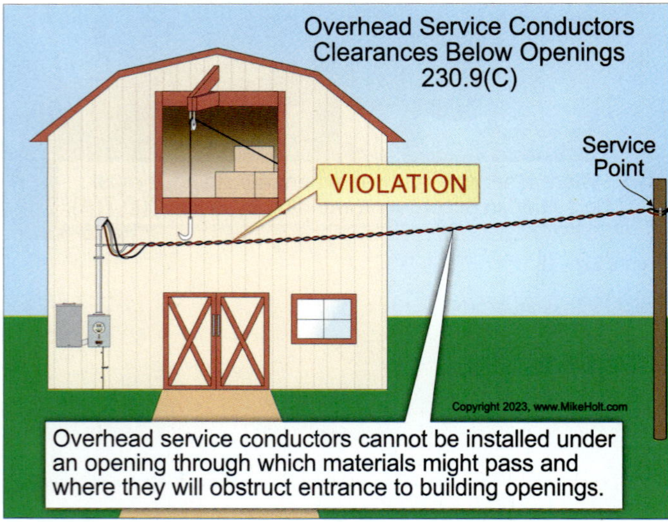

▶Figure 230–17

230.10 Vegetation as Support

Trees or other vegetation are not permitted to be used for the support of overhead service conductor spans or service disconnects. ▶Figure 230–18

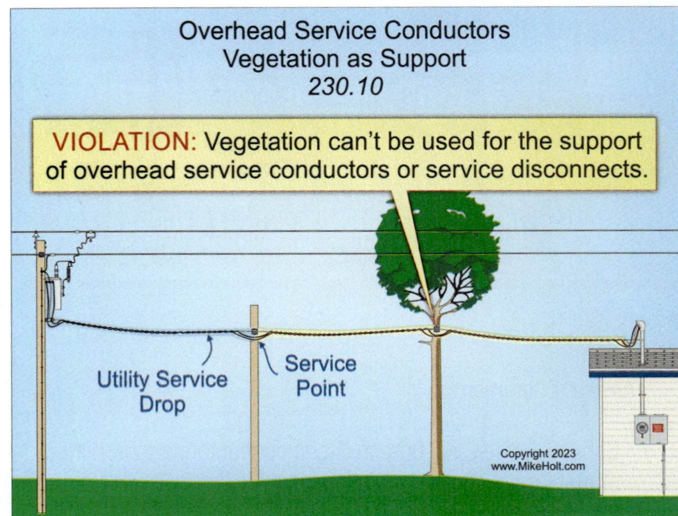

▶Figure 230–18

Part II. Overhead Service Conductors

According to Article 100, "Overhead Service Conductors" are the overhead conductors between the serving electric utility service point and the first point of connection to the service-entrance conductors at the building. ▶Figure 230–19

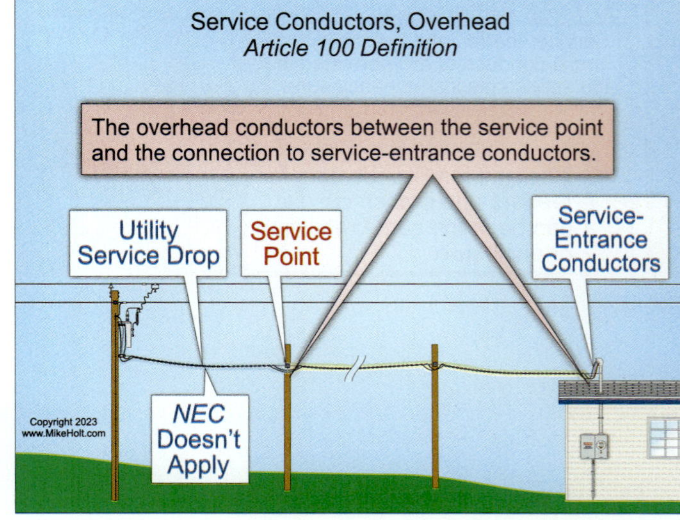

▶Figure 230–19

According to Article 100, "Service Point" is the point where the serving electric utility conductors connect to customer-owned premises wiring. ▶Figure 230–20

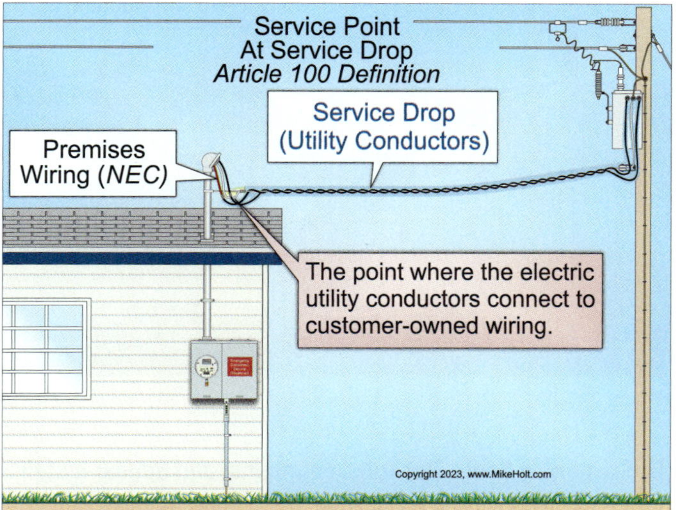

▶Figure 230–20

According to Article 100, "Service Drop" is the utility-owned overhead conductors between the serving electric utility transformer and the service point. ▶Figure 230–21

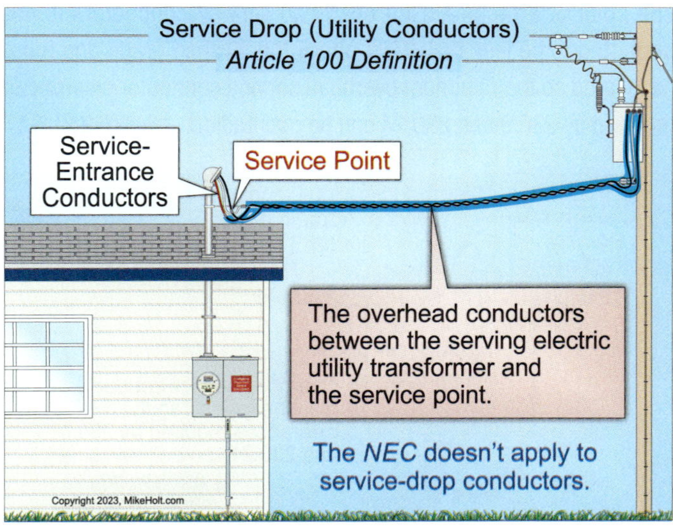

▶Figure 230–21

230.23 Overhead Service Conductor Size and Rating

(A) General. Overhead service conductors must have sufficient ampacity to carry the load as calculated in accordance with Parts II through V of Article 220.

(B) Phase Conductor Size. Overhead service conductors cannot be smaller than 8 AWG copper or 6 AWG aluminum.

Ex: Overhead service conductors can be as small as 12 AWG for limited-load installations.

(C) Neutral Conductor Size. The neutral conductor for overhead service conductors must be sized to carry the maximum unbalanced load in accordance with 220.61 and no smaller than required by 250.24(D)(1).

> **Warning**
>
> **WARNING:** The service neutral conductor size must not be smaller than that required by 250.24(D)(1) to ensure it has sufficiently low impedance and current-carrying capacity to safely carry fault current to facilitate the operation of the overcurrent protective device [250.4(A)(5)].

▶ Example

Question: What size overhead service neutral conductor is required for a structure with a 400A service supplied with 500 kcmil conductors if the maximum line-to-neutral load is no more than 100A?

(a) 1/0 AWG   (b) 2/0 AWG   (c) 3/0 AWG   (d) 4/0 AWG

Solution:

According to Table 310.16, a 3 AWG conductor rated 100A at 75°C [110.14(C)(1)(b)(1)] is sufficient to carry 100A of neutral current. However, the service neutral conductor cannot be smaller than 1/0 AWG according to Table 250.102(C)(1), based on the size/area of the 500 kcmil service conductors [250.24(D)].

Answer: (a) 1/0 AWG

230.24 Vertical Clearance for Overhead Service Conductors

Overhead service conductor spans must maintain vertical clearances as follows:

(A) Above Roofs. A minimum of 8 ft 6 in. above the surface of a roof for a minimum distance of 3 ft in all directions from the roof edge.

Ex 2: If the slope of the roof exceeds 4 in. of vertical rise for every 12 in. of horizontal run, the 120/208V or 120/240V overhead service conductor clearances can be reduced to 3 ft over the roof.

Ex 3: If no more than 6 ft of conductors pass over no more than 4 ft of roof overhang, the 120/208V or 120/240V overhead service conductor clearances over the roof overhang can be reduced to 18 in. ▶Figure 230–22

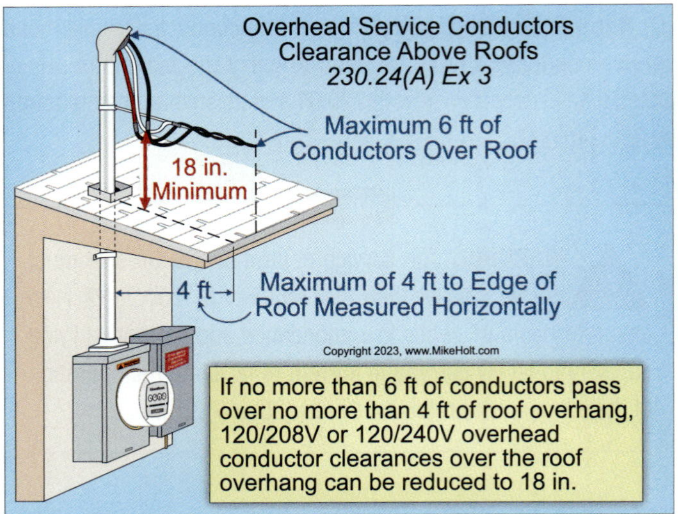

▶Figure 230–22

Ex 4: The 3-ft vertical clearance for overhead service conductors that extends from the roof does not apply when the point of attachment is on the side of the building below the roof.

Ex 5: If the voltage between conductors does not exceed 300V and the roof area is guarded or isolated, the clearance can be reduced to 3 ft.

(B) Above Grade. Overhead service conductor spans must maintain the following vertical clearances:

(1) 10 ft above finished grade, sidewalks, platforms, or projections that permit personal contact for circuits supplied by 120/208V or 120/240V.

(2) 12 ft above residential property and driveways, and commercial areas not subject to truck traffic for circuits supplied by 120/208V, 120/240V, or 277/480V. ▶Figure 230–23

(3) 15 ft above residential property and driveways, and commercial areas not subject to truck traffic for circuits supplied by a system having a voltage exceeding 300V to ground.

(4) 18 ft above public streets, alleys, roads, parking areas subject to truck traffic, driveways on other than residential property, and other areas traversed by vehicles such as those used for cultivation, grazing, forestry, and orchards.

(5) 24 ft 6 in. above tracks of railroads.

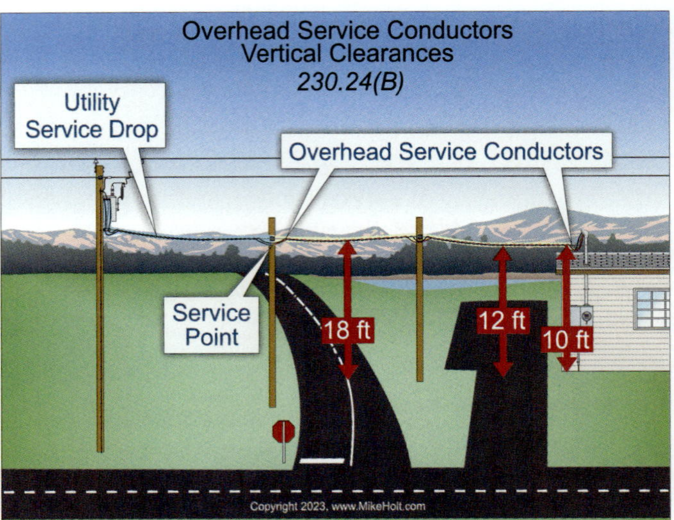

▶Figure 230–23

(D) Swimming Pools, Hot Tubs, Fountains, and Similar Installations. Overhead service conductors above pools, outdoor hot tubs, fountains, and similar installations must comply with the clearance requirements in 680.9.

230.26 Point of Attachment

The point of attachment for overhead service conductors is not permitted to be less than 10 ft above the finished grade and must be located so the minimum overhead service conductor clearances required by 230.9 and 230.24 can be maintained. ▶Figure 230–24

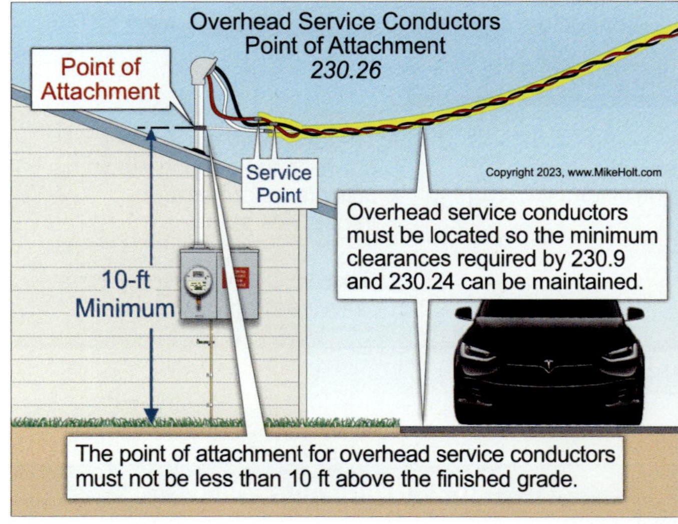

▶Figure 230–24

CAUTION: The point of attachment for conductors might need to be raised so the overhead service conductors will comply with the clearances from building openings required by 230.9 and from other areas as required by 230.24.

230.27 Means of Attachment

Open conductors must be attached to fittings identified for use with service conductors or to noncombustible, nonabsorbent insulators securely attached to the building.

230.28 Service Masts as Support

Masts used for the support of overhead service conductors or service drops must be installed in accordance with 230.28(A) and (B).

(A) Strength. If a mast is used for service drop or overhead service conductor support, it must have adequate mechanical strength, braces, or guy wires to withstand the strain caused by the conductors. ▶Figure 230–25

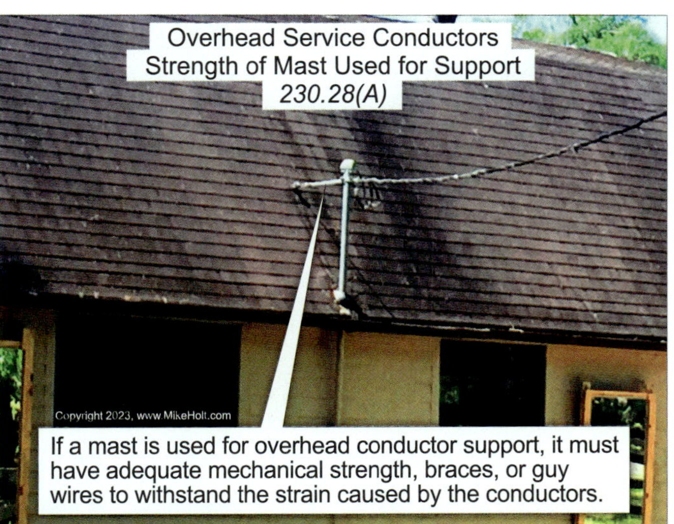

▶Figure 230–25

(B) Attachment. Conductors cannot be attached to a mast between a weatherhead or end of the conduit and a coupling if the coupling is above the last conduit support, or if the coupling is above the building. ▶Figure 230–26

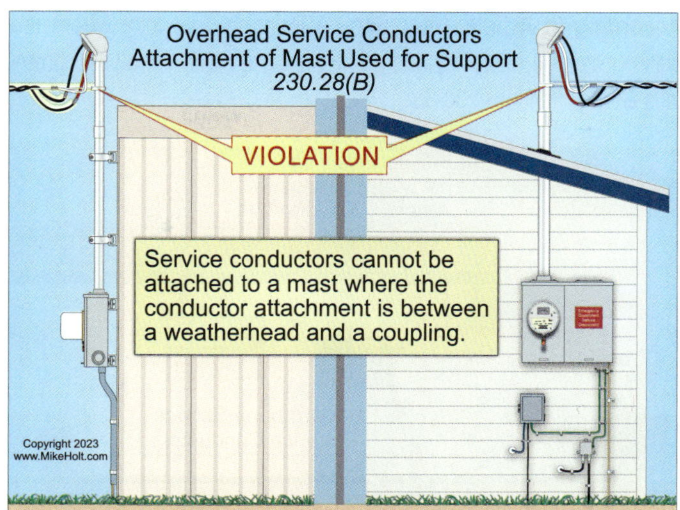

▶Figure 230–26

Author's Comment:

▶ Some local codes or utilities require a minimum 2 in. rigid metal conduit to be used for the service mast. In addition, many electric utilities contain specific requirements for the installation of the service mast.

Part III. Underground Service Conductors

According to Article 100, "Underground Service Conductors" are the underground conductors between the service point and the first point of connection to the service-entrance conductors in a terminal box, meter, or other enclosure, whether inside or outside the building wall. ▶Figure 230–27

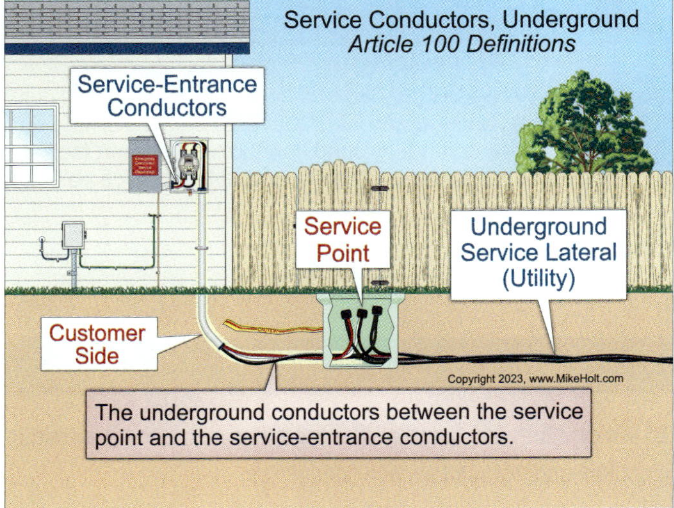

▶Figure 230–27

According to **Article 100,** "Service Point" is the point where the serving electric utility conductors connect to customer-owned premises wiring. ▶Figure 230–28

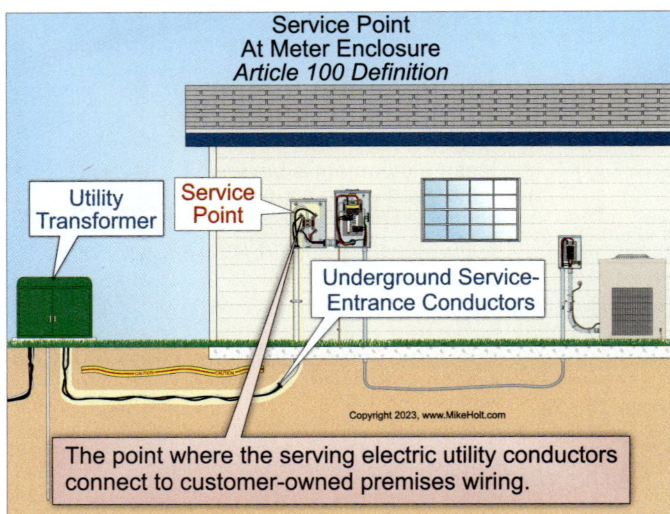

▶Figure 230–28

According to **Article 100,** "Service Lateral" is the utility-owned underground conductors between the serving electric utility transformer and the service point. ▶Figure 230–29

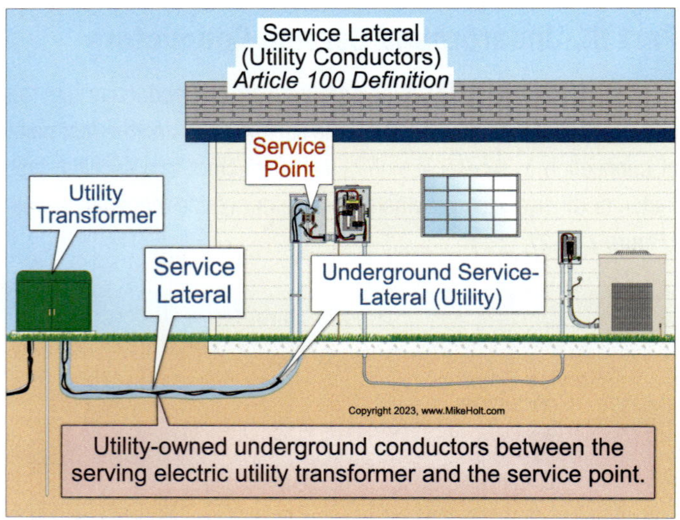

▶Figure 230–29

230.30 Installation

(B) Wiring Methods. Only the following wiring methods are permitted to contain underground service conductors:

(1) RMC conduit

(2) IMC conduit

(3) NUCC conduit

(4) HDPE conduit

(5) PVC conduit

(6) RTRC conduit

(7) IGS cable

(8) USE conductors or cables

(9) MV or MC cable identified for direct burial applications

(11) TC-ER cable identified for service entrance use and direct burial applications

230.31 Underground Service Conductor Ampacity

(A) General. Underground service conductors must have the ampacity to carry the load as calculated in accordance with Part II through Part V of Article 220.

(B) Phase Conductor Size. Underground service conductors are not permitted to be smaller than 8 AWG copper, or 6 AWG aluminum or copper-clad aluminum.

Ex: Underground service conductors can be as small as 12 AWG for limited-load installations.

(C) Neutral Conductor Size. The neutral conductor for underground service conductors must be sized to carry the maximum unbalanced load in accordance with 220.61 and not smaller than required by 250.24(D).

▶ **Example**

Question: *What size underground service neutral conductor is required for a structure with a 400A service supplied with 500 kcmil conductors if the maximum line-to-neutral load is no more than 100A?*

(a) 1/0 AWG   (b) 2/0 AWG   (c) 3/0 AWG   (d) 4/0 AWG

Solution:

According to Table 310.16, a 3 AWG conductor rated 100A at 75°C [110.14(C)(1)(b)(1)] can carry 100A of neutral current. However, the service neutral conductor must not be smaller than 1/0 AWG according to Table 250.102(C)(1), based on the size/area of the 500 kcmil service conductors [250.24(D)(1)].

***Answer:** (a) 1/0 AWG*

230.32 Protection Against Damage

Underground service conductors must be protected from physical damage in accordance with 300.5.

Part IV. Service-Entrance Conductors

According to Article 100, "Service-Entrance Conductors" are the conductors between the terminals of the service equipment and the service drop, overhead service conductors, service lateral, or underground service conductors. ▶Figure 230–30 and ▶Figure 230–31

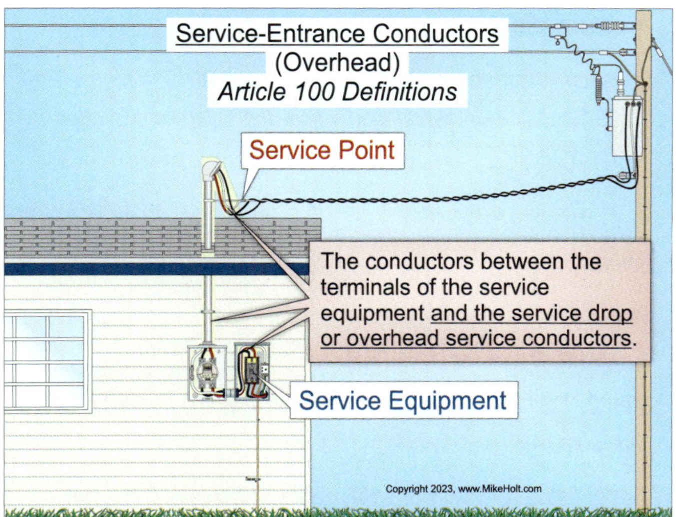

▶Figure 230–30

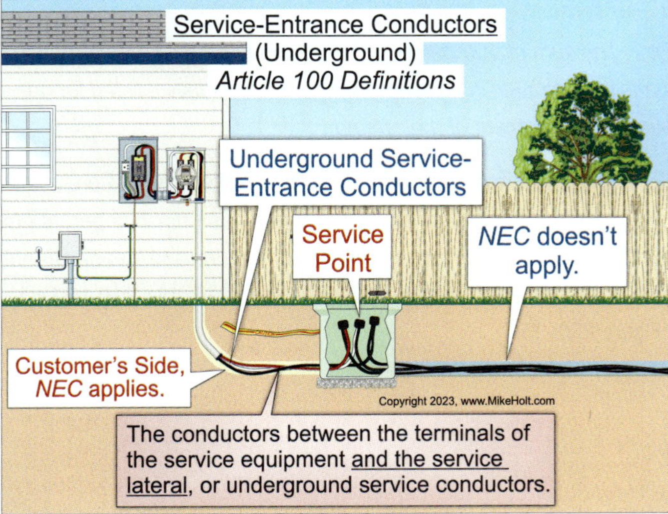

▶Figure 230–31

230.40 Number of Service-Entrance Conductor Sets

Each service drop, service lateral, or set of underground or overhead service conductors can only supply one set of service-entrance conductors.

Ex 1: A building with more than one occupancy can have one set of service-entrance conductors for each service, as permitted in 230.2, run to each occupancy. If the number of service disconnects does not exceed six, the requirements of 230.2(E) apply at each location.

Ex 2: Service conductors can supply two to six service disconnects in accordance with 230.71(B).

> **Author's Comment:**
>
> ▸ Underground sets of conductors 1/0 AWG and larger running to the same location and connected at their supply end, but not at their load end, are considered to supply one service [230.2].

Ex 5: One set of service-entrance conductors connected to the supply side of the normal service disconnect can supply standby power systems, fire pump equipment, fire and sprinkler alarms [230.82(5)], and solar PV systems [230.82(6)].

230.42 Conductor Sizing

(A) General. Service conductors must be sized to have an ampacity of not less than the largest of the calculations contained in 230.42(A)(1) or (2). ▶Figure 230–32

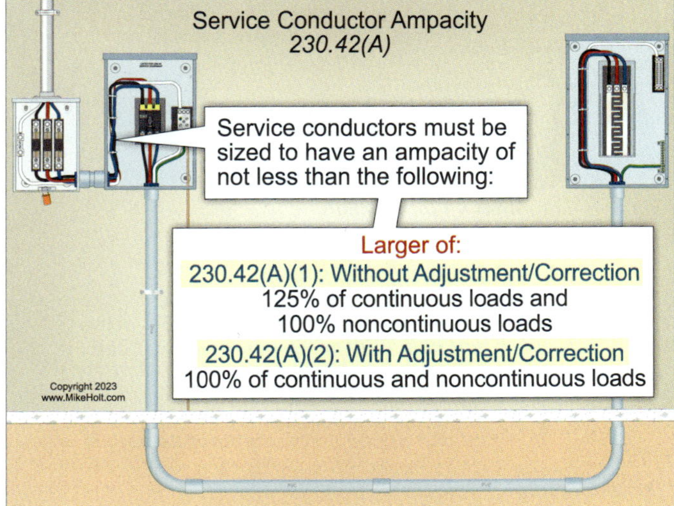

▶Figure 230–32

(1) Without Conductor Ampacity Correction/Adjustment. Service conductors must be sized to have an ampacity of not less than 125 percent of the continuous loads, plus 100 percent of the noncontinuous loads, based on the temperature rating of equipment in accordance with 110.14(C)(1) and Table 310.16, prior to conductor ampacity correction and/or adjustment. ▶Figure 230–33

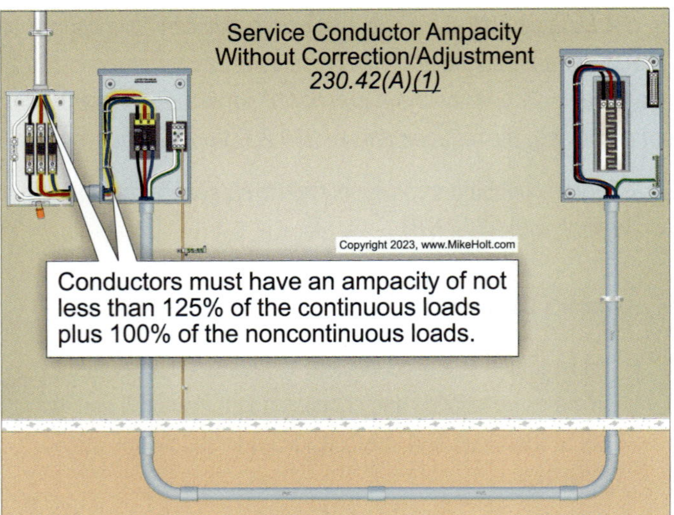

▶Figure 230–33

▶ Example 1

Question: What size conductors are required for a 180A continuous load where the equipment is rated for 75°C conductor?

(a) 1/0 AWG   (b) 2/0 AWG   (c) 3/0 AWG   (d) 4/0 AWG

Solution:

Step 1: *Minimum Conductor Ampacity.* ▶Figure 230–34

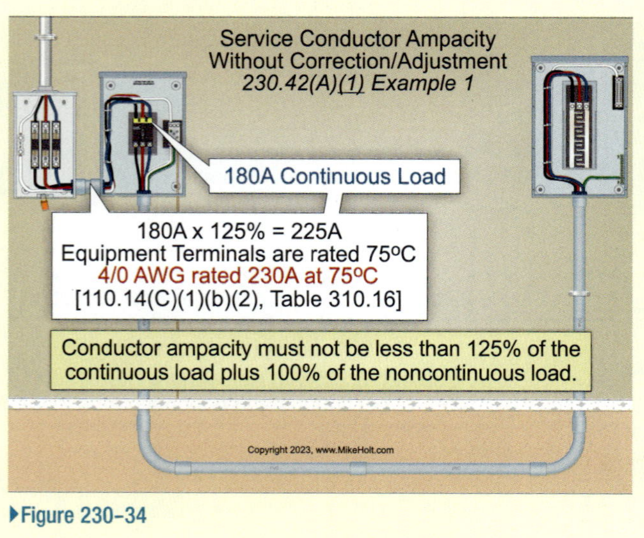

▶Figure 230–34

Minimum Conductor Ampacity = 180A × 125%
Minimum Conductor Ampacity = 225A

Step 2: *Conductor Size.*

Conductor Size = 4/0 AWG THWN-2, rated 230A [Table 310.16, 75°C column]

Answer: (d) 4/0 AWG

Ex 3: Neutral conductors are permitted to have an ampacity of 100 percent of the continuous and noncontinuous loads.

▶ Example 2

Question: What size neutral conductor rated 90°C is required for a 125A continuous neutral load where the equipment is rated for 75°C conductor?

(a) 1 AWG   (b) 2 AWG   (c) 3 AWG   (d) 4 AWG

Solution:

Step 1: The neutral conductor is sized to the 125A continuous load at 100 percent [230.2(A)(1) Ex 3].

Step 2: Size the conductors in accordance with 110.14(C)(1)(b)(2) and Table 310.16.

1 AWG has an ampacity of 130A [Table 310.16, 75°C column].

Answer: (a) 1 AWG

Ex 2: The sum of 100 percent of the continuous and noncontinuous loads if terminated in an overcurrent protective device listed for operation at 100 percent of their rating.

(2) With Conductor Ampacity Correction/Adjustment. Conductors must be sized to have an ampacity of not less than 100 percent of the total load after conductor ampacity correction and/or adjustment in accordance with Table 310.15(B)(1)(1) and Table 310.15(C)(1). ▶Figure 230–35

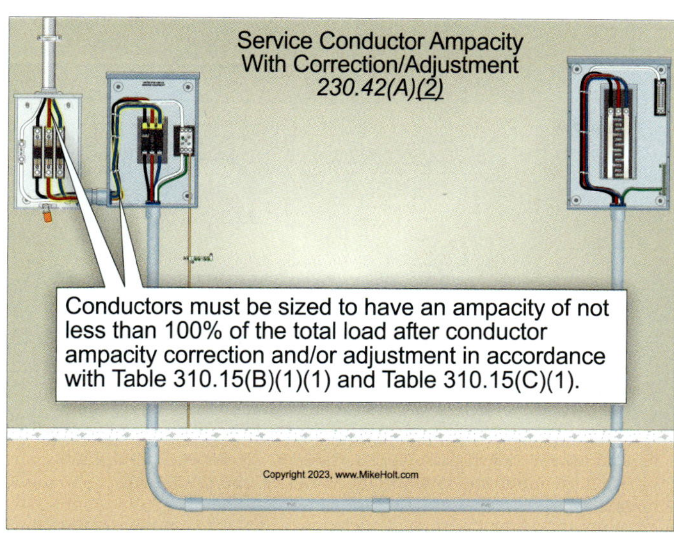

▶Figure 230–35

▶ Example 3

Question: *What size conductors rated 90°C are required for four current-carrying conductors supplying a 180A continuous load in an ambient temperature of 100°F where the equipment is rated for 75°C conductor?*

(a) 4/0 AWG   (b) 300 kcmil   (c) 500 kcmil   (d) 600 kcmil

Note: *According to 230.2(A), the service conductor size is determined by the larger of 230.2(A)(1) or (2).*

Solution:

Step 1: *The circuit conductors must have an ampacity of 180A after conductor ampacity temperature correction [Table 310.15(B)(1)(1)] and adjustment [Table 310.15(C)(1)] based on the conductor's insulation rating of 90°C. One way to find the conductor size is to determine the conductor ampacity required to supply a 180A continuous load at 100 percent after correction and adjustment.*

Conductor Ampacity at 90°C = Continuous Load at 100%/ (Correction × Adjustment)

Continuous Load = 180A

Correction [Table 310.15(B)(1)(1)] = 91% (100°F ambient temperature with 90°C Conductor)

Adjustment [Table 310.15(C)(1)] = 80% (four current-carrying conductors)

Conductor Ampacity at 90°C Column = 180A/(91% × 80%)
Conductor Ampacity at 90°C Column = 180A/73%
Conductor Ampacity at 90°C Column = 247A

Step 2: *Select the conductors from the 90°C column of Table 310.16 [110.14(C)(1)(b)(2)].* ▶Figure 230–36

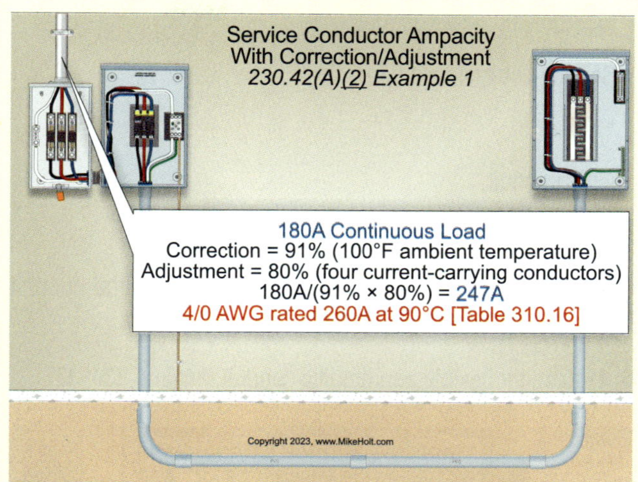

▶Figure 230–36

4/0 AWG is suitable because it has an ampacity of 260A at 90°C before any correction and adjustment.

Note: *According to 230.42(A), the service conductor size is determined by the larger of 230.42(A)(1) or (2). In this case, based on the conditions specified in this example, 4/0 AWG is the minimum size.*

Answer: *(a) 4/0 AWG*

(C) Neutral Conductor Size. The service neutral conductor must be sized to have an ampacity to carry the maximum unbalanced load in accordance with 220.61 and not smaller than required by 250.24(D).

> **Warning**
>
> **WARNING:** In no case can the service neutral conductor size be smaller than required by 250.24(D) to ensure it has sufficiently low impedance and current-carrying capacity to safely carry fault current to facilitate the operation of the overcurrent protective device.

230.43 Wiring Methods

Service-entrance conductors can be installed with any of the following wiring methods:

(1) Open wiring on insulators

(3) Rigid metal conduit

(4) Intermediate metal conduit

(5) Electrical metallic tubing

(6) Electrical nonmetallic tubing

(7) Service-entrance cables

(8) Wireways

(11) PVC conduit

(13) MC cable

(15) Flexible metal conduit or liquidtight flexible metal conduit in lengths not longer than 6 ft

(16) Liquidtight flexible nonmetallic conduit ▶Figure 230–37

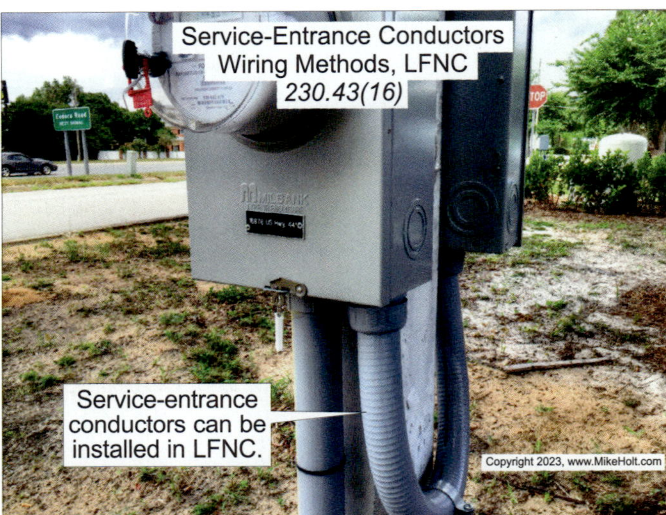

▶Figure 230–37

(17) High-density polyethylene conduit

(18) Nonmetallic underground conduit with conductors

(19) Reinforced thermosetting resin conduit

(20) TC-ER cable identified for use as service-entrance conductors

(21) Flexible bus system

230.46 Spliced and Tapped Connections

Pressure connectors, devices for splices and tap connections, and power distribution blocks installed on service conductors must be listed and marked "suitable for use on the line side of the service equipment" or equivalent. ▶Figure 230–38

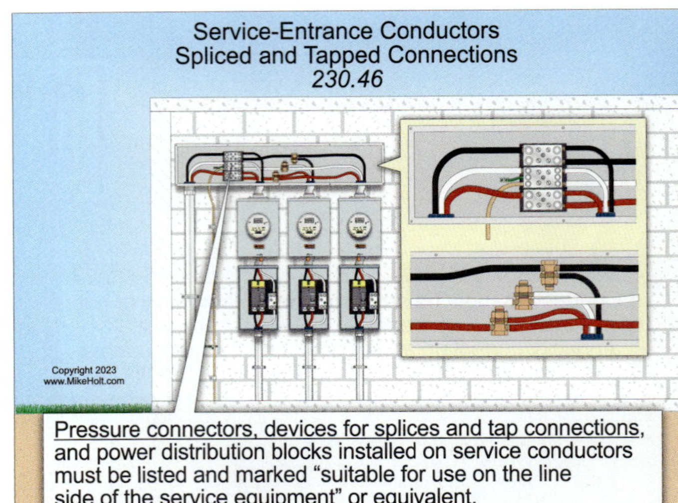

▶Figure 230–38

230.50 Protection Against Physical Damage

(A) Underground Service-Entrance Conductors. Underground service-entrance conductors must be protected against physical damage in accordance with 300.5. ▶Figure 230–39

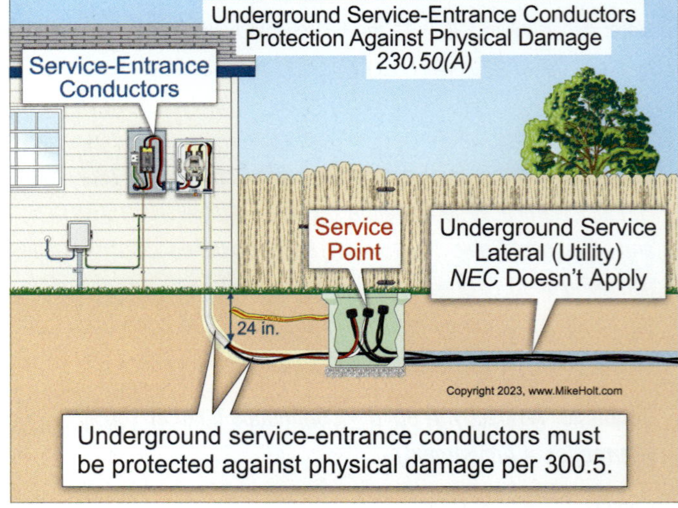

▶Figure 230–39

(B) Service-Entrance Cables Subject to Physical Damage.

(1) Service-Entrance Cables. Service-entrance cables that are subject to physical damage must be protected by any of the following: ▶Figure 230–40

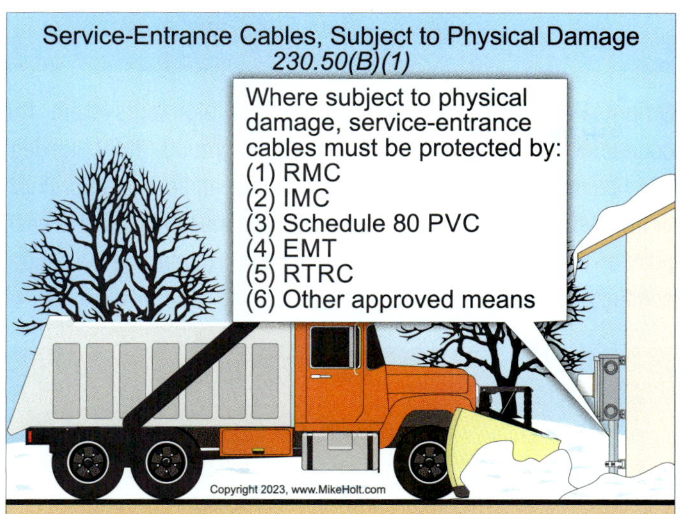

▶Figure 230–40

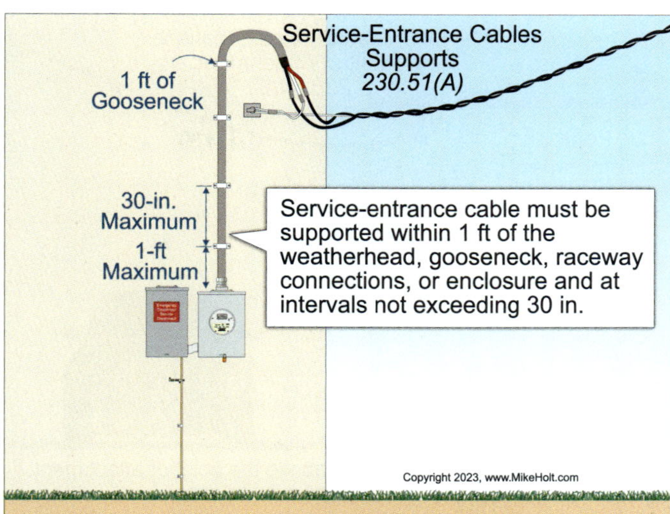

▶Figure 230–41

(1) Rigid metal conduit

(2) Intermediate metal conduit

(3) Schedule 80 PVC conduit

(4) Electrical metallic tubing

(5) Reinforced thermosetting resin conduit

(6) Other means approved by the authority having jurisdiction

(2) Other Than Service-Entrance Cable. Individual open conductors and cables, other than service-entrance cables, are not permitted to be installed within 10 ft of grade level or where exposed to physical damage.

230.51 Cable Supports

(A) Service-Entrance Cable Supports. Service-entrance cable must be supported within 1 ft of the weatherhead, gooseneck, raceway connections, or enclosure. Supports must be at intervals not exceeding 30 in. ▶Figure 230–41

230.53 Raceways to Drain

Where exposed to the weather or embedded in masonry, raceways enclosing service-entrance conductors must be listed or approved for use in wet locations and arranged to drain.

230.54 Overhead Service Locations

(A) Service Head. Raceways for service drops or overhead service conductors must have a weatherhead listed for wet locations.

(B) Service-Entrance Cable. Service-entrance cables must be equipped with a weatherhead listed for wet locations.

Ex: Type SE cable is permitted to be formed into a gooseneck and taped with a self-sealing weather-resistant tape. ▶Figure 230–42

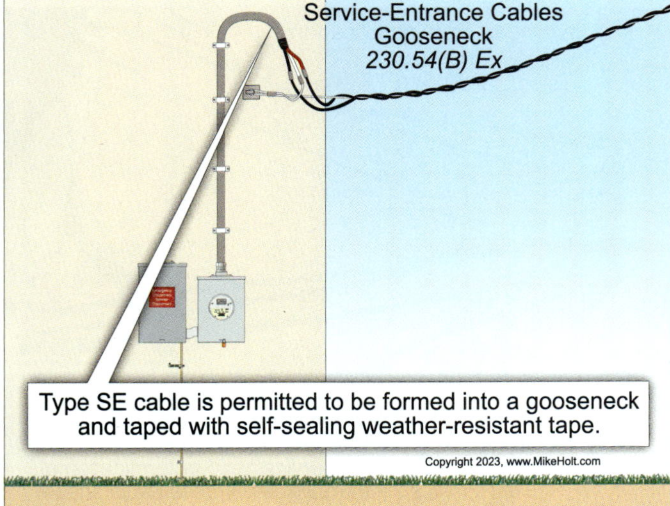

▶Figure 230–42

(C) Above the Point of Attachment. Service weatherheads on raceways or service-entrance cables must be above the point of attachment [230.26] for service-drop or overhead service conductors. ▶Figure 230–43

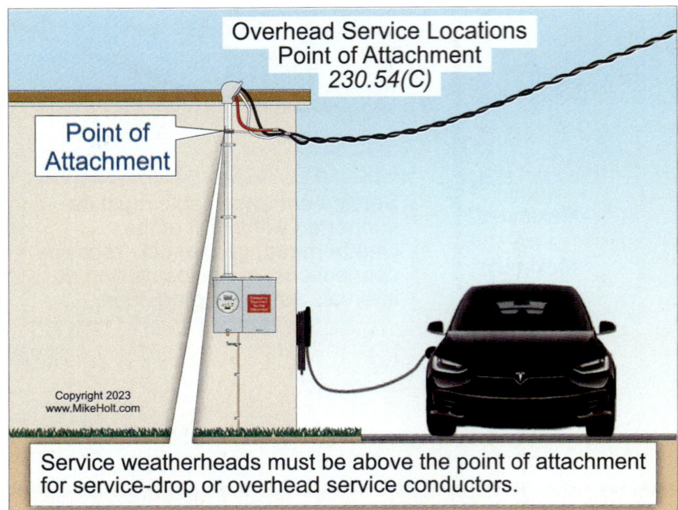

Service weatherheads must be above the point of attachment for service-drop or overhead service conductors.

▶Figure 230–43

Ex: If it is impractical to locate the service head above the point of attachment, it must be within 2 ft of the point of attachment.

(D) Secured. Service-entrance cables must be held securely in place.

(E) Opposite Polarity Through Separately Bushed Holes. Service heads must provide a bushed opening, and phase conductors must be in separate openings.

(F) Drip Loops. Drip loop conductors must be connected to the service-drop or overhead service conductors below the service head or termination of the service-entrance cable sheath. ▶Figure 230–44

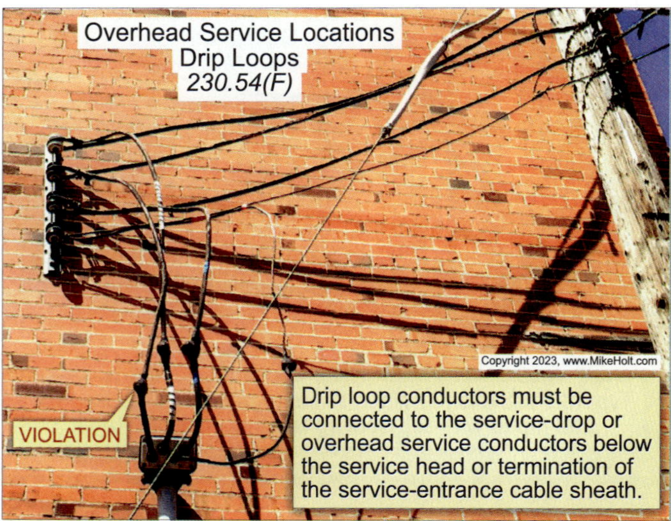

Drip loop conductors must be connected to the service-drop or overhead service conductors below the service head or termination of the service-entrance cable sheath.

▶Figure 230–44

(G) Arranged so Water Will Not Enter. Service-entrance and overhead service conductors must be arranged to prevent water from entering the service disconnect.

230.56 High-Leg Conductor Identification

On a 4-wire, delta-connected, three-phase high-leg system, the conductor with the higher phase voltage-to-ground (208V high-leg) must be durably and permanently marked by an orange outer finish or other effective means. Such identification must be placed at each point on the system where both a connection is made, and the neutral conductor is present [110.15]. ▶Figure 230–45 and ▶Figure 230–46

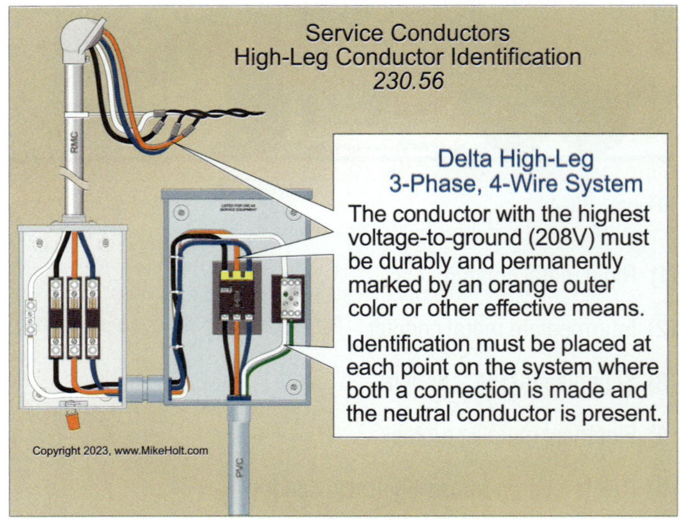

▶Figure 230–45

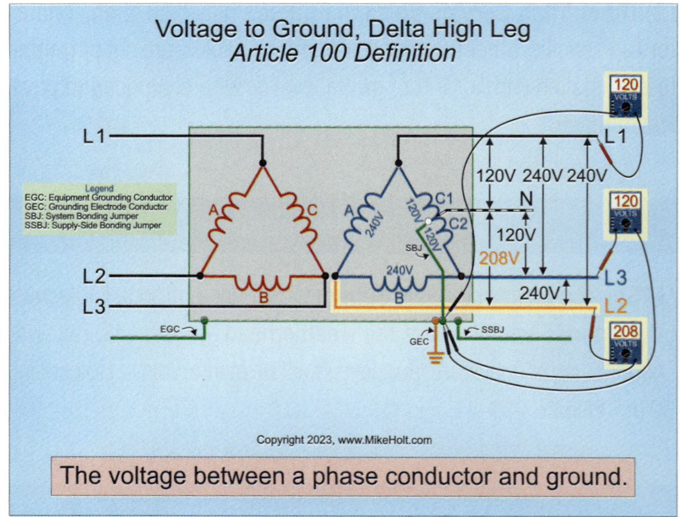

The voltage between a phase conductor and ground.

▶Figure 230–46

Author's Comment:

▶ The high-leg conductor is also called the "Wild Leg" or "Stinger Leg."

▸ Since 1975, panelboards supplied by a 4-wire, delta-connected, three-phase system must have the high-leg (208V) conductor terminate to the "B" (center) phase of a panelboard [408.3(E)]. For many years, the high-leg marking of larger conductors was usually done with orange phasing tape, but individual conductors are now manufactured with orange insulation in almost all sizes.

▸ The ANSI standard for meter equipment requires the high-leg conductor (208V to neutral) to terminate on the "C" (right) phase of the meter socket enclosure. This is because the demand meter needs 120V which comes from the "B" phase. Hopefully, the electric utility lineman is not colorblind and does not inadvertently cross the "orange" high-leg (208V) conductor with the red (120V) service conductor at the weatherhead. It has happened before... ▸Figure 230–47

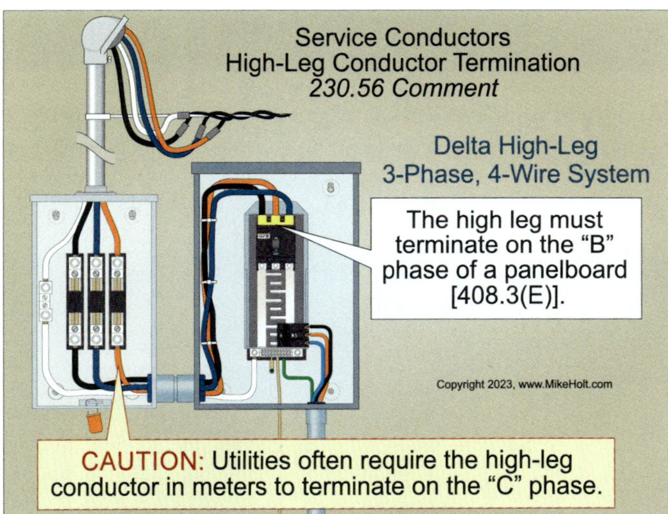

▸Figure 230–47

Part V. Service Disconnect—General

230.62 Service Equipment—Barriers

(C) Barriers. Barriers must be placed on energized uninsulated phase service busbar or service terminals exposed to inadvertent contact when the service disconnect is in the open position. ▸Figure 230–48

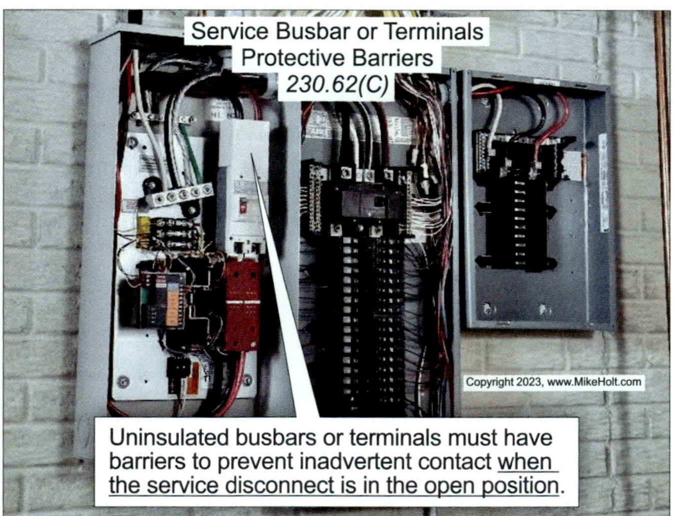

▸Figure 230–48

Author's Comment:

▸ The line side of the service disconnect will have energized parts—even with the disconnect in the open position. Barriers provide some measure of safety against inadvertent contact with line-side energized parts.

230.66 Marking for Service Equipment

(A) Service Equipment Marking. The service disconnect must be marked to identify it as suitable for use as service equipment. ▸Figure 230–49

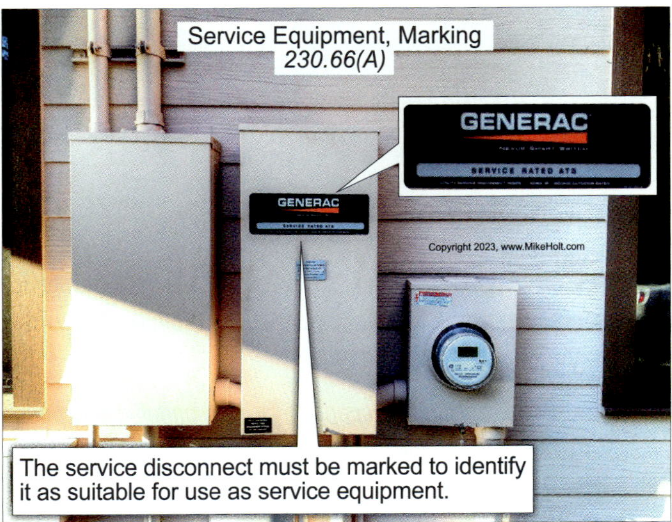

▸Figure 230–49

According to Article 100, "Service Equipment" is the circuit breaker or switch connected to the serving electric utility and intended to disconnect the power from the serving electric utility. ▶Figure 230–50 and ▶Figure 230–51

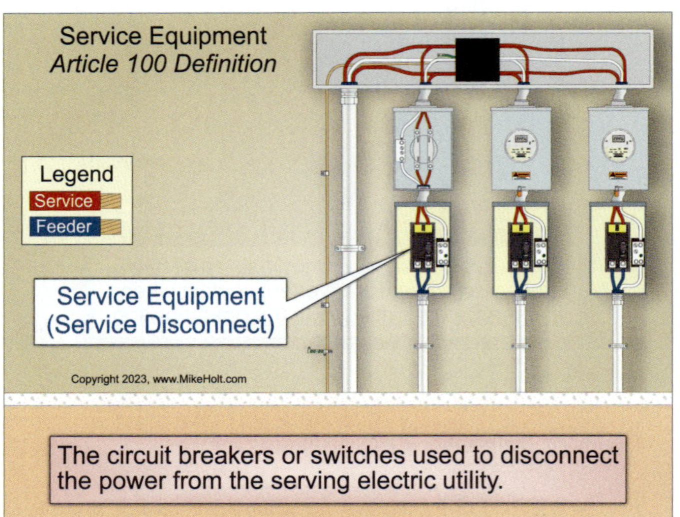

▶Figure 230–50

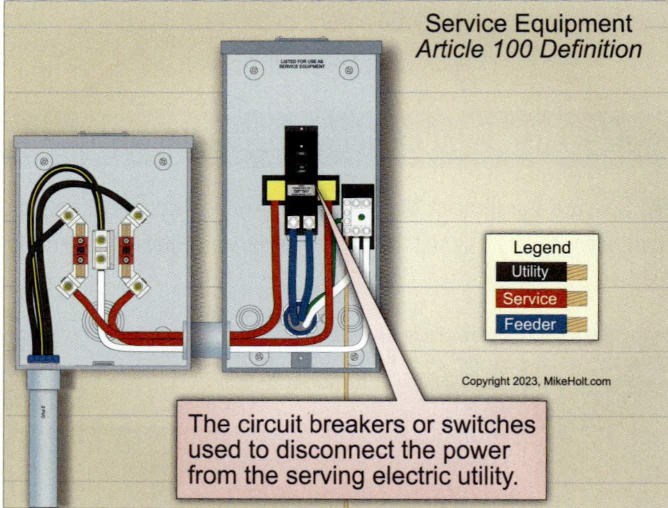

▶Figure 230–51

(B) Meter Socket Listing. Meter sockets are not considered service equipment and must be listed and rated for the voltage and current rating of the service. ▶Figure 230–52

Ex: Meter socket enclosures supplied by, and under the exclusive control of, a serving electric utility are not required to be listed.

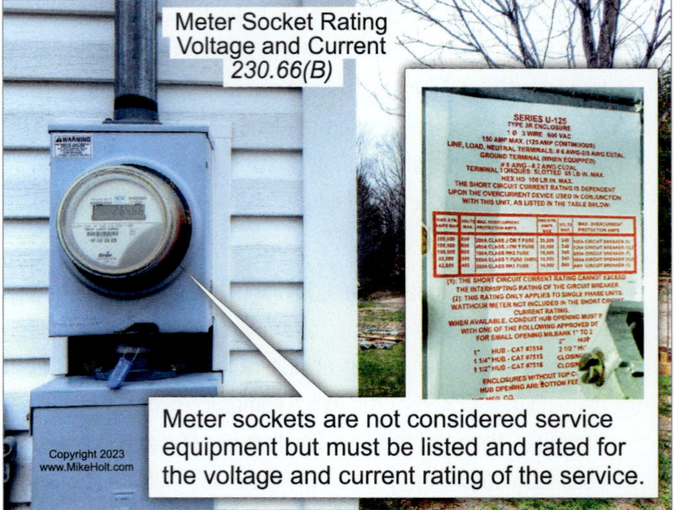

▶Figure 230–52

230.67 Surge Protection

(A) Surge-Protective Device. Where a service supplies <u>any of the following occupancies</u>, a surge-protective device must be provided:

(1) Dwelling units ▶Figure 230–53

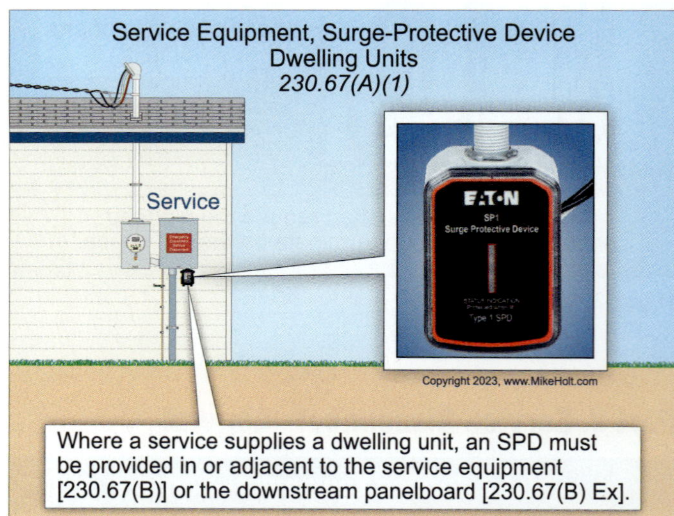

▶Figure 230–53

(2) Dormitory units

(3) Guest rooms and guest suites of hotels and motels

(4) Areas of nursing homes and limited care facilities used exclusively as patient sleeping rooms

(B) SPD Location. The surge-protective device must be an integral part of the service disconnect or be immediately adjacent to the service disconnect.

Ex: The surge-protective device is permitted to be at the downstream panelboard.

Author's Comment:

▸ An example of the application of this exception is where there is an exterior meter main that feeds an interior panel. The SPD could be installed at the interior panel using the exception.

▸ See Parts I and II of Article 242 for installation requirements that apply to SPDs.

(C) SPD Type. The surge-protective device must be a Type 1 or Type 2 SPD.

(D) Service Equipment Replacement. Where service equipment is replaced, surge protection must be installed.

(E) SPD Discharge Current Rating. SPDs must have a nominal discharge current rating (In) of not less than 10 kA. ▸Figure 230–54

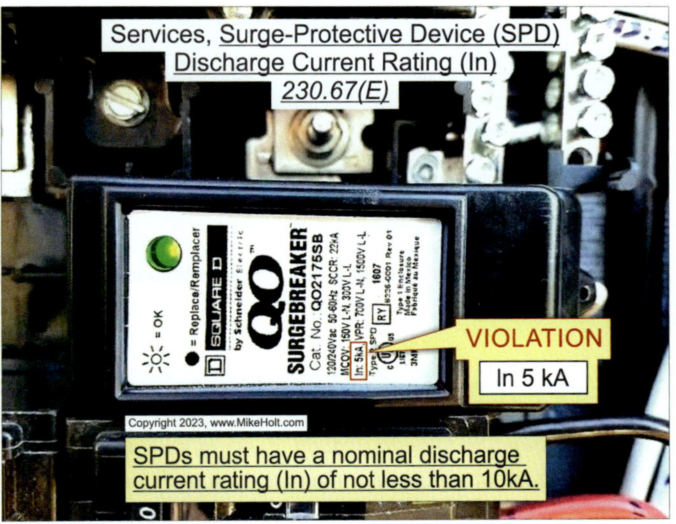

▸Figure 230–54

Author's Comment:

▸ Lead lengths of conductors to the SPD should be kept as short as possible to reduce let-through voltages.

Part VI. Service Disconnect—Disconnecting Means

230.70 Service Disconnect Requirements

The service disconnect must open all phase conductors.

(A) Location.

(1) Readily Accessible. The service disconnect must be placed at a readily accessible location either outside the building or inside nearest the point of service conductor entry.

> **Warning**
>
> **WARNING:** Because service-entrance conductors do not have short-circuit or ground-fault protection, they must be limited in length when installed inside a building. Some local jurisdictions have a specific requirement as to the maximum length permitted within a building. ▸Figure 230–55

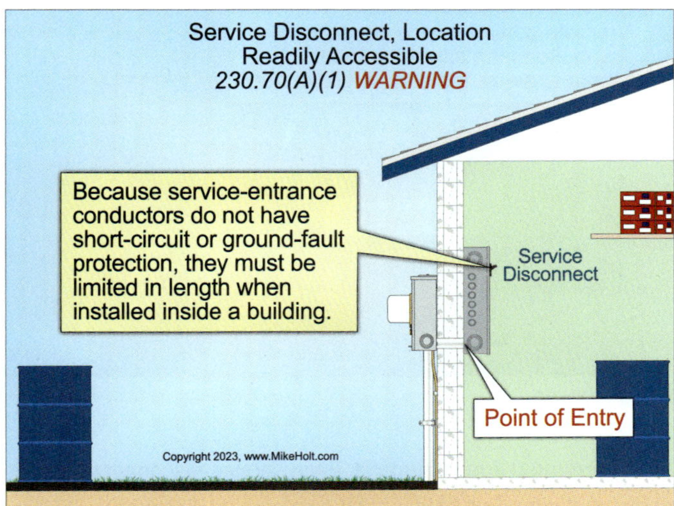

▸Figure 230–55

(2) Bathroom Areas. Service disconnects are not permitted to be installed in a bathroom area. ▸Figure 230–56

(3) Remote Control. A remote-control device (such as a pushbutton for a shunt-trip breaker) used to activate the service disconnect cannot serve as the service disconnect. The service disconnect, not the remote-control device, must be at a readily accessible location either outside the building, or if inside, nearest the point of entrance of the service conductors as required by 230.70(A)(1). ▸Figure 230–57

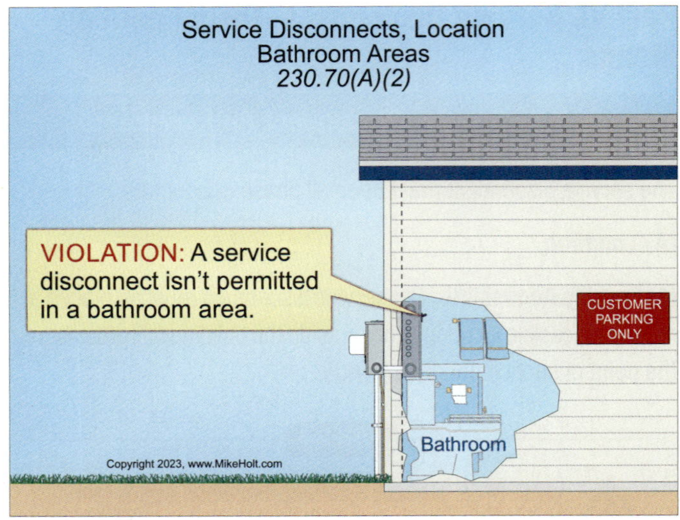

▶Figure 230–56

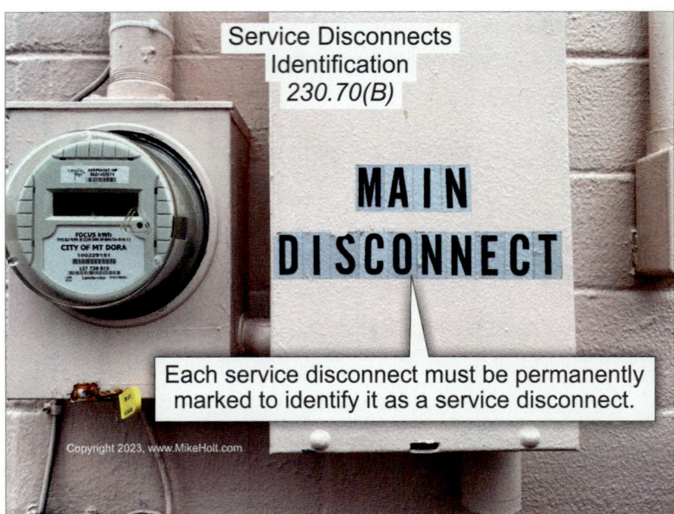

▶Figure 230–58

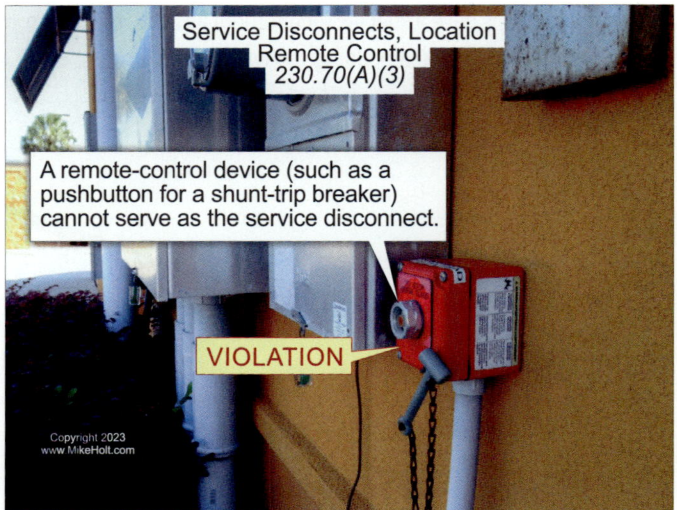

▶Figure 230–57

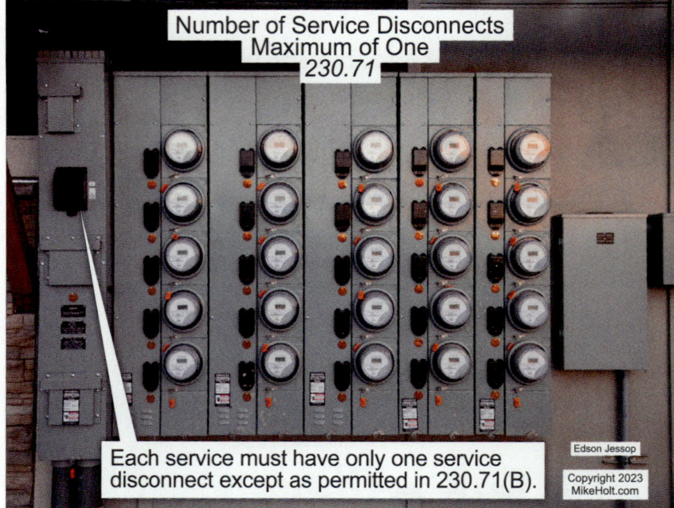

▶Figure 230–59

(B) Disconnect Identification. Each service disconnect must be permanently marked to identify it as a service disconnect. ▶Figure 230–58

230.71 Number of Service Disconnects

Each service must have only one service disconnect except as permitted in 230.71(B). ▶Figure 230–59

(B) Two to Six Service Disconnecting Means. Each service can have up to six service disconnects in accordance with 230.71(B)(1) through (5).

> **Caution**
>
> **CAUTION:** This rule limits six disconnects for each service or set of service-entrance conductors. For example, if the building has more than one service as permitted by 230.2, then there can be more than six service disconnects at the building. ▶Figure 230–60

The two to six service disconnects can consist of a combination of any of the following:

(1) Separate enclosures with a service disconnect in each enclosure

(2) Panelboards with a service disconnect in each panelboard

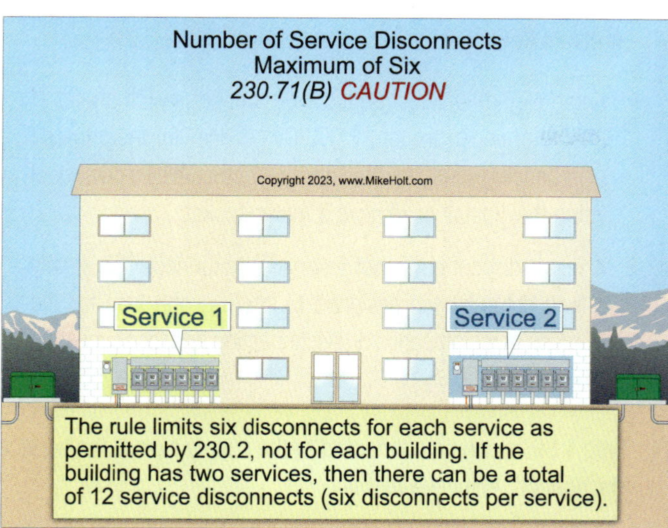

▶Figure 230–60

(3) Switchboard(s) where there is only one service disconnect in each separate vertical section <u>with barriers provided between each vertical section from the adjacent section</u>

(4) Switchgear, <u>transfers switches</u>, or metering centers where each service disconnect is in a separate compartment

(5) <u>Metering centers with a service disconnect upstream in a separate compartment of each metering center</u>

Ex: Existing service equipment in compliance with previous editions of this Code *that permitted multiple service disconnects in a single enclosure is permitted to contain a maximum of six service disconnects.*
▶Figure 230–61

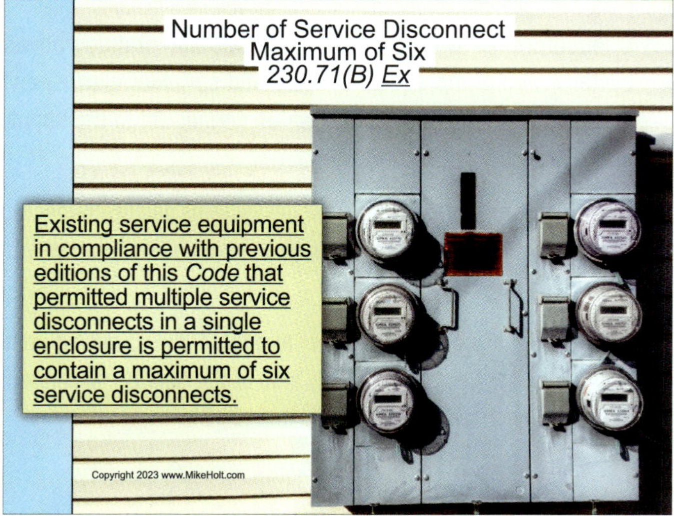

▶Figure 230–61

230.72 Grouping of Service Disconnects

(A) Two to Six Disconnects. The service disconnects for each service must be grouped and marked to indicate the load served. ▶Figure 230–62

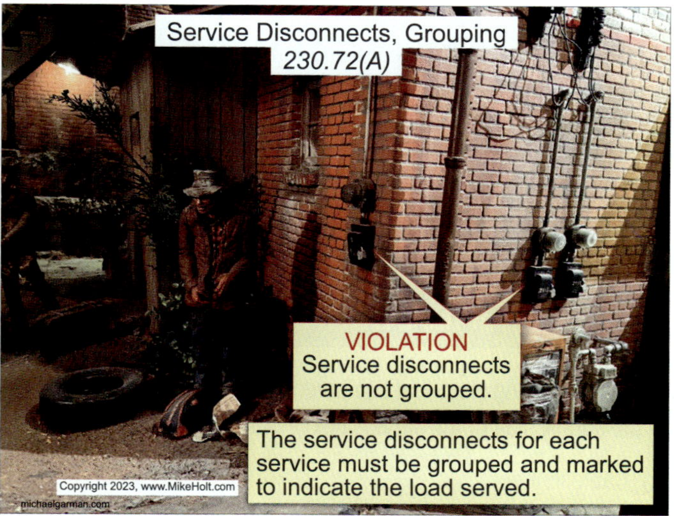

▶Figure 230–62

(B) Additional Service Disconnecting Means. To minimize the possibility of simultaneous interruption of power, the disconnect for fire pumps [Article 695], emergency systems [Article 700], legally required standby systems [Article 701], or optional standby systems [Article 702] must be remote from the service disconnect(s) for normal service.

Author's Comment:

▶ Because emergency systems are just as important as fire pumps and standby systems, they need to have the same safety precautions to prevent unintended interruption of the supply of electricity.

▶ The authority having jurisdiction is responsible for determining what a sufficiently remote distance is for an additional service disconnect.

230.79 Rating of Disconnect

The service disconnect for a building must have an ampere rating of not less than the calculated load according to Article 220, and in no case can it be less than:

(A) One-Circuit Installation. For installations consisting of a single branch circuit, the disconnect must have an ampere rating of not less than 15A.

(B) Two-Circuit Installation. For installations consisting of two 2-wire branch circuits, the disconnect must have an ampere rating of not less than 30A.

(C) One-Family Dwelling. For a one-family dwelling, the disconnect must have an ampere rating of not less than 100A.

(D) Other Installations. For other installations, the disconnect must have an ampere rating of not less than 60A.

230.82 Connected on Supply Side of the Service Disconnect

Only the following electrical equipment is permitted to be connected to the supply side of the service disconnect:

(1) Cable limiters.

(2) Meters and meter sockets rated not less than 1000V.

(3) Meter disconnect switches are permitted to be connected to the supply side of the service disconnect and must have a short-circuit current rating equal to or greater than the available fault current. They must be legibly field marked on the exterior in a manner suitable for the environment as follows: METER DISCONNECT—NOT SERVICE EQUIPMENT. ▶Figure 230–63

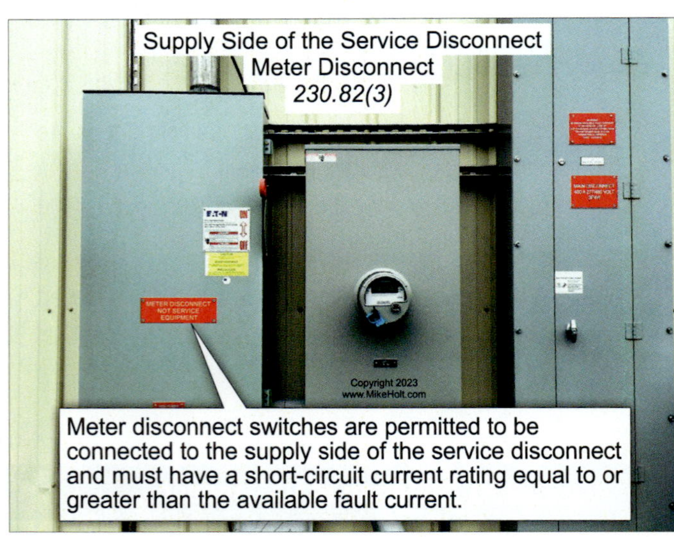

▶Figure 230–63

Author's Comment:

▶ Some electric utilities require a disconnect switch ahead of the meter enclosure for 277/480V services for the purpose of enhancing safety for the serving electric utility's personnel when they install or remove a meter socket.

▶ A meter disconnect is not a service disconnect. It is simply a load break switch designed to interrupt the load for the purpose of maintenance or disconnection and/or connection of a meter.

(4) Type 1 SPDs can be connected to the supply side of the service disconnect. ▶Figure 230–64

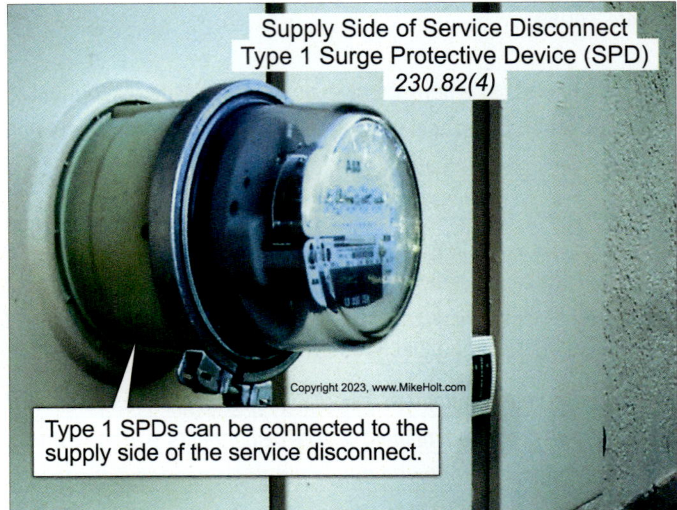

▶Figure 230–64

(5) Conductors for legally required and optional standby power systems, fire pump equipment, fire and sprinkler alarms, and energy management systems can be connected to the supply side of the service disconnect.

(6) Solar PV systems and energy storage systems can be connected to the supply side of the service disconnect in accordance with 700.11(D). ▶Figure 230–65

(10) Emergency disconnects for one- and two-family dwelling units can be connected to the supply side of the service disconnect in accordance with 230.85(B)(2) and (B)(3).

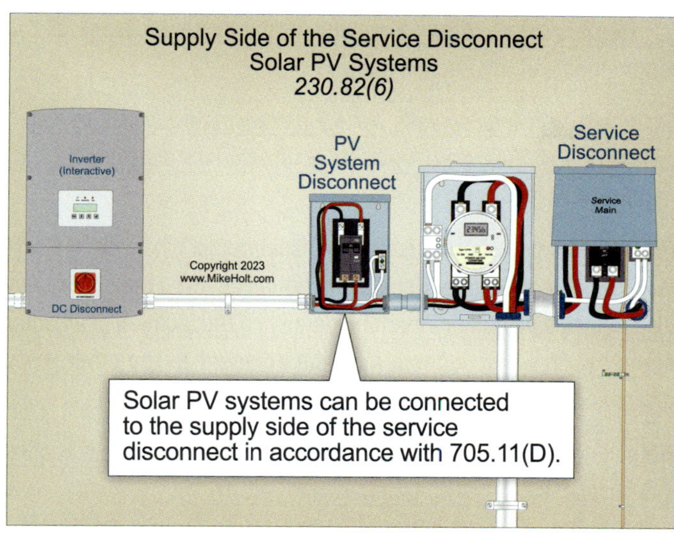

▶Figure 230–65

(11) Meter-mounted transfer switches are permitted to be connected to the supply side of the service disconnect and must have a short-circuit current rating equal to or greater than the available fault current. A meter-mounted transfer switch must be listed and capable of transferring the load served. A meter-mounted transfer switch must be marked on its exterior in the following manner: ▶Figure 230–66

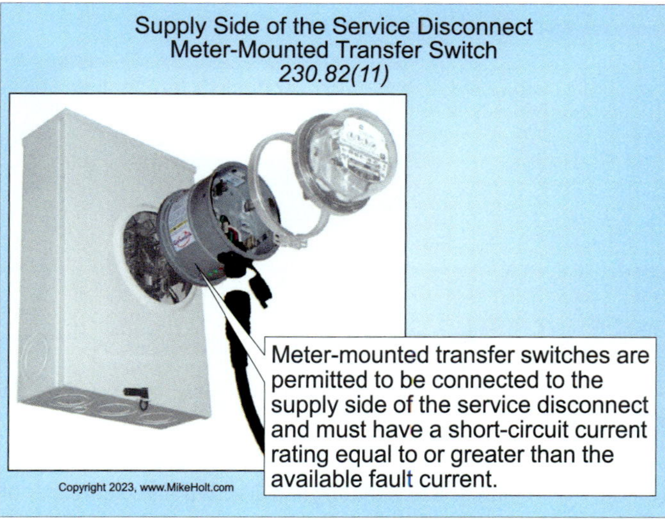

▶Figure 230–66

(a) Meter-mounted transfer switch

(b) Not service equipment

For one- and two-family dwelling units, an emergency disconnect must be installed for first responders and others in accordance with 230.85(A) through (E).

(A) General.

(1) Location. The required emergency disconnect must be installed at a readily accessible outdoor location within sight of the dwelling unit. ▶Figure 230–67

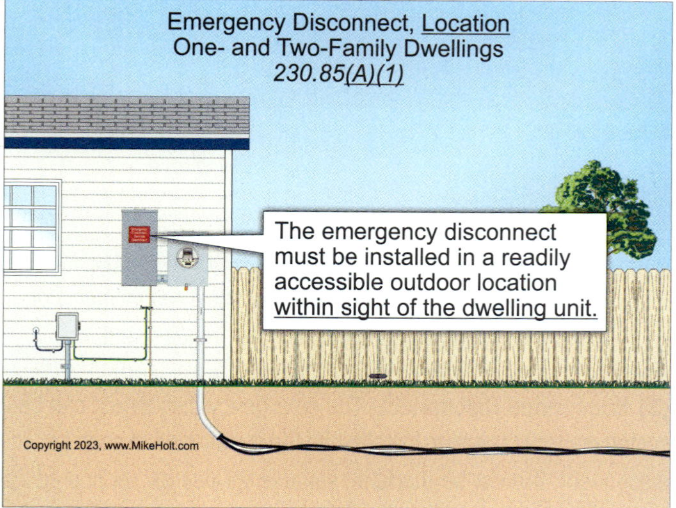

▶Figure 230–67

According to Article 100, "Within Sight" means that it is visible and not more than 50 ft from the location of the equipment.

Ex: Where the requirements of 225.41 are met, this section does not apply.

(2) Rating. The emergency disconnect must have a short-circuit current rating equal to or greater than the available fault current.

(3) Grouping. If more than one emergency disconnect is provided, they must be grouped.

(B) Type of Emergency Disconnect. Each emergency disconnect must be one of the following types:

(1) Service Disconnect. The emergency disconnect can be the service disconnect required by 230.70. ▶Figure 230–68

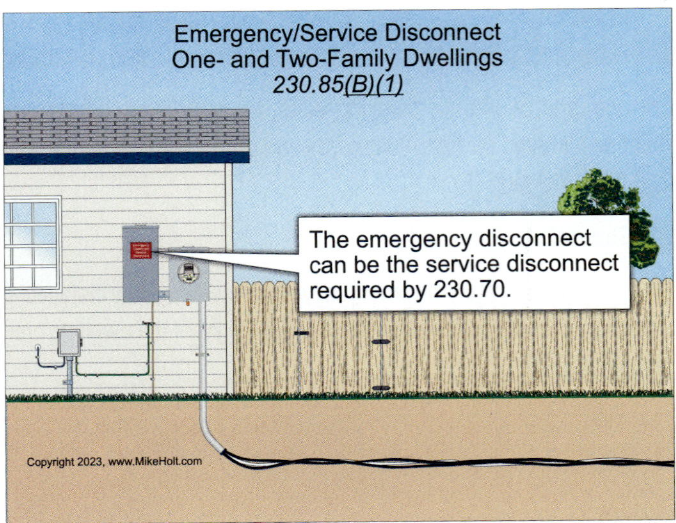

▶Figure 230–68

Author's Comment:

▸ An automatic transfer switch that is rated for service equipment can be used to meet the service disconnect requirements of 230.70 and the emergency disconnect requirement.

(3) Nonservice Disconnect. The emergency disconnect can be a switch or circuit breaker, installed on the supply side of each service disconnect. It must be marked "suitable for use as service equipment," but not marked as "suitable only for use as service equipment."

Author's Comment:

▸ A transfer switch is not listed as a "switch" or a "circuit breaker." Therefore, it is not permitted to be used as an emergency disconnect ahead of service equipment.

Note 1: Conductors between the emergency disconnect and the service disconnect in 230.85(2) and 230.85(3) are service conductors.

Note 2: Equipment marked "Suitable only for use as service equipment" has a factory marking of "Service Disconnect."

Author's Comment:

▸ The emergency disconnect in 230.85(3) cannot be marked "Suitable only for use as service equipment" because it would require the equipment to be modified after leaving the factory by removing the marking "Service Disconnect" and removing the factory installed main bonding jumper.

(C) Replacement. Where a service disconnect is replaced, all the requirements of this section apply.

Ex: Where only meter sockets, service-entrance conductors, or related raceways and fittings are replaced, an emergency disconnect is not required.

(D) Identification of Other Isolation Disconnects. Where disconnects for other energy source systems are not adjacent to the emergency disconnect, a plaque or directory identifying the location of all other energy source disconnects must be adjacent to the emergency disconnect.

Note: For examples of other energy source system disconnecting means, see 445.19, 480.7, 705.20, and 706.15.

(E) Marking.

(1) Marking Text. The disconnect must be marked as follows:

(1) Service conductors terminating in an outdoor service disconnect must be marked: "EMERGENCY DISCONNECT, SERVICE DISCONNECT." ▶Figure 230–69

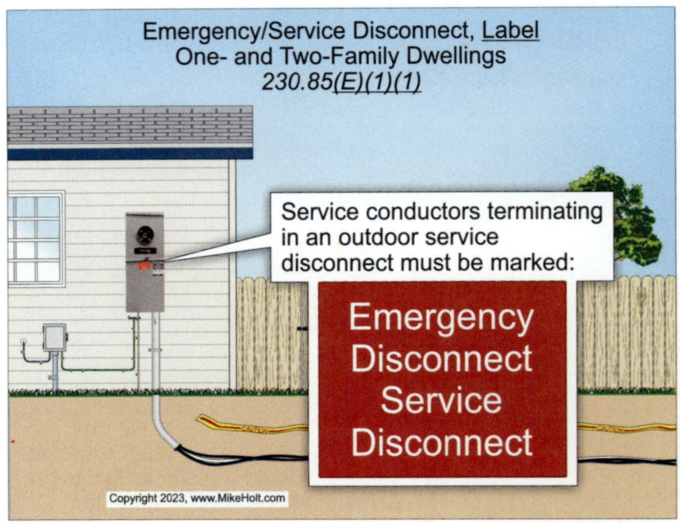

▶Figure 230–69

(3) Service conductors terminating in a switch or circuit breaker on the load side of the meter and supply side of the service disconnect must be marked: "EMERGENCY DISCONNECT, NOT SERVICE EQUIPMENT."

Author's Comment:

▶ When replacing a service, list item (3) permits replacing the interior service equipment and install an "EMERGENCY DISCONNECT, NOT SERVICE EQUIPMENT" on the outside of the building without having to change the location of the existing service bonding and grounding requirements contained in 250.24.

(2) Marking Location and Size. Markings must be permanently affixed and sufficiently durable to withstand the environment involved in accordance with 110.21(B) and comply with following:

(1) The marking or labels must be on the outside front of the disconnect with a red background and white text.

(2) The letters must be at least ½ in. high.

Part VII. Service Conductor Overcurrent Protection

230.90 Overload Protection—Where Required

Each service phase conductor must have overload protection. ▶Figure 230–70

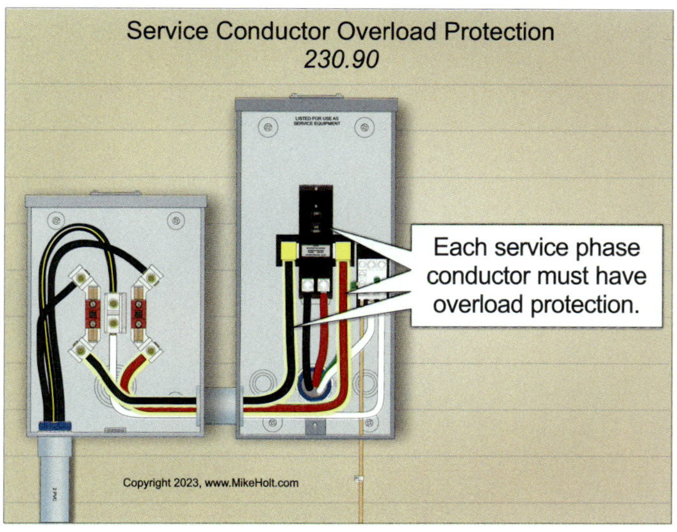

▶Figure 230–70

Author's Comment:

▶ The service overcurrent protective device provides overload protection for the line side of service conductors, but not short-circuit and ground-fault protection because that protection can only be provided at the supply end of a circuit.

(A) Overcurrent Protective Device Rating. The rating of the overcurrent protective device must not be greater than the ampacity of the service phase conductors. ▶Figure 230–71

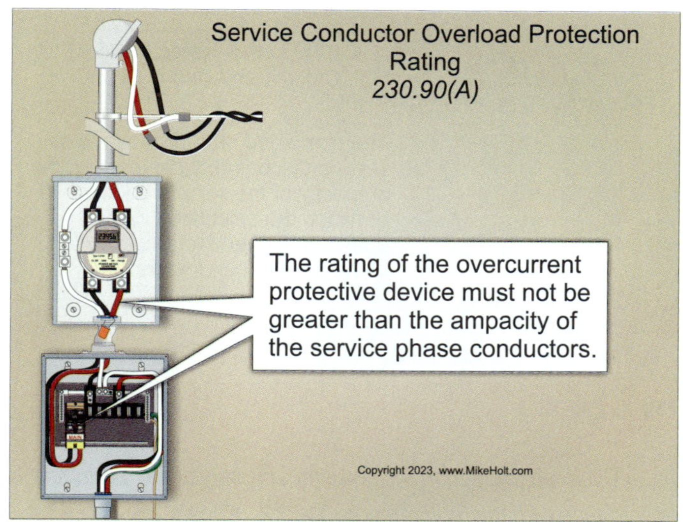

▶Figure 230–71

Ex 2: If the ampacity of the phase conductors does not correspond with the standard rating of overcurrent protective devices as listed in 240.6(A), the next higher overcurrent protective device can be used if it does not exceed 800A [240.4(B)]. ▶Figure 230–72

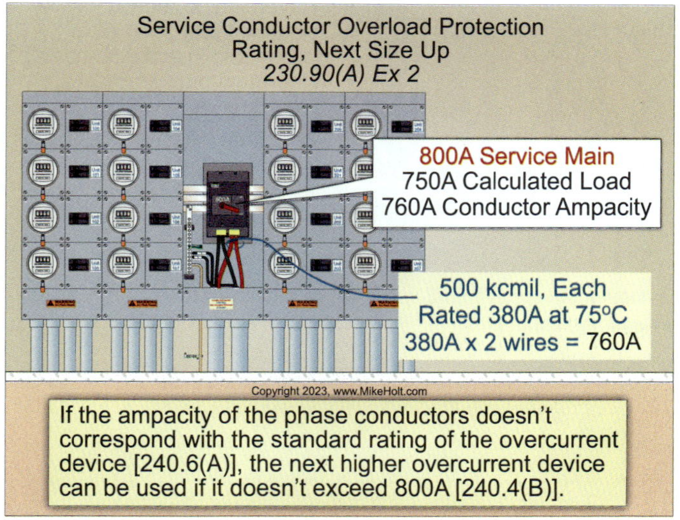

▶Figure 230–72

Ex 3: The combined ratings of two to six service disconnects can exceed the ampacity of the service conductors provided the calculated load does not exceed the ampacity of the service conductors in accordance with Article 220. ▶Figure 230–73

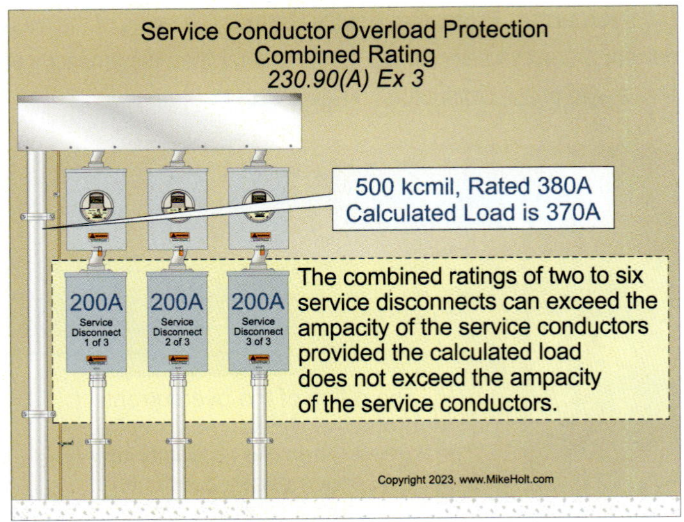

▶Figure 230–73

Ex 5: Overload protection for dwelling unit services is permitted in accordance with the requirements 310.12. ▶Figure 230–74

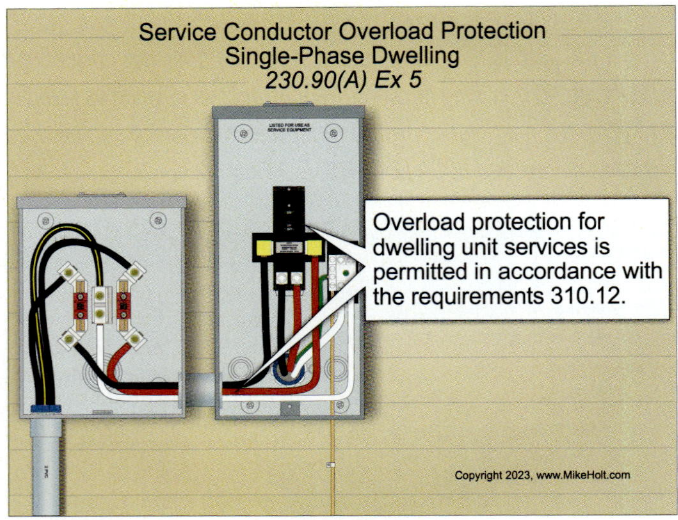

▶Figure 230–74

▸ The service disconnect fuse or circuit breaker only supplies overload protection for the line-side service conductors, but not short-circuit and ground-fault protection.

(B) Service Grounded Conductor. The service grounded conductor can terminate on a circuit breaker that simultaneously opens all conductors of the circuit.

230.91 Location

The service overcurrent protective device must be an integral part of the service disconnect or be immediately adjacent to the service disconnect. Where fuses are used as the service overcurrent protective device, the disconnect must be ahead of the supply side of the fuses.

230.95 Ground-Fault Protection of Equipment

Each service disconnect rated 1000A or more supplied by a 4-wire, three-phase, 277/480V wye-connected system must be provided with ground-fault protection of equipment. The rating of the service disconnect is based on the rating of the largest fuse that can be installed or the circuit breaker's highest continuous current trip setting.

OVERCURRENT PROTECTION

Introduction to Article 240—Overcurrent Protection

Article 240 covers the general requirements for overcurrent protection and the installation requirements of overcurrent protective devices—typically circuit breakers or fuses. Overcurrent protection is installed to protect the circuit if the current reaches a value that will cause damage to conductors, conductor insulation, or equipment. Some topics covered in our material for Article 240 include:

- Protection of Conductors and Cords
- Standard Ampere Ratings
- Supplementary Overcurrent Protection
- Location in the Circuit
- Location in the Premises
- Enclosure Requirements
- Fuse Requirements
- Breaker Requirements

This article consists of eight parts:

- Part I. General
- Part II. Location
- Part III. Enclosures
- Part IV. Disconnecting and Guarding
- Part V. Plug Fuses
- Part VI. Cartridge Fuses
- Part VII. Circuit Breakers
- Part VIII. Supervised Industrial Installations

According to Article 100, "Overcurrent" is the current that is in excess of the conductor's ampacity caused by an overload, short circuit, or ground fault. ▶Figure 240–1

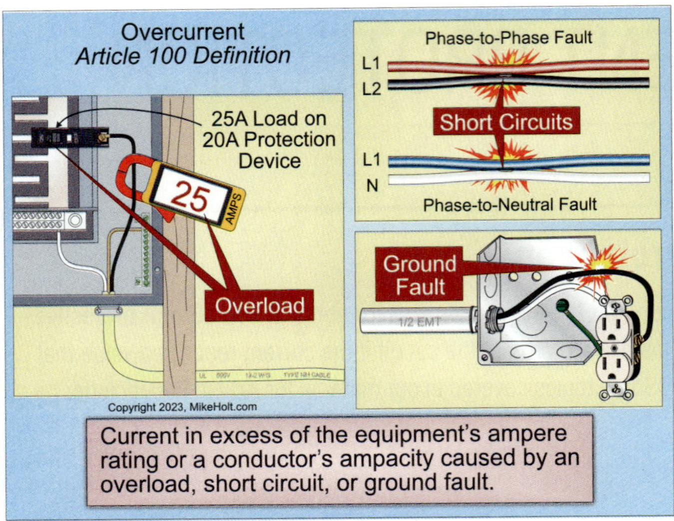

▶Figure 240–1

According to Article 100, "Overcurrent Protective Device" is a device capable of providing protection from an overload, short circuit, or ground fault for service, feeder, and branch circuits.

"Ground Fault" is an unintentional electrical connection between a phase conductor and equipment grounding conductors, metal parts of enclosures, metal raceways, or metal equipment. ▶Figure 240–2

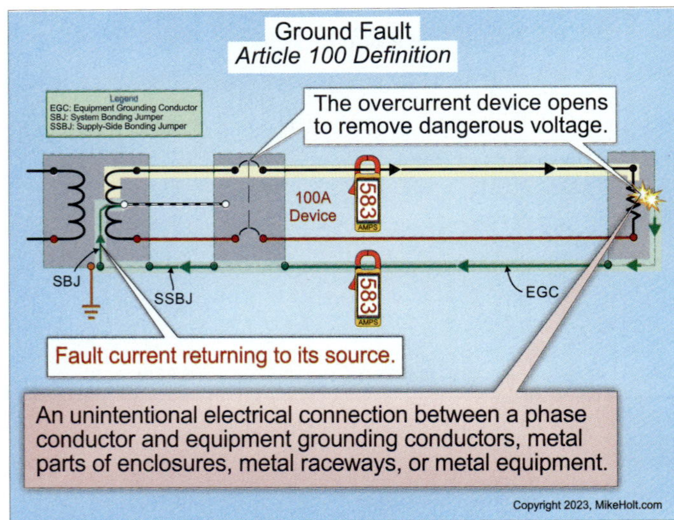

▶Figure 240–2

According to Article 100, "Overload" occurs when equipment operates above its current rating or current in excess of a conductor's ampacity. A short circuit or ground fault is not an overload. ▶Figure 240–3

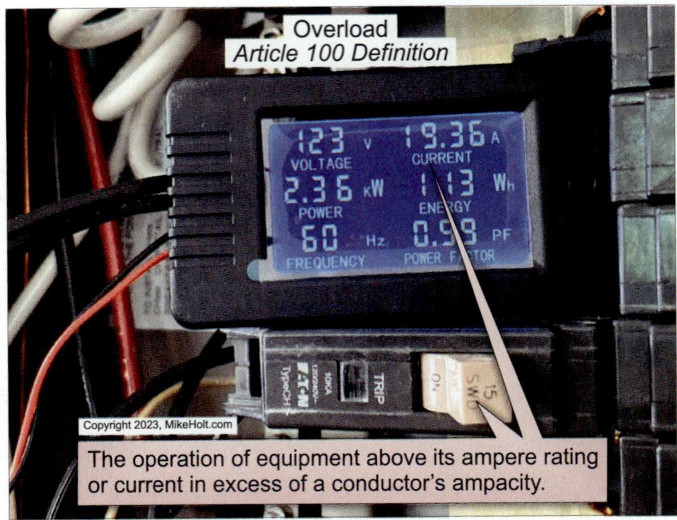

▶Figure 240–3

According to Article 100, "Short Circuit" is an abnormal connection of relatively low impedance, whether made accidentally or intentionally, between two or more points of different potential. ▶Figure 240–4

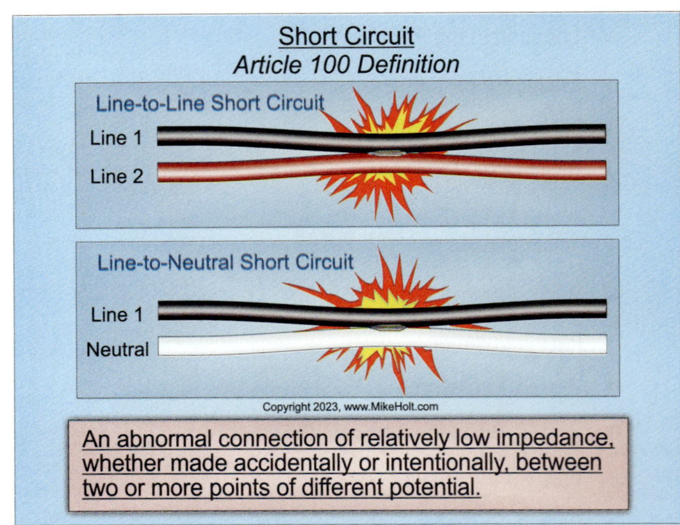

▶Figure 240–4

Part I. General

240.1 Scope

Article 240 covers the general requirements for overcurrent protection of conductors and the installation requirements of overcurrent protective devices. ▶Figure 240–5

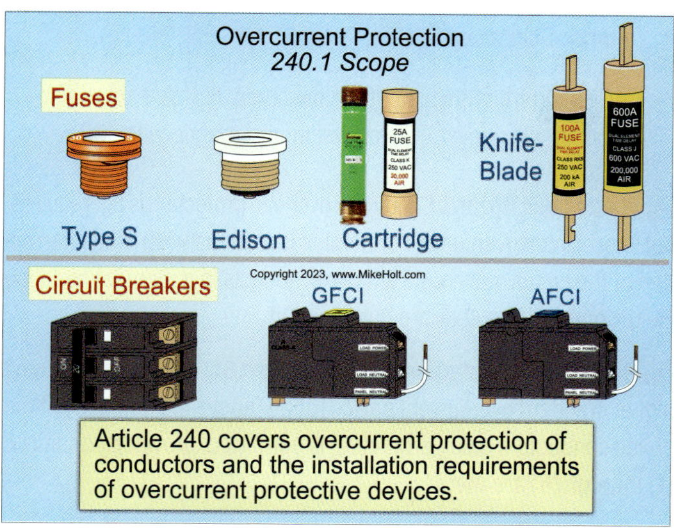

▶Figure 240–5

Note 1: An overcurrent protective device protects the circuit by opening the device when the current reaches a value that will cause excessive or dangerous temperature rise (overheating) in conductors.

Note 2: Overcurrent protective devices must have an interrupting rating sufficient for the maximum possible fault current available on the line-side terminals of the equipment [110.9]. Electrical equipment must have a short-circuit current rating that permits the circuit's overcurrent protective device to clear short circuits or ground faults without extensive damage to the circuit's electrical components [110.10].

Author's Comment:

▶ Perhaps one of the most critical points to understand is that a fault or other overcurrent condition will eventually occur even in the best electrical system. Our job is to ensure the overcurrent protection equipment can handle the conditions safely with little or no damage. Proper overcurrent protection is a critical step in this process.

240.3 Other Articles (Overcurrent Protection of Equipment)

The following equipment and their conductors must be protected against overcurrent in accordance with the article for that type of equipment:

Table 240.3—Other Articles

Equipment	Article	Section
Air-Conditioning Equipment	440	440.22
Appliances	422	All
Audio Circuits	640	640.9
Branch Circuits	210	210.20
Class 1 Power-Limited Circuits	724	724.43
Class 2 Power-Limited Circuits	725	All
Feeder Conductors	215	215.3
Flexible Cords	240	240.5(B)(1)
Fire Alarms	760	All
Fire Pumps	695	All
Fixed Electric Space-Heating Equipment	424	424.3(B)
Fixture Wire	240	240.5(B)(2)
Panelboards	408	408.36
Service Conductors	230	230.90(A)
Transformers	450	450.3

240.4 Overcurrent Protection of Conductors

Overcurrent protection for conductors is required in accordance with their ampacities as specified in 310.14, except as permitted by (A) through (H). ▶Figure 240–6 and ▶Figure 240–7

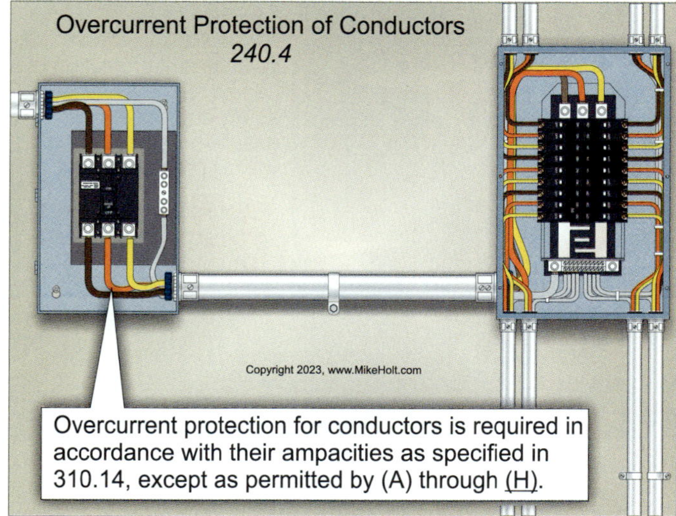

▶Figure 240–6

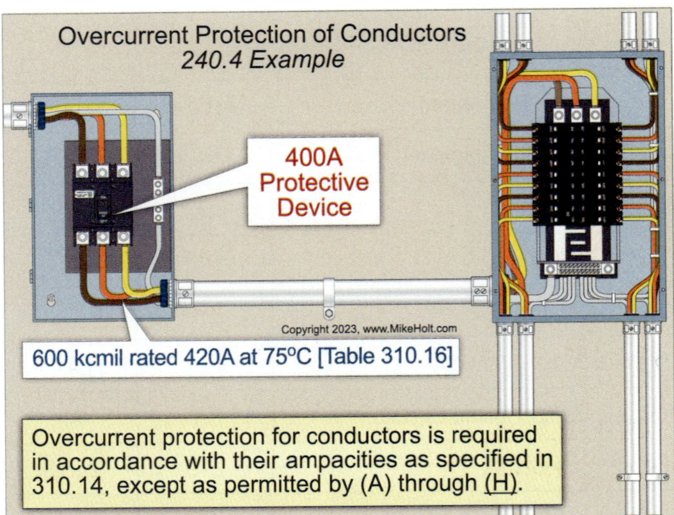

▶Figure 240–7

Author's Comment:

▸ Table 310.16 contains conductor ampacities based on up to three current-carrying conductors in a raceway with ambient temperatures of 86°F or 30°C at up to 2000V. If any other conditions apply (such as more than three current-carrying conductors, or a different ambient temperature), the ampacities found in Table 310.16 must be corrected in accordance with 310.15(B) and adjusted in accordance with 310.15(C).

▸ Overcurrent protection of conductors is a critical safety component to ensure an electric circuit will fail properly. Bypassing overcurrent protection is extremely dangerous to persons and property. ▶Figure 240–8

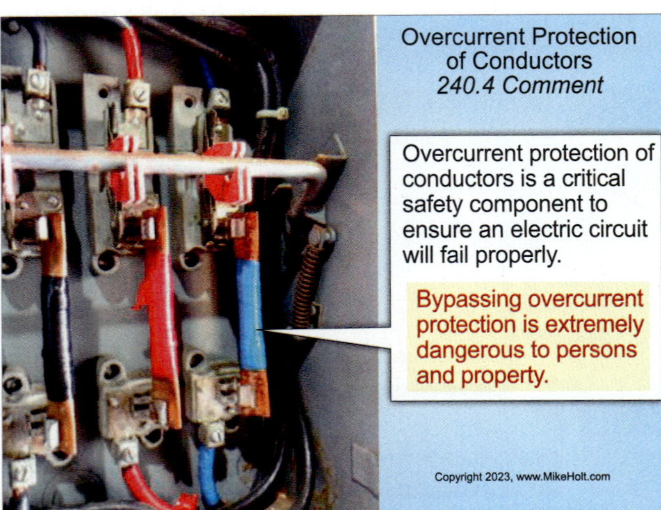

▶Figure 240–8

Author's Comment:

▸ Overcurrent protection of flexible cords, flexible cables, and fixture wires must be provided in accordance with 240.5.

(A) Power Loss Hazard. Conductor overload protection is not required, but short-circuit overcurrent protection is required where the interruption of the circuit will create a hazard, such as in a material-handling electromagnet circuit or fire pump circuit.

(B) Overcurrent Protective Devices Rated 800A or Less. The next higher standard overcurrent device rating (above the ampacity of the phase conductors being protected) is permitted, provided conditions (1) through (3) are met:

(1) The conductors are not part of a branch circuit supplying more than one receptacle for cord-and-plug-connected loads.

(2) The ampacity of a conductor after the application of ambient temperature correction [Table 310.15(B)(1)(1)], conductor bundling adjustment [Table 310.15(C)(1)], or both, does not correspond with the standard rating of a fuse or circuit breaker identified in 240.6(A).

(3) The next higher standard overcurrent protective device rating from 240.6(A) does not exceed 800A.

In accordance with 240.4(B)(1), if the overcurrent protective device is an adjustable trip device, it is permitted to be set to a value that does not exceed the next higher standard value above the ampacity of the conductors being protected when in compliance with 240.6(C).

▶ Example 1

Question: According to Table 310.16, what is the maximum size overcurrent protective device that can be used to protect 500 kcmil conductors where each conductor has an ampacity of 380A at 75°C?
▶Figure 240–9

(a) 300A   (b) 350A   (c) 400A   (d) 500A

Answer: (c) 400A [240.6(A)]

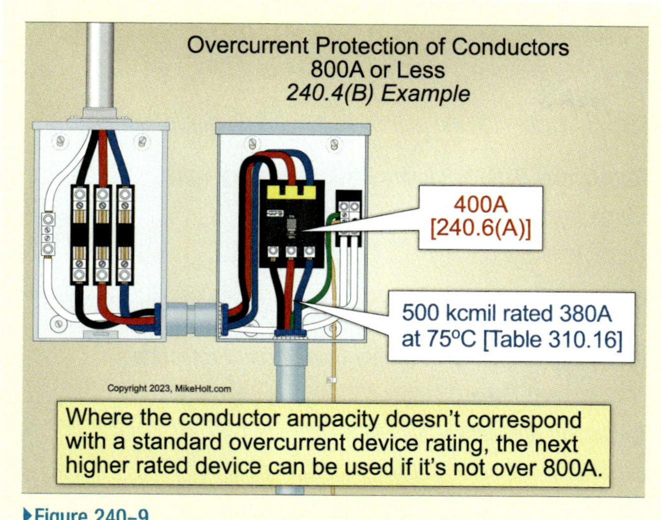

▶Figure 240–9

(C) Overcurrent Protective Devices Rated Over 800A. If the circuit's overcurrent protective device exceeds 800A, the conductor ampacity, after the application of ambient temperature correction [310.15(B)(1)(1)], conductor spacing adjustment [Table 310.15(C)(1)], or both, must have an ampere rating or setting of not less than the rating of the overcurrent protective device defined in 240.6.

▶ **Example 2**

Question: What is the minimum size of conductors, paralleled in three conductors per phase, allowed to be protected by a 1,200A overcurrent protective device? ▶**Figure 240–10**

(a) 400 kcmil   (b) 500 kcmil   (c) 600 kcmil   (d) 750 kcmil

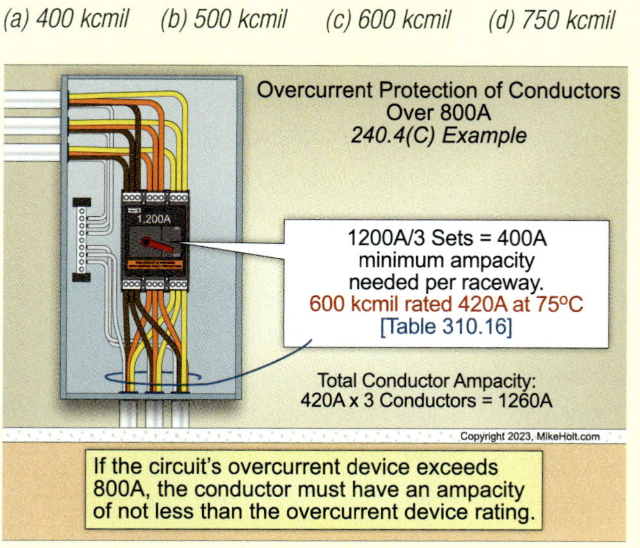

▶Figure 240–10

Solution:

The total ampacity of the three parallel conductor sets must be equal to or greater than 1,200A [240.4(C)]. The ampacity for each conductor within the parallel set must be equal to or greater than 400A (1,200A/3 raceways).

Conductor Size = 600 kcmil conductors per phase rated 420A at 75°C [110.14(C)(1)(b)(2) and Table 310.16]

Total Conductor Ampacity = 420A × 3 conductors
Total Conductor Ampacity = 1,260A, okay for a 1,200A overcurrent protective device

Answer: *(c) 600 kcmil*

(D) Small Conductors. Overcurrent protection for conductors is not permitted to exceed the following values, except as permitted in 240.4(E) or (G): ▶Figure 240–11

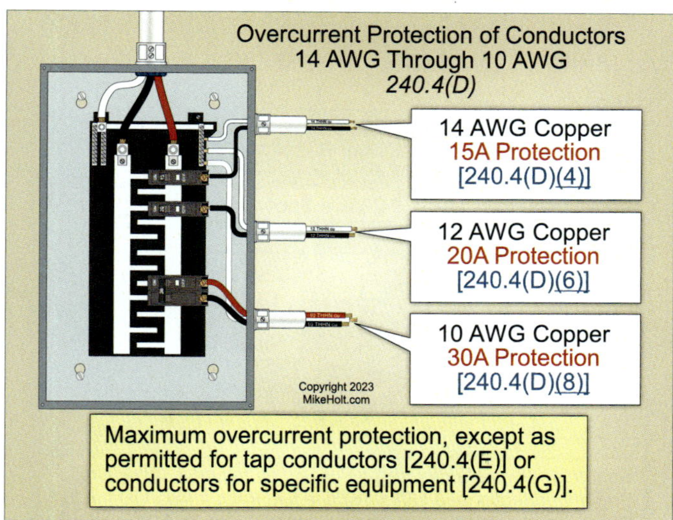

▶Figure 240–11

(1) 18 AWG copper—7A

(2) 16 AWG copper—10A

(4) 14 AWG copper—15A

(5) 12 AWG aluminum and copper-clad aluminum—15A

(6) 12 AWG copper—20A

(7) 10 AWG aluminum and copper-clad aluminum—25A

(8) 10 AWG copper—30A

(E) Tap Conductors. Tap conductors must have overcurrent protection in accordance with the following:

(1) Household ranges, cooking appliances, and other loads [210.19(D)]

(2) Fixture wire [240.5(B)(2)]

(3) Location in circuit [240.21]

(F) Transformer Secondary Conductors. For a 2-wire, single-voltage system and delta/delta, 3-wire systems, the primary overcurrent protective device sized in accordance with 450.3(B) is considered suitable to protect the secondary conductors, provided it does not exceed the value determined by multiplying the secondary conductor ampacity by the secondary-to-primary transformer voltage ratio.

▶ **Example 3**

Question: What is the minimum size secondary conductor required for a single-phase, 1.50 kVA, 480V to 120V transformer that is protected with a 5A fuse on the primary? ▶**Figure 240–12**

(a) 18 AWG   (b) 16 AWG   (c) 14 AWG   (d) 12 AWG

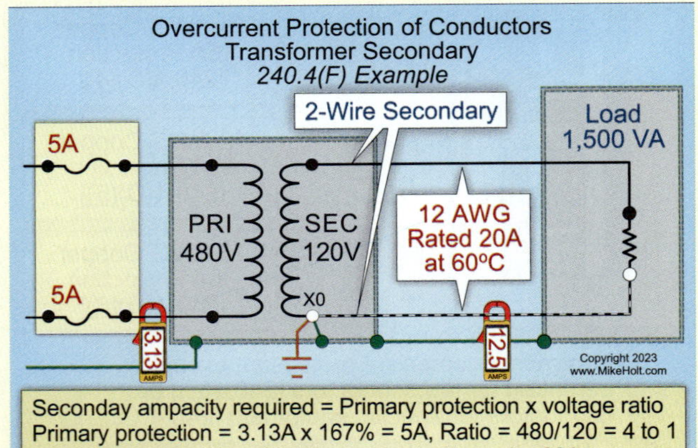

▶Figure 240–12

Solution:

Step 1: *Determine the primary current.*

VA/E

VA = 1,500 VA

E = 480V

Primary Current = 1,500 VA/480V

Primary Current = 3.13A

Step 2: *Determine the primary overcurrent protective device rating [450.3(B)].*

Primary Overcurrent Protection = 3.13A × 167%

Primary Overcurrent Protection = 5.23A or a 5A Fuse

Step 3: *Determine the primary-to-secondary transformer ratio.*

Transformer Ratio = Primary Volts/Secondary Volts

Transformer Ratio = 480V/120V

Transformer Ratio = 4 to 1

Step 4: *Determine the secondary conductor minimum ampacity.*

Secondary Ampacity = Primary Overcurrent Protection × Transformer Ratio

Secondary Ampacity = 5A × 4

Secondary Ampacity = 20A

Use 12 AWG conductor rated 20A at 60°C [110.14(C)(1)(a)(2) and Table 310.16].

Answer: *(d) 12 AWG*

(G) Overcurrent Protection for Specific Applications. Overcurrent protection for conductors for specific equipment must comply with the requirements referenced in Table 240.4(G).

Author's Comment:

▸ Table 240.4(G) indicates that overcurrent protection for conductors for specific applications like air-conditioning, the requirements of Article 440 may be applied. For motors, the overcurrent protection requirements of Article 430 may be applied.

▸ In accordance with "*UL Guide Information LZFE,*" heating and cooling equipment terminations are based on the 75°C conductor ampacities in accordance with Table 310.16.

▶ **Air Conditioner Example**

Question: What size branch-circuit conductor and overcurrent protective device are required for an air conditioner when the nameplate indicates the minimum circuit ampacity is 24A, and the maximum overcurrent protection is 40A? Terminals are rated 75°C. ▶**Figure 240–13**

(a) 12 AWG, 20A OCPD   (b) 12 AWG, 30A OCPD
(c) 12 AWG, 40A OCPD   (d) 12 AWG, 50A OCPD

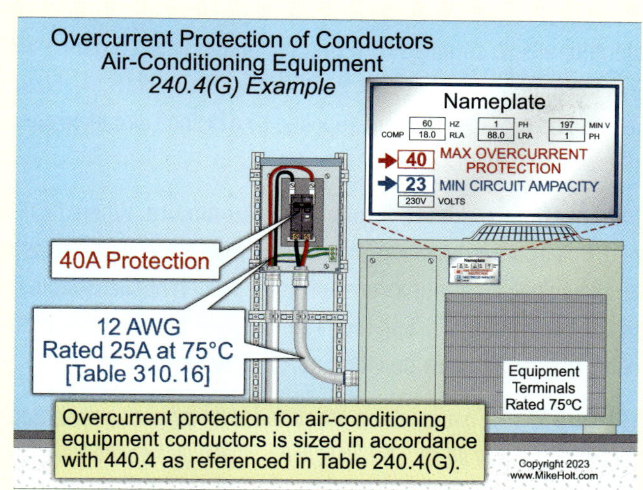

▶Figure 240–13

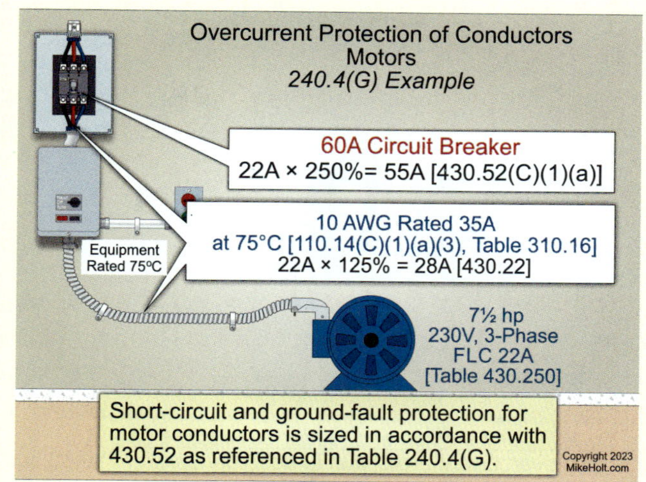

▶Figure 240–14

Solution:

The nameplate values for listed air-conditioning equipment are used to size the branch-circuit conductors and short-circuit overcurrent protective device [440.4(B)]. No calculation is required.

Conductor: A 12 AWG conductor is suitable because it has an ampacity of 25A at 75°C [110.14(C)(1)(a)(3) and Table 310.16].

Protection: The air conditioner branch-circuit short-circuit protection is sized to the nameplate maximum overcurrent protection of 40A.

A 40A circuit breaker is permitted to protect a 12 AWG conductor rated 25A at 75°C in accordance with 110.14(C)(1)(a)(3), 240.4(G), and 440.4(B).

Answer: (c) 12 AWG, 40A OCPD

▶ Motor Example

Question: What size branch-circuit conductor and overcurrent protective device (circuit breaker) are required for a 7½ hp, 230V, three-phase motor? Terminals are rated 75°C. ▶Figure 240–14

(a) 10 AWG, 20A OCPD   *(b) 10 AWG, 30A OCPD*
(c) 10 AWG, 40A OCPD   *(d) 10 AWG, 60A OCPD*

Solution:

Step 1: Determine the branch-circuit conductor size at 125 percent of the motor's FLC [430.22, and Table 430.250].

FLC = 22A [Table 430.250]

Conductor = 22A × 125%
Conductor = 28A [430.22]
Conductor = 10 AWG which is rated 35A at 75°C [110.14(C)(1)(a)(3) and Table 310.16]

Step 2: Determine the branch-circuit overcurrent protection size at 250 percent of the motor's FLC [Table 430.52(C)(1), 430.52(C)(1)(a), and Table 430.250].

Inverse Time Circuit Breaker = 22A × 250%
Inverse Time Circuit Breaker = 55A

A 60A inverse time circuit breaker is permitted to protect the 10 AWG conductor in accordance with 240.4(G), Table 430.52(C)(1), and 430.52(C)(1)(a).

Answer: (d) 10 AWG, 60A OCPD

(H) Dwelling Unit Service and Feeder Conductors. Dwelling unit service and feeder conductors can have overcurrent protection in accordance with 310.12. ▶Figure 240–15 and ▶Figure 240–16

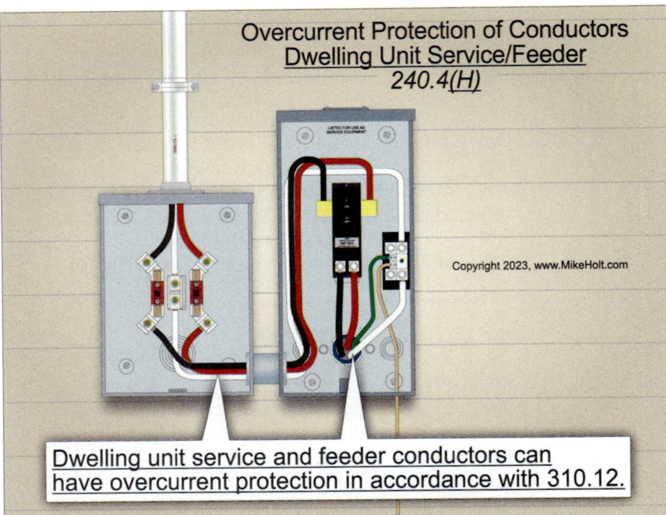

▶Figure 240–15

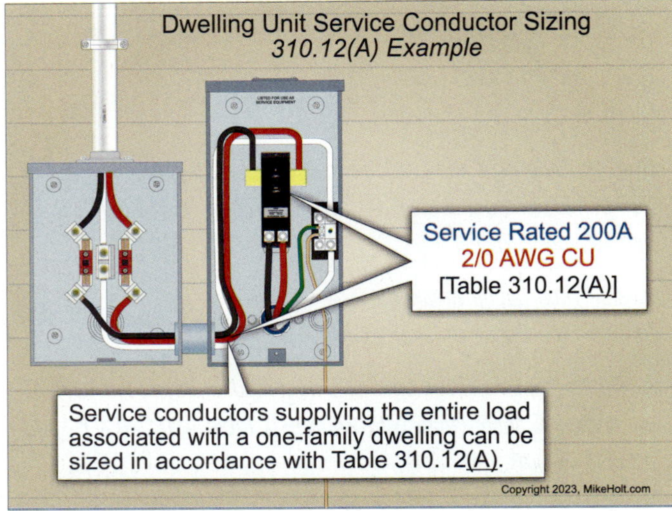

▶Figure 240–16

240.5 Overcurrent Protection of Flexible Cords, Flexible Cables, and Fixture Wires

Flexible cord (including tinsel cord and extension cords) and fixture wires must be protected against overcurrent by either 240.5(A) or (B).

(A) Ampacities. Flexible cord must be protected by an overcurrent protective device in accordance with its ampacity as specified in Table 400.5(A)(1) and Table 400.5(A)(2). Fixture wire must be protected against overcurrent in accordance with its ampacity as specified in Table 402.5. Supplementary overcurrent protection, as covered in 240.10, is an acceptable means for providing this protection.

(B) Branch-Circuit Overcurrent Device. Flexible cord must be protected, where supplied by a branch circuit, in accordance with one of the methods described in 240.5(B)(1), (B)(3), or (B)(4). Fixture wire must be protected, where supplied by a branch circuit, in accordance with 240.5(B)(2).

(1) Supply Cord of Listed Appliance or Luminaire. Where flexible cord or tinsel cord is approved for, and used with, a specific listed appliance or luminaire, it is considered protected when applied within the appliance or luminaire listing requirements. For the purposes of this section, a luminaire may be either portable or permanent.

(2) Fixture Wire. Fixture wire is permitted to be tapped to the branch-circuit conductor of a branch circuit in accordance with the following:

(1) 15A or 20A circuits—18 AWG, up to 50 ft of run length

(2) 15A or 20A circuits—16 AWG, up to 100 ft of run length

(3) 20A circuits—14 AWG and larger

(4) 30A circuits—14 AWG and larger

(5) 40A circuits—12 AWG and larger

(6) 50A circuits—12 AWG and larger

(3) Extension Cord Sets. Flexible cord used in listed extension cord sets is considered protected when applied within the extension cord listing requirements.

240.6 Standard Ampere Ratings

(A) Fuses and Fixed-Trip Circuit Breakers. The standard ampere ratings for fuses and inverse time circuit breakers are shown in Table 240.6(A). Additional standard ampere ratings for fuses are 1A, 3A, 6A, and 601A. ▶Figure 240–17

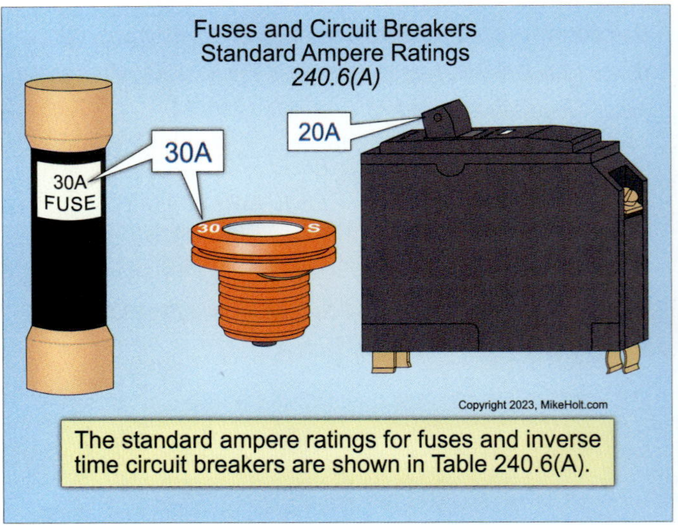

▶Figure 240–17

Table 240.6(A) Standard Ampere Ratings for Fuses and Inverse Time Circuit Breakers Standard Ampere Ratings

10	15	20	25	30
35	40	45	50	60
70	80	90	100	110
125	150	175	200	225
250	300	350	400	450
500	600	700	800	1000
1200	1600	2000	2500	3000

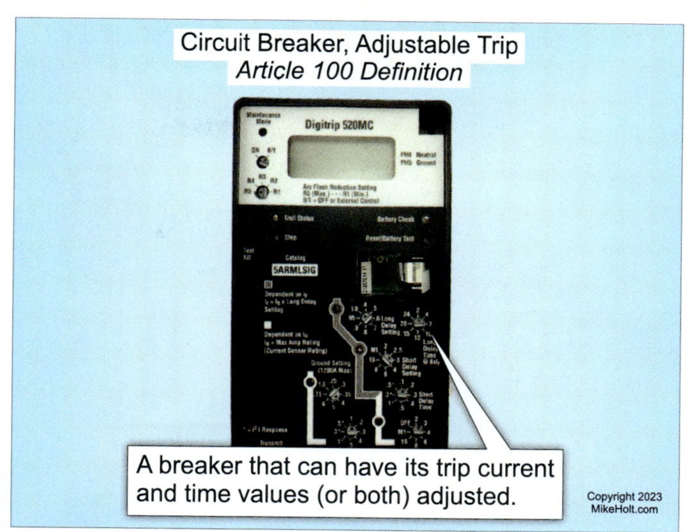

▶Figure 240–18

(B) Adjustable Trip Circuit Breakers, Without Restricted Access. The ampere rating of an adjustable trip circuit breaker without restricted access is equal to its maximum long-time pickup current setting.

(C) Adjustable Trip Circuit Breakers, Local Restricted Access. The ampere rating of adjustable trip circuit breakers with restricted access to the adjusting means is equal to the adjusted long-time pickup current settings. Restricted access is achieved by one of the following methods:

(1) Locating behind removable and sealable covers over the adjusting means

(2) Locating behind bolted equipment enclosure doors

(3) Locating behind locked doors accessible only to qualified personnel

(4) Being password protected with the password only accessible to qualified personnel

According to Article 100, "Adjustable Trip Circuit Breaker" permits the circuit breaker to be set to trip at various values of current, time (or both), within a predetermined range. ▶Figure 240–18

(D) Adjustable-Trip Circuit Breakers, Remotely Accessible. A circuit breaker(s) that can be adjusted remotely to modify the adjusting means is permitted to have an ampere rating(s) that is equal to the adjusted current setting (long-time pickup setting).

Remote access must be achieved by one of the following methods:

(1) Connected directly through a local nonnetworked interface.

(2) Connected through a networked interface complying with one of the following methods:

    a. The circuit breaker and associated software for adjusting the settings are identified as being evaluated for cybersecurity.

    b. A cybersecurity assessment of the network is completed. Documentation of the assessment and certification must be made available to those authorized to inspect, operate, and maintain the system.

Note 3: Cybersecurity is a specialized field requiring constant, vigilant attention to security vulnerabilities that could arise due to software defects, system configuration changes, or user interactions. Installation of devices that can be secured is an important first step but not sufficient to guarantee a secure system.

240.10 Supplementary Conductor Overcurrent Protection

Supplementary overcurrent protective devices are not permitted to be used as the required branch-circuit overcurrent protective device. ▶Figure 240–19

A supplementary overcurrent protective device is not required to be readily accessible.

According to Article 100, "Supplementary Overcurrent Protective Device" is a device intended to provide limited overcurrent protection for specific applications and utilization equipment. This limited overcurrent protection is in addition to the overcurrent protection provided in the required branch circuit by the branch-circuit overcurrent protective device.

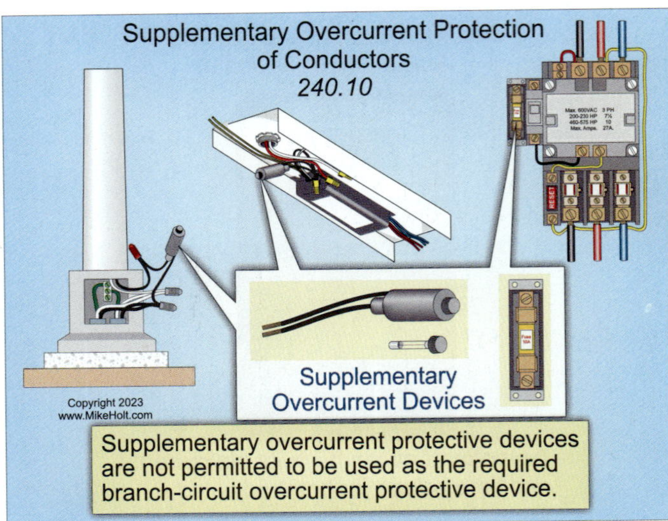

▶Figure 240–19

240.13 Ground-Fault Protection of Equipment

(A) General. Ground-fault protection of equipment must be provided for service disconnects [230.95] and feeder disconnects [215.10] rated 1000A or more supplied from a 4-wire, three-phase, 277/480V wye-connected system in accordance with 230.95.

According to Article 100, "Ground-Fault Protection of Equipment" is a system intended to provide overcurrent protection of equipment from ground faults by opening the overcurrent protective device at current levels less than those required to protect conductors from damage. This type of protective system is not intended to protect people, only connected equipment.

> **Author's Comment:**
>
> ▸ Ground-fault protection of equipment is not required for emergency power systems [700.31] or legally required standby power systems [701.31].
>
> ▸ Do not confuse ground-fault protection of equipment (GFPE) with ground-fault circuit interrupter (GFCI) protection for personnel.

240.15 Overcurrent Protective Device, Handle Ties

(B) Circuit Breaker. Circuit breakers protecting a circuit must automatically open all phase conductors of the circuit during an overcurrent condition, except as follows:

(1) Multiwire Branch Circuits. Individual single-pole breakers with handle ties identified for the purpose are permitted to protect each phase conductor of a multiwire branch circuit. ▶Figure 240–20

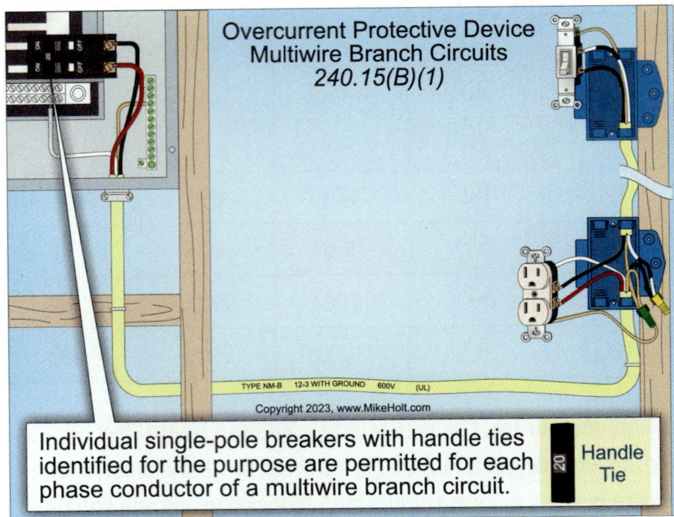

▶Figure 240–20

According to Article 100, "Identified" means recognized as suitable for a specific purpose, function, or environment by listing, labeling, or other means approved by the authority having jurisdiction. This means handle ties made from nails, screws, wires, or other nonconforming materials are not permitted to serve as a handle tie. ▶Figure 240–21

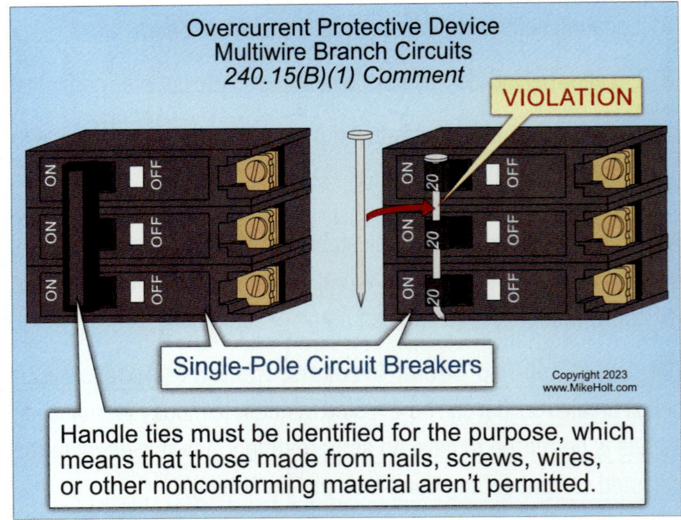

▶Figure 240–21

(2) Line-to-Line Loads, Single-Phase. Individual single-pole circuit breakers rated 120/240V with handle ties identified for the purpose are permitted to protect each phase conductor of a single-phase line-to-line load. ▶Figure 240–22

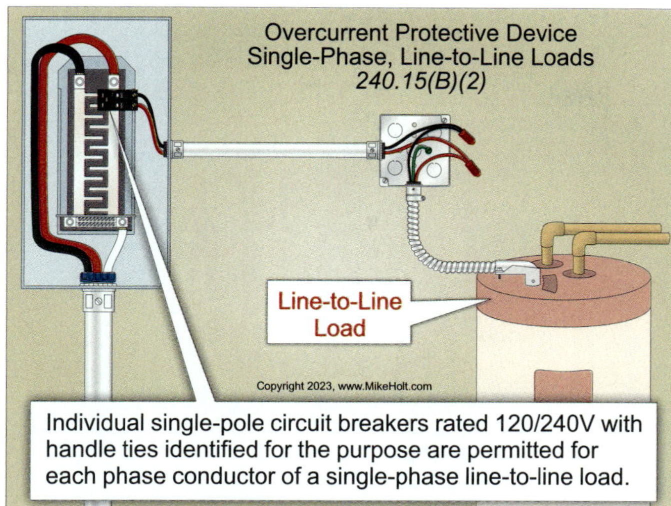

▶Figure 240–22

(3) Line-to-Line Loads, Three-Phase. Individual single-pole circuit breakers rated 120/240V with handle ties identified for the purpose are permitted for each phase conductor of a three-phase line-to-line load. ▶Figure 240–23

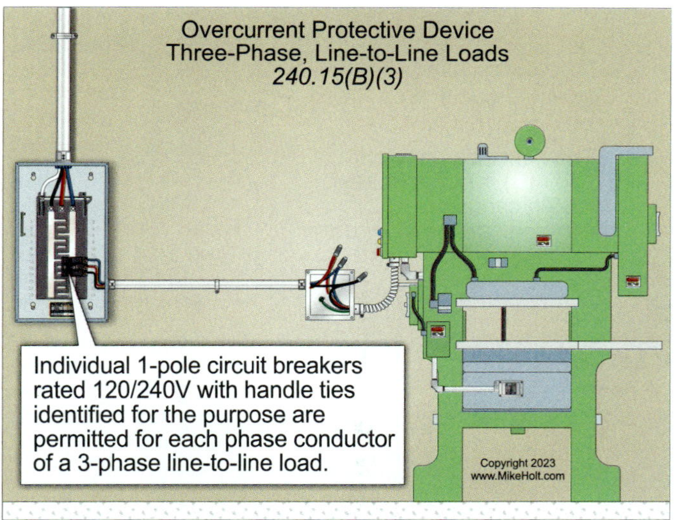

▶Figure 240–23

Author's Comment:

▶ A delta high-leg 120/240V system has the B phase conductor rated at 208V to ground, which could be used on a 2-pole line-to-line load if the circuit breaker has a straight 240V voltage rating [240.85]. In addition, see the provisions in 240.22 for connecting the neutral conductor in series with an overcurrent protective device if all circuit conductors open simultaneously.

Part II. Location of Overcurrent Protective Device

240.21 Location of Overcurrent Protective Device in Circuit

Overcurrent protection must be provided at the point where conductors receive their supply, except as permitted by (A) through (H). ▶Figure 240–24

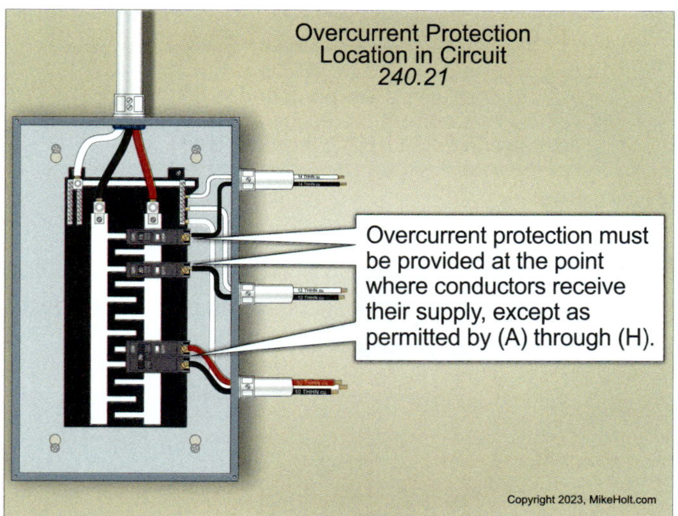

▶Figure 240–24

Conductors supplied in accordance with 240.21(A) through (H) are not permitted to supply another conductor. ▶Figure 240–25

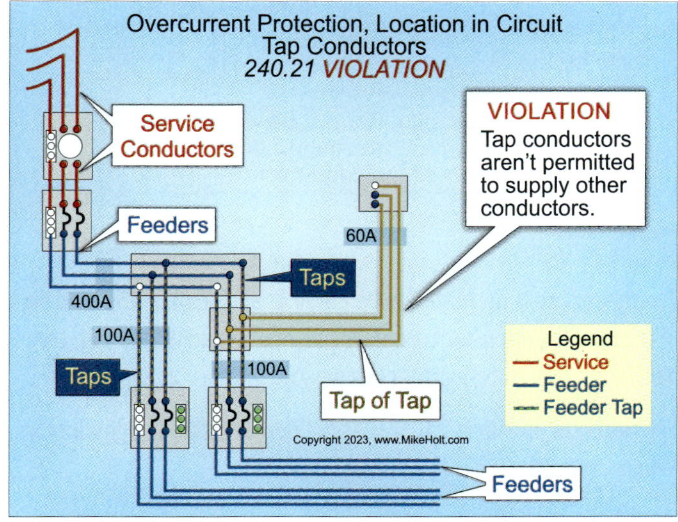

▶Figure 240–25

(B) Feeder Taps. Feeder conductors are permitted to be tapped, without overcurrent protection at the tap, as specified in 240.21(B)(1) through (B)(5). ▶Figure 240–26

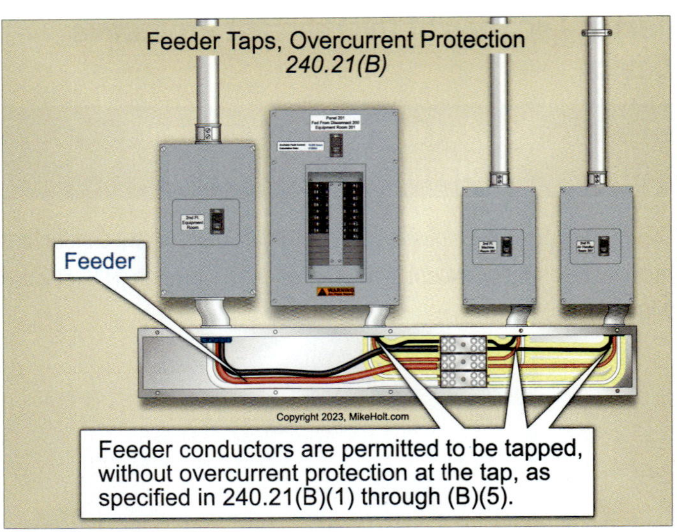

▶Figure 240–26

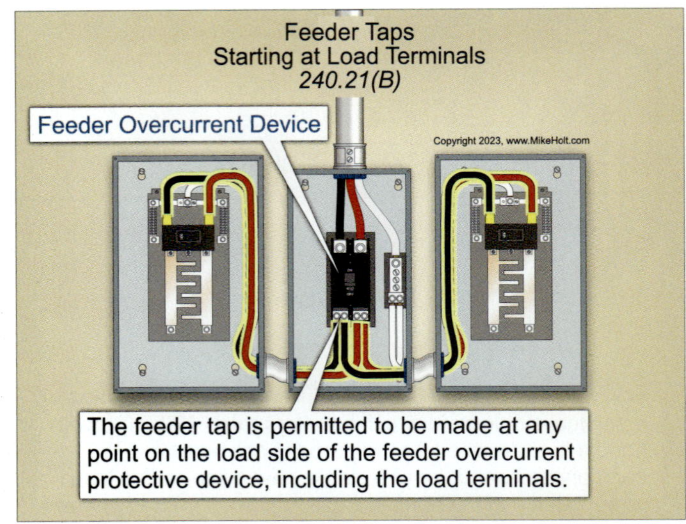

▶Figure 240–28

According to Article 100, "Tap Conductor" is a conductor, other than a service conductor, with overcurrent protection rated more than the ampacity of the conductor. ▶Figure 240–27

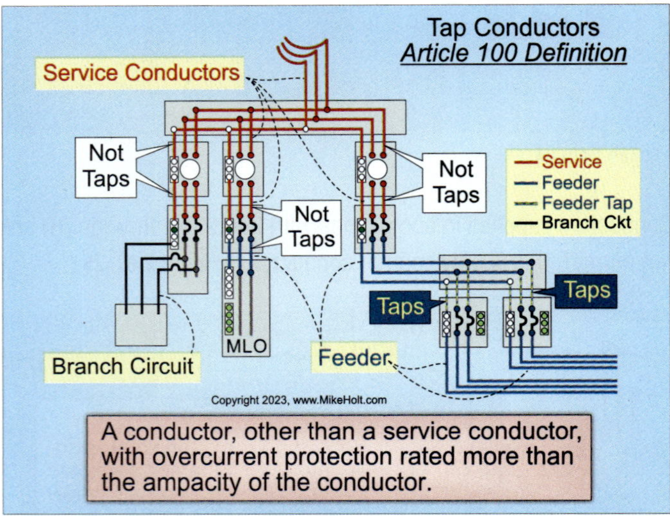

▶Figure 240–27

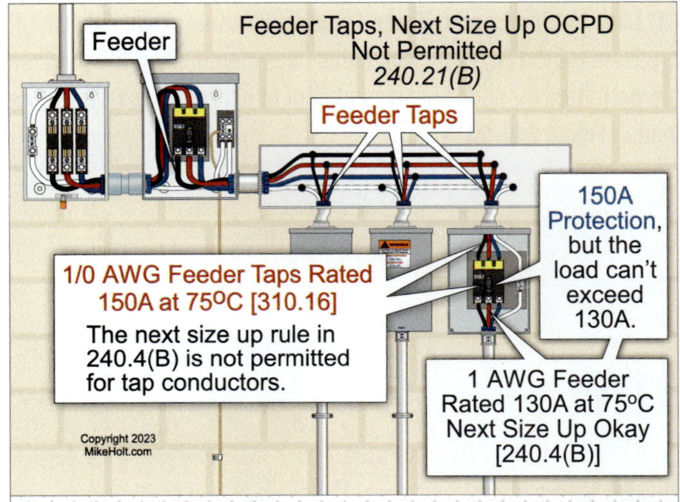

▶Figure 240–29

The feeder tap is permitted to be made at any point on the load side of the feeder overcurrent protective device, including the load terminals of the overcurrent protective device. ▶Figure 240–28

The next size up rule in 240.4(B) is not permitted for tap conductors. ▶Figure 240–29

(1) Feeder Tap Not Over 10 Feet. Tap conductors up to 10 ft long are permitted when they comply with the following:

(1) Tap conductors have an ampacity of not less than: ▶Figure 240–30

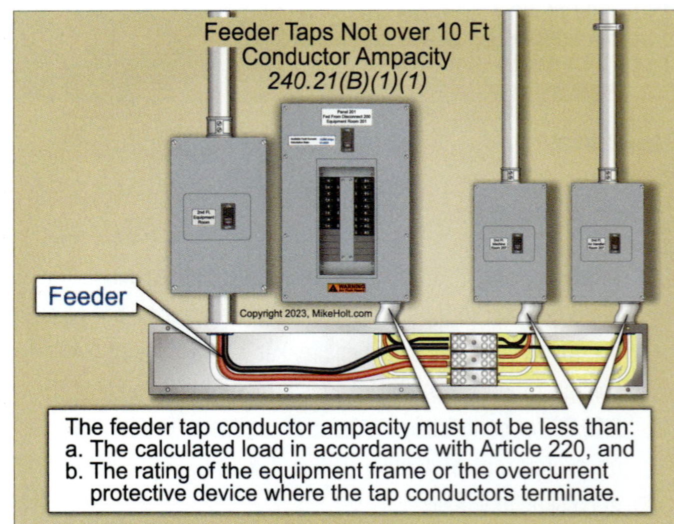

▶Figure 240–30

a. The calculated load in accordance with Article 220, and

b. The rating of the equipment frame or the overcurrent protective device where the tap conductors terminate.

(2) The tap conductors do not extend beyond the equipment they supply.

(3) Except at the point of connection, tap conductors must be installed within a raceway.

(4) Tap conductors that leave the enclosure where the tap is made must have an ampacity of not less than 10 percent of the rating of the feeder overcurrent protective device. ▶Figure 240–31

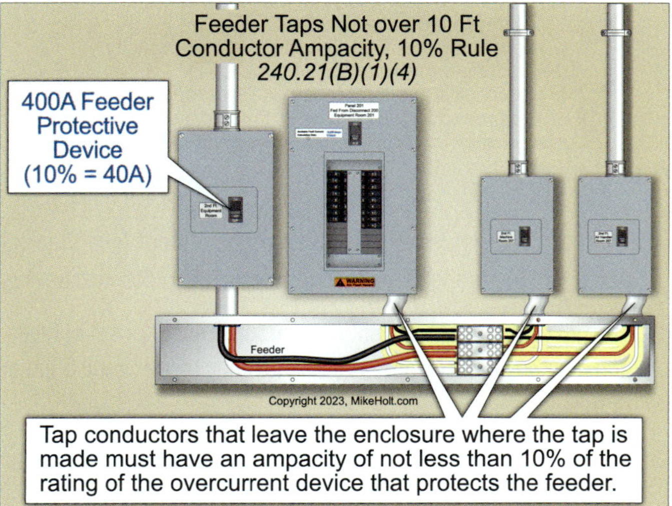

▶Figure 240–31

Note: If a tap supplies a panelboard, the tap conductors must terminate in an overcurrent protective device in accordance with 408.36. ▶Figure 240–32

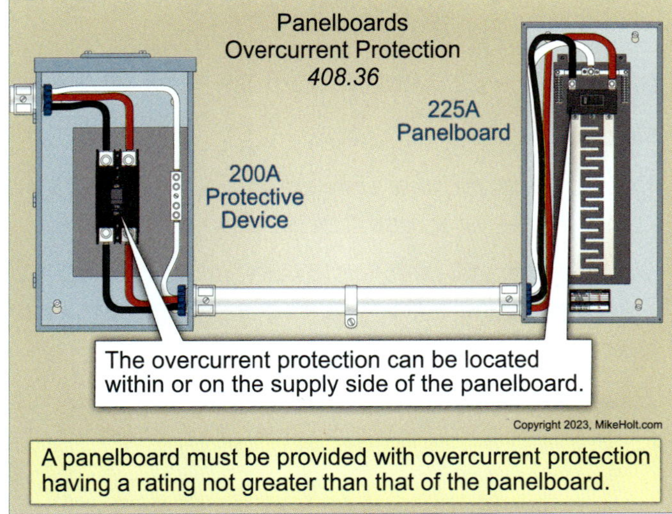

▶Figure 240–32

10-Foot Tap Rule

▶ 10-Foot Tap Rule Example 1

Question: What size 10-ft tap conductor is needed from a 400A circuit breaker to supply a 200A panelboard where the equipment is rated for 75°C conductor? ▶Figure 240–33

(a) 1/0 AWG   (b) 2/0 AWG   (c) 3/0 AWG   (d) 4/0 AWG

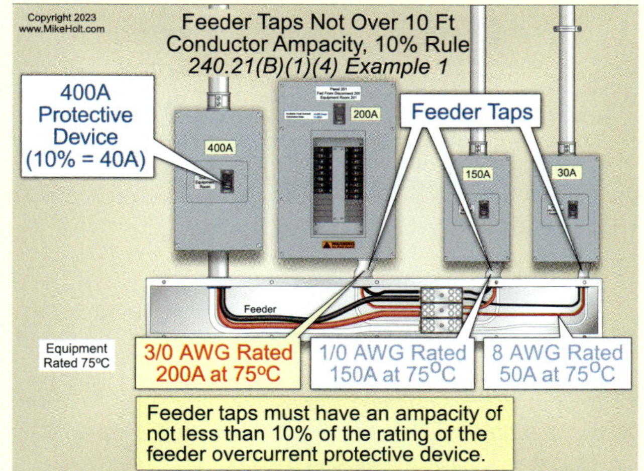

▶Figure 240–33

Solution:

10% of 400A = 40A minimum conductor ampacity

3/0 AWG is rated 200A at 75°C [110.14(C)(1)(b)(2) and Table 310.16] which is greater than 10 percent of the rating of the 400A overcurrent protective device.

Answer: (c) 3/0 AWG

▶ 10-Foot Tap Rule Example 2

Question: What size 10-ft tap conductor is needed from a 400A circuit breaker to supply a 150A feeder disconnect where the equipment is rated for 75°C conductor? ▶Figure 240–34

(a) 1/0 AWG   (b) 2/0 AWG   (c) 3/0 AWG   (d) 4/0 AWG

Solution:

10% of 400A = 40A minimum conductor ampacity

1/0 AWG is rated 150A at 75°C [110.14(C)(1)(b)(2) and Table 310.16] which is greater than 10 percent of the rating of the 400A overcurrent protective device.

Answer: (a) 1/0 AWG

• • •

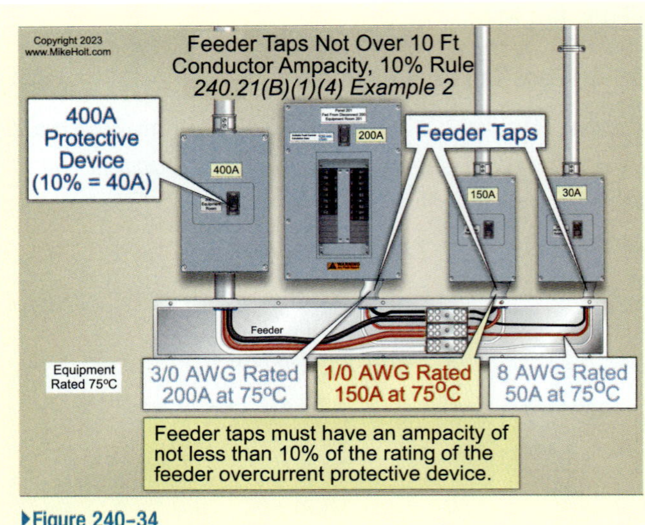

▶Figure 240–34

▶ 10-Foot Tap Rule Example 3

Question: What size 10-ft tap conductor is needed from a 400A circuit breaker to supply a 30A feeder disconnect where the equipment is rated for 75°C conductor? ▶Figure 240–35

(a) 8 AWG   *(b) 6 AWG*   *(c) 4 AWG*   *(d) 3 AWG*

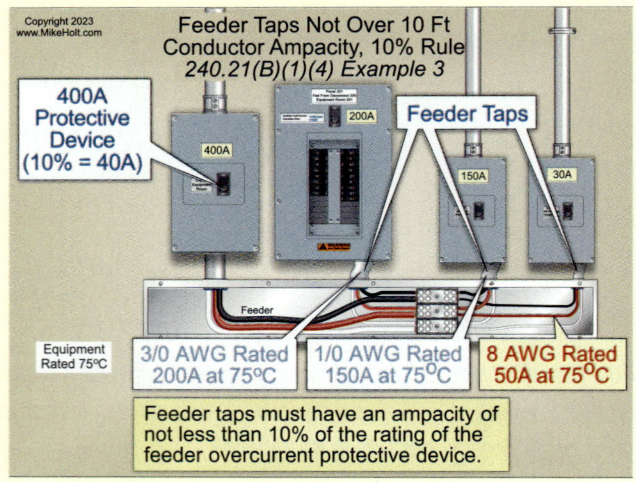

▶Figure 240–35

Solution:

10% of 400A = 40A minimum conductor ampacity

8 AWG is rated 50A at 75°C [110.14(C)(1)(a)(3) and Table 310.16] which is greater than 10 percent of the rating of the 400A overcurrent protective device.

Answer: (a) 8 AWG

(2) Feeder Tap Not Over 25 Feet. Tap conductors up to 25 ft long are permitted when they comply with the following: ▶Figure 240–36

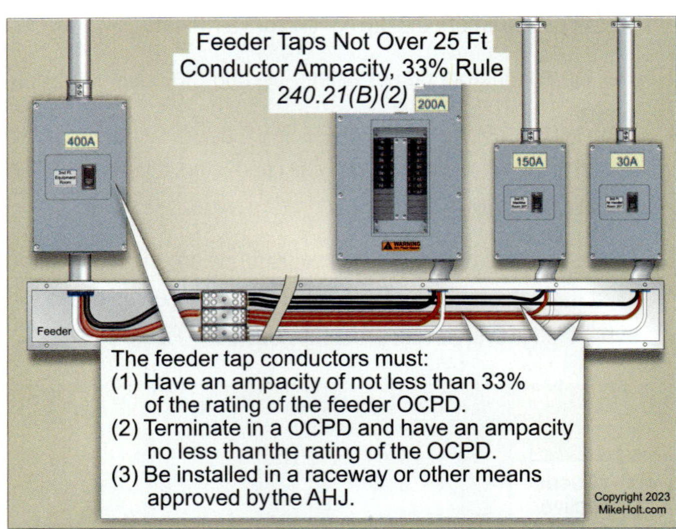

▶Figure 240–36

(1) The tap conductors must have an ampacity not less than 33 percent of the rating of the feeder overcurrent protective device.

(2) The tap conductors terminate in a circuit breaker or set of fuses, and have an ampacity no less than the rating of the circuit breaker or fuse.

(3) The tap conductors must be installed in a raceway or other means approved by the authority having jurisdiction.

25-Foot Tap Rule

▶ 25-Foot Tap Example 1

Question: What size 25-ft tap conductor is needed from a 400A circuit breaker to supply a 200A panelboard where the equipment is rated for 75°C conductor? ▶Figure 240–37

(a) 1/0 AWG   *(b) 2/0 AWG*   *(c) 3/0 AWG*   *(d) 4/0 AWG*

Solution:

The tap conductor must have a minimum rating of no less than 133A (33 percent of the rating of the 400A overcurrent protective device).

3/0 AWG is rated 200A at 75°C [110.14(C)(1)(b) and Table 310.16] which is greater than 133A (⅓ the rating of the 400A overcurrent protective device) and equal to the 200A disconnect.

Answer: (c) 3/0 AWG

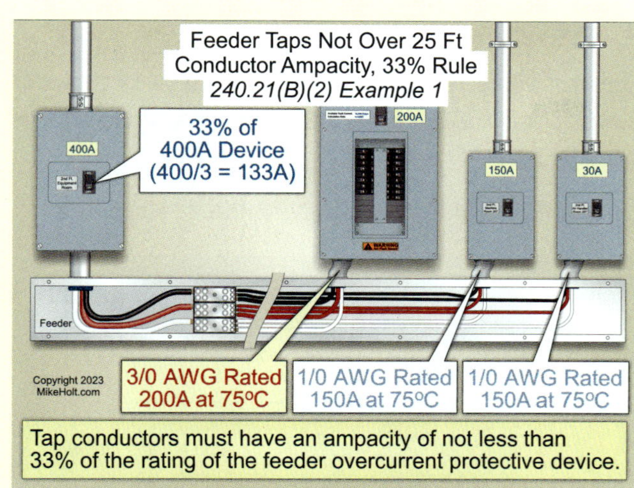

▶Figure 240–37

▶ 25-Foot Tap Example 2

Question: *What size 25-ft tap conductor is needed from a 400A circuit breaker to supply a 150A feeder disconnect where the equipment is rated for 75°C conductor?* ▶**Figure 240–38**

(a) 1/0 AWG   (b) 2/0 AWG   (c) 3/0 AWG   (d) 4/0 AWG

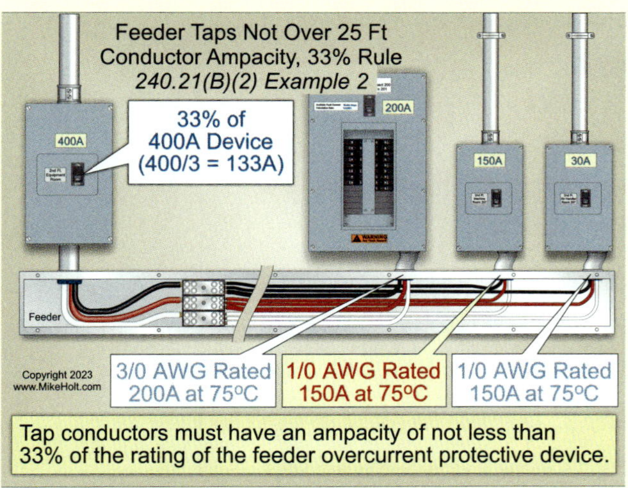

▶Figure 240–38

Solution:

The tap conductor must have a minimum rating of no less than 133A (33 percent of the rating of the 400A overcurrent protective device).

1/0 AWG is rated 150A at 75°C [110.14(C)(1)(b) and Table 310.16] which is greater than 133A (⅓ the rating of the 400A overcurrent protective device) and equal to the 150A disconnect.

Answer: *(a) 1/0 AWG*

▶ 25-Foot Tap Example 3

Question: *What size 25-ft tap conductor is needed from a 400A circuit breaker to supply a 30A feeder disconnect where the equipment is rated for 75°C conductor?* ▶**Figure 240–39**

(a) 3 AWG   (b) 2 AWG   (c) 1 AWG   (d) 1/0 AWG

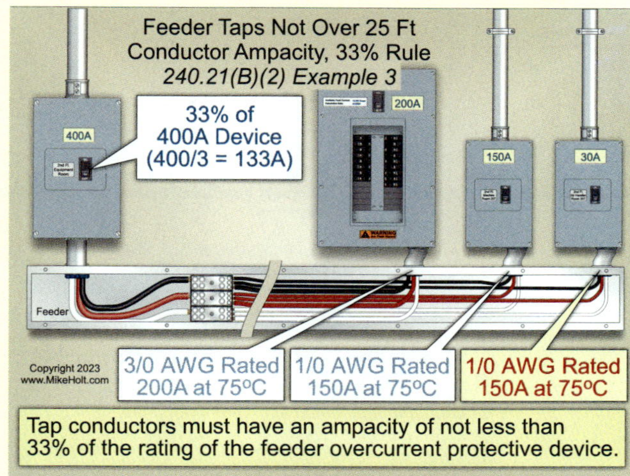

▶Figure 240–39

Solution:

The tap conductor must have a minimum rating of no less than 133A (33 percent of the rating of the 400A overcurrent protective device).

1/0 AWG is rated 150A at 75°C [110.14(C)(1)(a) and Table 310.16] which is greater than 133A (⅓ the rating of the 400A overcurrent protective device) and greater than the 30A disconnect main breaker.

Answer: *(d) 1/0 AWG*

(5) Outside Feeder Taps. Outside tap conductors can be of unlimited length if they comply with the following: ▶**Figure 240–40**

(2) The tap conductors terminate in a circuit breaker or set of fuses and have an ampacity of no less than the rating of the circuit breaker or fuse.

Author's Comment:

▶ The feeder overcurrent protective device provides short-circuit and ground-fault protection for the tap conductors and the tap termination overcurrent protective device provides overload protection. ▶**Figure 240–41**

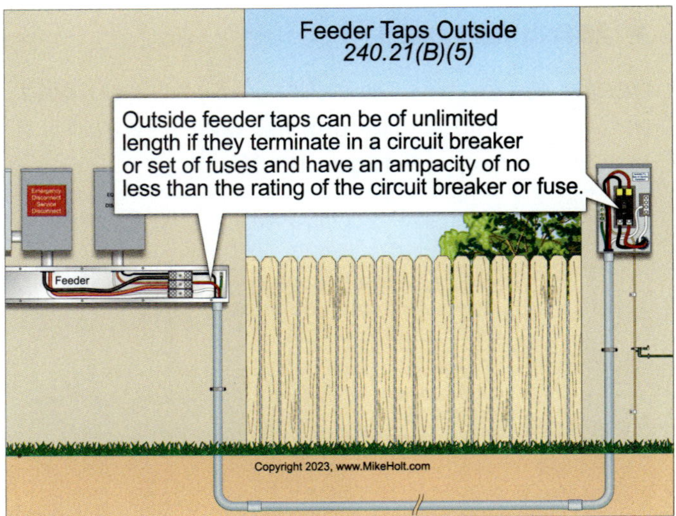

▶Figure 240–40

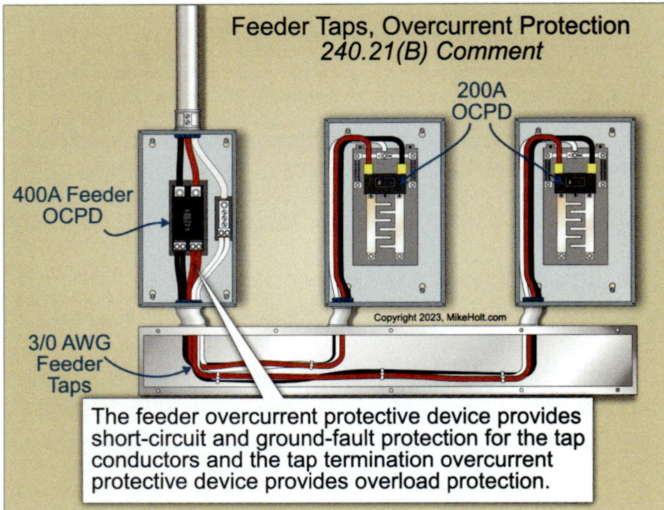

▶Figure 240–41

(C) Transformer Secondary Conductors. The secondary terminals of a transformer can supply multiple sets of secondary conductors. The next size up rule in 240.4(B) is not permitted for transformer secondary conductors.

(1) Protection by Primary Overcurrent Protective Device. The primary overcurrent protective device sized in accordance with 450.3(B) is considered suitable to protect the secondary conductors of a 2- or 3-wire (single-voltage) system, provided the primary overcurrent protective device does not exceed the value determined by multiplying the secondary conductor ampacity by the secondary-to-primary transformer voltage ratio.

Question: *What is the minimum size secondary conductor required for a single-phase, 1.50 kVA, 480V-to-120V transformer that is protected with a 5A fuse?* ▶Figure 240–42

(a) 14 AWG   (b) 12 AWG   (c) 10 AWG   (d) 8 AWG

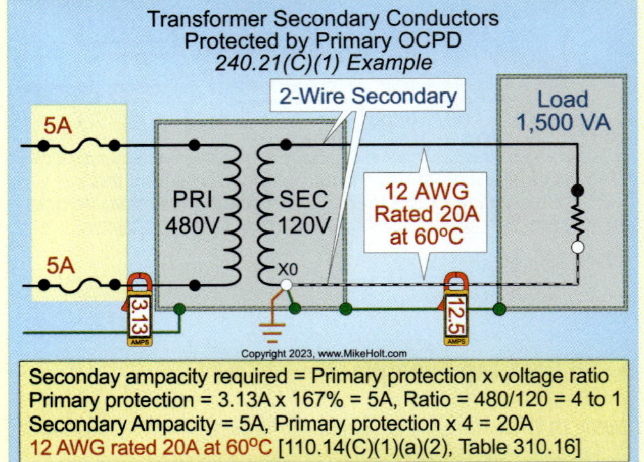

▶Figure 240–42

Solution:

Step 1: *Determine the primary current.*

VA/E
VA = 1,500 VA
E = 480V

Primary Current = 1,500 VA/480V
Primary Current = 3.13A

Step 2: *Determine the primary overcurrent protective device [450.3(B)].*

Primary Overcurrent Protection = 3.13A × 167%
Primary Overcurrent Protection = 5.22A or 5A Fuse

Step 3: *Determine the primary-to-secondary transformer ratio.*

Ratio = Primary Volts/Secondary Volts
Ratio = 480V/120V
Ratio = 4 to 1

Step 4: *Determine the secondary conductor minimum ampacity.*

Secondary Ampacity = Primary Overcurrent Protection × Ratio
Secondary Ampacity = 5A × 4
Secondary Ampacity = 20A

Use a 12 AWG conductor rated 20A at 60°C [110.14(C)(1)(a)(2) and Table 310.16].

Answer: *(b) 12 AWG*

(2) Secondary Conductors Not Over 10 Feet. Secondary conductors up to 10 ft long are permitted when they comply with the following:

(1) The secondary conductors must have an ampacity of not less than: ▶Figure 240–43

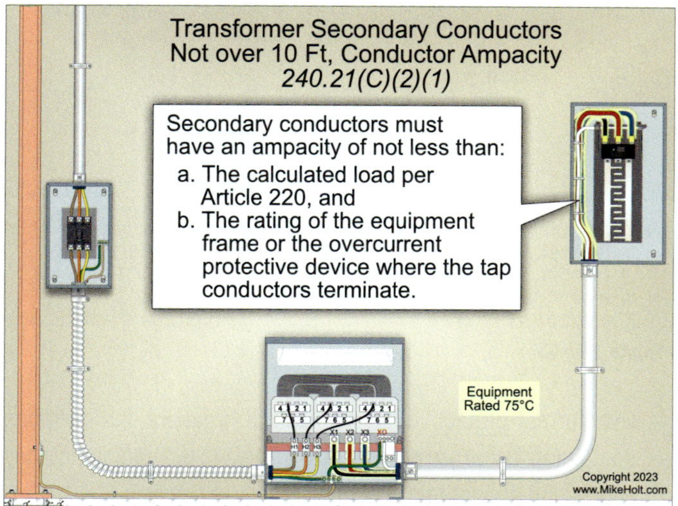

▶Figure 240–43

a. The calculated load in accordance with Article 220, and

b. The rating of the equipment frame or the overcurrent protective device where the tap conductors terminate.

(3) The secondary conductors are enclosed in a raceway.

Note: See 408.36 for overcurrent protection of panelboards.

Author's Comment:

▶ When a panelboard is supplied from a transformer, the overcurrent protection for the panelboard must be on the secondary side of the transformer. The overcurrent protection can be in an enclosure ahead of the panelboard or within the panelboard. ▶Figure 240–44

(4) Outside Secondary Conductors of Unlimited Length. Outside secondary conductors can be of unlimited length if they comply with the following: ▶Figure 240–45

(2) The outside secondary conductors terminate in a circuit breaker or set of fuses and have an ampacity of no less than the rating of the circuit breaker or fuse.

(6) Secondary Conductors Not Over 25 Feet. Secondary conductors up to 25 ft long are permitted when they comply with the following: ▶Figure 240–46

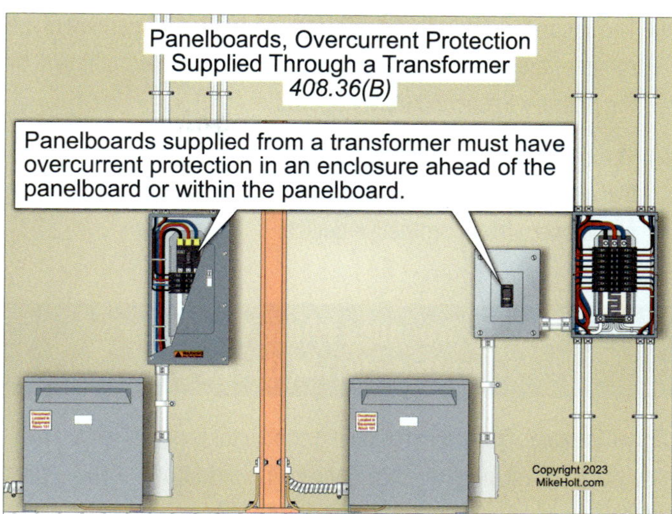

▶Figure 240–44

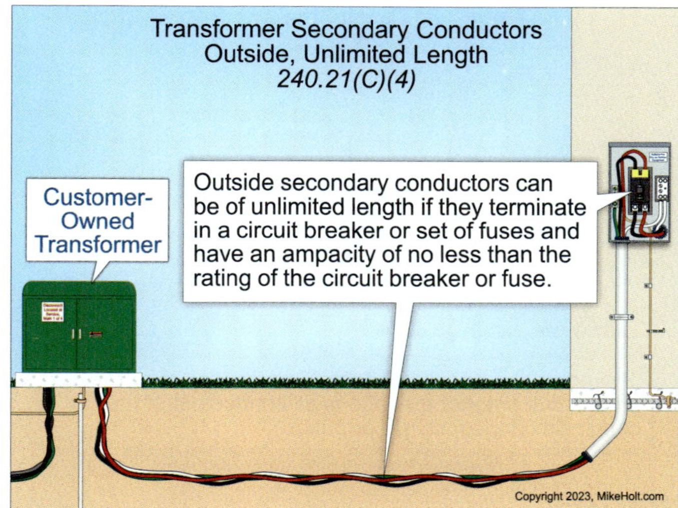

▶Figure 240–45

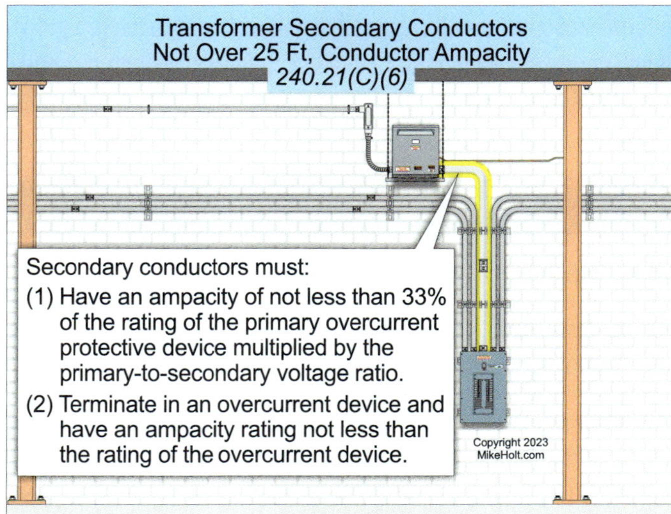

▶Figure 240–46

(1) The secondary has an ampacity of not less than 33 percent of the rating of the primary overcurrent protective device multiplied by the primary-to-secondary voltage ratio.

(2) The secondary conductors terminate in an overcurrent protective device and have an ampacity rating not less than the rating of the overcurrent protective device.

240.22 Grounded-Phase Conductor on Overcurrent Device

Circuit Breaker. The grounded-phase conductor is permitted to terminate on a circuit breaker that opens all conductors of the circuit simultaneously (2- or 3-pole). ▶Figure 240–47

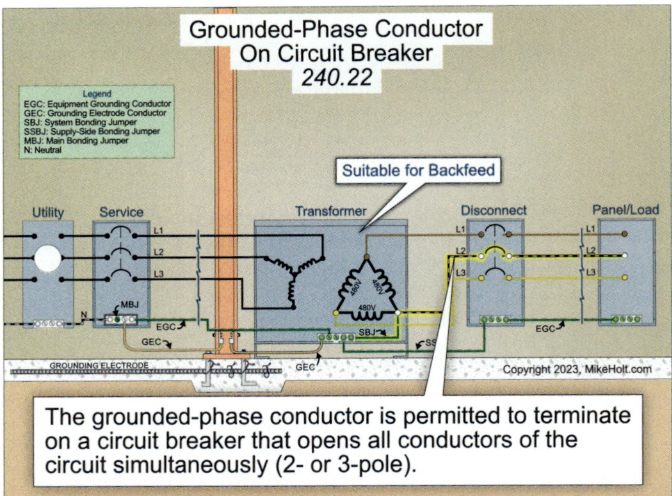

▶Figure 240–47

Fusible Disconnect. The grounded-phase conductor is not permitted to terminate on a fuse of a fusible disconnect because the grounded-phase conductor cannot be opened simultaneously with the other fuses in the disconnect.

240.24 Location of Overcurrent Protective Devices

(A) Accessibility.

Readily Accessible. Circuit breakers and switches containing fuses must be readily accessible.

Maximum Height of Handle. The center of the grip of the operating handle of the switch or circuit breaker in its highest position, is not permitted to be more than 6 ft 7 in. above the floor or working platform except as permitted in the following applications: ▶Figure 240–48

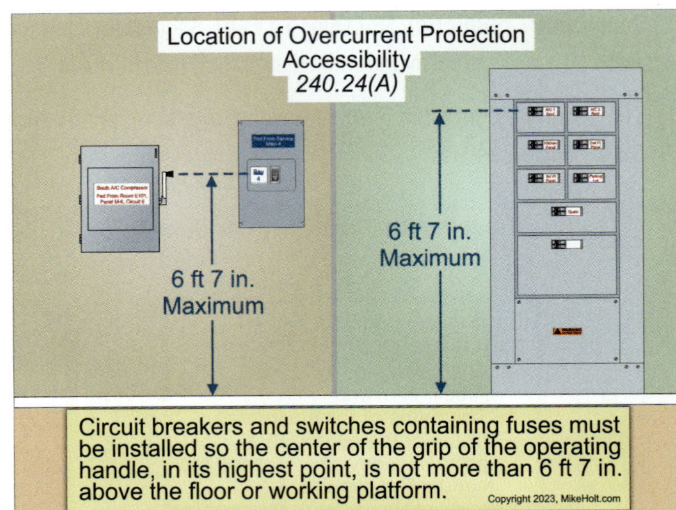

▶Figure 240–48

(4) Overcurrent protective devices (circuit breakers and switches containing fuses) are permitted to be next to the equipment they supply and are not required to be readily accessible.

(C) Not Exposed to Physical Damage. Overcurrent protective devices are not permitted to be exposed to physical damage.

(D) Not in Vicinity of Easily Ignitible Material. Overcurrent protective devices cannot be near easily ignitible material, such as in clothes closets. ▶Figure 240–49

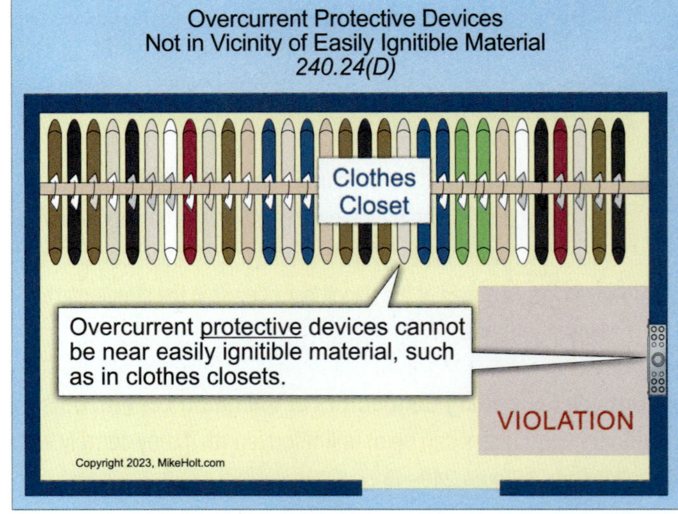

▶Figure 240–49

(E) Not in Bathroom Areas. Overcurrent protective devices are not permitted to be installed in bathroom areas, showering facilities, or locker rooms with showering facilities. ▶Figure 240–50

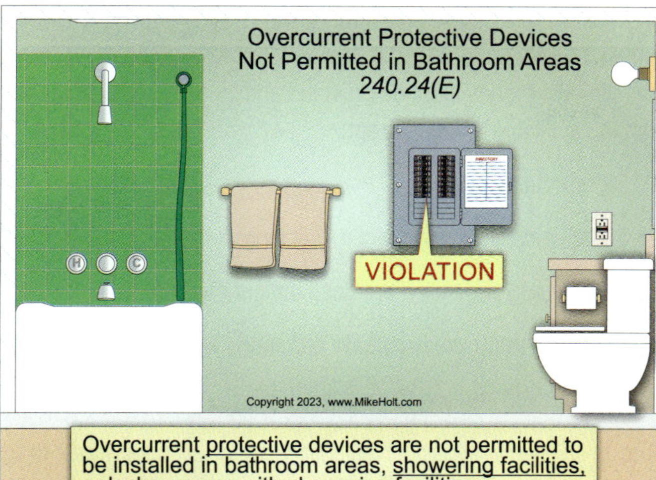

▶Figure 240–50

Author's Comment:

▶ The service disconnect switch is not permitted to be installed in a bathroom area even in commercial or industrial facilities [230.70(A)(2)].

(F) Not Over Steps. Overcurrent protective devices are not permitted to be located over steps of a stairway. ▶Figure 240–51

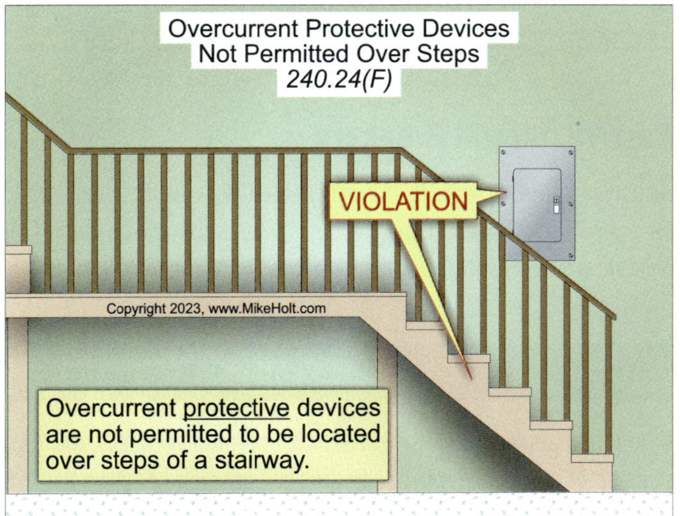

▶Figure 240–51

Author's Comment:

▶ In accordance with 110.26(A)(6), the working space must be level and flat for the entire depth and width of the required working space. Clearly, it is difficult for electricians to safely work on electrical equipment that is on uneven surfaces such as over stairways.

Part III. Enclosures Containing Overcurrent Protective Devices

240.33 Vertical Position, Enclosures

Fuses. Enclosures containing fuses must be mounted in a vertical position.

Circuit Breakers. Enclosures containing circuit breakers must be mounded vertically if the circuit-breaker handle is operated vertical. See 240.81. ▶Figure 240–52

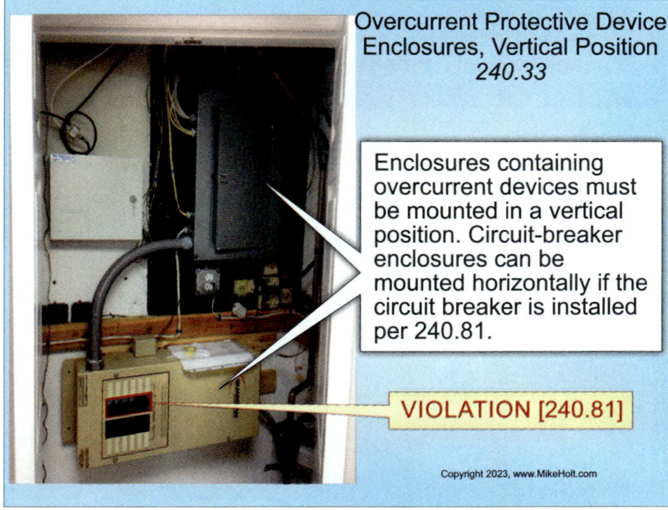

▶Figure 240–52

Author's Comment:

▶ Section 240.81 specifies that where circuit-breaker handles are operated vertically, the "up" position of the handle must be the "on" position. So, in effect, an enclosure that contains one row of circuit breakers can be mounted horizontally, but an enclosure that contains a panelboard with multiple circuit breakers on opposite sides of each other must be mounted vertically.

Part V. Plug Fuses, Fuseholders, and Adapters

240.51 Edison-Base Fuses

(A) Classification. Edison-base fuses are classified to operate at not more than 125V and have an ampere rating of not more than 30A. ▶Figure 240–53

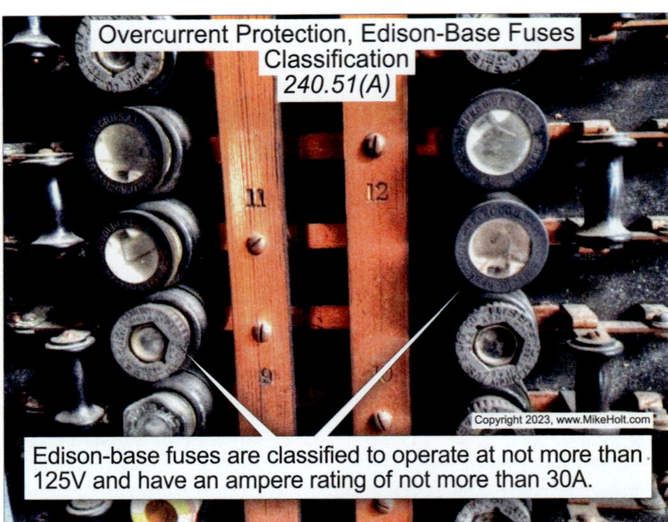

▶Figure 240–53

(B) Replacement Only. Edison-base fuses are permitted only for replacement in an existing installation if there is no evidence of tampering or over fusing. ▶Figure 240–54

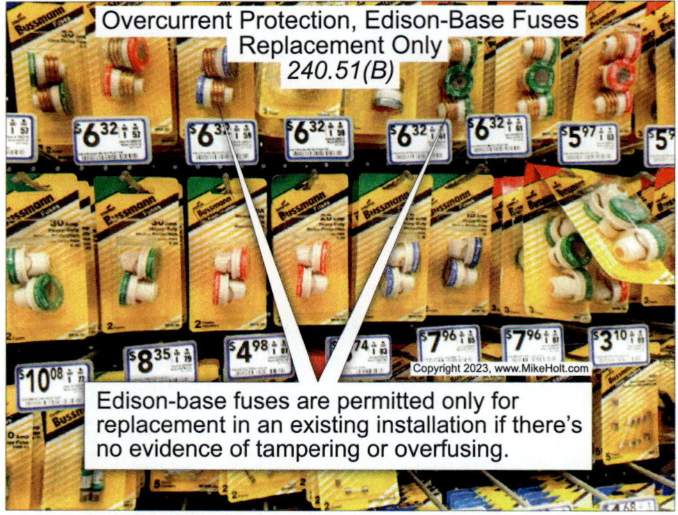

▶Figure 240–54

Part VI. Cartridge Fuses and Fuseholders

240.67 Arc-Energy Reduction—Fuses

Fuses rated 1200A or greater must be installed as follows:

(A) Documentation. Documentation must be available to those authorized to design, install, operate, or inspect the installation as to the location of the fuses. Documentation must be provided to demonstrate that the method chosen to reduce clearing time is set to operate at a value below the available arcing current.

(B) Method to Reduce Clearing Time. A fuse must have a clearing time of 0.07 seconds or less at the available arcing current, or one of the following means must be provided and be set to operate at less than the available arcing current:

(1) Differential relaying

(2) Energy-reducing maintenance switching with local status indicator

(3) Energy-reducing active arc-flash mitigation system

(4) Current-limiting, electronically actuated fuses

(5) An approved equivalent means

Note 1: An energy-reducing maintenance switch allows a worker to set a disconnect switch to reduce the clearing time while working within an arc-flash boundary as defined in NFPA 70E, *Standard for Electrical Safety in the Workplace*, and then to set the disconnect switch back to a normal setting after the potentially hazardous work is complete.

Note 2: An energy-reducing active arc-flash mitigation system helps in reducing arcing duration in the electrical distribution system. No change in the disconnect switch or the settings of other devices is required during maintenance when a worker is working within an arc-flash boundary as defined in NFPA 70E, *Standard for Electrical Safety in the Workplace*.

Note 3: IEEE 1584, *IEEE Guide for Performing Arc-Flash Hazard Calculations,* provides guidance in determining arcing current.

Part VII. Circuit Breakers

According to Article 100, "Circuit Breaker" is a device designed to be opened and closed manually, but opens automatically during an overcurrent event without damage to itself. ▶Figure 240–55

240.81 Indicating

When the handle of a circuit breaker is operated vertically, the "up" position of the handle must be in the "on" position. ▶Figure 240–56

240.83 Markings

(D) Used as Switches. Circuit breakers used to switch 120V or 277V fluorescent lighting circuits must be listed and marked "SWD" or "HID." Circuit breakers used to switch high-intensity discharge lighting circuits must be listed and marked "HID." ▶Figure 240–57

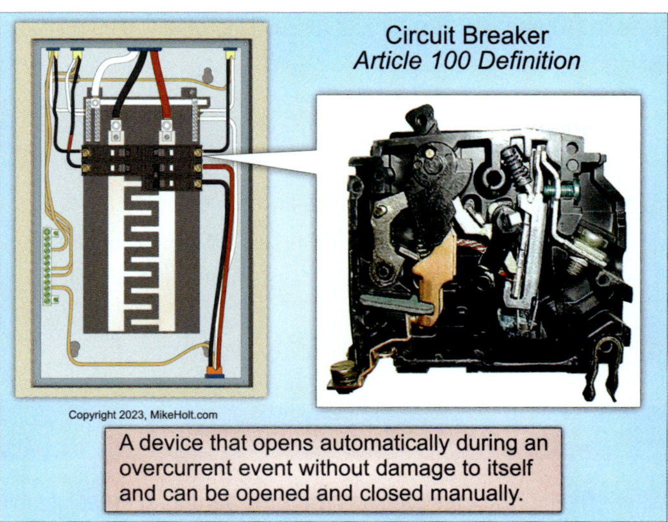

Circuit Breaker
Article 100 Definition

A device that opens automatically during an overcurrent event without damage to itself and can be opened and closed manually.

▶Figure 240–55

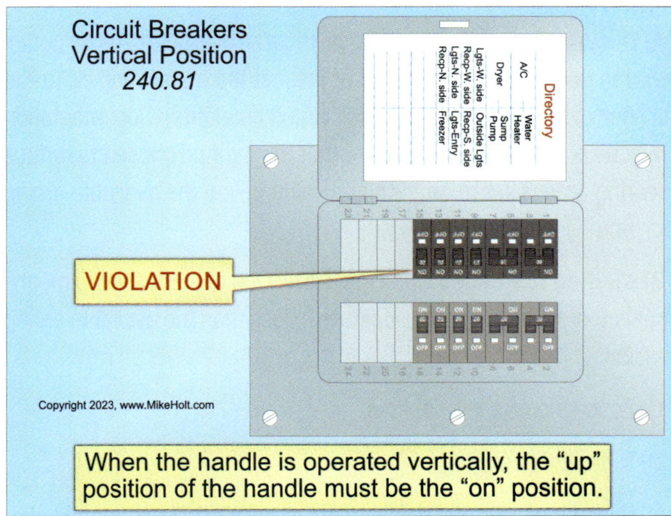

Circuit Breakers
Vertical Position
240.81

When the handle is operated vertically, the "up" position of the handle must be the "on" position.

▶Figure 240–56

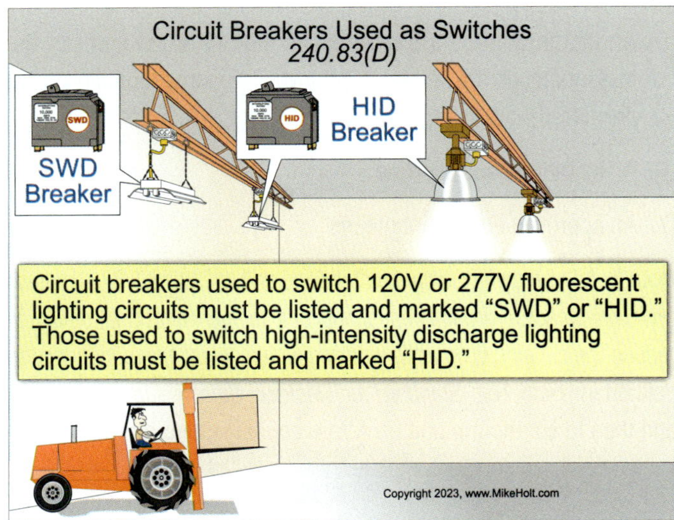

Circuit Breakers Used as Switches
240.83(D)

Circuit breakers used to switch 120V or 277V fluorescent lighting circuits must be listed and marked "SWD" or "HID." Those used to switch high-intensity discharge lighting circuits must be listed and marked "HID."

▶Figure 240–57

Straight Voltage Rating Circuit Breaker. A circuit breaker with a straight voltage rating (such as 240V or 480V) is permitted on a circuit if the nominal voltage between any two conductors (line-to-neutral or line-to-line) does not exceed the circuit breakers' voltage rating. ▶Figure 240–58

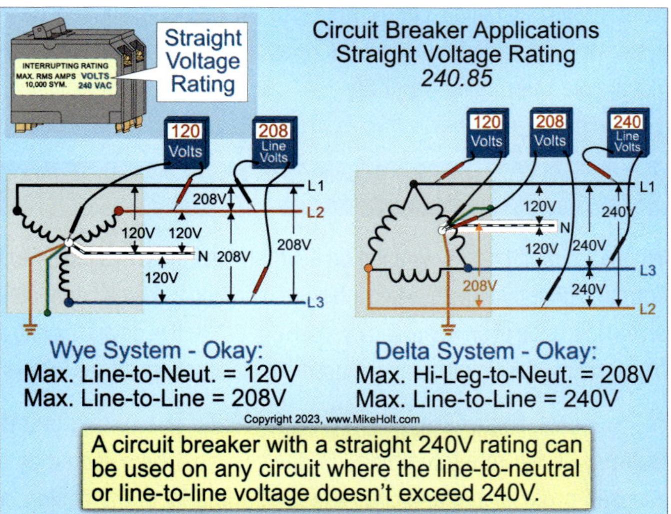

▶Figure 240–58

Slash Voltage Rating Circuit Breaker. A circuit breaker with a slash rating (such as 120/240V or 277/480V) is only permitted if the nominal voltage of any one conductor to ground does not exceed the lower of the two values, and the nominal voltage between any two conductors does not exceed the higher value. ▶Figure 240–59

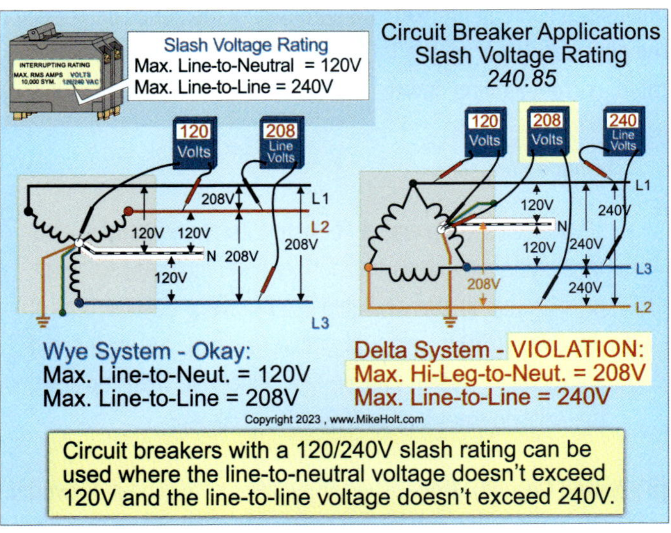

▶Figure 240–59

Author's Comment:

▶ A 120/240V slash circuit breaker is not permitted to be used on the high-leg of a 4-wire, three-phase, 120/240V delta-connected system because the line-to-ground voltage of the high-leg is 208V, which exceeds the 120V line-to-ground voltage rating of a 120/240V slash circuit breaker.

Note: When installing circuit breakers on corner-grounded delta systems, consideration needs to be given to the circuit breakers' individual pole-interrupting capability.

240.86 Series Ratings

Where a circuit breaker is used on a circuit having an available fault current higher than the marked interrupting rating by being connected on the load side of an approved overcurrent protective device having a higher rating, the circuit breaker must meet the requirements as follows:

(A) Selected Under Engineering Supervision in Existing Installations. Series rated combination devices must be selected by a licensed professional engineer engaged primarily in the design or maintenance of electrical installations. The selection must be documented and stamped by the professional engineer.

This documentation must be available to those authorized to design, install, inspect, maintain, and operate the system. This series combination rating, including identification of the upstream overcurrent protective device(s), must be field marked on the end-use equipment. For calculated applications, the engineer must ensure the downstream circuit breakers that are part of the series combination remain passive during the interruption period of the line side, fully rated, current-limiting device.

Author's Comment:

▶ Upgrades or replacement of existing components in an electrical system (such as transformers and motors) can create an increase in the available fault current beyond that of the existing overcurrent protection system. An engineered series rated system can be less expensive than replacing the existing electrical system.

(B) Tested Combinations. The combination of the line-side overcurrent protective device and the load-side circuit breaker(s) are tested and marked on the end-use equipment, such as switchboards and panelboards.

Note to (A) and (B): See 110.22 for marking of series combination systems.

Author's Comment:

▶ Section 240.86(A) is used for an engineered series rated system in an existing installation. Section 240.86(B) can be used for a tested combination system in a new or existing installation.

240.87 Arc-Energy Reduction—Circuit Breakers

Where the highest continuous current trip setting of an adjustable trip circuit breaker is rated or can be adjusted to 1200A or higher, 240.87(A) through 240.87(C) applies:

(A) Documentation. Documentation must be available to those authorized to design, install, operate, or inspect the installation as to the location of the arc-energy reduction circuit breaker(s). Documentation must be provided to demonstrate that the method chosen to reduce clearing time is set to operate at a value below the available arcing current.

(B) Method to Reduce Clearing Time. One of the following means must be provided and set to operate at less than the available arcing current:

(1) Zone-selective interlocking

(2) Differential relaying

(3) Energy-reducing maintenance switching with local status indicator

(4) Energy-reducing active arc-flash mitigation system

(5) An instantaneous trip setting (temporary adjustment of the instantaneous trip setting to achieve arc-energy reduction is not permitted)

(6) An instantaneous override

(7) An approved equivalent means

Note 1: An energy-reducing maintenance switch [240.87(B)(3)] allows a worker to set a circuit breaker trip unit to "no intentional delay" to reduce the clearing time while working within an arc-flash boundary as defined in NFPA 70E, *Standard for Electrical Safety in the Workplace*, and then to set the trip unit back to a normal setting after the potentially hazardous work is complete.

Note 2: An energy-reducing active arc-flash mitigation system [240.87(B)(4)] helps in reducing arcing duration in the electrical distribution system. No change in the circuit breaker or the settings of other devices is required during maintenance when a worker is working within an arc-flash boundary as defined in NFPA 70E, *Standard for Electrical Safety in the Workplace*.

Note 3: An instantaneous trip [240.87(B)(5)] is a function that causes a circuit breaker to trip with no intentional delay when currents exceed the instantaneous trip setting or current level. If arcing currents are above the instantaneous trip level, the circuit breaker will trip in the minimum possible time.

Note 4: IEEE 1584, *IEEE Guide for Performing Arc-Flash Hazard Calculations*, provides guidance in determining arcing current.

OVERVOLTAGE PROTECTION

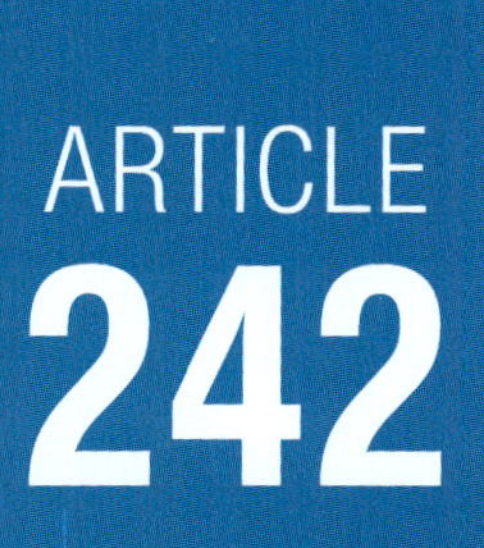

Introduction to Article 242—Overvoltage Protection

This article provides the general, installation, and connection requirements for overvoltage protection and overvoltage protective devices (surge-protective devices or SPDs). Surge-protective devices are installed to reduce transient voltages present on the premises electrical system to protect electronic safety equipment such as smoke detectors, AFCIs, GFCIs, and electronic breakers from damage. Some topics covered in this material for Article 242 include:

▸ Short-Circuit Current Rating

▸ SPD Types

▸ Location

▸ Conductor Routing and Sizing

According to Article 100, "Surge Protection Device (SPD)" is a protective device intended to limit transient voltages by diverting or limiting surge current and preventing its continued flow while remaining capable of repeating these functions. ▸Figure 242–1 and ▸Figure 242–2

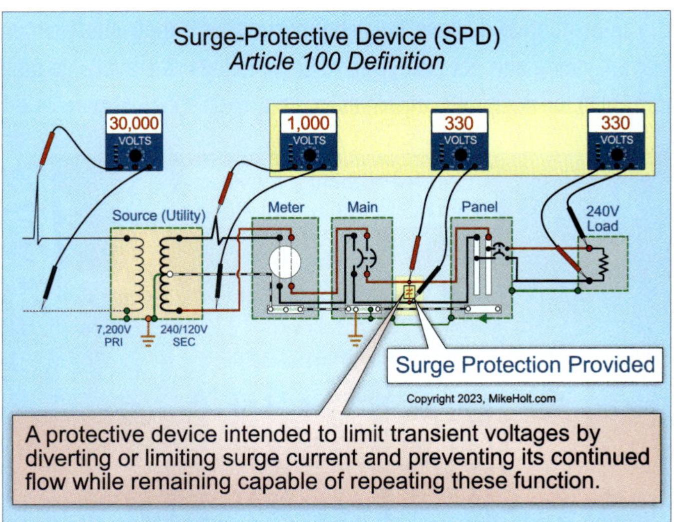

▸Figure 242–1

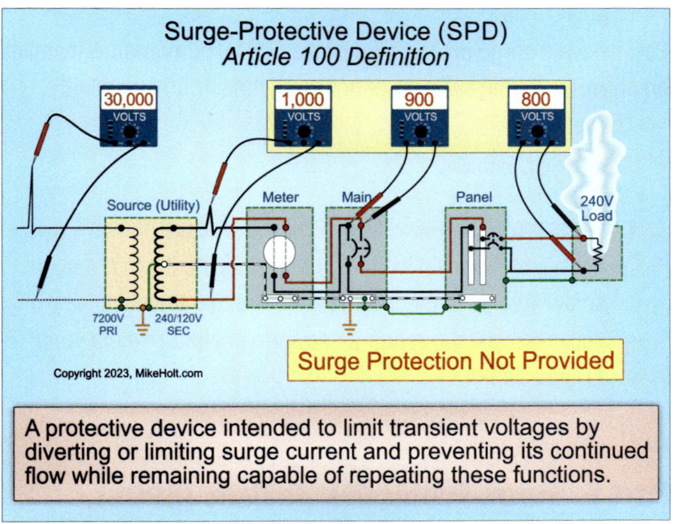

▸Figure 242–2

Part I. General

242.1 Scope

Part I of this article provides the general, installation, and connection requirements for overvoltage protection and overvoltage protective devices. Table 242.3 covers specific equipment and locations where surge-protective devices are required. ▶Figure 242–3

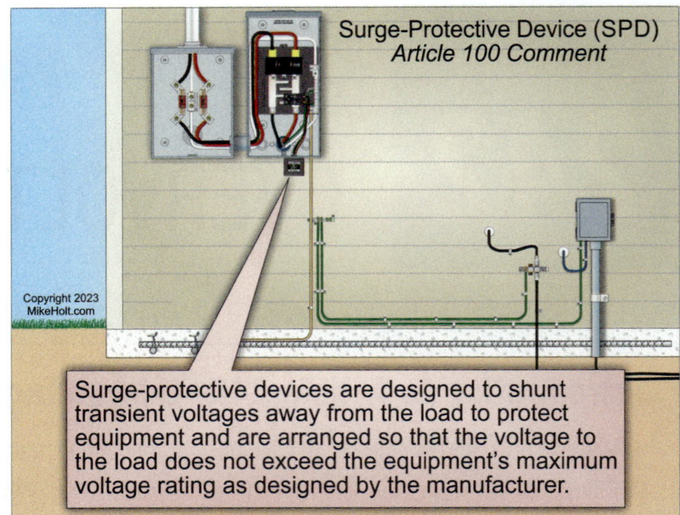

▶Figure 242–4

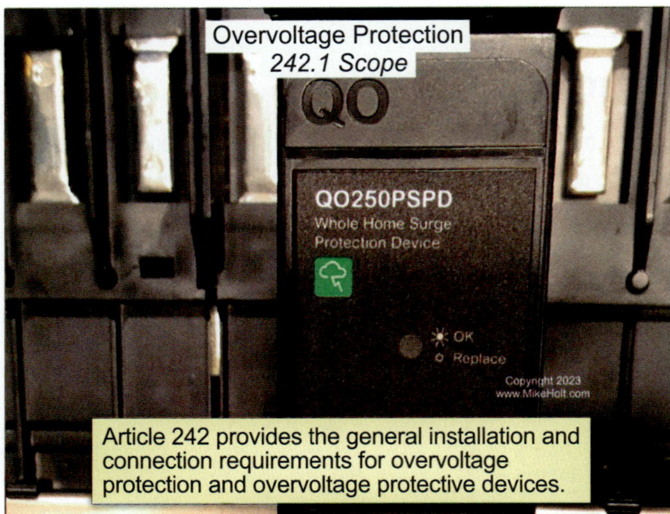

▶Figure 242–3

Part II covers surge-protective devices (SPDs) permanently installed on premises wiring systems of not more than 1000V, nominal.

Author's Comment:

▶ Surge-protective devices are designed to shunt transient voltages away from the load to protect equipment and arranged so the voltage to the load does not exceed the equipment's maximum voltage rating as designed by the manufacturer. ▶Figure 242–4

Part II. Surge-Protective Devices (SPDs), 1000V or Less

242.6 Listing

Surge-protective devices must be listed.

Author's Comment:

▶ In accordance with UL 1449, "*Standard for Surge-Protective Devices*," these units are intended to limit the maximum extent of transient voltage surges on power lines to specified values. They are not intended to function as lightning arresters. The adequacy of the voltage suppression level to protect connected equipment from voltage surges has not been evaluated.

242.8 Short-Circuit Current Rating

Surge-protective devices must be marked with their short-circuit current rating and not permitted to be installed if the available fault current at the equipment terminals exceeds that rating. ▶Figure 242–5

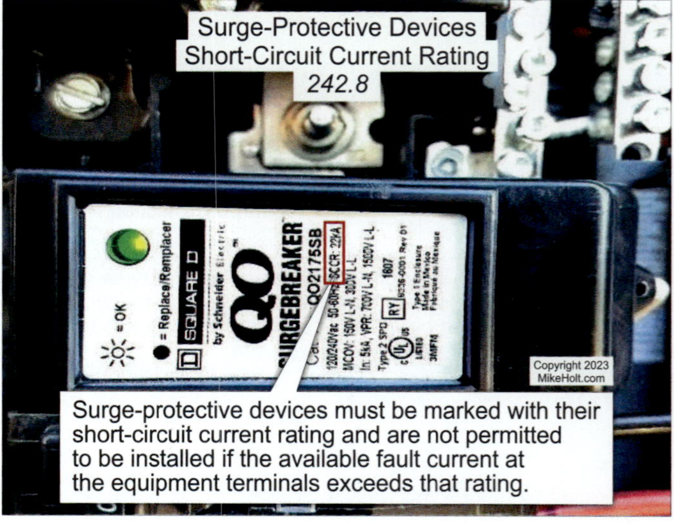

▶Figure 242–5

WARNING: Surge-protective devices are susceptible to failure at high fault currents. A hazardous condition is present if the short-circuit current rating of a surge-protective device is less than the available fault current. See 110.10.

242.9 Indicating

A surge-protective device must provide indication that it is functioning properly. ▶Figure 242–6

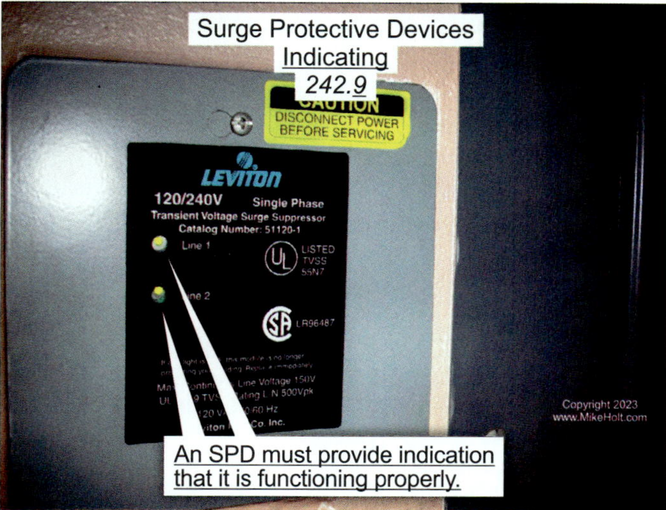

▶Figure 242–6

242.12 Uses Not Permitted

A surge-protective device is not permitted to be used:

(1) In circuits that exceed 1000V

(2) In ungrounded systems, impedance grounded systems, or corner-grounded delta systems unless listed specifically for use on these systems

(3) If the voltage rating of the surge-protective device is less than the maximum continuous phase-to-ground voltage available at the point of connection

242.13 Type 1 SPDs—Supply Side of Service Equipment

According to Article 100, "Type 1 SPD" is listed for the installation at or ahead of the service disconnect. ▶Figure 242–7

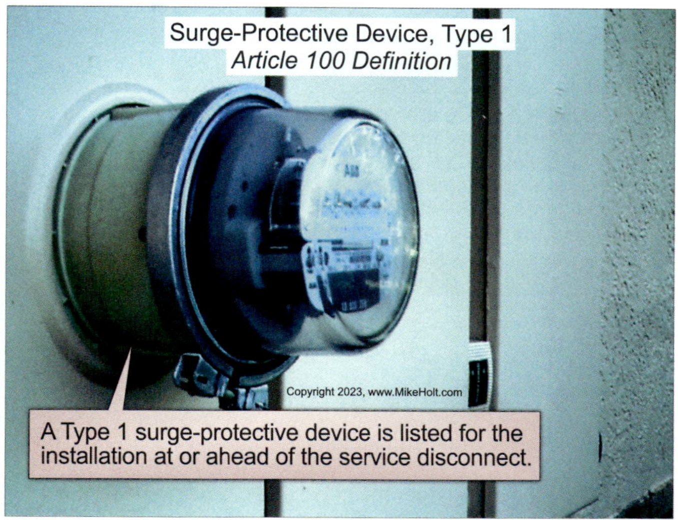

▶Figure 242–7

(A) Installation. Type 1 surge-protective devices can be connected as follows:

(1) On the supply side of the service disconnect [230.82(4)] ▶Figure 242–8

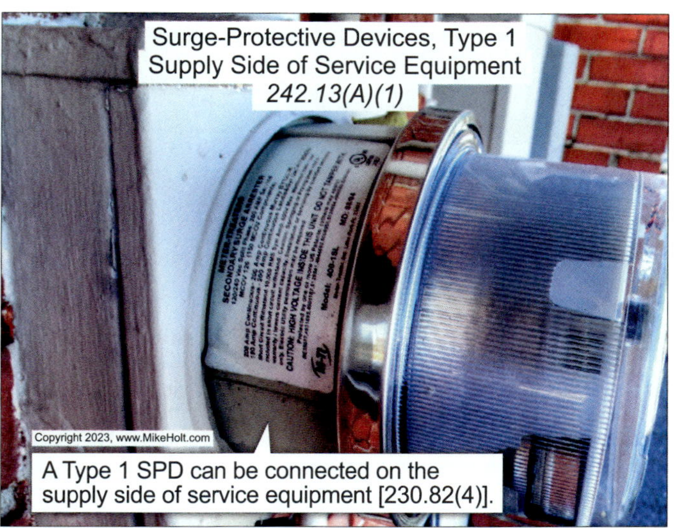

▶Figure 242–8

(2) On the load side of the service equipment as per 242.14

(B) Supply Side of Service. Type 1 SPDs on the supply side of service equipment must be connected as follows: ▶Figure 242–9

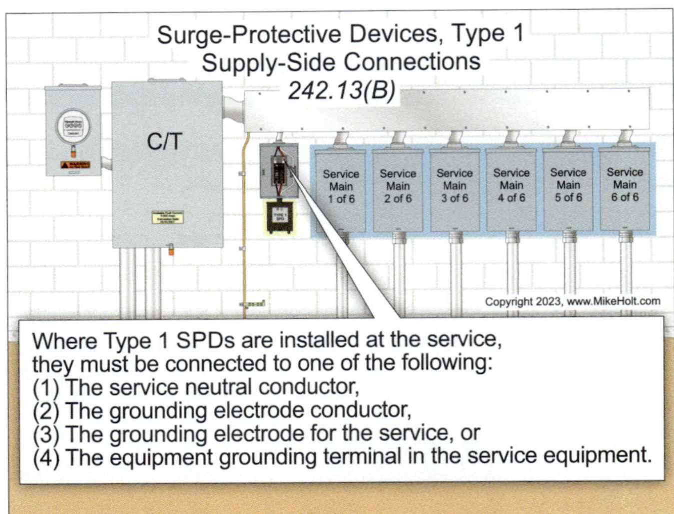

▶Figure 242–9

(1) Service neutral conductor

(2) Grounding electrode conductor

(3) Grounding electrode for the service

(4) Equipment grounding terminal in the service equipment

242.14 Type 2 SPDs—Feeder Circuits

According to Article 100, "Type 2 SPD" is listed for the installation on the load side of the service disconnect. ▶Figure 242–10

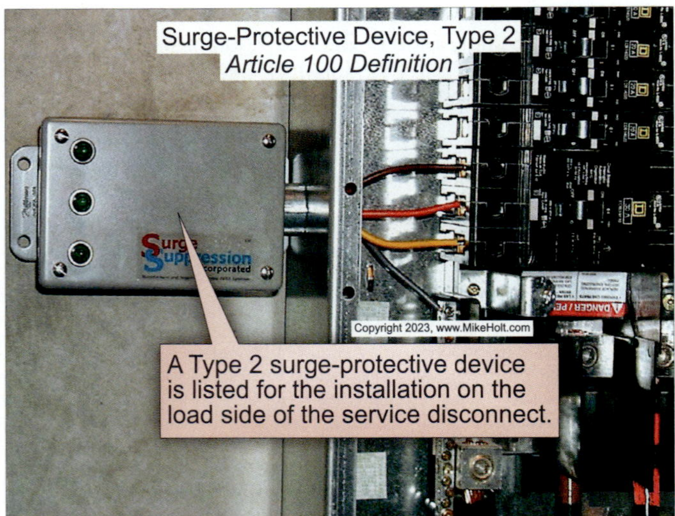

▶Figure 242–10

(A) Load Side of Service Disconnect. Type 2 surge-protective devices must be connected to the load side of the service disconnect. ▶Figure 242–11

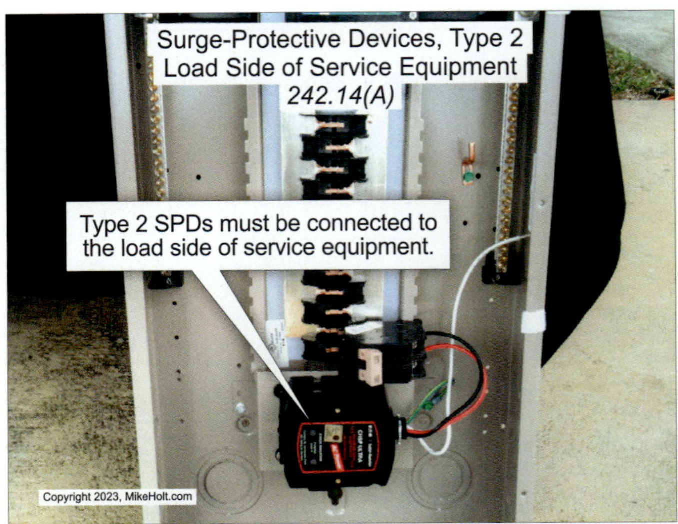

▶Figure 242–11

▶ Only one conductor can be connected to a terminal unless the terminal is identified for multiple conductors [110.14(A)]. ▶Figure 242–12

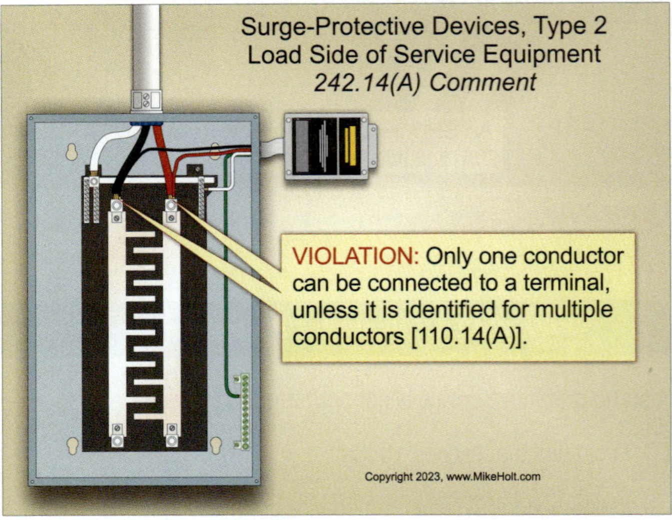

▶Figure 242–12

(B) Feeder-Supplied Remote Buildings. Type 2 surge-protective devices must be connected anywhere on the load side of the remote building disconnecting means. ▶Figure 242–13

(C) Separately Derived Systems. Type 2 surge-protective devices must be connected anywhere on the load side of the separately derived system disconnect overcurrent protective device.

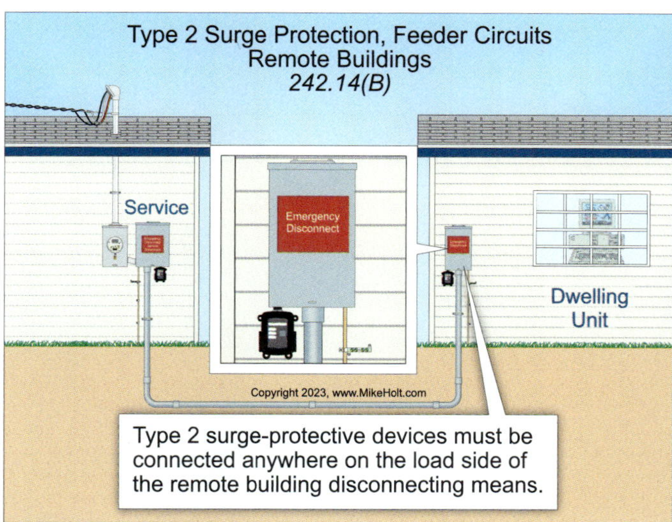

▶Figure 242–13

242.20 Number Required

If installed, the surge-protective device must be connected to each phase conductor of the circuit.

242.24 Routing of Surge-Protective Device Conductors

Surge-protective device conductors are not permitted to be any longer than necessary, and unnecessary bends must be avoided. ▶Figure 242–14

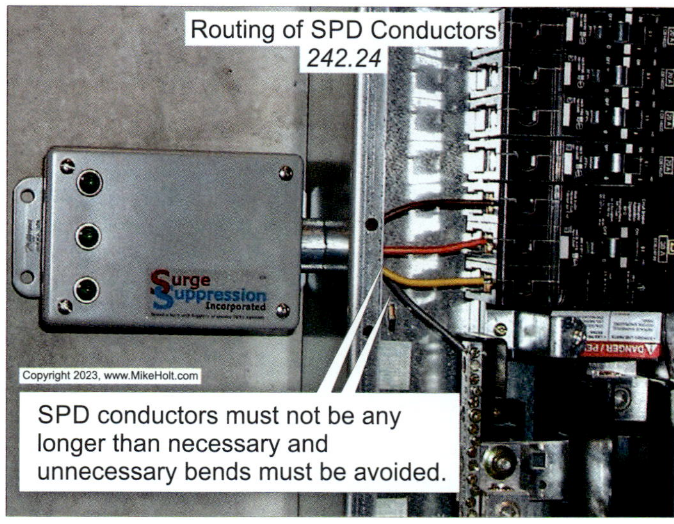

▶Figure 242–14

Author's Comment:

▶ Shorter conductors and minimal bends will improve the performance of the surge-protective device by helping to reduce conductor impedance during high-frequency transient events.

Introduction to Article 250—Grounding and Bonding

Article 250 covers the general requirements for bonding and grounding electrical installations. The terminology used in this article has been a source of much confusion over the years so pay careful attention to the definitions pertaining to Article 250. Understanding the difference between bonding and grounding will help you correctly apply the provisions of this article. Because of the massive size and scope of Article 250, Figure 250.1 in the *NEC* is provided as a reference for the locations of the different types of rules. Of the ten parts contained in this article only parts one through seven are covered in this material. Some topics covered in this material include:

- ▶ General Requirements for Grounding and Bonding
- ▶ Objectionable Current
- ▶ Protection of Clamps and Fittings
- ▶ System Grounding Requirements
- ▶ Bonding Jumpers
- ▶ Generator Bonding
- ▶ Grounding Electrode System
- ▶ Service Equipment Bonding
- ▶ Piping System and Structural Steel Bonding
- ▶ Equipment Grounding Conductors (EGCs)

This article consists of ten parts:

- ▶ Part I. General
- ▶ Part II. System Grounding
- ▶ Part III. Grounding Electrode System and Grounding Electrode Conductor (GEC)
- ▶ Part IV. Enclosure, Raceway, and Service Cable Connections
- ▶ Part V. Bonding
- ▶ Part VI. Equipment Grounding Conductors (EGC)
- ▶ Part VII. Methods of EGC Connections
- ▶ Part VIII. Direct-Current Systems
- ▶ Part IX. Instruments, Meters, and Relays
- ▶ Part X. Grounding of Systems and Circuits of over 1000 Volts

Part I. General

250.1 Scope

Article 250 covers the general requirements for grounding and bonding electrical installations. ▶Figure 250–1

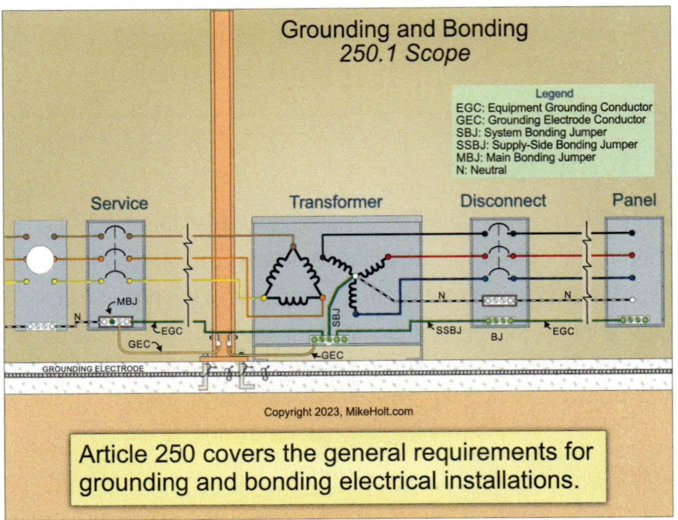

▶Figure 250–1

Author's Comment:

▸ There are two completely different concepts being covered in this article: "grounding" which is the connection to the Earth, and "bonding" which is connecting conductive metal parts together to ensure electrical conductivity between metal parts. ▶Figure 250–2

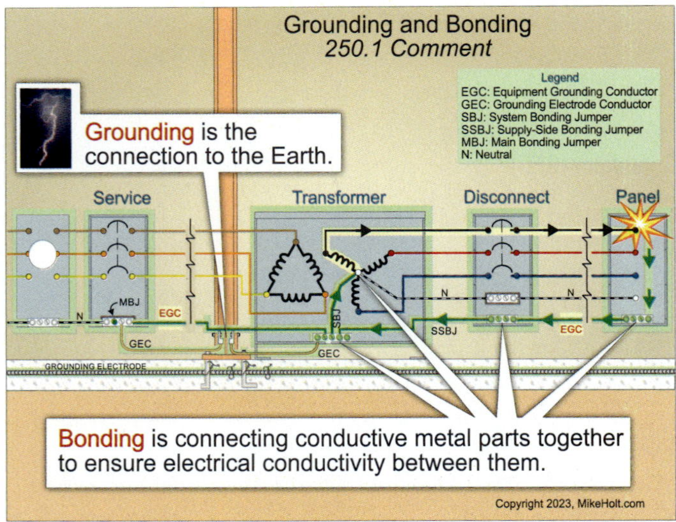

▶Figure 250–2

According to Article 100, "Bonding" means connected to establish electrical continuity and conductivity. ▶Figure 250–3

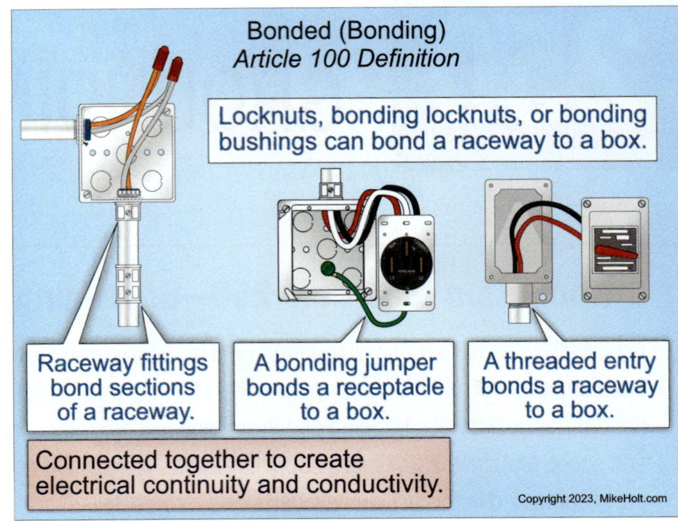

▶Figure 250–3

According to Article 100, "Grounding" means the connection to the Earth (ground) or to a conductive body that extends the ground connection. ▶Figure 250–4

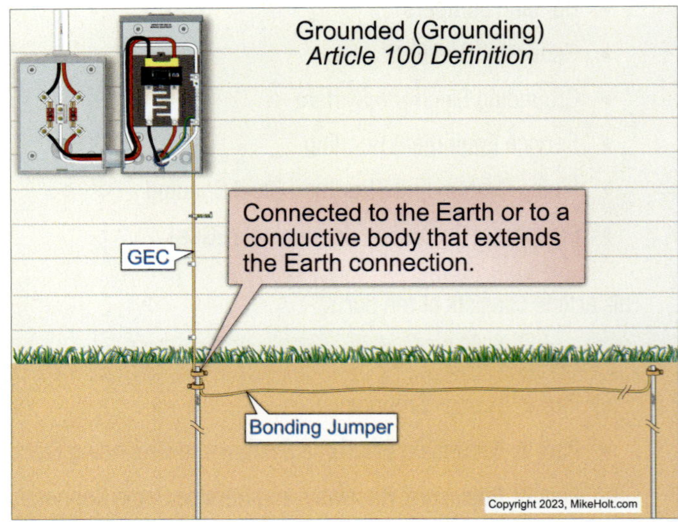

▶Figure 250–4

According to Article 100, "Ground" means the Earth. ▶Figure 250–5

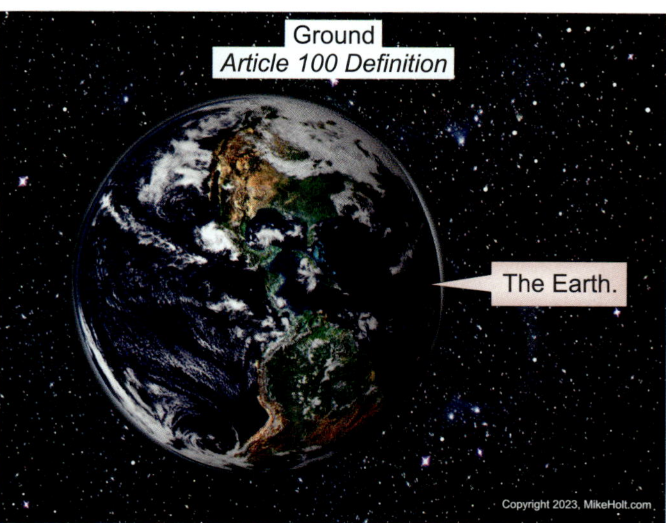

▶Figure 250–5

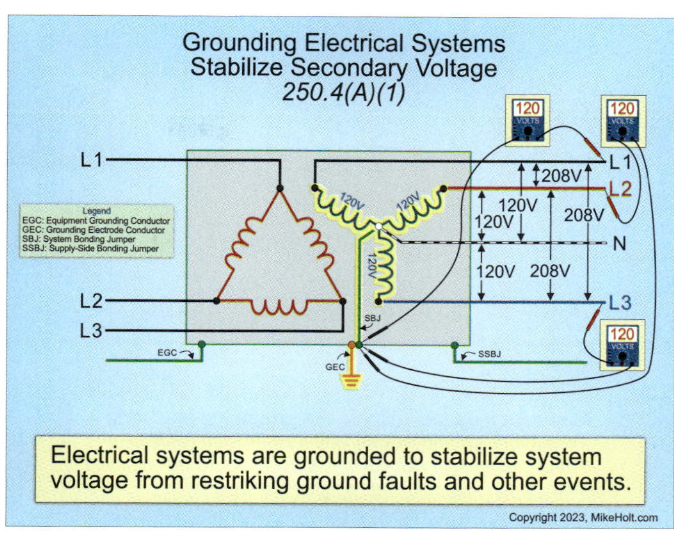

▶Figure 250–7

250.4 Performance Requirements for Grounding and Bonding

(A) Grounded Systems.

(1) Grounding of Electrical Systems.

Reduce Inducted Voltage. Electrical systems are grounded to the Earth to reduce induced voltage on the system conductors from indirect lightning strikes. ▶Figure 250–6

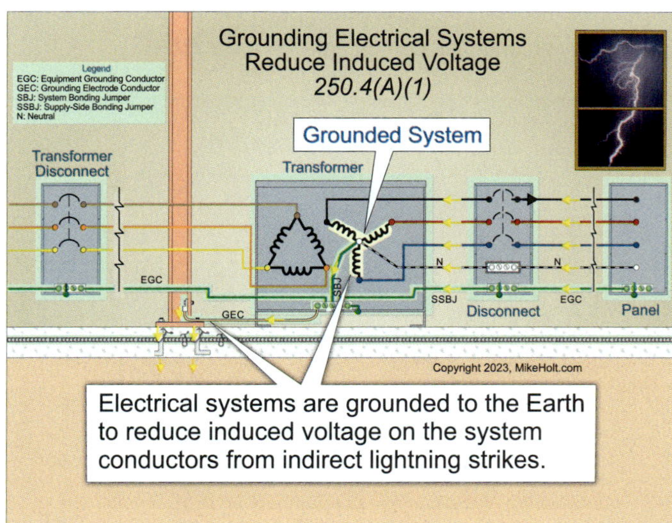

▶Figure 250–6

Stabilize System Voltage. Electrical systems are grounded to stabilize system voltage from restricting ground faults and other events. ▶Figure 250–7

▸ System grounding reduces induced voltage from indirect lightning. It stabilizes system voltage from restriking ground faults, thereby ensuring longer insulation life for motors, transformers, and other electrical equipment. ▶Figure 250–8

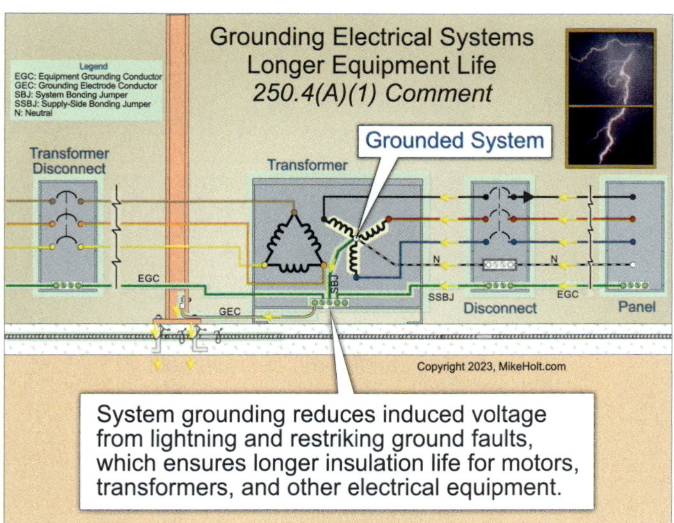

▶Figure 250–8

Note 1: To reduce induced voltage, the grounding electrode conductors should not be any longer than necessary, and unnecessary bends and loops should be avoided. ▶Figure 250–9 and ▶Figure 250–10

(2) Grounding Metal Parts of Equipment. Metal parts of electrical equipment must be bonded together and grounded to the Earth to reduce induced voltage on the metal parts from indirect lightning strikes. ▶Figure 250–11

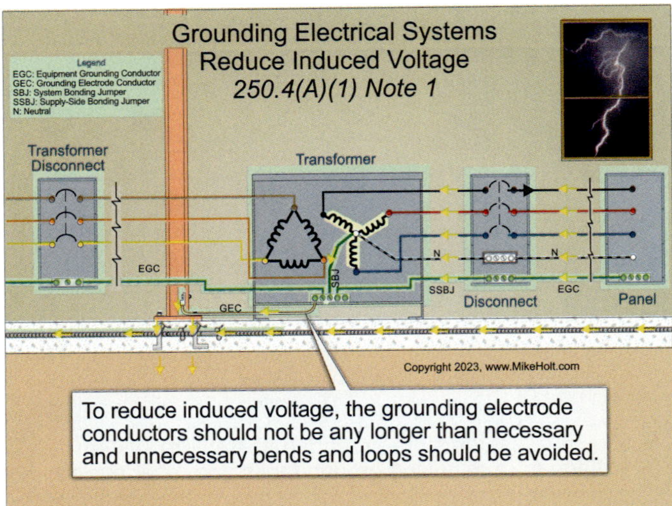

▶Figure 250–9

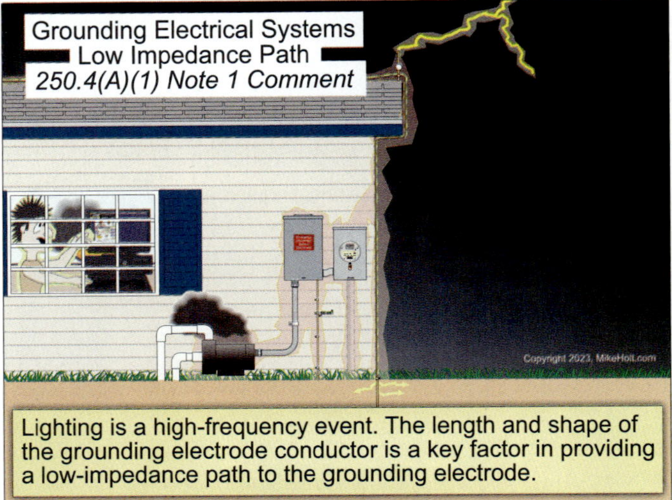

▶Figure 250–10

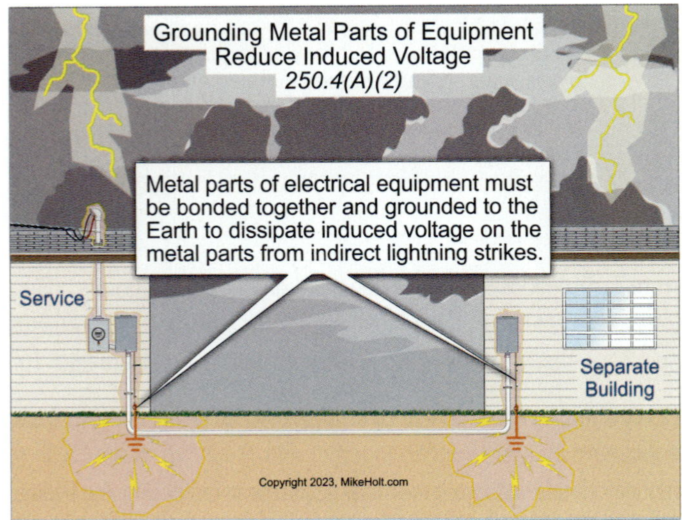

▶Figure 250–11

DANGER: Failure to ground metal parts to the Earth can result in millions of volts of induced voltage on the metal parts generated by an indirect lightning strike. This energy seeks a path to the Earth within the building—possibly resulting in a fire and/or electric shock from a side flash. ▶Figure 250–12

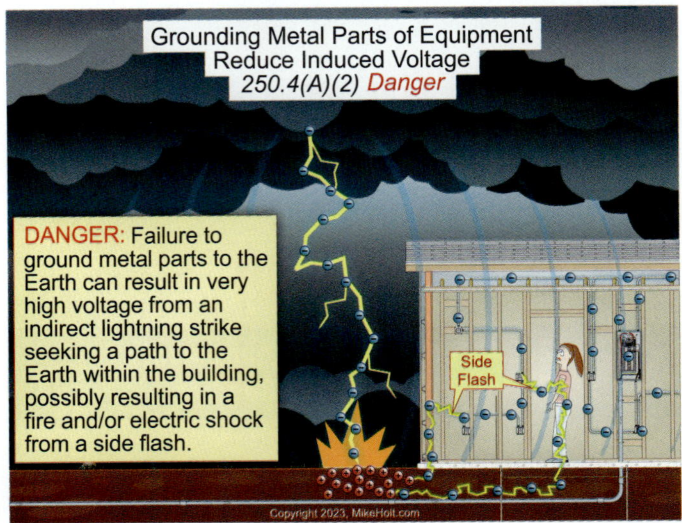

▶Figure 250–12

(3) Bonding Metal Parts of Equipment to Establish an Effective Ground-Fault Current Path. Metal parts of raceways, cables, and enclosures must be bonded together and to the source to establish an effective ground-fault current path. ▶Figure 250–13

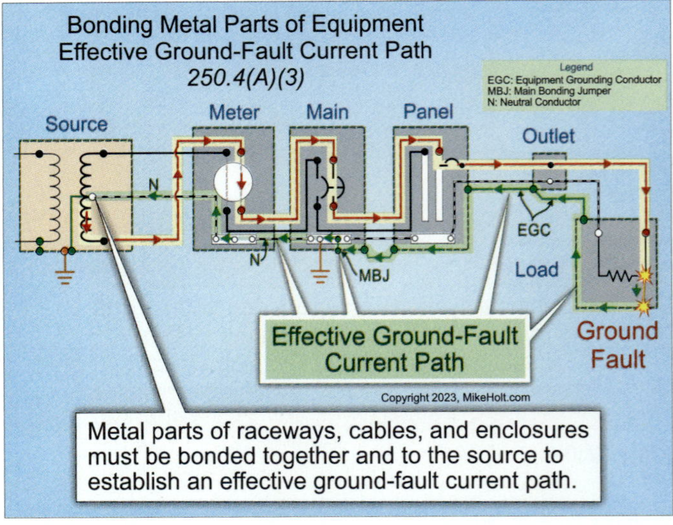

▶Figure 250–13

According to Article 100, "Effective Ground-Fault Current Path" is an intentionally constructed low-impedance conductive path designed to carry fault current from the point of a ground fault to the source for the purpose of opening the circuit overcurrent protective device. ▶Figure 250–14

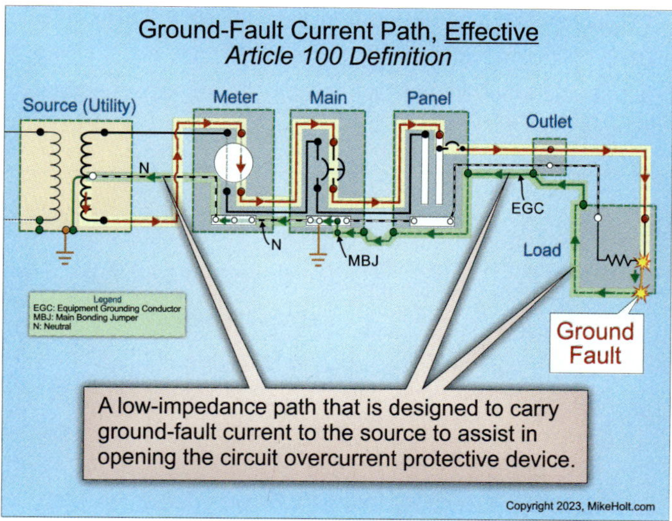

▶Figure 250–14

Author's Comment:

▶ The purpose of the effective ground-fault current path is to quickly remove dangerous voltage on metal parts from a ground fault. The effective ground-fault current path must have sufficiently low impedance to the source so fault current will quickly rise to a level that will open the circuit overcurrent protective device. ▶Figure 250–15

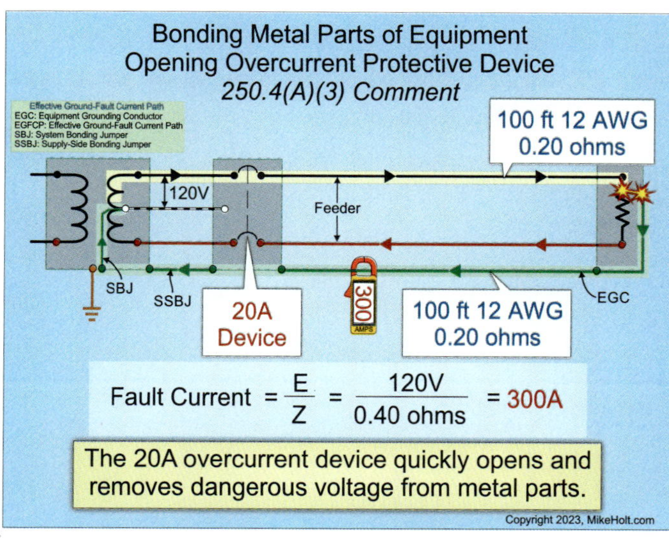

$$\text{Fault Current} = \frac{E}{Z} = \frac{120V}{0.40 \text{ ohms}} = 300A$$

▶Figure 250–15

▶ The time it takes for an overcurrent protective device to open is dependent on the magnitude of the fault current. A higher fault current value will result in a shorter clearing time for the overcurrent protective device. For example, a 20A overcurrent protective device with an overload of 40A (two times the 20A rating) takes 25 to 150 seconds to open. The same device at 100A (five times the 20A rating) trips in 5 to 20 seconds. ▶Figure 250–16

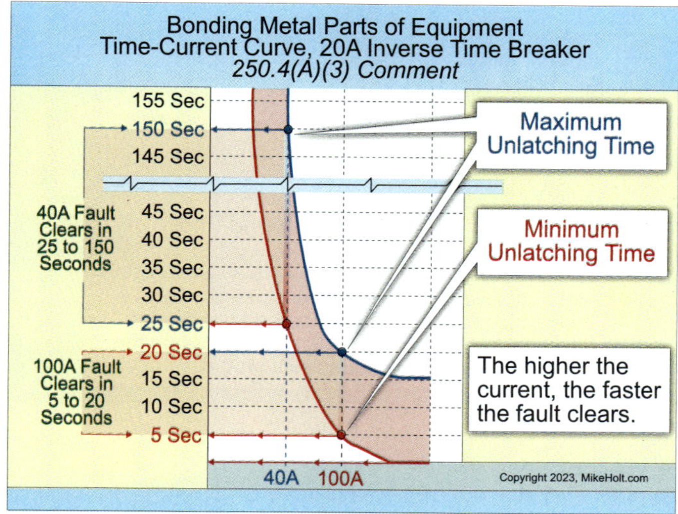

▶Figure 250–16

(4) Bonding Metal Piping and Structural Steel. Metal piping systems and exposed structural steel that is likely to become energized must be bonded to the source to facilitate opening of the circuit overcurrent protective device during a ground fault. ▶Figure 250–17

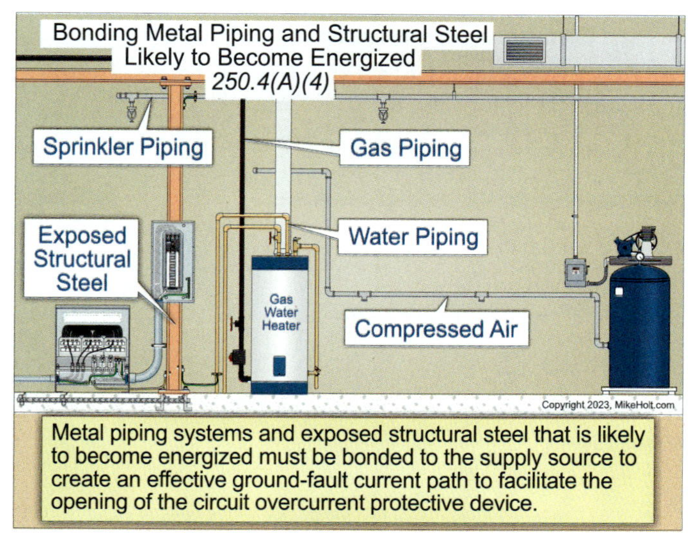

▶Figure 250–17

(5) Effective Ground-Fault Current Path.

Opening Overcurrent Protective Device. Metal raceways, cables, and enclosures must be bonded together and to the source to create an effective ground-fault current path to facilitate the opening of the circuit overcurrent protective device. ▶Figure 250–18

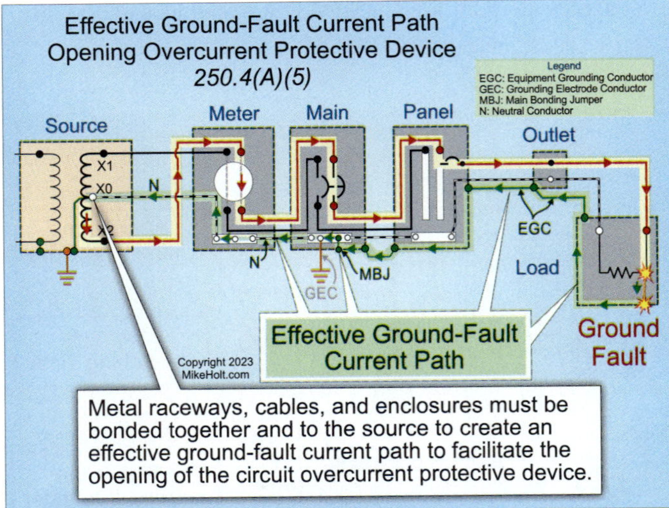

▶Figure 250–18

Earth Not Suitable. The Earth cannot not serve as an effective ground-fault current path because of the high contact resistance of the ground rod to the Earth. An equipment grounding conductor of a type recognized in 250.118 is required for all circuits. ▶Figure 250–19

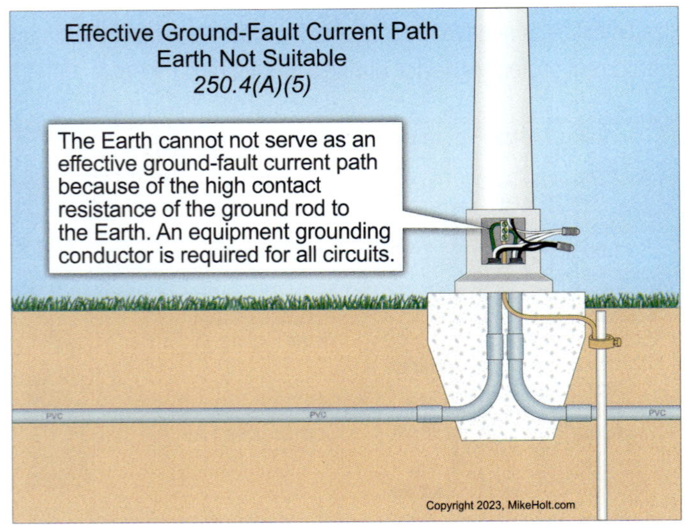

▶Figure 250–19

DANGER: Earth grounding does not remove dangerous touch voltage because the contact resistance of a grounding electrode (like a ground rod) to the Earth is so high, very little fault current returns to the source. As a result, the circuit overcurrent protective device will not open, and all metal parts associated with the electrical installation, metal piping, and structural building steel will become—and remain—energized. ▶Figure 250–20

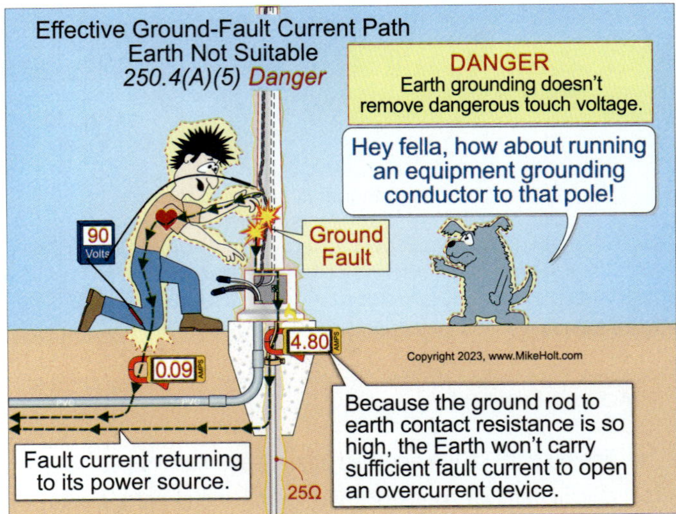

▶Figure 250–20

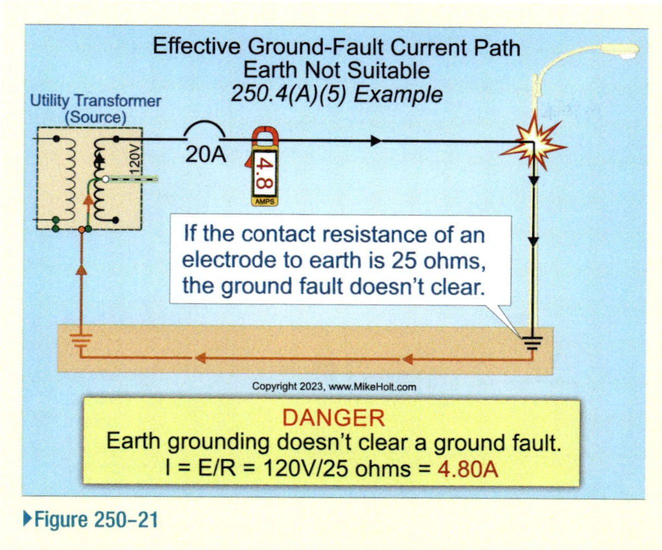

▶Figure 250–21

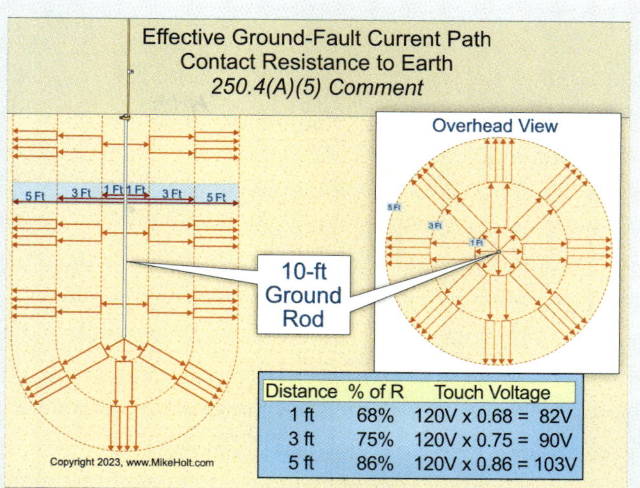

Distance	% of R	Touch Voltage
1 ft	68%	120V x 0.68 = 82V
3 ft	75%	120V x 0.75 = 90V
5 ft	86%	120V x 0.86 = 103V

▶Figure 250–22

Earth Shells

According to ANSI/IEEE 142, *Recommended Practice for Grounding of Industrial and Commercial Power Systems* (Green Book) [4.1.1], the resistance of the soil outward from a 10-ft ground rod is equal to the sum of the series resistances of the Earth shells. The shell nearest the ground rod has the highest resistance, and each shell further out has progressively larger areas and lower resistances. Do not be concerned if you do not understand this statement, just review the table below.

Distance from Rod	Soil Contact Resistance
1 ft (Shell 1)	68% of total contact resistance
3 ft (Shells 1 and 2)	75% of total contact resistance
5 ft (Shells 1, 2, and 3)	86% of total contact resistance

Contact Resistance. The Earth is an excellent conductor due to an almost limitless number of parallel paths over which electrons can flow. However, the problem lies in the contact resistance between the grounding electrode and the Earth. The surface area of the electrode contacting the Earth is minimal compared to the Earth itself.

Since voltage is directly proportional to resistance (Ohm's Law), the voltage gradient of the Earth around an energized rod (assuming a 120V ground fault) will be as follows: ▶Figure 250–22 and ▶Figure 250–23

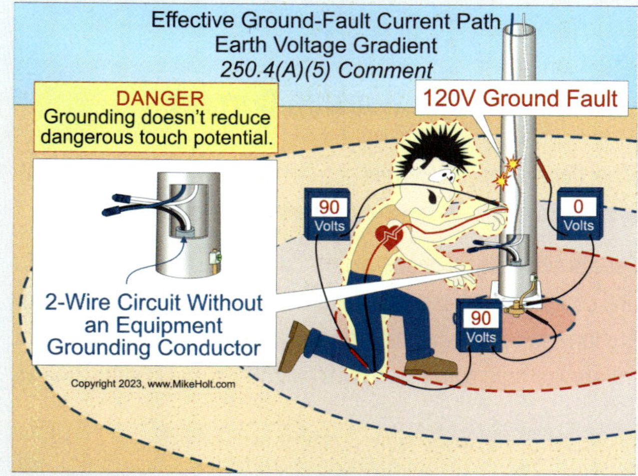

▶Figure 250–23

Distance from Rod	Soil Contact Resistance	Voltage Gradient
1 ft (Shell 1)	68%	82V
3 ft (Shells 1 and 2)	75%	90V
5 ft (Shells 1, 2, and 3)	86%	103V

250.6 Objectionable Current

(A) Arranged to Prevent Objectionable Current. Electrical systems and equipment must be installed in a manner that prevents objectionable current from flowing on metal parts. ▶Figure 250–24

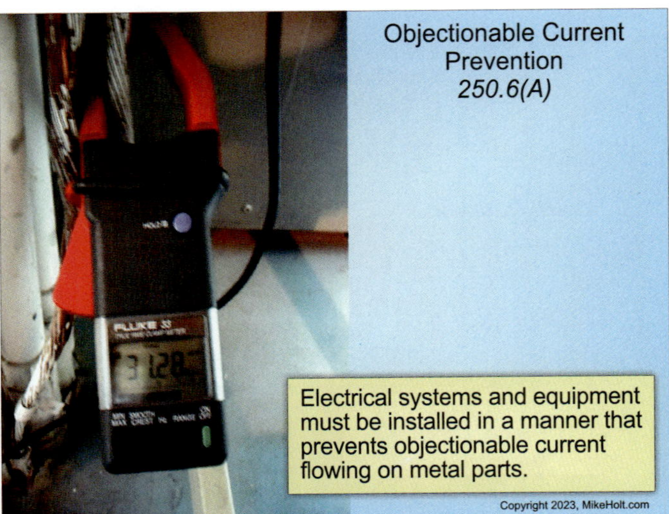

▶Figure 250–24

Objectionable Current

Objectionable neutral current occurs because of improper neutral-to-case connections or wiring errors that violate 250.24(B).

Panelboards. Objectionable neutral current will flow on metal parts and equipment grounding conductor when the neutral conductor is connected to the metal case of a panelboard on the load side of the service equipment in violation of 250.24(B). ▶Figure 250–25

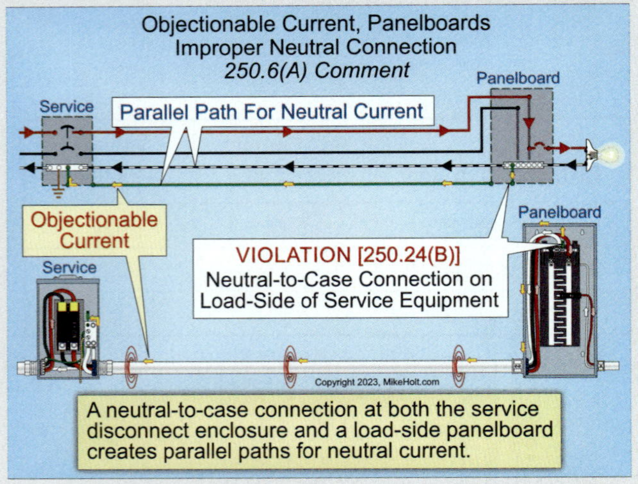

▶Figure 250–25

Transformers. Objectionable neutral current will flow on metal parts if the neutral conductor is connected to the circuit equipment grounding conductor at both the transformer and any other location on the load side of the system bonding jumper in violation of 250.30(A)(1). ▶Figure 250–26

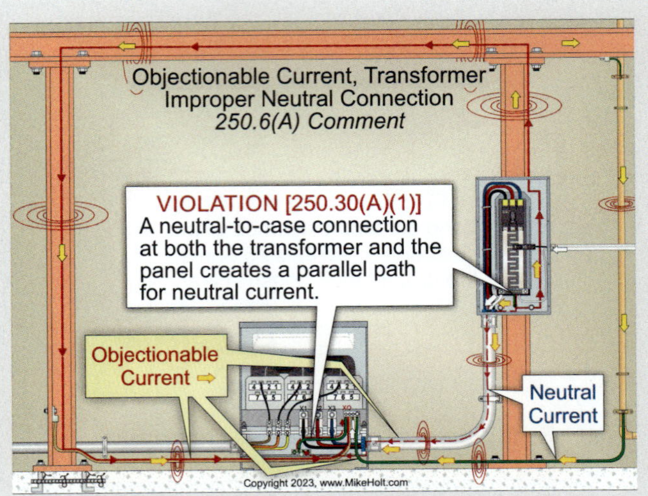

▶Figure 250–26

Generators. Objectionable neutral current will flow on metal parts and the equipment grounding conductor if a generator is connected to a transfer switch with a solidly connected neutral, and a neutral-to-case connection is made at the generator in violation of 250.30(A). ▶Figure 250–27

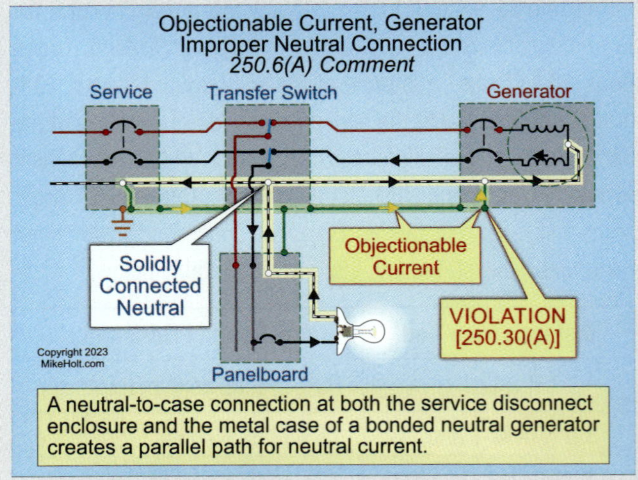

▶Figure 250–27

Disconnects. Objectionable neutral current will flow on metal parts and the equipment grounding conductor if the neutral conductor is connected to the metal case of a remote building disconnect that is not part of the service disconnect in violation of 250.32(B)(1). ▶Figure 250–28

Wiring Errors. Objectionable neutral current will flow on metal parts and equipment grounding conductors if the neutral conductor from one system is used as the neutral conductor for a different system. ▶Figure 250–29

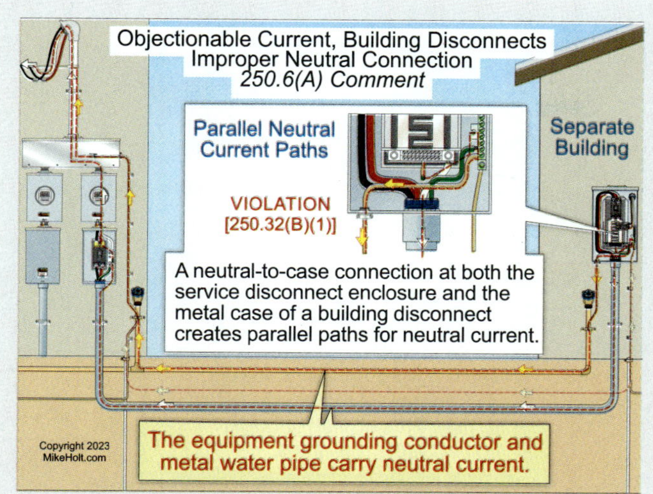

▶Figure 250–28

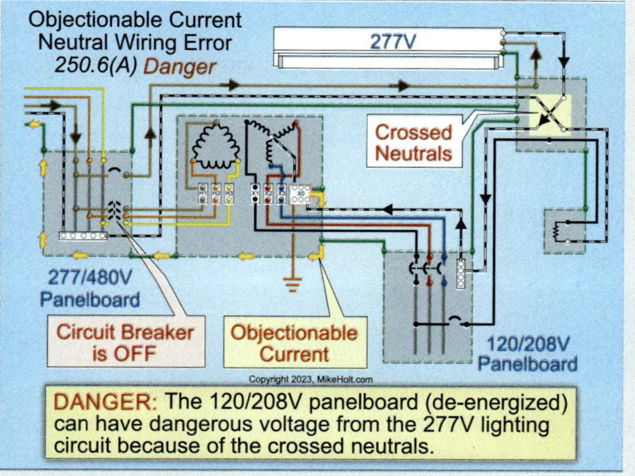

▶Figure 250–29

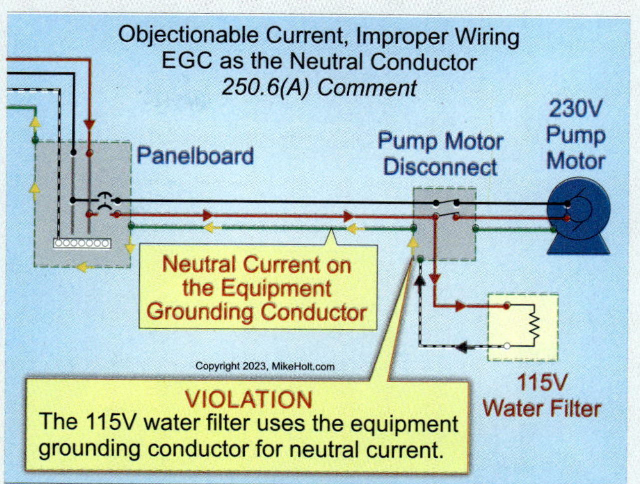

▶Figure 250–30

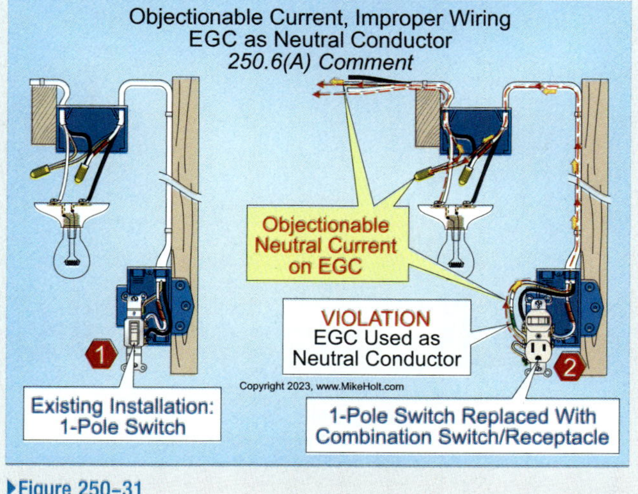

▶Figure 250–31

Improper Wiring. Objectionable neutral current will flow on the equipment grounding conductor if the circuit equipment grounding conductor is used as a neutral conductor, such as where:

▶ A 230V time-clock motor is replaced with a 115V time-clock motor, and the circuit equipment grounding conductor is used for neutral return current.

▶ A 115V water filter is wired to a 240V well-pump motor circuit, and the circuit equipment grounding conductor is used for neutral return current. ▶Figure 250–30

▶ The circuit equipment grounding conductor is used for neutral return current. ▶Figure 250–31

Dangers of Objectionable Current

Objectionable neutral current on metal parts can cause electric shock, fires, and the improper operation of electronic equipment and overcurrent protective devices such as GFPEs, GFCIs, SPGFCIs, and AFCIs.

Shock Hazard. When objectionable neutral current flows on metal parts or the equipment grounding conductor, electric shock—and even death—can occur from the elevated voltage. ▶Figure 250–32 and ▶Figure 250–33

•••

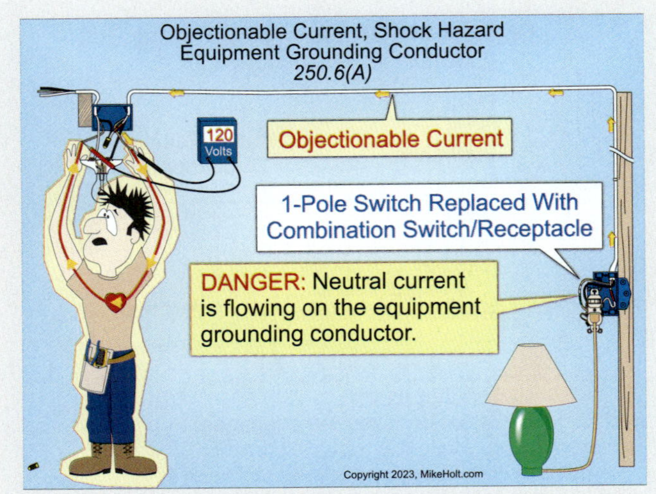

▶Figure 250–32

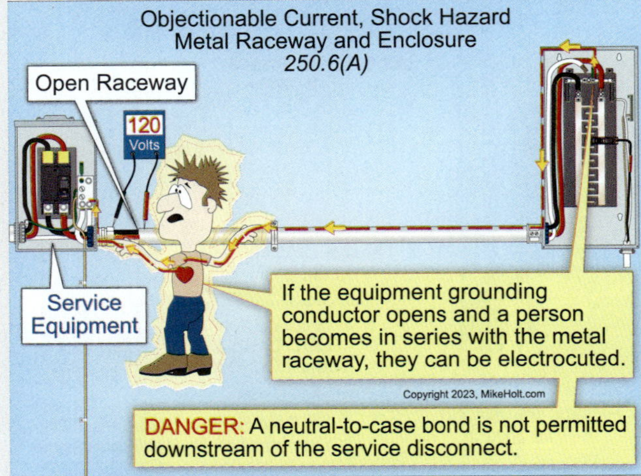

▶Figure 250–33

Fire Hazard. When objectionable neutral current flows on metal parts, a fire can ignite adjacent combustible material. Heat is generated whenever current flows, particularly over high-resistance parts. In addition, arcing at loose connections is especially dangerous in areas containing easily ignitible and explosive gases, vapors, or dust. ▶Figure 250–34

Operation of Overcurrent Protective Devices. When objectionable neutral current travels on metal parts, electronic overcurrent protective devices equipped with ground-fault protection can trip because some neutral current flows on the circuit equipment grounding conductor—instead of on the neutral conductor.

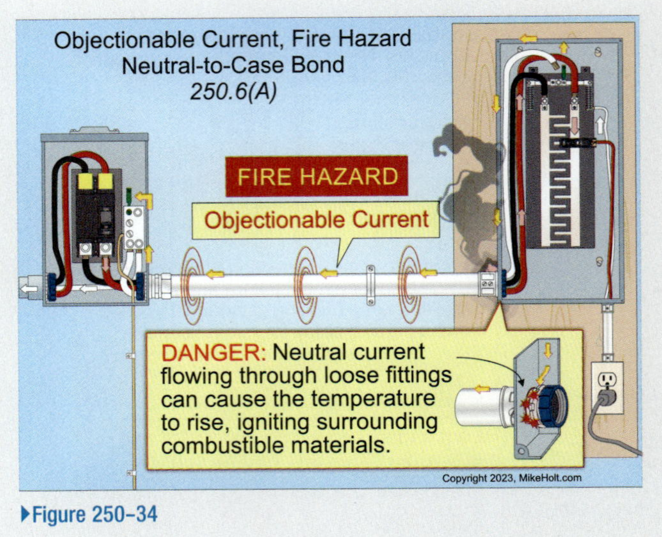

▶Figure 250–34

(C) Currents Not Classified as Objectionable Currents. Currents resulting from abnormal conditions such as ground faults and currents resulting from required grounding and bonding connections, are not classified as objectionable current for the purposes specified in 250.6(A) and (B).

250.8 Connection of Grounding and Bonding Conductors

(A) Permitted Methods. Equipment grounding conductors, grounding electrode conductors, and bonding jumpers must be connected by one or more of the following methods:

(1) Listed pressure connectors ▶Figure 250–35

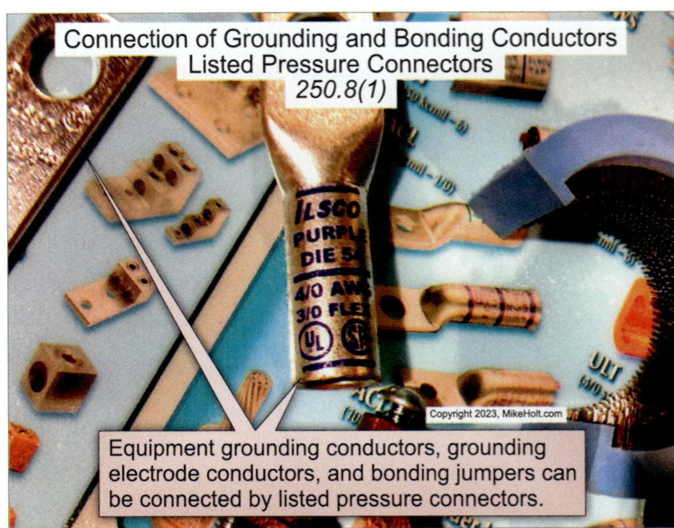

▶Figure 250–35

(2) Terminal bars

(3) Pressure connectors listed for grounding and bonding

(4) Exothermic welding

(5) Machine screws that engage at least two threads or are secured with a nut

(6) Thread-forming machine screws that engage at least two threads in the enclosure

(7) Connections that are part of a listed assembly

(8) Other listed means

Author's Comment:

▶ The requirements contained in 250.8 only apply to the termination of conductors—not the termination of grounding and bonding terminals.

According to Article 100, "Listed" means equipment or materials included in a list published by a recognized testing laboratory acceptable to the authority having jurisdiction.

250.10 Protection of Ground Clamps and Fittings

Ground clamps and fittings subject to physical damage must be protected. ▶Figure 250–36

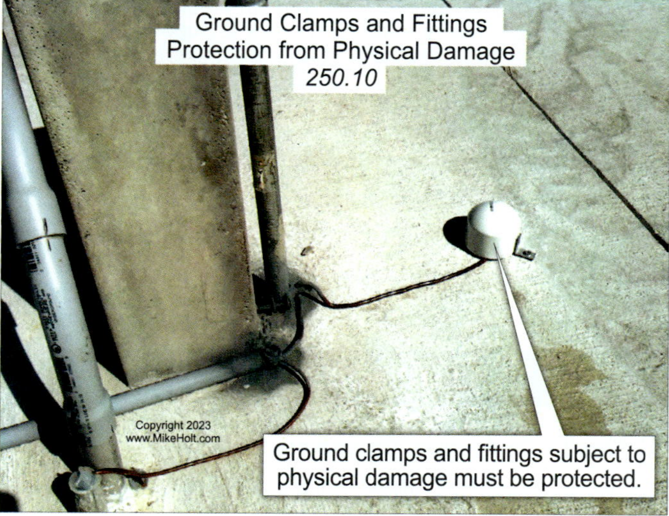

▶Figure 250–36

250.12 Clean Surfaces

Nonconductive coatings (such as paint) on equipment to be bonded or grounded must be removed to ensure electrical continuity, or the termination fittings must be designed to make such removal unnecessary.

Author's Comment:

▶ Fittings such as locknuts are designed to cut through nonconductive coatings and establish the intended electrical continuity when they are properly tightened.

▶ The tarnish on copper water pipe need not be removed before making a termination because copper-oxide does not interfere with the copper conductor conductivity.

Part II. System Grounding and Bonding

250.20 Systems Required to be Grounded

(A) Systems Below 50V. The secondary of a transformer operating below 50V is not required to be bonded or grounded unless the transformer's primary supply is from: ▶Figure 250–37

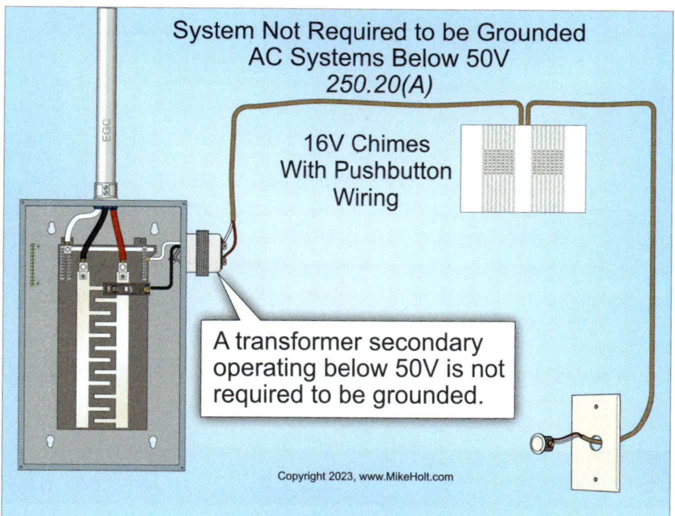

▶Figure 250–37

(1) A 277V or 480V system

(2) An ungrounded system

(B) Systems 50V to 1000V. The following systems must be grounded if the neutral conductor is used as a circuit conductor:

(1) Single-phase systems ▶Figure 250–38

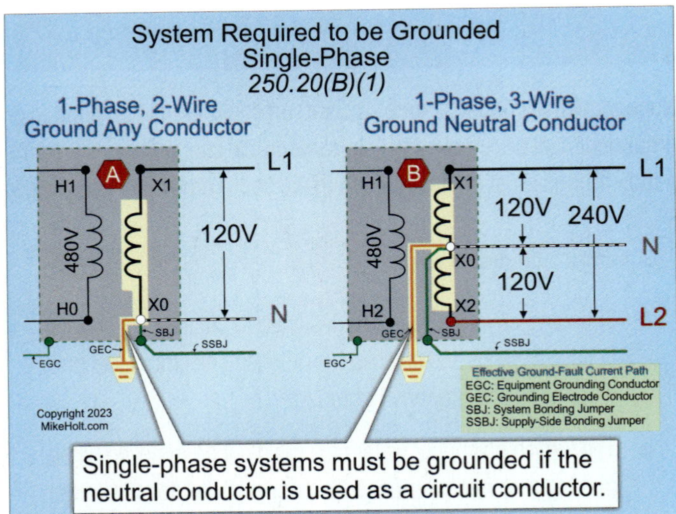

▶Figure 250–38

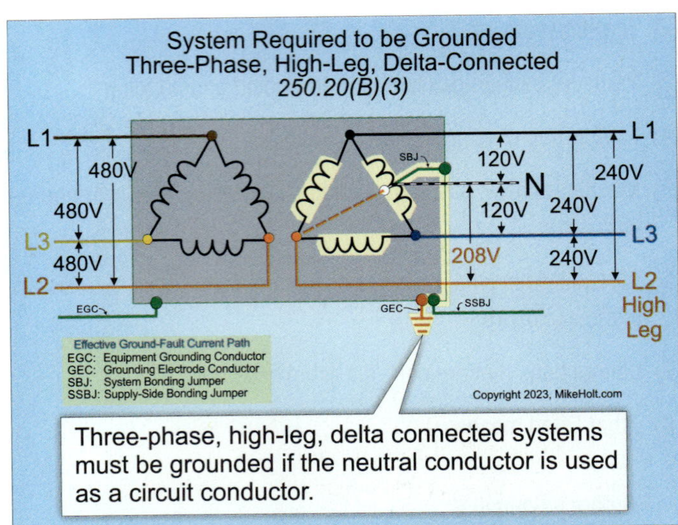

▶Figure 250–40

(2) Three-phase, wye-connected systems ▶Figure 250–39

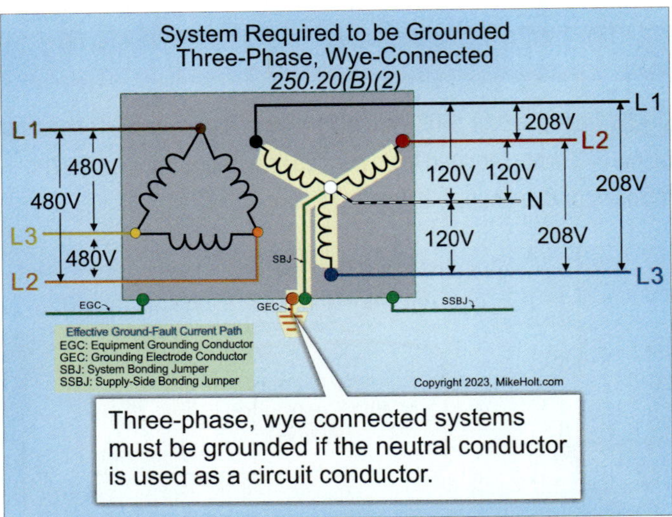

▶Figure 250–39

(3) Three-phase, high-leg delta-connected systems ▶Figure 250–40

250.21 Ungrounded Systems

(B) Ground Detectors. Ungrounded systems from 50V to 1000V or less are not required to be grounded if:

(1) The ungrounded systems operating between 120V and 1000V as permitted in 250.21(A) must have a secondary ground detector sensing equipment.

(2) The secondary ground detection sensing equipment must be connected as close as practicable to where the system receives its supply. ▶Figure 250–41

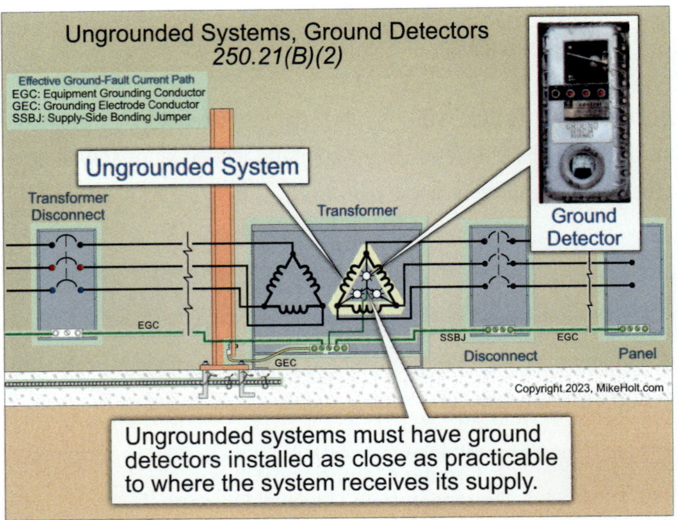

▶Figure 250–41

(C) Marking. Ungrounded systems must be legibly marked "CAUTION UNGROUNDED SYSTEM OPERATING — _____ VOLTS BETWEEN CONDUCTORS" with sufficient durability to withstand the environment involved at the source or first disconnect of the system.

250.24 Service Grounding

(A) Service Equipment, Grounding. A premises wiring system supplied by a grounded service must have a grounding electrode conductor connected to the service neutral conductor in accordance with the following:

(1) General. The grounding electrode conductor connection to the neutral conductor at service equipment must be made at any accessible point from the load end of the overhead service conductors, service drop, underground service conductors, or service lateral to the terminal or bus to which the service neutral conductor is connected at the service disconnect. ▶Figure 250–42

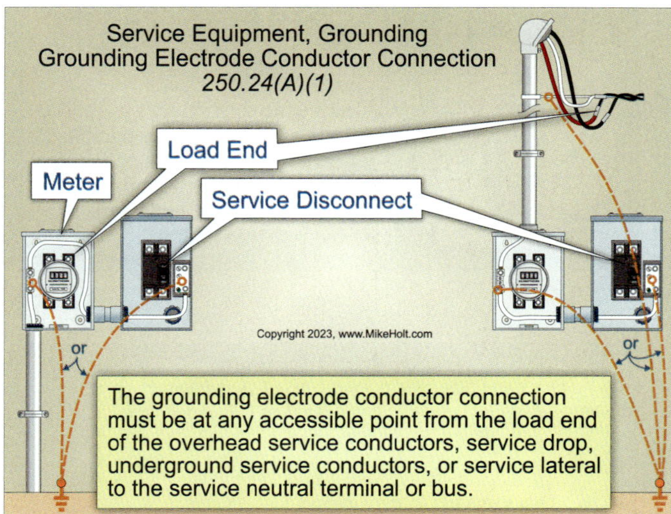

▶Figure 250–42

Author's Comment:

▶ Some inspectors require the grounding electrode conductor connection to the service neutral conductor to be made at the meter socket enclosure, while others insist the connection be made only within the service disconnect. Grounding at either location complies with this rule, but be sure you know the local utility company's policy on connections inside the meter socket.

(4) Service Equipment, Main Bonding Jumper. If the main bonding jumper specified in 250.28 is a wire or busbar, the grounding electrode conductor is permitted to terminate to the equipment grounding terminal, bar, or bus to which the main bonding jumper is connected, instead of the neutral terminal.

(B) Load-Side Bonding Connections. A neutral conductor cannot be connected to metal parts of equipment or the equipment grounding conductor(s) on the load side of the service disconnect. ▶Figure 250–43

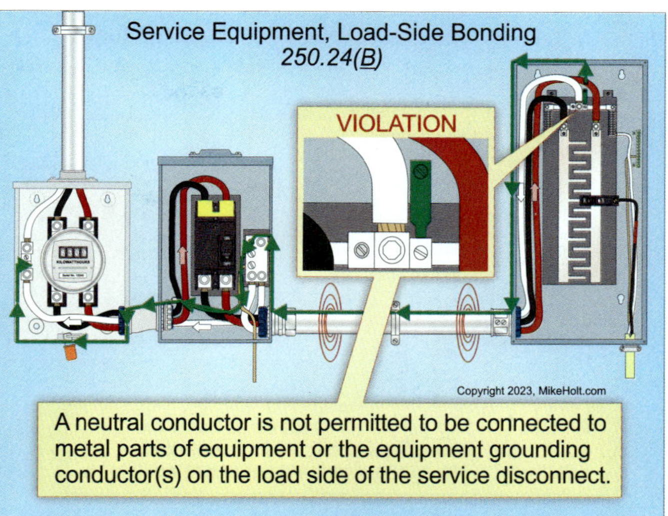

▶Figure 250–43

Author's Comment:

▶ If a neutral-to-case connection is made on the load side of the service disconnect, objectionable neutral current will flow on conductive metal parts of electrical equipment [250.6(A)]. Objectionable neutral current on metal parts of electrical equipment can be extremely dangerous. It does not take much current to cause electric shock or death (from ventricular fibrillation), as well as a fire. ▶Figure 250–44

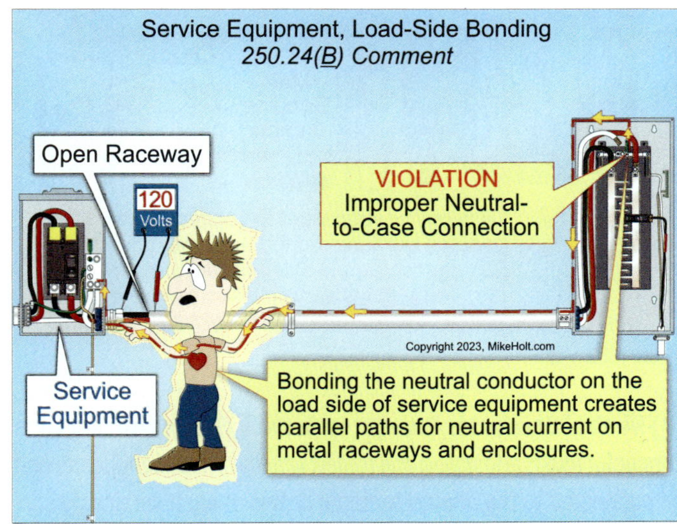

▶Figure 250–44

(C) Main Bonding Jumper. A main bonding jumper is required to bond the equipment grounding conductor to the neutral conductor in each service disconnect enclosure in accordance with 250.28. ▶Figure 250–45

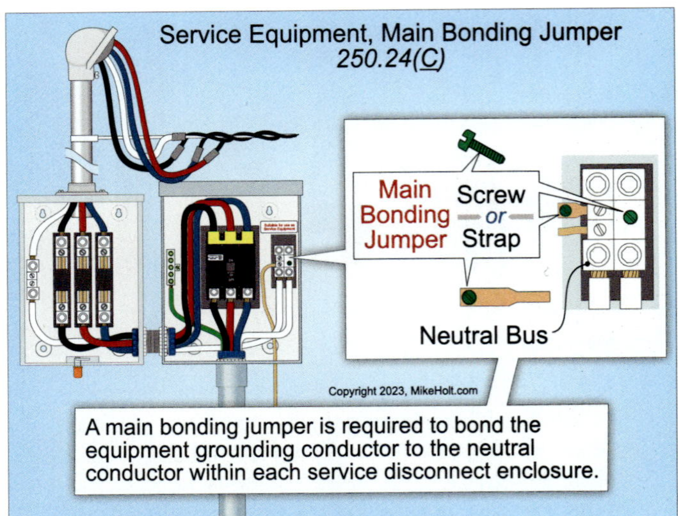

▶Figure 250–45

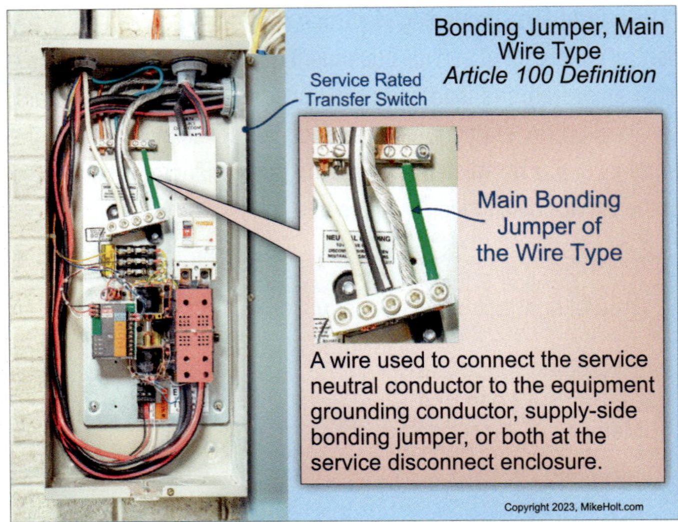

▶Figure 250–47

According to Article 100, "Main Bonding Jumper" is a wire, screw, or busbar used to connect the service neutral conductor to the equipment grounding conductor, supply-side bonding jumper (or both) at the service disconnect enclosure. ▶Figure 250–46 and ▶Figure 250–47

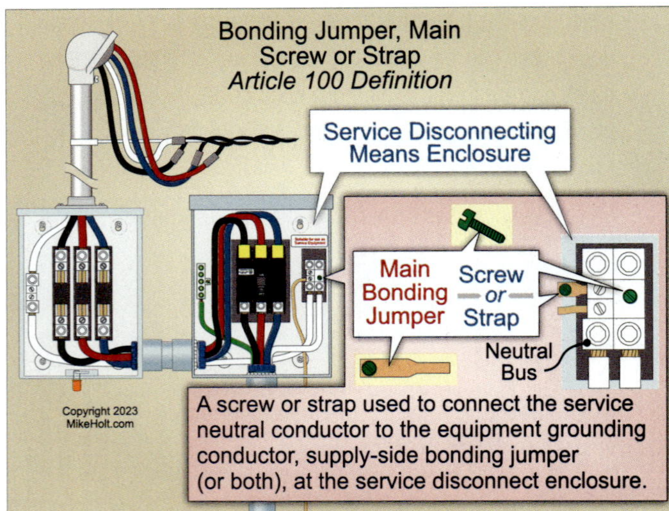

▶Figure 250–46

(D) Neutral Conductor Brought to Service Equipment. A neutral conductor must be installed and routed with the phase conductors and be connected to the neutral terminal or bus at each service disconnect enclosure. ▶Figure 250–48 and ▶Figure 250–49

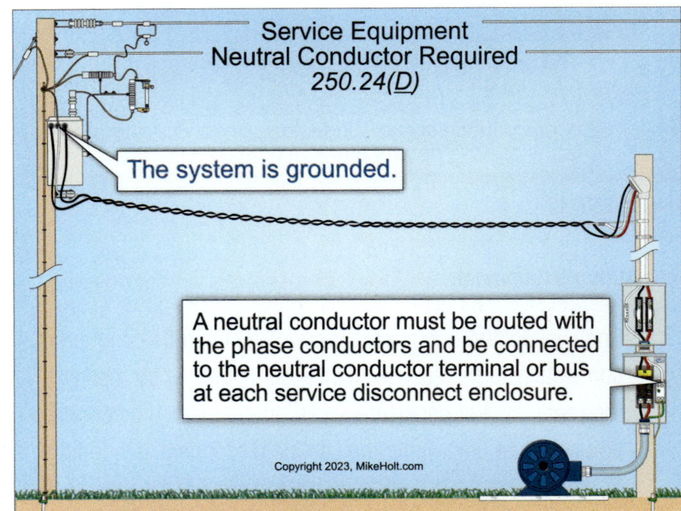

▶Figure 250–48

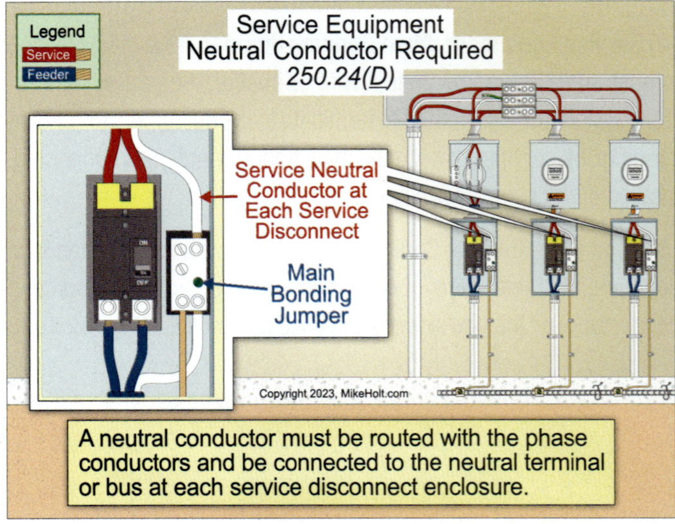

▶Figure 250–49

Author's Comment:

▸ A neutral conductor must be routed with the phase conductors and connected to the neutral conductor terminal or bus at each service disconnect enclosure, regardless of whether line-to-neutral loads are supplied.

▸ The service neutral conductor provides the effective ground-fault current path to the source to remove dangerous voltage from a ground fault by opening the circuit overcurrent protective device [250.4(A)(3) and 250.4(A)(5)]. ▸Figure 250–50

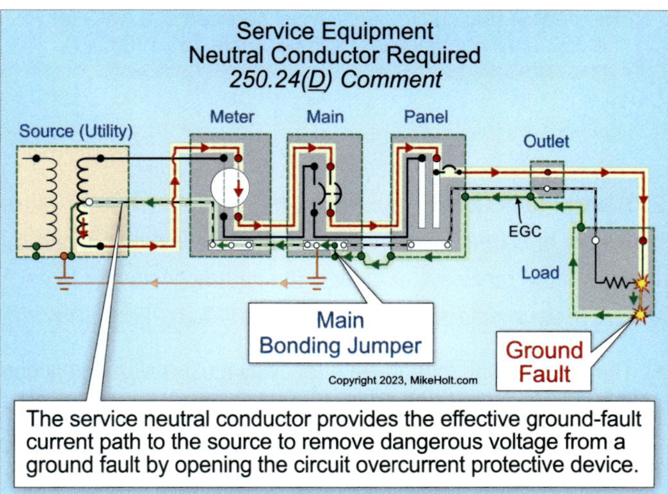

▸Figure 250–50

Author's Comment:

▸ The main bonding jumper is a vital component of bonding. It facilitates the operation of overcurrent protective devices and is a critical part of the grounding system since it bonds the neutral conductor, service enclosure, and the equipment grounding conductor to the grounding electrode system via the grounding electrode conductor.

Danger

DANGER: f the neutral conductor is opened, dangerous voltage may be present on metal parts under normal conditions, providing the potential for electric shock. If the Earth's ground resistance is 25Ω and the load's resistance is 25Ω, the voltage drop across each of these resistances will be half of the voltage source. Since the neutral is connected to the service disconnect, all metal parts will be elevated 60V above the Earth's voltage for a 120/240V system. ▸Figure 250–51

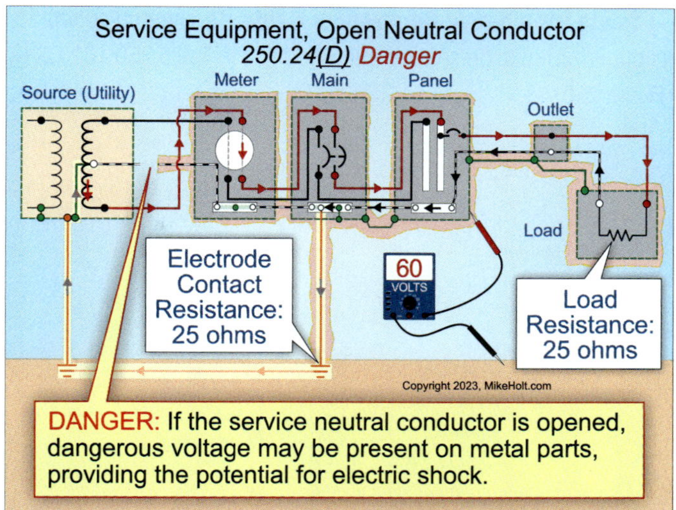

▸Figure 250–51

Danger

DANGER: Dangerous voltage from a ground fault will not be removed from metal parts, metal piping, and structural steel if the service-disconnect enclosure is not connected to the service neutral conductor. This is because the contact resistance of a grounding electrode to the Earth is so great that insufficient ground-fault current returns to the source if that is the only ground-fault current return path available to open the circuit overcurrent protective device. ▸Figure 250–52

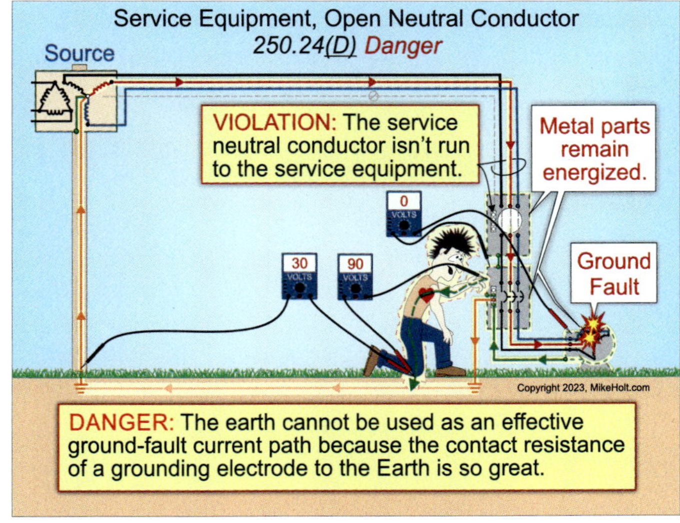

▸Figure 250–52

The neutral conductor(s) must be sized in accordance with 250.24(D)(1) and (2) as follows:

(1) Sizing for a Single Raceway or Cable. The neutral conductor is not permitted to be smaller than specified in Table 250.102(C)(1). ▶Figure 250–53

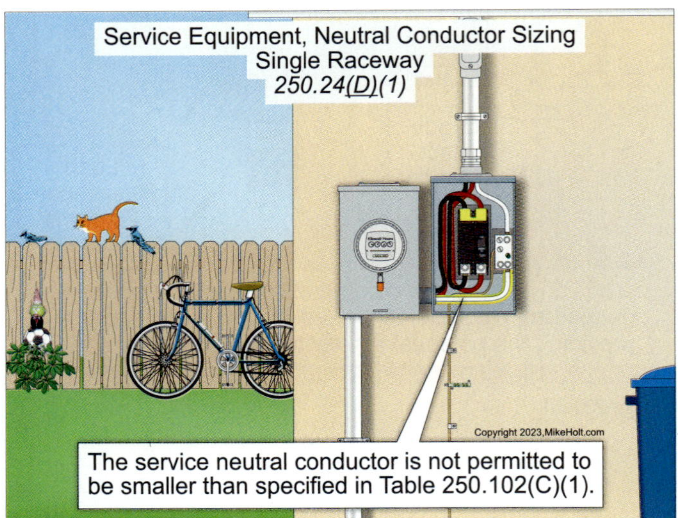

▶Figure 250–53

Author's Comment:

▶ In addition, the neutral conductor must have the capacity to carry the maximum unbalanced neutral current in accordance with 220.61.

▶ **Example**

Question: What is the minimum size copper service neutral conductor required when the service phase conductors are 4/0 AWG? ▶**Figure 250–54**

(a) 3 AWG   (b) 2 AWG   (c) 1 AWG   (d) 1/0 AWG

Solution:

2 AWG [Table 250.102(C)(1)]

Answer: *(b) 2 AWG*

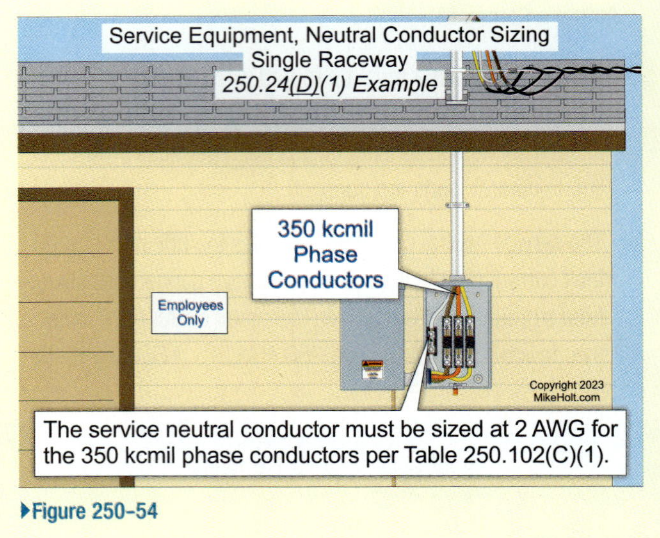

▶Figure 250–54

(2) Neutral Conductors Connected in Parallel in Two or More Raceways or Cables. If service conductors are installed in parallel in two or more raceways or cables, the neutral conductor in each raceway must be sized in accordance with 250.24(D)(2)(a) or (D)(2)(b).

(a) The neutral conductor in each raceway must be sized in accordance with Table 250.102(C)(1), based on the circular mil area of the largest phase conductor in each raceway, but not smaller than 1/0 AWG.

(b) The neutral conductors must be sized based on the sum of the circular mil areas of the largest phase conductors from each set connected in parallel in each raceway in accordance with Table 250.102(C)(2)(2).

Note: See 310.10(G) for neutral conductors connected in parallel.

(3) Delta-Connected Service. The grounded conductor of a three-phase, 3-wire delta service must have an ampacity of not less than that of the phase conductors.

(E) Grounding Electrode Conductor. The grounding electrode conductor at service equipment must be sized in accordance with 250.66. ▶Figure 250–55 and ▶Figure 250–56

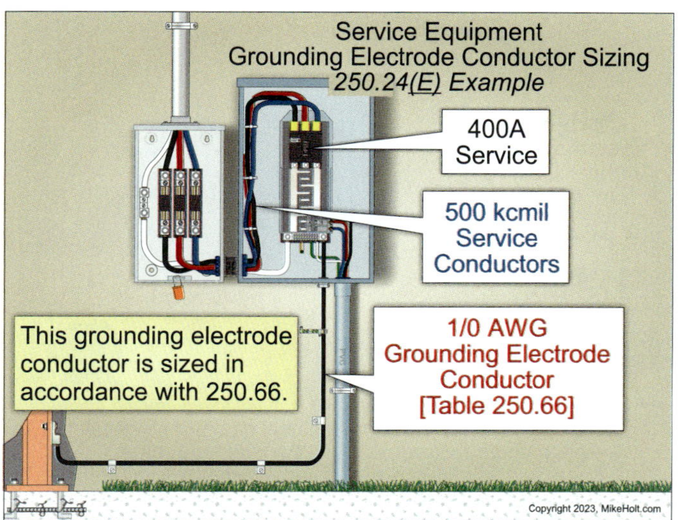

▶Figure 250–55

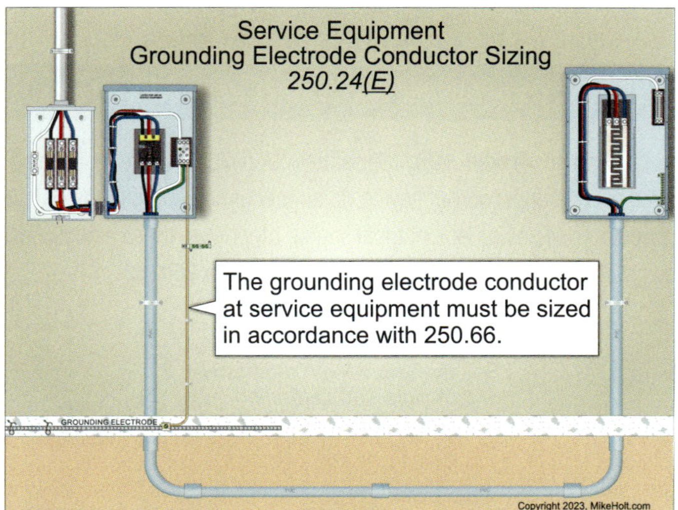

▶Figure 250–56

250.28 Main Bonding Jumper and System Bonding Jumper

Main and system bonding jumpers must be installed as follows:

(A) Material. The bonding jumper can be a wire, bus, or screw. ▶Figure 250–57

(B) Construction. If the bonding jumper is a screw, it must be identified with a green finish visible when the screw is installed.

(C) Attachment. Main and system bonding jumpers must terminate to a device by any one of the methods contained in 250.8(A).

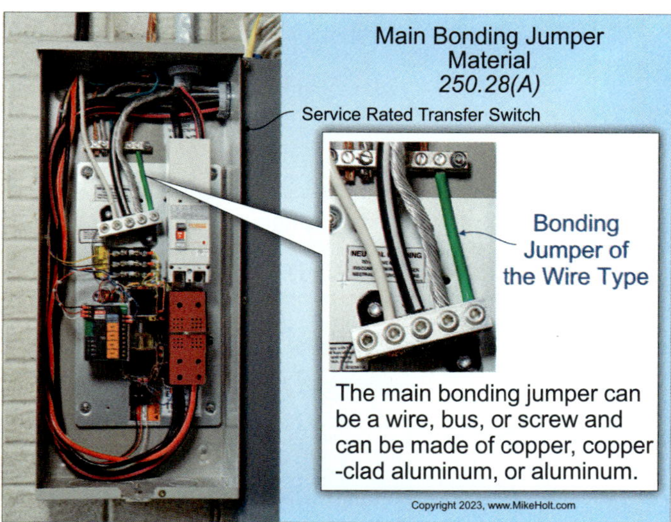

▶Figure 250–57

(D) Size.

(1) Main and system bonding jumpers of the wire type must not be sized smaller than specified in Table 250.102(C)(1). ▶Figure 250–58 and ▶Figure 250–59

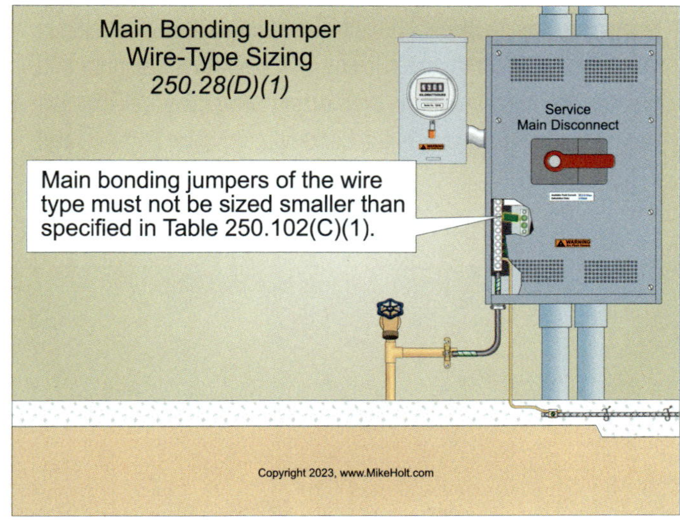

▶Figure 250–58

Author's Comment:

▶ The primary purpose of the main and system bonding jumpers is to create a path for fault current to flow from a fault to the source to open the circuit overcurrent protective device.

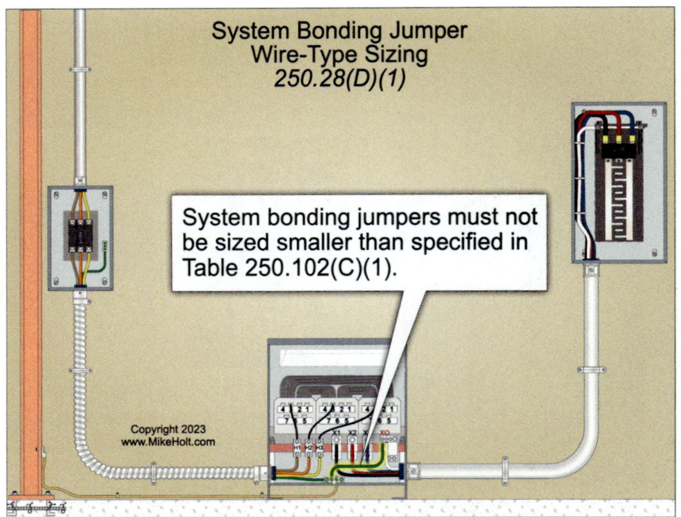

▶Figure 250–59

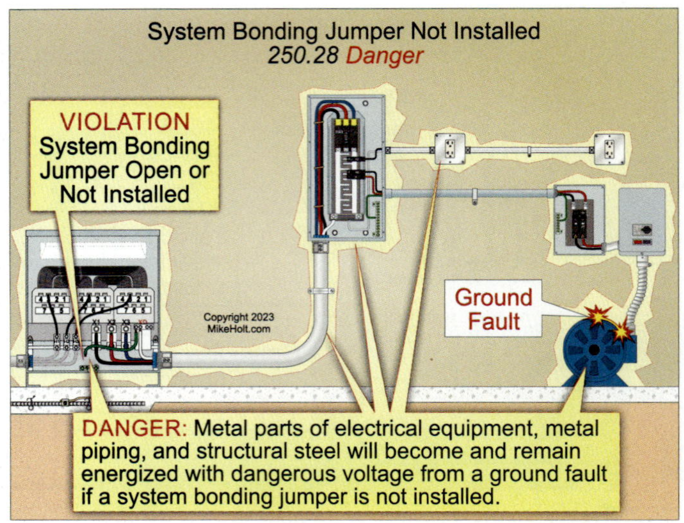

▶Figure 250–61

Danger

DANGER: Metal parts of electrical equipment, as well as metal piping and structural steel, will become and remain energized with dangerous voltage from a ground fault if a main bonding jumper or system bonding jumper is not installed. A missing main or system bonding jumper causes an opening in the effective ground-fault current path back to the source and creates a condition where overcurrent protective devices will not open during a ground-fault condition. ▶Figure 250–60 and ▶Figure 250–61

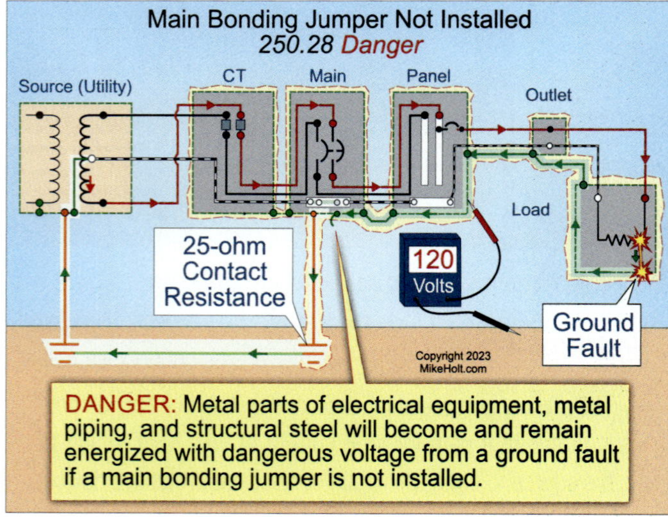

▶Figure 250–60

250.30 Transformer Separately Derived Systems

According to Article 100, "Separately Derived System" is an electrical power supply output having no direct connection(s) to the circuit conductors of any other electrical source other than those established by grounding and bonding connections. ▶Figure 250–62

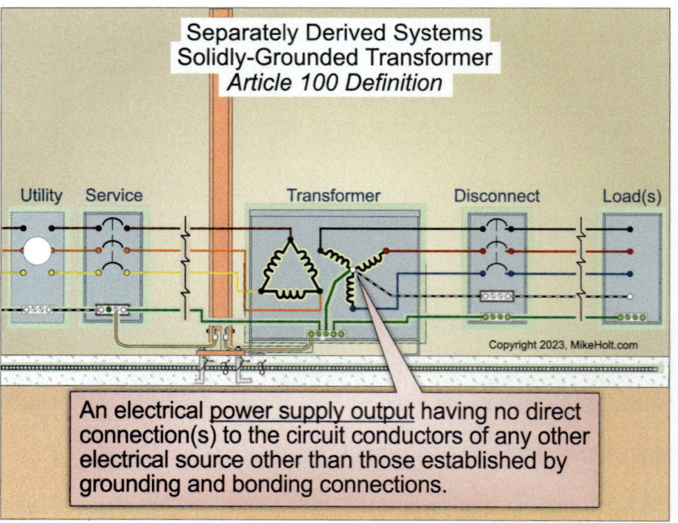

▶Figure 250–62

▶ Transformers, other than autotransformers, are separately derived because the primary conductors have no direct electrical connection from the circuit conductors of one system to the circuit conductors of another.

(A) Grounded Systems. Separately derived transformer systems must be bonded and grounded in accordance with 250.30(A)(1) through (A)(8). A neutral-to-case connection is not permitted to be made on the load side of the system bonding jumper.

A neutral conductor is not permitted to be connected to metal parts of equipment or equipment grounding conductors on the load side of the system bonding jumper.

(1) System Bonding Jumper. A system bonding jumper must be installed at the secondary neutral point or the secondary disconnect neutral terminal, but not both. The system bonding jumper must comply with 250.28 and sized in accordance with 250.102(C). ▶Figure 250–63

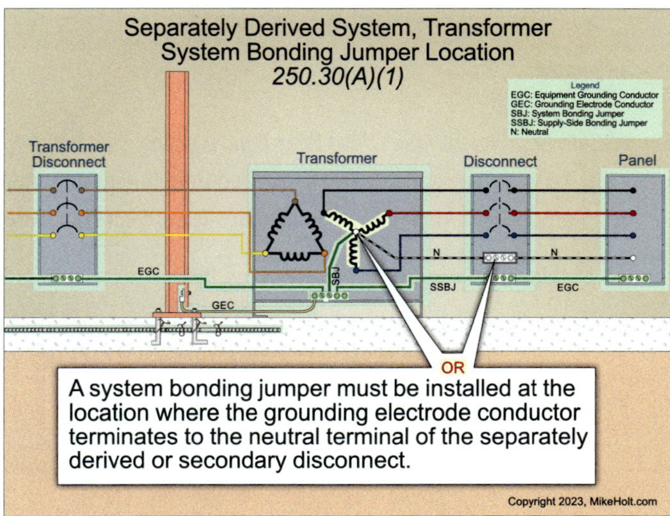

▶Figure 250–63

Author's Comment:

▶ Section 250.30(A)(5) requires the termination of a grounding electrode conductor to the same point where the system bonding jumper has been installed.

According to Article 100, "System Bonding Jumper" is the connection between the neutral conductor or grounded-phase conductor and the equipment grounding conductor, supply-side bonding jumper, or both at a transformer separately derived system. ▶Figure 250–64

Ex 2: If a building or structure is supplied by a feeder from an outdoor transformer separately derived system, a system bonding jumper at both the source and the first disconnect is permitted if doing so does not establish a parallel path for the neutral current. The neutral conductor is not permitted to be smaller than the size specified for the system bonding jumper, and it is not required to be larger than the phase conductor(s).

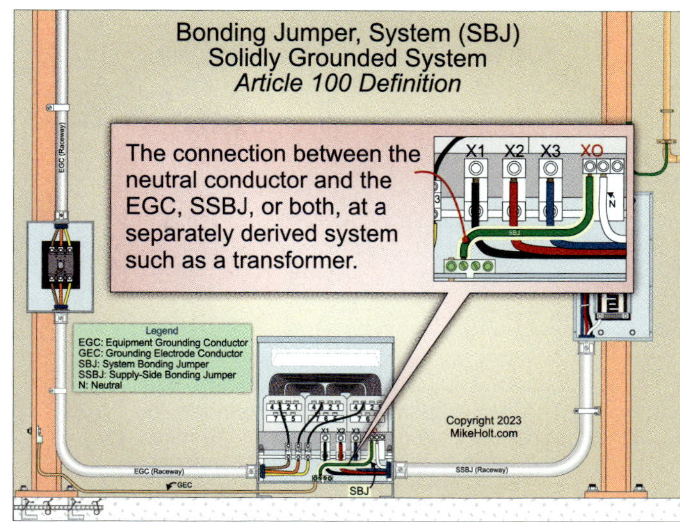

▶Figure 250–64

(a) System Bonding Jumper at Source. The system bonding jumper connects the secondary neutral point of the system to the metal enclosure of the transformer separately derived system. ▶Figure 250–65

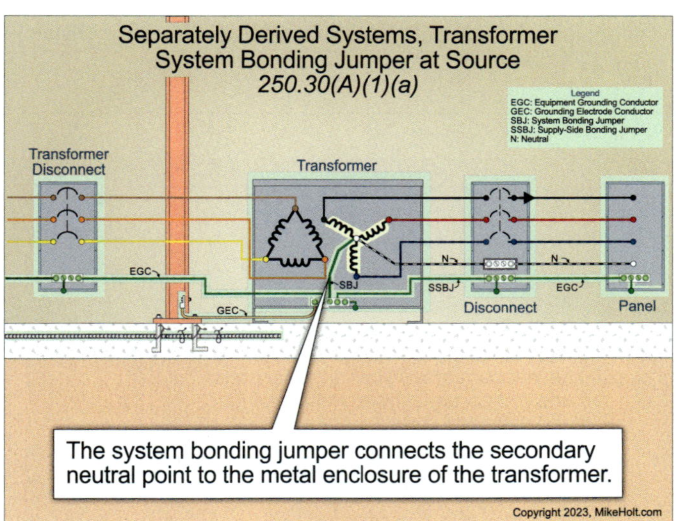

▶Figure 250–65

(b) System Bonding Jumper at First Disconnecting Means. The system bonding jumper connects the neutral conductor of the transformer secondary to the metal enclosure at the secondary disconnect. ▶Figure 250–66

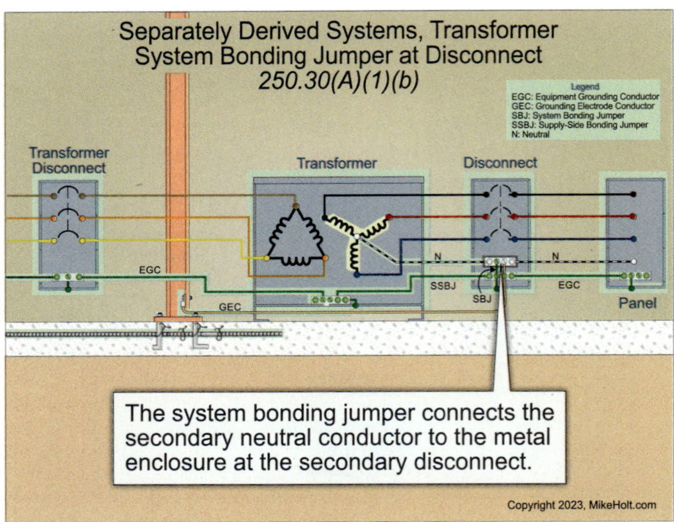

▶Figure 250–66

Caution

CAUTION: Dangerous objectionable neutral current will flow on conductive metal parts of electrical equipment, metal piping, and structural steel in violation of 250.6(A). ▶Figure 250–67

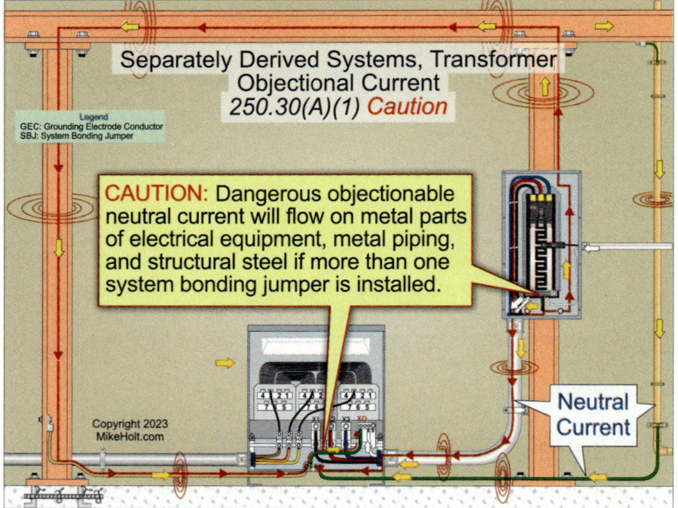

▶Figure 250–67

(2) Supply-Side Bonding Jumper to Disconnect.

Nonflexible Metal Raceway. A nonflexible metal raceway can be used as a supply-side bonding jumper if installed from the transformer enclosure to the secondary disconnect enclosure. ▶Figure 250–68

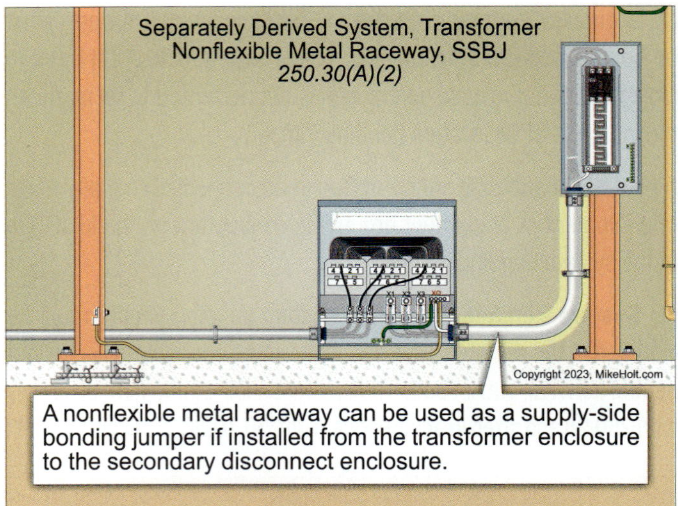

▶Figure 250–68

Supply-Side Bonding Jumper of the Wire-Type. A supply-side bonding jumper of the wire-type can be used if installed from the transformer enclosure grounding terminal to the secondary disconnect enclosure grounding terminal. ▶Figure 250–69

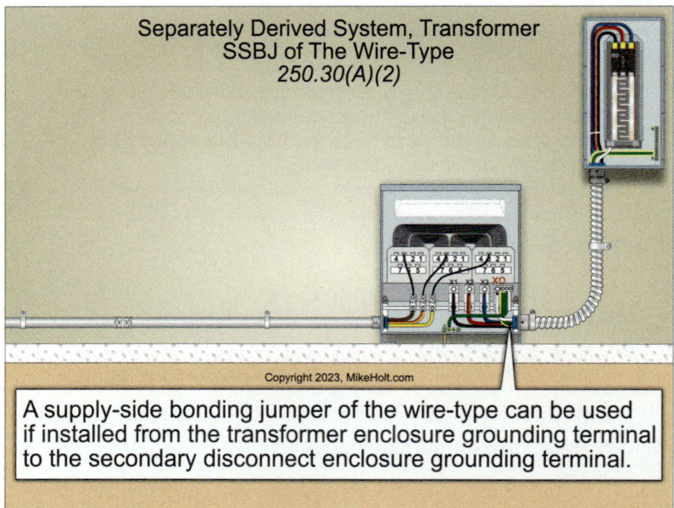

▶Figure 250–69

Author's Comment:

▶ The supply-side bonding jumper can be RMC, IMC, or EMT run between the transformer separately derived system enclosure and the secondary system disconnect enclosure. A nonmetallic or flexible raceway must have a supply-side bonding jumper of the wire type.

---

(1) A supply-side bonding jumper of the wire type must be sized in accordance with 250.102(C) based on the size or area of the secondary phase conductors in the raceway or cable.

▶ Example 1

Question: What size supply-side bonding jumper is required for flexible metal conduit containing 300 kcmil transformer secondary conductors?
▶Figure 250–70

(a) 4 AWG   (b) 2 AWG   (c) 1/0 AWG   (d) 3/0 AWG

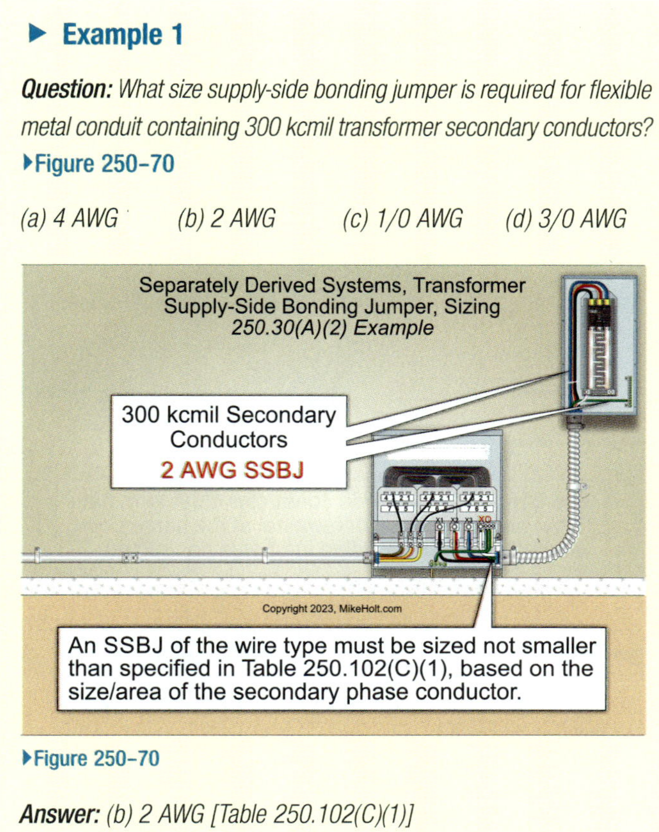

▶Figure 250–70

Answer: (b) 2 AWG [Table 250.102(C)(1)]

(3) Neutral Conductor Size. The neutral conductor between the transformer separately derived system and the secondary system disconnect is not required to be larger than the phase conductors. If the system bonding jumper is installed at the secondary system disconnect, instead of at the transformer separately derived system, the following apply:

(a) Single Raceway. A secondary neutral conductor must be run from the transformer separately derived system to the secondary system disconnect, and the secondary neutral conductor must be sized in accordance with Table 250.102(C)(1) based on the size or area of the secondary phase conductor.

▶ Example 2

Question: What size neutral conductor is required for a 75 kVA transformer with 250 kcmil secondary conductors? ▶Figure 250–71

(a) 2 AWG   (b) 1/0 AWG   (c) 4/0 AWG   (d) 250 kcmil

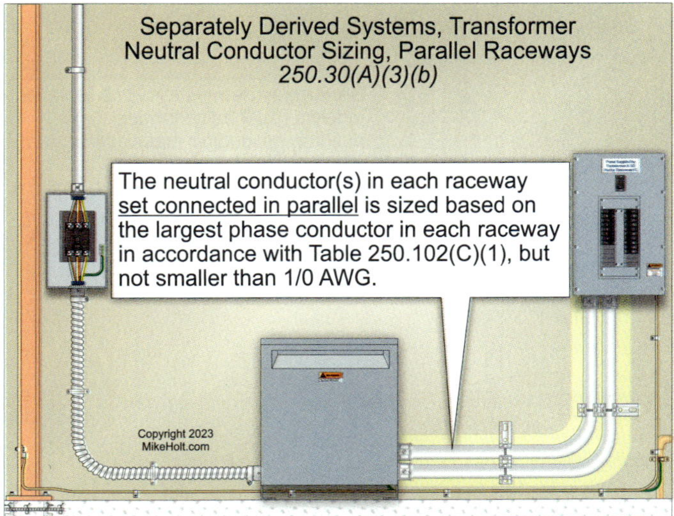

▶Figure 250–71

Answer: (a) 2 AWG [Table 250.102(C)(1)]

(b) Paralleled in Two or More Raceways or Cables. The neutral conductor(s) in each raceway or cable set connected in parallel is sized based on the largest phase conductor in each raceway or cable in accordance with Table 250.102(C)(1), but not smaller than 1/0 AWG.
▶Figure 250–72

▶Figure 250–72

> ### ▶ Example 3
>
> **Question:** *The minimum secondary neutral conductor size for a 112.50 kVA transformer is _____ if the secondary paralleled phase conductors are 3/0 AWG kcmil.*
>
> *(a) 4 AWG in each raceway*　*(b) 2 AWG in each raceway*
> *(c) 1/0 AWG in each raceway*　*(d) 3/0 AWG in each raceway*
>
> **Solution:**
>
> **Step 1:** *Determine the equivalent area for two 3/0 AWG conductors from Chapter 9, Table 8:*
>
> *3/0 AWG = 167,800 circular mils*
>
> *2 conductors × 167,800 cmil = 335,600 cmil [Table 250.102(C)(1)]*
>
> **Step 2:** *Size the neutral conductor in each raceway to Table 250.102(C)(1) based on 3/0 AWG phase conductors per raceway: 2 AWG.*
>
> **Step 3:** *The minimum parallel conductor is 1/0 in accordance with 310.10(G): 1/0 AWG.*
>
> **Answer:** *(c) 1/0 AWG in each raceway*

(4) Grounding Electrode. Separately derived transformer system installed indoors must be grounded to the building grounding electrode system in accordance with 250.30(C). ▶Figure 250–73

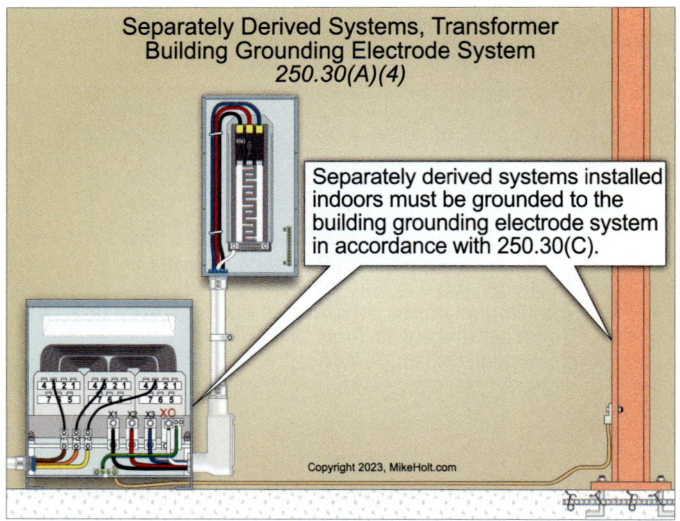

▶Figure 250–73

Separately derived transformer systems located outdoors must be grounded in accordance with 250.30(C).

(5) Grounding Electrode Conductor. The grounding electrode conductor for a transformer separately derived system must be sized in accordance with 250.66.

The grounding electrode conductor must terminate to the neutral conductor at the same point where the system bonding jumper is connected. ▶Figure 250–74

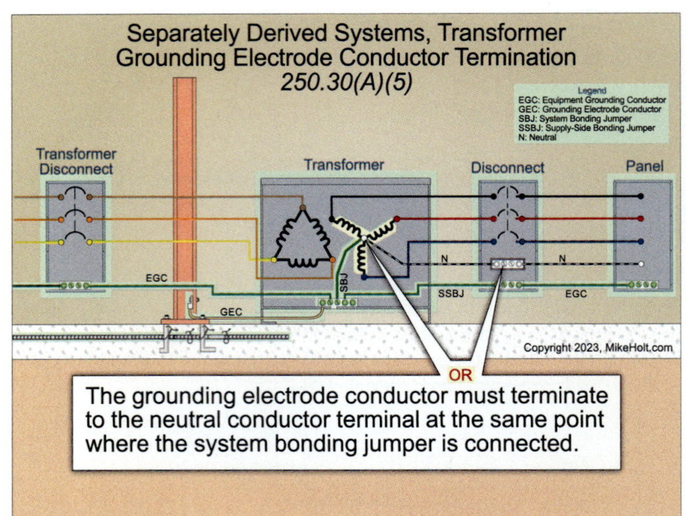

▶Figure 250–74

> **Author's Comment:**
>
> ▶ To prevent objectionable neutral current from flowing onto metal parts [250.6], the grounding electrode conductor must originate at the same point on the transformer separately derived system as where the system bonding jumper is connected [250.30(A)(1)].

Ex 1: If the system bonding jumper is a wire or busbar [250.30(A)(1)], the grounding electrode conductor can terminate at the grounding terminal, bar, or bus where the system bonding jumper terminates, instead of on the neutral terminal. ▶Figure 250–75

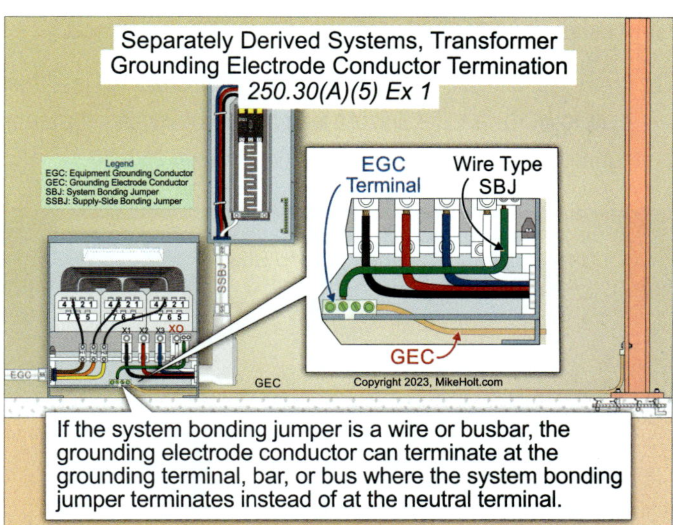

▶Figure 250–75

▶ Grounding Electrode Conductor Example 1

Question: *What size grounding electrode conductor is required for a 45 kVA, three-phase, 480V to 120/208V transformer when the secondary conductors are sized at 1/0 AWG?* ▶**Figure 250–76**

(a) 6 AWG   (b) 4 AWG   (c) 3 AWG   (d) 2 AWG

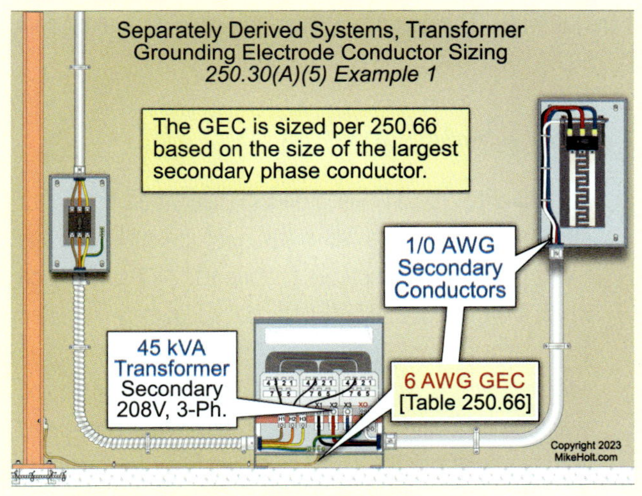

▶Figure 250–76

Answer: *(a) 6 AWG [Table 250.66]*

▶ Grounding Electrode Conductor Example 2

Question: *What size grounding electrode conductor is required for a 75 kVA, three-phase, 480V to 120/208V transformer when the secondary conductors are sized at 4/0 AWG?* ▶**Figure 250–77**

(a) 6 AWG   (b) 4 AWG   (c) 3 AWG   (d) 2 AWG

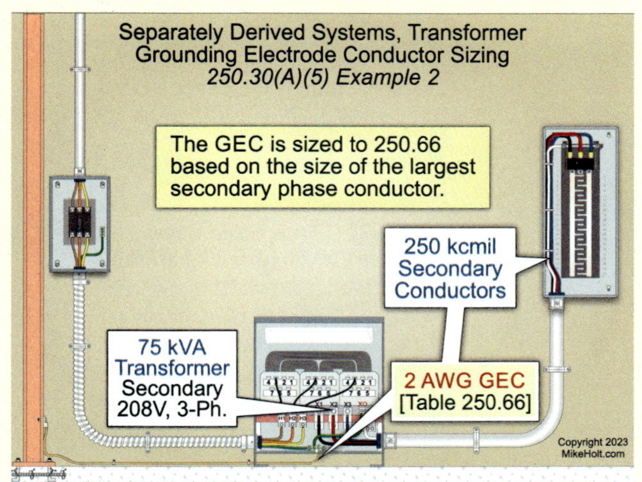

▶Figure 250–77

Answer: *(d) 2 AWG [Table 250.66]*

▶ Grounding Electrode Conductor Example 3

Question: *What size grounding electrode conductor is required for a 112.50 kVA, three-phase, 480V to 120/208V transformer when the secondary conductors are sized at 600 kcmil?* ▶**Figure 250–78**

(a) 1/0 AWG   (b) 2/0 AWG   (c) 3/0 AWG   (d) 4/0 AWG

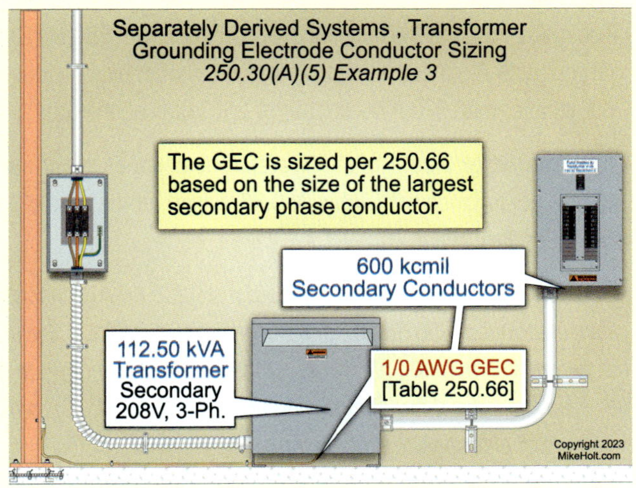

▶Figure 250–78

Answer: *(b) 2/0 AWG*

(6) Common Grounding Electrode Conductor, Multiple Separately Derived Transformer Systems. Where there are multiple separately derived transformer systems, a grounding electrode conductor tap from each of them to a common grounding electrode conductor is permitted. This connection must be made at the same point on the transformer separately derived system secondary as where the system bonding jumper is connected [250.30(A)(1)]. ▶Figure 250–79

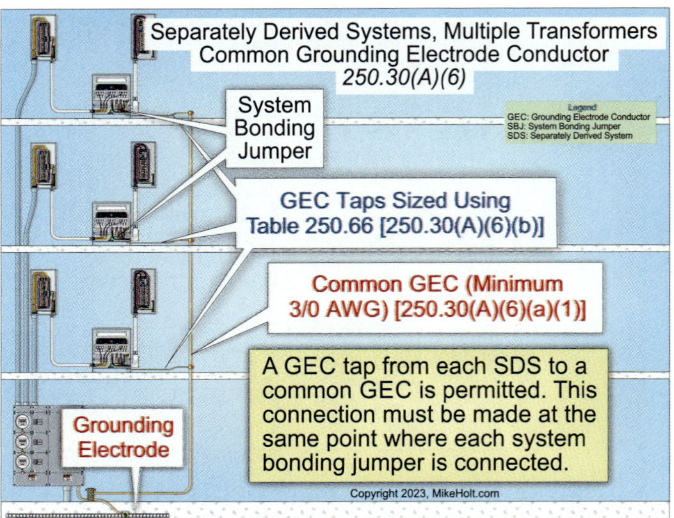

▶Figure 250–79

(a) Common Grounding Electrode Conductor. The common grounding electrode conductor can be any of the following:

(1) An unspliced conductor not smaller than 3/0 AWG copper or 250 kcmil aluminum

(2) Interior metal water pipe not more than 5 ft from the point of entrance to the building [250.68(C)(1)]

(3) The metal frame of the building in accordance with 250.68(C)(2) or connected to the grounding electrode system by a conductor not smaller than 3/0 AWG copper or 250 kcmil aluminum

(b) Tap Conductor Size. Grounding electrode conductor taps must be sized in accordance with Table 250.66, based on the area of the largest secondary phase conductor.

Ex: If the only electrodes present are ground rods [250.66(A)], concrete-encased electrodes [250.66(B)], or ground rings [250.66(C)], the size of the common grounding electrode conductor is not required to be larger than the largest conductor required by 250.66(A), (B), or (C) for the type of electrode that is present.

(c) Connections. Tap connections to the common grounding electrode conductor must be made at an accessible location by any of the following methods:

(1) A connector listed as "bonding and grounding equipment."

(2) Listed connections to aluminum or copper busbars not less than ¼ in. thick × 2 in. wide, and of a length to accommodate the terminations necessary for the installation. ▶Figure 250–80

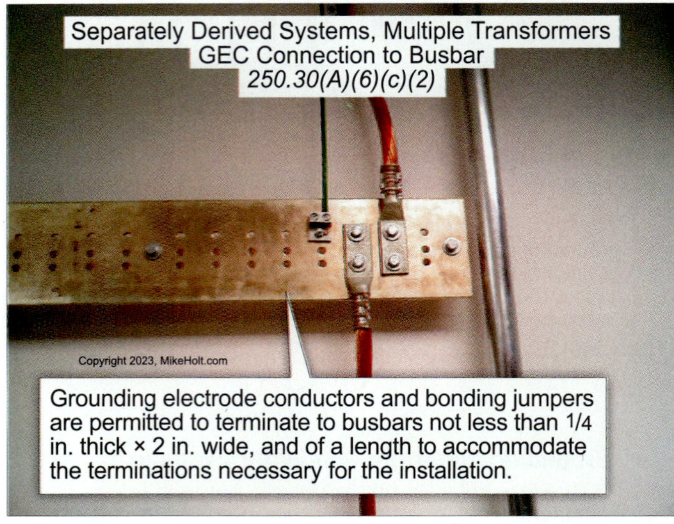

Grounding electrode conductors and bonding jumpers are permitted to terminate to busbars not less than 1/4 in. thick × 2 in. wide, and of a length to accommodate the terminations necessary for the installation.

▶Figure 250–80

(3) Exothermic Welding. Tap grounding electrode conductors must remain without a splice or joint.

(7) Installation. The grounding electrode conductor must comply with 250.64(A), (B), (C), and (E).

Author's Comment:

▶ According to 250.64, the grounding electrode conductor must be copper where within 18 in. of the surface of the Earth [250.64(A)], securely fastened to the surface on which it is carried [250.64(B)(1)], and adequately protected if exposed to physical damage [250.64(B)(2) and (3)]. In addition, ferrous metal enclosures enclosing a grounding electrode conductor must be made electrically continuous from the point of attachment to cabinets or equipment to the grounding electrode [250.64(E)].

(C) Outdoor Source. If located outdoors, the grounding electrode connection must be made at the transformer separately derived system. ▶Figure 250–81

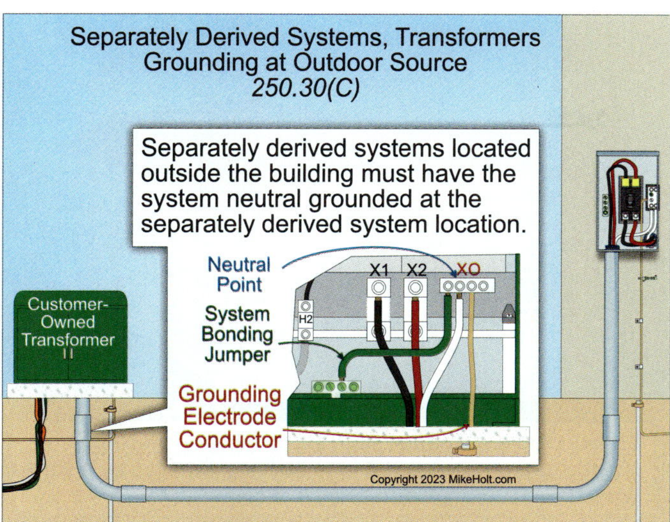

▶Figure 250–81

Generator Separately Derived Systems

According to Article 100, "Separately Derived System" is an electrical power supply output having no direct connection(s) to the circuit conductors of any other electrical source other than those established by grounding and bonding connections. ▶Figure 250–82

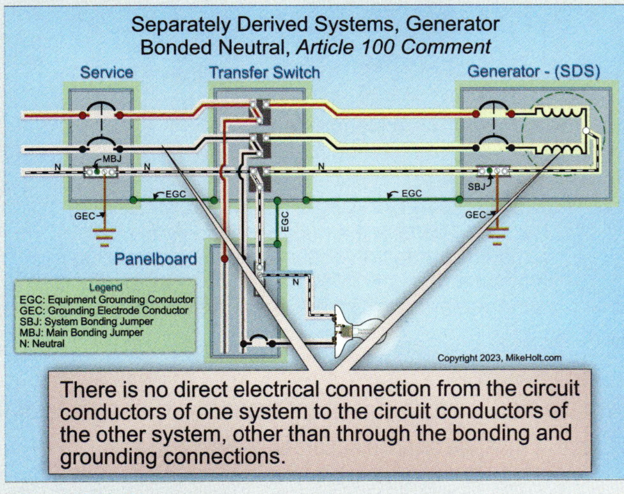

▶Figure 250–82

(A) Grounded Systems. A generator with a disconnect supplying a switched-neutral transfer switch must be bonded and grounded in accordance with the following. ▶Figure 250–83

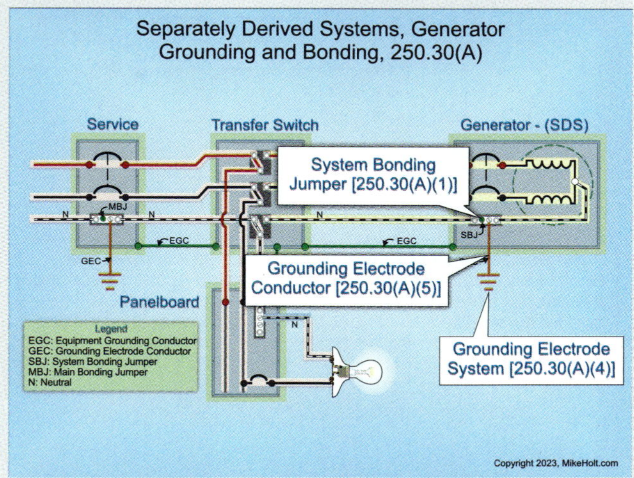

▶Figure 250–83

(1) System Bonding Jumper. A system bonding jumper must be installed at the secondary neutral point.

(4) Grounding Electrode. A separately derived generator system installed indoors must be grounded to the building grounding electrode system. Separately derived generator systems located outdoors must have the grounding electrode connection made at the generator separately derived system in accordance with 250.30(C).

(5) Grounding Electrode Conductor. The grounding electrode conductor must terminate to the neutral terminal where the system bonding jumper is connected.

Ex 1: If the system bonding jumper is a wire or busbar, the grounding electrode conductor can terminate at the generator equipment grounding terminal.

According to 250.30 Note 1, a generator with a transfer switch that does not open the neutral is not a generator separately derived system. This is because the neutral from the generator has a direct connection with the service neutral conductor, and is not required to be bonded or grounded in accordance with 250.30. ▶Figure 250–84

• • •

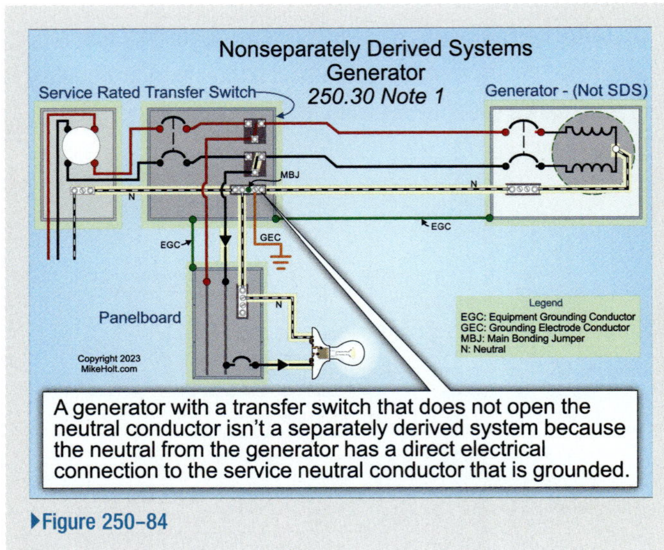

▶Figure 250–84

250.32 Buildings Supplied by a Feeder

(A) Grounding Electrode System and Conductor. A building supplied by a feeder must have a grounding electrode conductor connected to a grounding electrode system in accordance with Part III of Article 250. ▶Figure 250–85

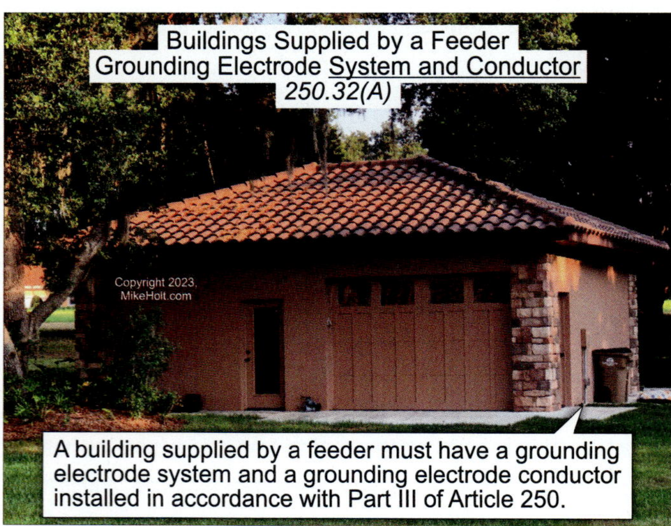

▶Figure 250–85

Ex: A grounding electrode system and grounding electrode conductor is not required for a building if it is supplied by a single branch circuit or multiwire branch circuit. ▶Figure 250–86

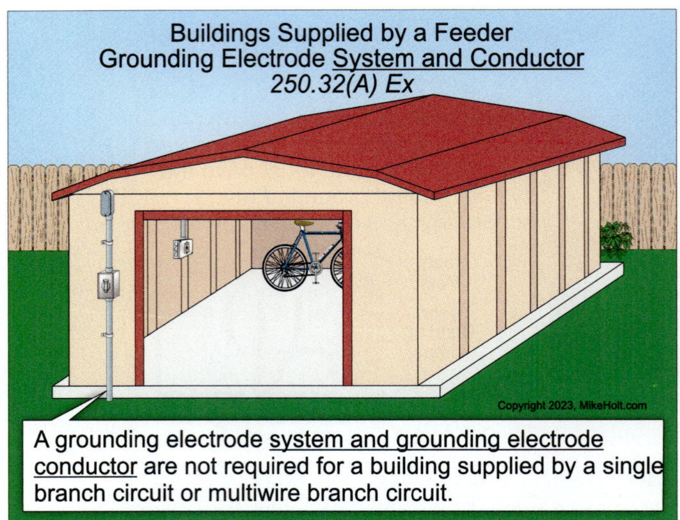

▶Figure 250–86

(B) Equipment Grounding Conductor.

(1) The metal parts of the building disconnect must be connected to the feeder equipment grounding conductor of a type described in 250.118(A). ▶Figure 250–87

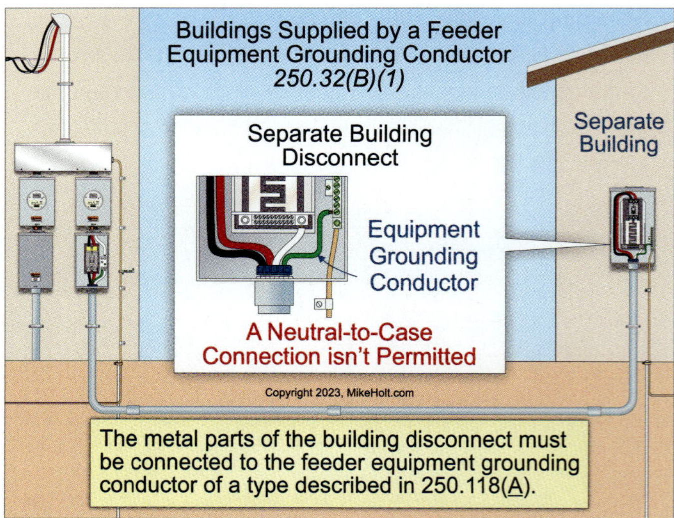

▶Figure 250–87

Where the supply circuit equipment grounding conductor is of the wire type, it must be sized in accordance with 250.122.

> **Caution**
>
> **CAUTION:** To prevent dangerous objectionable neutral current from flowing on metal parts [250.6(A)], the supply circuit neutral conductor is not permitted to be connected to the remote building disconnect metal enclosure. [250.142(B)]. ▶Figure 250–88

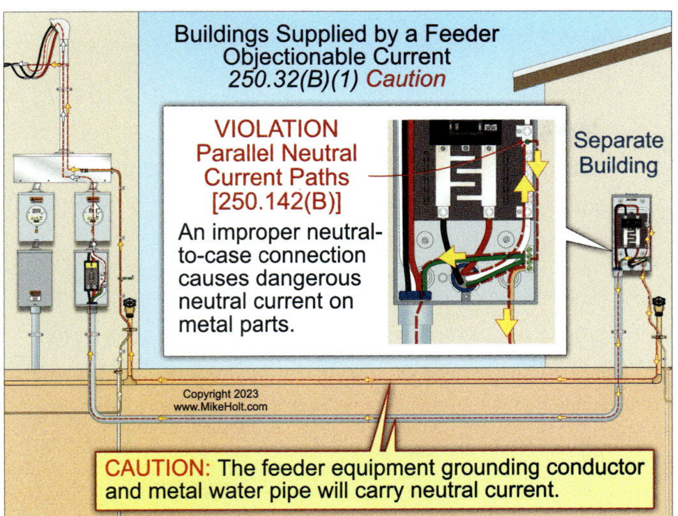

▶Figure 250–88

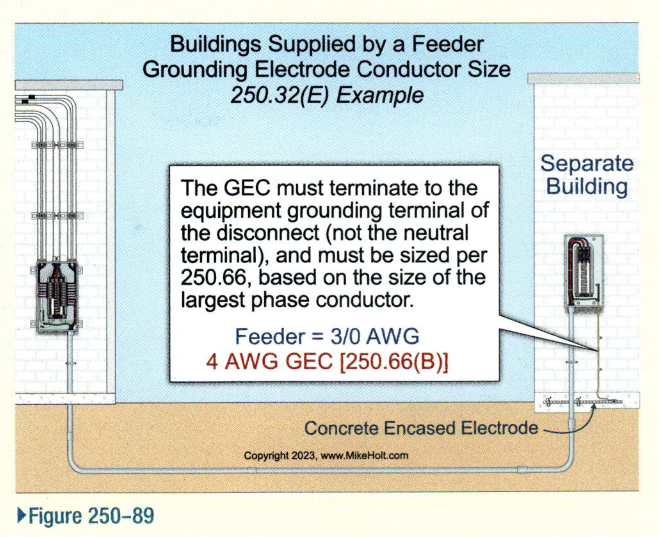

▶Figure 250–89

Ex 1: The neutral conductor can serve as the ground-fault return path for the building disconnect for existing installations where there are no continuous metallic paths between buildings and structures, ground-fault protection of equipment is not installed on the supply side of the circuit, and the neutral conductor is sized no smaller than the larger of:

(1) The maximum unbalanced calculated neutral load in accordance with 220.61

(2) The minimum equipment grounding conductor size in accordance with 250.122

(E) Grounding Electrode Conductor Size. The grounding electrode conductor must terminate to the equipment grounding terminal of the disconnect (not the neutral terminal) and must be sized in accordance with 250.66.

> ▶ **Example**
>
> **Question:** *What size grounding electrode conductor is required for a building disconnect supplied with a 3/0 AWG feeder with a concrete-encased electrode?* ▶Figure 250–89
>
> *(a) 4 AWG   (b) 2 AWG   (c) 1 AWG   (d) 1/0 AWG*
>
> **Answer:** *(a) 4 AWG*
>
> **Note:** *If the grounding electrode conductor is connected to a concrete-encased electrode(s), the portion of the conductor that connects only to the concrete-encased electrode(s) is not required to be larger than 4 AWG copper [250.66(B)].*

Author's Comment:

▶ If the grounding electrode conductor is connected to a rod(s), the portion of the conductor that connects only to the rod(s) is not required to be larger than 6 AWG copper [250.66(A)].

250.36 Impedance Grounded Systems—480V to 1000V

To limit ground-fault current to a low value, an impedance grounded system with a <u>grounding impedance device</u>, typically a resistor, is permitted to be installed on three-phase systems of 480V up to 1000V where all the following conditions are met: ▶Figure 250–90

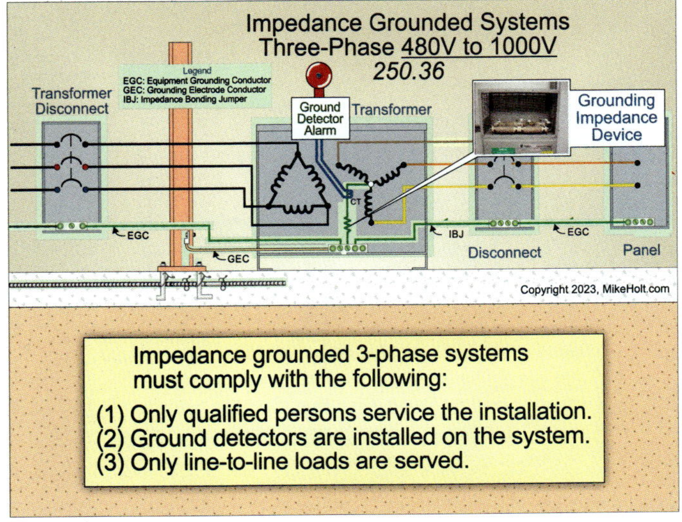

▶Figure 250–90

(1) Conditions of maintenance and supervision ensure that only qualified persons service the installation.

(2) Ground detectors are installed on the system.

(3) Only line-to-line loads are served.

Note: Impedance grounding is an effective tool for reducing arc-flash hazards, see Annex O of NFPA 70E, *Standard for Electrical Safety in the Workplace.* ▶Figure 250–91

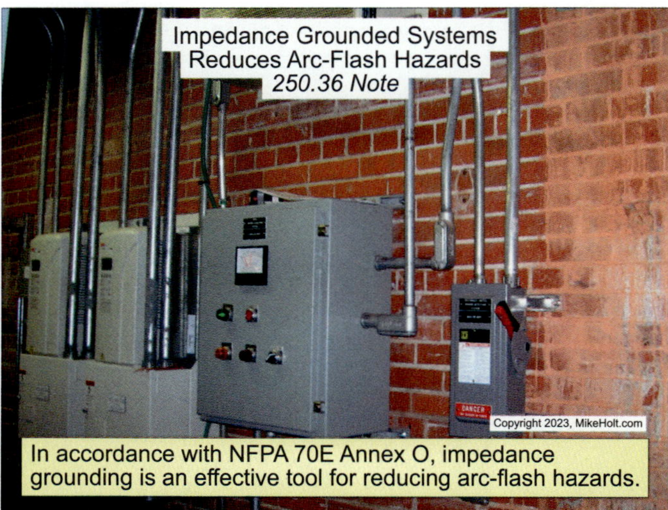

▶Figure 250–91

According to Article 100, "Impedance Grounded System" is an electrical system that is grounded by bonding the system neutral point to the metal parts of the enclosure through an impedance device. ▶Figure 250–92

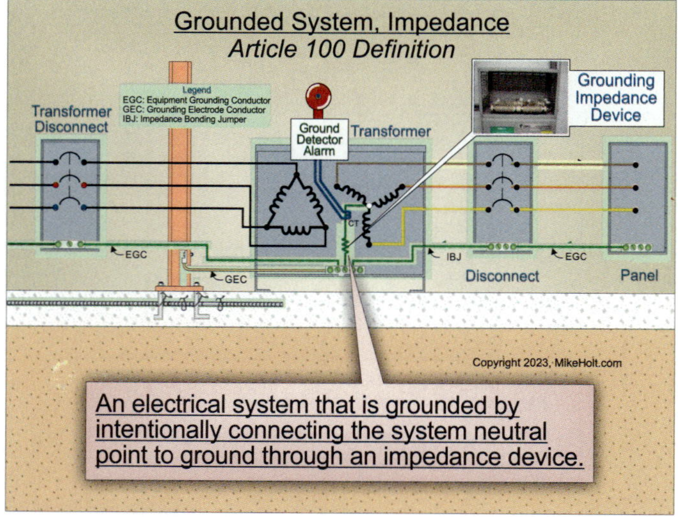

▶Figure 250–92

▸ Impedance grounded systems are generally referred to as "high-resistance grounded systems" in the industry. These systems are generally used where sudden interruption of power will create increased hazards and when a reduction of incident energy is needed for worker safety.

▸ High-resistance grounding will insert an impedance in the ground return path and will typically limit the fault current to 10A or less, leaving insufficient fault energy and thereby reducing the arc-flash hazard level. High-resistance grounding will not affect arc-flash energy for line-to-line faults NFPA 70E, *Standard for Electrical Safety in the Workplace.*

(A) Grounding Impedance Device Location. A grounding impedance device must be installed between the impedance grounding conductor and the transformer secondary neutral point. ▶Figure 250–93

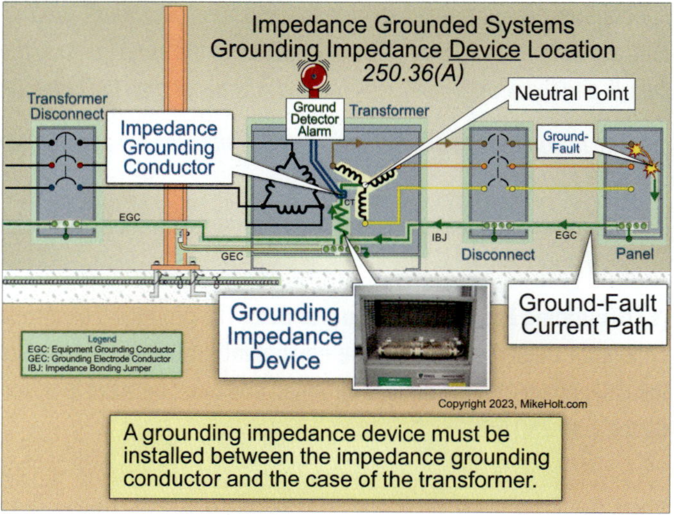

▶Figure 250–93

According to Article 100, "Impedance Grounding Conductor" is a conductor that connects the system neutral point to the impedance device in an impedance grounded system. ▶Figure 250–94

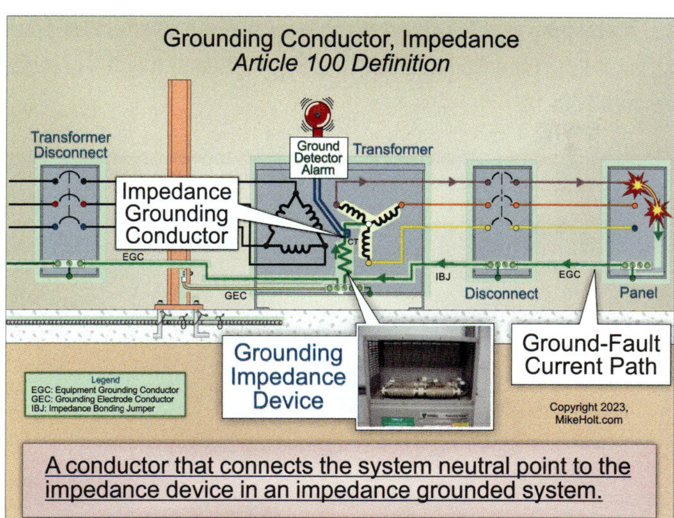

▶Figure 250–94

Part III. Grounding Electrode System and Grounding Electrode Conductor

250.50 Grounding Electrode System

According to Article 100, "Grounding Electrode" is a conducting object used to make a direct electrical connection to the Earth [250.50 through 250.70]. ▶Figure 250–95

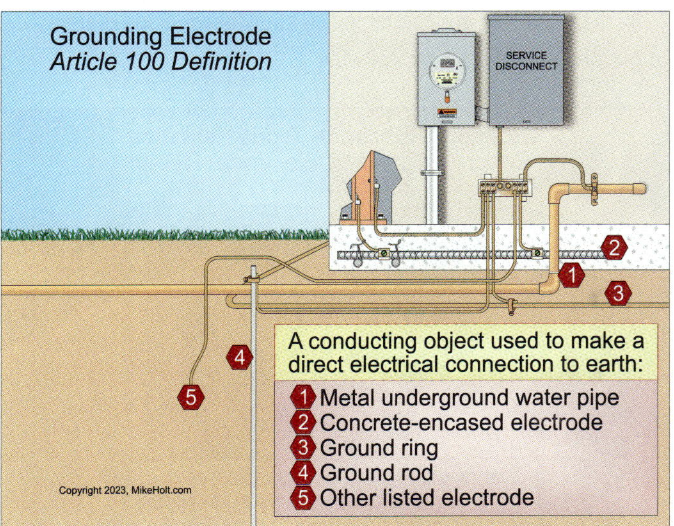

▶Figure 250–95

A grounding electrode system is comprised of bonding together the grounding electrodes described in 250.52(A)(1) through (A)(8) that are present at a building or structure. ▶Figure 250–96

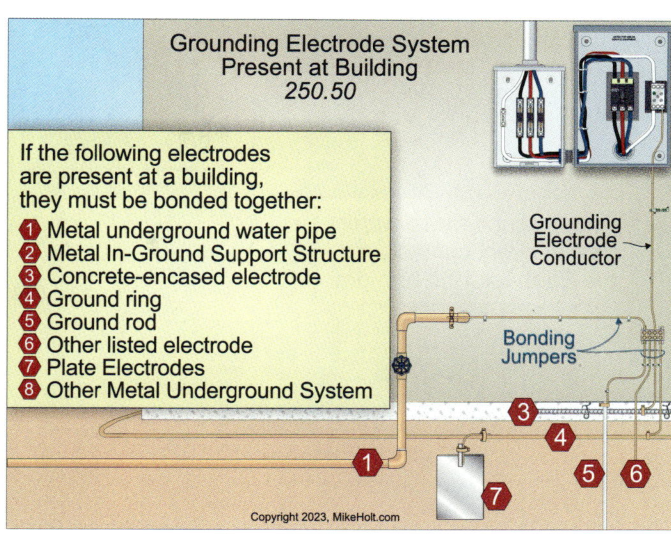

▶Figure 250–96

Ex: Concrete-encased electrodes are not required for existing buildings or structures if the <u>rebar</u> is not accessible without chipping up the concrete. ▶Figure 250–97

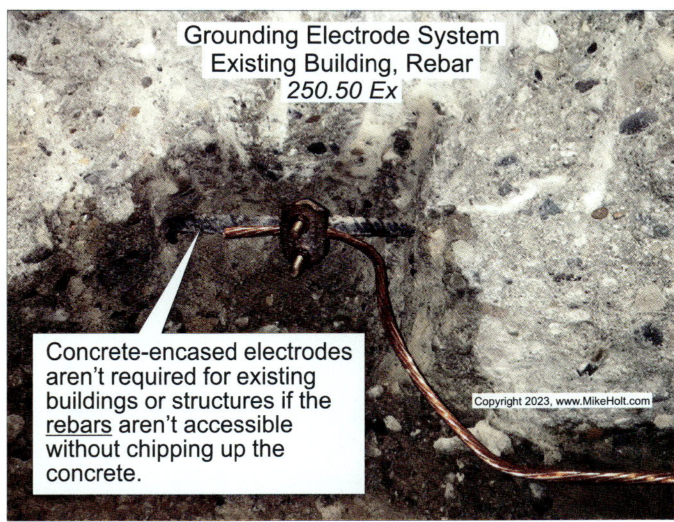

▶Figure 250–97

250.52 Grounding Electrode Types

(A) Electrodes Permitted.

(1) Underground Metal Water Pipe Electrode. Underground metal water pipe in direct contact with the Earth for 10 ft or more. ▶Figure 250–98

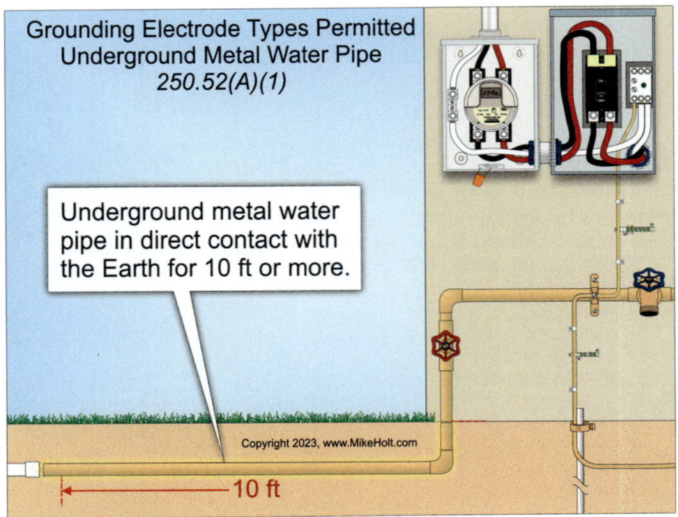

▶Figure 250–98

Author's Comment:

▶ Controversy about using metal underground water piping as a grounding electrode has existed since the early 1900s. The water industry believes that neutral current flowing on water piping corrodes the metal. For more information, contact the American Water Works Association about their report, *Effects of Electrical Grounding on Pipe Integrity and Shock Hazard*, Catalog No. 90702, 1.800.926.7337. ▶Figure 250–99

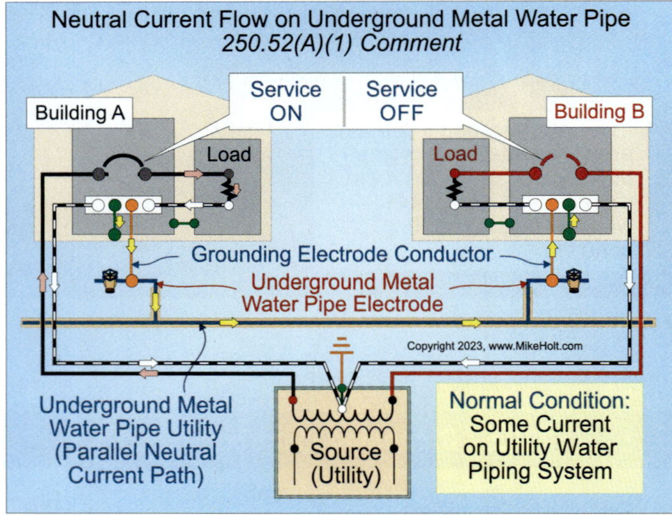

▶Figure 250–99

▶ Where there is a common metal underground water piping system, it is possible for the service neutral to be open and not show any symptoms that are typically associated with open service neutrals. This can create a dangerous condition for water workers who open the underground water pipe when it is acting as the service neutral.

(2) Metal In-Ground Support Structure(s). Metal in-ground support structure(s) in direct contact with the Earth vertically for 10 ft or more. ▶Figure 250–100

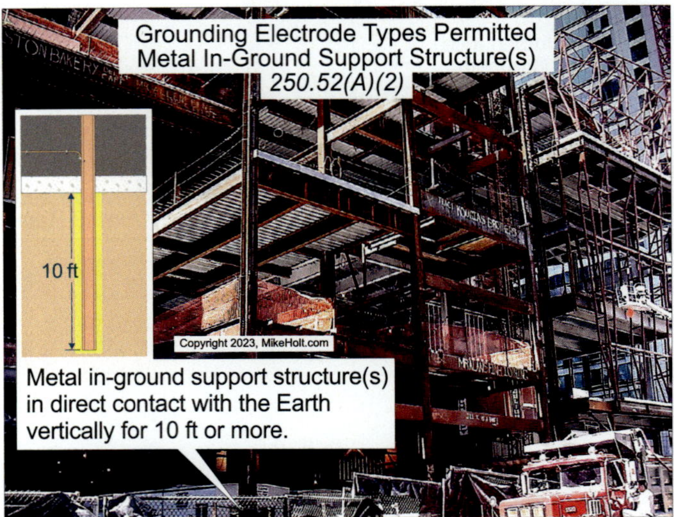

▶Figure 250–100

Note: Metal in-ground support structures include—but are not limited to—pilings, casings, and other structural metal.

(3) Concrete-Encased Electrode. Concrete-encased electrodes must be one of the following:

(1) Rebar. One or more pieces of conductive rebar of not less than ½ in. diameter that are connected by steel tie wires to create a 20 ft or greater length. ▶Figure 250–101

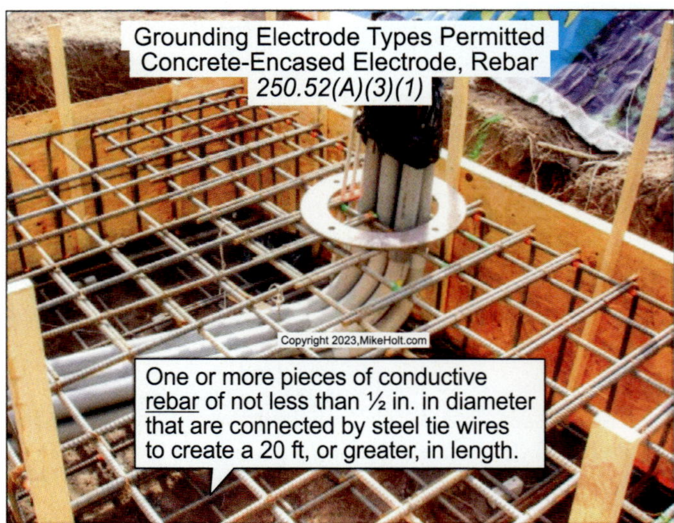

▶Figure 250–101

(2) Conductor. A bare copper conductor not smaller than 4 AWG and 20 ft or greater in length. ▶Figure 250–102

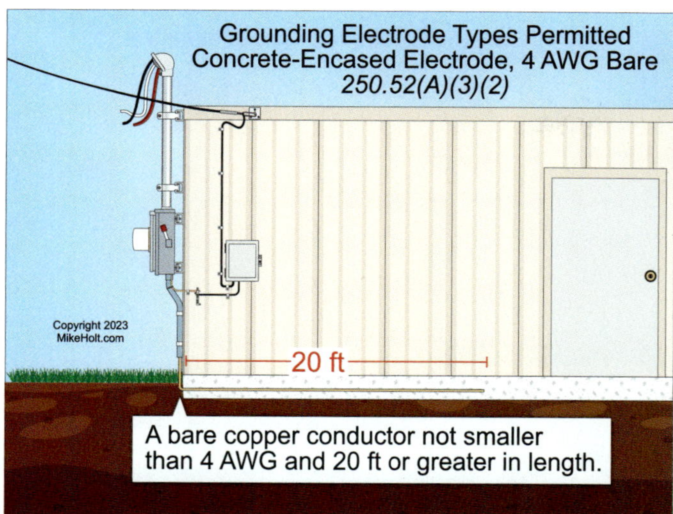

▶Figure 250–102

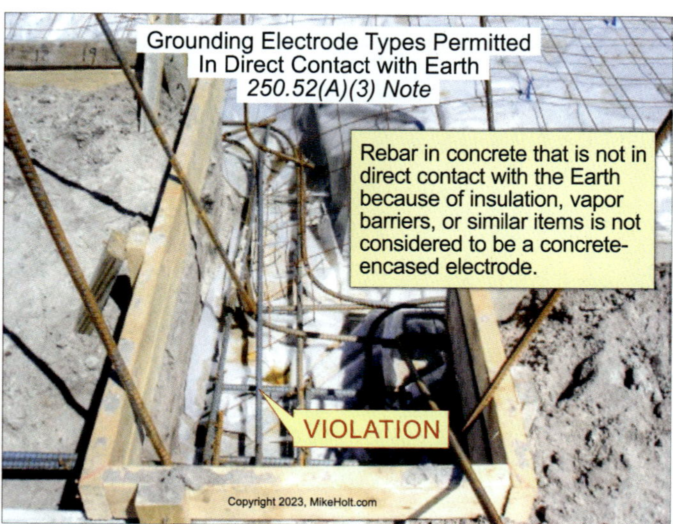

▶Figure 250–104

Rebar or Conductor. The rebar or bare copper conductor used as part of the concrete-encased electrode must be encased by at least 2 in. of concrete that is in direct contact with the Earth. ▶Figure 250–103

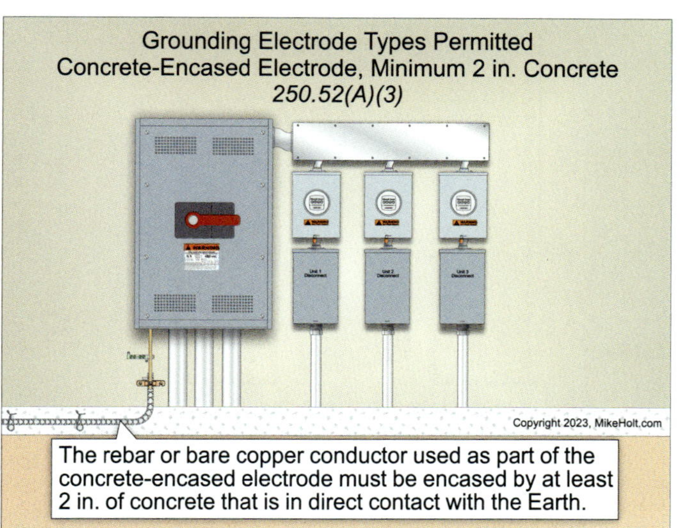

▶Figure 250–103

The concrete-encased electrode can be horizontal or vertical within a foundation or footing that is in direct contact with the Earth. If multiple concrete-encased electrodes are present at a building, only one is required to serve as a grounding electrode.

Note: Rebar in concrete that is not in direct contact with the Earth because of insulation, vapor barriers, or similar items is not considered to be a concrete-encased electrode. ▶Figure 250–104

Author's Comment:

▶ A grounding electrode conductor connected to a concrete-encased grounding electrode is not required to be larger than 4 AWG copper [250.66(B)].

▶ A concrete-encased grounding electrode is also called a "Ufer Ground," named after a consultant working for the U.S. Army during World War II. The technique Herbert G. Ufer created was necessary because the site needing grounding had no underground water table and little rainfall. The desert site was a series of bomb storage vaults near Flagstaff, Arizona. This type of grounding electrode generally offers the lowest ground resistance for the cost. In fact, Mr. Ufer's method is so effective that ground rods are not necessary!

(4) Ground Ring. A direct buried bare copper conductor not smaller than 2 AWG encircling a building. ▶Figure 250–105

Author's Comment:

▶ A ground ring encircling a building must not be installed less than 30 in. below the surface of the Earth [250.53(F)].

(5) Ground Rod.

(2) Ground rods at least 8 ft in length in contact with the Earth. ▶Figure 250–106

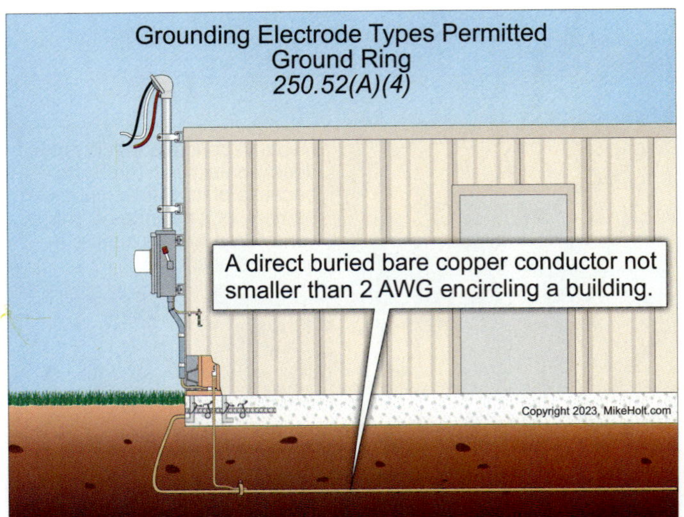

▶Figure 250–105

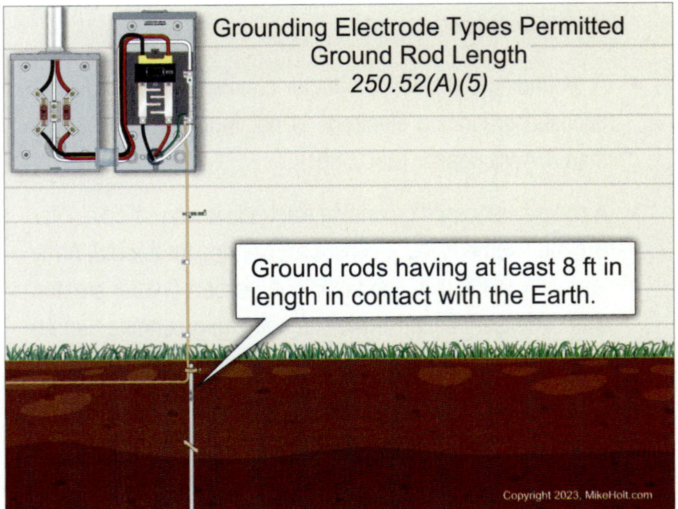

▶Figure 250–106

Author's Comment:

▸ The grounding electrode conductor, if it is the sole connection to the rod(s), is not required to be larger than 6 AWG copper [250.66(A)].

▸ The diameter of a ground rod has an insignificant effect on the contact resistance of a rod(s) to the Earth. However, larger diameter rods (¾ in. and 1 in.) are sometimes installed where mechanical strength is desired, or is needed to compensate for the loss of the electrode's metal due to corrosion.

(6) Listed Electrode. Other listed grounding electrodes. ▶Figure 250–107

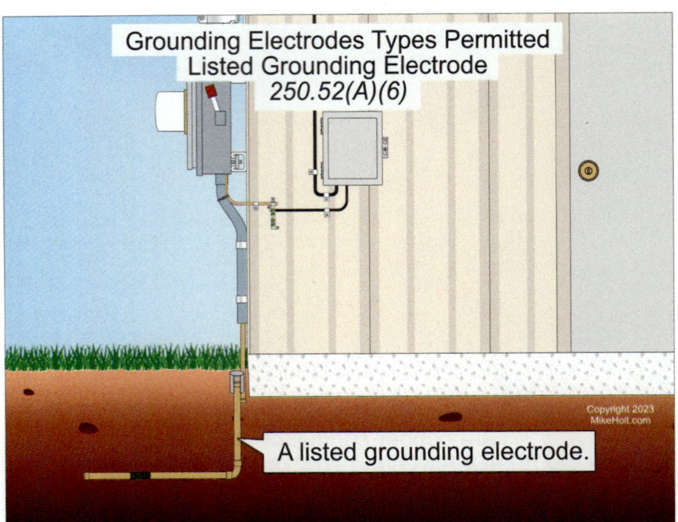

▶Figure 250–107

(7) Plate Electrode. A steel plate of not less than ¼ in. thick with an exposed surface area of not less than 288 sq inches (2 ft). ▶Figure 250–108

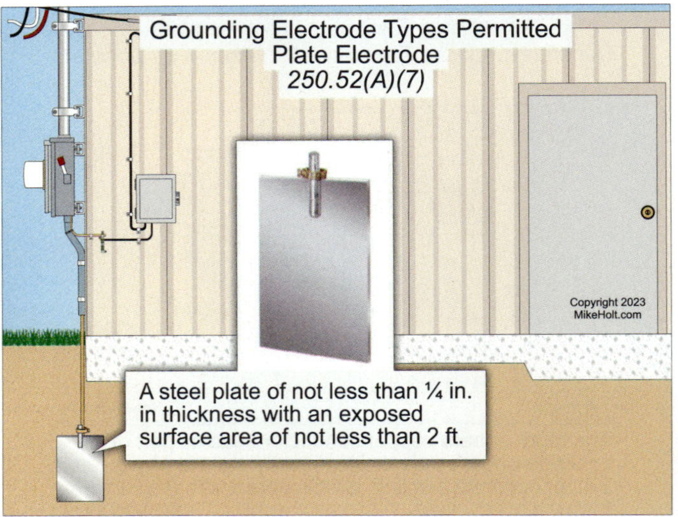

▶Figure 250–108

(8) Metal Underground Systems. Metal underground piping and metal well casings. ▶Figure 250–109

Author's Comment:

▸ The grounding electrode conductor to the metal underground system must be sized in accordance with Table 250.66.

(B) Not Permitted for Use as a Grounding Electrode.

(1) Underground metal gas piping systems are not permitted to be used as a grounding electrode. ▶Figure 250–110

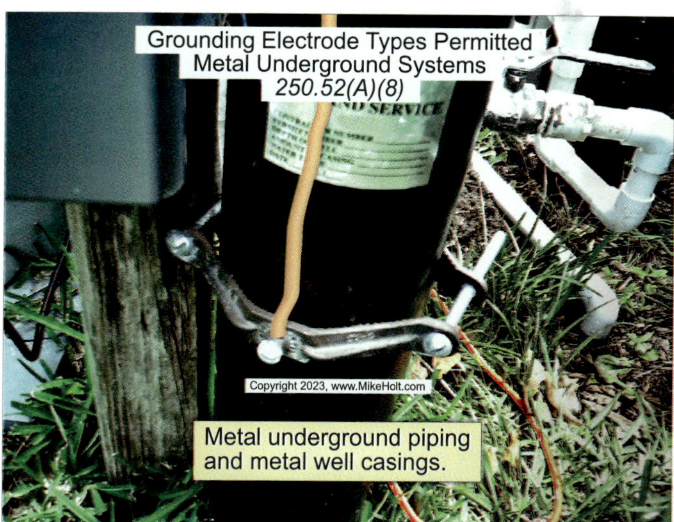

▶Figure 250–109

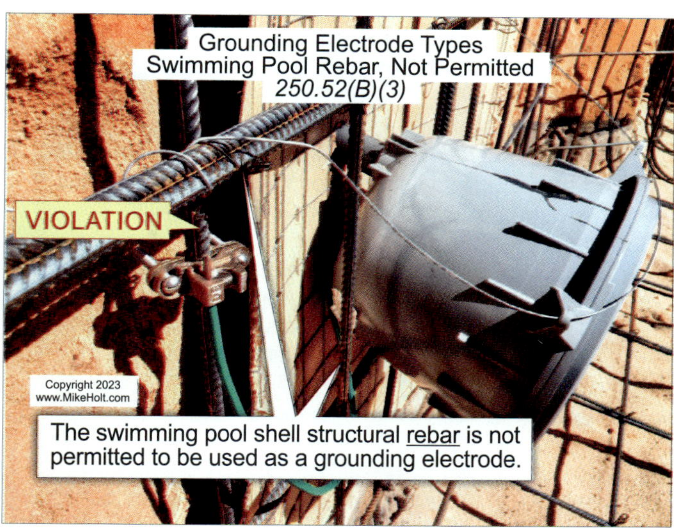

▶Figure 250–111

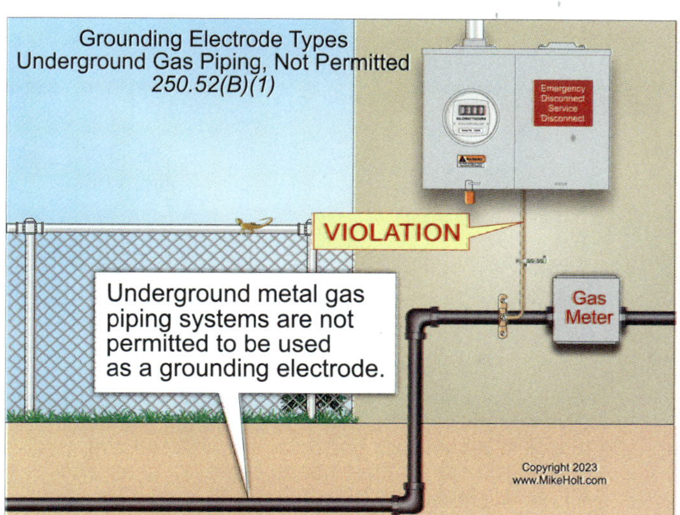

▶Figure 250–110

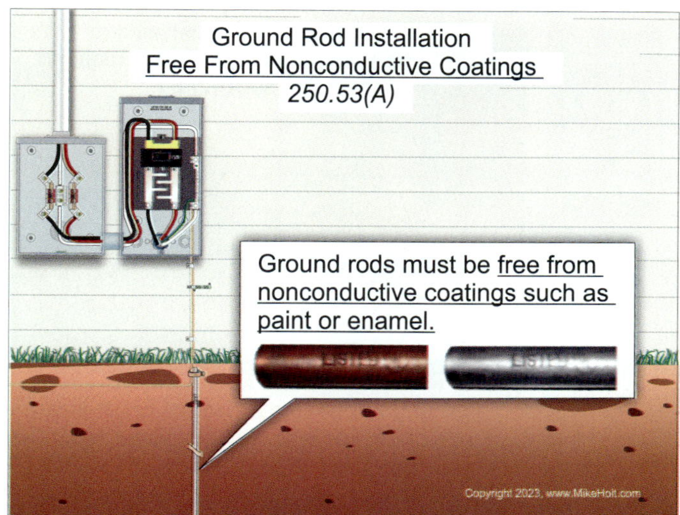

▶Figure 250–112

(2) Aluminum is not permitted to be used as a grounding electrode.

(3) The swimming pool shell structural rebar described in 680.26(B)(1) and (B)(2) is not permitted to be used as a grounding electrode. ▶Figure 250–111

250.53 Grounding Electrode Installation

(A) Ground Rods. Ground rods must be free from nonconductive coatings such as paint or enamel. ▶Figure 250–112

(1) Below Permanent Moisture Level. If practicable, rod, pipe, and plate electrodes must be embedded below the permanent moisture level.

(2) Supplemental Electrode. A single ground rod must be supplemented by an additional electrode. The supplemental electrode must be bonded to: ▶Figure 250–113

(1) Another ground rod

(2) The grounding electrode conductor

(3) The service neutral conductor

(4) A nonflexible metal service raceway

(5) The service-disconnect enclosure

Ex: A single ground rod having a contact resistance to the Earth of 25Ω or less is not required to have a supplemental electrode. ▶Figure 250–114

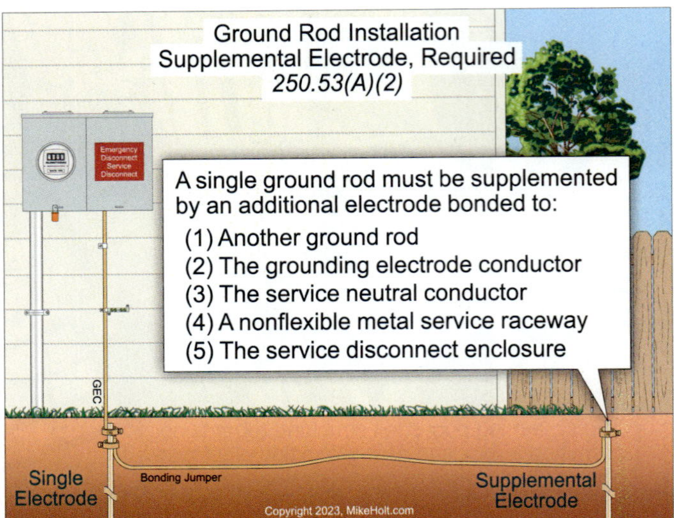

▶Figure 250–113

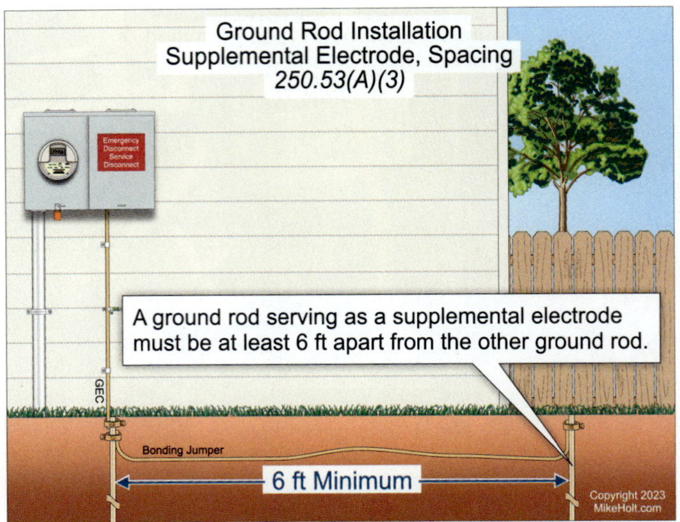

▶Figure 250–115

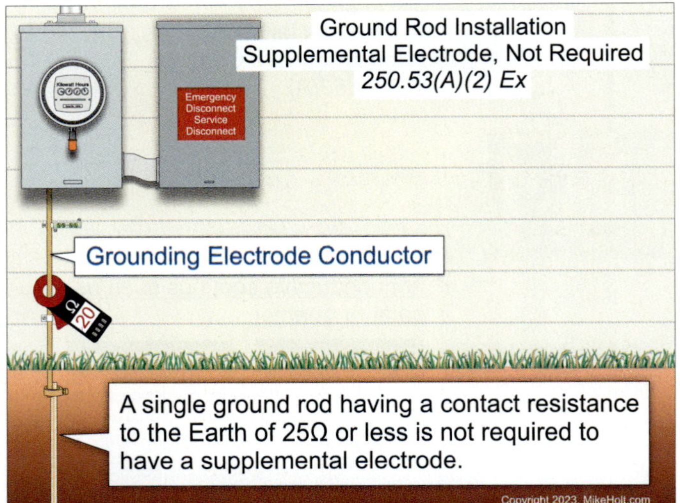

▶Figure 250–114

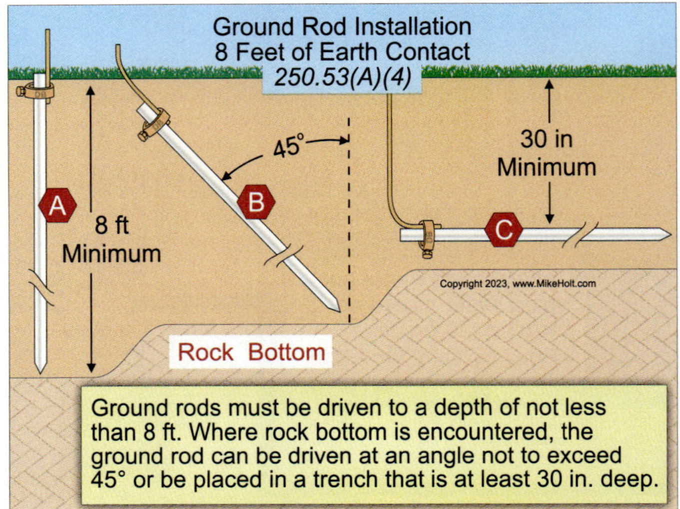

▶Figure 250–116

(3) Supplemental Ground Rod, Spacing. A ground rod serving as a supplemental electrode must be at least 6 ft apart from the other ground rod. ▶Figure 250–115

4) Rod Electrodes. Ground rods must be driven to a depth of not less than 8 ft. Where rock bottom is encountered, the ground rod can be driven at an angle not to exceed 45 degrees or be placed in a trench that is at least 30 in. deep. ▶Figure 250–116

The upper end of the ground rod must be flush with or below ground level, unless the grounding electrode conductor attachment is protected against physical damage as specified in 250.10. ▶Figure 250–117

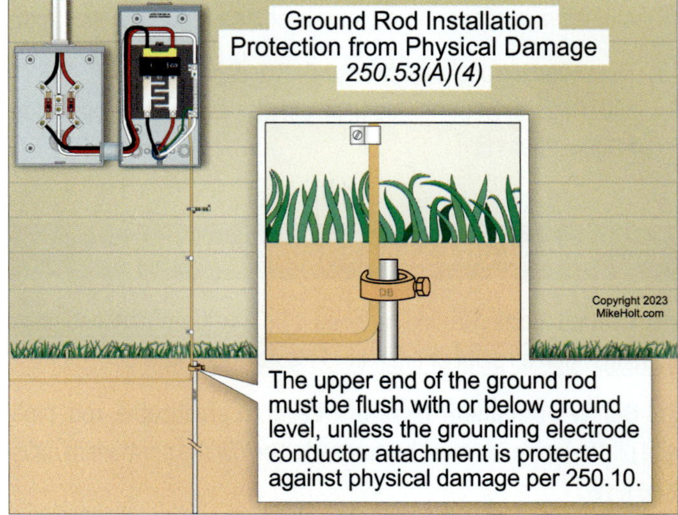

▶Figure 250–117

Author's Comment:

▸ When the grounding electrode attachment fitting is underground (below ground level), it must be listed for direct soil burial [250.70(A)].

(5) Plate Electrode. Plate electrodes must be installed no less than 30 in. below the surface of the Earth. ▸Figure 250–118

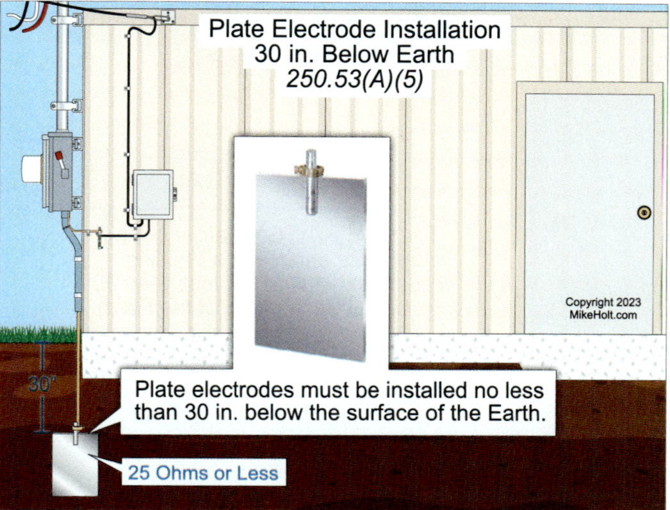

▸Figure 250–118

(B) Electrode Spacing. The building grounding electrode(s) must be at least 6 ft from other grounding electrode systems, such as the lightning protection grounding electrode(s). ▸Figure 250–119

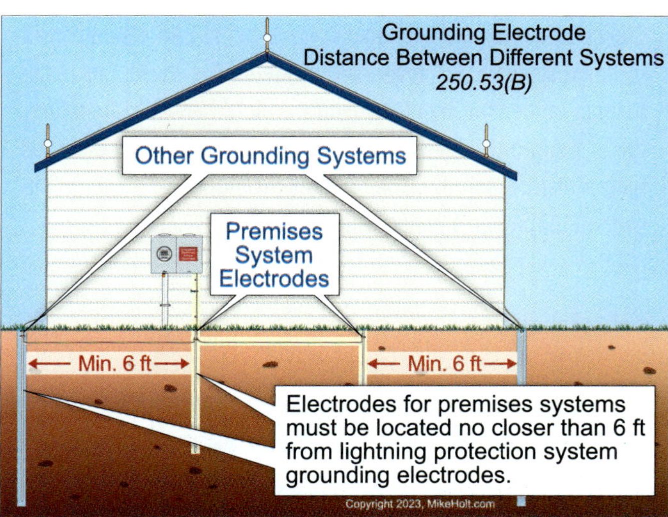

▸Figure 250–119

(C) Grounding Electrode Bonding Jumper. Grounding electrode bonding jumpers must be copper when within 18 in. of the Earth [250.64(A)]. Exposed grounding electrode bonding jumpers must be securely fastened to the surface and protected from physical damage [250.64(B)]. Grounding electrode bonding jumpers installed in metal raceways must be bonded at both ends [250.64(E)]. The bonding jumper to each electrode must be sized in accordance with 250.66. ▸Figure 250–120

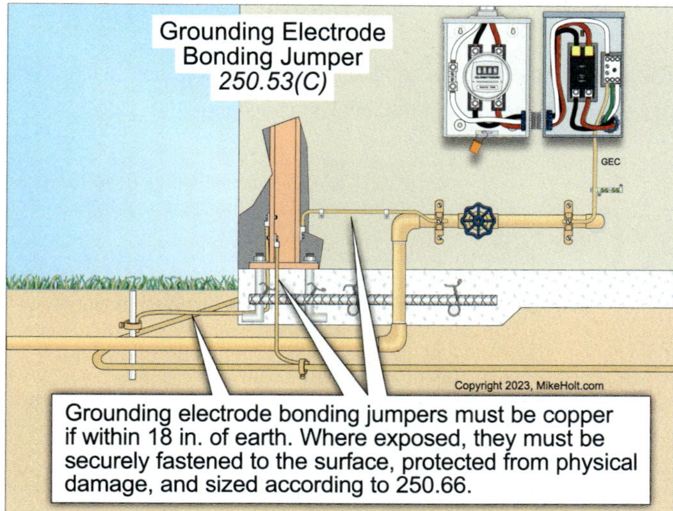

▸Figure 250–120

When the grounding electrode conductor termination is encased in concrete or buried, the termination fittings must be listed for this purpose [250.70(A)].

(D) Underground Metal Water Pipe Electrode.

(1) Continuity. The continuity of interior metal water piping systems must not rely on water meters or filtering devices. ▸Figure 250–121

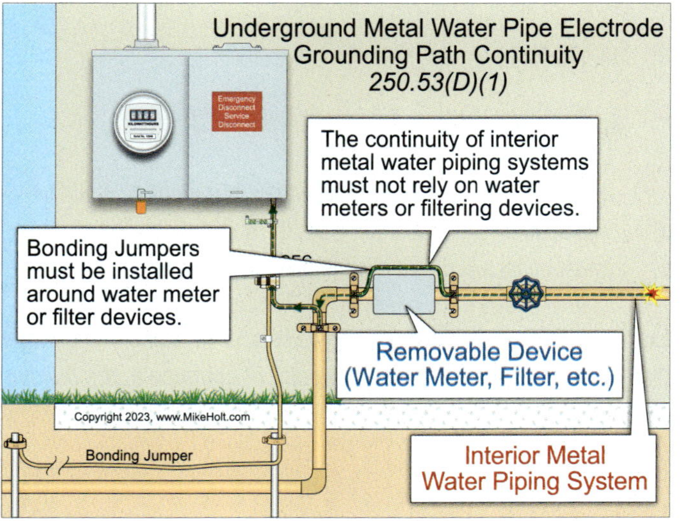

▸Figure 250–121

(2) Water Pipe Supplemental Electrode. When an underground metal water pipe grounding electrode is present, it must be supplemented by any of the following electrodes:

▸ Metal frame of the building electrode [250.52(A)(2)]

▸ Concrete-encased electrode [250.52(A)(3)]

▸ Rod electrode [250.52(A)(5)]

▸ Other type of listed electrode [250.52(A)(6)]

▸ Metal underground piping electrode [250.52(A)(8)]

The grounding electrode conductor for the supplemental electrode must be bonded to any of the following: ▸Figure 250–122

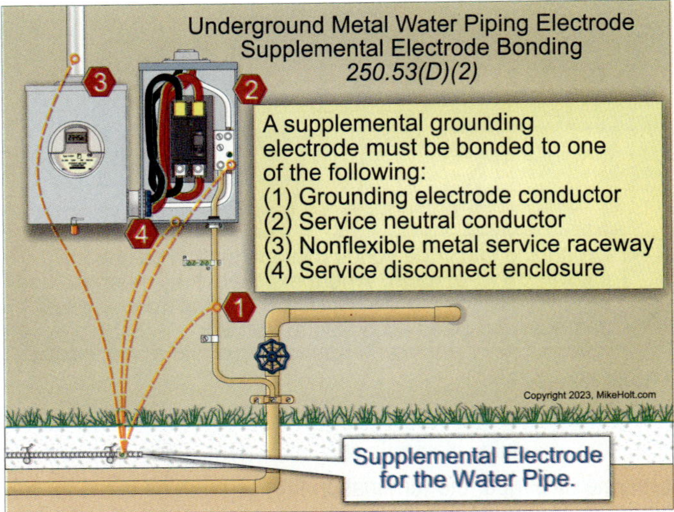

▸Figure 250–122

(1) Grounding electrode conductor

(2) Service neutral conductor

(3) Nonflexible metal service raceway

(4) Service-disconnect enclosure

Author's Comment:

▸ Because a metal underground waterpipe electrode could be replaced by a plastic water pipe, the supplemental electrode must be installed as if it is the only electrode for the system.

Ex: The supplemental electrode can be bonded to interior metal water piping not more than 5 ft from the point of entrance to the building [250.68(C)(1)].

(E) Supplemental Rod Electrode Bonding Jumper Size. The grounding electrode bonding jumper to a ground rod that serves as a water pipe supplemental electrode is not required to be larger than 6 AWG copper.

(F) Ground Ring. The bare 2 AWG or larger copper conductor encircling a building [250.52(A)(4)] must be installed not less than 30 in. below the surface of the Earth. ▸Figure 250–123

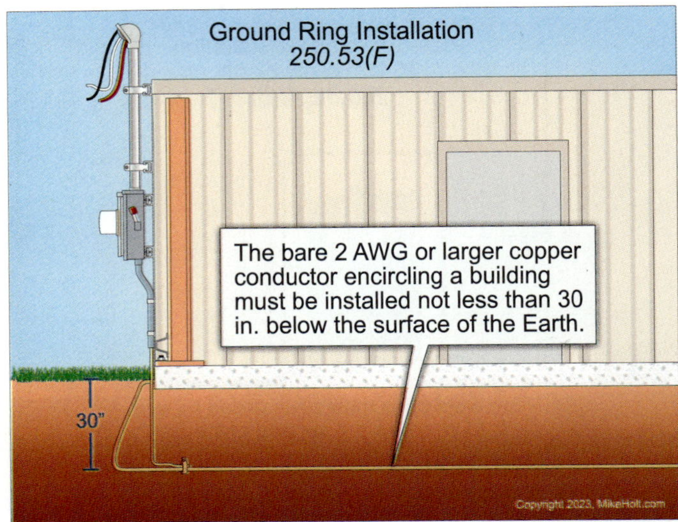

▸Figure 250–123

Soil Resistivity

The contact resistance of an electrode to the Earth is impacted by soil resistivity, which varies throughout the world. Soil resistivity is influenced by electrolytes, which consist of moisture, minerals, and dissolved salts. Because soil resistivity changes with moisture content, the contact resistance of a grounding system to the Earth varies with the seasons.

250.54 Auxiliary Grounding Electrodes

Grounding electrodes that are not required by the *NEC* are called "auxiliary electrodes" and connected to the equipment grounding conductors. Since they serve no purpose related to the electrical safety addressed by the *Code*, they have no *NEC* requirements. ▸Figure 250–124

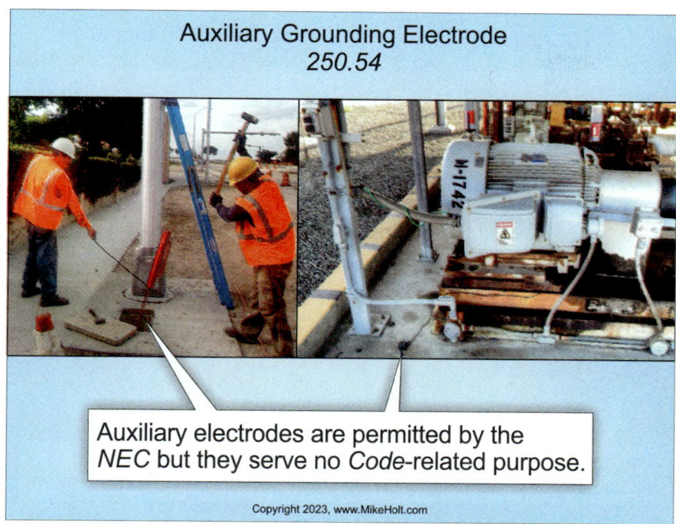

▶Figure 250–124

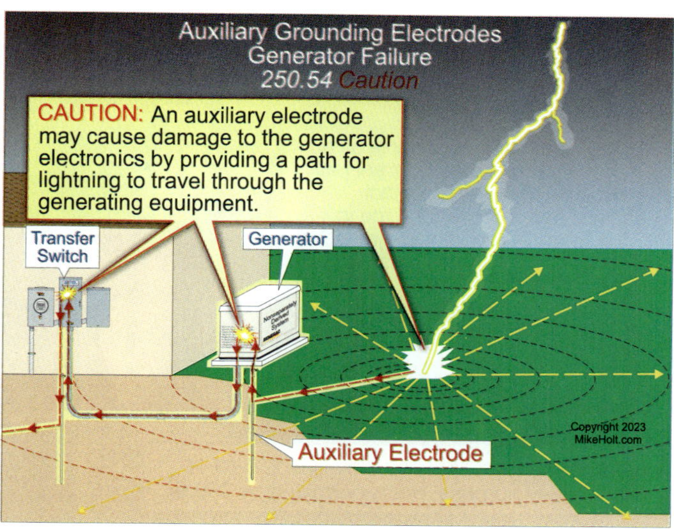

▶Figure 250–126

If an auxiliary electrode is installed, it is not required to be bonded to the building grounding electrode system, to have the grounding conductor sized to 250.66, nor must it comply with the 25Ω single ground rod requirement of 250.53(A)(2) Ex. ▶Figure 250–125

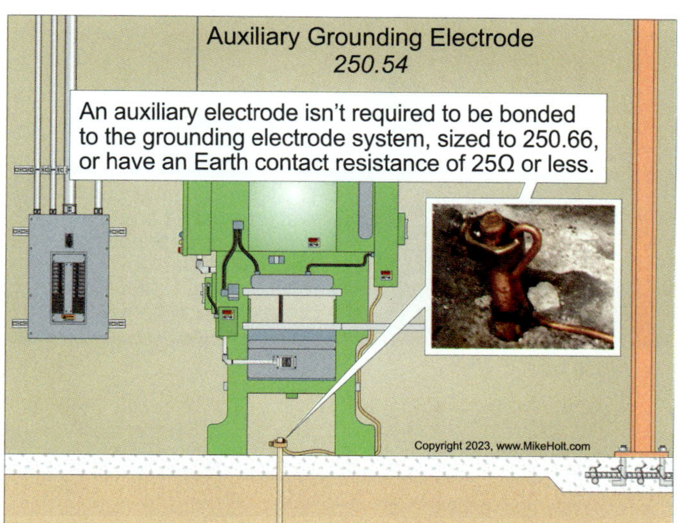

▶Figure 250–125

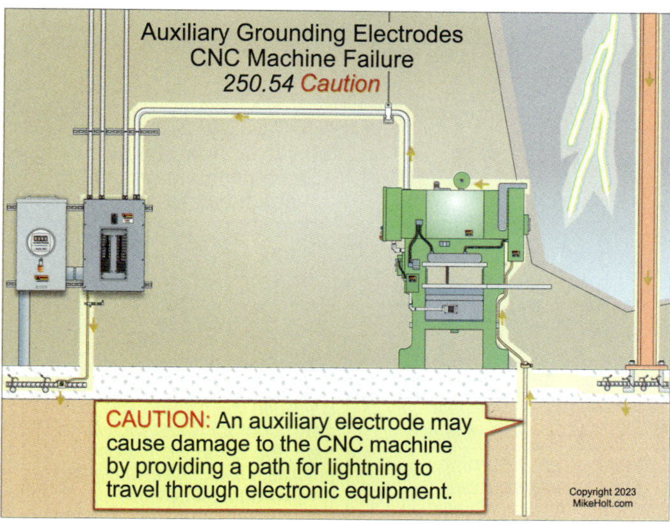

▶Figure 250–127

The Earth is not to be considered the effective ground-fault current path specified in 250.4(A)(5). ▶Figure 250–128

> **Caution**
>
> **CAUTION:** An auxiliary electrode may cause damage to the generator electronics by providing a path for lightning to travel through the generating equipment. ▶Figure 250–126 and ▶Figure 250–127

> **Danger**
>
> **DANGER:** Because the contact resistance of an electrode to the Earth is so great, very little fault current returns to the source if the Earth is the only fault-current return path. As a result, the circuit overcurrent protective device will not open and clear the ground fault, and all metal parts associated with the electrical installation, metal piping, and structural building steel will become and remain energized. ▶Figure 250–129

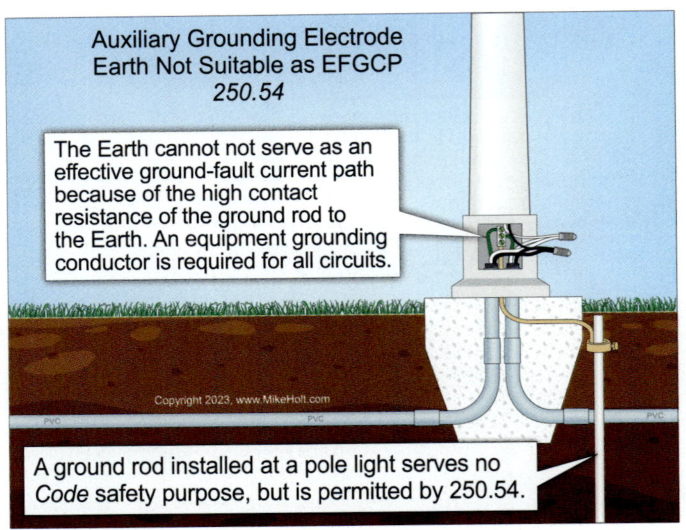

▶Figure 250–128

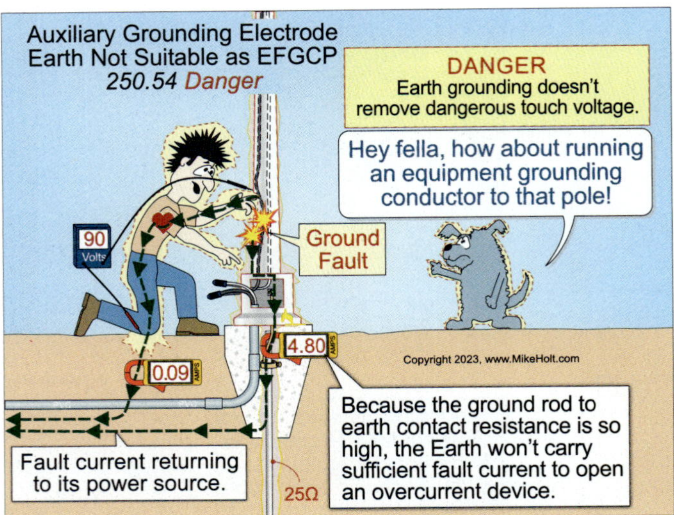

▶Figure 250–129

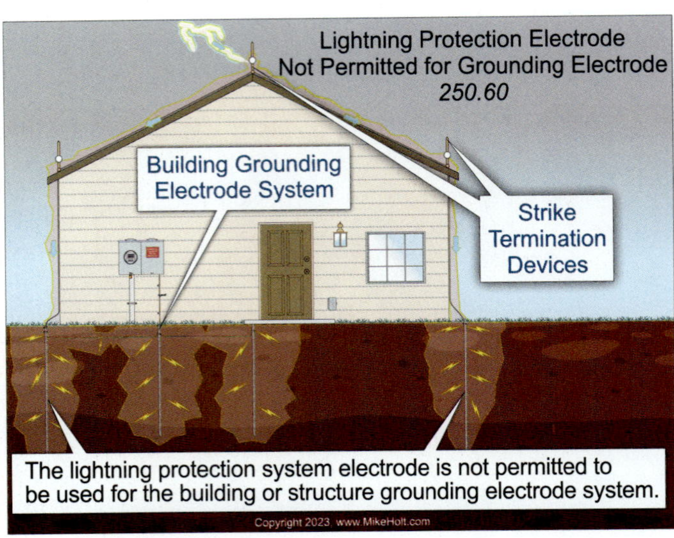

▶Figure 250–130

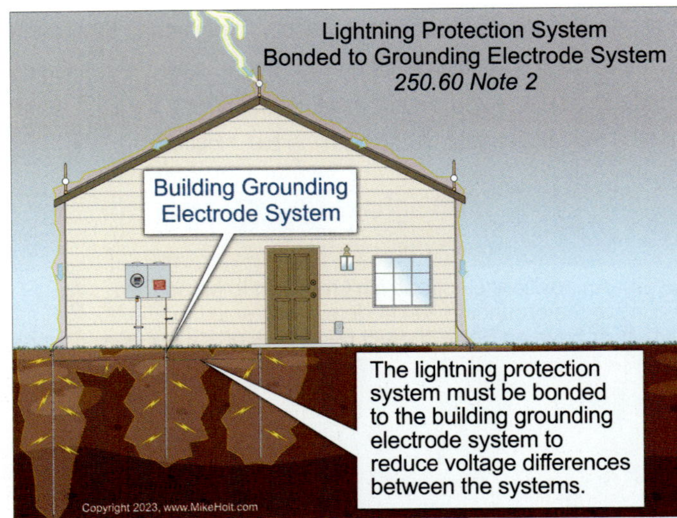

▶Figure 250–131

250.60 Lightning Protection Electrode

The lightning protection system electrode is not permitted to be used for the building or structure grounding electrode system required for service equipment [250.24(A)(1)], separately derived systems [250.30], or remote building feeder disconnect [250.32(A)]. ▶Figure 250–130

Note 1: See 250.106 for the bonding requirements of the lightning protection system to the building or structure grounding electrode system.

Note 2: Bonding together of all separate grounding electrodes will limit voltage differences between them and their associated wiring systems. ▶Figure 250–131

250.62 Grounding Electrode Conductor

Grounding electrode conductors can be copper, aluminum or copper-clad aluminum.

250.64 Grounding Electrode Conductor Installation

(A) Aluminum Conductors or Copper-Clad Aluminum.

(1) Aluminum or copper-clad aluminum grounding electrode conductors are not permitted to be installed in direct contact with concrete.

(3) Aluminum or copper-clad aluminum grounding electrode conductors are not permitted to terminate within 18 in. of the Earth.

(B) Conductor Protection. If exposed, a grounding electrode conductor must be securely fastened to the surface on which it is carried.

(1) Not Exposed to Physical Damage. Grounding electrode conductors sized 6 AWG and larger not subject to physical damage can be installed exposed along the surface if securely fastened. ▶Figure 250–132

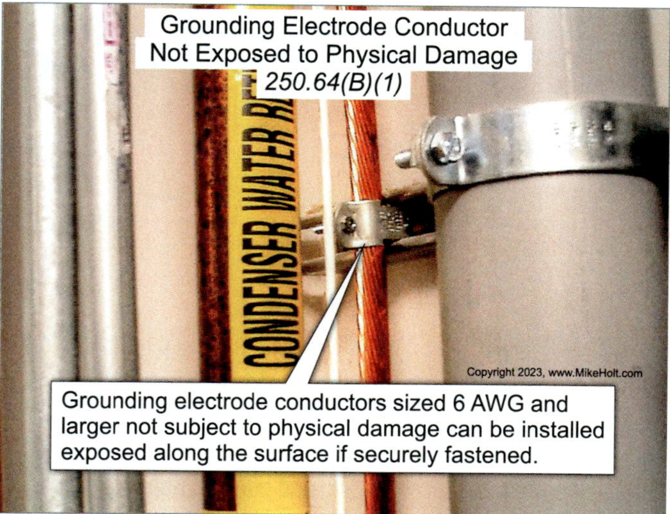

▶Figure 250–132

(2) Exposed to Physical Damage. Grounding electrode conductors sized 6 AWG and larger and exposed to physical damage must be protected in rigid metal conduit (RMC), intermediate metal conduit (IMC), electrical metallic tubing (EMT) Schedule 80 rigid polyvinyl chloride conduit (PVC), reinforced thermosetting resin conduit Type XW (RTRC-XW), or cable armor. ▶Figure 250–133

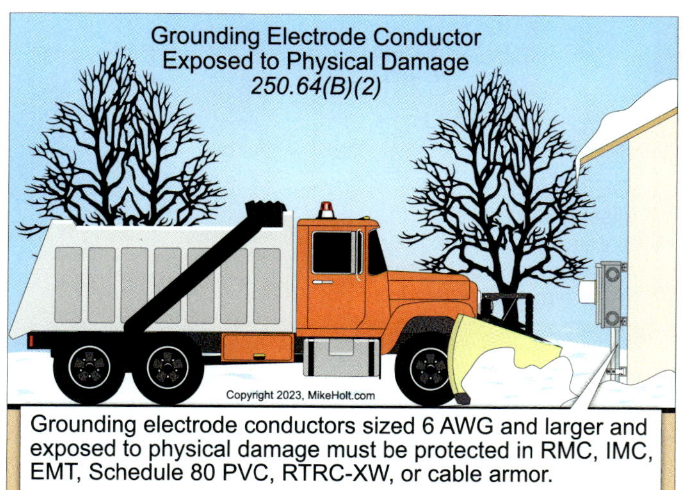

▶Figure 250–133

(3) 8 AWG and Smaller. Grounding electrode conductors 8 AWG and smaller must be installed in RMC, IMC, Schedule 80 PVC, RTRC-XW, EMT, or cable armor.

> **Author's Comment:**
>
> ▶ While Table 250.66 permits the use of 8 AWG copper as the grounding electrode conductor for the phase conductor typically used for a 100A service, using a GEC smaller than 6 AWG is not common.
>
> ▶ Where grounding electrode conductors are installed in RMC, IMC, or EMT, the metal raceways must be bonded at both ends per 250.64(E).

(4) Burial Depth Not Required. Grounding electrode conductors and bonding jumpers in contact with the Earth are not required to comply with the cover requirements of 300.5, but must be protected where subject to physical damage. ▶Figure 250–134

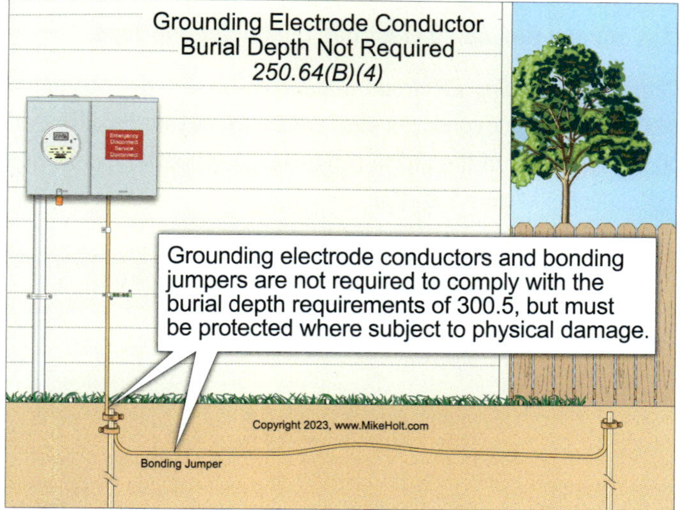

▶Figure 250–134

(C) Continuous. Grounding electrode conductor(s) must be installed without a splice or joint except by:

(1) Irreversible compression-type connectors or exothermic welding ▶Figure 250–135

(2) Busbars connected together

(3) Bolted, riveted, or welded connections to the structural metal frames of buildings

(4) Threaded, welded, brazed, soldered, or bolted-flange connections to metal water piping

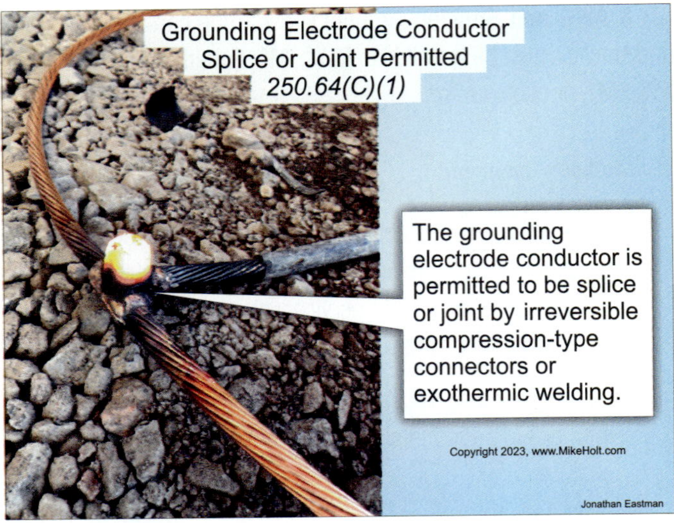

▶Figure 250–135

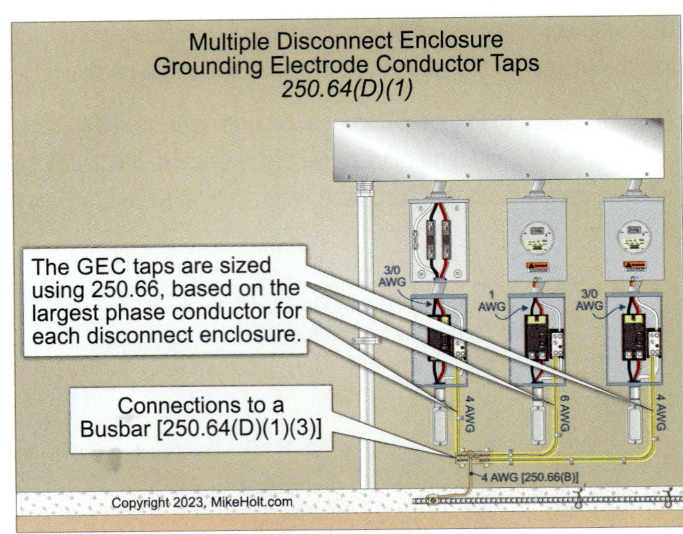

▶Figure 250–137

(D) Multiple Disconnect Enclosures. If a building contains two or more service or building feeder disconnects, the grounding electrode connections must comply with the following:

(1) Common Grounding Electrode Conductor and Taps.

Common Grounding Electrode Conductor. An unspliced common grounding electrode conductor sized in accordance with 250.66 based on the total area of the phase conductor(s) supplying the service disconnects. ▶Figure 250–136

The grounding electrode conductor taps must be connected to the common grounding electrode by any of the following methods:

(1) Exothermic welding

(2) Connectors listed as grounding and bonding equipment

(3) Connections to a busbar not less than ¼ in. thick × 2 in. wide that is securely fastened and installed in an accessible location ▶Figure 250–138

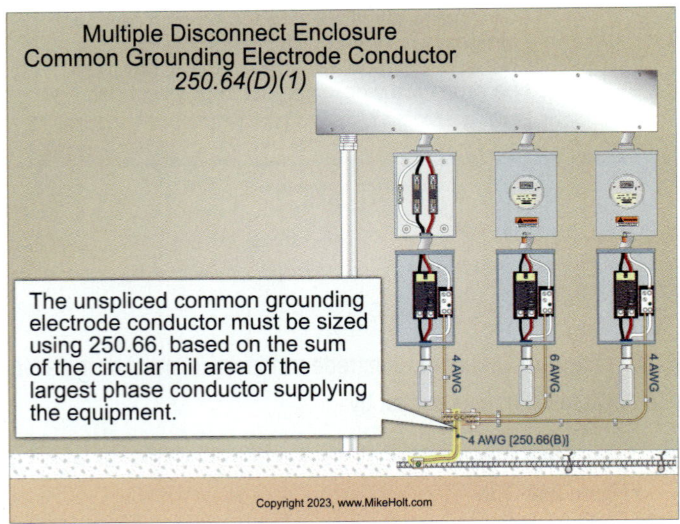

▶Figure 250–136

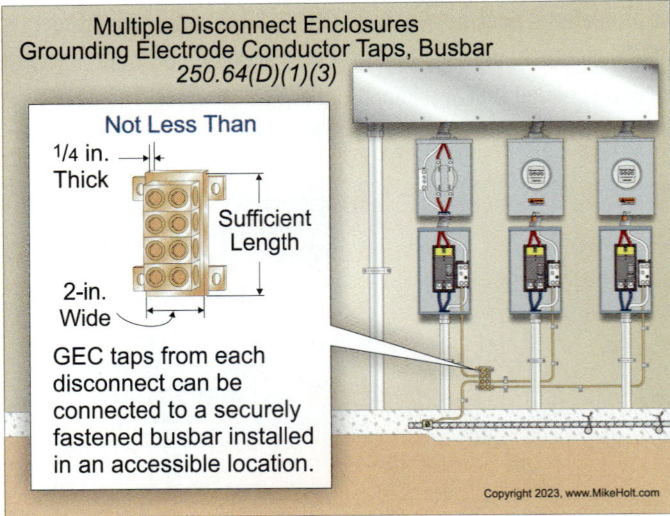

▶Figure 250–138

Grounding Electrode Taps. Grounding electrode conductor taps from each disconnect must be sized no smaller than specified in Table 250.66 and connected to the common grounding electrode conductor. ▶Figure 250–137

(2) Individual Grounding Electrode Conductors. A grounding electrode conductor from each service disconnect sized in accordance with 250.66 based on the phase conductor(s) supplying the service disconnect. ▶Figure 250–139

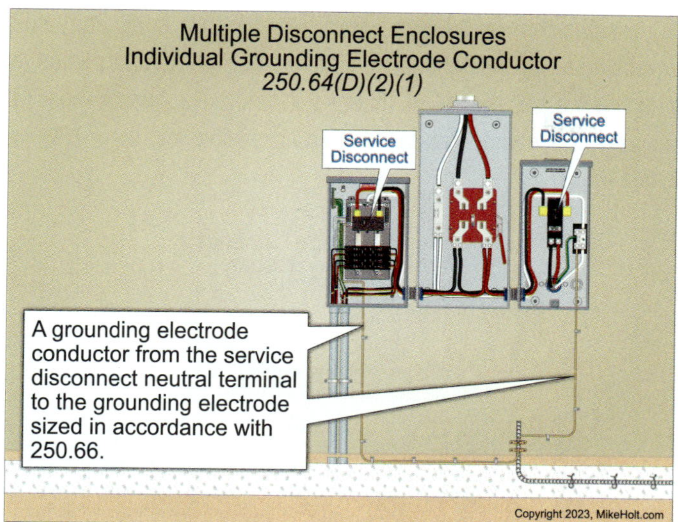

▶Figure 250–139

(3) Supply Side of Disconnects. A grounding electrode conductor on the supply side of the service disconnects, sized in accordance with 250.66 based on the phase conductor(s) supplying the service connected to:

(1) The service neutral conductor ▶Figure 250–140

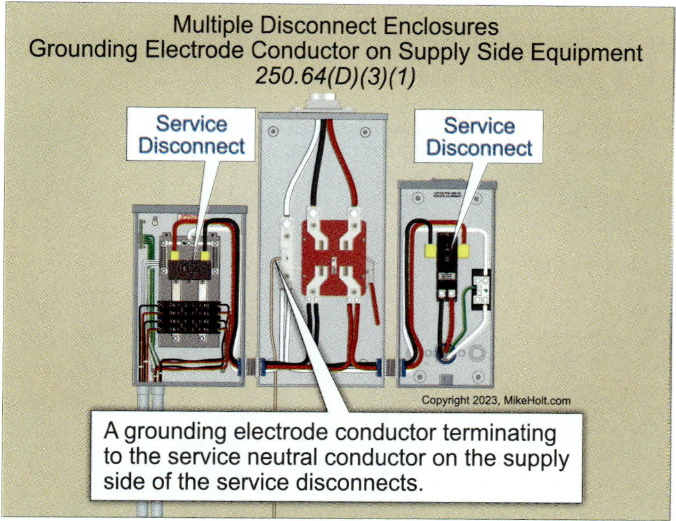

▶Figure 250–140

(2) The equipment grounding conductor of the feeder circuit

(3) The supply-side bonding jumper

(E) Ferrous Raceways, Cable Armor, and Enclosures Containing Grounding Electrode Conductors.

(1) General. Ferrous metal raceways containing the grounding electrode conductor must have each end of the raceway bonded to the grounding electrode conductor. ▶Figure 250–141

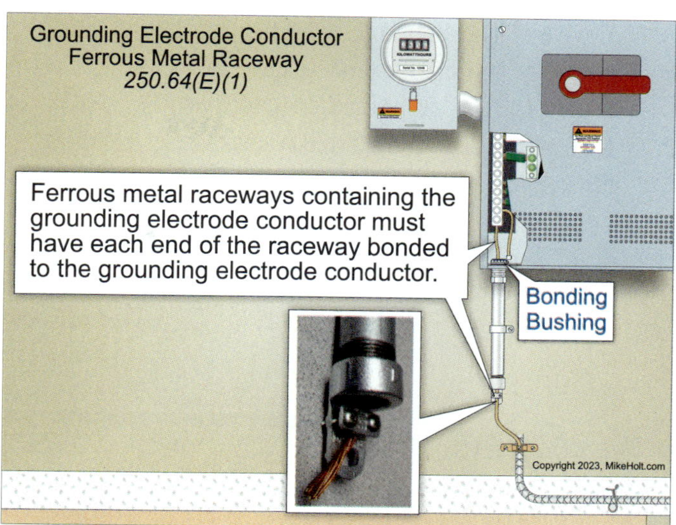

▶Figure 250–141

(2) Methods. Ferrous metal raceways must be bonded in accordance with 250.92(B)(2) through (B)(4).

(3) Size. Bonding jumpers for ferrous metal raceways must be sized no smaller than the grounding electrode conductor in the raceway. ▶Figure 250–142

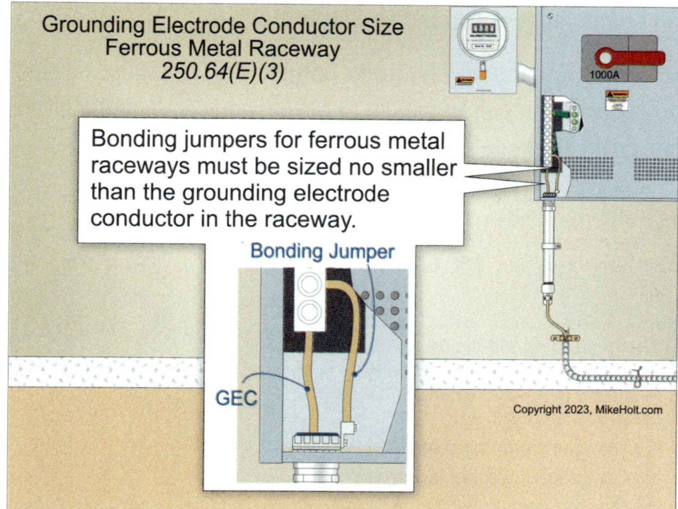

▶Figure 250–142

Author's Comment:

▶ Nonferrous metal raceways, such as aluminum rigid metal conduit, enclosing the grounding electrode conductor are not required to meet the "bonding each end of the raceway to the grounding electrode conductor" provisions of this section.

▶ To save of time and effort, install the grounding electrode conductor in a PVC raceway suitable for the application. Schedule 40 PVC can be used for exposed work [352.10(G)], but Schedule 80 PVC is required in areas subject to physical damage [250.64(B)(2)(3) and 352.10(K)]. ▶Figure 250–143

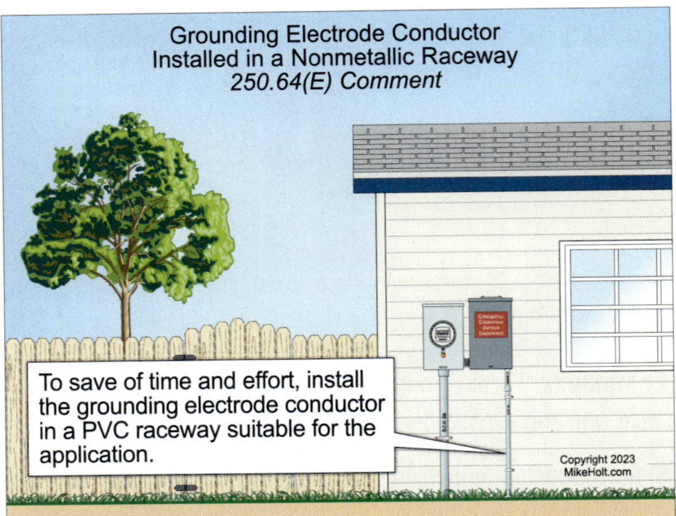

▶Figure 250–143

(F) Termination to Grounding Electrode.

(1) Single Grounding Electrode Conductor. The grounding electrode conductor can terminate to any grounding electrode of the grounding electrode system. ▶Figure 250–144

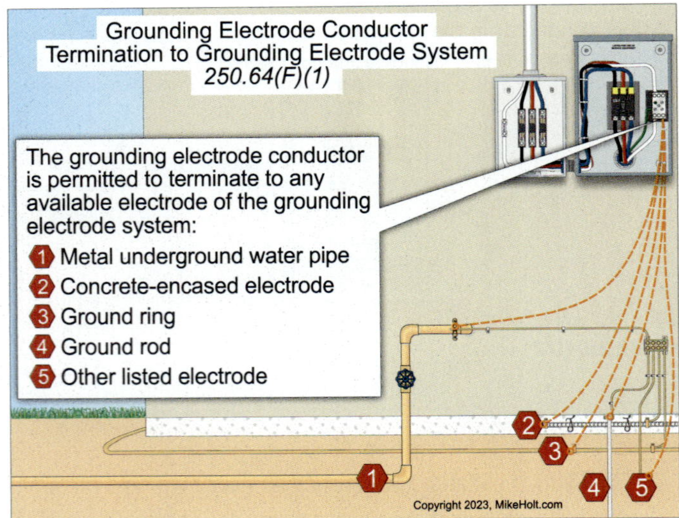

▶Figure 250–144

(2) Multiple Grounding Electrode Conductors. Where multiple grounding electrode conductors are installed, each one can terminate to any grounding electrode of the grounding electrode system.

(3) Termination to Busbar. Grounding electrode conductors and grounding electrode bonding jumpers are permitted to terminate to a busbar not less than ¼ in. thick × 2 in. wide. The busbar must be securely fastened and installed in an accessible location. ▶Figure 250–145

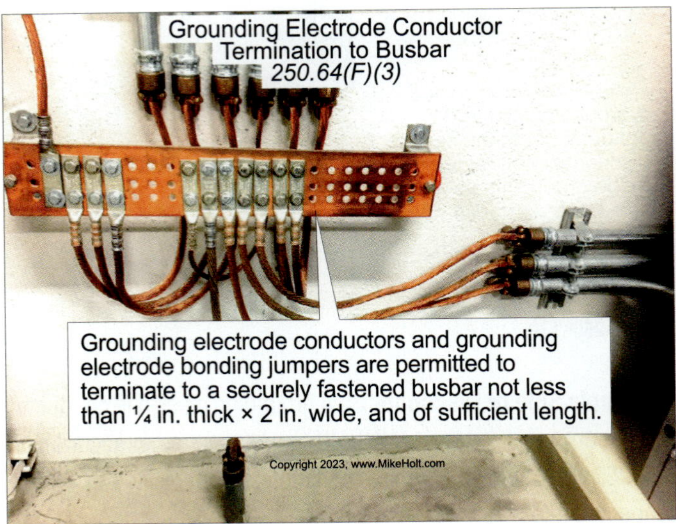

▶Figure 250–145

(G) Equipment with Ventilation Openings. Grounding electrode conductors are not permitted to be installed through ventilation openings of enclosures. ▶Figure 250–146

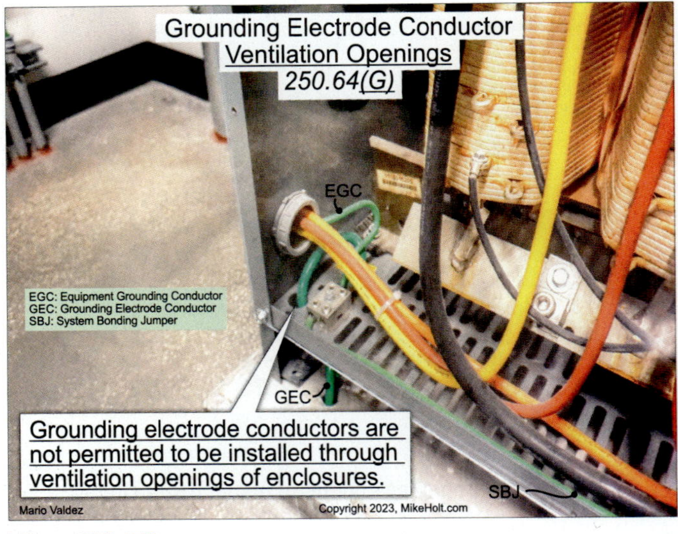

▶Figure 250–146

250.66 Sizing Grounding Electrode Conductors

According to Article 100, "Grounding Electrode Conductor" is the conductor used to connect the system neutral conductor, grounded-phase conductor, or equipment to the grounding electrode system. ▶Figure 250–147

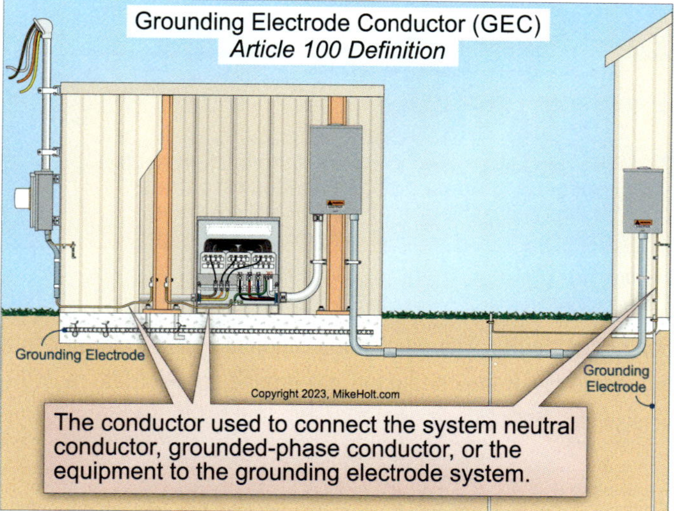

▶Figure 250–147

Except as permitted in 250.66(A) through (C), grounding electrode conductors must be sized in accordance with Table 250.66. ▶Figure 250–148

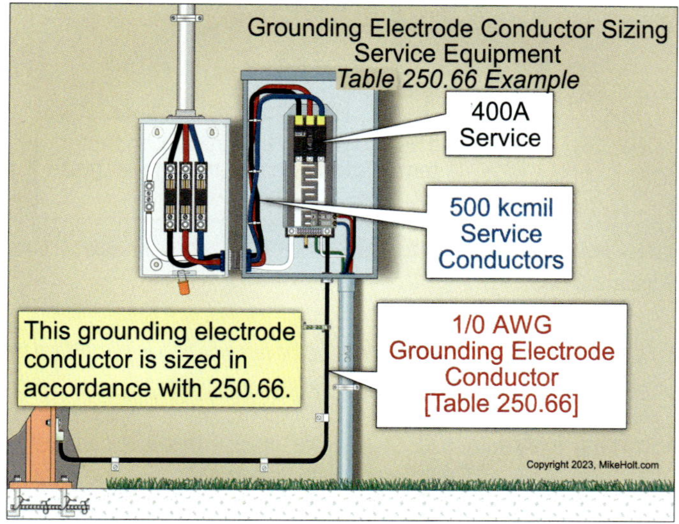

▶Figure 250–148

▶ Grounding Electrode Conductor, Transformer

Question: *What size grounding electrode conductor is required for a 112.50 kVA, three-phase, 480V to 120/208V transformer when the secondary conductors are sized at 600 kcmil?* ▶Figure 250–149

(a) 1/0 AWG   (b) 2/0 AWG   (c) 3/0 AWG   (d) 4/0 AWG

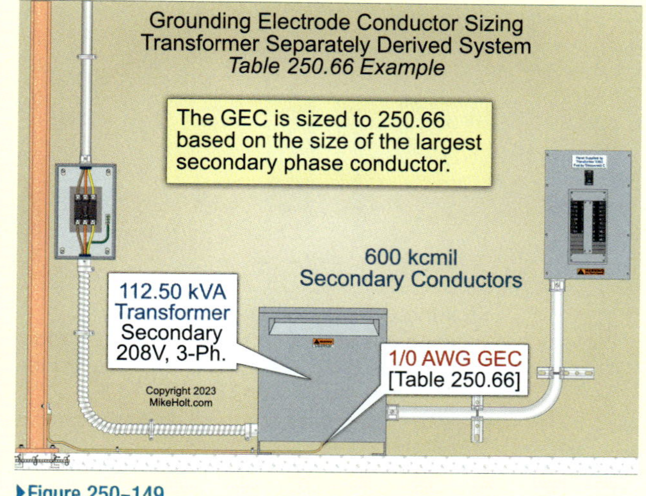

▶Figure 250–149

Answer: *(a) 1/0 AWG*

(A) Ground Rods. If a grounding electrode conductor or grounding electrode bonding jumper only connects to a ground rod [250.52(A)(5)], the grounding electrode conductor is not required to be larger than 6 AWG copper. ▶Figure 250–150

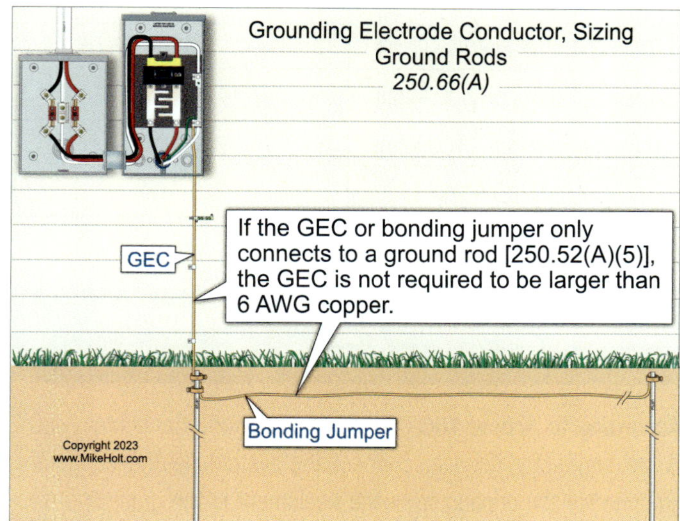

▶Figure 250–150

(B) Concrete-Encased Grounding Electrodes. If a grounding electrode conductor or bonding jumper only connects to a concrete-encased electrode [250.52(A)(3)], the grounding electrode conductor is not required to be larger than 4 AWG copper. ▶Figure 250–151

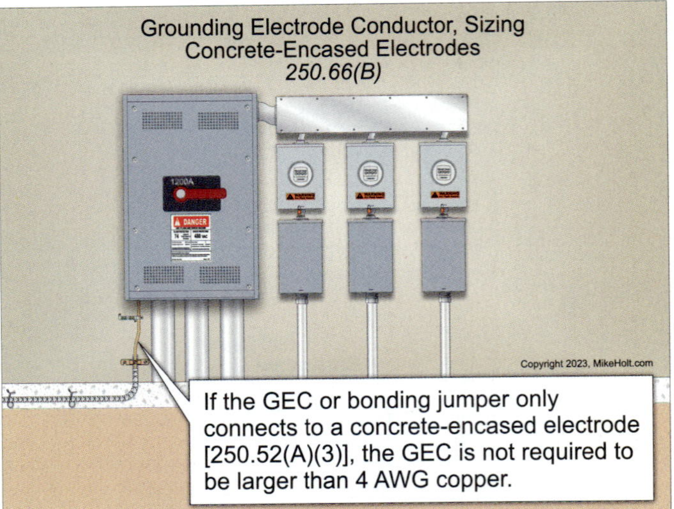

▶Figure 250–151

Table 250.66 Grounding Electrode Conductor

AWG or Area of Parallel Copper Conductors	Copper Grounding Electrode Conductor
2 AWG or Smaller	8 AWG
1 or 1/0 AWG	6 AWG
2/0 or 3/0 AWG	4 AWG
Over 3/0 through 350 kcmil	2 AWG
Over 350 through 600 kcmil	1/0 AWG
Over 600 through 1100 kcmil	2/0 AWG
Over 1100 kcmil	3/0 AWG

250.68 Grounding Electrode Conductor Connection to Grounding Electrodes

According to Article 100, "Grounding Electrode Conductor (GEC)" is the conductor used to connect the system neutral conductor, grounded-phase conductor, or the equipment to the grounding electrode system. ▶Figure 250–152

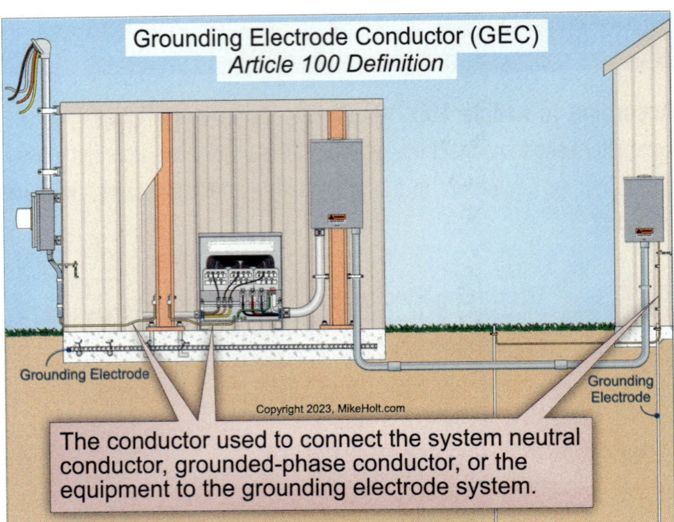

▶Figure 250–152

(A) Accessibility. The mechanical elements used to terminate a grounding electrode conductor to a grounding electrode must be accessible. ▶Figure 250–153

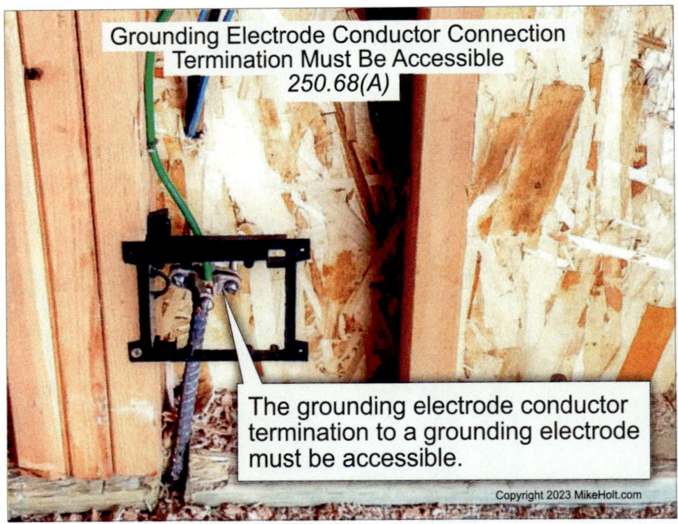

▶Figure 250–153

Ex 1: The grounding electrode conductor termination is permitted to be encased in concrete or buried. ▶Figure 250–154

According to Article 100, "Accessible" means that it is capable of being removed or exposed without damaging the building structure or finish, or not permanently closed in or blocked by the building structure, other electrical equipment, other building systems, or the building finish.

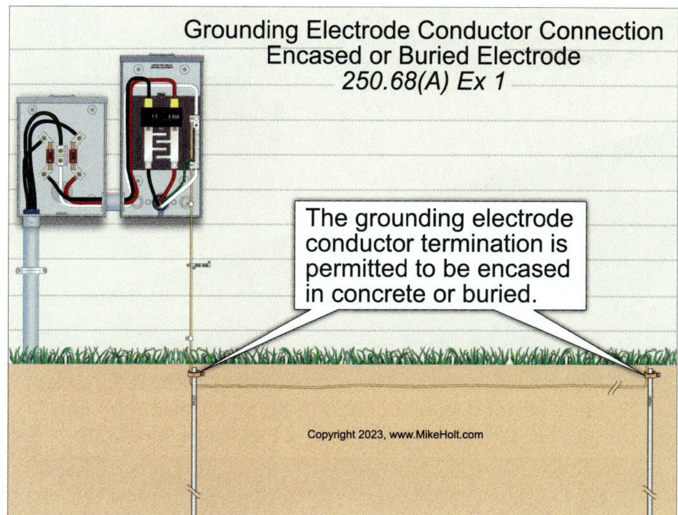

▶Figure 250–154

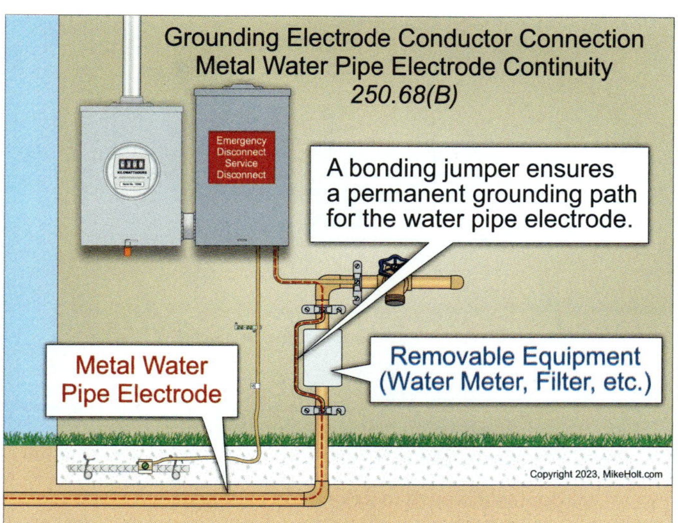

▶Figure 250–155

Author's Comment:

▶ If the grounding electrode attachment fitting is encased in concrete or buried in the Earth, it must be listed for direct soil burial [250.70(A)].

▶ In accordance with "*UL Guide Information KDER*," all grounding electrode connectors that are marked as suitable for direct burial use are also suitable for concrete encasement.

(B) Integrity of Underground Metal Water Pipe Electrode. A bonding jumper must be installed around insulated joints and equipment likely to be disconnected for repairs or replacement for an underground metal water piping system used as a grounding electrode. The bonding jumper must be of sufficient length to allow the removal of such equipment, while retaining the integrity of the grounding path. ▶Figure 250–155

According to Article 100, "Bonding Jumper" is a conductor that ensures electrical conductivity by connecting metal parts of equipment together. ▶Figure 250–156

(C) Grounding Electrode Conductor Connections. Grounding electrode conductors and bonding jumpers are permitted to terminate at the following locations and to be used to extend the connection to an electrode(s):

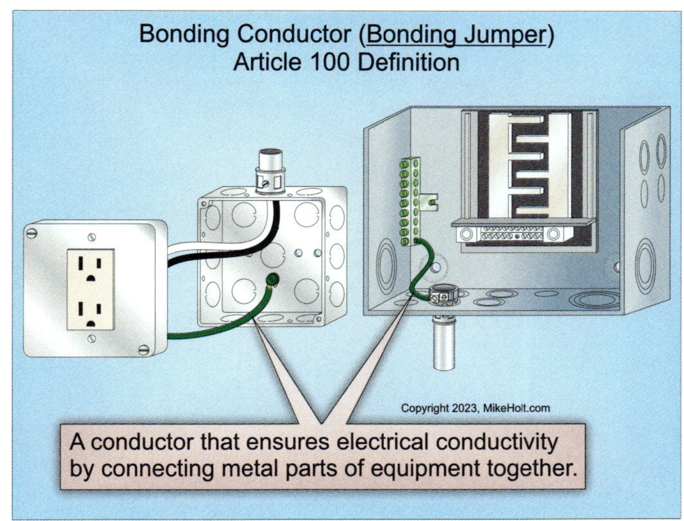

▶Figure 250–156

(1) Interior Metal Water Piping. Interior metal water piping that is electrically continuous with a metal underground water pipe electrode and is not more than 5 ft from the point of entrance to the building, as measured along the water piping, can be used to extend the connection to electrodes. Interior metal water piping more than 5 ft from the point of entrance to the building, as measured along the water piping, is not permitted to be used as a conductor to interconnect electrodes of the grounding electrode system. ▶Figure 250–157

(2) Metal Structural Frame. The metal structural frame of a building can be used as a grounding electrode conductor. ▶Figure 250–158

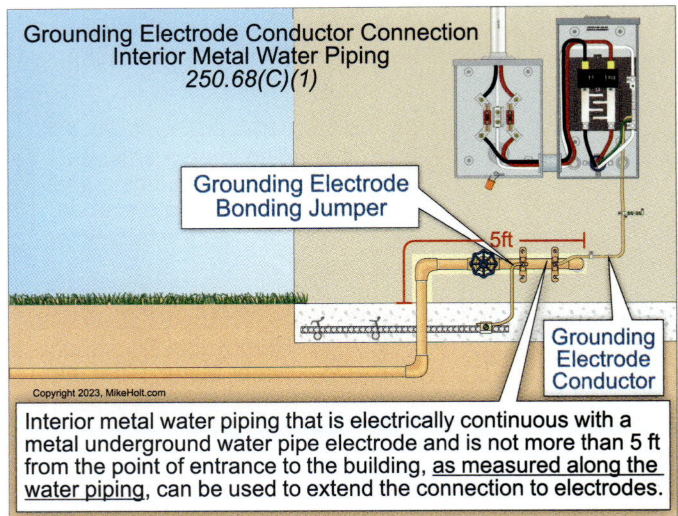

▶Figure 250–157

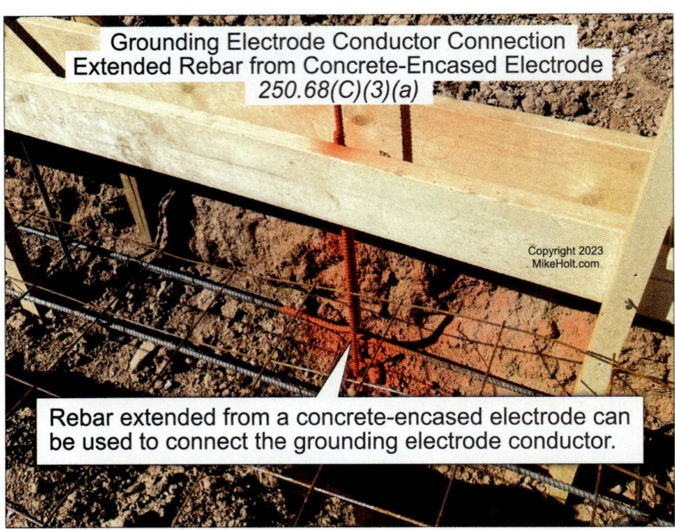

▶Figure 250–159

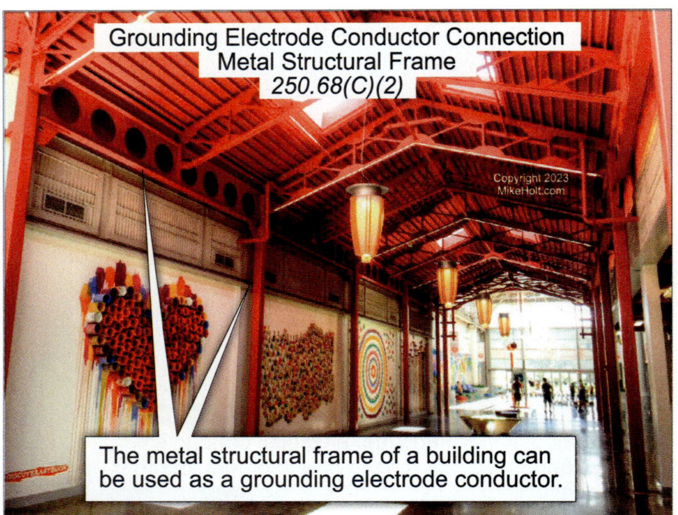

▶Figure 250–158

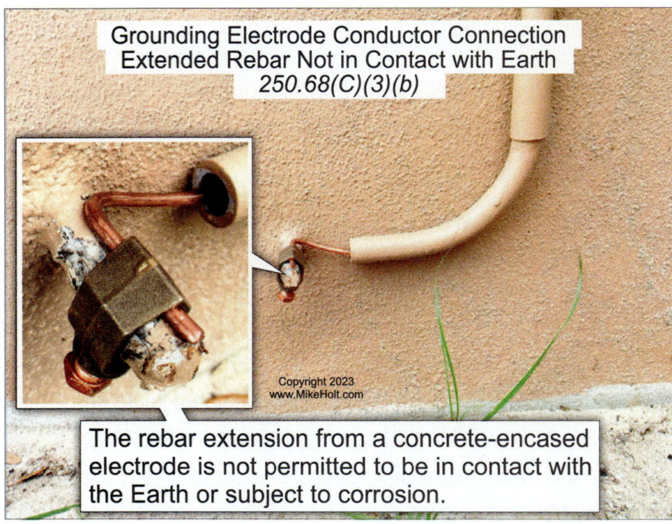

▶Figure 250–160

(3) Rebar from Concrete-Encased Electrode. A rebar-type concrete-encased electrode [250.52(A)(3)] with rebar extended to an accessible location above the concrete foundation or footing is permitted under the following conditions:

(a) Rebar extended to an accessible location to connect a grounding electrode conductor is permitted if the extension is connected to a rebar-type grounding electrode by steel tie wires or other effective means. ▶Figure 250–159

(b) The rebar extension from a concrete-encased electrode is not permitted to be in contact with the Earth or subject to corrosion. ▶Figure 250–160

(c) The rebar extension is not permitted to be used as a conductor to interconnect the electrodes of grounding electrode systems.

250.70 Grounding Electrode
Conductor Termination Fittings

(A) General.

Termination. The grounding electrode conductor must terminate to the grounding electrode by exothermic welding, listed lugs, listed pressure connectors, listed clamps, or other means listed for the grounding electrode and the grounding electrode conductor. ▶Figure 250–161

Direct Burial or Concrete Encasement. When the termination to a grounding electrode encased in concrete or buried, the termination fitting must be listed for direct soil burial. ▶Figure 250–162

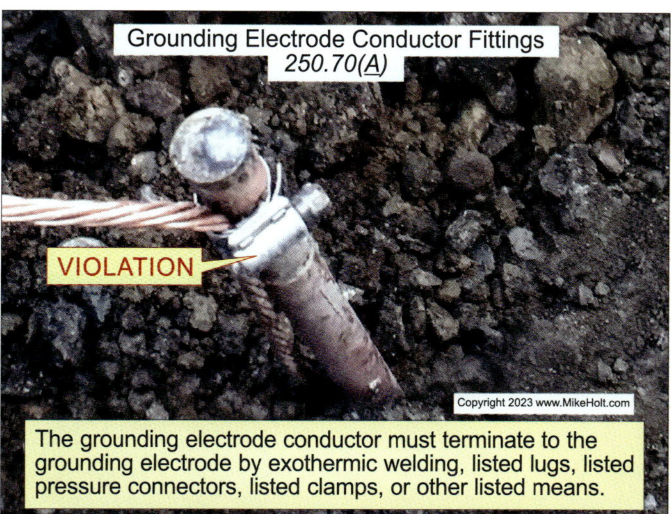

▶Figure 250–161

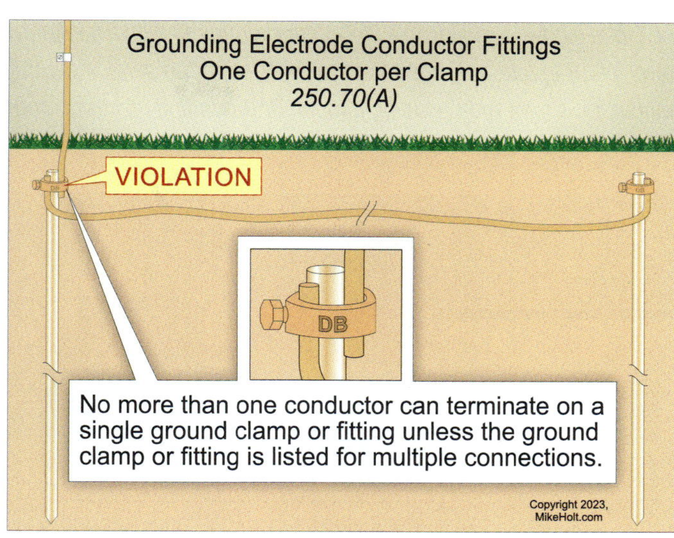

▶Figure 250–163

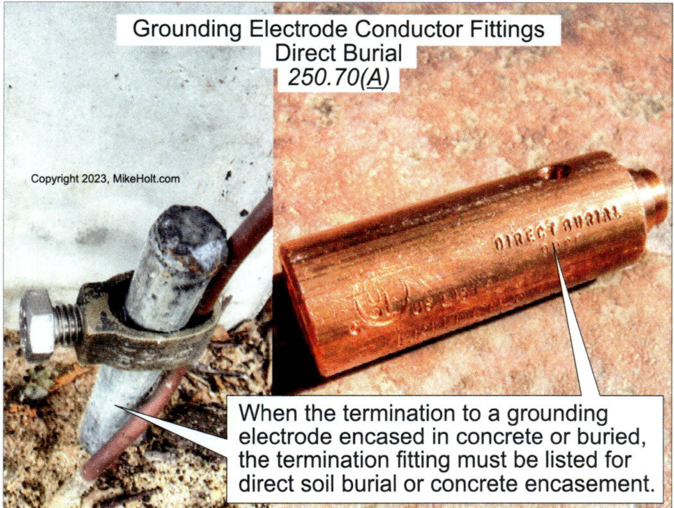

▶Figure 250–162

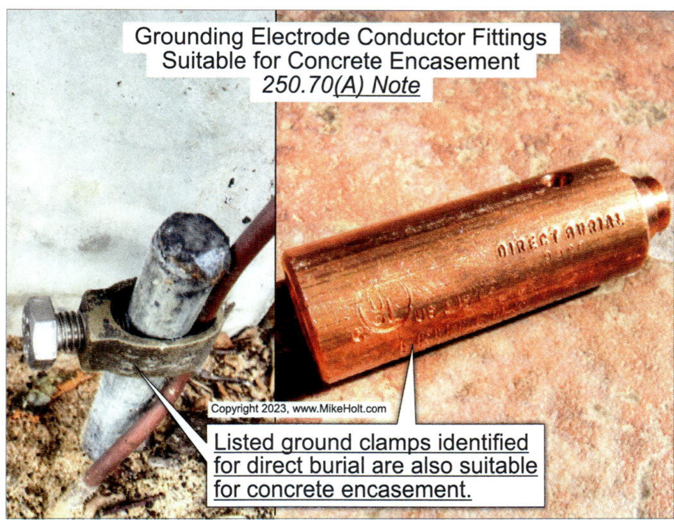

▶Figure 250–164

Only One Conductor. No more than one conductor can terminate on a single ground clamp or fitting, unless the ground clamp or fitting is listed for multiple connections. ▶Figure 250–163

Note: Listed ground clamps identified for direct burial are also suitable for concrete encasement. ▶Figure 250–164

Part IV. Enclosure and Raceway

250.80 Service Raceways and Enclosures

Metal raceways and enclosures containing service conductors must be connected to the service neutral conductor. ▶Figure 250–165

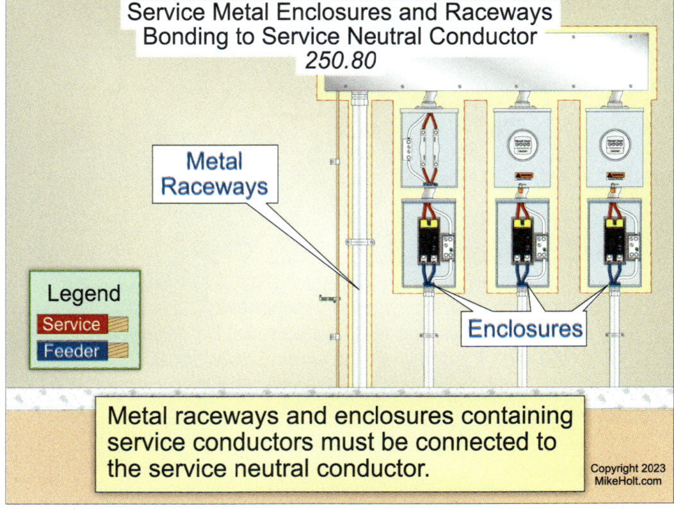

▶Figure 250–165

Ex: Metal elbows installed in a PVC underground run with a minimum cover of 18 in. are not required to be bonded to the service neutral conductor, supply-side bonding jumper, or grounding electrode conductor. ▶Figure 250–166

Ex 2: Short sections of metal raceways used for the support or physical protection of cables are not required to be connected to the circuit equipment grounding conductor.

Ex 3: Metal elbows are not required to be bonded if the metal elbows have a minimum cover of 18 in. or are encased in not less than 2 in. of concrete. ▶Figure 250–168

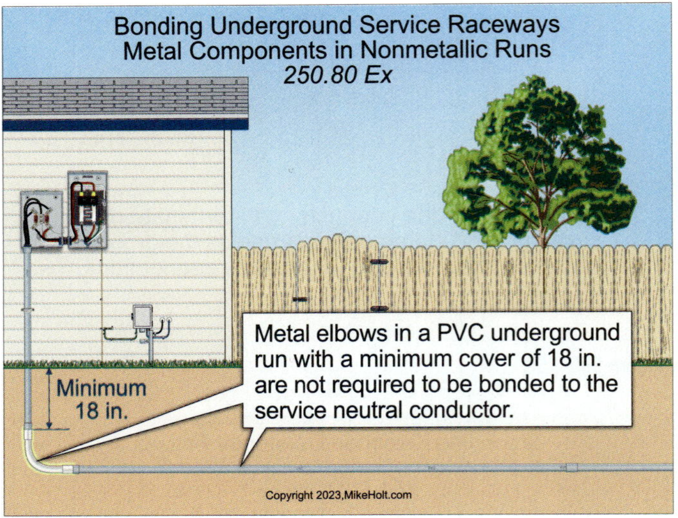

▶Figure 250–166

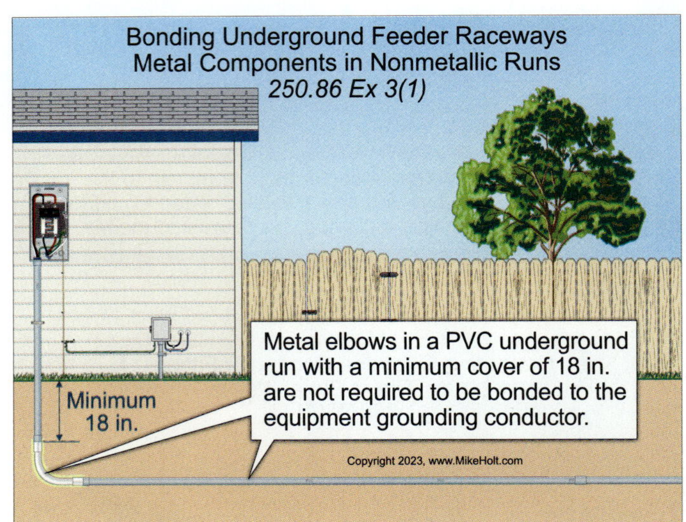

▶Figure 250–168

250.86 Other than Service Enclosures and Raceways

Metal raceways and enclosures containing feeder and branch circuit conductors must be connected to the circuit equipment grounding conductor. ▶Figure 250–167

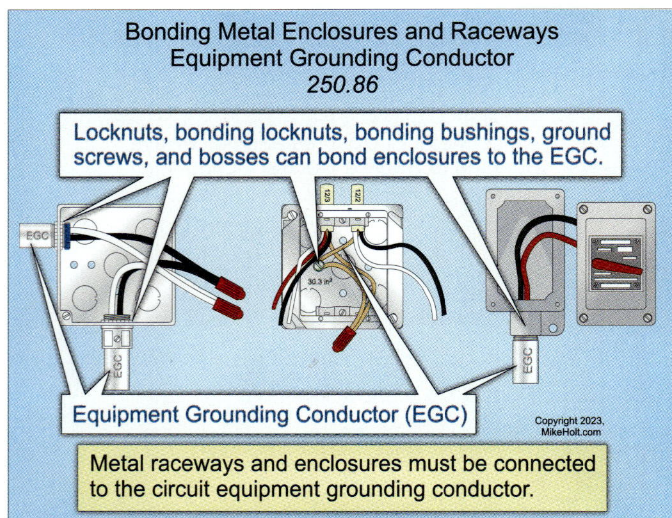

▶Figure 250–167

Part V. Bonding

250.92 Bonding Metal Service Raceways and Enclosures

(A) Metal Raceways and Enclosures. Metal raceways and enclosures containing service conductors must be bonded in accordance with 250.92(B). ▶Figure 250–169

According to Article 100, "Service Conductors" are conductors from the serving electric utility service point to the service disconnect. ▶Figure 250–170

(B) Methods of Bonding Raceways. Metal raceways and enclosures containing service conductors must be bonded by one of the following methods:

(1) Service Neutral. Bonding metal raceways and enclosures to the service neutral conductor. ▶Figure 250–171

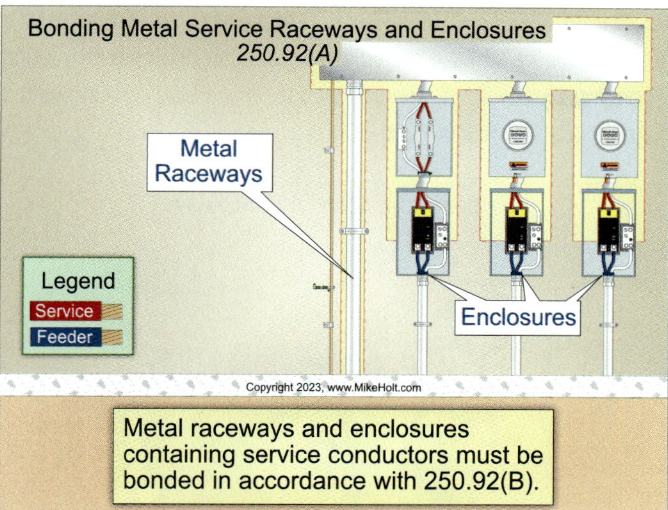

▶Figure 250–169

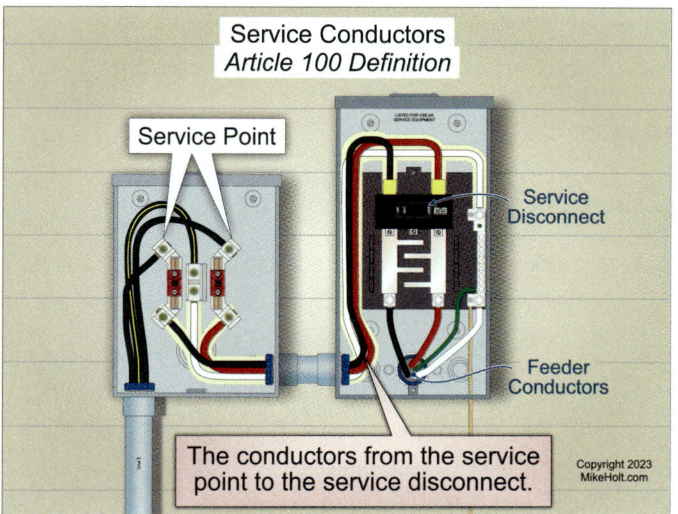

▶Figure 250–170

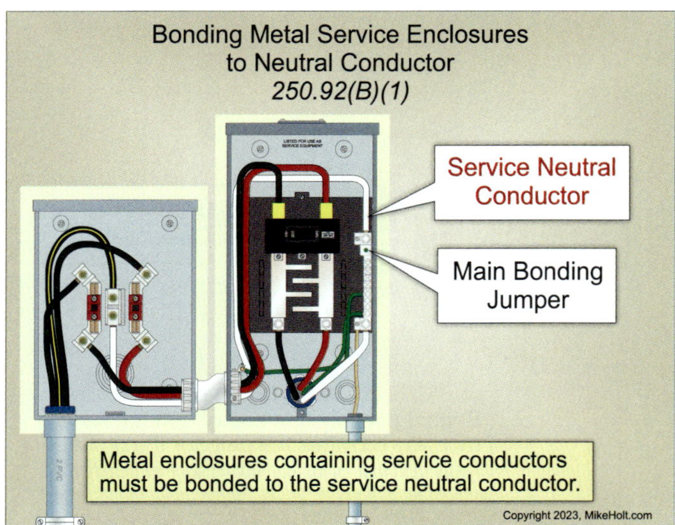

▶Figure 250–171

Author's Comment:

▶ A main bonding jumper is required to bond the service disconnect to the service neutral conductor [250.24(C) and 250.28].

▶ A supply-side bonding jumper can be used to bond metal service raceways to the neutral conductor.

▶ At the service disconnect, the service neutral conductor provides the effective ground-fault current path to the source [250.24(D)].

▶ A supply-side bonding jumper is not required to be installed in PVC conduit containing service-entrance conductors [250.142(A)(1) and 352.60 Ex 2]. ▶Figure 250–172

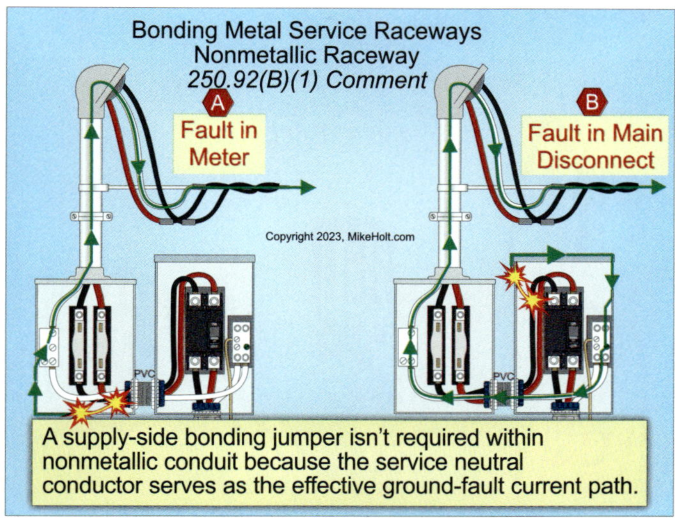

▶Figure 250–172

(2) Threaded Entries. Bonding by tightening wrenchtight threaded couplings, threaded entries, or listed threaded hubs on enclosures. ▶Figure 250–173

(3) Threadless Fittings. Bonding by terminating metal raceways to threadless fittings. ▶Figure 250–174

(4) Other Listed Fittings. Bonding by the use of bonding-type locknuts, bonding wedges, or bonding bushings with bonding jumpers to the service neutral conductor as follows:

Ring Knockouts. Metal service raceways that terminate to a metal enclosure with ringed knockouts require a bonding fitting with a bonding jumper to the service neutral conductor. ▶Figure 250–175

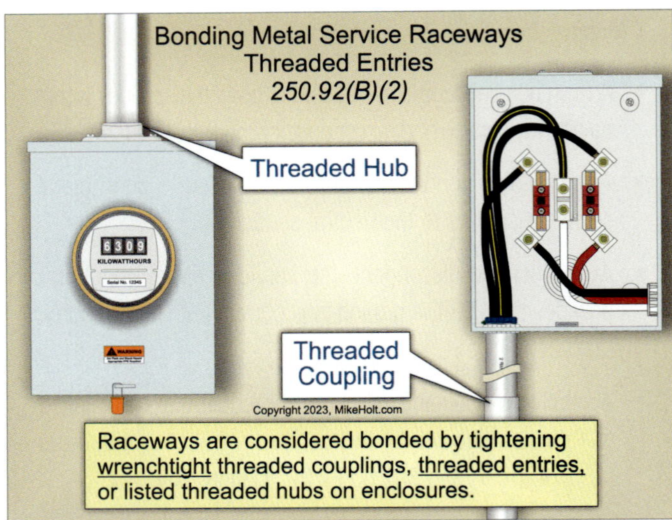

▶Figure 250–173

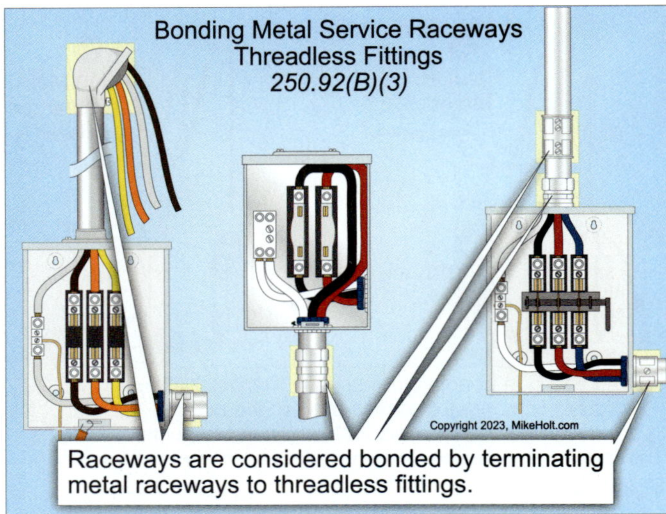

▶Figure 250–174

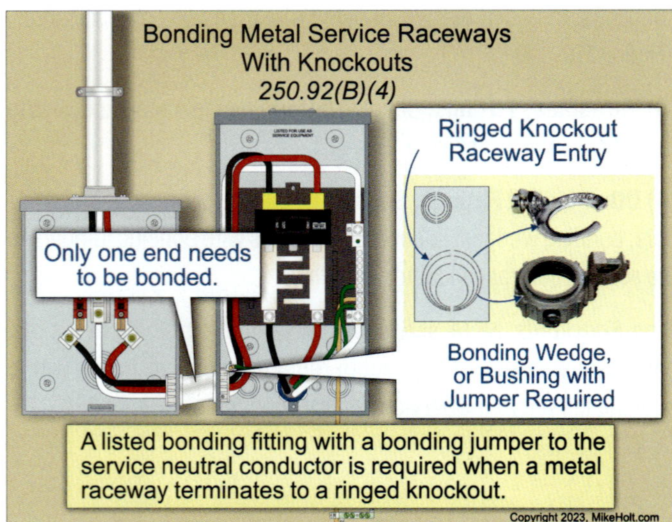

▶Figure 250–175

No Ringed Knockout. Metal service raceways that terminate to a metal enclosure without ringed knockouts can be bonded by using a bonding-type locknut, bonding wedge, or bonding bushing with a bonding jumper. ▶Figure 250–176

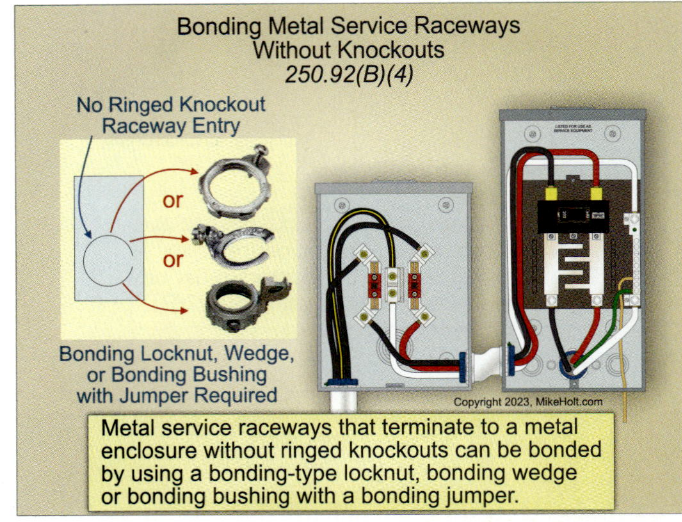

▶Figure 250–176

Author's Comment:

▶ A bonding locknut differs from a standard locknut in that it contains a bonding screw with a sharp point that drives into the metal enclosure to ensure a solid connection.

▶ Bonding one end of a service raceway to the service neutral is all that is necessary to provide a low-impedance fault current path to the source required by 250.4(A)(3) and (A)(5). ▶Figure 250–177

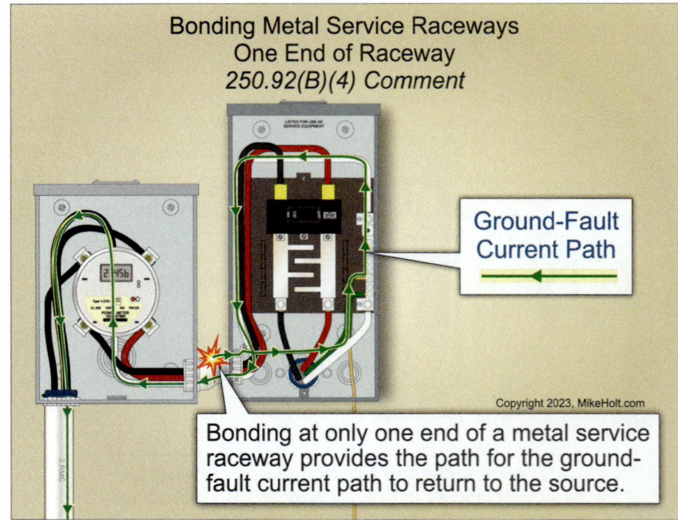

▶Figure 250–177

250.94 Bonding for Communications Systems

According to Article 100, "Intersystem Bonding Termination" is a device that provides a means to connect intersystem bonding conductors for communications systems to the grounding electrode system in accordance with 250.94. ▶Figure 250–178

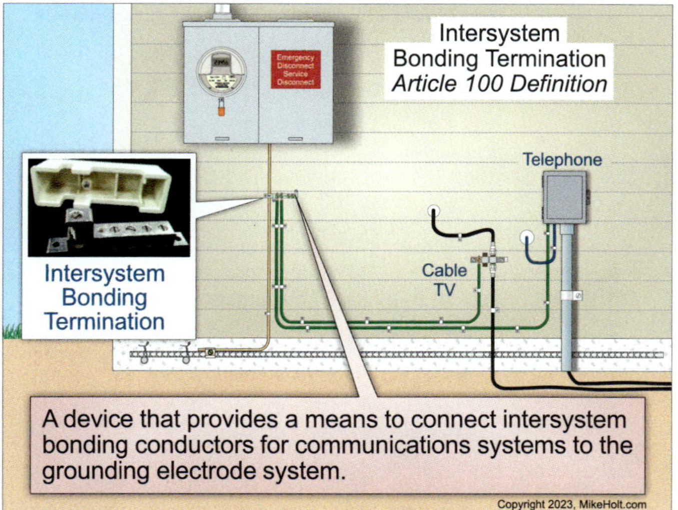

▶Figure 250–178

(A) Intersystem Bonding Termination Device. An intersystem bonding termination device must be installed at the service equipment, meter enclosures, or at the disconnect for a building supplied by a feeder and meet all the following requirements:

(1) Be accessible for connection and inspection. ▶Figure 250–179

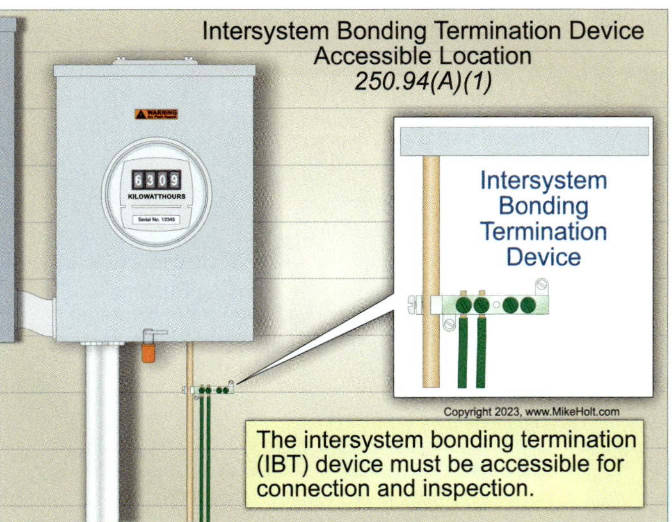

▶Figure 250–179

(2) Have a capacity for at least three intersystem bonding conductors.

(3) Be installed not to interfere with the opening of any enclosure.

(4) The intersystem bonding termination device (ITB) must be:

(a) Securely mounted to the <u>metal</u> service disconnect enclosure, <u>metal</u> meter enclosure, <u>metal</u> service raceway, or the grounding electrode conductor. ▶Figure 250–180

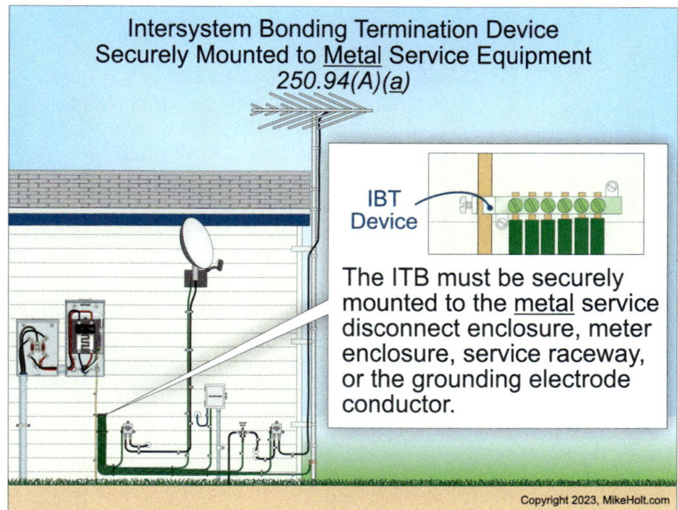

▶Figure 250–180

(b) Securely mounted to the <u>metal</u> remote building feeder disconnect enclosure or grounding electrode conductor. ▶Figure 250–181

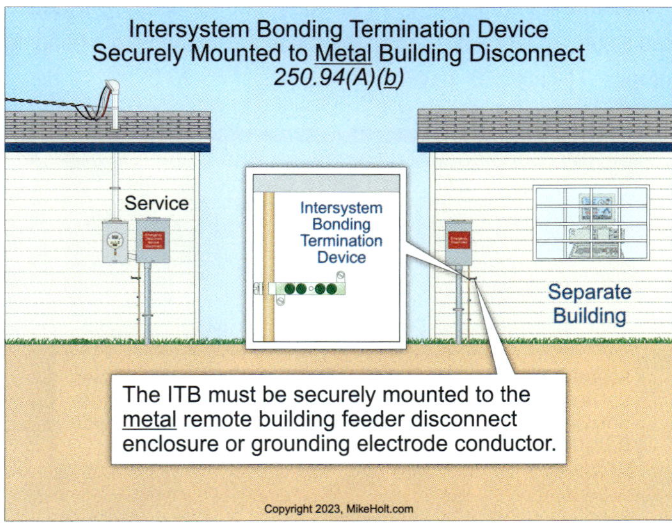

▶Figure 250–181

(5) Listed as grounding and bonding equipment.

Ex: An intersystem bonding termination device is not required where communications systems are not likely to be used.

Note: Communications systems within the scope of Chapter 8 (telephone, antennas, and CATV) must be bonded to the intersystem bonding termination device. ▶Figure 250–182

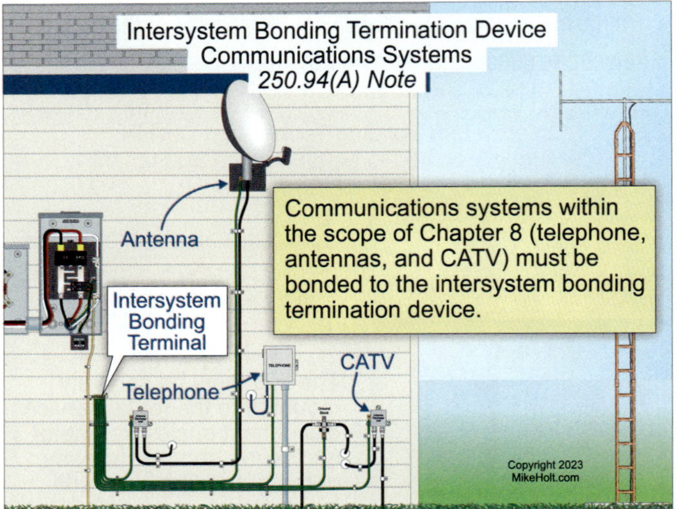

▶Figure 250–182

250.97 Bonding Metal Raceways and Metal Cables Containing 277V and 480V Circuits

Metal raceways and metal cables containing feeder or branch circuit conductors (operating at 277V or 480V) and terminating at ringed knockouts, must be bonded to the metal enclosure with a bonding jumper. ▶Figure 250–183

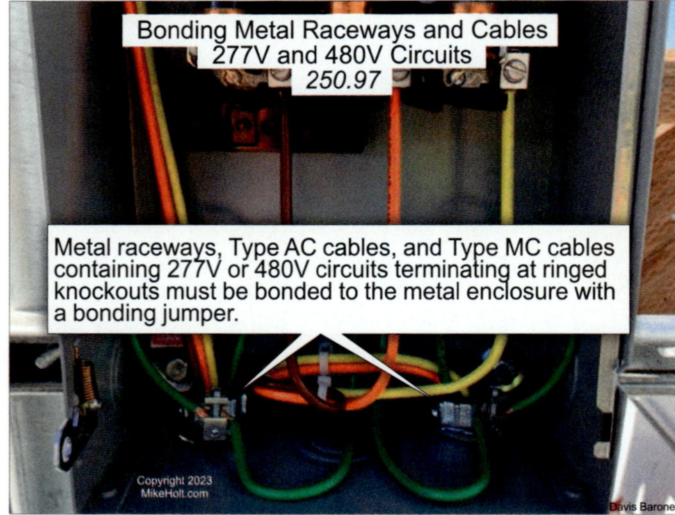

▶Figure 250–183

▸ Bonding jumpers for raceways and cables containing 277V or 480V circuits are required at ringed knockout terminations to ensure the ground-fault current path has the capacity to safely conduct the maximum ground-fault current likely to be imposed [110.10, 250.4(A)(5), and 250.96(A)]. Ringed knockouts are not listed to withstand the heat generated by a 277V ground fault, which generates five times as much heat as does a 120V ground fault. ▶Figure 250–184

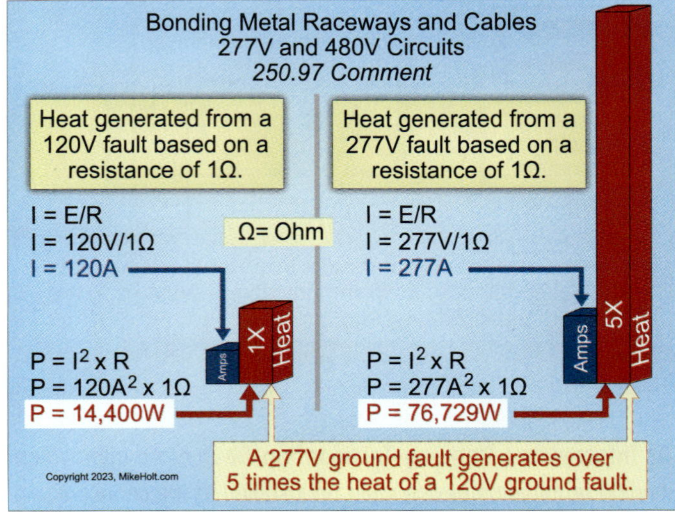

▶Figure 250–184

Ex: A bonding jumper is not required if reducing washers or ringed knockout are not encountered at metal raceway and metal cable terminations. ▶Figure 250–185

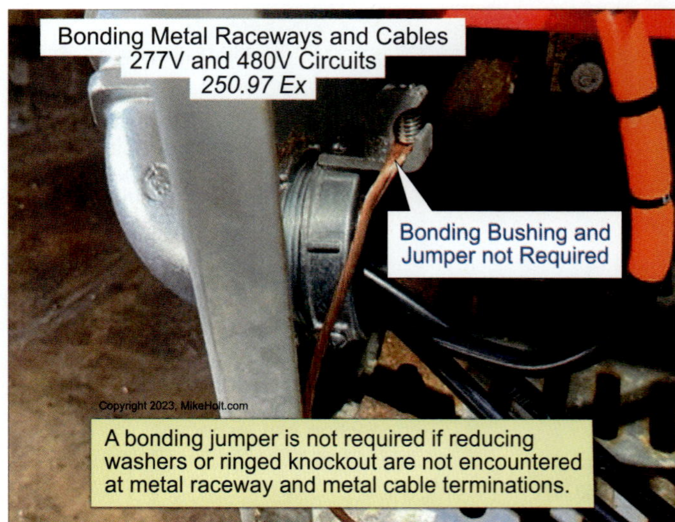

▶Figure 250–185

250.98 Bonding Loosely Jointed Metal Raceways

Metal raceways with expansion fittings, expansion-deflection fittings, deflection fittings, or telescoping sections must be made electrically continuous using equipment bonding jumpers. ▶Figure 250–186

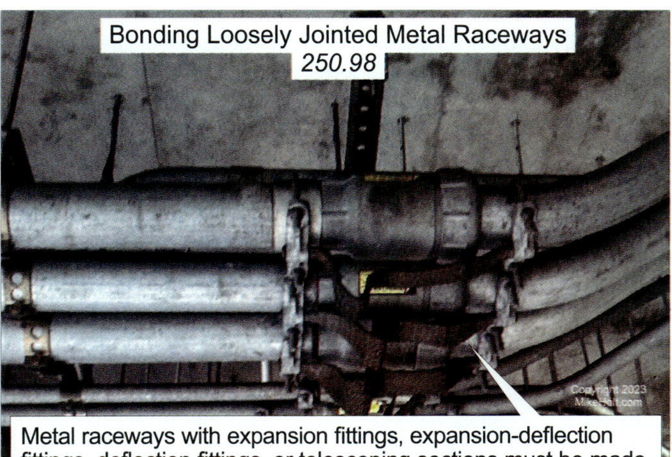

▶Figure 250–186

According to Article 100, "Equipment Bonding Jumper" is the conductor used to ensure electrical continuity between two or more portions of the equipment grounding conductor.

250.100 Bonding in Hazardous (Classified) Locations

Bonding in hazardous (classified) locations must be installed using one of the methods in 250.92(B)(2) through (4), whether or not an equipment grounding conductor of the wire type is installed.

250.102 Bonding Jumper Sizing

(C) Supply-Side Bonding Jumper Sizing.

According to Article 100, "Supply-Side Bonding Jumper" is the conductor installed on the supply side of a service, within the service equipment, or separately derived system that ensures conductivity between metal parts required to be electrically connected. ▶Figure 250–187, ▶Figure 250–188, and ▶Figure 250–189

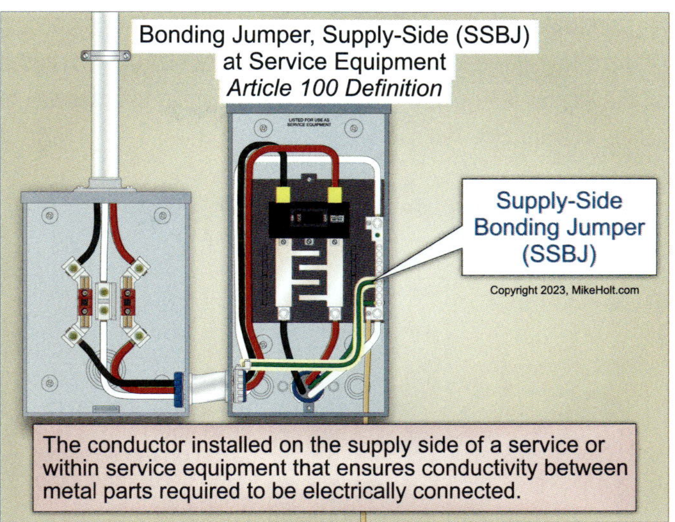

▶Figure 250–187

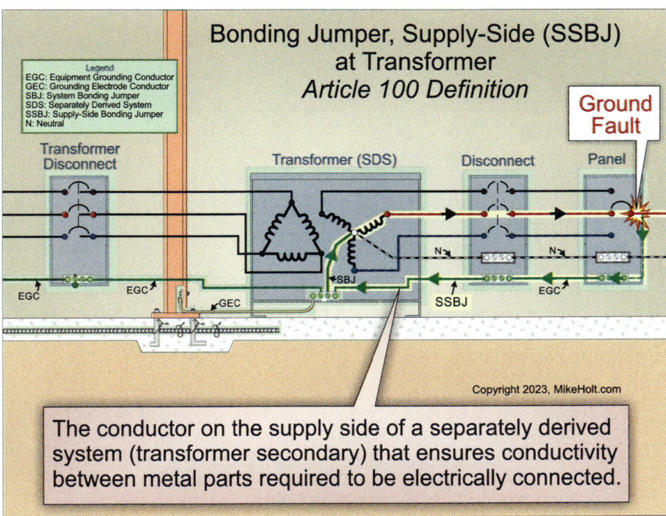

▶Figure 250–188

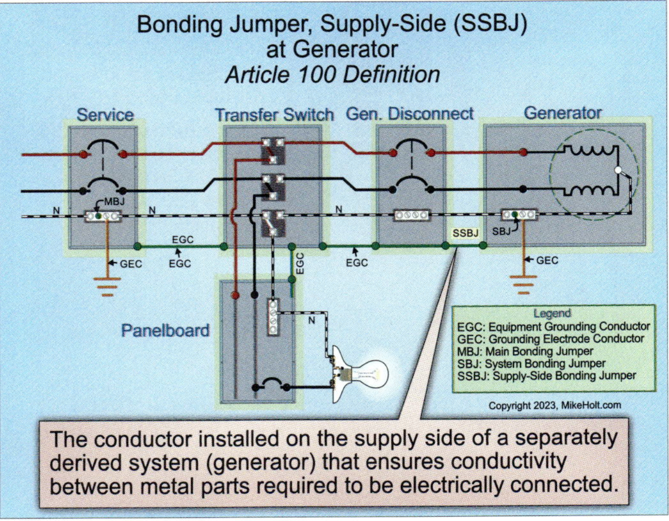

▶Figure 250–189

(1) Conductors in Single Raceway or Cable. Supply-side bonding jumpers must be sized in accordance with Table 250.102(C)(1) based on the size or area of the phase conductor within the raceway or cable. ▶Figure 250–190

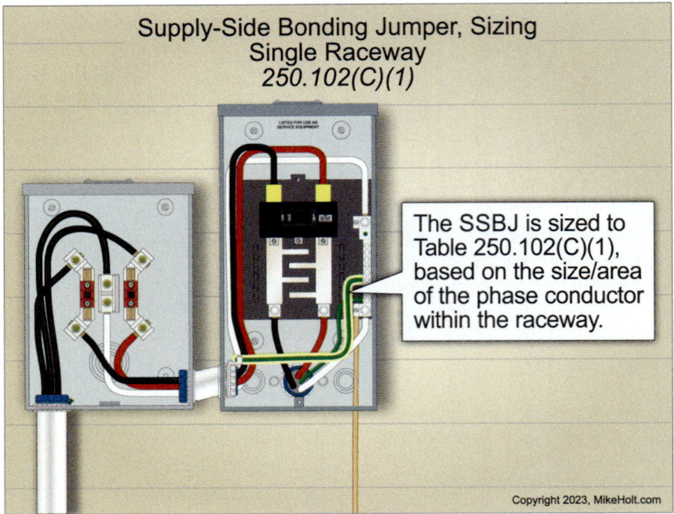

▶Figure 250–190

> ▶ **Example 1**
>
> *Question: What size copper single supply-side bonding jumper is required for a raceway containing 3/0 AWG copper service conductors?*
> ▶Figure 250–191
>
> *(a) 1 AWG   (b) 2 AWG   (c) 3 AWG   (d) 4 AWG*

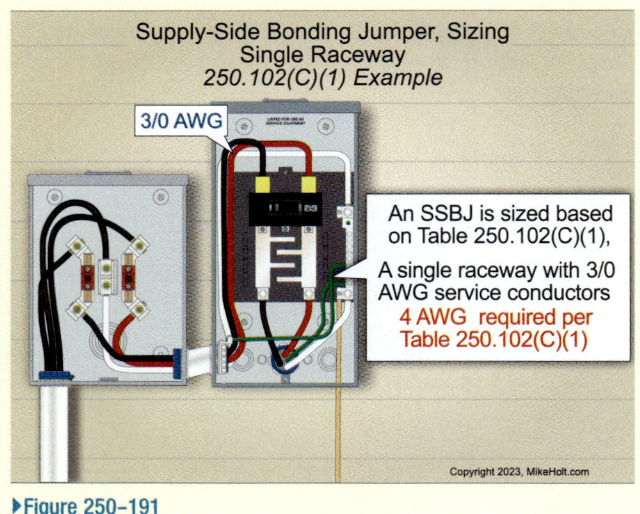

> ▶Figure 250–191
>
> ***Answer:** (d) 4 AWG*

(2) Parallel Conductors in Multiple Raceways or Cables. If the phase conductors are <u>connected in parallel</u> in multiple raceways or cables, the supply-side bonding jumper must be sized in accordance with either of the following:

(1) Individual Bonding Jumper for Each Raceway. An individual bonding jumper for each raceway or cable must be selected from Table 250.102(C)(1) based on the size or area of the largest phase conductors in each raceway or cable. ▶Figure 250–192

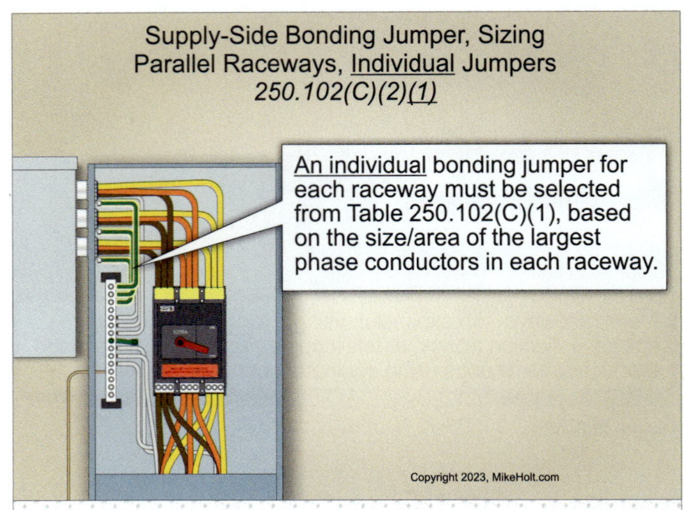

▶Figure 250–192

> ▶ **Example 2**
>
> *Question: What size individual copper supply-side bonding jumper is required for each of three metal raceways, if each raceway contains 600 kcmil copper service conductors in parallel?* ▶Figure 250–193
>
> *(a) 2 AWG   (b) 1 AWG   (c) 1/0 AWG   (d) 2/0 AWG*
>
> *Solution:*
>
> *A single supply-side bonding jumper is permitted for multiple raceways based on the area of the supply-side 600 kcmil phase conductors.*
>
> ***Answer:** (c) 1/0 AWG*

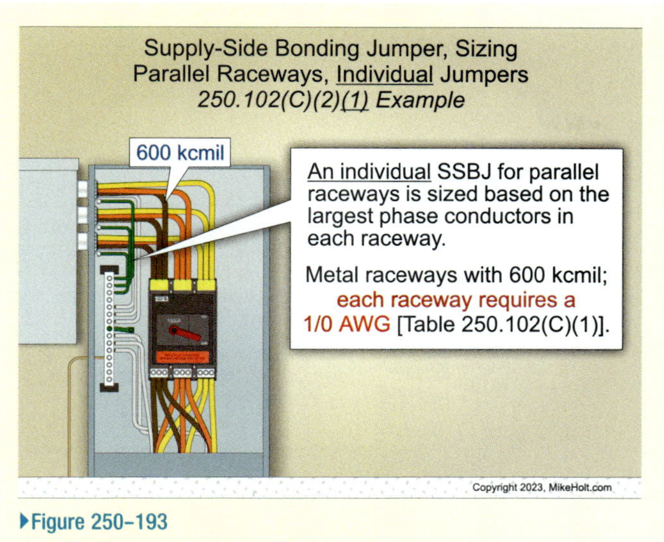

▶Figure 250–193

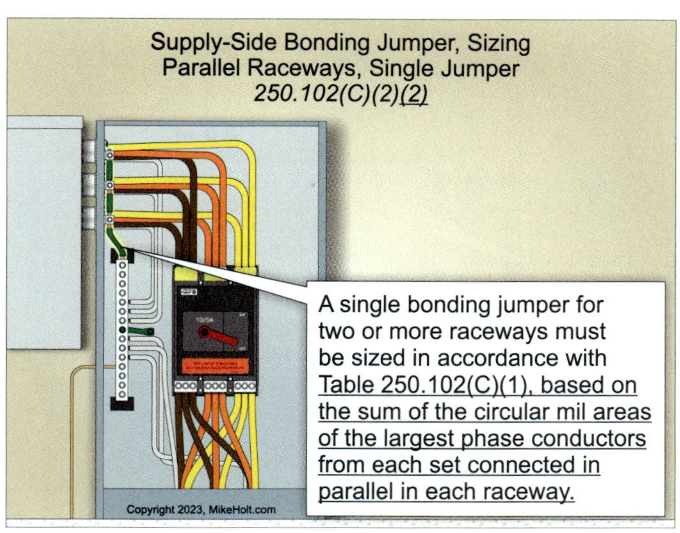

▶Figure 250–194

Table 250.102(C)(1) Neutral Conductor, Main Bonding Jumper, System Bonding Jumper, and Supply-Side Bonding Jumper

Size of Largest Phase Conductor Per Raceway or Equivalent Area for Parallel Conductors	Size of Bonding Jumper or Neutral Conductor	
Copper	Aluminum or Copper-Clad Aluminum	Copper-Aluminum
2 or smaller	1/0 or smaller	8 CU–6 AL
1 or 1/0	2/0 or 3/0	6 CU–4 AL
2/0 or 3/0	Over 3/0 250 kcmil	4 CU–2 AL
Over 3/0–350 kcmil	Over 250–500 kcmil	2 CU–1/0 AL
Over 350–600 kcmil	Over 500–900 kcmil	1/0 CU–3/0 AL
Over 600–1100 kcmil	Over 900–1750 kcmil	2/0 CU–4/0 AL
Over 1100 kcmil	Over 1750 kcmil	See Note 1

If the total area of the parallel phase conductors exceeds 1100 kcmil, then the size of the single bonding jumper is not permitted to be sized less than 12.5 percent of the total are of the parallel phase conductors.

(2) Single Bonding Jumper for All Raceways. A single bonding jumper for two or more raceways or cables containing parallel conductors must be sized in accordance with Table 250.102(C)(1), based on the sum of the circular mil areas of all parallel phase conductors.

▶Figure 250–194

▶ Example 3

Question: *What size single copper supply-side bonding jumper is required for all three metal raceways, if each raceway contains 600 kcmil copper service conductors in parallel?* ▶Figure 250–195

(a) 4/0 AWG (b) 250 kcmil (c) 300 kcmil (d) 350 kcmil

Solution:

A single bonding jumper for two or more raceways or cables containing parallel conductors must be sized in accordance with Table 250.102(C)(1), based on the sum of the circular mil areas of all parallel phase conductors.

If the total area of the phase conductors exceeds 1,100 kcmil, then the size of the single bonding jumper is not permitted to be sized less than 12.5 percent of the total are of the parallel phase conductors.

Step 1: *Each raceway has 600 kcmil phase conductors.*

Step 2: *Total are of three 600 kcmil phase conductors = 1,800 kcmil.*

Step.3: *SSBJ sized to 12.5 percent of 1,800 kcmil x 12.5% = 225 kcmil.*

Answer: *(b) 250 kcmil*

Note 1: The term "supply conductors" includes phase conductors that do not have overcurrent protection on their supply side and terminate at the service disconnect or the first disconnect of a separately derived system.

Note 2: See Chapter 9, Table 8 for the circular mil area of conductors 18 AWG through 4/0 AWG.

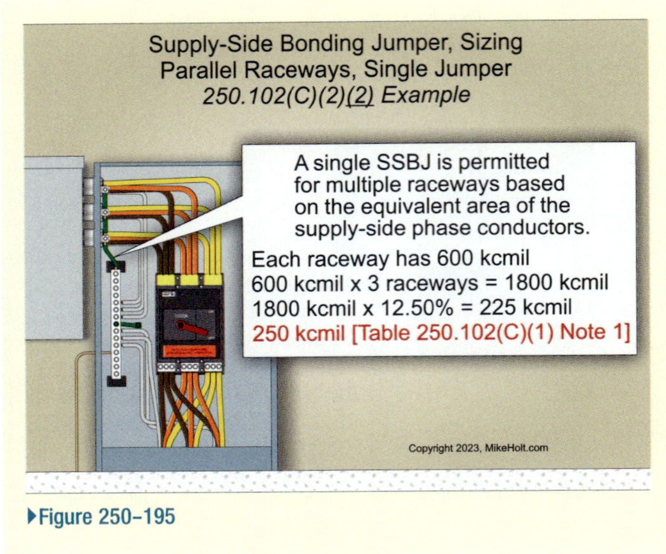

▶Figure 250–195

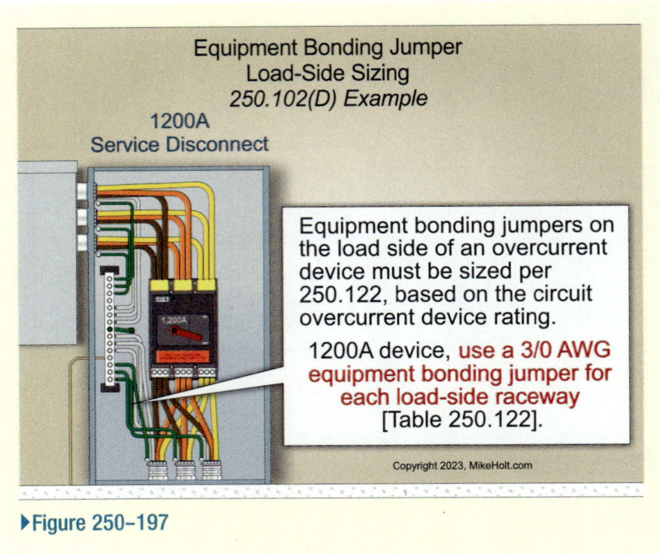

▶Figure 250–197

(D) Load-Side Bonding Jumper Sizing. Bonding jumpers on the load side of feeder and branch-circuit overcurrent protective devices are sized in accordance with 250.122. ▶Figure 250–196

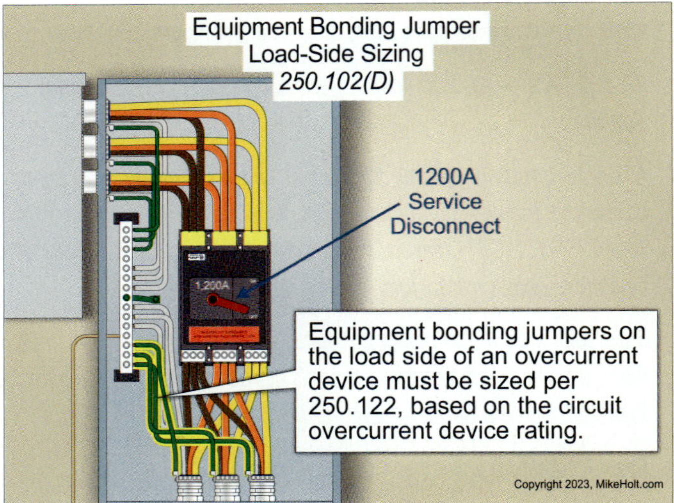

▶Figure 250–196

▶ **Example 4**

Question: What size equipment bonding jumper is required for each metal raceway where the circuit conductors are protected by a 1,200A overcurrent protective device? ▶**Figure 250–197**

(a) 1/0 AWG   (b) 2/0 AWG   (c) 3/0 AWG   (d) 4/0 AWG

Answer: *(c) 3/0 AWG [Table 250.122]*

If a single bonding jumper is used to bond two or more metal raceways, it must be sized in accordance with 250.122, based on the rating of the largest circuit overcurrent protective device.

(E) Installation of Bonding Jumpers.

(2) Outside a Raceway. Equipment bonding jumpers installed outside a raceway must be routed with the raceway, and the conductor cannot exceed 6 ft in length. ▶Figure 250–198

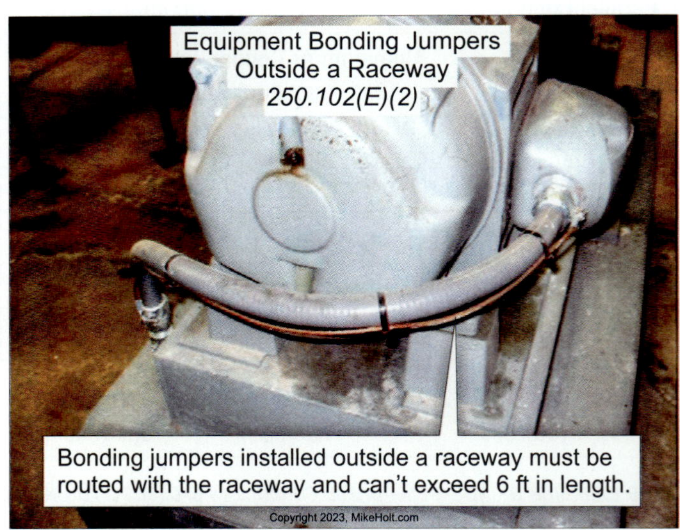

▶Figure 250–198

250.104 Bonding of Piping Systems and Exposed Structural Metal

(A) Metal Water Piping System. Electrically continuous metal water piping systems and metal sprinkler piping must be bonded in accordance with 250.104(A)(1), (A)(2), or (A)(3).

(1) Buildings Supplied by a Service. Electrically continuous metal water piping must be bonded to any one of the following: ▶Figure 250–199

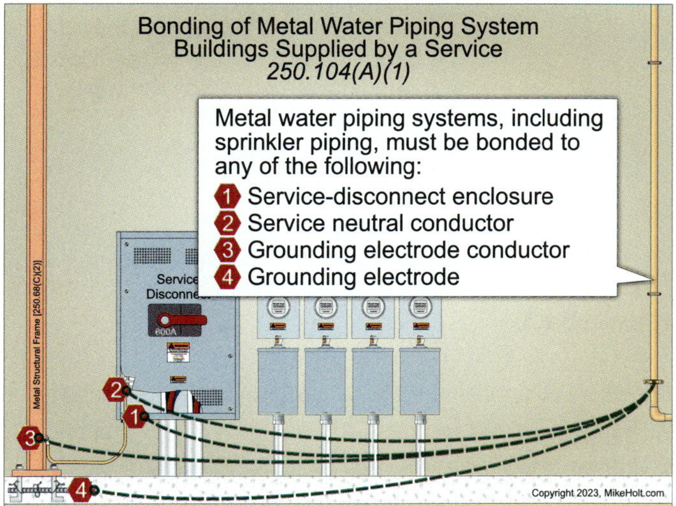

▶Figure 250–199

(1) Service-disconnect enclosure

(2) Service neutral conductor

(3) Grounding electrode conductor if of sufficient size

(4) One of the grounding electrodes of the grounding electrode system if the grounding electrode conductor or bonding jumper to the electrode is of sufficient size

Author's Comment:

▸ The intent of this rule is to remove dangerous voltage on metal parts from a ground fault to electrically conductive metal water piping systems and metal sprinkler piping.

Metal water piping system bonding jumpers must be sized in accordance with Table 250.102(C)(1), based on the size or area of the service phase conductors. They are not required to be larger than 3/0 AWG copper or 250 kcmil aluminum or copper-clad aluminum, except as permitted in 250.104(A)(2) and (A)(3).

▶ Example

Question: What size bonding jumper is required for a metal water piping system if the 300 kcmil service conductors are paralleled in two raceways? ▶Figure 250–200

(a) 1/0 AWG   (b) 2/0 AWG   (c) 3/0 AWG   (d) 4/0 AWG

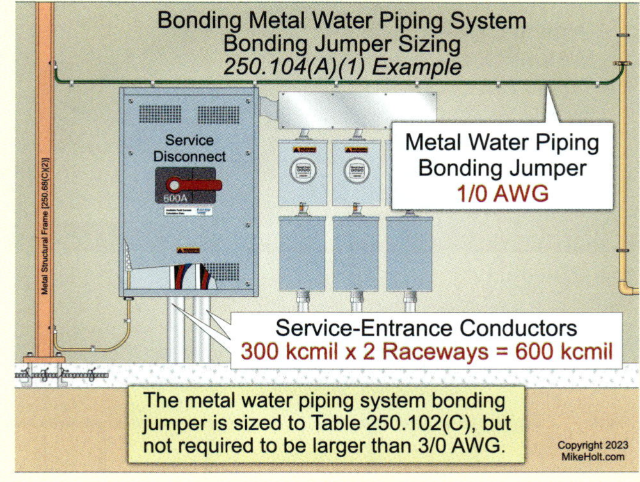

▶Figure 250–200

Solution:

A 1/0 AWG bonding jumper is required based on the 600 kcmil conductors (300 kcmil × 2 raceways) [250.102(C)(1)].

Answer: (a) 1/0 AWG

Author's Comment:

▸ Bonding is not required for isolated sections of metal water piping connected to a nonmetallic water piping system. In fact, these isolated sections of metal piping should not be bonded because they could become a shock hazard under certain conditions if they were bonded. ▶Figure 250–201

(2) Bonding Multiple-Occupancy Buildings. When an electrically continuous metal water piping system in an individual occupancy is metallically isolated from other occupancies in a building, the metal water piping system for that occupancy can be bonded to the equipment grounding terminal of the occupancy's switchgear, switchboard, or panelboard. The bonding jumper must be sized in accordance with 250.122 [250.102(D)]. ▶Figure 250–202

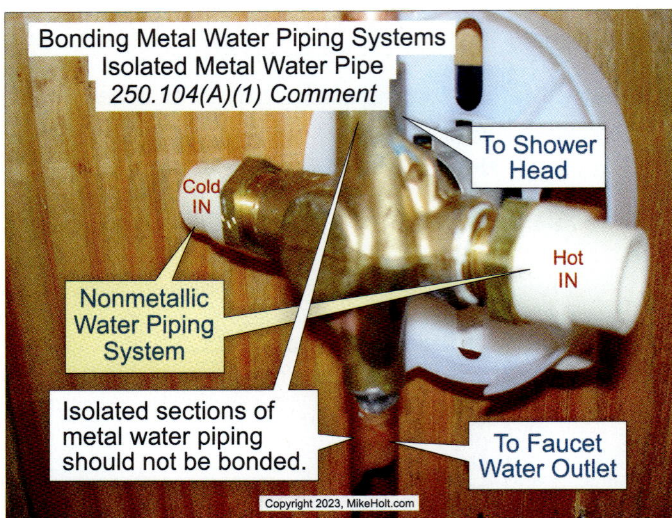

▶Figure 250–201

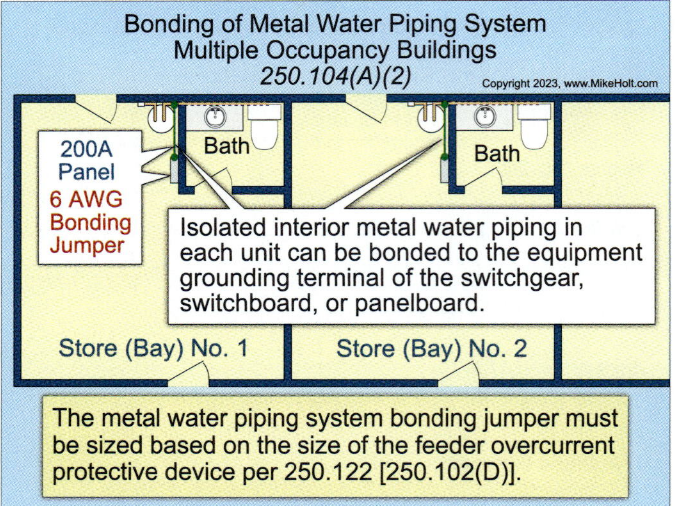

▶Figure 250–202

(3) Buildings Supplied by a Feeder. The metal water piping system of a building supplied by a feeder must be bonded to one of the following:

(1) The equipment grounding terminal of the building's disconnect enclosure

(2) The feeder equipment grounding conductor

(3) One of the building's grounding electrodes of the grounding electrode system if the grounding electrode or bonding jumper to the electrode is of sufficient size

The bonding jumper is sized in accordance with 250.102(D) and is not required to be larger than the largest feeder phase or branch-circuit conductor supplying the building.

(B) Bonding Other Metal-Piping Systems. Metal-piping systems in or attached to a building must be bonded. The piping is considered bonded when it is connected to an appliance that is connected to the circuit equipment grounding conductor. ▶Figure 250–203

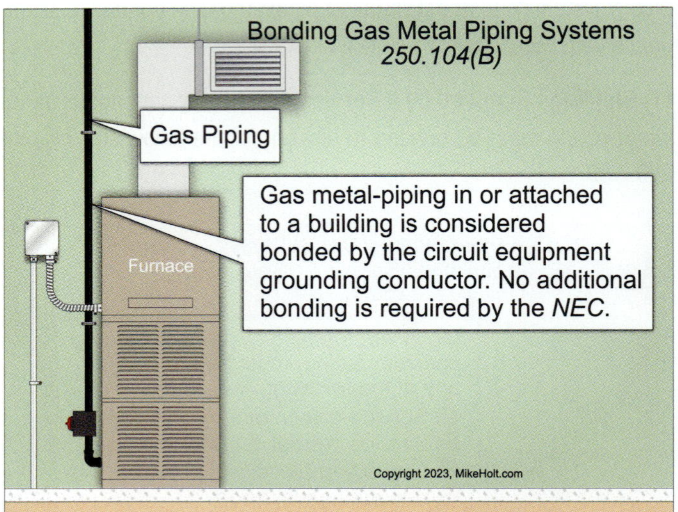

▶Figure 250–203

Note 2: Additional information for gas piping systems can be found in NFPA 54, *National Fuel Gas Code* and NFPA 780, *Standard for the Installation of Lightning Protection Systems.* ▶Figure 250–204

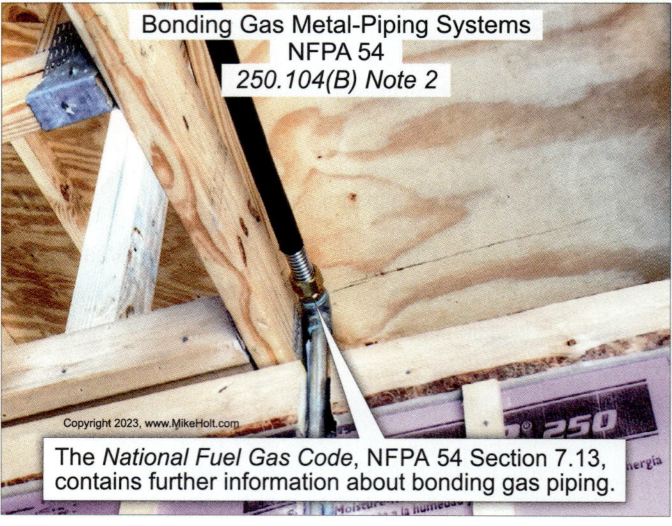

▶Figure 250–204

Author's Comment:

▶ According to the *National Fuel Gas Code*, NFPA 54, section 7.12, you only need to bond CSST tubing if it is not of the "arc-resistant jacket type." See https://www.gastite.com/us/products/flashshield/flashshieldplus_csst/

(C) Bonding Exposed Structural Metal. Exposed structural metal that is interconnected to form a metal building frame must be bonded to any of the following: ▶Figure 250–205

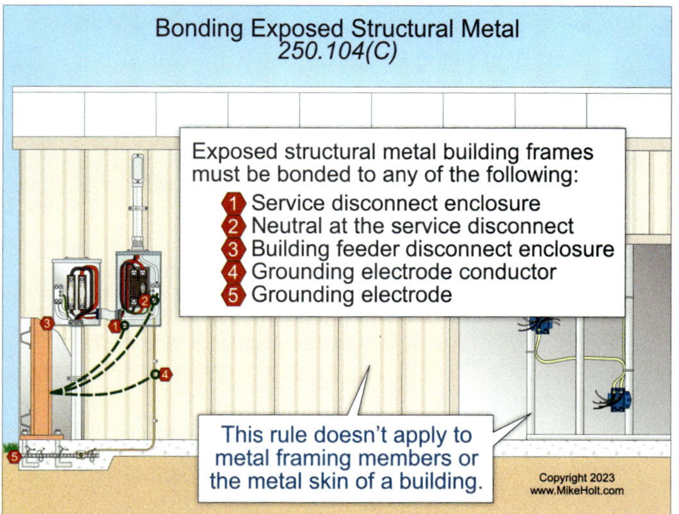

▶Figure 250–205

(1) The service-disconnect enclosure

(2) The neutral at the service disconnect

(3) The building's disconnect enclosure for those supplied by a feeder

(4) The grounding electrode conductor sized in accordance with Table 250.102(C)(1)

(5) One of the grounding electrodes of the grounding electrode system if the grounding electrode conductor or bonding jumper to the electrode is sized in accordance with Table 250.102(C)(1)

The structural metal bonding conductor must be sized in accordance with Table 250.102(C)(1) based on the size or area of the supply phase conductors. It is not required to be larger than 3/0 AWG copper or 250 kcmil aluminum or copper-clad aluminum. The bonding jumper must be copper where within 18 in. of the surface of the Earth [250.64(A)], be securely fastened to the surface on which it is carried [250.64(B)], be adequately protected if exposed to physical damage [250.64(B)], and bonded at both ends if inside a metal raceway [250.64(E)]. In addition, all points of attachment must be accessible, except as permitted in 250.68(A) Ex 2.

(D) Transformers. Metal water piping systems and structural metal that is interconnected to form a building frame must be bonded to the transformer secondary winding in accordance with 250.104(D)(1) through (D)(3).

(1) Bonding Metal Water Pipe. Metal water piping systems in the area served by a transformer must be bonded to the secondary neutral conductor where the grounding electrode conductor is connected at the transformer. ▶Figure 250–206

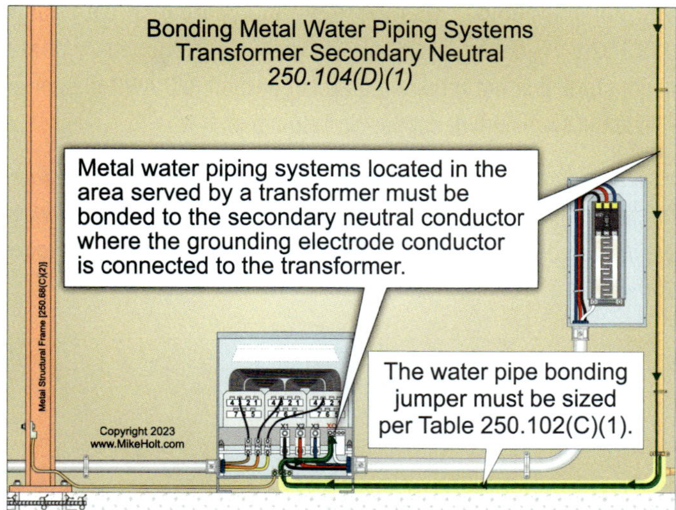

▶Figure 250–206

The bonding jumper must be sized in accordance with Table 250.102(C)(1) based on the size or area of the secondary phase conductors. It is not required to be larger than 3/0 AWG copper or 250 kcmil aluminum or copper-clad aluminum.

Ex 2: The metal water piping system can be bonded to the metal structural building frame if it serves as the grounding electrode [250.52(A)(2)] or grounding electrode conductor [250.68(C)(2)] for the transformer. ▶Figure 250–207

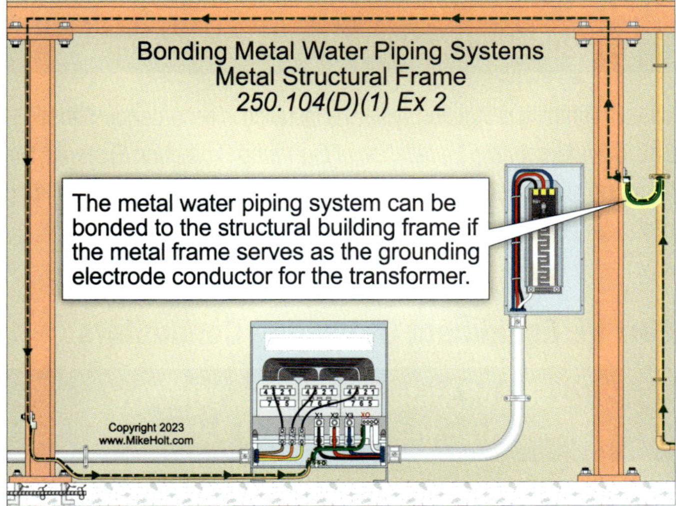

▶Figure 250–207

(2) Bonding Exposed Structural Metal. Exposed structural metal that is interconnected to form the building frame in the area served by a transformer must be bonded to the secondary neutral conductor where the grounding electrode conductor is connected at the transformer.

The bonding jumper must be sized in accordance with Table 250.102(C)(1) based on the size or area of the secondary phase conductors. It is not required to be larger than 3/0 AWG copper or 250 kcmil aluminum or copper-clad aluminum.

Ex 1: Bonding to the transformer is not required if the metal structural frame serves as the grounding electrode [250.52(A)(2)] or grounding electrode conductor [250.68(C)(2)] for the transformer. ▶Figure 250–208

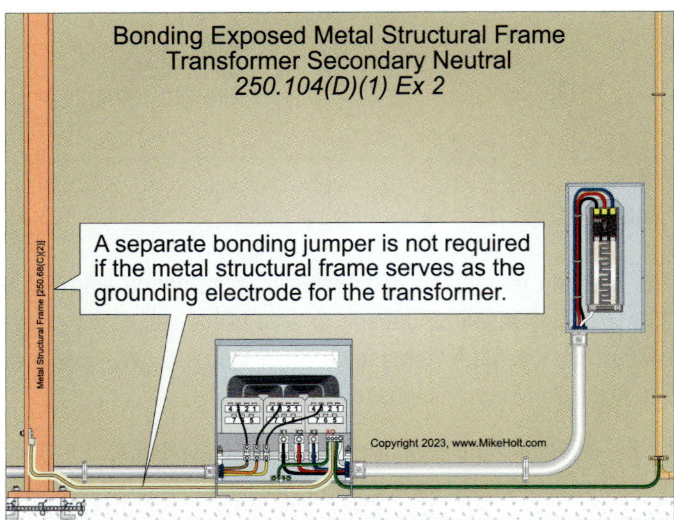

▶Figure 250–208

250.106 Lightning Protection Systems

When a lightning protection system is installed in accordance with NFPA 780, *Standard for the Installation of Lightning Protection Systems*, the lightning protection electrode system must be bonded to the building grounding electrode system. ▶Figure 250–209

Part VI. Equipment Grounding Conductors

250.109 Metal Enclosures, Effective Ground-Fault Current Path

Metal enclosures can be used to connect bonding jumpers or equipment grounding conductors together to become a part of an effective ground-fault current path. ▶Figure 250–210

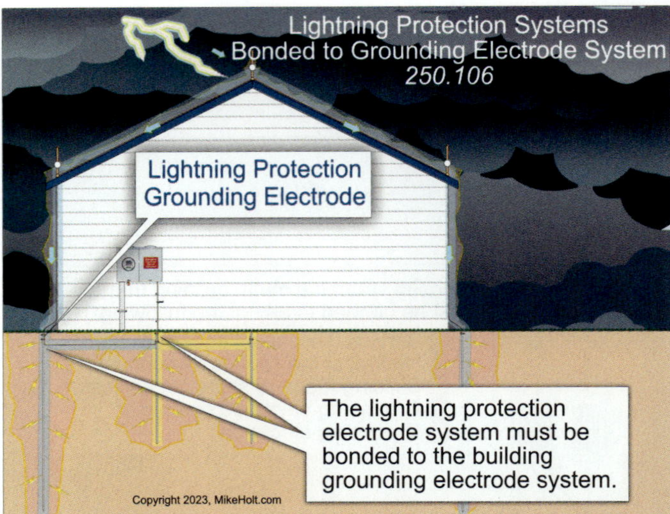

▶Figure 250–209

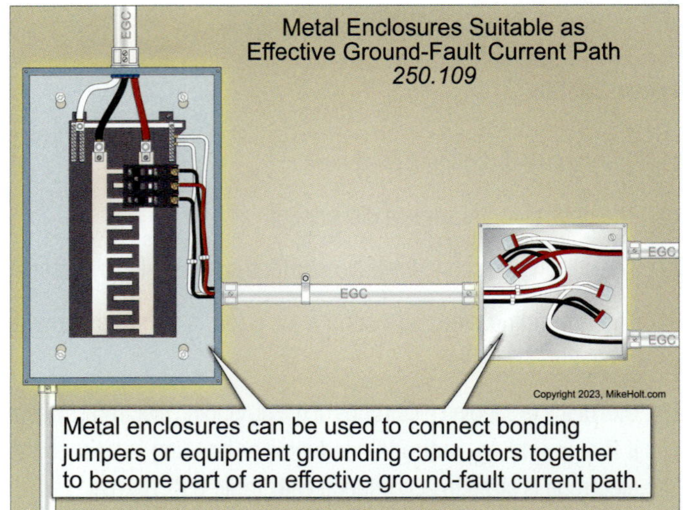

▶Figure 250–210

Metal covers, metal plaster rings, and metal extension rings must be attached to metal enclosures to ensure an effective ground-fault current path. ▶Figure 250–211

250.114 Equipment Connected by Cord and Plug

Metal parts of cord-and-plug-connected equipment must be connected to the equipment grounding conductor of the circuit supplying the equipment under any of the following conditions:

Ex: Listed tools, appliances, and equipment covered in 250.114 list items (2) through (4) are not required to be connected to an equipment grounding conductor if protected by a system of double insulation or its equivalent. Double-insulated equipment must be distinctively marked.

(1) In hazardous (classified) locations [Articles 500 through 517]

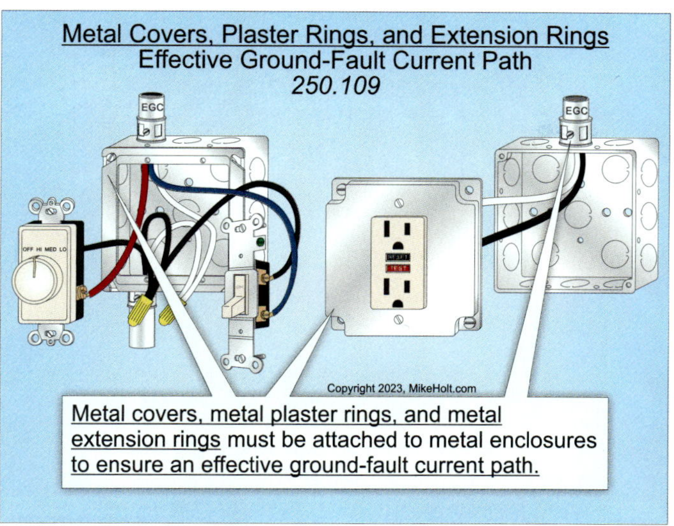

▶Figure 250–211

(2) If operated at over 150V to ground

Ex 1 to (2): Motors that are guarded.

Ex 2 to (2): Metal frames of exempted electrically heated appliances.

(3) In residential occupancies:

   a. Refrigerators, freezers, ice makers, and air conditioners

   b. Clothes-washing, clothes-drying, or dish-washing machines, ranges, kitchen waste disposals, sump pumps, and electrical aquarium equipment

   c. Hand-held (stationary or fixed) and light industrial motor-operated tools

   d. Motor-operated hedge clippers, lawn mowers, snow-blowers, and wet scrubbers

   e. Portable handlamps and portable luminaires

(4) In other than residential occupancies:

   a. Refrigerators, freezers, ice makers, and air conditioners

   b. Clothes-washing, clothes-drying or dish-washing machines, IT equipment, sump pumps, and electrical aquarium equipment

   c. Hand-held (stationary or fixed) and light industrial motor-operated tools

   d. Motor-operated hedge clippers, lawn mowers, snow-blowers, and wet scrubbers

   e. Portable handlamps and portable luminaires

f. Appliances used in damp or wet locations or by persons standing on the ground, standing on metal floors, or working inside metal tanks or boilers

g. Tools likely to be used in wet or conductive locations

Ex: Tools and portable handlamps or portable luminaires likely to be used in wet or conductive locations are not required to be connected to an equipment grounding conductor if supplied through an isolating transformer with an ungrounded secondary of not over 50V.

250.118 Types of Equipment Grounding Conductors

According to Article 100, "Equipment Grounding Conductor" is the conductive path(s) that is part of an effective ground-fault current path. ▶Figure 250–212 and ▶Figure 250–213

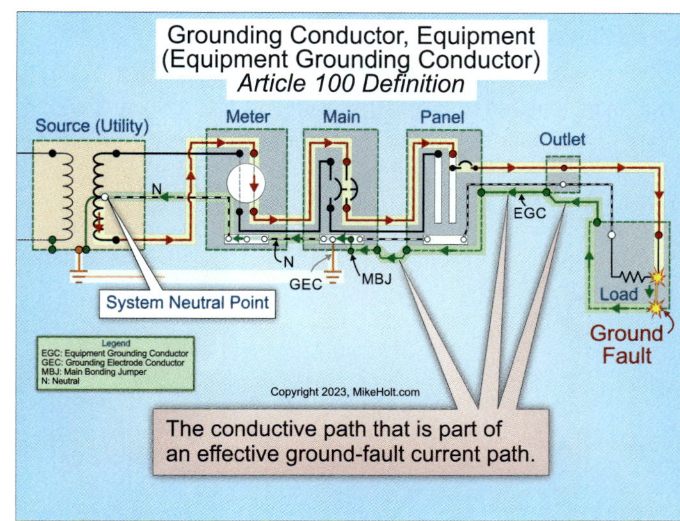

▶Figure 250–212

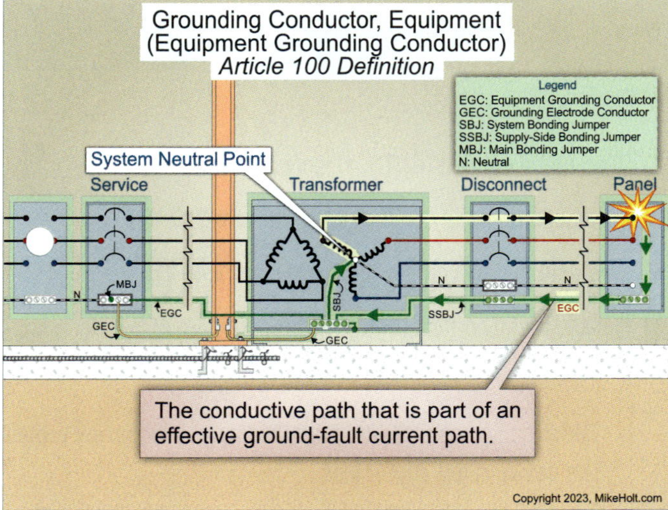

▶Figure 250–213

(A) Permitted. The equipment grounding conductor can be any one of the following types: ▶Figure 250–214

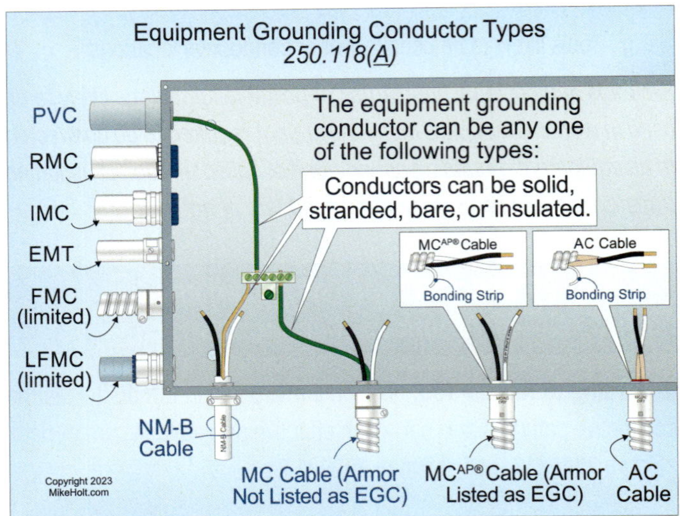

▶Figure 250–214

(1) Conductor sized in accordance with 250.122 ▶Figure 250–215

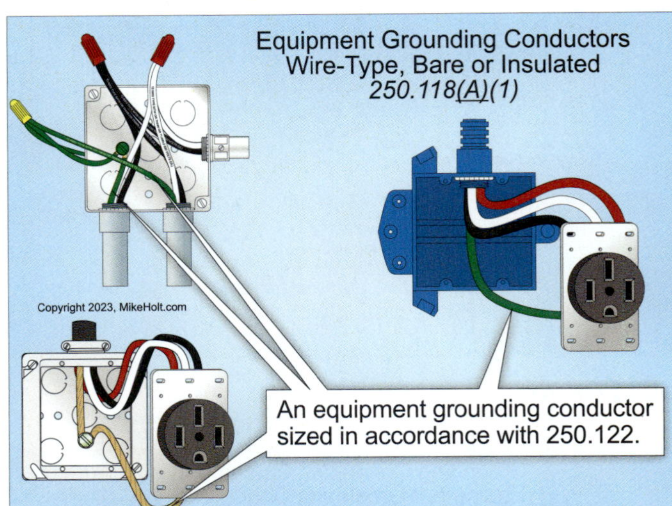

▶Figure 250–215

(2) Rigid metal conduit (RMC) ▶Figure 250–216

(3) Intermediate metal conduit (IMC) ▶Figure 250–217

(4) Electrical metallic tubing (EMT) ▶Figure 250–218

(5) Flexible metal conduit (FMC), where: ▶Figure 250–219

   a. The raceway terminates in listed fittings.

   b. The circuit conductors are protected by an overcurrent protective device rated 20A or less.

   c. The size of the flexible metal conduit does not exceed 1¼ in.

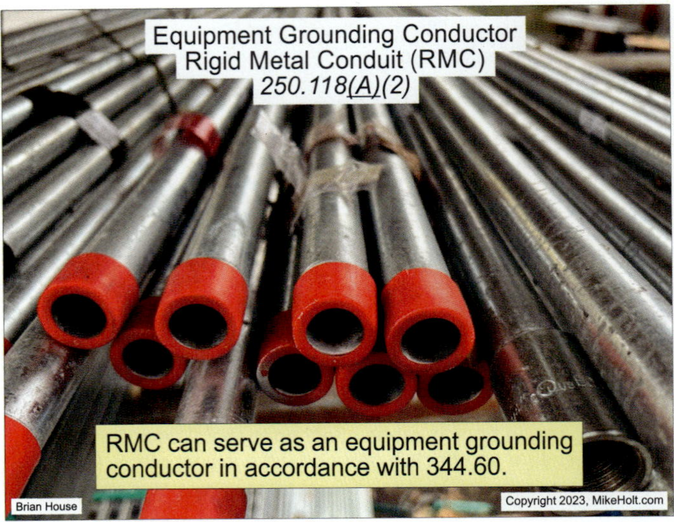

▶Figure 250–216

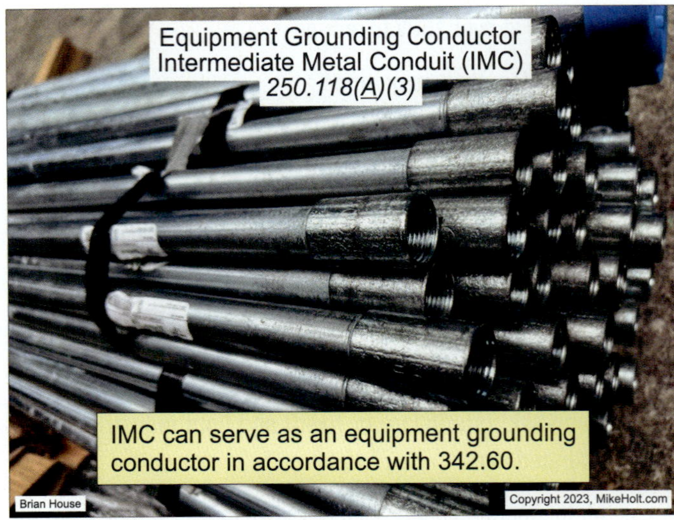

▶Figure 250–217

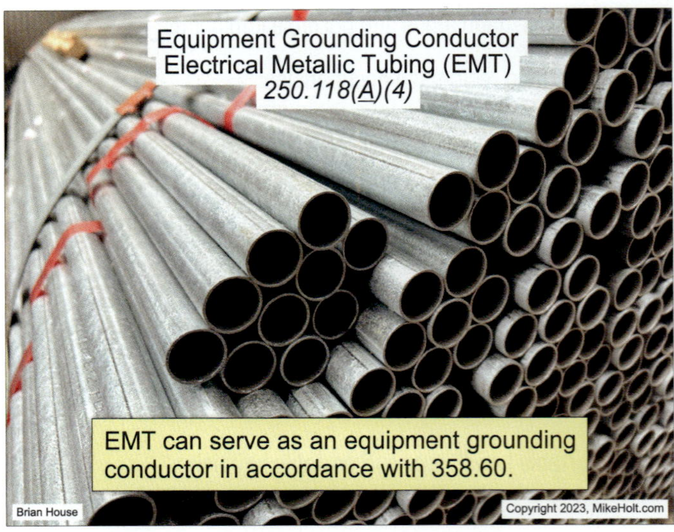

▶Figure 250–218

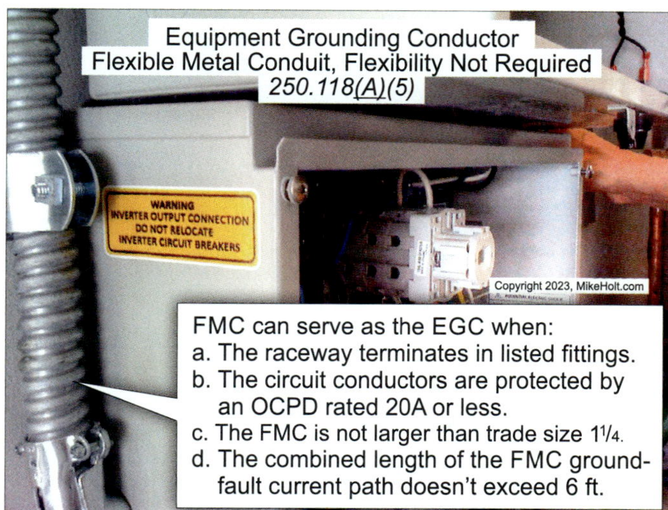

▶Figure 250–219

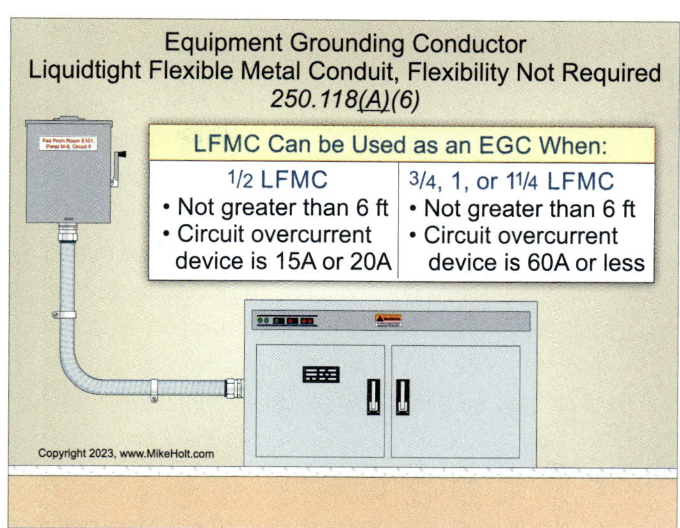

▶Figure 250–221

d. The combined length of the flexible metal conduit in the same effective ground-fault current path does not exceed 6 ft.

e. If flexibility is required to minimize the transmission of vibration from equipment or to provide flexibility for equipment that requires movement after installation, an equipment grounding conductor or a bonding jumper of the wire type must be installed with the circuit conductors in accordance with 250.102(E). ▶Figure 250–220

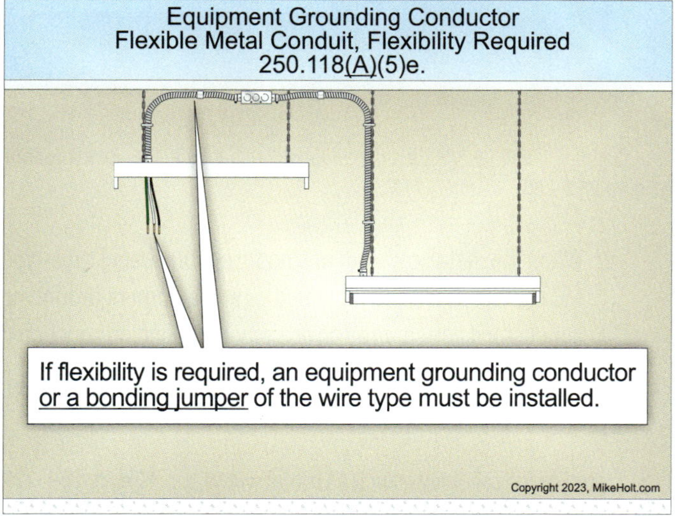

▶Figure 250–220

(6) Liquidtight flexible metal conduit (LFMC), where: ▶Figure 250–221

a. The raceway terminates in listed fittings.

b. For ½ in., the circuit conductors are protected by overcurrent protective devices rated 20A or less.

c. For ¾ through 1¼ in., the circuit conductors are protected by overcurrent protective devices rated 60A or less.

d. The combined length of the liquidtight flexible metal conduit in the same effective ground-fault current path does not exceed 6 ft.

e. If flexibility is required to minimize the transmission of vibration from equipment or to provide flexibility for equipment that requires movement after installation, an equipment grounding conductor of the wire type or a bonding jumper must be installed with the circuit conductors in accordance with 250.102(E).

(8) Type AC cable ▶Figure 250–222

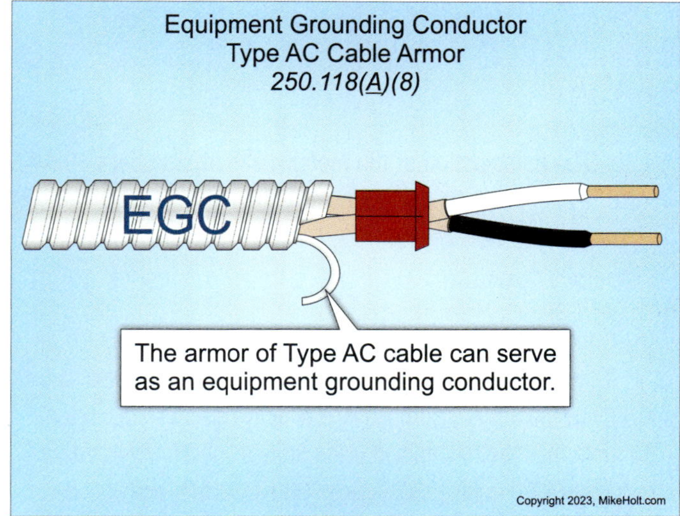

▶Figure 250–222

▶ The internal aluminum bonding strip of Type AC cable is not an equipment grounding conductor, but it allows the interlocked armor of the cable to serve as an equipment grounding conductor because it reduces the impedance of the armored spirals to ensure a ground fault will be cleared. It is the aluminum bonding strip in combination with the cable armor that creates the circuit equipment grounding conductor. Once the bonding strip exits the cable it can be cut off because it no longer serves any purpose.

(10) Type MC cable as follows:

    a. The equipment grounding conductor of the wire-type contained in Type MC cable. ▶Figure 250–223

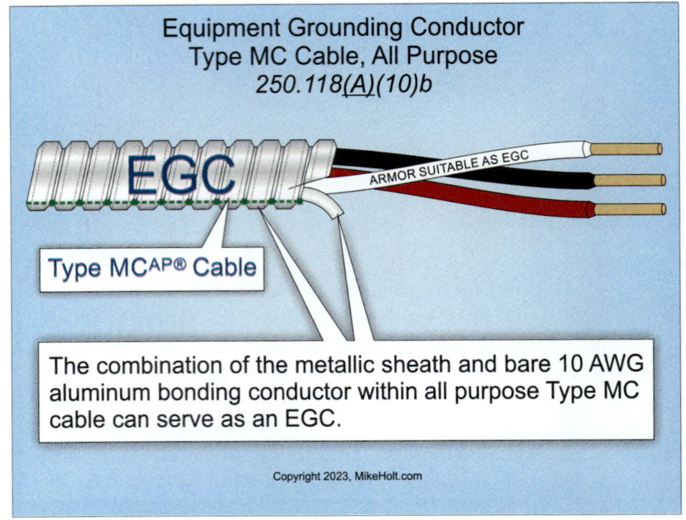

▶Figure 250–224

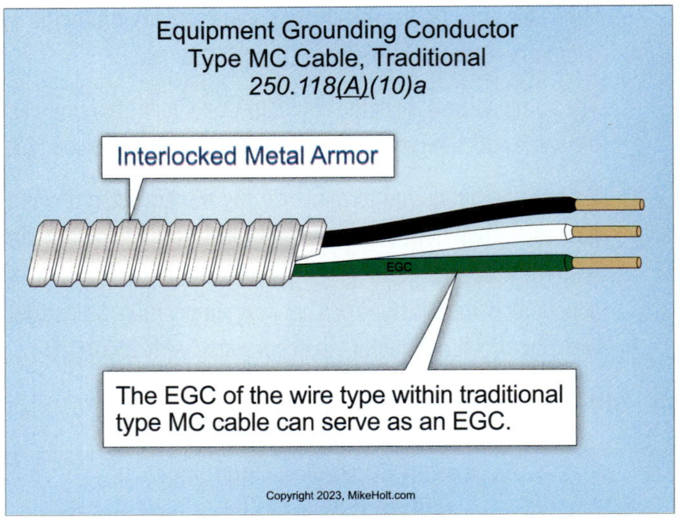

▶Figure 250–223

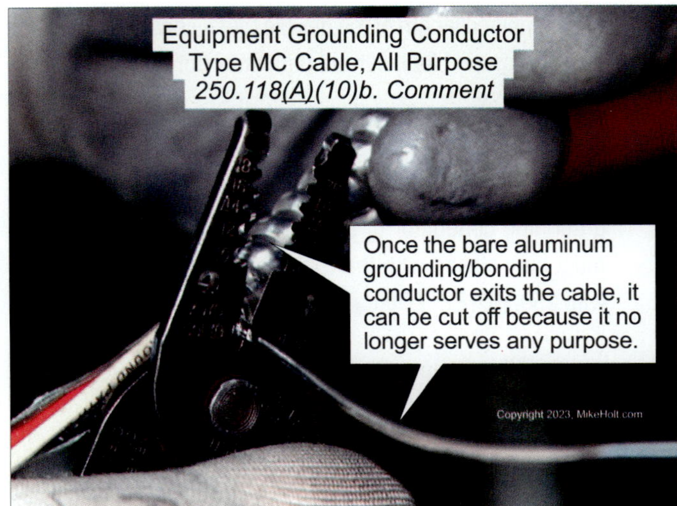

▶Figure 250–225

    b. The combination of the metallic sheath and bare 10 AWG aluminum bonding/grounding conductor. ▶Figure 250–224

    c. When the metallic sheath of smooth or corrugated tube-type MC cable is listed and identified as an equipment grounding conductor it can serve as an equipment grounding conductor.

▶ Once the bare aluminum grounding/bonding conductor of Type MC cable exits the cable, it can be cut off because it no longer serves any purpose. The effective ground-fault current path must be maintained using fittings specifically listed for Type MC^AP® cable [330.6]. See 300.12, 300.15, and 330.108. ▶Figure 250–225

(11) Metal cable trays in accordance with 392.10 and 392.60 ▶Figure 250–226

(13) Listed metal raceways, such as metal wireways ▶Figure 250–227

(14) Surface metal raceways listed for grounding ▶Figure 250–228

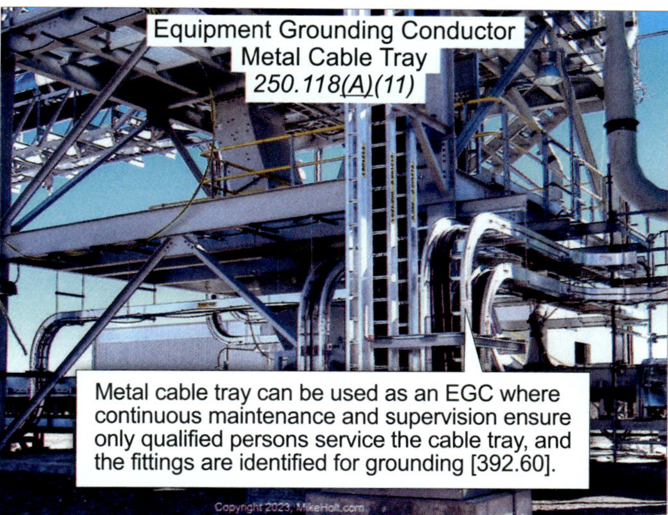

▶Figure 250–226

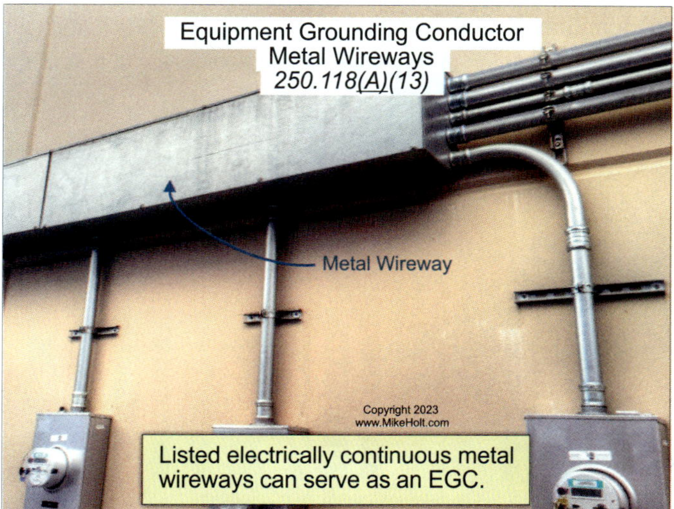

▶Figure 250–227

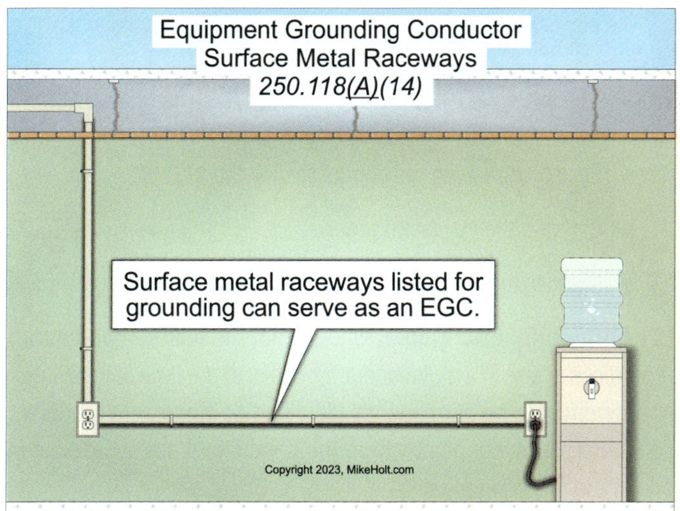

▶Figure 250–228

According to Article 100, "Effective Ground-Fault Current Path" is an intentionally constructed low-impedance conductive path designed to carry ground-fault current during a ground-fault event to the power source. The purpose of the effective ground-fault current path is to assist in opening the circuit overcurrent protective device in the event of a ground fault. ▶Figure 250–229

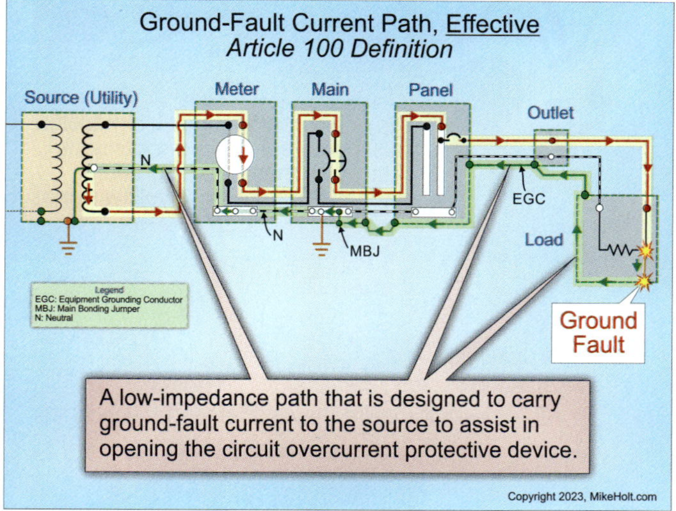

▶Figure 250–229

Author's Comment:

▶ According to "*UL Guide Information DWTT*," listed offset nipples and metal fittings for metal cable, conduit, and tubing are considered suitable for grounding circuits where installed in accordance with the *NEC*, except as noted for flexible metal conduit fittings and liquid-tight flexible metal conduit fittings.

250.119 Identification of Wire-Type Equipment Grounding Conductors

(A) General. Unless required to be insulated in this *Code*, equipment grounding conductors can be bare or covered.

Conductors 6 AWG and Smaller. Insulated equipment grounding conductors 6 AWG and smaller, must have a continuous outer finish that is either green or green with one or more yellow stripes. ▶Figure 250–230

Conductors with insulation that is green or green with one or more yellow stripes are not permitted to be used as phase or neutral conductors.

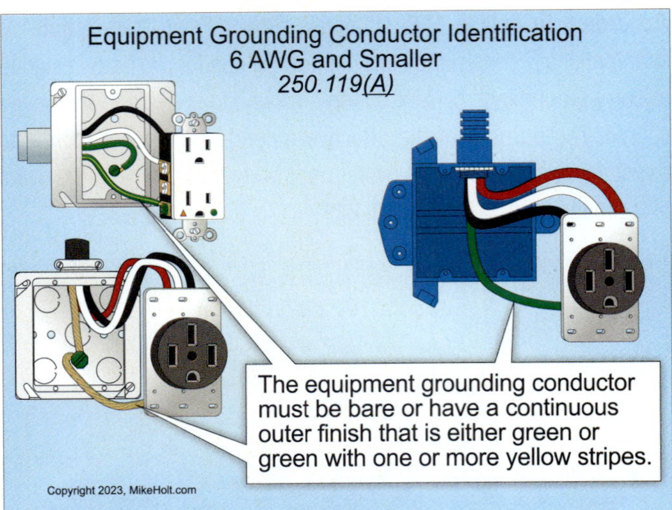

▶Figure 250–230

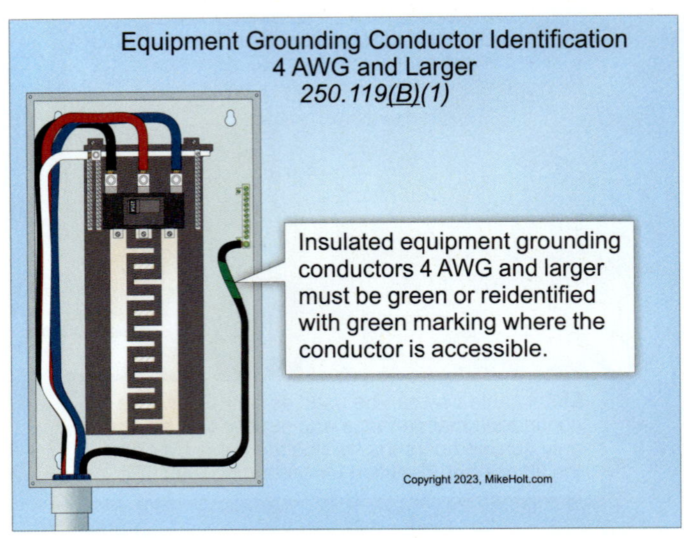

▶Figure 250–232

Author's Comment:

▶ The *NEC* does not require the color green to identify the grounding electrode conductor. ▶Figure 250–231

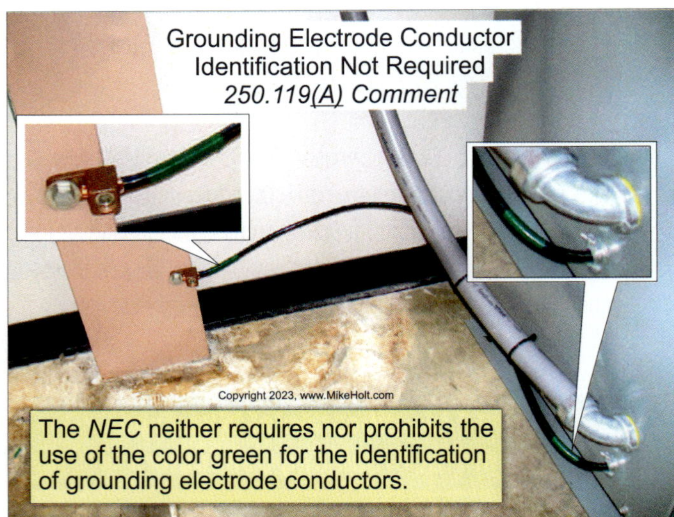

▶Figure 250–231

(B) Conductors 4 AWG and Larger. Insulated equipment grounding conductors 4 AWG and larger, must comply with 250.119(B)(1) and (B)(2).

(1) Identified Where Accessible. Insulated equipment grounding conductors 4 AWG and larger that do not comply with 250.119(A) must be reidentified with green marking in accordance with 250.119(B)(2) where the conductor is accessible. ▶Figure 250–232

(2) Identification at Terminals. The equipment grounding conductor identification at terminations must comply with one of the following: ▶Figure 250–233

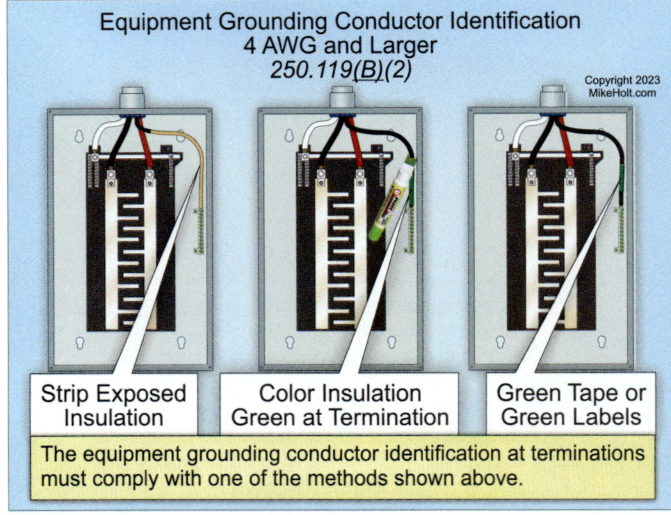

▶Figure 250–233

a. Bare by removing the conductor insulation.

b. Coloring the insulation green.

c. Marking the insulation with green tape or green adhesive labels.

(C) Multiconductor Cable. One or more insulated conductors, regardless of size in a multiconductor cable, at the time of installation are permitted to be permanently identified as equipment grounding conductors at every point where the conductors are accessible by one of the following means:

(1) Stripping the insulation from the entire exposed length.

(2) Coloring the exposed insulation green.

(3) Marking the exposed insulation with green tape or green adhesive labels and must encircle the conductor.

250.120 Equipment Grounding Conductor Installation

(A) Fittings Made Tight. The termination fitting for raceways, cable trays, or cable armor must be made tight using suitable tools.

(B) Aluminum and Copper-Clad Aluminum Conductors. Aluminum and copper-clad aluminum equipment grounding conductors must comply with the following:

(1) Aluminum and copper-clad aluminum equipment grounding conductors are not permitted to be installed where subject to corrosive conditions or in direct contact with concrete, masonry, or the Earth.

(2) Aluminum and copper-clad aluminum equipment grounding conductors are permitted within 18 in. of the bottom of any enclosure.

(3) Aluminum and copper-clad aluminum equipment grounding conductors are not permitted to terminate within 18 in. of the Earth.

250.122 Sizing Wire-Type Equipment Grounding Conductors

(A) General. Equipment grounding conductors must be sized in accordance with Table 250.122 and are not required to be larger than the largest circuit phase conductors. ▶Figure 250–234

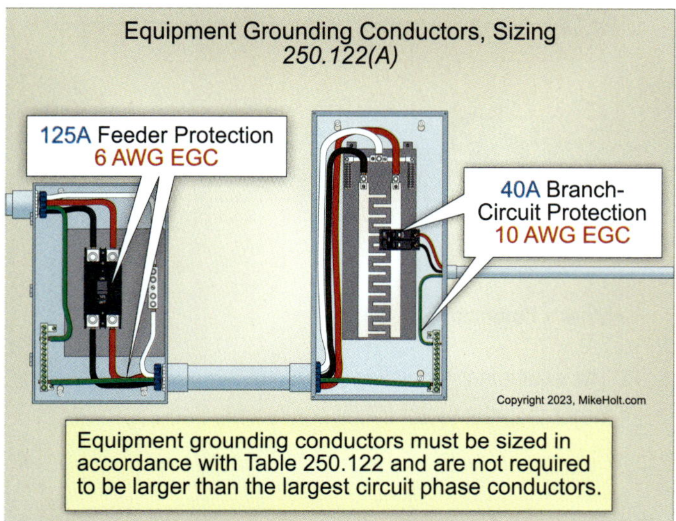

▶Figure 250–234

Table 250.122 Sizing Equipment Grounding Conductor

Overcurrent Protective Device Rating	Copper Conductor
15A	14 AWG
20A	12 AWG
25A–60A	10 AWG
70A–100A	8 AWG
110A–200A	6 AWG
225A–300A	4 AWG
350A–400A	3 AWG
450A–500A	2 AWG
600A	1 AWG
700A–800A	1/0 AWG
1000A	2/0 AWG
1200A	3/0 AWG

Note: Where necessary to comply with 250.4(A)(5) or (B)(4), the equipment grounding conductor might be required to be sized larger than given in this table.

(B) Increased in Size. If the phase conductors are larger than required by the *NEC*, such as for voltage drop consideration, the wire-type equipment grounding conductors must be proportionately increased in size based on the circular mil area of the phase conductors. ▶Figure 250–235

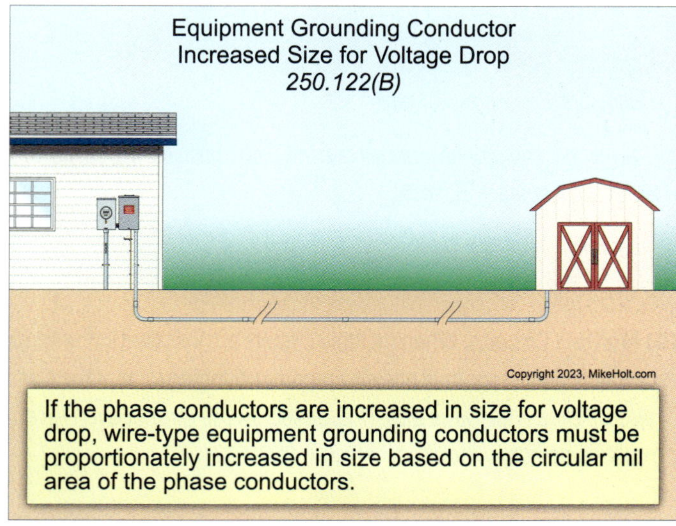

▶Figure 250–235

Ex: Equipment grounding conductors can be sized by a qualified person.

▶ Example 1

Question: *If the phase conductors for a 40A circuit are increased in size from 8 AWG to 6 AWG due to voltage drop, the circuit equipment grounding conductor must be increased in size from 10 AWG to ______.* ▶Figure 250–236

(a) 8 AWG   (b) 6 AWG   (c) 4 AWG   (d) 3 AWG

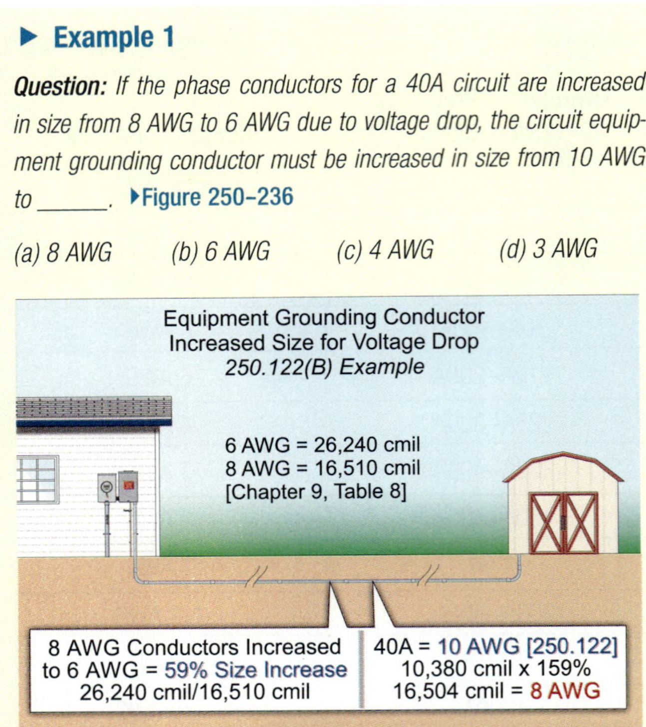

▶Figure 250–236

Solution:

The circular mil area of 6 AWG is 59 percent more than 8 AWG (26,240 cmil/16,510 cmil) [Chapter 9, Table 8].

According to Table 250.122, the circuit equipment grounding conductor for a 40A overcurrent protective device will be 10 AWG (10,380 cmil), but the circuit equipment grounding conductor for this circuit must be increased in size by a multiplier of 159 percent.

Conductor Size = 10,380 cmil × 159%

Conductor Size = 16,504 cmil

The circuit equipment grounding conductor must be increased to 8 AWG [Chapter 9, Table 8].

Answer: *(a) 8 AWG*

(C) Multiple Circuits. When multiple circuits are installed in the same raceway or cable tray, only one equipment grounding conductor, sized in accordance with Table 250.122, based on the largest overcurrent protective device is required. ▶Figure 250–237

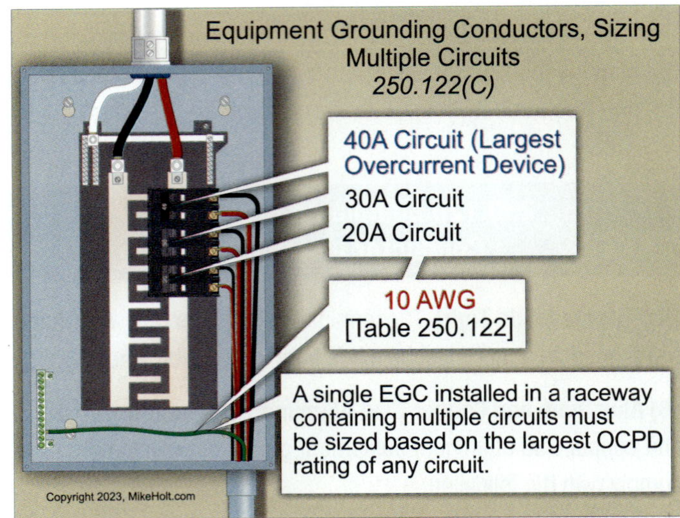

▶Figure 250–237

(D) Motor Branch Circuits. Equipment grounding conductors for motor circuits must be sized in accordance with 250.122(D)(1) or (D)(2).

(1) General. The equipment grounding conductor for a motor is sized in accordance with 250.122(A), based on the rating of the motor circuit branch-circuit short-circuit and ground-fault protective device. ▶Figure 250–238

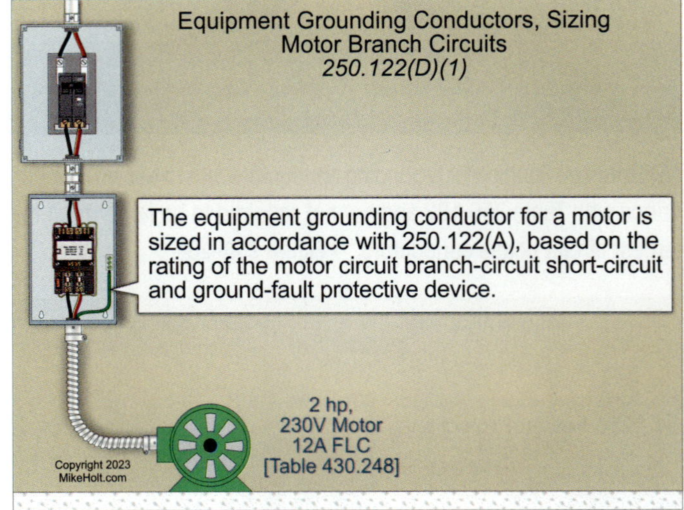

▶Figure 250–238

Author's Comment:

▶ The equipment grounding conductor is not required to be larger than the motor circuit conductors. See 250.122(A).

▶ Example 2

Question: What size equipment grounding conductor of the wire type is required for a 14 AWG motor branch circuit [430.22], protected with a 2-pole, 40A circuit breaker in accordance with 430.22 and 430.52(C)(1)? ▶Figure 250–239

(a) 14 AWG   (b) 12 AWG   (c) 10 AWG   (d) 8 AWG

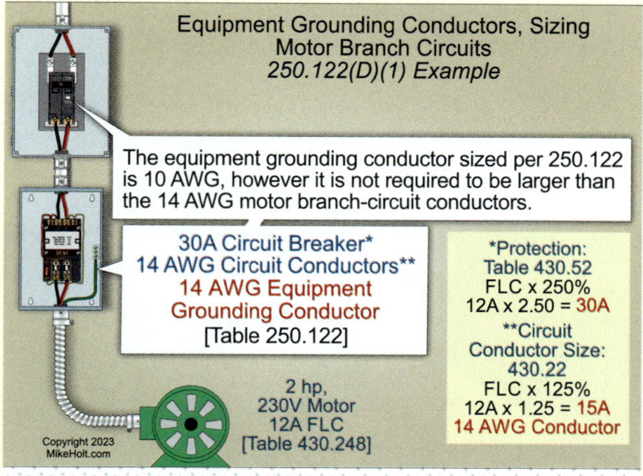

▶Figure 250–239

Solution:

The equipment grounding conductor sized to 250.122 is 10 AWG [250.122(D)(1)], however it is not required to be larger than the 14 AWG motor branch-circuit conductors [250.122(A)].

Answer: *(a) 14 AWG*

(F) Parallel Conductors. Where circuit conductors are installed in parallel in accordance with 310.10(G), an equipment grounding conductor of the wire type must be installed in accordance with the following:

(1) Raceways or Cable Trays.

(a) Parallel Conductors in a Single Raceway. Parallel conductors installed in a single raceway, require a wire-type equipment grounding conductor sized in accordance with Table 250.122.

(b) Parallel Conductors in Multiple Raceways. Parallel conductors installed in multiple raceways require a wire-type equipment grounding conductor in each raceway sized in accordance with Table 250.122. ▶Figure 250–240 and ▶Figure 250–241

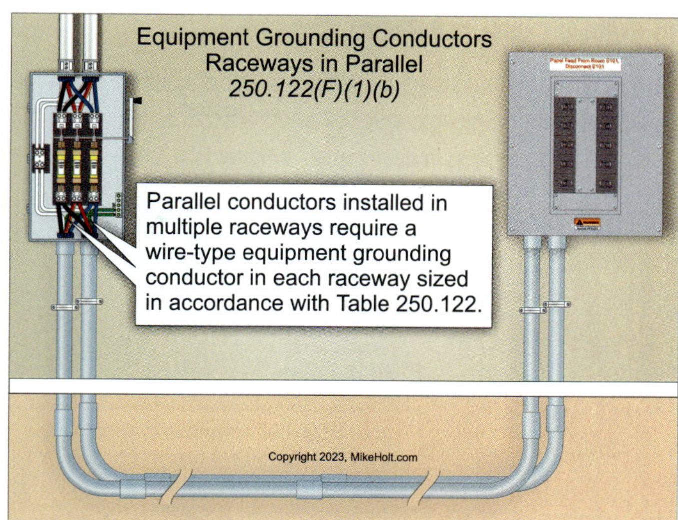

▶Figure 250–240

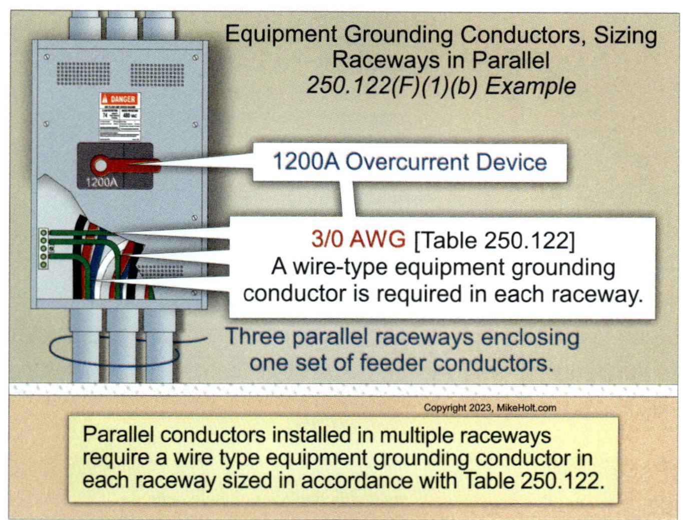

▶Figure 250–241

▶ Example 3

Question: What size aluminum equipment grounding conductor of the wire type is required for a 4,000A feeder containing twelve parallel sets of 600 kcmil aluminum conductors per phase in PVC conduit?

(a) 750 kcmil   (b) 800 kcmil   (c)1,000 kcmil   (d) 1,250 kcmil

Solution:

According to Table 250.122, the equipment grounding conductor in each raceway must not be smaller than 750 kcmil, which is larger than the individual phase conductors!

Answer: *(a) 750 kcmil*

(2) Multiple Cables in Parallel.

(a) If parallel conductors are installed in multiple cables, a wire-type equipment grounding conductor sized in accordance with Table 250.122 is required in each cable. ▶Figure 250–242

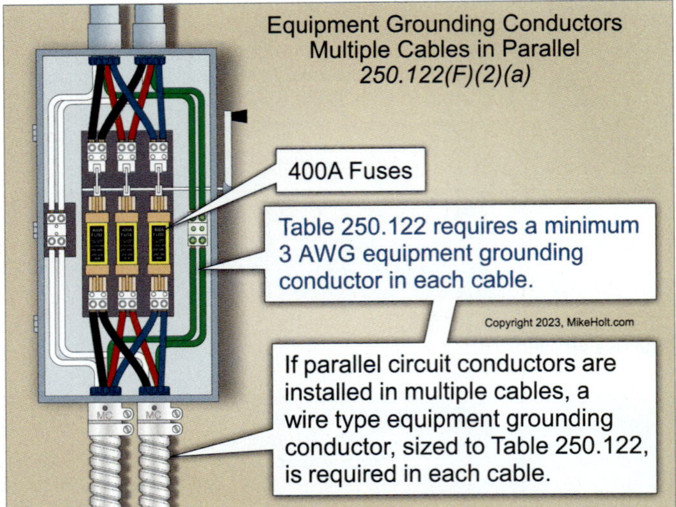

▶Figure 250–242

(G) Feeder Tap Conductors. Equipment grounding conductors for feeder taps must be sized in accordance with Table 250.122 based on the ampere rating of the overcurrent protective device on the supply side of the tap. The feeder equipment grounding conductor for the feeder tap is not required to be larger than the tap conductors. ▶Figure 250–243

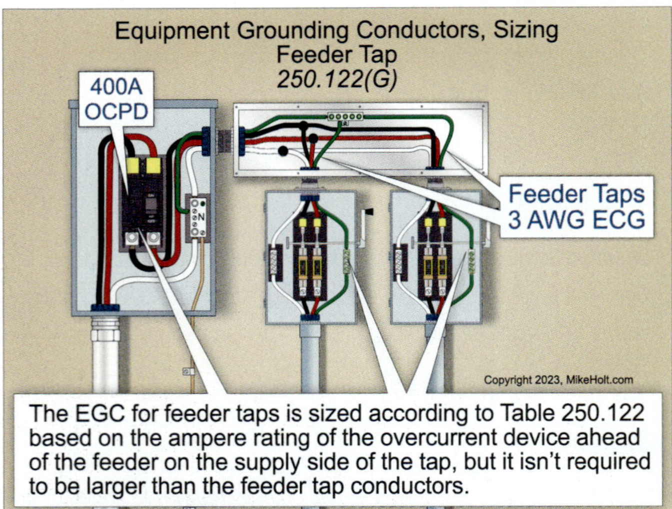

▶Figure 250–243

Part VII. Equipment Grounding Conductor Connections

250.134 Equipment Connected by Permanent Wiring Methods

Except as permitted for services or separately derived systems [250.142(A)], metal parts of equipment, raceways, and enclosures must be connected to an equipment grounding conductor by connecting the metal parts to an equipment grounding conductor of a type 250.118.

Ex 2: For direct-current circuits, the equipment grounding conductor is permitted to be run separately from the circuit conductors. ▶Figure 250–244

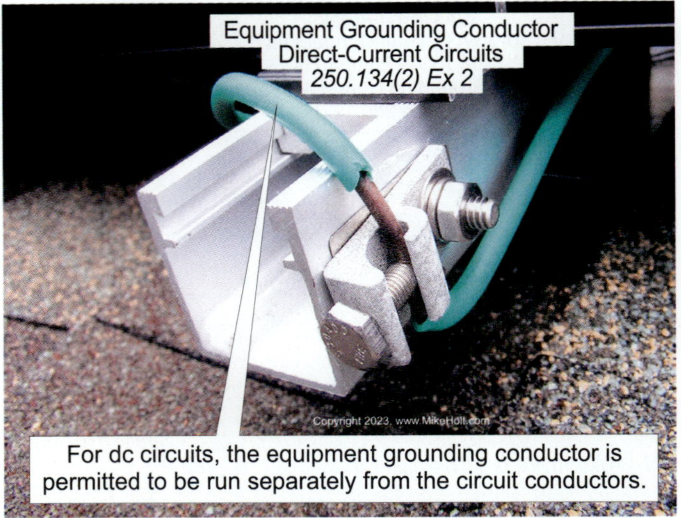

▶Figure 250–244

250.138 Cord-and-Plug-Connected

(A) Equipment Grounding Conductor. Metal parts of cord-and-plug-connected equipment must be connected to an equipment grounding conductor that terminates to a grounding-type attachment plug. ▶Figure 250–245

250.140 Frames of Ranges, Ovens, and Clothes Dryers

The frames of electric ranges, wall-mounted ovens, counter-mounted cooking units, and clothes dryers must be connected to the circuit equipment grounding conductor in accordance with 250.140(A) or (B).

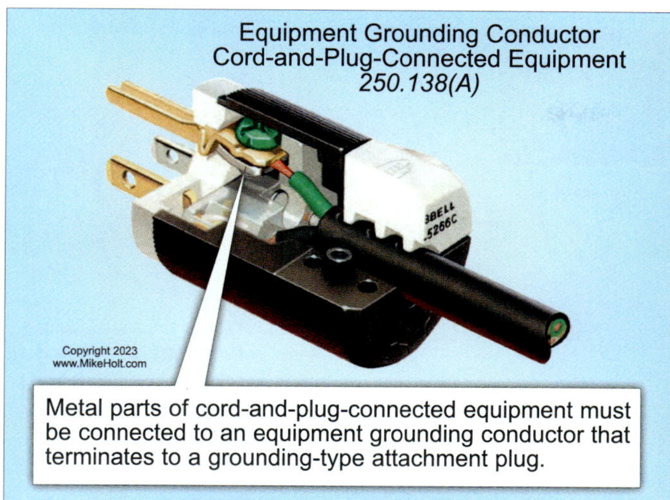

Metal parts of cord-and-plug-connected equipment must be connected to an equipment grounding conductor that terminates to a grounding-type attachment plug.

▶Figure 250–245

(A) Equipment Grounding Conductor. The circuit supplying electric ranges, ovens, cooktops, and clothes dryers must include an equipment grounding conductor connected to the frame of the appliance. ▶Figure 250–246

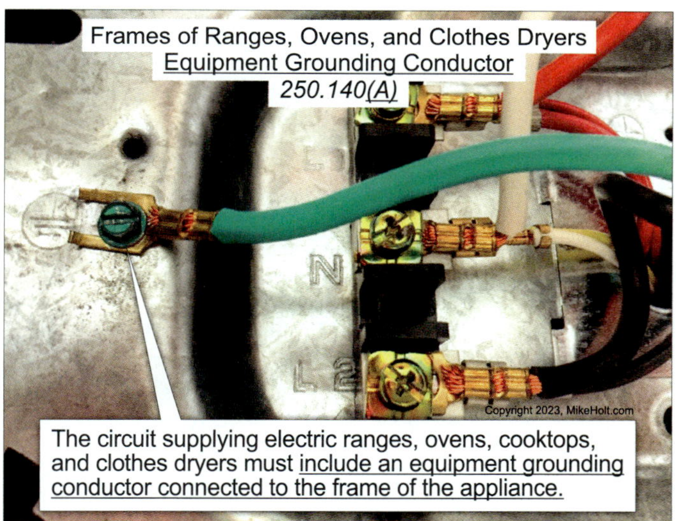

The circuit supplying electric ranges, ovens, cooktops, and clothes dryers must include an equipment grounding conductor connected to the frame of the appliance.

▶Figure 250–246

(B) Neutral Conductor. For existing installations, if an equipment grounding conductor is not present in the outlet box, the frames of electric ranges, ovens, cooktops, and clothes dryers must be connected to the neutral conductor. ▶Figure 250–247

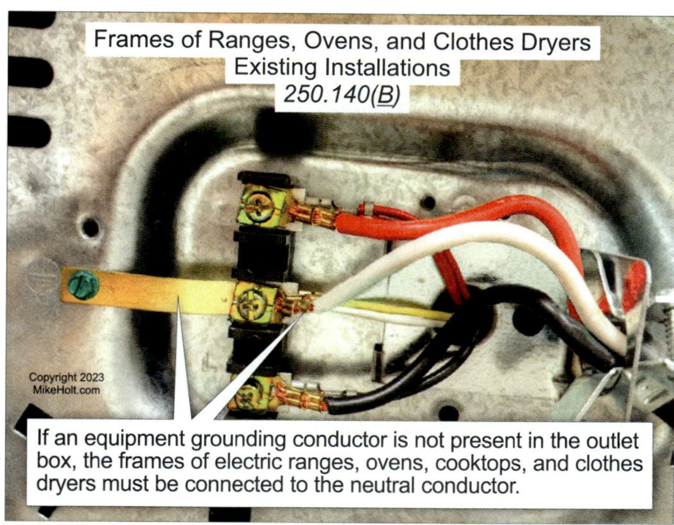

If an equipment grounding conductor is not present in the outlet box, the frames of electric ranges, ovens, cooktops, and clothes dryers must be connected to the neutral conductor.

▶Figure 250–247

250.146 Connecting Receptacle Grounding Terminal to an Equipment Grounding Conductor

An equipment bonding conductor is required to connect the grounding terminals of a receptacle to a metal box, except as permitted in 250.146(A) through (D). ▶Figure 250–248

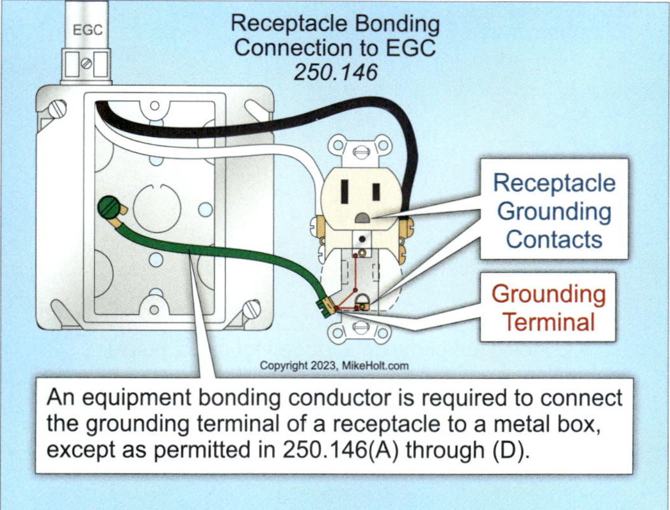

An equipment bonding conductor is required to connect the grounding terminal of a receptacle to a metal box, except as permitted in 250.146(A) through (D).

▶Figure 250–248

Author's Comment:

▶ The *NEC* does not restrict the position of the receptacle grounding terminal—it can be up, down, or sideways. *Code* proposals to specify the mounting position of receptacles have always been rejected. ▶Figure 250–249

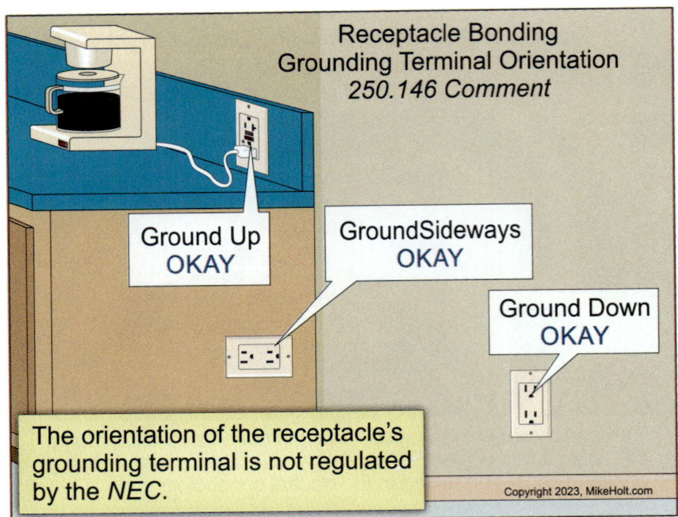

▶Figure 250–249

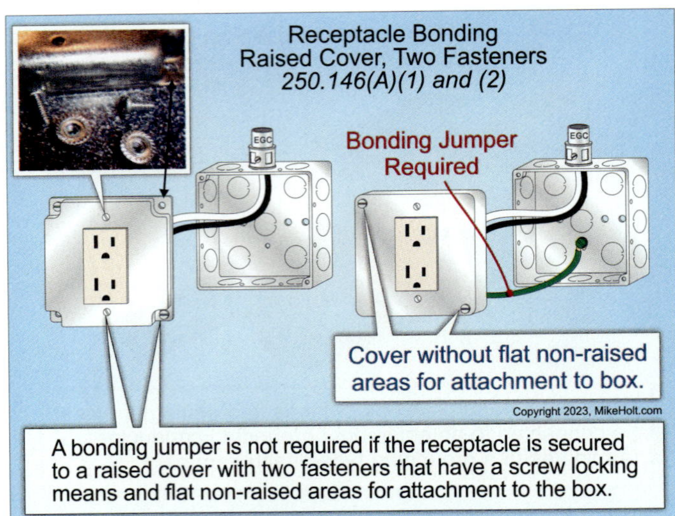

▶Figure 250–251

(A) Surface-Mounted Box. A bonding jumper is not required for a receptacle having direct metal-to-metal contact between the receptacle mounting strap and a surface metal box. To ensure sufficient metal-to-metal contact, at least one of the insulating retaining washers on the yoke screw must be removed. ▶Figure 250–250

(B) Self-Grounding Receptacles. A bonding jumper is not required for a self-grounding receptacle mounted to a metal box. ▶Figure 250–252

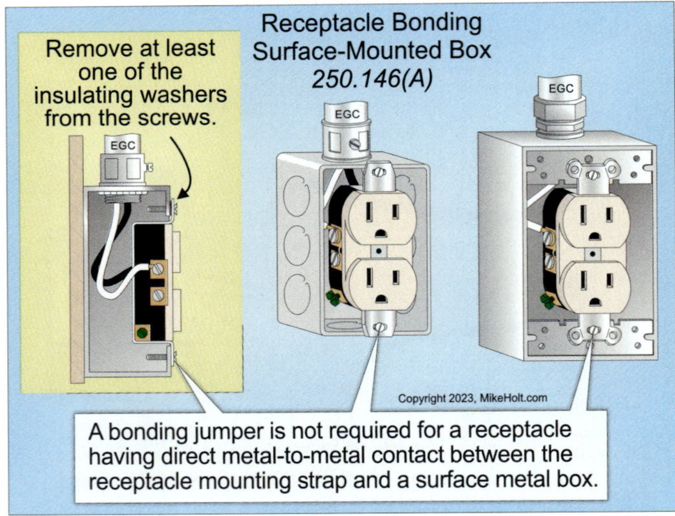

▶Figure 250–250

A bonding jumper is not required for a receptacle installed on a raised cover under both of the following conditions:

(1) The receptacle is attached to the metal cover with at least two fasteners that have a thread locking, or screw or nut locking means.

(2) The cover mounting holes are on a flat non-raised portion of the cover. ▶Figure 250–251

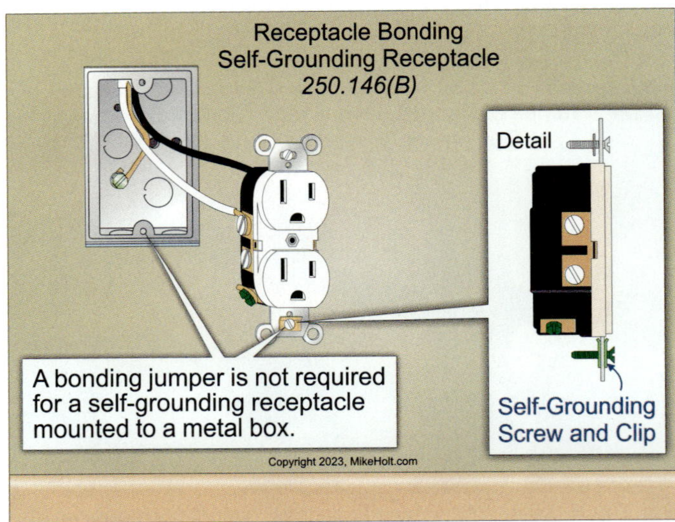

▶Figure 250–252

Author's Comment:

▶ Receptacle yokes listed as self-grounding are considered bonded through the supporting screws connected to the metal box. ▶Figure 250–253

(C) Floor Boxes. Metal floor boxes must establish the bonding path between the receptacle yoke and a metal box.

(D) Isolated Ground Receptacles. The grounding terminal of an isolated ground receptacle must be connected to an insulated equipment grounding conductor. ▶Figure 250–254

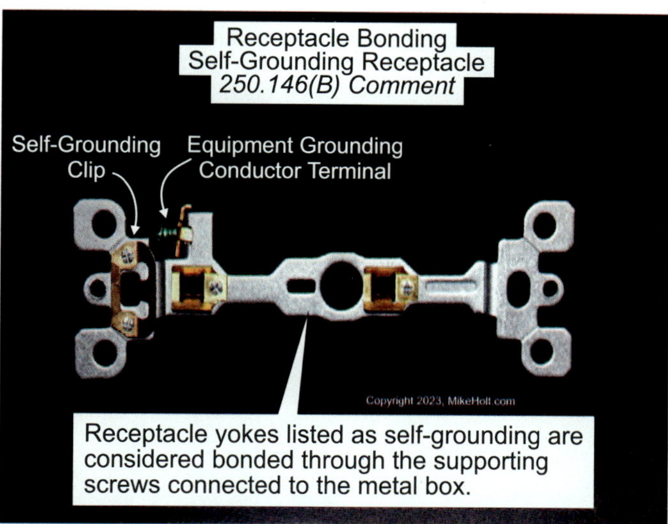

▶Figure 250–253

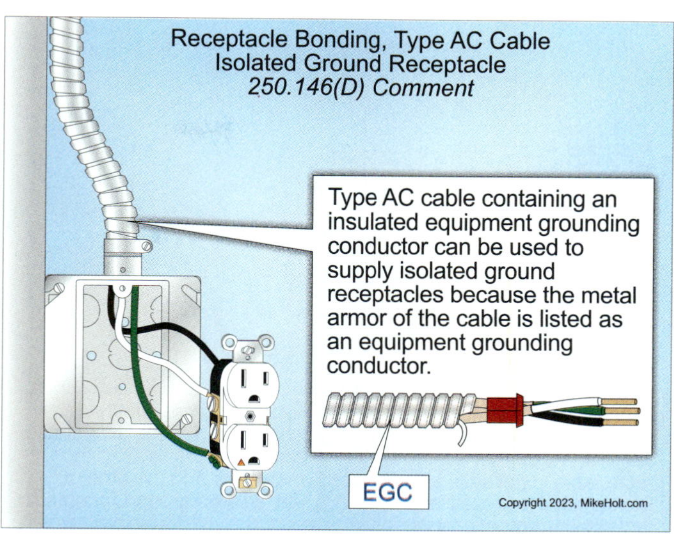

▶Figure 250–255

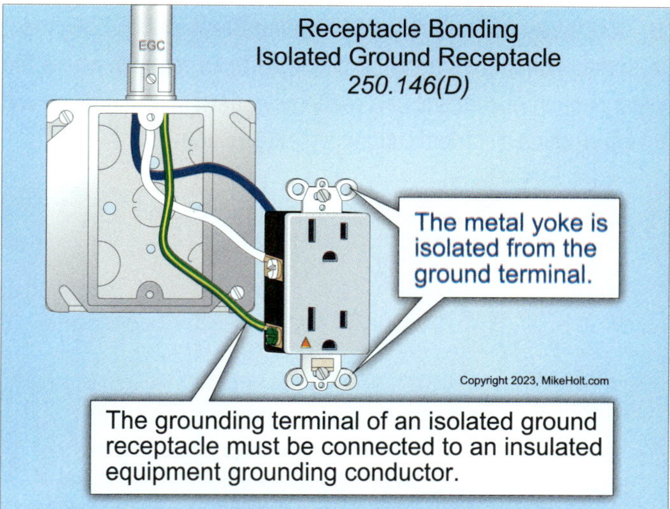

▶Figure 250–254

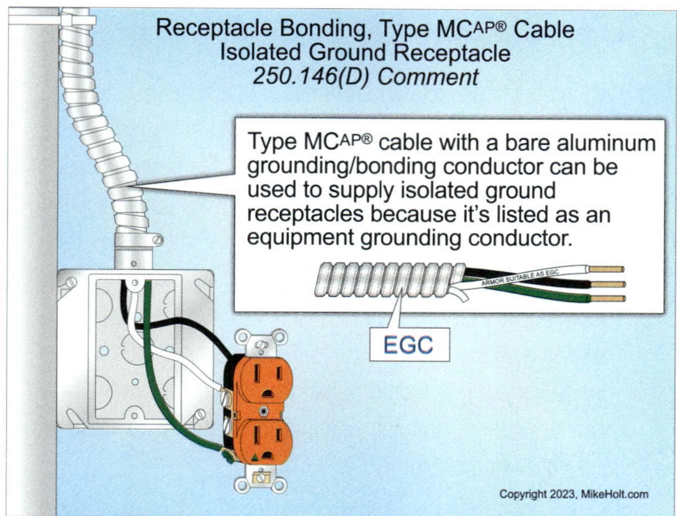

▶Figure 250–256

Author's Comment:

▸ Type AC cable containing an insulated equipment grounding conductor can be used to supply isolated ground receptacles because the metal armor of the cable is listed as an equipment grounding conductor [250.118(A)(8)]. ▶Figure 250–255

▸ Type MCAP® cable with a 10 AWG bare aluminum grounding/bonding conductor can be used to supply isolated ground receptacles because it is listed as an equipment grounding conductor [250.118(A)(10)(b)].

▸ An interlocked Type MCAP® cable is an acceptable wiring method to use for an isolated ground receptacle. ▶Figure 250–256

Caution

CAUTION: Type MC Cable. The metal armor sheath of traditional interlocked Type MC cable containing an insulated equipment grounding conductor is not listed as an equipment grounding conductor. Therefore, this wiring method with a single equipment grounding conductor cannot supply an isolated ground receptacle. Type MC cable with two insulated equipment grounding conductors is acceptable since one bonds to the metal box, and the other one connects to the isolated ground receptacle. ▶Figure 250–257

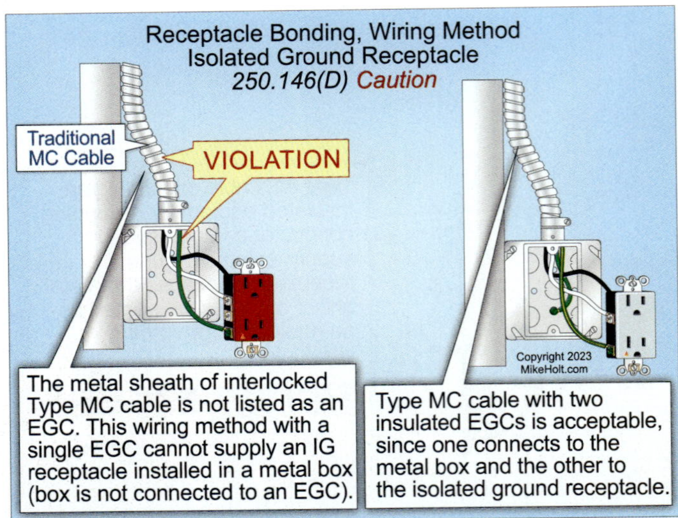

▶Figure 250–257

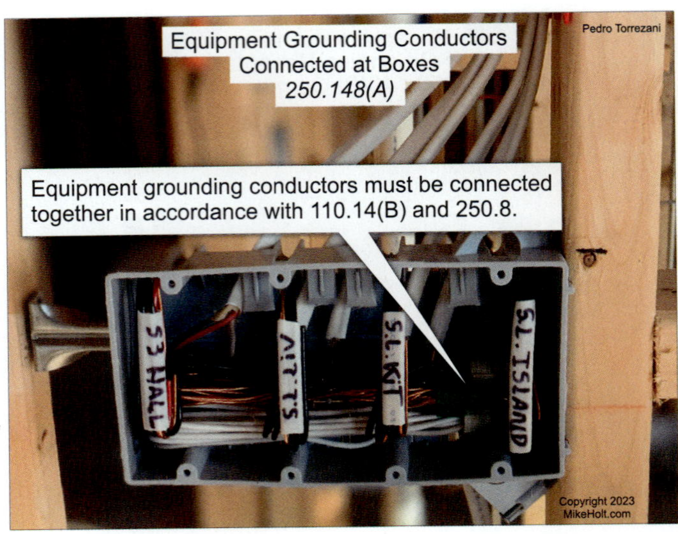

▶Figure 250–258

Author's Comment:

▶ When should an isolated ground receptacle be installed and how should the isolated ground system be designed? These questions are design issues and are not answered based on the *NEC* alone [90.2(C)]. In most cases, using isolated ground receptacles is a waste of money. For example, IEEE 1100, *Powering and Grounding Electronic Equipment* (Emerald Book) section 8.5.3.2 states, "The results from the use of the isolated ground method range from no observable effects, the desired effects, or worse noise conditions than when standard equipment bonding configurations are used to serve electronic load equipment."

▶ Few electrical installations truly require an isolated ground system. For those systems that can benefit from one, engineering opinions differ as to what is a proper design. Making matters worse—of those properly designed, few are correctly installed, and even fewer are properly maintained.

250.148 Continuity and Attachment of Equipment Grounding Conductors in Boxes

If circuit conductors are spliced or terminate to equipment in a box, the equipment grounding conductor must comply with 250.148(A) through (D).

(A) Connections and Splices. Equipment grounding conductors must be connected together in accordance with 110.14(B) and 250.8.

▶Figure 250–258

(B) Continuity of Equipment Grounding Conductors. Equipment grounding conductors must be connected in a manner where the disconnection or removal of a receptacle, device, or luminaire will not interrupt its electrical continuity. ▶Figure 250–259

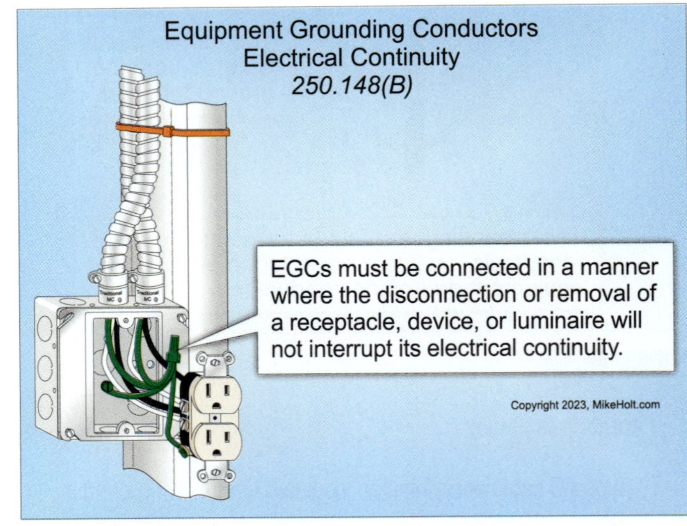

▶Figure 250–259

(C) Metal Boxes. Bonding jumpers and equipment grounding conductors must be connected to the metal box by a device that serves no other purpose. ▶Figure 250–260 and ▶Figure 250–261

Ex: The circuit equipment grounding conductor for an isolated ground receptacle [250.146(D)] is not required to be bonded to other equipment grounding conductors or metal box. ▶Figure 250–262

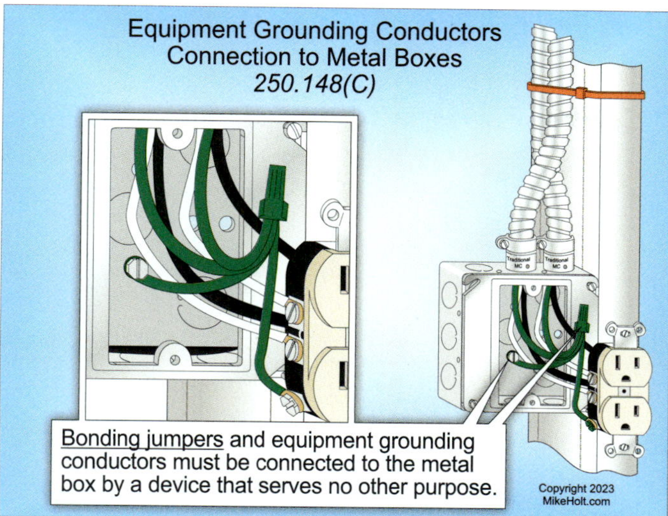

▶Figure 250–260

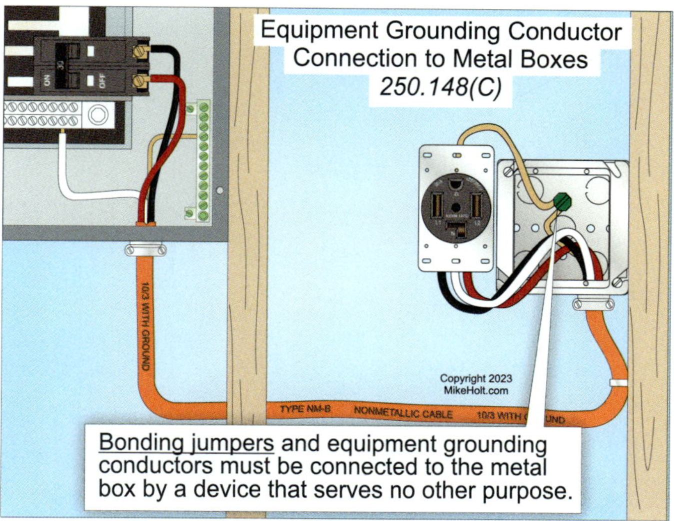

▶Figure 250–261

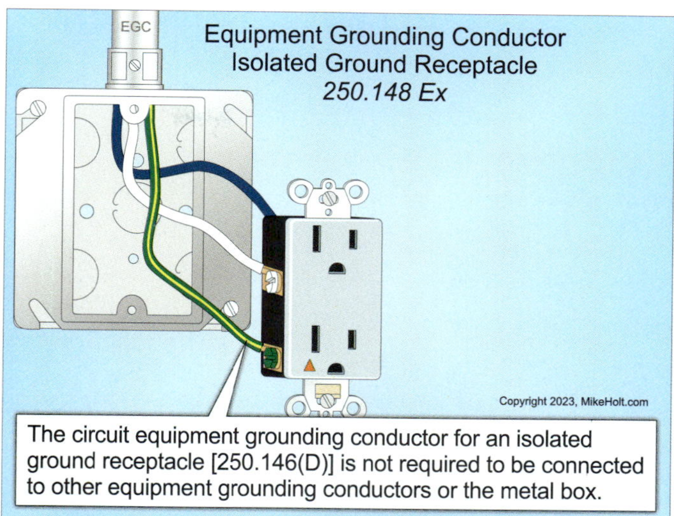

▶Figure 250–262

(D) Nonmetallic Boxes. One or more equipment grounding conductors brought into a nonmetallic outlet box shall be arranged to provide a connection to any fitting or device in that box requiring connection to an equipment grounding conductor.

WIRING METHODS AND MATERIALS

Introduction to Chapter 3—Wiring Methods and Materials

Chapter 3 of the *Code* is divided into fifty-one articles containing the general rules for wiring and sizing circuits, overcurrent protection of conductors, overvoltage protection of equipment, and bonding and grounding. The rules in this chapter apply to all electrical installations covered by the *NEC*—except as modified in Chapters 5, 6, 7, or specifically referenced in Chapter 8 [90.3].

This chapter can be thought of as the rough in phase of a job because it is primarily focused on the wiring methods and materials used to rough out an installation. Every article in this chapter deals with a different method or material used to get wiring from point "A" to point "B" in a system. The Chapter 3 articles covered by this material are:

Wiring Method Articles

▸ **Article 300—General Requirements for Wiring Methods and Materials.** Article 300 contains the general requirements for all wiring methods included in the *Code*, except for Class 2 power-limited, fire alarm and coaxial cables, which are covered in Chapters 7 and 8.

▸ **Article 310—Conductors for General Wiring.** This article contains the general requirements for conductors such as insulation markings, ampacity ratings, and conductor use. There is also a section that addresses single-family dwelling service and feeder conductors exclusively. Article 310 does not apply to conductors that are part of flexible cords, fixture wires, or conductors that are an integral part of equipment [90.7 and 310.1].

▸ **Article 312—Cabinets, Cutout Boxes, and Meter Socket Enclosures.** Article 312 covers the installation and construction specifications for cabinets and meter socket enclosures.

▸ **Article 314—Outlet, Device, Pull, and Junction Boxes; Conduit Bodies; Fittings; and Handhole Enclosures.** Installation requirements for outlet boxes, pull and junction boxes, as well as conduit bodies and handhole enclosures are contained in this article.

Cable Articles

Articles 320 through 340 address specific types of cables. If you take the time to become familiar with the various types of cables, you will be able to:

▸ Understand what is available for doing the work.

▸ Recognize cable types having special *NEC* requirements.

▸ Avoid buying cable you cannot install due to *Code* requirements you cannot meet with that wiring method.

. . .

Here is a brief overview of the cable articles covered in this material:

▸ **Article 320—Armored Cable (Type AC).** Armored cable is an assembly of insulated conductors, 14 AWG through 1 AWG, individually wrapped with waxed paper. The conductors are contained within a flexible metal (steel or aluminum) spiral sheath that interlocks at the edges. Armored cable looks like flexible metal conduit. Many electricians call this metal cable "BX®."

▸ **Article 330—Metal-Clad Cable (Type MC).** Metal-clad cable encloses insulated conductors in a metal sheath of corrugated, smooth copper or aluminum tubing, or spiral interlocked steel or aluminum. The physical characteristics of Type MC cable make it a versatile wiring method permitted in almost any location and for almost any application. The most used Type MC cable is the interlocking kind, which looks like armored cable or flexible metal conduit.

▸ **Article 334—Nonmetallic-Sheathed Cable (Type NM).** Nonmetallic-sheathed cable is commonly referred to by its trade name "Romex®." It encloses two, three, or four insulated conductors, 14 AWG through 2 AWG, within a nonmetallic outer jacket. Because this cable is manufactured in this manner, it contains a separate (usually bare) equipment grounding conductor. Nonmetallic-sheathed cable is commonly used for residential wiring applications but may sometimes be permitted for use in commercial occupancies.

▸ **Article 336—Power and Control Tray Cable (Type TC).** Power and control tray cable is flexible, inexpensive, and easily installed. It provides very limited physical protection for the conductors, so the installation restrictions are rigorous. Its low cost and relative ease of installation make it a common wiring method for industrial applications.

▸ **Article 338—Service-Entrance Cable (Types SE and USE).** Service-entrance and underground service-entrance cables can be a single conductor or a multiconductor assembly within an overall nonmetallic outer jacket or covering. These cables are most often used for services not over 1000V but are also permitted for feeders and branch circuits. When used as a service conductor(s) or a service-entrance conductor(s), pre-manufactured Type "SE" cable assemblies will typically contain two insulated phase conductors and a bare neutral conductor. When permitted for use as a feeder or branch circuit, Type SE cable is usually designated as Type "SER" and will contain the same three conductors as Type SE but a fourth conductor (which is insulated) will be added to serve as the neutral conductor.

▸ **Article 340—Underground Feeder and Branch-Circuit Cable (Type UF).** Underground feeder cable is a moisture-, fungus-, and corrosion-resistant cable suitable for direct burial in the Earth and is available in sizes 14 AWG through 4/0 AWG [340.104]. Multiconductor UF cable is covered in molded plastic that surrounds the insulated conductors.

Raceway Articles

Articles 342 through 390 address specific types of raceways. Refer to Article 100 for the definition of a raceway. If you take the time to become familiar with the various types of raceways, you will be able to:

▸ Understand what is available for doing the work.

▸ Recognize raceway types having special *Code* requirements.

▸ Avoid buying a raceway you cannot install due to *NEC* requirements you cannot meet with that wiring method.

Here is a brief overview of the raceway articles included in this material:

▸ **Article 342—Intermediate Metal Conduit (IMC).** Intermediate metal conduit is a circular metal raceway with the same outside diameter as rigid metal conduit. The wall thickness of this type of conduit is less than that of rigid metal conduit, so it has a larger interior cross-sectional area for holding conductors. Intermediate metal conduit is lighter and less expensive than rigid metal conduit and is approved by the *Code* for use in the same applications as rigid metal conduit. This type of conduit also uses a different steel alloy, which makes it stronger than rigid metal conduit, even though the walls are thinner.

▶ **Article 344—Rigid Metal Conduit (RMC).** Rigid metal conduit is like intermediate metal conduit, except the wall thickness is larger, so it has a smaller interior cross-sectional area. This type of conduit is heavier than intermediate metal conduit and is permitted for use in the same applications as intermediate metal conduit (IMC).

▶ **Article 348—Flexible Metal Conduit (FMC).** Flexible metal conduit is a raceway of circular cross section made of a helically wound, interlocked metal strip of either steel or aluminum. It is commonly called "Greenfield" (after its inventor) or "Flex."

▶ **Article 350—Liquidtight Flexible Metal Conduit (LFMC).** Liquidtight flexible metal conduit is a raceway of circular cross section with an outer liquidtight, nonmetallic, sunlight-resistant jacket over an inner flexible metal core, with associated couplings, connectors, and fittings. It is listed for the installation of electrical conductors. This type of conduit is commonly called "Seal-Tite®" or simply "liquidtight." Liquidtight flexible metal conduit is similar in construction to flexible metal conduit, but it has an outer thermoplastic covering.

▶ **Article 352—Rigid Polyvinyl Chloride Conduit (PVC).** Rigid polyvinyl chloride conduit is a nonmetallic raceway of circular cross section with integral or associated couplings, connectors, and fittings. It is listed for the installation of electrical conductors.

▶ **Article 356—Liquidtight Flexible Nonmetallic Conduit (LFNC).** Liquidtight flexible nonmetallic conduit (commonly referred to as "Carflex®") is a raceway of circular cross section with an outer liquidtight, nonmetallic, sunlight-resistant jacket over an inner flexible core, with associated couplings, connectors, and fittings.

▶ **Article 358—Electrical Metallic Tubing (EMT).** Electrical metallic tubing is a nonthreaded thinwall raceway of circular cross section designed for the physical protection and routing of conductors and cables. Compared to rigid metal conduit and intermediate metal conduit, electrical metallic tubing is relatively easy to bend, cut, and ream. EMT is not threaded, so all connectors and couplings are of the threadless type. It is available in a range of colors, such as red and blue.

▶ **Article 362—Electrical Nonmetallic Tubing (ENT).** Electrical nonmetallic tubing is a pliable, corrugated, circular raceway made of PVC. It is often referred to as "Smurf Pipe" or "Smurf Tube," because it was only available in blue when it was first available. The nickname is a reference to the children's cartoon characters "The Smurfs." It is now available in many other colors.

▶ **Article 376—Metal Wireways.** A metal wireway is a sheet metal trough with hinged or removable covers making the electrical conductors and cables housed and protected inside accessible. Metal wireways must be installed as complete and contiguous systems.

▶ **Article 380—Multioutlet Assemblies.** A multioutlet assembly is a surface, flush, or freestanding raceway designed to hold conductors and receptacles. It is assembled in the field or at the factory.

▶ **Article 386—Surface Metal Raceways.** A surface metal raceway is a metal raceway intended to be mounted to a surface with associated accessories, in which conductors are placed after the raceway has been installed as a complete system.

Cable Trays

▶ **Article 392—Cable Trays.** A cable tray system is a unit or assembly of units or sections with associated fittings forming a structural system used to securely fasten or support cables and raceways. A cable tray is not a raceway. It is a support system for raceways, cables, and enclosures.

Notice as you read through the various wiring methods that the *NEC* attempts to use similar section numbering for similar topics from one article to the next. It uses the same digits after the decimal point in the section numbers for the same topic. This makes it easier to locate the specific requirements of a particular article. For example, the rules for securing and supporting can be found in the section ending with ".30" of each article.

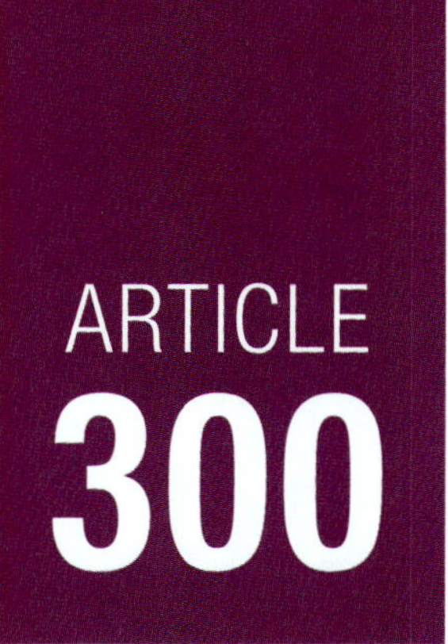

ARTICLE 300

GENERAL REQUIREMENTS FOR WIRING METHODS AND MATERIALS

Introduction to Article 300—General Requirements for Wiring Methods and Materials

Article 300 contains the general requirements for all installed wiring methods included in the *NEC*. Because the *Code* is an installation standard this article does not apply where these wiring methods are integral parts of electrical equipment.

Because Article 300 contains the general requirements for wiring methods and materials, you must have a solid understanding of these rules to correctly and safely install the wiring methods included in Chapter 3. Some topics covered in this material include:

- ▶ Conductors
- ▶ Terminations
- ▶ Burial Depth
- ▶ Electrical and Mechanical Continuity of Raceways and Cables
- ▶ Securing and Supporting
- ▶ Length of Free Conductors
- ▶ Induced Currents in Steel Enclosures
- ▶ Spread of Fire

Part I. General Requirements

300.1 Scope

(A) All Wiring Installations. Article 300 contains the general requirements for wiring methods and materials for power and lighting. ▶Figure 300–1

Author's Comment:

- ▶ The requirements contained in Article 300 do not apply to Class 2 power-limited circuits, fire alarm circuits, optical fiber cables, or coaxial cable, unless they are specifically reference in the appropriate article.

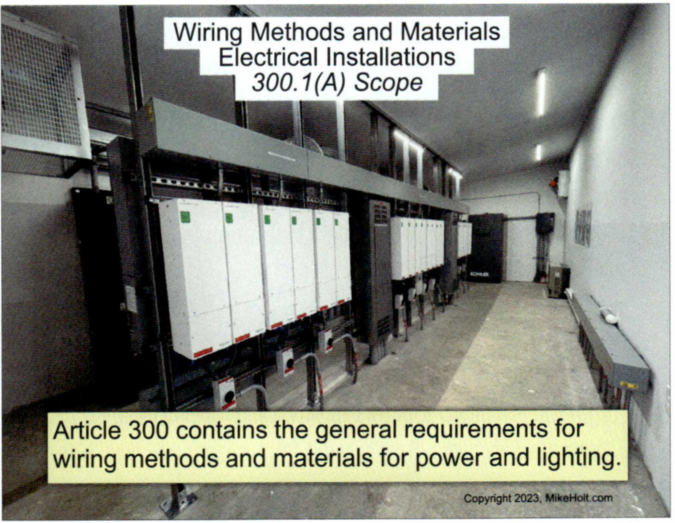

▶Figure 300–1

(B) Integral Parts of Equipment. The requirements contained in Article 300 do not apply to the integral parts of electrical equipment. ▶Figure 300–2

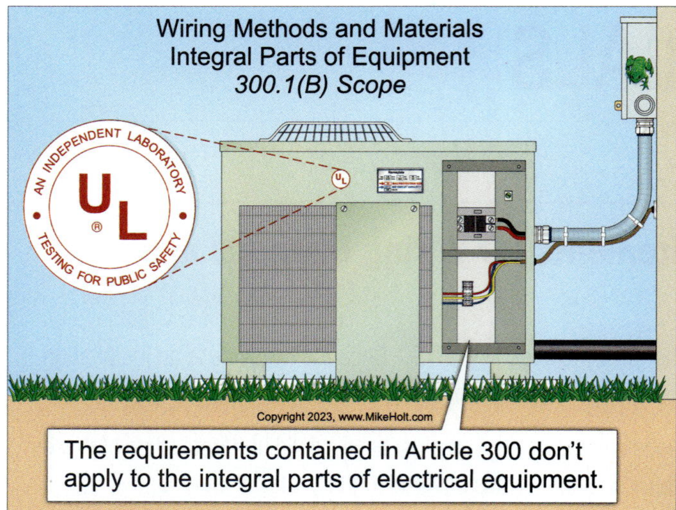

▶Figure 300–2

Author's Comment:

▸ Integral wiring of equipment is covered by various product standards and not the *NEC*. It is the intent of this *Code* that the factory-installed internal wiring of equipment processed by a qualified testing laboratory does not need to be inspected [90.7].

300.3 Conductors

(A) Conductors. Conductors must be installed in a Chapter 3 wiring method, such as raceways, cables, or cable trays. ▶Figure 300–3

(B) Conductors Grouped Together. All conductors of a circuit, including the neutral and equipment grounding conductors, must be installed together in the same raceway, <u>conduit body</u>, cable, trench, or cable tray except as permitted by 330.3(B)(1) through (4). ▶Figure 300–4

Author's Comment:

▸ The equipment grounding conductor must be grouped together with the circuit conductors to provide a low impedance path during a short-circuit or ground-fault event. ▶Figure 300–5

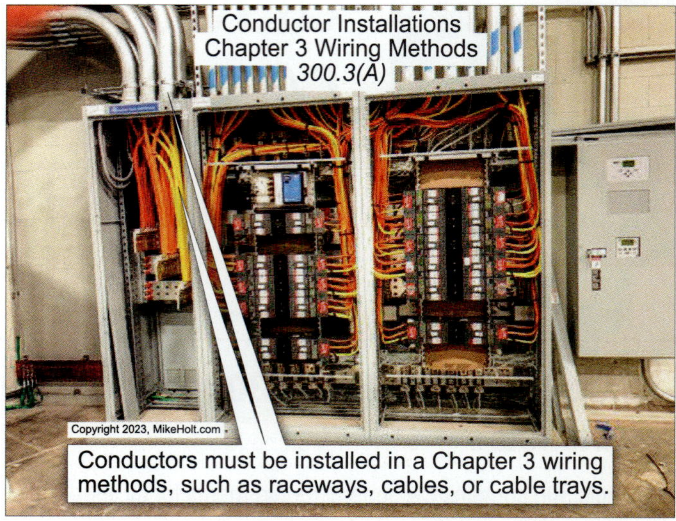

▶Figure 300–3

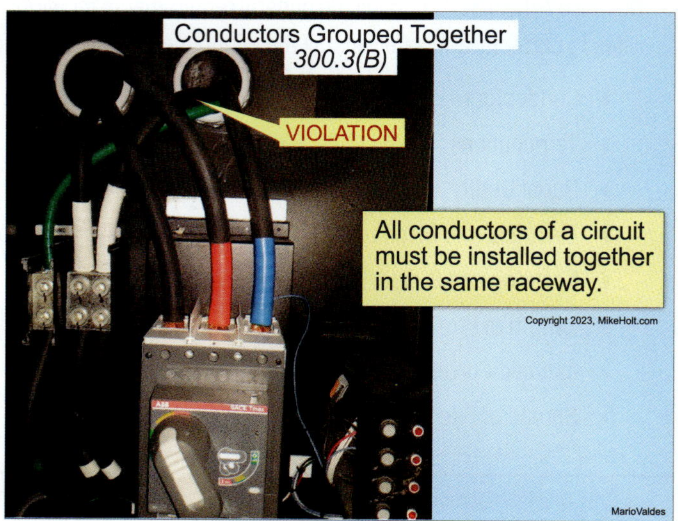

▶Figure 300–4

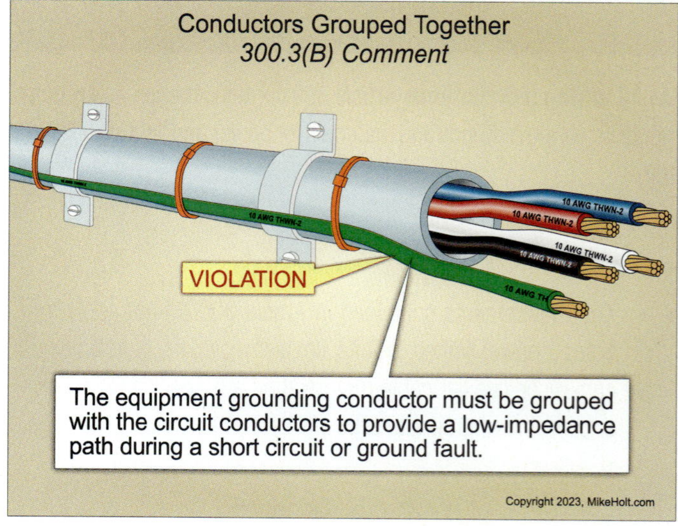

▶Figure 300–5

(1) Paralleled Installations. All conductors of a parallel set must be installed within the same raceway, cable, or cable tray in accordance with 310.10(G). ▶Figure 300–6

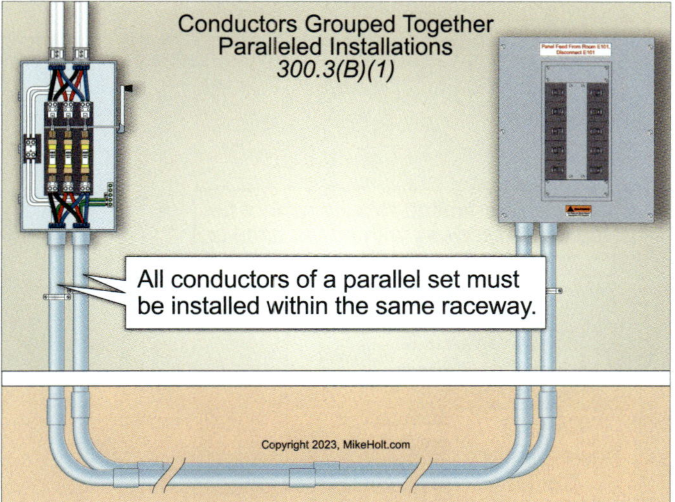

▶Figure 300–6

Connections, taps, or extensions made from paralleled conductors must connect to all conductors of the paralleled set.

Author's Comment:

▶ Grouping all phase, neutral, and equipment grounding and bonding conductors of the circuit helps minimize the inductive heating of the surrounding steel raceways and enclosures for alternating-current circuits. See 300.20(A). ▶Figure 300–7

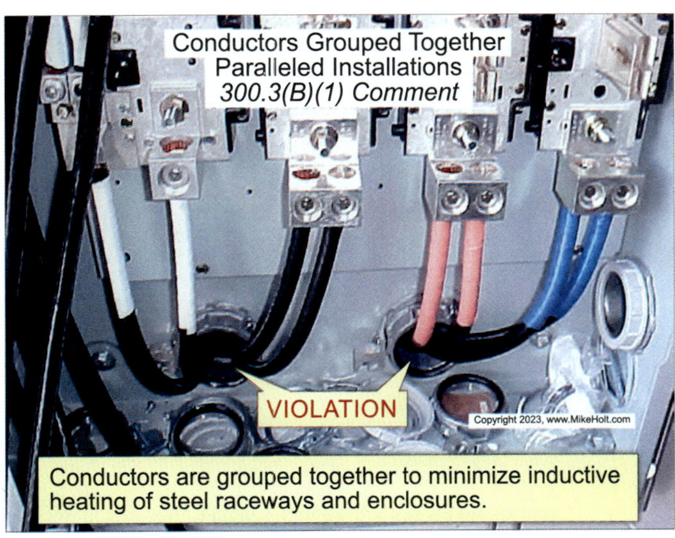

▶Figure 300–7

Ex: Isolated parallel phase and neutral conductors can be installed in individual underground nonmetallic raceways (Phase A in raceway 1, Phase B in raceway 2, and so forth) as permitted by 300.5(I) Ex 2, if the installation complies with 300.20(B). ▶Figure 300–8

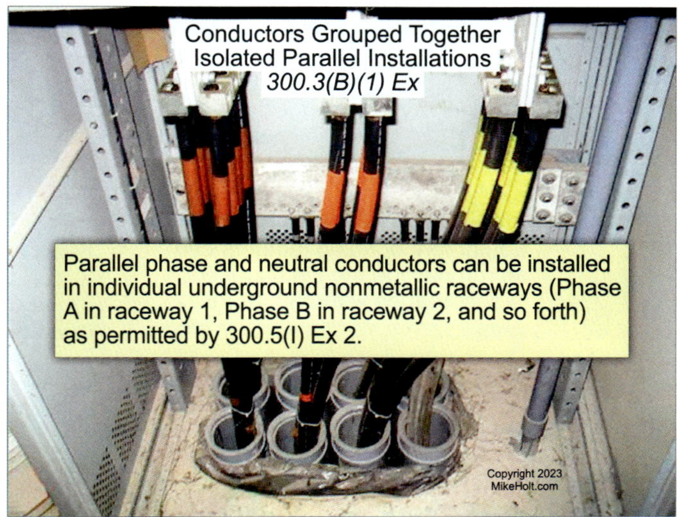

▶Figure 300–8

(2) Bonding Jumpers Outside the Raceway. Equipment bonding jumpers for dc circuits can be run separately from the circuit conductors in accordance with 250.134(2) Ex 2. ▶Figure 300–9

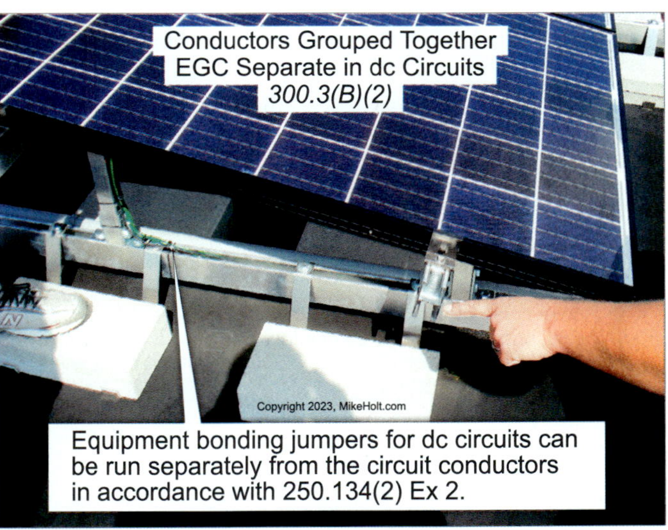

▶Figure 300–9

Equipment bonding jumpers can be run outside the circuit raceway in accordance with 250.102(E)(2). ▶Figure 300–10

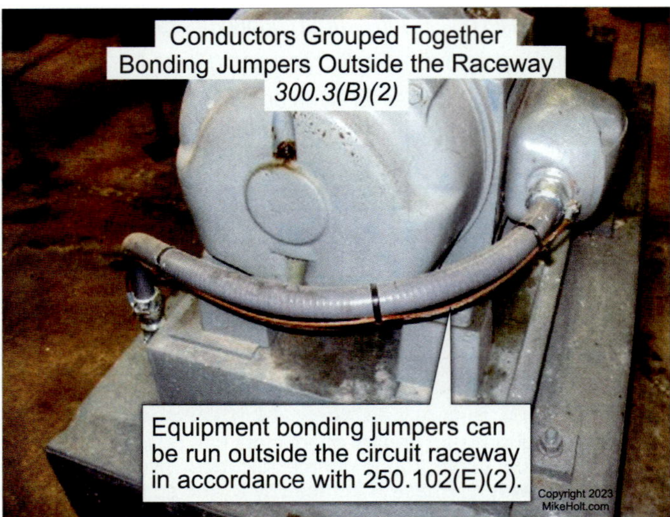

▶Figure 300–10

(C) Mixing Conductors of Different Voltage Systems.

(1) Voltage Insulation Rating. Power conductors can occupy the same raceway, cable, or enclosure if all conductors have an insulation voltage rating not less than the maximum circuit voltage. ▶Figure 300–11

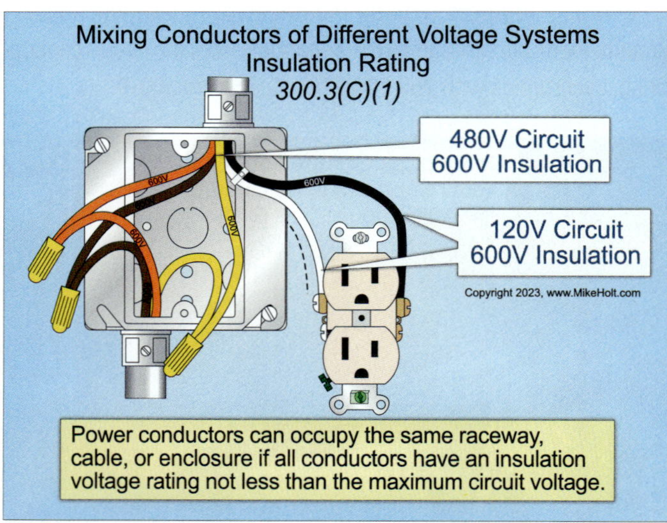

▶Figure 300–11

Author's Comment:

▸ The maximum circuit voltage in the raceway is what determines the minimum voltage rating for the insulation of the conductors—not the maximum insulation voltage of the conductors in the raceway. For example, a 120/240V circuit installed in a raceway with 600V insulated conductors must have all conductors with a minimum insulation voltage rating of 240V not 600V.

Note 1: Class 2 power-limited circuits must be separated from power circuits in raceways, so the higher-voltage conductors do not accidentally energize the Class 2 power-limited circuits [725.136(A)]. ▶Figure 300–12

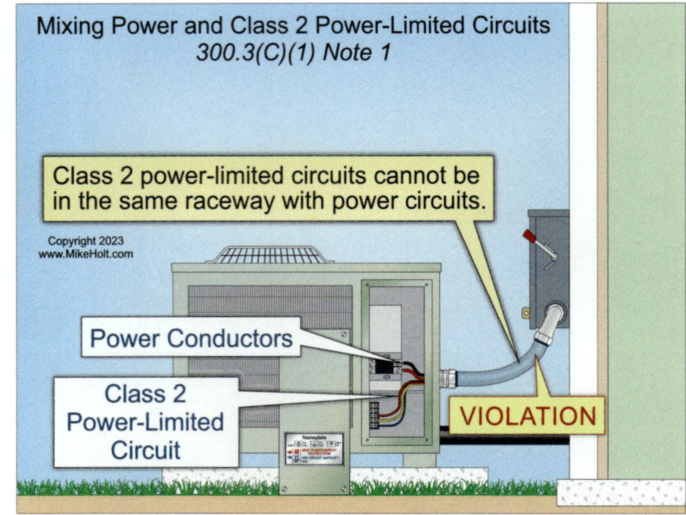

▶Figure 300–12

300.4 Protection Against Physical Damage

Where subject to physical damage, conductors, raceways, and cables must be protected in accordance with 300.4(A) through (H).

(A) Cables and Raceways Through Wood Members.

Author's Comment:

▸ When the following wiring methods are installed through wood members, they must comply with 300.4(A)(1) or (2).

▸ Armored Cable, Article 320
▸ Electrical Metallic Tubing, Article 358
▸ Electrical Nonmetallic Tubing, Article 362
▸ Flexible Metal Conduit, Article 348
▸ Liquidtight Flexible Metal Conduit, Article 350
▸ Liquidtight Flexible Nonmetallic Conduit, Article 356
▸ Metal-Clad Cable, Article 330
▸ PVC Conduit, Article 352
▸ Nonmetallic-Sheathed Cable, Article 334
▸ Service-Entrance Cable, Article 338
▸ Underground Feeder and Branch-Circuit Cable, Article 340

(1) Bored Holes in Wood Members. Holes through wood framing members for cables or raceways must be not less than 1¼ in. from the edge of the wood member. If the edge of a drilled hole in a wood framing member is less than 1¼ in. from the edge of the framing member, a steel plate ¹⁄₁₆ in. thick of sufficient length and width must be installed to protect the wiring method from screws and nails. ▶Figure 300–13

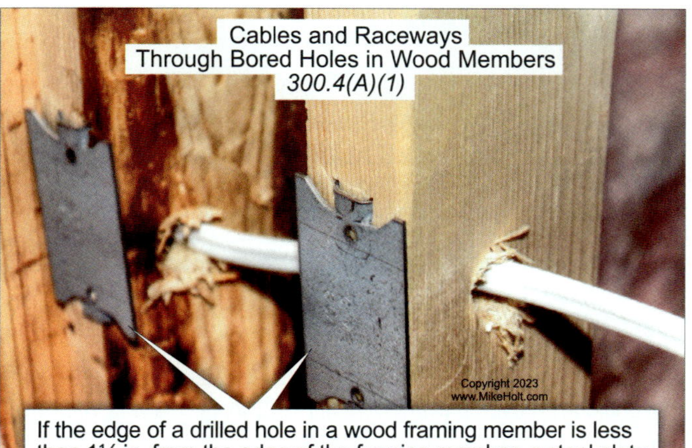

If the edge of a drilled hole in a wood framing member is less than 1¼ in. from the edge of the framing member, a steel plate ¹/₁₆ in. thick of enough length and width must be installed to protect the wiring method from screws and nails.

▶Figure 300–13

Ex 1: A steel plate is not required to protect rigid metal conduit, intermediate metal conduit, PVC conduit, reinforced thermosetting resin conduit (RTRC), or electrical metallic tubing.

(2) Notches in Wood Members. If notching of wood framing members for cables and raceways is permitted by the building code, a ¹⁄₁₆ in. thick steel plate of sufficient length and width must be installed to protect the wiring method laid in those wood notches from penetration by screws and nails. ▶Figure 300–14

Ex 1: A steel plate is not required to protect rigid metal conduit, intermediate metal conduit, PVC conduit, or electrical metallic tubing.

Caution

CAUTION: Many wood and metal framing members (especially joists and beams) have specific drilling and/or notching instructions meant to maintain structural integrity. Building code requirements limit the diameter of the hole to ⅓ the depth of the joist framing member. Notching is limited to ¼ the depth of joist framing members in accordance with the IBC 2308, *International Building Code* and IRC 5208, *International Residential Code*.

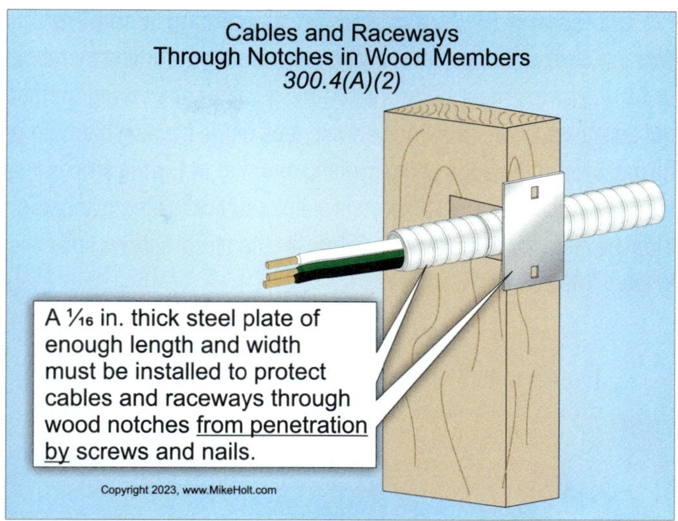

▶Figure 300–14

(B) Nonmetallic-Sheathed Cable and Electrical Nonmetallic Tubing Through Metal Framing Members.

(1) Type NM Cable, Metal Framing Members. If Type NM cable passes through factory or field-made openings in metal framing members, the cable must be protected by listed bushings or grommets that cover all metal edges. The protection fitting must be securely fastened in the opening before the installation of the cable. ▶Figure 300–15

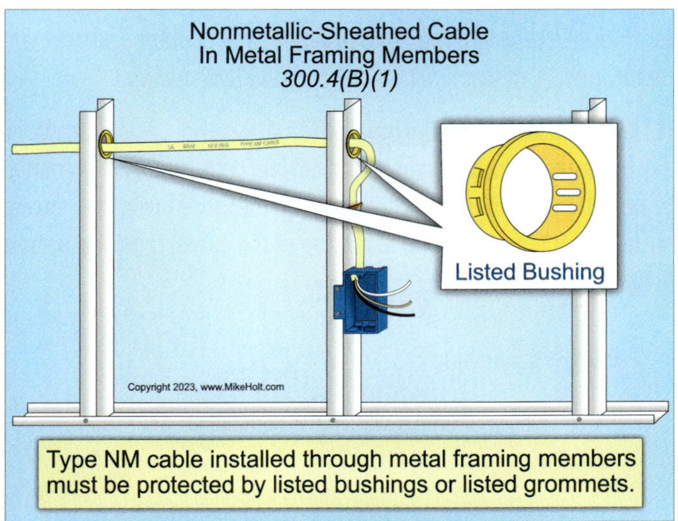

▶Figure 300–15

(2) Type NM Cable and Electrical Nonmetallic Tubing. If nails or screws are likely to penetrate Type NM cable or electrical nonmetallic tubing, a steel sleeve, steel plate, or steel clip not less than ¹⁄₁₆ in. thick must be installed to protect the cable or tubing.

Ex: A listed and marked steel plate less than ¹⁄₁₆ in. thick that provides equal or better protection against nail or screw penetration is permitted.

(D) Cables and Raceways Parallel to Framing Members and Furring Strips. Cables or raceways run parallel to framing members or furring strips must be protected by installing the wiring method not less than 1¼ in. from the nearest edge of the framing member or furring strip. If the edge of the framing member or furring strip is less than 1¼ in. away, a ¹⁄₁₆ in. thick steel plate of sufficient length and width must be installed to protect the wiring method from screws and nails. ▶Figure 300–16

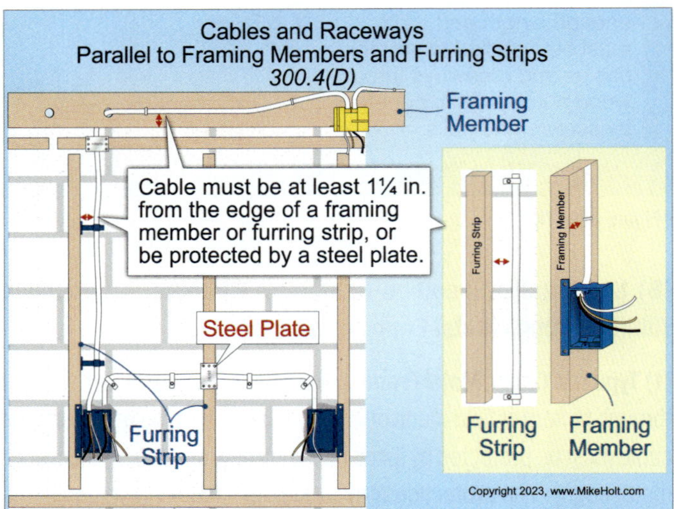

▶Figure 300–16

Ex 1: Protection is not required for rigid metal conduit, intermediate metal conduit, PVC conduit, or electrical metallic tubing.

(E) Wiring Under Metal-Corrugated Roof Decking. Cables, raceways, and boxes under metal-corrugated sheet roof decking are not permitted to be within 1½ in. of the roof decking, measured from the lowest surface of the roof decking to the top of the cable, raceway, or box. ▶Figure 300–17

Author's Comment:

▶ A similar requirement applies to luminaires installed in or under roof decking [410.10(F)].

Note: Raceways or cables installed under metal roof decking might be penetrated by screws or other mechanical devices designed to "hold down" the waterproof membrane or roof insulating material.

Ex 1: Spacing from roof decking does not apply to rigid metal conduit and intermediate metal conduit with listed steel or malleable iron fittings and boxes.

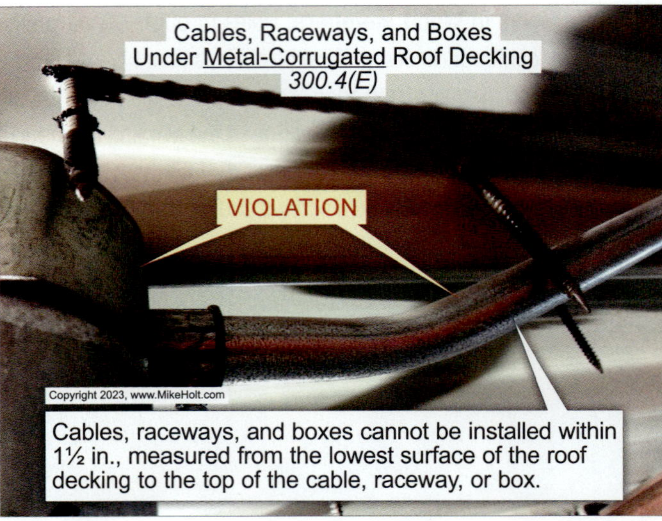

▶Figure 300–17

Ex 2: The 1½ in. spacing is not required where metal-corrugated sheet roof decking is covered with a minimum of 2 in. of concrete, measured from the top of the corrugated roofing.

(G) Raceway Termination Fittings. Raceways containing insulated circuit conductors 4 AWG and larger that enter a cabinet, box, enclosure, or raceway must be protected prior to the installation of the conductors as follows:

(1) An identified raceway fitting providing a smoothly rounded insulating surface. ▶Figure 300–18

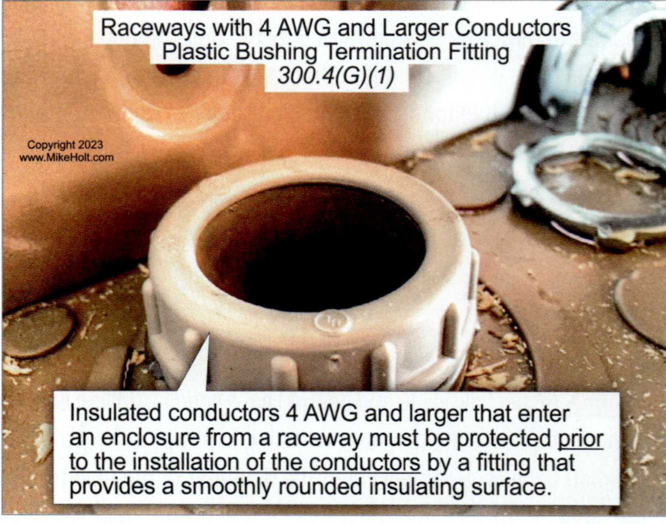

▶Figure 300–18

(2) A listed metal raceway fitting with smoothly rounded edges. ▶Figure 300–19

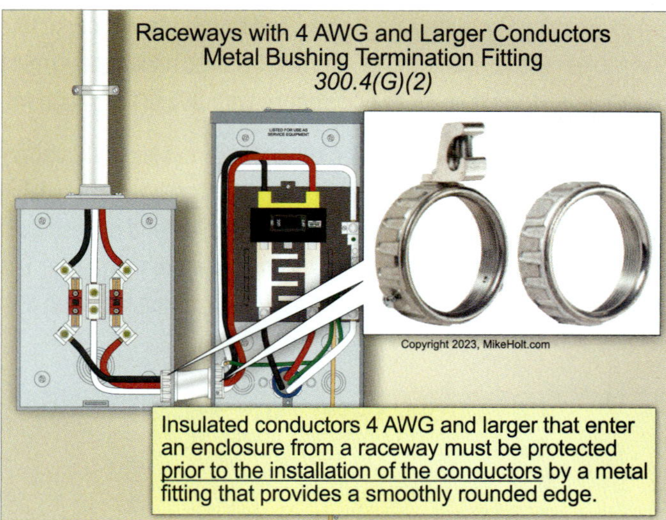

▶Figure 300–19

Conduit bushings constructed of metal can be used to secure a fitting or raceway.

(H) Structural Joints. A listed expansion/deflection fitting, or other means approved by the authority having jurisdiction, must be used where a raceway crosses a structural joint intended for expansion, contraction, or deflection.

300.5 Underground Installations

(A) Minimum Burial Cover Requirements. When cables or raceways are installed underground, they must have a minimum burial cover in accordance with Table 300.5(A). ▶Figure 300–20

	Column 1 UF or USE Cables or Conductors	Column 2 RMC or IMC	Column 3 EMT or Nonmetallic Raceways	Column 4 Residential 15A & 20A GFCI 120V Branch Ckts
Dwelling Unit Driveway and Parking Area	18 in.	18 in.	18 in.	12 in.
Under Roadway Driveway Parking Lot	24 in.	24 in.	24 in.	24 in.
Other Locations	24 in.	6 in.	18 in.	12 in.

▶Figure 300–20

▶ There are no burial cover requirements for raceways underneath a building. ▶Figure 300–21

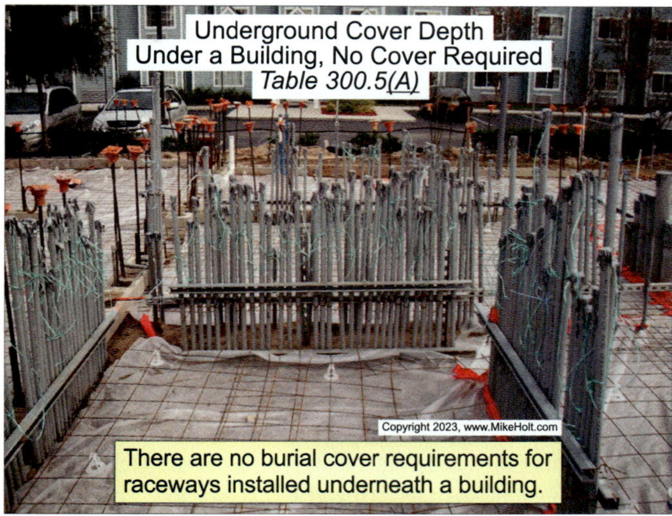

▶Figure 300–21

	Column 1 Buried Cables	Column 2 RMC or IMC	Column 3 EMT or Nonmetallic Raceways
Location			
Under Building	0	0	0
Dwelling Unit	24/12*	6	18
Dwelling Unit Driveway	18/12*	6	18/12*
Under Roadway	24	24	24
Other Locations	24	6	18

Table 300.5(A) Minimum Cover Requirements in Inches

Residential branch circuits rated 120V or less with GFCI protection and maximum protection of 20A.

See the table in the NEC for full details.

Note 1 to Table 300.5: "Cover" is measured as the shortest distance from the top of the underground cable or raceway to the top surface of finished grade. ▶Figure 300–22

Note 6 to Table 300.5: Directly buried electrical metallic tubing (EMT) must comply with 358.10.

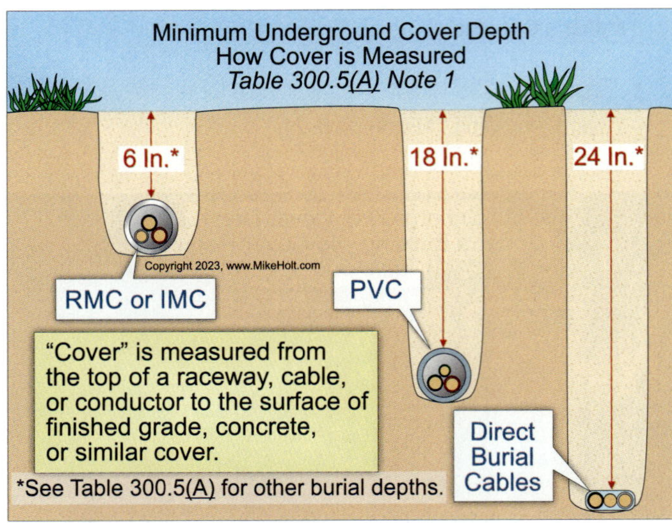

▶Figure 300–22

(B) Wet Locations. Cables and insulated conductors installed in raceways and enclosures underground must be listed as suitable for a wet location in accordance with 310.10(C). ▶Figure 300–23

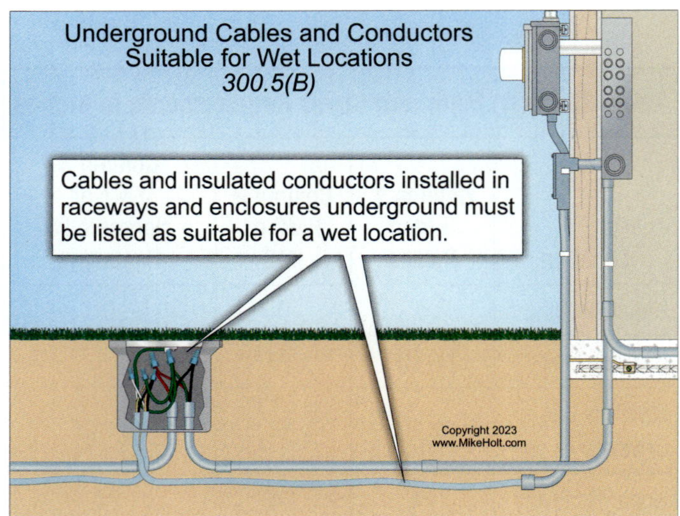

▶Figure 300–23

According to Article 100, "Wet Location" includes installations underground, in concrete slabs in direct contact with the Earth, locations subject to saturation with water, and unprotected locations exposed to weather. See 300.9 for raceways in wet locations above ground.

(C) Cables and Conductors Under Buildings. Cables and conductors installed under a building must be installed within a raceway that extends past the outside walls of the building.

Ex 2: Type MC cable listed for direct burial or concrete encasement is permitted under a building without installation within a raceway [330.10(A)(5) and 330.10(A)(11)].

(D) Protecting Underground Cables and Conductors. Conductors and cables such as Types MC, UF, and USE installed underground must be protected from damage in accordance with 300.5(1) through (4).

(1) Emerging from Grade. Type UF and USE cables and conductors that emerge from grade must be protected against physical damage. Protection below grade is required to extend no less than the cover requirements of Table 300.5 and not more than 18 in. The protection above grade must extend to a height of not less than 8 ft. ▶Figure 300–24

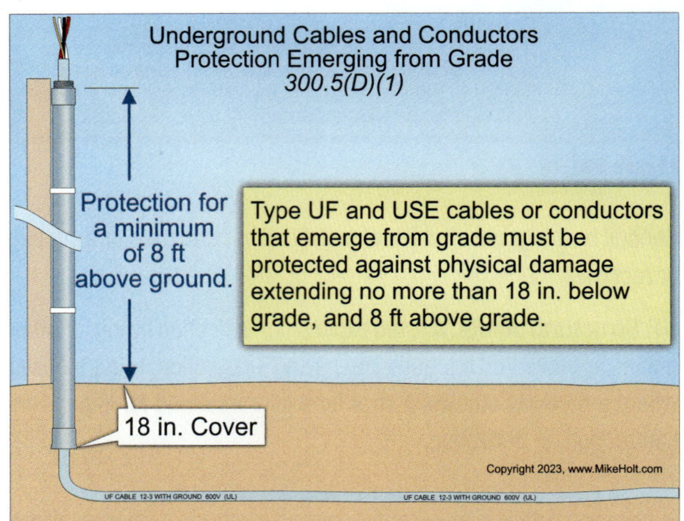

▶Figure 300–24

Author's Comment:

▶ Where a raceway is subject to physical damage, the conductors must be installed in EMT, RMC, IMC, RTRC-XW, or Schedule 80 PVC conduit [300.5(D)(4)].

(2) Conductors Entering Buildings. Underground conductors and cables that enter a building must be protected to the point of entrance.

(3) Underground Service Conductors. Underground service-entrance conductors (USE) must have their location identified by a warning ribbon placed in the trench at least 12 in. above the underground conductors. ▶Figure 300–25

Author's Comment:

▶ The *NEC* does not require a warning ribbon for conductors under the exclusive control of the utility [90.2(D)(5)].

▶ The requirements for a warning ribbon do not apply to underground service conductors that are installed in a raceway or encased in concrete

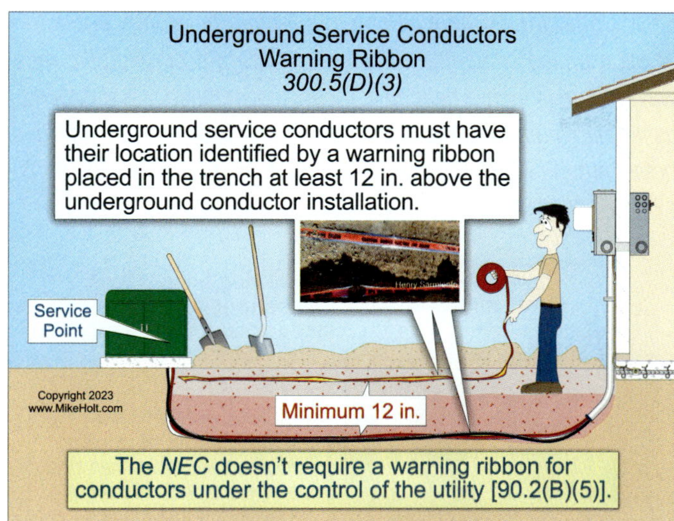

▶Figure 300–25

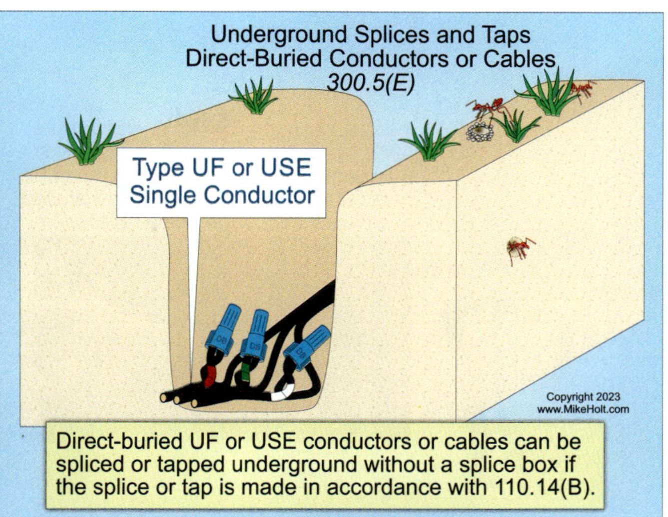

▶Figure 300–27

(4) Raceway Damage. Where an underground raceway emerging from grade is subject to physical damage, the conductors must be installed in EMT, RMC, IMC, RTRC-XW, or Schedule 80 PVC conduit.
▶Figure 300–26

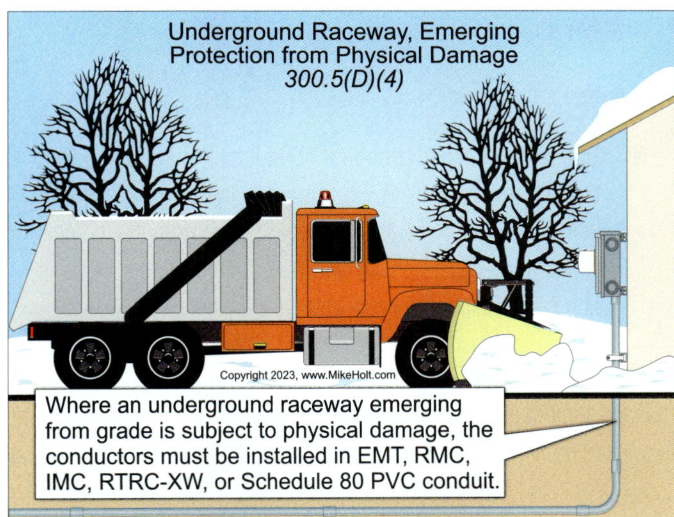

▶Figure 300–26

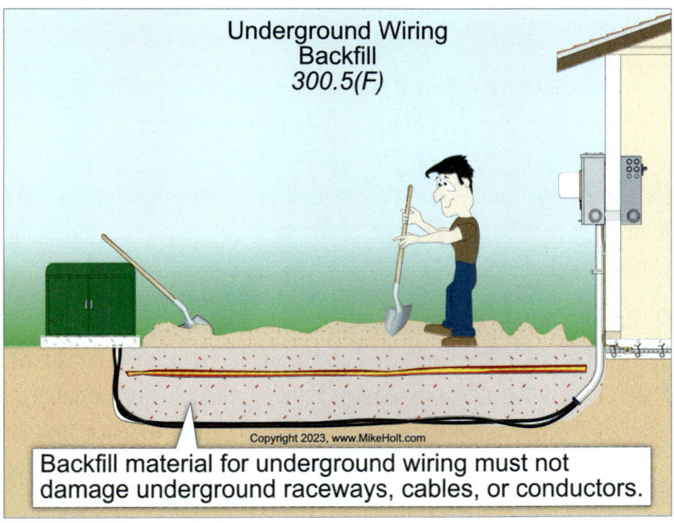

▶Figure 300–28

(E) Underground Splices and Taps. Direct-buried UF or USE conductors or cables can be spliced or tapped underground without a splice box [300.15(G)], if the splice or tap is made in accordance with 110.14(B). ▶Figure 300–27

(F) Backfill. Backfill material for underground wiring must not damage underground raceways, cables, or conductors. ▶Figure 300–28

Author's Comment:

▶ Large rocks, chunks of concrete, steel rods, mesh, and other sharp-edged objects are not permitted to be used for back-filling material because they can damage the underground conductors, cables, or raceways.

(G) Raceway Seals. If moisture might contact energized live parts through an underground raceway, a seal identified for use with the cable or conductor insulation must be installed at either or both ends of the raceway [225.27 and 230.8]. ▶Figure 300–29

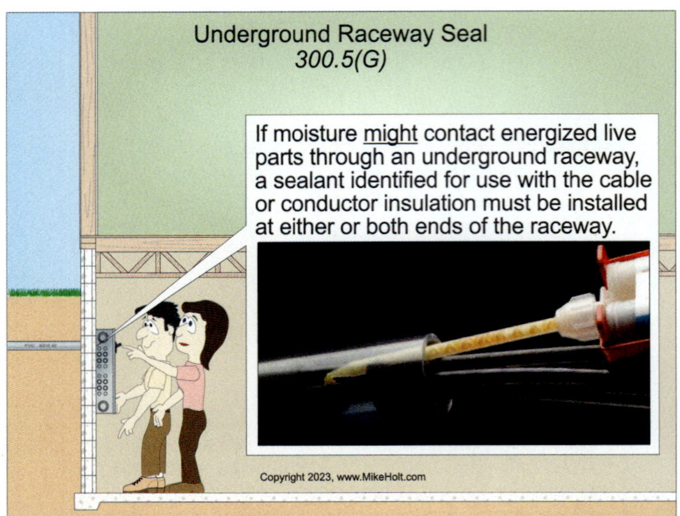

▶Figure 300–29

Author's Comment:

▶ Moisture is a common problem for equipment downhill from the supply or in underground equipment rooms.

(H) Bushing. Raceways that terminate underground must have a bushing or fitting at the end of the raceway to protect emerging cables or conductors.

(I) Conductors Grouped Together. Underground conductors of the same circuit (including the neutral and equipment grounding conductor) must be installed inside the same raceway, multiconductor cable, or near each other in the same trench. See 300.3(B). ▶Figure 300–30

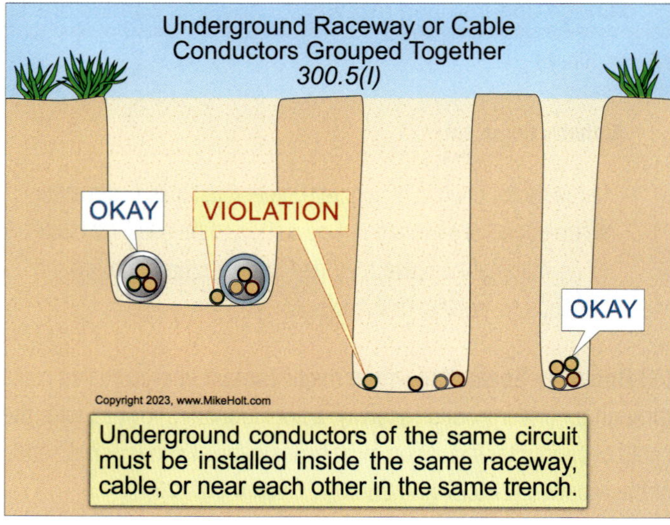

▶Figure 300–30

Ex 2: Underground parallel conductors can have the conductors of each phase or neutral installed in separate nonmetallic raceways where inductive heating at raceway terminations is reduced by using aluminum locknuts and cutting a slot between the individual holes through which the conductors pass as required by 300.20(B).
▶Figure 300–31

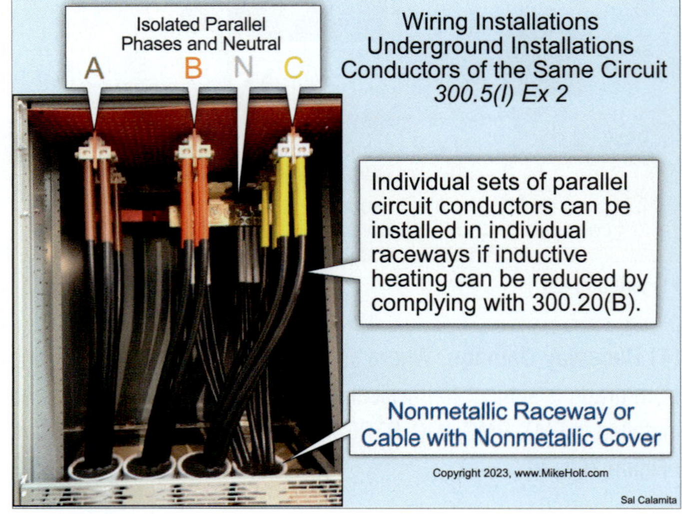

▶Figure 300–31

Author's Comment:

▶ Separating phase and neutral conductors in individual PVC conduits makes it easier to terminate larger parallel installations, but it also results in elevated electromagnetic fields (EMF). Keeping the phase and neutral conductors close to each other helps reduce circuit impedance.

(J) Earth Movement. Direct-buried conductors, cables, or raceways that are subject to movement by settlement or frost must be arranged to prevent damage to conductors or equipment connected to the wiring.

300.6 Protection Against Corrosion

Raceways, cable trays, cable armor, boxes, cable sheathing, cabinets, enclosures, elbows, couplings, fittings, supports, and support hardware must be suitable for the environment.

(A) Steel Equipment. Steel raceways, cables, cable trays, cabinets, enclosures, fittings, and support hardware must be protected against corrosion by a coating of approved corrosion-resistant material.
▶Figure 300–32

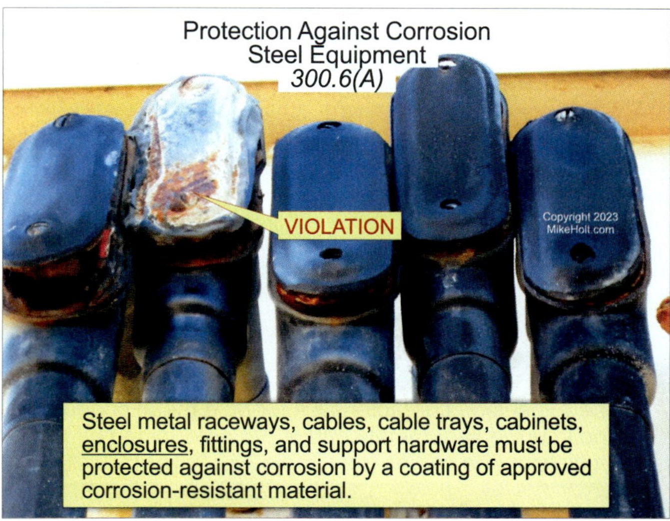

▶Figure 300–32

Author's Comment:

▶ In accordance with "*UL Guide Information DYIX*," supplementary corrosion protection is required when a steel raceway transitions from concrete encasement to the soil. ▶Figure 300–33

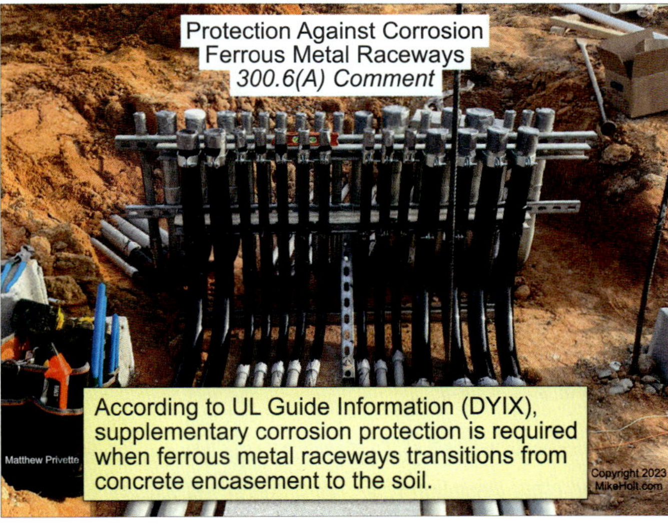

▶Figure 300–33

Where corrosion protection is required and IMC or RMC is threaded in the field, the threads must be coated with an approved electrically conductive, corrosion-resistant compound.

300.7 Raceways Exposed to Different Temperatures

(A) Sealing. If a raceway is subjected to different temperatures and where condensation is known to be a problem, the raceway must be filled with a material approved by the authority having jurisdiction that will prevent the circulation of warm air to a colder section of the raceway. Sealants must be identified for use with cable insulation, conductor insulation, a bare conductor, a shield, or other components.
▶Figure 300–34 and ▶Figure 300–35

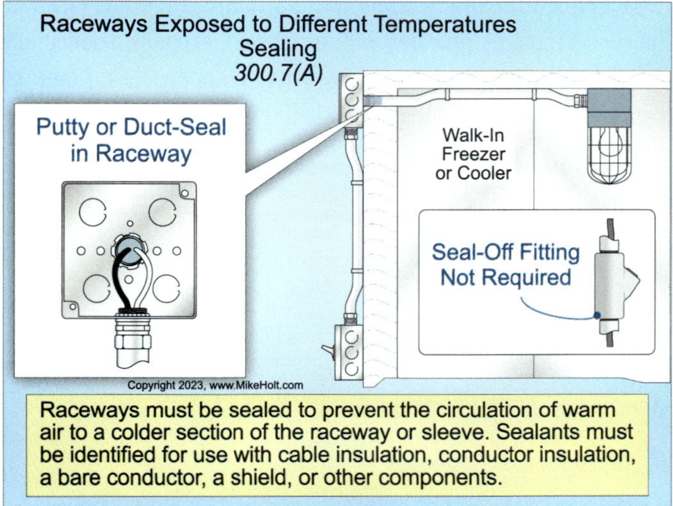

▶Figure 300–34

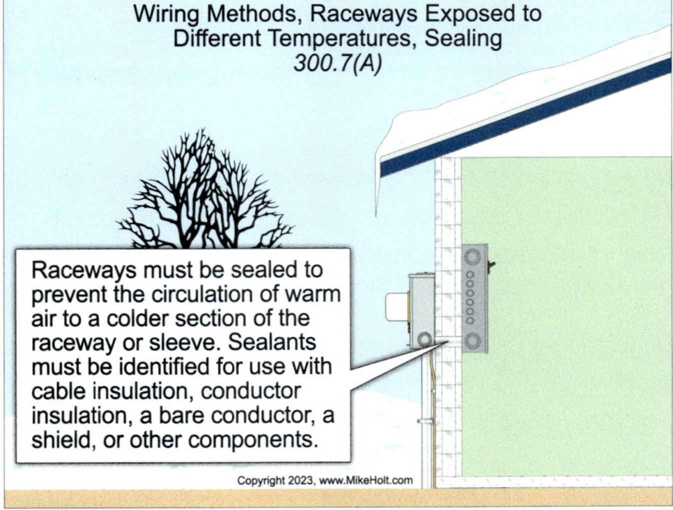

▶Figure 300–35

▶ One common product used for this is electrical duct seal and it is so identified. There are other identified products such as Polywater's FST Duct Sealant. Typical expanding foams used to seal buildings are not identified for this application.

According to Article 100, "Identified" means marked suitable for the purpose by the manufacturer, and recognized as suitable for a specific purpose, function, use, environment, or application.

(B) Expansion, Expansion-Deflection, and Deflection Fittings. Raceways must be provided with expansion, expansion-deflection, or deflection fittings where necessary to compensate for thermal expansion, deflection, and contraction. ▶Figure 300–36

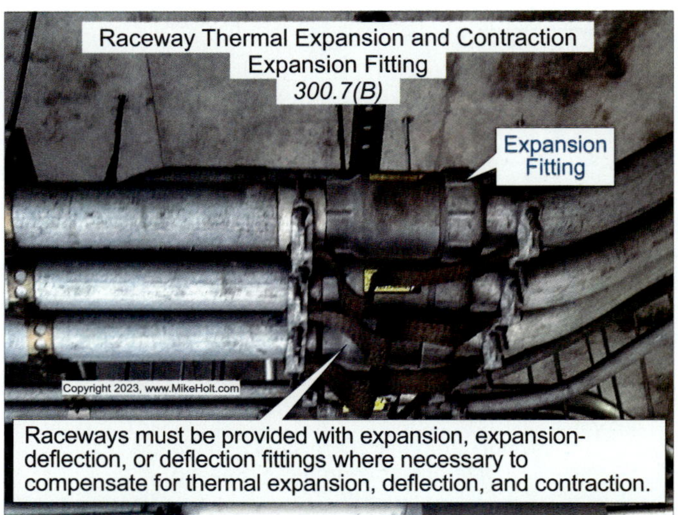

▶Figure 300–36

Note 1: Table 352.44(A) provides the expansion characteristics for PVC conduit. The expansion characteristics for rigid metal conduit and intermediate metal is determined by multiplying the values from Table 352.44(A) by 0.20. ▶Figure 300–37

Note 2: For information on expansion and expansion-deflection fittings, see NEMA FB 2.40, *Installation Guidelines for Expansion and Expansion/Deflection Fittings.*

300.9 Raceways in Wet Locations Above Grade

The interior of raceways installed in wet locations above ground is considered a wet location. Insulated conductors and cables installed in raceways in above ground wet locations must be listed for use in wet locations in accordance with 310.10(C). ▶Figure 300–38

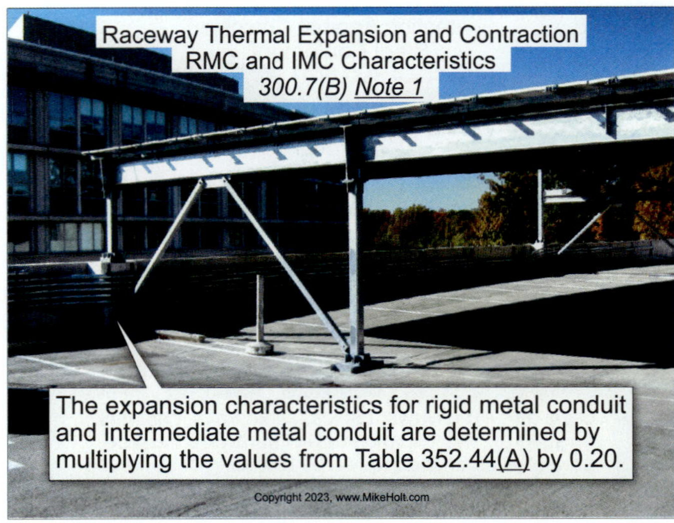

▶Figure 300–37

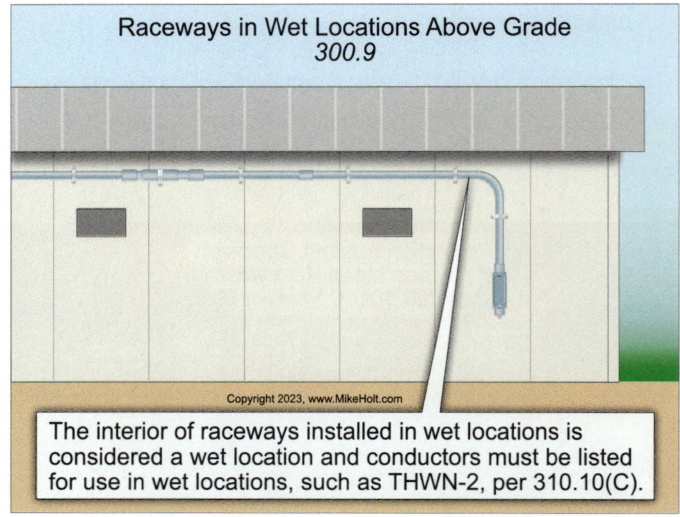

▶Figure 300–38

▶ In addition to 310.10(C), Table 310.4(A)(1) can be used to find other insulation types permitted in wet locations.

According to Article 100, "Wet Location" means installations underground or in concrete slabs in contact with the Earth, and locations subject to water spray or exposed to weather.

300.10 Electrical Continuity

Metal raceways, cable armor, and metal enclosures must be metallically joined together to provide electrical continuity [250.4(A)(3)]. ▶Figure 300–39

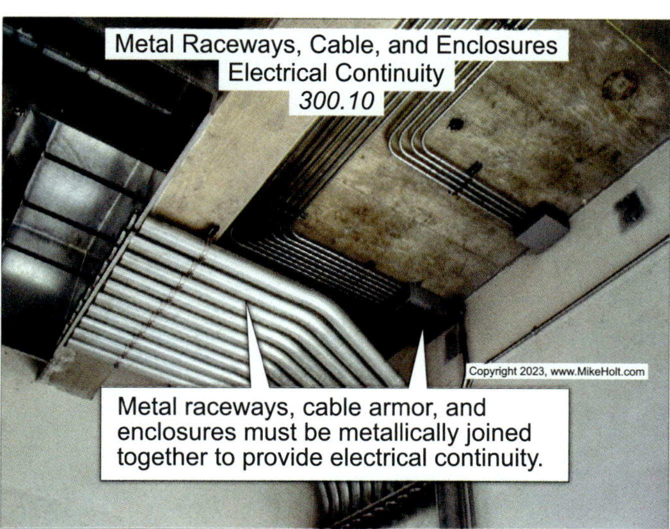

▶Figure 300–39

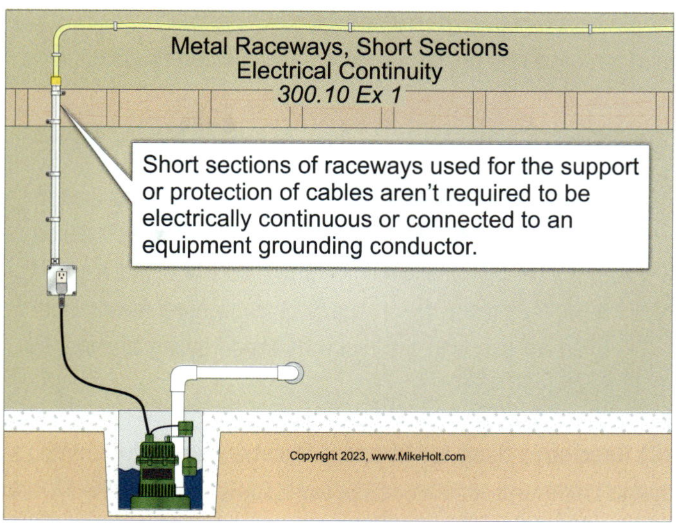

▶Figure 300–41

Author's Comment:

▶ The purpose of electrical continuity between metal parts is to establish the effective ground-fault current path necessary to open the circuit overcurrent protective device in the event of a ground fault [250.4(A)(5)]. ▶**Figure 300–40**

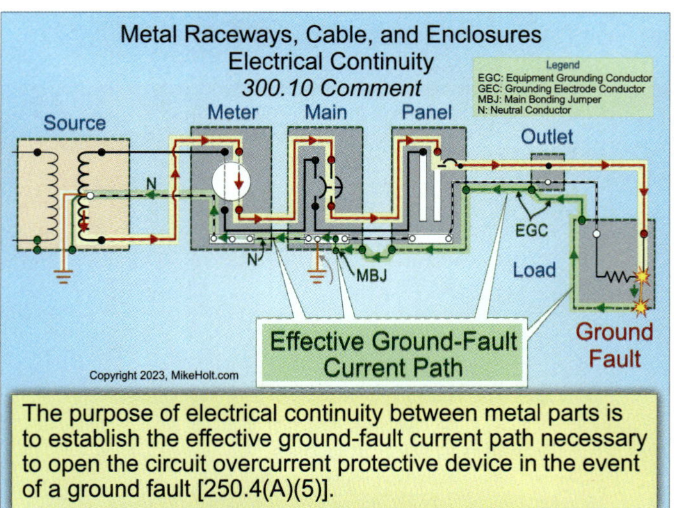

▶Figure 300–40

Ex 1: Short lengths of metal raceways used for the support or protection of cables are not required to be electrically continuous or connected to the circuit equipment grounding conductor [250.86 Ex 2 and 300.12 Ex 1]. ▶**Figure 300–41**

300.11 Securing and Supporting

(A) Secured in Place. Raceways, cable assemblies, and enclosures must be securely fastened in place.

(B) Wiring Systems Installed Above Suspended Ceilings. Ceiling-support wires or the ceiling grid are not permitted to support raceways or cables. Independent support wires secured at both ends can be used to support raceways or cables. ▶**Figure 300–42**

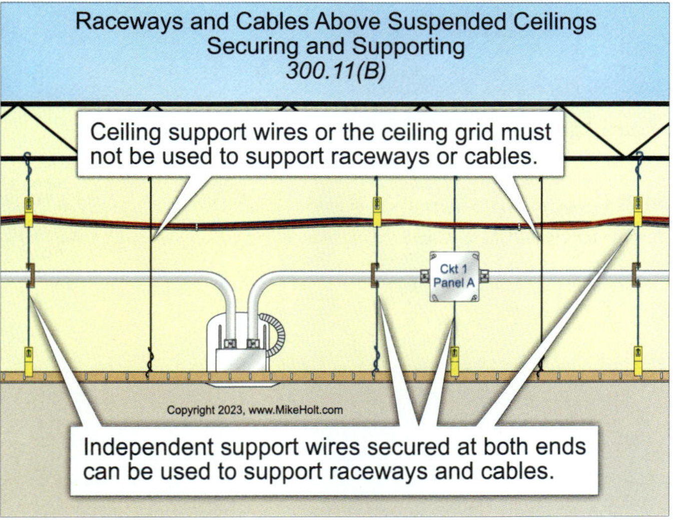

▶Figure 300–42

(1) Fire-Rated Assemblies. Electrical wiring within the cavity of a fire-rated ceiling assembly must be supported by independent support wires attached to the ceiling assembly. The independent support wires must be distinguishable from the suspended-ceiling support wires by color, tagging, or other effective means.

Ex: Electrical wiring can be supported by ceiling-support wires if installed in accordance with the ceiling system manufacturer's instructions.

Author's Comment:

▸ Outlet boxes [314.23(D)] and luminaires can be secured to the suspended-ceiling grid if the luminaire is securely fastened to the ceiling-framing members by mechanical means such as bolts, screws, rivets, clips or other securing means identified for use with the type of ceiling-framing member(s) used [410.36(B)].

(C) Raceways Used for Support. Raceways are not permitted to support raceways or cables, except as follows: ▸Figure 300–43 and ▸Figure 300–44

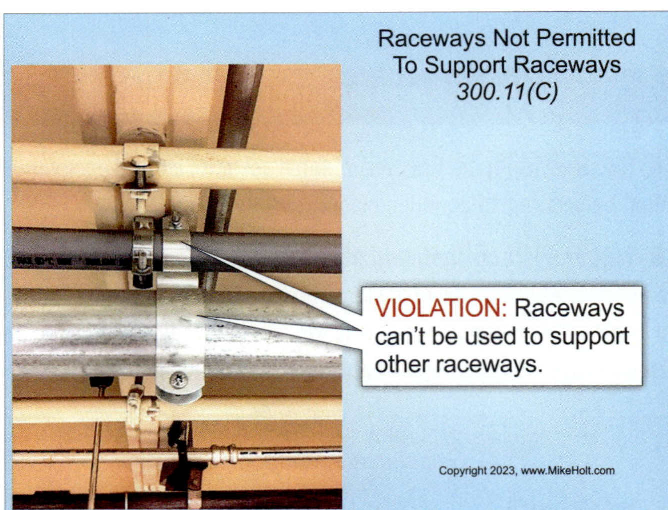

▸Figure 300–43

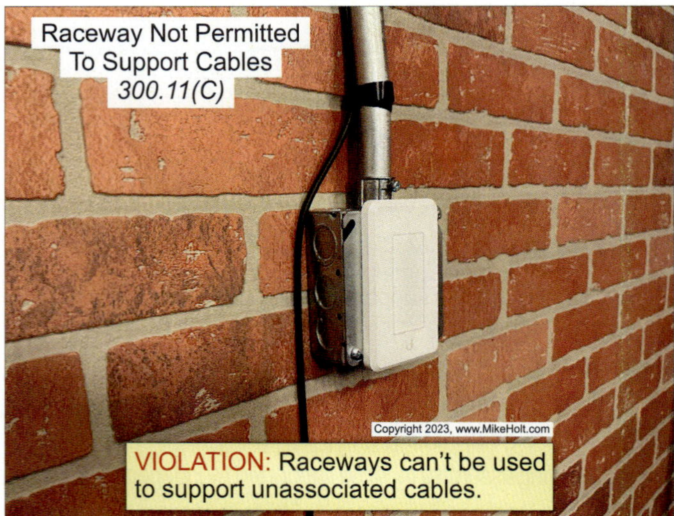

▸Figure 300–44

(2) Class 2 Power-Limited Cables. Class 2 power-limited cables can be supported by the raceway that supplies power to the equipment controlled by the Class 2 power-limited cable. ▸Figure 300–45

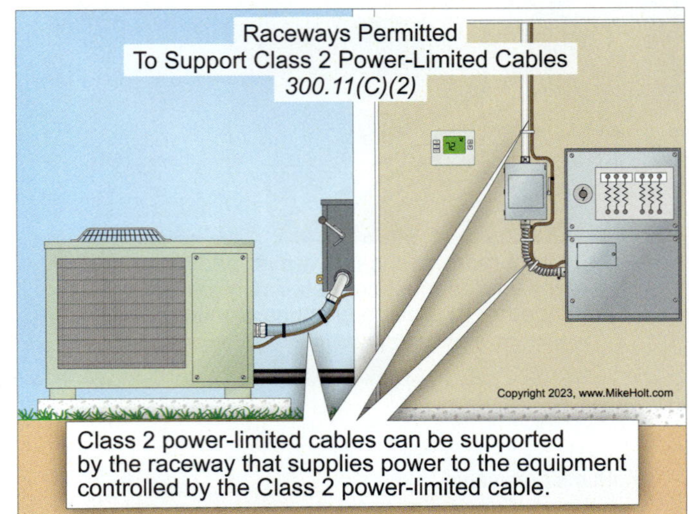

▸Figure 300–45

(3) Boxes. Raceways are permitted to support boxes in accordance with 314.23.

(D) Cables Not Used as Means of Support. Cables are not permitted to support raceways or cables. ▸Figure 300–46

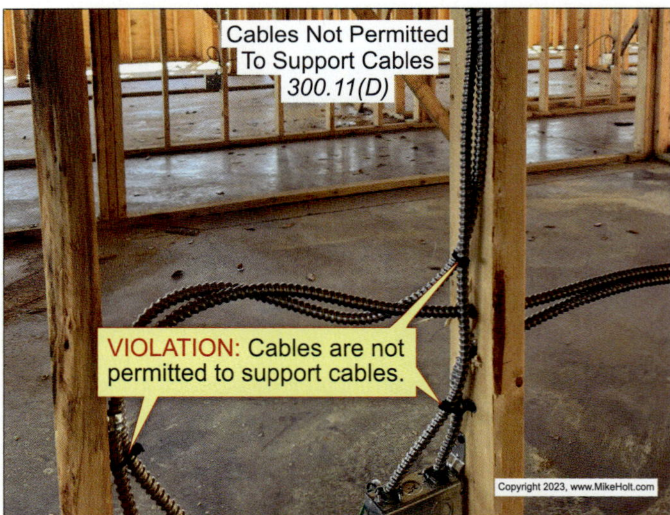

▸Figure 300–46

300.12 Mechanical Continuity

Raceways and cable sheaths must be mechanically continuous between boxes, cabinets, conduit bodies, fittings, or other enclosures. ▸Figure 300–47 and ▸Figure 300–48

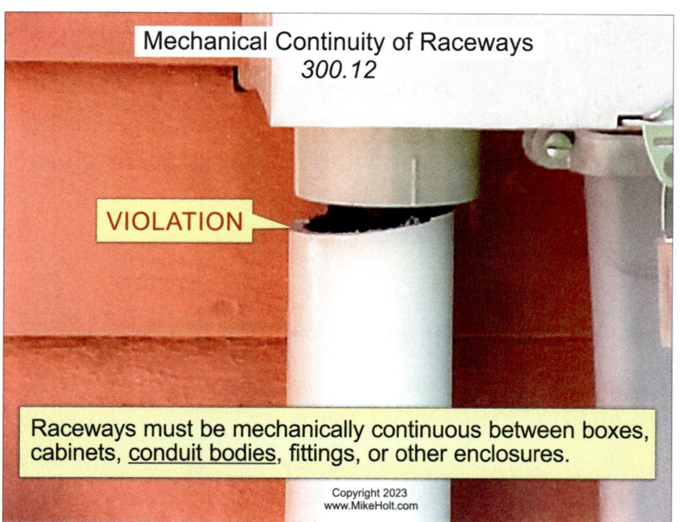

Raceways must be mechanically continuous between boxes, cabinets, <u>conduit bodies</u>, fittings, or other enclosures.

▶Figure 300–47

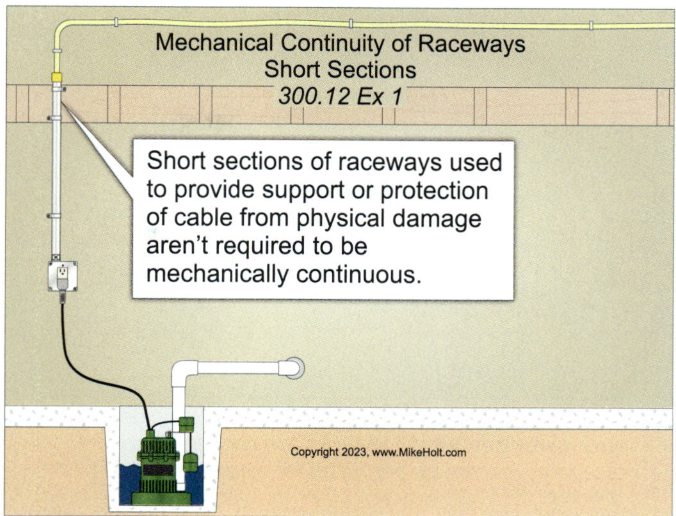

▶Figure 300–49

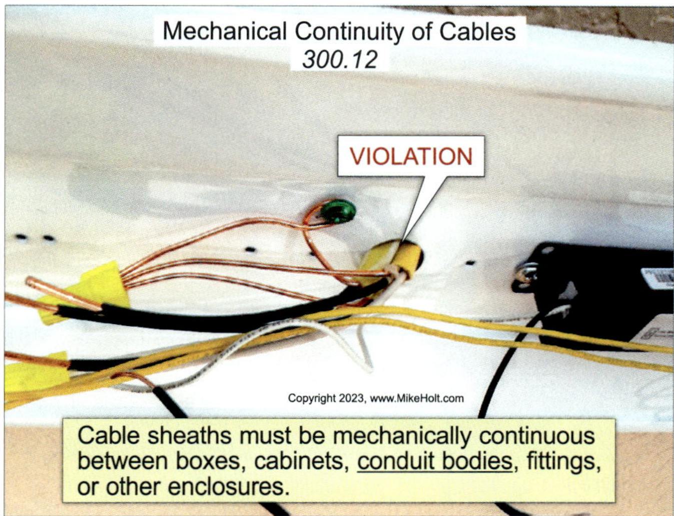

Cable sheaths must be mechanically continuous between boxes, cabinets, <u>conduit bodies</u>, fittings, or other enclosures.

▶Figure 300–48

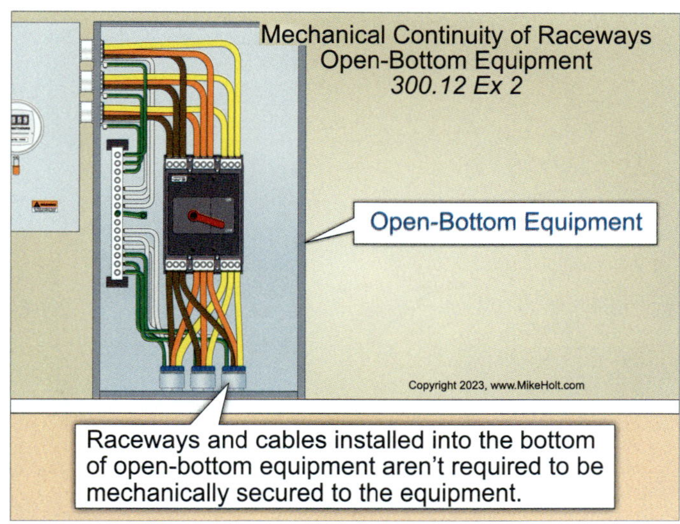

Raceways and cables installed into the bottom of open-bottom equipment aren't required to be mechanically secured to the equipment.

▶Figure 300–50

Ex 1: Short sections of raceways used to provide support or protection of cables from physical damage aren't required to be mechanically continuous [250.86 Ex 2 and 300.10 Ex 1]. ▶Figure 300–49

Ex 2: Raceways and cables installed into the bottom of open-bottom equipment such as switchboards, motor control centers, floor- or pad-mounted transformers aren't required to be mechanically secured to the equipment. ▶Figure 300–50

300.13 Mechanical and Electrical Continuity of Conductors—Splices and Pigtails

(A) Conductor Splices. Conductor splices and taps must be made inside enclosures in accordance with 300.15. Splices are not permitted in raceways, except as permitted for wireways in accordance with 376.56. ▶Figure 300–51

(B) Device Removal—Neutral Continuity. Continuity of the neutral conductor of a multiwire branch circuit is not permitted to be interrupted by the removal of a wiring device. ▶Figure 300–52

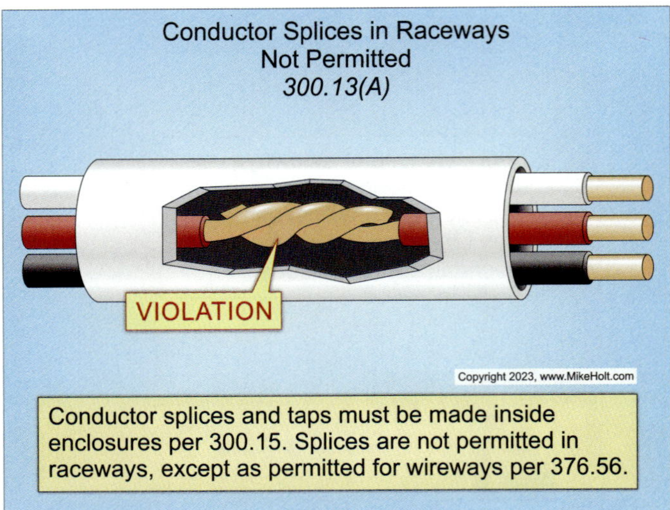

Conductor splices and taps must be made inside enclosures per 300.15. Splices are not permitted in raceways, except as permitted for wireways per 376.56.

▶Figure 300–51

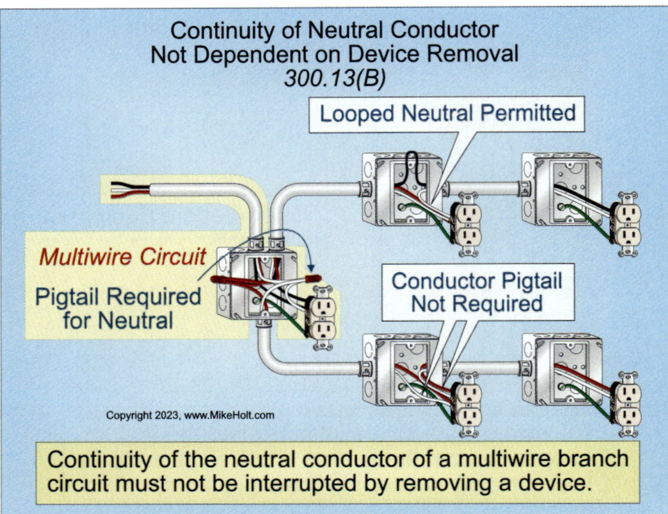

Continuity of the neutral conductor of a multiwire branch circuit must not be interrupted by removing a device.

▶Figure 300–52

Author's Comment:

▶ For multiwire applications, the neutral conductors must be spliced together, and a pigtail must be provided for the wiring device.

▶ The opening of the phase conductors or the neutral conductor of a 2-wire circuit while a device is replaced, does not cause a safety hazard, so pigtailing those conductors is not required [110.14(B)].

CAUTION: If the continuity of the neutral conductor of a multiwire circuit is interrupted (opened), the resulting over- or undervoltage can cause a fire and/or destruction of electrical equipment.

▶ Hazard of Open Neutral Example

Example: *If the neutral conductor is interrupted on a 3-wire, 120/240V multiwire circuit that supplies a 1,200W, 120V hair dryer and a 600W, 120V television, it will cause the 120V television to momentarily operate at 160V before it burns up. This can be determined as follows:* ▶Figure 300–53 *and* ▶Figure 300–54

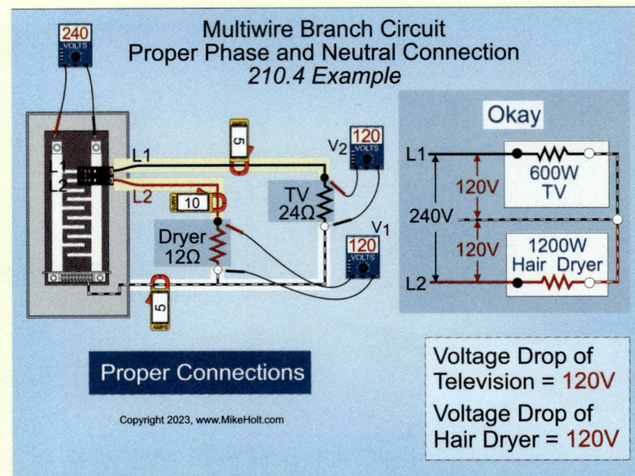

▶Figure 300–53

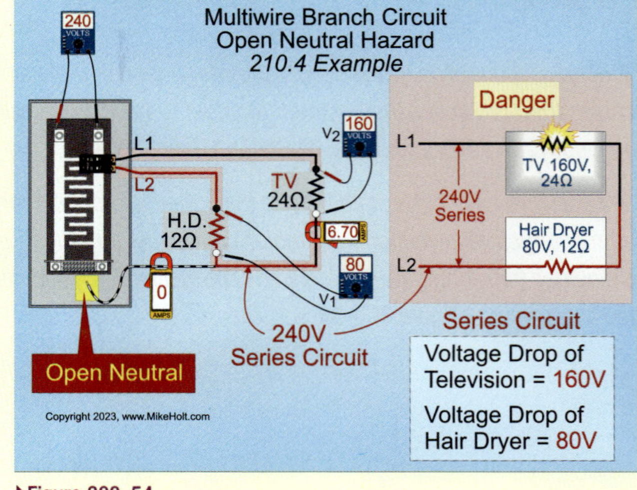

▶Figure 300–54

Step 1: Determine the resistance of each appliance.

$R = E^2/P$

R of Hair Dryer = $120V^2/1,200W$

R of Hair Dryer = 12Ω

R of Television = $120V^2/600W$

R of Television = 24Ω

Step 2: Determine the current of the circuit.

$I = Volts/Resistance$

Volts = 240V

$R = 12\Omega + 24\Omega$

$R = 36\Omega$

$I = 240V/36\Omega$

$I = 6.70A$

Step 3: Determine the operating voltage for each appliance.

$Volts = I \times R$

$I = 6.70A$

$R = 12\Omega$ for the hair dryer and 24Ω for the television.

Voltage of Hair Dryer = $6.70A \times 12\Omega$

Voltage of Hair Dryer = 80V

Voltage of Television = $6.70A \times 24\Omega$

Voltage of Television = 160V

300.14 Conductor Length at Boxes

At least 6 in. of <u>spliced or unspliced</u> conductor, measured from the point in the box where the conductors enter the enclosure, must be provided for conductor splices or terminations. ▶Figure 300–55

Boxes with openings less than 8 in. at any dimension must have at least 6 in. of conductor, measured from the point where the conductors enter the box, and at least 3 in. of conductor outside the box. ▶Figure 300–56

300.15 Boxes or Fittings, Splices and Terminations

A box must be installed at each <u>conductor</u> splice point or <u>conductor</u> termination point, except as permitted by 300.15(A) through (L): ▶Figure 300–57 and ▶Figure 300–58

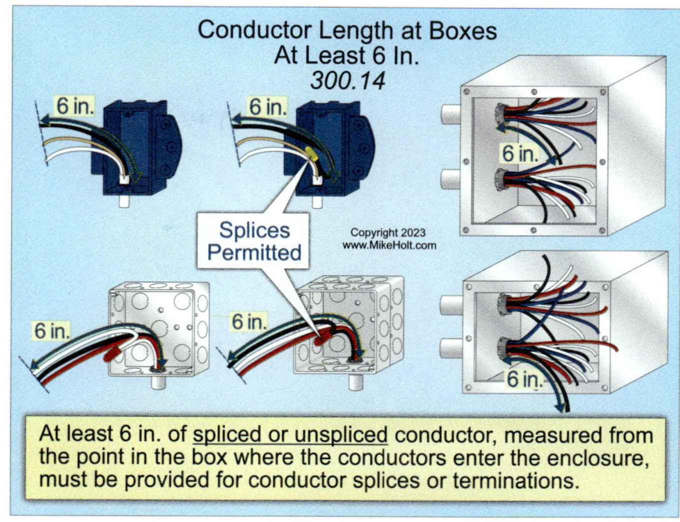

At least 6 in. of <u>spliced or unspliced</u> conductor, measured from the point in the box where the conductors enter the enclosure, must be provided for conductor splices or terminations.

▶Figure 300–55

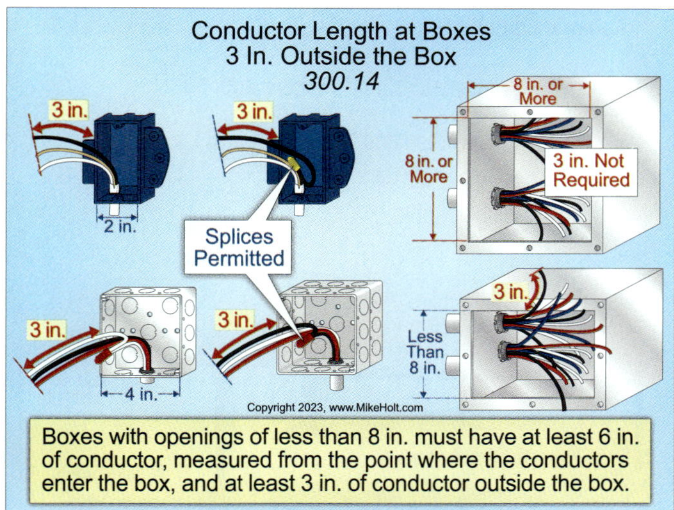

Boxes with openings of less than 8 in. must have at least 6 in. of conductor, measured from the point where the conductors enter the box, and at least 3 in. of conductor outside the box.

▶Figure 300–56

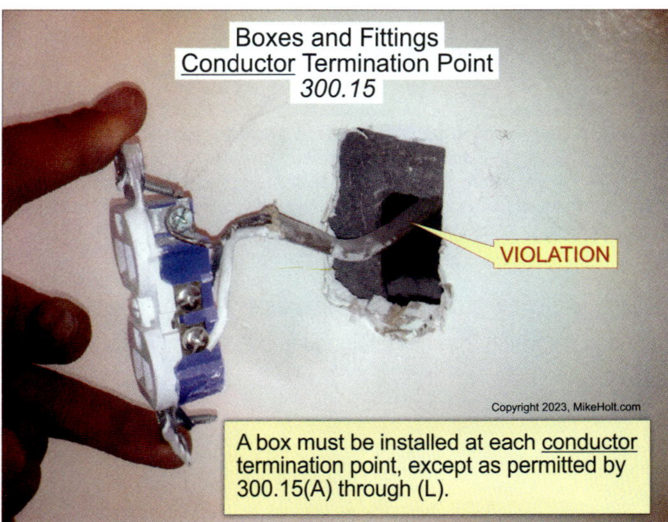

A box must be installed at each <u>conductor</u> termination point, except as permitted by 300.15(A) through (L).

▶Figure 300–57

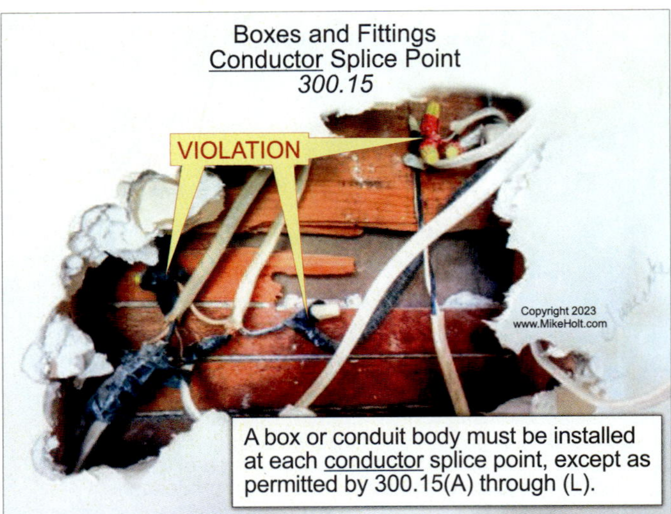

▶Figure 300–58

Author's Comment:

▶ Boxes are not required for: ▶Figure 300–59

- Class 2 Power-Limited Circuits, 725.3
- Coaxial Cable, 800.3
- Optical Fiber Cable, 770.3

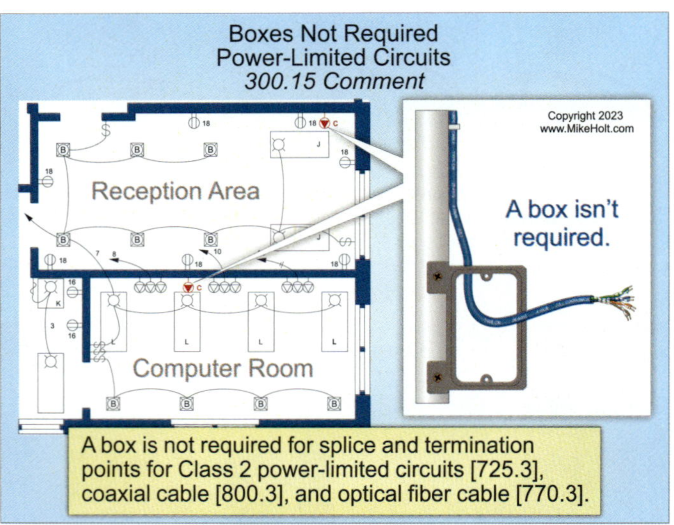

▶Figure 300–59

Fittings and connectors must only be used with the specific wiring methods for which they are designed and listed. ▶Figure 300–60

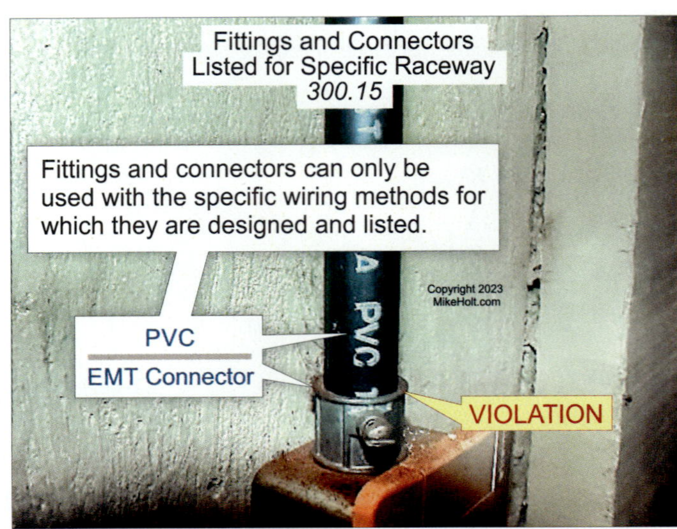

▶Figure 300–60

Author's Comment:

▶ Type NM cable connectors are not permitted to be used with Type AC cable. Electrical metallic tubing fittings are not permitted to be used with rigid metal conduit or intermediate metal conduit unless listed for the purpose.

▶ PVC conduit couplings and connectors are permitted to be installed with electrical nonmetallic tubing if the proper glue is used in accordance with the manufacturer's instructions [110.3(B)]. See 362.48.

(A) Wiring Methods with Interior Access. A box is not required for wiring methods with removable covers such as wireways, multioutlet assemblies, and surface raceways.

(G) Underground Conductor and Cable Splices. A box is not required where a splice is made underground if Type UF or USE conductors are spliced with a splicing device listed for direct burial. ▶Figure 300–61

Author's Comment:

▶ The only conductors permitted to be direct buried are Type UF [340.10(1)] and Type USE [338.10(B)(4)(b)(2)].

300.17 Number and Size of Conductors in a Raceway

Raceways must be large enough to permit the installation and removal of conductors without damaging their insulation.

Note: See the "xxx.22" section of the specific raceway wiring method for more information about the number of conductors permitted.

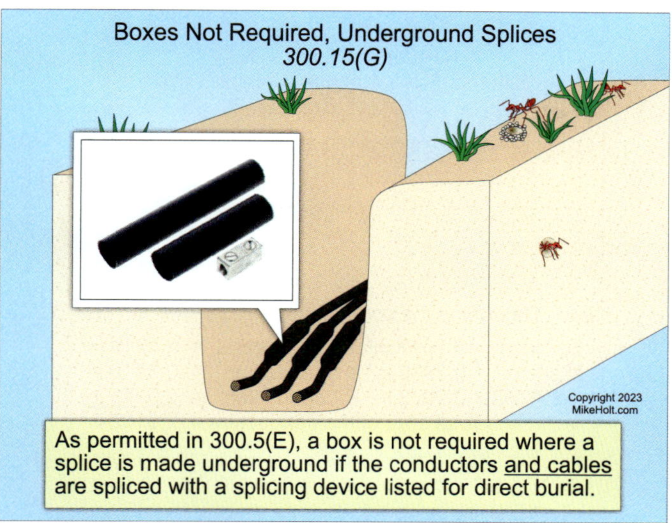

▶Figure 300–61

Author's Comment:

▶ When all conductors within a raceway are the same size, same insulation type, number of conductors permitted, or raceway size, use Annex C [Note (1) of Chapter 9].

▶ Example 1

Question: How many 12 AWG, THWN-2 conductors can be installed in ¾ EMT? ▶Figure 300–62

(a) 10　　　*(b) 12*　　　*(c) 14*　　　*(d) 16*

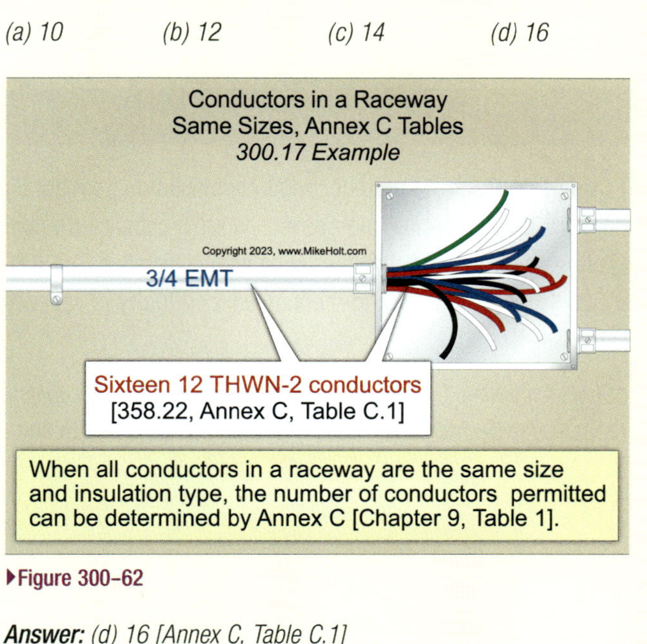

▶Figure 300–62

Answer: (d) 16 [Annex C, Table C.1]

Author's Comment:

▶ When different size conductors are installed in a raceway, conductor fill is limited to the percentages in Table 1 and Note (6) of Chapter 9. ▶Figure 300–63

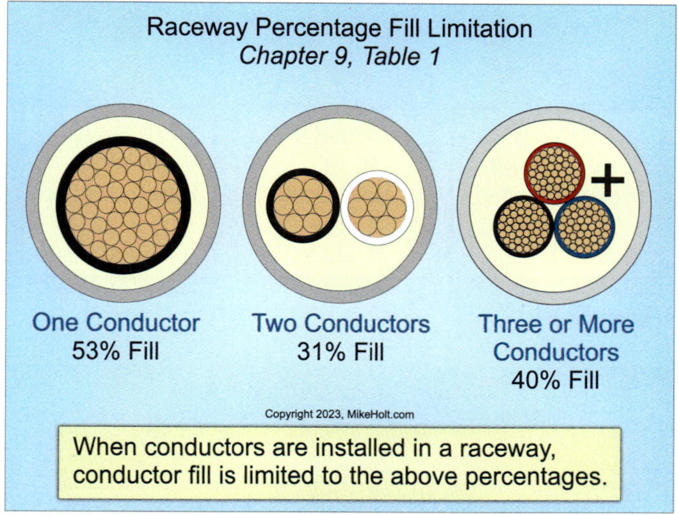

▶Figure 300–63

Chapter 9, Table 1	
Number	**Percent Fill**
1 Conductor	53%
2 Conductors	31%
3 or More	40%

The above percentages are based on conditions where the length of the conductor and number of raceway bends are within reasonable limits [Chapter 9, Table 1, Table Note 1].

Author's Comment:

▶ Follow these steps for sizing raceways:

　▶ **Step 1:** When sizing a raceway, first determine the total area needed for the conductors (Chapter 9, Table 5 for insulated conductors and Chapter 9, Table 8 for bare conductors). ▶Figure 300–64

　▶ **Step 2:** Select the raceway from Chapter 9, Table 4 in accordance with the percent fill listed in Chapter 9, Table 1. ▶Figure 300–65

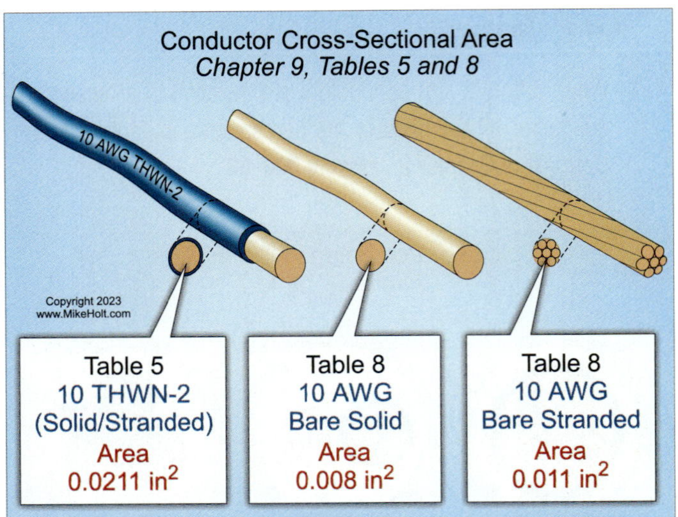

▶Figure 300–64

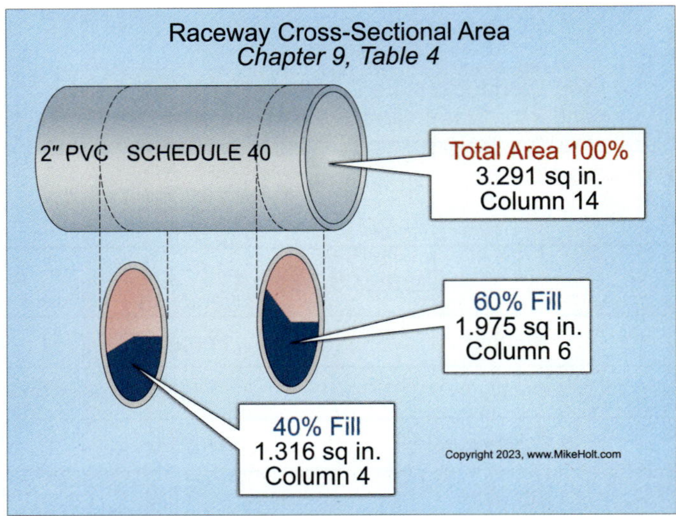

▶Figure 300–65

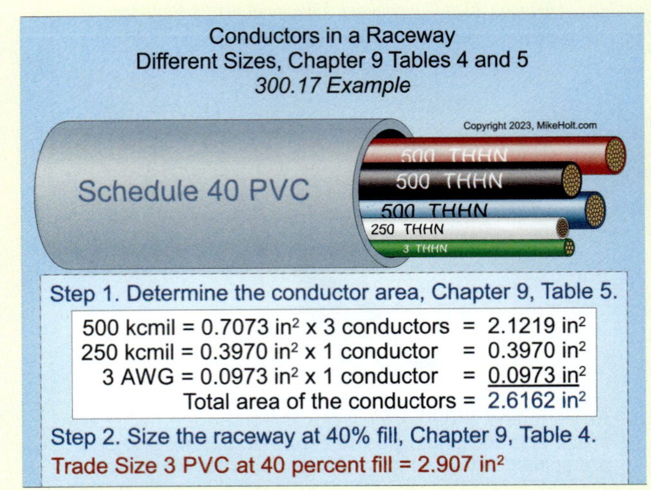

▶Figure 300–66

500 kcmil THWN-2	0.7073 in.² × 3 =	2.1219 in.²
250 kcmil THWN-2	0.3970 in.² × 1 =	0.3970 in.²
3 AWG THWN-2	0.0973 in.² × 1 =	+0.0973 in.²
Total Area of Conductors =		2.6162 in.²

Step 2: Select the raceway at 40 percent fill [Chapter 9, Table 1 and Table Note (6), and Table 4].

Use 3 in. schedule 40 PVC because there are 2.907 sq in. of conductor fill at 40 percent.

Answer: (c) 3 in.

300.18 Raceway Installations

(A) Complete Runs. To protect conductor insulation from abrasion during installation, raceways must be mechanically completed between the pulling points before conductors or cables are installed. See 300.10 and 300.12 for electrical and mechanical continuity of raceways. ▶Figure 300–67

Ex: Short sections of raceways used for the protection of cables are not required to be complete between pulling points. ▶Figure 300–68

▶ **Example 2**

Question: *What size Schedule 40 PVC conduit is required for the following conductors?* ▶Figure 300–66

- *3–500 kcmil THWN-2*
- *1–250 kcmil THWN-2*
- *1–3 AWG THWN-2*

(a) 1 in.   (b) 2 in.   (c) 3 in.   (d) 4 in.

Solution:

Step 1: *Determine the total area needed for the conductors [Chapter 9, Table 5].*

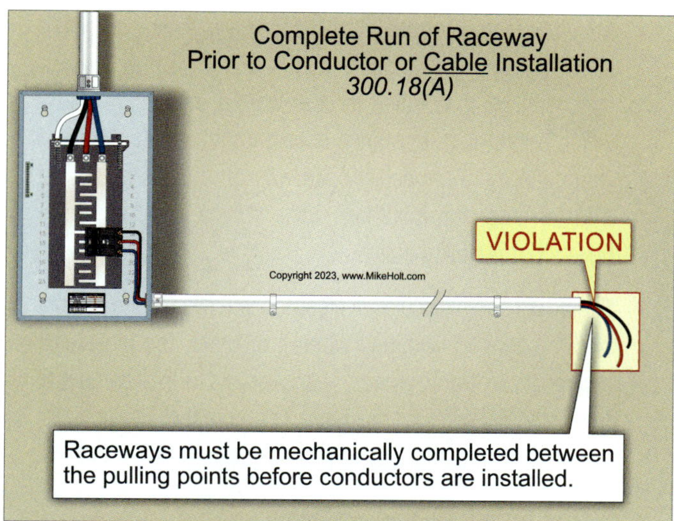

▶Figure 300–67

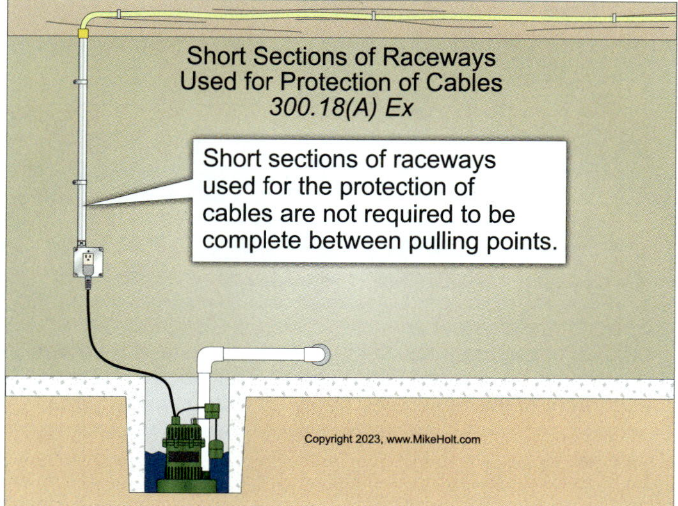

▶Figure 300–68

300.19 Supporting Conductors in Vertical Raceways

(A) Spacing Intervals. If the vertical rise of a raceway exceeds the values of Table 300.19(A), each conductor must be supported at the top or as close to the top as practical. Intermediate support must also be provided in increments not exceeding the values of Table 300.19(A).
▶Figure 300–69

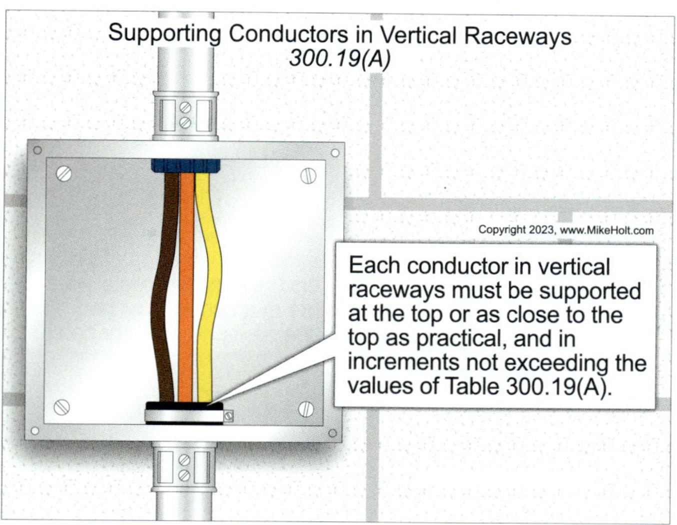

▶Figure 300–69

Author's Comment:

▶ A great deal of weight accumulates in long vertical runs of conductors and can cause them to drop out of the raceway (sometimes called a "runaway") if they are not properly secured. There have been many cases where conductors in a vertical raceway were released from the pulling "basket" or "grip" (at the top) without being secured. Sheer weight and gravity take over, accelerating the conductors down and out of the raceway and injuring those at the bottom of the installation.

300.20 Reducing Inductive Heating

(A) Conductors Grouped Together. To minimize the induction heating of steel raceways, enclosures, and metal parts, all conductors of a circuit (including any neutral and equipment grounding conductors) must be installed in the same raceway or cable. See 250.102(E), 300.3(B), 300.5(I), and 392. 20(C). ▶Figure 300–70 and ▶Figure 300–71

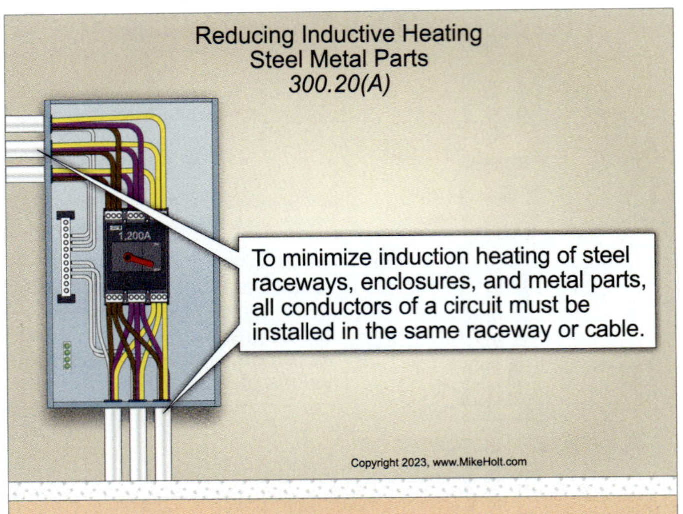

▶Figure 300–70

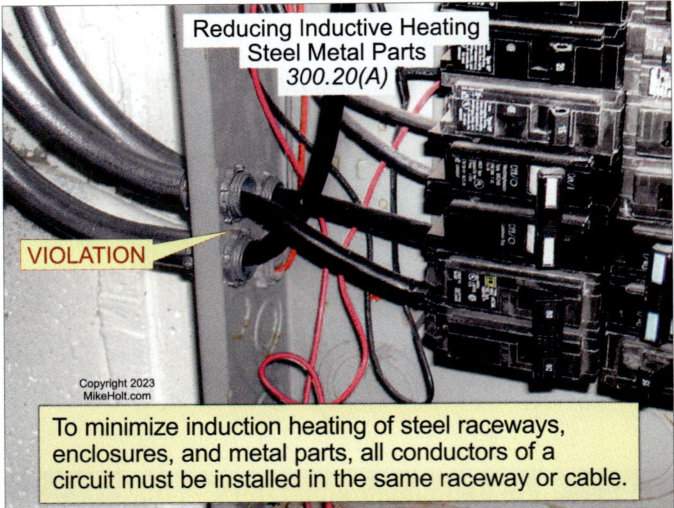

▶Figure 300–71

Author's Comment:

▶ When alternating current flows through a conductor, a pulsating or varying magnetic field is created around the conductor. This magnetic field is constantly expanding and contracting with the amplitude of the alternating current. In the United States, the frequency is 60 cycles per second (Hz). Since alternating current reverses polarity 120 times per second, the magnetic field that surrounds the conductor also reverses direction 120 times per second. This expanding and collapsing magnetic field induces eddy currents in the steel parts that surround the conductors, causing them to heat up due to hysteresis heating.

▶ Magnetic materials naturally resist rapidly changing magnetic fields. The resulting friction produces its own heat (hysteresis heating), in addition to eddy current heating. A metal which offers high resistance is said to have high magnetic "permeability." Permeability can vary on a scale of 100 to 500 for magnetic materials, while nonmagnetic materials have a permeability of one.

▶ Simply put, the molecules of steel and iron align to the polarity of the magnetic field, and when it reverses, the molecules reverse their polarity as well. This back-and-forth alignment of the molecules heats up the metal. The more the current flows, the more the heat increases in steel parts. ▶Figure 300–72

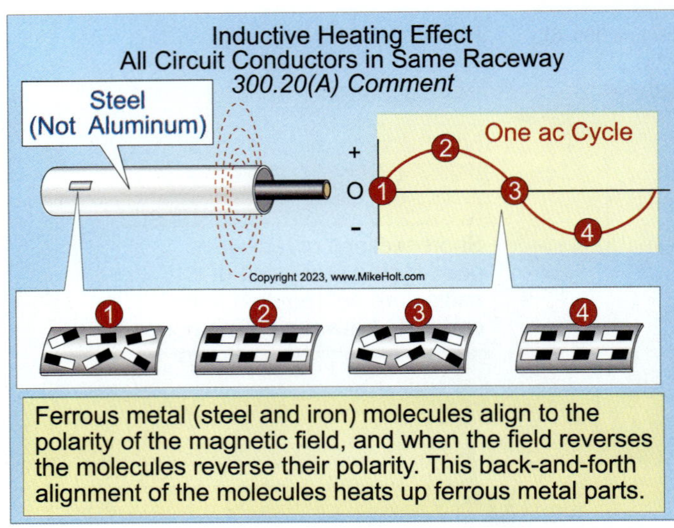

▶Figure 300–72

Author's Comment:

▶ When conductors of the same circuit are grouped together, the magnetic fields of the different conductors tend to cancel each other out, resulting in a reduced magnetic field around them. The smaller magnetic field reduces induced currents in steel raceways or enclosures, which reduces the hysteresis heating of the surrounding metal enclosure.

(B) Single Conductors. Where a single conductor or a parallel set of a conductors enter an enclosure, the inductive heating effects on the metal enclosure must be minimized by cutting slots between the individual holes through which the conductors pass, or by passing the conductors through the same wall opening. ▶Figure 300–73 and ▶Figure 300–74

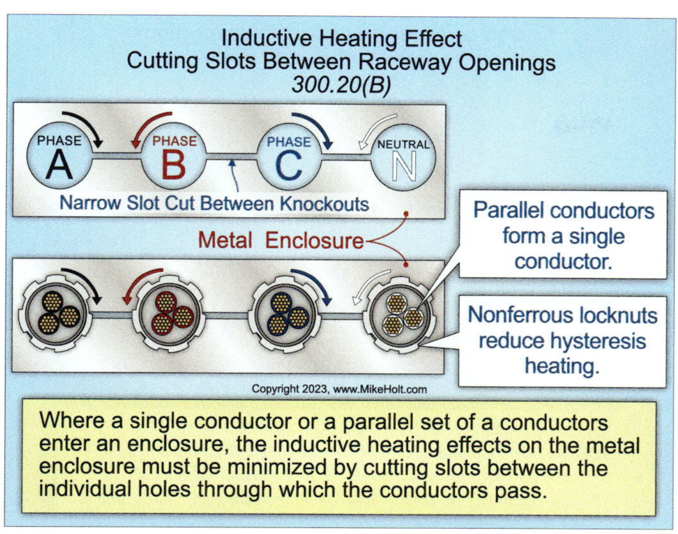

▶Figure 300–73

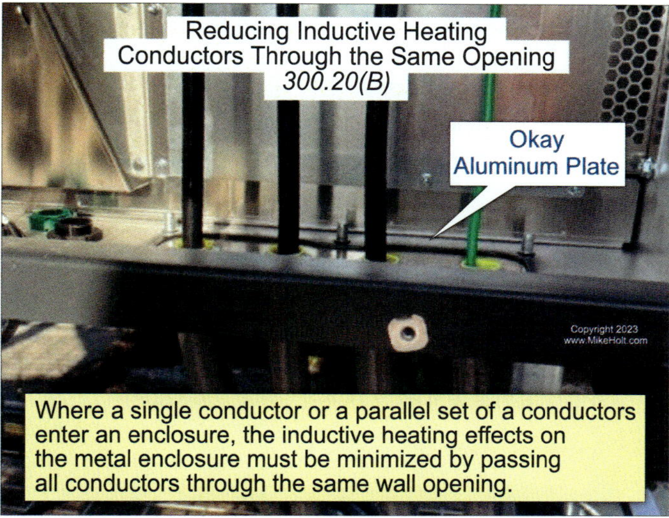

▶Figure 300–74

Author's Comment:

▶ When single conductors are installed in nonmetallic raceways as permitted in 300.5(I) Ex 2, the inductive heating of the metal enclosure can be minimized by using aluminum locknuts and by cutting a slot between the individual holes through which the conductors pass.

Note: Because aluminum is a nonmagnetic metal, aluminum parts do not heat up due to hysteresis heating.

300.21 Spread of Fire or Products of Combustion

Electrical circuits and equipment must be installed in such a way that the spread of fire or products of combustion will not be substantially increased. Openings around electrical penetrations into or through fire-resistant-rated walls, partitions, floors, or ceilings must be firestopped using approved methods to maintain the fire-resistance rating. ▶Figure 300–75

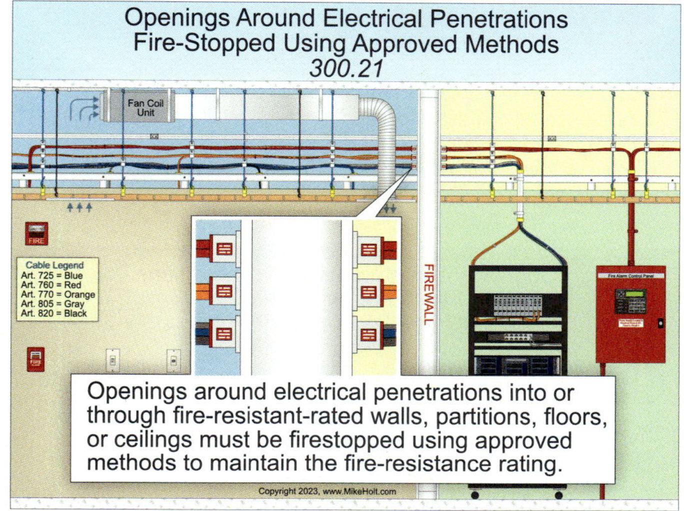

▶Figure 300–75

Author's Comment:

▶ Fire-stopping materials are listed for the specific types of wiring methods and fire-rated assembly they penetrate. For example, MC cable will have a different fire penetration detail when passing through a fire wall than will EMT. ▶Figure 300–76 and ▶Figure 300–77

Note: Directories of electrical construction materials published by recognized testing laboratories contain listing and installation restrictions necessary to maintain the fire-resistive rating of assemblies. Building codes also have restrictions on penetrations on opposite sides of a fire-resistance-rated wall. Outlet boxes must have a horizontal separation of not less than 24 in. when installed on opposite sides in a fire-rated assembly, unless an outlet box is listed for closer spacing or protected by fire-resistant "putty pads" in accordance with the manufacturer's instructions. ▶Figure 300–78 and ▶Figure 300–79

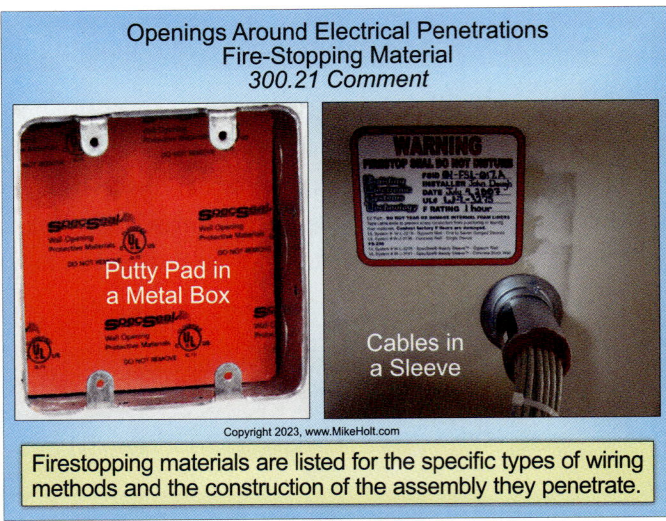

Firestopping materials are listed for the specific types of wiring methods and the construction of the assembly they penetrate.

▶Figure 300–76

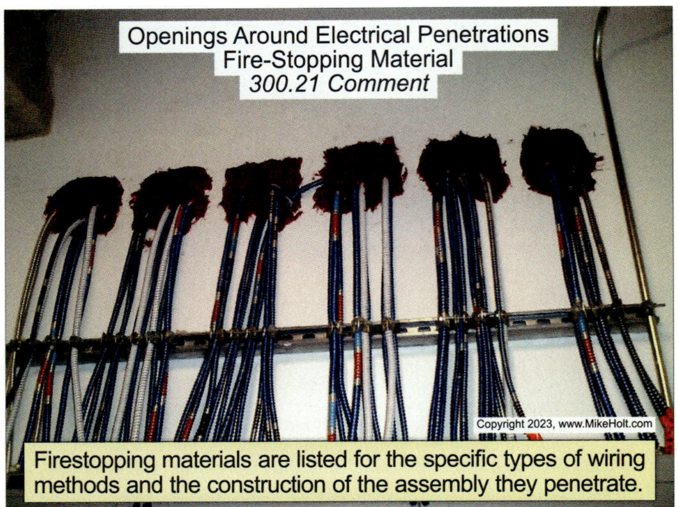

Firestopping materials are listed for the specific types of wiring methods and the construction of the assembly they penetrate.

▶Figure 300–77

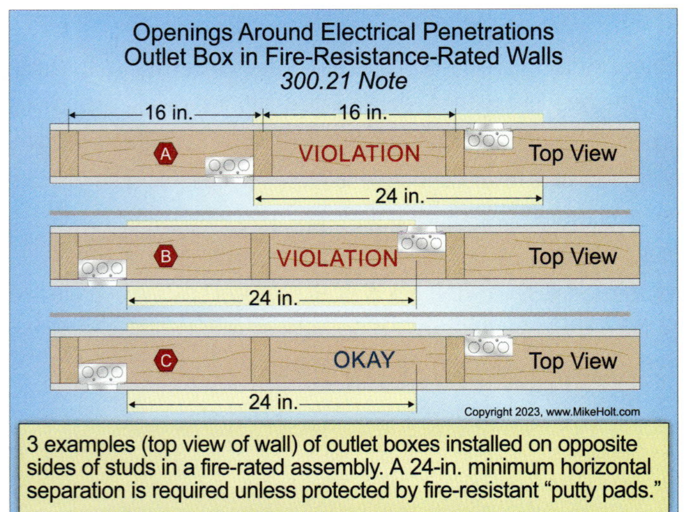

3 examples (top view of wall) of outlet boxes installed on opposite sides of studs in a fire-rated assembly. A 24-in. minimum horizontal separation is required unless protected by fire-resistant "putty pads."

▶Figure 300–78

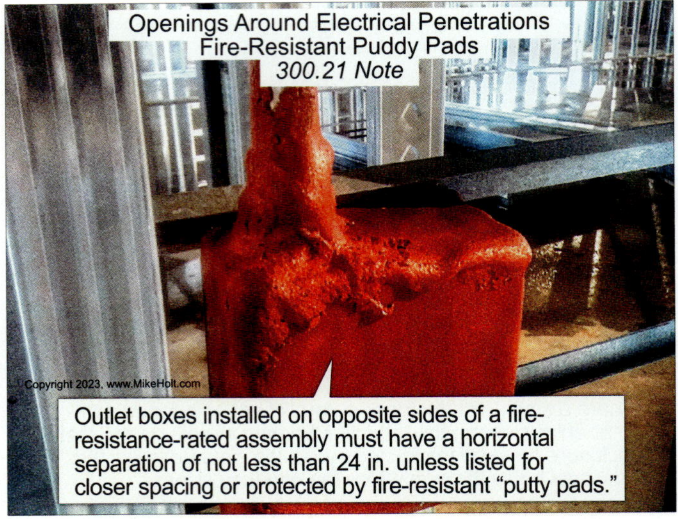

Outlet boxes installed on opposite sides of a fire-resistance-rated assembly must have a horizontal separation of not less than 24 in. unless listed for closer spacing or protected by fire-resistant "putty pads."

▶Figure 300–79

Author's Comment:

▸ Boxes installed in fire-resistance-rated assemblies must be listed for the purpose. If steel boxes are used, they must be secured to the framing member. Cut-in type boxes are not permitted.

▸ Building code requirements restrict penetrations on a fire-rated assembly section of 100 sq ft to 100 sq in. of allowable penetrations. If a 4 × 4 metal box has 16 sq in., then only six boxes (100/16 = 6.25) are allowed in that section of fire wall in accordance with IBC 714.4.2, *International Building Code*.

▸ This requirement also applies to:

  ▸ Class 2 Power-Limited Circuits, 725.3(B)
  ▸ Coaxial Cable, 800.26
  ▸ Fire Alarms, 760.3(A)
  ▸ Optical Fiber Cable, 770.26

300.22 Wiring in Ducts and Plenum Spaces

The requirements of this section apply to the installation and uses of electrical wiring and equipment in ducts used for dust or vapor removal, ducts specifically fabricated for environmental air, and plenum spaces used for environmental air.

(A) Ducts Used for Dust or Vapor. Wiring methods are not permitted to be installed in ducts that transport dust or flammable vapors. ▶Figure 300–80

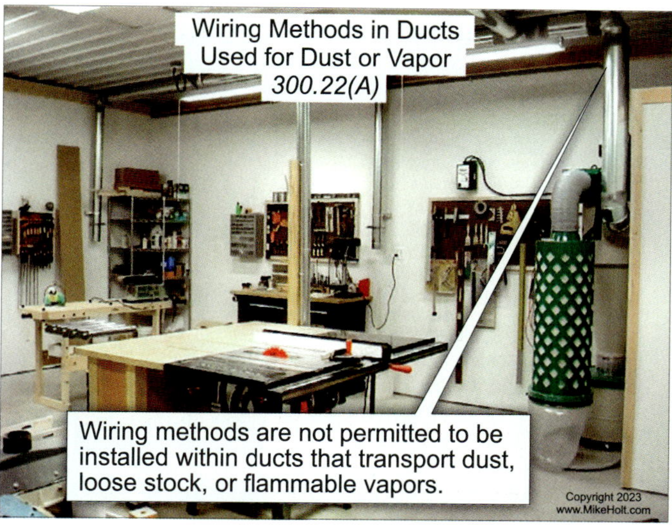

▶Figure 300–80

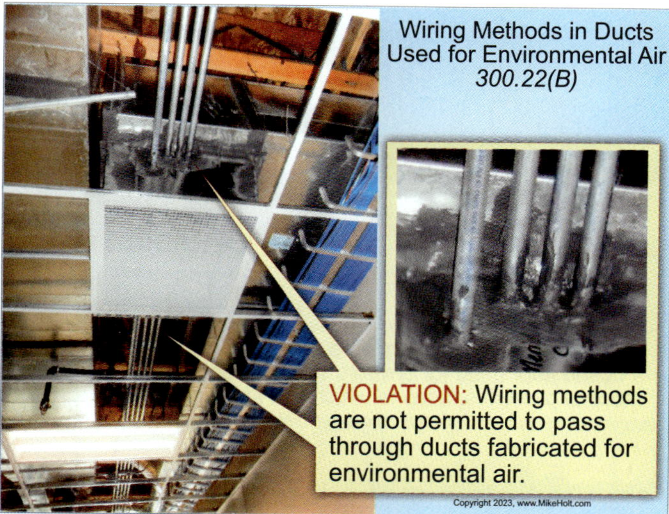

▶Figure 300–82

(B) Ducts Fabricated for Environmental Air. Equipment and wiring methods are only permitted within a duct fabricated to transport environmental air if the equipment is necessary for the direct action upon (or sensing of) the contained air. ▶Figure 300–81 and ▶Figure 300–82

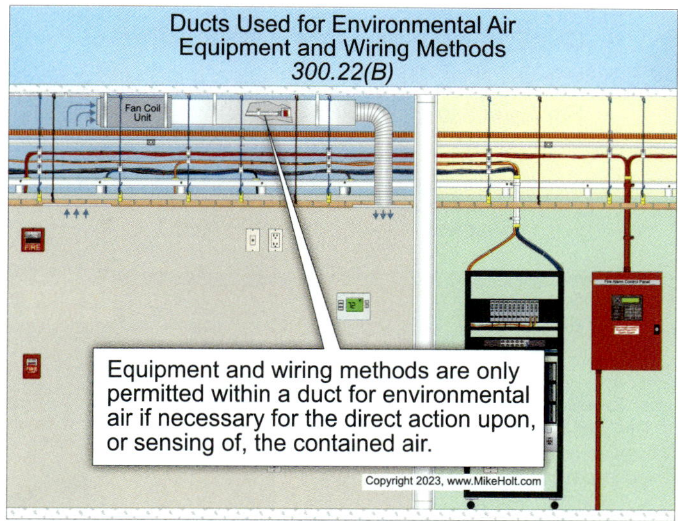

▶Figure 300–81

Type MC cable without an overall nonmetallic covering and metal raceways can be installed in ducts fabricated to transport environmental air. Flexible metal conduit in lengths not exceeding 4 ft can be used to connect physically adjustable equipment and devices within the fabricated duct.

Ex: Wiring methods and cabling systems, listed for use in plenum spaces, can be installed in ducts specifically fabricated for environmental air-handling purposes under both of the following conditions: ▶Figure 300–83

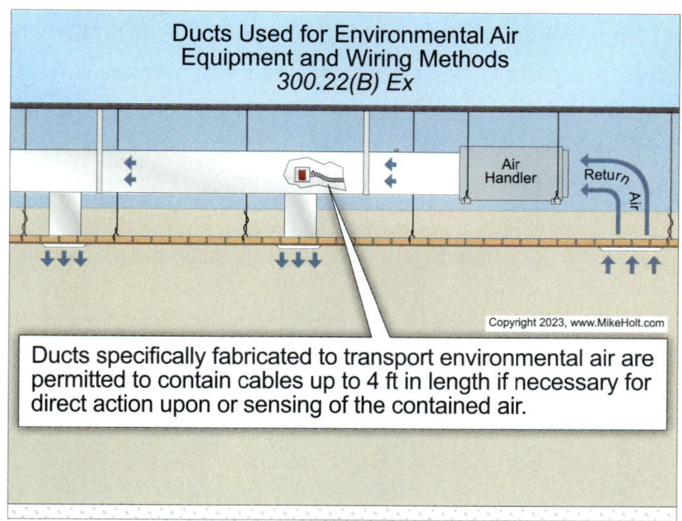

▶Figure 300–83

(1) The wiring methods or cabling systems are necessary to connect to equipment or devices associated with the direct action upon, or sensing of, the contained air.

(2) The total length of such wiring methods or cabling systems does not exceed 4 ft.

(C) Plenum Spaces for Environmental Air. This section applies only to the space above a suspended ceiling or below a raised floor used for environmental air. It does not apply to habitable rooms or areas of buildings, the prime purpose of which is not air handling.

Note 1: The spaces or cavities above a suspended ceiling and below a raised floor used for environmental air are examples of the type of plenum spaces to which this section applies. ▶Figure 300–84

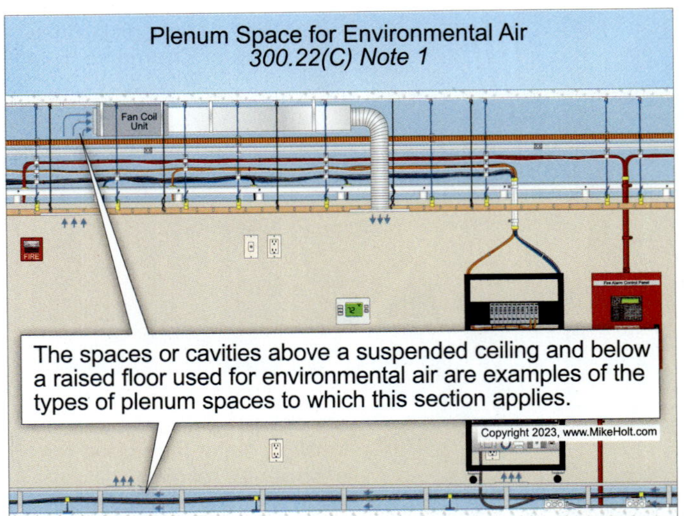

▶Figure 300–84

(1) Wiring Methods. Metal raceways, Type AC cable, Type MC cable without a nonmetallic cover, electrical metallic tubing, intermediate metal conduit, rigid metal conduit, flexible metal conduit, or (where accessible) surface metal raceways or metal wireways with metal covers are permitted to be installed in the plenum space. ▶Figure 300–85

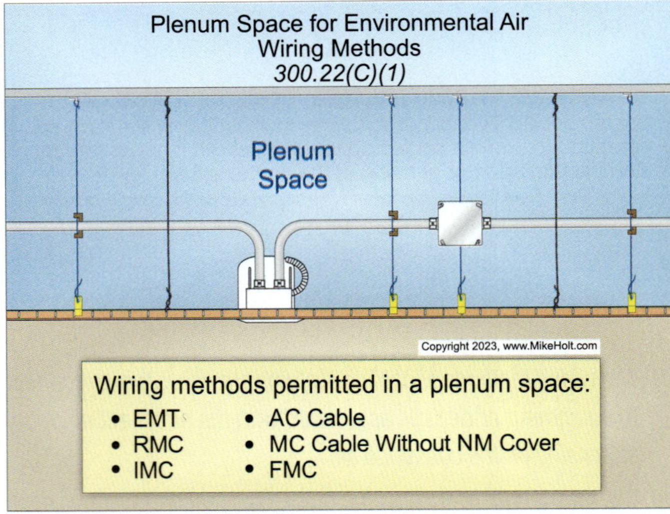

▶Figure 300–85

Cable ties for securing and supporting cables must be listed for use in a plenum space. ▶Figure 300–86

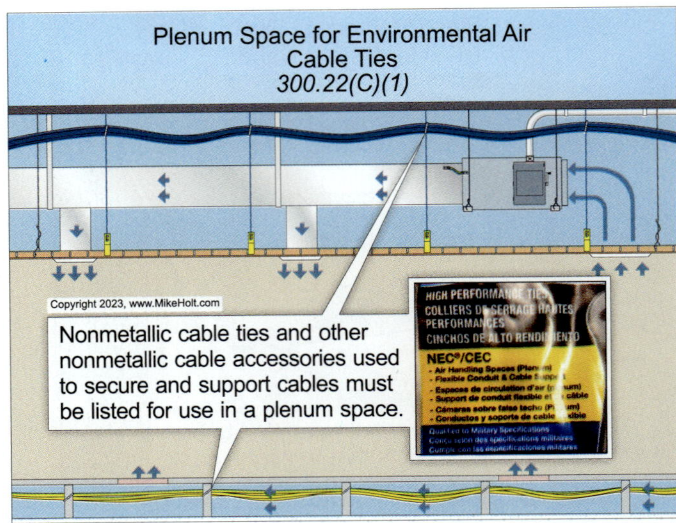

▶Figure 300–86

Author's Comment:

▸ Plenum-rated Chapter 7 and Chapter 8 wiring methods are permitted in plenum spaces according to the following: ▶Figure 300–87

  ▹ Class 2 Power-Limited Cables, 725.3(B)
  ▹ Coaxial Cables, 800.3(C)
  ▹ Fire Alarm Cables, 760.3(B) Ex 2

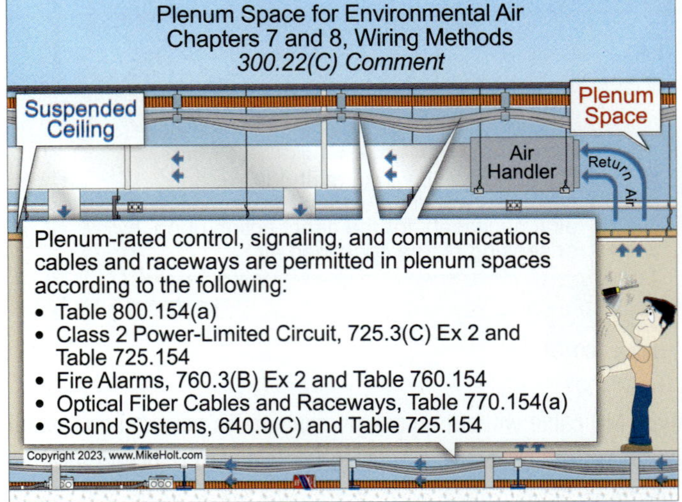

▶Figure 300–87

(2) Cable Tray Systems.

(a) Metal Cable Tray Systems. Metal cable tray systems can be installed to support the wiring methods permitted to be installed in a plenum space. ▶Figure 300–88

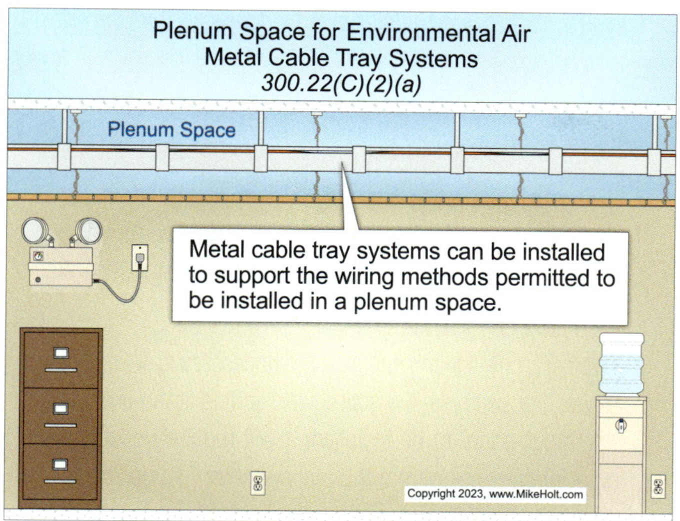

▶Figure 300–88

(3) Equipment. Electrical equipment with a metal enclosure, or a nonmetallic enclosure listed for use in an air-handling space, can be installed in a plenum space. ▶Figure 300–89

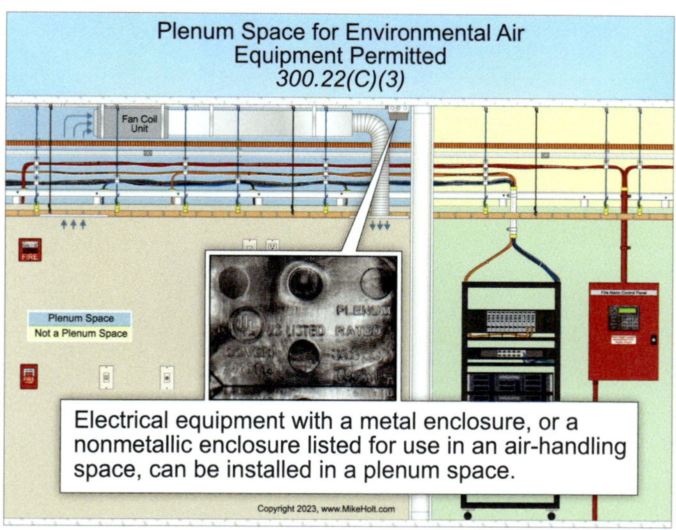

▶Figure 300–89

Author's Comment:

▸ Examples of electrical equipment permitted in plenum spaces are air handlers, junction boxes, and dry-type transformers, although transformers are not permitted to be rated over 50 kVA when in hollow spaces [450.13(B)].

300.23 Panels Designed to Allow Access

Cables, raceways, and equipment installed behind suspended-ceiling panels must be located so the panels can be removed to give access to electrical equipment. ▶Figure 300–90

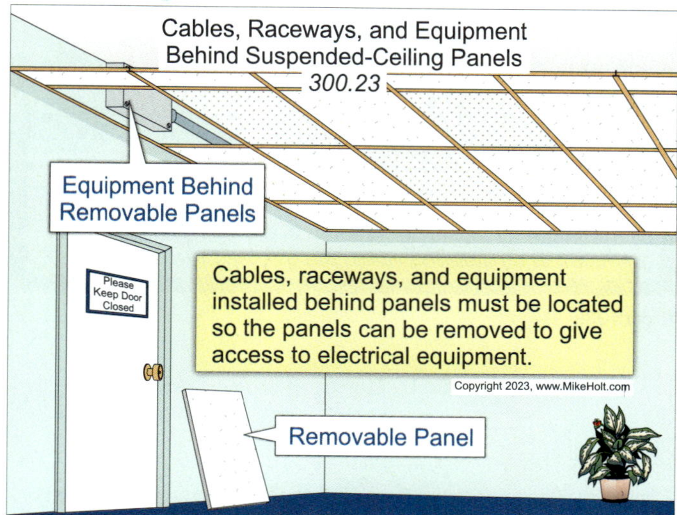

▶Figure 300–90

Author's Comment:

▸ Access to equipment is not permitted to be hindered by an accumulation of cables that prevent the removal of suspended-ceiling panels. Chapter 7 and Chapter 8 wiring methods must be located and supported so the suspended-ceiling panels can be moved to provide access to electrical equipment.

  ▸ Class 2 Power-Limited Circuits, 725.21
  ▸ Coaxial Cable, 800.21
  ▸ Fire Alarm Cable, 760.21
  ▸ Optical Fiber Cable, 770.21

300.25 Exit Stair Towers

Where an exit stair tower is required to have a fire-resistance rating, only the wiring methods serving equipment permitted by the authority having jurisdiction in the exit stair tower are permitted to be installed within the exit stair tower. ▶Figure 300–91

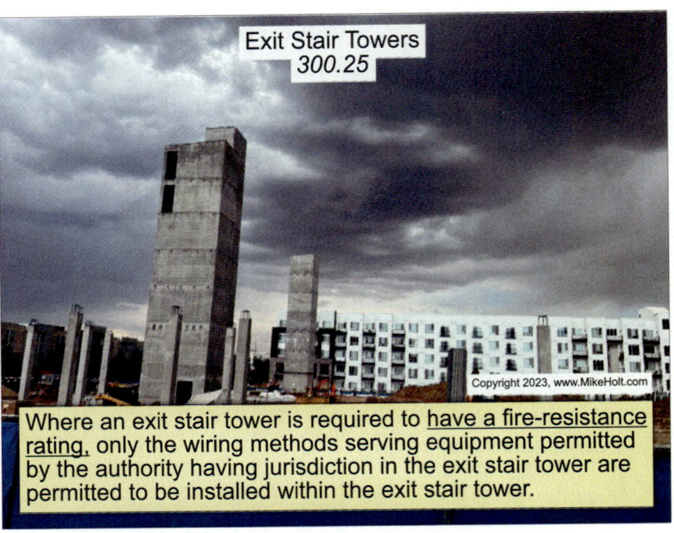

Where an exit stair tower is required to <u>have a fire-resistance rating,</u> only the wiring methods serving equipment permitted by the authority having jurisdiction in the exit stair tower are permitted to be installed within the exit stair tower.

▶Figure 300–91

Ex: Egress lighting located outside exterior doorways from the exit stair tower can be supplied from a circuit located inside the exit stair tower.

Author's Comment:

▸ Fire-resistance rating is a defined term in the *International Building Code*. The fire-rating rules for walls surrounding a stair tower are much more stringent and serve to "separate" it from the main building.

▸ Typically, only lighting and heat are necessary to serve a stair tower. For example, if a stair tower landing is the only place for a sub-panel to be installed, it will require documented special permission from the authority having jurisdiction.

Note: For more information, refer to NFPA 101, *Life Safety Code*, 7.1.3.2.1(10)(b).

CONDUCTORS FOR GENERAL WIRING

Introduction to Article 310—Conductors for General Wiring

This article contains the general requirements for conductors such as their insulation markings, ampacity ratings, and conditions of use. It does not apply to conductors that are part of flexible cords, fixture wires, or to those that are an integral part of equipment [90.7 and 300.1(B)]. Some topics covered in this material include:

- ▸ Conductor Size and Material
- ▸ Insulation Types
- ▸ Conductor Identification and Marking
- ▸ Conductor Ampacity

Article 310 consists of three parts:

- ▸ Part I. General
- ▸ Part II. Construction Specifications
- ▸ Part III. Installation

Part I. General

310.1 Scope

Article 310 contains the general requirements, insulation markings, ampacity, and conditions of use for conductors rated up to 2000V. ▸Figure 310–1

Note: For flexible cords and cables, see Article 400. For fixture wires, see Article 402.

310.3 Conductors, Minimum Size and Material

(A) Minimum Size Conductors. The minimum sizes of conductors are 14 AWG copper or 12 AWG aluminum or copper-clad aluminum, except as permitted elsewhere in this *Code*.

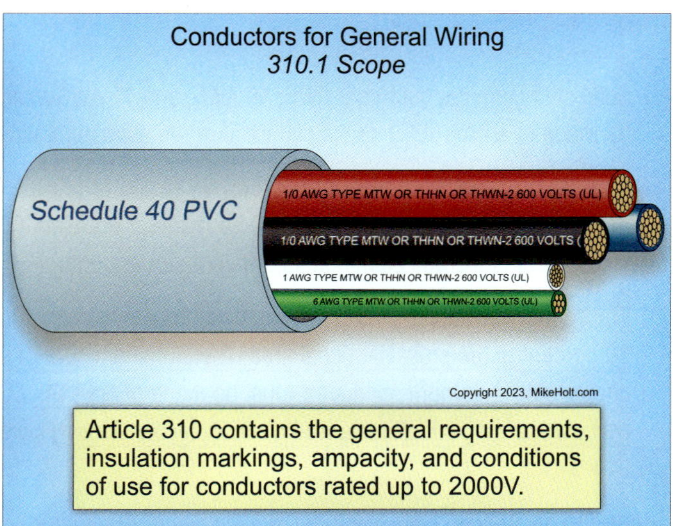

▸Figure 310–1

Author's Comment:

▸ There is a misconception that 12 AWG copper is the smallest conductor permitted for commercial or industrial facilities. Although it is not true based on *NEC* rules, it might be a job specification or local code requirement.

▸ Conductors smaller than 14 AWG are permitted to be installed for Class 1 power-limited circuits [724.43], fixture wire [402.6], and motor control circuits [Table 430.72(B)].

(B) Conductor Material. Conductors must be copper, aluminum, or copper-clad aluminum. Aluminum and copper-clad aluminum conductors must comply with the following: ▸Figure 310–2

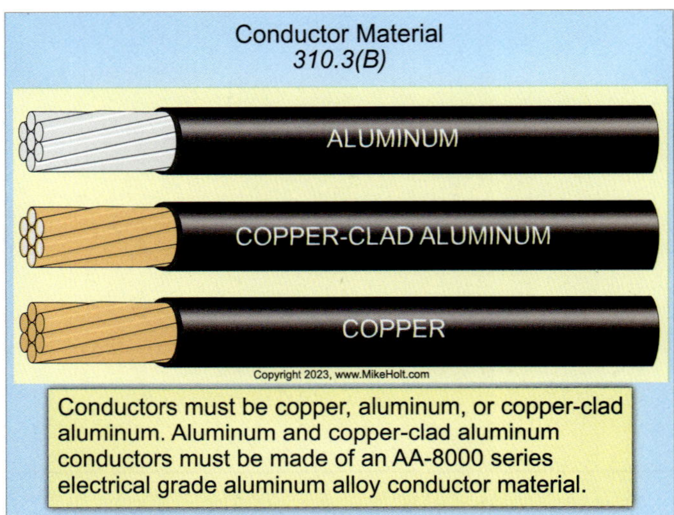

▸Figure 310–2

(1) Solid aluminum conductors 8 AWG, 10 AWG, and 12 AWG must be made of an AA-8000 series electrical grade aluminum alloy conductor material.

(2) Stranded aluminum conductors must be made of an AA-8000 series electrical grade aluminum alloy conductor material.

(3) The copper of a copper-clad aluminum conductor only makes up 10 percent of the cross-sectional area. The aluminum core of a copper-clad aluminum conductor must be made of an AA-8000 series electrical grade aluminum alloy conductor material. ▸Figure 310–3

According to Article 100, "Copper-Clad Aluminum Conductor" is drawn from a copper-clad aluminum rod, with the copper metallurgically bonded to an aluminum core. ▸Figure 310–4

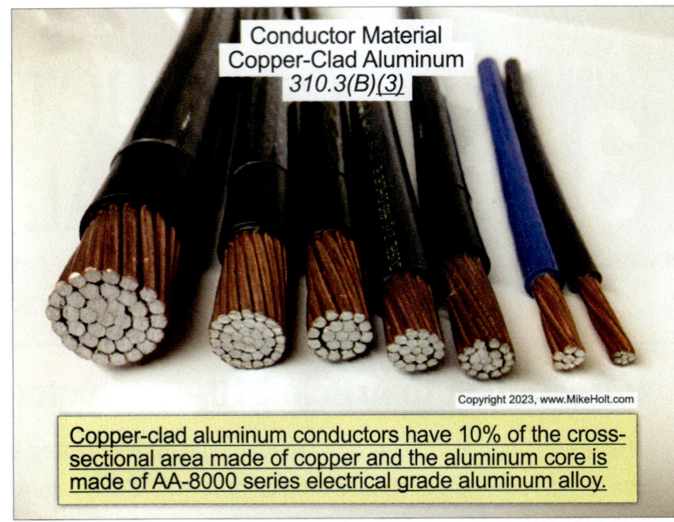

▸Figure 310–3

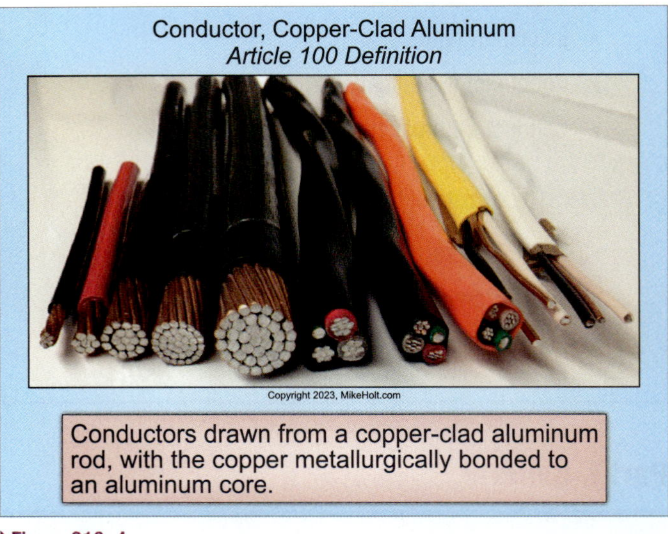

▸Figure 310–4

(4) Copper-clad aluminum conductor material must be listed.

(C) Stranded Conductors. Conductors 8 AWG and larger installed in a raceway must be stranded to be solid, unless specifically permitted or required elsewhere in this *Code*. ▸Figure 310–5

Author's Comment:

▸ According to 250.120(C), exposed equipment grounding conductors 8 AWG and smaller for direct-current circuits [250.134(2) Ex 2], such as those required by 690.45 for solar PV systems, are permitted to be run separately from the circuit conductors. Where an 8 AWG or smaller exposed equipment grounding conductor is subject to physical damage, it must be installed in a raceway or cable.

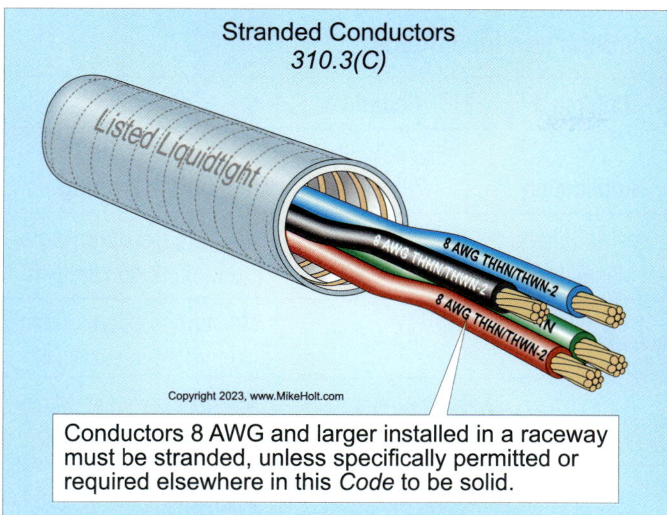

▶Figure 310–5

> ▶ A grounding electrode conductor is an example of where an 8 AWG and larger solid conductor can be installed in a raceway when it is required to be protected from physical damage [250.64(B)].

(D) Insulated. Conductors must be insulated, unless specifically permitted to be bare. ▶Figure 310–6

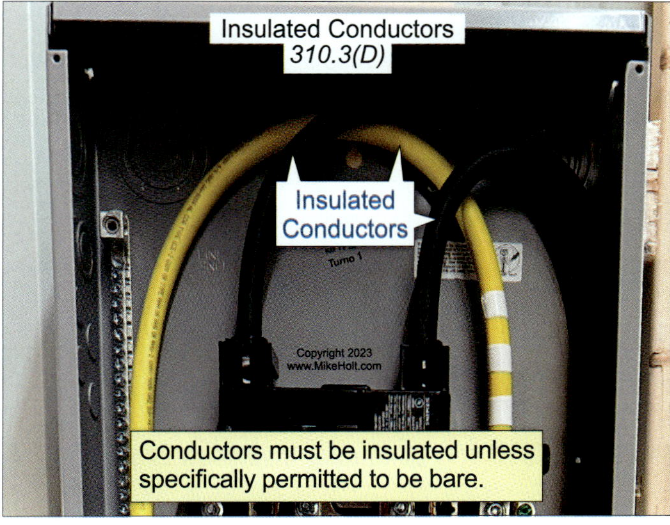

▶Figure 310–6

Part II. Construction Specifications

310.4 Conductor Construction and Application

Table 310.4(1) provides information on conductor insulation properties such as letter type, maximum operating temperature, application, insulation, and outer cover properties. ▶Figure 310–7

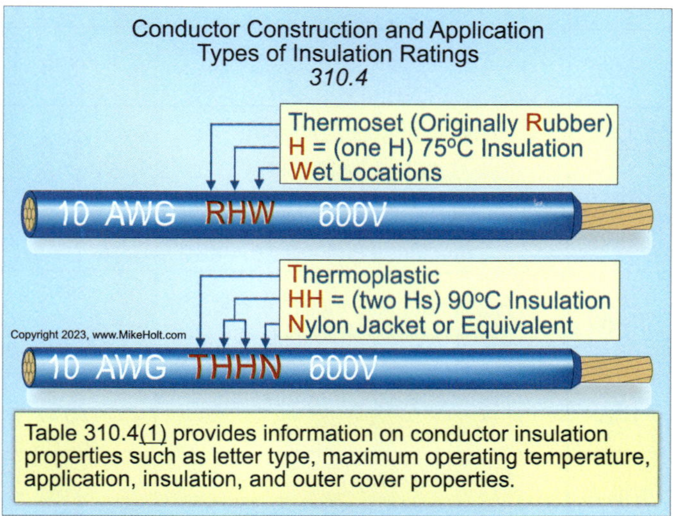

▶Figure 310–7

Author's Comment:

> ▶ The following explains the lettering on conductor insulation [Table 310.4(1)]:
>
> > ▶ No H   60°C insulation rating
> > ▶ H   75°C insulation rating
> > ▶ HH   90°C insulation rating permitted in dry locations
> > ▶ -2   90°C insulation rating permitted in wet locations
> > ▶ N   Nylon outer cover
> > ▶ T   Thermoplastic insulation
> > ▶ U   Underground
> > ▶ W   Permitted in wet or damp locations
> > ▶ X   Thermoset insulation
> > ▶ R   Rubber insulation

Table 310.4(1) Conductor Applications and Insulations

Type Letter	Column 2 Insulation	Column 3 Max. Operating Temperature	Column 4 Application	Column 5 Sizes Available AWG or kcmil	Column 6 Outer Covering
RHH	Flame-retardant thermoset	90°C	Dry and damp locations	14–2000	Moisture-resistant, flame-retardant, nonmetallic
RHW	Flame-retardant, moisture-resistant thermoset	75°C	Dry and wet locations	14–2000	Moisture-resistant, flame-retardant, nonmetallic
RHW-2	Flame-retardant, moisture-resistant thermoset	90°C	Dry and wet locations	14–2000	Moisture-resistant, flame-retardant, nonmetallic
THHN	Flame-retardant, heat-resistant thermoplastic	90°C	Dry and damp locations	14–1000	Nylon jacket or equivalent
THHW	Flame-retardant, moisture- and heat-resistant thermoplastic	75°C 90°C	Dry and wet locations	14–1000	None
THW	Flame-retardant, moisture- and heat-resistant thermoplastic	75°C	Dry, damp, and wet locations	14–2000	None
THW-2	Flame-retardant, moisture- and heat-resistant thermoplastic	90°C	Dry, damp, and wet locations	14–1000	None
THWN	Flame-retardant, moisture- and heat-resistant thermoplastic	75°C	Dry, damp, and wet locations	14–1000	Nylon jacket or equivalent
THWN-2	Flame-retardant, moisture- and heat-resistant thermoplastic	90°C	Dry, damp, and wet locations	14–1000	Nylon jacket or equivalent
TW	Flame-retardant, moisture-resistant thermoplastic	60°C	Dry, damp, and wet locations	14–2000	None
USE	Heat- and moisture-resistant	75°C	See Article 338	14–2000	Moisture-resistant nonmetallic
USE-2	Heat- and moisture-resistant	90°C	See Article 338	14–2000	Moisture-resistant nonmetallic

Author's Comment:

- It is common to see conductors with a multiple insulation rating, such as THHN/THWN. This type of conductor can be used in a dry location at the THHN 90°C ampacity. If it is used in a wet location, you must adhere to the THWN ampacity rating of the 75°C column of Table 310.16 for THWN insulation types. ▶Figure 310–8

- When a "–2" is at the end of an insulation type (such as THWN-2), the conductor has a maximum operating temperature of 90°C and is suitable to be installed in a dry or wet location. ▶Figure 310–9

▶ **Table 310.4(1) Conductor Insulation Example**

Question: Which of the following describe(s) Type THHN insulation?

(a) Thermoplastic insulation
(b) Suitable for dry or damp locations
(c) A maximum operating temperature of 90°C
(d) all of these

Answer: (d) all of these

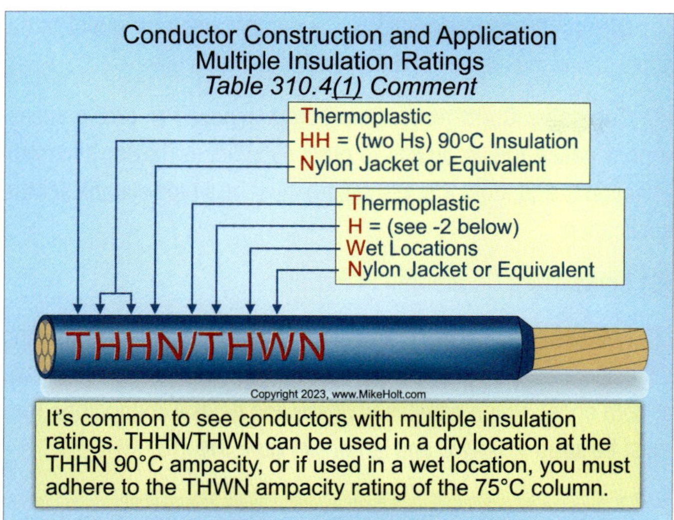

▶Figure 310–8

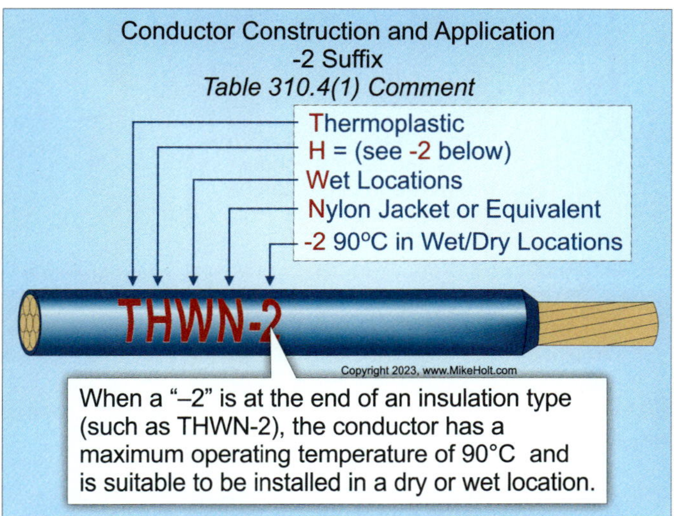

▶Figure 310–9

310.6 Conductor Identification

(A) Neutral Conductor. Insulated neutral conductors must be identified white or gray in accordance with 200.6.

(B) Equipment Grounding Conductor. Insulated equipment grounding conductors must be identified green or green with yellow stripe in accordance with 250.119.

(C) Identification of Phase Conductors. Phase conductor insulation can be any color but white [200.7] or green [250.119]. ▶Figure 310–10

Where premises wiring is supplied from more than one nominal voltage system, branch-circuit phase conductors must be identified in accordance with 210.5(C), and feeders must be identified in accordance with 215.12(C).

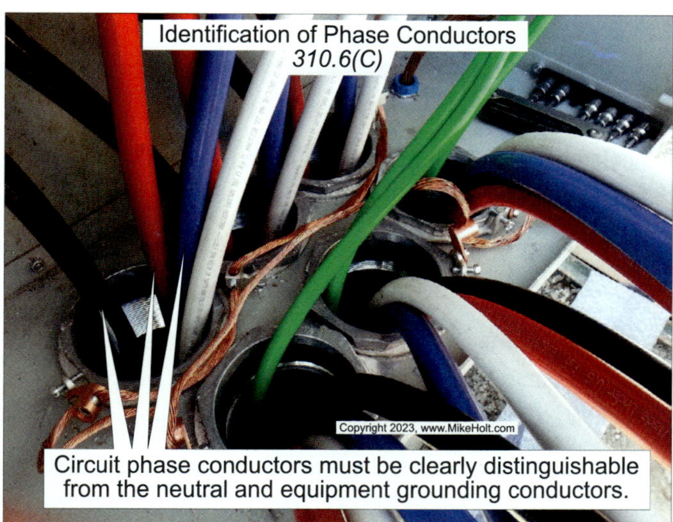

Circuit phase conductors must be clearly distinguishable from the neutral and equipment grounding conductors.

▶Figure 310–10

Ex: Conductor identification is permitted in accordance with 200.7.

Author's Comment:

▶ Although the *NEC* does not require a specific color code for phase conductors, electricians often use the following color system: ▶Figure 310–11

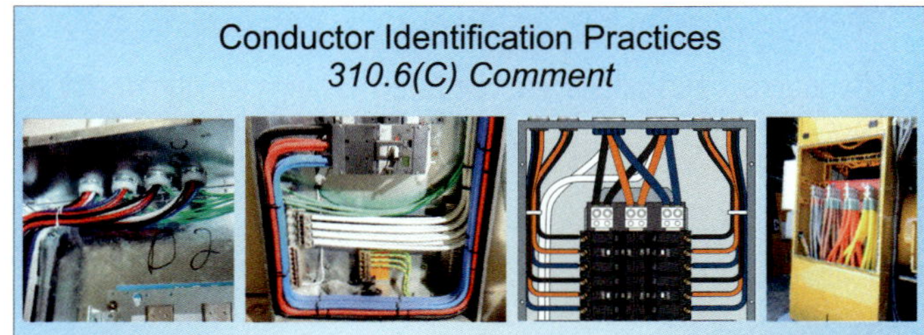

▶Figure 310–11

▶ 120/240V, single-phase—black, red, and white

▶ 120/208V, three-phase—black, red, blue, and white

▶ 120/240V, three-phase—(high-leg) black, orange, blue, and white

▶ 277/480V, three-phase—brown, orange, yellow, and gray; or, brown, purple, yellow, and gray

Part III. Installation

310.10 Uses Permitted

Conductors described in Table 310.4(1) are permitted for use in any of the wiring methods covered in Chapter 3.

(A) Dry Locations. Insulated conductors used in dry locations can be any of the types identified in Table 310.4.

(B) Dry and Damp Locations. Insulated conductors typically used in dry and damp locations include THHN, THHW, THWN, THWN-2, and XHHW.

(C) Wet Locations. Insulated conductors typically used in wet locations include THHW, THWN, THWN-2, XHHW, XHHW-2, XHHN, XHWN, and XHWN-2. Cables must be moisture impervious and listed for wet locations.

> **Author's Comment:**
>
> ▸ The letter "W" found on the insulation types indicate it is suitable for wet locations.

(D) Locations Exposed to Direct Sunlight. Insulated conductors or cables exposed to the direct rays of the sun must comply with the following:

(1) Conductors and cables must be listed as being sunlight resistant. ▸Figure 310–12

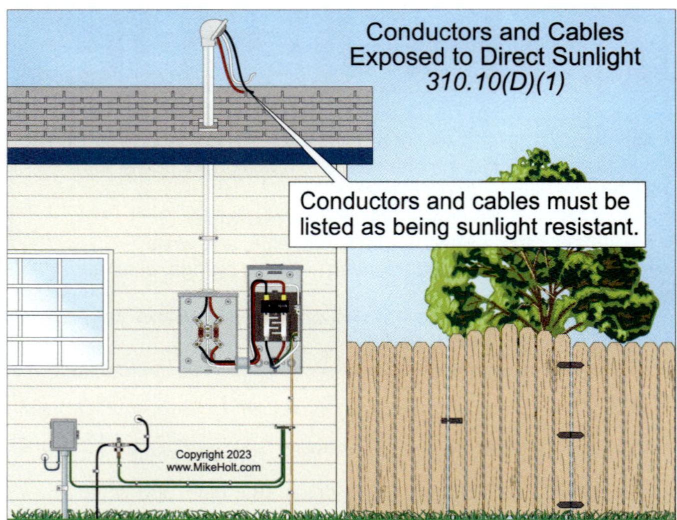

▸Figure 310–12

(2) Conductors and cables must be covered with insulating material (such as tape or sleeving) that is listed as being sunlight resistant.

(E) Direct Burial Conductors. Conductors used for direct burial applications must be of a type identified for such use.

(F) Corrosive Conditions. Conductors exposed to oils, greases, vapors, gases, fumes, liquids, or other substances (having a harmful effect on the conductor or insulation) must be a type suitable for the application.

(G) Conductors Connected in Parallel.

(1) 1/0 AWG and Larger. Phase, neutral, and equipment grounding conductors are permitted to be connected in parallel (electrically joined at both ends). When paralleling phase and neutral conductors, they must be sized 1/0 AWG and larger. ▸Figure 310–13

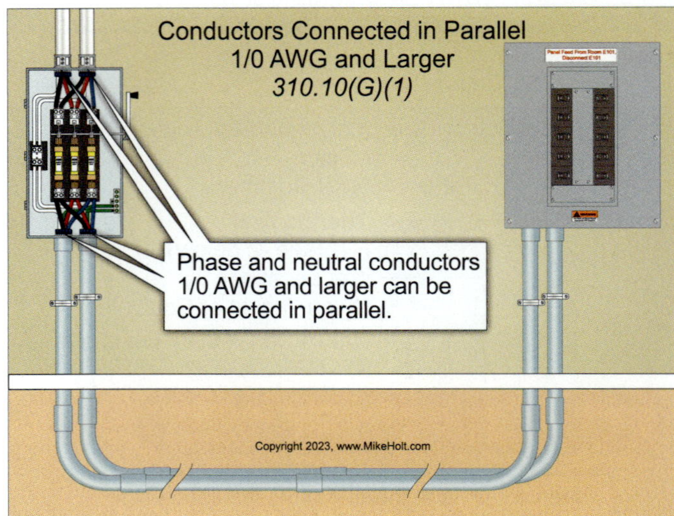

▸Figure 310–13

> **Author's Comment:**
>
> ▸ When conductors are installed in parallel (electrically joined at both ends), the current flow will be evenly distributed between the individual parallel conductors.

(2) Conductor and Installation Characteristics. All parallel phase conductors, neutral conductors, equipment grounding conductors, and supply-side bonding jumpers must comply with the following: ▸Figure 310–14

(1) Be the same length.

(2) Be the same conductor material (copper, aluminum, or copper-clad aluminum).

(3) Be the same size in circular mil area (minimum 1/0 AWG).

(4) Have the same type of insulation.

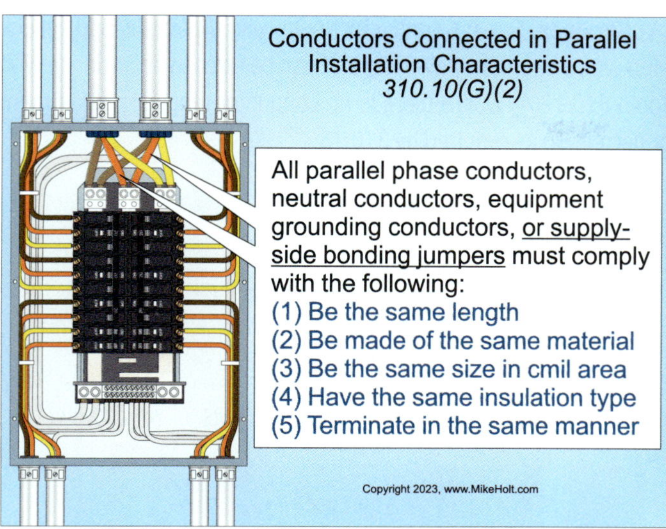

▶Figure 310–14

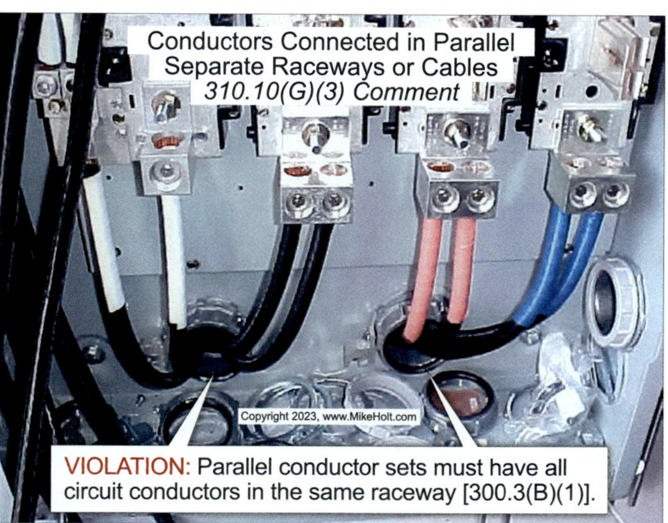

▶Figure 310–16

(5) Terminate in the same manner (set screw versus compression fitting).

(3) Separate Raceways or Cables. The raceways or cables for parallel circuits must have the same number of conductors and electrical characteristics (metallic versus nonmetallic). ▶Figure 310–15

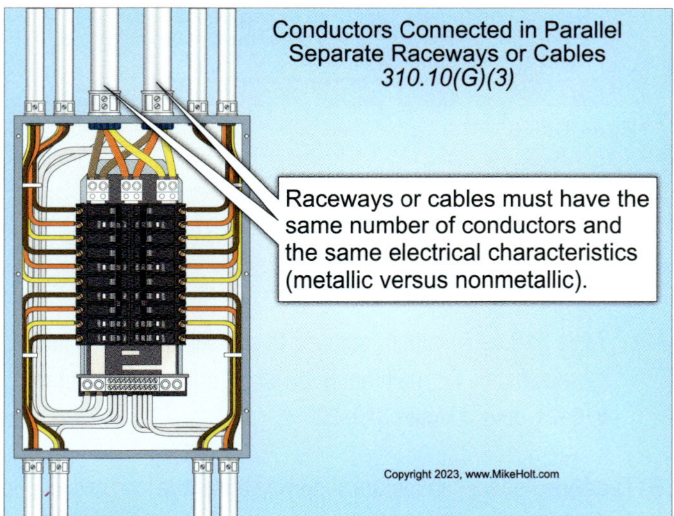

▶Figure 310–15

Conductors that comprise one paralleled set are not required to have the same physical characteristics as another paralleled set. ▶Figure 310–17

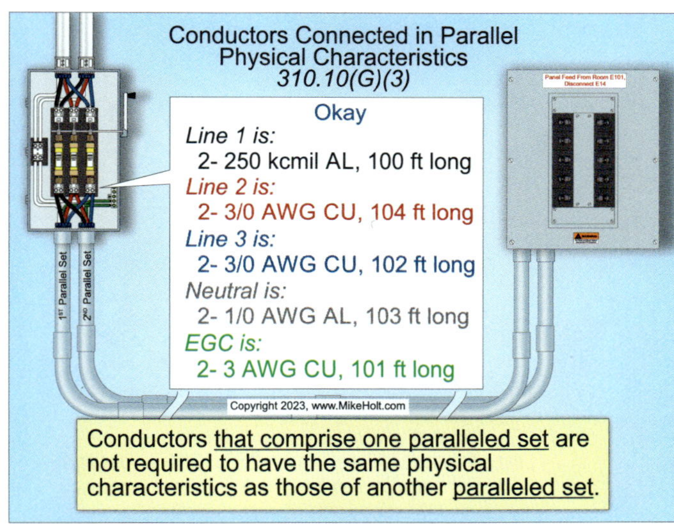

▶Figure 310–17

(4) Conductor Ampacity Correction or Adjustment.

Ambient Temperature over 86°F. Where conductors are installed in an ambient temperature greater 86°F, the conductor ampacity (based on the 90°C column of Table 310.16), must be corrected in accordance with 310.15(B)(1).

Four or More Current-Carrying Conductors. Where four or more current-carrying conductors are installed in a raceway or cable, the conductor ampacity (based on the 90°C column of Table 310.16), must be adjusted in accordance with 310.15(C)(1). ▶Figure 310–18

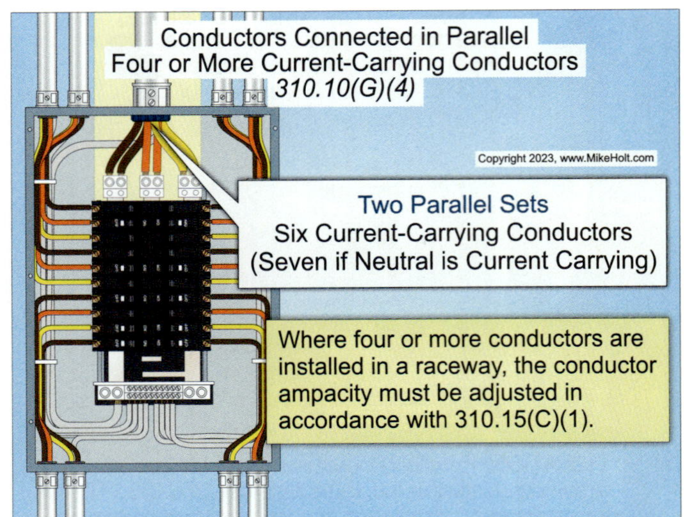

▶Figure 310–18

(5) Equipment Grounding Conductors. Equipment grounding conductors must be sized in accordance with 250.122(F), but they are not required to be 1/0 AWG and larger. ▶Figure 310–19

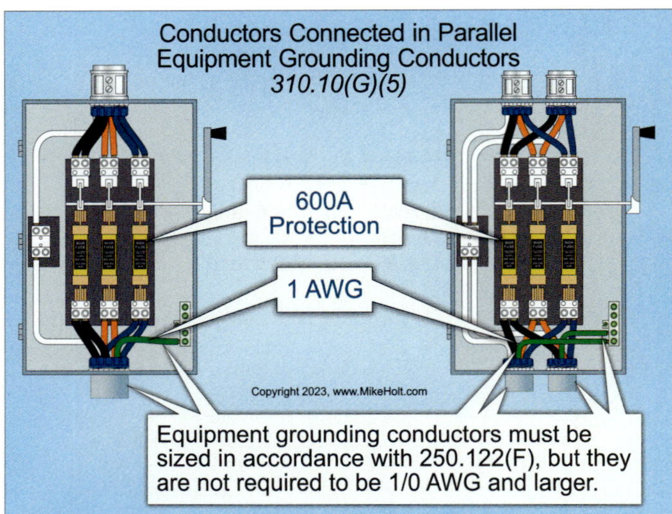

▶Figure 310–19

(6) Bonding Jumpers. Supply-side bonding jumpers must be sized in accordance with 250.102(C) and load-side bonding jumpers must be sized in accordance with 250.102(D), but they are not required to be 1/0 AWG and larger.

310.12 Dwelling Services and Feeders

Dwelling unit services and feeders can be sized in accordance with the following:

(A) Services. Service conductors supplying the entire load associated with a one-family dwelling unit can be sized in accordance with Table 310.12(A) where there is no conductor ampacity adjustment or correction as required by 310.15.

▶ **Example 1**

Question: What size service conductors are required if the calculated load for a single-family dwelling unit requires a service disconnect rated 200A? ▶Figure 310–20

(a) 1/0 AWG   (b) 2/0 AWG   (c) 3/0 AWG   (d) 4/0 AWG

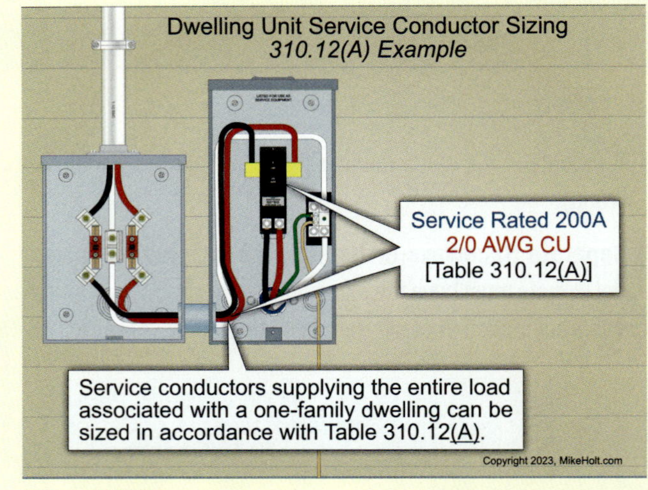

▶Figure 310–20

Answer: (b) 2/0 AWG [Table 310.12(A)]

Author's Comment:

▸ Table 310.12(A) cannot be used to size service conductors for two-family or multifamily dwelling buildings. ▶Figure 310–21 and ▶Figure 310–22

(B) Feeders. Feeder conductors supplying the entire load associated with an individual dwelling unit can be sized in accordance with Table 310.12(A). ▶Figure 310–23, ▶Figure 310–24, and ▶Figure 310–25

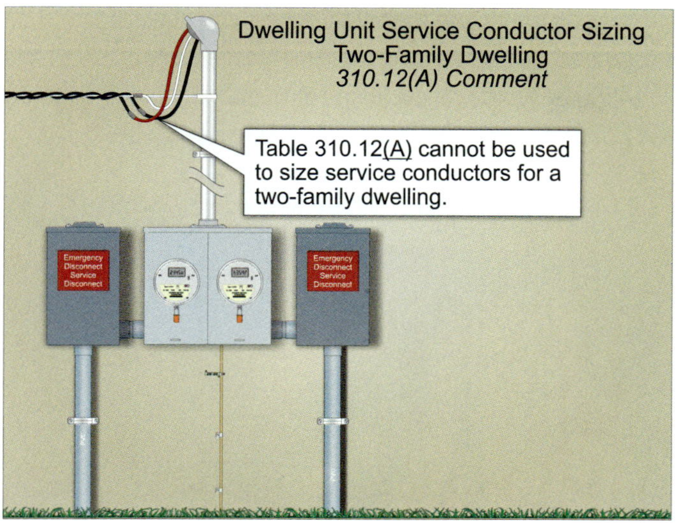

▶Figure 310–21

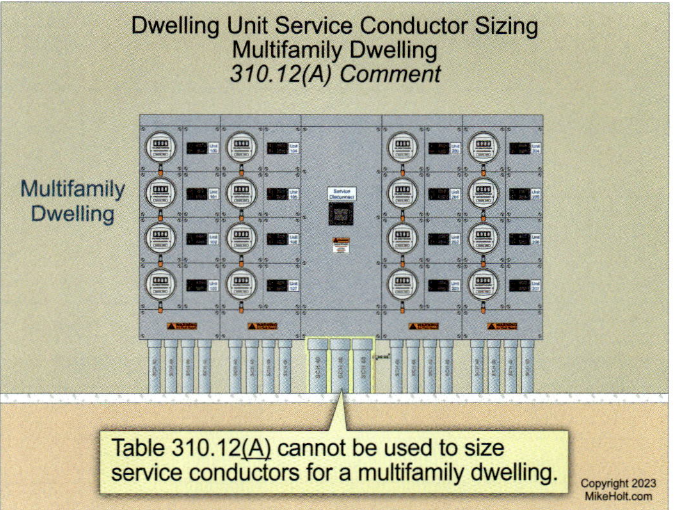

▶Figure 310–22

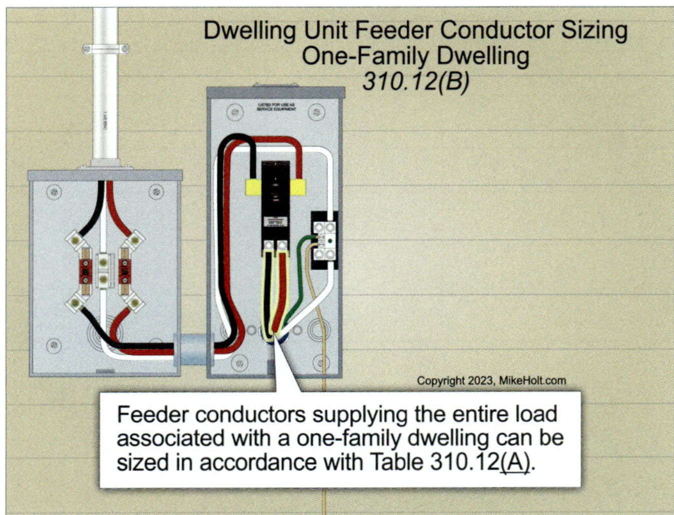

▶Figure 310–23

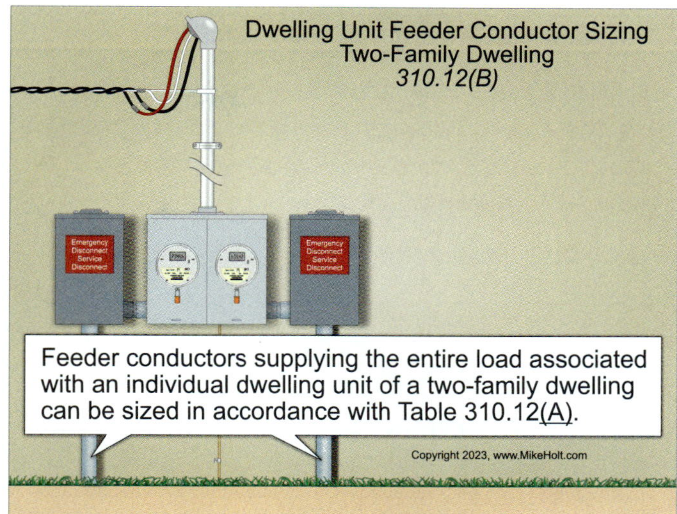

▶Figure 310–24

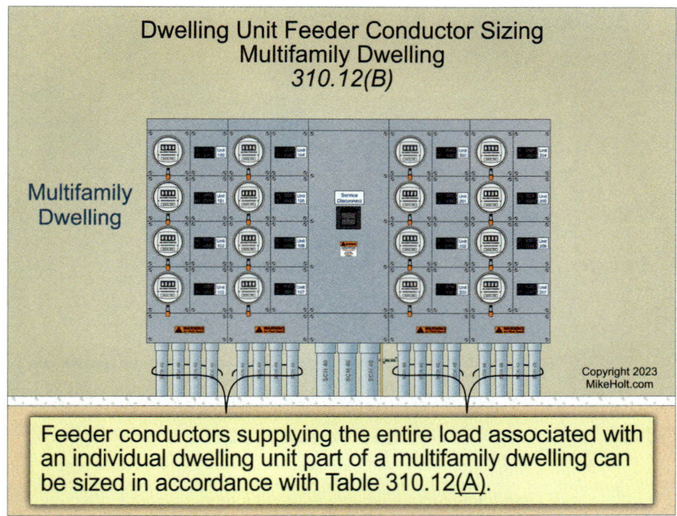

▶Figure 310–25

▶ Example 2

Question: *What size feeder conductors are required if the calculated load for a single-family dwelling unit requires a service disconnect rated 200A, and the feeder conductors carry the entire load of the dwelling unit?* ▶Figure 310–26

(a) 1/0 AWG   (b) 2/0 AWG   (c) 3/0 AWG   (d) 4/0 AWG

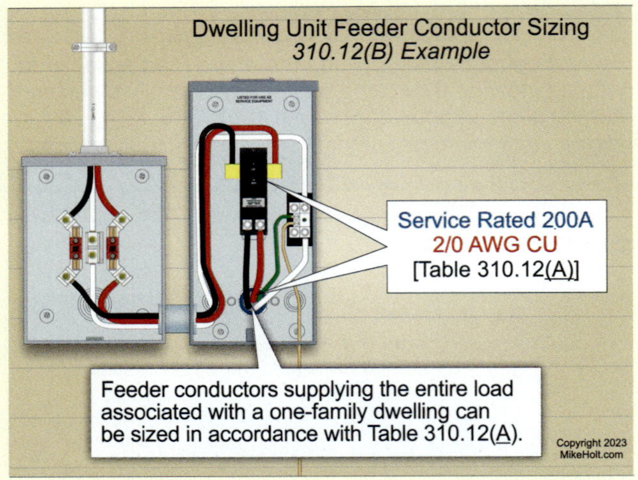

▶Figure 310–26

Answer: *(b) 2/0 AWG [Table 310.12(A)]*

(C) Feeder Conductors Not Greater Than Service Conductors.
The feeder conductor ampacity for an individual dwelling unit is not required to be larger than the service conductor. ▶Figure 310–27

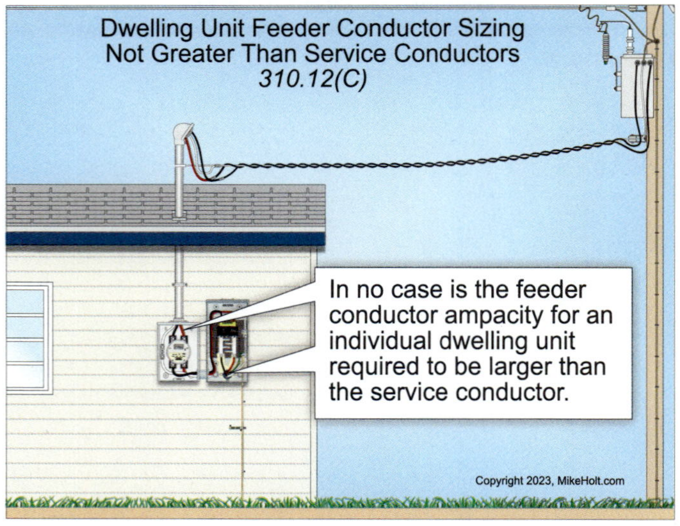

▶Figure 310–27

(D) Neutral Conductors. Neutral conductors are permitted to be sized smaller than the phase conductors if the requirements of 220.61 and 230.42(C) for service conductors, or the requirements of 215.2(A)(2) and 220.61 for feeder conductors are met. ▶Figure 310–28

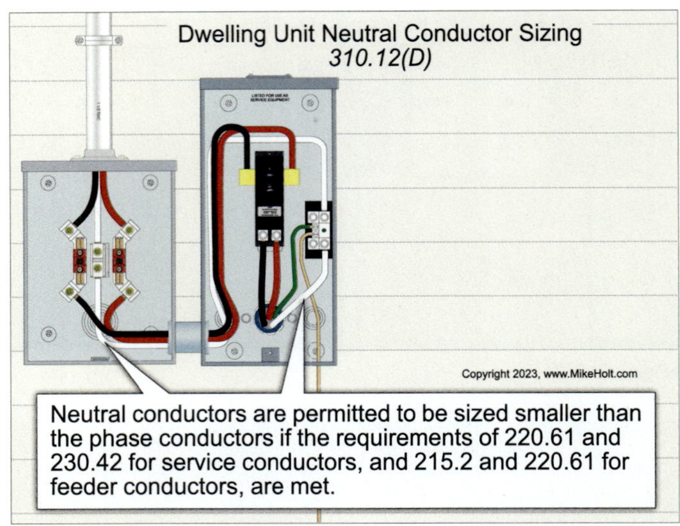

▶Figure 310–28

Table 310.12(A) Single-Phase Dwelling Services and Feeders		
Service or Feeder Rating	Copper	Aluminum or Copper-Clad Aluminum
100A	4 AWG	2 AWG
110A	3 AWG	1 AWG
125A	2 AWG	1/0 AWG
150A	1 AWG	2/0 AWG
175A	1/0 AWG	3/0 AWG
200A	2/0 AWG	4/0 AWG
225A	3/0 AWG	250 kcmil
250A	4/0 AWG	300 kcmil
300A	250 kcmil	350 kcmil
350A	350 kcmil	500 kcmil
400A	400 kcmil	600 kcmil

310.14 Ampacities for Conductors Rated 0V to 2000V

(A) General Requirements.

(1) Tables or Engineering Supervision. The ampacity of a conductor can be determined either by using the tables contained in the *NEC* as corrected and adjusted in accordance with 310.15, or under engineering supervision as provided in 310.14(B).

According to Article 100, "Ampacity" is equal to the maximum current (in amperes) a conductor can carry continuously under its conditions of use without exceeding its temperature rating. ▶Figure 310–29

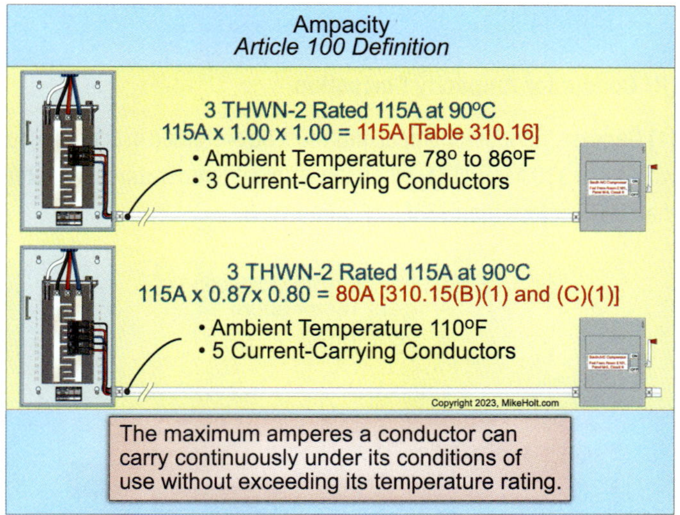

▶Figure 310–29

(2) Conductor Ampacity—Lower Rating. Where more than one ampacity applies to part of the circuit because of temperature correction [Table 310.15(B)(1)(1)] or adjustment factors [Table 310.15(C)(1)], the lowest ampacity value must be used for the total circuit. ▶Figure 310–30

Ex: When different ampacities apply to parts of a circuit because of temperature correction [Table 310.15(B)(1)(1)] or adjustment factors [Table 310.15(C)(1)], the higher ampacity can apply for the entire circuit if the length of the lower ampacity does not exceed the lesser of 10 ft or 10 percent of the total circuit's length. ▶Figure 310–31

(3) Insulation Temperature Limitation. Conductors are not permitted to be used where the operating temperature exceeds that designated for the type of insulated conductor involved.

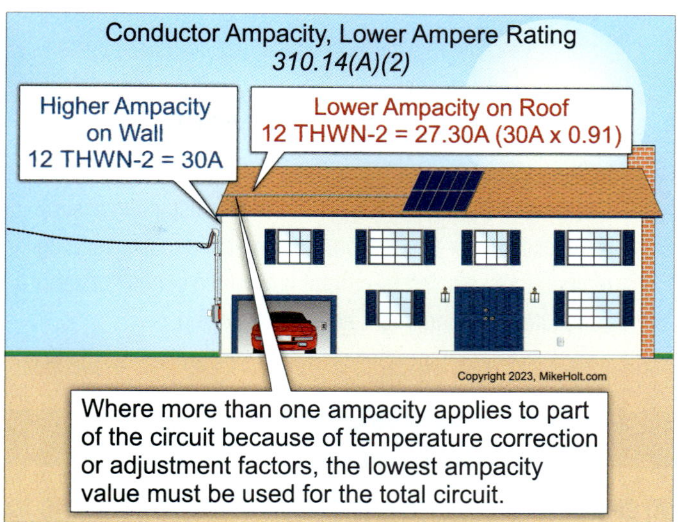

▶Figure 310–30

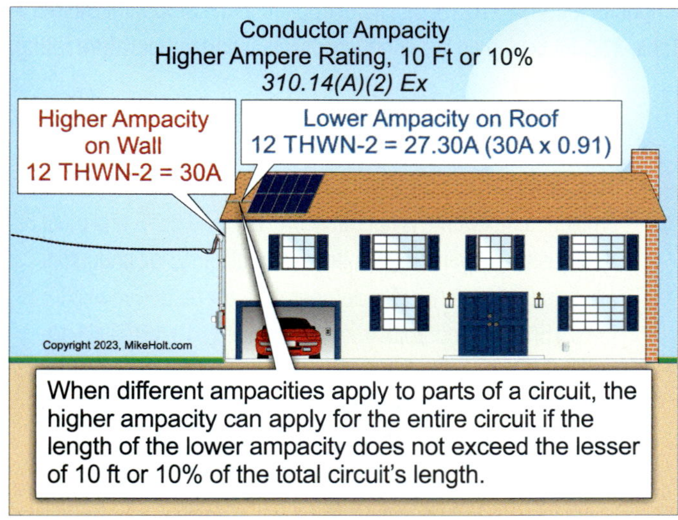

▶Figure 310–31

Note 1: The insulation temperature rating of Table 310.4(1) insulated conductors is the maximum temperature a conductor can withstand over a prolonged time period without serious degradation. The main factors to consider for conductor operating temperature include:

(1) Ambient temperature that may vary along the conductor length, as well as from time to time [Table 310.15(B)(1)(1)].

(2) Heat generated internally in the conductor as the result of load current flow.

(3) The rate at which generated heat dissipates into the ambient medium.

(4) Adjacent load-carrying conductors that have the effect of raising the ambient temperature and impeding heat dissipation [Table 310.15(C)(1)].

310.15 Ampacity Tables

(A) General. Ampacities for conductors are contained in Table 310.16.

The temperature ampacity correction [310.15(B)(1)] and adjustment ampacity factors [310.15(C)(1)] are applied to the ampacities listed in Table 310.16, based on the conductor's insulation temperature rating.

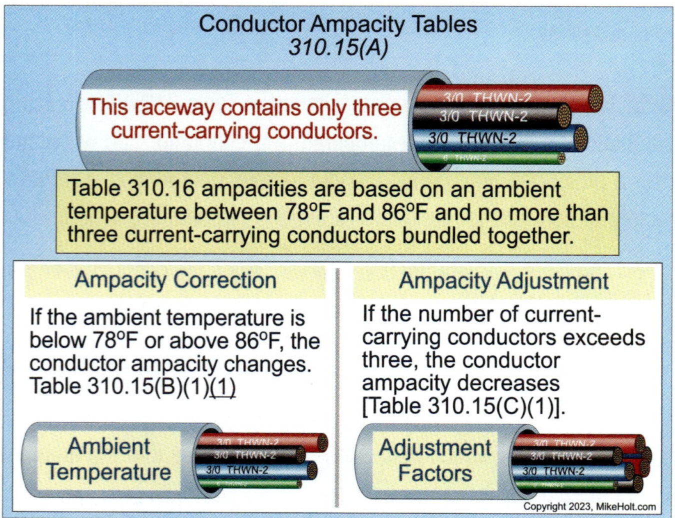

▶Figure 310–32

The corrected or adjusted conductor ampacity must not exceed the temperature rating of the equipment terminations of 110.14(C).

(B) Conductor Ampacity Correction.

(1) General. Conductor ampacities must be corrected in accordance with Table 310.15(B)(1)(1) when the ambient temperature is greater than 86°F or less than 78°F. ▶Figure 310–33

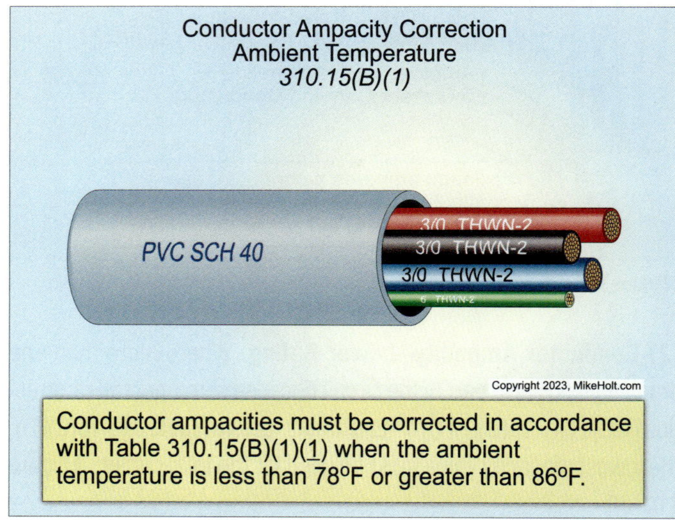

▶Figure 310–33

Corrected Conductor Ampacity—Ambient Temperature Correction Formula:

Corrected Ampacity = Table 310.16 Ampacity × Ambient Correction Factor

Table 310.15(B)(1)(1) Ambient Temperature Correction Factors Based on 30°C (86°F) and 90°C Insulation

Ambient Temperature °F	Ambient Temperature °C	Correction Factor 90°C Conductors
50°F or less	10°C or less	1.15
51–59°F	11–15°C	1.12
60–68°F	16–20°C	1.08
69–77°F	21–25°C	1.04
78–86°F	26–30°C	1.00
87–95°F	31–35°C	0.96
96–104°F	36–40°C	0.91
105–113°F	41–45°C	0.87
114–122°F	46–50°C	0.82

▶ Ambient Temperature Below 86°F Example

Question: What is the ampacity of a 12 AWG, THWN-2 conductor when installed in an ambient temperature of 50°F? ▶Figure 310–34

(a) 20A   (b) 25A   (c) 31A   (d) 35A

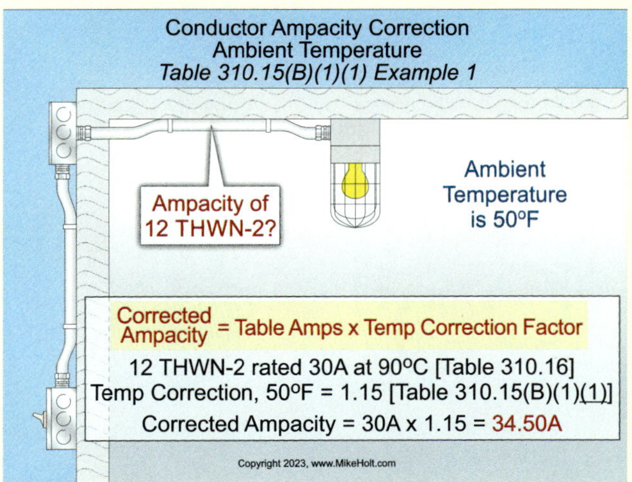

▶Figure 310–34

Solution:

The conductor ampacity for 12 AWG, THWN-2 is 30A at 90°C [Table 310.16].

The correction factor for a 90°C conductor installed in an ambient temperature of 50°F is 1.15 [Table 310.15(B)(1)(1)].

Corrected Ampacity = 30A × 115%
Corrected Ampacity = 34.50A, round to 35A

Note: Ampacity increases when the ambient temperature is less than 86°F.

Answer: (d) 35A

▶ Ambient Temperature Above 86°F Example

Question: What is the ampacity of a 6 AWG, THWN-2 conductor installed in an ambient temperature of 122°F? ▶Figure 310–35

(a) 35A   (b) 53A   (c) 62A   (d) 75A

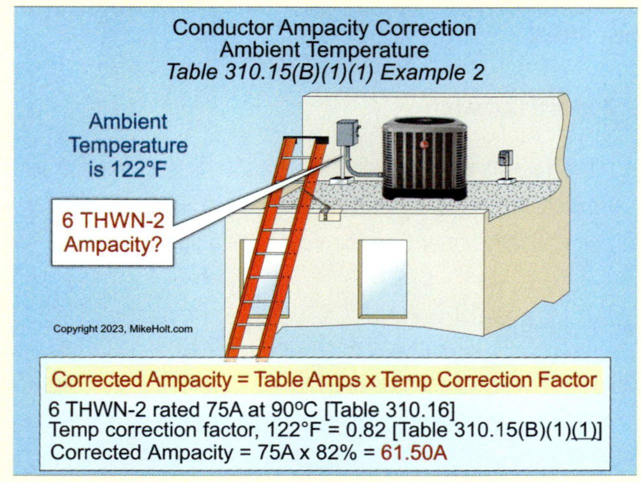

▶Figure 310–35

Solution:

The conductor ampacity for 6 AWG, THWN-2 is 75A at 90°C [Table 310.16].

The correction factor for a 90°C conductor installed in an ambient temperature of 122°F is 0.82 [Table 310.15(B)(1)(1)].

Corrected Ampacity = 75A × 82%
Corrected Ampacity = 61.50A, round to 62A

Answer: (c) 62A

(2) Raceways and Cables Exposed to Sunlight on Rooftops. Where raceways or cables are exposed to direct sunlight and located less than ¾ in. above the roof, a temperature of 60°F (33°C) must be added to the outdoor ambient temperature to determine the ambient temperature correction in accordance with Table 310.15(B)(1)(1). ▶Figure 310–36

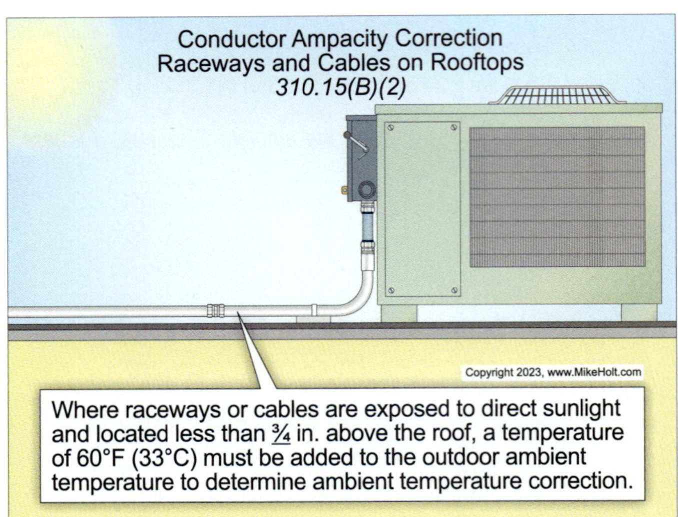

▶Figure 310–36

Author's Comment:

▶ The reason for the temperature adder is because the air inside raceways and cables that are in direct sunlight is significantly hotter than the surrounding air.

▶ Example

Question: What is the ampacity of a 6 AWG, THWN-2 in a raceway ½ in. above the roof, where the ambient temperature is 90°F? ▶Figure 310–37

(a) 40A *(b) 41A* *(c) 42A* *(d) 44A*

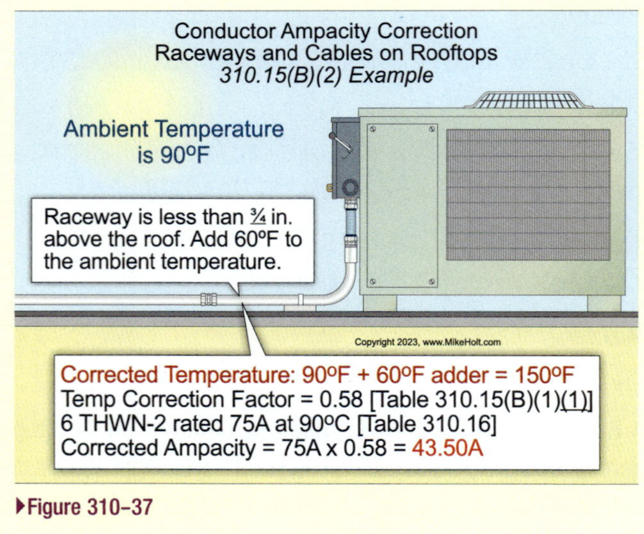

▶Figure 310–37

Solution:

Corrected Temperature = 90°F + 60°F adder [310.15(B)(2)]
Corrected Temperature = 150°F

The temperature correction factor for 150°F = 0.58 [Table 310.15(B)(1)(1)]

6 AWG, THWN-2 is rated 75A at 90°C [Table 310.16]

Corrected Ampacity = 75A × 58%
Corrected Ampacity = 43.50A, round to 44A

Answer: *(d) 44A*

Ex: Type XHHW-2 insulated conductors are not subject to the rooftop temperature adder.

Note 1: The *ASHRAE Handbook—Fundamentals* (www.ashrae.org) is one source for the ambient temperatures in various locations.

(C) Conductor Ampacity Adjustment.

(1) Four or More Current-Carrying Conductors.

Author's Comment:

▶ Conductor ampacity reduction is required when four or more current-carrying conductors are bundled together because heat generated by current flow is not able to dissipate as quickly as when there are fewer current-carrying conductors. ▶Figure 310–38

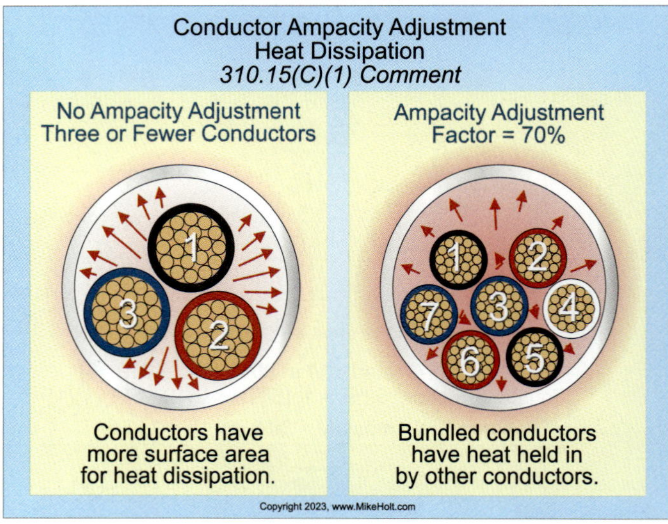

▶Figure 310–38

Conductors in Raceways or Cables. Where four or more current-carrying conductors are within a raceway or cable, the conductor ampacities contained in Table 310.16 in the 90°C column must be adjusted in accordance with Table 310.15(C)(1). ▶Figure 310–39

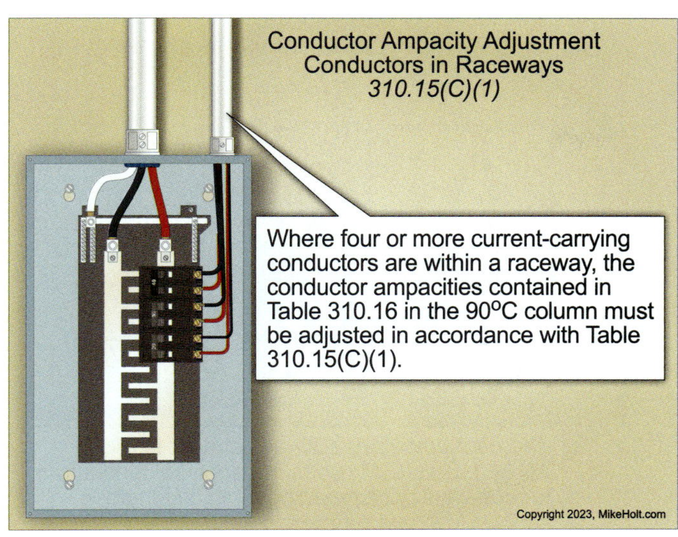

▶Figure 310–39

Table 310.15(C)(1) Conductor Ampacity Adjustment for More Than Three Current–Carrying Conductors

Number of Conductors[1]	Adjustment
4–6	80%
7–9	70%
10–20	50%
21–30	45%
31–40	40%
41 and above	35%

[1] *Does not include conductors that cannot be energized at the same time.*

Cables Bundled Together. Where cables are bundled together without maintaining spacing for more than 24 in., the conductor ampacities contained in Table 310.16 in the 90°C column must be adjusted in accordance with Table 310.15(C)(1). ▶Figure 310–40

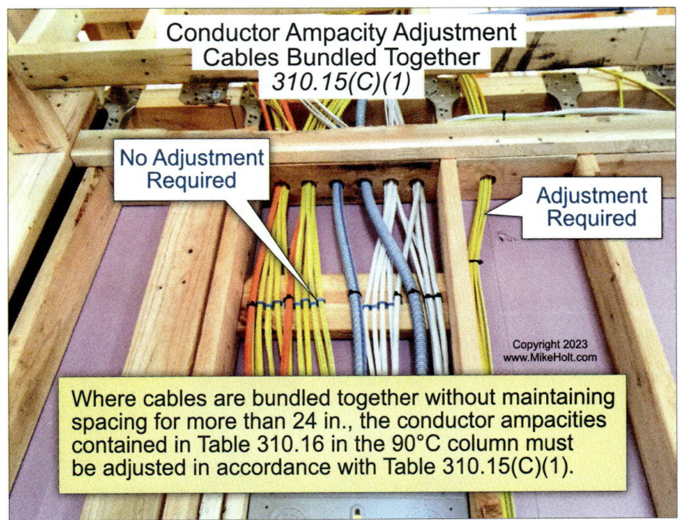

▶Figure 310–40

Author's Comment:

▶ The neutral conductor is not considered a current-carrying conductor for the purposes of conductor ampacity adjustment [310.15(C)(1)] under the conditions specified in 310.15(E)(1).

▶ Equipment grounding conductors are never considered current carrying [310.15(F)].

▶ Ampacity Adjustment Example 1

Question: *What is the adjusted ampacity of four current-carrying 12 AWG, THWN-2 conductors in a raceway?* ▶Figure 310–41

(a) 20A   (b) 24A   (c) 29A   (d) 32A

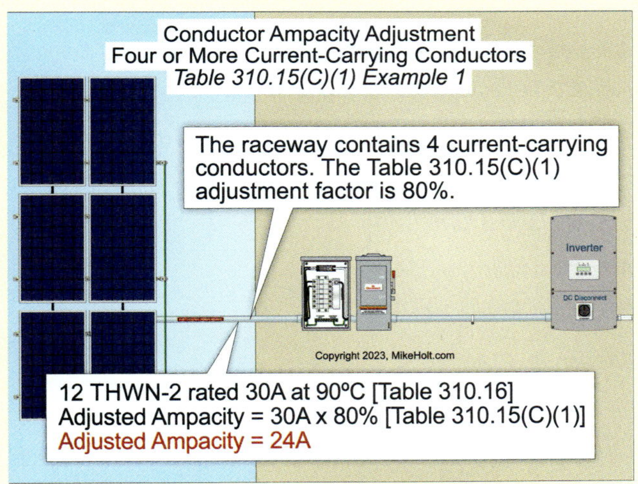

▶Figure 310–41

Solution:

Adjusted Ampacity = Table 310.16 Ampacity × Bundled Ampacity Adjustment Factor from Table 310.15(C)(1)

12 AWG, THWN-2 is rated 30A at 90°C [Table 310.16].

The adjustment factor for four current-carrying conductors is 80 percent [Table 310.15(C)(1)].

Adjusted Ampacity = 30A × 80%

Adjusted Ampacity = 24A

Answer: *(b) 24A*

▶ Ampacity Adjustment Example 2

Question: *What is the adjusted ampacity of eight current-carrying 12 AWG, THWN-2 conductors in a raceway?* ▶**Figure 310–42**

(a) 16A   (b) 21A   (c) 35A   (d) 43A

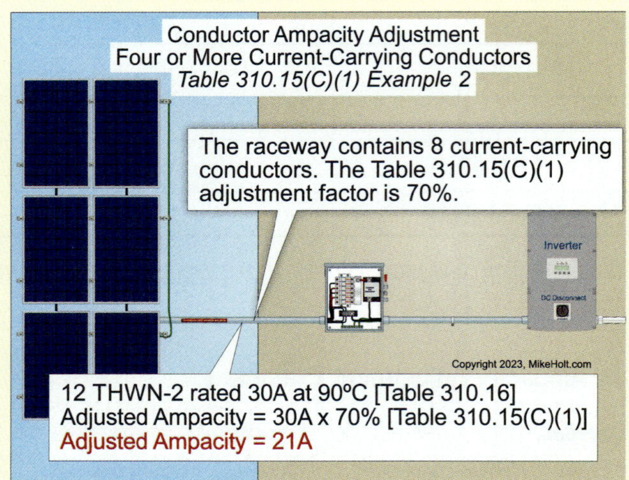

▶**Figure 310–42**

Solution:

Adjusted Ampacity = Table 310.16 Ampacity × Bundled Ampacity Adjustment Factor from Table 310.15(C)(1)

12 AWG, THWN-2 is rated 30A at 90°C [Table 310.16].

The adjustment factor for eight current-carrying conductors is 70 percent [Table 310.15(C)(1)].

Adjusted Ampacity = 30A × 70%

Adjusted Ampacity = 21A

Answer: *(b) 21A*

(a) Where conductors are installed in cable trays, 392.80 applies.

(b) Conductor ampacity adjustment from Table 310.15(C)(1) does not apply to conductors in raceways not exceeding 24 in. in length. ▶**Figure 310–43**

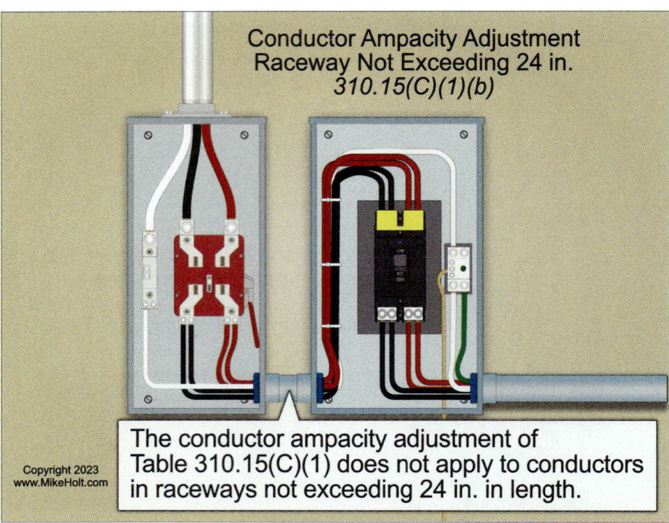

▶**Figure 310–43**

▶ Ampacity Adjustment—Raceway Not Exceeding 24 In. Example

Question: *What is the ampacity of five 3/0 AWG, THWN-2 conductors in a raceway that does not exceed 24 in. in length?* ▶**Figure 310–44**

(a) 150A   (b) 195A   (c) 205A   (d) 225A

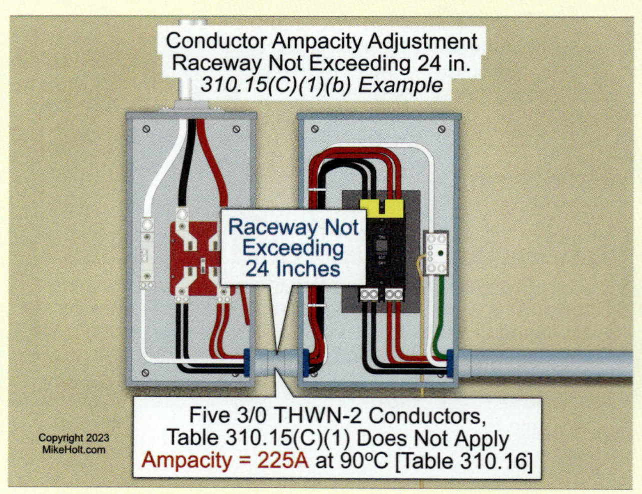

▶**Figure 310–44**

Solution:

3/0 AWG, THWN-2 is rated 225A at 90°C [Table 310.16].

Answer: *(d) 225A*

(d) The conductor ampacity adjustment of Table 310.15(C)(1) does not apply to conductors in Type AC or Type MC cable under all of the following conditions: ▶Figure 310–45

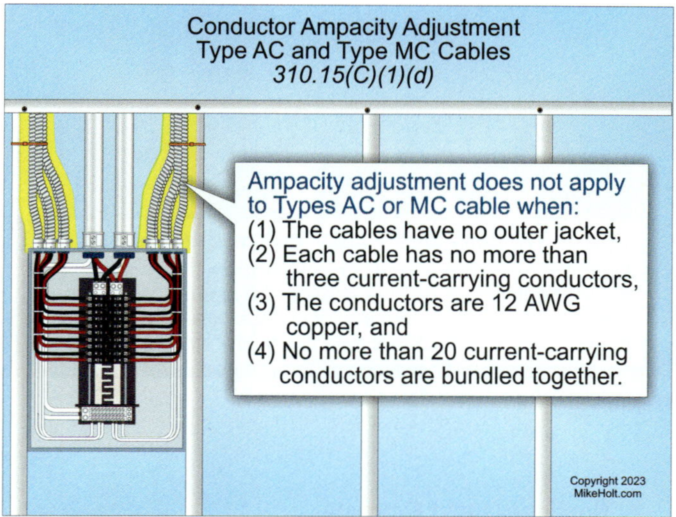

▶Figure 310–45

(1) The cables do not have an outer jacket.

(2) Each cable has no more than three current-carrying conductors.

(3) The conductors are 12 AWG copper.

(4) No more than twenty current-carrying conductors (ten 2-wire cables or six 3-wire cables) are bundled together.

Ex: Where more than twenty current-carrying conductors in Type AC or Type MC cable are bundled together for a continuous length longer than 24 in., a 60 percent adjustment factor can be applied.

(E) Neutral Conductor. Neutral conductors must be considered current carrying in accordance with the following:

(1) Not Considered Current Carrying. The neutral conductor of a 3-wire, single-phase, 120/240V system, or a 4-wire, three-phase, 120/208V or 277/480V wye-connected system, supplying linear loads is not considered a current-carrying conductor for the application of conductor ampacity adjustments in accordance with Table 310.15(C)(1). ▶Figure 310–46

(2) Considered Current Carrying. The neutral conductor of a 3-wire circuit from a 4-wire, three-phase, wye-connected system carries approximately the same current as the line-to-neutral load currents of the other conductors. It is considered a current-carrying conductor for conductor ampacity adjustments in accordance with Table 310.15(C)(1). ▶Figure 310–47

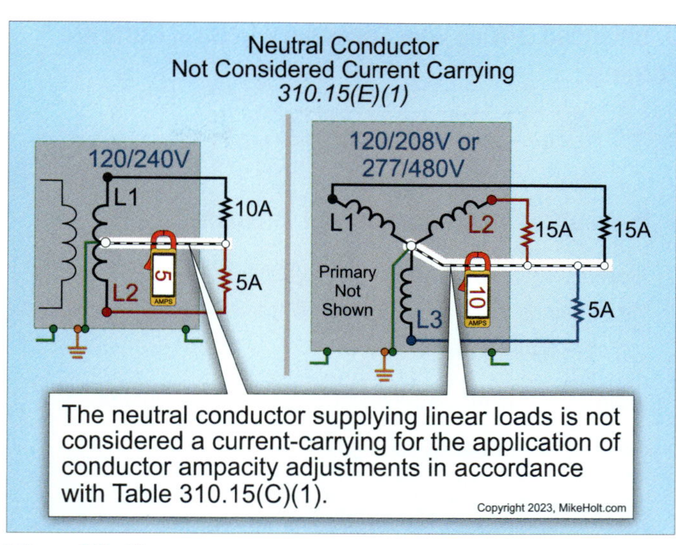

▶Figure 310–46

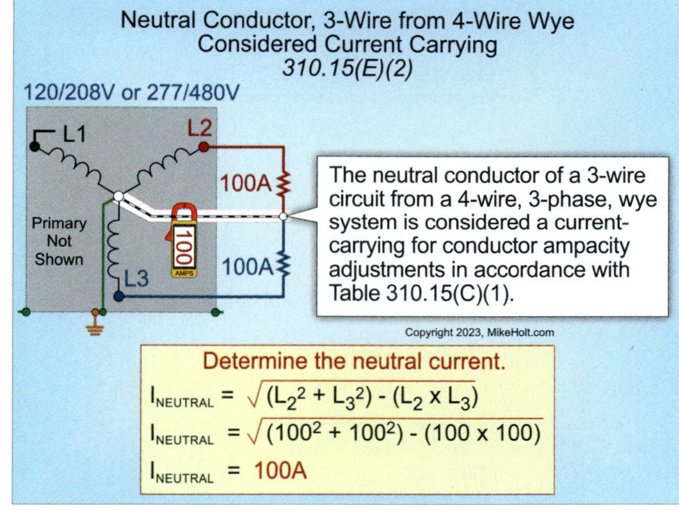

$$I_{NEUTRAL} = \sqrt{(L_2{}^2 + L_3{}^2) - (L_2 \times L_3)}$$
$$I_{NEUTRAL} = \sqrt{(100^2 + 100^2) - (100 \times 100)}$$
$$I_{NEUTRAL} = 100A$$

▶Figure 310–47

Unbalanced 3-Wire Wye Secondary Neutral Current Formula:

$$I_{Neutral} = \sqrt{[(I_{Line1}^2 + I_{Line2}^2) - (I_{Line1} \times I_{Line2})]}$$

▶ Neutral Conductor Current Example

Question: *What is the neutral current for two 16A, 120V circuits? The system is a 120/208V, three-phase, 4-wire, wye-connected system.* ▶Figure 310–48

(a) 8A   (b) 16A   (c) 32A   (d) 40A

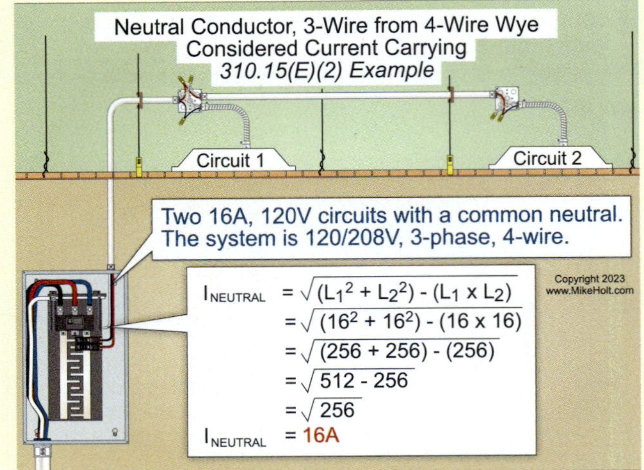

▶Figure 310–48

Solution:

$$I_{Neutral} = \sqrt{(I_{Line1}^2 + I_{Line2}^2) - (I_{Line1} \times I_{Line2})}$$
$$I_{Neutral} = \sqrt{(16^2 + 16^2) - (16 \times 16)}$$
$$I_{Neutral} = \sqrt{(512 - 256)}$$
$$I_{Neutral} = \sqrt{256}$$
$$I_{Neutral} = 16A$$

Answer: *(b) 16A*

(3) Considered Current Carrying. On a 4-wire, three-phase, wye circuit where the major portion of the load consists of nonlinear loads, the neutral conductor is considered a current-carrying conductor for conductor ampacity adjustments in accordance with Table 310.15(C)(1). ▶Figure 310–49

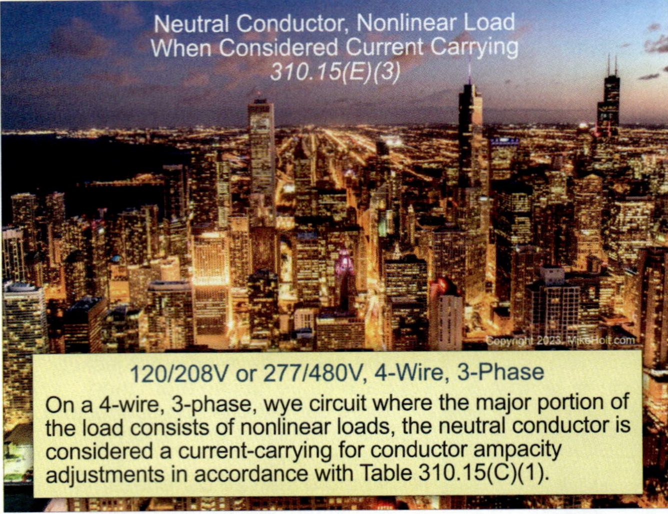

▶Figure 310–49

▶ Nonlinear Load Example

Question: *What size conductors rated 90°C are required for a circuit supplying a 44A nonlinear load where the equipment is rated for 75°C conductor?*

(a) 10 AWG   (b) 8 AWG   (c) 6 AWG   (d) 4 AWG

Solution:

Conductor Ampacity at 90°C = Actual Load/Adjustment

Actual Load = 44A

Adjustment [Table 310.15(C)(1)] = 80% (four current-carrying conductors)

Conductor Ampacity at 90°C Column = 44A/80%
Conductor Ampacity at 90°C Column = 55A
8 AWG is rated 55A at 90°C based on Table 310.16

Answer: *(b) 8 AWG*

According to **Article 100,** "Nonlinear Load" is a load where the shape of the current waveform does not follow the shape of the applied voltage waveform. ▶Figure 310–50 and ▶Figure 310–51

(F) Equipment Grounding and Bonding Conductor. Equipment grounding and bonding conductors are not considered current carrying for conductor ampacity adjustments in accordance with Table 310.15(C)(1). ▶Figure 310–52

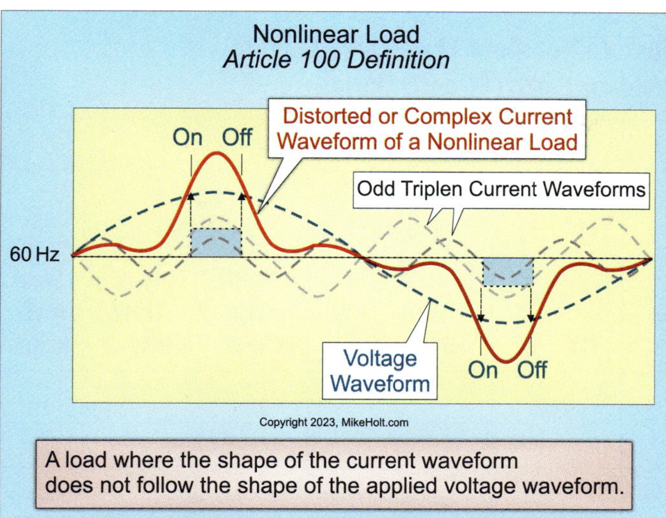

▶Figure 310–50

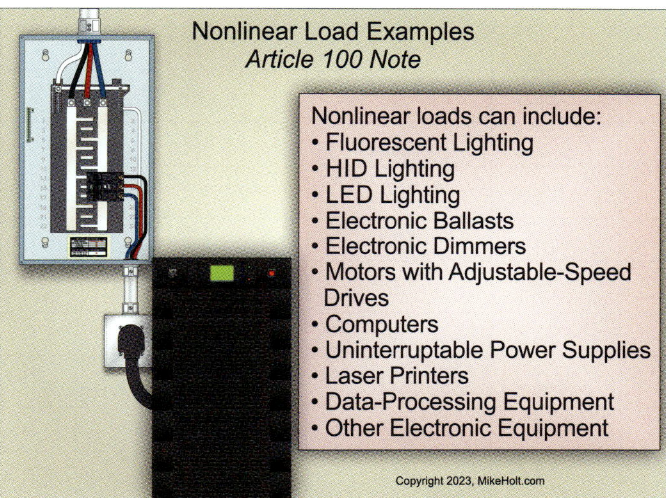

▶Figure 310–51

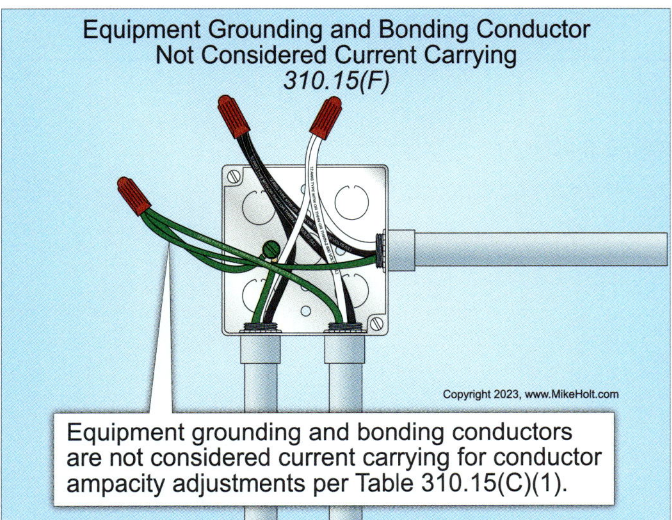

▶Figure 310–52

310.16 Ampacities of Insulated Conductors

The ampacities of conductors installed in raceways, cables, or directly buried (specified in Table 310.16) are based on the following conditions: ▶Figure 310–53

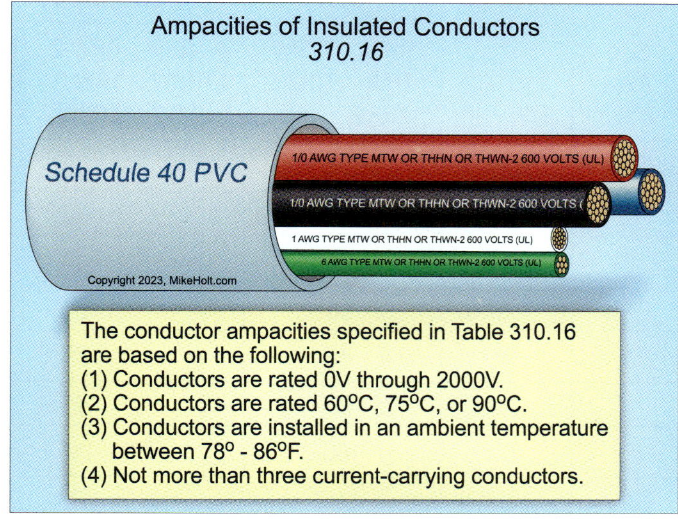

▶Figure 310–53

(1) Conductors are rated not over 2000V.

(2) Conductors are rated 60°C, 75°C, or 90°C.

(3) Conductors are installed in an ambient temperature between 78–86°F.

(4) There are not more than three current-carrying conductors.

	Copper			Aluminum			
	60°C (140°F)	75°C (167°F)	90°C (194°F)	60°C (140°F)	75°C (167°F)	90°C (194°F)	
Size AWG kcmil	TW UF	RHW THHW THW THWN XHHW USE	RHH RHW-2 THHN THHW THW-2 THWN-2 USE-2 XHHW XHHW-2	TW UF	THHN THW THWN XHHW	THHN THW–2 THWN-2 THHW XHHW XHHW–2	Size AWG kcmil
14	15	20	25				
12	20	25	30	15	20	25	12
10	30	35	40	25	30	35	10
8	40	50	55	35	40	45	8
6	55	65	75	40	50	55	6
4	70	85	95	55	65	75	4
3	85	100	115	65	75	85	3
2	95	115	130	75	90	100	2
1	110	130	145	85	100	115	1
1/0	125	150	170	100	120	135	1/0
2/0	145	175	195	115	135	150	2/0
3/0	165	200	225	130	155	175	3/0
4/0	195	230	260	150	180	205	4/0
250	215	255	290	170	205	230	250
300	240	285	320	195	230	260	300
350	260	310	350	210	250	280	350
400	280	335	380	225	270	305	400
500	320	380	430	260	310	350	500

Table 310.16 Ampacities of Insulated Conductors Not More Than Three Current-Carrying Conductors in Raceway, Cable, or Earth (Directly Buried)

Notes:

1. See 310.15(B) for ampacity correction factors where the ambient temperature is other than 30°C (86°F).

2. See 310.15(C)(1) for ampacity adjustment factors when more than three current-carrying conductors.

3. 310.16 must be referenced for conditions of use.

CABINETS, CUTOUT BOXES, AND METER SOCKET ENCLOSURES

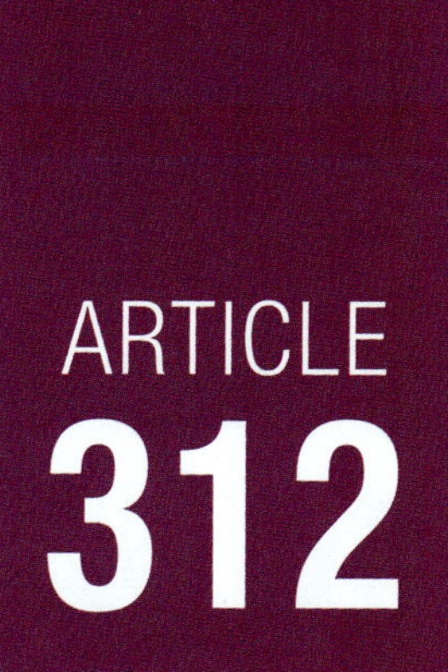

Introduction to Article 312—Cabinets, Cutout Boxes, and Meter Socket Enclosures

Article 312 covers the installation and construction specifications for cabinets for panelboards, cutout boxes for disconnects, and meter socket enclosures. Notice that these rules cover the cabinets and enclosures that contain electrical equipment such as panel boards—not the equipment itself. Some topics covered in this material include:

- ▶ Damp and Wet Locations
- ▶ Repairing Noncombustible Surfaces
- ▶ Deflection of Conductors
- ▶ Space in Enclosures
- ▶ Screws or Other Fasteners

This article consists of two parts:

- ▶ Part I. General
- ▶ Part II. Construction Specifications

Part I. General

312.1 Scope

Article 312 covers the installation and construction specifications for cabinets for panelboards, cutout boxes for disconnects, and meter enclosures. ▶Figure 312–1

According to Article 100, a "Cabinet" is a surface- or flush-mounted enclosure provided with a frame in which a door can be hung. ▶Figure 312–2

According to Article 100, a "Cutout Box" is an enclosure designed for surface mounting that has swinging doors or covers secured directly to and telescoping with the walls of the enclosure. ▶Figure 312–3

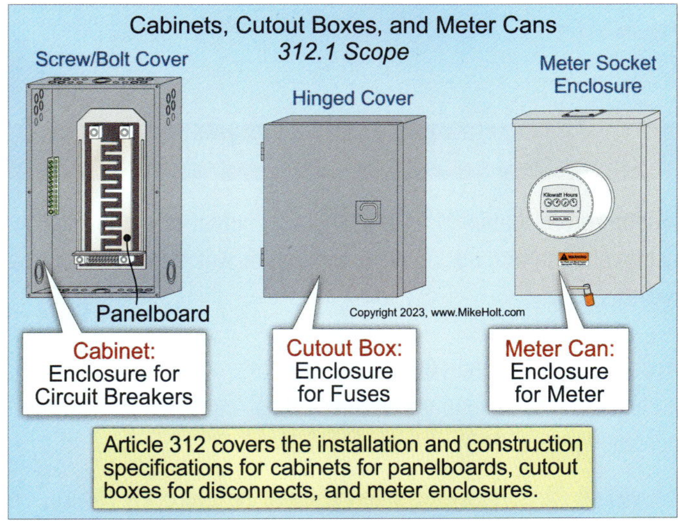

▶Figure 312–1

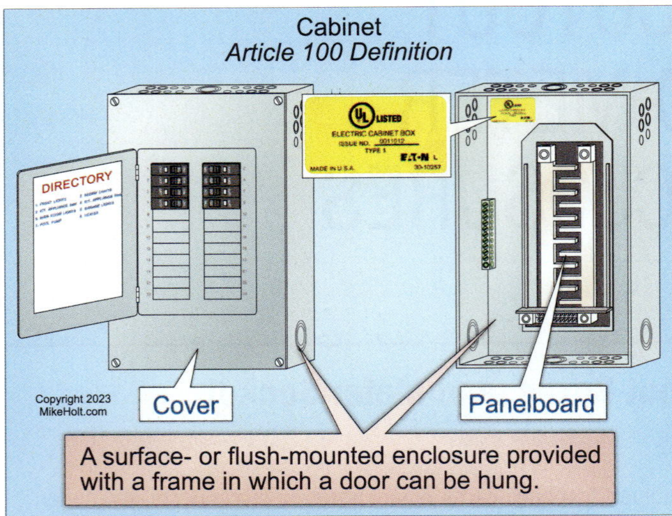

▶Figure 312–2

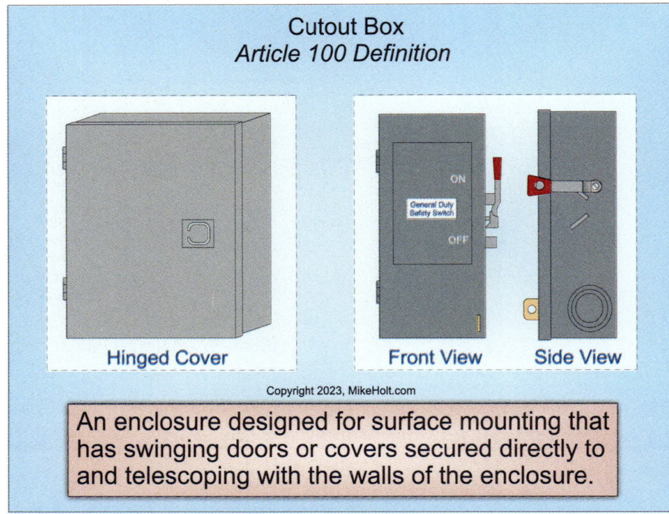

▶Figure 312–3

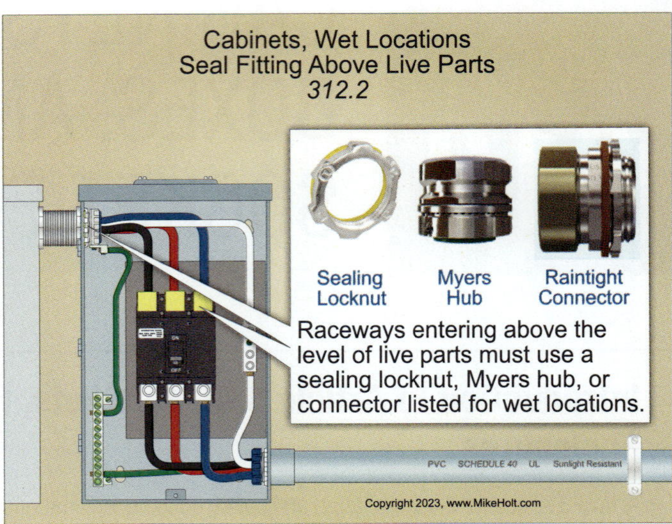

▶Figure 312–4

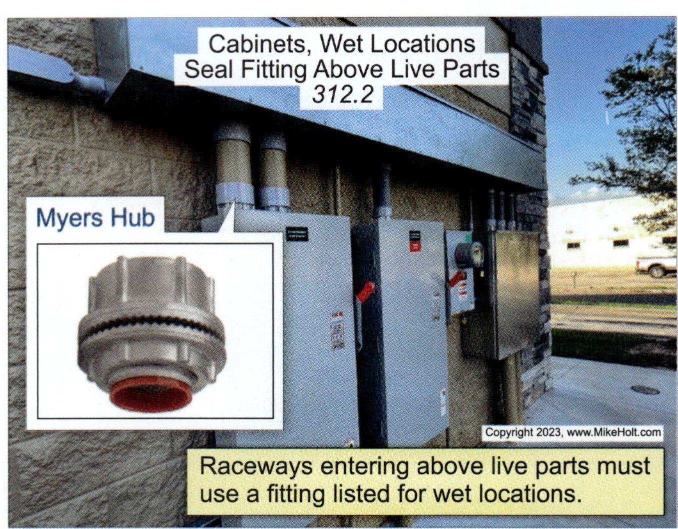

▶Figure 312–5

312.2 Damp or Wet Locations

Weatherproof. Cabinets for panelboards, cutout boxes for disconnects, and meter cans installed in damp or wet locations must be weatherproof.

According to Article 100, "Weatherproof" means constructed or protected so exposure to the weather will not interfere with successful operation [Article 100].

Above Live Parts. Raceways entering above the level of live parts (such as busbars and overcurrent devices) of cabinets, cutout boxes, and meter cans in wet locations must use a sealing locknut, Myers hub, or connector listed for wet locations. ▶Figure 312–4 and ▶Figure 312–5

Author's Comment:

▶ In accordance with "*UL Guide Information DWTT*," sealing locknuts are permitted on the outside or inside of the enclosure for RMC, IMC, or inside the enclosure for connectors if marked for this use on the fitting carton.

312.3 Position in Walls

Cabinets for panelboards installed in walls of noncombustible material must be installed so the front edge of the cabinet is set back no more than ¼ in. from the finished surface. In walls constructed of wood or other combustible material, cabinets for panelboards must be flush with the finished surface or project outward. ▶Figure 312–6

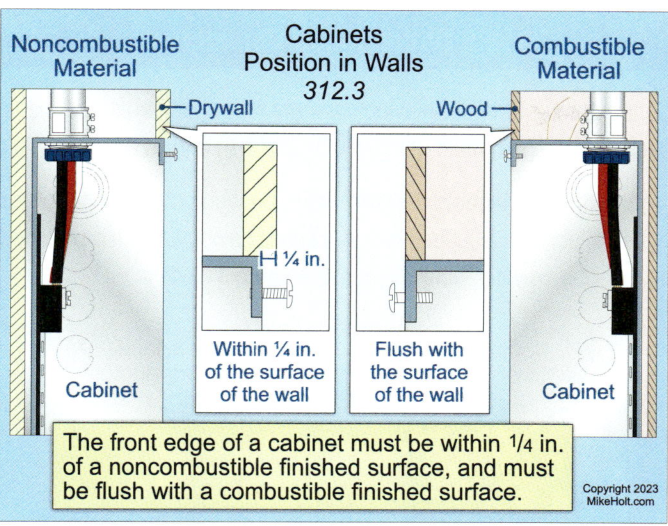

▶Figure 312–6

312.4 Repairing Gaps in Noncombustible Surfaces

Recessed cabinets for panelboards and cutout boxes in noncombustible surfaces (plaster, drywall, or plasterboard) must not have a gap of more than ⅛ in. around any edge of the cabinet. ▶Figure 312–7

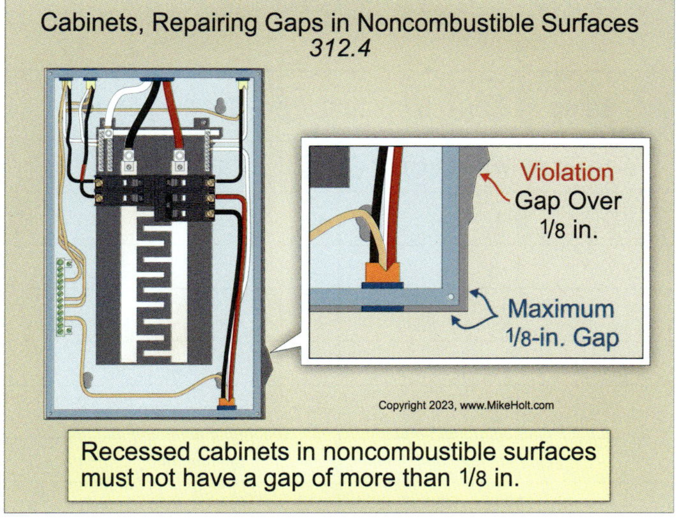

▶Figure 312–7

312.5 Cable Termination to Enclosures

(C) Cable Termination. Cables must be secured to the cabinet, cutout box, or meter socket enclosure with fittings listed for the cable type. See 300.12 and 300.15. ▶Figure 312–8 and ▶Figure 312–9

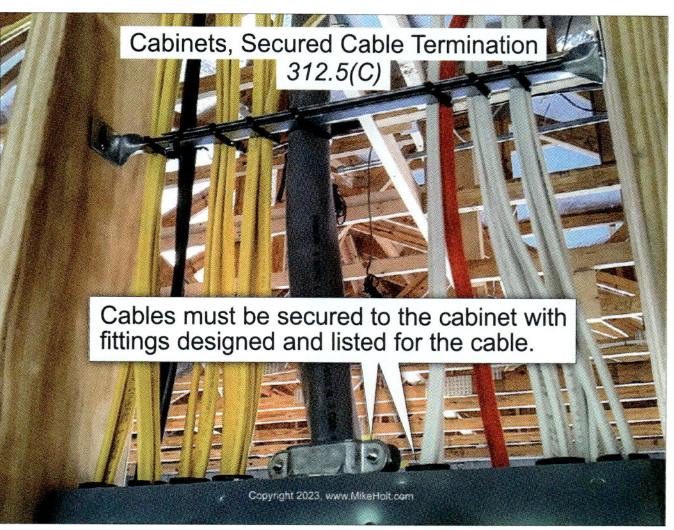

▶Figure 312–8

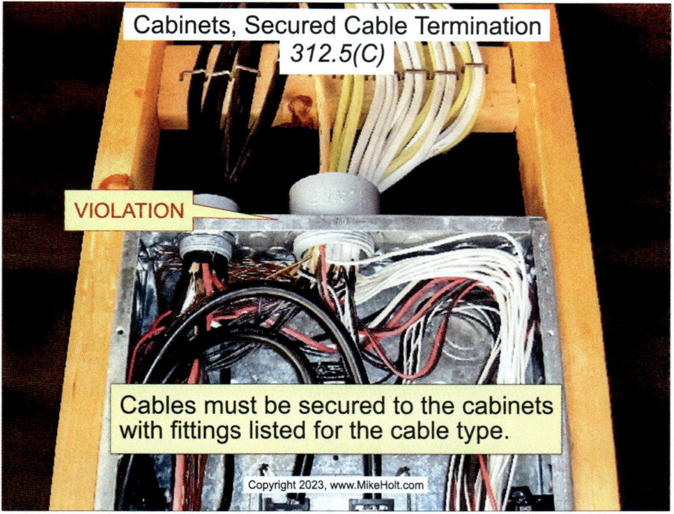

▶Figure 312–9

Author's Comment:

▶ In accordance with "*UL Guide Information PXJV,*" type NM cable clamps or cable connectors are only suitable for a single NM cable unless that clamp or connector is identified for more than one cable. Some Type NM cable clamps are listed for two or more Type NM cables within a single fitting. ▶Figure 312–10

Ex 1: Nonmetallic-sheathed cables are not required to be secured to the cabinet, cutout box, and meter socket enclosure if the cables enter the top of a surface-mounted enclosure through a nonflexible raceway not less than 18 in. or more than 10 ft long, if all the following conditions are met: ▶Figure 312–11

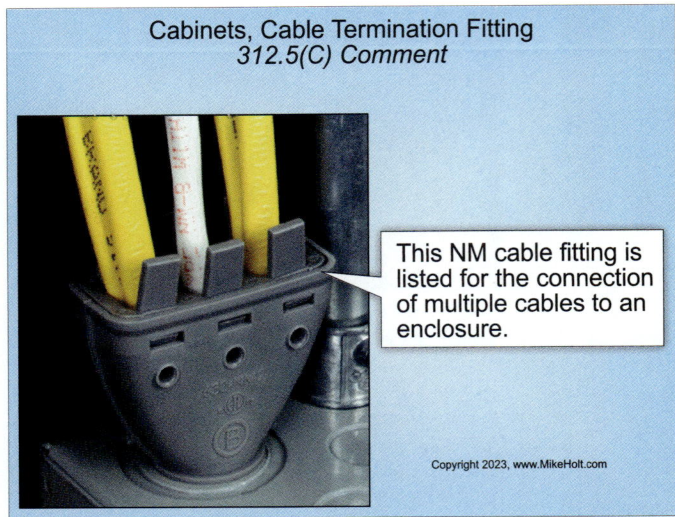

Cabinets, Cable Termination Fitting
312.5(C) Comment

▶Figure 312–10

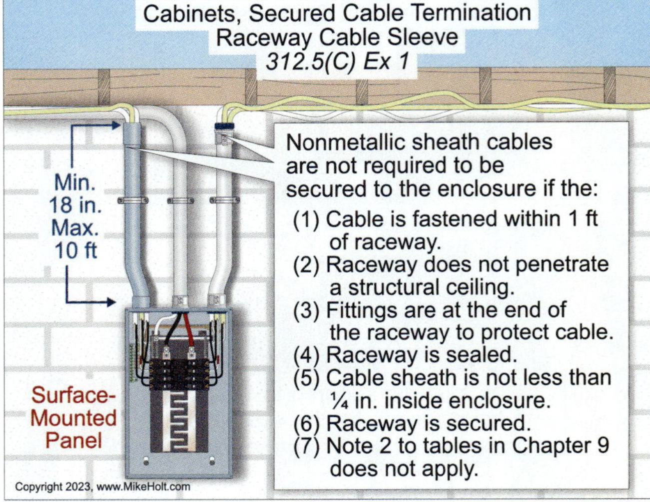

Cabinets, Secured Cable Termination
Raceway Cable Sleeve
312.5(C) Ex 1

▶Figure 312–11

(1) Each cable is fastened within 12 in. of the raceway.

(2) The raceway does not penetrate a structural ceiling.

(3) Fittings are provided on the raceway to protect the cables from abrasion.

(4) The raceway is sealed.

(5) Each cable sheath extends into the enclosure beyond the fitting not less than ¼ in.

(6) The raceway is properly secured.

(7) Where installed as conduit or tubing, Chapter 9, Table 1 Notes 5 and 9 apply. Note 2 to the tables in Chapter 9 does not apply to this condition.

312.6 Deflection of Conductors

Conductors entering or leaving cabinets for panelboards and meter socket enclosures must comply with 312.6(A) and 312.6(B).

(A) Width of Enclosures and Wireways. Conductors are not permitted to be deflected in a cabinet unless a space having a width is provided in accordance with Table 312.6(A). ▶Figure 312–12

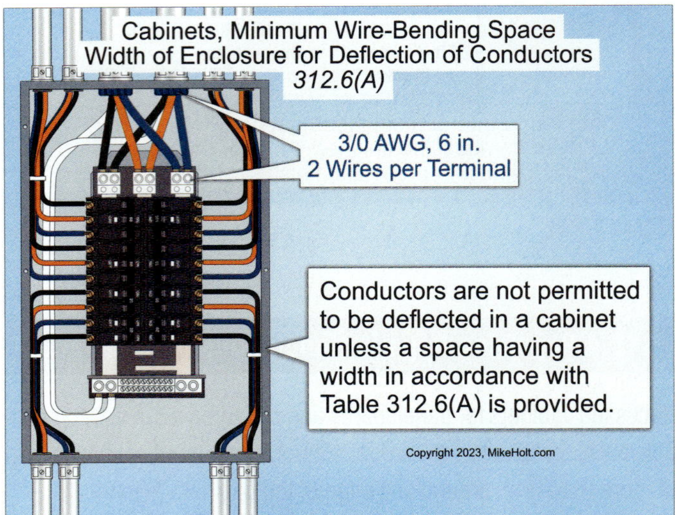

Cabinets, Minimum Wire-Bending Space
Width of Enclosure for Deflection of Conductors
312.6(A)

▶Figure 312–12

Table 312.6(A) Minimum Wire–Bending Space

Wire Size (AWG or kcmil)	Inches
8–6	1½
4–3	2
2	2½
1	3
1/0–2/0	3½
3/0–4/0	4
250	4½
300–350	5
400–500	6
600–700	8

(B) Wire-Bending Space at Terminals.

(2) Conductors Entering or Leaving Opposite Wall. Table 312.6(B)(2) applies where the conductor enters or leaves the cabinet through the wall opposite its terminal. ▶Figure 312–13

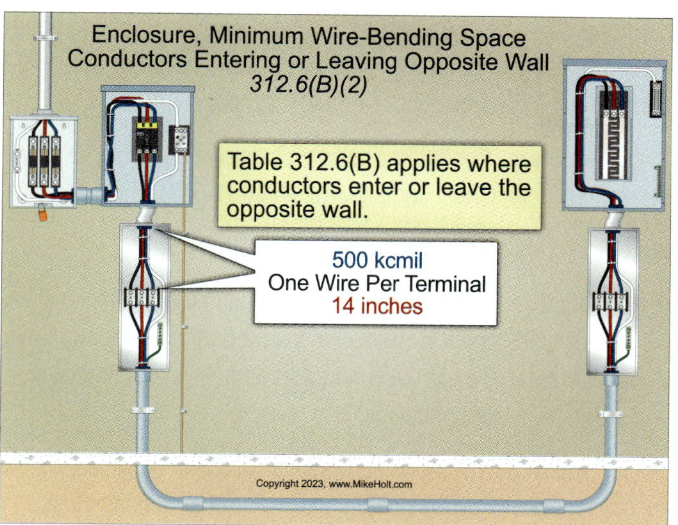

▶Figure 312–13

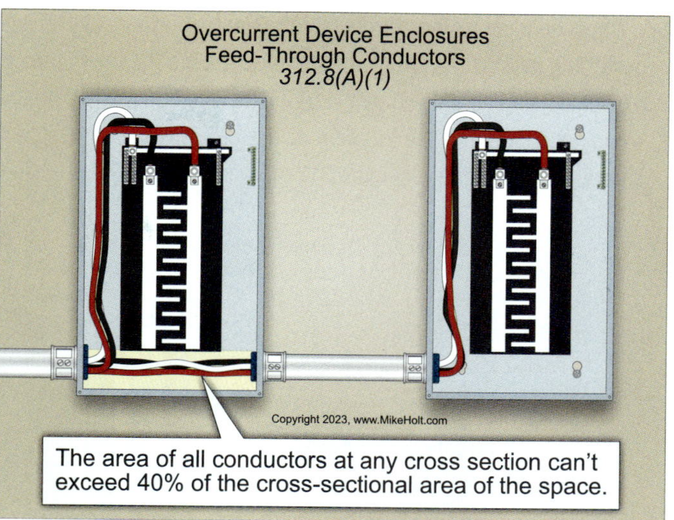

▶Figure 312–14

(2) The area of all conductors, splices, and taps installed at any cross section does not exceed 75 percent of the cross-sectional area of that space. ▶Figure 312–15

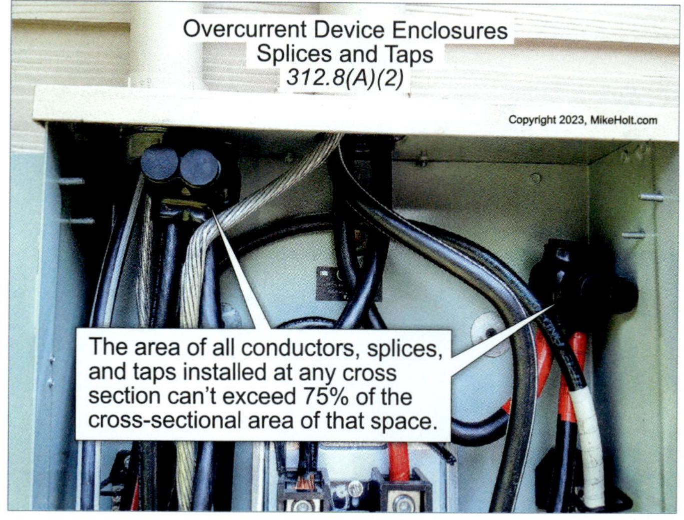

▶Figure 312–15

Table 312.6(B)(2) Minimum Wire–Bending Space	
Wire Size (AWG or kcmil)	Inches
2	3½
1	4½
1/0	5½
3/0	6½
250	8½
350	12
500	14
600	15

312.8 Overcurrent Device Enclosures

Cabinets for panelboards are permitted to contain wiring and other equipment as provided in 312.8 (A) and (B).

(A) Splices, Taps, and Feed-Through Conductors. The wiring space within cabinets for panelboards can be used for conductors feeding through, spliced, or tapped where all the conditions of (1), (2), and (3) are met:

(1) The area of all conductors at any cross section does not exceed 40 percent of the cross-sectional area of that space. ▶Figure 312–14

Author's Comment:

▶ The 40 percent and 75 percent requirements apply to all conductors, all splices, and all taps within the cross-sectional area, not just conductors, splice(s), or tap(s) being added.

(3) The bending space for conductors 4 AWG and larger complies with 314.28(A)(2).

(4) Where conductors feed through the cabinet, a permanently affixed warning label sufficiently durable to withstand the environment involved, and complying with 110.21(B), must be applied on the cabinet to identify the location of the disconnect for the feed-through conductors. ▶Figure 312–16

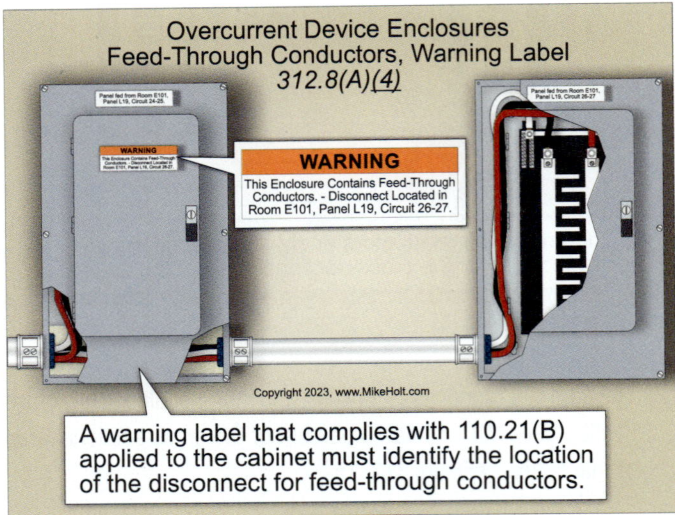

▶Figure 312–16

(B) Power Monitoring or Energy Management Equipment. The wiring space of enclosures for switches or overcurrent protective devices is permitted to contain power monitoring or energy management equipment where all the following conditions are met: ▶Figure 312–17

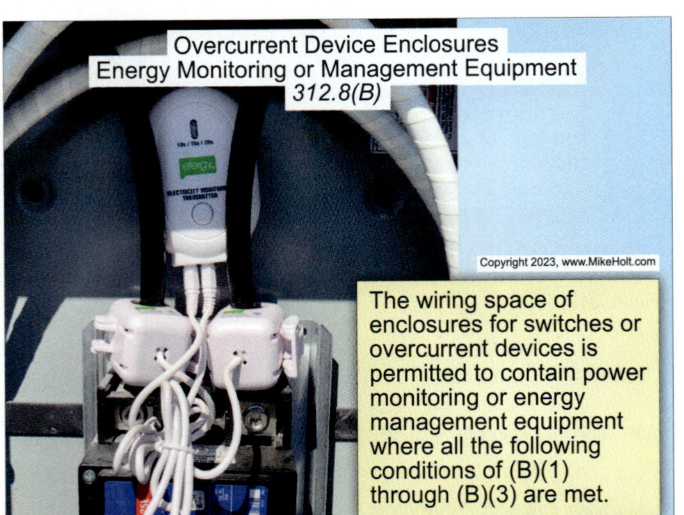

▶Figure 312–17

(1) Identification. Power monitoring or energy management equipment is identified either as a field installable accessory as part of the listed equipment, or is a listed kit evaluated for field installation in switch or overcurrent protective device enclosures.

(2) Area. The total area of all conductors, splices, taps, and equipment at any cross section of the wiring space does not exceed 75 percent of the cross-sectional area of that space.

(3) Conductors. Conductors used exclusively for control or instrumentation circuits must comply with either 312.8(B)(3)(a) or (b).

(a) Conductors must comply with 724.49.

(b) Conductors smaller than 18 AWG, but not smaller than 22 AWG for a single conductor and 26 AWG for a multiconductor cable, are permitted where the conductors and cable assemblies meet all the following conditions:

(1) Are within raceways or routed along one or more walls of the enclosure and secured at intervals not exceeding 10 in.

(2) Are secured within 10 in. of terminations.

(3) Are secured to prevent contact with current-carrying components within the enclosure.

(4) Are rated for the system voltage and not less than 600V.

(5) Have a minimum insulation temperature rating of 90°C.

312.10 Screws or Other Fasteners

Screws or other fasteners installed in the field that enter wiring spaces must be as provided by or specified by the manufacturer, or comply with the following:

(1) Screws must be machine type with blunt ends.

(2) Other fasteners must have blunt ends.

(3) Screws or other fasteners are not permitted to extend into the enclosure more than ¼ in. unless the end is protected with an approved means.

Ex to (3): Screws or other fasteners are permitted to extend into the enclosure not more than ⁷⁄₁₆ in. if within ³⁄₈ in. of an enclosure wall.

Part II. Construction Specifications

312.100 Enclosure Material

(A) Metal Enclosures. Metal enclosures within the scope of this article must be protected both inside and outside against corrosion. ▶Figure 312–18

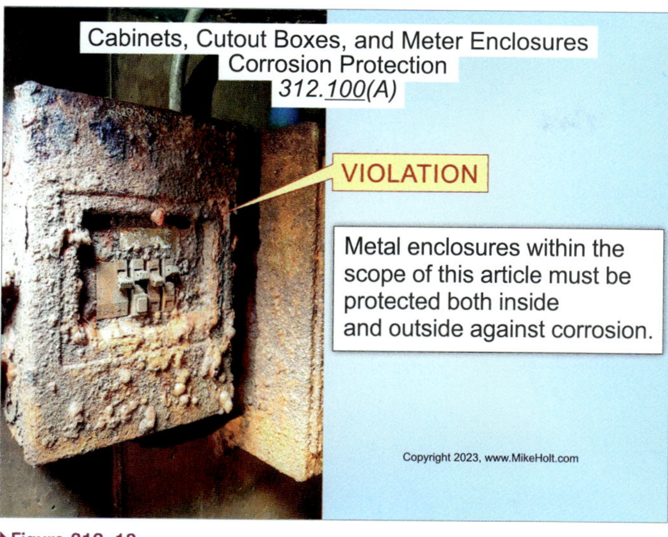

▶Figure 312–18

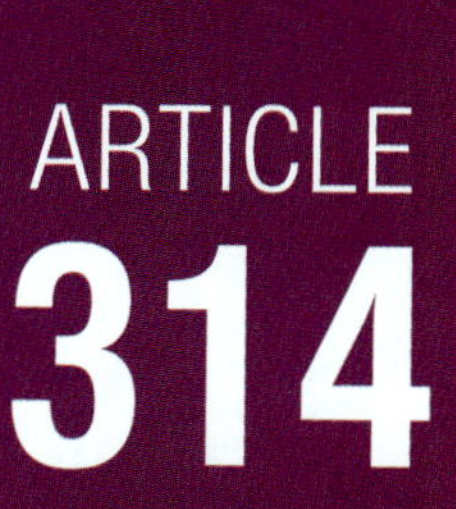

ARTICLE 314

BOXES, CONDUIT BODIES, AND HANDHOLE ENCLOSURES

Introduction to Article 314—Boxes, Conduit Bodies, and Handhole Enclosures

This article contains the installation requirements for outlet and device boxes, pull and junction boxes, conduit bodies, and handhole enclosures. Some topics covered in this material include:

- ▶ Round, Nonmetallic, and Metal Boxes
- ▶ Screws and Fasteners
- ▶ Number of Conductors in a Box or Conduit Body
- ▶ Conductor and Cables Entering Boxes
- ▶ Boxes Enclosing Devices or Equipment
- ▶ Surface- and Flush-Mounted Installations
- ▶ Repairing Noncombustible Surfaces Around Boxes
- ▶ Depth and Dimensions of Boxes
- ▶ Covers and Canopies
- ▶ Outlet Box, Pull Box, Junction Box, and Conduit Body Rules
- ▶ Accessibility

Article 314 consists of four parts:

- ▶ Part I. General
- ▶ Part II. Installation
- ▶ Part III. Use on Systems over 1000 Volts, Nominal (not covered in this material)
- ▶ Part IV. Construction Specifications

Part I. General

314.1 Scope

Article 314 contains the installation requirements for outlet boxes, pull and junction boxes, conduit bodies, and handhole enclosures. This article also includes installation requirements for fittings used to connect raceways and cables to boxes or conduit bodies. ▶Figure 314–1

314.3 Nonmetallic Boxes

Nonmetallic boxes can only be used with nonmetallic cables and raceways.

Ex 1: Metal raceways and metal cables entering nonmetallic boxes must be bonded to the circuit equipment grounding conductor. ▶Figure 314–2

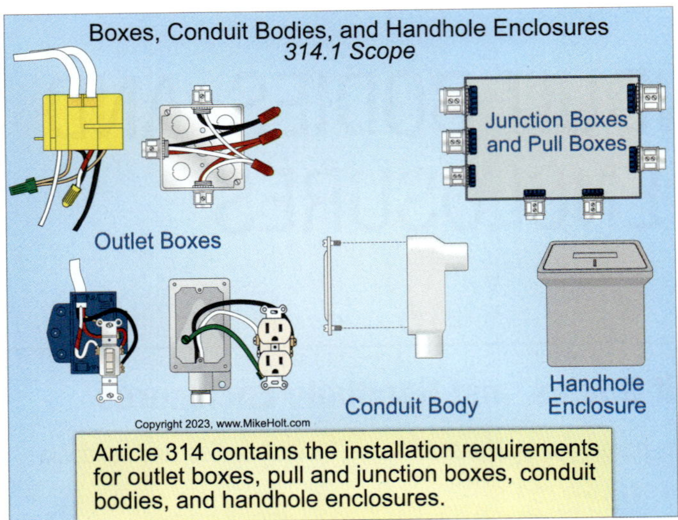

▶Figure 314–1

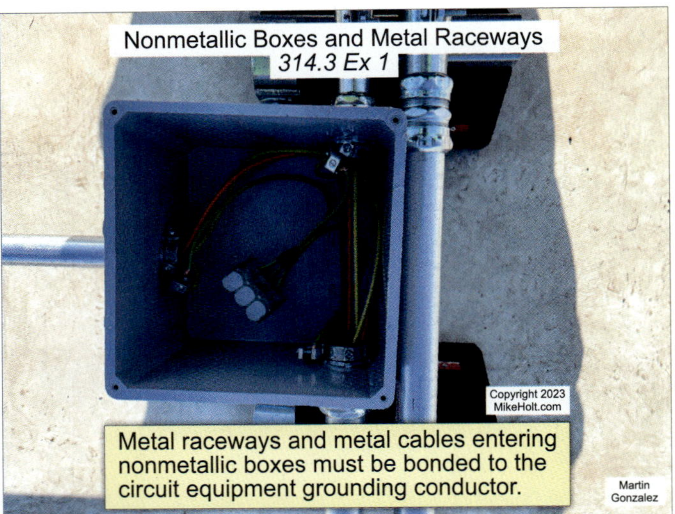

▶Figure 314–2

314.4 Metal Boxes

Metal boxes must be connected to the equipment grounding conductor in accordance with 250.148(C). ▶Figure 314–3

314.5 Screws or Other Fasteners

Screws or other fasteners installed in the field that enter a wiring space must be as provided by the manufacturer, specified by the manufacturer, or comply with the following:

(1) Screws must be machine type with blunt ends.

(2) Other fasteners must have blunt ends.

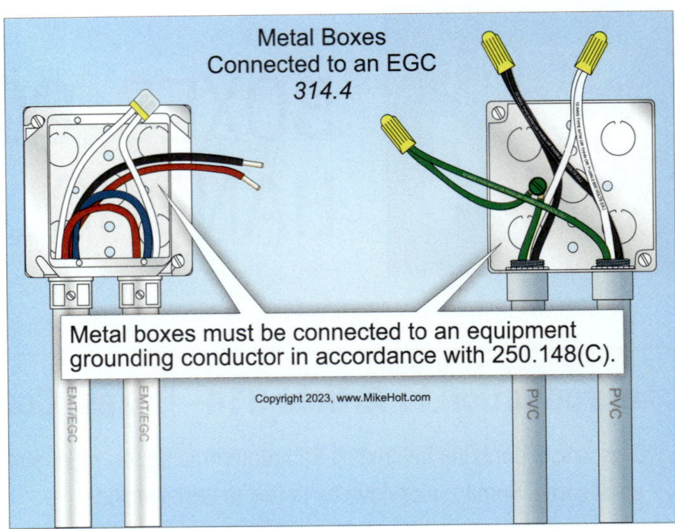

▶Figure 314–3

(3) Screws attaching a cover must extend no more than ⅜ in.

(4) Screws or other fasteners penetrating a cover must extend no more than ⁵⁄₁₆ in.

(5) Screws or other fasteners penetrating a wall of a box exceeding 100 cu in. must extend no more than ¼ in., or more than ⁷⁄₁₆ in. if within ⅜ in. of an adjacent box wall.

(6) Screws or other fasteners penetrating the wall of a box not exceeding 100 cu in. and not covered in 314.23(B)(1) must be made flush with the box interior.

(7) Screws or other fasteners penetrating the wall of a conduit body must be made flush with the conduit body interior.

Ex 1 to (3) through (6): A screw can be longer if the end of the screw is protected with an approved means.

Part II. Installation

314.15 Wet Locations

In wet locations boxes, conduit bodies, and raceway and cable connectors must be listed for use in wet locations. ▶Figure 314–4 and ▶Figure 314–5

314.16 Outlet Box Sizing

Boxes containing 6 AWG and smaller conductors must be sized in an approved manner to provide sufficient free space for all conductors, devices, and fittings. In no case can the volume of the box, as calculated in 314.16(A), be less than the volume requirement as calculated in 314.16(B). ▶Figure 314–6

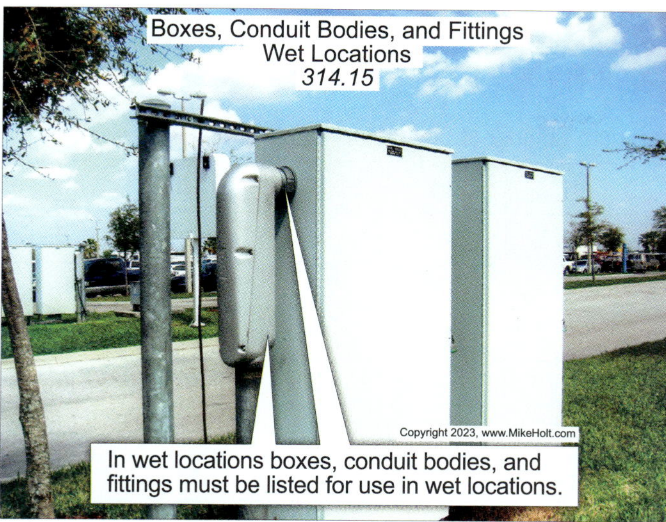

▶Figure 314–4

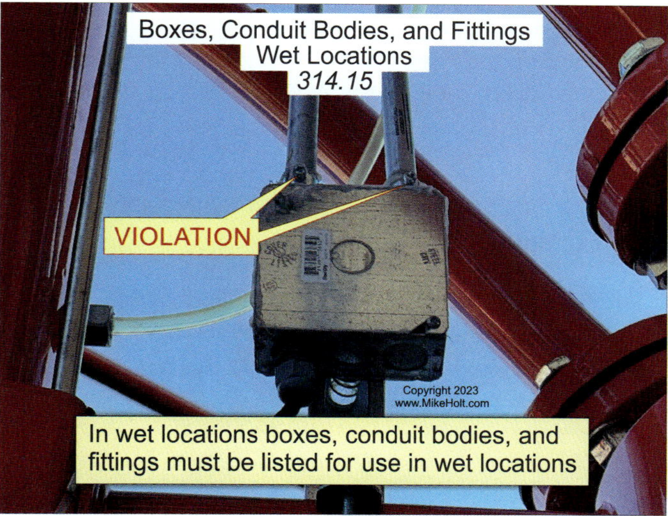

▶Figure 314–5

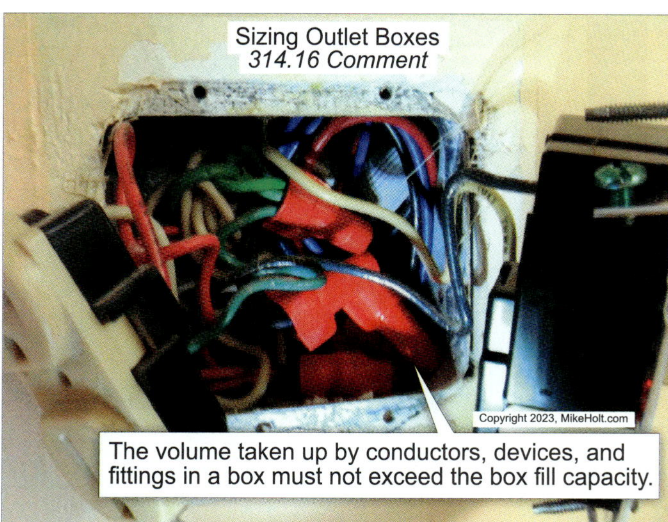

▶Figure 314–6

Author's Comment:

▸ The requirements for sizing boxes and conduit bodies containing conductors 4 AWG and larger are in 314.28, and those for sizing handhole enclosures are contained in 314.30(A). An outlet box is generally used for the attachment of devices and luminaires and has a specific amount of space (volume) for conductors, devices, and fittings. The volume taken up by conductors, devices, and fittings in a box must not exceed the box fill capacity.

Boxes and conduit bodies enclosing conductors 4 AWG or larger must also comply with the provisions of 314.28.

(A) Box Volume. The volume of a box is the total volume of its assembled parts including plaster rings, raised covers, and extension rings. The total volume includes only those parts marked with their volumes in cubic inches listed in Table 314.16(A). ▶Figure 314–7

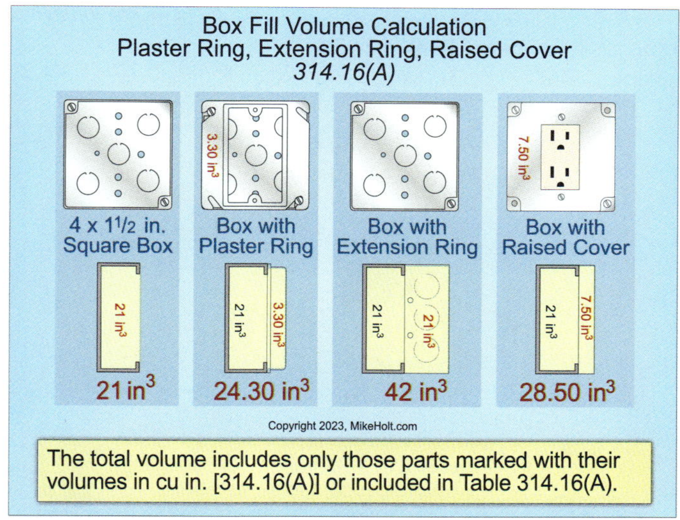

▶Figure 314–7

Table 314.16(A) Metal Boxes*

Box Trade Size		Minimum Volume	Maximum Number of Conductors (arranged by AWG size)					
in.	Box Shape	in³	18	16	14	12	10	8
(4 × 1¼)	round/octagonal	12.50	8	7	6	5	5	4
(4 × 1½)	round/octagonal	15.50	10	8	7	6	6	5
(4 × 2⅛)	round/octagonal	21.50	14	12	10	9	8	7
(4 × 1¼)	square	18.00	12	10	9	8	7	6
(4 × 1½)	square	21.00	14	12	10	9	8	7
(4 × 2⅛)	square	30.30	20	17	15	13	12	10
(41¹⁄₁₆ × 1¼)	square	25.50	17	14	12	11	10	8
(41¹⁄₁₆ × 1½)	square	29.50	19	16	14	13	11	9
(41¹⁄₁₆ × 2⅛)	square	42.00	28	24	21	18	16	14

Table 314.16(A) does not consider switches, receptacles, luminaire studs, luminaire hickeys, cable clamps, or equipment grounding conductors. ▶Figure 314–8

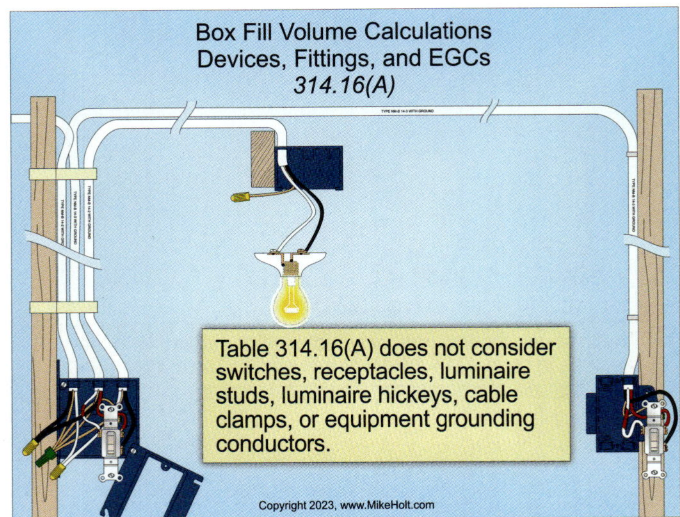

▶Figure 314–8

▶ Example

Question: What is the total box volume for a 4 in. × 4 in. × 1½ in. outlet box and a 4 in. × 4 in. × 1½ in. extension box with a domed cover marked with a 7.50 cu in. volume? ▶Figure 314–9

(a) 44.50 cu in. (b) 46.50 cu in.
(c) 47.50 cu in. (d) 49.50 cu in.

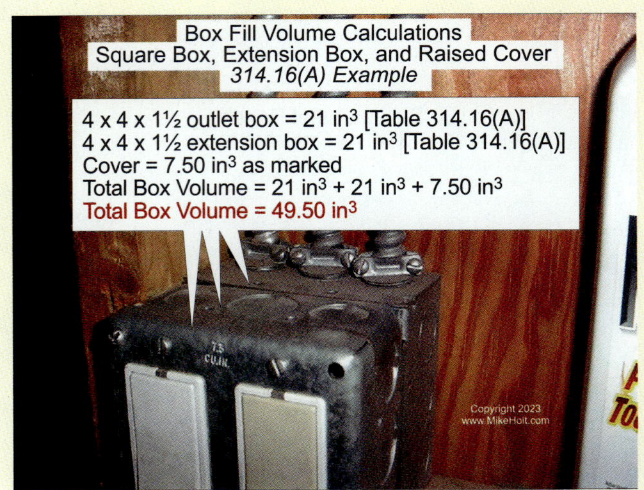

▶Figure 314–9

Solution:

*Volume of a 4 in. × 4 in. × 1½ in. Outlet Box = 21 cu in.
[Table 314.16(A)].*

*Volume of a 4 in. × 4 in. × 1½ in. Extension box = 21 cu in.
[Table 314.16(A)].*

Cover Volume = 7.50 cu in. as marked

Total Box Volume = 21 cu in. + 21 cu in. + 7.50 cu in.

Total Box Volume = 49.50 cu in.

Note: *Do not calculate the actual volume of a box contained in Table 314.16(A) since the table volume is based on the inside dimensions of the box, not the outside dimensions.*

Answer: *(d) 49.50 cu in.*

Where a box is provided with barriers, the volume is apportioned to each of the resulting spaces. Each barrier, if not marked with its volume, is considered to take up ½ cu in. if metal and 1 cu in. if nonmetallic.
▶Figure 314–10

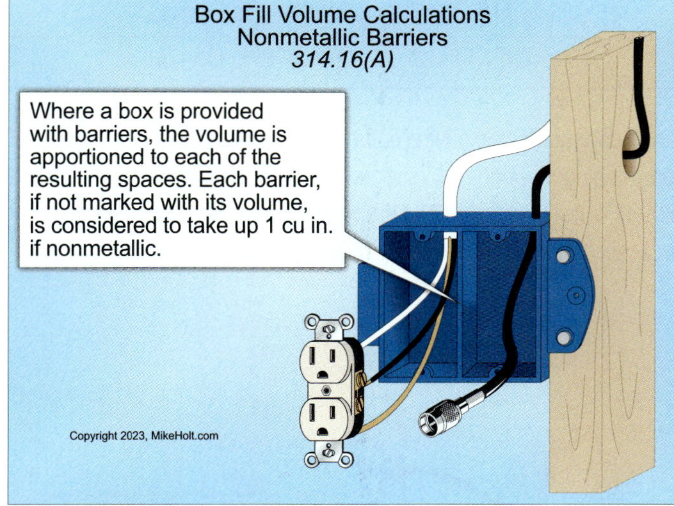

▶Figure 314–10

▶ When all the conductors in an outlet box are the same size (insulation does not matter), Table 314.16(A) can be used to determine the number of conductors permitted in the outlet box, or to determine the required outlet box size for the given number of conductors.

▶ If the outlet box contains switches, receptacles, luminaire studs, luminaire hickeys, cable clamps, or equipment grounding conductors, then allowance must be made for these items which are not reflected in Table 314.16(A).

▶ **Table 314.16(A) Example**

Question: *Which 4-in. square outlet box is the smallest permitted for three 12 AWG, THW conductors and six 12 AWG, THHN conductors?*
▶Figure 314–11

(a) 4 in. × 1¼ in. square 　　　 *(b) 4 in. × 1½ in. square*
(c) 4 in. × 2⅛ in. square 　　　 *(d) 4 in. × 2⅛ in. with extension*

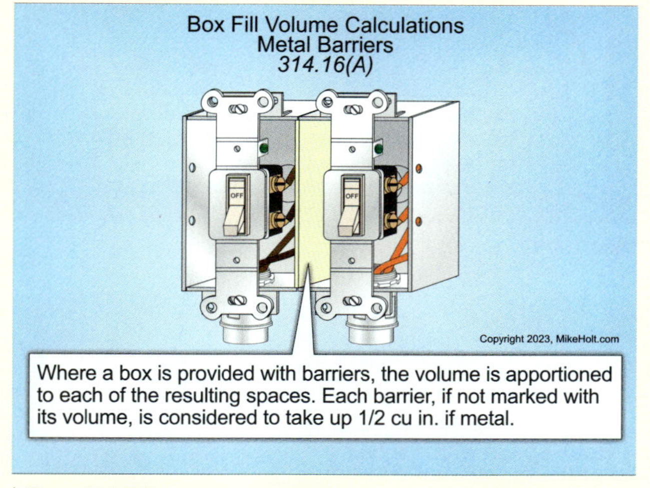

▶Figure 314–11

Answer: *(b) 4 in. × 1½ in. square*

(1) Standard Boxes. Metal boxes not marked with their volume must use the volume from Table 314.16(A).

(2) Nonmetallic Boxes. The volume for nonmetallic boxes must be legibly marked by the manufacturer.

(B) Box Fill Calculations. The calculated conductor volumes determined by 314.16(B)(1) through (B)(6) are added together using Table 314.16(B)(1) to determine the total volume of the conductors, devices, and fittings.

Raceway and cable fittings, including locknuts and bushings, are not counted for box fill calculations. ▶Figure 314–12

Each space within a box with a barrier must be calculated separately. ▶Figure 314–13

(1) Conductor Volume. Each conductor that originates outside the box and terminates or is spliced inside the box counts as a single conductor volume as shown in Table 314.16(B)(1). ▶Figure 314–14

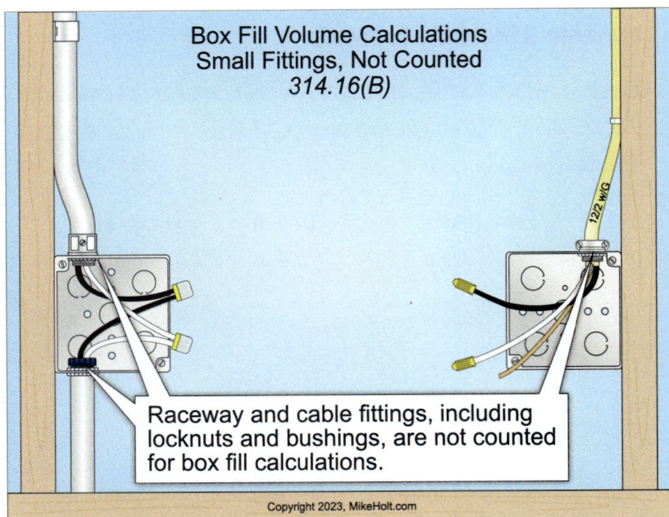

▶Figure 314–12

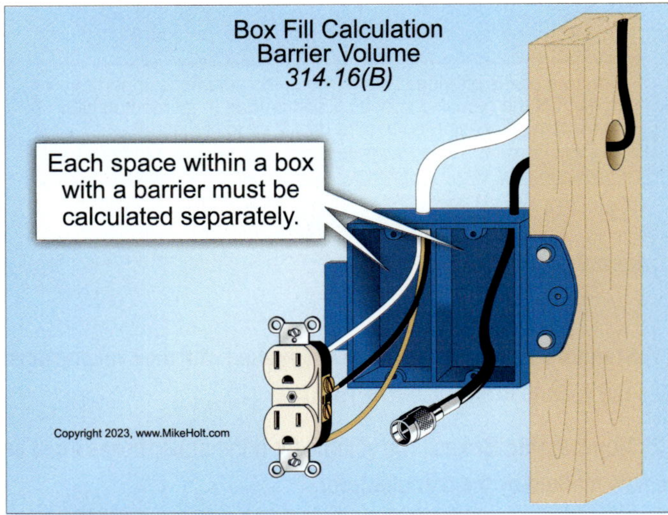

▶Figure 314–13

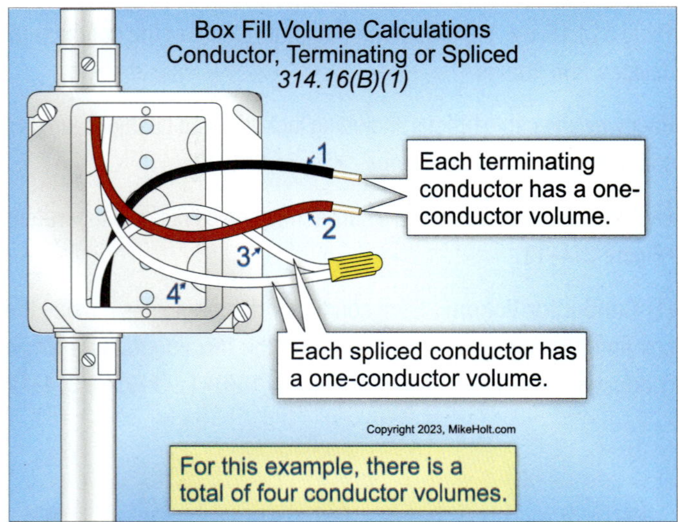

▶Figure 314–14

▸ Table 314.6(B)(1) lists the conductor cu in. volumes for 18 AWG through 6 AWG. For example, one 14 AWG conductor has a volume of 2 cu in. If a box has four 14 AWG conductors, the conductor volume is 8 cu in.

▸ Conductor insulation is not a factor for box fill calculations.

Table 314.16(B)(1) Volume Allowance Required per Conductor	
Conductor AWG Size	Free Space Required for Each Conductor (cu in.)
18	1.50
16	1.75
14	2.00
12	2.25
10	2.50
8	3.00
6	5.00

Each conductor loop having a total length of less than 12 in. is considered a single conductor volume, and each conductor loop having a length of not less than 12 in. is considered as two conductor volumes in accordance with Table 314.16(B)(1). ▶Figure 314–15

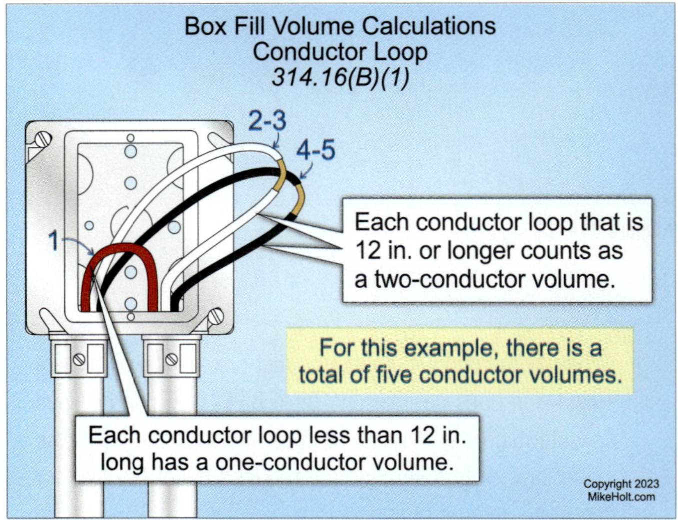

▶Figure 314–15

Author's Comment:

▸ At least 6 in. of conductor, measured from the point in the box where the conductor enters the enclosure, must be available at each point for conductor splices or terminations. ▸Figure 314–16

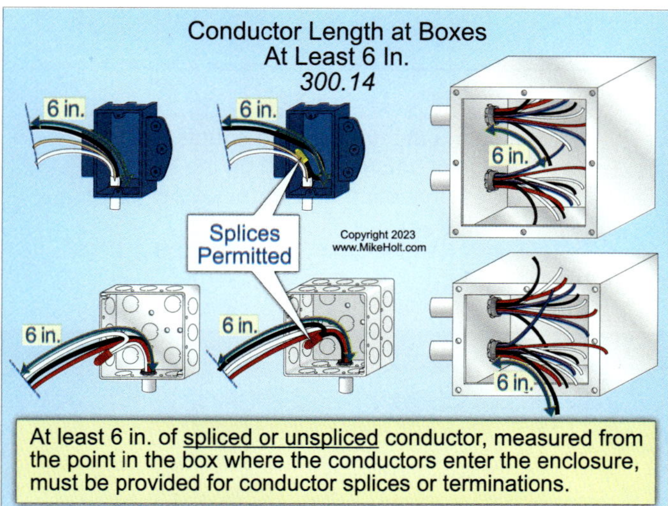

At least 6 in. of spliced or unspliced conductor, measured from the point in the box where the conductors enter the enclosure, must be provided for conductor splices or terminations.

▸Figure 314–16

▸ Boxes having openings of less than 8 in. in any dimension must have at least 6 in. of conductor, measured from the point where the conductor enters the box, and at least 3 in. of conductor outside the box. ▸Figure 314–17

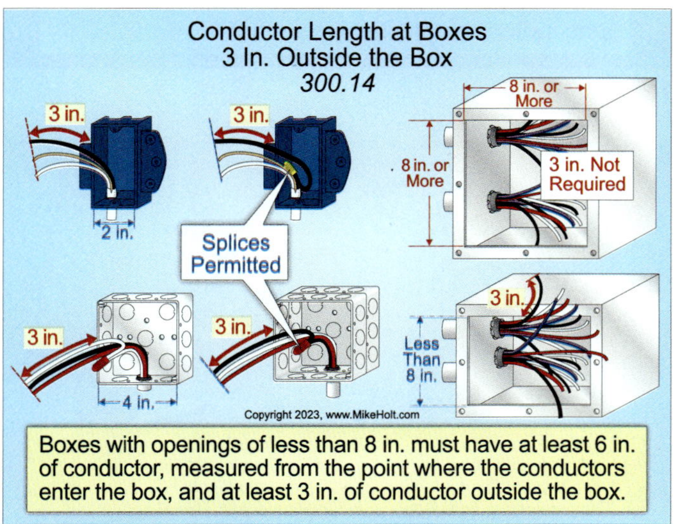

Boxes with openings of less than 8 in. must have at least 6 in. of conductor, measured from the point where the conductors enter the box, and at least 3 in. of conductor outside the box.

▸Figure 314–17

Conductors that originate and terminate within the box, such as pigtails and bonding jumpers, are not counted as a conductor volume. ▸Figure 314–18

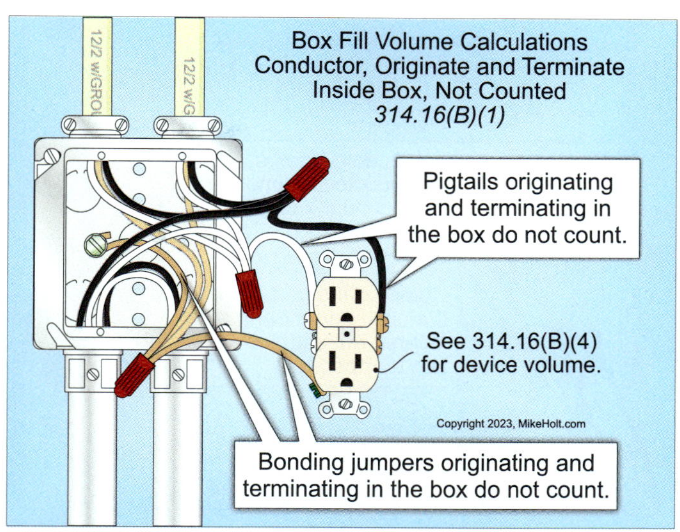

▸Figure 314–18

Ex: Equipment grounding conductors, circuit conductors, and not more than four fixture wires smaller than 14 AWG are not counted as a conductor volume if they enter the box from a domed luminaire or similar canopy, such as a ceiling paddle fan canopy. ▸Figure 314–19

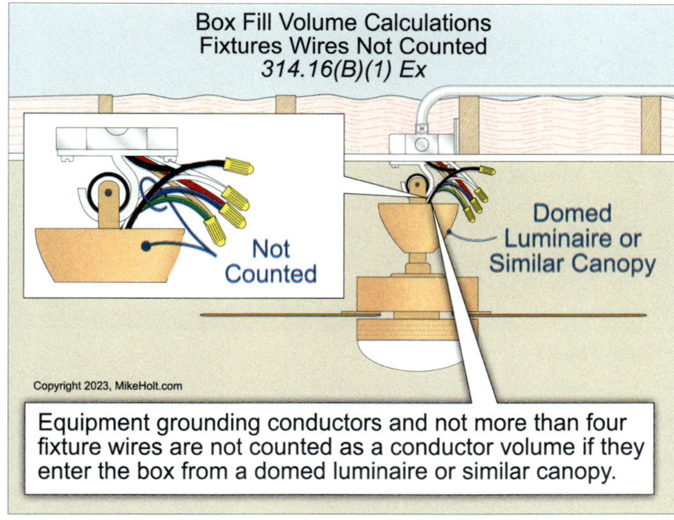

Equipment grounding conductors and not more than four fixture wires are not counted as a conductor volume if they enter the box from a domed luminaire or similar canopy.

▸Figure 314–19

(2) Cable Clamp Volume. Cable clamps that are part of the outlet box are counted as a single conductor volume based on the largest conductor in the box in accordance with Table 314.16(B)(1). ▸Figure 314–20

(3) Support Fitting Volume. Each luminaire stud or luminaire hickey counts as a single conductor volume based on the largest conductor that enters the box in accordance with Table 314.16(B)(1). ▸Figure 314–21

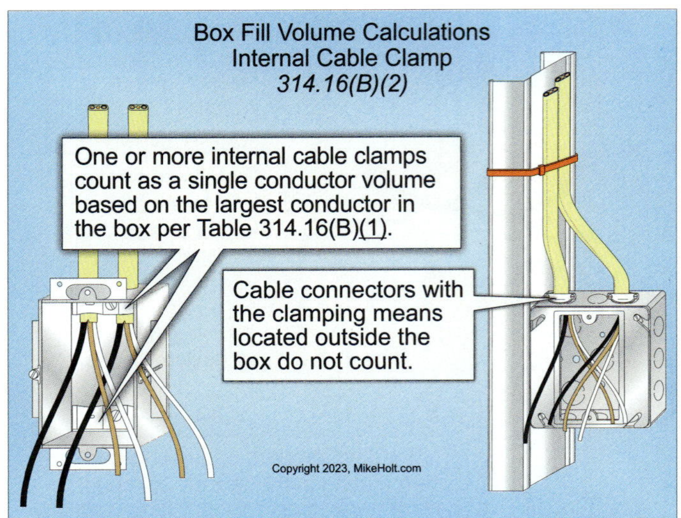

▶Figure 314–20

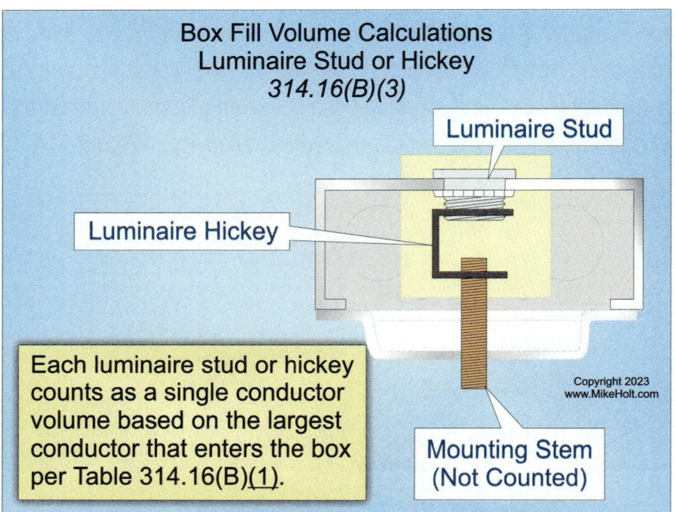

▶Figure 314–21

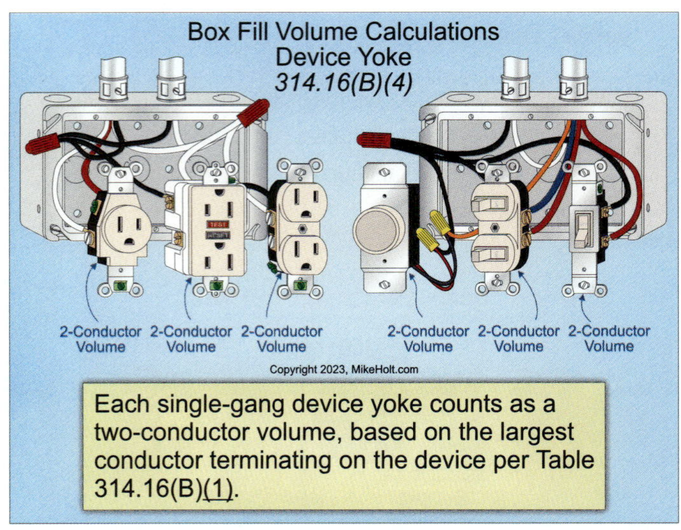

▶Figure 314–22

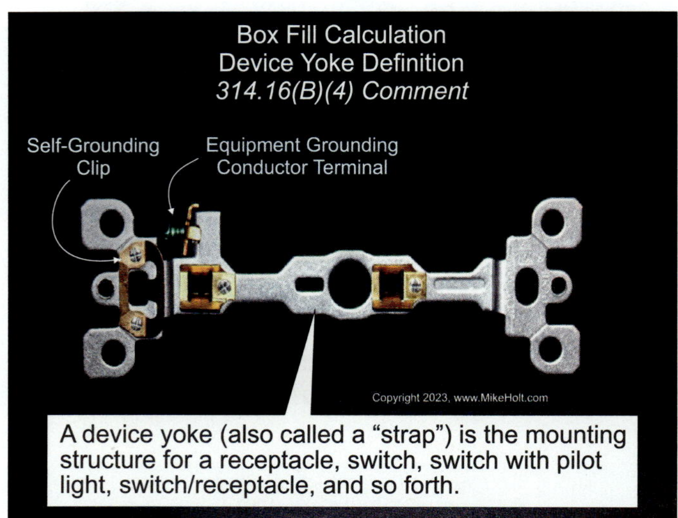

▶Figure 314–23

(4) Device Yoke Volume. Each single-gang device yoke counts as two conductor volumes based on the largest conductor that terminates on the device in accordance with Table 314.16(B)(1). ▶Figure 314–22

Author's Comment:

▶ A device yoke (also called a "strap") is the mounting structure for a receptacle, switch, switch with pilot light, switch/receptacle, and so forth. ▶Figure 314–23

Each device yoke wider than 2 in. counts as a two-conductor volume for each gang required for mounting, based on the largest conductor that terminates on the device in accordance with Table 314.16(B)(1). ▶Figure 314–24

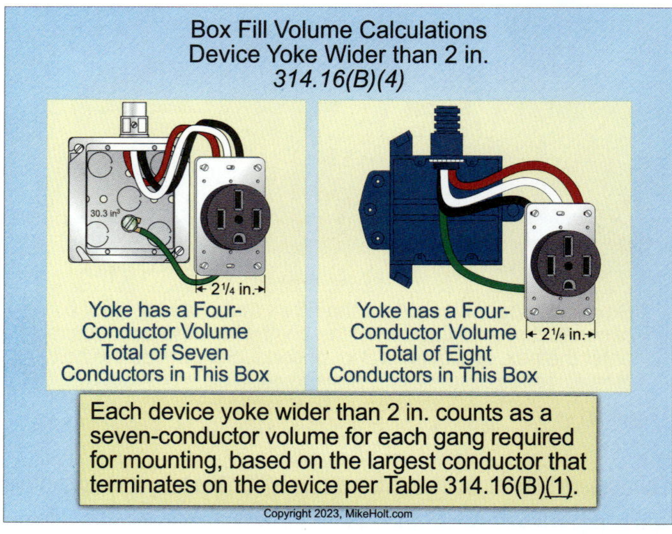

▶Figure 314–24

(5) Equipment Grounding Conductor Volume. Up to four equipment grounding conductors count as a single conductor volume, based on the largest equipment grounding conductor entering the box in accordance with Table 314.16(B)(1).

A ¼ volume allowance applies for each additional equipment grounding conductor that enters the box, based on the largest equipment grounding conductor. ▶Figure 314–25

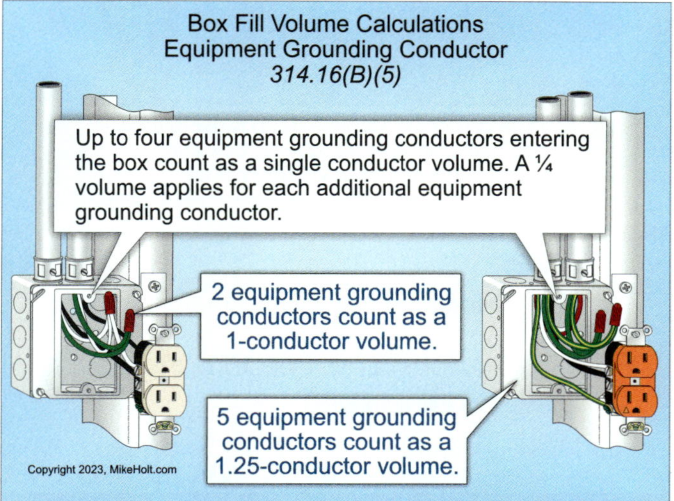

▶Figure 314–25

▶ Number of Conductors Example

Question: What is the volume fill for a 4-gang box containing four 14/2 NM cables and one 14/3 NM cable, three single-pole switches, and one three-way switch? ▶Figure 314–26

(a) 35.50 cu in. (b) 37.50 cu in.   (c) 39.50 cu in.   (d) 40.50 cu in.

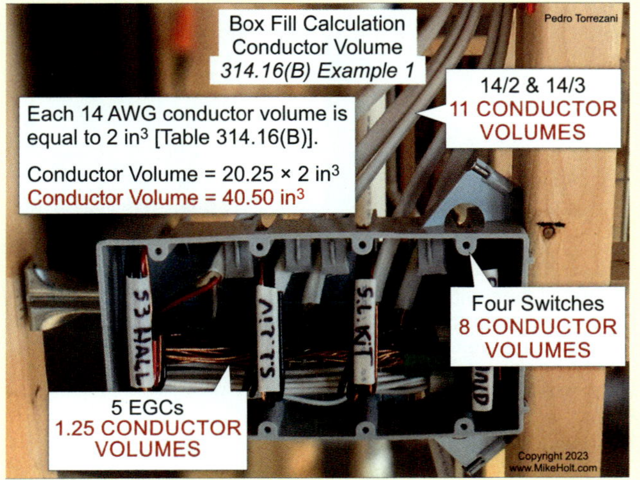

▶Figure 314–26

Solution:

Four 14/2 NM Cables	*8–14 AWG conductor volumes*
One 14/3 NM Cable	*3–14 AWG conductor volumes*
Five EGCs	*1.25–14 AWG conductor volumes*
Four Switches	*+ 8–14 AWG conductor volumes*
Total	*20.25–14 AWG conductor volumes*

Each 14 AWG conductor volume is equal to 2 cu in. [Table 312.6(B)(1)].

20.25 conductor volumes × 2 cu in. = 40.50 cu in.

Answer: *(d) 40.50 cu in.*

▶ Box Fill Example

Question: *How many 14 AWG conductors can be pulled through a 4-in. square × 2⅛ in. deep box with a plaster ring marked 3.60 cu in.? The box contains two receptacles, five 12 AWG conductors, and two 12 AWG equipment grounding conductors.* ▶Figure 314–27

(a) 4 conductors   *(b) 5 conductors*
(c) 6 conductors   *(d) 7 conductors*

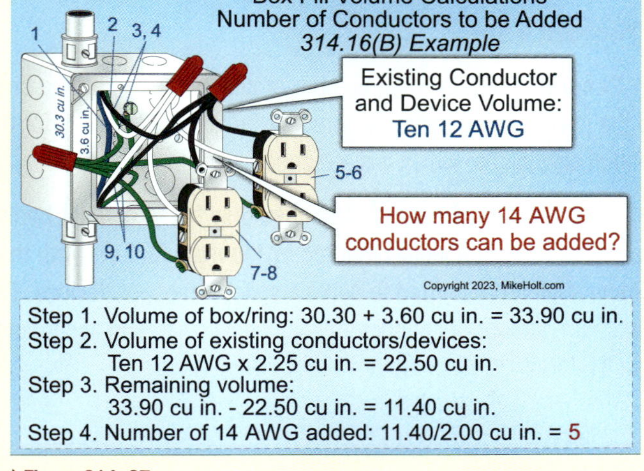

▶Figure 314–27

Solution:

Step 1: *Determine the volume of the box assembly [314.16(A)].*

Box Assembly Volume = Box 30.30 cu in. + 3.60 cu in. plaster ring
Box Assembly Volume = 33.90 cu in

• • •

Step 2: Determine the volume of the devices and conductors in the box.

Two–receptacles	4–12 AWG
Five–12 AWG conductors	5–12 AWG
Two–12 AWG equipment grounding conductors	1–12 AWG
	10–12 AWG

Total Device Volume and Conductors = 10–12 AWG × 2.25 cu in.
Total Device Volume and Conductors = 22.50 cu in.

Step 3: Determine the remaining volume permitted for the 14 AWG conductors (volume of the box minus the volume of the conductors).

Remaining Volume = 33.90 cu in. – 22.50 cu in.
Remaining Volume = 11.40 cu in.

Step 4: Determine the number of 14 AWG conductors (at 2.00 cu in. each) permitted in the remaining volume of 11.40 cu in.:

14 AWG = 2.00 cu in. each [Table 312.6(B)(1)]

11.40 cu in./2.00 cu in. = 5 conductors

Five 14 AWG conductors can be pulled through.

Answer: (b) 5 conductors

(C) Conduit Bodies.

(1) General. The maximum number of conductors permitted shall be the maximum number permitted by Table 1 of Chapter 9 for the conduit or tubing to which it is attached.

(2) With Splices, Taps, or Devices. Only those conduit bodies that are durably and legibly marked by the manufacturer with their volume shall be permitted to contain splices, taps, or devices. The maximum number of conductors shall be calculated in accordance with 314.16(B).

314.17 Cables That Enter Boxes

(B) Boxes. The installation of cables in boxes must comply with the following:

(2) Cables Entering Through Cable Clamps. Where cable assemblies (Type NM or UF) are used, the sheath must extend not less than ¼ in. inside the box and beyond the end of any cable clamp. ▶Figure 314–28

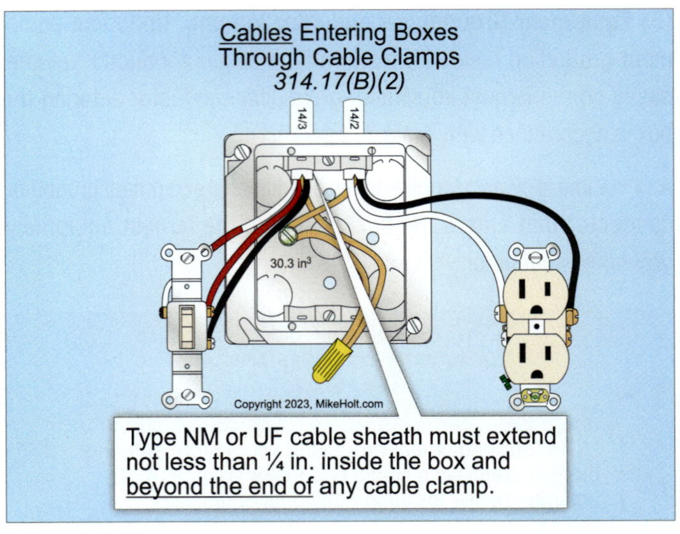

▶Figure 314–28

Author's Comment:

▶ Two Type NM cables can terminate in a single cable clamp if it is listed for this purpose.

314.20 Flush-Mounted Boxes

Noncombustible Walls and Ceilings. Installation within walls or ceilings finished with a noncombustible material must have the front edge of the box, plaster ring, extension ring, or listed extender set back no more than ¼ in. from the finished surface. ▶Figure 314–29

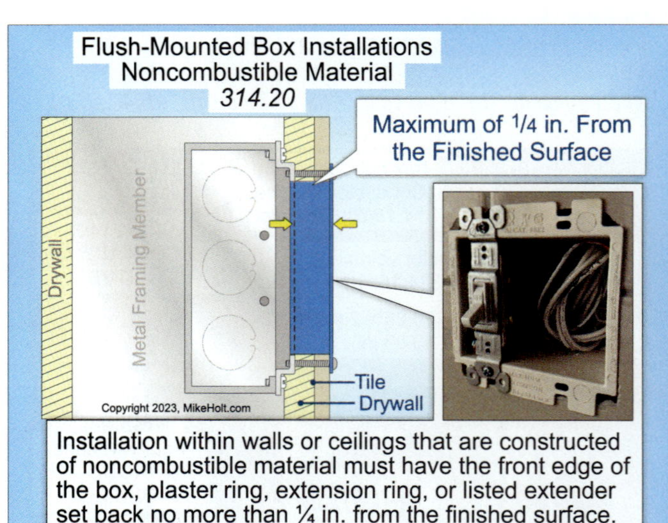

▶Figure 314–29

Combustible Walls and Ceilings. Installation within walls or ceilings constructed of wood or other combustible material must have the front edge of the box, plaster ring, extension ring, or listed extender extend to, or project out from, the finished surface. ▶Figure 314–30

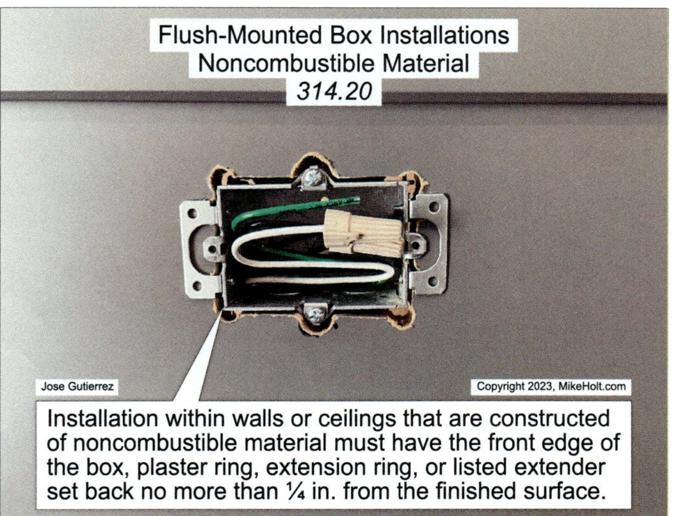

▶Figure 314–30

Author's Comment:

▶ Plaster rings and extension rings are available in a variety of depths to meet the above requirements.

▶ Final finished surfaces such as backsplashes and tile may need the use of listed extenders to meet the requirements of this section.

314.21 Repairing Noncombustible Surfaces

Gaps around boxes that are recessed in noncombustible surfaces (such as plaster, drywall, or plasterboard) must be repaired so there will be no gap greater than ⅛ in. at the edge of the box. ▶Figure 314–31

Author's Comment:

▶ Other examples of noncombustible surfaces include ceramic wall tile, ceramic or marble floor tile, brick, cinder block, and other types of masonry or stone. All these examples are subject to the requirements of 314.20 and 314.21.

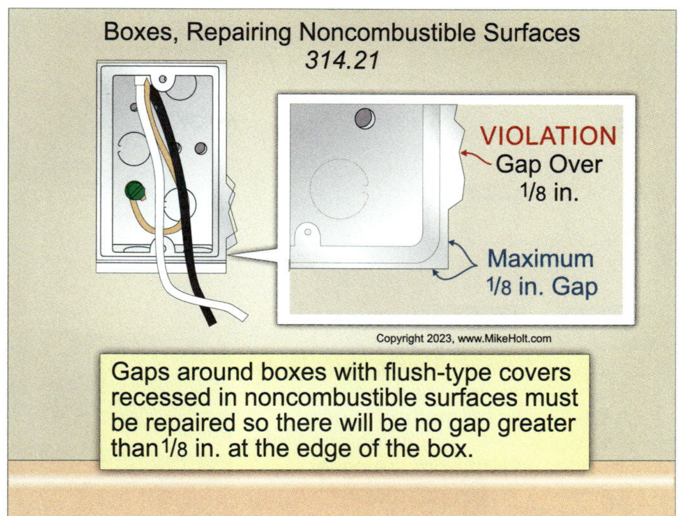

▶Figure 314–31

314.22 Surface Extensions

Surface extensions can only be made from an extension ring installed over a box. ▶Figure 314–32

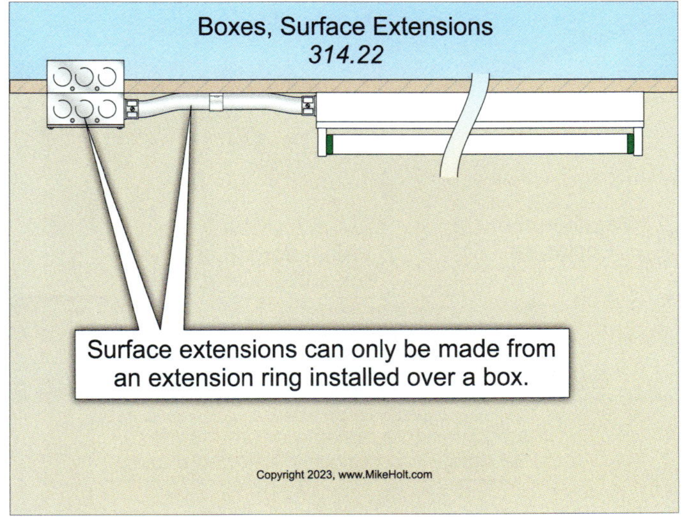

▶Figure 314–32

Ex: A surface extension can be made from the cover of a box if the cover is designed so it is unlikely to fall off if mounting screws become loose. The surface extension wiring method must be flexible to permit the removal of the cover, provide access to the box interior, and the equipment grounding continuity must be independent of the connection between the box and the cover. ▶Figure 314–33

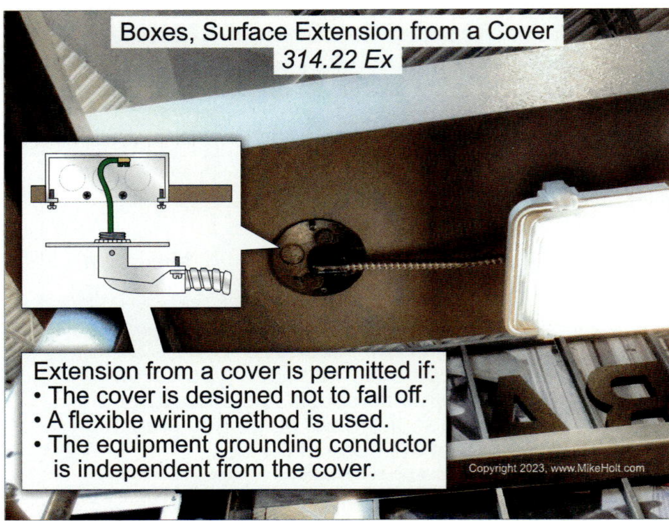

▶Figure 314–33

314.23 Securing Boxes

(A) Securing Boxes to Surface. Boxes secured to a building or other surface must be rigidly and securely fastened in place. ▶Figure 314–34

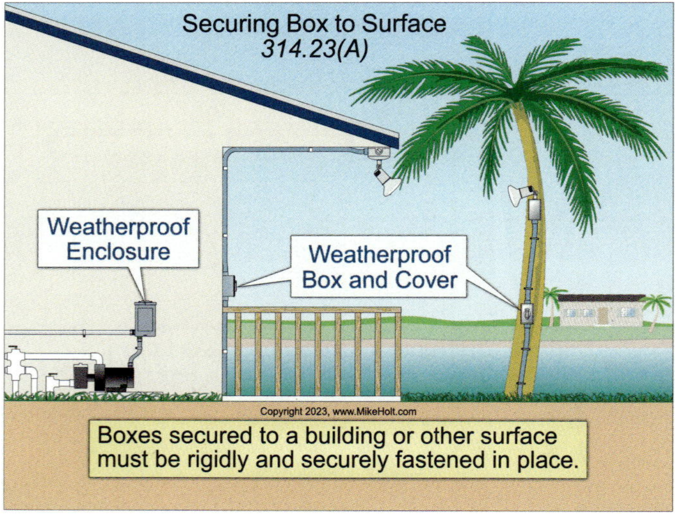

▶Figure 314–34

(B) Securing Boxes to Structural Member. A box can be secured to a structural member or from grade using a metal or wood brace.

(2) Braces. Boxes can be secured to a metal, plastic, or wood brace.

Metal Braces. Boxes can be secured to metal braces that has protection against corrosion. ▶Figure 314–35

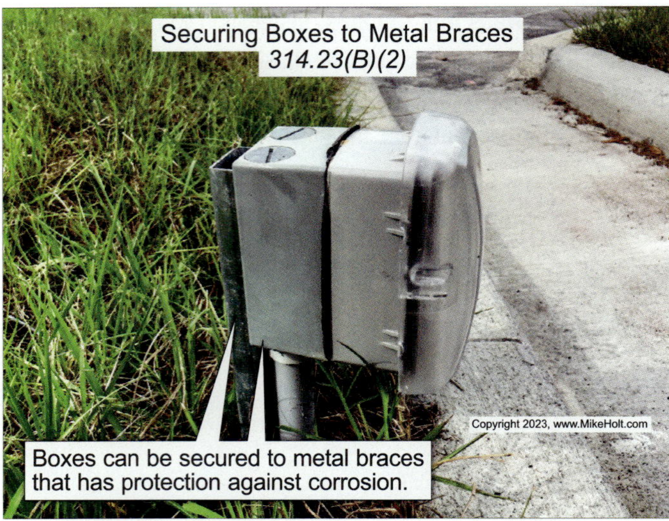

▶Figure 314–35

Wood Brace. Boxes can be secured to wood braces not less than a nominal 1 in. × 2 in. ▶Figure 314–36

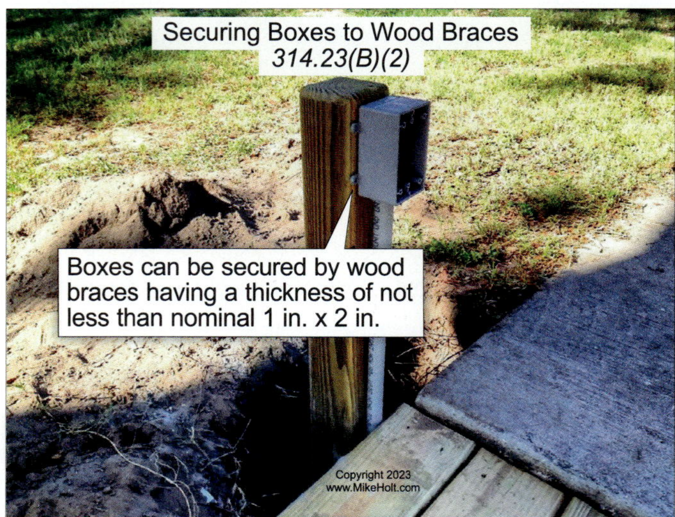

▶Figure 314–36

(C) Securing Boxes to Finished Surface. Boxes can be secured to a finished surface (drywall, plaster walls, or ceilings) by clamps or fittings identified for the purpose. ▶Figure 314–37

(D) Securing Boxes to Suspended-Ceiling. Outlet boxes can be secured to supporting elements of a suspended ceiling by any of the following methods:

(1) Ceiling Framing Members. An outlet box can be secured to suspended-ceiling framing members by bolts, screws, rivets, clips, or other means identified for the suspended-ceiling framing member(s). ▶Figure 314–38

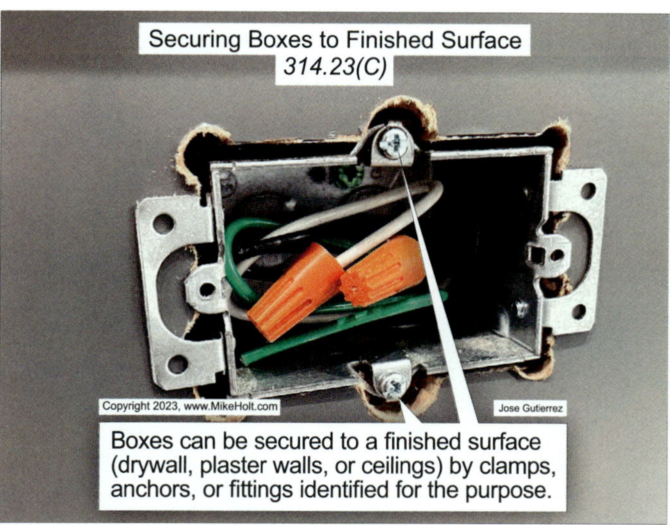

▶Figure 314–37

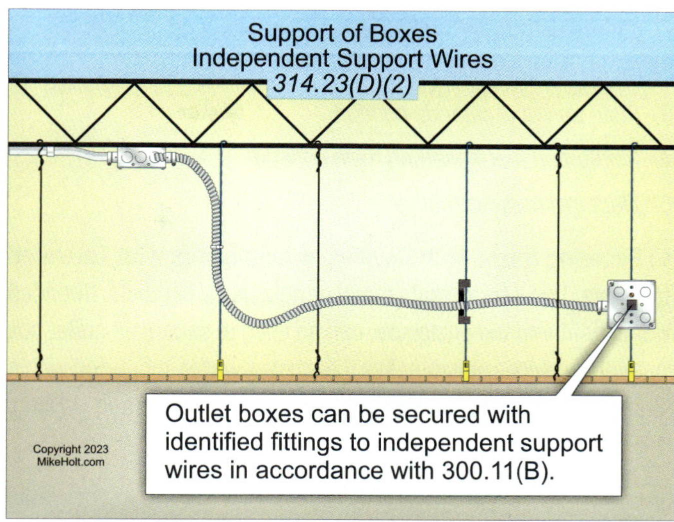

▶Figure 314–39

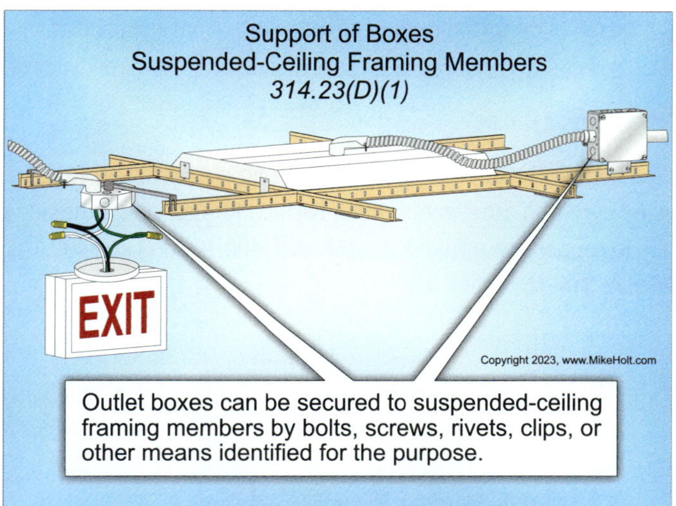

▶Figure 314–38

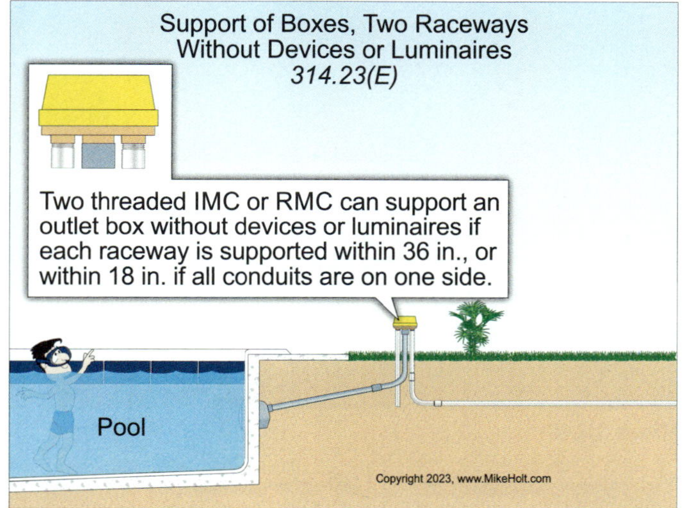

▶Figure 314–40

(2) Independent Support Wires. Outlet boxes can be secured with identified fittings to independent support wires in accordance with 300.11(B). ▶Figure 314–39

(E) Securing Boxes without Devices or Luminaires with Threaded Raceway. Two intermediate metal or rigid metal conduits, threaded wrenchtight into the enclosure, can be used to secure an outlet box that does not contain a device or luminaire if each raceway is supported within 36 in. of the box or within 18 in. of the box if all conduit entries are on the same side of the box. ▶Figure 314–40

Ex: The following wiring methods are permitted to support a conduit body with only one conduit entry, provided the size of the conduit body is not larger than the largest size of the conduit or tubing: ▶Figure 314–41

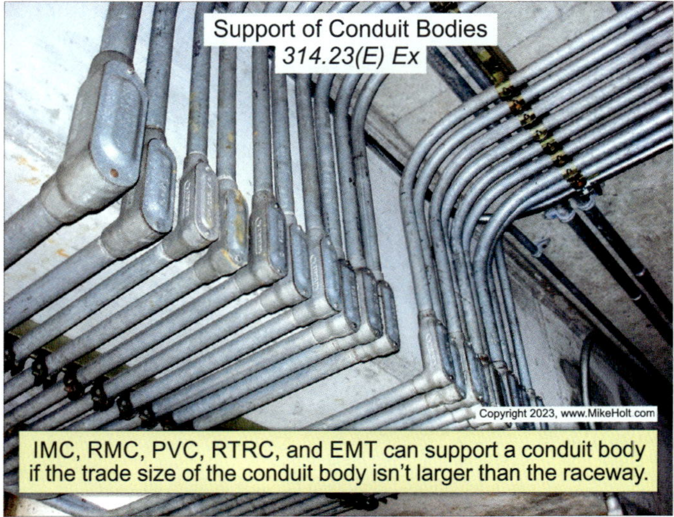

▶Figure 314–41

(1) Intermediate metal conduit

(2) Rigid metal conduit

(3) Rigid polyvinyl chloride conduit

(4) Reinforced thermosetting resin conduit

(5) Electrical metallic tubing

(F) Securing Boxes with Devices or Luminaires with Threaded Raceway. Two intermediate metal or rigid metal conduits, threaded wrenchtight into the enclosure, can be used to secure an outlet box containing devices or luminaires if each raceway is supported within 18 in. of the box. ▶Figure 314–42, ▶Figure 314–43, and ▶Figure 314–44

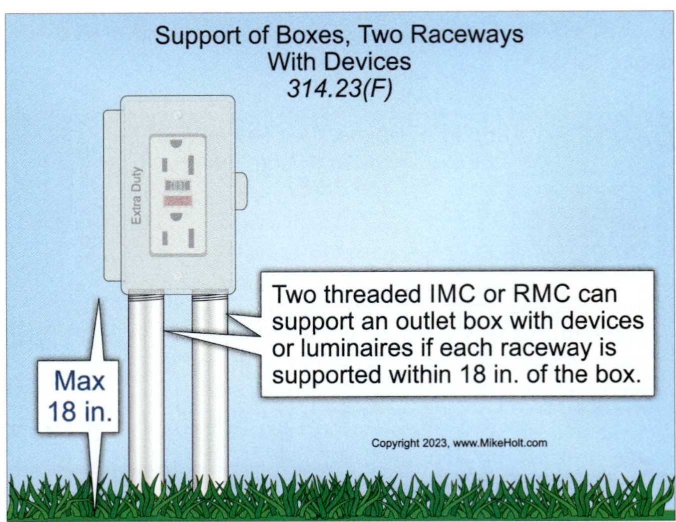

▶Figure 314–42

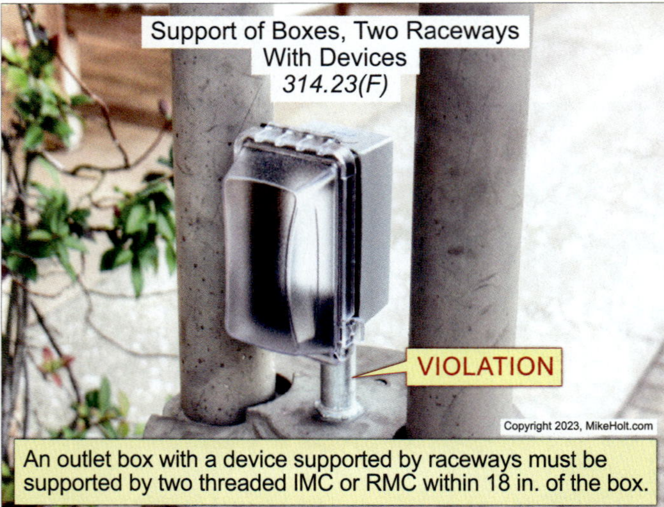

▶Figure 314–43

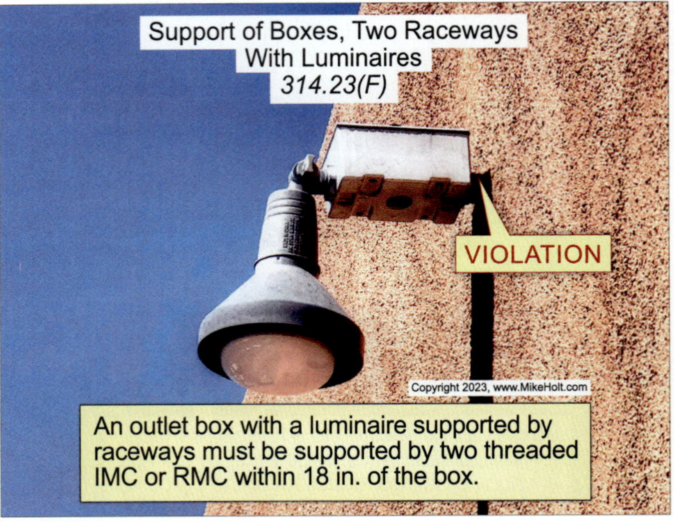

▶Figure 314–44

(G) Boxes in Concrete or Masonry. Boxes that are identified as suitably protected from corrosion can be embedded in concrete or masonry.

(H) Pendant Boxes.

(1) Flexible Cord. Boxes containing a hub are permitted to use a listed cord grip attachment fitting marked for use with a threaded hub to support a box from a flexible cord [400.10(A)(1) and 400.14]. ▶Figure 314–45

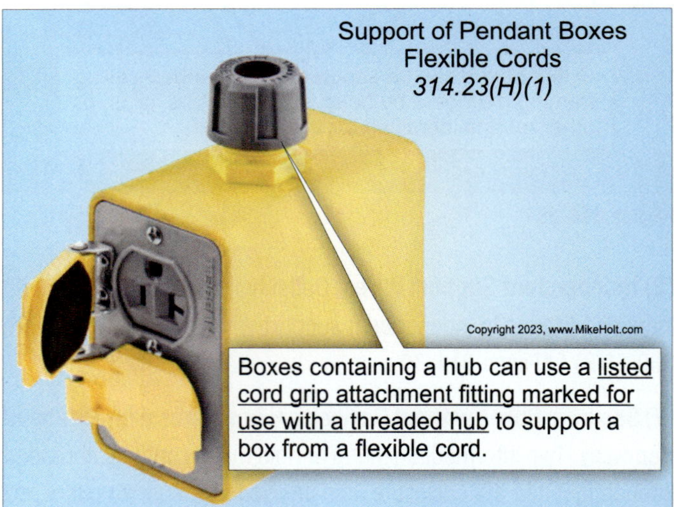

▶Figure 314–45

314.27 Box Requirements

(A) Boxes for Luminaires.

(1) Boxes for Luminaires in or on Vertical Surfaces. Boxes designed for the support of luminaires ($\frac{8}{32}$ screws for mounting) in or on a vertical surface must be identified and marked on the interior of the box to indicate the maximum weight of the luminaire that can be supported by the box if other than 50 lb. ▶Figure 314–46

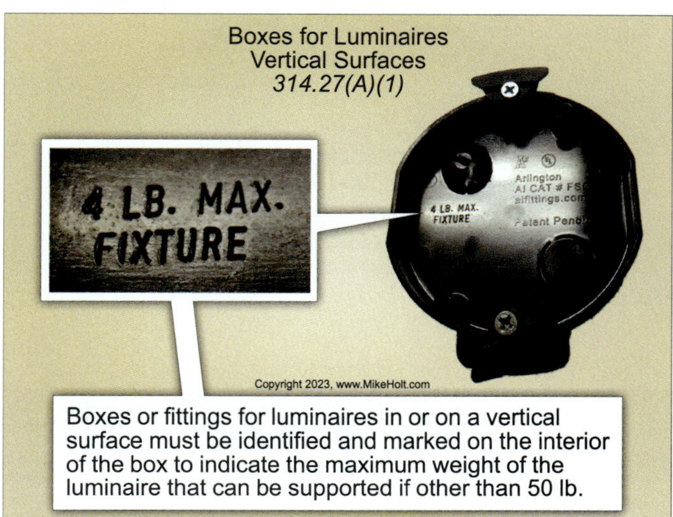

Boxes or fittings for luminaires in or on a vertical surface must be identified and marked on the interior of the box to indicate the maximum weight of the luminaire that can be supported if other than 50 lb.

▶Figure 314–46

Ex: A vertically mounted luminaire weighing no more than 6 lb can be supported to a device box or plaster ring ($\frac{6}{32}$ screws for mounting) secured to a device box, provided the luminaire or its supporting yoke is secured to the box with no fewer than two No. 6 or larger screws. ▶Figure 314–47

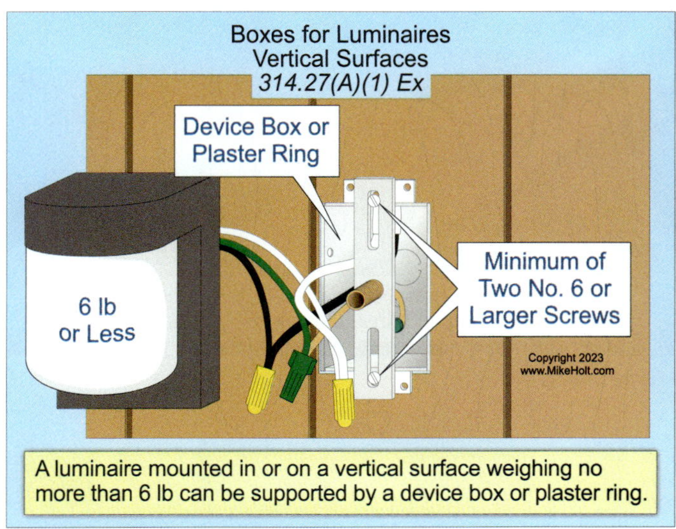

A luminaire mounted in or on a vertical surface weighing no more than 6 lb can be supported by a device box or plaster ring.

▶Figure 314–47

(2) Boxes for Luminaires in a Ceiling. Boxes for ceiling luminaires must be listed and marked to support a luminaire weighing a minimum of 50 lb.

Luminaires weighing more than 50 lb must be supported independently of the outlet box unless it is listed and marked on the interior of the box by the manufacturer for the maximum weight it can support. ▶Figure 314–48

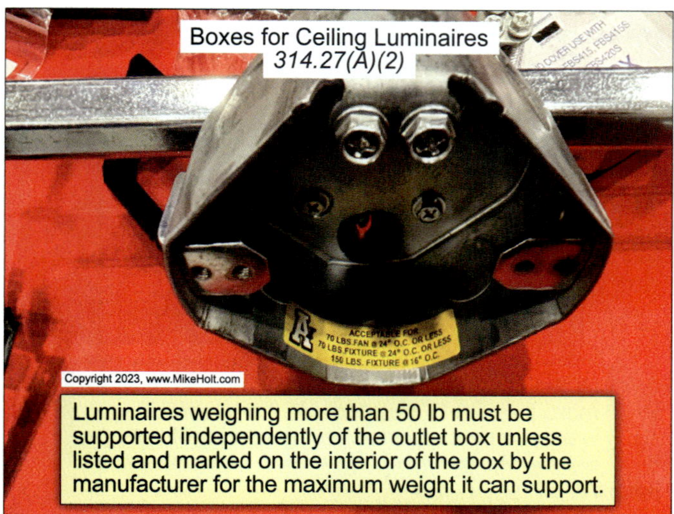

Luminaires weighing more than 50 lb must be supported independently of the outlet box unless listed and marked on the interior of the box by the manufacturer for the maximum weight it can support.

▶Figure 314–48

(B) Floor Boxes for Receptacles.

Floor boxes for receptacles must be specifically listed for the purpose. ▶Figure 314–49

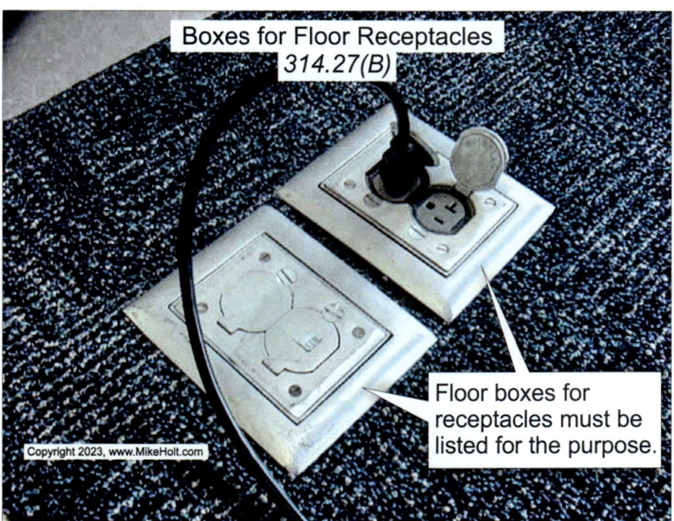

▶Figure 314–49

(C) Boxes for Paddle Fans. Outlet boxes for a ceiling paddle fan must be listed and marked <u>on the interior of the box</u> as suitable for the purpose and are not permitted to support a fan weighing more than 70 lb. Outlet boxes for a ceiling paddle fan that weighs more than 35 lb must include the maximum weight to be supported in the required marking. ▶Figure 314–50

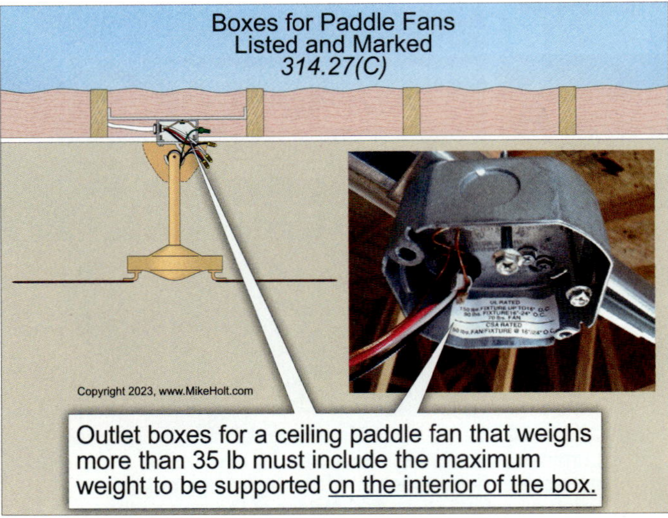

Outlet boxes for a ceiling paddle fan that weighs more than 35 lb must include the maximum weight to be supported <u>on the interior of the box.</u>

▶Figure 314–50

Ceiling-mounted outlet boxes in habitable rooms of a dwelling unit where a ceiling-suspended (paddle) fan could be installed must be listed for the support of a ceiling-suspended (paddle) fan. ▶Figure 314–51

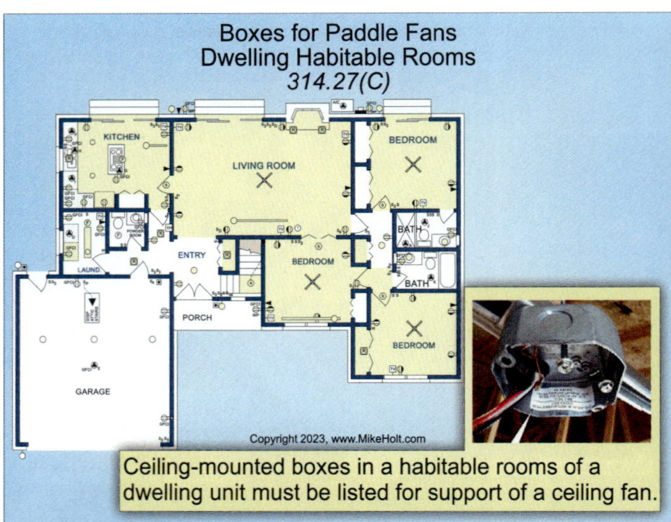

Ceiling-mounted boxes in a habitable rooms of a dwelling unit must be listed for support of a ceiling fan.

▶Figure 314–51

(D) Boxes for Utilization Equipment. Boxes used for the support of utilization equipment must be designed to support equipment that weighs a minimum of 50 lb [314.27(A)].

Ex: Utilization equipment weighing 6 lb or less can be supported by a box secured with two No. 6 or larger screws. ▶Figure 314–52

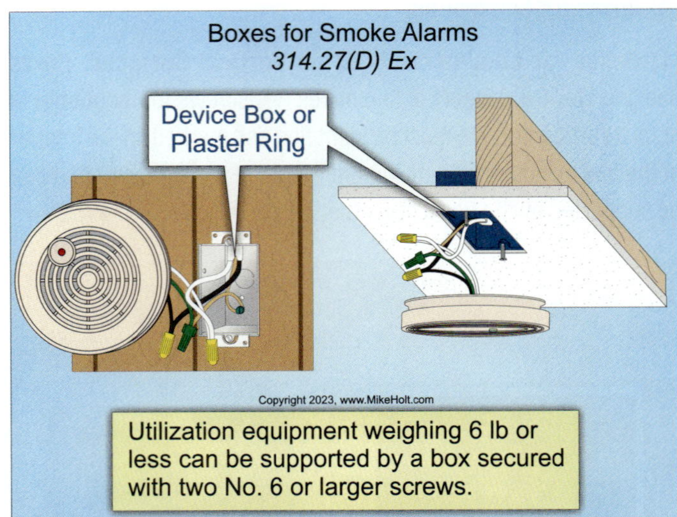

Utilization equipment weighing 6 lb or less can be supported by a box secured with two No. 6 or larger screws.

▶Figure 314–52

314.28 Pull Boxes, Junction Boxes, and Conduit Bodies

Boxes containing conductors 4 AWG and larger must be sized so the conductor insulation will not be damaged. ▶Figure 314–53 and ▶Figure 314–54

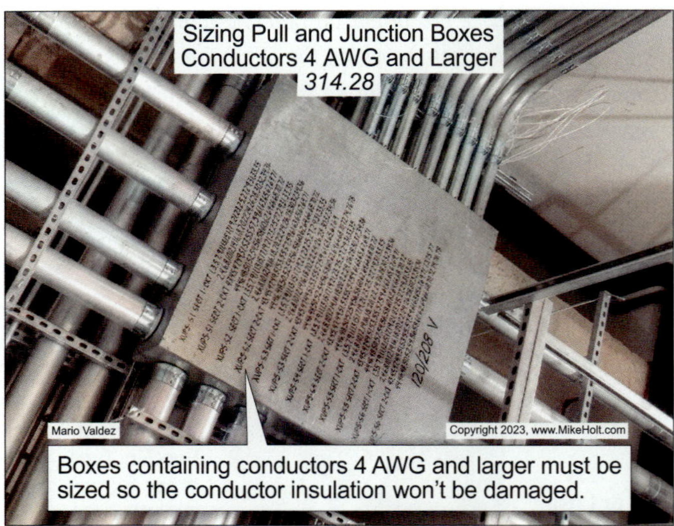

Boxes containing conductors 4 AWG and larger must be sized so the conductor insulation won't be damaged.

▶Figure 314–53

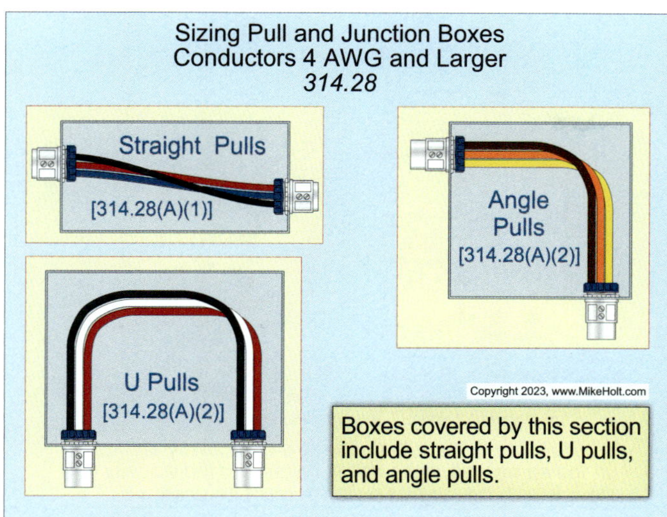

▶Figure 314–54

Author's Comment:

▸ The requirements for sizing boxes containing conductors 6 AWG and smaller are contained in 314.16.

▸ If conductors 4 AWG and larger enter a box or other enclosure, a fitting that provides a smooth, rounded, insulating surface (such as a bushing or adapter) is required to protect them from abrasion during and after installation [300.4(G)].

(A) Minimum Size. For raceways containing conductors 4 AWG and larger, the minimum dimensions of boxes and conduit bodies must comply with the following:

According to Article 100, "Conduit Body" is a fitting installed on a raceway that provides access to conductors through a removable cover. ▶Figure 314–55

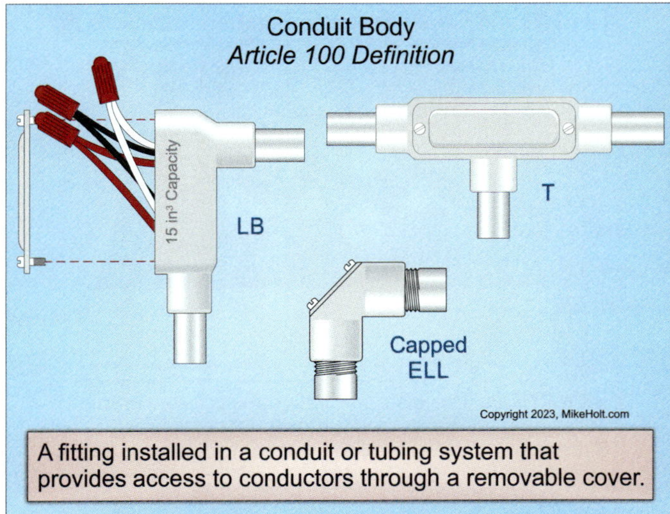

▶Figure 314–55

(1) Straight Pulls. The distance from where the raceway enters the box to the opposite wall of the box must be at least eight times the size of the largest raceway. ▶Figure 314–56

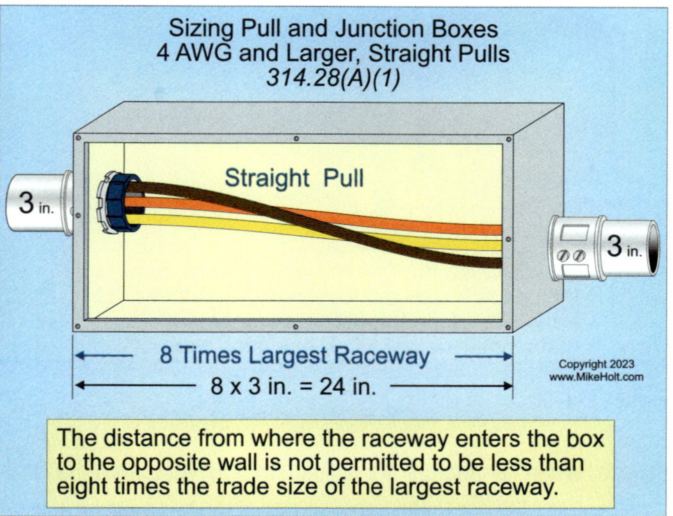

▶Figure 314–56

(2) Angle Pulls, U Pulls, or Splices

Angle Pulls. The distance from the raceway entry of the box to the opposite wall of the box must be at least six times the size of the largest raceway, plus the sum of the sizes of the remaining raceways on the same wall and row. ▶Figure 314–57

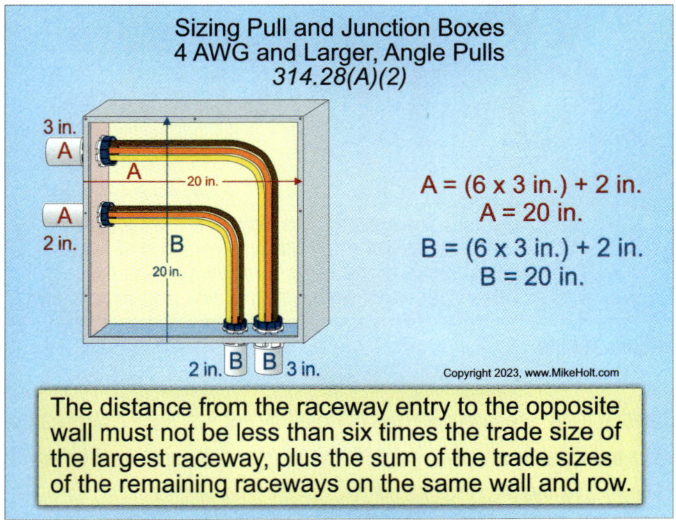

▶Figure 314–57

U Pulls. When a conductor enters and leaves from the same wall of the box, the distance from the raceway entry of the box to the opposite wall of the box must be at least six times the size of the largest raceway, plus the sum of the sizes of the remaining raceways on the same wall and row. ▶Figure 314–58

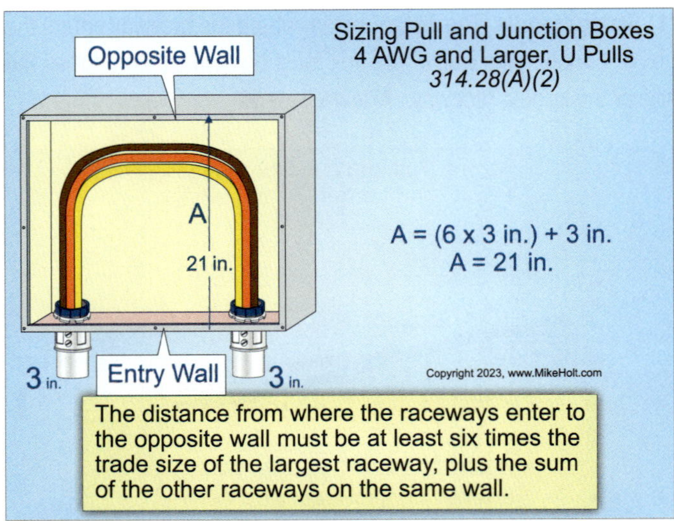

▶Figure 314–58

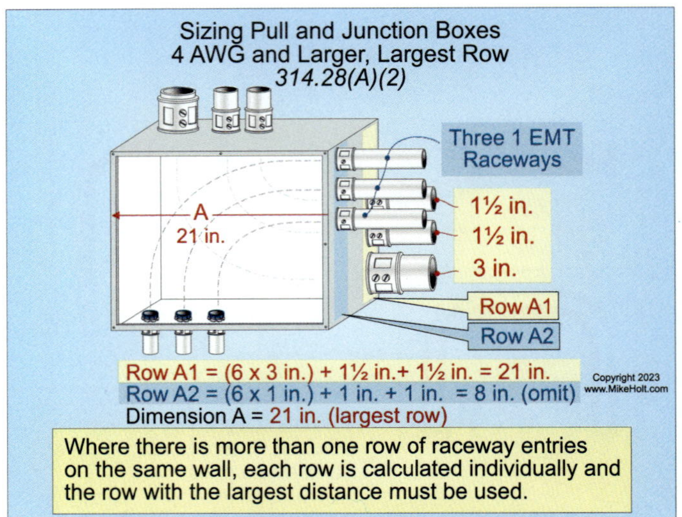

▶Figure 314–60

Splices. When conductors are spliced, the distance from the raceway's entry of the box to the opposite wall of the box must be at least six times the size of the largest raceway, plus the sum of the sizes of the remaining raceways on the same wall and row. ▶Figure 314–59

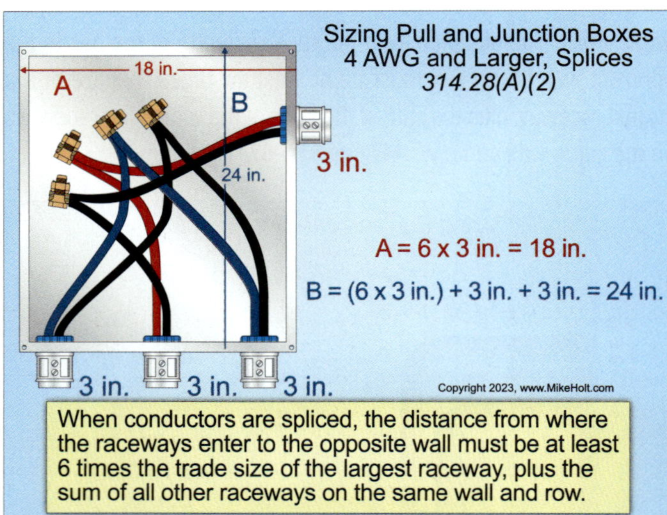

▶Figure 314–59

Rows. If there are multiple rows of raceway entries, each row is calculated individually and the row with the largest distance must be used. ▶Figure 314–60

Distance Between Raceways. The distance between raceway entries enclosing the same conductor must be at least six times the size of the largest raceway, measured between the raceway entry openings. ▶Figure 314–61 and ▶Figure 314–62

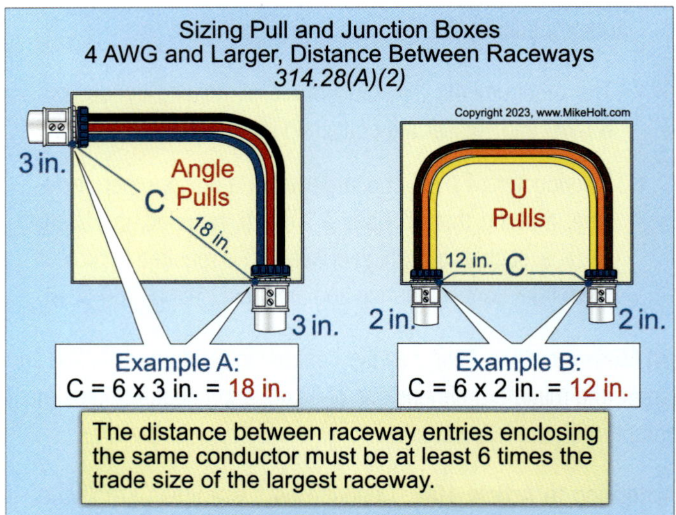

▶Figure 314–61

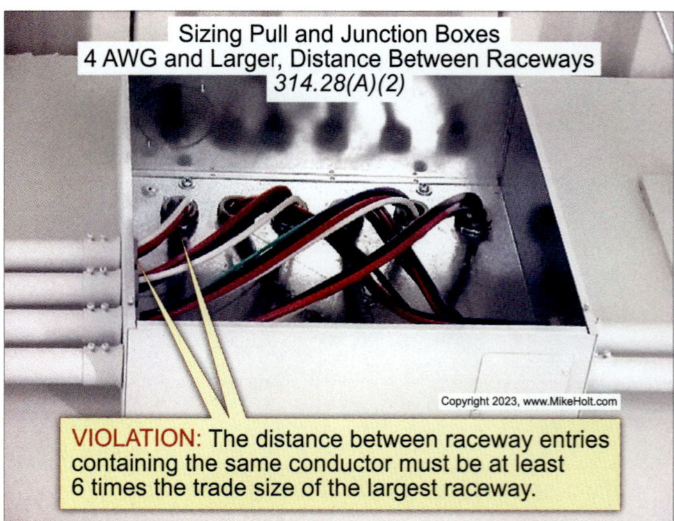

▶Figure 314–62

Ex: When conductors enter an enclosure or conduit body opposite a removable cover, the distance from that wall to the removable cover is not permitted to be less than the bending distance as contained in Table 312.6(A) for one conductor per terminal. ▶Figure 314–63 and ▶Figure 314–64

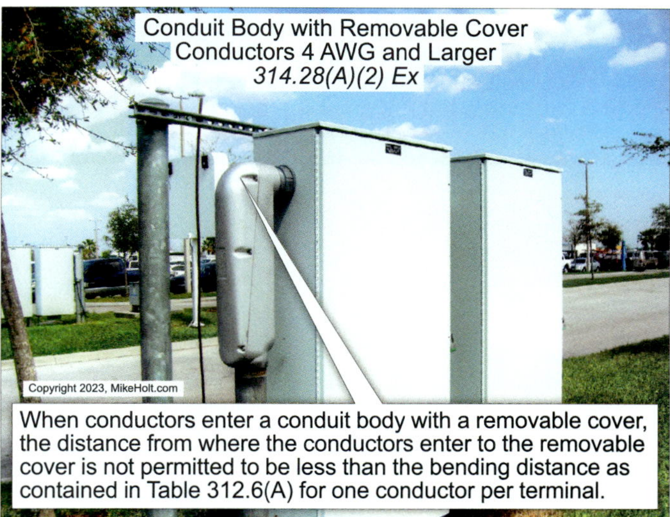

When conductors enter a conduit body with a removable cover, the distance from where the conductors enter to the removable cover is not permitted to be less than the bending distance as contained in Table 312.6(A) for one conductor per terminal.

▶Figure 314–63

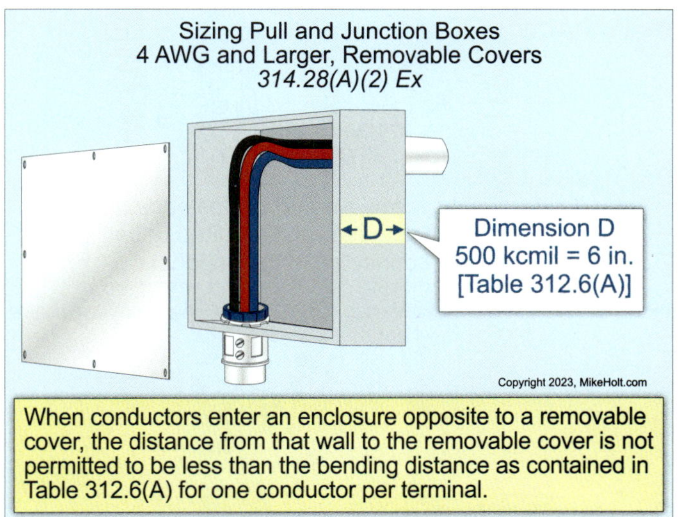

When conductors enter an enclosure opposite to a removable cover, the distance from that wall to the removable cover is not permitted to be less than the bending distance as contained in Table 312.6(A) for one conductor per terminal.

▶Figure 314–64

(3) Conduit Bodies, Smaller Dimension. The dimension of listed conduit bodies smaller than required in 314.28(A)(1) and (A)(2) must be marked by the manufacturer with the maximum size conductors permitted.

Note: The conductors marked by the manufacturer must be XHHW.

(B) Conductors in Pull or Junction Boxes. Pull boxes or junction boxes with any dimension over 6 ft must have all conductors cabled or racked in an approved manner.

Boxes, conduit bodies, and handhole enclosures must be installed so that wiring and devices contained within them can be rendered accessible in accordance with 314.29(A) and (B).

(A) In Buildings. Boxes and conduit bodies must be installed so the wiring and devices contained within the boxes and conduit bodies are accessible. ▶Figure 314–65

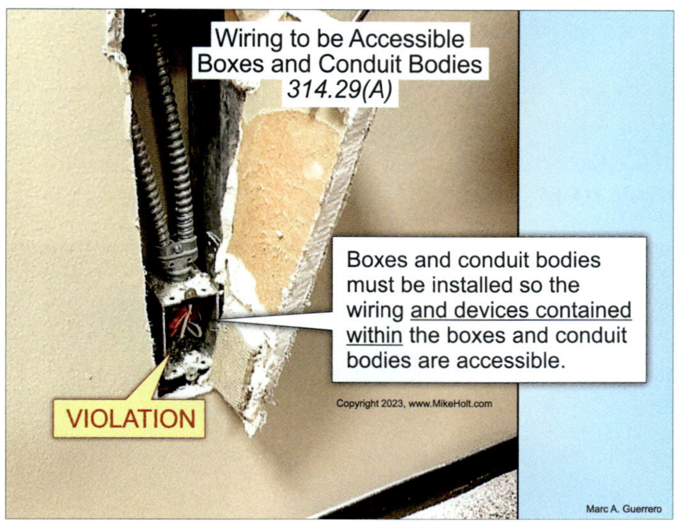

▶Figure 314–65

According to Article 100, "Accessible (as applied to wiring methods)" means capable of being removed or exposed without damaging the building structure or finish or not permanently closed in or blocked by the building structure, other electrical equipment, other building systems (piping, ducts, drains, or other mechanical systems), or the building finish. ▶Figure 314–66

(B) Handhold Enclosures. Handhole enclosures must be installed so that the wiring within is accessible without excavating sidewalks, paving, earth, or other substances used to establish the finished grade. ▶Figure 314–67

Handhole enclosures must be identified for underground use and be designed and installed to withstand all loads likely to be imposed on them. ▶Figure 314–68

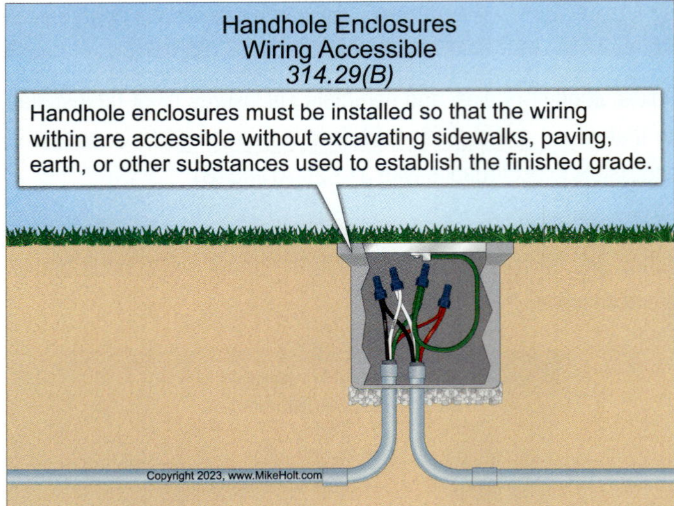

▶Figure 314–66

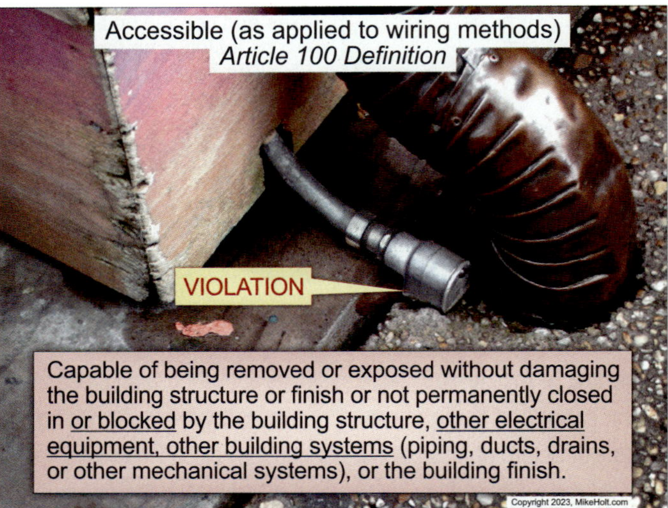

▶Figure 314–67

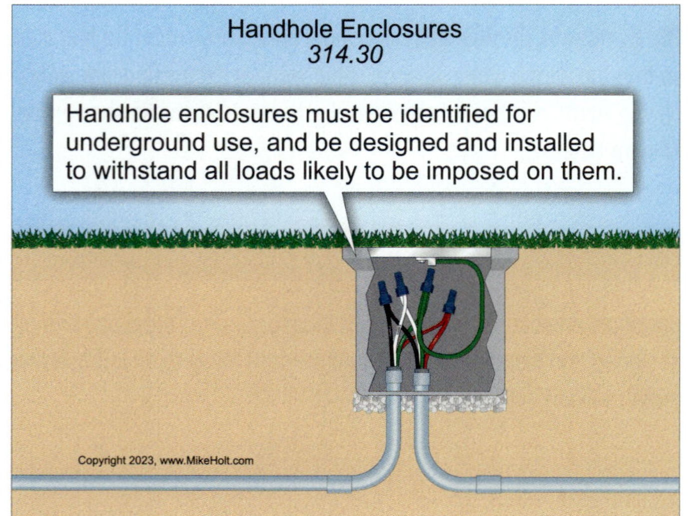

▶Figure 314–68

According to Article 100, a "Handhole Enclosure" is an underground enclosure with an open or closed bottom that is sized to allow personnel to reach into but not enter the enclosure. ▶Figure 314–69

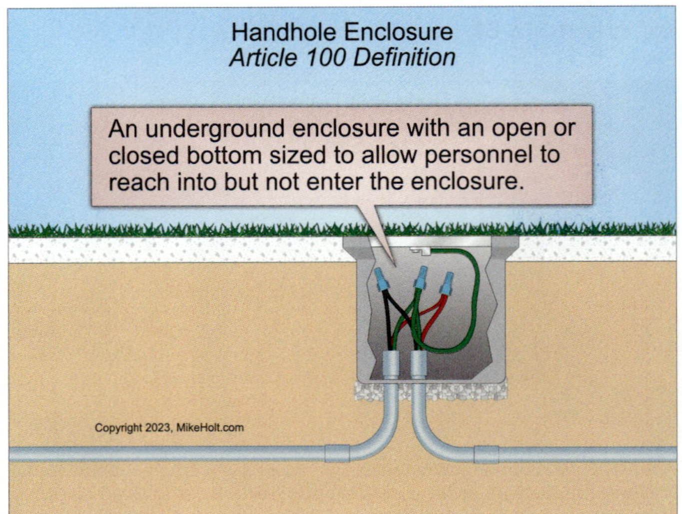

▶Figure 314–69

(B) Wiring Entries. Underground raceways and cables entering a handhole are not required to be mechanically connected to the handhole. ▶Figure 314–70

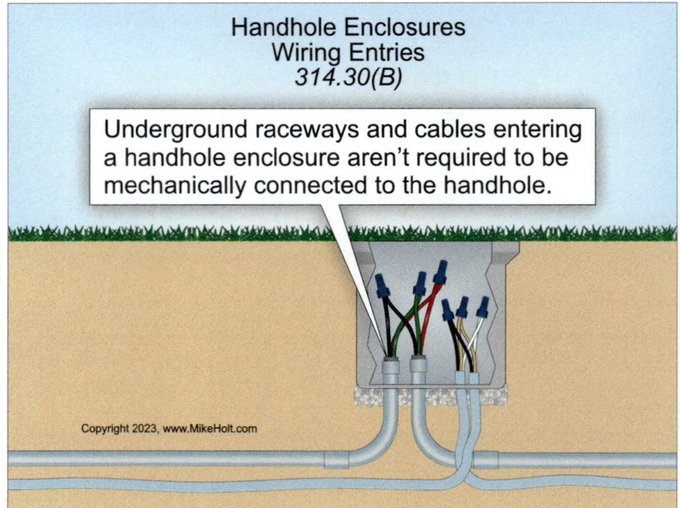

▶Figure 314–70

(C) Enclosure Wiring. Splices or terminations within a handhole must be listed for wet locations [110.14(B)]. ▶Figure 314–71

(D) Covers. Handhole covers must have an identifying mark or logo that prominently identifies the function of the handhole, such as "electric." Handhole covers must require the use of tools to open, or they must weigh over 100 lb. ▶Figure 314–72

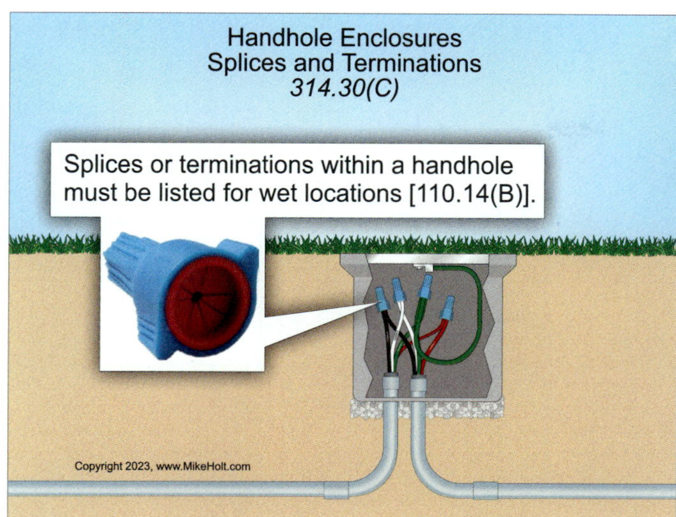

▶Figure 314–71

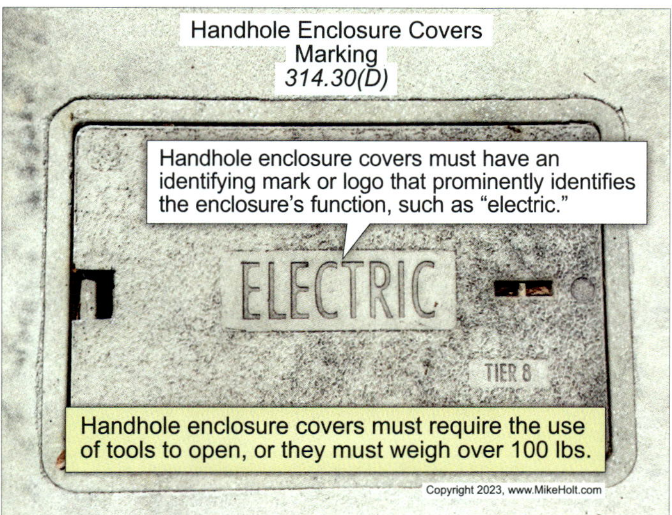

▶Figure 314–72

Metal covers and exposed conductive surfaces of handhole enclosures must be connected to the circuit equipment conductor in accordance with 250.96(A). ▶Figure 314–73

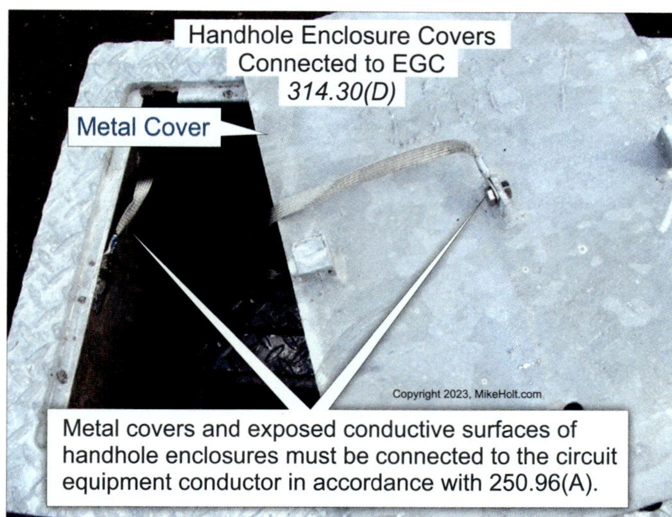

▶Figure 314–73

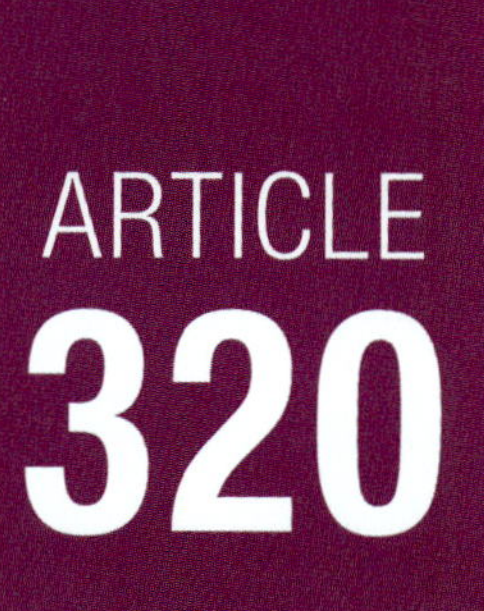

ARMORED CABLE (TYPE AC)

Introduction to Article 320—Armored Cable (Type AC)

Article 320 covers the use, installation, and construction specifications of armored cable (Type AC). AC cable is an assembly of up to four phase conductors and one neutral insulated conductor, sizes 14 AWG through 1 AWG, individually wrapped in a moisture-resistant, fire-retardant paper contained within a flexible spiral metal sheath. Some topics covered in this material include:

- ▶ Listing Requirements
- ▶ Uses Permitted
- ▶ Uses Not Permitted
- ▶ Installation in Accessible Roof Spaces
- ▶ Bending Radius
- ▶ Securing and Supporting
- ▶ Ampacity
- ▶ Construction
- ▶ Marking

This article consists of three parts:

- ▶ Part I. General
- ▶ Part II. Installation
- ▶ Part III. Construction Specifications

According to Article 100, "Type AC" is a fabricated assembly of conductors in a flexible interlocked metallic armor with an internal bonding strip in intimate contact with the armor for its entire length. ▶Figure 320–1

Part I. General

320.1 Scope

This article covers the use, installation, and construction specifications of armored cable, Type AC. ▶Figure 320–2

320.6 Listing Requirements

Type AC cable and associated fittings must be listed.

Part II. Installation

320.10 Uses Permitted

Type AC cable can be used or installed as follows:

(1) For feeders and branch circuits in both exposed and concealed installations.

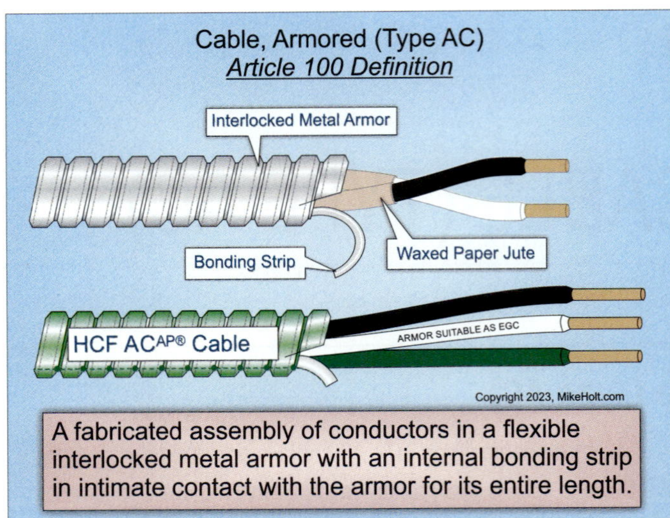

▶Figure 320–1

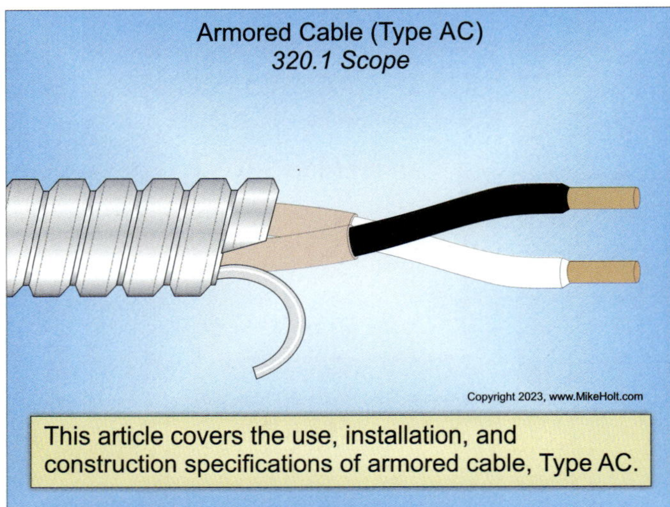

▶Figure 320–2

(2) In cable trays.

(3) In dry locations.

(4) Embedded in plaster in dry locations.

(5) In air voids of block walls where not exposed to excessive moisture or dampness.

Note: The "Uses Permitted" is not an all-inclusive list, which indicates other suitable uses are permitted if approved by the authority having jurisdiction.

Author's Comment:

▶ Type AC cable can also be installed in a plenum space in accordance with 300.22(C)(1).

320.12 Uses Not Permitted

Type AC cable is not permitted to be installed:

(1) Where subject to physical damage.

(2) In damp or wet locations.

(3) In air voids of block or tile walls where such walls are exposed or subject to excessive moisture or dampness.

(4) Where exposed to corrosive conditions.

(5) Embedded in plaster finish or concrete in wet or damp locations.

320.15 Exposed Work

Exposed Type AC cable, except as provided in 300.11(B), must closely follow the surface of the building finish or running boards. If installed on the bottom of floor or ceiling joists, it must be secured at every joist and must not be subject to physical damage. ▶Figure 320–3

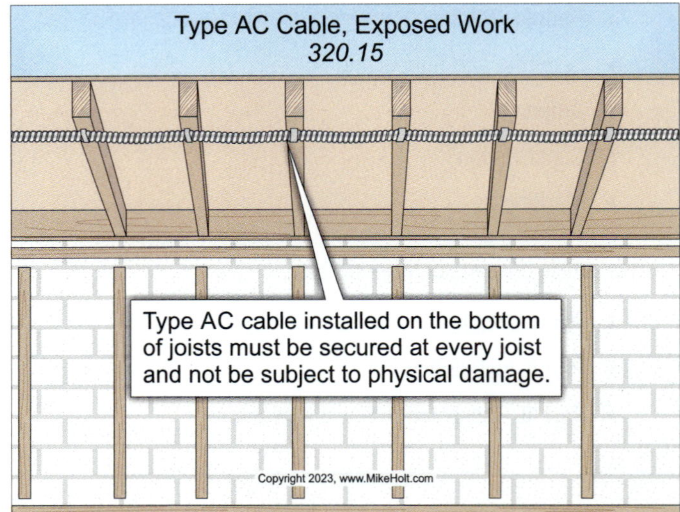

▶Figure 320–3

320.17 Through or Parallel to Framing Members

Type AC cable installed through or parallel to framing members or furring strips must be protected against physical damage from penetration by screws or nails by maintaining a 1¼ in. of separation between the cable and the nearest edge of a wood framing member or furring strip, or by a suitable metal plate in accordance with 300.4(A), (C), and (D). ▶Figure 320–4 and ▶Figure 320–5

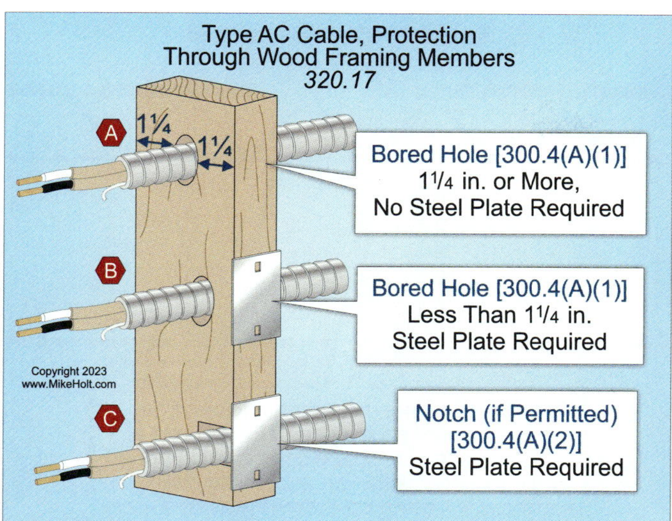

▶Figure 320–4

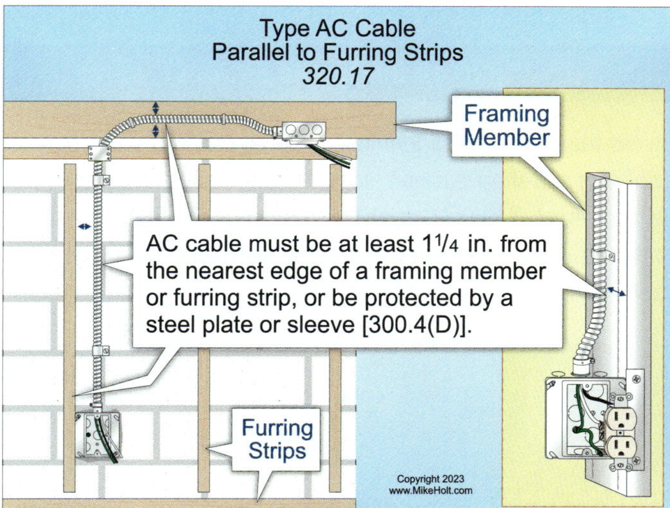

▶Figure 320–5

320.23 In Roof Spaces

(A) Cables Run Across the Top of <u>Framing Members</u>. Type AC cable in roof spaces within 6 ft of the nearest edge of the scuttle hole entrance run across the top of <u>framing members</u> must be protected by guard strips that are at least as high as the cable. ▶Figure 320–6

320.24 Bending Radius

Type AC cable is not permitted to be bent in a manner that will damage the cable. This is accomplished by limiting bending of the inner edge of the cable to a radius of not less than five times the diameter of the cable.

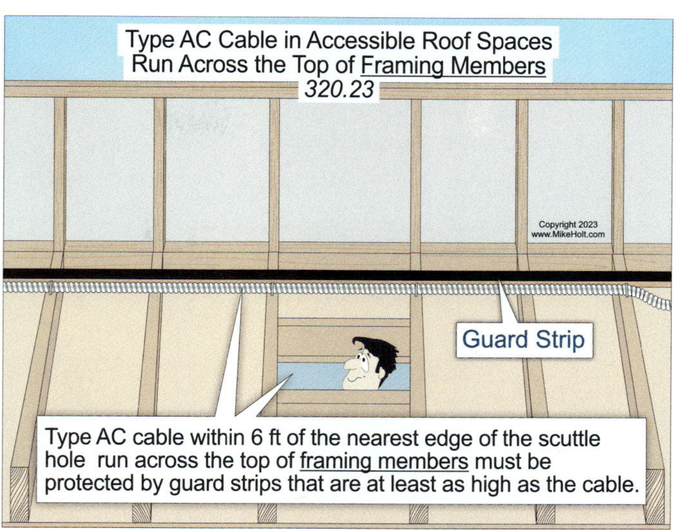

▶Figure 320–6

320.30 Securing and Supporting

(A) General. Type AC cable must be supported and secured by staples, cable ties listed and identified for securing and supporting, straps, hangers, similar fittings, or other approved means designed and installed so the cable is not damaged. ▶Figure 320–7

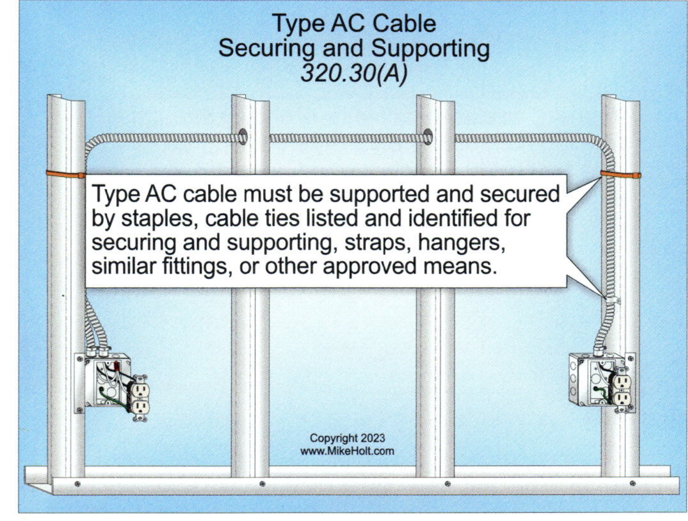

▶Figure 320–7

Type AC cable fittings are permitted as a means of cable support.

(B) Securing. Type AC cable must be secured within 12 in. of every outlet box, junction box, cabinet, or fitting and at intervals not exceeding 4½ ft. ▶Figure 320–8

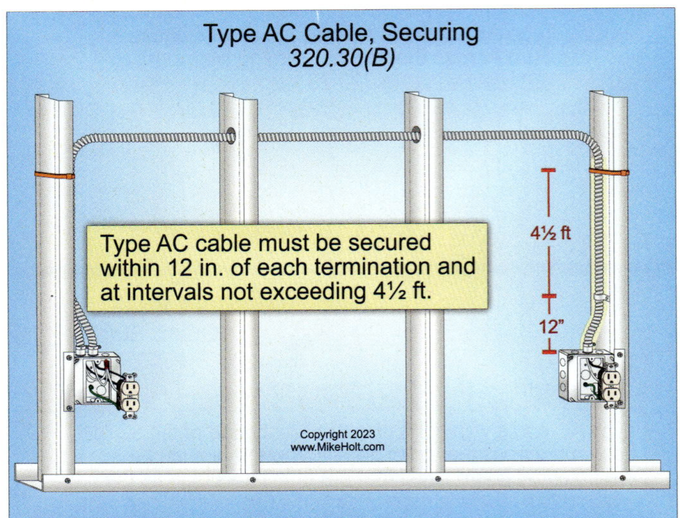

▶Figure 320–8

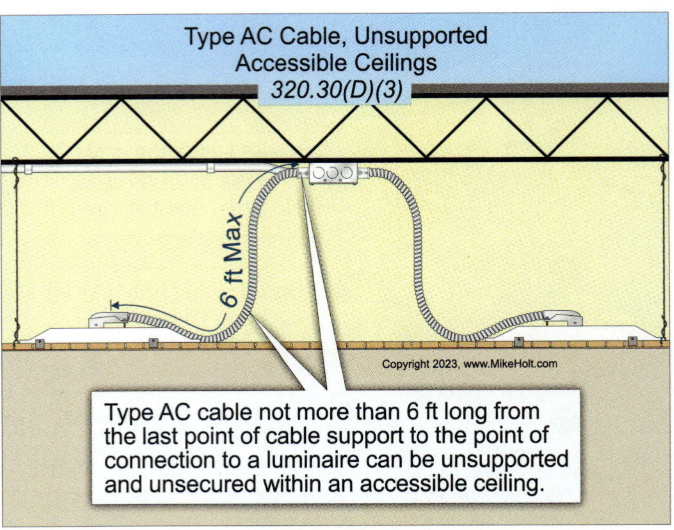

▶Figure 320–10

(C) Supporting. Type AC cable must be supported at intervals not exceeding 4½ ft. Cables installed horizontally through framing members are considered supported and secured if such support does not exceed 4½-ft intervals. ▶Figure 320–9

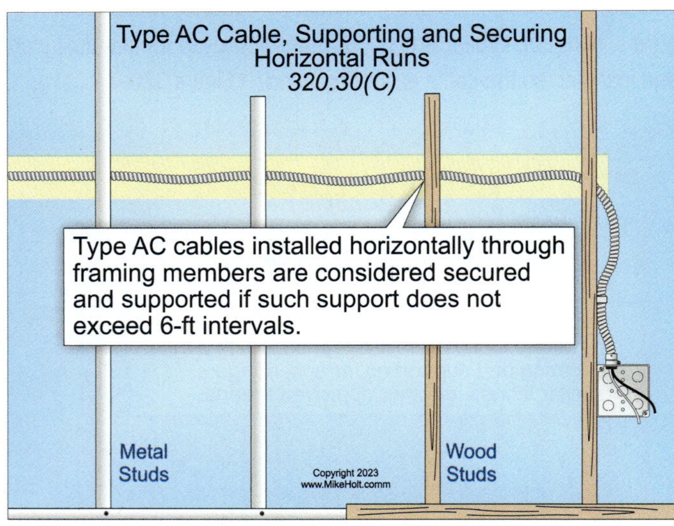

▶Figure 320–9

(D) Unsupported and Unsecured Cables.

(1) Type AC cable can be unsupported and unsecured where fished through concealed spaces.

(2) Type AC cable can be unsupported and unsecured where not more than 2 ft long at terminals and where flexibility is necessary.

(3) Type AC cable can be unsupported and unsecured where not more than 6 ft long from the last point of cable support or Type AC cable fitting to the point of connection to a luminaire within an accessible ceiling. ▶Figure 320–10

320.40 Boxes and Fittings

Unless the design of the termination fitting provides protection, an insulating anti-short bushing (sometimes called a "redhead") must be installed at all Type AC cable terminations. The termination fitting must permit the visual inspection of the anti-short bushing once the cable has been installed. ▶Figure 320–11

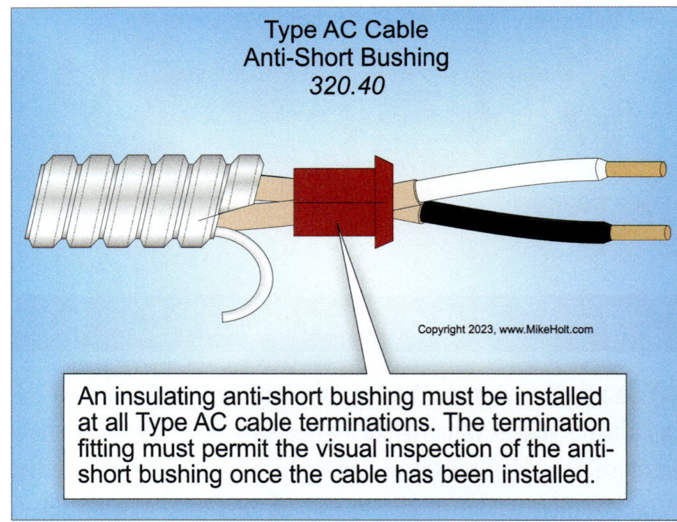

▶Figure 320–11

Author's Comment:

▶ To protect the conductors from abrasion, Type AC cable must terminate in boxes or fittings specifically listed for Type AC cable [300.15]. ▶Figure 320–12

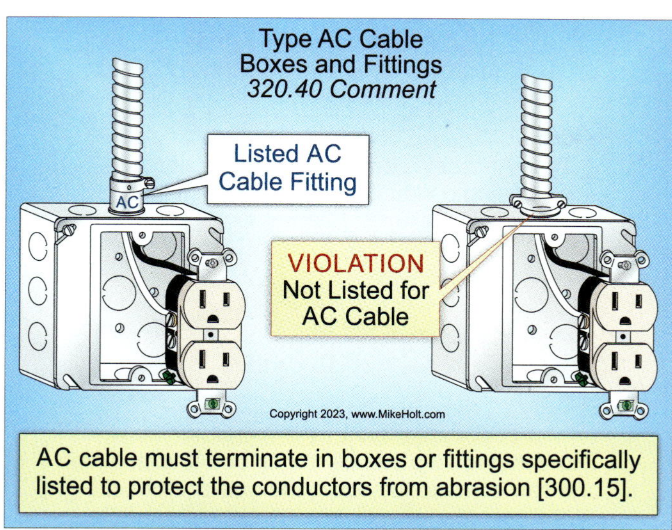

▶Figure 320–12

▶ The internal aluminum bonding strip within the cable serves no electrical purpose once it is outside the cable and can be cut off, but many electricians use it to secure the anti-short bushing to the cable. See 320.108.

320.80 Conductor Ampacity

The ampacity of Type AC cable must be determined in accordance with 310.14.

(A) Thermal Insulation. Where more than two Type AC cables are in contact with thermal insulation, caulking, or sealing foam, the ampacity of the conductors must be adjusted in accordance with Table 310.15(C)(1). ▶Figure 320–13

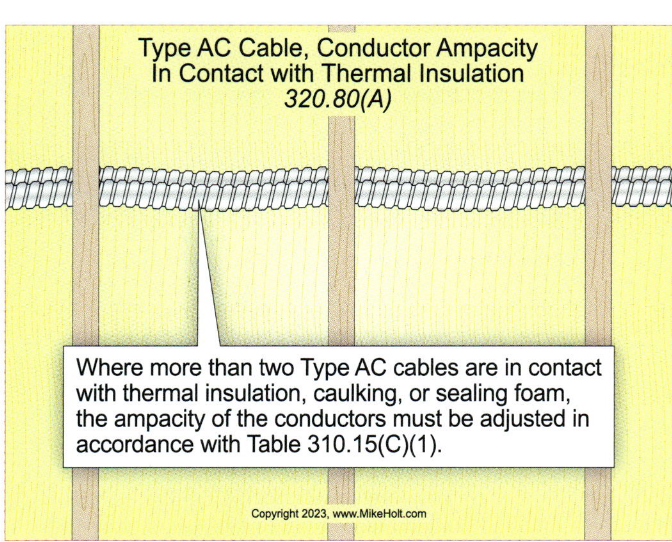

▶Figure 320–13

▶ Example

Question: *Is Type AC cable containing four 12 AWG current-carrying conductors suitable to be protected by a 20A circuit breaker?*

(a) Yes   (b) No

Solution:

Step 1: *Determine the ampacity of the circuit conductors in accordance with 310.16 and Table 310.15(C)(1).*

12 AWG is rated 30A at 90°C [Table 310.16].

Conductor Adjustment = 80% [Table 310.15(C)(1)]

Conductor Adjusted Ampacity = 30A × 80%
Conductor Adjusted Ampacity = 24A

Step 2: *Verify that the adjusted conductor ampacity can be protected by the 20A circuit breaker. In this case, 12 AWG is rated 24A after adjustment at 90°C and 20A at 60°C [240.4(D)].*

Answer: *(a) Yes*

Where more than two Type AC cables are bundled in contact with thermal insulation, caulk, or sealing foam, the conductor ampacity must be adjusted in accordance with Table 310.15(C)(1). ▶Figure 320–14

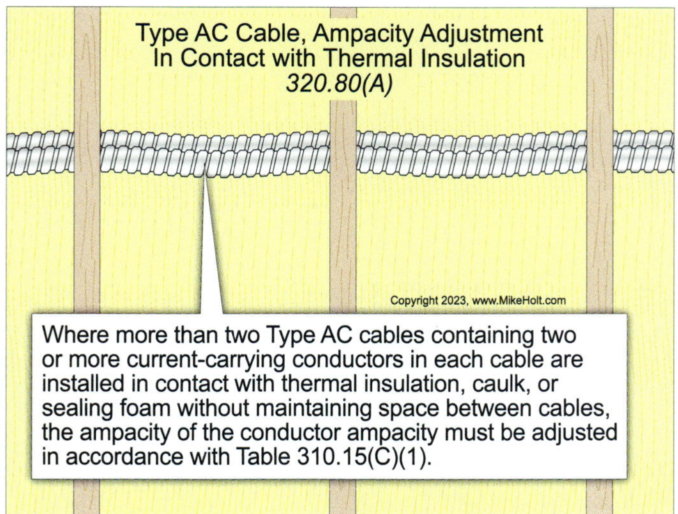

▶Figure 320–14

Author's Comment:

▶ Thermal insulation and similar materials impede the dissipation of heat from the cables. When Type AC cable is bundled in contact with insulation, caulking, or foam, the permission of 310.15(C)(1)(d) to ignore ampacity adjustments does not apply.

Part III. Construction Specifications

320.100 Construction

Type AC cable must have an armor of flexible metal tape with an internal aluminum bonding strip in intimate contact with the armor for its entire length.

Author's Comment:

▸ The best method of cutting Type AC cable is to use a tool specifically designed for the purpose, such as a rotary armor cutter.

▸ When cutting Type AC cable with a hacksaw, be sure to cut only one spiral of the cable and be careful not to nick the conductors. This is done by cutting the cable at an angle. Breaking the cable spiral (bending the cable very sharply), then cutting the cable with a pair of dikes is not a good practice.

320.108 Equipment Grounding Conductor

Type AC cable can serve as an equipment grounding conductor [250.118(A)(8)]. ▸Figure 320–15

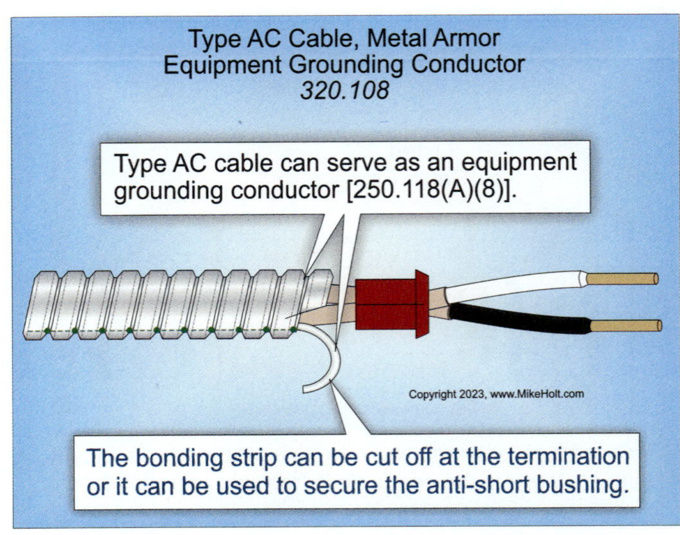

▸Figure 320–15

Author's Comment:

▸ The internal aluminum bonding strip is not an equipment grounding conductor, but it allows the interlocked armor to serve as one because it reduces the impedance of the armored spirals to ensure a ground fault will be cleared. It is the combination of the aluminum bonding strip and the cable armor that creates the equipment grounding conductor. Once the bonding strip exits the cable, it can be cut off because it no longer serves any purpose. The effective ground-fault current path must be maintained by using fittings specifically listed for Type AC cable [320.40]. See 300.12, 300.15, and 300.10.

330

METAL-CLAD CABLE (TYPE MC)

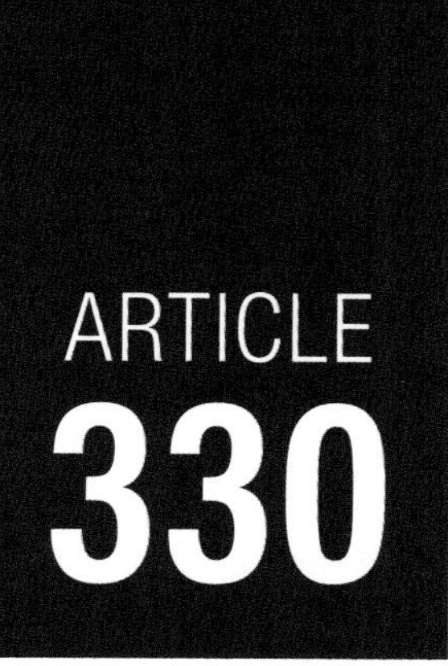

Introduction to Article 330—Metal-Clad Cable (Type MC)

This article covers the use, installation, and construction specifications of metal-clad cable (Type MC). Type MC cable is an assembly of any number of insulated conductors, 18 AWG through 2000 kcmil, with an overall polypropylene wrap enclosed in a metal sheath of either corrugated or smooth copper or aluminum tubing, or in spiral interlocked steel or aluminum. Some topics covered in this material include:

- ▶ Listing Requirements
- ▶ Uses Permitted
- ▶ Uses Not Permitted
- ▶ Installation in Accessible Roof Spaces
- ▶ Bending Radius
- ▶ Securing and Supporting
- ▶ Ampacity
- ▶ Construction
- ▶ Marking

Article 330 consists of three parts:

- ▶ Part I. General
- ▶ Part II. Installation
- ▶ Part III. Construction Specifications

According to Article 100, "Type MC" is a factory assembly of one or more insulated circuit conductors, with or without optical fiber members, enclosed in an armor of interlocking metal tape, or a smooth or corrugated metallic sheath. ▶Figure 330–1

Part I. General

330.1 Scope

Article 330 covers the use, installation, and construction specifications of metal-clad cable, Type MC. ▶Figure 330–2

330.6 Listing Requirements

Type MC cable and its fittings must be listed. ▶Figure 330–3

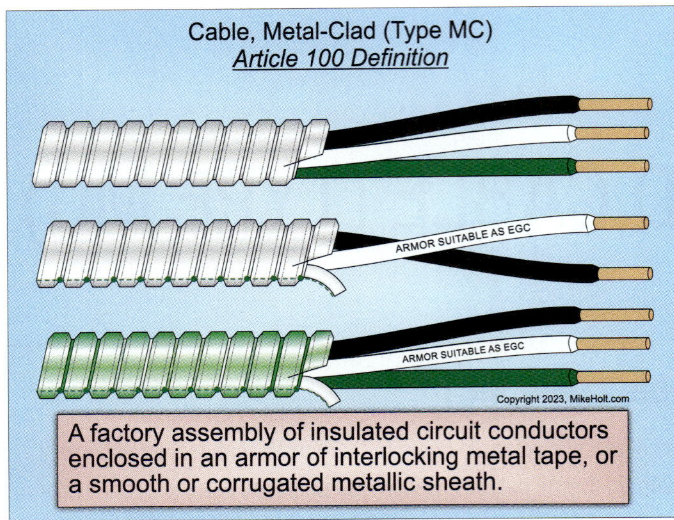

▶Figure 330–1

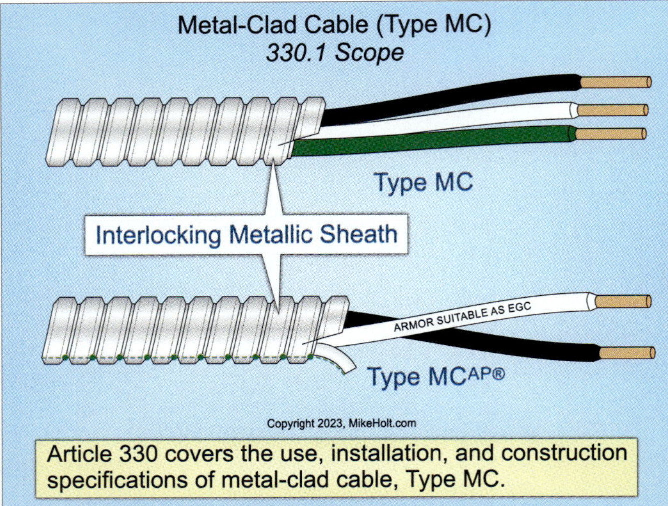

▶Figure 330–2

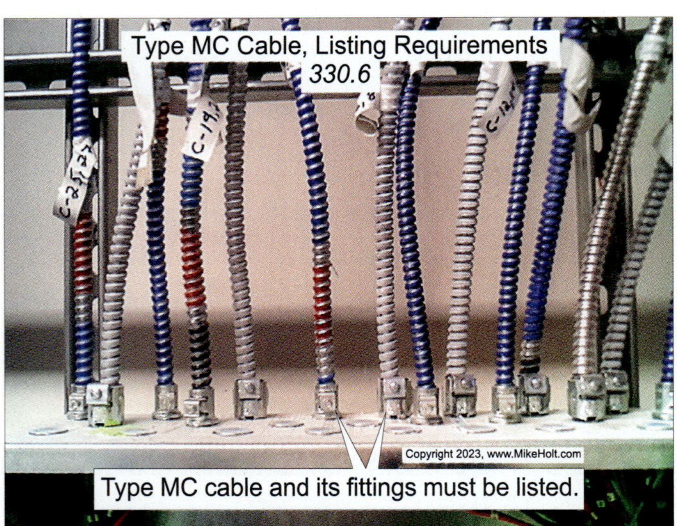

▶Figure 330–3

Author's Comment:

▸ Type MC cable is made with several types of metal sheaths. Steel and aluminum are the most common, but it is also available with a corrugated copper sheath or with a PVC outer jacket for use in environments requiring such protection. Fittings must be listed and identified for the specific type of MC cable being installed [300.15].

▸ Type MC AP® cable has a full-size equipment grounding conductor in intimate contact with the metal outer sheath armor throughout the cable's entire length. Type AC cable connectors can sometimes be used if the fitting (or the carton containing them) indicates they can also be used for the Type MC cable being installed.

▸ Section 320.40 requires anti-short bushing (red heads) at all terminations of Type AC cable. However, the *Code* does not require anti-short bushings at the termination of Type MC cable.

Part II. Installation

330.10 Uses Permitted

(A) General Uses. Type MC cable can be used:

(1) For branch circuits, feeders, and services

(2) For power, lighting, and power-limited circuits

(3) For indoor or outdoor locations

(4) Exposed or concealed

(5) To be directly buried (if identified for the purpose)

(6) In a cable tray (if identified for the purpose)

(7) In a raceway

(8) As aerial cable on a messenger

(9) In hazardous (classified) locations as permitted in 501.10(B)(5), 502.10(B)(4), and 503.10(A)(1)

(10) Embedded in plaster in dry locations

(11) In <u>damp</u> or wet locations, where a corrosion-resistant jacket is provided over the metallic sheath ▶Figure 330–4

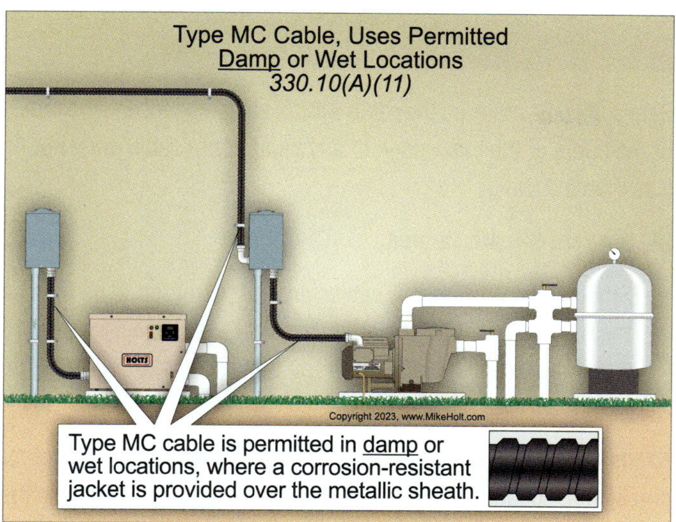

▶Figure 330–4

(B) Specific Uses.

(1) Cable Tray. Type MC cable can be installed in a cable tray in accordance with Article 392.

(2) Direct Buried. Direct-buried cables must be protected in accordance with 300.5.

(3) Installed as Service-Entrance Cable. Type MC cable is permitted to be used as service-entrance cable when installed in accordance with 230.43.

(4) Installed Outside Buildings. Type MC cable installed outside buildings must comply with 225.10, 396.10, and 396.12.

330.12 Uses Not Permitted

Type MC cable is not permitted to be used where:

(1) Subject to physical damage.

(2) Exposed to the destructive corrosive conditions in a. or b., unless the metallic sheath or armor is resistant to the conditions, or is protected by material resistant to the conditions:

   a. Direct burial in the Earth or embedded in concrete unless identified for the application.

   b. Exposed to cinder fills, strong chlorides, caustic alkalis, or vapors of chlorine or hydrochloric acids.

330.15 Exposed Work

Exposed runs of Type MC cable, except as provided in 300.11(B), must closely follow the surface of the building finish or running boards. Type MC cable installed on the bottom of floor or ceiling joists must be secured at every joist and not be subject to physical damage. ▶Figure 330–5

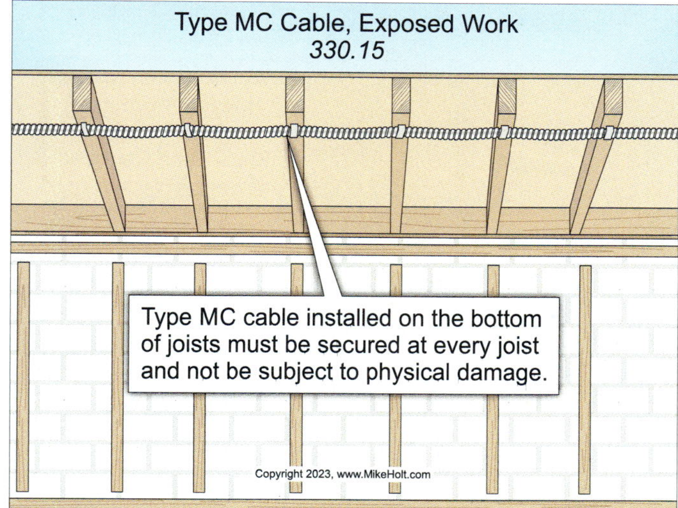

▶Figure 330–5

330.17 Through or Parallel to Framing Members

Type MC cable installed through or parallel to framing members or furring strips must be protected against physical damage from the penetration of screws or nails by maintaining a 1¼ in. separation from the nearest edge of a framing member or furring strip, or by installing a suitable metal plate in accordance with 300.4(A), (C), and (D). ▶Figure 330–6 and ▶Figure 330–7

330.23 In Roof Spaces

Type MC cable in roof spaces within 6 ft of the nearest edge of the scuttle hole run across the top of framing members must be protected by guard strips that are at least as high as the cable in accordance with 320.23. ▶Figure 330–8

  Understanding 2023 NEC Requirements for Solar PV and Energy Storage Systems | MikeHolt.com |

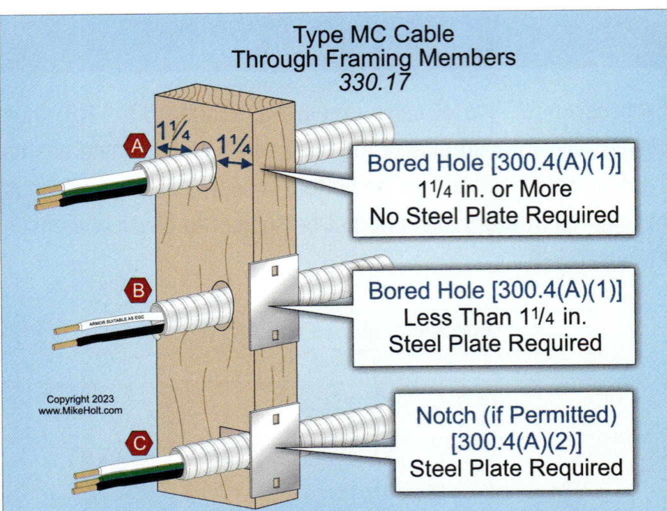

▶Figure 330–6

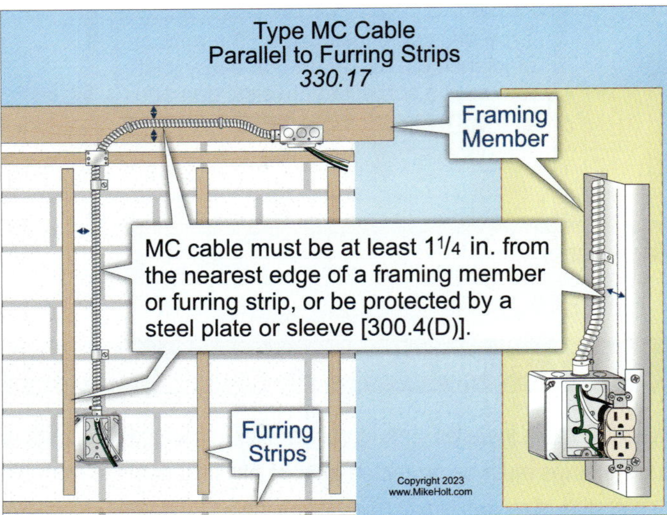

▶Figure 330–7

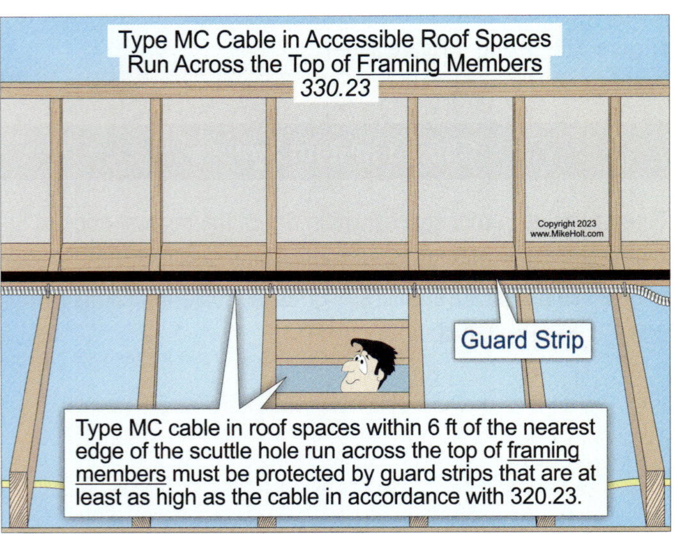

▶Figure 330–8

Bends must be made so the cable will not be damaged, and the radius of the curve of the inner edge of any bend at the cable must not be less than following:

(A) Smooth-Sheath Cables.

(1) Smooth-sheath Type MC cables are not permitted to be bent so the bending radius of the inner edge of the cable is less than 10 times the external diameter of the metallic sheath for cable up to ¾ in. in external diameter.

(B) Interlocked- or Corrugated-Sheath Armor. Interlocked- or corrugated-sheath Type MC cable is not permitted to be bent so the bending radius of the inner edge of the cable is less than seven times the external diameter of the cable.

(A) General. Type MC cable must be supported and secured by staples, cable ties listed and identified for securing and supporting, straps, hangers, similar fittings, or other approved means designed and installed so the cable is not damaged. ▶Figure 330–9

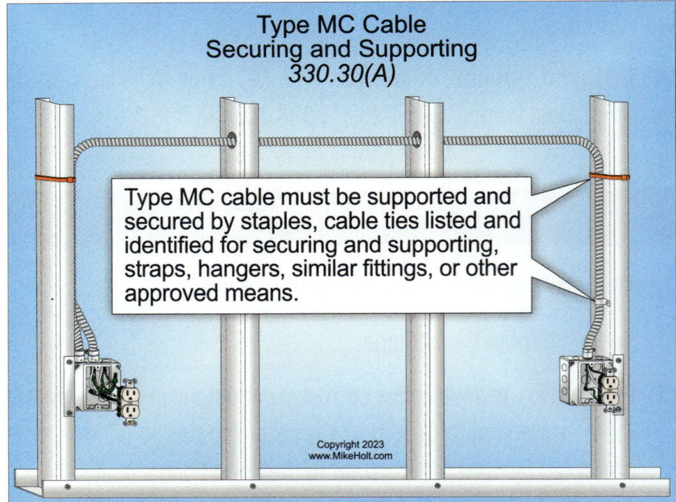

▶Figure 330–9

Type MC cable fittings are permitted as a means of cable support.

(B) Securing. Type MC cable with four or fewer conductors sized no larger than 10 AWG must be secured within 12 in. of every outlet box, junction box, cabinet, or fitting and at intervals not exceeding 6 ft. ▶Figure 330–10

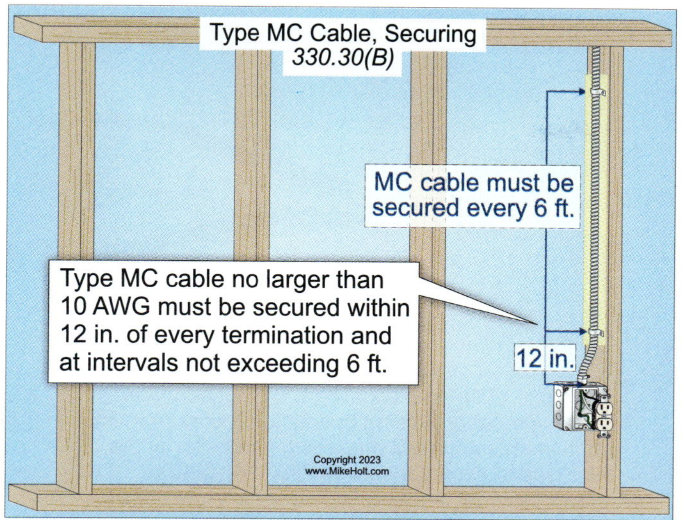

▶Figure 330–10

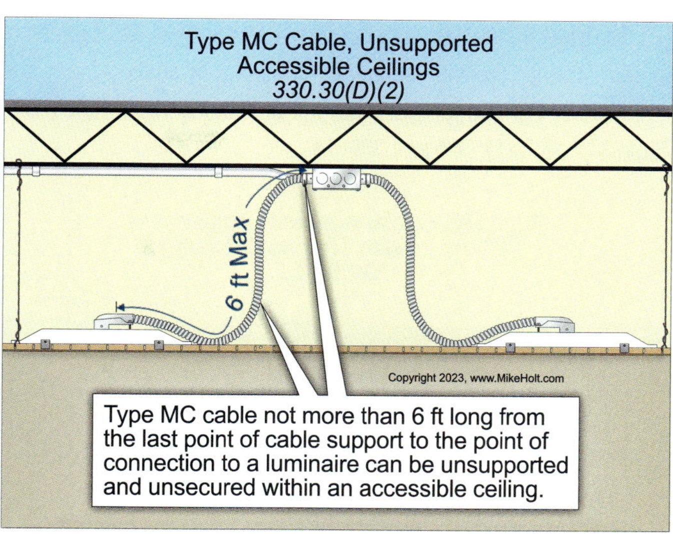

▶Figure 330–12

(C) Supporting. Type MC cable must be supported at intervals not exceeding 6 ft. Cables installed horizontally through framing members are considered secured and supported if such support does not exceed 6-ft intervals. ▶Figure 330–11

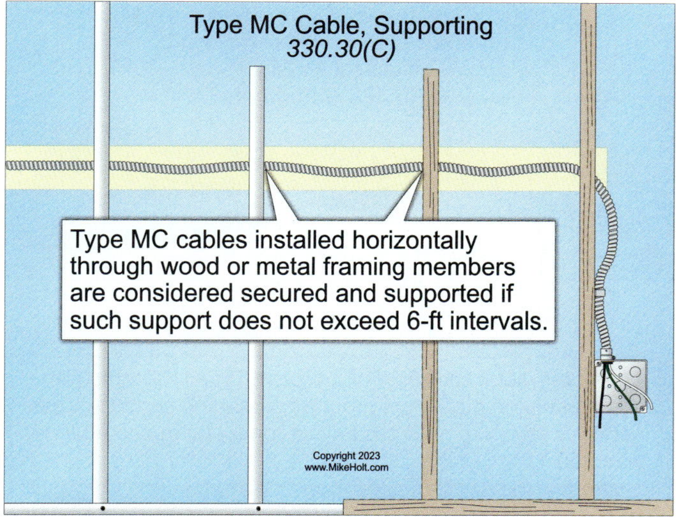

▶Figure 330–11

(D) Unsupported and Unsecured Cables.

(1) Type MC cable can be unsupported and unsecured where fished through concealed spaces in a finished building and support is impractical.

(2) Type MC cable can be unsupported and unsecured where not more than 6 ft long from the last point of cable support to the point of connection to a luminaire within an accessible ceiling. ▶Figure 330–12

(3) Type MC cable can be unsupported and unsecured where not more than 3 ft from the last point where it is securely fastened to provide flexibility for equipment that requires movement after installation, or to connect equipment where flexibility is necessary to minimize the transmission of vibration from the equipment. ▶Figure 330–13

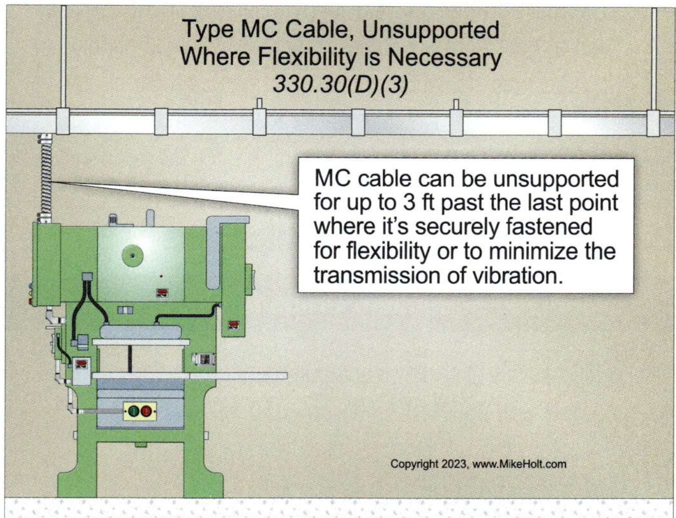

▶Figure 330–13

330.80 Conductor Ampacities

The ampacity of Type MC cable must be determined in accordance with 310.14.

(C) Thermal Insulation. Where more than two Type MC cables are in contact with thermal insulation, caulking, or sealing foam, the ampacity of the conductors must be adjusted in accordance with Table 310.15(C)(1). ▶Figure 330–14

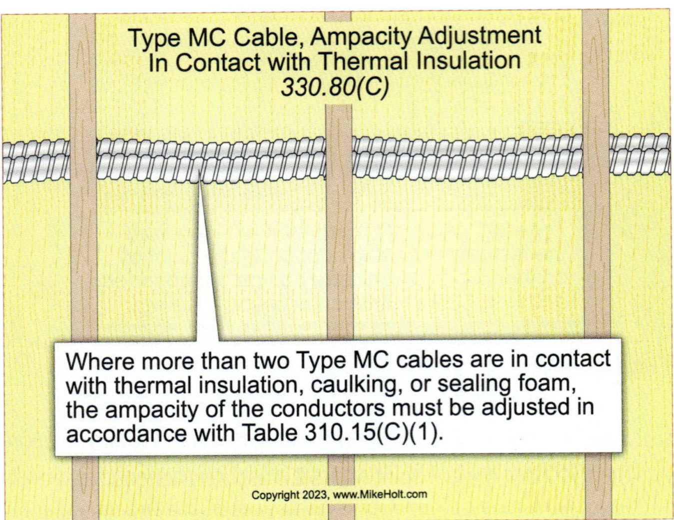

▶Figure 330–14

Author's Comment:

▸ Thermal insulation and similar materials impede the dissipation of heat from the cables. When MC cable is bundled in contact with insulation, caulking, or foam, the permission of 310.15(C)(1)(d) to ignore ampacity adjustments does not apply.

Part III. Construction Specifications

330.108 Equipment Grounding Conductor

If Type MC cable is to serve as an equipment grounding conductor, it must comply with 250.118(A)(10) and 250.122.

Author's Comment:

▸ The outer metal sheath of traditional interlocked Type MC cable is not permitted to serve as an equipment grounding conductor, so this cable must contain an equipment grounding conductor of the wire type in accordance with 250.118(A)(10)a. ▶Figure 330–15

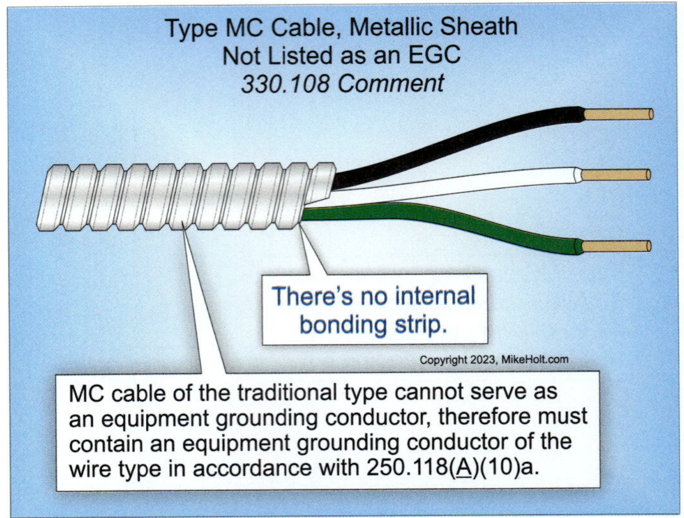

▶Figure 330–15

▸ The outer metal sheath of all-purpose Type MC cable with an uninsulated aluminum grounding/bonding conductor can serve as an equipment grounding conductor in accordance with 250.118(A)(10)b. ▶Figure 330–16

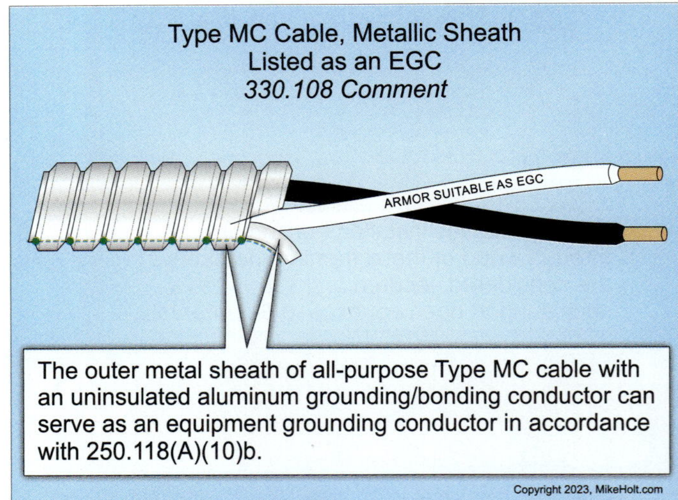

▶Figure 330–16

NONMETALLIC-SHEATHED CABLE (TYPE NM)

Introduction to Article 334—Nonmetallic-Sheathed Cable (Type NM)

Article 334 covers the use, installation, and construction specifications of nonmetallic-sheathed cable (Type NM). Type NM cable is an assembly of insulated conductors and an insulated or bare equipment grounding conductor, 14 AWG through 2AWG, with an overall nonmetallic flame-retardant sheath. This type of cable provides limited physical protection for the conductors inside the sheath, so its uses are limited by the building construction type. Its low cost and relative ease of installation makes it a common wiring method for residential and light commercial applications. Some topics covered in this material include:

- ▶ Listing Requirements
- ▶ Uses Permitted
- ▶ Uses Not Permitted
- ▶ Exposed Work
- ▶ Installation in Accessible Roof Spaces
- ▶ Bending Radius
- ▶ Securing and Supporting
- ▶ Ampacity
- ▶ Construction
- ▶ Marking

This article consists of three parts:

- ▶ Part I. General
- ▶ Part II. Installation
- ▶ Part III. Construction Specifications

According to Article 100, "Type NM" is a wiring method that encloses two or more insulated conductors within an outer nonmetallic jacket. ▶Figure 334–1

Author's Comment:

- ▶ It is the generally accepted practice in the electrical industry to call Type NM cable "Romex®," a registered trademark of the Southwire Company.

Part I. General

334.1 Scope

Article 334 covers the use, installation, and construction specifications of nonmetallic-sheathed cable, Type NM. ▶Figure 334–2

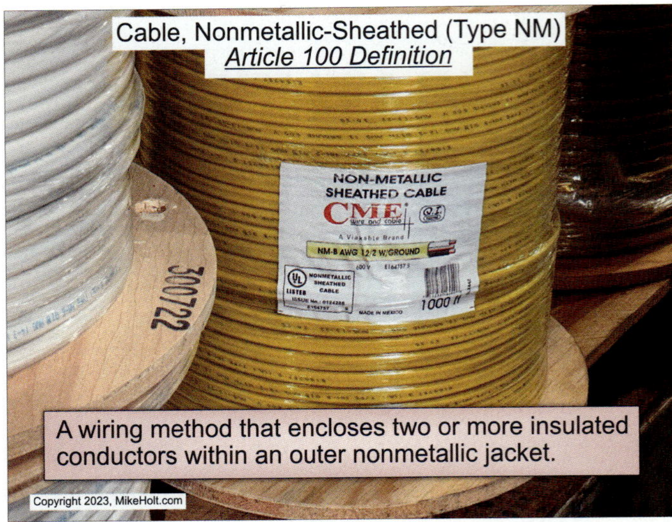

▶Figure 334–1

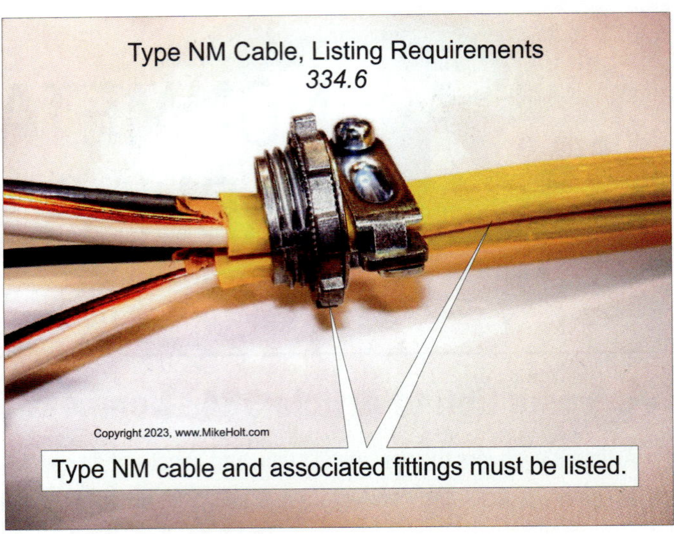

▶Figure 334–3

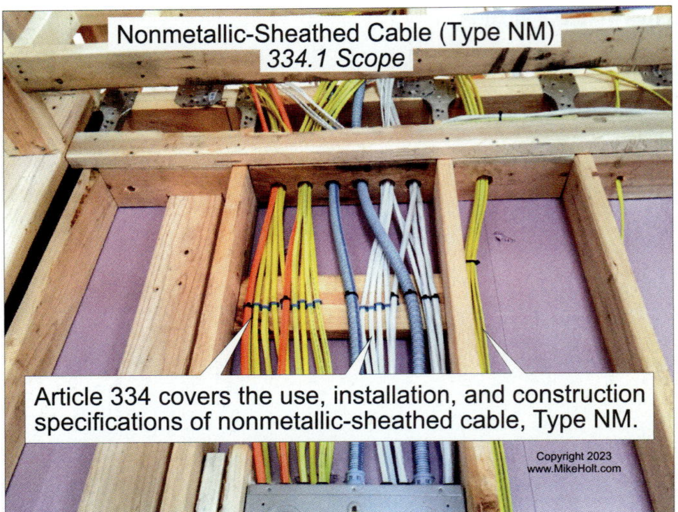

▶Figure 334–2

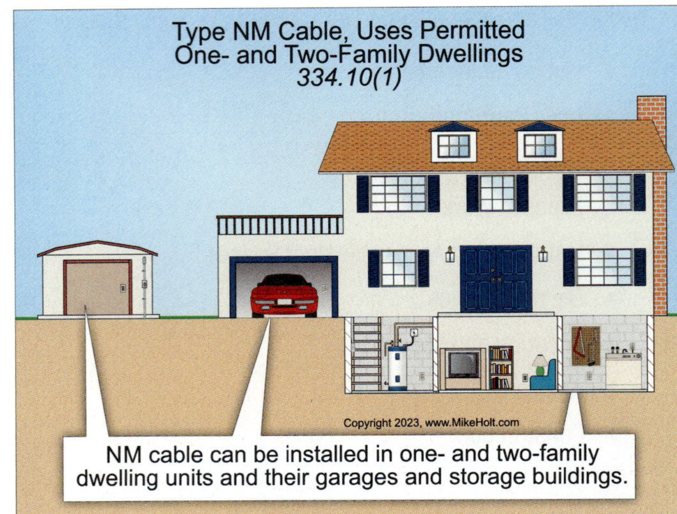

▶Figure 334–4

334.6 Listing Requirements

Type NM cable and associated fittings must be listed.   ▶Figure 334–3

Part II. Installation

334.10 Type NM Cable, Uses Permitted

Type NM cables is permitted in:

(1) One-family and two-family dwellings and their garages and storage buildings. ▶Figure 334–4

(2) Multifamily dwellings <u>and their detached garages</u> in buildings of Types III, IV, and V construction. ▶Figure 334–5

(3) Other buildings of Types III, IV, and V construction where the cable must be concealed within walls, floors, or ceilings that provide a thermal barrier of material with at least a 15-minute finish rating as identified in listings of fire-rated assemblies. ▶Figure 334–6

Note 1: For additional information on building code construction types, see NFPA 220, *Standard on Types of Building Construction*.

Note 2: See Annex E of the *NEC* for the determination of building types and the limits of the number of stories permitted for each type.

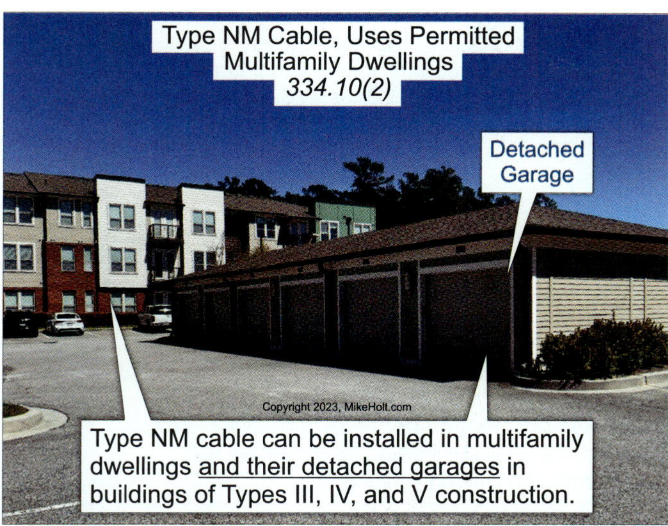

Type NM cable can be installed in multifamily dwellings <u>and their detached garages</u> in buildings of Types III, IV, and V construction.

▶Figure 334–5

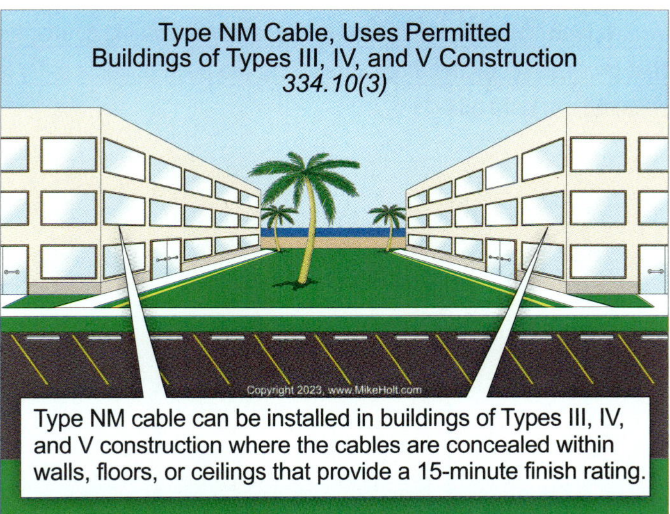

Type NM cable can be installed in buildings of Types III, IV, and V construction where the cables are concealed within walls, floors, or ceilings that provide a 15-minute finish rating.

▶Figure 334–6

334.12 Uses Not Permitted

(A) Locations. Type NM cable is not permitted:

(1) In any dwelling or structure not specifically permitted in 334.10(1), (2), (3), and (5)

(2) Exposed within a dropped or suspended ceiling in other than dwelling units ▶Figure 334–7

(3) As service-entrance cable

(4) In commercial garages having hazardous (classified) locations, as defined in 511.3

(5) In theaters and similar locations, except where permitted in 518.4(B)

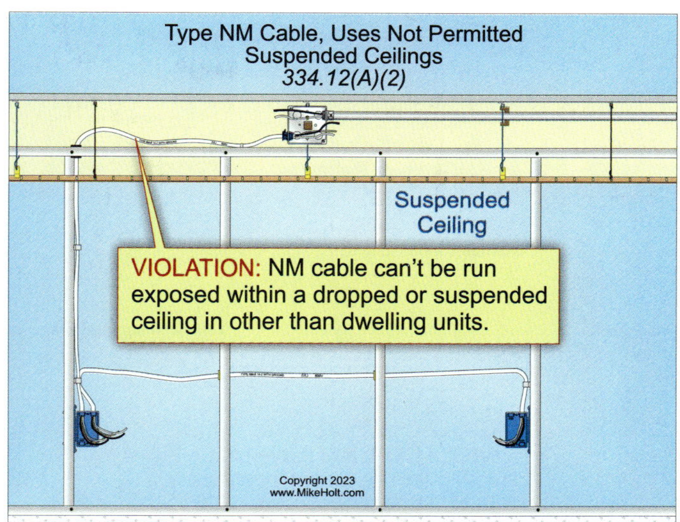

▶Figure 334–7

(6) In motion picture studios

(7) In storage battery rooms

(8) In hoistways, or on elevators or escalators

(9) Embedded in poured cement, concrete, or aggregate

(10) In any hazardous (classified) location, except where permitted by other sections in this *Code*

(B) Conditions. Type NM cable is not permitted to be used under the following conditions or in the following locations:

(1) If exposed to corrosive fumes or vapors

(2) If embedded in masonry, concrete, adobe, fill, or plaster

(3) In a shallow chase in masonry, concrete, or adobe and covered with plaster, adobe, or similar finish

(4) In wet or damp locations ▶Figure 334–8

Author's Comment:

▸ Raceways above the vapor barrier in ground floor slabs are not located in a wet location because the concrete is not in direct contact with the Earth [Article 100]. ▶Figure 334–9

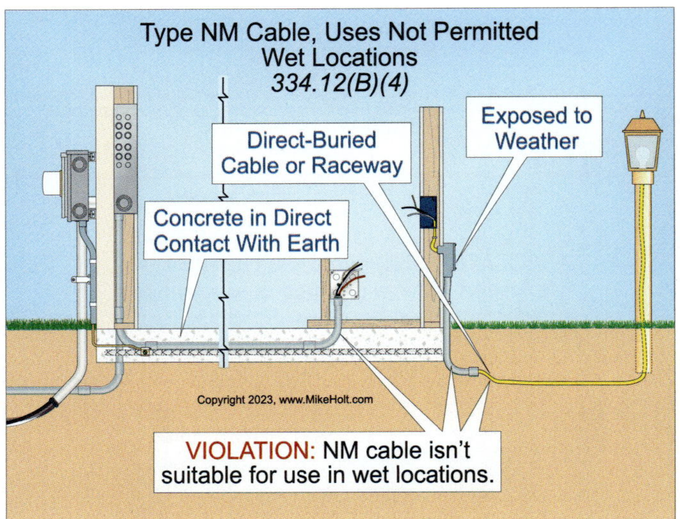

▶Figure 334–8

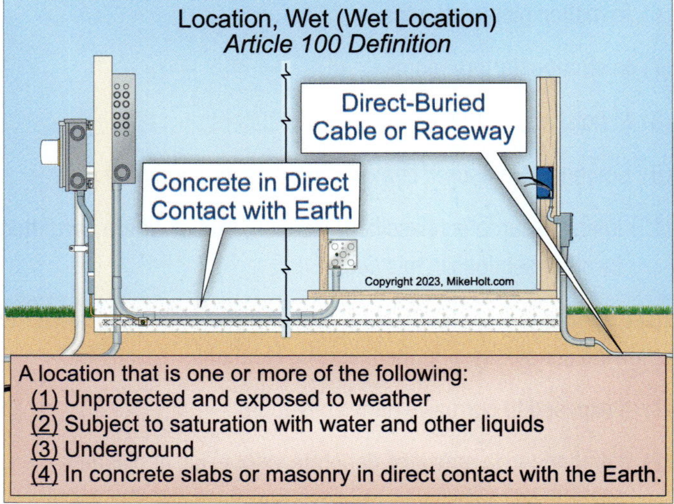

▶Figure 334–9

334.15 Exposed Work

Except as provided in 300.11(B), exposed Type NM cable can be installed as follows:

(A) Surface of the Building. Exposed Type NM cable must closely follow the surface of the building.

(B) Protected from Physical Damage. Nonmetallic-sheathed cable must be protected from physical damage by a raceway (Schedule 80 PVC, RMC, IMC, or EMT), guard strips, or other means approved by the authority having jurisdiction. ▶Figure 334–10

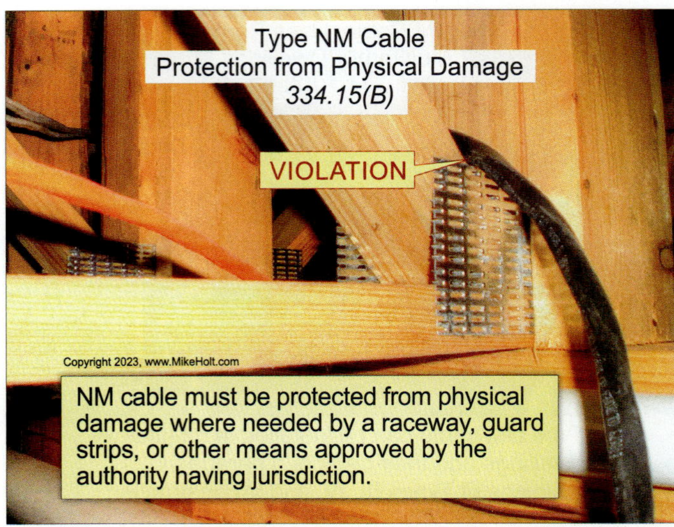

▶Figure 334–10

Where Type NM cable is installed in a raceway, a bushing or adapter that provides protection from abrasion at the point of cable entry is required. ▶Figure 334–11

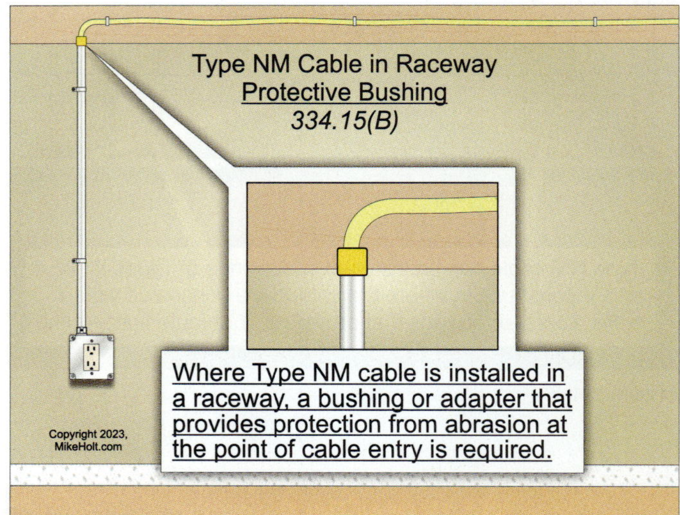

▶Figure 334–11

(C) In Unfinished Basements and Crawl Spaces. If Type NM cable is installed at angles with joists in unfinished basements and crawl spaces, cables containing conductors not smaller than two 6 AWG, or three 8 AWG, can be secured directly to the lower edges of the joists. Smaller cables must be installed through bored holes in joists or on running boards. ▶Figure 334–12

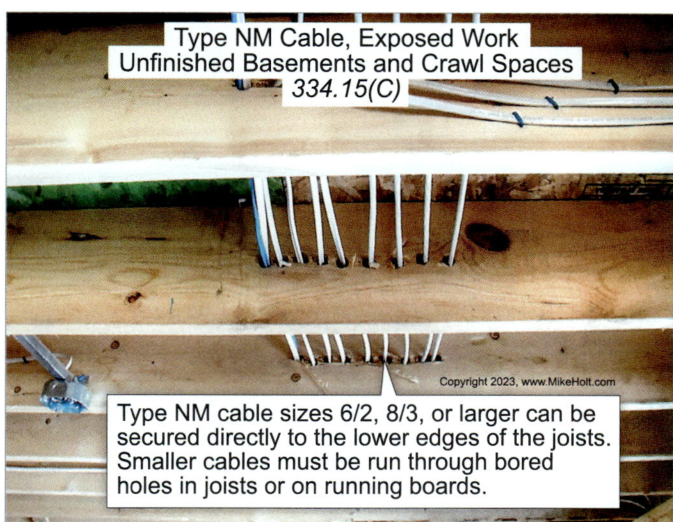

▶Figure 334–12

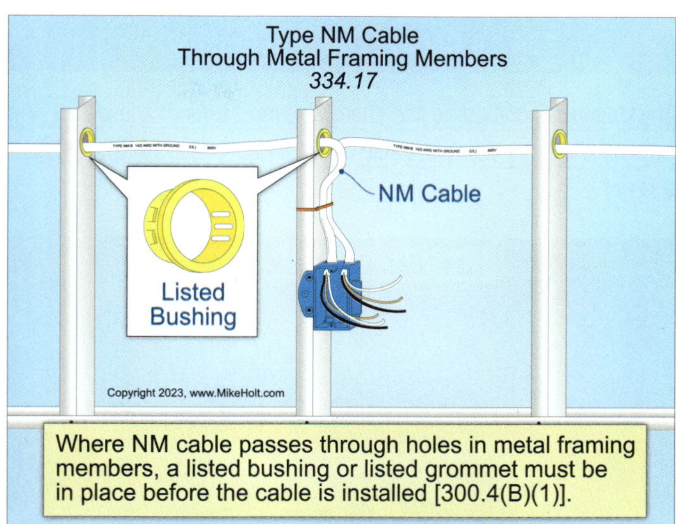

▶Figure 334–14

Type NM cable installed on a wall of an unfinished basement or crawl space subject to physical damage must be protected in accordance with 300.4, or be installed within a raceway with a nonmetallic bushing or adapter <u>that provides protection from abrasion</u> at the point where the cable enters the raceway. The cable must be secured within 12 in. of the point where it enters the raceway.

334.17 Through or Parallel to Framing Members

Cables installed through or parallel to framing members or furring strips must be protected by maintaining a 1¼ in. of separation between the cable and the nearest edge of a framing member, or by a suitable metal plate in accordance with 300.4(A), (C), and (D). ▶Figure 334–13, ▶Figure 334–14, and ▶Figure 334–15

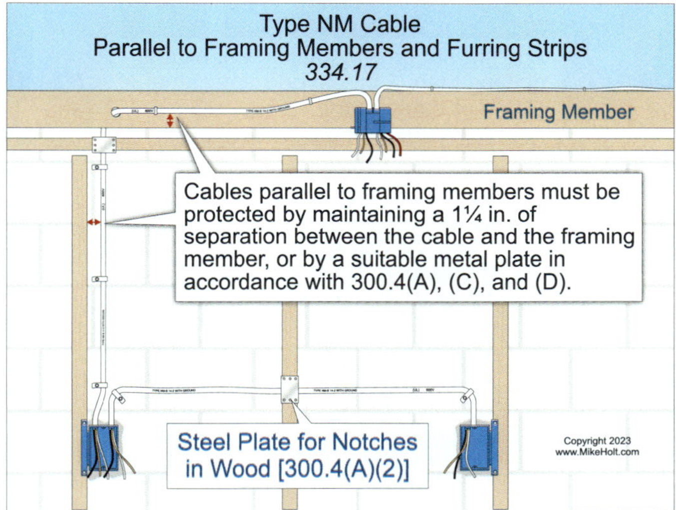

▶Figure 334–15

Author's Comment:

▶ The diameter of the holes bored must not exceed one-third the depth of the joist members and must not be any closer than 2 in. to the top, bottom, or any hole in the member. The referenced sections are in the IBC (International Building Code) section 2308.4, and the IRC (International Residential Code) section 502.8.

▶ If Type NM cable passes through factory or field openings in metal framing members, the cable must be protected by listed bushings or grommets that cover all metal edges [300.4(B)(1)]. The protection fitting must be securely fastened in the opening before installing the cable.

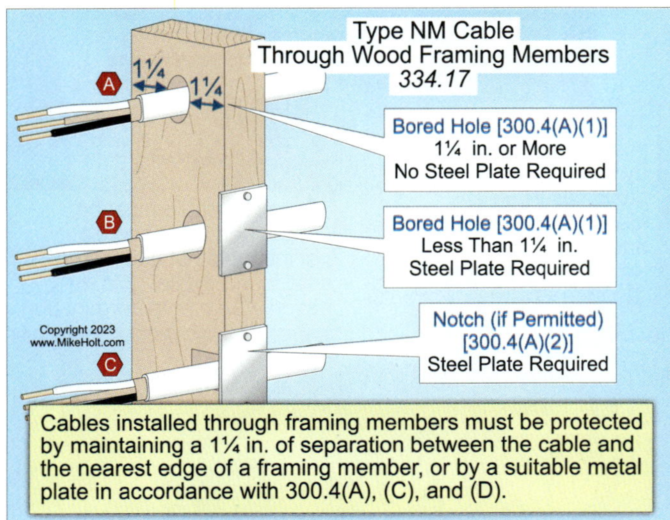

▶Figure 334–13

334.19 Cables Entering Enclosures

The sheath on nonmetallic-sheathed cable must extend no less than ¼ in. beyond any cable clamp or cable entry. ▶Figure 334–16 and ▶Figure 334–17

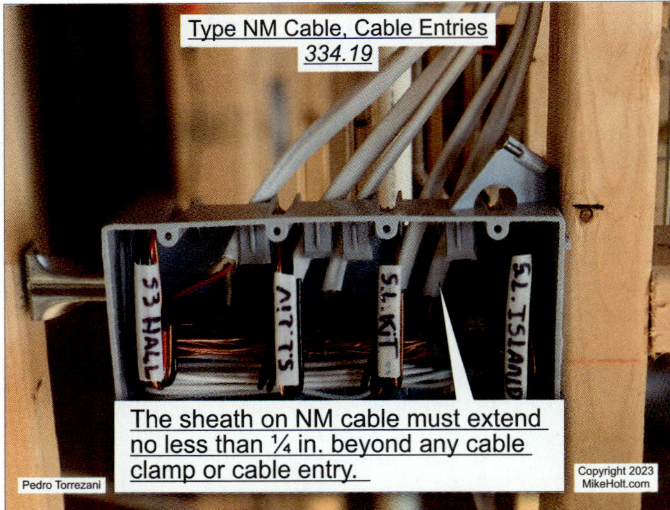

▶Figure 334–16

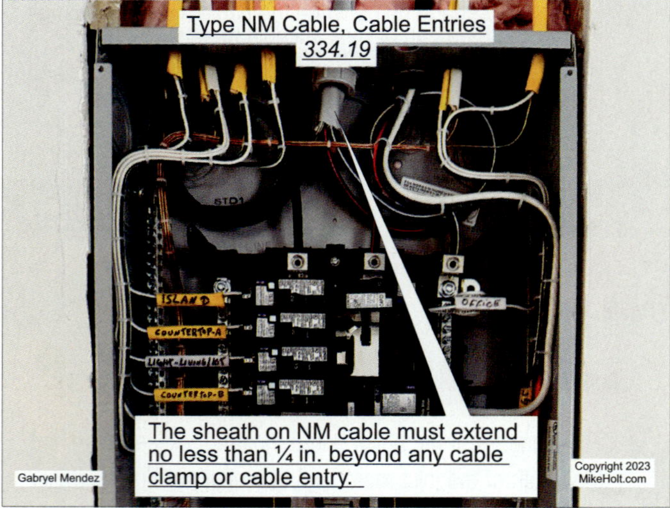

▶Figure 334–17

334.23 Accessible Roof Spaces

Type NM cable in roof spaces within 6 ft of the nearest edge of the scuttle hole run across the top of framing members must be protected by guard strips that are at least as high as the cable in accordance with 320.23. ▶Figure 334–18

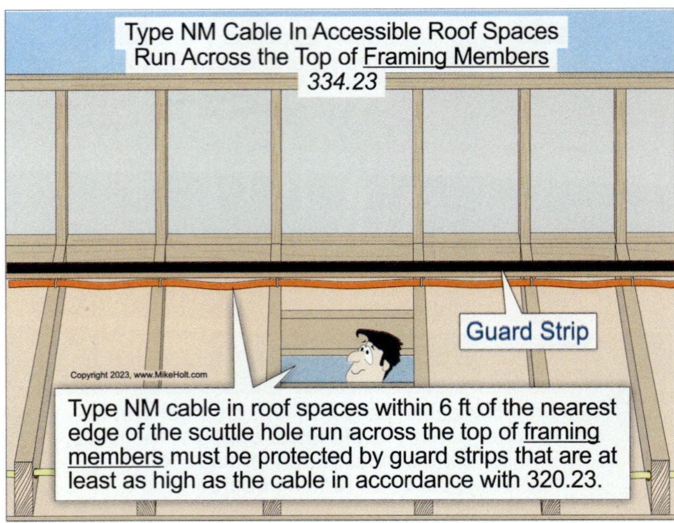

▶Figure 334–18

334.24 Bending Radius

Bends must be made so the cable will not be damaged, and the radius of the curve of any bend at the inner edge of the cable cannot be less than five times the major diameter of the cable.

334.30 Securing and Supporting

Type NM cable must be supported and secured by staples or straps, cable ties (listed and identified for securing and supporting), hangers or similar fittings at intervals not exceeding 4½ ft and within 12 in. of every cable entry termination into boxes, cabinets, or fittings. ▶Figure 334–19

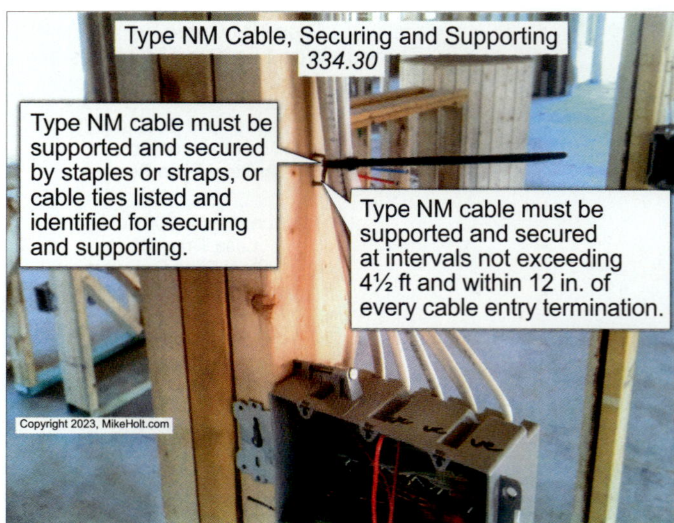

▶Figure 334–19

Author's Comment:

▶ Many times, there is a tendency to leave a length of sheathed NM cable in a box or enclosure (such as a panelboard) just to have "extra" cable. While this practice is not prohibited, the length of such sheathed cable cannot exceed 18 in. as measured along the surface of the cable.

Two-wire (flat) Type NM cable is not permitted to be stapled on edge. ▶Figure 334–20

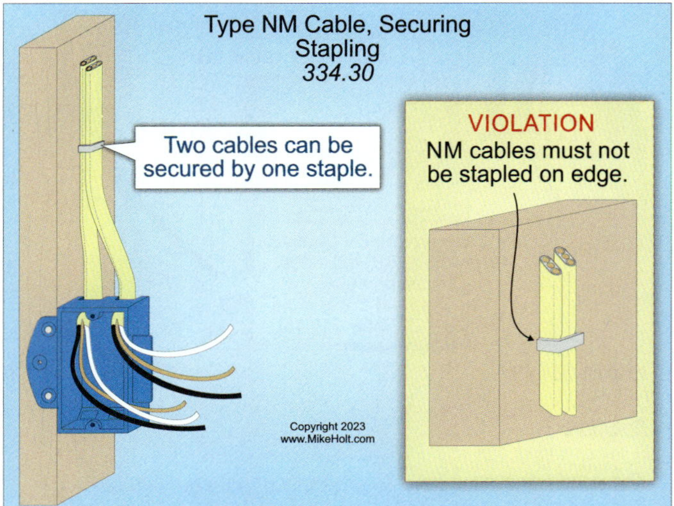

▶Figure 334–20

(A) Horizontal Runs. Type NM cable installed horizontally in bored or punched holes in wood or metal framing members, or notches in wooden members, is considered secured and supported if the distance between supports does not exceed 4½ ft, and the cable is secured within 1 ft of termination. ▶Figure 334–21

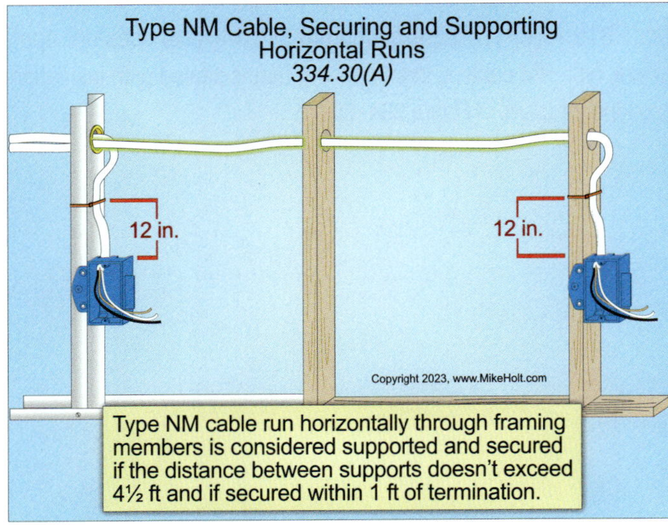

▶Figure 334–21

(B) Unsupported. Type NM cable can be unsupported in the following situations:

(1) Where the cable is fished between access points through concealed spaces in finished buildings, and support is impractical.

(2) Not more than 4½ ft of unsupported cable is permitted from the last point of support within an accessible ceiling for the connection of luminaires or equipment in a dwelling unit.

334.40 Boxes and Fittings

(B) NM Cable Interconnector Devices. A listed for use without a box nonmetallic-sheathed cable interconnector device can be installed in both exposed and concealed installations. ▶Figure 334–22

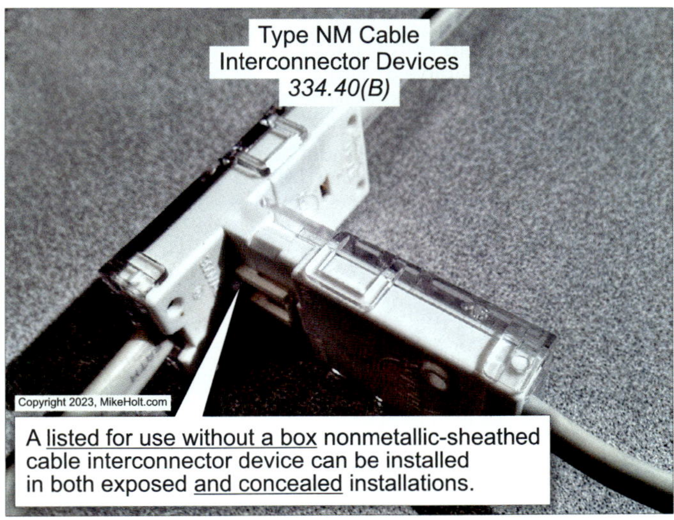

▶Figure 334–22

334.80 Conductor Ampacity

Type NM cable must be sized to the 60°C column of Table 310.16. Ampacity correction and adjustments are based on the 90°C conductor insulation rating.

▶ Example—Space Heating

Question: *What size conductor and overcurrent protective device are required for a 9,600W, 240V fixed electric space heater with a 3A, 240V blower motor?* ▶**Figure 334–23**

(a) 10 AWG/30A   *(b) 8 AWG/40A*
(c) 6 AWG/50A   *(d) 6 AWG/60A*

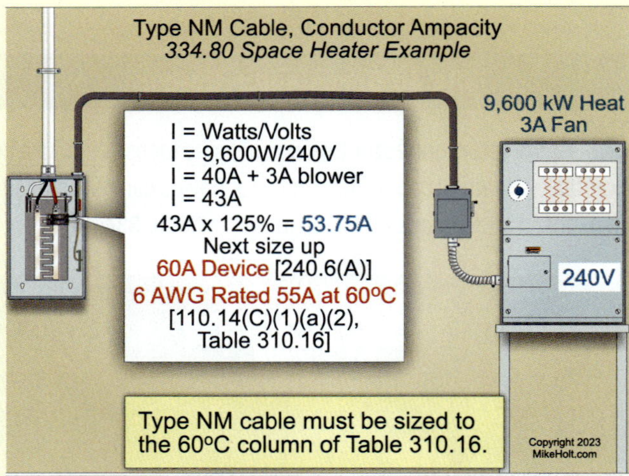

▶Figure 334–23

Solution:

Step 1: *Determine the total load.*

I = Watts/Volts
I = 9,600W/240V
I = 40A

Total Amperes = 40A (heat) + 3A (blower)
Total Amperes = 43A

Step 2: *Size the conductors at 125 percent of the total current load [110.14(C)(1)(a)(2), 210.19(A)(1), 424.4(B), and Table 310.16].*

Conductor = 43A × 125%
Conductor = 53.75A, round to 54A
Conductor = 6 AWG rated 55A at 60°C

Step 3: *Size the overcurrent protective device at 125 percent of the total current load [210.20(A), 240.4(B), and 240.6(A)].*

Overcurrent protection = 43A × 125%
Overcurrent protection = 53.75A, use the next size up: 60A [240.6(A)]

Use a 6 AWG conductor with a 60A overcurrent protective device.

Answer: *(d) 6 AWG/60A*

▶ Example EV Charger

Question: *What size Type NM cable is required for EV Charger rated 40A continuous load, where the cable is rated for 60°C conductor sizing?* ▶**Figure 334–24**

(a) 10 AWG   *(b) 8 AWG*   *(c) 6 AWG*   *(d) 4 AWG*

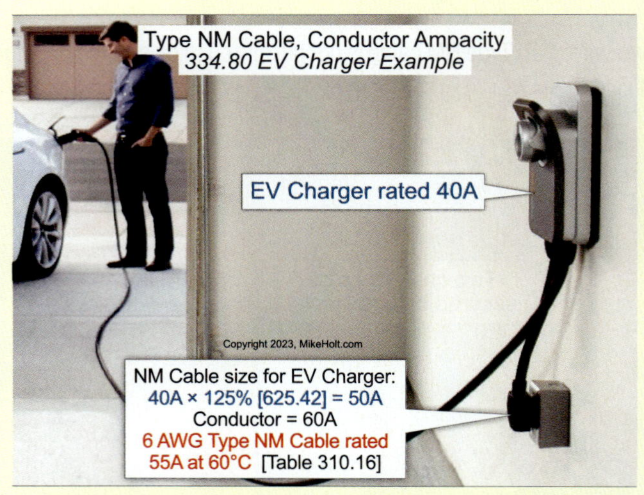

▶Figure 334–24

Solution:

The conductors must have an ampacity of not less than 50A (40A × 125% [625.42]).

6 AWG Type NM Cable rated 55A at 60°C [Table 310.16 and 334.80]

Answer: *(c) 6 AWG Type NM Cable*

If multiple Type NM cables pass through the same wood framing opening that is to be sealed with thermal insulation, caulking, or sealing foam, the ampacity of each conductor must be adjusted in accordance with Table 310.15(C)(1). The exception to 310.14(A)(2) does not apply where Type NM cable is in an opening that is sealed with insulation, caulking, or foam. ▶Figure 334–25

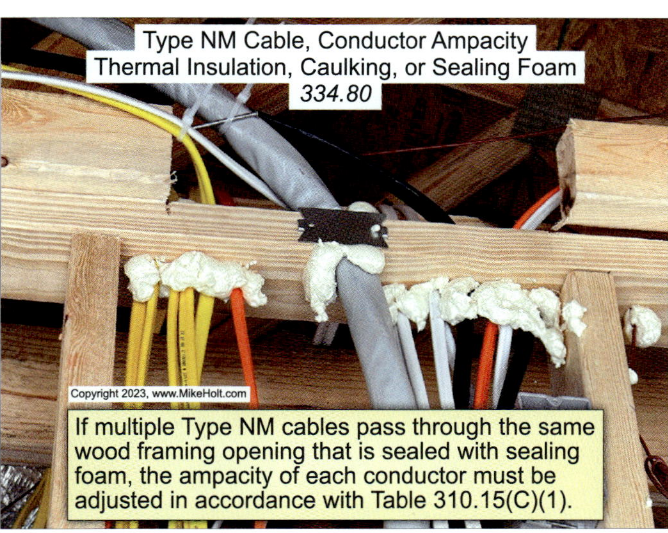

▶Figure 334–25

▶ Example

Question: *Can four Type NM cables, each containing two 14 AWG current-carrying conductors be protected by a 15A circuit breaker?*

(a) Yes   (b) No

Solution:

Step 1: *Determine the adjusted ampacity of the circuit conductors in accordance with Table 310.15(C)(1) and Table 310.16.*

14 AWG is rated 25A at 90°C [Table 310.16]

Conductor Adjustment = 70% [Table 310.15(C)(1)]

Conductor Adjusted Ampacity = 25A × 70%
Conductor Adjusted Ampacity = 17.50A

Step 2: *Verify that the adjusted conductor ampacity can be protected by the 15A circuit breaker. In this case, 14 AWG is rated 17.50A after adjustment at 90°C and 15A at 60°C [210.19(A) and 240.4(D)].*

Answer: *(a) Yes*

Part III. Construction Specifications

334.108 Equipment Grounding Conductor

Type NM cable must have an equipment grounding conductor of the wire-type. ▶Figure 334–26

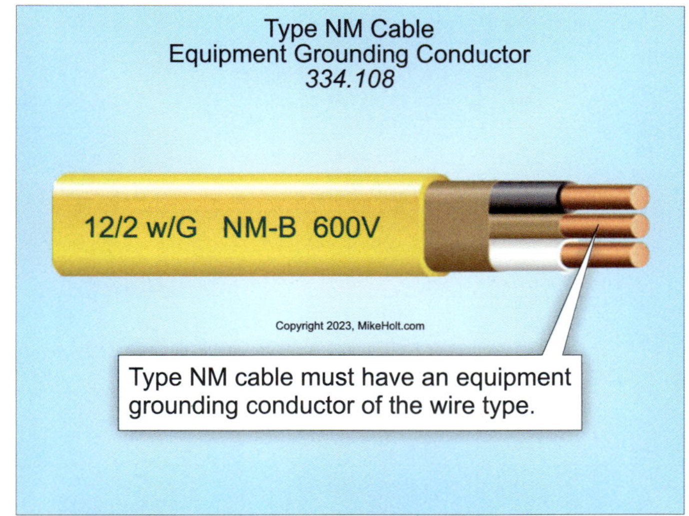

▶Figure 334–26

POWER AND CONTROL TRAY CABLE (TYPE TC)

Introduction to Article 336—Power and Control Tray Cable (Type TC)

This article covers the use and installation of power and control tray cable (Type TC). Type TC cable is flexible, inexpensive, and easily installed making it an attractive wiring method for industrial applications and for generators. Some topics covered in this material include:

- Listing Requirements
- Uses Permitted
- Uses Not Permitted
- Exposed Work
- Bending Radius
- Ampacity
- Construction
- Marking

Article 336 consists of three parts:

- Part I. General
- Part II. Installation
- Part III. Construction Specifications

According to Article 100, "Power and Control Tray (Type TC)" is a factory assembly of two or more insulated conductors (with or without associated bare or covered equipment grounding conductors) under a nonmetallic jacket. ▶Figure 336–1

Part I. General

336.1 Scope

This article covers the use and installation of power and control tray cable (Type TC). ▶Figure 336–2

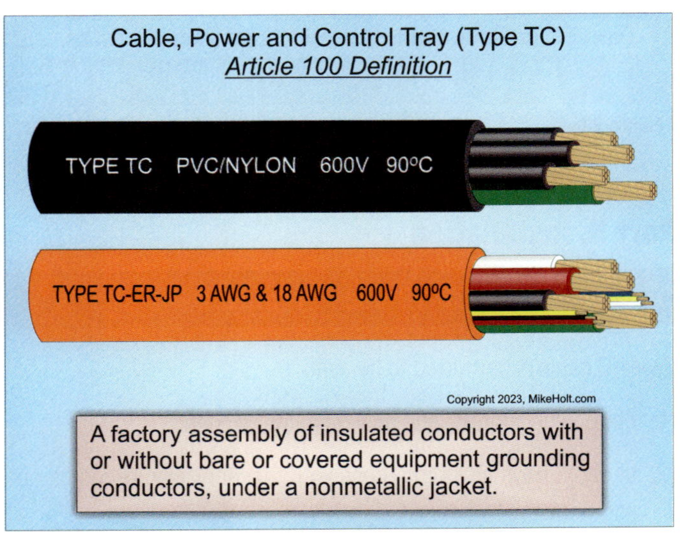

▶Figure 336–1

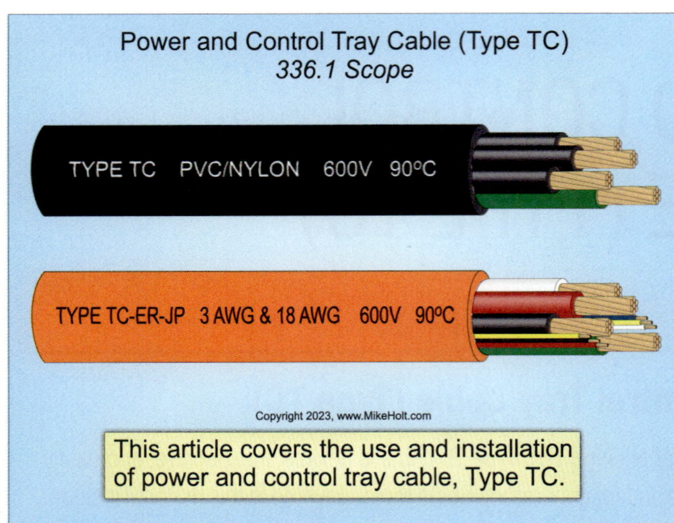

▶Figure 336–2

336.6 Listing Requirements

Type TC cable and associated fittings must be listed. ▶Figure 336–3

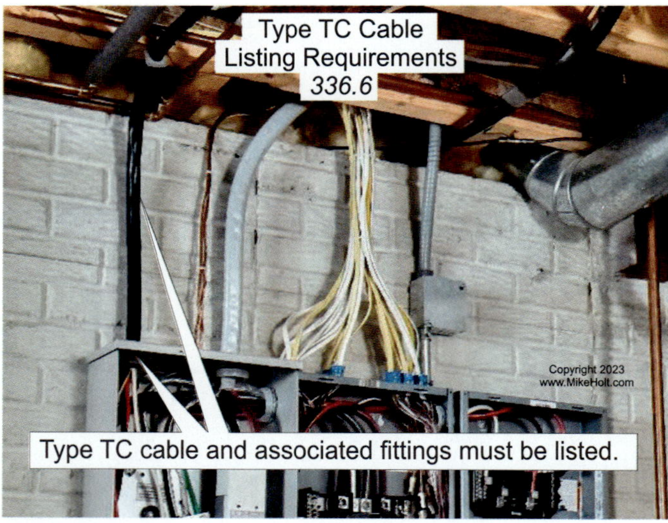

▶Figure 336–3

Part II. Installation

336.10 Uses Permitted

Type TC cable is permitted to be used:

(1) For power, lighting, and power-limited circuits

(2) In cable trays including those with mechanically discontinuous segments up to 1 ft

(3) In raceways

(4) In outdoor locations supported by a messenger wire

(5) For Class 1 power-limited circuits in accordance with Article 724

(7) Between a cable tray and equipment if it complies with 336.10(7)(a) through (f)

(8) In wet locations where the cable is resistant to moisture and corrosive agents

(9) Type TC-ER-JP cable containing both power conductors and control <u>circuits</u> must be installed in accordance with Part II of Article 334 for interior wiring and Part II of Article 340 for exterior wiring ▶Figure 336–4

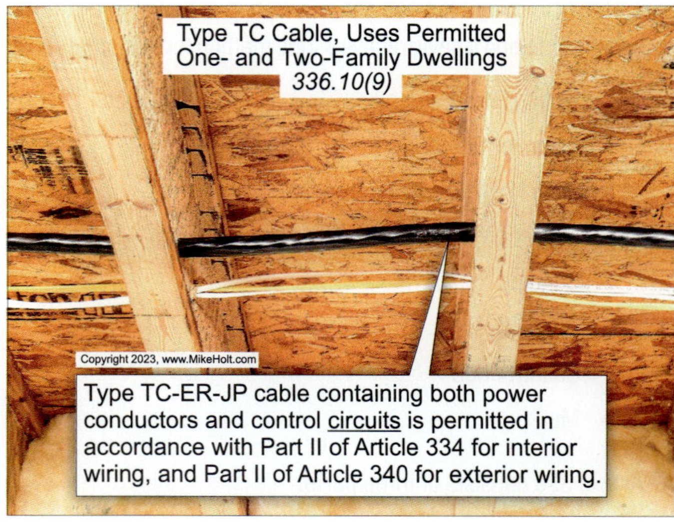

▶Figure 336–4

Author's Comment:

▶ In accordance with "*UL Guide Information QPOR*," for Type TC-ER-JP cable, the "ER" marking identifies it as suitable for exposed runs and the suffix "-JP" identifies it as being suitable for pulling through wood framing members.

▶ It is important to note that this permitted use only applies if the Type TC cable contains both power and control conductors. It is not a blanket permission to use this cable for dwelling unit branch circuits and feeders.

Ex: Where Type TC cable is used to connect a generator and its associated equipment, the cable ampacity limitations of 334.80 and 340.80 do not apply.

(10) Direct buried where identified for direct burial

(11) <u>In hazardous (classified) locations as permitted in this *Code*</u>

(12) <u>For service-entrance conductors where identified for such use and marked "Type TC-ER"</u>

336.12 Uses Not Permitted

Type TC cables are not permitted:

(1) Where exposed to physical damage

(2) Outside a raceway or cable tray system, except as permitted in 336.10(4), (7), (9), and (10)

(3) Exposed to the direct rays of the sun, unless identified as sunlight resistant

336.24 Bending Radius

Bends in Type TC cable must be made so the cable will not be damaged. Type TC cable without metal shielding must have a minimum bending radius as follows:

(1) Four times the overall diameter for cables 1 in. or less in diameter.

(2) Five times the overall diameter for cables larger than 1 in. but not more than 2 in. in diameter.

SERVICE-ENTRANCE CABLE (TYPES SE AND USE)

Introduction to Article 338—Service-Entrance Cable (Types SE and USE)

Article 338 covers the use, installation, and construction specifications of service-entrance cable (Types SE and USE). These cables can be a single conductor or a multiconductor assembly in sizes 14 AWG and larger for copper, and 12 AWG and larger for aluminum or copper-clad aluminum, within an overall nonmetallic outer jacket or covering. Some topics covered in this material include:

▶ Listing Requirements

▶ Uses Permitted

▶ Uses Not Permitted

▶ Bending Radius

▶ Construction

▶ Marking

This article consists of three parts:

▶ Part I. General

▶ Part II. Installation

▶ Part III. Construction Specifications

According to Article 100, "Service-Entrance Cable (Types SE and USE)" cable is a single or multiconductor cable with an overall covering. ▶Figure 338–1

Part I. General

338.1 Scope

Article 338 covers the use, installation, and construction specifications of service-entrance cable (Types SE and USE). ▶Figure 338–2

338.6 Listing Requirements

Types SE and USE cables and associated fittings must be listed. ▶Figure 338–3

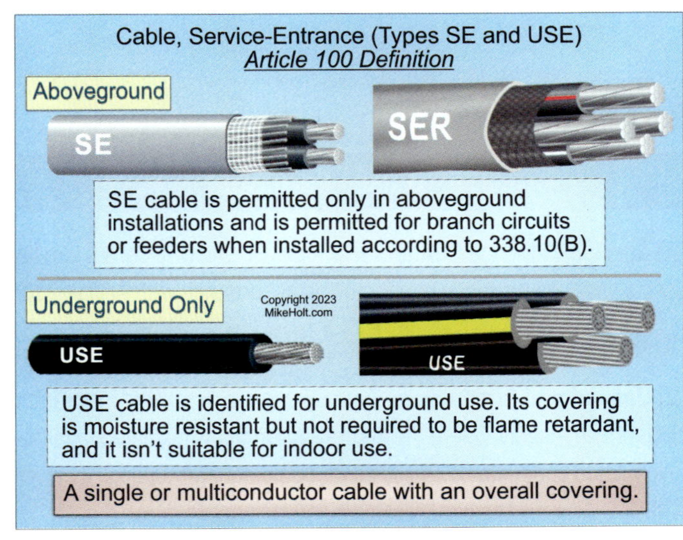

▶Figure 338–1

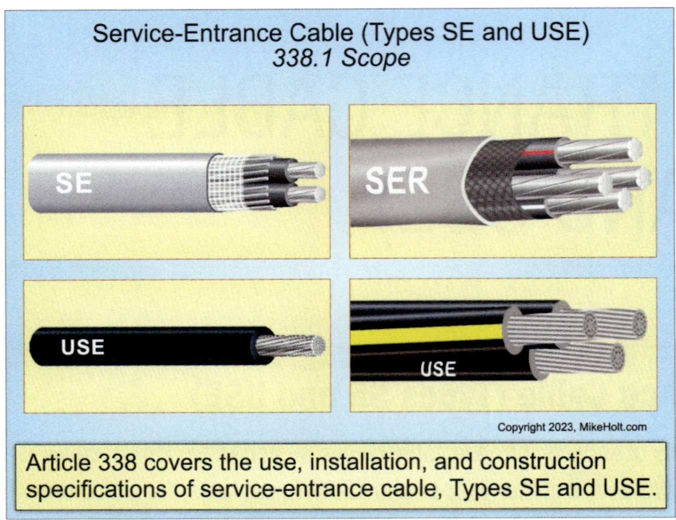

Service-Entrance Cable (Types SE and USE)
338.1 Scope

Article 338 covers the use, installation, and construction specifications of service-entrance cable, Types SE and USE.

▶Figure 338–2

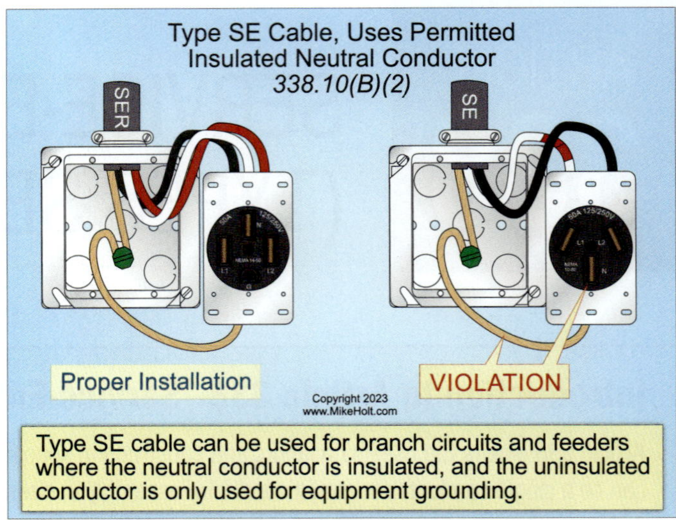

Type SE Cable, Uses Permitted
Insulated Neutral Conductor
338.10(B)(2)

Type SE cable can be used for branch circuits and feeders where the neutral conductor is insulated, and the uninsulated conductor is only used for equipment grounding.

▶Figure 338–4

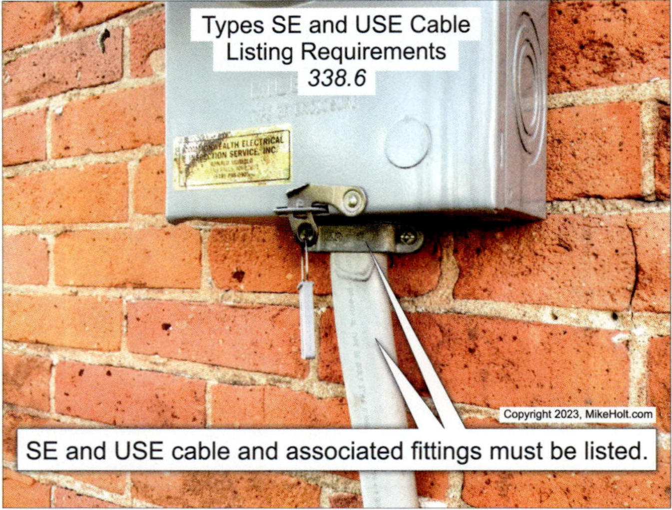

Types SE and USE Cable
Listing Requirements
338.6

SE and USE cable and associated fittings must be listed.

▶Figure 338–3

Part II. Installation

338.10 Uses Permitted

(A) Service-Entrance Conductors. Types SE and USE cables can be used as service-entrance conductors in accordance with Article 230.

(B) Branch Circuits or Feeders.

(2) Uninsulated Conductors. Type SE cable is permitted for branch circuits and feeders where the neutral conductor is insulated, and the uninsulated conductor is only used for equipment grounding. ▶Figure 338–4

(3) Temperature Limitations. Type SE cable is not permitted to be subjected to conductor temperatures exceeding its insulation rating.

(4) Installation Methods for Branch Circuits and Feeders.

(a) Interior Installations.

(1) Type SE cable used for interior branch circuit or feeder wiring must be installed in accordance with the same requirements as Type NM cable in Part II of Article 334, excluding 334.80. ▶Figure 338–5

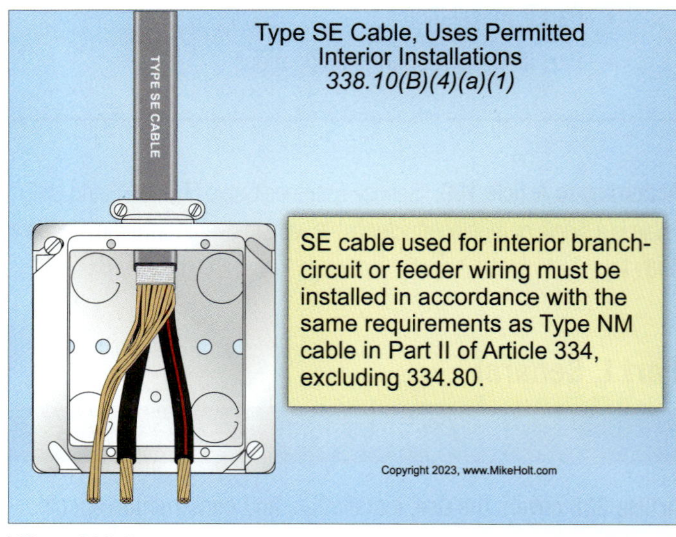

Type SE Cable, Uses Permitted
Interior Installations
338.10(B)(4)(a)(1)

SE cable used for interior branch-circuit or feeder wiring must be installed in accordance with the same requirements as Type NM cable in Part II of Article 334, excluding 334.80.

▶Figure 338–5

(2) Where more than two Type SE cables containing two or more current-carrying conductors in each cable are bundled in contact with thermal insulation, caulking, or sealing foam, the ampacity of each conductor must be adjusted in accordance with Table 310.15(C)(1).

(3) The ampacity of Type SE cable conductors 10 AWG and smaller, where installed in contact with thermal insulation or for conductor ampacity correction and/or adjustment, must be sized in accordance with 60°C (140°F) conductor temperature rating. The maximum conductor temperature rating ampacity may be used for adjustment and/or correction.

(b) Exterior Installations.

(1) Type USE cable must be installed in accordance with Part I of Article 225 and supported in accordance with 334.30.

(2) Where Type USE cable is run underground, the cable must comply with Part II of Article 340.

Author's Comment:

▸ In accordance with "*UL 44 Standard for Thermoset-Insulated Wires and Cables,*" when Type USE-2 is used in multiple ratings, such as RHH and RHW-2, it is taken as a single insulated conductor. The voltage rating on the USE-2 rating is 600V whereas the typical RHH/RHW-2 is rated at 1000V.

338.12 Uses Not Permitted

(A) Service-Entrance Cable. Type SE cable is not permitted under the following conditions or locations:

(1) Where subject to physical damage

(2) Underground with or without a raceway

(B) Underground Service-Entrance Cable. Type USE cable is not permitted:

(1) For interior wiring

(2) Above ground, except where protected against physical damage in accordance with 300.5(D)

338.24 Bending Radius

Bends in SE and USE cable must be made so the protective coverings of the cable are not damaged, and the radius of the curve of the inner edge is at least five times the major diameter of the cable.

UNDERGROUND FEEDER AND BRANCH-CIRCUIT CABLE (TYPE UF)

Introduction to Article 340—Underground Feeder and Branch-Circuit Cable (Type UF)

This article covers the use, installation, and construction specifications of underground feeder and branch-circuit cable (Type UF). Type UF cable is an assembly of conductors in sizes 14 AWG through 4/0 AWG [340.104] covered in a moisture-, fungus-, and corrosion-resistant sheath suitable for direct burial in the Earth. The sheath of multiconductor Type UF cable is a molded plastic that encases the insulated conductors. It can be difficult to strip off the sheath without damaging the conductor insulation or cutting yourself, so be careful. Some topics covered in this material include:

▸ Listing Requirements

▸ Uses Permitted

▸ Uses Not Permitted

▸ Bending Radius

▸ Construction

Article 340 consists of three parts:

▸ Part I. General

▸ Part II. Installation

▸ Part III. Construction Specifications

According to Article 100, "Underground Feeder Cable (Type UF)" is a factory assembly of insulated conductors with an integral or an overall covering of nonmetallic material suitable for direct burial in the Earth. ▸Figure 340–1

Part I. General

340.1 Scope

Article 340 covers the use, installation, and construction specifications of underground feeder and branch-circuit cable, Type UF. ▸Figure 340–2

340.6 Listing Requirements

Type UF cable and associated fittings must be listed.

Part II. Installation

340.10 Uses Permitted

Type UF cable is permitted:

(1) Underground in accordance with 300.5

(2) As a single conductor in a trench or raceway with circuit conductors

(3) For wiring in wet, dry, or corrosive locations

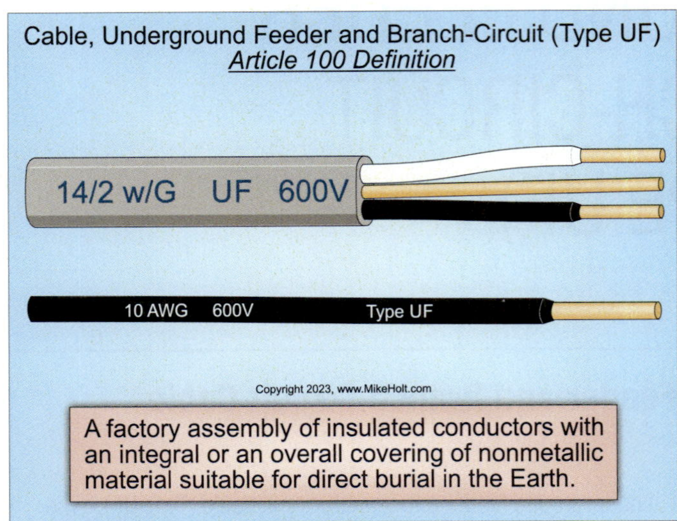

▶Figure 340–1

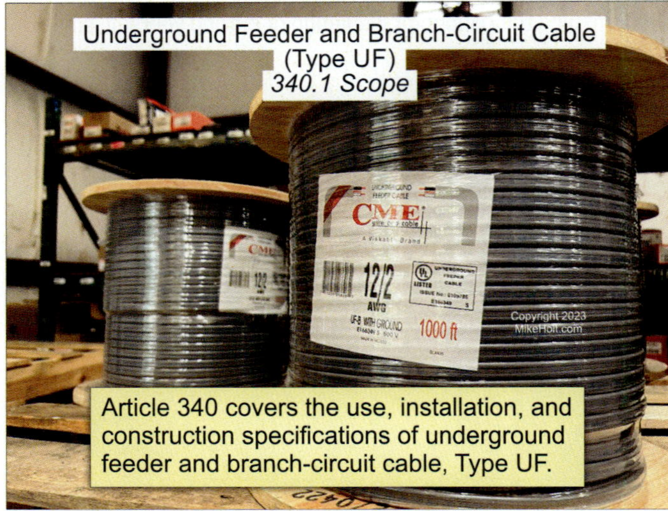

▶Figure 340–2

(4) Where installed as nonmetallic-sheathed cable, the installation must comply with Parts II and III of Article 334, except for 334.12(B)

340.12 Uses Not Permitted

Type UF cable is not permitted to be used:

(1) As service-entrance cable [230.43]

(2) In commercial garages [Article 511]

(3) In theaters [520.5]

(4) In motion picture studios [530.11]

(5) In storage battery rooms [Article 480]

(6) In hoistways [Article 620]

(7) In hazardous (classified) locations, except as specifically permitted by other articles in this *Code*

(8) Embedded in concrete

(9) Exposed to direct sunlight unless identified

Note: The sunlight-resistant marking on the outer jacket does not apply to the individual conductors.

(10) Where subject to physical damage ▶Figure 340–3

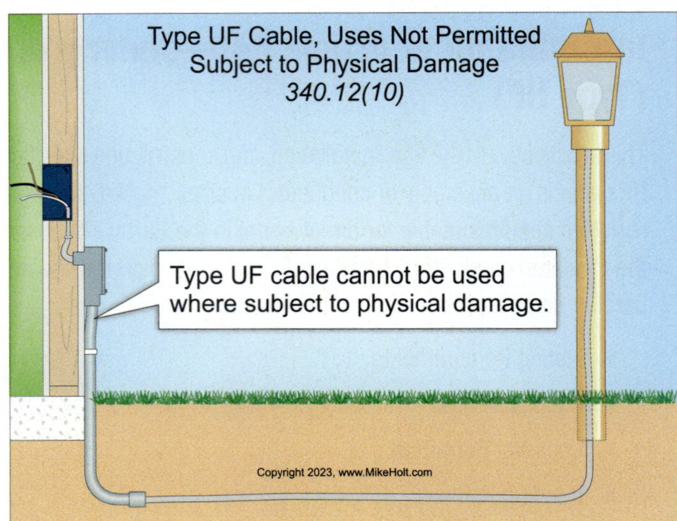

▶Figure 340–3

(11) As overhead cable, except where installed as messenger-supported wiring in accordance with Part II of Article 396

Author's Comment:

▶ UF cable is not permitted in ducts or plenum spaces [300.22(C)(1)], or in patient care spaces of health care facilities [517.13].

340.24 Bends

Bends must be made so the cable will not be damaged, and the radius of the curve of any bend at the inner edge of the cable must not be less than five times the major diameter of the cable.

340.80 Ampacity

The ampacity of conductors contained in Type UF cable is based on the 60°C insulation rating listed in Table 310.16.

Part III. Construction Specifications

340.108 Equipment Grounding Conductor

Type UF cable is permitted to have an insulated or bare equipment grounding conductor.

340.112 Insulation

The conductors of Type UF cable must be one of the moisture-resistant types listed in Table 310.4(1) that is suitable for branch-circuit wiring. If installed as a substitute wiring method for Type NM cable, the conductor insulation must be rated 90°C (194°F).

INTERMEDIATE METAL CONDUIT (IMC)

Introduction to Article 342—Intermediate Metal Conduit (IMC)

Article 342 covers the use, installation, and construction specifications of intermediate metal conduit (IMC) and associated fittings. IMC is a circular metal raceway that can be threaded and is available in trade sizes from ½ to 6. It has the same outside diameter as rigid metal conduit (RMC) [Article 344] but is made of a stronger metal which allows a thinner wall, making it lighter and providing a larger interior cross-sectional area for holding conductors. Some topics covered in this material include:

▸ Listing Requirements

▸ Uses Permitted

▸ Dissimilar Metals

▸ Bending, Reaming, and Threading

▸ Securing and Supporting

▸ Bushings

▸ Use as an Equipment Grounding Conductor

▸ Construction

This article consists of three parts:

▸ Part I. General

▸ Part II. Installation

▸ Part III. Construction Specifications

According to Article 100, "IMC" is a steel raceway of circular cross section that can be threaded with integral or associated couplings, listed for the installation of electrical conductors. ▸Figure 342–1

Author's Comment:

▸ The type of steel from which intermediate metal conduit is manufactured, the process by which it is made, and the corrosion protection applied are all equal (or superior) to that of rigid metal conduit.

Part I. General

342.1 Scope

Article 342 covers the use, installation, and construction specifications of intermediate metal conduit (IMC) and associated fittings. ▸Figure 342–2

342.6 Listing Requirements

Intermediate metal conduit and its associated fittings must be listed.

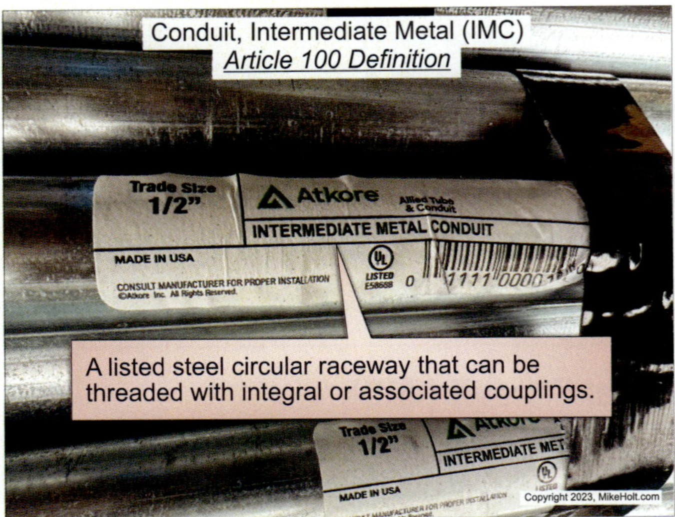

▶Figure 342–1

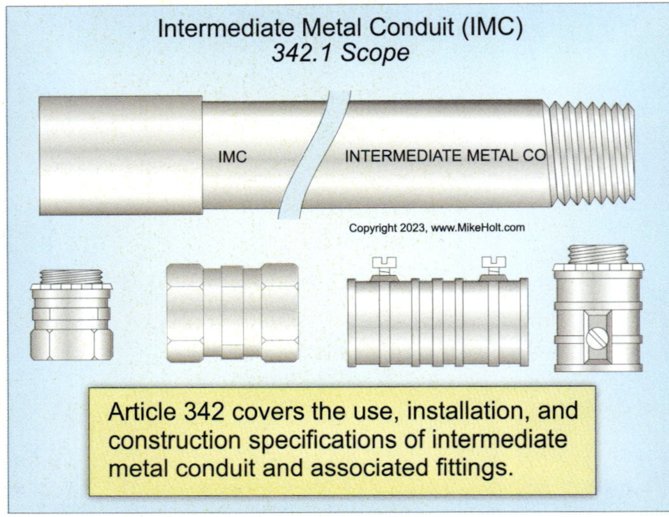

▶Figure 342–2

Author's Comment:

▸ Using listed IMC with listed fittings will ensure a low-impedance grounding path back to the supply source in case of a ground fault, and therefore the metal raceway itself can be used as an equipment grounding conductor [342.60].

Part II. Installation

342.10 Uses Permitted

(A) Atmospheric Conditions and Occupancies. IMC is permitted in all atmospheric conditions and occupancies.

(B) Corrosive Environments. IMC, elbows, couplings, and fittings can be installed in concrete, in direct contact with the Earth, in direct burial applications, or in areas subject to severe corrosive influences if provided with supplementary corrosion protection approved for the condition.

Note: See 300.6 for protection against corrosion.

Author's Comment:

▸ In accordance with "*UL Guide Information DYIX*," supplementary corrosion protection is required when IMC and associated fittings are buried in soil having a resistivity less than 2000Ω. In addition, supplementary corrosion protection is required at the point where IMC transitions from concrete encasement to the soil.

(E) Severe Physical Damage. IMC is permitted where subject to severe physical damage.

342.14 Dissimilar Metals

Where practical, contact of IMC with dissimilar metals should be avoided to prevent the deterioration of the metal because of galvanic action. Aluminum and stainless steel fittings and enclosures are permitted to be used with galvanized steel Type IMC where not subject to severe corrosive influences.

342.20 Trade Size

(A) Minimum. IMC smaller than trade size ½ is not permitted.

(B) Maximum. IMC larger than trade size 6 is not permitted.

342.22 Number of Conductors

The number of conductors in IMC is not permitted to exceed the percentage fill specified in Chapter 9, Table 1. Raceways must be large enough to permit the installation and removal of conductors without damaging the conductors' insulation.

Cables are permitted to be installed in IMC where such use is not prohibited by the respective cable articles. The number of cables must not exceed the percentage fill specified in Chapter 9, Table 1.

342.24 Bends

(A) How Made. Raceway bends are not permitted to be made in any manner that will damage the raceway or significantly change its internal diameter (no kinks).

(B) Degrees of Bends in One Run. To reduce the stress and friction on conductor insulation, the total degree of bends (including offsets) between pull points is not permitted to exceed 360 degrees. ▶Figure 342–3 and ▶Figure 342–4

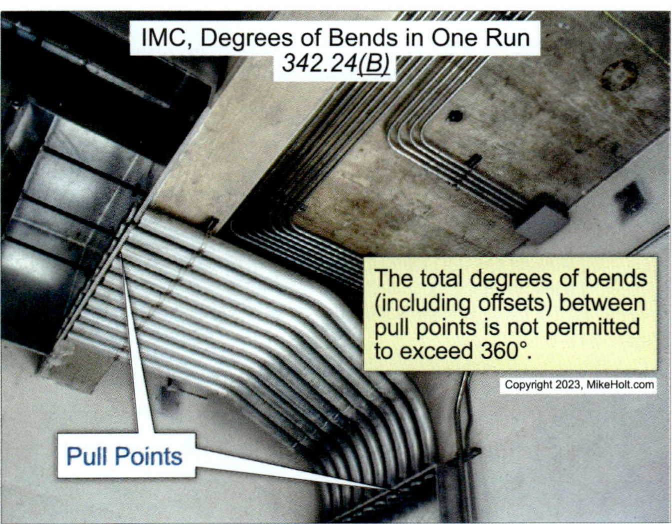

▶Figure 342–3

342.28 Reaming

When the raceway is cut in the field, reaming is required to remove the rough edges.

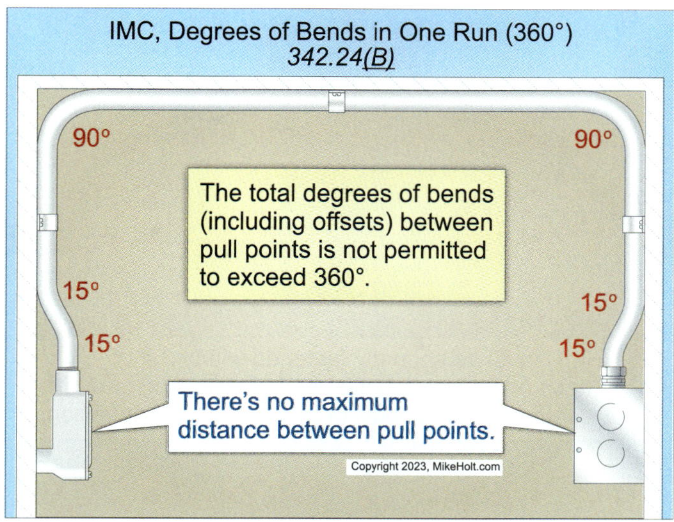

▶Figure 342–4

342.30 Securing and Supporting

IMC must be securely fastened in place and supported in accordance with 342.30(A) and (B).

(A) Securely Fastened. IMC must be secured in accordance with any of the following:

(1) Fastened within 3 ft of each outlet box, junction box, device box, cabinet, conduit body, or other conduit termination. ▶Figure 342–5

(2) When structural members do not permit the raceway to be secured within 3 ft of a box or termination fitting, the raceway must be secured within 5 ft of the termination. ▶Figure 342–6

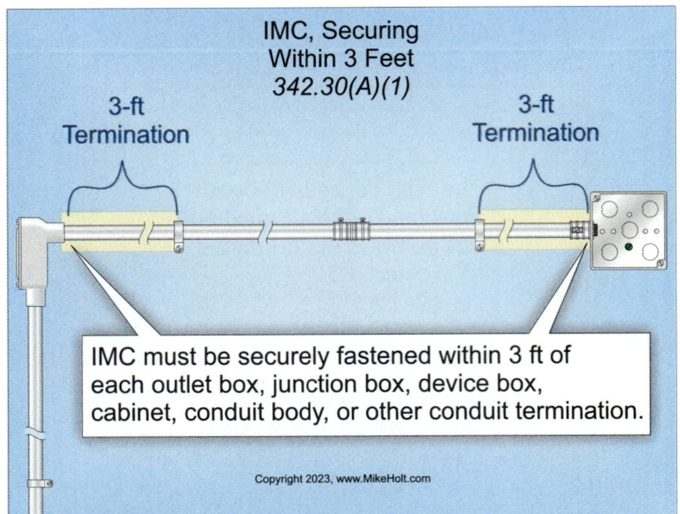

▶Figure 342–5

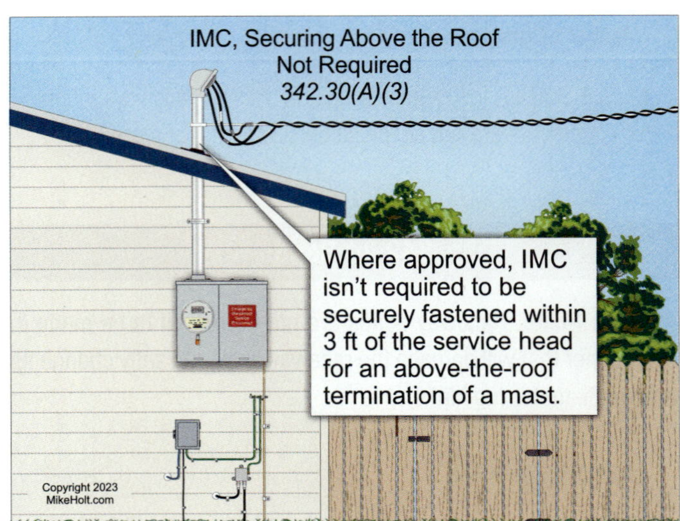

▶Figure 342–7

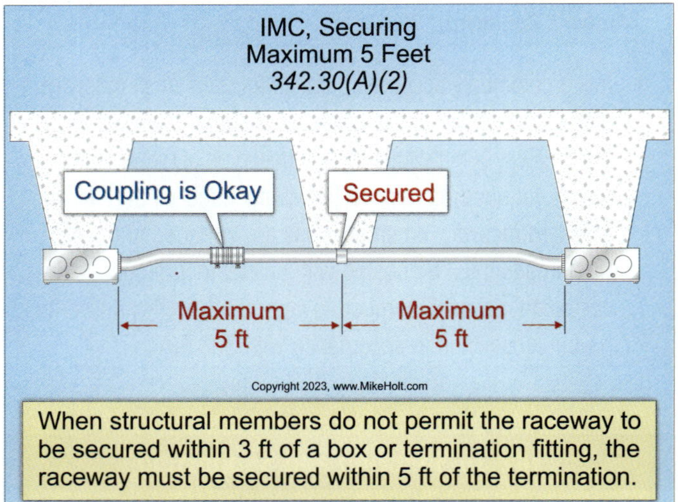

▶Figure 342–6

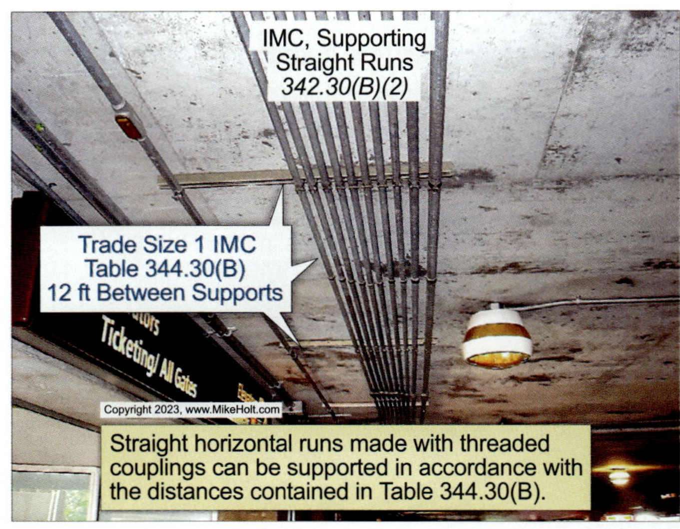

▶Figure 342–8

(3) Where approved, IMC is not required to be securely fastened within 3 ft of the service head for an above-the-roof termination of a mast. ▶Figure 342–7

(B) Supports.

(1) General. IMC must be supported at intervals not exceeding 10 ft.

(2) Straight Runs. Straight horizontal runs made with threaded couplings can be supported in accordance with the distances contained in Table 344.30(B). ▶Figure 342–8 and ▶Figure 342–9

(3) Vertical Risers. Exposed vertical risers of IMC for fixed equipment can be supported at intervals not exceeding 20 ft if the conduit is made up with threaded couplings, firmly supported, securely fastened at the top and bottom of the riser, and if no other means of support is available. ▶Figure 342–10

Table 344.30(B) Supports for Rigid Metal Conduit	
Trade Size	Support Spacing
½–¾	10 ft
1	12 ft
1¼–1½	14 ft
2–2½	16 ft
3 and larger	20 ft

(4) Horizontal Runs. IMC installed horizontally through framing members is considered supported and secured if such support does not exceed 10-ft intervals, and the conduit is secured within 3 ft of termination.

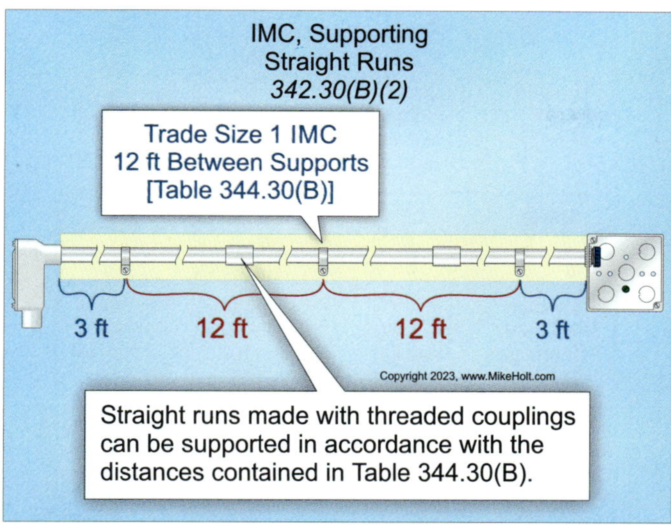

▶Figure 342–9

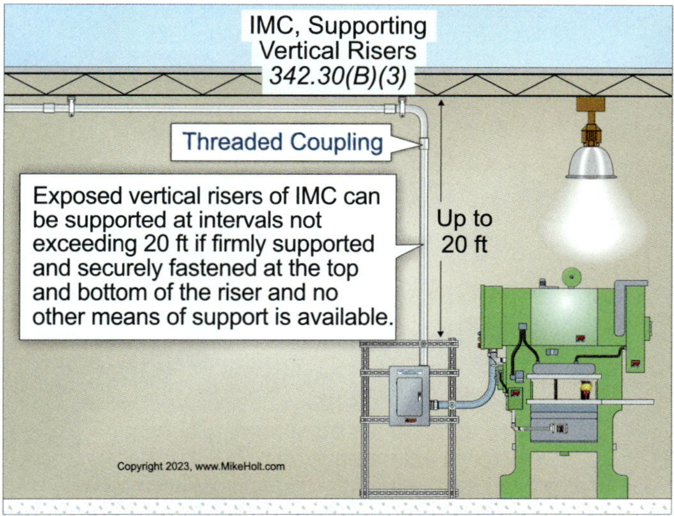

▶Figure 342–10

▸ IMC must be provided with expansion fittings where necessary to compensate for thermal expansion and contraction [300.7(B)]. The expansion characteristics for metal raceways are determined by multiplying the values from Table 352.44 by 0.20. Those for aluminum raceways are determined by multiplying the values from Table 352.44 by 0.40 [300.7(B) Note].

342.42 Couplings and Connectors

(A) Installation.

Effective Ground-Fault Path. Threadless couplings and connectors must be made up tight to maintain an effective ground-fault current path to safely conduct fault current in accordance with 250.4(A)(5), 250.96(A), and 300.10.

▸ Loose locknuts have been found to nearly disintegrate before a fault was cleared because loose termination fittings increase the impedance of the ground-fault current path.

Concrete Buried. If buried in concrete, threadless fittings must be of the concrete-tight type. ▶Figure 342–11

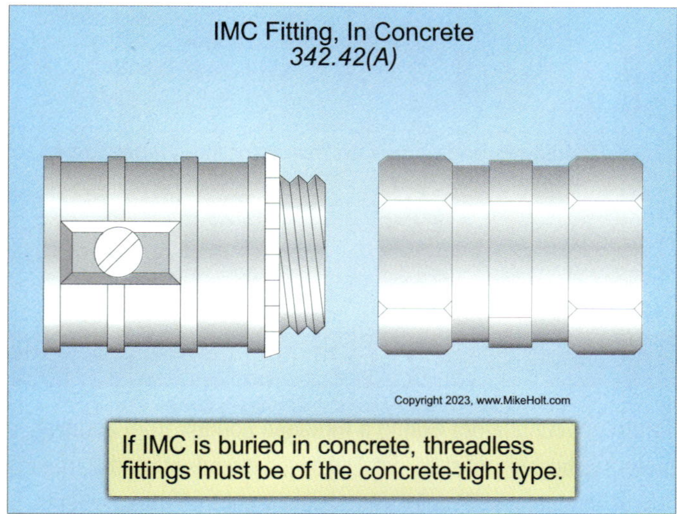

▶Figure 342–11

Wet Locations. Fittings installed in wet locations must be listed for use in wet locations to prevent moisture or water from entering or accumulating within the enclosure as required by 314.15. ▶Figure 342–12

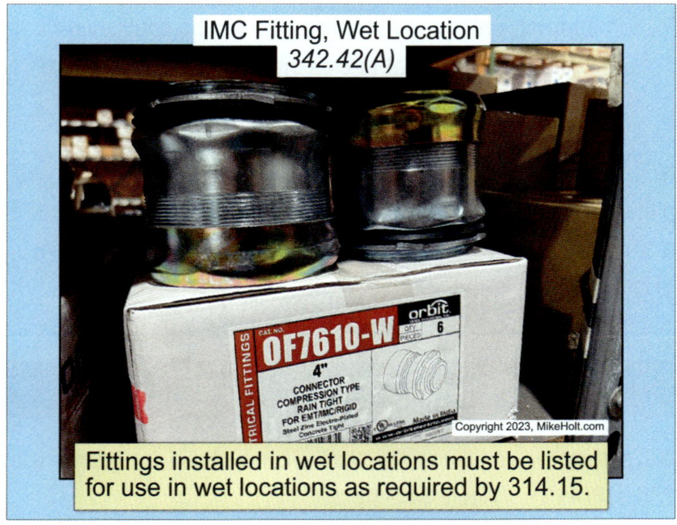

▶Figure 342–12

(B) Running Threads. Running threads are not permitted for the connection of couplings, but they are permitted at other locations. ▶Figure 342–13

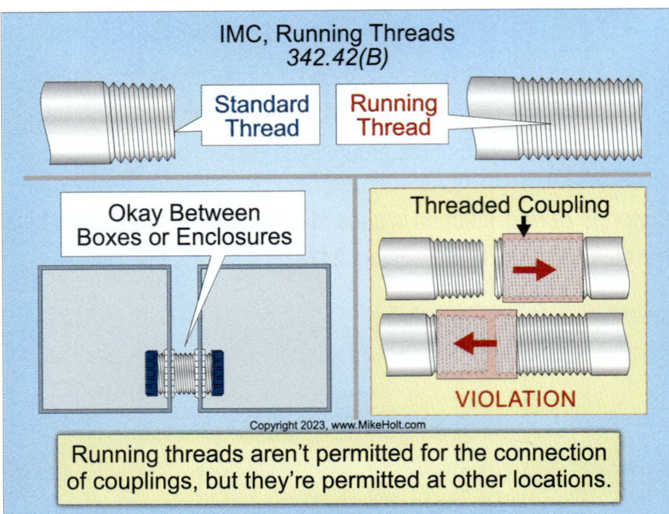

▶Figure 342–13

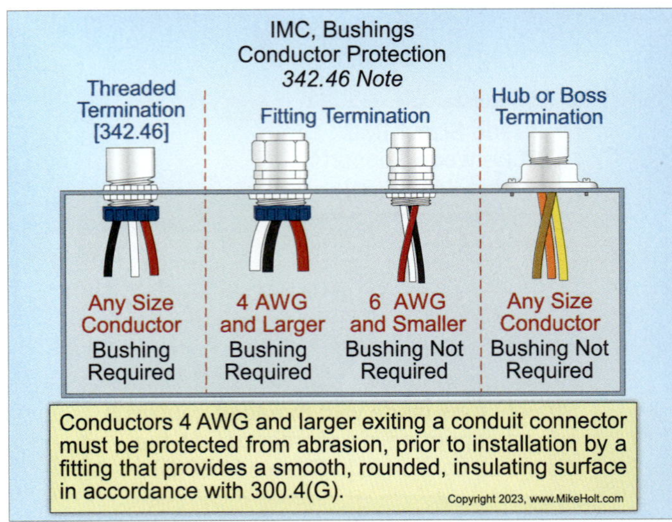

▶Figure 342–14

342.46 Bushings

To protect conductors exiting a threaded conduit from abrasion, a protective bushing must be installed on the threads of conduit (regardless of conductor size) unless the raceway enters a threaded entry in a box, fitting, or enclosure.

Author's Comment:

▶ In accordance with "*UL 514B Standard for Conduit, Tubing, and Cable Fittings*" section 5.4.1.1, a conduit fitting must be provided with a positive end stop for the conduit and a smooth rounded throat to protect against abrasion of insulation on conductors entering the conduit.

Note: Conductors 4 AWG and larger exiting a conduit connector must be protected from abrasion prior to the installation by a fitting that provides a smooth, rounded, insulating surface in accordance with 300.4(G). ▶Figure 342–14

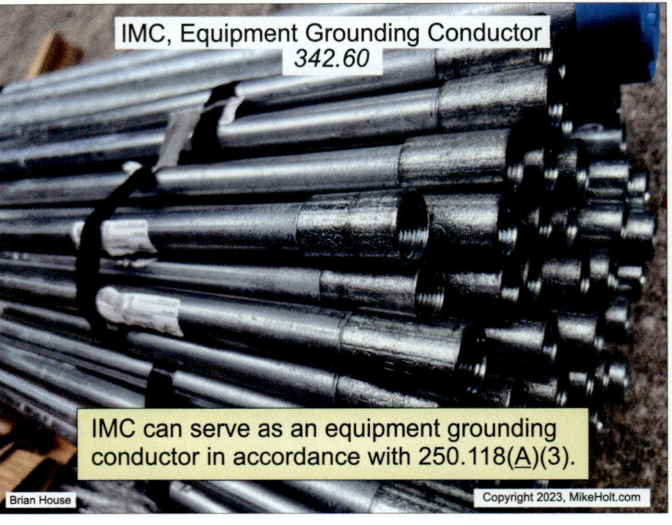

▶Figure 342–15

Author's Comment:

▶ The Steel Tube Institute and Georgia Tech provided studies that show ground-fault current paths travel effectively on metal raceways rather than on equipment grounding conductors. This is due to the eddy current and skin effect electrical characteristics of alternating current. Visit https://steeltubeinstitute.org for more information.

342.60 Equipment Grounding Conductor

IMC can serve an equipment grounding conductor in accordance with 250.118(A)(3). ▶Figure 342–15

RIGID METAL CONDUIT (RMC)

Introduction to Article 344—Rigid Metal Conduit (RMC)

This article covers the use, installation, and construction specifications of rigid metal conduit (RMC) and associated fittings. RMC, commonly called "rigid," has long been the standard raceway used to protect conductors from physical damage and from difficult environments. This type of conduit is available in trade sizes up to 6, can be threaded, and has the same outside diameter as intermediate metal conduit but has a thicker wall. It can be made of a variety of metals including steel, aluminum, red brass, and stainless steel. Some topics covered in this material include:

- Listing Requirements
- Uses Permitted
- Dissimilar Metals
- Size
- Bending, Reaming, and Threading
- Securing and Supporting
- Bushings
- Use as an Equipment Grounding Conductor
- Construction

Article 344 consists of three parts:

- Part I. General
- Part II. Installation
- Part III. Construction Specifications

According to Article 100, "Rigid Metal Conduit (RMC)" is a listed metal raceway of circular cross section with integral or associated couplings listed for the installation of electrical conductors. ▶Figure 344–1

Part I. General

344.1 Scope

Article 344 covers the use, installation, and construction specifications of rigid metal conduit (RMC) and associated fittings. ▶Figure 344–2

344.6 Listing Requirements

RMC and associated fittings must be listed. ▶Figure 344–3

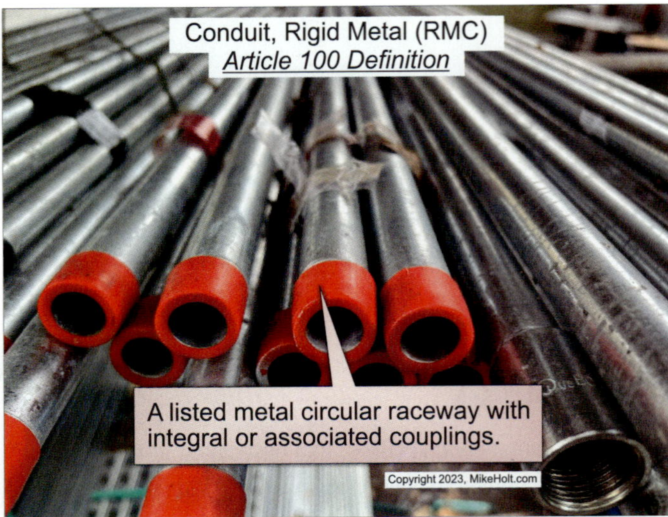

▶Figure 344–1

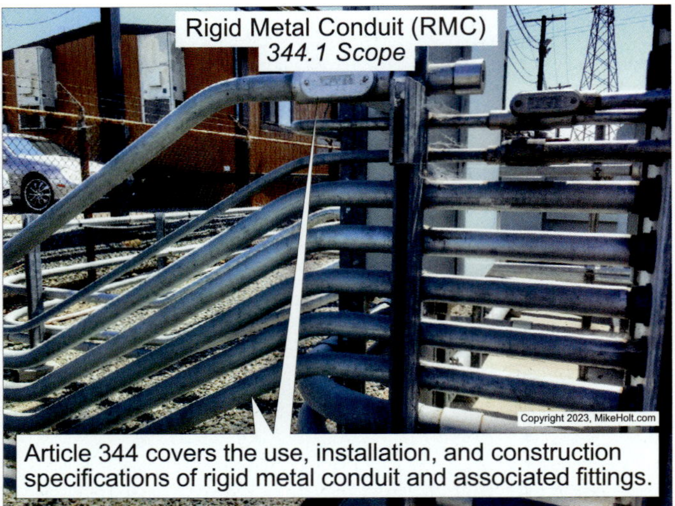

▶Figure 344–2

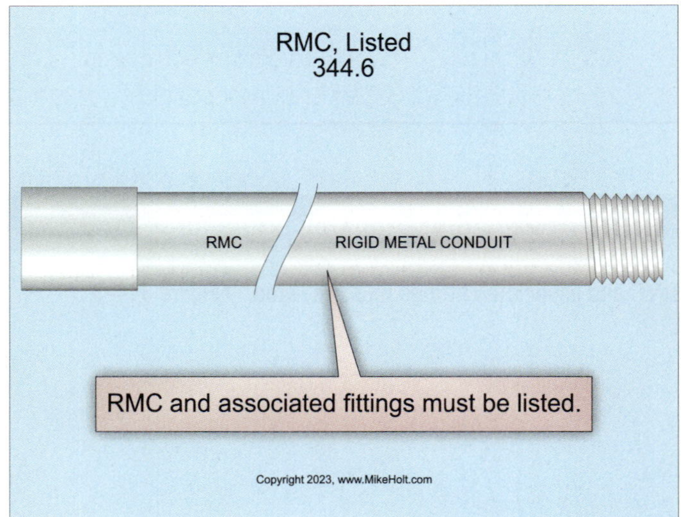

▶Figure 344–3

Author's Comment:

▸ Using listed RMC with listed fittings will ensure an effective low-impedance ground-fault current path back to the supply source in case of a ground fault. The metal raceway itself can therefore be used as an equipment grounding conductor [344.60].

Part II. Installation

344.10 Uses Permitted

(A) Atmospheric Conditions and Occupancies.

(1) RMC is permitted in all atmospheric conditions and occupancies.

(B) Corrosive Environments.

(1) RMC fittings, elbows, and couplings can be installed in concrete, in direct contact with the Earth, in direct burial applications, or in areas subject to severe corrosive influences if approved for the condition.

(D) Wet Locations. Support fittings (such as screws, straps, and so forth) installed in a wet location must be made of corrosion-resistant material or protected by corrosion-resistant coatings.

Note: See 300.6 for protection against corrosion.

Author's Comment:

▸ In accordance with "*UL Guide Information DYIX*," supplementary corrosion protection is required when RMC and associated fittings are buried in soil having a resistivity less than 2000Ω. In addition, supplementary corrosion protection is required at the point where RMC transitions from concrete encasement to the soil.

(E) Severe Physical Damage. RMC is permitted where subject to severe physical damage.

344.14 Dissimilar Metals

If practical, contact of RMC with dissimilar metals should be avoided to prevent the deterioration of the metal because of galvanic action. Aluminum and stainless steel fittings and enclosures are permitted to be used with galvanized steel rigid metal conduit where not subject to severe corrosive influences.

344.20 Trade Size

(A) Minimum. RMC smaller than trade size ½ is not permitted.

(B) Maximum. RMC larger than trade size 6 is not permitted.

344.22 Number of Conductors

The number of conductors in RMC is not permitted to exceed the percentage fill specified in Chapter 9, Table 1. Raceways must be large enough to permit the installation and removal of conductors without damaging the conductors' insulation.

Cables are permitted to be installed in RMC where such use is not prohibited by the respective cable articles. The number of cables must not exceed the percentage fill specified in Chapter 9, Table 1.

Author's Comment:

▶ See 300.17 for examples of how to size raceways when conductors are not all the same size.

344.24 Bends

(A) How Made. Raceway bends are not permitted to be made in any manner that will damage the raceway or significantly change its internal diameter (no kinks). The radius of the curve of any field bend to the centerline of the conduit is not permitted to be less than indicated in Chapter 9, Table 2.

Author's Comment:

▶ This is not a problem if you use a bender in accordance with the manufacturer's instructions.

(B) Degrees of Bends in One Run. To reduce stress and friction on conductor insulation, the total degrees of bends (including offsets) between pull points is not permitted to exceed 360 degrees. ▶Figure 344–4

Author's Comment:

▶ There is no maximum distance between pull boxes because this is a design issue, not a safety issue.

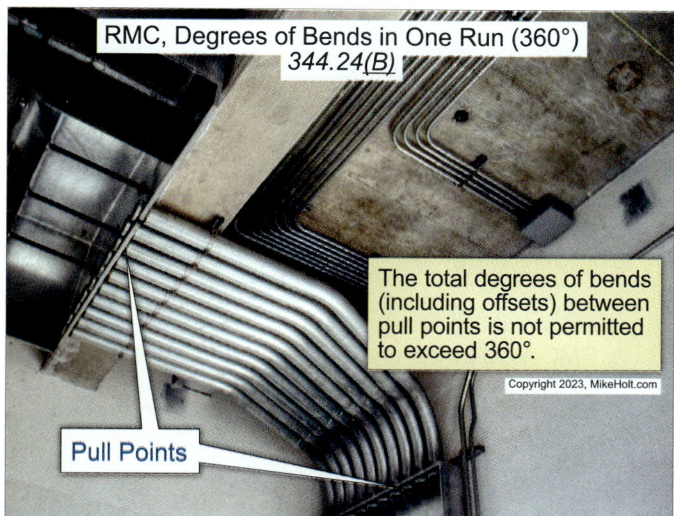

▶Figure 344–4

344.28 Reaming and Threading

When the raceway is cut in the field, reaming is required to remove the rough edges.

Author's Comment:

▶ It is a commonly accepted practice to ream small raceways with a screwdriver or the backside of pliers. However, when the raceway is cut with a three-wheel pipe cutter, a reaming tool is required to remove the sharp edge of the indented raceway. When conduit is threaded in the field, the threads must be coated with an electrically conductive, corrosion-resistant compound approved by the authority having jurisdiction in accordance with 300.6(A).

PVC-coated RMC must be threaded in accordance with manufacturer's instructions to prevent damage to the exterior coating.

344.30 Securing and Supporting

RMC must be securely fastened in place and supported in accordance with 344.30(A) and (B).

(A) Securely Fastened. RMC must be secured in accordance with any of the following:

(1) Fastened within 3 ft of each outlet box, junction box, device box, cabinet, conduit body, or other conduit termination. ▶Figure 344–5

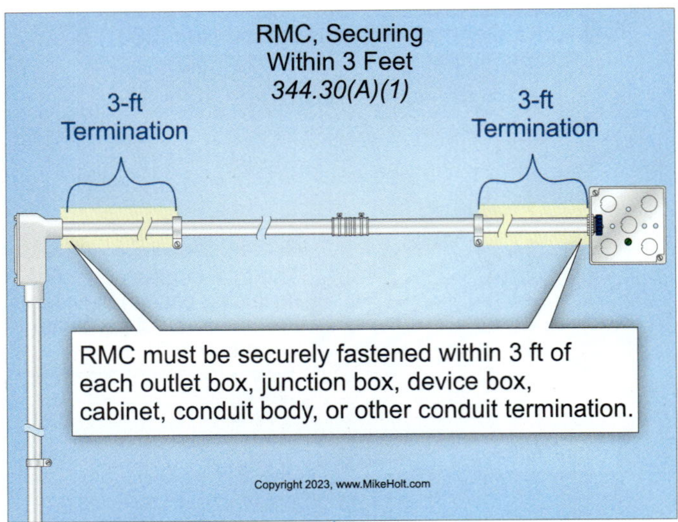

▶Figure 344–5

Author's Comment:

▸ Fastening is required within 3 ft of terminations—not within
3 ft of each coupling.

(2) When structural members do not permit the raceway to be secured
within 3 ft of a box or termination fitting, the raceway must be
secured within 5 ft of the termination. ▶Figure 344–6

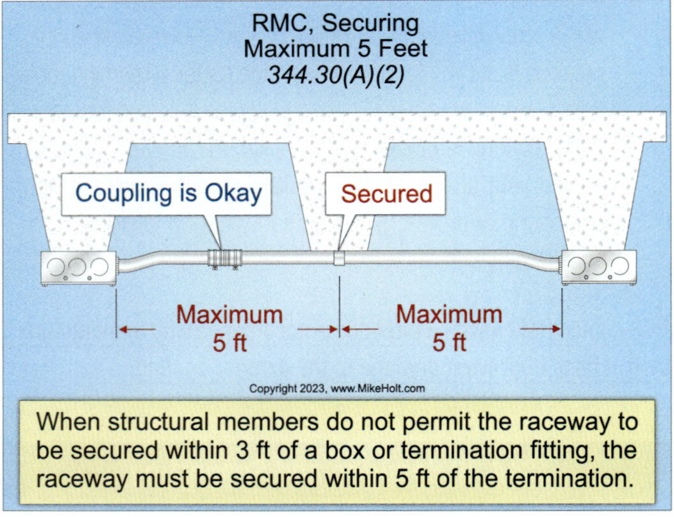

▶Figure 344–6

(3) Where approved, RMC is not required to be securely fastened
within 3 ft of the service head for an above-the-roof termination
of a mast. ▶Figure 344–7

(B) Supports.

(1) **General.** RMC must be supported at intervals not exceeding 10 ft.

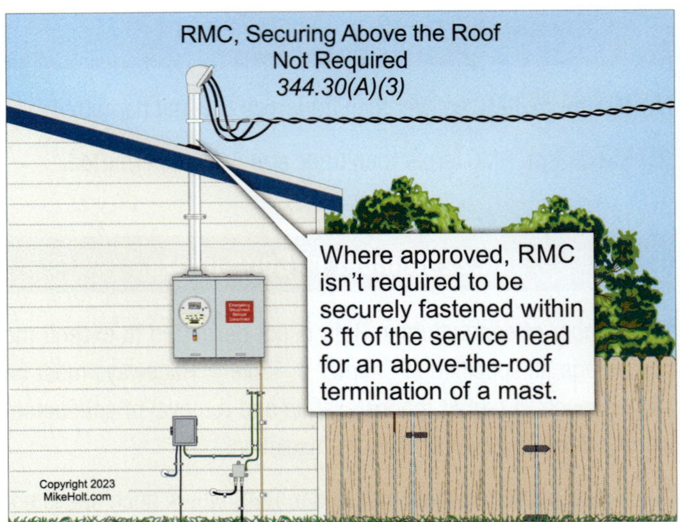

▶Figure 344–7

(2) **Straight Runs.** Straight runs made with threaded couplings can
be supported in accordance with the distances contained in Table
344.30(B). ▶Figure 344–8

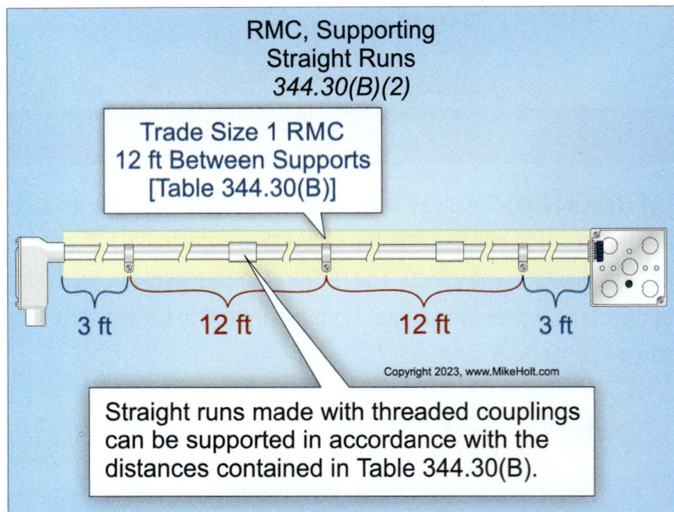

▶Figure 344–8

Table 344.30(B) Supports for Rigid Metal Conduit	
Trade Size	**Support Spacing**
½–¾	10 ft
1	12 ft
1¼–1½	14 ft
2–2½	16 ft
3 and larger	20 ft

(3) Vertical Risers. Exposed vertical risers for fixed equipment can be supported at intervals not exceeding 20 ft if the conduit is made up with threaded couplings, firmly supported, securely fastened at the top and bottom of the riser, and if no other means of support is available. ▶Figure 344–9

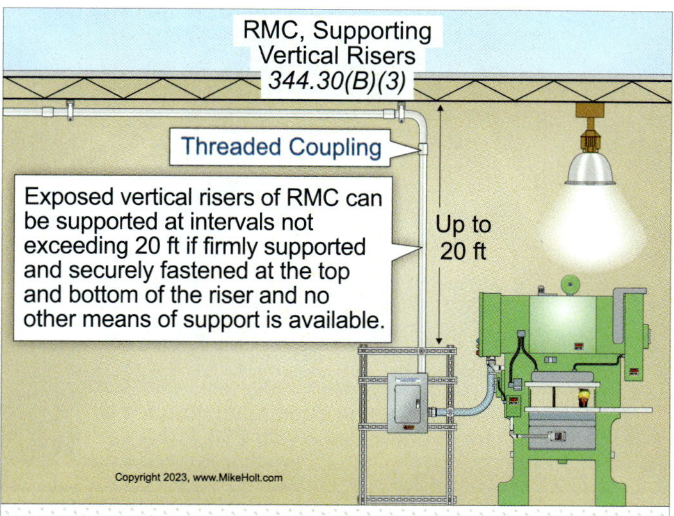

▶Figure 344–9

(4) Horizontal Runs. Conduits installed horizontally through framing members are considered supported and secured if such support does not exceed 10-ft intervals, and the conduit is secured within 3 ft of termination.

344.42 Couplings and Connectors

(A) Installation. Threadless couplings and connectors must be made up tight to maintain an effective ground-fault current path to safely conduct fault current in accordance with 250.4(A)(5), 250.96(A), and 300.10.

Buried in Concrete. If buried in concrete, threadless fittings must be of the concrete-tight type. ▶Figure 344–10

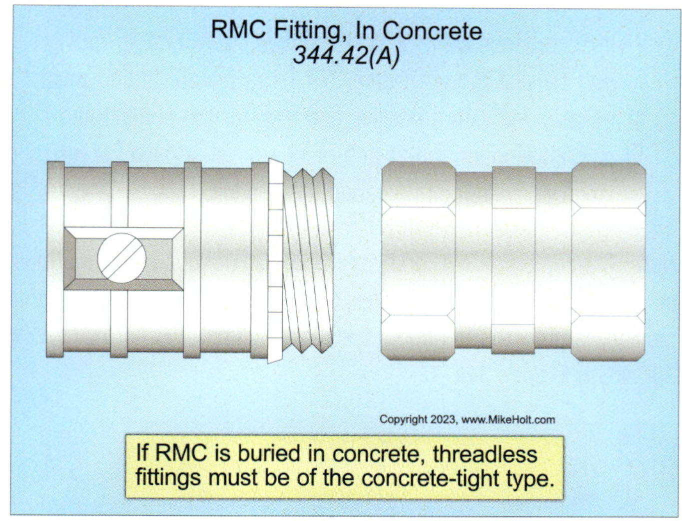

▶Figure 344–10

Wet Locations. If installed in wet locations, fittings must be listed for use in wet locations and prevent moisture or water from entering or accumulating within the enclosure in accordance with 314.15.

(B) Running Threads. Running threads are not permitted for the connection of couplings, but they are permitted at other locations. ▶Figure 344–11

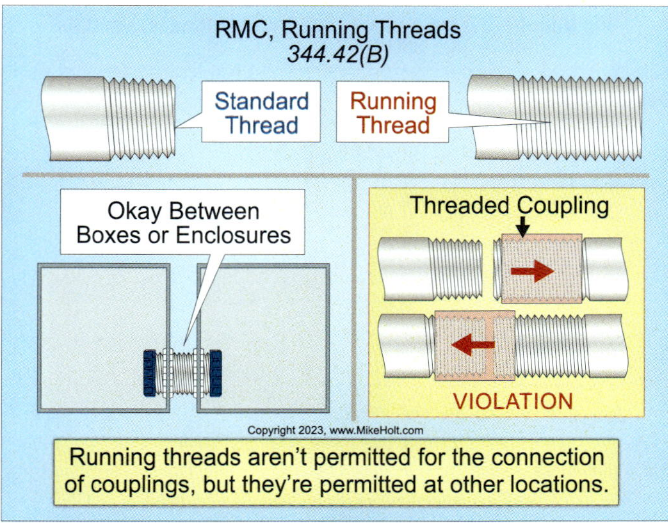

▶Figure 344–11

344.46 Bushings

To protect conductors exiting a threaded conduit from abrasion, a bushing must be installed on the threads of conduit (regardless of conductor size) unless the raceway enters a threaded entry in a box, fitting, or enclosure.

Author's Comment:

▸ In accordance with *"UL 514B Standard for Conduit, Tubing, and Cable Fittings"* section 5.4.1.1, a conduit fitting must be provided with a positive end stop for the conduit and a smooth rounded throat to protect against abrasion of insulation on conductors entering the conduit.

Note: Conductors 4 AWG and larger exiting a conduit connector must be protected from abrasion, prior to the installation by a fitting that provides a smooth, rounded, insulating surface in accordance with 300.4(G). ▸Figure 344–12

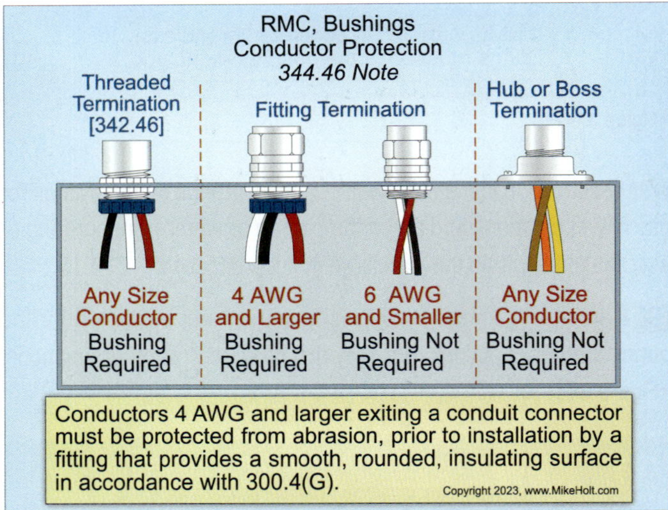

▸Figure 344–12

344.60 Equipment Grounding Conductor

RMC can serve an equipment grounding conductor in accordance with 250.118(A)(2). ▸Figure 344–13

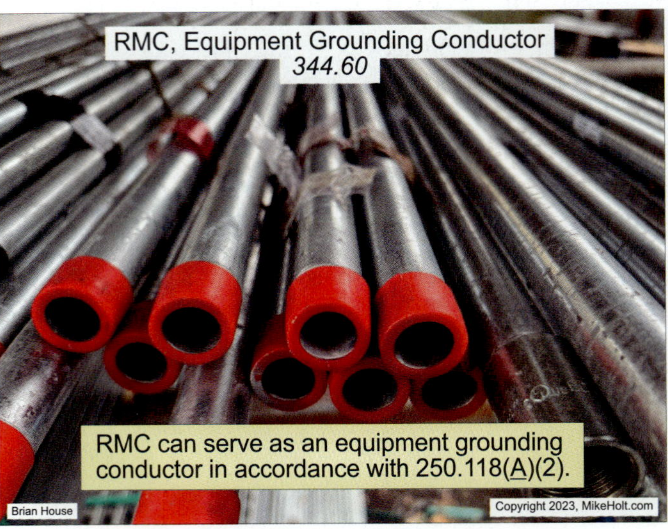

▸Figure 344–13

Author's Comment:

▸ The Steel Tube Institute and Georgia Tech provided studies that show ground-fault current paths travel effectively on metal raceways rather than on equipment grounding conductors. This is due to the eddy current and skin effect electrical characteristics of alternating current. Visit https://steeltubeinstitute.org for more information.

ARTICLE 348

FLEXIBLE METAL CONDUIT (FMC)

Introduction to Article 348—Flexible Metal Conduit (FMC)

Article 348 covers the use, installation, and construction specifications for flexible metal conduit (FMC) and associated fittings. FMC, commonly called "flex" or sometimes "Greenfield" (after its inventor), is a raceway made a spiral interlocked steel or aluminum strip. It is primarily used where flexibility is necessary or where equipment moves, shakes, or vibrates. Some topics covered in this material include:

▶ Listing Requirements

▶ Uses Permitted

▶ Uses Not Permitted

▶ Size

▶ Bending and Trimming

▶ Securing and Supporting

▶ Couplings and Connectors

▶ Splices and Taps

▶ Use as an Equipment Grounding Conductor

This article consists of two parts:

▶ Part I. General

▶ Part II. Installation

According to Article 100, "Flexible Metal Conduit (FMC)" is a raceway of circular cross section made of a helically wound, formed, interlocked metal strip, and listed for the installation of electrical conductors. ▶Figure 348–1

Part I. General

348.1 Scope

Article 348 covers the use, installation, and construction specifications for flexible metal conduit (FMC) and associated fittings. ▶Figure 348–2

348.6 Listing Requirements

Flexible metal conduit and associated fittings must be listed.

Part II. Installation

348.10 Uses Permitted

FMC is permitted to be installed exposed or concealed.

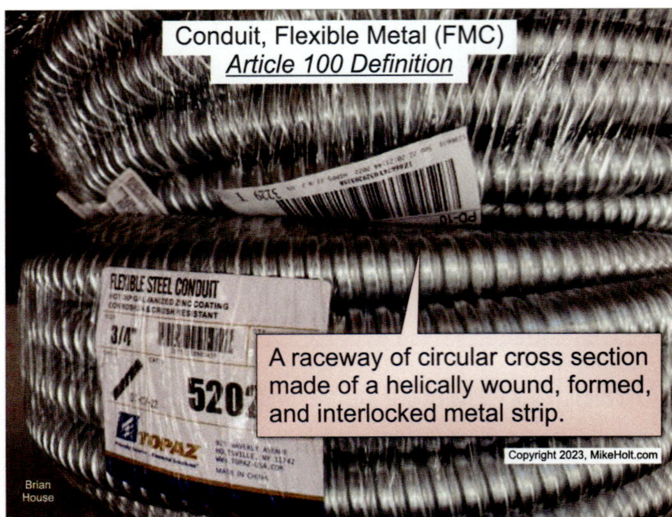

▶Figure 348–1

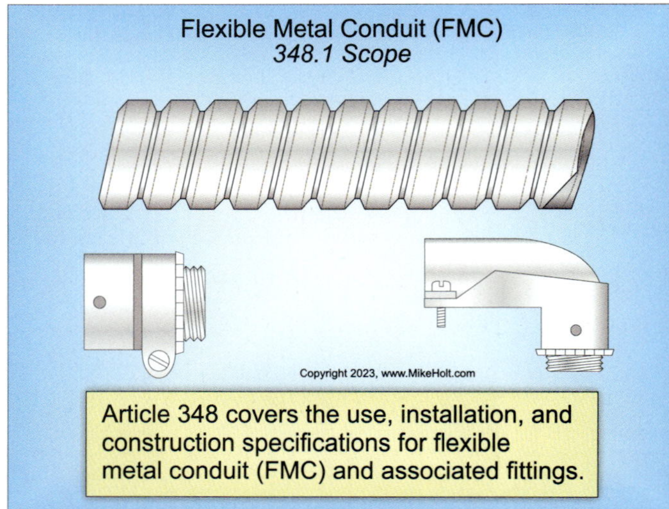

▶Figure 348–2

348.12 Uses Not Permitted

FMC is not permitted:

(1) In wet locations ▶Figure 348–3

(2) In hoistways, other than as permitted in 620.21(A)(1)

(3) In storage battery rooms

(4) In any hazardous (classified) location, except as permitted by 501.10(B)

(5) Exposed to material having a deteriorating effect on the installed conductors

(6) Underground or embedded in poured concrete ▶Figure 348–4

(7) Where subject to physical damage

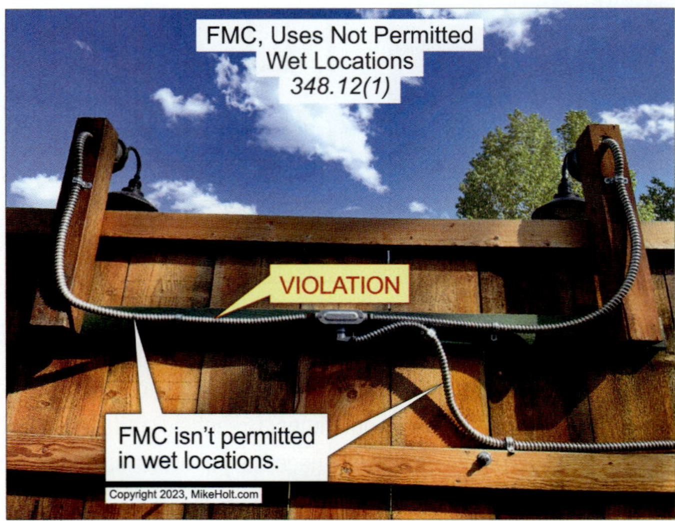

▶Figure 348–3

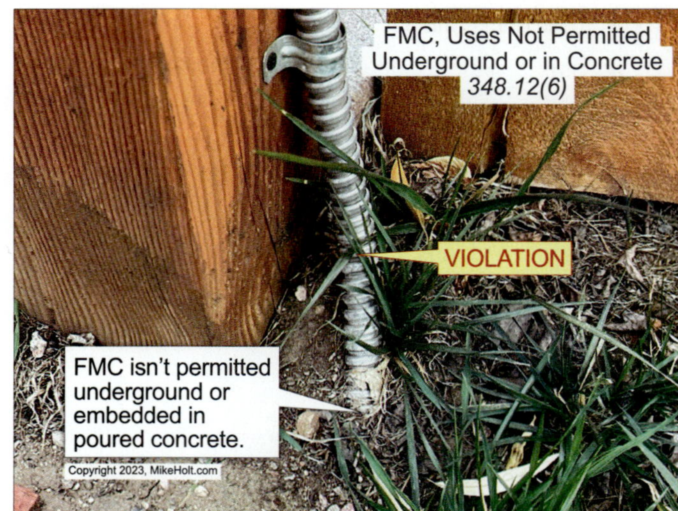

▶Figure 348–4

348.20 Trade Size

(A) Minimum. Trade size ½. However, trade size ⅜ is permitted for the following applications

(1) For enclosing the leads of motors

(2) Not exceeding 6 ft in length for any of the following: ▶Figure 348–5

   a. For utilization equipment

   b. As part of a listed assembly

   c. For luminaire tap connections in accordance with 410.117(C)

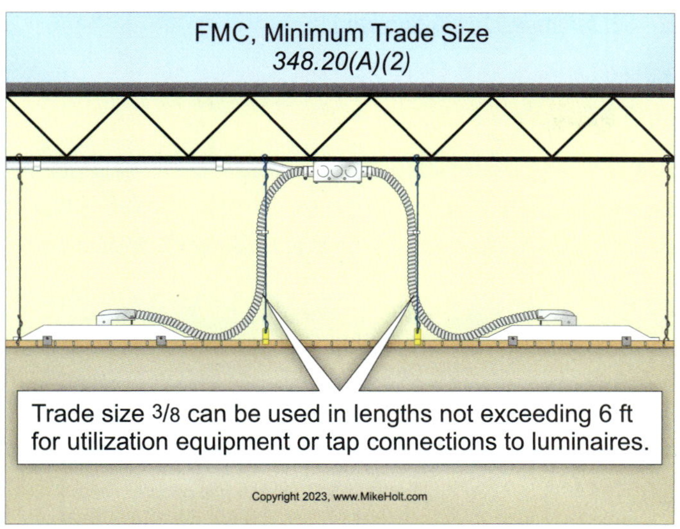

▶Figure 348–5

(5) As part of a listed assembly used to interconnect luminaires per 410.137(C)

(B) Maximum. Trade size 4.

348.22 Number of Conductors

FMC size ½ in. and larger must be large enough to permit the installation and removal of conductors without damaging the conductors' insulation. When all conductors within a raceway are the same size and insulation, the number of conductors permitted can be found in Annex C for the raceway type.

The number of conductors in FMC is not permitted to exceed the percentage fill specified in Chapter 9, Table 1. Raceways must be large enough to permit the installation and removal of conductors without damaging the conductor insulation.

▶ Example 1

Question: How many 6 AWG, THWN-2 conductors can be installed in 1 FMC?

(a) 2 conductors　　　　　　*(b) 4 conductors*
(c) 6 conductors　　　　　　*(d) 8 conductors*

Answer: (c) 6 conductors [Annex C, Table C.3]

Author's Comment:

▶ See 300.17 for examples of how to size raceways when conductors are not all the same size.

Trade Size 3/8. The number and size of conductors in 3/8 FMC must comply with Table 348.22.

▶ Example 2

Question: How many 12 AWG, THWN-2 conductors can be installed in 3/8 Type FMC that uses outside fittings?

(a) 2 conductors　　　　　　*(b) 3 conductors*
(c) 4 conductors　　　　　　*(d) 5 conductors*

Solution:

One insulated, covered or bare, equipment grounding conductor of the same size is permitted with the circuit conductors. See the "" note at the bottom of Table 348.22.*

Answer: (b) 3 conductors [Table 348.22]

Cables can be installed in FMC if the total area of cables does not exceed the allowable percentage fill specified in Chapter 9, Table 1.

348.24 Bends

(A) How Made. Bends must be made so the conduit will not be damaged, and its internal diameter will not be effectively reduced. The radius of the curve of the inner edge of any field bend is not permitted to be less than shown in Chapter 9, Table 2, using the column "Other Bends."

Author's Comment:

▶ A ½ FMC has a bending radius of 4 in. from the curve of the inner edge [Chapter 9 Table 2]. If the bending radius is exceeded, the conduit will be compromised and a new section will be required to be installed.

(B) Degrees of Bends in One Run. To reduce the stress and friction on conductor insulation, the total degrees of bends (including offsets) between pull points is not permitted to exceed 360 degrees.

348.28 Trimming

The cut ends of FMC must be trimmed to remove the rough edges, but is not necessary if fittings are threaded into the convolutions.

348.30 Securing and Supporting

(A) Securely Fastened. FMC must be securely fastened by a means approved by the authority having jurisdiction within 1 ft of termination, and it must be secured and supported at intervals not exceeding 4½ ft. ▶Figure 348–6

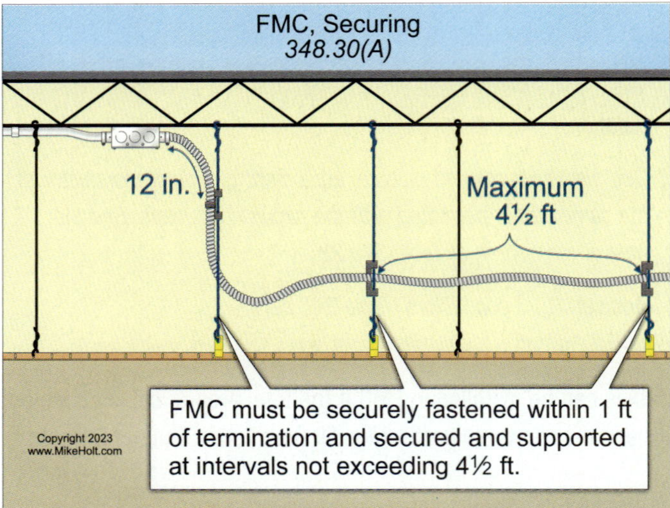

▶Figure 348–6

Where cable ties are used to secure and support Type FMC, they must be listed and identified for securing and supporting.

Ex 1: FMC is not required to be securely fastened or supported where fished between access points through concealed spaces and supporting is impractical.

Ex 2: If flexibility is necessary after installation, unsecured lengths from the last point of securement are not permitted to exceed: ▶Figure 348–7

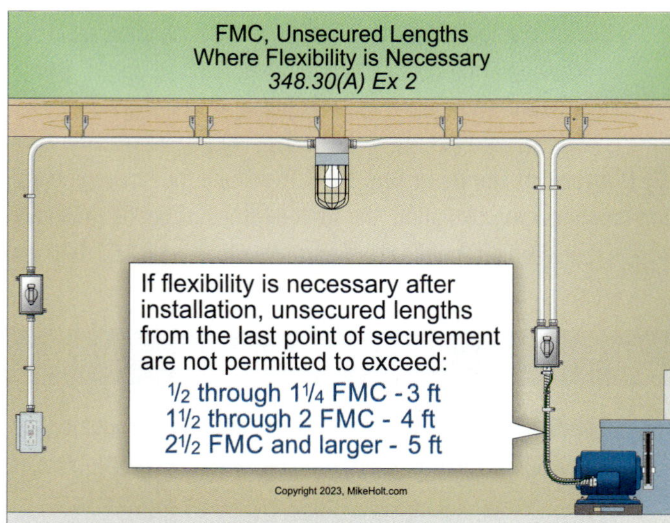

▶Figure 348–7

(1) *3 ft for trade sizes ½ through 1¼*

(2) *4 ft for trade sizes 1½ through 2*

(3) *5 ft for trade sizes 2½ and larger*

Ex 4: FMC can be unsecured within an accessible ceiling for lengths not exceeding 6 ft from the last point of securement. Listed FMC fittings are considered a means of securement and support. ▶Figure 348–8

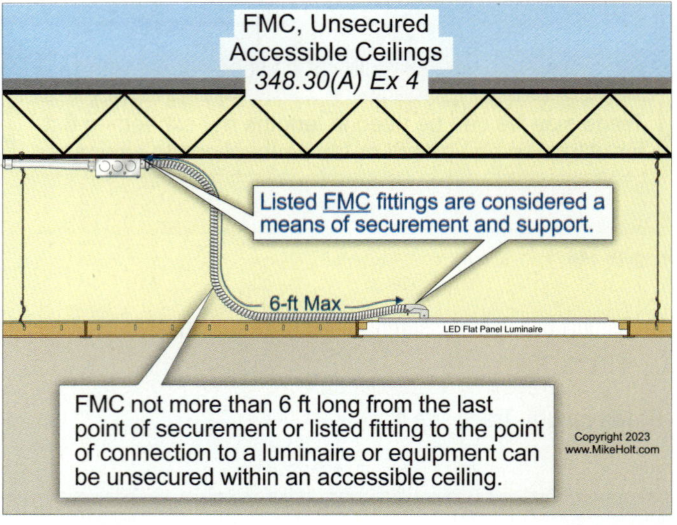

▶Figure 348–8

(B) Horizontal Runs. FMC installed horizontally through framing members is considered supported and secured if such support does not exceed 4½ ft and the raceway is secured within 1 ft of terminations. ▶Figure 348–9

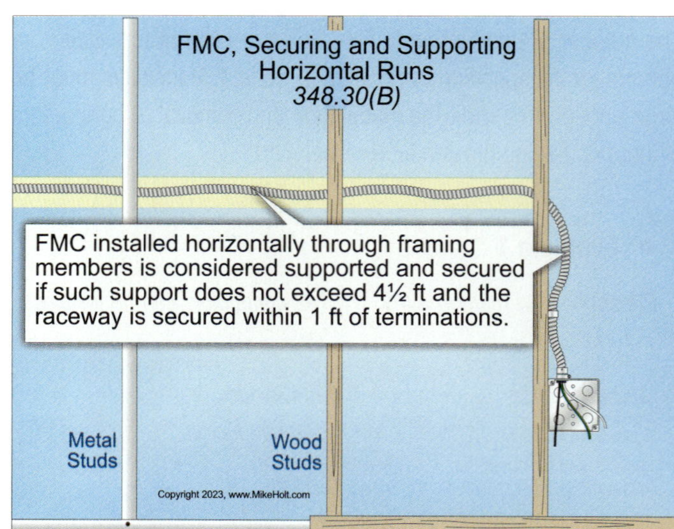

▶Figure 348–9

348.42 Couplings and Connectors

Angle connectors are not permitted to be concealed inside drywall or concrete.

348.60 Equipment Grounding and Bonding Conductors

(A) Fixed Installation. If flexibility is not necessary after installation or vibration is not a concern, the metal armor of FMC can serve as an equipment grounding conductor in accordance with 250.118(A)(5).
▶Figure 348–10

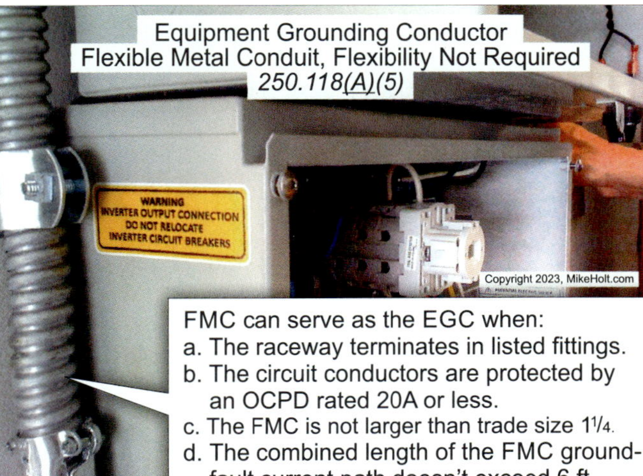

▶Figure 348–10

(B) Flexible Installation. If flexibility is necessary to minimize the transmission of vibration from equipment, or to provide flexibility for equipment that requires movement after installation, an equipment grounding conductor of the wire type must be installed with the circuit conductors. ▶Figure 348–11

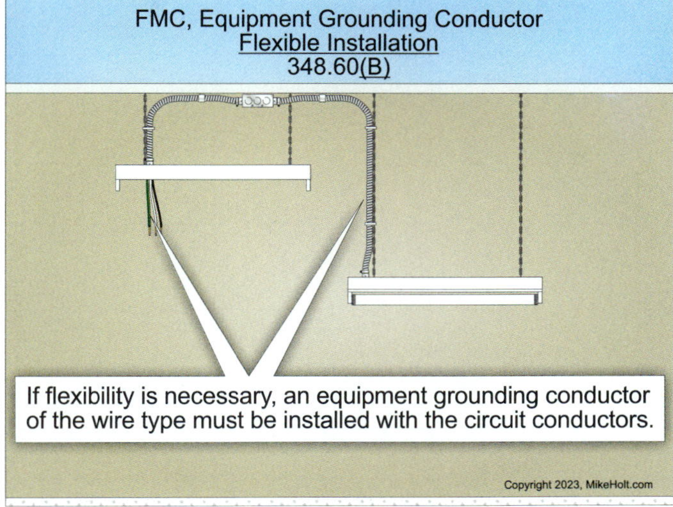

▶Figure 348–11

(D) Equipment Bonding Jumpers. The equipment bonding jumper can be installed inside or outside the flexible metal conduit. Where installed outside the FMC, the length of the equipment bonding jumper is not permitted to exceed 6 ft and must be routed with the flexible metal conduit in accordance with 250.102(E)(2).

LIQUIDTIGHT FLEXIBLE METAL CONDUIT (LFMC)

Introduction to Article 350—Liquidtight Flexible Metal Conduit (LFMC)

This article covers the use, installation, and construction specifications of liquidtight flexible metal conduit (LFMC) and associated fittings. LFMC, with its associated connectors and fittings, is a flexible raceway commonly available in trade size ½ and larger. It is used for connections to equipment that vibrates or must be occasionally moved. LFMC is commonly called "Seal-Tite®" or "liquidtight." It is similar in use and construction to flexible metal conduit but has an outer liquidtight thermoplastic covering that provides protection from liquids and some corrosive effects. Some topics covered in this material include:

▸ Listing Requirements

▸ Uses Permitted

▸ Uses Not Permitted

▸ Size

▸ Number of Conductors

▸ Bending and Trimming

▸ Securing and Supporting

▸ Couplings and Connectors

▸ Splices and Taps

▸ Grounding and Bonding

Article 350 consists of three parts:

▸ Part I. General

▸ Part II. Installation

▸ Part III. Construction Specifications

According to Article 100, "Liquidtight Flexible Metal Conduit (LFMC)" is a raceway of circular cross section, having an outer liquidtight, nonmetallic, sunlight-resistant jacket over an inner flexible metal core, with associated connectors and fittings, listed for the installation of electrical conductors. ▸Figure 350–1

Part I. General

350.1 Scope

Article 350 covers the use, installation, and construction specifications of liquidtight flexible metal conduit (LFMC) and associated fittings. ▸Figure 350–2

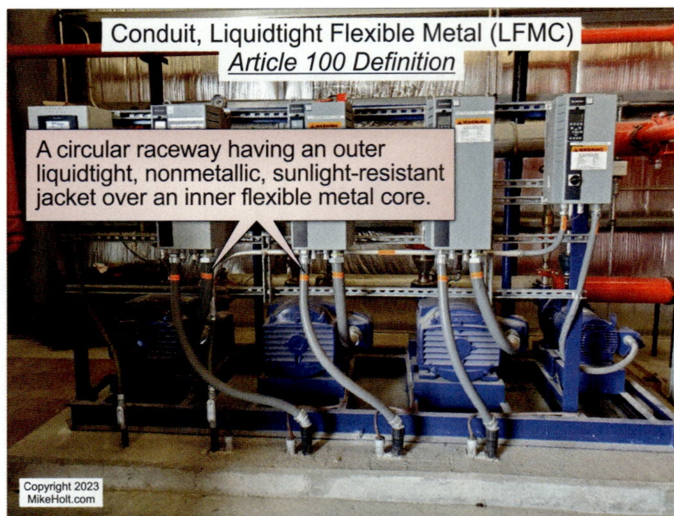

▶Figure 350–1

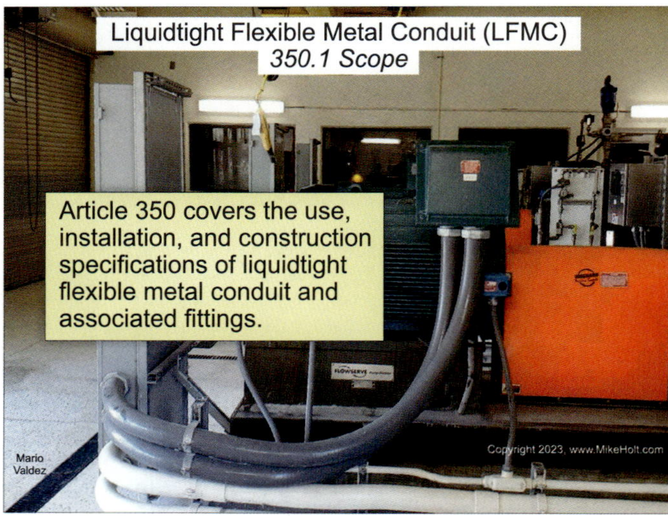

▶Figure 350–2

350.6 Listing Requirements

LFMC and its associated fittings must be listed.

Author's Comment:

▶ In accordance with "*UL 360 Standard for Liquidtight Flexible Metal Conduit,*" listed LFMC will have an internal copper strip that bonds the inner flexible metal core to each convolution of the raceway.

Part II. Installation

350.10 Uses Permitted

Listed LFMC is permitted, either exposed or concealed, at any of the following locations:

(1) If flexibility is required

(2) In hazardous (classified) locations in accordance with Chapter 5

(3) For direct burial if listed and marked for this purpose ▶Figure 350–3

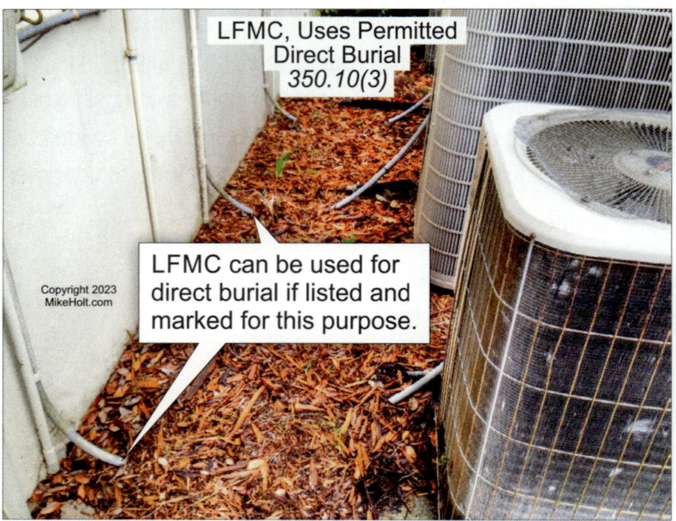

▶Figure 350–3

350.12 Uses Not Permitted

LFMC must not be used where subject to physical damage. ▶Figure 350–4

350.20 Trade Size

(A) Minimum. LFMC smaller than trade size ½ is not permitted to be used.

Ex: LFMC can be smaller than trade size ½ if installed in accordance with 348.20(A).

(B) Maximum. LFMC larger than trade size 4 is not permitted to be used.

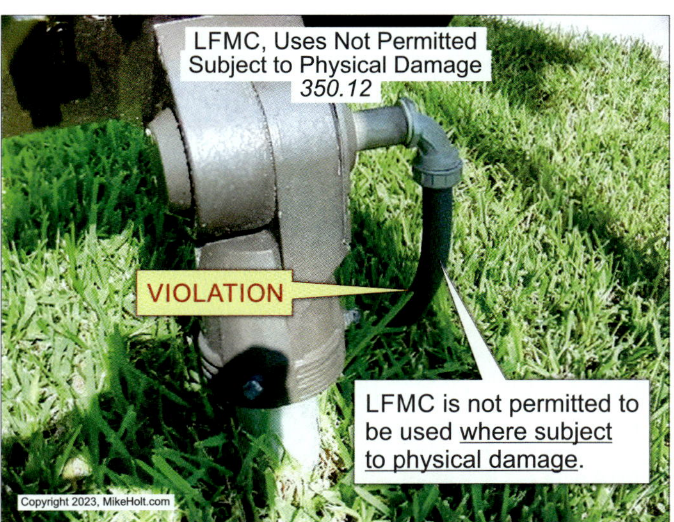

▶Figure 350–4

350.22 Number of Conductors

(A) Raceways ½ and Larger. Raceways must be large enough to permit the installation and removal of conductors without damaging the insulation. When all conductors within a raceway are the same size and insulation, the number of conductors permitted can be found in Annex C for the raceway type.

▶ Example 1

Question: How many 6 AWG, THHN conductors can be installed in 1 LFMC? ▶Figure 350–5

(a) 2 conductors

(b) 4 conductors

(c) 6 conductors

(d) 7 conductors

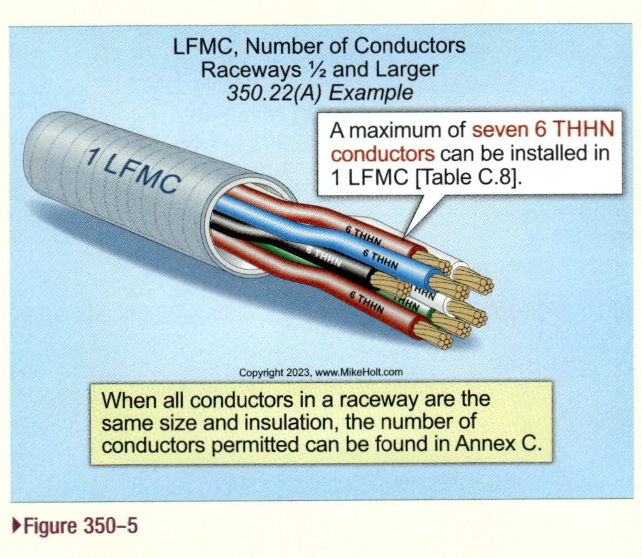

▶Figure 350–5

Answer: (d) 7 conductors [Annex C, Table C.8]

▶ See 300.17 for examples of how to size raceways when conductors are not all the same size.

Cables can be installed in LFMC if the number of cables does not exceed the allowable percentage fill specified in Chapter 9, Table 1.

(B) Raceways Trade Size ⅜. The number and size of conductors in trade size ⅜ LFMC must comply with Table 348.22.

▶ Example 2

Question: How many 12 AWG, THWN-2 conductors can be installed in ⅜ LFMC that uses outside fittings?

(a) 2 conductors

(b) 3 conductors

(c) 4 conductors

(d) 5 conductors

Solution:

One insulated, covered or bare, equipment grounding conductor of the same size is permitted with the circuit conductors. See the "" note at the bottom of Table 348.22.*

Answer: (b) 3 conductors [Table 348.22]

350.24 Bends

(A) How Made. Bends must be made so the conduit will not be damaged, and the internal diameter will not be effectively reduced.

(B) Degrees of Bends in One Run. To reduce the stress and friction on conductor insulation, the total degrees of bends (including offsets) between pull points is not permitted to exceed 360 degrees. ▶Figure 350–6

350.28 Trimming

Cut ends of LFMC must be trimmed both inside and outside the raceway to remove rough edges.

350.30 Securing and Supporting

LFMC must be securely fastened in place and supported in accordance with 350.30(A) and (B).

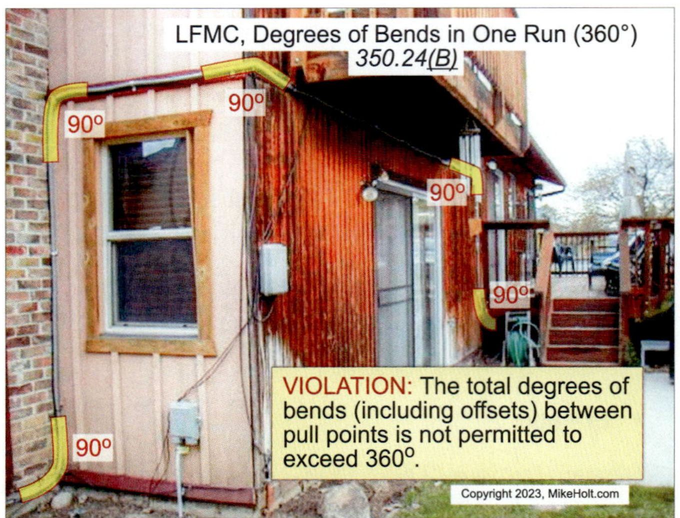

▶Figure 350–6

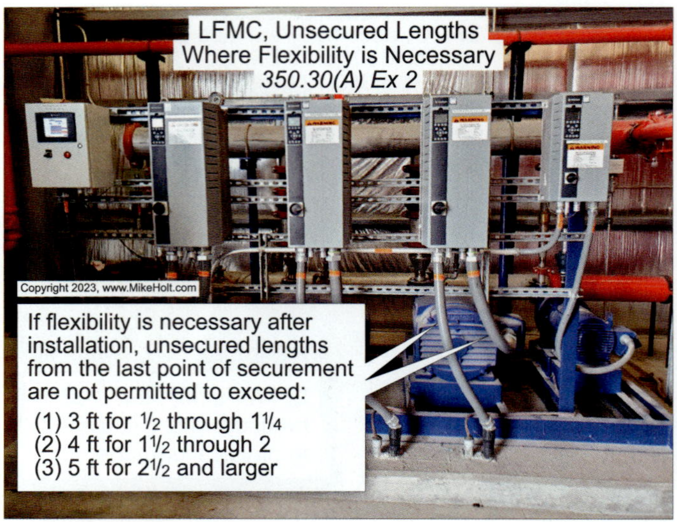

▶Figure 350–8

(A) Securely Fastened. LFMC must be securely fastened by a means approved by the authority having jurisdiction within 1 ft of termination. They must be secured and supported at intervals not exceeding 4½ ft. ▶Figure 350–7

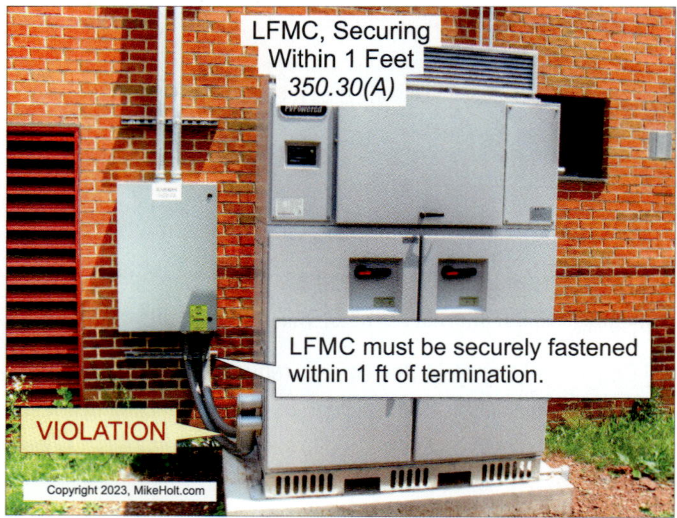

▶Figure 350–7

Where cable ties are used for securing LFMC, they must be listed and identified for securement and support.

Ex 1: LFMC is not required to be securely fastened or supported where fished between access points through concealed spaces and supporting is impractical.

Ex 2: If flexibility is necessary after installation, unsecured lengths from the last point of securement are not permitted to exceed: ▶Figure 350–8

(1) 3 ft for trade sizes ½ through 1¼

(2) 4 ft for trade sizes 1½ through 2

(3) 5 ft for trade sizes 2½ and larger

Ex 4: LFMC can be unsecured within an accessible ceiling for lengths not exceeding 6 ft from the last point of securement. ▶Figure 350–9

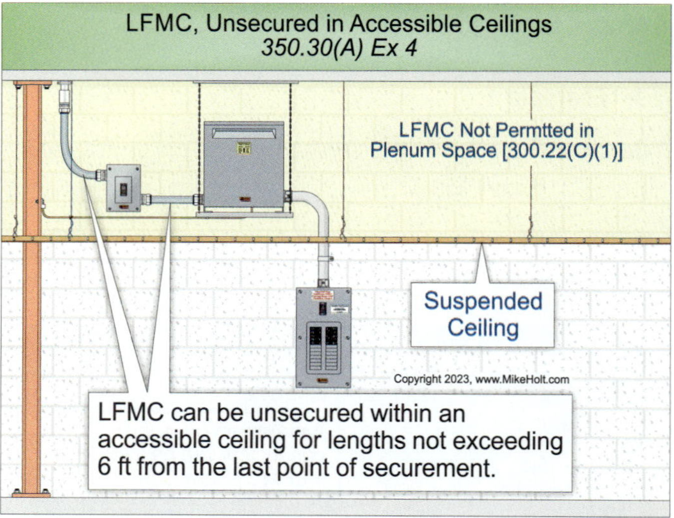

▶Figure 350–9

LFMC fittings are permitted as a means of securement and support.

Author's Comment:

▶ This last sentence following the four exceptions means that the use of LFMC fittings as the means of securing and supporting only applies to installations made using one of the four exceptions. It should not be interpreted as permission to use these fittings to secure and support LFMC in all applications.

(B) Horizontal Runs. LFMC installed horizontally through framing members is considered supported and secured if such support does not exceed 4½ ft, and the raceway is secured within 1 ft of termination.

350.60 Equipment Grounding and Bonding Conductors

(A) Fixed Installations. If flexibility is not necessary after installation, and vibration is not a concern, the metal armor of liquidtight flexible metal conduit can serve as an equipment grounding conductor in accordance with 250.118(A)(6). ▶Figure 350–10

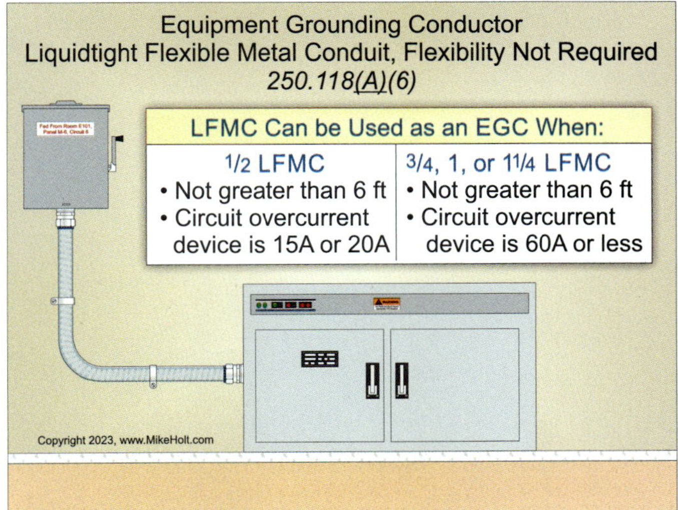

▶Figure 350–10

(B) Flexible Installations. If flexibility is necessary to minimize the transmission of vibration from equipment, or to provide flexibility for equipment that requires movement after installation, an equipment grounding conductor of the wire type must be installed with the circuit conductors. ▶Figure 350–11

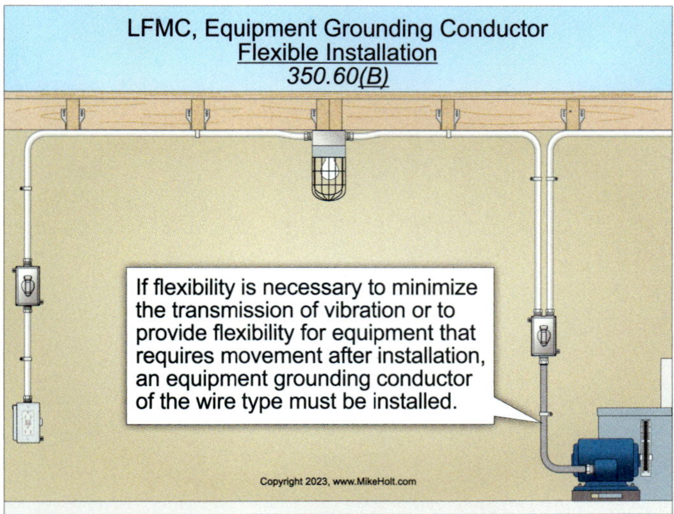

▶Figure 350–11

(D) Equipment Bonding Jumper. The equipment bonding jumper can be installed inside or outside the liquidtight flexible metal conduit. Where the bonding jumper is installed outside the LFMC, the length of the equipment bonding jumper cannot exceed 6 ft, and it must be routed with the liquidtight flexible metal conduit in accordance with 250.102(E)(2).

RIGID POLYVINYL CHLORIDE CONDUIT (PVC)

Introduction to Article 352—Rigid Polyvinyl Chloride Conduit (PVC)

Article 352 covers the use, installation, and construction specifications of polyvinyl chloride conduit (PVC) and associated fittings. PVC is a rigid nonmetallic conduit that is available in trade sizes ½ to 6. Two wall thicknesses ("schedules") are available. Schedule 40 PVC is used in most applications that are not subject to physical damage. Schedule 80 PVC, which has the same outside diameter but a thicker wall, is used where resistance to physical damage is required. This type of conduit is inexpensive, lightweight, and easily installed. It is permitted in concrete, corrosive areas, underground, and in wet locations. Some topics covered in this material include:

- ▸ Listing Requirements
- ▸ Uses Permitted
- ▸ Uses Not Permitted
- ▸ Size
- ▸ Number of Conductors
- ▸ Bending and Trimming
- ▸ Securing and Supporting
- ▸ Expansion Fittings
- ▸ Bushings and Joints
- ▸ Splices and Taps
- ▸ Grounding and Bonding

This article consists of three parts:

- ▸ Part I. General
- ▸ Part II. Installation
- ▸ Part III. Construction Specifications

According to Article 100, "Polyvinyl Chloride Conduit (PVC)" is a rigid nonmetallic raceway of circular cross section with integral or associated couplings, connectors, and fittings listed for the installation of electrical conductors. ▶Figure 352–1

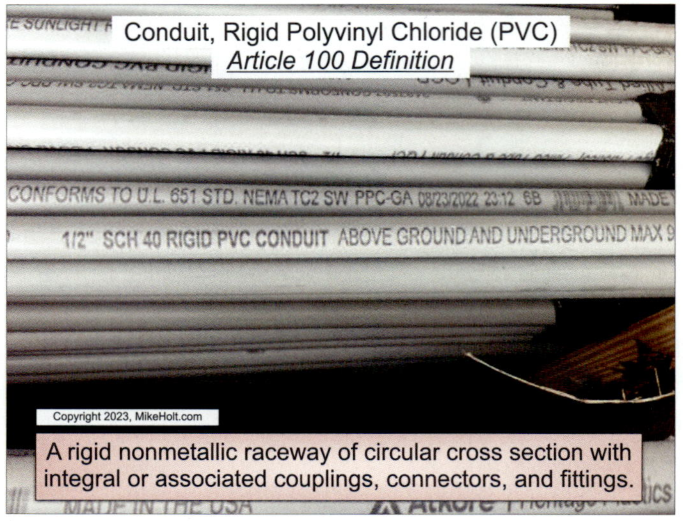

▶Figure 352–1

Part I. General

Article 352 covers the use, installation, and construction specifications of polyvinyl chloride conduit (PVC) and associated fittings. ▶Figure 352–2

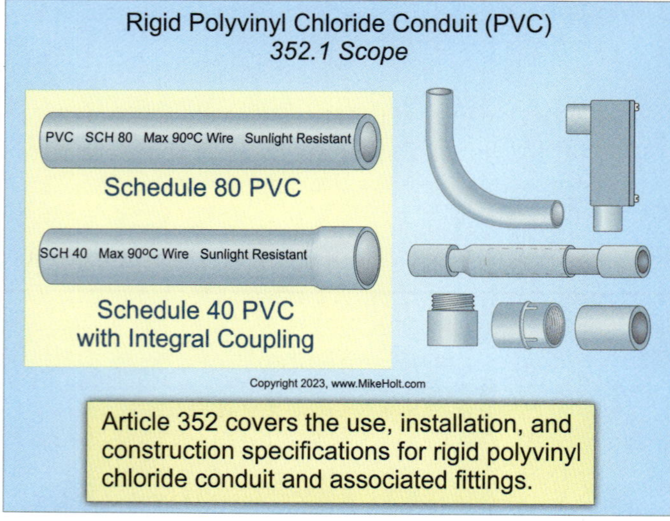

▶Figure 352–2

PVC conduit, factory elbows, and associated fittings are required to be listed.

Part II. Installation

PVC conduit is permitted in the following applications:

Note: In extreme cold, PVC conduit can become brittle and is more susceptible to physical damage.

(A) Concealed. PVC conduit is permitted to be concealed within walls, floors, or ceilings.

(B) Encased in Concrete. PVC conduit is permitted to be encased in concrete. ▶Figure 352–3

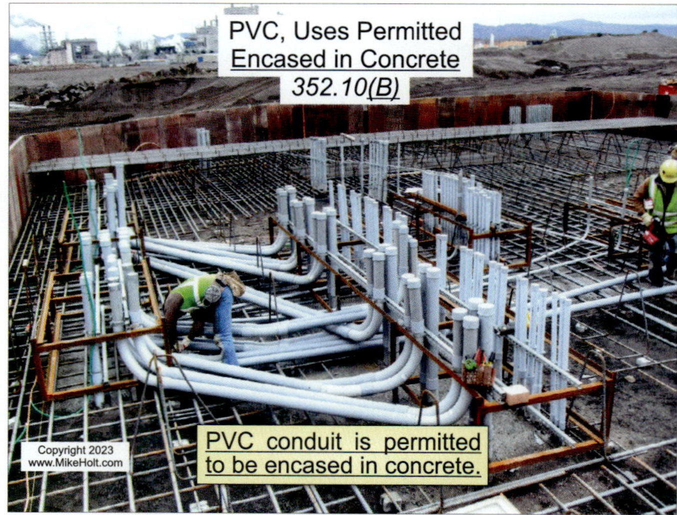

▶Figure 352–3

(C) Corrosive Influences. PVC conduit is permitted in areas subject to severe corrosion for which the material is specifically approved by the authority having jurisdiction.

(E) Wet Locations. PVC conduit is permitted in wet locations such as dairies, laundries, canneries, car washes, and other areas frequently washed. It is also permitted in outdoor locations. Support fittings (such as straps, screws, and bolts) must be made of corrosion-resistant materials or protected with a corrosion-resistant coating in accordance with 300.6(A).

(F) Dry and Damp Locations. PVC conduit is permitted in dry and damp locations except where limited in 352.12.

(G) Exposed. Schedule 40 PVC conduit is permitted to be installed in exposed locations where the raceway is not subject to physical damage. ▶Figure 352–4

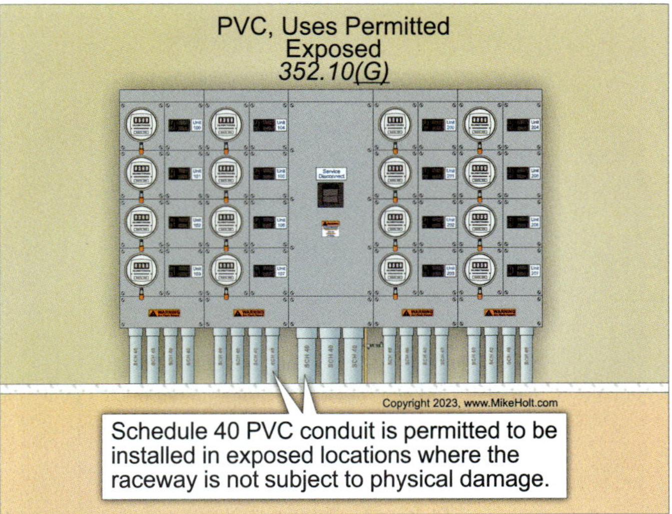

▶Figure 352–4

Note: PVC Schedule 80 conduit is identified for use in areas subject to physical damage.

(H) Underground. PVC conduit is permitted to be direct buried and underground encased in concrete.

(K) Physical Damage. Where subject to physical damage, Schedule 80 PVC and associated fitting must be used. ▶Figure 352–5

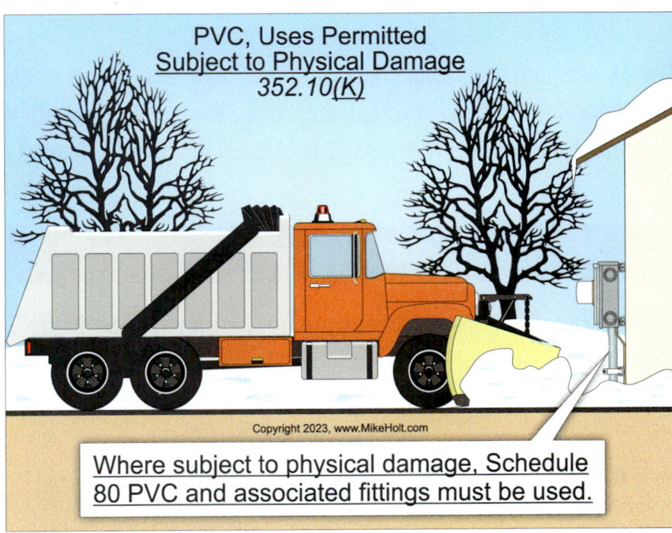

▶Figure 352–5

Note: All listed PVC conduit fittings are suitable for connection to both Schedule 40 and Schedule 80 PVC conduit.

352.12 Uses Not Permitted

PVC conduit is not permitted in the following environments:

(A) Hazardous (Classified) Locations. PVC conduit is not permitted to be used in hazardous (classified) locations except as permitted by 501.10(A)(1)(1) Ex, 501.10(B)(1)(6), 502.10(B)(7), 503.10(A)(1), 504.20, 514.8 Ex 2, and 515.8(A).

(B) Support of Luminaires. PVC conduit is not permitted to be used for the support of luminaires or other equipment.

(C) Physical Damage. PVC conduit is not permitted to be used where subject to physical damage unless installed in Schedule 80 PVC [352.10(K)]. ▶Figure 352–6

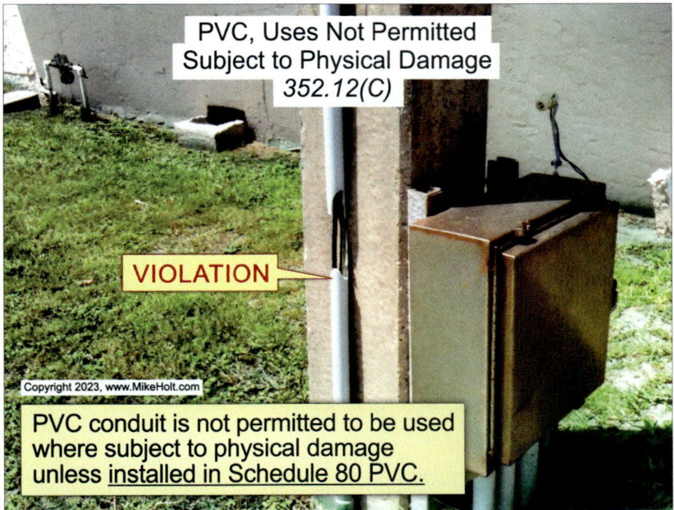

▶Figure 352–6

Author's Comment:

▶ Schedule 40 PVC conduit is not identified for use where subject to physical damage, but Schedule 80 PVC conduit is [352.10(K)].

(D) Ambient Temperature. PVC conduit is not permitted to be installed if the ambient temperature exceeds 50°C (122°F).

Author's Comment:

▶ PVC conduit and fittings are not permitted to be installed in environmental air spaces (plenums) [300.22(C)].

352.20 Trade Size

(A) Minimum. PVC conduit smaller than trade size ½ is not permitted.

(B) Maximum. PVC conduit larger than trade size 6 is not permitted.

352.22 Number of Conductors

Raceways must be large enough to permit the installation and removal of conductors without damaging the conductors' insulation. The number of conductors is not permitted to exceed the percentage fill specified in Chapter 9, Table 1.

When all conductors within a raceway are the same size and insulation, the number of conductors permitted can be found in Annex C for the raceway type.

▶ Example 1

Question: How many 4/0 AWG, THWN conductors can be installed in 2 Schedule 40 PVC conduit? ▶Figure 352–7

(a) 2 conductors
(b) 4 conductors
(c) 6 conductors
(d) 8 conductors

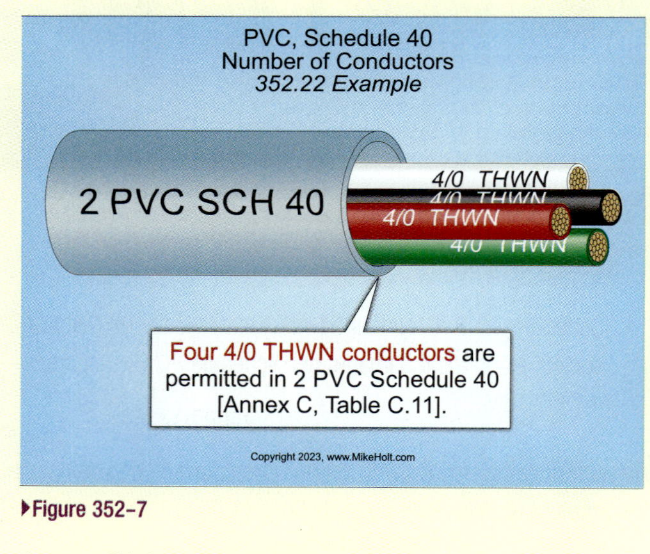

▶Figure 352–7

Answer: (b) 4 conductors [Annex C, Table C.11]

Author's Comment:

▸ Schedule 80 PVC conduit has the same outside diameter as Schedule 40, but the wall thickness is greater which results in a reduced interior area for conductor fill.

▶ Example 2

Question: How many 4/0 AWG, THWN conductors can be installed in 2 Schedule 80 PVC conduit? ▶Figure 352–8

(a) 2 conductors
(b) 3 conductors
(c) 4 conductors
(d) 5 conductors

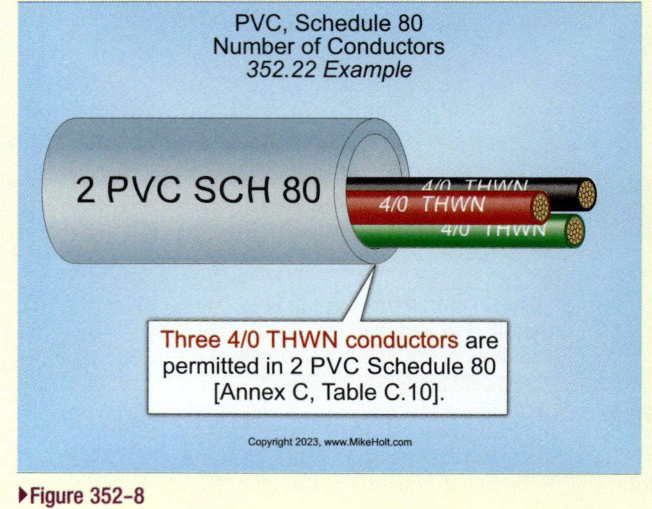

▶Figure 352–8

Answer: (b) 3 conductors [Annex C, Table C.10]

Author's Comment:

▸ See 300.17 for examples of how to size raceways when conductors are not all the same size.

Cables are permitted to be installed in PVC where such use is not prohibited by the respective cable articles. The number of cables must not exceed the percentage fill specified in Chapter 9, Table 1.

352.24 Bends

(A) How Made. Raceway bends are not permitted to be made in any manner that will damage the raceway or significantly change its internal diameter (no kinks).

Author's Comment:

▸ PVC can be bent by hand, with a heat gun, or a heat box. Just make sure you do not damage the PVC.

(B) Degrees of Bends in One Run. To reduce the stress and friction on conductor insulation, the total degrees of bends (including offsets) between pull points is not permitted to exceed 360 degrees. ▶Figure 352–9

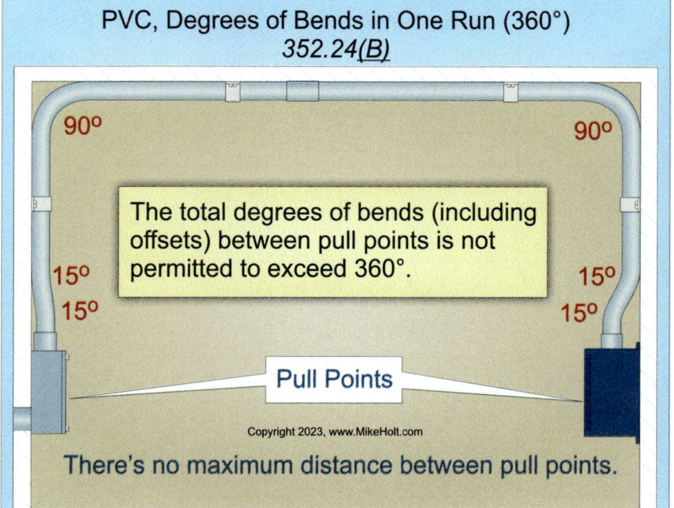

▶Figure 352–9

352.28 Trimming

The cut ends of PVC conduit must be trimmed (inside and out) to remove the burrs and rough edges.

Author's Comment:

▶ Trimming PVC conduit is very easy since most of the burrs will rub off with your fingers, and a knife will smooth the rough edges.

352.30 Securing and Supporting

PVC conduit must be fastened and supported in accordance with 352.30(A) and (B) so movement from thermal expansion and contraction is permitted.

(A) Securely Fastened. PVC conduit must be secured within 3 ft of every box, cabinet, or termination fitting (such as a conduit body). ▶Figure 352–10

(B) Supports. PVC conduit must be supported at intervals not exceeding the values in Table 352.30(B). The raceway must be fastened in a manner that permits movement from thermal expansion or contraction. ▶Figure 352–11

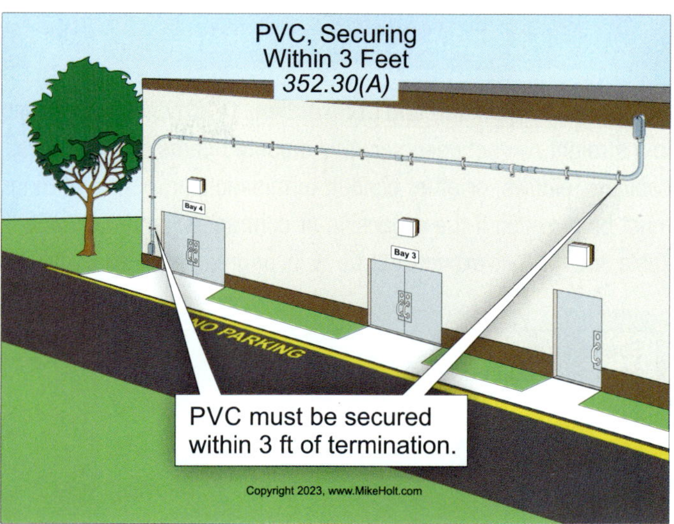

▶Figure 352–10

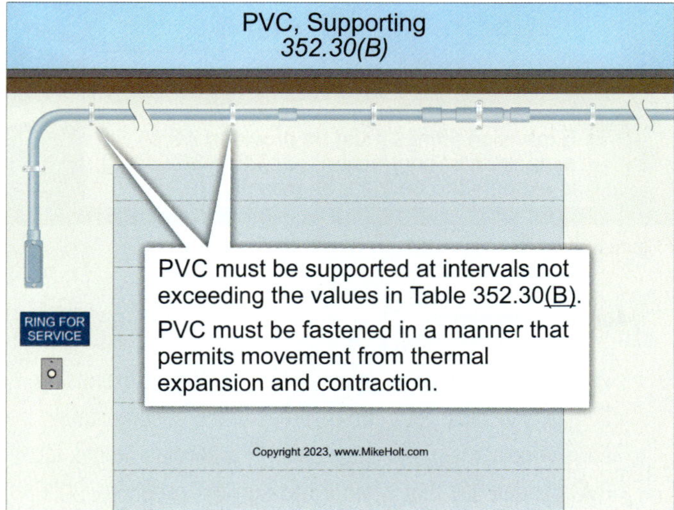

▶Figure 352–11

Table 352.30(B) Support of Rigid PVC	
Trade Size	Support Spacing
½–1	3 ft
1¼–2	5 ft
2½–3	6 ft
3½–5	7 ft
6	8 ft

PVC conduit installed horizontally through framing members is considered supported and secured if such support does not exceed Table 352.30(B) requirements, and the raceway is secured within 3 ft of termination.

352.44 Expansion Fittings

(A) Thermal Expansion and Contraction. If PVC conduit is installed in a straight run between securely mounted items such as boxes, cabinets, elbows, or other conduit terminations, expansion fittings must be provided if the expansion or contraction length change in Table 352.44(A) is expected to be ¼ in. or greater. ▶Figure 352–12

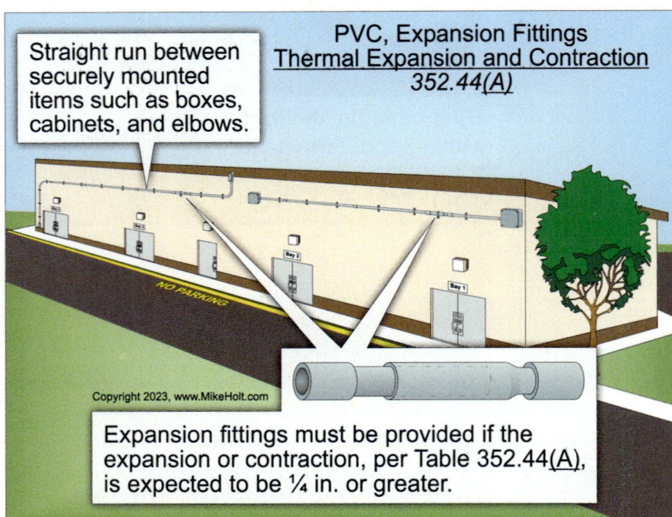

▶Figure 352–12

Author's Comment:

▶ When determining the number and setting of expansion fittings, you must read the manufacturer's documentation. For example, instructions for Carlon® expansion fittings for PVC conduit say that when it has sunlight exposure, 30°F must be added to the high ambient temperature.

(B) Earth Movement. When necessary to compensate for earth settling or movement (including frost heave), expansion fittings above ground must be installed.

Note: See 300.5(J).

Table 352.44(A) Expansion Characteristics of PVC Rigid Nonmetallic Conduit Coefficient of Thermal Expansion

Temperature Change (°C)	Length of Change of PVC Conduit (mm/m)	Temperature Change (°F)	Length Change of PVC Conduit (in./100 ft)
5	0.30	5	0.20
10	0.61	10	0.41
15	0.91	15	0.61
20	1.22	20	0.81
25	1.52	25	1.01
30	1.83	30	1.22
35	2.13	35	1.42
40	2.43	40	1.62
45	2.74	45	1.83
50	3.04	50	2.03
55	3.35	55	2.23
60	3.65	60	2.43
65	3.95	65	2.64
70	4.26	70	2.84
75	4.56	75	3.04
80	4.87	80	3.24
85	5.17	85	3.45
90	5.48	90	3.65
95	5.78	95	3.85
100	6.08	100	4.06

352.46 Bushings

A protective bushing or adapter shall be provided to protect the wire from abrasion unless the box, fitting, or enclosure design provides equivalent protection. ▶Figure 352–13

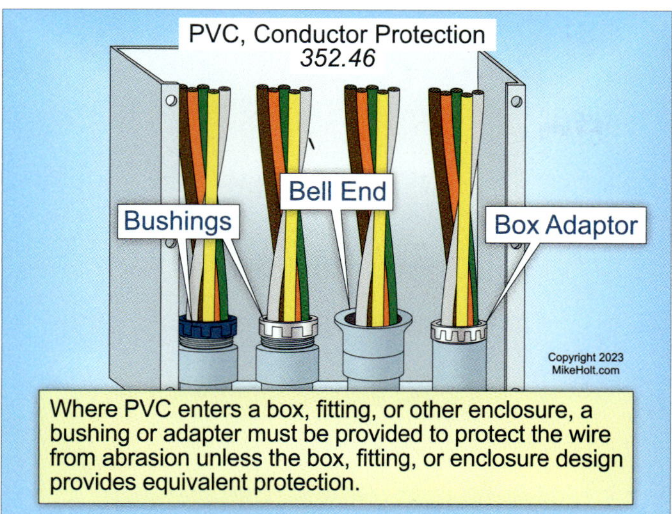

▶Figure 352–13

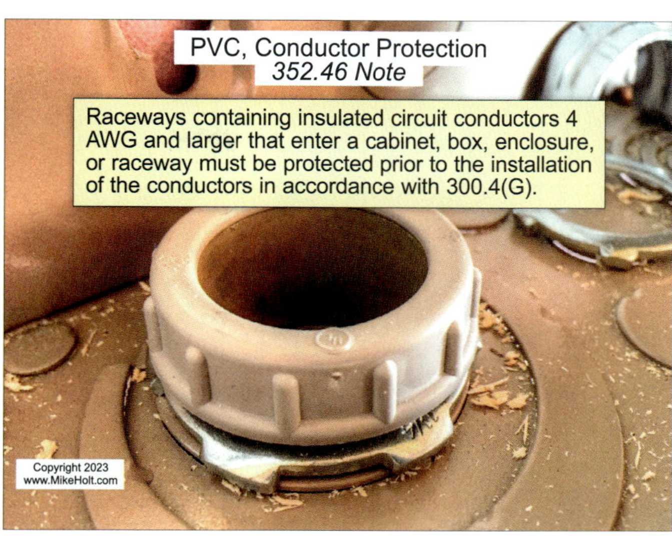

▶Figure 352–14

Author's Comment:

▸ In accordance with *"UL 651 Standard for Schedule 40 and 80 PVC Conduit and Fittings"* section 5.1.2, the inner and outer surfaces of a fitting are not permitted to be subject to peeling, scaling, or flaking and must be smooth and free from blisters, cracks, or other defects. The fitting must have a smooth, rounded inlet hole to afford protection to the conductors. In the case of a molded product, excess flashing must be removed from the mold line of all interior surfaces so there are no sharp edges or obstructions to the passage of wiring or mating products in the intended use of the product.

Note: Conductors 4 AWG and larger that enter an enclosure must be protected from abrasion (during and after installation) by a fitting that provides a smooth, rounded insulating surface (such as an insulating bushing), unless the design of the box, fitting, or enclosure provides equivalent protection in accordance with 300.4(G). ▶Figure 352–14

352.48 Joints

Joints, such as couplings and connectors, must be made in a manner approved by the authority having jurisdiction.

Author's Comment:

▸ Follow the manufacturers' instructions for the raceway, fittings, and glue. Some glue requires the raceway surface to be cleaned with a solvent before it is applied. After applying glue to both surfaces, a quarter turn of the fitting is required.

352.60 Equipment Grounding Conductor

An equipment grounding conductor must be installed within PVC when metal parts of equipment require a connection to an equipment grounding conductor. ▶Figure 352–15

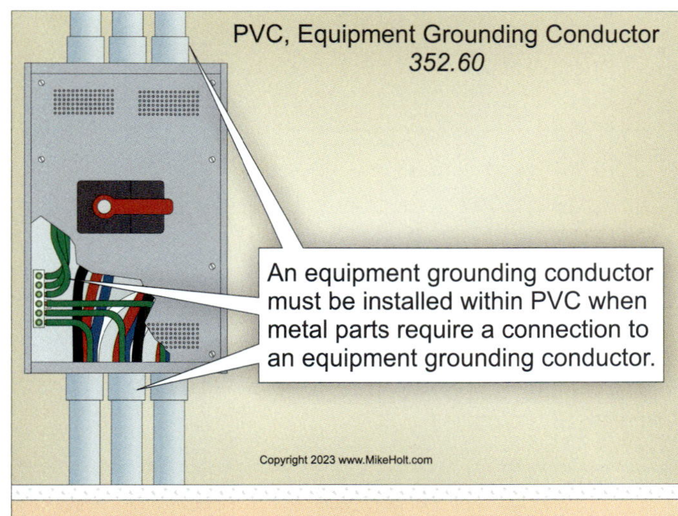

▶Figure 352–15

Ex 2: An equipment grounding conductor is not required in PVC conduit where the service neutral conductor is bonded to service equipment in accordance with 250.142(A). ▶Figure 352–16

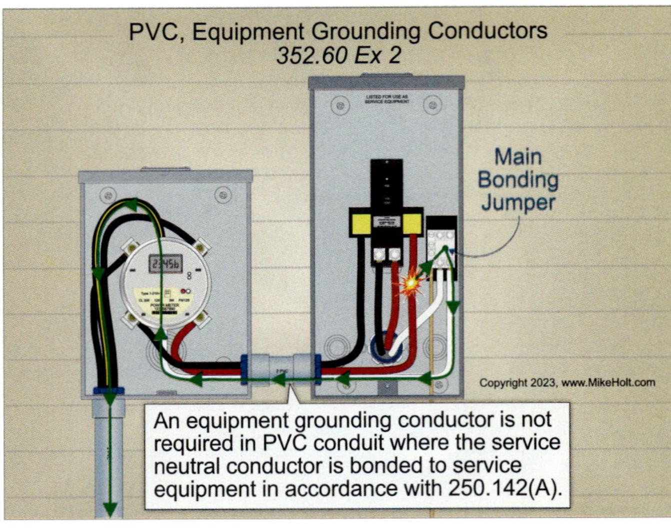

▶Figure 352–16

LIQUIDTIGHT FLEXIBLE NONMETALLIC CONDUIT (LFNC)

Introduction to Article 356—Liquidtight Flexible Nonmetallic Conduit (LFNC)

This article covers the use, installation, and construction specifications of liquidtight flexible nonmetallic conduit (LFNC) and associated fittings. LFNC has an inner flexible core with an outer liquidtight, nonmetallic, sunlight-resistant jacket. It is available in trade sizes ½ to 4 and is sometimes referred to as "Carflex®." Some topics covered in this material include:

- Listing Requirements
- Uses Permitted
- Uses Not Permitted
- Size
- Number of Conductors
- Bending and Trimming
- Securing and Supporting
- Couplings and Connectors
- Grounding and Bonding

Article 356 consists of three parts:

- Part I. General
- Part II. Installation
- Part III. Construction Specifications

According to Article 100, "Liquidtight flexible nonmetallic conduit (LFNC)" is a raceway of circular cross section with an outer liquidtight, nonmetallic, sunlight-resistant jacket over a flexible inner core, with associated couplings, connectors, and fittings, listed for the installation of electrical conductors. ▶Figure 356–1

Part I. General

356.1 Scope

Article 356 covers the use, installation, and construction specifications of liquidtight flexible nonmetallic conduit (LFNC) and associated fittings. ▶Figure 356–2

356.6 Listing Requirements

LFNC and its associated fittings must be listed.

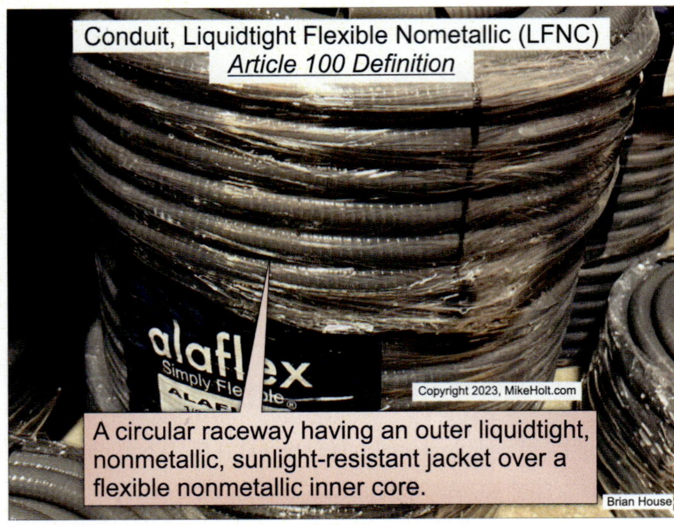

▶Figure 356–1

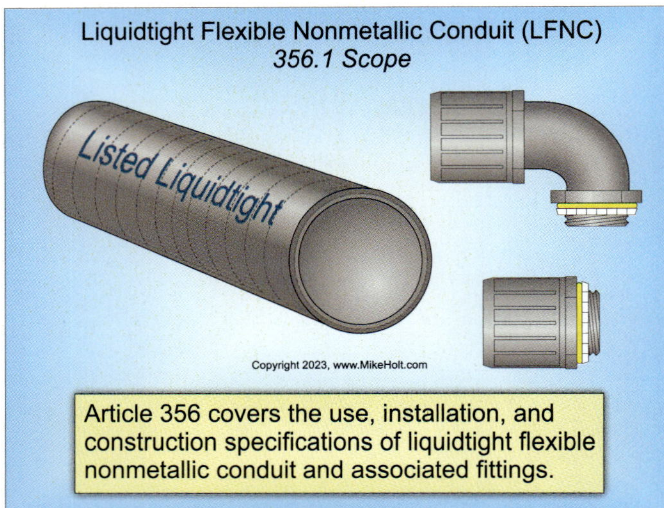

▶Figure 356–2

Part II. Installation

356.10 Uses Permitted

Listed LFNC is permitted (either exposed or concealed) at any of the following purposes and locations:

(1) If flexibility is required.

(2) If protection from liquids, vapors, machine oils, or solids is required.

(3) Outdoors, if listed and marked for this purpose.

(4) Directly buried in the Earth if listed and marked for this purpose.
▶Figure 356–3

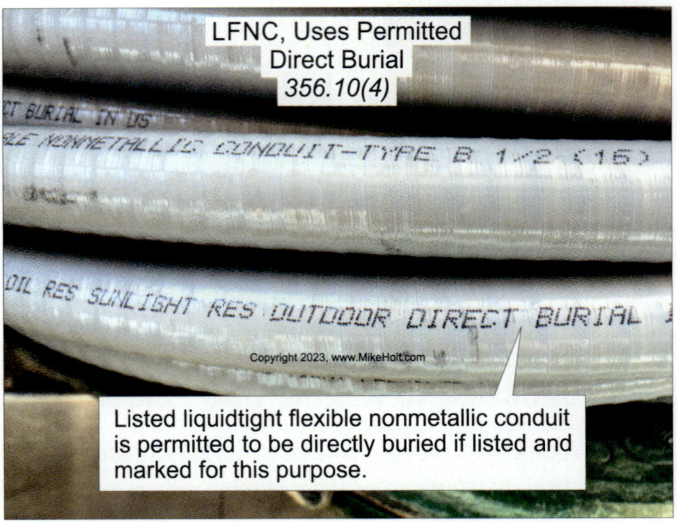

▶Figure 356–3

(5) Installed in lengths over 6 ft if secured in accordance with 356.30.

(7) Encasement in concrete if listed for direct burial.

(8) In locations subject to severe corrosive influences as covered in 300.6 where listed for exposure to specific chemicals.

(9) Conductors or cables rated at a temperature higher than the listed temperature rating of LFNC conduit are permitted to be installed in LFNC, provided the conductors or cables are not operated at a temperature higher than the listed temperature rating of the LFNC.

Note: Extreme cold can cause some types of nonmetallic conduits to become brittle and therefore more susceptible to damage from physical contact.

356.12 Uses Not Permitted

LFNC is not permitted:

(1) Where subject to physical damage

(2) If the ambient temperature and/or conductor temperature exceeds its listing

(3) Longer than 6 ft, except if approved by the authority having jurisdiction as essential for a required degree of flexibility

(4) In any hazardous (classified) location except as permitted by 501.10(B)(2), 502.10(A)(2) and (B)(2), and 504.20

356.20 Trade Size

(A) Minimum. LFNC smaller than trade size ½ is not permitted, except as in the following applications:

(1) Enclosing the leads of motors [430.245(B)]

(2) For tap connections to lighting fixtures in accordance with 410.117(C) for trade size ⅜

(B) Maximum. LFNC larger than trade size 4 is not permitted.

356.22 Number of Conductors

Raceways must be large enough to permit the installation and removal of conductors without damaging the conductors' insulation. The number of conductors is not permitted to exceed the percentage fill specified in Chapter 9, Table 1.

When all conductors within a raceway are the same size and insulation, the number of conductors permitted can be found in Annex C for the raceway type.

▶ **Example**

Question: *How many 8 AWG, THHN conductors can be installed in ¾ LFNC-B?* ▶Figure 356–4

(a) 2 conductors
(b) 4 conductors
(c) 6 conductors
(d) 8 conductors

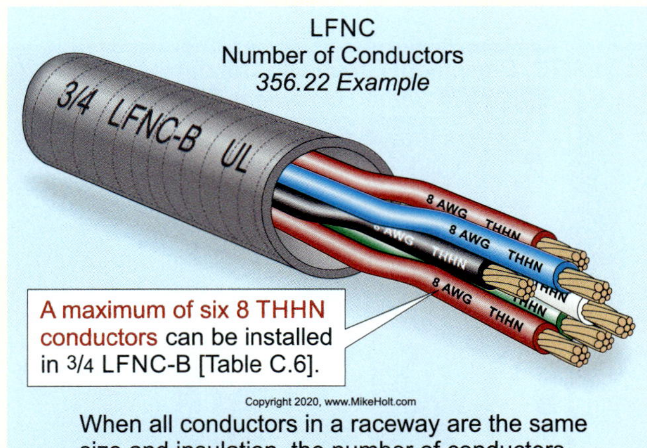

▶Figure 356–4

Answer: *(c) 6 conductors [Annex C, Table C.6]*

▸ See 300.17 for examples of how to size raceways when conductors are not all the same size.

Cables can be installed in LFNC if the number of cables does not exceed the allowable percentage fill specified in Chapter 9, Table 1.

356.24 Bends

(A) How Made. Raceway bends are not permitted to be made in any manner that will damage the raceway or significantly change its internal diameter (no kinks).

(B) Degrees of Bends in One Run. To reduce the stress and friction on conductor insulation, the total degrees of bends (including offsets) between pull points is not permitted to exceed 360 degrees.

356.30 Securing and Supporting

LFNC must be securely fastened and supported in accordance with any of the following:

(1) The conduit must be securely fastened at intervals not exceeding 3 ft and within 1 ft of termination when installed in lengths longer than 6 ft. ▶Figure 356–5

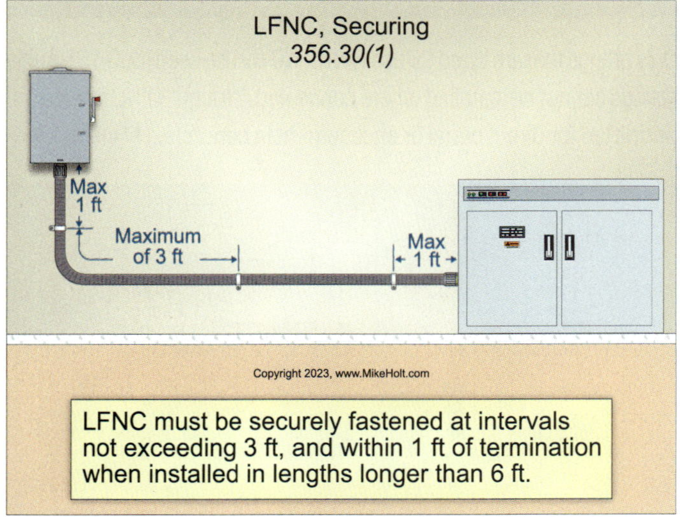

▶Figure 356–5

Where cable ties are to be used to secure and support LFNC, they must be listed for the application, securing, and supporting.

(2) Securing or supporting is not required if LFNC is fished or installed in lengths not exceeding 3 ft at terminals if flexibility is required.

(3) Runs of LFNC installed horizontally through framing members are considered supported and secured if such support does not exceed 3 ft, and the raceway is secured within 1 ft of termination.

(4) Securing or supporting LFNC is not required if installed in lengths not exceeding 6 ft from the last point where the raceway is securely fastened for connections within an accessible ceiling to a luminaire(s) or other equipment. For the purposes of this allowance, listed fittings are considered support. ▶Figure 356–6

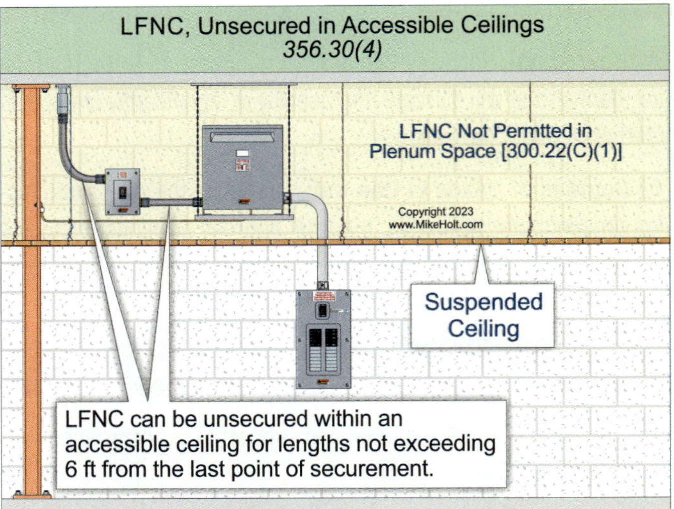

▶Figure 356–6

356.42 Fittings

Only fittings that are listed for use with LFNC can be used [300.15]. Angle fittings cannot be installed where concealed. Straight LFNC fittings are permitted for direct burial or encasement in concrete. ▶Figure 356–7

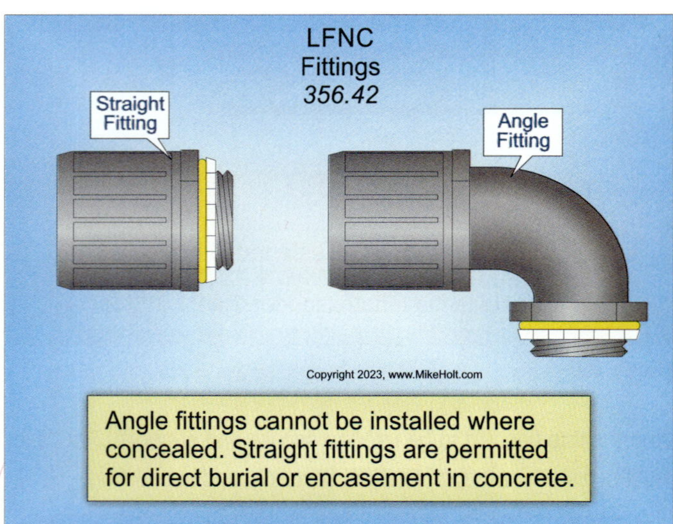

▶Figure 356–7

356.60 Equipment Grounding Conductor

An equipment grounding conductor must be installed within LFNC when metal parts of equipment require a connection to an equipment grounding conductor. ▶Figure 356–8

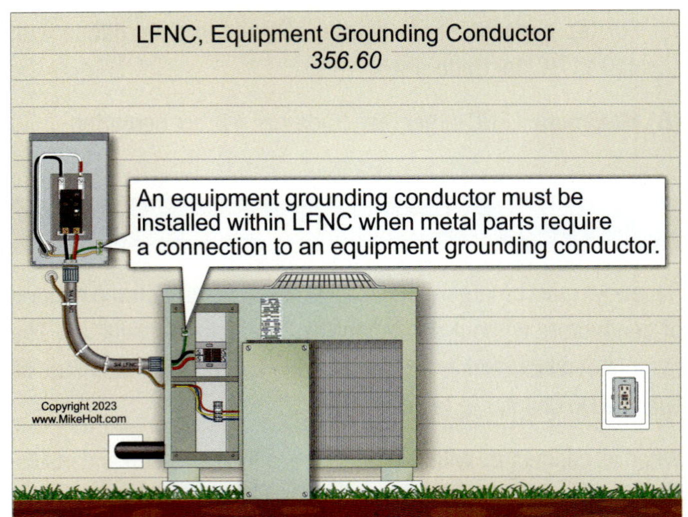

▶Figure 356–8

Author's Comment:

▶ An equipment grounding conductor is not required to be installed in a nonmetallic raceway supplying nonmetallic equipment because there is nothing in the nonmetallic box that requires a connection to an equipment grounding conductor. ▶Figure 356–9

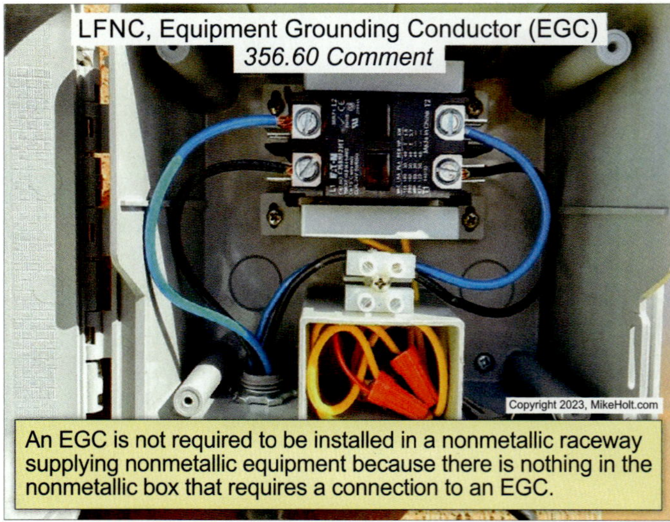

▶Figure 356–9

ELECTRICAL METALLIC TUBING (EMT)

Introduction to Article 358—Electrical Metallic Tubing (EMT)

Article 358 covers the use, installation, and construction specifications of electrical metallic tubing (EMT) and associated fittings. EMT is a lightweight metal tubing that is easy to bend, cut, and ream but it cannot be threaded. It is the most common raceway used in commercial and industrial installations. Some topics covered in this material include:

- Listing Requirements
- Uses Permitted
- Dissimilar Metals
- Size
- Number of Conductors
- Bending, Reaming, and Threading
- Securing and Supporting
- Use as an Equipment Grounding Conductor
- Construction

This article consists of three parts:

- Part I. General
- Part II. Installation
- Part III. Construction Specifications

According to Article 100, "Electrical Metallic Tubing (EMT)" is an unthreaded thinwall circular metallic raceway used for the installation of electrical conductors. When joined together with listed fittings and enclosures as a complete system, it is a reliable wiring method providing both physical protection for conductors as well an effective ground-fault current path. ▶Figure 358–1

Part I. General

358.1 Scope

Article 358 covers the use, installation, and construction specifications of electrical metallic tubing (EMT) and associated fittings. ▶Figure 358–2

358.6 Listing Requirements

EMT and associated fittings must be listed. ▶Figure 358–3

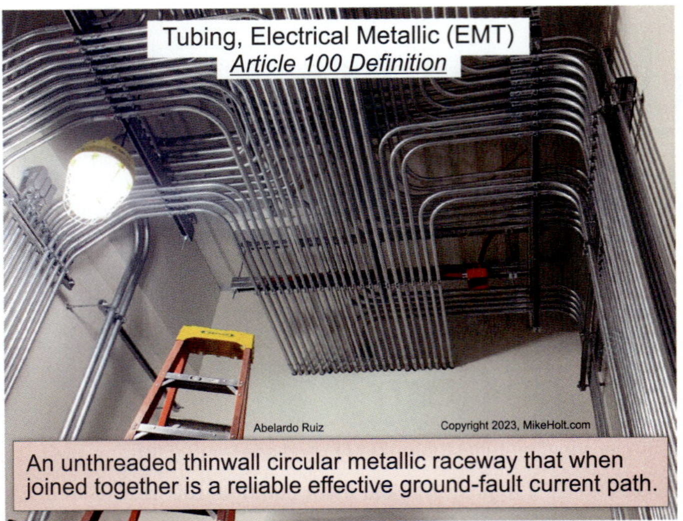

▶Figure 358–1

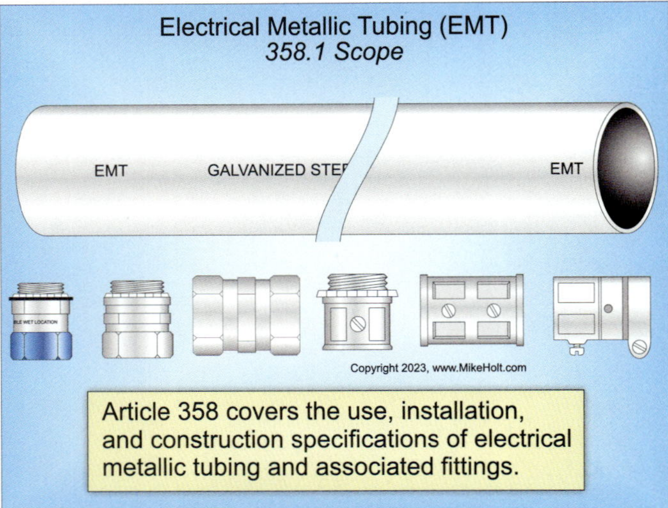

▶Figure 358–2

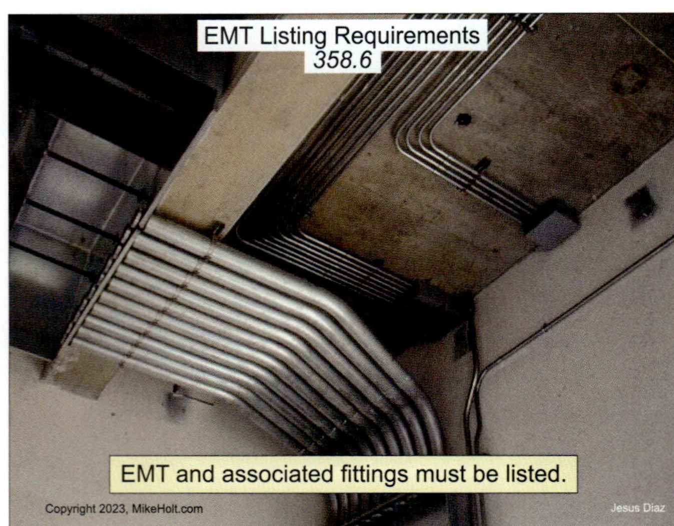

▶Figure 358–3

Part II. Installation

358.10 Uses Permitted

(A) Exposed and Concealed. EMT is permitted to be used exposed and concealed for the following applications:

(1) In concrete and in direct contact with the Earth <u>with fittings identified for direct burial</u>

(2) In dry, damp, or wet locations

(3) In any hazardous (classified) location as permitted by other articles in this *Code* ▶Figure 358–4

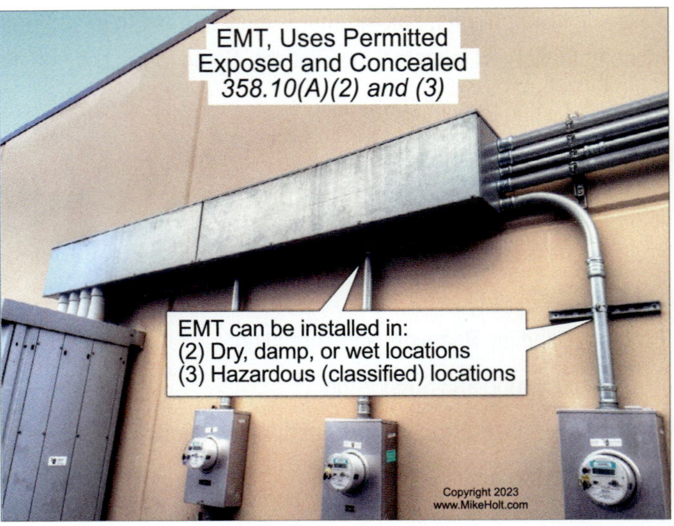

▶Figure 358–4

(B) Corrosive Environments.

(1) Galvanized Steel. Galvanized and stainless steel EMT, elbows, and fittings can be installed in concrete, in direct contact with the Earth, or in areas subject to severe corrosive influences. In addition, they must be protected by corrosion protection and approved as suitable for the condition.

> **Author's Comment:**
>
> ▶ In accordance with "*UL Guide Information FJMX*," supplementary corrosion protection is required when EMT and associated fittings are buried. In addition, supplementary corrosion protection is required at the point where EMT transitions from concrete encasement to the soil.

(D) Wet Locations. Support fittings (such as screws, straps, and so forth) installed in a wet location must be made of corrosion-resistant material.

Note: See 300.6 for protection against corrosion.

Author's Comment:

▶ If installed in wet locations, fittings for EMT must be listed for use in wet locations and prevent moisture or water from entering or accumulating within the enclosure in accordance with 314.15 [358.42].

358.12 Uses Not Permitted

EMT is not permitted to be used under the following conditions:

(1) Where subject to severe physical damage ▶Figure 358–5

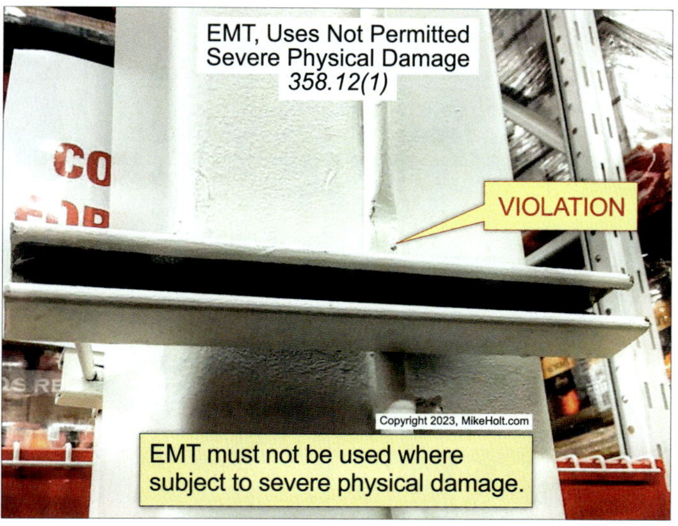

▶Figure 358–5

(2) For the support of luminaires or other equipment ▶Figure 358–6

358.20 Trade Size

(A) Minimum. EMT smaller than trade size ½ is not permitted.

(B) Maximum. EMT larger than trade size 6 is not permitted.

358.22 Number of Conductors

Raceways must be large enough to permit the installation and removal of conductors without damaging the conductors' insulation. The number of conductors is not permitted to exceed the percentage fill specified in Chapter 9, Table 1.

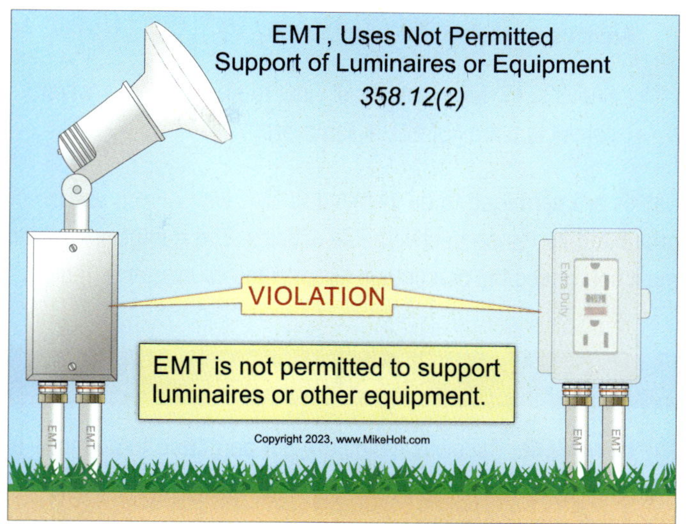

▶Figure 358–6

When all conductors within a raceway are the same size and insulation, the number of conductors permitted can be found in Annex C for the raceway type.

▶ **Example**

Question: How many 12 AWG, THHN conductors can be installed in 1 EMT? ▶Figure 358–7

(a) 23 conductors   (b) 24 conductors
(c) 25 conductors   (d) 26 conductors

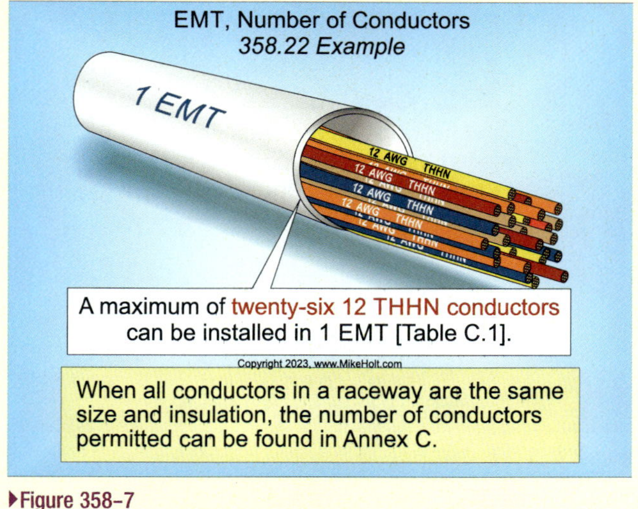

▶Figure 358–7

Answer: (d) 26 conductors [Annex C, Table C.1]

Author's Comment:

▸ See 300.17 for examples of how to size raceways when conductors are not all the same size.

Cables are permitted to be installed in EMT where such use is not prohibited by the respective cable articles. The number of cables must not exceed the percentage fill specified in Chapter 9, Table 1.

358.24 Bends

(A) How Made. Raceway bends are not permitted to be made in any manner that will damage the raceway or significantly change its internal diameter (no kinks).

Author's Comment:

▸ This is generally not a problem because typical EMT benders are made to comply with this requirement.

(B) Degrees of Bends in One Run. To reduce the stress and friction on conductor insulation, the total degrees of bends in the tubing (including offsets) between pull points cannot exceed 360 degrees. ▸Figure 358–8

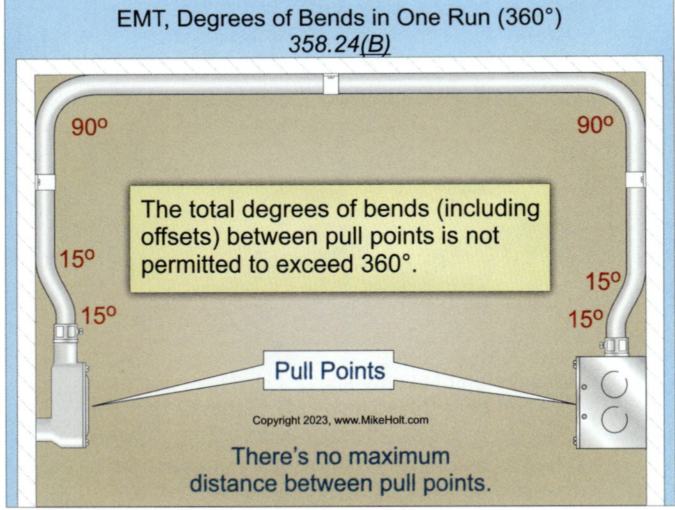

▸Figure 358–8

Author's Comment:

▸ There is no maximum distance between pull boxes because this is a design issue, not a safety issue.

358.28 Reaming

(A) Reaming. Reaming to remove the burrs and rough edges is required when the raceway is cut. ▸Figure 358–9

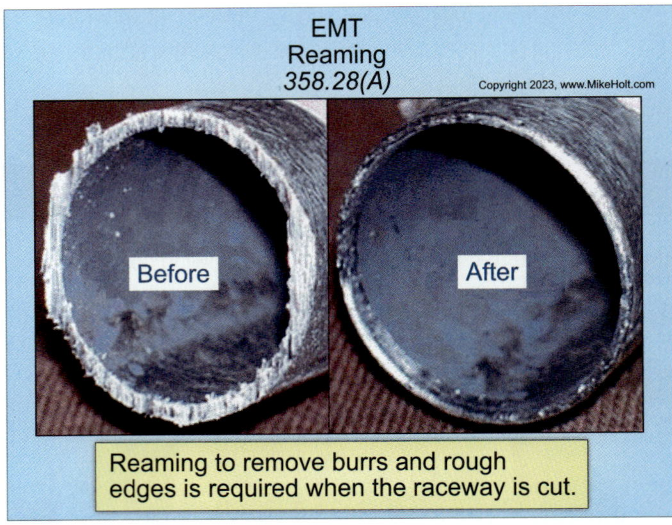

▸Figure 358–9

Author's Comment:

▸ It is considered an accepted practice to ream small raceways with a screwdriver or lineman's pliers.

358.30 Securing and Supporting

(A) Securely Fastened. EMT must be securely fastened in place and supported in accordance with the following: ▸Figure 358–10

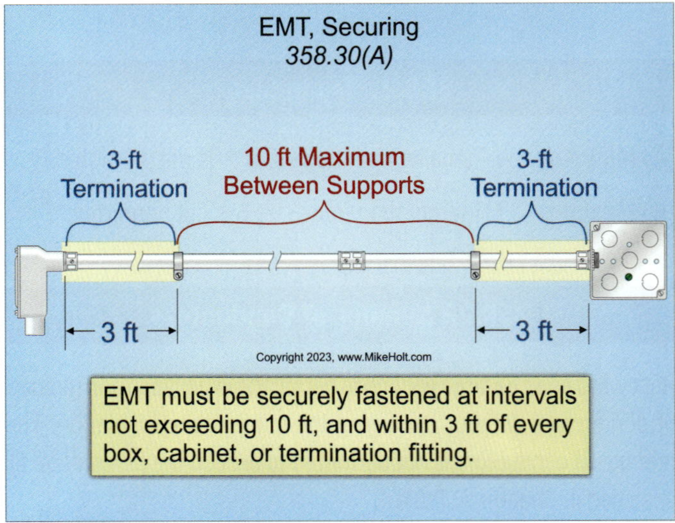

▸Figure 358–10

(1) EMT must be securely fastened at intervals not exceeding 10 ft.

(2) The tubing must be securely fastened within 3 ft of every box, cabinet, or termination fitting.

Author's Comment:

▸ Fastening is required within 3 ft of termination, not within 3 ft of a coupling.

Ex 1: When structural members do not permit the raceway to be secured within 3 ft of a box or termination fitting, an unbroken raceway can be secured within 5 ft of a box or termination fitting. ▸Figure 358–11

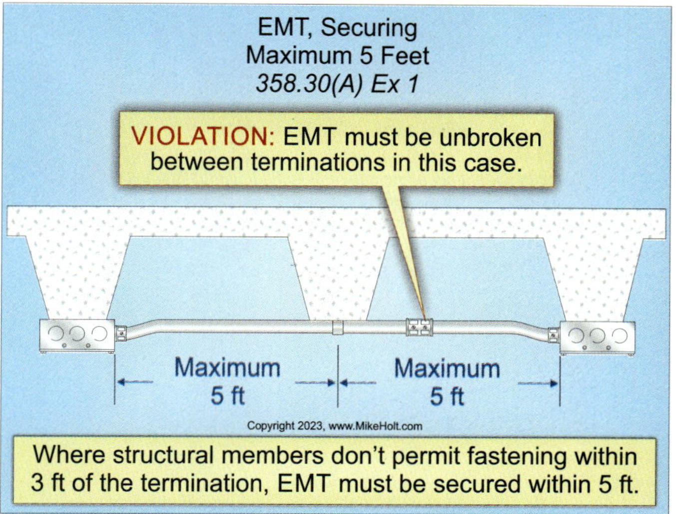

▸Figure 358–11

(B) Horizontal Runs. EMT installed horizontally through framing members is considered supported and secured if such support does not exceed 10 ft, and the raceway is secured within 3 ft of termination. ▸Figure 358–12

358.42 Couplings and Connectors

Couplings and connectors must be made up tight to maintain an effective ground-fault current path to safely conduct fault current in accordance with 250.4(A)(5), 250.96(A), and 300.10.

Buried in Concrete. Couplings and connectors buried in concrete must be of the concrete-tight type. ▸Figure 358–13

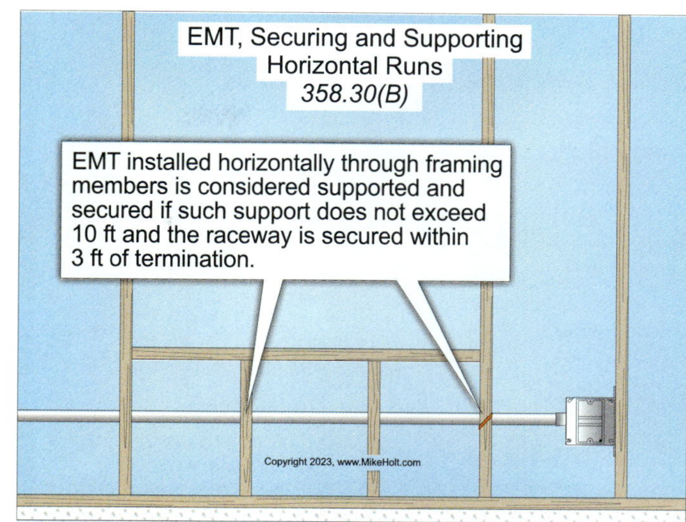

▸Figure 358–12

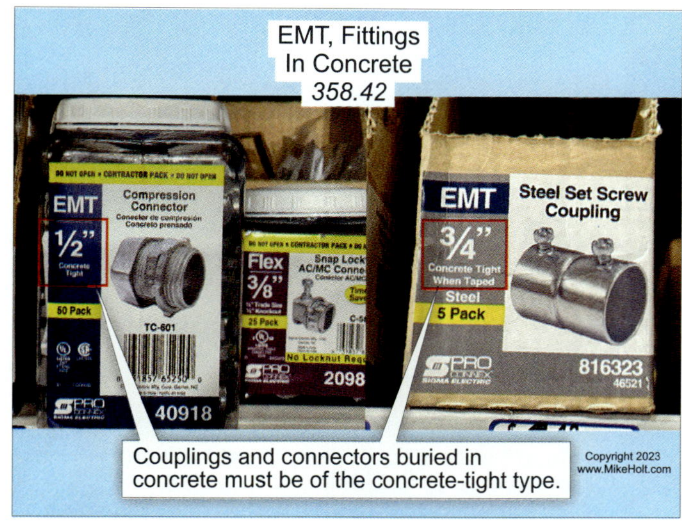

▸Figure 358–13

Wet Locations. Couplings and connectors in wet locations must be listed for use in wet locations. ▸Figure 358–14 and ▸Figure 358–15

Author's Comment:

▸ In accordance with "*UL Guide Information DWTT,*" some EMT fittings are marked on the carton as "concrete-tight when taped" and can be used in concrete.

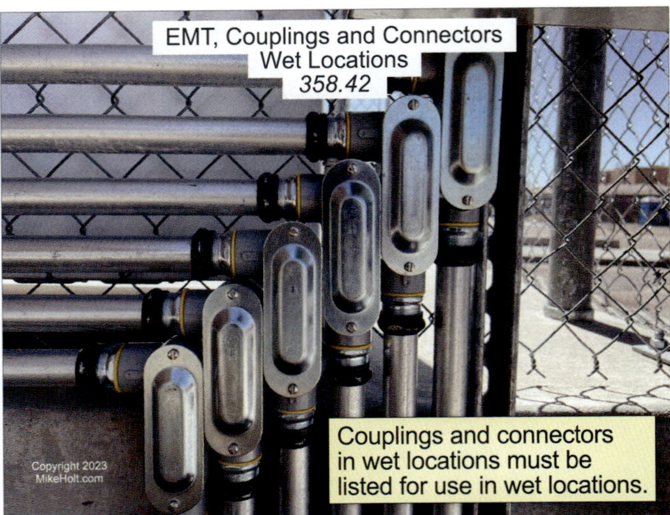

▶Figure 358–14

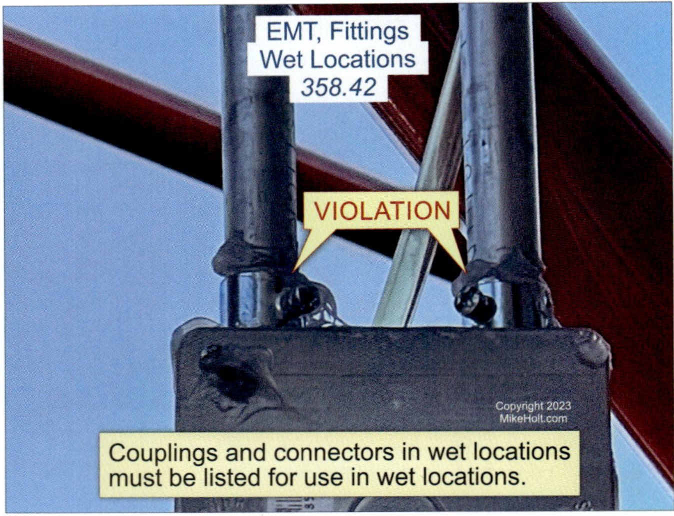

▶Figure 358–15

358.60 Equipment Grounding Conductor

EMT can serve as an equipment grounding conductor [250.118(A)(4)].
▶Figure 358–16

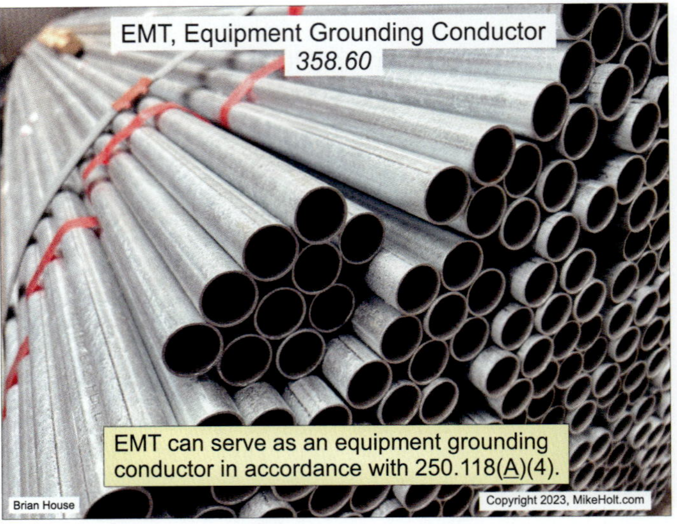

▶Figure 358–16

ELECTRICAL NONMETALLIC TUBING (ENT)

Introduction to Article 362—Electrical Nonmetallic Tubing (ENT)

This article covers the use, installation, and construction specifications of electrical nonmetallic tubing (ENT) and associated fittings. ENT is a nonmetallic, pliable, corrugated, circular raceway. It is often referred to as "Smurf Pipe" or "Smurf Tube" after the cartoon characters by the same name because it was only available in blue when it was first available, but now comes in additional colors. This type of tubing is fragile and is not sunlight resistant, so it has limited uses. Some topics covered in this material include:

- ▶ Listing Requirements
- ▶ Uses Permitted
- ▶ Uses Not Permitted
- ▶ Size
- ▶ Number of Conductors
- ▶ Bending and Trimming
- ▶ Securing and Supporting
- ▶ Bushings
- ▶ Use as an Equipment Grounding Conductor

Article 362 consists of three parts:

- ▶ Part I. General
- ▶ Part II. Installation
- ▶ Part III. Construction Specifications

According to Article 100, "Electrical Nonmetallic Tubing (ENT)" is a pliable, corrugated, circular raceway of circular cross section with integral or associated couplings, connectors, and fittings that are listed for the installation of electrical conductors. It is composed of a material that is resistant to moisture and chemical atmospheres, and it is also flame retardant. ▶Figure 362–1

Part I. General

362.1 Scope

Article 362 covers the use, installation, and construction specifications of electrical nonmetallic tubing (ENT) and associated fittings. ▶Figure 362–2

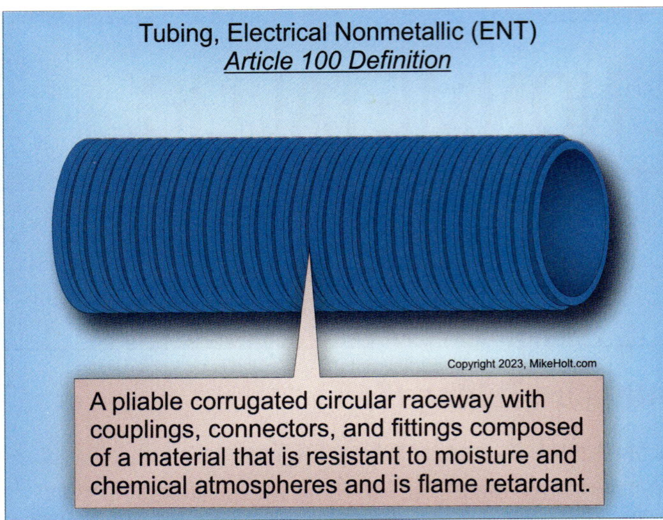

▶Figure 362–1

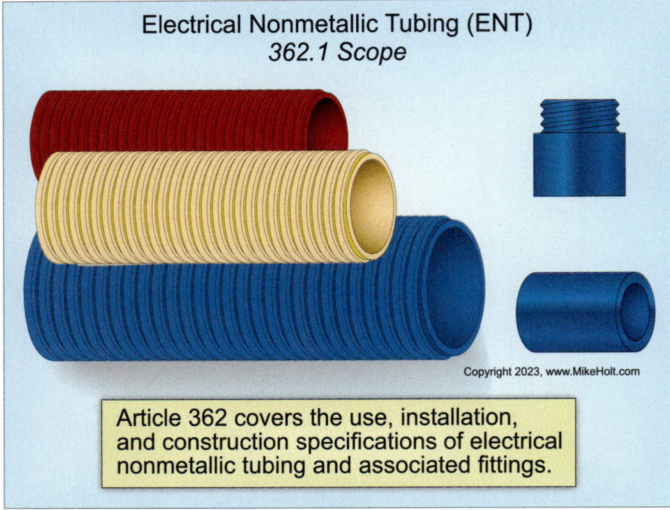

▶Figure 362–2

362.6 Listing

ENT and its associated fittings must be listed.

Author's Comment:

▸ ENT fittings are interchangeable with PVC fittings however, the proper glue (blue) must be applied for the joints.

Part II. Installation

362.10 Uses Permitted

Electrical nonmetallic tubing is permitted as follows:

(1) In buildings not exceeding three floors. ▶Figure 362–3

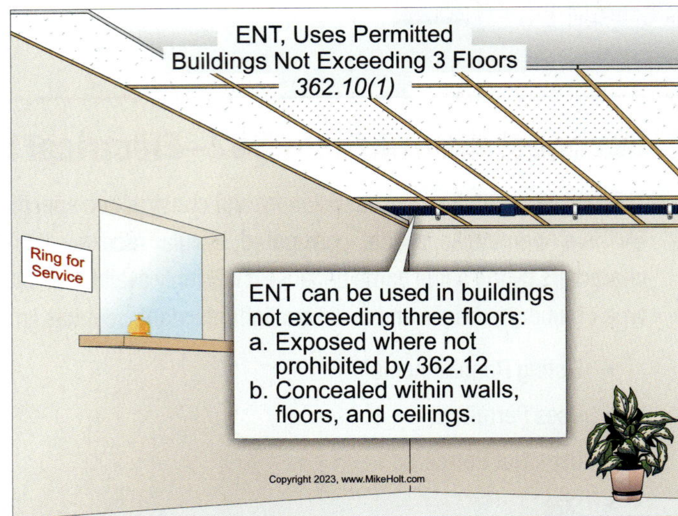

▶Figure 362–3

a. Exposed, where not prohibited by 362.12

b. Concealed within walls, floors, and ceilings

(2) In buildings exceeding three floors, where installed concealed within combustible or noncombustible walls, floors, or ceilings that provide a thermal barrier having a 15-minute finish rating, as identified in listings of fire-rated assemblies. ▶Figure 362–4

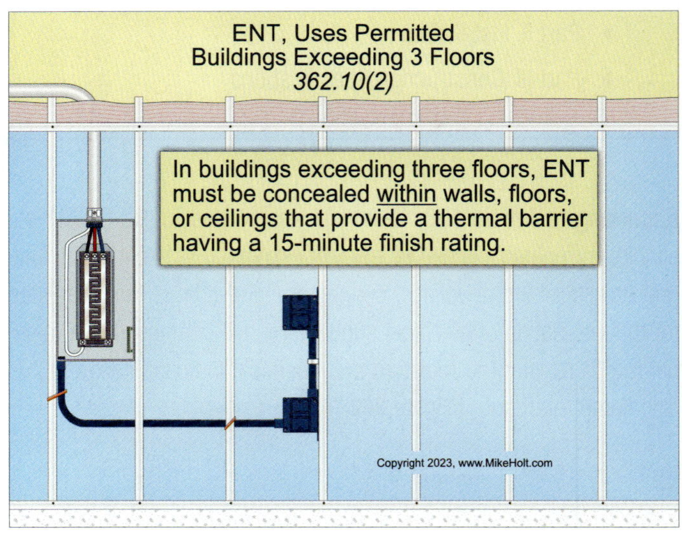

▶Figure 362–4

Ex to (2): If an approved automatic fire protective system is installed on all floors, electrical nonmetallic tubing is permitted exposed or concealed in buildings of any height. ▶Figure 362–5

Ex to (5): If an approved automatic fire protective system is installed on all floors, ENT is permitted above a suspended ceiling that does not have a 15-minute finish rated thermal barrier. ▶Figure 362–7

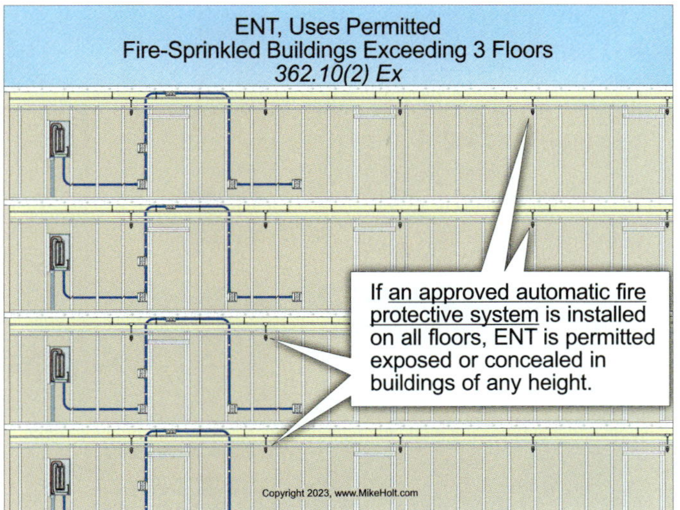

▶Figure 362–5

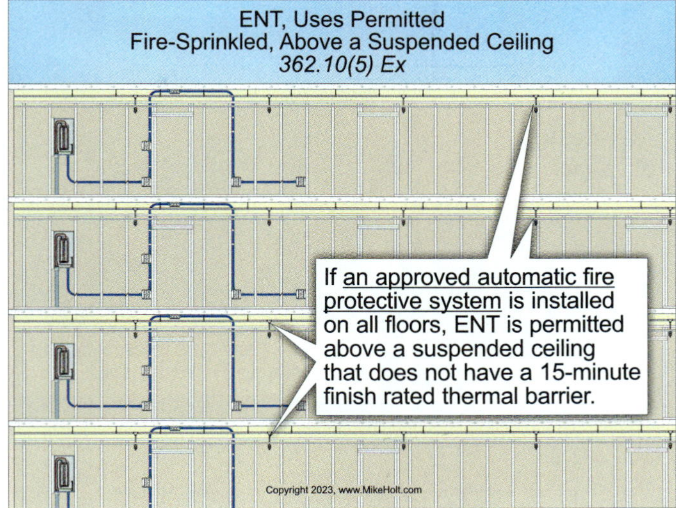

▶Figure 362–7

Author's Comment:

▶ ENT is not permitted above a suspended ceiling used as a plenum space [300.22(C)].

(3) In severe corrosive and chemical locations [300.6] when identified for this use.

(4) In dry and damp concealed locations if not prohibited by 362.12.

(5) Above a suspended ceiling if the suspended ceiling provides a thermal barrier having a 15-minute finish rating, as identified in listings of fire-rated assemblies. ▶Figure 362–6

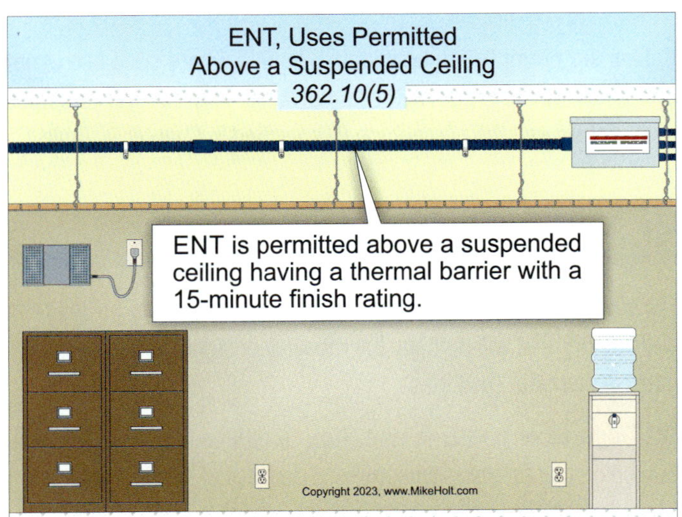

▶Figure 362–6

(6) Encased in poured concrete floors, ceilings, walls, and slabs.

(7) Embedded in a concrete slab provided fittings identified for the purpose are used.

(8) In wet locations or in a concrete slab on or below grade with fittings listed for the purpose.

362.12 Uses Not Permitted

ENT is not permitted to be used in the following applications:

(1) In any hazardous (classified) location, except as permitted by 504.20 and 505.15(A).

(2) For the support of luminaires or equipment. See 314.23.

(3) If the ambient temperature exceeds 50°C (122°F).

(4) For direct burial in the Earth.

Author's Comment:

▶ Electrical nonmetallic tubing is permitted to be encased in concrete [362.10(6)].

(5) Exposed in buildings over three floors, except as permitted by 362.10(1), 362.10(5) Ex, and 362.10(8).

(6) In assembly occupancies or theaters, except as permitted by 518.4 and 520.5.

(7) Exposed to the direct rays of the sun. ▶Figure 362–8

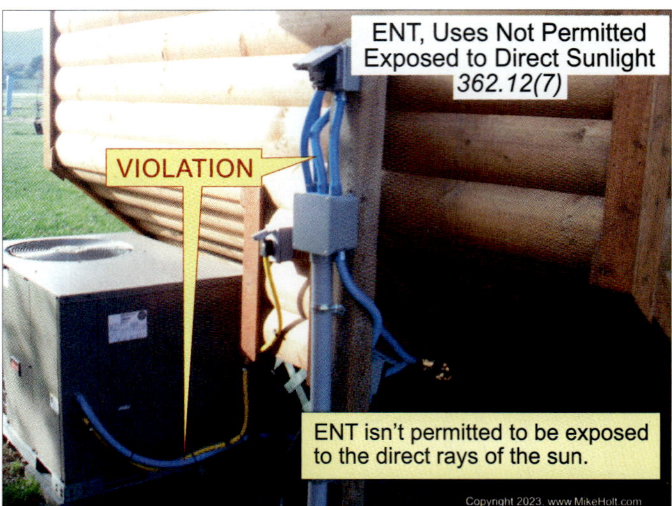

▶Figure 362–8

Author's Comment:

▸ Exposing electrical nonmetallic tubing to direct sunlight for an extended time may result in the product becoming brittle, unless it is listed to resist the effects of ultraviolet (UV) radiation.

(8) Where subject to physical damage.

Author's Comment:

▸ Electrical nonmetallic tubing is prohibited in ducts, plenum spaces [300.22(C)], and patient care space circuits in health care facilities [517.13(A)].

362.20 Trade Sizes

(A) Minimum. Electrical nonmetallic tubing smaller than trade size ½ is not permitted.

(B) Maximum. Electrical nonmetallic tubing larger than trade size 2½ is not permitted.

362.22 Number of Conductors

Raceways must be large enough to permit the installation and removal of conductors without damaging the conductors' insulation. The number of conductors is not permitted to exceed the percentage fill specified in Chapter 9, Table 1.

When all conductors within a raceway are the same size and insulation, the number of conductors permitted can be found in Annex C for the raceway type.

▶ **Example**

Question: How many 12 AWG, THHN conductors can be installed in ½ ENT? ▶Figure 362–9

(a) 2 conductors   (b) 4 conductors
(c) 6 conductors   (d) 8 conductors

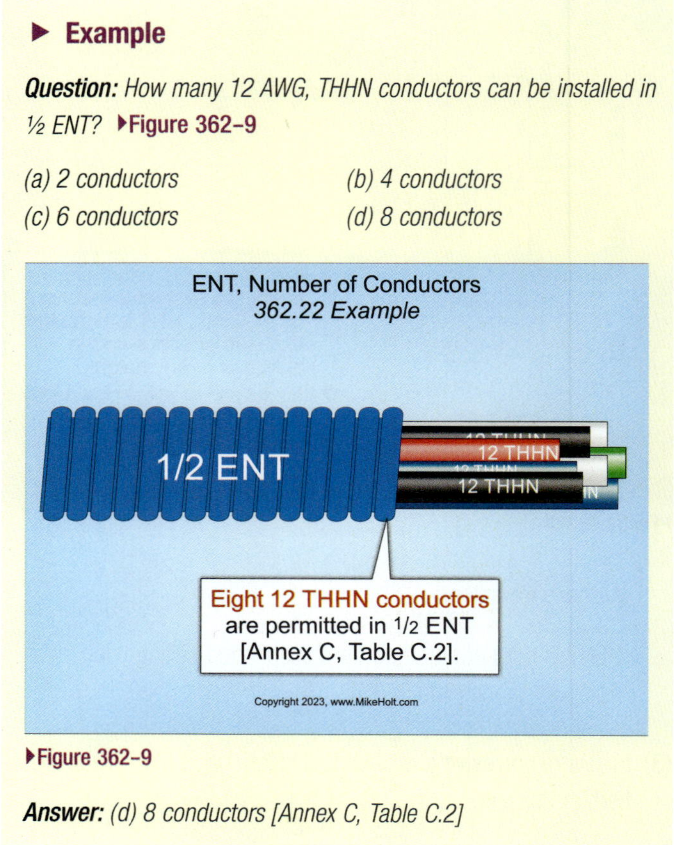

▶Figure 362–9

Answer: (d) 8 conductors [Annex C, Table C.2]

Author's Comment:

▸ See 300.17 for examples of how to size raceways when conductors are not all the same size.

Cables are permitted to be installed in ENT where such use is not prohibited by the respective cable articles. The number of cables must not exceed the percentage fill specified in Chapter 9, Table 1.

362.24 Bends

(A) How Made. Raceway bends are not permitted to be made in any manner that will damage the raceway or significantly change its internal diameter (no kinks).

(B) Degrees of Bends in One Run. To reduce the stress and friction on conductor insulation, the total degrees of bends in the tubing (including offsets) between pull points cannot exceed 360 degrees.

362.28 Trimming

The cut ends of electrical nonmetallic tubing must be trimmed (inside and out) to remove the burrs and rough edges.

Author's Comment:

▸ Trimming electrical nonmetallic tubing is very easy since most of the burrs will rub off with your fingers, and a knife will smooth the rough edges.

362.30 Securing and Supporting

ENT must be securely fastened in place by an approved means and supported in accordance with 362.30(A) and (B).

(A) Securely Fastened. ENT must be secured within 3 ft of every box, cabinet, or termination fitting (such as a conduit body) and at intervals not exceeding 3 ft. ▸Figure 362–10

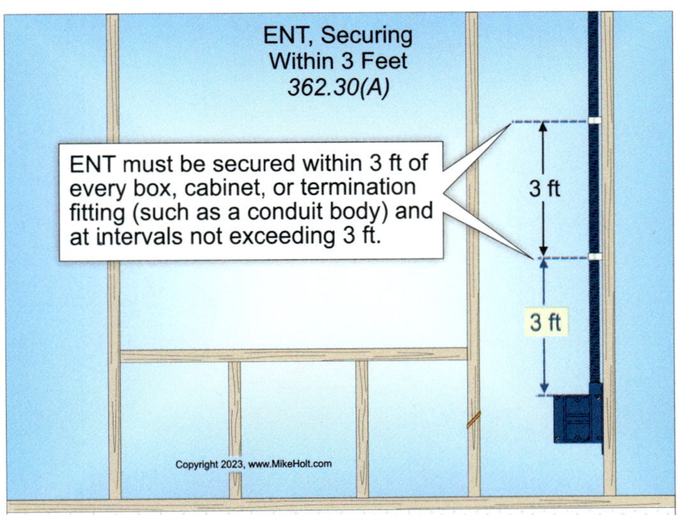

▸Figure 362–10

Where cable ties are to be used to secure and support electrical nonmetallic tubing, they must be listed as suitable for the application, securing, and supporting. ▸Figure 362–11

Ex 2: Lengths not exceeding 6 ft from the last point of support if the raceway is securely fastened within an accessible ceiling to luminaire(s) or other equipment.

Ex 3: If fished between access points through concealed spaces and securing is impractical.

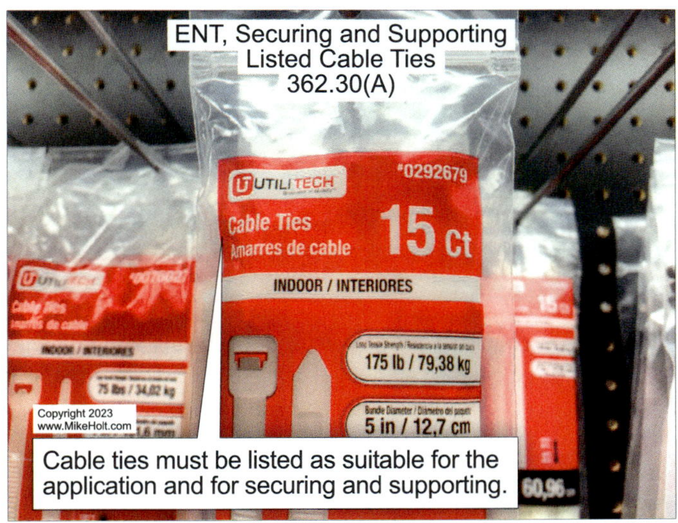

▸Figure 362–11

(B) Horizontal Runs. ENT installed horizontally through framing members is considered supported and secured if such support does not exceed 3 ft, and the raceway is secured within 3 ft of terminations. ▸Figure 362–12

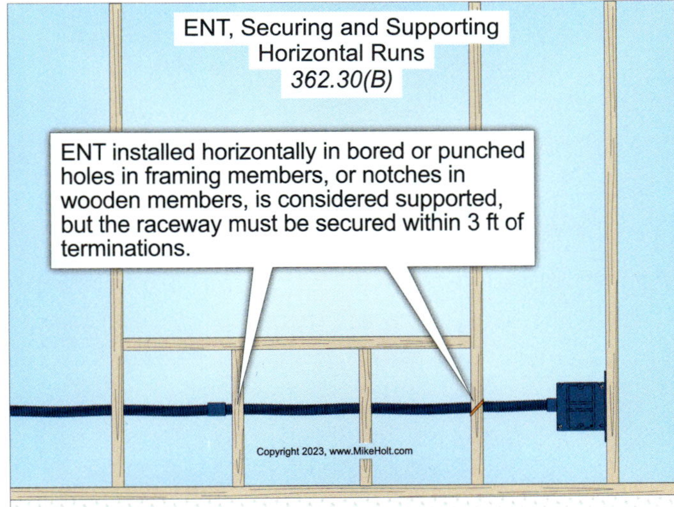

▸Figure 362–12

362.46 Bushings

Where ENT enters a box, fitting, or other enclosure, a bushing or adapter must be provided to protect the wire from abrasion, unless the box fitting or enclosure design provides equivalent protection.

Note: Conductors 4 AWG and larger that enter an enclosure must be protected from abrasion (during and after installation) by a fitting that provides a smooth, rounded insulating surface (such as an insulating bushing), unless the design of the box, fitting, or enclosure provides equivalent protection in accordance with 300.4(G).

362.48 Joints

Joints such as couplings and connectors must be made in a manner approved by the authority having jurisdiction.

362.60 Equipment Grounding Conductor

An equipment grounding conductor must be installed within ENT when metal parts of equipment require a connection to an equipment grounding conductor. ▶Figure 362–13

Ex 2: The equipment grounding conductor is not required where the neutral conductor is used as part of the effective ground-fault current path as permitted in 250.142.

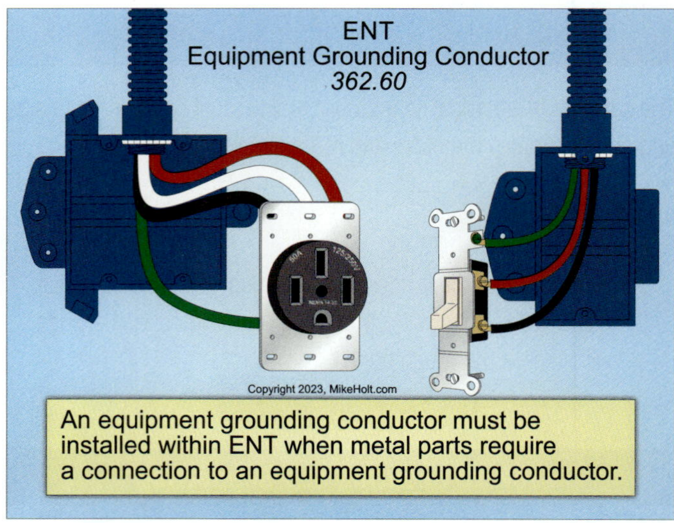

▶Figure 362–13

METAL WIREWAYS

Introduction to Article 376—Metal Wireways

Article 376 covers the use, installation, and construction specifications of metal wireways and associated fittings. Metal wireways are commonly used where access to conductors inside a raceway is required to make terminations, splices, or taps to several devices at a single location. They are often incorrectly called "auxiliary gutters" or "gutters" in the field. Wireways and auxiliary gutters are similar in design but a wireway is a raceway [Article 100] while an auxiliary gutter [Article 366] is not—it is a supplemental enclosure for wiring. Some topics covered in this material include:

- Uses Permitted
- Uses Not Permitted
- Size and Number of Conductors
- Securing and Supporting
- Splices, Taps, and Power Distribution Blocks
- Use as an Equipment Grounding Conductor
- Construction

This article consists of three parts:

- Part I. General
- Part II. Installation
- Part III. Construction Specifications

According to Article 100, "Metal Wireway" is a sheet metal trough with hinged or removable covers for housing and protecting electrical conductors and cable, and in which conductors are placed after the raceway has been installed. ▶Figure 376–1

Part I. General

376.1 Scope

Article 376 covers the use, installation, and construction specifications of metal wireways and associated fittings. ▶Figure 376–2

Part II. Installation

376.10 Uses Permitted

Wireways are permitted to be used in the following manners:

(1) Exposed

(2) In any hazardous (classified) location as permitted by other articles in the *Code*

(3) In wet locations where listed for the purpose ▶Figure 376–3

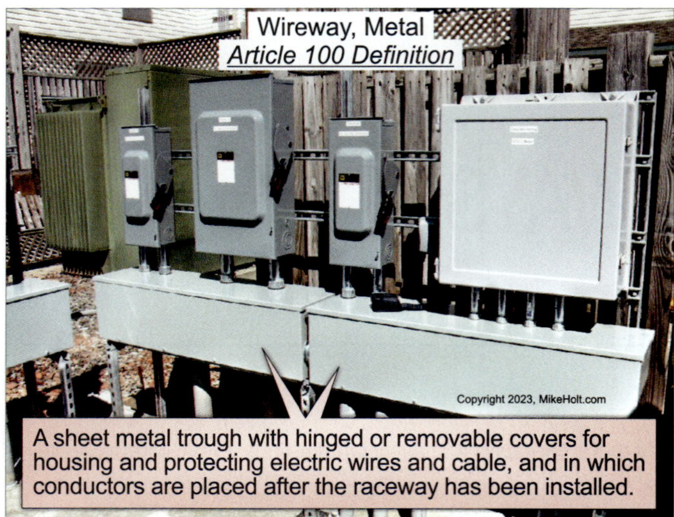

▶Figure 376–1

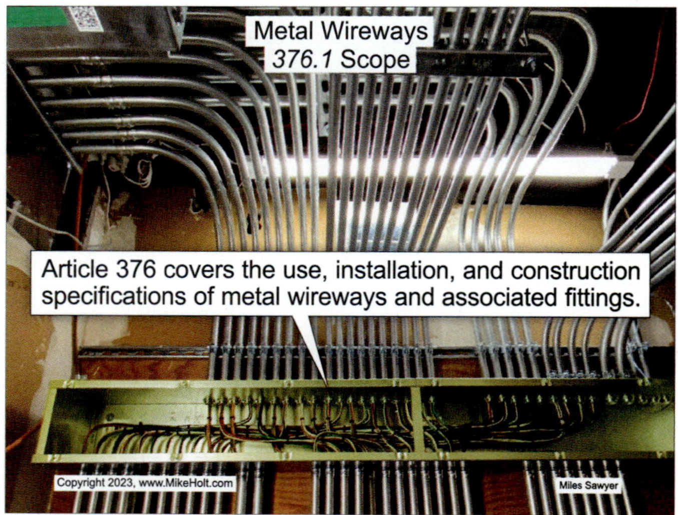

▶Figure 376–2

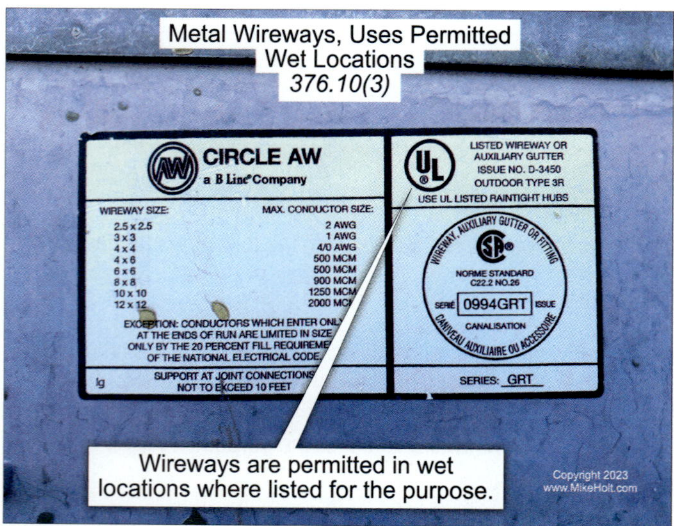

▶Figure 376–3

▸ Wireways are not required to be listed in damp or dry locations.

(4) Unbroken through walls, partitions, and floors

376.12 Uses Not Permitted

Wireways are not permitted to be used:

(1) Where subject to severe physical damage

(2) Where subject to severe corrosive environments

376.20 Conductors Connected in Parallel

Where conductors are installed in parallel as permitted in 310.10(G), the parallel conductors must be installed in groups consisting of not more than one conductor per phase or neutral to prevent current imbalance in the paralleled conductors due to inductive reactance. ▶Figure 376–4

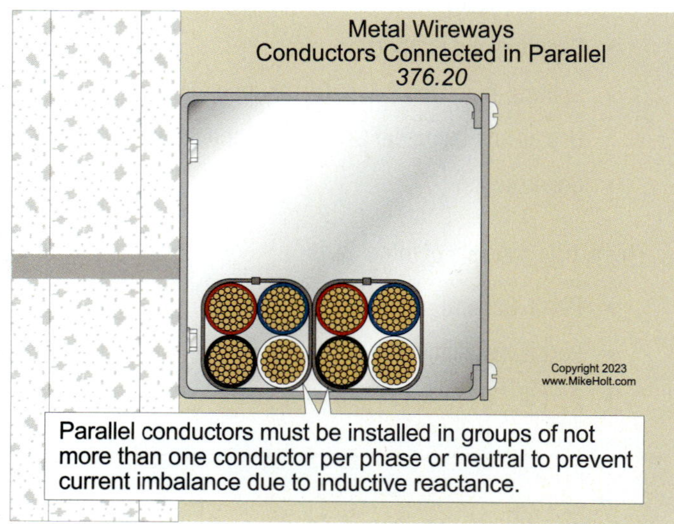

▶Figure 376–4

Note: The purpose of having all parallel conductor sets within the same group is to prevent current imbalance in the paralleled conductors due to inductive reactance.

376.21 Size of Conductors

Conductors are not permitted to be larger than that for which the wireway is designed. ▶Figure 376–5

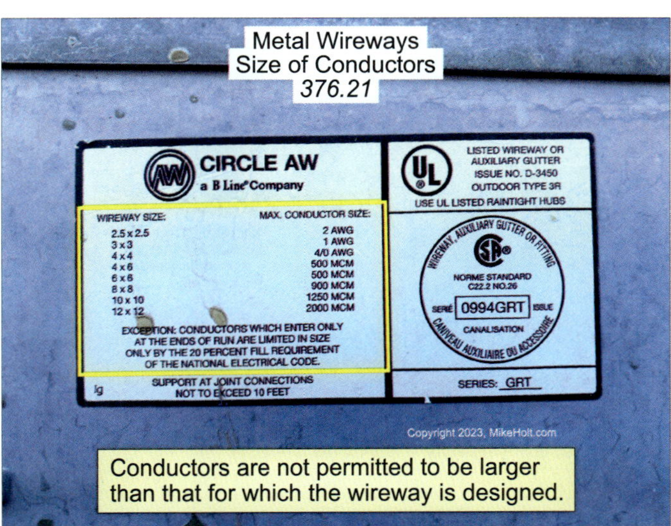

▶Figure 376–5

376.22 Number of Conductors and Ampacity

(A) Number of Conductors. The maximum number of conductors permitted in a wireway is limited to 20 percent of the cross-sectional area of the wireway. ▶Figure 376–6

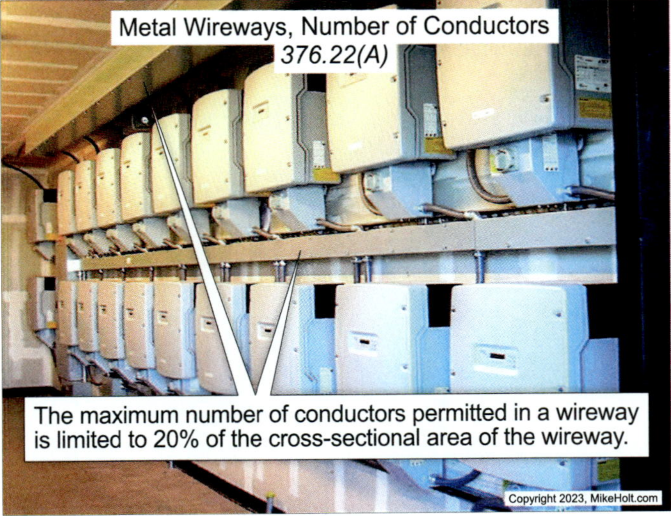

▶Figure 376–6

Author's Comment:

▶ Splices and taps, including conductors, are not permitted to fill more than 75 percent of the wiring space at any cross section [376.56(A)].

▶ Wireway Conductor Fill Example 1

Question: *What is the maximum conductor fill permitted for a 6 in. × 6 in. wireway?* ▶Figure 376–7

(a) 7.20 sq in.   (b) 15 sq in.   (c) 21.50 sq in.   (d) 36 sq in.

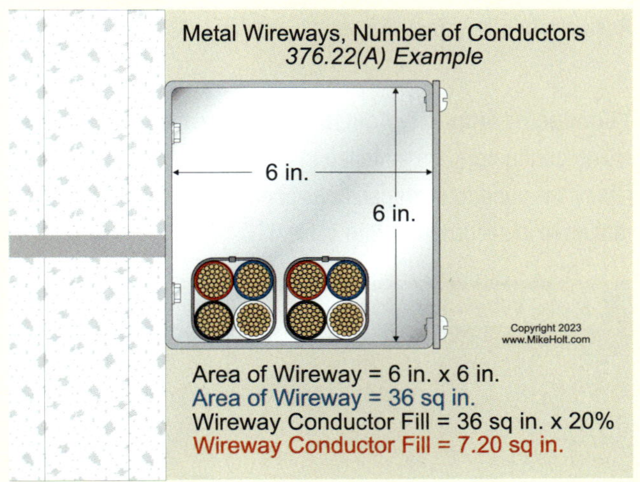

▶Figure 376–7

Solution:

36 sq in. × 20% = 7.20 sq in.

Answer: *(a) 7.20 sq in.*

▶ Wireway Conductor Fill Example 2

Question: *What is the minimum size wireway suitable for three 500 kcmil THWN-2, one 250 kcmil THWN-2, and four 4/0 AWG THWN-2 conductors?*

(a) 4 in. × 4 in. (16 sq in.)   (b) 6 in. × 6 in. (36 sq in.)
(c) 8 in. × 8 in. (64 sq in.)   (d) 10 in. × 10 in. (100 sq in.)

Solution:

Find the conductor area [Chapter 9, Table 5].

500 kcmil THWN-2 = 0.7073 sq in. × 3 conductors
500 kcmil THWN-2 = 2.1219 sq in.

250 kcmil THWN-2 = 0.3970 sq in.

4/0 AWG THWN-2 = 0.3237 sq in. × 4 conductors
4/0 AWG THWN-2 = 1.2948 sq in.

Total Conductor Area = 3.8137 sq in.

The wireway must not be filled to over 20 percent of its cross-sectional area [376.22(A)]. Twenty percent is equal to one-fifth, so we can multiply the required conductor area by five to find the minimum square inch area required.

• • •

Conductor Area × 5 = Required Wireway Minimum Area

3.8137 sq in. × 5 = 19.07 sq in. (less than 36 sq in.)

A 6 in. × 6 in. wireway has a cross-sectional area of 36 sq in. and will be large enough.

Answer: *(b) 6 in. × 6 in. (36 sq in.)*

(B) Conductor Ampacity Adjustment. When more than 30 current-carrying conductors are installed in any cross-sectional area of the wireway, the conductor ampacity, as contained in Table 310.16, must be adjusted in accordance with Table 310.15(C)(1). ▶Figure 376–8

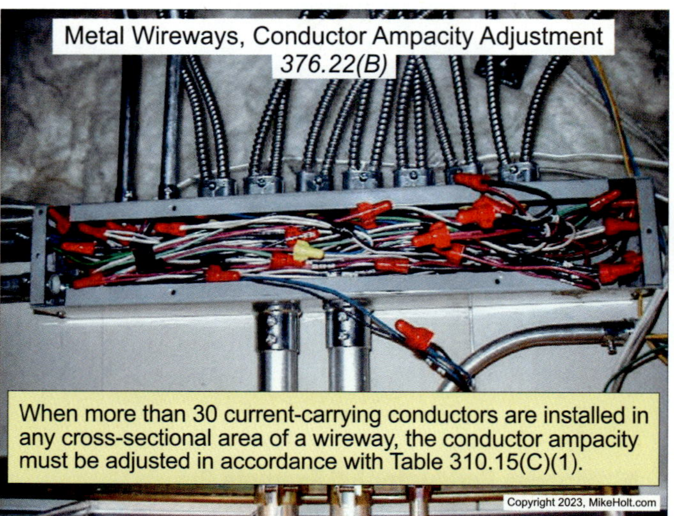

▶Figure 376–8

▶ **Wireway—Conductor Ampacity Adjustment Example**

Question: What is the ampacity of 8 AWG THWN-2 conductors if there are thirty-one current carrying conductors in the cross-sectional area of a wireway? ▶Figure 376–9

(a) 20A　　　*(b) 22A*　　　*(c) 29A*　　　*(d) 32A*
Solution:

Adjusted Ampacity = Table 310.16 Ampacity × Bundled Ampacity Adjustment Factor from Table 310.10.15(C)(1)

8 AWG THWN-2 is rated 55A at 90°C [Table 310.16].

The adjustment factor for thirty-one current-carrying conductors is 40 percent [Table 310.15(C)(1)].

Adjusted Ampacity = 55A × 40%
Adjusted Ampacity = 22A

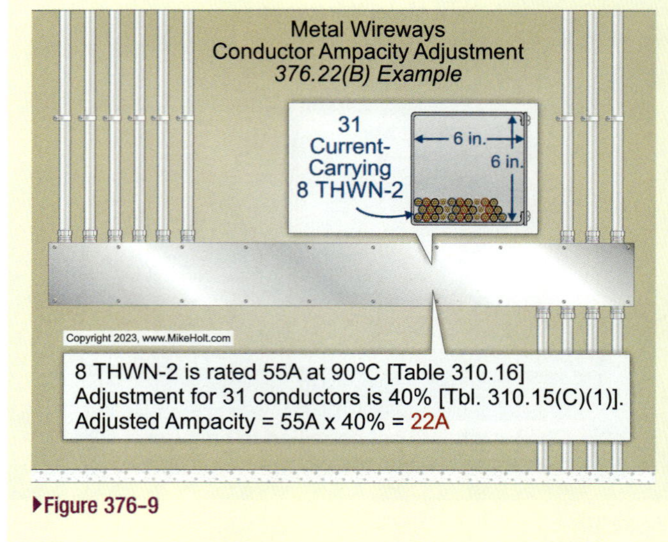

▶Figure 376–9

Answer: *(b) 22A*

376.23 Wireway Sizing

(A) Conductor Bending Space. Where conductors are bent more than 30 degrees in a wireway, the wireway must be sized to the conductor bending space requirements contained in Table 312.6(A), based on one wire per terminal. ▶Figure 376–10

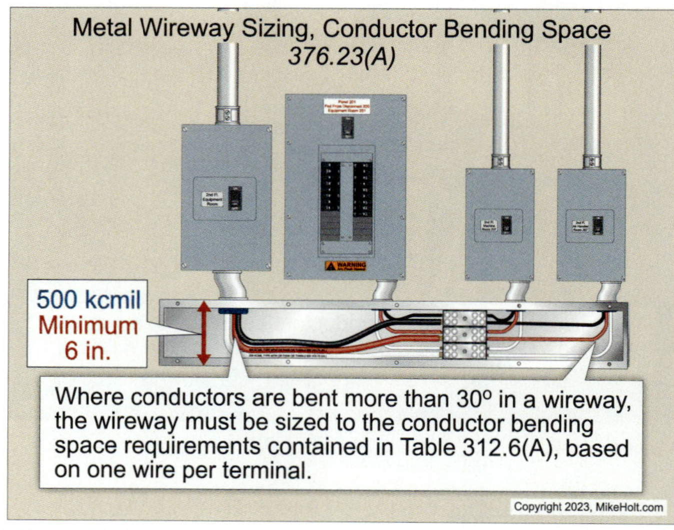

▶Figure 376–10

▶ Wireway Bending Space Example

Question: What minimum size wireway is suitable for three 500 kcmil THWN-2 conductors from the first disconnect, three 3/0 AWG THWN-2 conductors from the panelboard, and three 1/0 AWG THWN-2 conductors from the other disconnect? ▶Figure 376–11

(a) 4 in.   *(b) 6 in.*   *(c) 8 in.*   *(d) 10 in.*

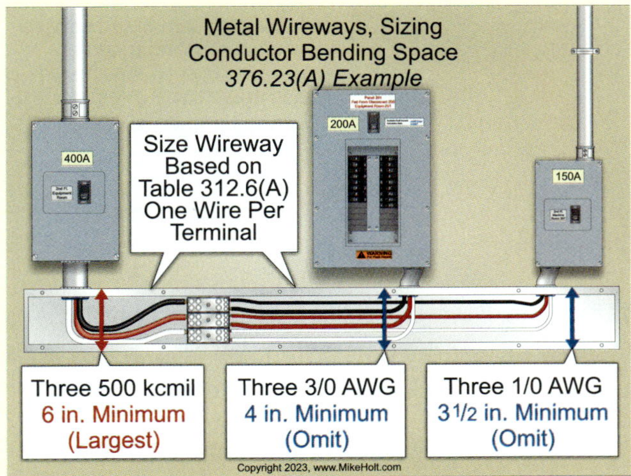

▶Figure 376–11

Solution:

According to Table 312.6(A), based on one wire per terminal, the wireway must be large enough to accommodate the bending space required for the largest conductor. In this application, it is based on the 500 kcmil conductors [376.23(A)].

Answer: (b) 6 in.

(B) Metal Wireways Used as Pull Boxes. Where insulated conductors 4 AWG or larger are pulled through a wireway, the wireway must be sized in accordance with 314.28(A)(1) for straight pulls and 314.28(A)(2) for angle pulls. ▶Figure 376–12

376.30 Supports

Wireways must be supported in accordance with 376.30(A) and (B).

(A) Horizontal Support. If installed horizontally, metal wireways must be supported at each end and at intervals not exceeding 5 ft. The distance between supports must not exceed 10 ft. ▶Figure 376–13

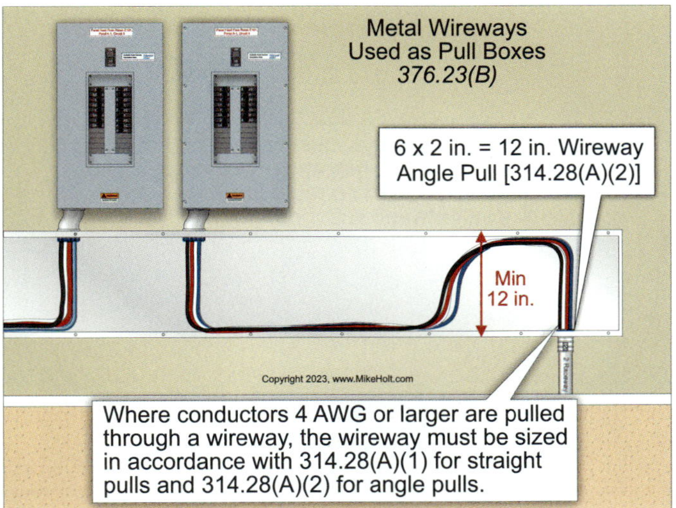

▶Figure 376–12

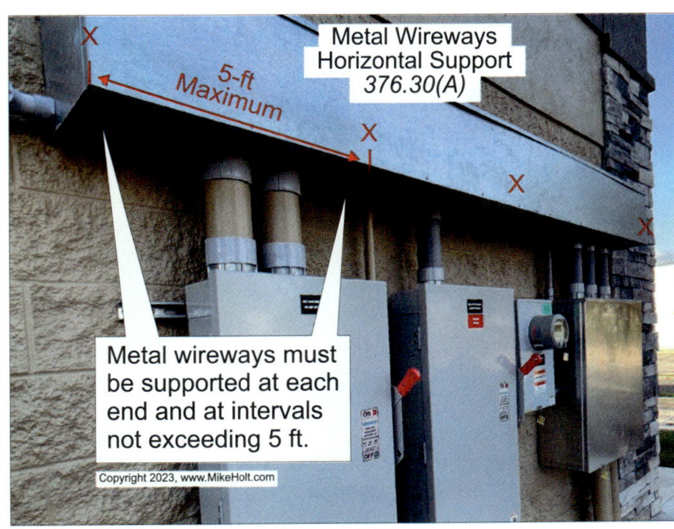

▶Figure 376–13

(B) Vertical Support. If installed vertically, metal wireways must be securely supported at intervals not exceeding 15 ft and with no more than one joint between supports. ▶Figure 376–14

376.56 Splices, Taps, and Power Distribution Blocks

(A) Splices and Taps. Splices and taps in metal wireways must be accessible and not permitted to fill the wireway to more than 75 percent of the wireway's cross-sectional area. ▶Figure 376–15

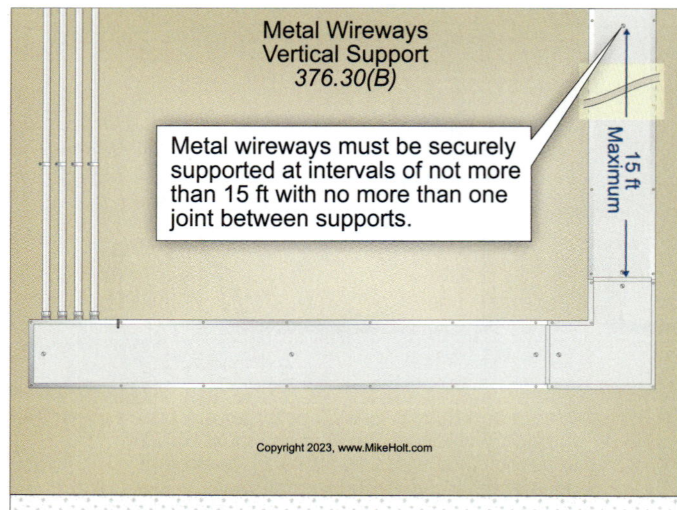

▶Figure 376–14

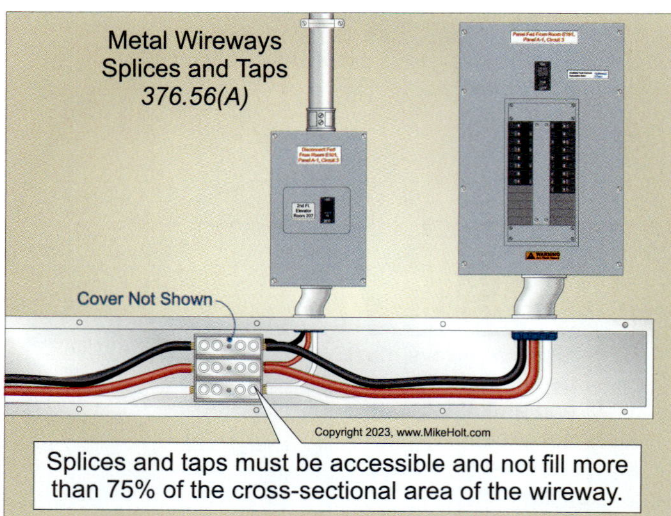

▶Figure 376–15

(B) Power Distribution Blocks.

(1) Installation. Power distribution blocks installed in wireways must be listed. If installed on the supply side of the service disconnect, they must be marked "SUITABLE FOR USE ON THE LINE SIDE OF SERVICE DISCONNECT" or equivalent. ▶Figure 376–16

(2) Size of Enclosure. In addition to the wiring space requirements [376.56(A)], the power distribution block must be installed in a metal wireway not smaller than specified in the instructions for the power distribution block.

(3) Wire-Bending Space. Wire-bending space at the terminals of power distribution blocks must comply with 312.6(B).

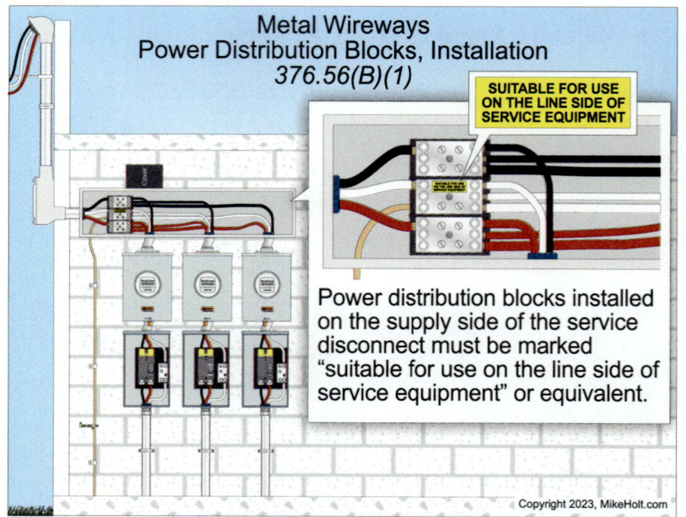

▶Figure 376–16

(4) Live Parts. Power distribution blocks are not permitted to have uninsulated exposed live parts in the metal wireway after installation, whether the wireway cover is installed or not. ▶Figure 376–17

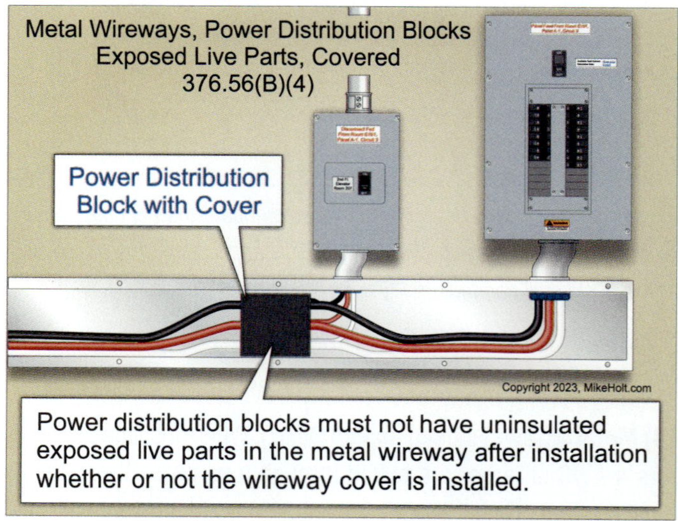

▶Figure 376–17

(5) Conductors. Conductors must be installed so the terminals of the power distribution block are not obstructed. ▶Figure 376–18

376.60 Equipment Grounding Conductor

Listed metal wireways are permitted to serve as an equipment grounding conductor in accordance with 250.118(A)(13). ▶Figure 376–19

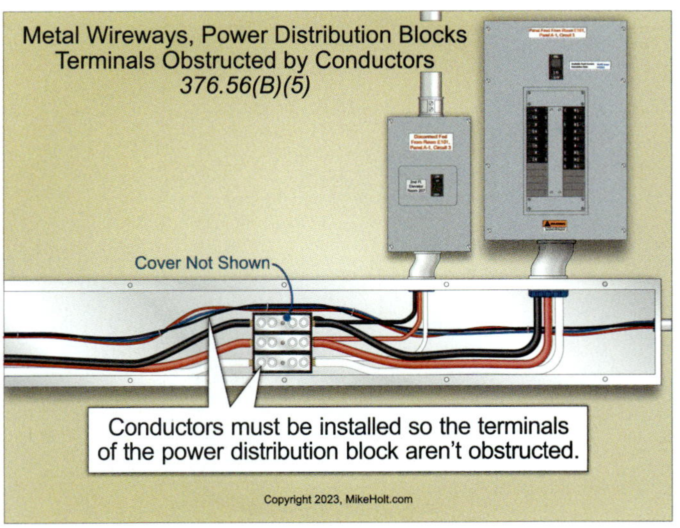

▶Figure 376–18

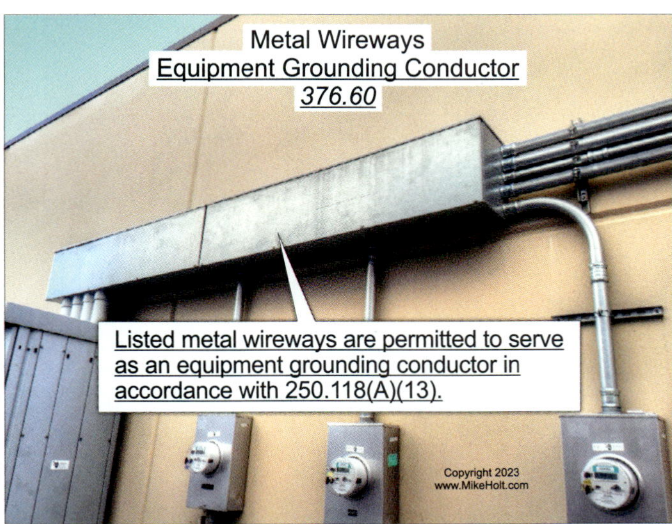

▶Figure 376–19

Introduction to Article 380—Multioutlet Assemblies

This article covers the use and installation requirements for multioutlet assemblies. A multioutlet assembly is a surface, flush, or free-standing raceway designed to hold conductors and receptacles. It can be assembled in the field or at the factory and is not required to be listed. Some topics covered in this material include:

▶ Uses Permitted

▶ Uses Not Permitted

▶ Insulated Conductors

Article 380 consists of two parts:

▶ Part I. General

▶ Part II. Installation

According to Article 100, "Multioutlet Assembly" is a surface, flush, or freestanding assembly containing receptacles. ▶Figure 380–1

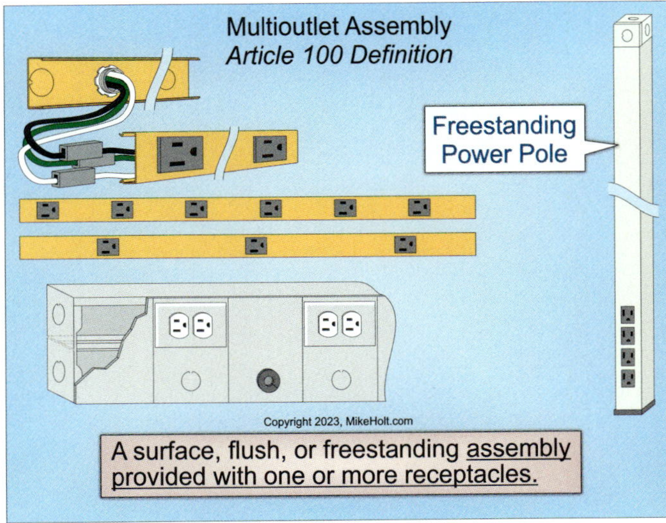

▶Figure 380–1

Author's Comment:

▶ Portable assemblies such as power strips are relocatable power taps—not multioutlet assemblies. ▶Figure 380–2

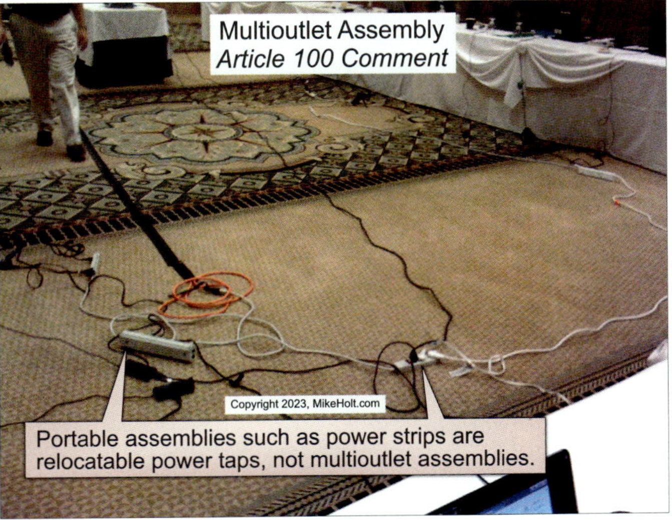

▶Figure 380–2

Part I. General

380.1 Scope

Article 380 covers the use and installation requirements for multioutlet assemblies. ▶Figure 380–3

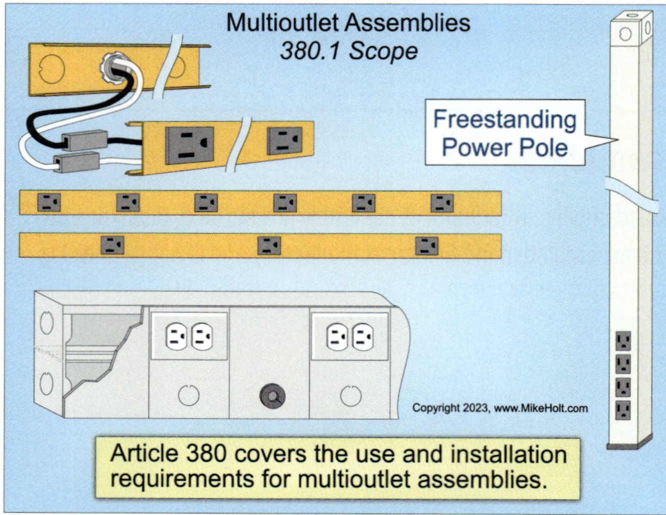

▶Figure 380–3

Part II. Installation

380.10 Uses Permitted

Multioutlet assemblies are only permitted in dry locations.

380.12 Uses Not Permitted

A multioutlet assembly must not be installed as follows:

(1) Concealed

(2) Where subject to severe physical damage

(3) If the voltage is 300V or more between conductors, unless the metal has a thickness of not less than 0.04 in

(4) Where subject to corrosive vapors

(5) In hoistways

(6) In any hazardous (classified) location except as permitted elsewhere in this *Code*

(7) Where cord-and-plug-connected

380.76 Through Partitions

Metal multioutlet assemblies can pass through a dry partition provided no receptacle is concealed in the wall, and the cover of the exposed portion of the system can be removed.

ARTICLE 386
SURFACE METAL RACEWAYS

Introduction to Article 386—Surface Metal Raceways

Article 386 covers the use, installation, and construction specifications of surface metal raceways and associated fittings. Surface metal raceways are often used where exposed traditional raceway systems are not aesthetically pleasing and raceway concealment is not economically feasible. They come in several colors and shapes and may be referred to as "Wiremold®" in the field. Some topics covered in this material include:

- ▶ Listing Requirements
- ▶ Uses Permitted
- ▶ Uses Not Permitted
- ▶ Size and Number of Conductors
- ▶ Securing and Supporting
- ▶ Equipment Grounding Conductor Connections

This article consists of three parts:

- ▶ Part I. General
- ▶ Part II. Installation
- ▶ Part III. Construction Specifications

According to Article 100, "Surface Metal Raceway" is a raceway with associated fittings in which conductors are placed after the raceway has been installed as a complete system. ▶Figure 386–1

Part I. General

386.1 Scope

Article 386 covers the use, installation, and construction specifications of surface metal raceways and associated fittings. ▶Figure 386–2

Author's Comment:

- ▶ Surface metal raceways are available in different shapes and sizes and can be mounted on walls, ceilings, or floors.

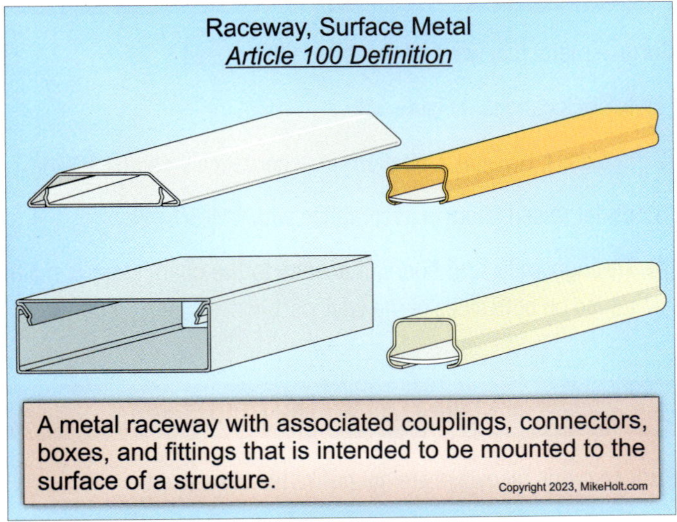

▶Figure 386–1

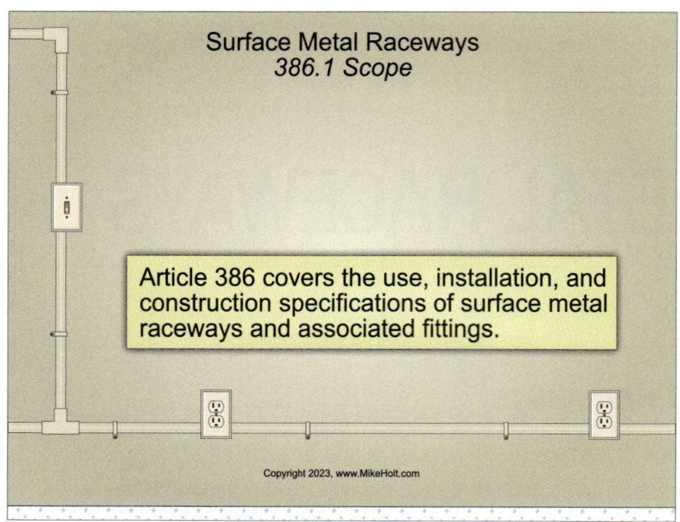

▶Figure 386–2

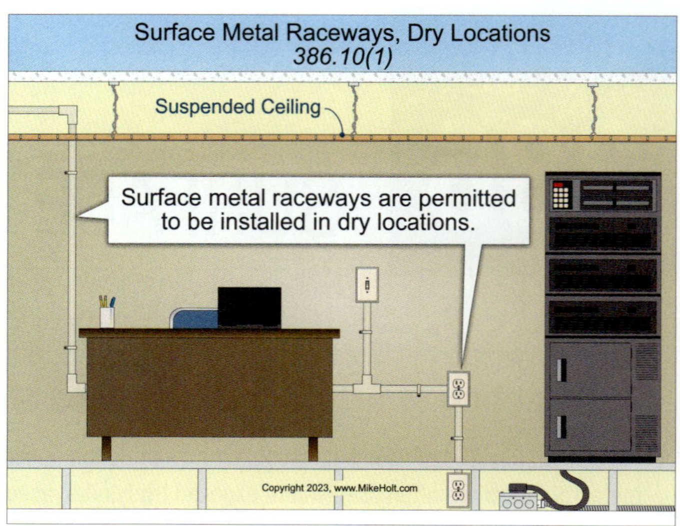

▶Figure 386–3

386.6 Listing Requirements

Surface metal raceways and associated fittings must be listed.

Author's Comment:

▸ Enclosures for switches, receptacles, luminaires, and other devices are identified by the markings on their packaging, which specify the type of surface metal raceway that can be used with the enclosure.

Part II. Installation

386.10 Uses Permitted

Surface metal raceways are permitted to be used:

(1) In dry locations ▶Figure 386–3

(2) In Class I, Division 2 locations in accordance with 501.10(B)(3)

(3) Under raised floors in accordance with 645.5(E)(2)

(4) Through walls and floors, if access to the conductors is maintained on both sides of the wall, partition, or floor

386.12 Uses Not Permitted

Surface metal raceways are not permitted to be used:

(1) Where subject to severe physical damage unless approved by the authority having jurisdiction

(2) If the voltage is 300V or more between conductors unless the metal has a thickness of not less than 0.04 in.

(3) Where subject to corrosive vapors

(4) In hoistways

(5) If concealed, except as permitted in 386.10

386.21 Size of Conductors

The maximum size conductor permitted in a surface metal raceway cannot be larger than that for which the raceway is designed.

386.22 Number of Conductors

The number of conductors installed in a surface metal raceway must not be more than the number for which the raceway is designed.

Author's Comment:

▸ The size and number of conductors permitted is marked on the raceway or on the package.

The ampacity adjustment factors of Table 310.15(C)(1) do not apply to conductors installed in surface metal raceways if all the following conditions are met: ▶Figure 386–4

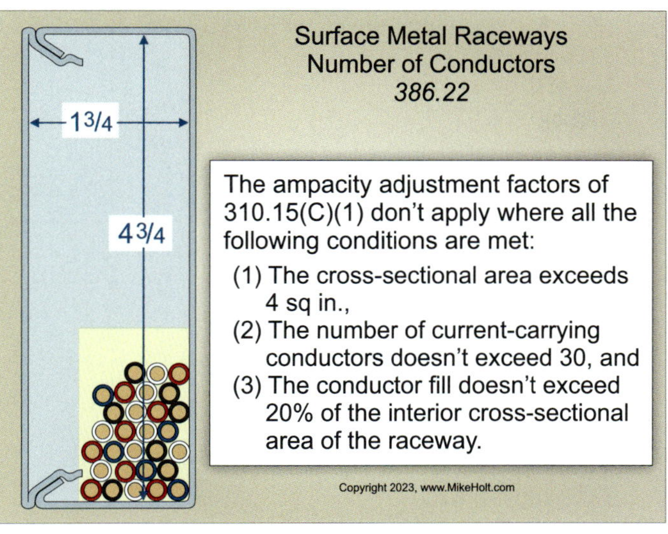

▶Figure 386–4

(1) The cross-sectional area of the raceway exceeds 4 sq in.

(2) The number of current-carrying conductors does not exceed 30.

(3) The sum of the cross-sectional areas of all contained conductors does not exceed 20 percent of the interior cross-sectional area of the raceway.

386.30 Securing and Supporting

Surface metal raceways and fittings must be supported in accordance with the manufacturer's instructions. ▶Figure 386–5

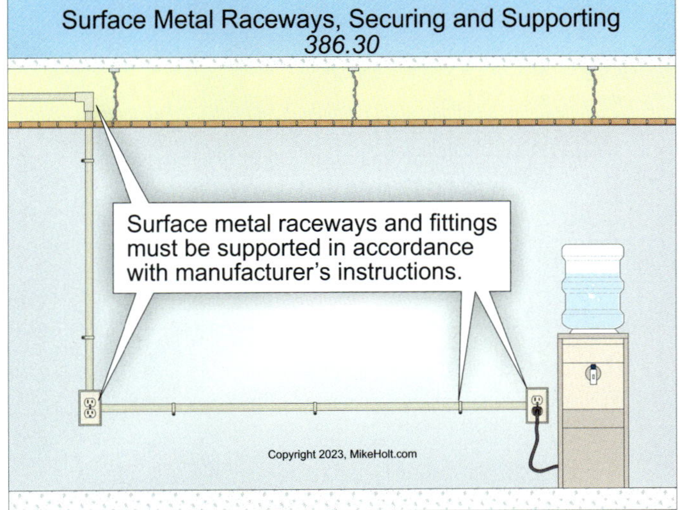

▶Figure 386–5

386.56 Splices and Taps

Splices and taps must be accessible and they, along with any conductors, must not fill the raceway to more than 75 percent of its cross-sectional area.

386.60 Equipment Grounding Conductor

Surface metal raceway fittings must be mechanically and electrically joined together in a manner that does not subject the conductors to abrasion. Surface metal raceways that allow a transition to another wiring method (such as knockouts for connecting raceways) must have a means for the termination of an equipment grounding conductor.

A surface metal raceway is suitable as an equipment grounding conductor in accordance with 250.118(A)(14). ▶Figure 386–6

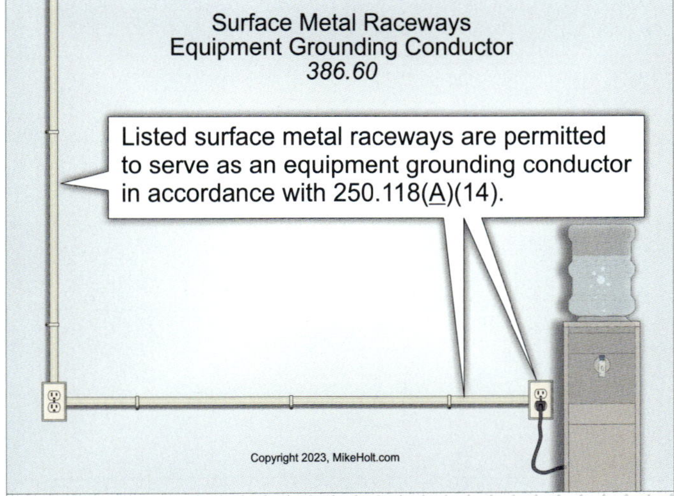

▶Figure 386–6

CABLE TRAYS

Introduction to Article 392—Cable Trays

This article covers cable tray systems including ladder, ventilated trough, ventilated channel, solid bottom, and other similar structures. A cable tray system is a unit or an assembly of units or sections with associated fittings forming a structural system used to securely fasten or support cables and raceways. Some topics covered in this material include:

- Uses Permitted
- Uses Not Permitted
- Cable Tray Installation
- Conductor Installation
- Number of Conductors
- Securing and Supporting
- Expansion Splice Plates
- Grounding and Bonding
- Conductor Ampacity

This article consists of three parts:

- Part I. General
- Part II. Installation
- Part III. Construction Specifications

According to Article 100, "Cable Tray System" is a unit, assembly of units, or sections with associated fittings forming a rigid structural system used to securely fasten or support cables and raceways. ▶Figure 392–1

Part I. General

392.1 Scope

Article 392 covers cable tray systems, ladder, ventilated trough, ventilated channel, solid bottom, and other similar structures. ▶Figure 392–2

Part II. Installation

392.10 Uses Permitted

Cable trays can be used as a support system for wiring methods containing branch circuits, feeders, service conductors, and Chapters 7 and 8 wiring methods. ▶Figure 392–3

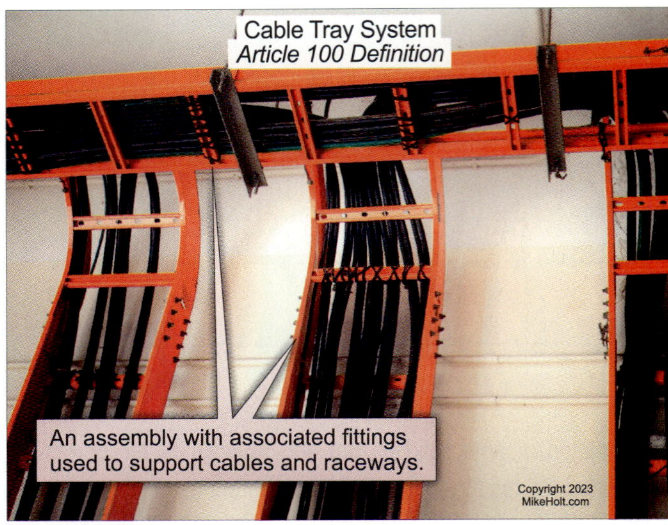

▶Figure 392–1

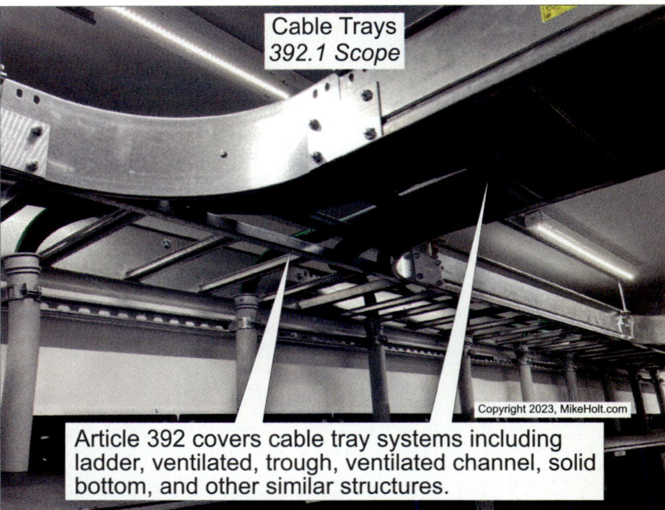

▶Figure 392–2

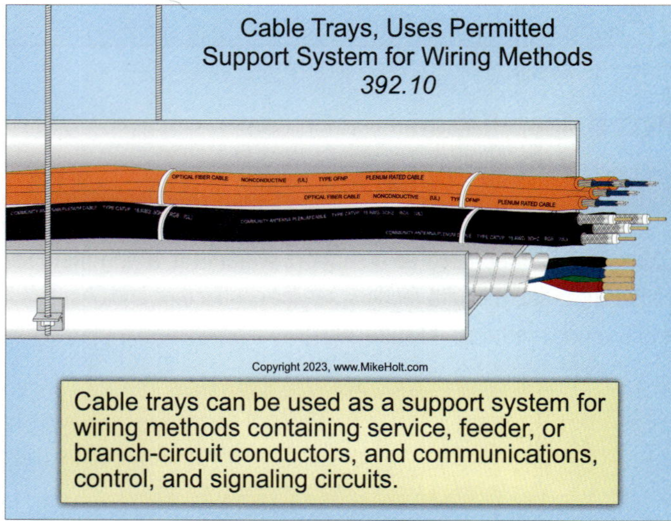

▶Figure 392–3

Single insulated <u>cables and</u> insulated conductors are only permitted in cable trays when installed in accordance with 392.10(B)(1).

▸ Cable trays used to support service-entrance conductors must be installed in accordance with 230.44.

(A) Wiring Methods. Any of the wiring methods contained in Table 392.10(A) can be installed in a cable tray.

Table 392.10(A) Wiring Methods	
Wiring Method	**Article/Section**
Armored cable	320
Coaxial cables	800 and 820
Class 2 power-limited cables	722 and 725
Coaxial cables	800 and 820
Electrical metallic tubing	358
Electrical nonmetallic tubing	362
Fire alarm cables	722 and 760
Flexible metal conduit	348
Instrumentation tray cable	341
Intermediate metal conduit	342
Liquidtight flexible metal conduit	350
Liquidtight flexible nonmetallic conduit	356
Metal-clad cable	330
Nonmetallic-sheathed cable	334
Polyvinyl chloride (PVC) conduit	352
Power and control tray cable	336
Power-limited fire alarm cable	722 and 760
Power-limited tray cable	Table 725.154 and 725.179(E) and 725.135(H)
Rigid metal conduit	344
Service-entrance cable	338
Underground feeder and branch-circuit cable	340

(B) In Industrial Establishments.

(1) Single-Conductor Cables and Insulated Conductors. Where conditions of maintenance and supervision ensure that only qualified persons service the installed cable tray system, single-conductor cables, and single insulated conductors can be installed in accordance with the following: ▸Figure 392–4

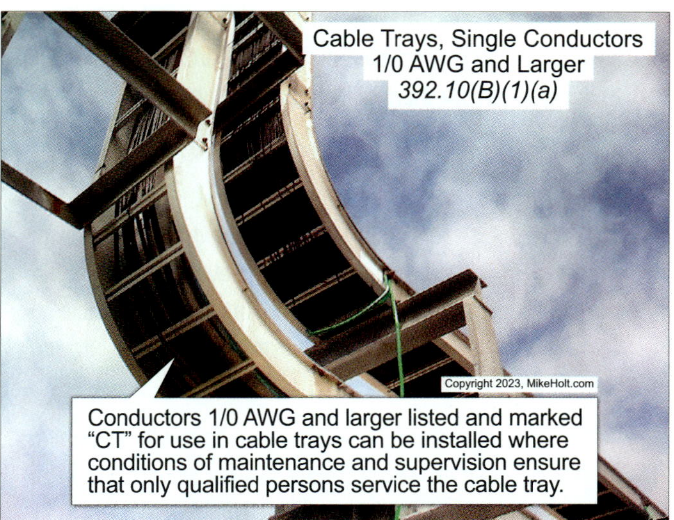

▸Figure 392–4

(a) 1/0 AWG and larger listed and marked for use in cable trays.

(c) Equipment grounding conductors must be 4 AWG and larger.

(C) Hazardous (Classified) Locations. Cable trays in hazardous (classified) locations must contain only the cable types and raceways permitted by this *Code* for the application.

392.12 Uses Not Permitted

Cable tray systems are not permitted in hoistways or where subject to severe physical damage.

392.18 Cable Tray Installations

(A) Complete System. Cable trays must be installed as a complete system, except that mechanically discontinuous segments between cable tray runs (or between cable tray runs and equipment) are permitted. The system must provide for the support of the cables and raceways in accordance with their corresponding articles. ▸Figure 392–5

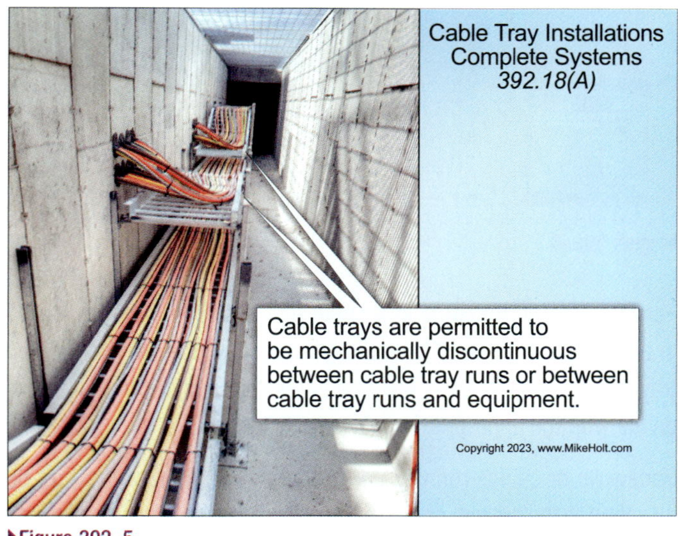

▸Figure 392–5

A bonding jumper, sized in accordance with 250.102 and installed in accordance with 250.96, must bond the sections of metal cable tray, or the cable tray and raceway or equipment.

(B) Completed Before Installation. Each run of cable tray must be completed before the installation of cables or conductors.

(D) Through Partitions and Walls. Cable trays can extend through partitions and walls, or vertically through platforms and floors, if the installation is made in accordance with the firestopping requirements of 300.21.

(E) Exposed and Accessible. Cable trays must be exposed and accessible, except as permitted by 392.18(D).

(F) Adequate Access. Sufficient space must be provided and maintained about cable trays to permit adequate access for installing and maintaining the cables.

(G) Raceways, Cables, and Boxes Supported from Cable Trays. In industrial facilities where conditions of maintenance and supervision ensure only qualified persons will service the installation, cable tray systems can support raceways, cables, boxes, and conduit bodies. ▸Figure 392–6

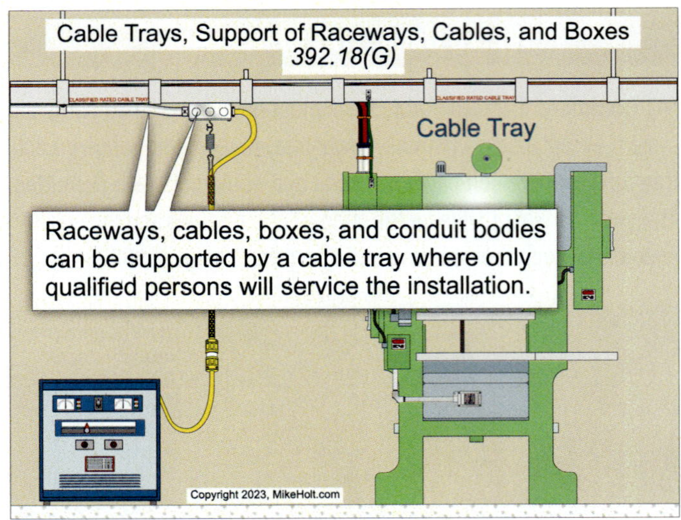

▶Figure 392–6

For raceways terminating at a cable tray, a listed cable tray clamp or adapter must be used to securely fasten the raceway to the cable tray system. The raceway must be supported and secured in accordance with the appropriate raceway article.

Raceways or cables running parallel to a cable tray system can be attached to the bottom or side of the cable tray system. The raceway or cable must be fastened and supported in accordance with the appropriate raceway or cable article.

Boxes and conduit bodies attached to the bottom or side of a cable tray system must be fastened and supported in accordance with 314.23.

(H) Marking. Cable trays containing conductors operating at over 600V must have a permanent, legible warning notice carrying the wording, "DANGER—HIGH VOLTAGE—KEEP AWAY" placed in a readily visible position on all cable trays, with the spacing of warning notices not to exceed 10 ft. The danger marking(s) or labels must comply with 110.21(B).

392.20 Cable and Conductor Installation

(C) Connected in Parallel. To prevent unbalanced current in paralleled conductors due to inductive reactance, all circuit conductors of a parallel set (phase and neutral [310.10(G)]) must be bundled together and secured to prevent excessive movement due to fault-current magnetic forces.

(D) Single Conductors. Conductors not connected in parallel must be installed in a single layer unless the conductors are bound together.

392.30 Securing and Supporting

(A) Cable Trays. Cable trays must be supported in accordance with the manufacturers' instructions.

(B) Cables and Conductors. Cables and conductors must be secured to and supported by the cable tray system in accordance with the following:

(4) Cable ties must be listed and identified for the application and for securement and support.

392.44 Expansion Splice Plates

Expansion splice plates for cable trays must be provided where necessary to compensate for thermal expansion and contraction.

> **Author's Comment:**
>
> ▶ Thermal expansion is an issue without the installation of raceway expansion joints and often overlooked. For the raceway to properly serve its function, it must be able to expand, as well as contract, and expansion joints provide the ability to do so.
>
> ▶ This *Code* section gives no guidance as to how to determine the need for an expansion splice plate, but there is a National Electrical Manufacturer's Association (NEMA) document available as a free download that may assist. This document is titled, *NEMA VE2, Cable Tray Installation Guidelines*.

392.46 Bushed Conduit and Tubing

A box is not required where cables or conductors are installed in a bushed raceway used for support, protection against physical damage, or where conductors or cables transition to a raceway from the cable tray. ▶Figure 392–7

(A) Through Bushed Conduit or Tubing. Individual conductors or multiconductor cables with nonmetallic sheaths can enter enclosures where they are terminated through nonflexible bushed conduit or tubing installed for their protection, provided they are secured at the point of transition from the cable tray and the raceway is sealed at the outer end using an approved means to prevent debris from entering the equipment through the raceway.

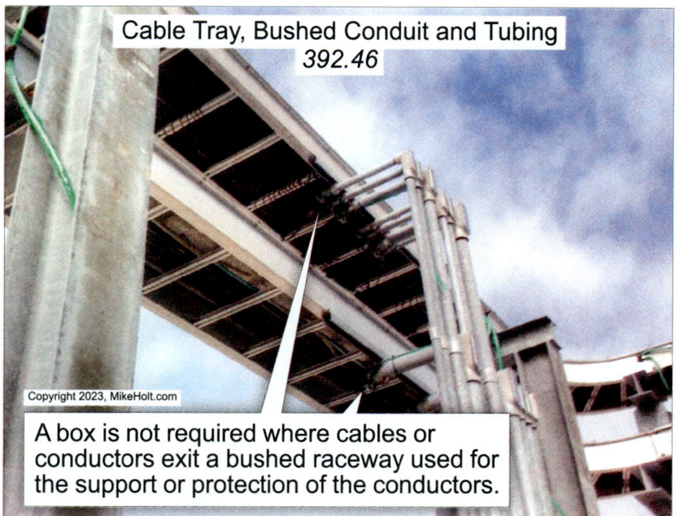

A box is not required where cables or conductors exit a bushed raceway used for the support or protection of the conductors.

▶Figure 392–7

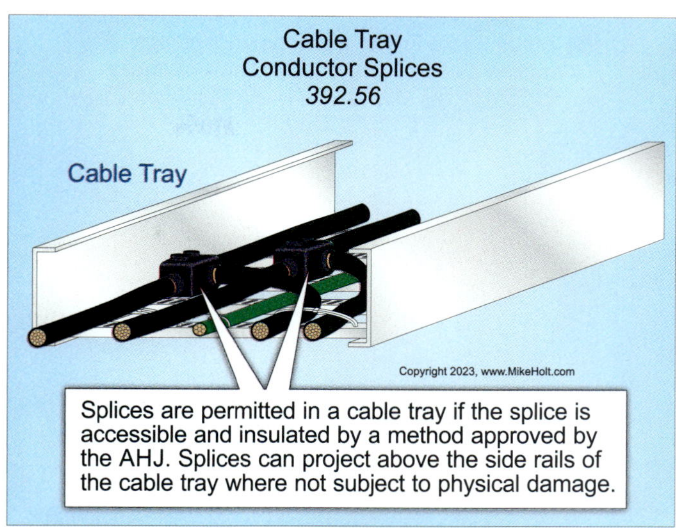

Splices are permitted in a cable tray if the splice is accessible and insulated by a method approved by the AHJ. Splices can project above the side rails of the cable tray where not subject to physical damage.

▶Figure 392–8

(B) Flanged Connections. Individual conductors or multiconductor cables with entirely nonmetallic sheaths can enter enclosures through openings associated with flanges from cable trays where the cable tray is attached to the flange and the flange is mounted directly to the equipment. The openings must be made so the conductors are protected from abrasion and must be sealed or covered to prevent debris from entering the enclosure through them.

Note: One method of preventing debris from entering the enclosure is to seal the outer end of the raceway or the opening with duct seal.

392.56 Cable Splices

Splices are permitted in a cable tray if they are accessible and insulated by a method approved by the authority having jurisdiction. Splices can project above the side rails of the cable tray if not subject to physical damage. ▶Figure 392–8

392.60 Equipment Grounding Conductor

(A) Used as an Equipment Grounding Conductor. Metal cable trays can be used as equipment grounding conductors where continuous maintenance and supervision ensure that only qualified persons will service the cable tray system. ▶Figure 392–9

Metal cable trays containing single conductors must be bonded together to ensure they have the capacity to conduct safely any fault current likely to be imposed on them in accordance with 250.96(A).

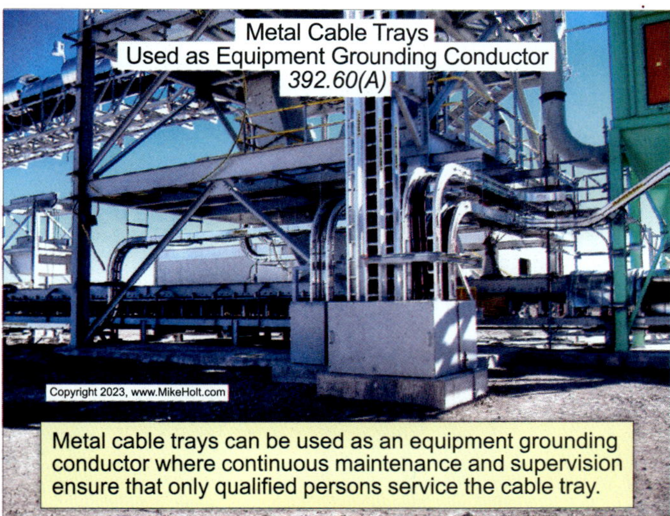

Metal cable trays can be used as an equipment grounding conductor where continuous maintenance and supervision ensure that only qualified persons service the cable tray.

▶Figure 392–9

(B) Serve as an Equipment Grounding Conductor. Metal cable trays can serve as equipment grounding conductors where the following requirements have been met:

(1) Identified as Equipment Grounding Conductor. Where metal cable trays and fittings are identified as an equipment grounding conductor. ▶Figure 392–10

(4) Bonding. Cable tray sections, fittings, and connected raceways must be bonded to each other to ensure electrical continuity and the capacity to conduct safely any fault current likely to be imposed on them [250.96(A)]. This is accomplished by using bolted mechanical connectors or bonding jumpers sized in accordance with 250.102. ▶Figure 392–11

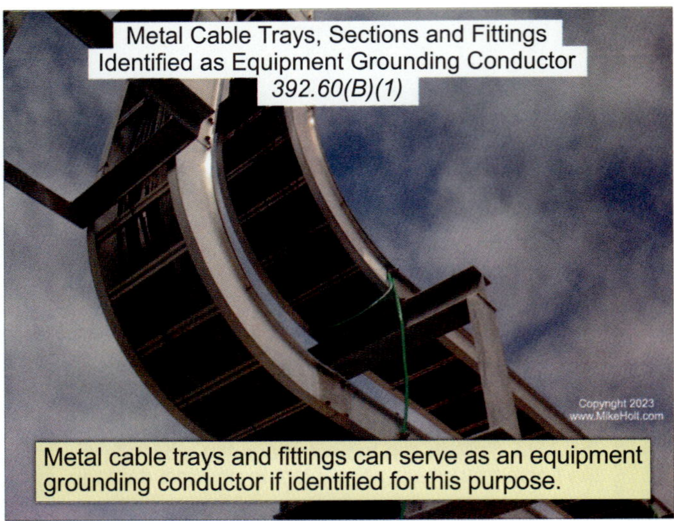

▶Figure 392–10

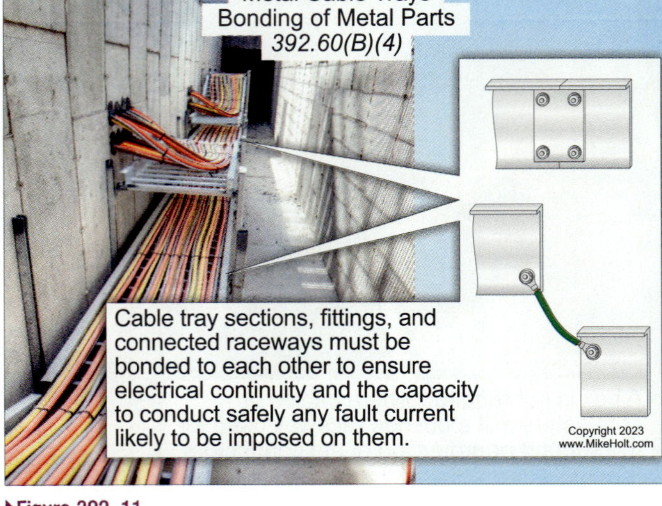

▶Figure 392–11

4 EQUIPMENT FOR GENERAL USE

Introduction to Chapter 4—Equipment for General Use

With the first three chapters of the *NEC* behind you, this fourth one is necessary for building a solid foundation in general equipment installations. Some examples of general equipment include but are not limited to luminaires, heaters, motors, air-conditioning units, generators, and transformers. The articles in Chapter 4 help you apply the first three chapters to installations involving general equipment. You must understand the first four chapters of the *Code* to properly apply these requirements to Chapters 5, 6, and 7, and at times to Chapter 8.

Chapter 4 is arranged in the following manner:

▶ **Article 400—Flexible Cords.** Article 400 covers the general requirements, applications, and construction specifications for flexible cords.

▶ **Article 402—Fixture Wires.** This article covers the general requirements and construction specifications for fixture wires.

▶ **Article 404—Switches.** The requirements of Article 404 apply to switches of all types. These include snap (toggle) switches, dimmer switches, fan switches, knife switches, circuit breakers, and automatic switches such as time clocks, timers, and switches and circuit breakers used for disconnects.

▶ **Article 406—Receptacles and Attachment Plugs (Caps).** This article covers the rating, type, and installation of receptacles and attachment plugs. It also covers flanged surface inlets.

▶ **Article 408—Switchboards and Panelboards.** Article 408 covers specific requirements for switchboards, panelboards, and distribution boards that supply lighting and power circuits.

> **Author's Comment:**
>
> ▶ See Article 100 for the definitions of "Panelboard" and "Switchboard."

▶ **Article 445—Generators.** Article 445 contains the electrical installation requirements for both portable and stationary generators, both of which are required to be listed [445.6]. Installation requirements such as where they can be located, nameplate markings, conductor ampacity, and disconnects are also covered.

▶ **Article 450—Transformers.** This article covers the installation of transformers. Understanding the overcurrent protection requirements in Table 450.3(B) and the disconnect location is important to provide protection properly.

▶ **Article 480—Storage Batteries.** Article 480 covers stationary installations of storage batteries.

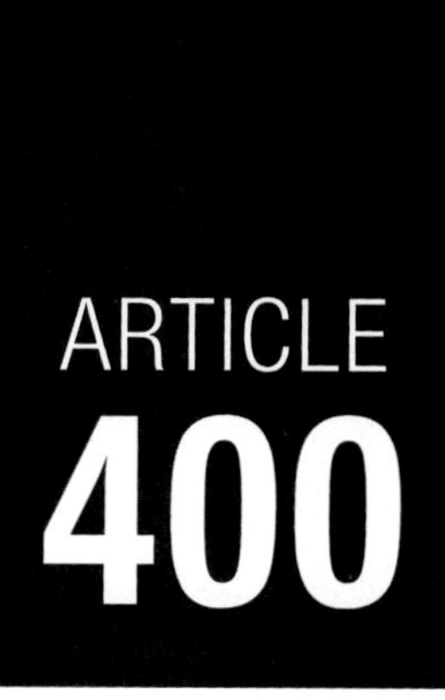

ARTICLE 400

FLEXIBLE CORDS

Introduction to Article 400—Flexible Cords

Article 400 covers the general requirements, applications, and construction specifications for flexible cords as contained in Table 400.4. The *NEC* does not consider flexible cords to be a wiring method like those addressed in Chapter 3 because they are not used as part of the wiring in the construction of a building. This article has four parts, but only two are within the scope of this material. Some of the topics covered here include:

▸ Suitability

▸ Types

▸ Ampacities

▸ Uses Permitted

▸ Uses Not Permitted

▸ Splices

▸ Overcurrent Protection

▸ Protection from Damage

▸ Construction

▸ Equipment Grounding Conductor

This article consists of four parts:

▸ Part I. General

▸ Part II. Construction Specifications

▸ Part III. Portable Cables 600V, up to 2000V, Nominal (not covered)

▸ Part IV. Portable Power Feeder Cables Over 2000V, Nominal (not covered)

400.1 Scope

Article 400 covers the general requirements, applications, and construction specifications for flexible cords as contained in Table 400.4. ▸Figure 400–1

According to Article 100, a "Flexible Cord" is a two or more insulated conductors enclosed in a flexible covering. ▸Figure 400–2

400.3 Suitability

Flexible cords (as well as their fittings) must be suitable for the use and location. ▸Figure 400–3

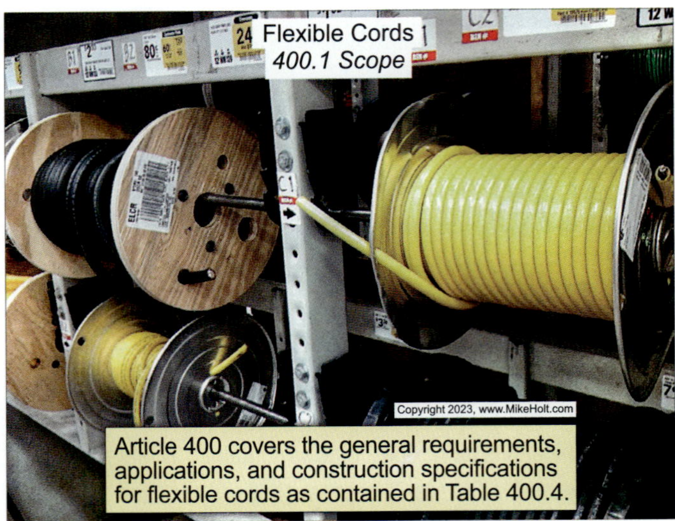

▶Figure 400–1

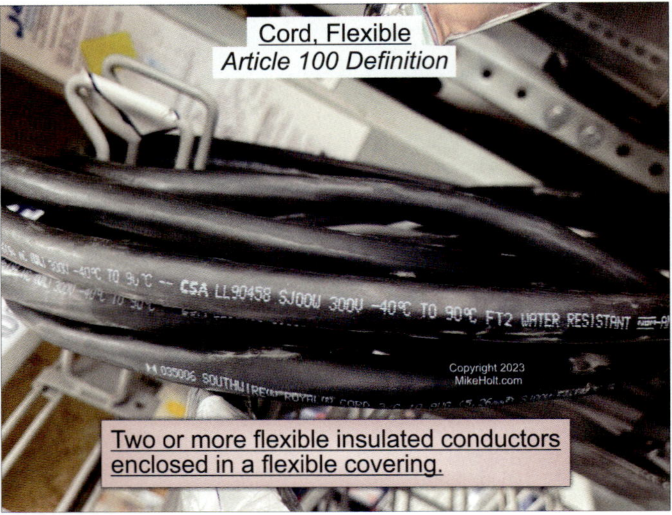

▶Figure 400–2

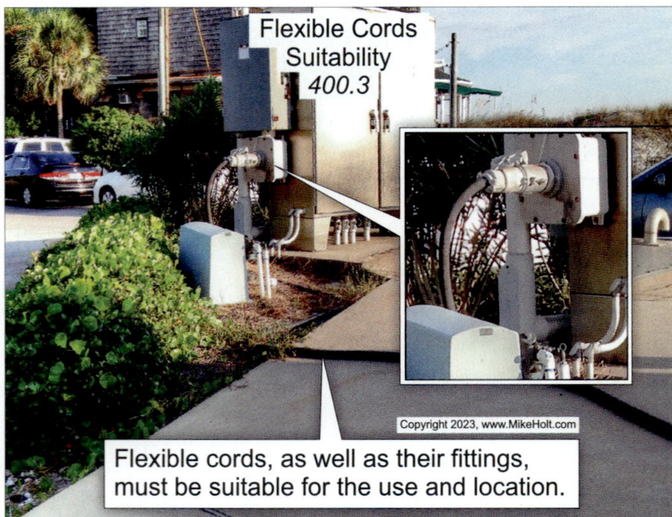

▶Figure 400–3

400.4 Types of Flexible Cords

The use of flexible cords must conform to the descriptions contained in Table 400.4.

Author's Comment:

▶ The suffix "W" at the end of a flexible cord type designates it is sunlight resistant and suitable for wet locations [Table 400.4, Note 9].

▶ Flexible cords have conductor stranding other than Class B or C require the use of terminations specifically identified for the stranding in the flexible cord or cable [110.14].

400.5 Ampacity of Flexible Cords

(A) Ampacity Tables. Table 400.5(A)(1) lists the ampacities for individual conductors inside manufactured flexible cords. Table 400.5(A)(2) lists the ampacities for overall cord assemblies with not more than three current-carrying conductors in an ambient temperature of not more than 86°F.

400.10 Uses Permitted

(A) Uses Permitted. Flexible cords within the scope of this article can be used for:

(1) Pendant boxes [314.23(H)(1)], pendant lampholders, pendant luminaires, and pendant receptacles [210.50(A)]

(2) Wiring of luminaires [410.24(A) and 410.62(B)]

(3) Connection of portable luminaires, portable and mobile signs, or appliances ▶Figure 400–4

(4) Elevator cables

(5) Wiring of cranes and hoists

(6) Connection of utilization equipment to facilitate frequent interchange [422.16] ▶Figure 400–5

(7) Prevention of the transmission of noise or vibration [422.16]

(8) Appliances where the fastening means and mechanical connections are specifically designed to permit ready removal for maintenance and repair, and the appliance is intended or identified for flexible cord connections [422.16] ▶Figure 400–6

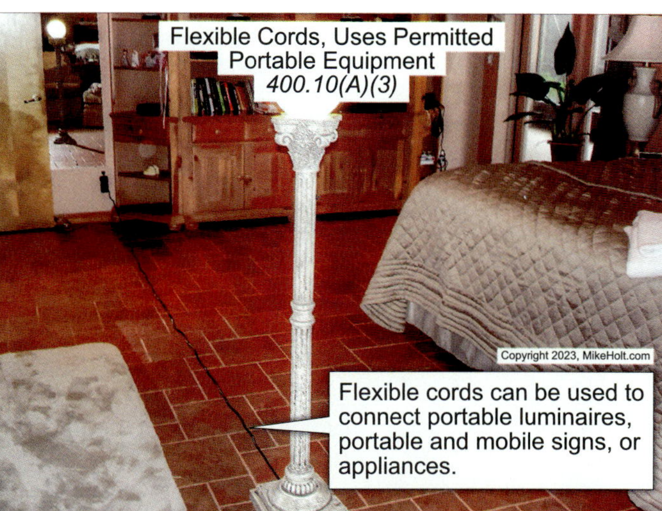

▶Figure 400–4

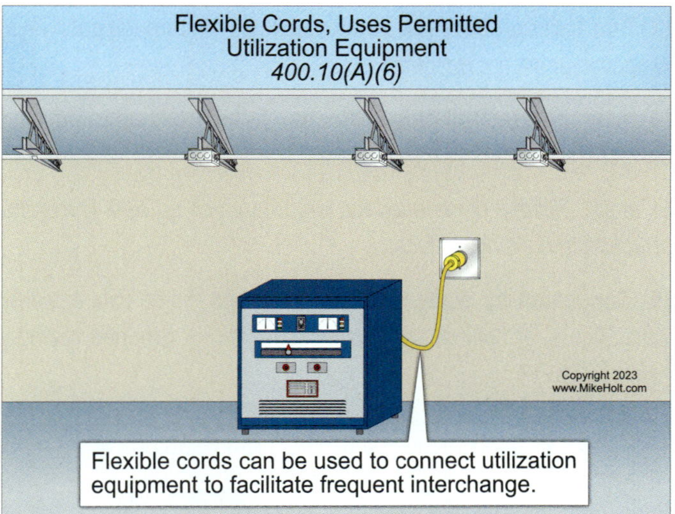

▶Figure 400–5

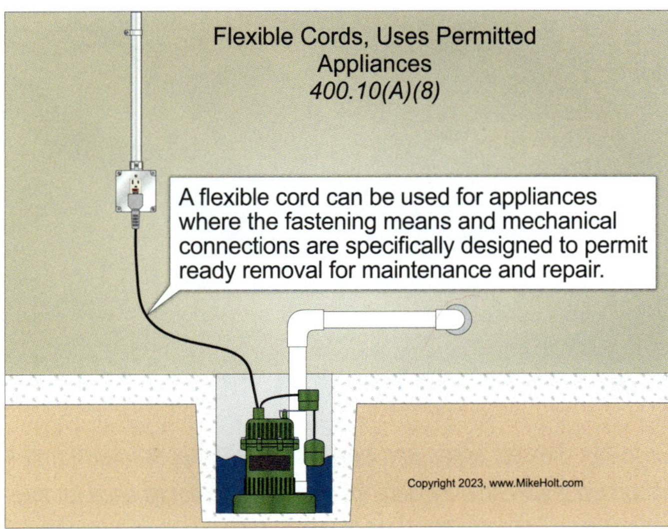

▶Figure 400–6

Author's Comment:

▶ Appliances fastened in place cannot be connected by a flexible cord unless the appliances are specifically identified to be used with a flexible cord [422.16]. ▶Figure 400–7

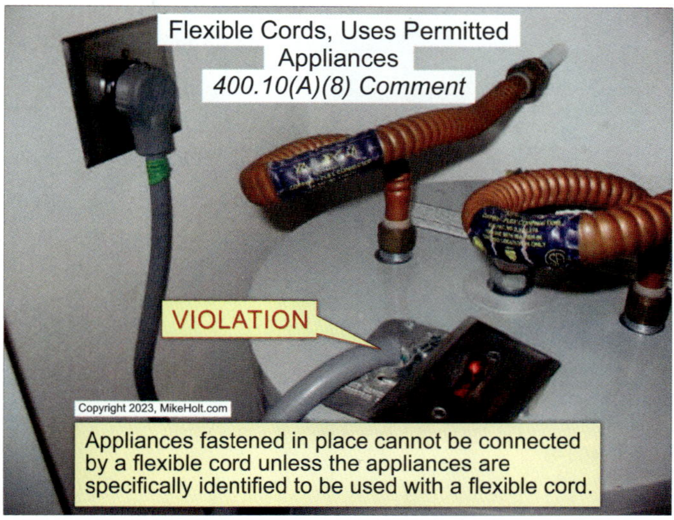

▶Figure 400–7

(9) Connection of moving parts

(B) Attachment Plugs. Attachment plugs are required for flexible cords used on portable luminaires, portable and mobile signs, or appliances [400.10(A)(3) and 422.16]; utilization equipment to facilitate its frequent interchange [400.10(A)(6) and 422.16]; and appliances specifically designed to permit ready removal for maintenance and repair and identified for flexible cord connection [400.10(A)(8) and 422.16]. ▶Figure 400–8

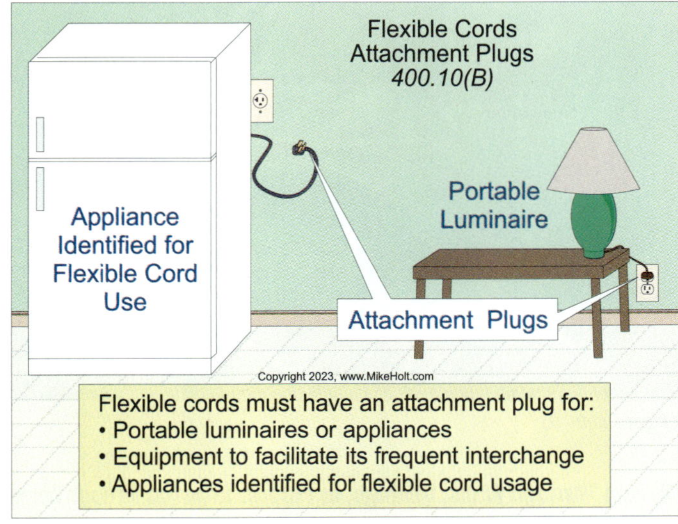

▶Figure 400–8

According to Article 100, "Attachment Plug" means a wiring device at the end of a flexible cord intended to be inserted into a receptacle to make an electrical connection. ▶Figure 400–9

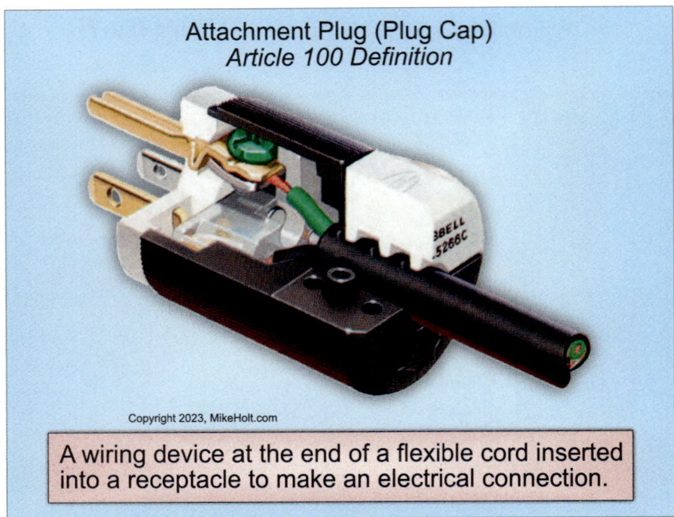

▶Figure 400–9

400.12 Uses Not Permitted

Unless specifically permitted in 400.10, flexible cords, cord sets (extension cords), and power-supply cords are not permitted for the following:

(1) Substitute for Fixed Wiring. As a substitute for fixed wiring. ▶Figure 400–10

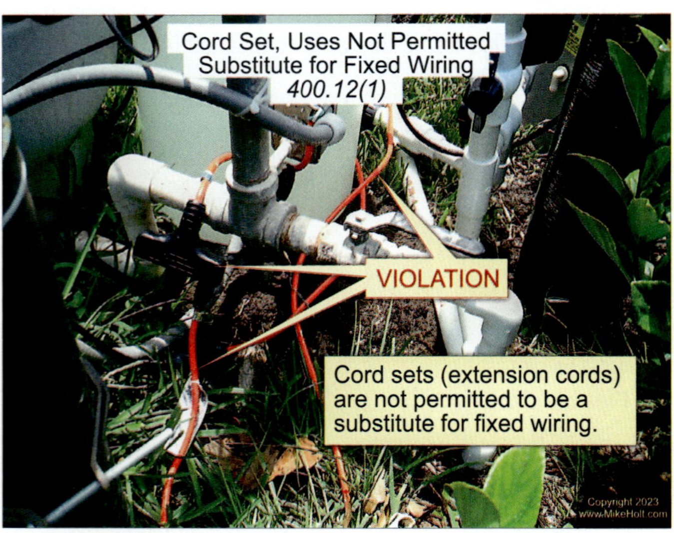

▶Figure 400–10

(2) Run Through Walls, Ceilings, or Floors. To be run through holes in walls, ceilings, or floors. ▶Figure 400–11

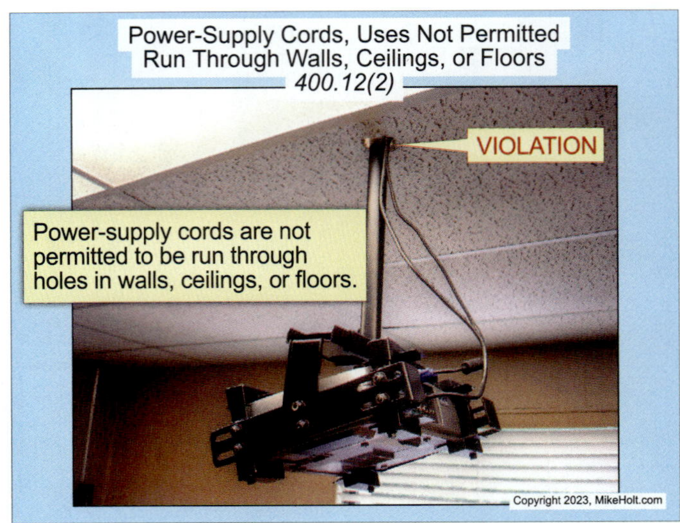

▶Figure 400–11

(3) Run Through Doors or Windows. To be run through doorways, windows, or similar openings.

(4) Attached to Building Surfaces. To be attached to building surfaces.

Ex to (4): Flexible cords used for temporary wiring [590.4] may be attached to building surfaces.

(5) Concealed by Walls, Floors or Ceilings. To be concealed by walls, floors, or ceilings, or above suspended or dropped ceilings. ▶Figure 400–12

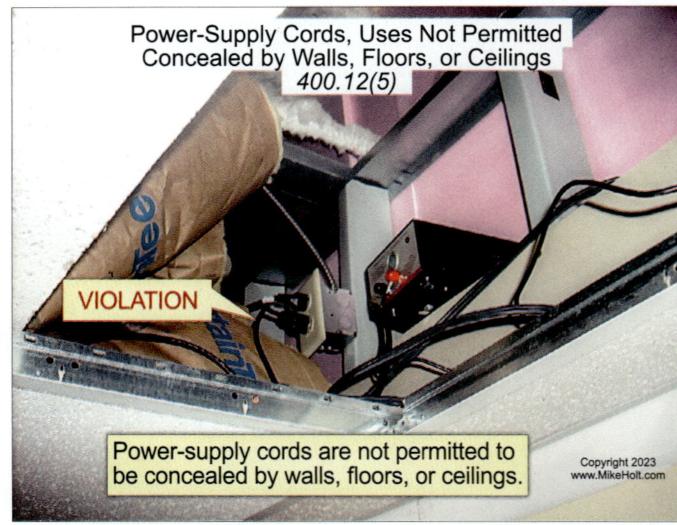

▶Figure 400–12

Ex to (5): Flexible cords and power-supply cords are permitted if contained within an enclosure for use in other spaces used for environmental air as permitted by 300.22(C)(3).

(6) Installed in Raceways. To be installed in raceways, except as permitted by 400.17.

(7) Subject to Physical Damage. Where they are subject to physical damage.

400.13 Splices

Flexible cords must be installed continuous without splices or taps in 400.10(A) applications.

400.14 Pull at Joints and Terminals

Flexible cords must be connected to devices and fittings so that tension is not transmitted to joints or terminals. ▶Figure 400–13

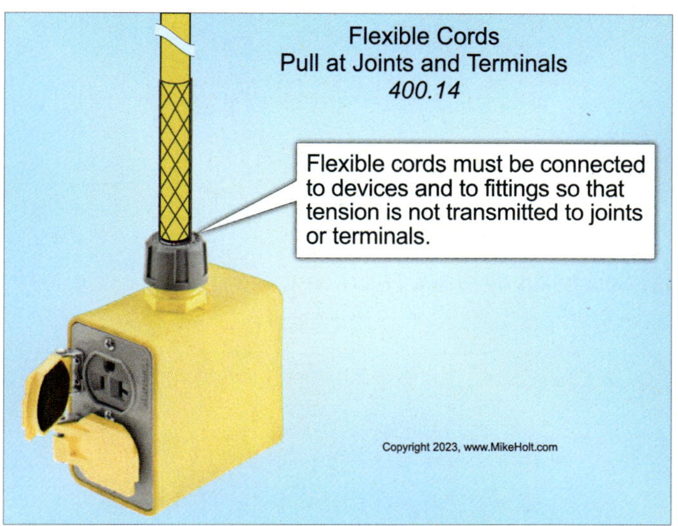

▶Figure 400–13

Note: This can be accomplished by knotting the cord, winding it with tape, or by using support or strain-relief fittings. ▶Figure 400–14

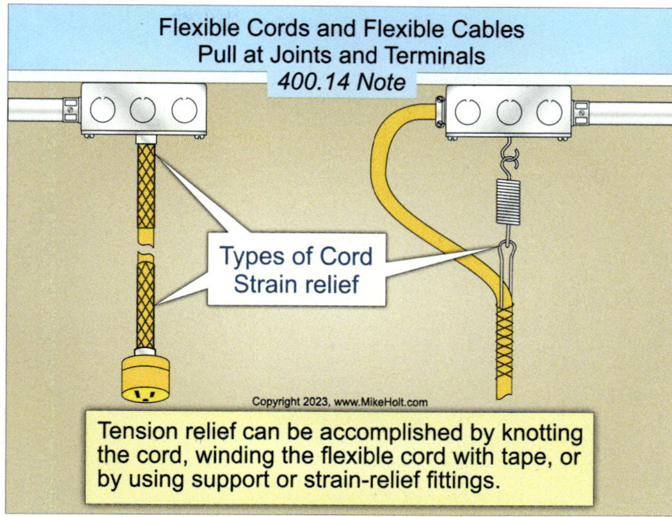

▶Figure 400–14

400.17 Protection from Damage

Flexible cords must be protected by bushings or fittings where passing through holes in covers, outlet boxes, or similar enclosures.

FIXTURE WIRES

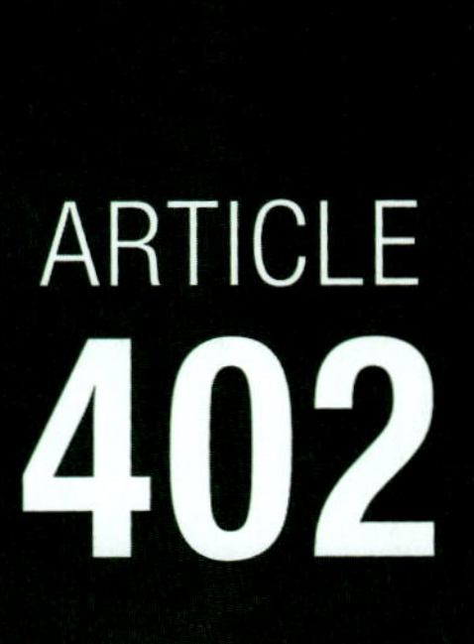

Introduction to Article 402—Fixture Wires

This article covers the general requirements and construction specifications for fixture wires. Fixture wires must be of a type and size listed in Table 402.3. Some topics covered in this material include:

- ▸ Types
- ▸ Ampacities
- ▸ Minimum Size
- ▸ Identification
- ▸ Uses Permitted
- ▸ Uses Not Permitted
- ▸ Overcurrent Protection

402.1 Scope

Article 402 covers the general requirements and construction specifications for fixture wires. ▸**Figure 402–1**

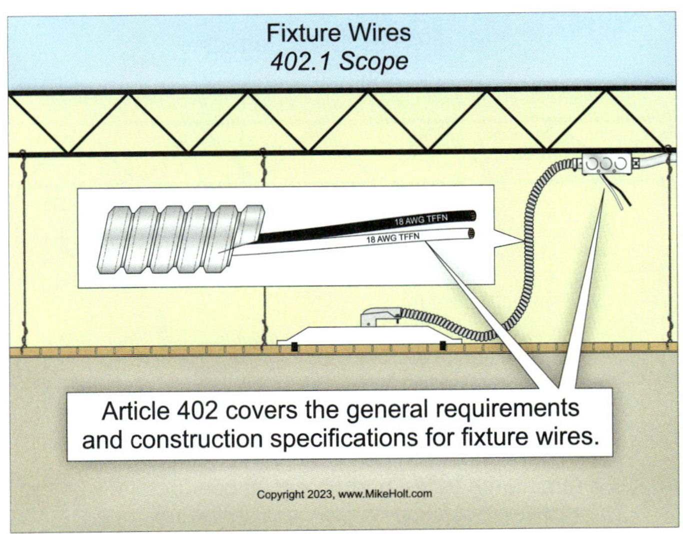

▸**Figure 402–1**

402.2 Other Articles

Fixture wires must comply with this article and with the applicable provisions of other articles of this *Code*.

Note: See Part VI of Article 410 for application in luminaires.

402.3 Types

Fixture wires must be a type contained in Table 402.3.

402.5 Ampacity of Fixture Wires

The ampacities of fixture wires are as follows:

402.6 Minimum Size

Fixture wires are not permitted to be smaller than 18 AWG.

Table 402.5 Ampacity for Fixture Wires	
Wire AWG	Wire Ampacity
18	6A
16	8A
14	17A
12	23A
10	28A

402.7 Raceway Size

Raceways must be large enough to permit the installation and removal of conductors without damaging the conductors' insulation. The number of fixture wires permitted in a single raceway must not exceed the percentage fill specified in Chapter 9, Table 1.

Author's Comment:

▸ When all conductors within a raceway are the same size and insulation, the number of conductors permitted can be found in Annex C for the raceway type.

▸ **Example**

Question: How many 18 AWG, TFFN conductors can be installed in ½ electrical metallic tubing? ▸**Figure 402–2**

(a) 22 conductors *(b) 24 conductors*
(c) 26 conductors *(d) 28 conductors*

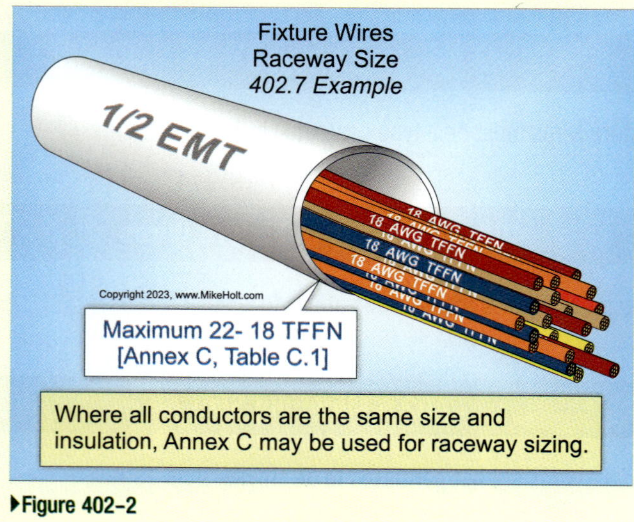

▸Figure 402–2

Answer: (a) 22 conductors [Annex C, Table C.1]

Author's Comment:

▸ See 300.17 for examples on how to size raceways when conductors are not all the same size.

402.8 Neutral Conductor

Fixture wire used as a neutral conductor must be identified by continuous white stripes.

402.10 Uses Permitted

Fixture wires are permitted for:

(1) Installation in luminaires and similar equipment where enclosed or protected and not subject to bending or twisting in use.

(2) Connecting luminaires to the branch-circuit conductors. ▸**Figure 402–3**

Author's Comment:

▸ Fixture wires can also be used for elevators and escalators [620.11(C)] and Class 1 Power-Limited Circuits [724.49(B)].

402.12 Uses Not Permitted

Fixture wires are not permitted to be used for branch-circuit wiring.

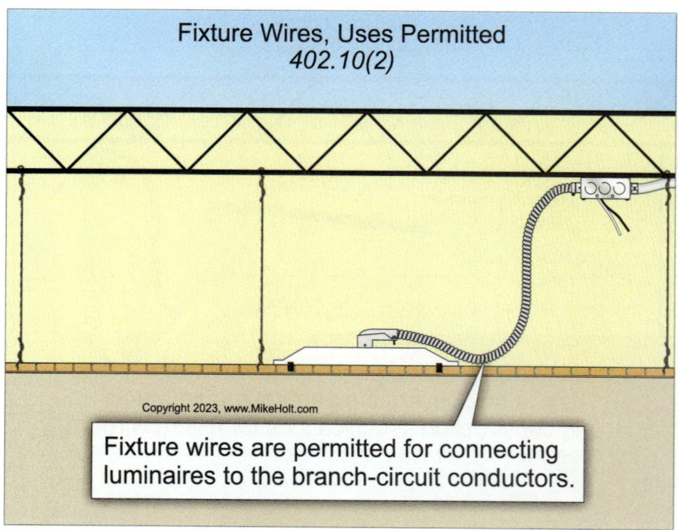

▸Figure 402–3

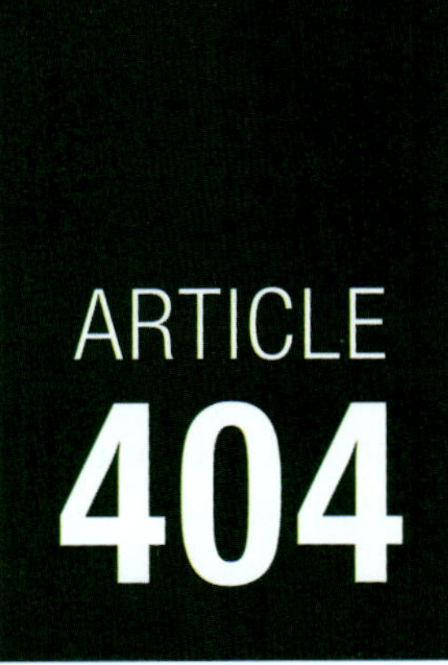

ARTICLE 404

SWITCHES

Introduction to Article 404—Switches

Article 404 covers all types of switches, switching devices, and circuit breakers such as snap (toggle) switches, dimmer switches, fan switches, disconnect switches, circuit breakers, and automatic switches such as those used for time clocks and timers. Some topics covered in this material include:

- ▸ Switch Connection Types
- ▸ Enclosures
- ▸ Position and Connection of Switches
- ▸ Mounting
- ▸ Circuit Breakers as Switches
- ▸ Rating and Use of Switches
- ▸ Construction Specifications

This article consists of two parts:

- ▸ Part I. General
- ▸ Part II. Construction Specifications

Part I. Installation

404.1 Scope

The requirements of Article 404 apply to all types of switches, switching devices, and circuit breakers. ▸**Figure 404–1**

Article 404 does not cover wireless control equipment to which circuit conductors are not connected. ▸**Figure 404–2**

Note: See 210.70 for additional information related to branch circuits that include switches or listed wall-mounted control devices.

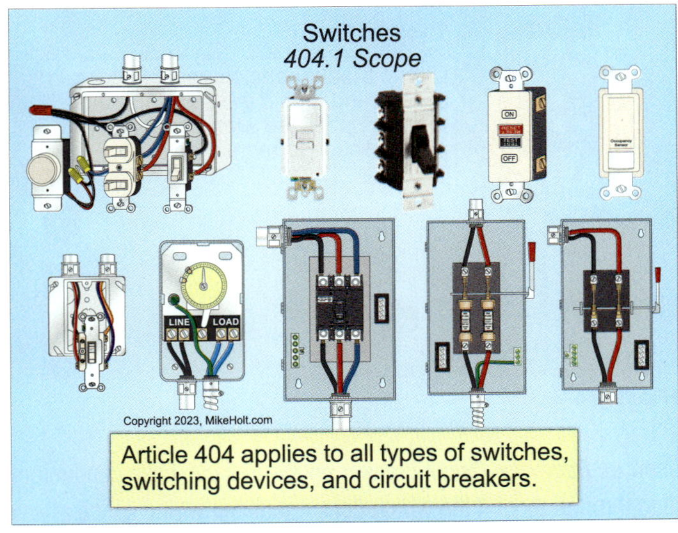

▸Figure 404–1

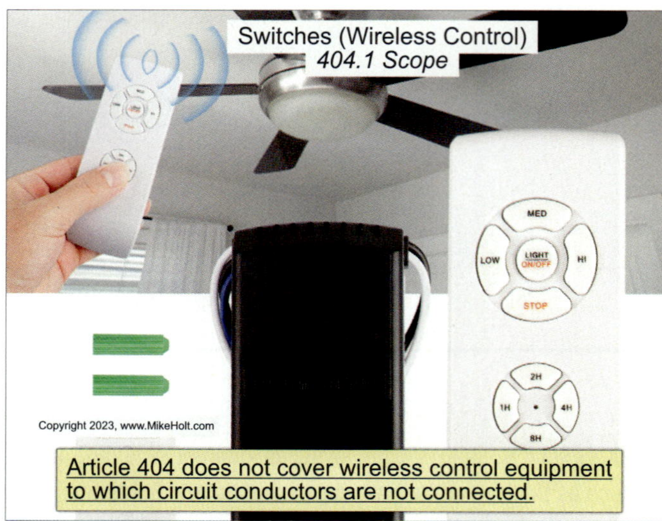

▶Figure 404–2

404.3 Circuit Breaker Enclosures

(A) General. Circuit breakers must be mounted in an enclosure listed for the intended use.

(B) Used as a Raceway, Taps, or Splices.

Splices and Taps. Circuit-breaker enclosures can contain splices and taps if the splices and/or taps do not fill the wiring space at any cross section to more than 75 percent. ▶Figure 404–3

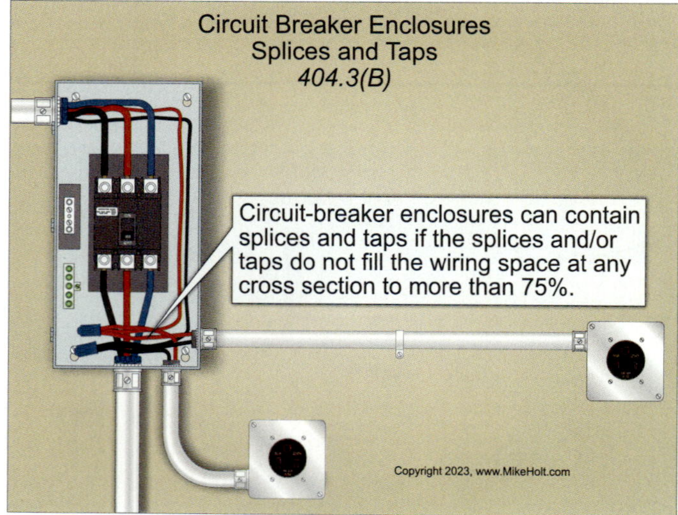

▶Figure 404–3

Used as Raceway. Circuit-breaker enclosures can have conductors feed through them if the wiring does not fill the wiring space at any cross section to more than 40 percent in accordance with 312.8.

404.4 Damp or Wet Locations

(A) Surface-Mounted Switches or Circuit Breakers. Surface-mounted switches or circuit breakers in damp or wet locations must be installed in a weatherproof enclosure. ▶Figure 404–4

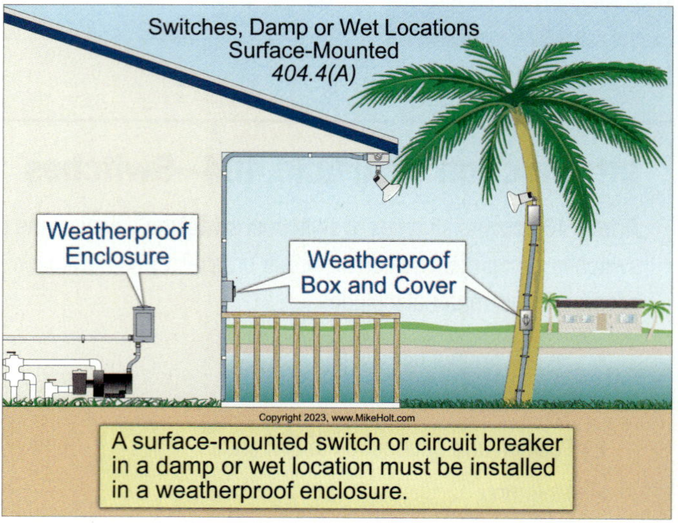

▶Figure 404–4

(B) Flush-Mounted Switches or Circuit Breakers. Flush-mounted switches or circuit breakers in damp or wet locations must have a weatherproof cover. ▶Figure 404–5

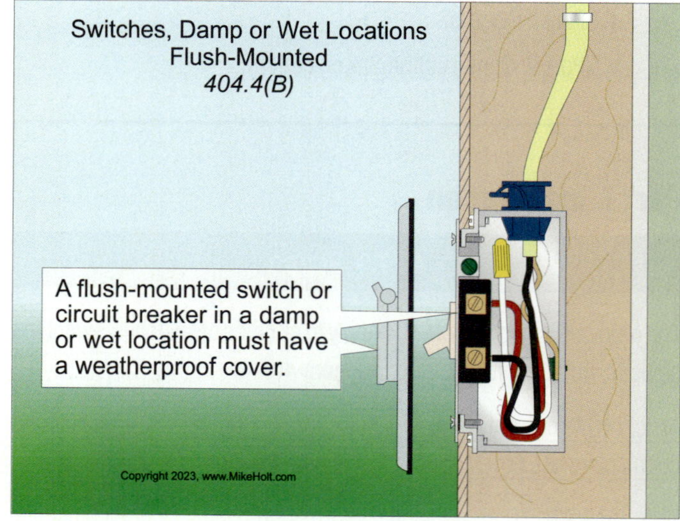

▶Figure 404–5

(C) Switches Within Tub and Shower Spaces. Switches are not permitted to be installed within tub or shower spaces unless installed as part of a listed tub or shower assembly. ▶Figure 404–6

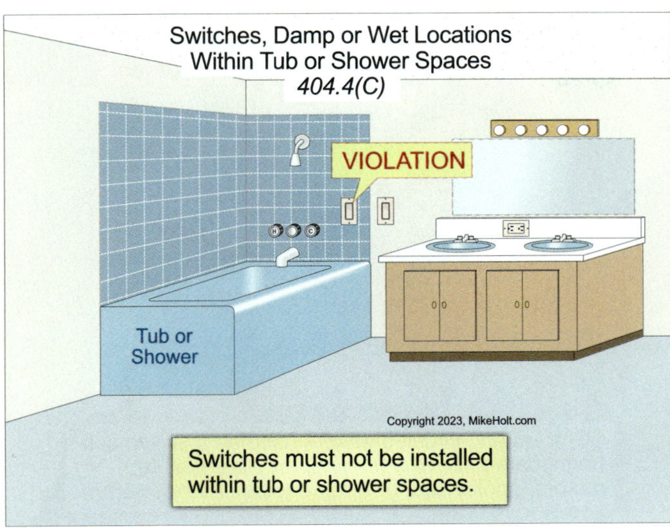

▶Figure 404–6

Author's Comment:

▸ The *Code* does not specify how far outside a tub or shower space a switch must be.

404.7 Indicating

Switches must be marked to indicate if the switch is in the "on" or "off" position.

When a switch or circuit breaker is operated vertically, the "up" position of the circuit breaker handle must be the "on" position. ▶Figure 404–7

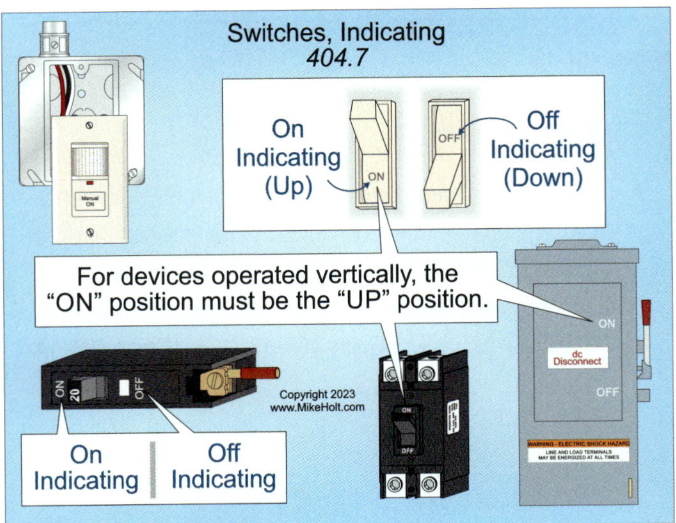

▶Figure 404–7

Ex 1: 3-way and 4-way switches, are not required to be marked "on" or "off."

(C) Connection of Switches. Single-throw knife switches must be connected so their blades are de-energized when the switch is in the "open" position.

Author's Comment:

▸ In accordance with "*UL 98 Standard for Enclosed and Dead-Front Switches*" section 6.7.1.11, a switch of the knife-blade type must be so arranged that the blades will be de-energized when the switch is open.

404.8 Accessibility and Grouping

(A) Location. Switches and the switch handle of circuit breakers must be capable of being operated from a readily accessible location.

Maximum Height. The center of the grip of the operating handle of a switch or circuit breaker when in its highest position is not permitted to be more than 6 ft 7 in. above the floor or working platform except as follows: ▶Figure 404–8

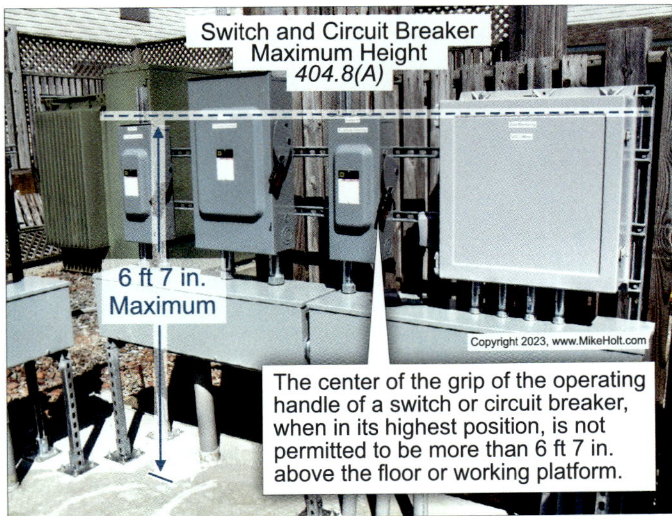

▶Figure 404–8

Author's Comment:

▸ There are no requirements for a minimum height above the floor or working platform for switches or circuit breakers. ▶Figure 404–9

(1) On busways, fusible switches and circuit breakers can be located at the same level as the busway where suitable means is provided to operate the handle of the device from the floor. ▶Figure 404–10

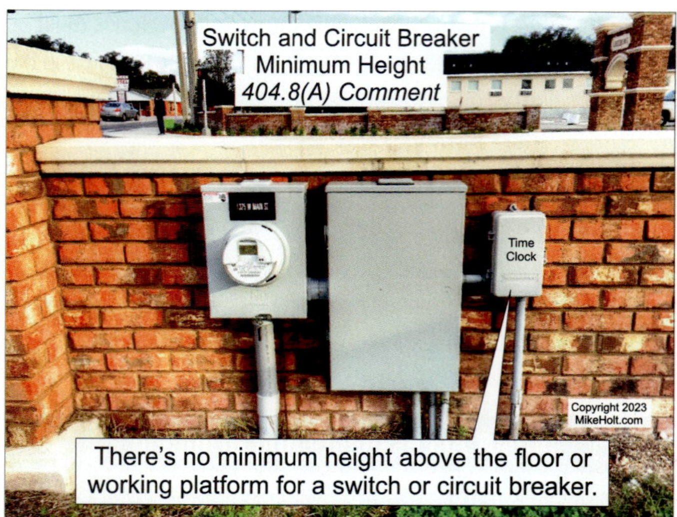

▶Figure 404–9

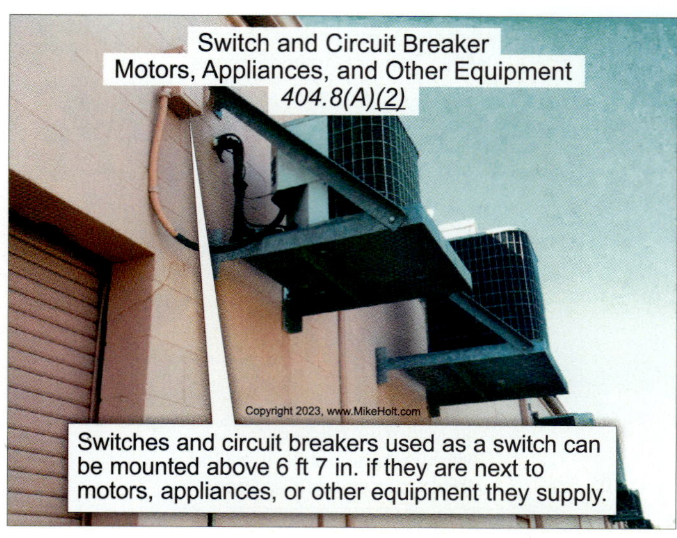

▶Figure 404–11

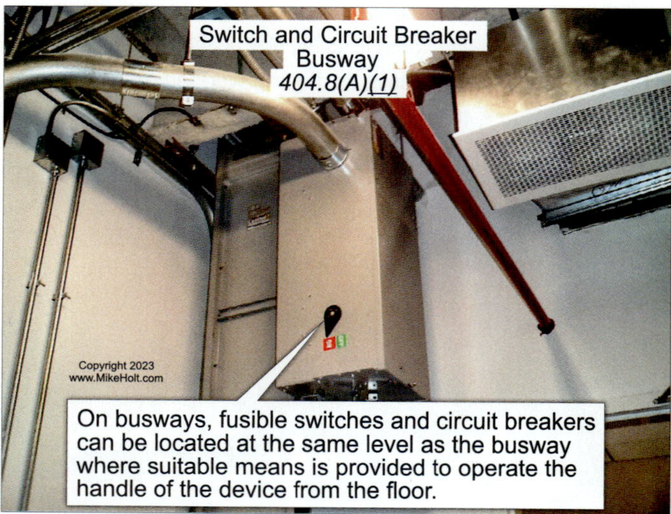

▶Figure 404–10

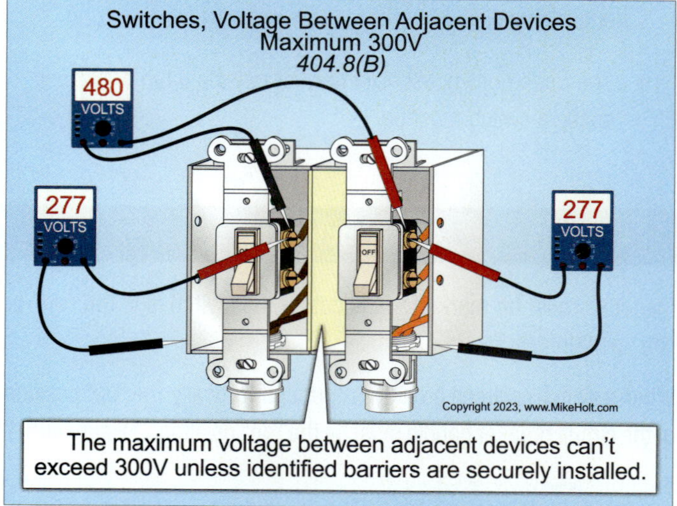

▶Figure 404–12

(2) Switches and circuit breakers can be mounted above 6 ft 7 in. if they are next to motors, appliances, or other equipment they supply. ▶Figure 404–11

(B) Voltage Between Devices. Snap switches are not permitted to be in enclosures with other switches or receptacles if the voltage between adjacent devices exceeds 300V, unless the devices are installed in enclosures equipped with securely installed barriers identified for the purpose between adjacent devices. ▶Figure 404–12

Author's Comment:

▶ The voltage between devices is a function of the difference in voltage between the conductors. When adjacent devices are connected to different systems (such as 120/208V and 277/480V), the voltage difference between the devices can be as much as 381V. ▶Figure 404–13 and ▶Figure 404–14

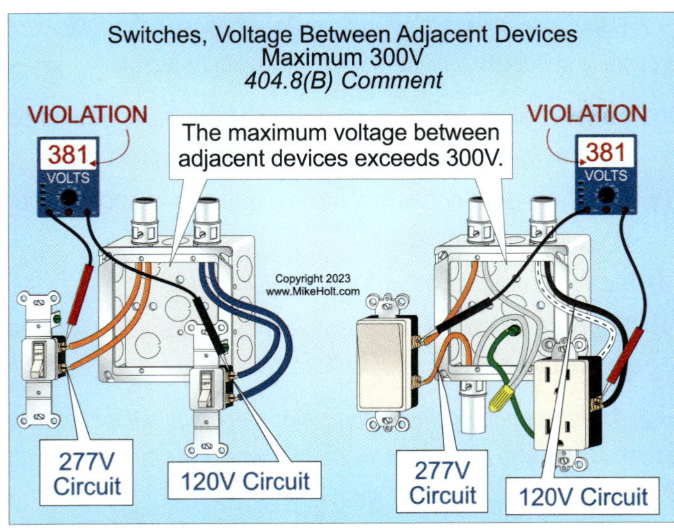

▶Figure 404–13

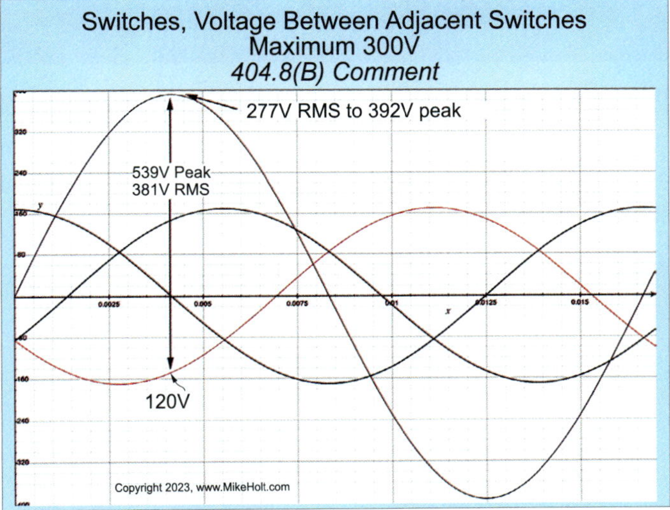

▶Figure 404–14

404.9 General-Use Snap Switches, Dimmers, and Control Switches

(A) Faceplates. Faceplates for switches, dimmers, and control switches must completely cover the outlet box opening. Where flush mounted, the faceplate must seat against the wall surface. ▶Figure 404–15

(B) Equipment Grounding Conductor. Switches, dimmers, and control switches and metal faceplates must be connected to the circuit equipment grounding conductor using either of the following methods:

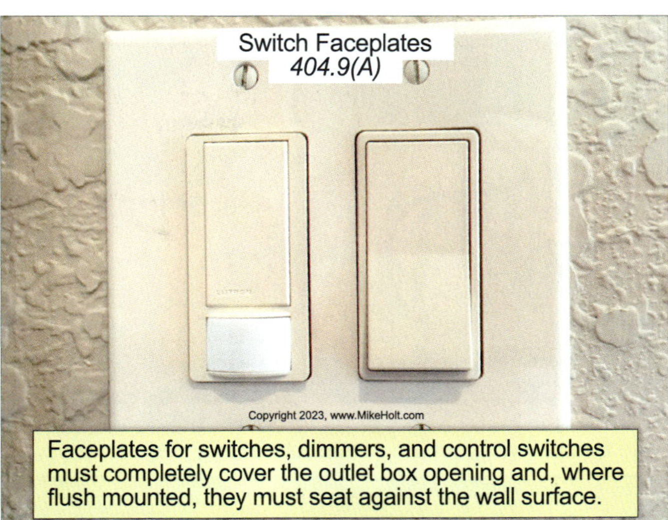

▶Figure 404–15

(1) Metal Boxes.

Metal Faceplates. Metal faceplates must be connected to the circuit equipment grounding conductor (metal faceplates secured with metal screws to the switch). ▶Figure 404–16

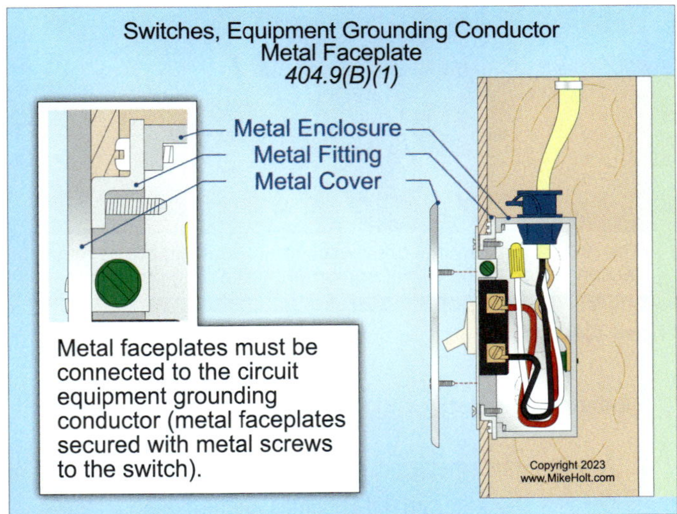

▶Figure 404–16

Switch. Switches in metal boxes or metal covers are connected to the equipment grounding conductor using metal screws [250.109]. ▶Figure 404–17

(2) Nonmetallic Boxes. The grounding terminal of a switch in nonmetallic boxes must be connected to the circuit equipment grounding conductor. ▶Figure 404–18

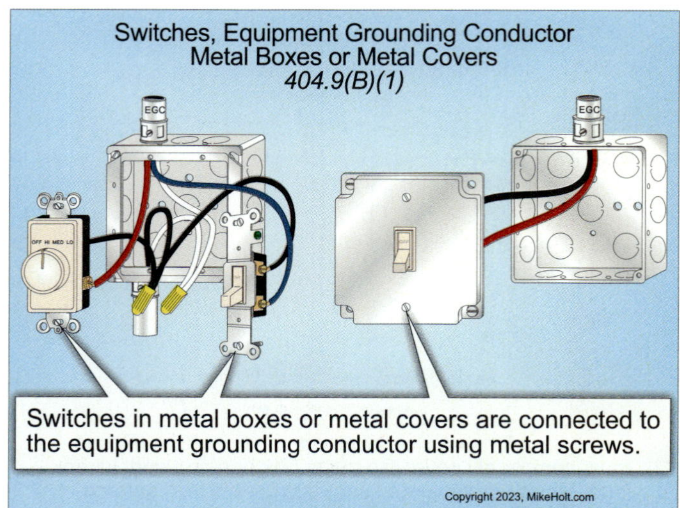

▶Figure 404–17

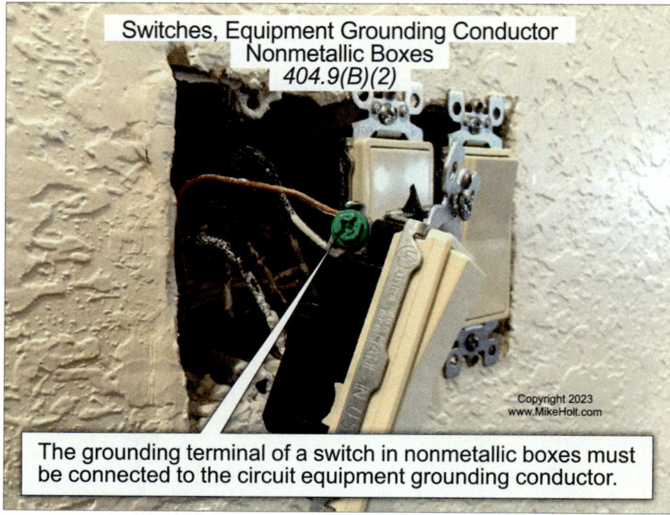

▶Figure 404–18

Author's Comment:

▶ A switch with a metal faceplate installed in a nonmetallic box poses a shock hazard if it becomes energized. An effective ground-fault current path must be provided by connecting the metal faceplate with metal screws to a switch that is connected to an equipment grounding conductor [250.109].

Ex 1: Where no means exists within the box for bonding to an equipment grounding conductor, or if the wiring method at the existing switch does not contain an equipment grounding conductor, a switch without such a connection to the equipment grounding conductor is permitted for replacement purposes only. A switch installed under this exception must have a faceplate that is nonmetallic and noncombustible with nonmetallic screws, or the replacement switch must be GFCI protected.

Ex 2: Listed assemblies are not required to be bonded to an equipment grounding conductor if all the following conditions are met:

(1) The device is provided with a nonmetallic faceplate and designed such that no metallic faceplate replaces the one provided.

(2) The device does not have a mounting means to accept other configurations of faceplates.

(3) The device is equipped with a nonmetallic yoke.

(4) Parts of the device that are accessible after the faceplate is installed are manufactured of nonmetallic material.

Ex 3: An equipment grounding conductor is not required for bonding a snap switch with an integral nonmetallic enclosure complying with 300.15(E).

404.10 Mounting of Snap Switches, Dimmers, and Control Switches

(B) Box Mounted. General-use snap switches, dimmers, and control switches mounted in boxes that are set back from the finished surface must be installed so the extension plaster ears are seated against the surface. ▶Figure 404–19

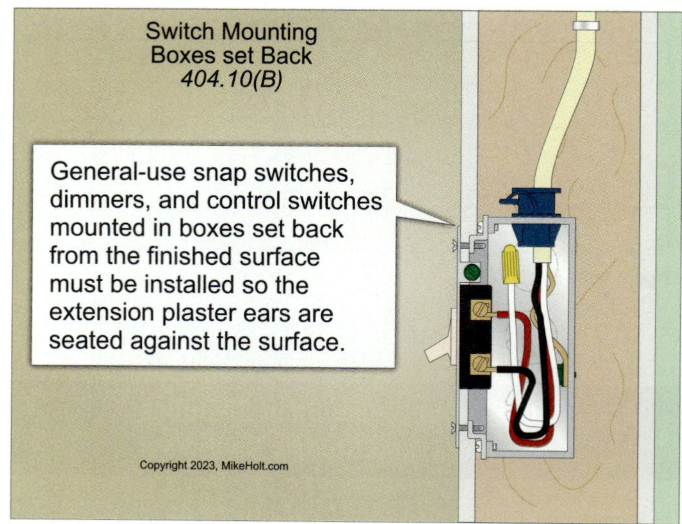

▶Figure 404–19

Screws used for the purpose of attaching a device to a box must be of the type provided with a listed device, machine screws having 32 threads per in., or part of listed assemblies or systems in accordance with the manufacturer's instructions. ▶Figure 404–20

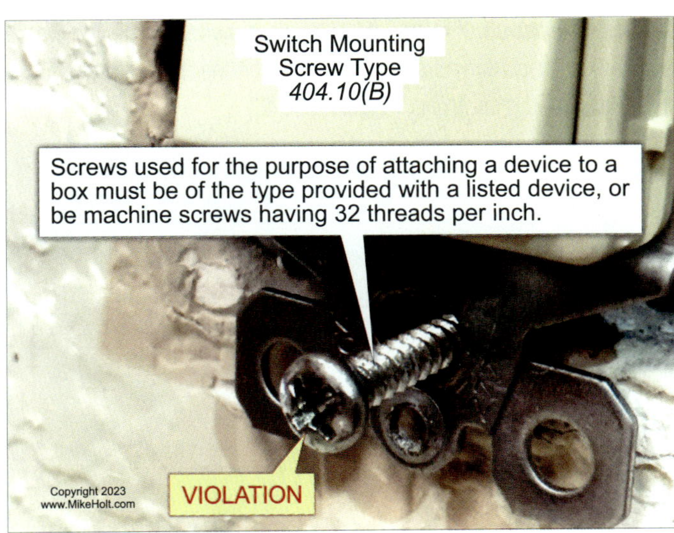

▶Figure 404–20

Author's Comment:

▶ In walls or ceilings of noncombustible material (such as drywall), boxes are not permitted to be set back more than ¼ in. from the finished surface. In walls or ceilings with combustible surfaces, boxes must be flush with, or project slightly from, the finished surface [314.20]. There must not be any gaps of more than ⅛ in. at the edge of the box [314.21].

404.12 Bonding of Enclosures

Metal enclosures for switches and circuit breakers must be connected to an equipment grounding conductor of a type recognized in 250.118(A) [250.4(A)(3)].

Metal enclosures for switches and circuit breakers used as service equipment must be bonded to the service neutral conductor via the main bonding jumper to provide an effective ground-fault current path [250.92(A)].

Where nonmetallic enclosures are used with metal raceways or metal-armored cables, they must comply with 314.3 Ex 1 or Ex 2.

404.14 Rating and Use of Snap Switches

General-Use Snap Switches. General-use snap switches must be listed and marked with their ratings as indicated.

According to Article 100, "General-Use Snap Switch" is constructed to be installed in a device box or a box cover.

(A) Alternating-Current General-Use Snap Switches. General-use snap switches are permitted to control:

(4) Motor loads not exceeding 80 percent of the ampere rating of the switch at its rated voltage [430.109(C)(2)].

(5) Electronic ballasts, self-ballasted lamps, compact fluorescent lamps, and LED lamp loads with their associated drivers, not exceeding 20A and not exceeding the ampere rating of the switch at the voltage applied

(C) CO/ALR Snap Switches. Aluminum conductors connected to snap switches rated 20A or less must be marked CO/ALR.

(D) Snap Switch Terminations. Snap switch terminations must be installed in accordance with the following:

(1) 15A and 20A snap switches not marked CO/ALR can only be used with copper and copper-clad aluminum conductors.

(2) Switch terminals marked CO/ALR can be used with aluminum, copper, and copper-clad aluminum conductors.

(F) Dimmer and Electronic Control Switches. General-use dimmer switches, timer switches, and occupancy sensors are only permitted to control connected loads, such as permanently installed incandescent luminaires, unless listed for the control of other loads. ▶Figure 404–21

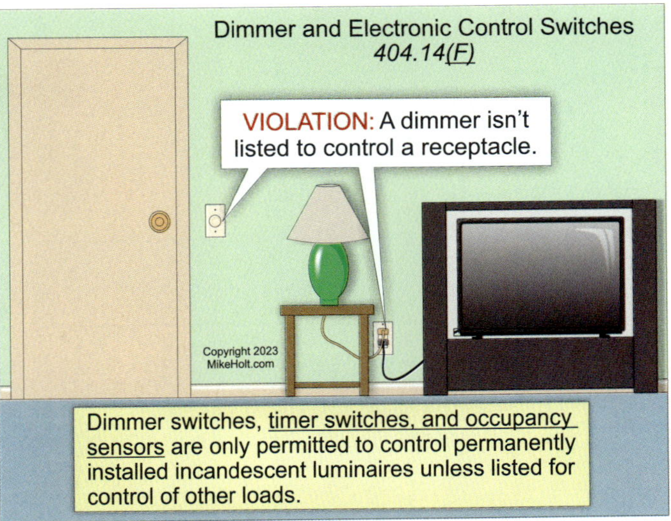

▶Figure 404–21

Such switches must be marked by the manufacturer with their current and voltage ratings and used for loads not exceeding their ampere rating at the voltage applied.

Part II. Construction Specifications

404.20 Switch Marking

(A) Markings. Switches must be marked with the current, voltage, and if horsepower rated, the maximum rating for which they are designed. ▶Figure 404–22

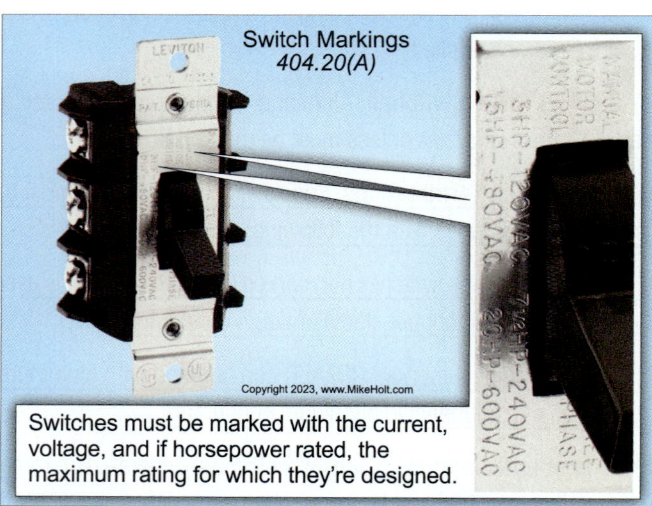

Switches must be marked with the current, voltage, and if horsepower rated, the maximum rating for which they're designed.

▶Figure 404–22

(B) Off Indication. If in the off position, a switching device with a marked "off" position must completely disconnect all phase conductors of the load it controls. ▶Figure 404–23

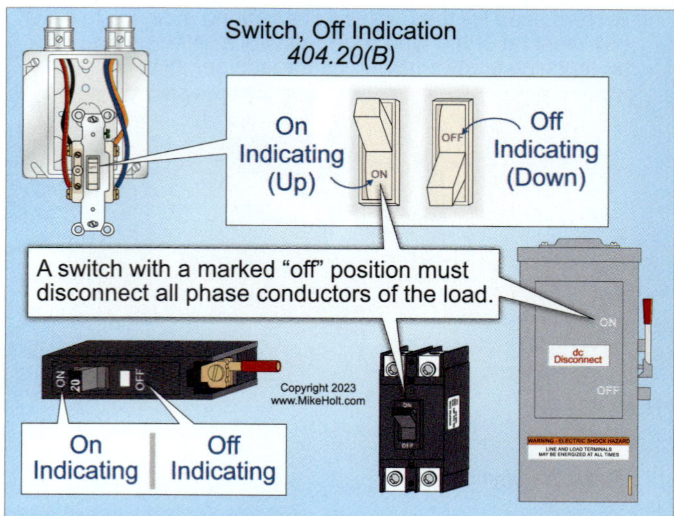

▶Figure 404–23

RECEPTACLES, ATTACHMENT PLUGS, AND FLANGED INLETS

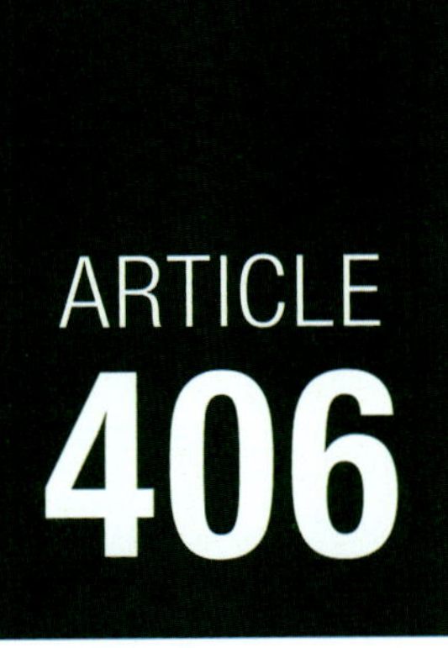

Introduction to Article 406—Receptacles, Attachment Plugs, and Flanged Inlets

This article covers the rating, type, and installation of receptacles, attachment plugs, and flanged inlets. There are many types of receptacles such as self-grounding, isolated ground, tamper resistant, weather resistant, GFCIs and AFCIs, energy controlled, work surface and countertop assemblies, USBs, surge protectors, and so on. Some topics covered in this material include:

▸ Receptacle Types and Ratings

▸ Mounting

▸ Faceplates

▸ Flanged Surface Devices, Cord Connectors, and Attachment Plugs

▸ Damp or Wet Locations

▸ Equipment Grounding Conductor Terminals

▸ Tamper-Resistant Receptacles

According to Article 100, "Receptacle" is a contact device installed at an outlet for the connection of an attachment plug or equipment designed to mate with the contact device. ▸**Figure 406–1**

A single receptacle contains one contact device on the same yoke or strap. A multiple receptacle has more than one contact device on the same yoke or strap. ▸**Figure 406–2**

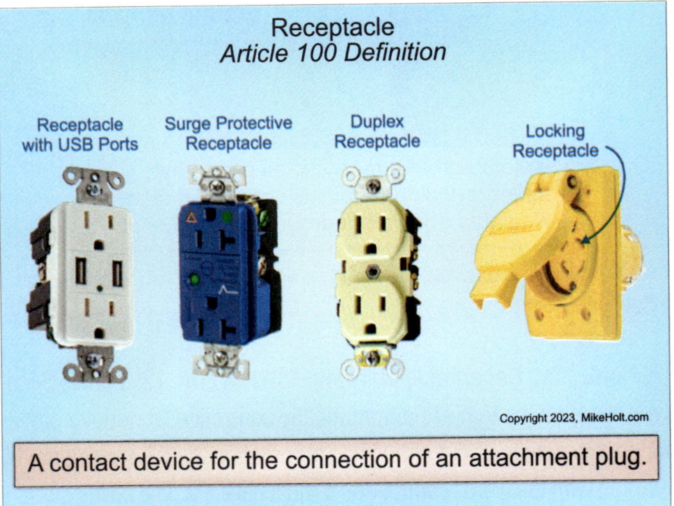

▸Figure 406–1

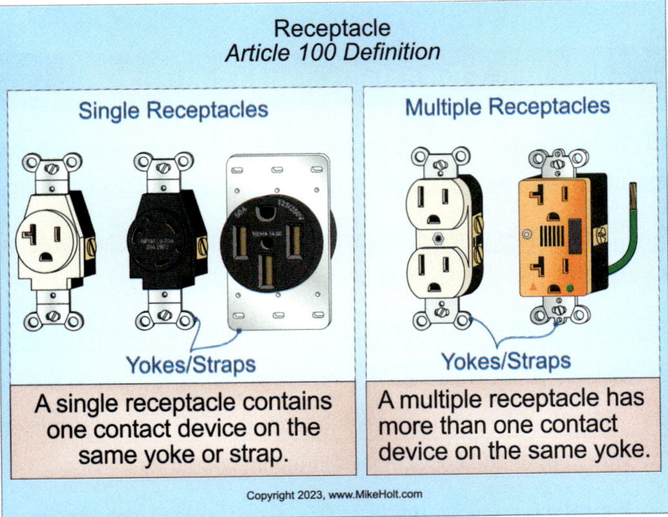

▸Figure 406–2

Author's Comment:

▸ A yoke (also called a "strap") is the metal mounting structure for such items as receptacles, switches, switches with pilot lights, and switch/receptacles to name a few.

Note: A duplex receptacle is an example of a multiple receptacle with two receptacles on the same yoke or strap.

406.1 Scope

Article 406 covers the rating, type, and installation of receptacles, attachment plugs, and flanged inlets. ▸**Figure 406–3**

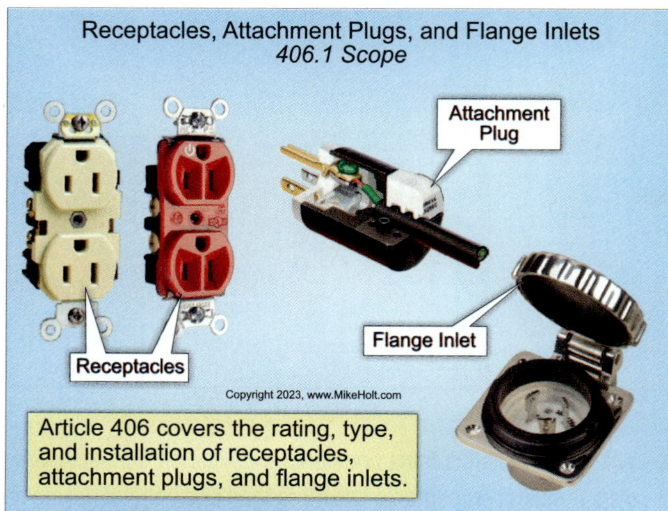

▸Figure 406–3

406.3 Receptacle Rating and Type

(A) Receptacles. Receptacles must be listed and marked with the manufacturer's name or identification, voltage rating, and ampere rating.

(C) CO/ALR Receptacles. Aluminum conductors connected to receptacles rated 20A or less must be marked CO/ALR.

(D) Receptacle Terminations. Receptacle terminations must be in accordance with the following:

(1) 15A and 20A receptacles not marked CO/ALR can only be used with copper and copper-clad aluminum conductors.

(2) Receptacle terminals marked CO/ALR can be used with aluminum, copper, and copper-clad aluminum conductors.

(E) Isolated Ground Receptacles. Isolated ground receptacles must be identified by an orange triangle on the face of the receptacle. ▸**Figure 406–4**

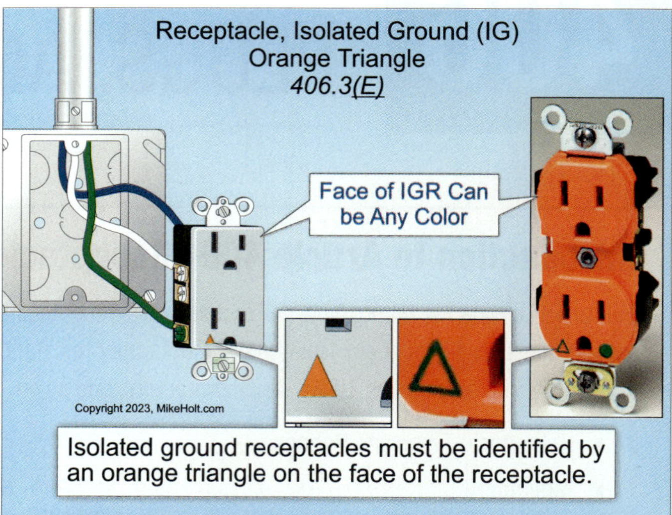

▸Figure 406–4

(1) Isolated ground receptacles must have their grounding terminals connected to an insulated equipment grounding conductor in accordance with 250.146(D). ▸**Figure 406–5**

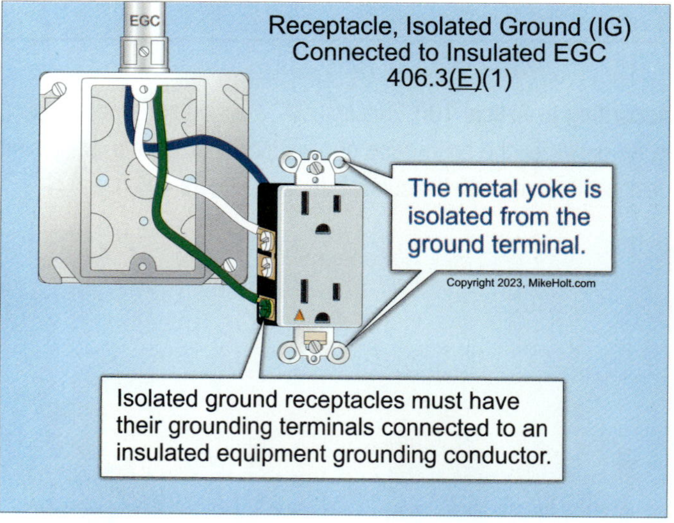

▸Figure 406–5

(F) Controlled Receptacle Marking. 15A and 20A, 125V nonlocking-type receptacles that are automatically controlled to remove power for energy management or building automation must be permanently marked with the word "controlled." It must have a visible power symbol on the receptacle after installation. ▸**Figure 406–6**

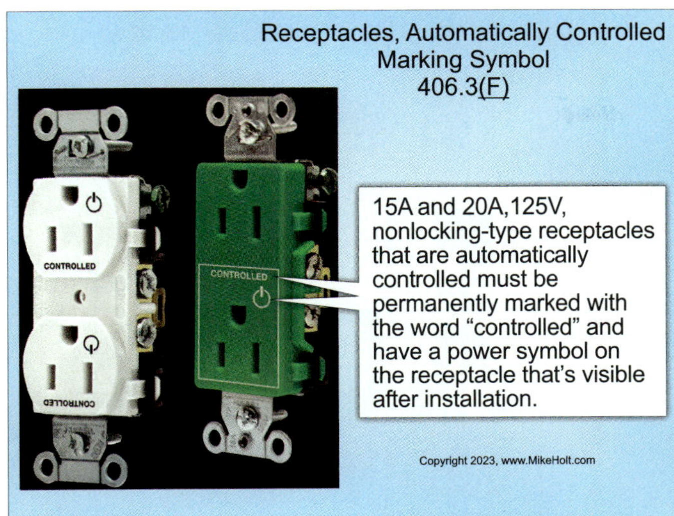

▶Figure 406–6

Author's Comment:

▶ ICC Energy Code C405.6 and ASHREA 90.1 section 8.4 requires "Automatic Receptacle Control" to reduce electrical power demands on commercial buildings from cord-and-plug-connected loads such as cell phone chargers, computer monitors, task lighting, and other equipment that consume energy even in the off state.

406.4 General Installation Requirements

(A) Grounding Type. Receptacles installed on 15A and 20A branch circuits must be of the grounding type, except as permitted for 2-wire receptacle replacements in 406.4(D)(2). ▶Figure 406–7

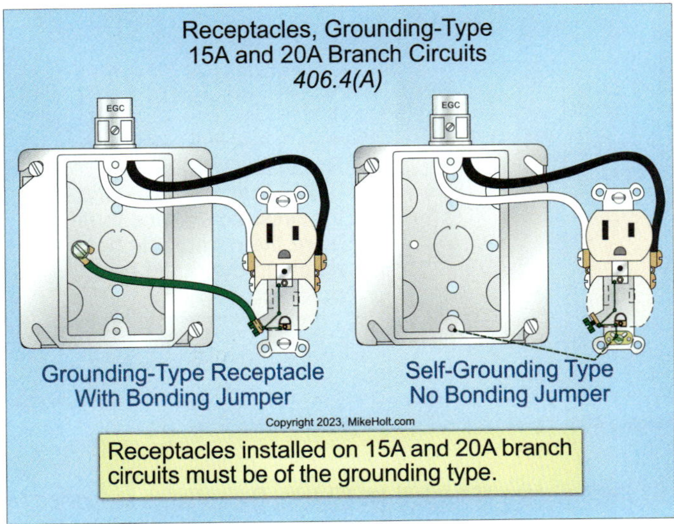

▶Figure 406–7

Grounding-type receptacles must be installed on circuits rated in accordance with Table 210.21(B)(1) for single receptacles and Table 210.21(B)(2) or Table 210.21(B)(3) for two or more receptacles.

Table 210.21(B)(3) Receptacle Ratings

Circuit Rating	Receptacle Rating
15A	15A
20A	15A or 20A
30A	30A
40A	40A or 50A
50A	50A

(C) Methods of Connection to Equipment Grounding Conductor.
The receptacle grounding terminal must be connected to the equipment grounding conductor of the circuit supplying the receptacle in accordance with 250.146. ▶Figure 406–8

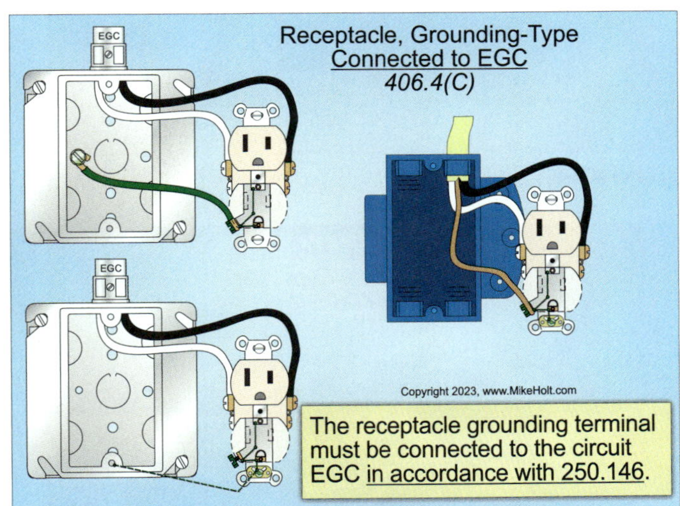

▶Figure 406–8

Cord connectors must be connected to the circuit equipment grounding conductor.

Note 1: For acceptable types of equipment grounding conductors see 250.118(A).

Note 2: See 250.130 for extensions of existing branch circuits.

406.5 Receptacle Mounting

Receptacles must be installed in outlet boxes that are securely fastened in place in accordance with 314.23.

Author's Comment:

▸ Boxes containing a hub can be supported from a flexible cord connected to fittings that prevent tension from being transmitted to joints or terminals [400.14 and 314.23(H)(1)].

Screws used for attaching a receptacle to a box must be a type provided with a listed receptacle or machine screws having 32 threads per in. ▸**Figure 406–9** and ▸**Figure 406–10**

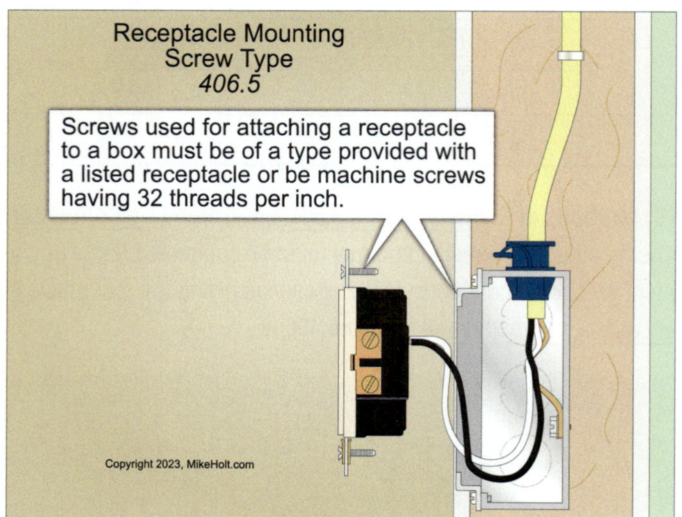

▸Figure 406–9

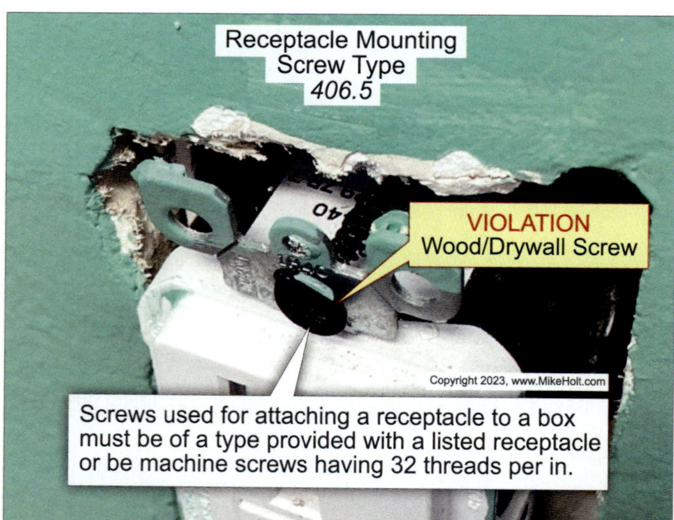

▸Figure 406–10

(A) Boxes Set Back. Receptacles in outlet boxes that are set back from the finished surface must have the receptacle held rigidly to the finished surface. ▸**Figure 406–11**

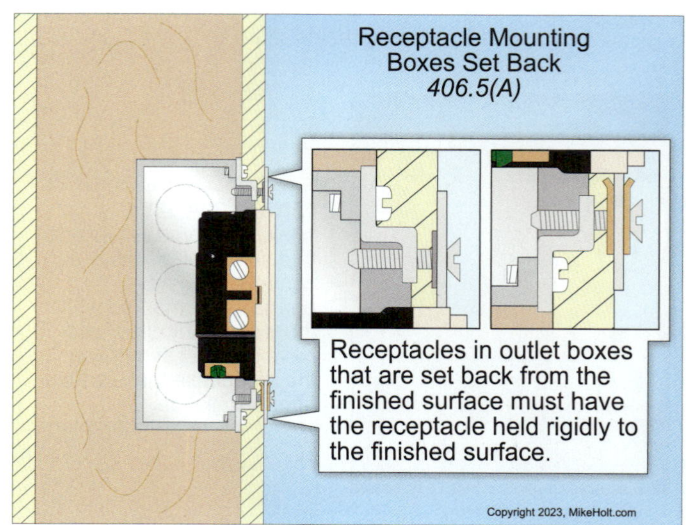

▸Figure 406–11

Author's Comment:

▸ In walls or ceilings of noncombustible material (such as drywall) outlet boxes are not permitted to be set back more than ¼ in. from the finished surface. In walls or ceilings of combustible material, outlet boxes must be flush with the finished surface [314.20]. There must not be any gaps of more than ⅛ in. at the edge of the outlet box [314.21].

(B) Boxes Flush with Surface. Receptacles in outlet boxes that are flush with the finished surface must have the receptacle held rigidly to the outlet box or raised cover. ▸**Figure 406–12**

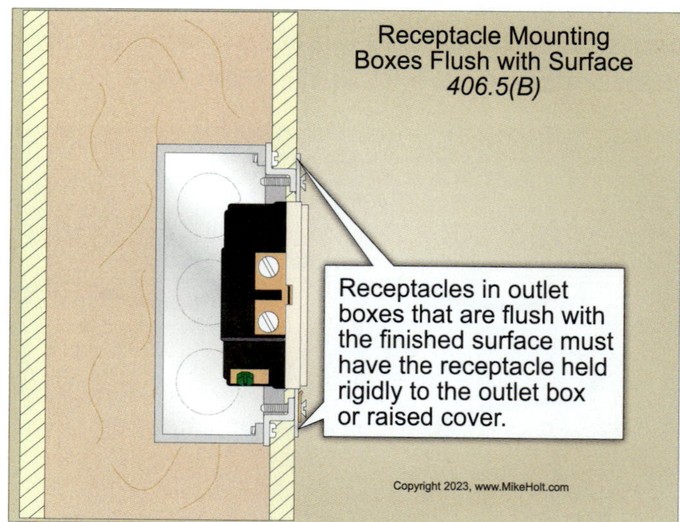

▸Figure 406–12

(C) Receptacles Mounted on Covers. Receptacles supported by a cover must be held rigidly to the cover with at least two screws. ▸**Figure 406–13**

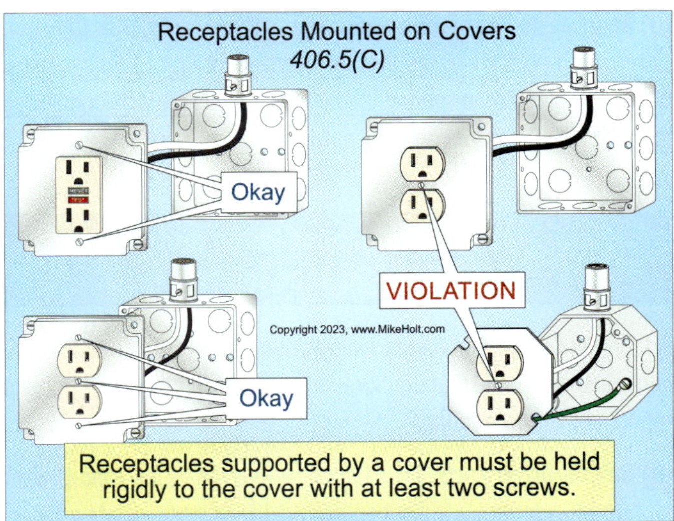

Receptacles supported by a cover must be held rigidly to the cover with at least two screws.

▶Figure 406–13

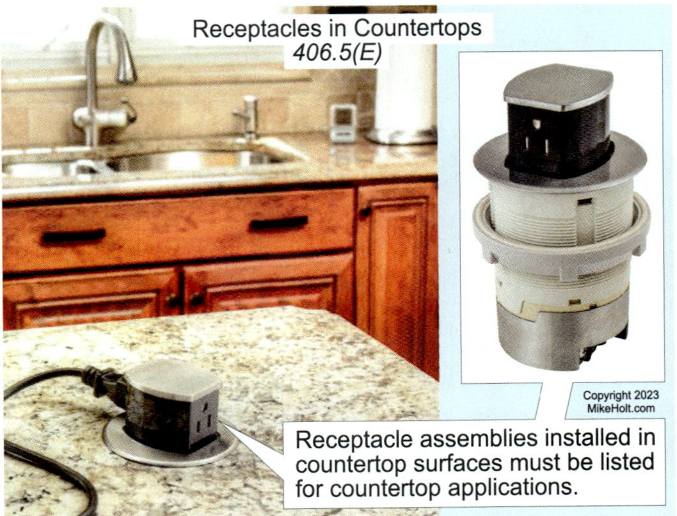

Receptacle assemblies installed in countertop surfaces must be listed for countertop applications.

▶Figure 406–14

(D) Position of Receptacle Faces. Receptacles must be flush with (or project from) the faceplates.

(E) Receptacles in Countertops. Receptacle assemblies installed in countertop surfaces must be listed for countertop applications. ▶Figure 406–14

(F) Receptacles in Work Surfaces. Receptacle assemblies listed for work surfaces or countertops can be installed in a work surface.

(G) Receptacle Orientation.

(1) Countertop and Work Surfaces. Receptacles are not permitted to be installed in a face-up position in or on countertop surfaces or work surfaces unless listed for countertop surface or work surface applications. ▶Figure 406–15

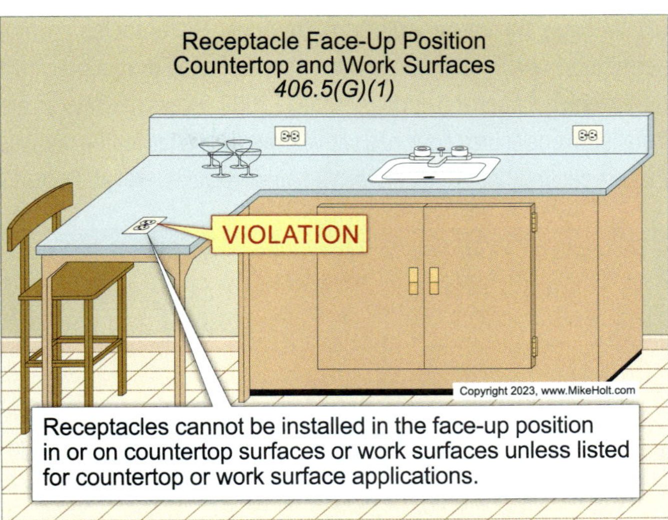

Receptacles cannot be installed in the face-up position in or on countertop surfaces or work surfaces unless listed for countertop or work surface applications.

▶Figure 406–15

(2) Under Sinks. Receptacles are not permitted to be installed in a face-up position in the area below a sink.

Author's Comment:

▶ The position of the ground terminal of a receptacle is not specified in the *NEC* so it can be up, down, or to the side. Proposals to specify the mounting position of the ground terminal have been rejected throughout many *Code* revision cycles. ▶Figure 406–16

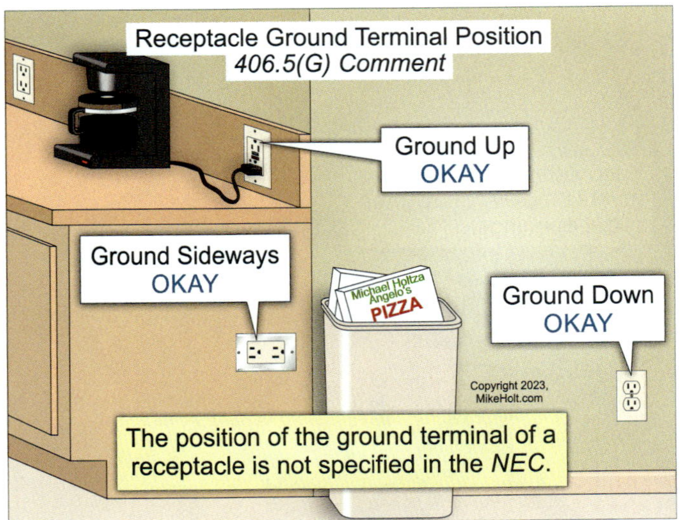

The position of the ground terminal of a receptacle is not specified in the *NEC*.

▶Figure 406–16

(J) Voltage Between Adjacent Devices. Receptacles are not permitted to be in enclosures with other switches or receptacles if the voltage between the devices exceeds 300V, unless the devices are installed in enclosures equipped with barriers identified for the purpose that are securely installed between adjacent devices. ▶**Figure 406–17**

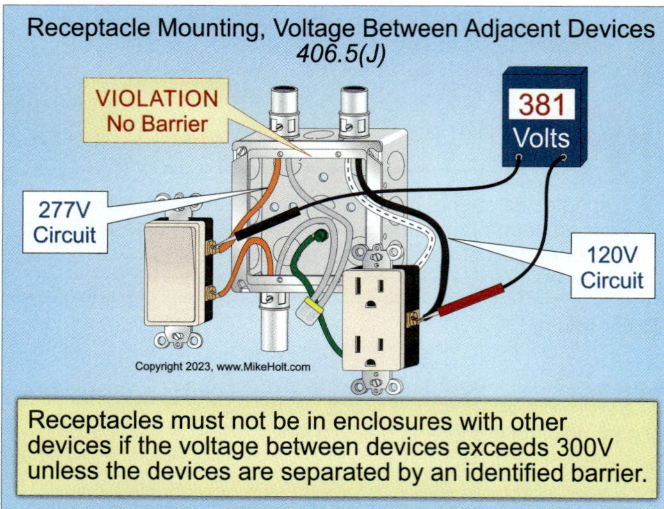

▶Figure 406–17

406.6 Receptacle Faceplates

Faceplates for receptacles must completely cover the outlet openings and press against the mounting surface. ▶**Figure 406–18**

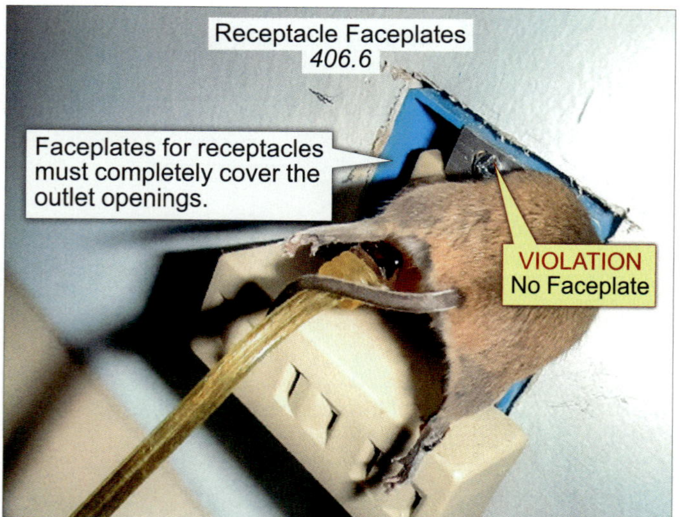

▶Figure 406–18

(D) Receptacle Faceplates with Integral Night Light/USB Charger. Listed receptacle faceplates with an integral night light, USB charger (or both) that rely solely on spring-tensioned contacts must be connected to only brass or copper alloy receptacle terminal screws.

406.7 Attachment Plugs and Flanged Surface Inlets

Attachment plugs and flanged inlets must be listed for the purpose and marked with the manufacturer's name (or identification), voltage rating, and ampere rating.

(B) No Energized Parts. Attachment plugs must be installed so their prongs, blades, or pins are not energized unless inserted into an energized receptacle or flexible cord. ▶**Figure 406–19**

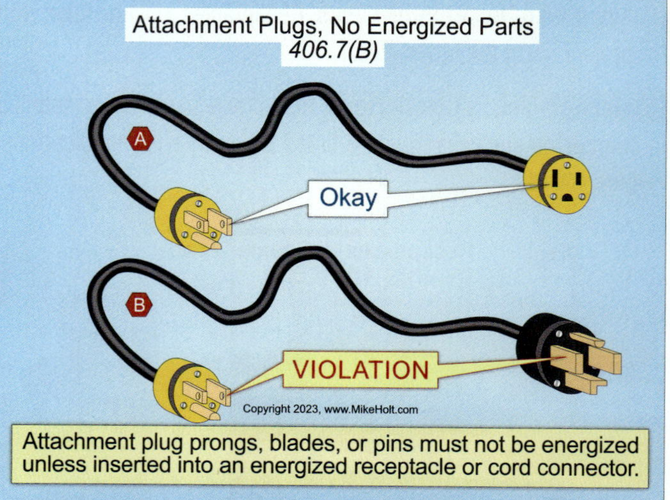

▶Figure 406–19

(D) Flanged Surface Inlet. A flanged surface inlet must be installed so the prongs, blades, or pins are not energized unless an energized cord connector is inserted into the inlet. ▶**Figure 406–20**

According to Article 100, "Cord Connector" is a contact device terminated to a flexible cord that accepts an attachment plug or other insertion.

406.9 Receptacles in Damp or Wet Locations

(A) Damp Locations. Receptacles installed in a damp location must be the weather-resistant (WR) type. It must be installed in an enclosure that is weatherproof when an attachment plug is not inserted (damp location rated) or the attachment plug is inserted when the cover is closed (wet location rated). ▶**Figure 406–21**

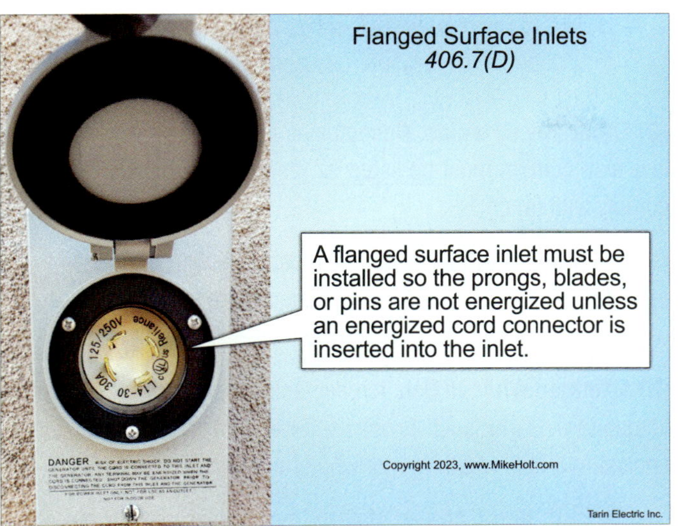

▶Figure 406–20

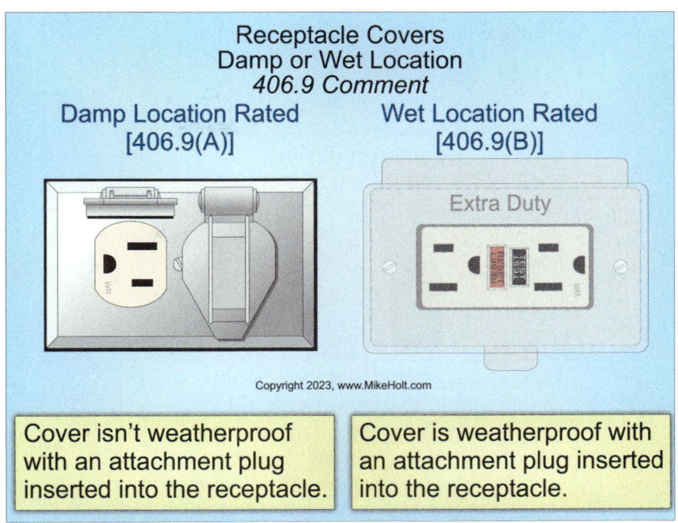

▶Figure 406–22

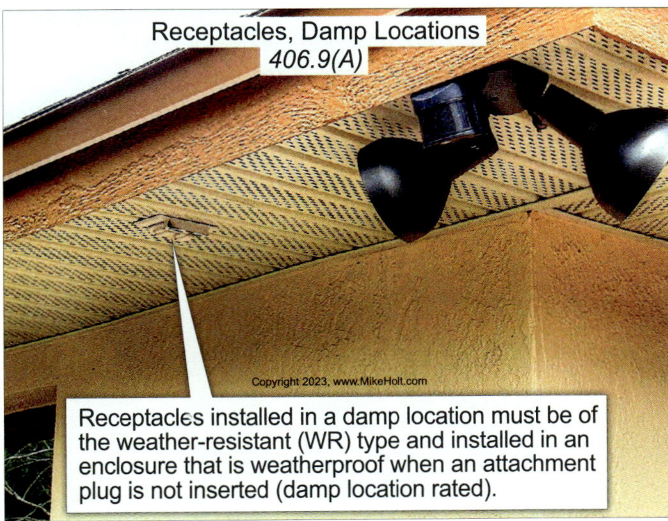

▶Figure 406–21

An example of a damp location is one where a receptacle is under roofed open porches, canopies, or marquees, and not subjected to beating rain or water runoff.

Hinged covers of outlet box hoods must be able to open at least 90 degrees or fully open (if the cover is not designed to open 90 degrees from the closed to open position) after installation.

Author's Comment:

▶ The main difference between the cover for a 15A or 20A receptacle in a damp location [406.9(A)] or wet location [406.9(B)] is whether it is weather resistant when the attachment plug is inserted. ▶Figure 406–22

(B) Wet Locations.

(1) 15A and 20A Receptacles. 15A and 20A receptacles installed in a wet location must be within an enclosure that is weatherproof when an attachment plug is inserted using an outlet box hood identified as "extra duty." ▶Figure 406–23

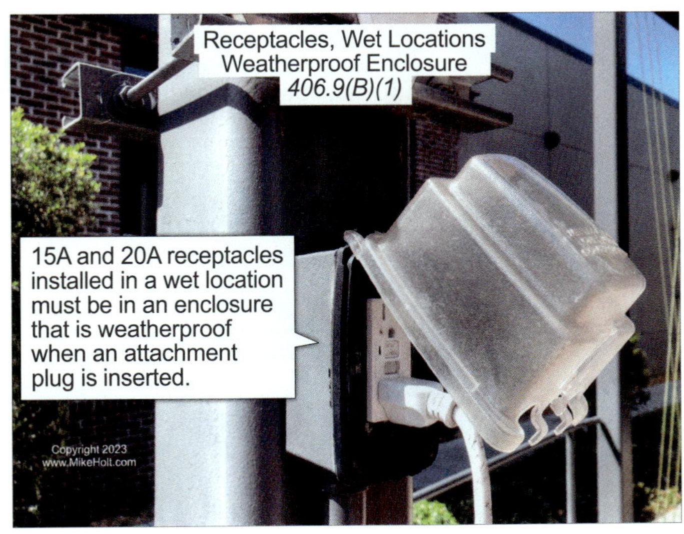

▶Figure 406–23

Hinged covers of outlet box hoods must be able to open at least 90 degrees or fully open (if the cover is not designed to open 90 degrees from the closed to open position) after installation. ▶Figure 406–24

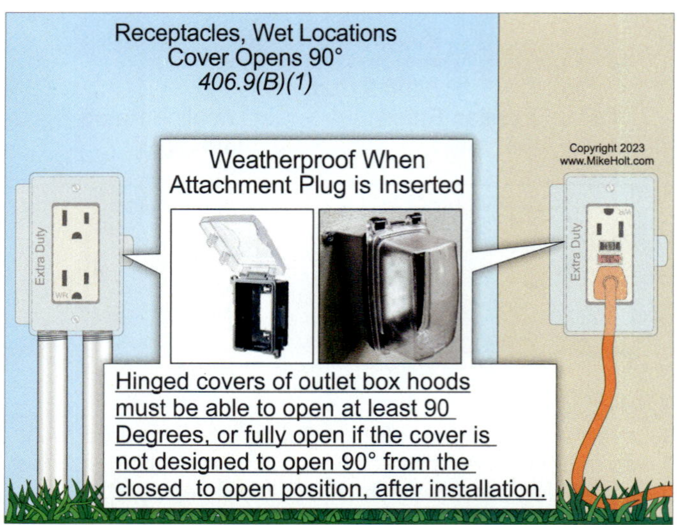

▶Figure 406–24

Nonlocking-type 15A and 20A receptacles in a wet location must be listed as weather-resistant (WR) type. ▶Figure 406–25

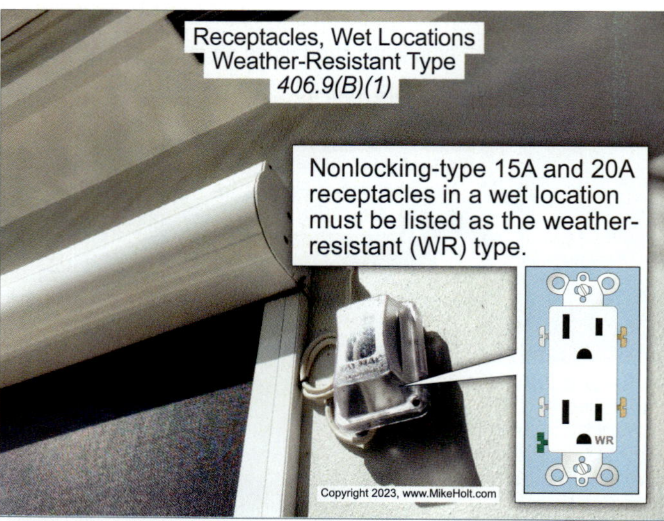

▶Figure 406–25

▶ A wet location is an area subject to saturation with water and unprotected locations exposed to weather [Article 100].

(2) Other Receptacles. Receptacles rated 30A or more installed in a wet location must <u>be listed as the weather-resistant type and</u> comply with (a) or (b).

(a) Unattended While in Use. A receptacle where the load is not attended while in use must be in an enclosure that is weatherproof when an attachment plug is inserted.

(b) Attended While in Use. A receptacle that will only be used while someone is nearby, such as one used with portable tools, can use an enclosure that is weatherproof when the cover is closed.

(C) Bathtub and Shower Space. Receptacles are not permitted <u>inside a tub or shower or</u> within 3 ft horizontally from any outside edge of a bathtub or shower stall. This includes <u>the space measured vertically from the floor</u> to 8 ft vertically above the top of the bathtub rim or shower stall threshold. ▶Figure 406–26

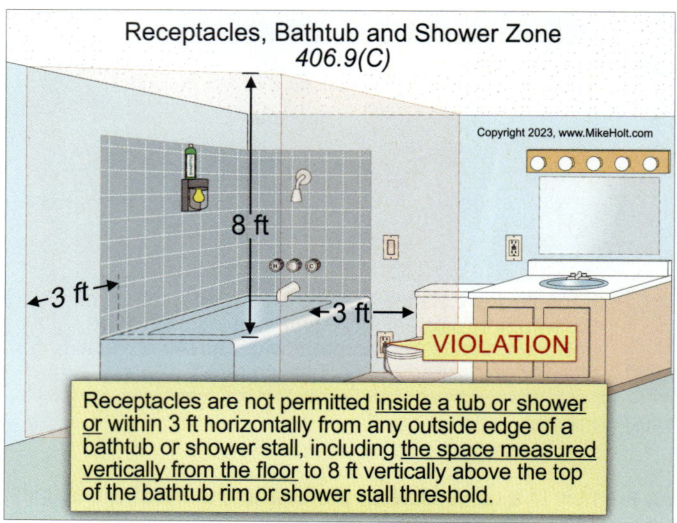

▶Figure 406–26

Ex 1: Receptacles for hydromassage bathtubs installed in accordance with 680.73 are permitted to be installed in the prohibited receptacle zone. ▶Figure 406–27

Ex 2: In dwelling unit bathrooms with less than the required zone, the bathroom sink receptacle, required by 210.52(D), is permitted to be located on the furthest wall opposite the bathtub rim or shower stall threshold. ▶Figure 406–28

Ex 4: In dwelling unit bathrooms, a single receptacle for an electronic toilet or electronic bidet seat is permitted in the prohibited receptacle zone if the receptacle is not in the space between the toilet and the bathtub or shower. ▶Figure 406–29

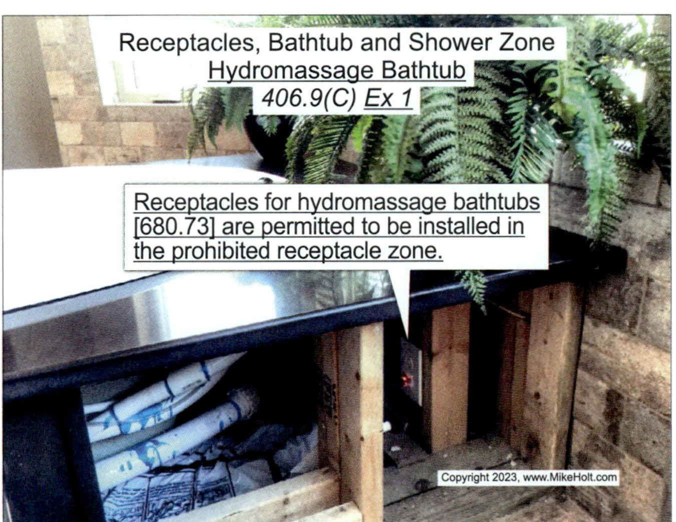

▶Figure 406–27

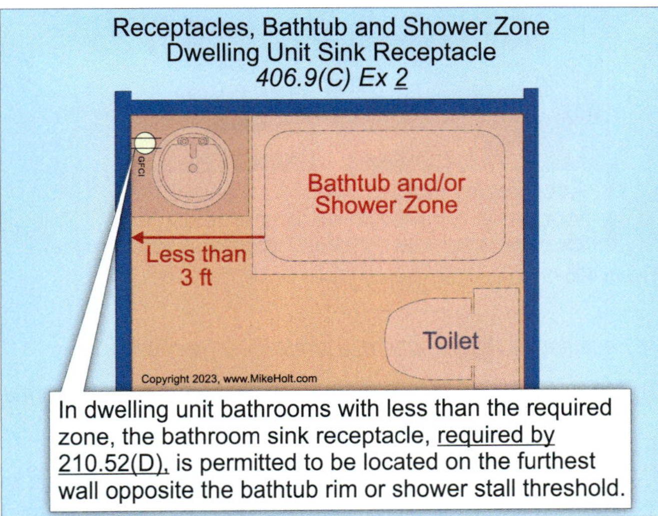

▶Figure 406–28

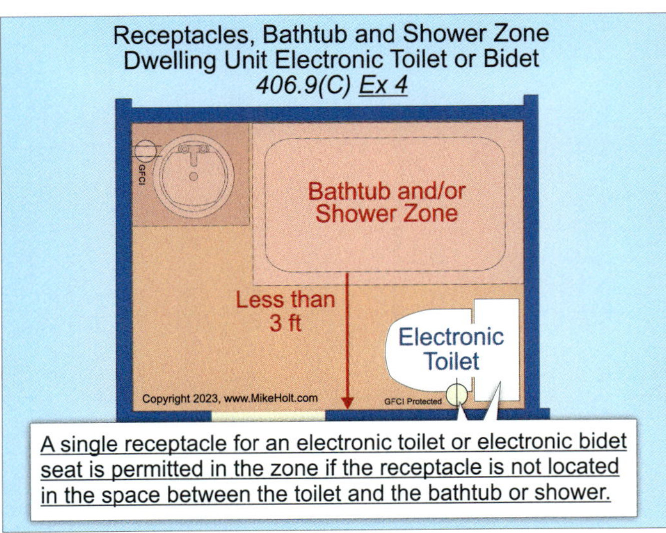

▶Figure 406–29

406.11 Connecting Receptacle Grounding Terminal to Equipment Grounding Conductor

The grounding terminal of receptacles must be connected to an equipment grounding conductor in accordance with 250.146.

406.12 Tamper-Resistant Receptacles

Nonlocking-type 15A and 20A receptacles in the following areas must be tamper resistant "TR" in:

Author's Comment:

▸ Inserting an object into one slot of a tamper-resistant receptacle does not open the internal shutter mechanism. Simultaneous pressure applied to the polarized slots is required to insert the plug. ▶Figure 406–30

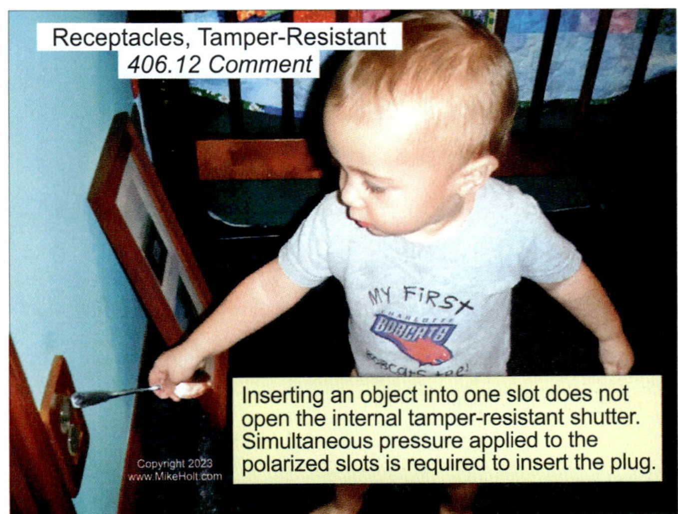

▶Figure 406–30

(1) Dwelling units, boathouses, mobile homes, and manufactured homes, including their attached or detached garages and accessory buildings, and common areas of multifamily dwellings

(2) Hotel and motel guest rooms and guest suites, and their common areas

(3) Childcare facilities

Author's Comment:

▸ A childcare facility is a building or portions of a building used for educational, supervision, or personal care services for five or more children seven years in age or less [Article 100].

(4) In preschools and education facilities

Author's Comment:

▸ This applies to all educational facilities including high schools, colleges, vocational schools, universities, and so forth.

(5) Clinics, medical and dental offices, outpatient facilities, and the following spaces:

a. Business offices accessible to the general public

b. Lobbies and waiting spaces

c. Spaces of nursing homes and limited care facilities used exclusively as patient sleeping rooms

(6) Places of awaiting transportation, gymnasiums, skating rinks, fitness centers, and auditoriums

(7) Dormitory units

(8) Residential care/assisted living facilities, social and substance abuse rehabilitation facilities, and group homes

(9) Foster care facilities, nursing homes, and psychiatric hospitals

(10) Areas and common areas of agricultural buildings accessible to the general public

Note 3: Areas of agricultural buildings frequently converted to hospitality areas include petting zoos, stables, and buildings used for recreation or educational purposes.

Ex to (1) through (10): Receptacles in the following locations are not required to be tamper resistant:

(1) Receptacles which are more than 5½ ft above the floor. ▸**Figure 406–31**

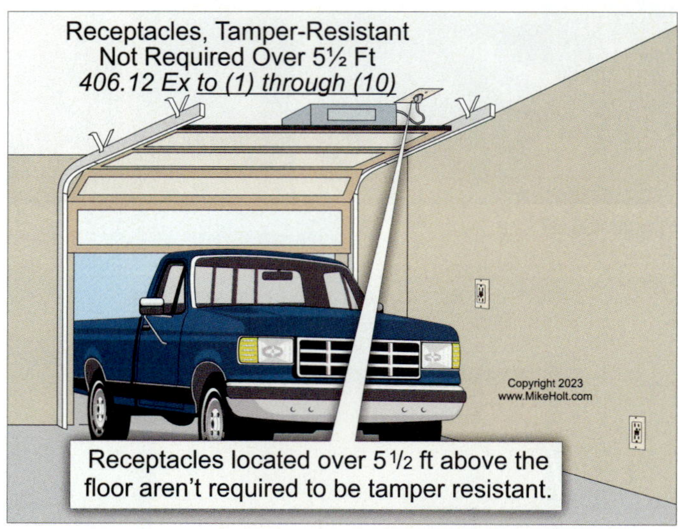

▸Figure 406–31

(2) Receptacles that are part of a luminaire or appliance.

(3) A receptacle within dedicated space for an appliance that in normal use is not easily moved.

(4) Nongrounding receptacles installed as permitted in 406.4(D)(2)(a).

SWITCHBOARDS AND PANELBOARDS

Introduction to Article 408—Switchboards and Panelboards

Article 408 covers the specific requirements for switchboards and panelboards that control power and lighting circuits. Since these rules address the equipment at the heart of the premises electrical system, take some time to become familiar with them. Some topics covered in this material include:

- Support and Arrangement of Busbars and Conductors
- Circuit Identification
- Clearance from Conductors Entering Enclosures
- Short-Circuit Current Ratings
- Unused Openings
- Replacement Panelboards
- Damp or Wet Locations
- Locations
- Energy Management Systems
- Enclosures
- Grounding and Grounded Conductor Terminations
- Orientation

This article consists of four parts:

- Part I. General
- Part II. Switchboards and Switchgear
- Part III. Panelboards
- Part IV. Construction Specifications

Author's Comment:

▶ The slang term in the electrical field for a panelboard is "the guts." The requirements for panelboards are contained in Article 408.

Part I. General

408.1 Scope

Article 408 covers the requirements for switchboards and panelboards that control power and lighting circuits. ▶Figure 408–1

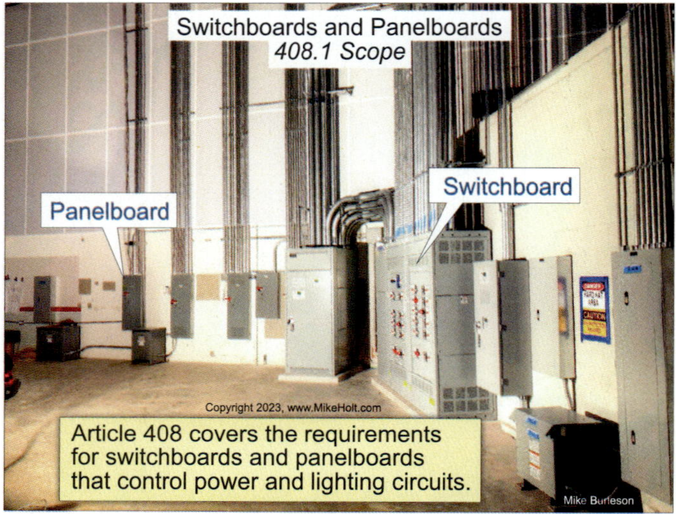

▶Figure 408–1

408.3 Arrangement of Busbars and Conductors

According to Article 100, "Panelboard" is an assembly with buses and overcurrent protective devices designed to be placed in a cabinet or enclosure. ▶Figure 408–2 .

(E) Bus Arrangement.

(1) Alternating-Current Phase Arrangement. Panelboards supplied by a 4-wire, delta-connected, three-phase (high-leg) system must have the high-leg conductor (which operates at 208V to ground) terminate to the "B" phase of the panelboard. ▶Figure 408–3

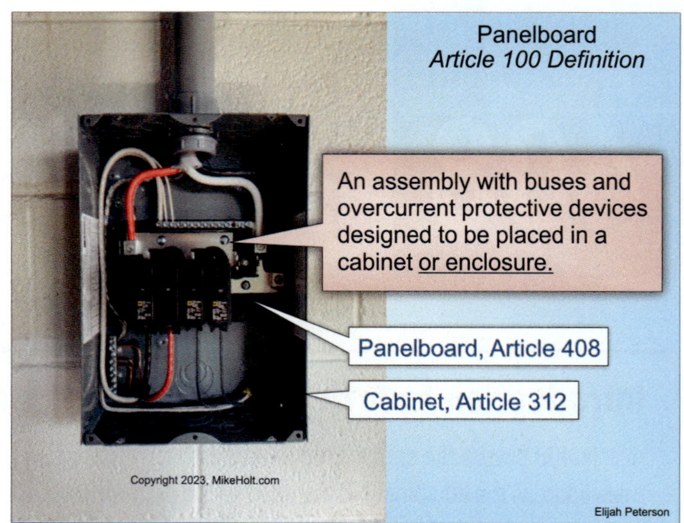

▶Figure 408–2

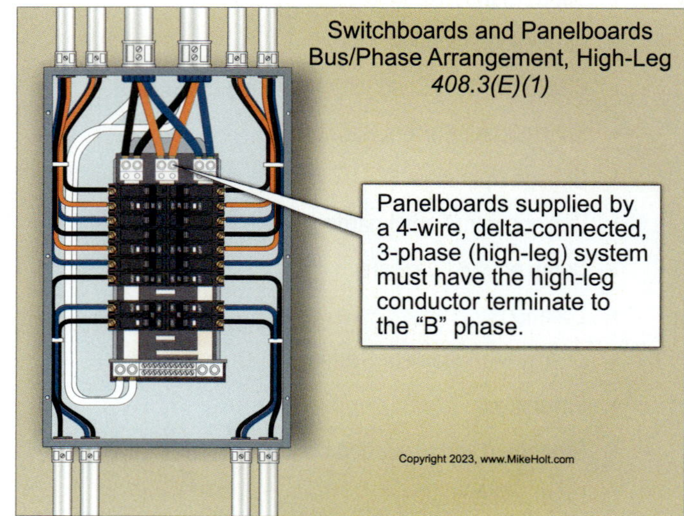

▶Figure 408–3

Note: On a 4-wire, delta-connected, three-phase system, where the midpoint of one phase winding of the secondary is grounded, the conductor with the resulting 208V to ground (high-leg) must be durably and permanently marked by an outer finish (insulation) that is orange in color or other effective means [110.15]. Such identification must be placed at each point where a connection is made if the neutral conductor is present [230.56]. ▶Figure 408–4

Warning

⚠ **WARNING:** The ANSI standard for meter equipment requires the high-leg conductor (208V to neutral) to terminate on the "C" (right) phase of the meter socket enclosure. This is because the demand meter needs 120V which it gets from the "B" phase.

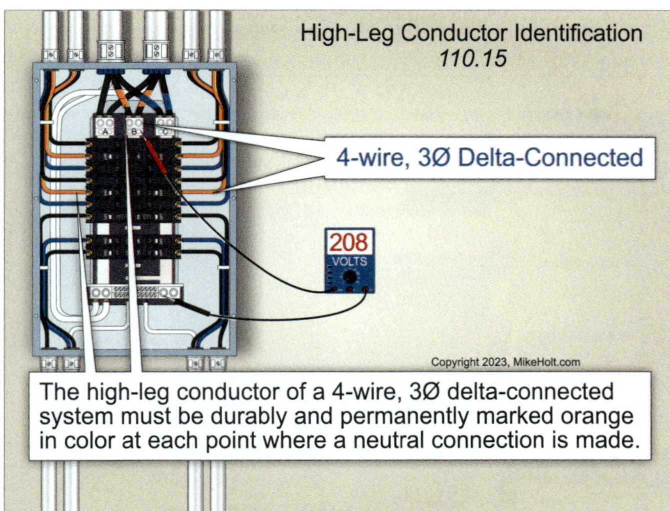

The high-leg conductor of a 4-wire, 3Ø delta-connected system must be durably and permanently marked orange in color at each point where a neutral connection is made.

▶Figure 408–4

Warning

WARNING: When replacing equipment in existing facilities that contain a high-leg conductor, use care to ensure the high-leg conductor is replaced in the original phase position. Prior to 1975, the high-leg conductor was required to terminate on the "C" phase of panelboards and switchboards. Failure to re-terminate the high-leg in accordance with the existing installation can result in 120V circuits being inadvertently connected to the 208V high-leg, with disastrous results. ▶Figure 408–5

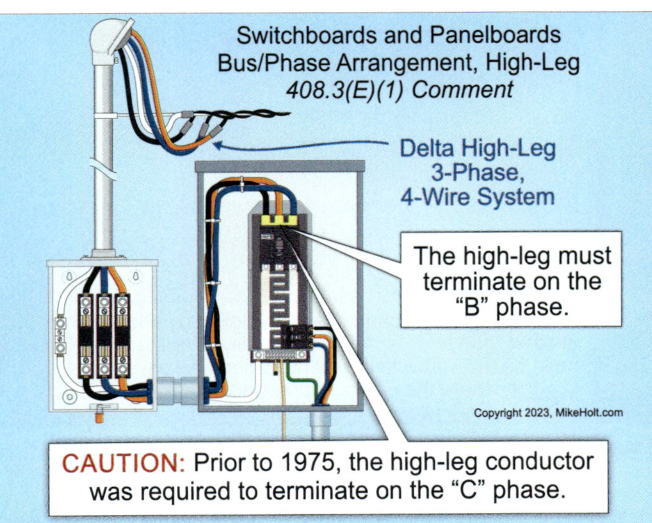

▶Figure 408–5

(F) Switchboard and Panelboard Identification.

(1) High-Leg Identification. A switchboard or panelboard containing a 4-wire, delta-connected system where the midpoint of one phase winding is grounded, must have a label that is legibly and permanently field marked as follows: "CAUTION _______ PHASE HAS _______ VOLTS TO GROUND" ▶Figure 408–6

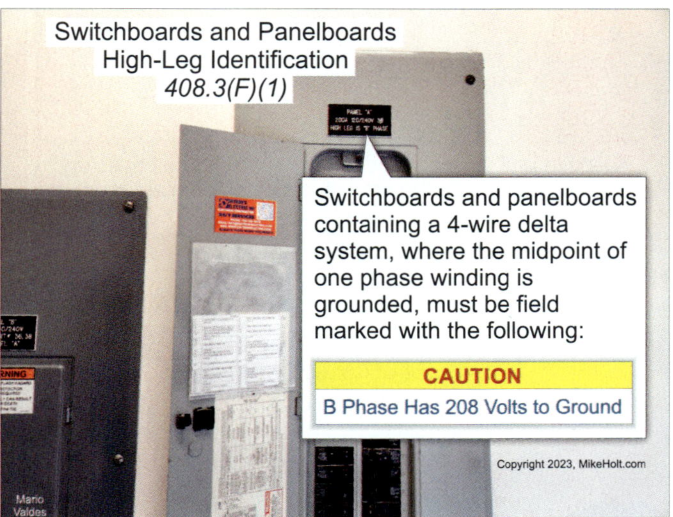

▶Figure 408–6

(G) Wire Bending Space. The minimum wire bending space at terminals provided in switchboards and panelboards must comply with 312.6.

408.4 Circuit Directory and Description

(A) Circuit Descriptions. Circuits and circuit modifications must be provided with a legible and permanent description on a circuit directory.

(1) Switchboard. The circuit description must be located at each circuit breaker in a switchboard.

(2) Panelboard. The circuit description must be located on the face, inside, or in an approved location adjacent to the panel door. ▶Figure 408–7

(3) Purpose of Circuit Description. The circuit description must be clear and specific to the purpose or use of each circuit, including spare positions for unused overcurrent protective devices. ▶Figure 408–8

(4) Circuit Description Details. The circuit description must have a degree of detail and clarity that is unlikely to result in confusion between circuits.

(5) Transient Conditions. The circuit description must not be dependent on transient conditions of occupancy such as "Dad's Office." ▶Figure 408–9

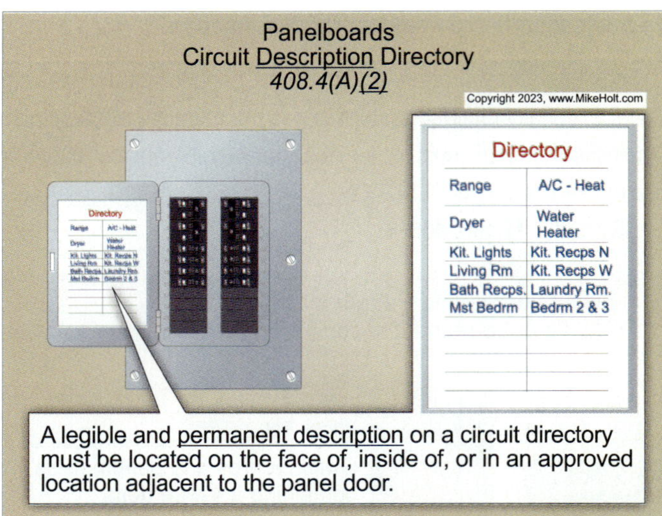

A legible and permanent description on a circuit directory must be located on the face of, inside of, or in an approved location adjacent to the panel door.

▶Figure 408–7

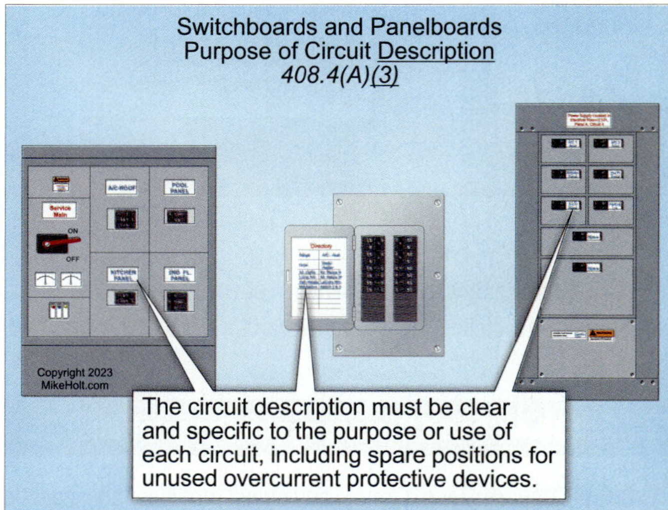

The circuit description must be clear and specific to the purpose or use of each circuit, including spare positions for unused overcurrent protective devices.

▶Figure 408–8

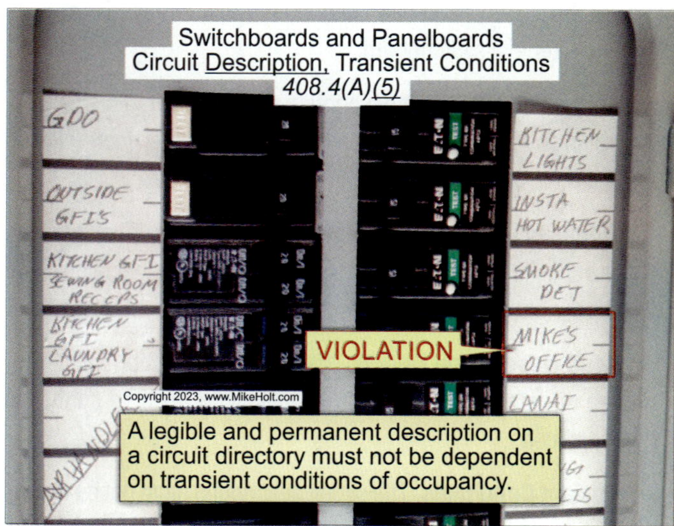

A legible and permanent description on a circuit directory must not be dependent on transient conditions of occupancy.

▶Figure 408–9

(6) Abbreviations and Symbols. The circuit description must be clear in explaining abbreviations and symbols when used. ▶Figure 408–10

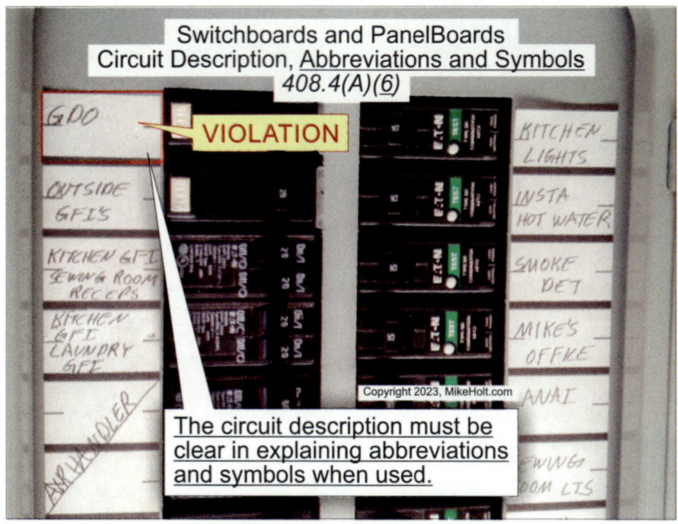

The circuit description must be clear in explaining abbreviations and symbols when used.

▶Figure 408–10

(B) Description of Source of Supply. Switchboards and panelboards supplied by a feeder, in other than one- family or two-family dwelling units, must be marked as follows:

(1) With the identification and physical location where the power supply originates. ▶Figure 408–11

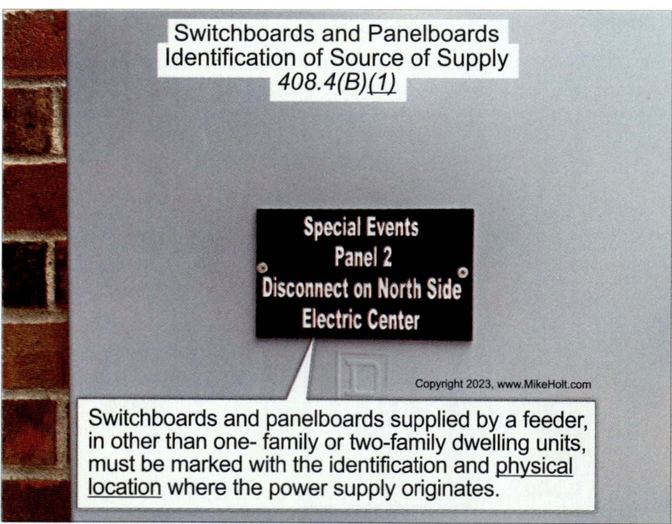

Switchboards and panelboards supplied by a feeder, in other than one- family or two-family dwelling units, must be marked with the identification and physical location where the power supply originates.

▶Figure 408–11

(2) With a permanent label that withstands the environment involved in accordance with 110.22(A).

(3) A method that is not handwritten must be used.

408.5 Clearance for Conductors Entering Bus Enclosures

If raceways enter a switchboard, floor-standing panelboard, or similar enclosure, the raceways (including end fittings) are not permitted to rise more than 3 in. above the bottom of the enclosure.

408.6 Short-Circuit Current Rating

Switchboards and panelboards must have a short-circuit current rating not less than the available fault current on the line side of the equipment. In other than one- and two-dwelling units, the available fault current and the date the calculation was performed must be marked on the enclosure. The marking must be sufficiently durable to withstand the environment involved in accordance with 110.21(B)(3). ▶**Figure 408–12**

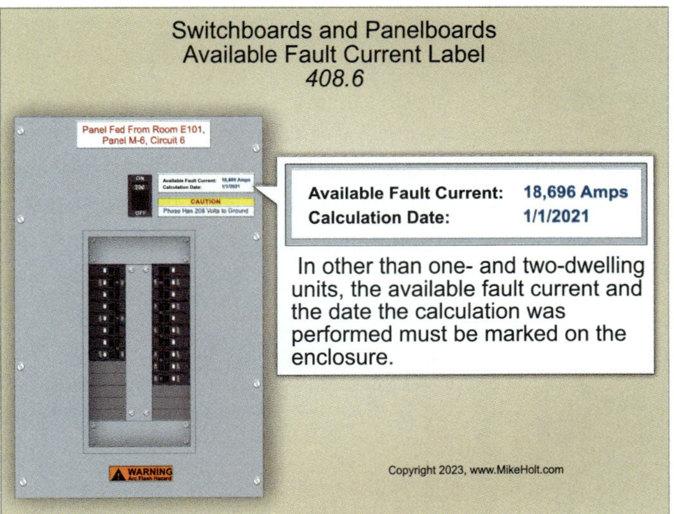

▶Figure 408–12

408.7 Unused Openings

Unused openings for circuit breakers must be closed using identified closures (or other approved means) which provide protection substantially equivalent to the wall of the enclosure. ▶**Figure 408–13**

408.9 Replacement Panelboards

(B) Panelboards Not Listed for the Specific Enclosure.

10,000A and Greater. If the available fault current is greater than 10,000A, the completed work must be field labeled.

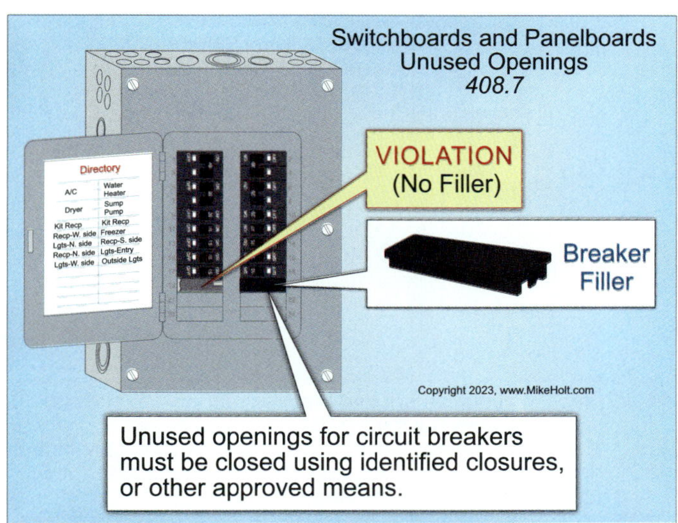

▶Figure 408–13

According to Article 100, "Field Labeled" is defined as "equipment or materials which have a label, symbol, or other identifying mark of a field evaluation body (FEB) indicating the equipment or materials were evaluated and found to comply with the requirements described in the accompanying field evaluation report."

"Field Evaluation Body (FEB)" is an organization (or part of an organization) that performs field evaluations of electrical equipment and materials.

Not Over 10,000A. If the available fault current is 10,000A or less, the replacement panelboard must be identified for the application. Any previously applied listing marks on the cabinet that pertain to the panelboard must be removed.

Part II. Switchboards

408.18 Clearances

(A) From Ceiling. For other than a totally enclosed switchboard, a space of not less than 3 ft must be provided between the top of the switchboard and any combustible ceiling unless a noncombustible shield is provided between the switchboard and the ceiling.

(B) Around Switchboards. Clearances around switchboards must comply with 110.26.

(C) Connections. Each section of equipment that requires rear or side access to make field connections must be so marked by the manufacturer on the front of the equipment. Section openings requiring rear or side access must comply with the workspace and access to workspace requirements of 110.26. ▶**Figure 408–14**

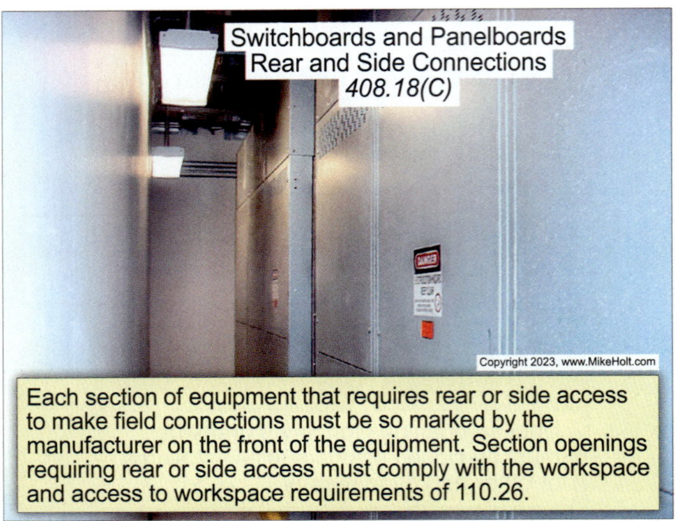

▶Figure 408–14

Part III. Panelboards

408.30 Panelboard Rating

The panelboard rating must not be less than the minimum feeder capacity as determined by load calculations in accordance with Article 220, as applicable.

408.36 Overcurrent Protection

Panelboards must be provided with overcurrent protection within or at any point on the supply side of the panelboard with a rating not greater than the panelboard. ▶Figure 408–15

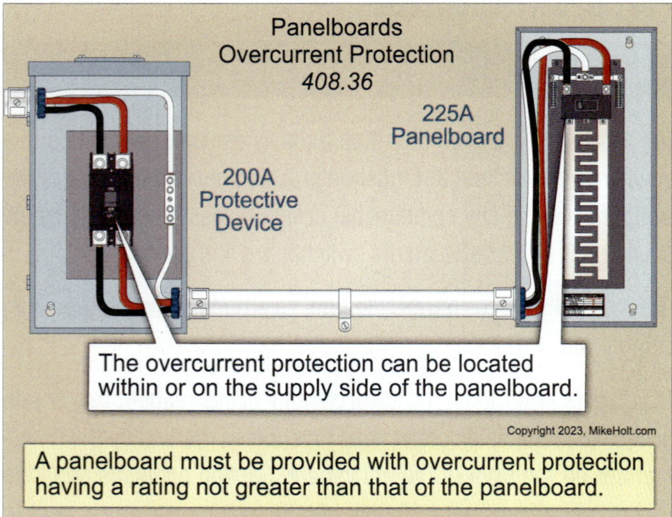

▶Figure 408–15

(B) Panelboards Supplied by a Transformer. When a panelboard is supplied from a transformer, as permitted in 240.21(C), the overcurrent protection for the panelboard can be in an enclosure ahead of the panelboard or within the panelboard. ▶Figure 408–16

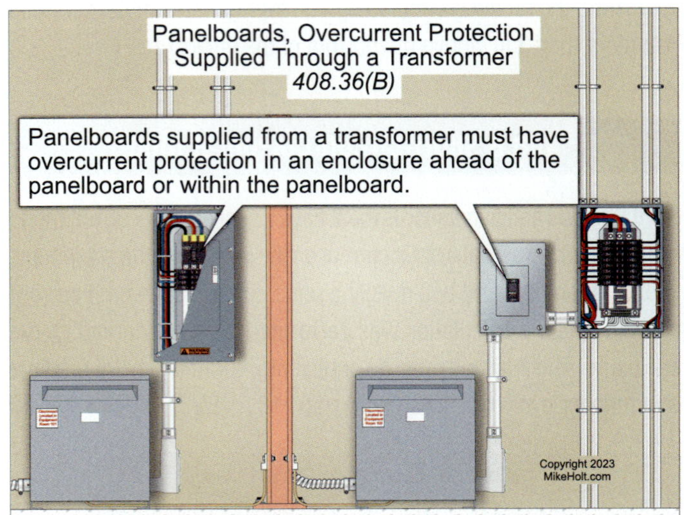

▶Figure 408–16

(D) Back-Fed Devices. Plug-in circuit breakers that are backfed must be secured in place by a fastener that requires other than a pull to release the breaker from the panelboard. ▶Figure 408–17

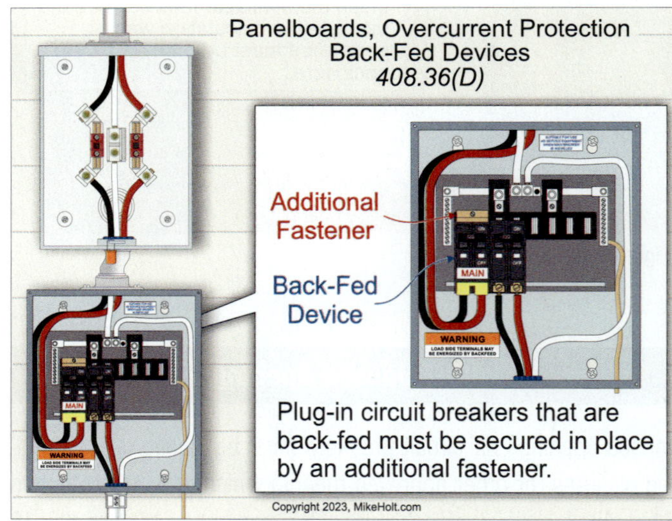

▶Figure 408–17

Author's Comment:

▶ The purpose of the breaker fastener is to prevent the circuit breaker from being accidentally removed from the panelboard while energized, thereby exposing someone to dangerous voltage.

CAUTION: Circuit breakers marked "Line" and "Load" must be installed in accordance with listing or labeling instructions [110.3(B)]. These types of devices are therefore not permitted to be backfed.

408.37 Panelboards in Damp or Wet Locations

Cabinets for panelboards installed in damp or wet locations must be weatherproof in accordance with 312.2.

408.38 Enclosure

Panelboards must be mounted in cabinets, cutout boxes, or identified enclosures and must have dead-front covers.

408.40 Equipment Grounding Conductor

Where equipment grounding conductors of the wire-type enter an enclosed panelboard, they must terminate to a grounding terminal bar within the enclosed panelboard. ▶Figure 408–18

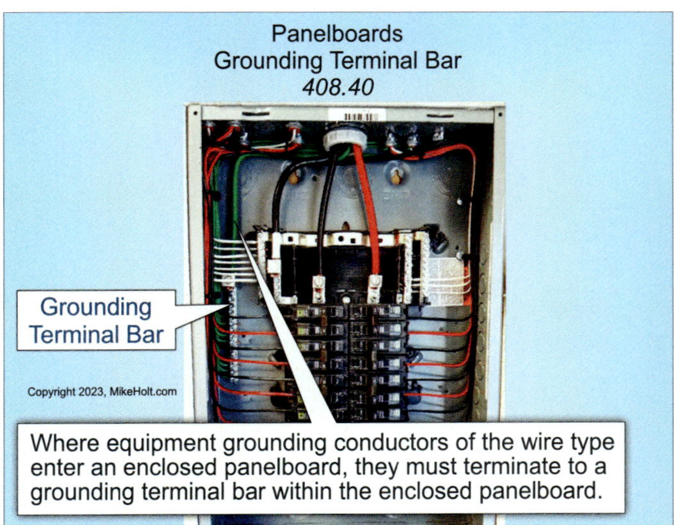

▶Figure 408–18

Equipment grounding conductors are not permitted to terminate on the neutral terminal bar except as permitted by 250.142(D) for services and 250.30(A) for separately derived systems. ▶Figure 408–19

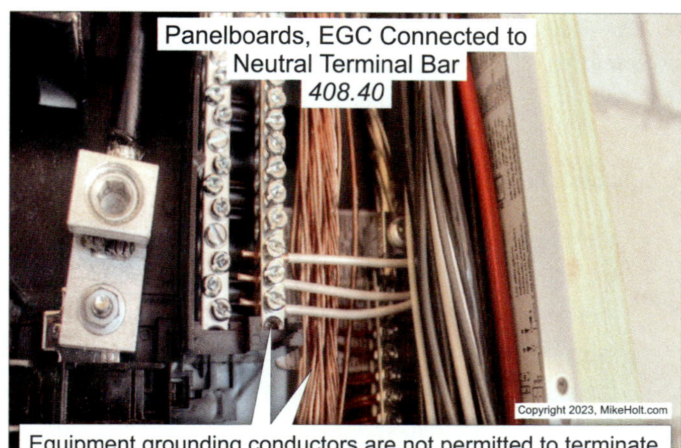

▶Figure 408–19

CAUTION: Many panelboards are rated for use as service disconnects, which means they are supplied with a main bonding jumper [250.28]. This screw or strap is not permitted to be installed except when the panelboard is used for a service disconnect [250.24(B)] or separately derived system [250.30(A)(1)].

408.41 Neutral Conductor Terminations

Each neutral conductor within a panelboard must terminate in an individual terminal. ▶Figure 408–20

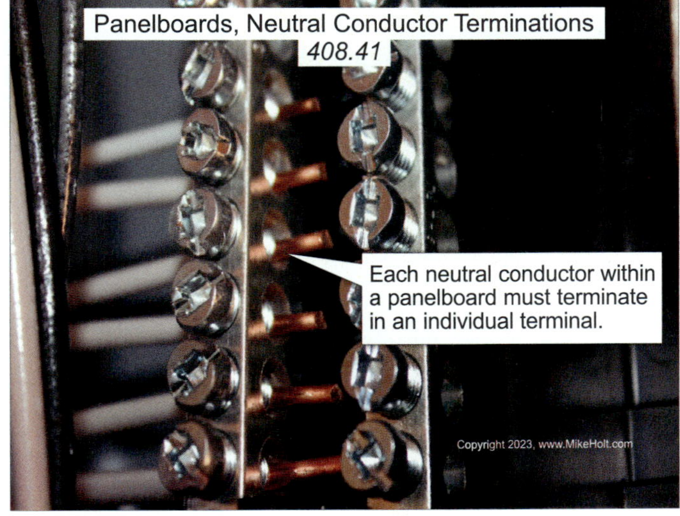

▶Figure 408–20

Ex: Neutral conductors run in parallel are permitted to terminate to a single terminal if the terminal is identified for more than one conductor [110.14(A)]

Author's Comment:

▶ If two neutral conductors are connected to the same terminal, and someone removes one of them, the other neutral conductor might unintentionally be removed as well. If that happens to the neutral conductor of a multiwire circuit, it can result in excessive line-to-neutral voltage for one of the circuits, as well as undervoltage for the other. See 300.13(B) of this material for details. ▶**Figure 408–21**

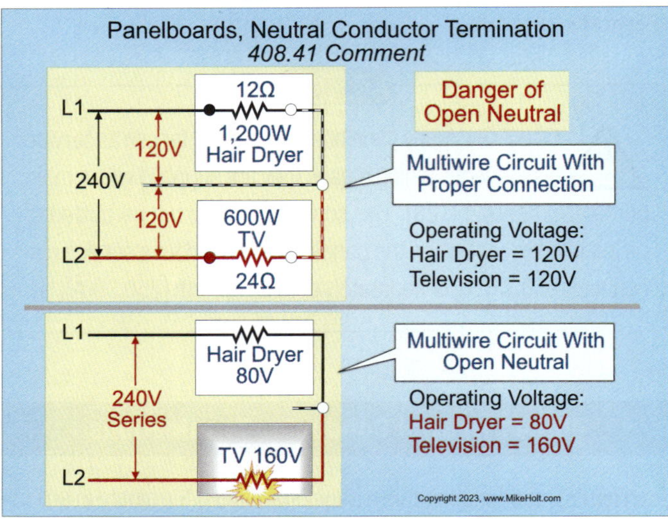

▶Figure 408–21

408.43 Panelboard Orientation

408.43 Panelboard Orientation

Panelboards are not permitted to be installed in the face-up <u>or face-down</u> position. ▶Figure 408–22

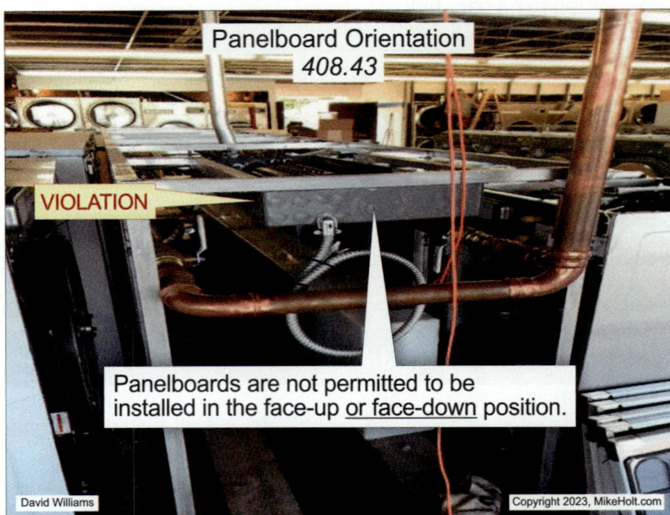

▶Figure 408–22

GENERATORS

Introduction to Article 445—Generators

This article contains the installation and other requirements for generators and generator sets. Rules located here include such things as where generators can be installed, nameplate markings, conductor ampacity, transference of power, and disconnect requirements. Some topics covered in this material include:

- ▸ Installation Locations
- ▸ Marking
- ▸ Overcurrent Protection
- ▸ Conductor Ampacity
- ▸ Disconnecting Means and Emergency Shutdown
- ▸ Portable Generators

445.1 Scope

Article 445 contains the installation requirements for generators.
▸Figure 445–1

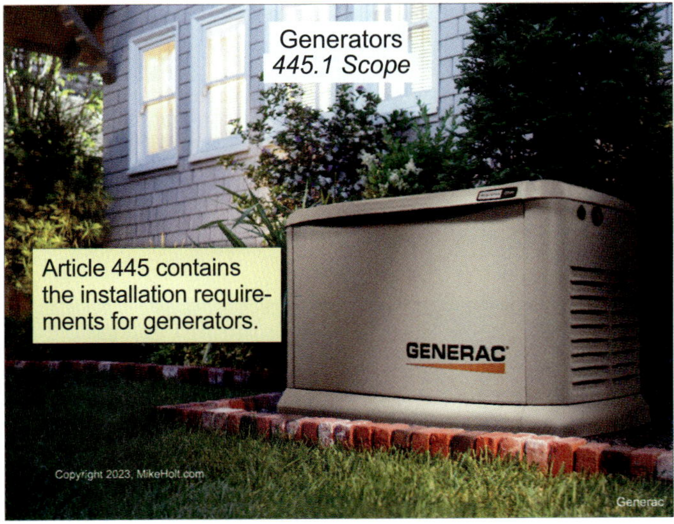

▸Figure 445–1

According to Article 100, "Generator" is a machine that converts mechanical energy into electrical energy by means of a prime mover. ▸Figure 445–2

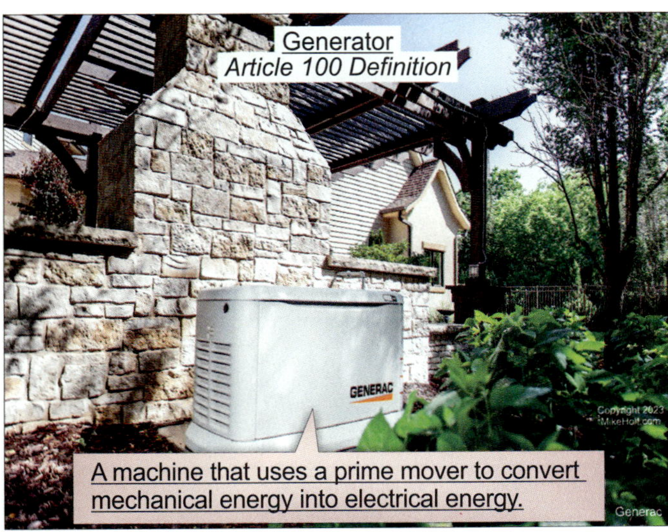

▸Figure 445–2

According to Article 100, "Prime Mover" is a machine that supplies mechanical horsepower to a generator. ▶Figure 445–3

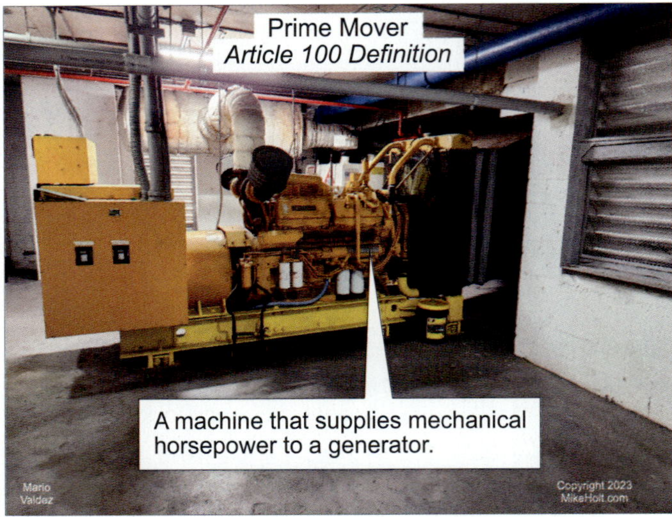

▶Figure 445–3

445.6 Listing

Stationary generators must be listed. ▶Figure 445–4

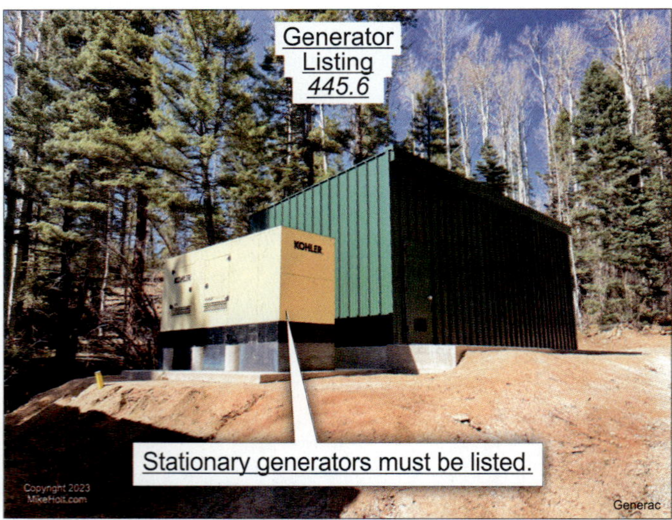

▶Figure 445–4

445.11 Marking

The generators nameplate must include the manufacturer's name, rated frequency, number of phases, rating in kilowatts or kilovolt-amperes, power factor, and the volts and amperes. ▶Figure 445–5

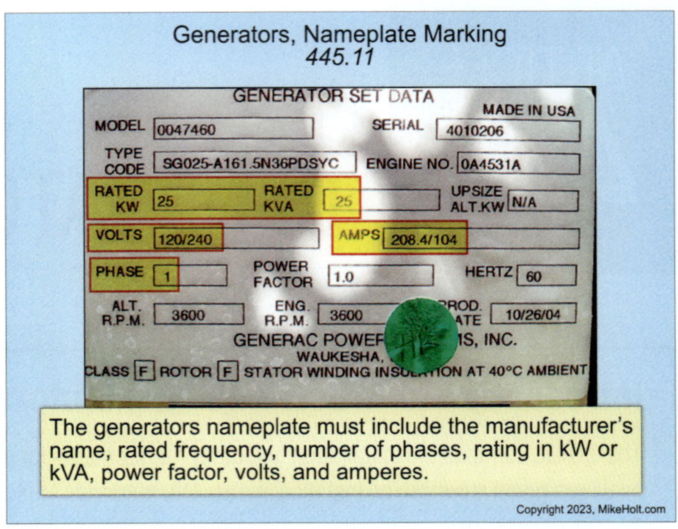

▶Figure 445–5

Markings by the manufacturer must indicate whether the neutral is bonded to the frame or not. If the manufacturer bonding is modified in the field, field marking is required to indicate if the neutral is bonded to the frame. ▶Figure 445–6

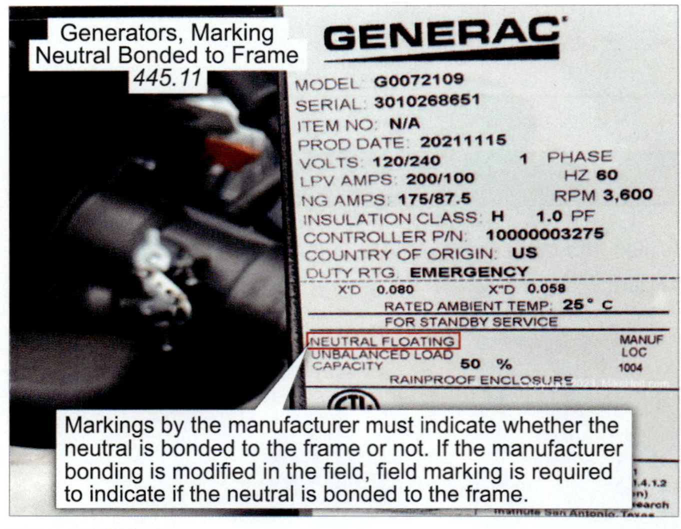

▶Figure 445–6

445.13 Conductor Ampacity

(A) General. The ampacity of the conductors from the generator winding to the first overcurrent protective device must not be less than 115 percent of the generator's nameplate current rating. ▶Figure 445–7

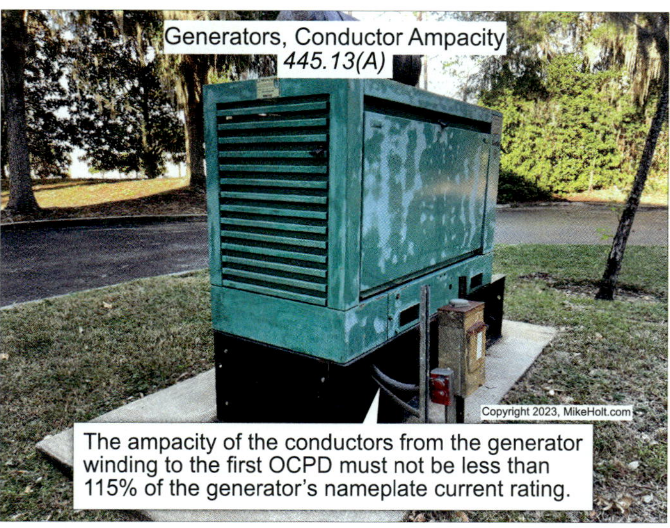

▶Figure 445–7

Author's Comment:

▶ Since the overcurrent protective device is typically part of the generator, this 115-percent rule applies to the generator manufacturer—not the field installer.

▶ Conductors from the load side of the generator OCPD to the transfer switch are sized to the generator's overcurrent protective device rating in accordance with 240.4. ▶Figure 445–8

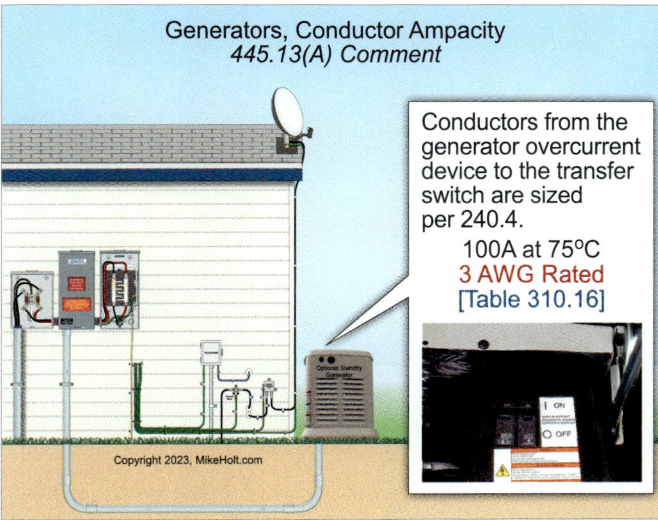

▶Figure 445–8

445.18 Disconnecting Means

(A) Disconnect Required. Each fixed generator must have a disconnect that is capable of being locked in the open position in accordance with 110.25. ▶Figure 445–9

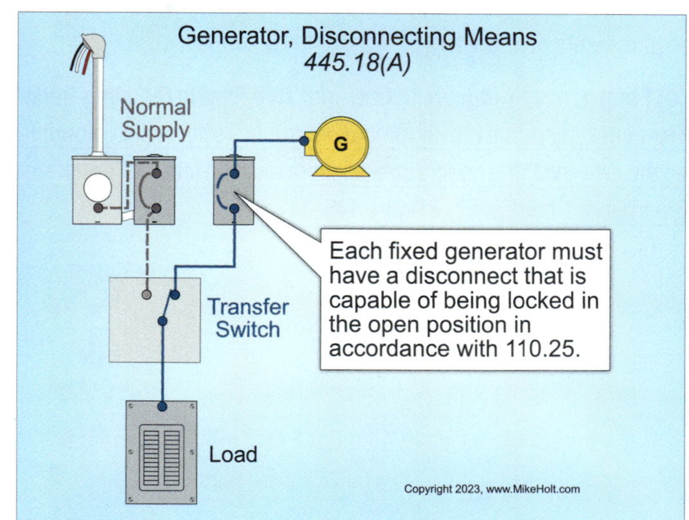

▶Figure 445–9

445.19 Emergency Shutdown of Prime Mover

(B) Commercial and Industrial Installations. Generators with greater than 15 kW rating must be provided with a remote emergency stop switch to shut down the prime mover. ▶Figure 445–10

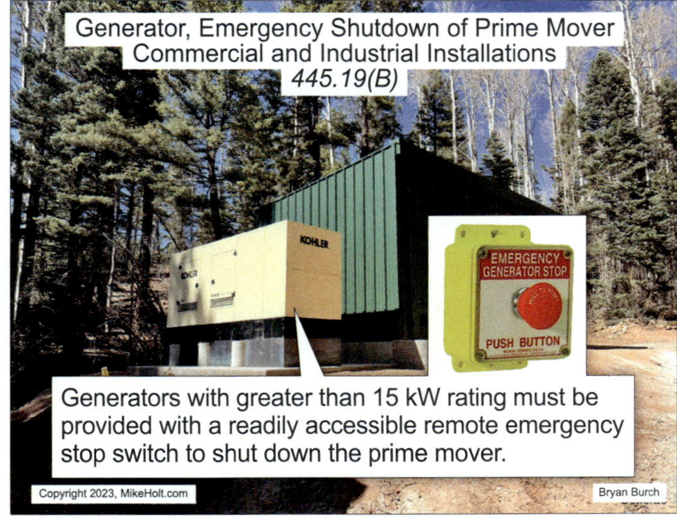

▶Figure 445–10

Location. The remote emergency stop switch must be located outside the equipment room or generator enclosure at a readily accessible location. The remote emergency stop switch is permitted to be mounted on the exterior of the generator enclosure.

Labeling. The remote emergency stop switch must be labeled "Generator Emergency Shutdown," and the label shall meet the requirements of 110.21(B).

(C) Emergency Shutdown in One- and Two-Family Dwelling Units. The generator prime mover remote emergency stop switch mounted on the exterior of the generator enclosure must be labeled "Generator Emergency Shutdown." ▶Figure 445–11

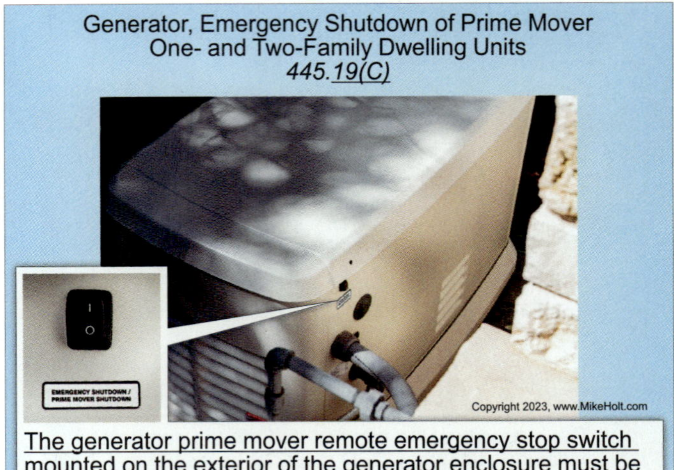

The generator prime mover remote emergency stop switch mounted on the exterior of the generator enclosure must be labeled "Generator Emergency Shutdown."

▶Figure 445–11

450 TRANSFORMERS

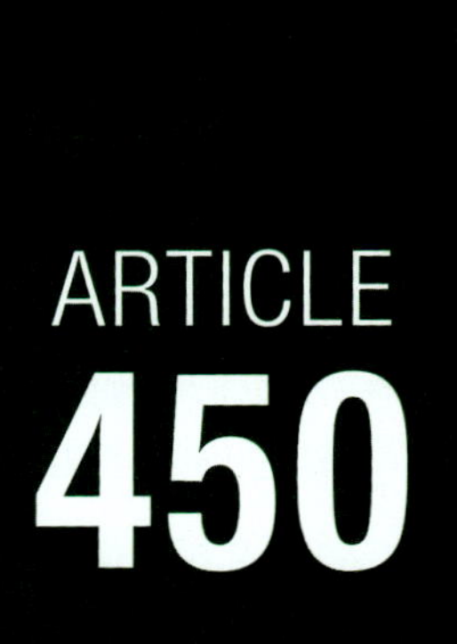

Introduction to Article 450—Transformers

Article 450 covers the installation requirements for transformers supplying power and lighting loads. Those types of transformers not covered by these rules are listed in the "Scope" section of this article. While the *NEC* does not provide design criteria for transformers, it does give an extensive set of rules to ensure a properly selected transformer can be installed and perform as intended by the designer. Several sections of this article fall outside the scope of this material and will not be covered. Some covered topics include:

▶ Overcurrent Protection

▶ Ventilation

▶ Grounding and Bonding

▶ Accessibility

▶ Disconnect Requirements

▶ Transformer Types

This article consists of three parts:

▶ Part I. General

▶ Part II. Installation

▶ Part III. Transformer Vaults

450.1 Scope

Article 450 covers the installation requirements of all transformers other than the following: ▶Figure 450–1

1. Current transformers.

2. Transformers that constitute a component part of another apparatus.

3. Transformers that are an integral part of an X-ray, high-frequency, or electrostatic-coating apparatus.

4. Transformers for Class 2 and Class 3 power-limited circuits.

5. Transformers for signs.

6. Transformers for electric-discharge lighting.

7. Transformers for power-limited fire alarm circuits.

8. Transformers used for research, development, or testing.

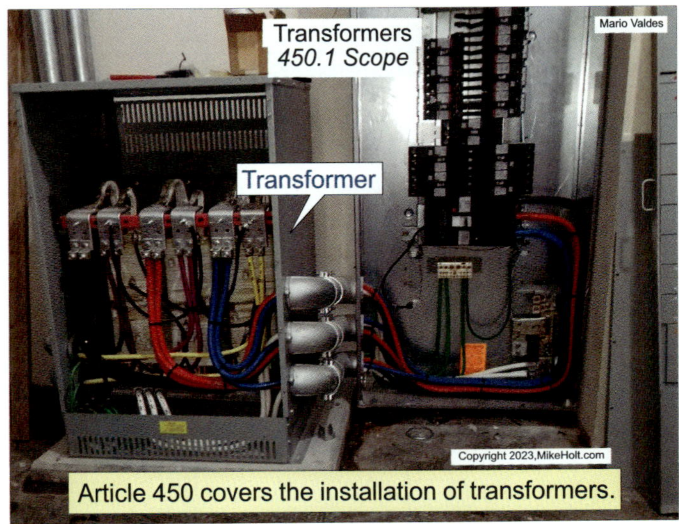

▶Figure 450–1

According to Article 100, a "Transformer" uses electromagnetic induction to convert current and voltage in a primary circuit into current and voltage in a secondary circuit. ▶**Figure 450–2**

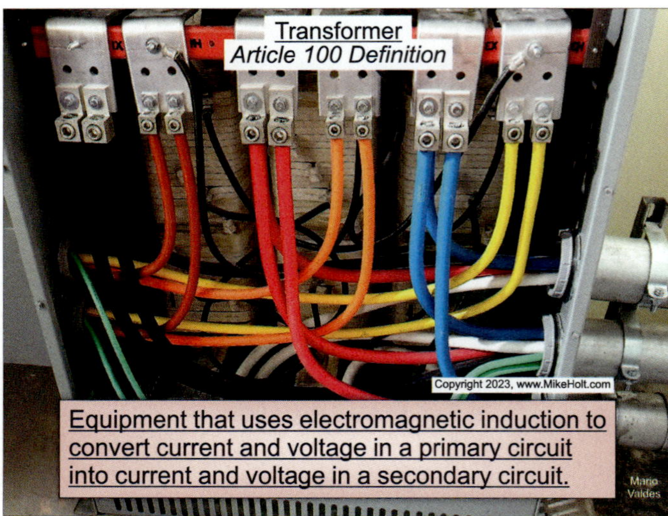

▶Figure 450–2

450.3 Primary Overcurrent Protection

(B) Transformer 1,000V or Less. Transformers' primary only overcurrent protective device must have the primary overcurrent protective device sized in accordance with Table 450.3(B) based on the primary nameplate current rating and its applicable notes.

Table 450.3(B) Primary Protection Only	
Primary Current Rating	**Maximum Protection**
Less than 2A	300%
2A to 9A	167%
More Than 9A	125%[1]

Note 1: Transformers with a primary current rating of 9A (or more) are permitted to use the "next size up" rule when 125 percent of the primary current does not correspond to the standard rating of a fuse or circuit breaker listed in 240.6(A).

▶ **Primary Only Protection—Primary Current Less than 2A Example**

Question: What is the maximum primary only overcurrent protective device rating for a 750 VA, single-phase, 480V transformer? ▶Figure 450–3

(a) 3A   *(b) 6A*   *(c) 10A*   *(d) 15A*

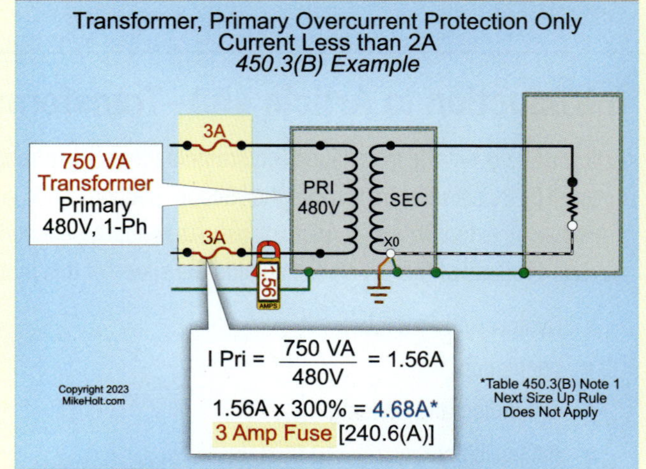

▶Figure 450–3

Solution:

Primary Current = Transformer VA Rating/Primary Voltage
Primary Current = 750 VA/480V
Primary Current = 1.56A

Primary Protection = Primary Current × Table 450.3(B) Percentage
Primary Protection = 1.56A × 300%
Primary Protection = 4.68A

Use a 3A overcurrent protective device [240.6(A) and Table 450.3(B)].

Answer: *(a) 3A*

▶ Primary Only Protection—Primary Current 2A to 9A Example

Question: What is the maximum primary only overcurrent protective device rating for a 2 kVA, single-phase, 240V transformer? ▶**Figure 450–4**

(a) 3A   (b) 6A   (c) 10A   (d) 15A

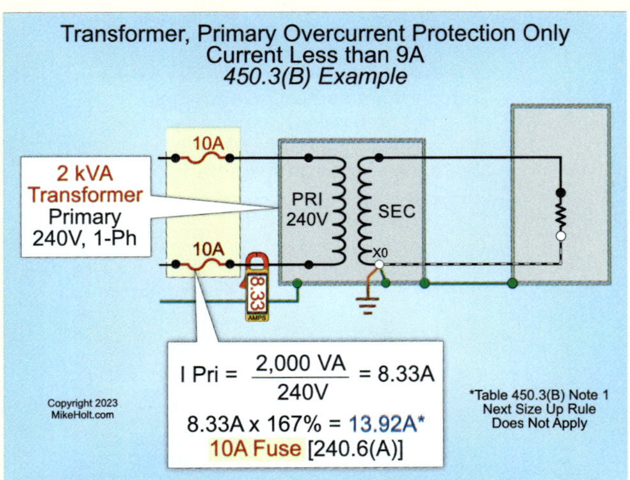

▶Figure 450–4

Solution:

Primary Current = Transformer VA Rating/Primary Voltage
Primary Current = 2,000 VA/240V
Primary Current = 8.33A

Primary Protection = Primary Current × Table 450.3(B) Percentage
Primary Protection = 8.33A × 167%
Primary Protection = 13.92A

Use a 10A overcurrent protective device [240.6(A) and Table 450.3(B)].

Answer: *(c) 10A*

▶ Primary Only Protection—Primary Current Greater than 9A Example

Question: What is the maximum primary only overcurrent protective device rating for a 30 kVA, three-phase, 480V to 120/208V transformer? ▶**Figure 450–5**

(a) 40A   (b) 45A   (c) 50A   (d) 60A

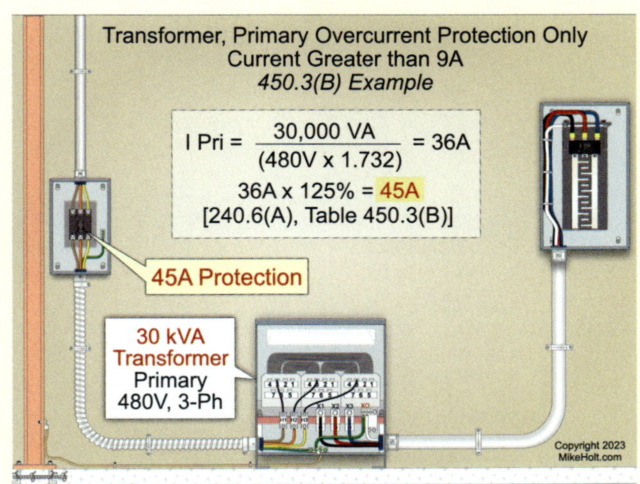

▶Figure 450–5

Solution:

Primary Current = Transformer VA Rating/ (Primary Voltage × 1.732)
Primary Current = 30,000 VA/(480V × 1.732)
Primary Current = 30,000 VA/831.36V)
Primary Current = 36A

Primary Protection = Primary Current × Table 450.3(B) Percentage
Primary Protection = 36A × 125%
Primary Protection = 45A

Use a 45A overcurrent protective device [240.6(A) and Table 450.3(B)].

Answer: *(b) 45A*

▶ Primary Only Protection—Primary Current Greater than 9A, Note 1 Example

Question: What is the maximum primary only overcurrent protective device rating for a 45 kVA, three-phase, 480V to 120/208V transformer? ▶Figure 450–6

(a) 50A   (b) 60A   (c) 70A   (d) 100A

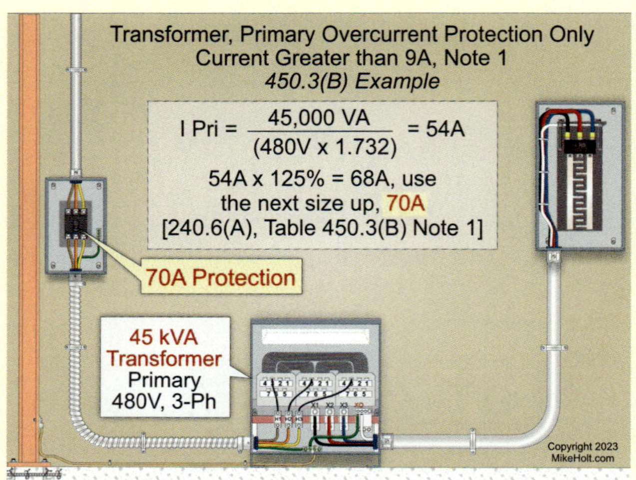

▶Figure 450–6

Solution:

Primary Current = Transformer VA Rating/(Primary Voltage × 1.732)

Primary Current = 45,000 VA/(480V × 1.732)

Primary Current = 45,000 VA/831.36V

Primary Current = 54A

Primary Protection = Primary Current × Table 450.3(B) Percentage

Primary Protection = 54A × 125%

Primary Protection = 68A

Use a 70A overcurrent protective device [240.6(A) and Table 450.3(B) Note 1].

*Answer: (c) 70A **

**According to Note 1 of Table 450.3(B), transformers having a primary current rating of 9A or more are permitted to use the "next size up" rule when 125 percent of the primary current does not correspond to the standard rating of a fuse or nonadjustable circuit breaker listed in 240.6(A). This Note does not require the next size up protection, it permits the use of the next size up protective device.*

450.9 Ventilation

Transformers with ventilating openings must be installed so they are not blocked by walls or other obstructions. The required clearances from the ventilation openings must be clearly marked on the transformer. ▶Figure 450–7

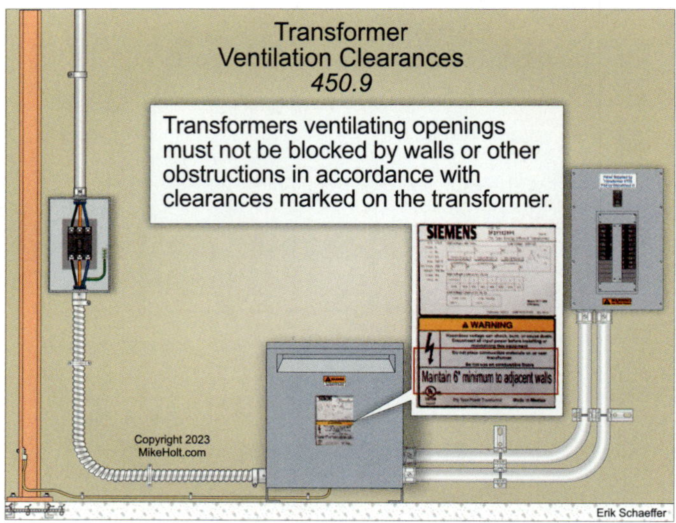

▶Figure 450–7

The top surface of transformers that are horizontal and readily accessible must be marked to prohibit storage.

450.10 Grounding and Bonding

(A) Dry-Type Transformer Enclosures. A grounding terminal bar must be installed inside the transformer enclosure in accordance with 250.12, but not on or over any vented portions of the transformer case. ▶Figure 450–8

450.13 Transformer Accessibility

(A) Open Installations. Dry-type transformers are required to be readily accessible, unless located on open walls or columns. ▶Figure 450–9

(B) Above Suspended Ceilings. Dry-type transformers are required to be readily accessible, unless rated not more than 50 kVA installed in hollow spaces of building, such as above a suspended ceiling. ▶Figure 450–10

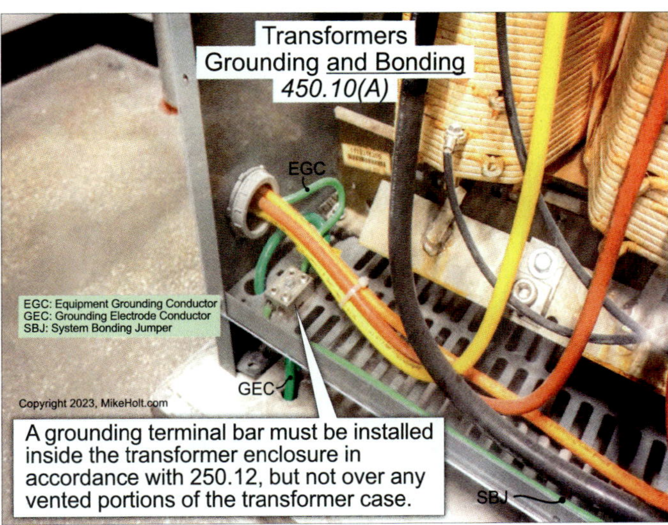

▶Figure 450–8

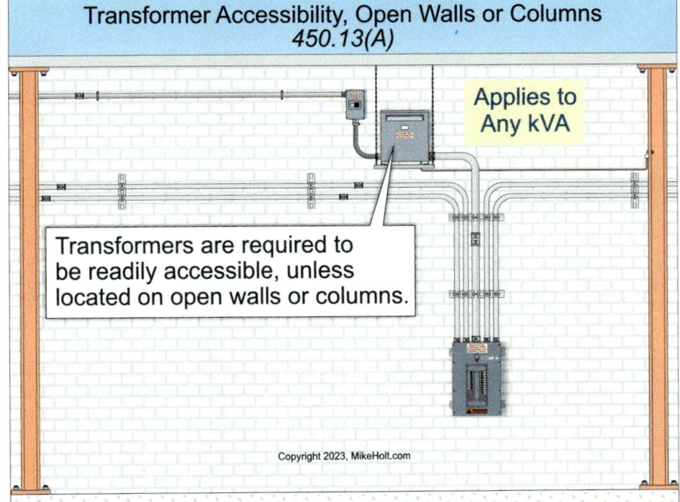

▶Figure 450–9

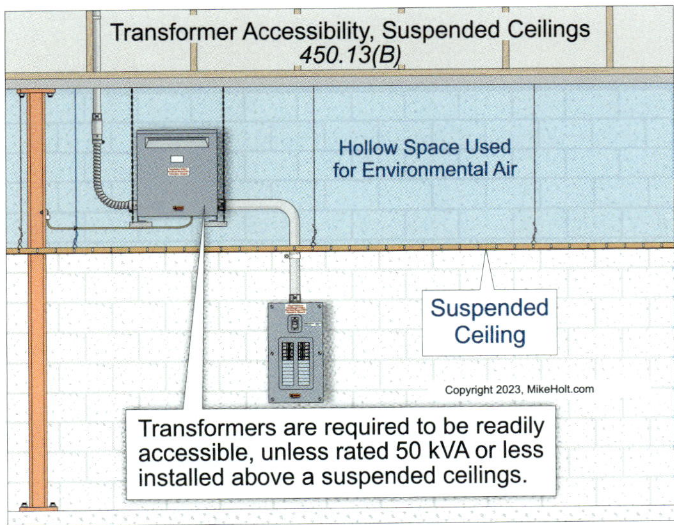

▶Figure 450–10

450.14 Disconnecting Means

Within Sight. A transformer must have a disconnect located within sight of the transformer. ▶Figure 450–11

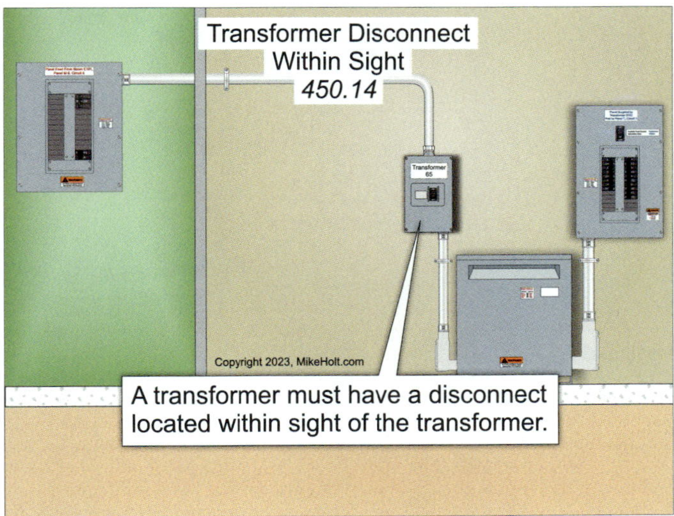

▶Figure 450–11

Not Within Sight. Where the disconnect is in a remote location (not within sight of the transformer), it must be capable of being locked in the open position in accordance with 110.25. The location must be field marked on the transformer. ▶Figure 450–12

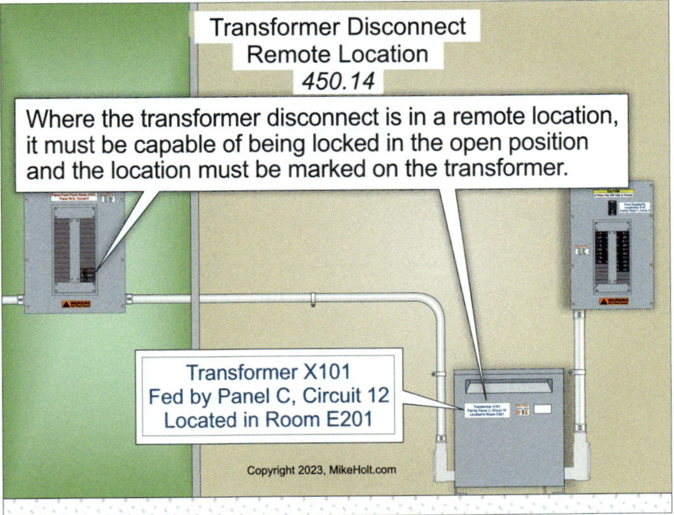

▶Figure 450–12

According to Article 100, "Within Sight" means it is visible and not more than 50 ft from the location of the equipment. ▶Figure 450–13

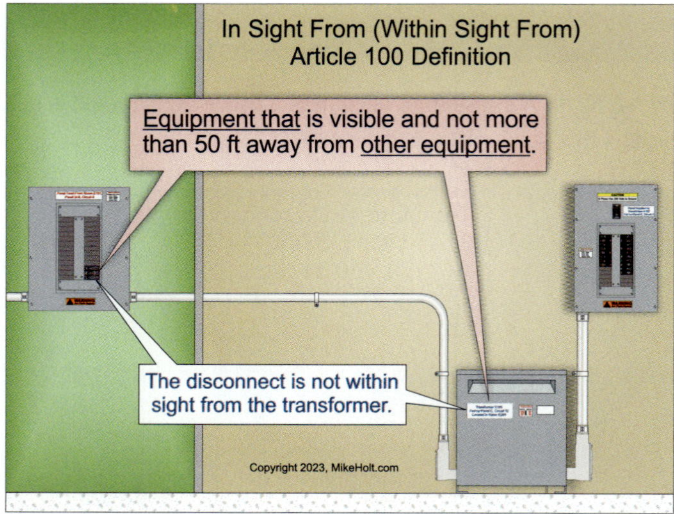

▶Figure 450–13

STATIONARY STANDBY BATTERIES

Introduction to Article 480—Stationary Standby Batteries

The provisions of this article apply to all installations of stationary standby batteries having a capacity greater than 1 kWh. That is a small battery capacity and, with the many improvements in technology, these systems are much more common than they were just a few years ago. Systems such as uninterruptible power supplies, emergency power and lighting systems, and stand-alone power systems are a few of the many applications for this article. All of these types of battery systems involve highly specialized areas of knowledge found in standards other than the *NEC*. Some topics covered in this material include:

▸ Battery and Cell Terminations

▸ Overcurrent Protection

▸ Support Systems

▸ Locations

▸ Ventilation

▸ Interconnection

480.1 Scope

The provisions of Article 480 apply to <u>all installations of</u> stationary standby batteries having a capacity greater than 1 kWh. ▸Figure 480–1

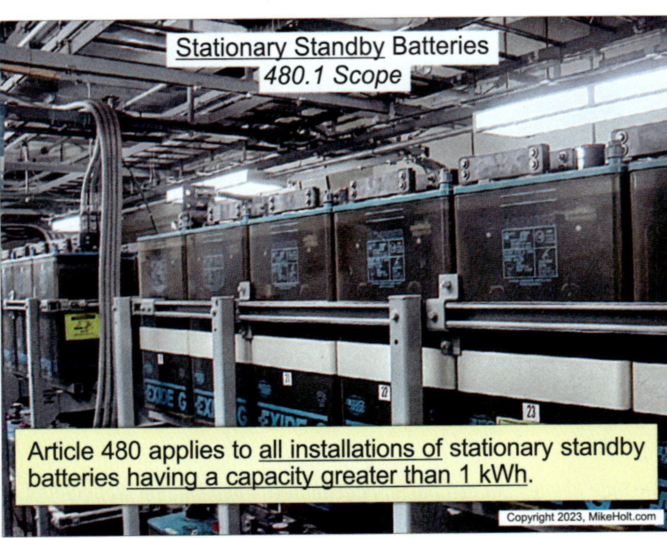

▸Figure 480–1

According to Article 100, "Battery" is a single cell or a group of cells connected together electrically in series, parallel, or a combination of both. ▸Figure 480–2

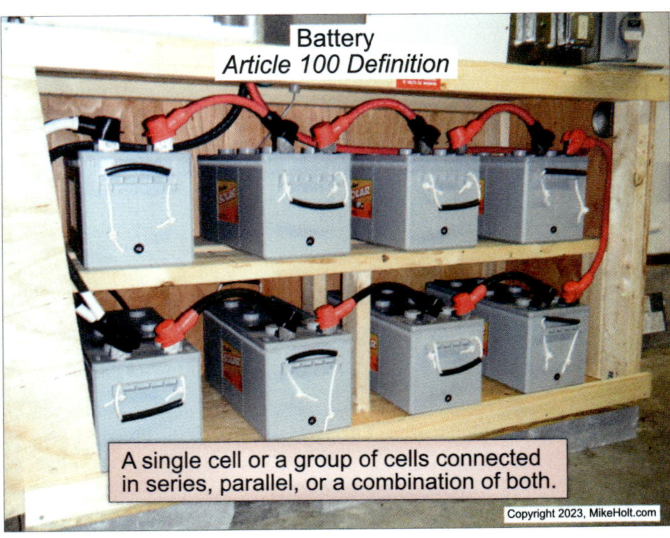

▸Figure 480–2

Note 1: See Article 706 for the installation requirements for energy storage systems.

According to Article 100, "Energy Storage System" is a system capable of storing energy and providing it to the premises wiring system or electric utility supply. ▶Figure 480–3

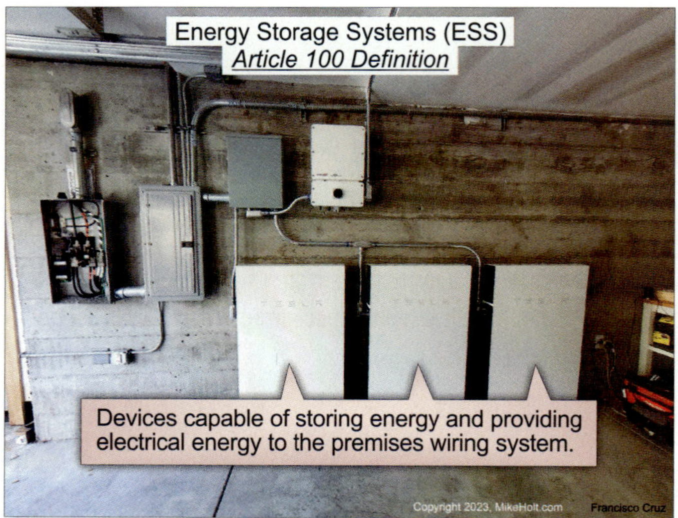

▶Figure 480–3

480.4 Battery and Cell Terminations

(A) Dissimilar Metals. Where connections between dissimilar metals occur, antioxidant material must be used <u>where recommended by the battery manufacturer's installation instruction manual.</u> ▶Figure 480–4

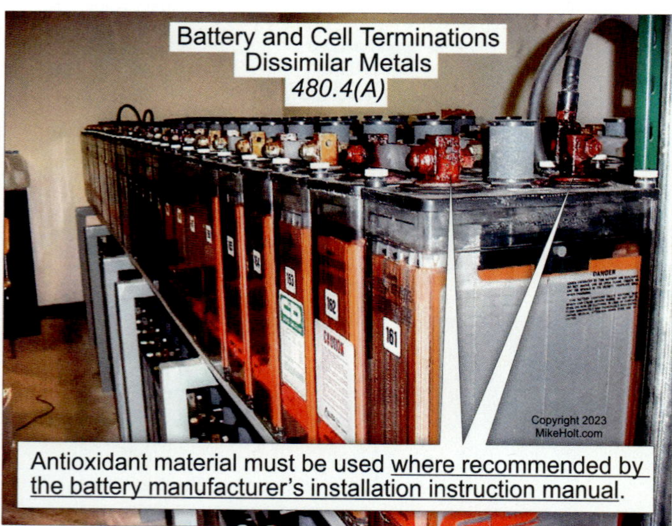

▶Figure 480–4

(C) Battery Terminals. Electrical connections to the battery and cable(s) between cells on separate levels or racks to the battery must not put mechanical strain on the battery terminals. ▶Figure 480–5

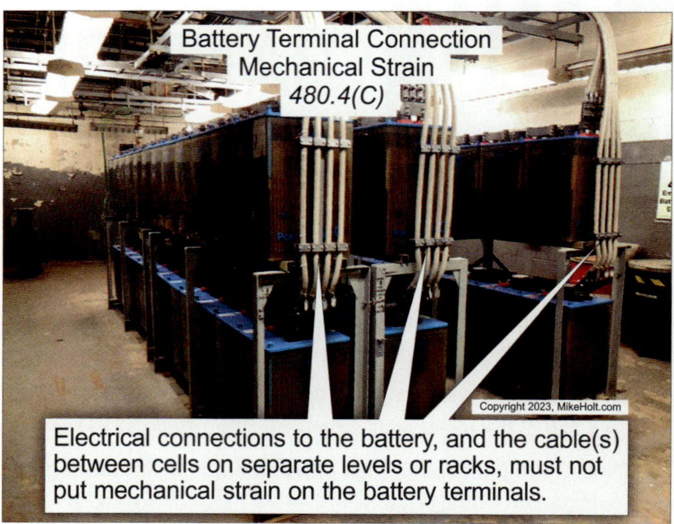

▶Figure 480–5

Note: Conductors are commonly pre-formed to eliminate stress on battery terminations. Fine-stranded cables may also eliminate the stress on battery terminations. See the manufacturer's instructions for guidance.

(D) Accessibility. The terminals of all cells or multicell units must be readily accessible for readings, inspections, and cleaning where required by the equipment design. ▶Figure 480–6

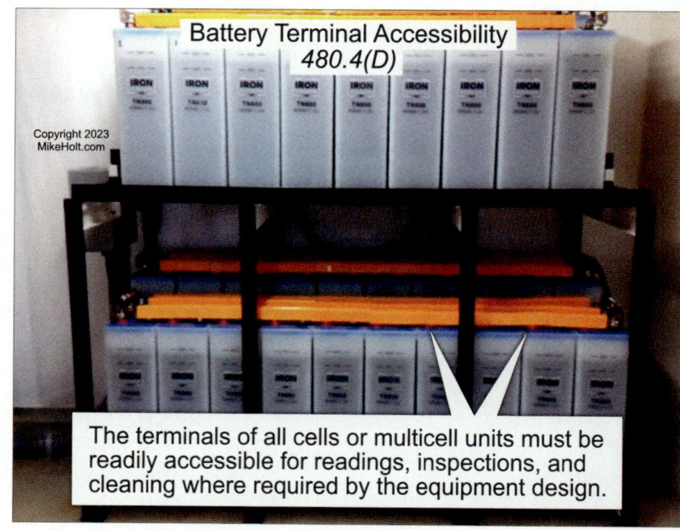

▶Figure 480–6

One side of transparent battery containers must be readily accessible for inspection of the internal components. ▶Figure 480–7

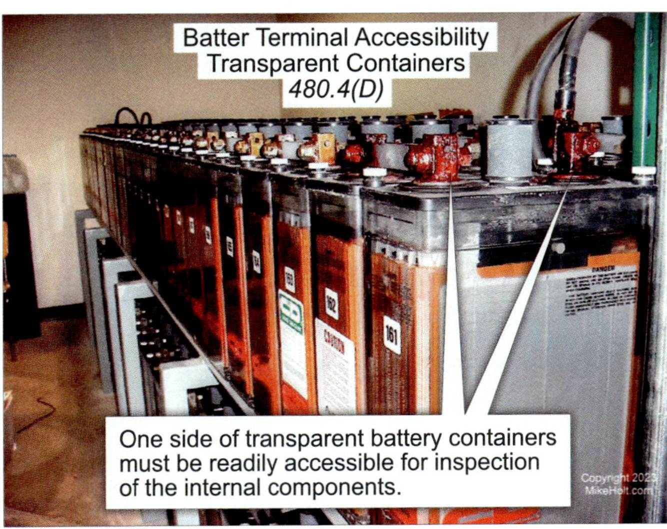

▶Figure 480–7

480.9 Battery Support Systems

For battery chemistries with corrosive electrolyte, the structure that supports the battery must be resistant to deteriorating action by the electrolyte. Metallic structures must have nonconducting support members for the cells or constructed with a continuous insulating material. ▶Figure 480–8

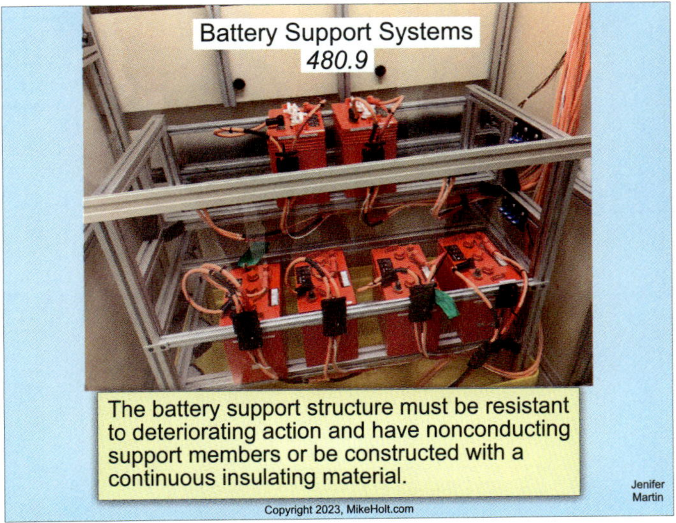

▶Figure 480–8

480.10 Battery Locations

(A) Ventilation. Provisions must permit sufficient diffusion and ventilation of battery gases to prevent the accumulation of an explosive mixture. ▶Figure 480–9

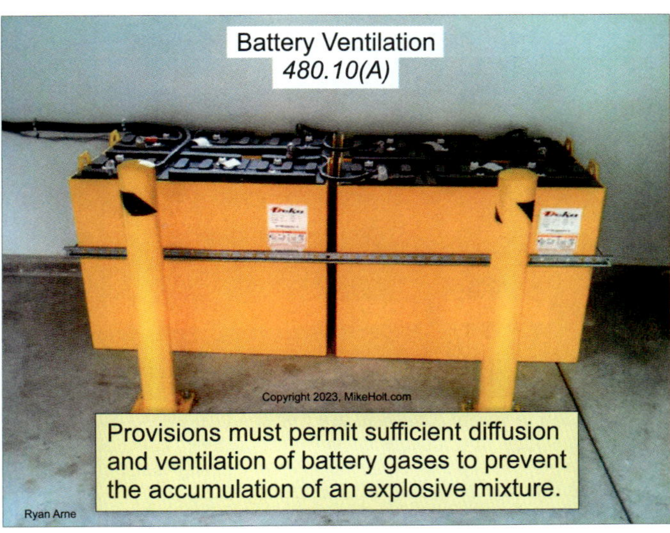

▶Figure 480–9

(C) Working Space for Stationary Standby Batteries. Spaces around stationary standby batteries must be in accordance with 110.26 as measured from the edge of the battery cabinet, rack, or tray. ▶Figure 480–10

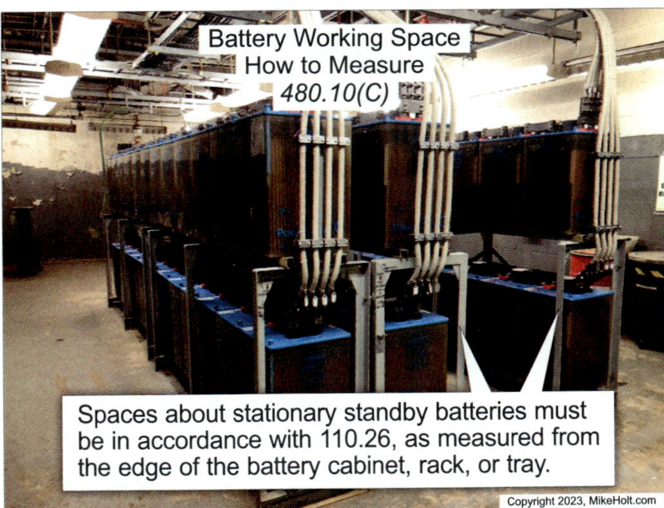

▶Figure 480–10

(D) Top Terminal Batteries. Where top terminal batteries are installed on tiered racks, working space in accordance with the battery manufacturer's instructions must be provided between the highest point on a cell and the row or ceiling above that point. ▶Figure 480–11

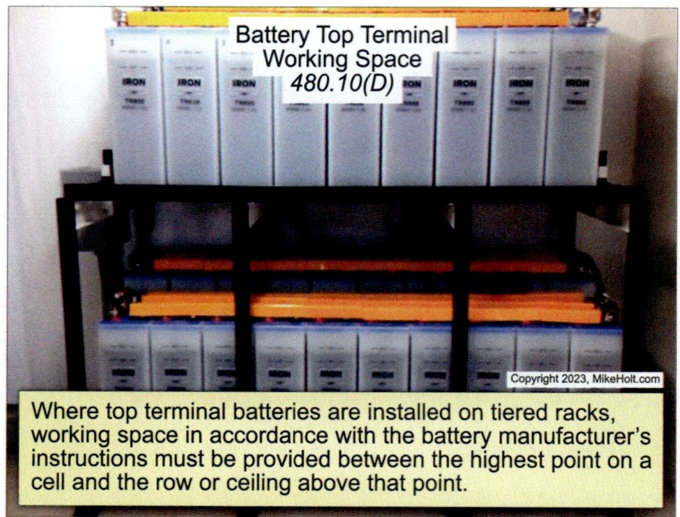

Where top terminal batteries are installed on tiered racks, working space in accordance with the battery manufacturer's instructions must be provided between the highest point on a cell and the row or ceiling above that point.

▶Figure 480–11

(E) Egress. Personnel doors intended for entrance to or egress from rooms designated as battery rooms must open 90 degrees in the direction of egress. They must be equipped with listed panic or listed fire exit hardware.

(G) Illumination. The working space around a stationary standby battery must have illumination that is not only controlled by automatic means.

480.12 Battery Interconnections

Minimum Size, 2/0 AWG. Flexible cables (as shown in Table 400.4) in sizes 2/0 AWG and larger are permitted within the battery enclosure from battery terminals to a nearby junction box where they must be connected to an approved wiring method.

Listed and Identified. Battery cables must be listed and identified for the environmental conditions.

Fine-Stranded Cables. Terminals for flexible fine-stranded cables must be identified for use in accordance with 110.14.

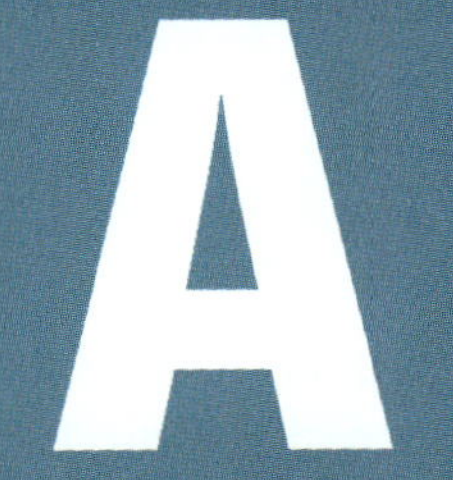

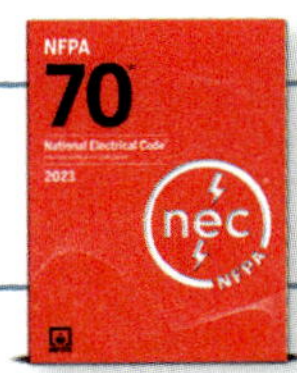

Please use the 2023 *Code* book to answer the following questions.

1. Installations used to export electric power from vehicles to premises wiring or for _______ current flow is covered by the *NEC*.

   (a) emergency
   (b) primary
   (c) bidirectional
   (d) secondary

2. The maximum current, in amperes, that a conductor can carry continuously under the conditions of use without exceeding its temperature rating is known as its _______.

   (a) short-circuit rating
   (b) ground-fault rating
   (c) ampacity
   (d) all of these

3. _______ is a raceway of circular cross section made of a helically wound, formed, interlocked metal strip.

   (a) Type MC cable
   (b) Type AC cable
   (c) LFMC
   (d) FMC

4. Off-road, self-propelled electric vehicles, such as _______ are not considered electric vehicles.

   (a) industrial trucks, hoists, and lifts
   (b) golf carts and airline ground support equipment
   (c) tractors and boats
   (d) all of these

5. A(An) _______ is a system consisting of a monitor(s), communications equipment, a controller(s), a timer(s), or other device(s) that monitors and/or controls an electrical load or a power production or storage source.

   (a) energy management system
   (b) power distribution system
   (c) energy storage system
   (d) interconnected power production system

6. Earth, as used in the *NEC* best describes the term _______.

   (a) bonded
   (b) ground
   (c) effective ground-fault current path
   (d) guarded

7. A system or circuit conductor that is intentionally grounded is called a(an) _______.

   (a) grounding conductor
   (b) unidentified conductor
   (c) grounded conductor
   (d) grounding electrode conductor

8. A functionally grounded system has an electrical ground reference for operational purposes that is not _______ grounded.

   (a) effectively
   (b) sufficiently
   (c) solidly
   (d) any of these

9. A handhole enclosure is an enclosure for use in underground systems, provided with an open or closed bottom, and sized to allow personnel to ______.

   (a) enter and exit freely
   (b) reach into but not enter
   (c) have full working space
   (d) visually examine the interior

10. The operating mode for power production or microgrids that allows energy to be supplied to loads that are disconnected from an electric power production and distribution network or other primary power source defines the term ______.

    (a) island mode
    (b) isolation mode
    (c) emergency mode
    (d) standby mode

11. A ______ is an electric power system capable of operating in island mode and capable of being interconnected to an electric power production and distribution network or other primary source while operating in interactive mode.

    (a) tandem system
    (b) primary system
    (c) microgrid
    (d) dual function system

12. The ______ is the neutral point.

    (a) common point on a wye-connection in a polyphase system
    (b) midpoint on a single-phase, 3-wire system
    (c) midpoint of a single-phase portion of a 3-phase delta system
    (d) any of these

13. A PV ______ is a complete, environmentally protected unit consisting of solar cells and other components, designed to produce dc power.

    (a) interface
    (b) battery
    (c) module
    (d) cell bank

14. A contact device installed at an outlet for the connection of an attachment plug is known as a(an) ______.

    (a) attachment point
    (b) tap
    (c) receptacle
    (d) wall plug

15. A duplex receptacle is an example of a multiple receptacle that has two receptacles on the same ______.

    (a) yoke or strap
    (b) strap
    (c) device
    (d) cover plate

16. A ______ system is an electrical power supply output, other than a service, having no direct connection(s) to circuit conductors of any other electrical source other than those established by grounding and bonding connections.

    (a) separately derived
    (b) classified
    (c) direct
    (d) emergency

17. A service drop is defined as the overhead conductors between the serving utility and the ______.

    (a) service equipment
    (b) service point
    (c) grounding electrode conductor
    (d) equipment grounding conductor

18. General requirements for the examination and approval, installation and use, access to and spaces about electrical conductors and equipment; enclosures intended for personnel entry; and tunnel installations are within the scope of ______.

    (a) Article 800
    (b) Article 300
    (c) Article 110
    (d) Annex J

19. Equipment servicing and electrical preventive maintenance shall be performed in accordance with the original equipment manufacturer's instructions and ______.

    (a) information included in the listing information
    (b) applicable industry standards,
    (c) as approved by the authority having jurisdiction
    (d) any of these

20. Each disconnecting means shall be legibly marked to indicate its purpose unless located and arranged so ______.

    (a) that it can be locked out and tagged
    (b) it is not readily accessible
    (c) the purpose is evident
    (d) that it operates at less than 300 volts-to-ground

21.   _______ at other than dwelling units shall be legibly field marked with the available fault current, include the date the fault-current calculation was performed, and be of sufficient durability to withstand the environment involved.

(a) Service equipment
(b) Sub panels
(c) Motor control centers
(d) all of these

22.   Working space distances for enclosed live parts shall be measured from the _______ of equipment if the live parts are enclosed.

(a) enclosure or opening
(b) front or back
(c) mounting pad
(d) footprint

23.   The minimum height of working spaces shall be clear and extend from the grade, floor, or platform to a height of _______ ft or the height of the equipment, whichever is greater.

(a) 3 ft
(b) 6 ft
(c) 6½ ft
(d) 7 ft

24.   All service equipment, switchboards, panelboards, and motor control centers shall be _______.

(a) located in dedicated spaces
(b) protected from damage
(c) in weatherproof enclosures
(d) located in dedicated spaces and protected from damage

25.   Surge-protective devices shall be installed in or adjacent to distribution equipment, connected to the _______ side of the feeder that contains branch circuit overcurrent protective device(s) that supply dwelling units, dormitory units, and guest rooms and suites.

(a) line
(b) load
(c) supply
(d) line or supply

26.   Where dwelling units are supplied by a feeder and the distribution equipment is _______, the required Type 1 or Type 2 SPD shall be installed.

(a) replaced
(b) repaired
(c) due for maintenance
(d) replaced or repaired

27.   The point of attachment of overhead premises wiring to a building shall in no case be less than _______ above finished grade.

(a) 8 ft
(b) 10 ft
(c) 12 ft
(d) 15 ft

28.   The vertical clearance of final spans of overhead conductors above or within _______ measured horizontally of platforms, projections, or surfaces that will permit personal contact shall be maintained in accordance with 225.18.

(a) 3 ft
(b) 6 ft
(c) 8 ft
(d) 10 ft

29.   Overhead branch-circuit and feeder conductors shall not be installed beneath openings through which materials may be moved, such as openings in farm and commercial buildings, and shall not be installed where they obstruct _______ these openings.

(a) entrance to
(b) egress from
(c) access to
(d) a safe descent from

30.   In accordance with Article 225—Outside Branch Circuits and Feeders, the two to six disconnects for a disconnecting means for a building supplied by a feeder shall be _______.

(a) the same size
(b) grouped
(c) in the same enclosure
(d) of the same manufacturer

31. The emergency disconnecting means for one- and two-family dwellings supplied by an outside feeder shall be marked as EMERGENCY DISCONNECT and the marking or labels shall ______.

    (a) be located on the outside front of the disconnect enclosure
    (b) have a red background with white text
    (c) have lettering at least ½ in. high
    (d) all of these

32. Where a service ______ enters a building or structure, it shall be sealed in accordance with 300.5(G) and 300.7(A).

    (a) raceway
    (b) cable assembly
    (c) cable tray
    (d) any of these

33. Where the voltage between conductors does not exceed 300 and the roof has a slope of 4 in. in 12 in. or greater, a reduction in clearance to ______ over the roof is permitted.

    (a) 3 ft
    (b) 4 ft
    (c) 5 ft
    (d) 8 ft

34. Underground service conductors shall have ______.

    (a) adequate mechanical strength
    (b) no splices
    (c) 90°C conductors
    (d) sufficient ampacity for the loads calculated

35. The minimum service-entrance conductor size shall have an ampacity not less than the maximum load to be served after the application of any ______ factors.

    (a) adjustment
    (b) correction
    (c) demand
    (d) adjustment or correction

36. On a three-phase, 4-wire, delta-connected service where the midpoint of one phase winding is grounded, the service conductor having the higher phase voltage-to-ground shall be durably and permanently marked by an outer finish that is ______ in color, or by other effective means, at each termination or junction point.

    (a) orange
    (b) red
    (c) blue
    (d) any of these

37. The surge-protective device (SPD) required for a dwelling unit shall be ______.

    (a) Type 1 or 2
    (b) Type 2 or 3
    (c) Type 3
    (d) Type 4

38. The additional service disconnecting means for fire pumps, emergency systems, legally required standby, or optional standby services shall be installed remote from the one to six service disconnecting means for normal service to minimize the possibility of ______ interruption of supply.

    (a) intentional
    (b) accidental
    (c) simultaneous
    (d) prolonged

39. In grounded systems, normally noncurrent-carrying electrically conductive materials that are likely to become energized shall be connected ______ in a manner that establishes an effective ground-fault current path.

    (a) together
    (b) to the electrical supply source
    (c) to the closest grounded conductor
    (d) together and to the electrical supply source

40. For grounded systems, the earth ______ considered an effective ground-fault current path.

    (a) shall be
    (b) shall not be
    (c) is
    (d) is not

41. The grounding electrode conductor connection shall be made at any accessible point from the load end of the overhead service conductors, ______ to the terminal or bus to which the grounded service conductor is connected at the service disconnecting means.

    (a) service drop
    (b) underground service conductors
    (c) service lateral
    (d) any of these

42. A grounded conductor shall not be connected to normally noncurrent-carrying metal parts of equipment, to equipment grounding conductor(s), or be reconnected to ground on the load side of the ______ except as otherwise permitted.

    (a) service disconnecting means
    (b) distribution panel
    (c) switchgear
    (d) switchboard

43. A grounding electrode conductor, sized in accordance with ______, shall be used to connect the equipment grounding conductors, the service-equipment enclosures, and, if the system is grounded, the grounded service conductor to the grounding electrode(s).

    (a) 250.66
    (b) 250.102(C)(1)
    (c) 250.122
    (d) 310.16

44. Tap connections to a common grounding electrode conductor for multiple separately derived systems shall be made at an accessible location by ______.

    (a) a connector listed as grounding and bonding equipment
    (b) listed connections to aluminum or copper busbars
    (c) the exothermic welding process
    (d) any of these

45. Rod and pipe grounding electrodes shall not be less than ______ in length.

    (a) 6 ft
    (b) 8 ft
    (c) 10 ft
    (d) 20 ft

46. ______ electrodes shall be free from nonconductive coatings such as paint or enamel.

    (a) Rod
    (b) Pipe
    (c) Plate
    (d) all of these

47. Where a metal underground water pipe is used as a grounding electrode, the continuity of the grounding path or the bonding connection to interior piping shall not rely on ______ and similar equipment.

    (a) bonding jumpers
    (b) water meters or filtering devices
    (c) grounding clamps
    (d) all of these

48. Ferrous metal raceways for grounding electrode conductors shall be ______ continuous from the point of attachment to cabinets or equipment to the grounding electrode.

    (a) electrically
    (b) physically
    (c) mechanically
    (d) integrally

49. The grounding electrode conductor is permitted to be run to any ______ available in the grounding electrode system.

    (a) panelboards
    (b) bonding jumper
    (c) switchgear
    (d) convenient grounding electrode

50. A metal water pipe grounding electrode conductor sized at ______ is required for a 400A service supplied with 500 kcmil conductors.

    (a) 1 AWG
    (b) 1/0 AWG
    (c) 2/0 AWG
    (d) 3/0 AWG

51. A metal water pipe grounding electrode conductor sized at ______ is required for a service supplied with 350 kcmil conductors.

    (a) 6 AWG
    (b) 3 AWG
    (c) 2 AWG
    (d) 1/0 AWG

52. At existing buildings or structures, an intersystem bonding termination is not required if other acceptable means of bonding exists. An external accessible means for bonding communications systems together can be by the use of a(an) ______.

    (a) nonflexible metal raceway
    (b) exposed grounding electrode conductor
    (c) connection to a grounded raceway or equipment approved by the authority having jurisdiction
    (d) any of these

53. Receptacle yokes or contact devices designed and ______ as self-grounding can, in conjunction with the supporting screws, establish the equipment bonding between the device yoke and a flush-type box.

    (a) approved
    (b) advertised
    (c) listed
    (d) installed

54. Rigid metal conduit that is directly buried outdoors shall have at least ______ of cover.

    (a) 6 in.
    (b) 12 in.
    (c) 18 in.
    (d) 24 in.

55. All conductors of the same circuit shall be ______, unless otherwise specifically permitted in the *Code*.

    (a) bonded
    (b) grounded
    (c) the same size
    (d) in the same raceway or cable or be in close proximity in the same trench

56. Where independent support wires of a suspended ceiling assembly are used to support raceways, cable assemblies, or boxes above a ceiling, they shall be secured at ______ end(s).

    (a) one
    (b) both
    (c) the line and load
    (d) at the attachment to the structural member

57. Cable wiring methods shall not be used as a means of support for ______.

    (a) other cables
    (b) raceways
    (c) nonelectrical equipment
    (d) any of these

58. A box or conduit body shall not be required for splices and taps in ______ conductors and cables as long as the splice is made with a splicing device that is identified for the purpose.

    (a) direct-buried
    (b) exposed
    (c) concealed
    (d) none of these

59. Electrical installations in hollow spaces shall be made so as to not increase the spread of fire, such as boxes installed in a wall cavity on opposite sides of a fire-rated wall where a minimum horizontal separation of ______ usually applies between boxes.

    (a) 6 in.
    (b) 12 in.
    (c) 18 in.
    (d) 24 in.

60. No wiring of any type shall be installed in ducts used to transport ______.

    (a) dust
    (b) flammable vapors
    (c) loose stock
    (d) all of these

61. Electrical equipment with a metal enclosure, or electrical equipment with a nonmetallic enclosure listed for use within an air-handling space and having low ______ release properties are permitted to be installed in other spaces used for environmental air.

    (a) resistance
    (b) impedance
    (c) and high temperature
    (d) smoke and heat

62. Cables, raceways, and ______ installed behind suspended-ceiling panels shall be arranged and secured to allow access to the electrical equipment.

    (a) equipment
    (b) appliances
    (c) cords
    (d) conductors

63. Where an exit enclosure (stair tower) is required to have a fire-resistance rating, only electrical wiring methods serving equipment permitted by the ______ in the exit enclosure shall be installed within the exit enclosure.

    (a) fire code official
    (b) building code official
    (c) authority having jurisdiction
    (d) electrical engineer

64. Solid aluminum conductors of 8 AWG, 10 AWG, and 12 AWG shall be made of an AA-______ series electrical grade aluminum alloy conductor material.

    (a) 1,350
    (b) 2,000
    (c) 6,000
    (d) 8,000

65. Insulated conductors with letter designation of ______, are permitted in a wet location with a maximum operating temperature of 90°C.

    (a) USE
    (b) RHW
    (c) XHWN
    (d) THWN-2

66. Insulated conductors and cables used in ______ shall be any of the types identified in this *Code*.

    (a) dry and damp locations
    (b) dry locations
    (c) damp locations
    (d) wet and damp locations

67. In general, the minimum size conductor permitted for parallel installations is ______.

    (a) 10 AWG
    (b) 4 AWG
    (c) 1 AWG
    (d) 1/0 AWG

68. Parallel conductors shall have the same ______.

    (a) length
    (b) conductor material
    (c) size in circular mil area
    (d) all of these

69. Type ______ insulated conductors shall not be subject to ampacity adjustment where installed exposed to direct sunlight on a rooftop.

    (a) THW-2
    (b) XHHW-2
    (c) THWN-2
    (d) RHW-2

70. A(An) ______ conductor that carries only the unbalanced current from other conductors of the same circuit shall not be required to be counted when applying the provisions of 310.15(C)(1).

    (a) neutral
    (b) ungrounded
    (c) grounding
    (d) bonded

71. On a 4-wire, three-phase wye circuit where the major portion of the neutral load consists of ______ loads, the neutral conductor shall be considered a current-carrying conductor.

    (a) 240V
    (b) 277V
    (c) nonlinear
    (d) linear

72. Screws or other fasteners installed in the field that enter wiring spaces of outlet, device, pull, or junction boxes, shall be permitted to be longer than specified in 314.5(3) through (6) if the end of the screw is protected with ______ means.

    (a) a listed
    (b) an approved
    (c) an identified
    (d) any of these

73. Boxes, conduit bodies, and fittings installed in wet locations shall be listed for use in ______ locations.

    (a) wet
    (b) damp
    (c) dry
    (d) corrosive

74. Where cable assemblies with nonmetallic sheaths are used, the sheath shall extend not less than ______ inside the box and beyond any cable clamp.

    (a) ¼ in.
    (b) ⅜ in.
    (c) ½ in.
    (d) ¾ in.

75. Pull boxes or junction boxes with any dimension over ______ shall have all conductors cabled or racked in an approved manner.

    (a) 3 ft
    (b) 6 ft
    (c) 9 ft
    (d) 12 ft

76. Handhole enclosure covers shall require the use of tools to open, or they shall weigh over ______.

    (a) 45 lb
    (b) 70 lb
    (c) 100 lb
    (d) 200 lb

77. Type AC cable and associated fittings shall be ______.

    (a) identified
    (b) approved
    (c) listed
    (d) labeled

78. Smooth-sheath Type MC cable with an external diameter not greater than ¾ in. shall have a bending radius not less than ______ times the external diameter of the cable.

    (a) five
    (b) ten
    (c) twelve
    (d) thirteen

79. Type MC cable fittings shall be permitted as a means of cable support.

    (a) True
    (b) False

80. Type MC cable containing four or fewer conductors, sized no larger than 10 AWG, shall be secured within ______ of every box, cabinet, fitting, or other cable termination.

    (a) 8 in.
    (b) 12 in.
    (c) 18 in.
    (d) 24 in.

81. Type TC cable can be used ______.

    (a) for power, lighting, control, and signal circuits
    (b) in cable trays including those with mechanically discontinuous segments up to 1 ft
    (c) for Class 1 control circuits as permitted in Parts II and III of Article 725
    (d) all of these

82. For interior installations of Type SE cable with ungrounded conductor sizes ______ and smaller, where installed in thermal insulation, the ampacity shall be in accordance with 60°C (140°F) conductor temperature rating.

    (a) 14 AWG
    (b) 12 AWG
    (c) 10 AWG
    (d) 8 AWG

83. Running threads shall not be used on IMC for connection at ______.

    (a) couplings
    (b) terminal adapters
    (c) enclosures
    (d) threadless connectors

84. Where IMC enters a box, fitting, or other enclosure, ______ shall be provided to protect the wire from abrasion unless the design of the box, fitting, or enclosure affords equivalent protection.

    (a) a bushing
    (b) duct seal
    (c) electrical tape
    (d) seal fittings

85. RMC shall be securely fastened within ______ of each outlet box, junction box, device box, cabinet, conduit body, or other conduit termination.

    (a) 3 ft
    (b) 4 ft
    (c) 5 ft
    (d) 6 ft

86. Threadless couplings and connectors used with RMC buried in masonry or concrete shall be the _______ type.

    (a) raintight
    (b) wet and damp location
    (c) nonabsorbent
    (d) concrete tight

87. All cut ends of LFMC conduit shall be _______ inside and outside to remove rough edges.

    (a) sanded
    (b) trimmed
    (c) brushed
    (d) any of these

88. PVC conduit shall be permitted to be _______.

    (a) encased in concrete
    (b) used for the support of luminaires
    (c) installed in movie theaters
    (d) none of these

89. Article _______ covers the use, installation, and construction specifications for liquidtight flexible nonmetallic conduit (LFNC) and associated fittings.

    (a) 300
    (b) 334
    (c) 350
    (d) 356

90. Securing or supporting of LFNC is not required where installed in lengths not exceeding _______ from the last point where the raceway is securely fastened for connections within an accessible ceiling to a luminaire(s) or other equipment.

    (a) 3 ft
    (b) 6 ft
    (c) 8 ft
    (d) 10 ft

91. Article _______ covers the use, installation, and construction specifications for electrical metallic tubing (EMT) and associated fittings.

    (a) 334
    (b) 350
    (c) 356
    (d) 358

92. The use of EMT shall be permitted in concrete in direct contact with the earth, in direct burial applications with fittings identified for direct burial, or in areas subject to severe _______ influences, where installed in accordance with 358.10(B).

    (a) corrosive
    (b) weather
    (c) sunlight
    (d) none of these

93. Galvanized steel and stainless steel EMT, elbows, couplings, and fittings can be installed in concrete, in direct contact with the earth, or in areas subject to severe corrosive influences where _______.

    (a) protected by corrosion protection
    (b) made of aluminum
    (c) made of stainless steel
    (d) listed for wet locations

94. ENT and fittings can be _______, provided fittings identified for this purpose are used.

    (a) encased in poured concrete floors, ceilings, walls, and slabs
    (b) embedded in a concrete slab on grade where the tubing is placed on sand or approved screenings
    (c) installed in wet locations as permitted in 362.10
    (d) any of these

95. Surface metal raceway enclosures providing a transition from other wiring methods shall have a means for connecting a(an) _______ conductor.

    (a) grounded
    (b) ungrounded
    (c) equipment grounding
    (d) all of these

96. Where single conductor cables comprising each phase, neutral, or grounded conductor of a circuit are connected in parallel in a cable tray, the conductors shall be installed _______, to prevent current imbalance in the paralleled conductors due to inductive reactance.

    (a) in groups consisting of not more than three conductors per phase or neutral, or grounded conductor
    (b) in groups consisting of not more than one conductor per phase, neutral, or grounded conductor
    (c) as individual conductors securely bound to the cable tray
    (d) in separate groups

97. Cable _______ made and insulated by approved methods can be located within a cable tray provided they are accessible and do not project above the side rails where the splices may be subject to physical damage.

    (a) connections
    (b) jumpers
    (c) splices
    (d) conductors

98. The ampacity of 14 AWG fixture wire is _______.

    (a) 6A
    (b) 8A
    (c) 10A
    (d) 17A

99. Surface-mounted switches or circuit breakers in a damp or wet location shall be enclosed in a _______ enclosure or cabinet that complies with 312.2.

    (a) weatherproof
    (b) rainproof
    (c) watertight
    (d) raintight

100. Receptacles and cord connectors that have equipment grounding conductor contacts shall have those contacts connected to _______.

    (a) the enclosure
    (b) a bonding bushing
    (c) an equipment grounding conductor
    (d) any of these

Introduction to Chapter 6—Special Equipment

Chapter 6, which covers special equipment, is the second of the three *NEC* chapters dealing with special equipment requirements. Special equipment is that, by the nature of its use, construction, or unique nature, have special installation requirements to safeguard people and property from the hazards of electricity arising from its use. This chapter contains 27 articles addressing special equipment used for things like electric signs, swimming pools, and solar PV systems. Many of the Chapter 6 articles are outside of the scope of this material, however, we do cover the following:

▶ **Article 625—Electric Vehicle Power Transfer System.** An electrically powered vehicle needs a dedicated charging circuit and that is where Article 625 comes in. It provides the requirements for the electrical equipment needed to charge automotive-type electric and hybrid vehicles including cars, bikes, and buses.

▶ **Article 690—Solar Photovoltaic (PV) Systems.** This article focuses on reducing the electrical hazards that may arise from installing and operating a solar PV system, to the point where it can be considered safe for property and people. The requirements of the *NEC* Chapters 1 through 4 apply to these installations, except as specifically modified here.

▶ **Article 691—Large-Scale Solar Photovoltaic (PV) Electric Supply Stations.** Article 691 covers large-scale PV electric supply stations with a generating capacity of 5000 kW or more and not under exclusive utility control.

ELECTRIC VEHICLE POWER TRANSFER SYSTEM

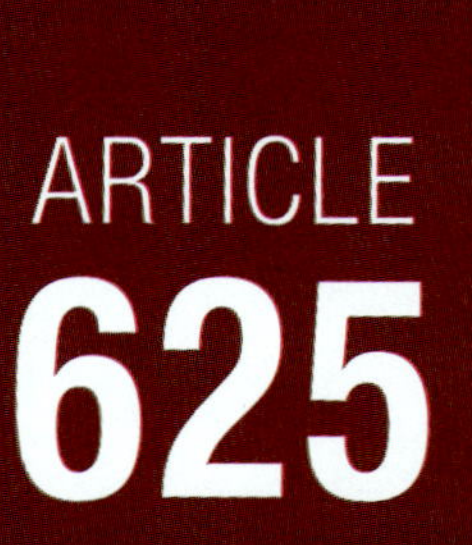

Introduction to Article 625—Electric Vehicle Power Transfer System

Electric vehicles have been around for a long time. Anyone who has worked in a factory or warehouse, or visited a big box store, has probably encountered an electric lift truck. And, of course, we are all familiar with golf carts. These and other off-road vehicles have charging requirements that are easily accommodated by small charging systems.

But today, a new challenge has emerged and is becoming increasingly common. That challenge is the electrically powered passenger vehicle, bus, truck, and motorcycle. Such vehicles, especially an electric car or bus, can weigh considerably more than a golf cart and just moving one takes a proportionately larger motor. In fact, many designs use multiple drive motors.

Those motors are powered by batteries. Adding to the battery sizing requirement are other demands. For example:

▸ These vehicles must be able to travel at highway speeds over distances roughly comparable to those traveled by their internal combustion engine counterparts.

▸ These vehicles have powered accessories that you typically will not find on a golf cart, such as air-conditioning, electric windows, stereo systems, windshield wipers, security systems, and window defrosters.

▸ These vehicles are expected to start in summer heat and in brutal winter cold.

The battery system for an electrically powered passenger vehicle is therefore considerably larger than that for a golf cart or other typical off-road electric vehicle. Consequently, the charging system must have the capability of delivering far more power than the one needed for a typical off-road electric vehicle.

An electrically powered passenger vehicle needs a dedicated charging circuit. Article 625 defines the requirements for the installation of the electrical equipment needed to charge automotive-type electric and hybrid vehicles including cars, motorcycles, and buses.

Part I. General

625.1 Scope

Article 625 covers the installation of conductors and equipment associated with an electric vehicle for the purposes of charging, power export, or bidirectional current flow. ▸Figure 625–1 and ▸Figure 625–2

According to Article 100, "Electric Vehicle" is an on-road use automobile, bus, truck, van, neighborhood electric vehicle and motorcycle primarily powered by an electric motor. ▸Figure 625–3

Note: Off-road, self-propelled electric industrial trucks, hoists, lifts, transports, golf carts, airline ground support equipment, tractors, and boats are not electric vehicles for the purpose of the *NEC*. ▸Figure 625–4

625.6 Listed

Electric vehicle power transfer system equipment for the purposes of charging, power export, or bidirectional current flow must be listed. ▸Figure 625–5

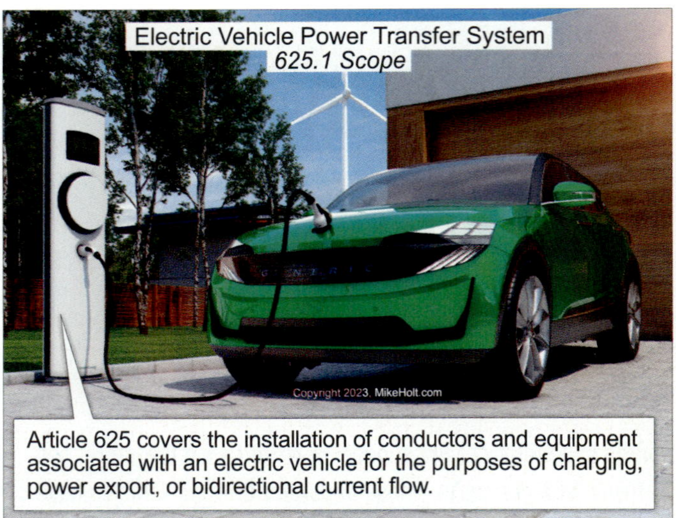

Article 625 covers the installation of conductors and equipment associated with an electric vehicle for the purposes of charging, power export, or bidirectional current flow.

▶Figure 625–1

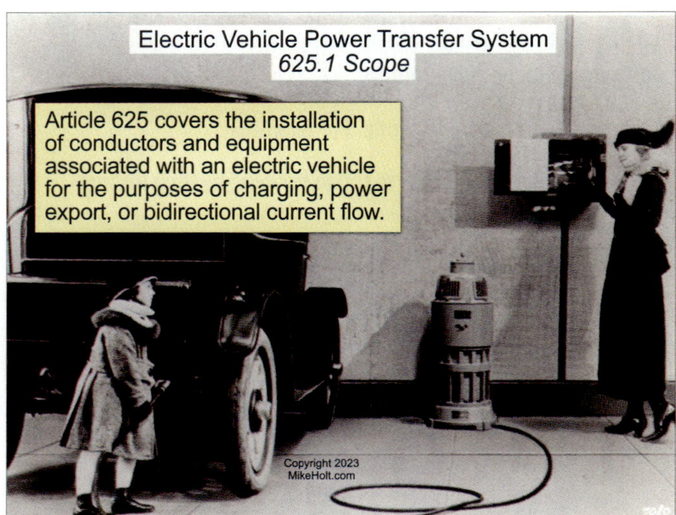

▶Figure 625–2

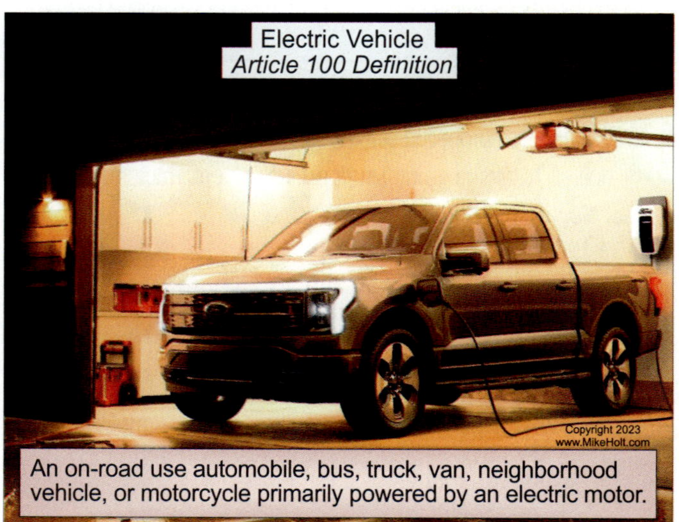

▶Figure 625–3

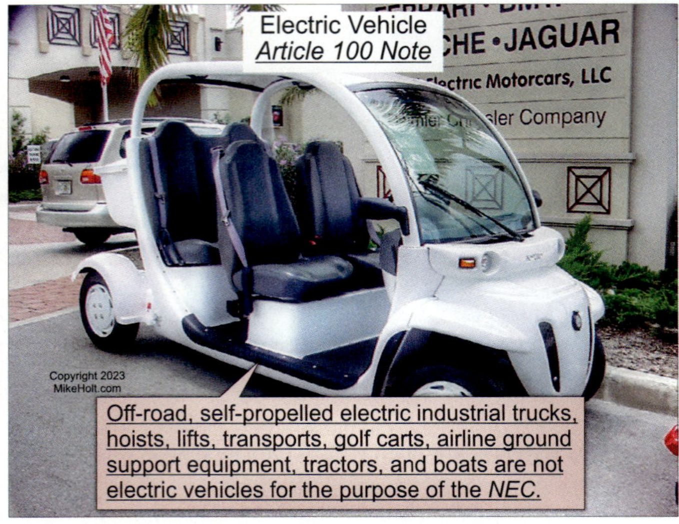

▶Figure 625–4

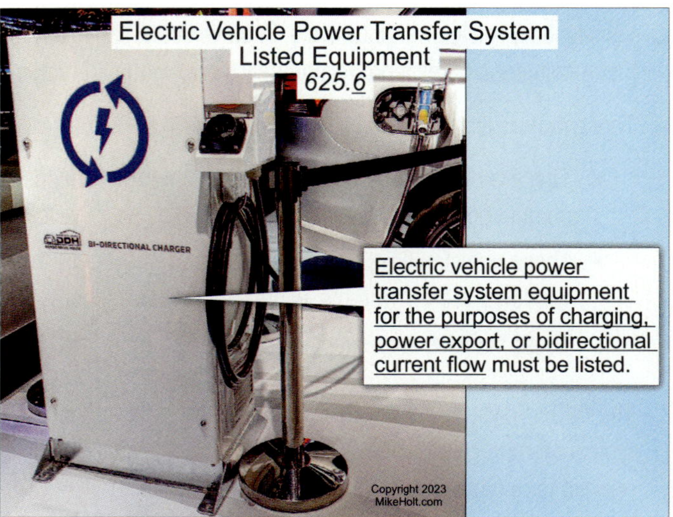

▶Figure 625–5

Part III. Installation

625.40 Electric Vehicle Branch Circuit

The branch circuit for electric vehicle supply equipment <u>rated greater than 16A or 120V</u> must be supplied by an individual branch circuit. ▶Figure 625–6

According to Article 100, "Electric Vehicle Supply Equipment (EVSE)" includes the conductors, electric vehicle connectors, attachment plugs, personnel protection system, devices, and power outlets installed for the purpose of transferring energy between the premises wiring and the electric vehicle. ▶**Figure 625–7**

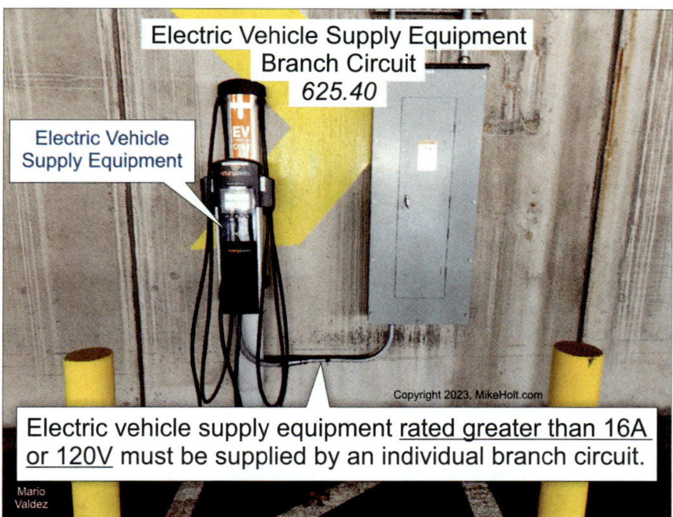

▶Figure 625–6

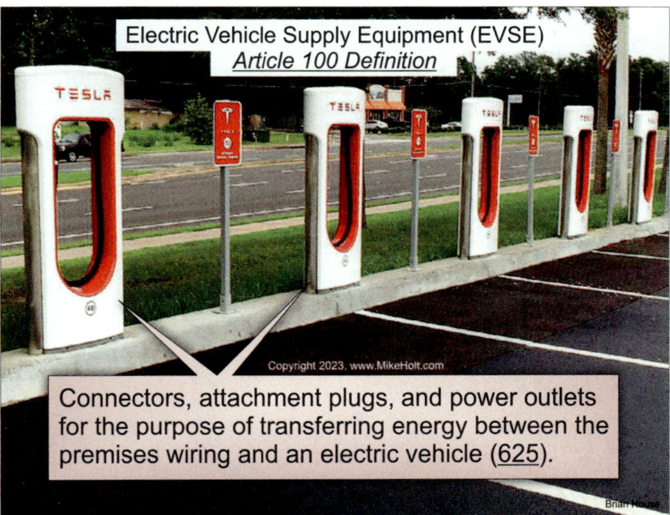

▶Figure 625–7

According to Article 100, "Individual Branch Circuit" is a branch circuit that supplies only one utilization equipment.

Ex: A single branch circuit is permitted to supply more than one electric vehicle supply equipment when the loads are managed by an energy management system in accordance with 625.42(A) or (B).

625.41 Overcurrent Protection

Overcurrent protection must be sized at no less than 125 percent of the electric vehicle supply equipment current rating. ▶Figure 625–8

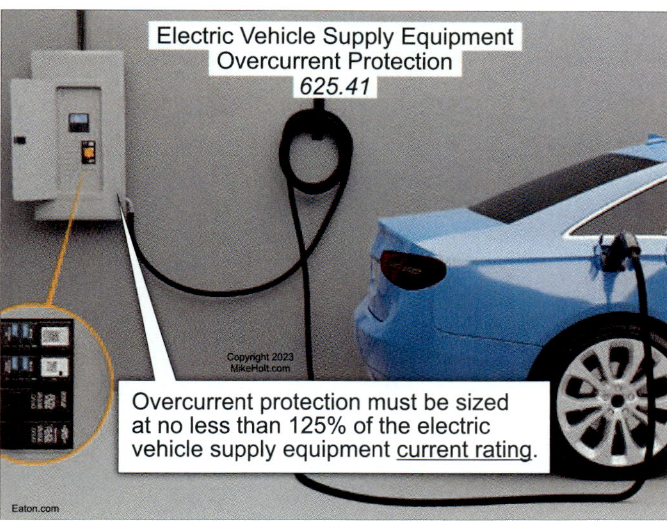

▶Figure 625–8

▶ **Example**

Question: What size overcurrent protection device is required for EVSE (EV Charger) rated 40A? ▶Figure 625–9

(a) 40A   (b) 50A   (c) 60A   (d) 70A

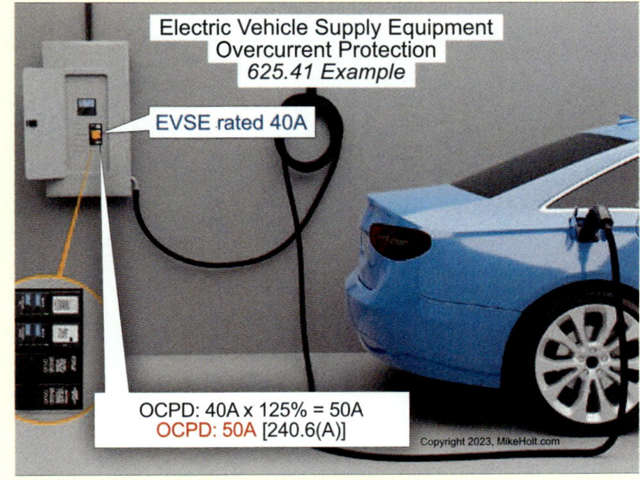

▶Figure 625–9

Solution:

The OCPD must have an ampere rating of not less than 50A (40A × 125%).

Answer: *(b) 50A*

625.42 Load

Electric vehicle supply equipment is considered a continuous load. ▶Figure 625–10

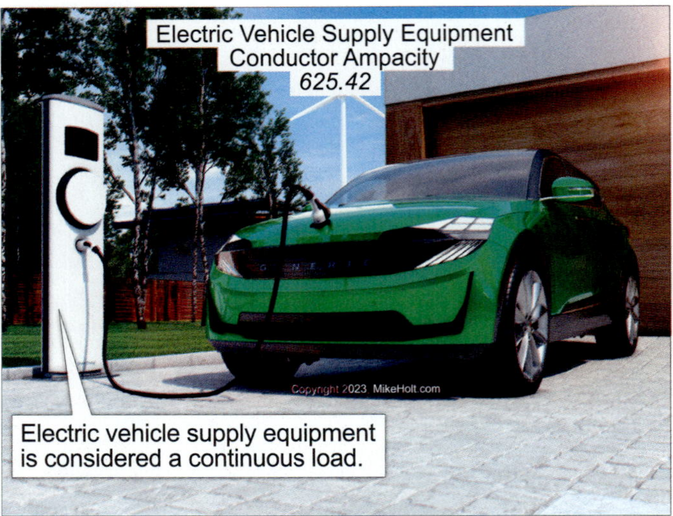

▶Figure 625–10

▶ Conductor Ampacity Example

Question: *What's the minimum conductor ampacity size for an EVSE (EV Charger) rated 40A?* ▶**Figure 625–11**

(a) 10 AWG   *(b) 8 AWG*   *(c) 6 AWG*   *(d) 4 AWG*

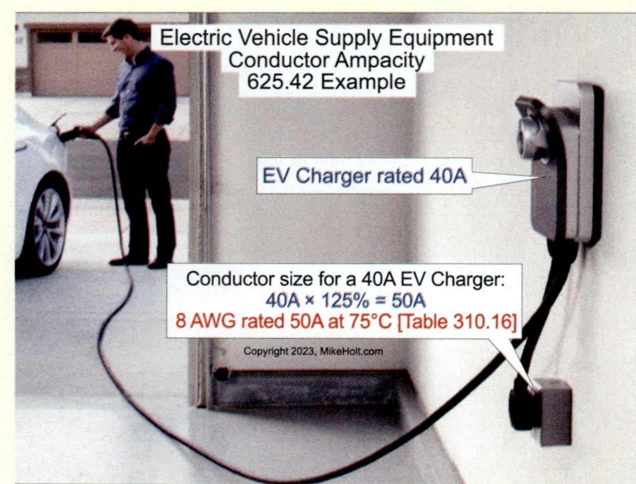

▶Figure 625–11

Solution:

The conductor must have an ampacity of not less than 50A (40A × 125%).

8 AWG rated 50A at 75°C [Table 310.16]

Answer: *(c) 6 AWG*

▶ Type NM Cable Example

Question: *What's the minimum type NM cable ampacity size required for an EVSE (EV Charger) rated 40A?* ▶**Figure 625–12**

(a) 10 AWG   *(b) 8 AWG*   *(c) 6 AWG*   *(d) 4 AWG*

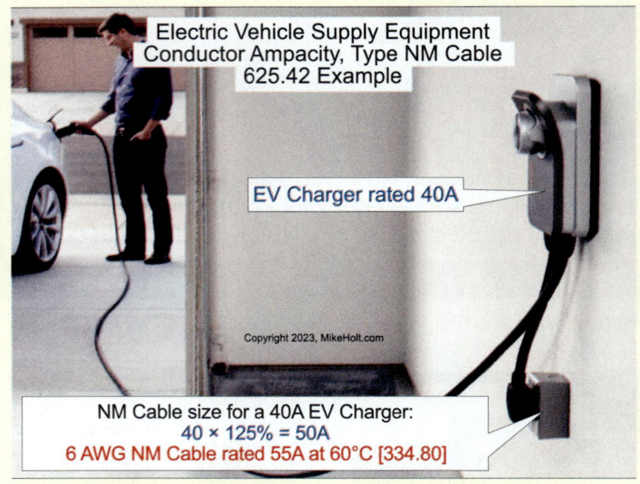

▶Figure 625–12

Solution:

The type NM cable must have an ampacity of not less than 50A (40A × 125%) at 60°C in accordance with 334.80.

6 AWG NM Cable rated 55A at 60°C [Table 310.16]

Answer: *(c) 6 AWG NM Cable*

(A) Energy Management System. Where an energy management system is used to control the electric vehicle supply equipment, the load is not included when sizing feeders and service conductors in accordance with 750.30(C)(1)(1). ▶**Figure 625–13**

> **Author's Comment:**
>
> ▶ An EV energy management system prevents the need for a service upgrade to an existing electrical system and EVSE is installed.

(B) Electric Vehicle Supply Equipment with Adjustable Settings. The adjustable ampere setting in accordance with manufacturers of electric vehicle supply equipment must appear on the rating label with sufficient durability to withstand the environment involved.

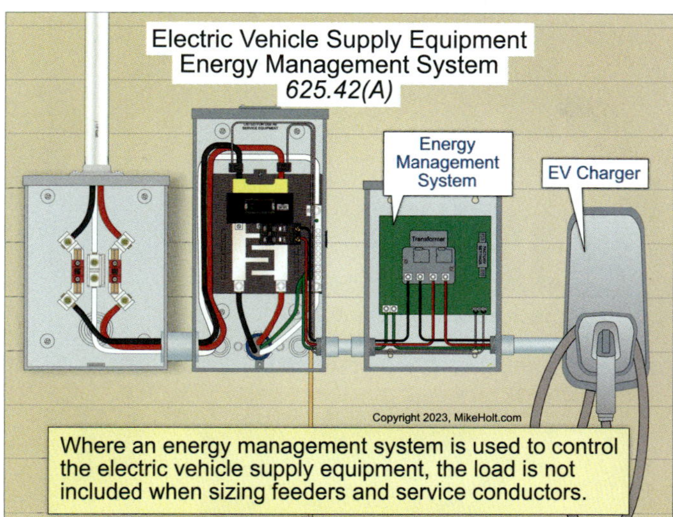

▶Figure 625–13

625.43 Disconnecting Means

Electric vehicle supply equipment (EVSE) rated more than 60A must have a disconnect installed at a readily accessible location. ▶**Figure 625–14**

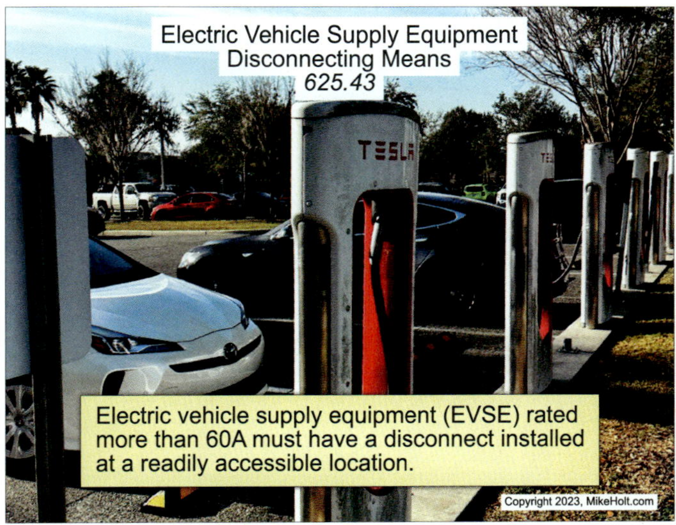

▶Figure 625–14

If the disconnect for the electric vehicle equipment is remote from the electric vehicle supply equipment or wireless power transfer equipment, a plaque must be placed on the equipment denoting the location of the disconnect.

The remote disconnect must be capable of being locked in the open position with provisions for locking to remain in place whether the lock is installed or not in accordance with 110.25.

625.48 Interactive Equipment

Electric vehicle supply equipment that incorporates a power export function as an interactive (grid tied) optional standby system or a bidirectional power feed must be listed and marked as suitable for that purpose. ▶Figure 625–15

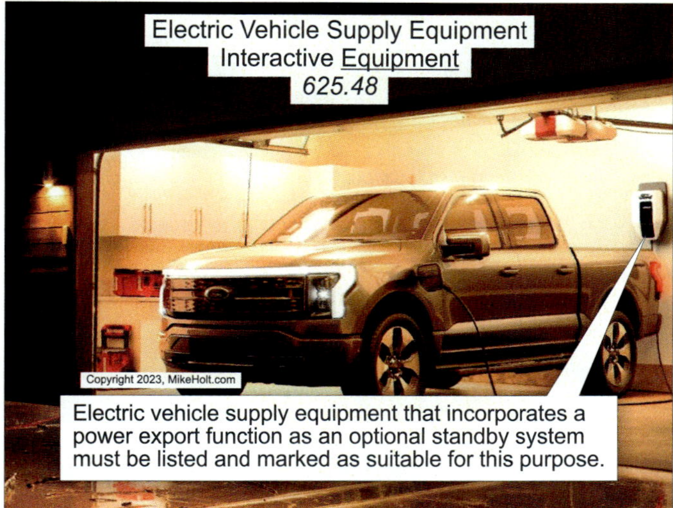

▶Figure 625–15

When an electric vehicle is used as an optional standby system, the interconnection to premises wiring must be in accordance with Parts I and II of Article 705 apply.

Note 1: See UL 1741, *Inverters, Converters, Controllers and Interconnection System Equipment for Use with Distributed Energy Resources*, for further information on supply equipment.

Note 2: See UL 9741, *Bidirectional Electric Vehicle (EV) Charging System Equipment*, for vehicle interactive (grid tied) systems.

Note 3: See SAE J3072, *Standard for Interconnection Requirements for Onboard, Utility-Interactive Inverter Systems*, for further information.

625.49 Island Mode

Electric vehicle power export equipment and bidirectional electric vehicle supply equipment that incorporate a power export function are permitted to be a part of an interconnected power system operating in island mode.

According to Article 100, "Island Mode" is the operating mode for power production equipment that is disconnected from an electric utility. ▶Figure 625–16

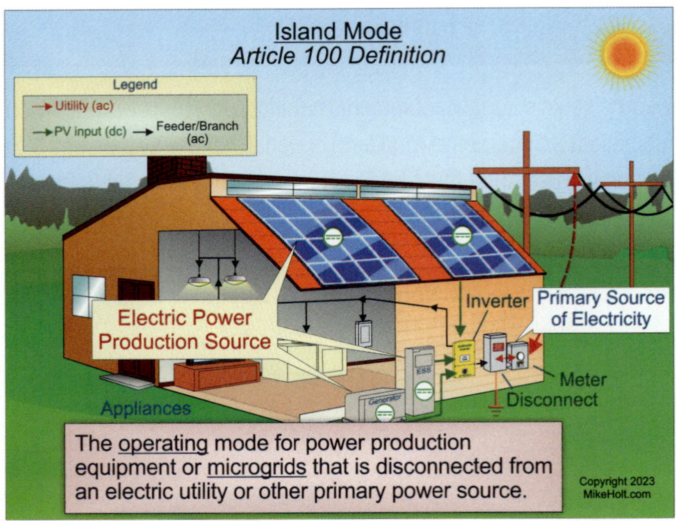

▶Figure 625–16

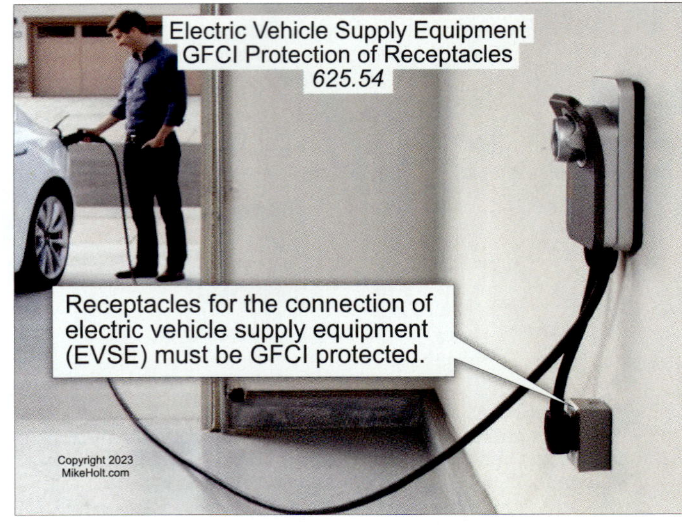

▶Figure 625–17

625.52 Ventilation

The ventilation requirement for charging an electric vehicle in an indoor enclosed space is determined by any of the following:

(A) Ventilation Not Required. Mechanical ventilation is not required where the electric vehicle supply equipment is listed for charging electric vehicles indoors without ventilation.

(B) Ventilation Required. Mechanical ventilation is required where the electric vehicle supply equipment is listed for charging electric vehicles with ventilation for indoor charging. The ventilation must include both supply and exhaust equipment permanently installed and located to intake and vent directly to the outdoors.

625.54 GFCI

Receptacles for the connection of electric vehicle supply equipment must be GFCI protected. ▶Figure 625–17

Author's Comment:

▶ GFCI breakers or receptacles typically used in dwelling units are not suitable for back feeding. That prohibits their use for a bidirectional EVSE. This GFCI requirement only applies to cord-and-plug-connected EVSE, making hard-wired EVSE the only type suitable for bidirectional use.

Part IV. Wireless Power Transfer Equipment

According to Article 100, "Wireless Power Transfer Equipment (WPTE)" is used to transferring energy between premises wiring and an electric vehicle without physical electrical contact. ▶Figure 625–18

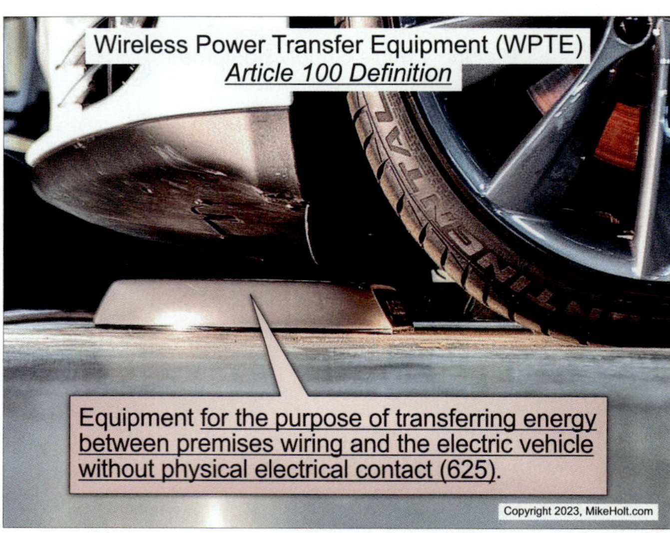

▶Figure 625–18

625.101 Grounding

The primary pad base plate must be of a nonferrous metal and connected to the circuit equipment grounding conductor unless double-insulated.

625.102 Installation

(A) General. The control pad must comply with 625.102(B). and the primary pad must comply with 625.102(C).

(B) Control Box. The control box enclosure must be suitable for the environment and mounted not less than 18 in. above the floor level for indoor locations or 24 in. above grade level for outdoor locations.

The control box must be mounted in:

(1) Pedestal

(2) Wall or pole

(3) Building or structure

(4) Raised concrete pad

(C) Primary Pad. The primary pad must be secured to the surface or embedded in the surface with its top flush with or below the surface and:
▶Figure 625–19

(1) Where located in an area requiring snow removal, it must not be located on or above the surface.

Ex: Where installed on private property where snow removal is done manually, the primary pad is permitted to be installed on or above the surface.

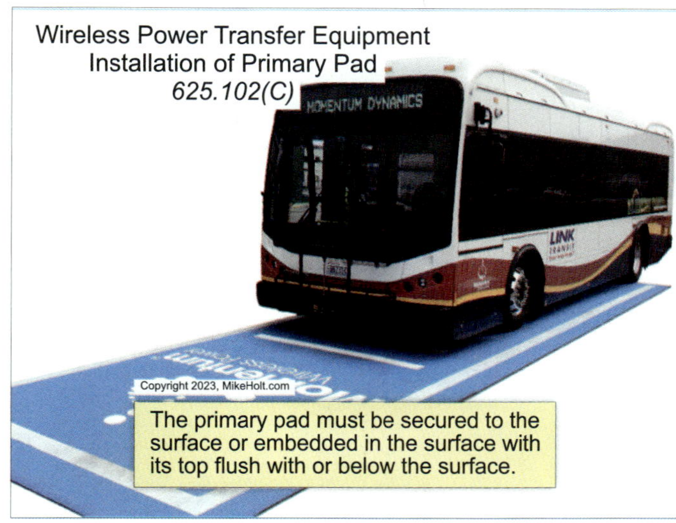

▶Figure 625–19

(2) The primary pad enclosure must be suitable for the environment; if located in an area subject to severe climatic conditions (e.g. flooding), the enclosure must be suitably for those conditions.

(D) Protection of Cords and Cables to the Primary Pad. The output cable to the primary pad must be secured in place over its entire length for the purpose of restricting its movement and to prevent strain at the connection points. If installed in conditions where drive-over could occur, the cable must be provided with supplemental protection.

(E) Other Wiring Systems. Other wiring systems and fittings specifically listed for use on the WPTE are permitted.

SOLAR PHOTOVOLTAIC (PV) SYSTEMS

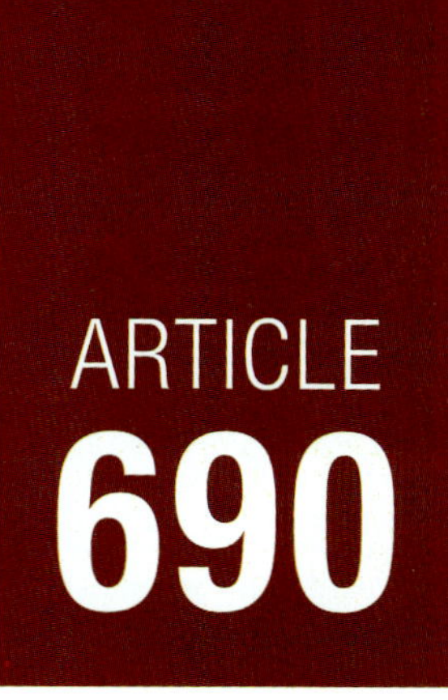

Introduction to Article 690—Solar Photovoltaic (PV) Systems

You have seen, or maybe own, devices powered by photovoltaic cells such as night lights, car coolers, and toys. These generally consist of a small solar module powering a small device running on a few volts and a fraction of an ampere. A solar PV system that powers a building or interconnects with an electric utility operates on the same principals but on a much larger scale.

Solar PV systems that provide electrical power to an electrical system are complex. There are many issues that require expert knowledge in electrical, structural, and architectural issues.

The purpose of the *NEC* is to safeguard persons and property from the hazards arising from the use of electricity [90.2(C)]. Article 690 is focused on the electrical hazards that may arise from installing and operating a PV system. It consists of eight parts.

The general *Code* requirements of Chapters 1 through 4 also apply to these installations, except as specifically modified by this article [90.3].

Part I. General

690.1 Scope

The requirements contained in Article 690 apply to solar photovoltaic (PV) systems other than those covered by Article 691. ▶Figure 690–1

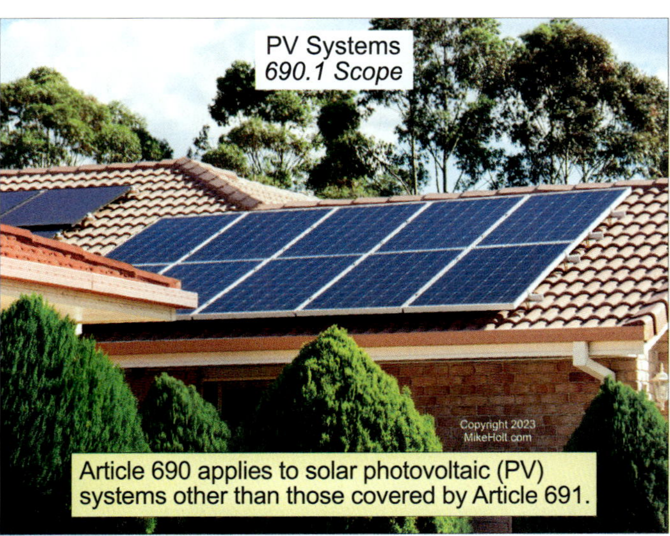

▶Figure 690–1

According to Article 100, a "Photovoltaic (PV) System" is the combination of components, circuits, and equipment up to and including the PV system disconnect, that converts solar energy into electrical energy. ▶Figure 690–2

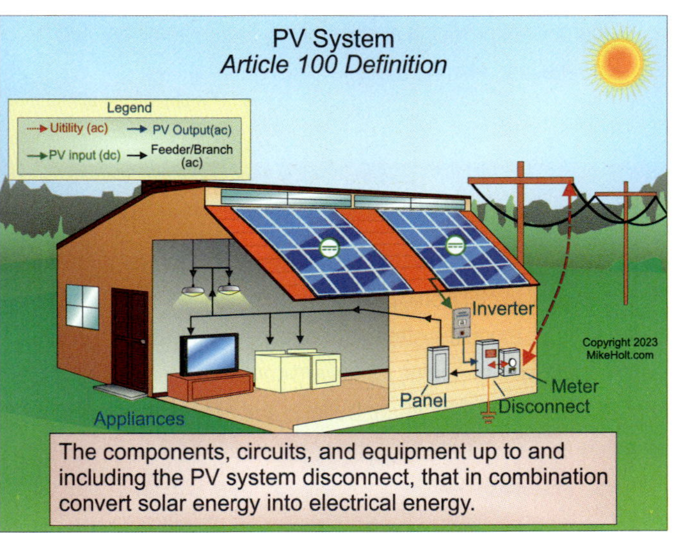

▶Figure 690–2

Note 1: See *NEC* Figure 690.1.

Note 2: Article 691 covers the installation of large-scale PV electric supply stations with an inverter generating capacity of 5000 kW and more, and not under the electric utility control. ▶**Figure 690–3**

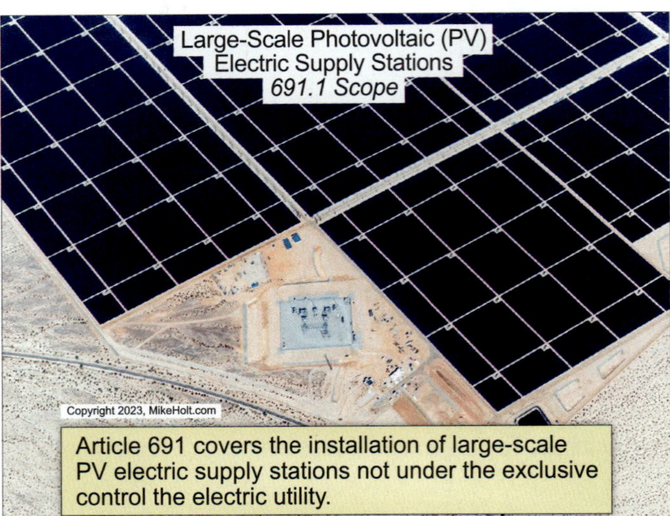

▶Figure 690–3

According to Article 100, the "Inverter Generating Capacity" is equal to the sum of parallel-connected inverter maximum continuous output power at 40C in watts, kilowatts, volt-amperes, or kilovolt-amperes.

Author's Comment:

▸ Large-scale PV supply stations have specific design and safety features unique to these facilities and are for the sole purpose of providing electric supply to a system operated by a regulated electric utility.

690.4 General Requirements

(B) Listed or Field Labeled Equipment. Components of the PV system including underlined electronic power converters, inverters, PV modules, ac modules, ac module systems, dc combiners, dc-to-dc converters, PV rapid shutdown equipment, PV hazard control equipment, PV hazard control systems, dc circuit controllers, and charge controllers must be listed or be evaluated for the application and have a field label applied. ▶**Figure 690–4**

According to Article 100, a "DC Combiner" is an enclosure that includes devices for the parallel connection of two or more PV system dc circuits. ▶**Figure 690–5**

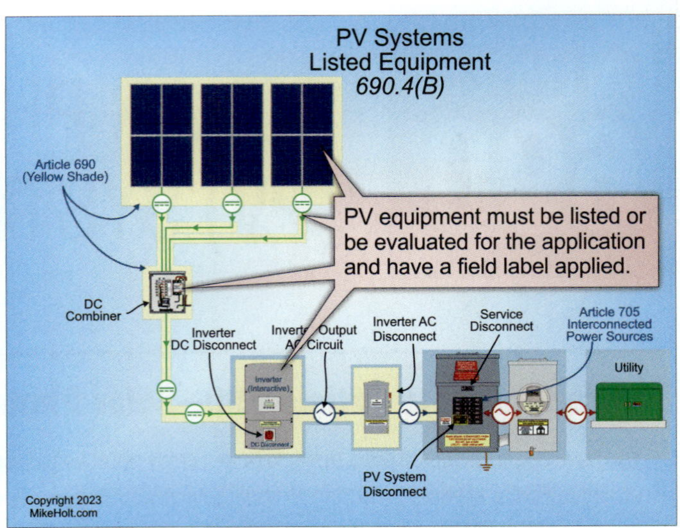

▶Figure 690–4

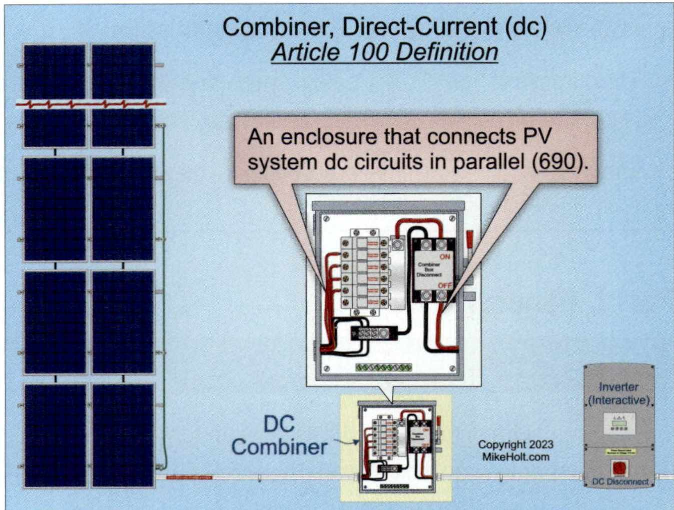

▶Figure 690–5

According to Article 100, a "DC-to-DC Converter" can provide an output dc voltage and current at a higher or lower value than the input dc voltage and current. ▶**Figure 690–6**

An "Electronic Power Converter" is a device that uses power electronics to convert one form of electrical power into another form of electrical power. Examples of electronic power converters include, but are not limited to, inverters and dc-to-dc converters. ▶**Figure 690–7**

An "Inverter" changes direct current to alternating current. ▶**Figure 690–8**

A "PV Module" is a unit of environmentally protected solar cells and components designed to produce dc power. ▶**Figure 690–9**

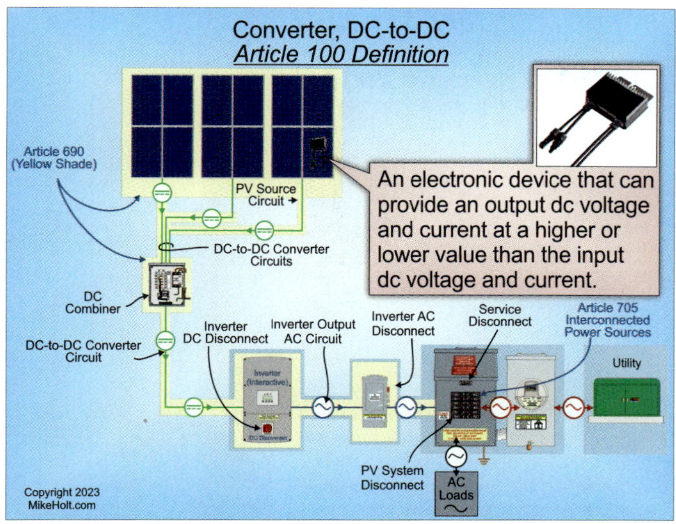

▶Figure 690–6

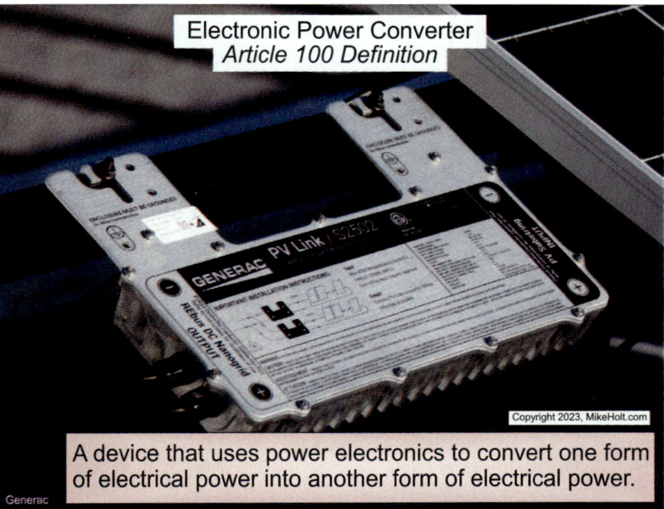

▶Figure 690–7

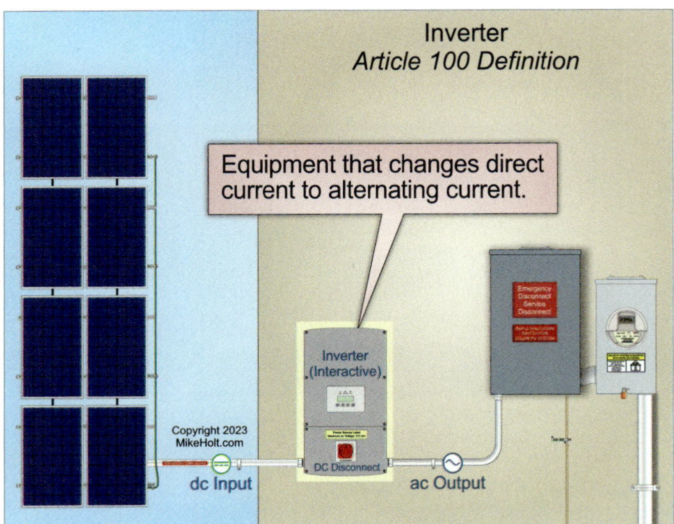

▶Figure 690–8

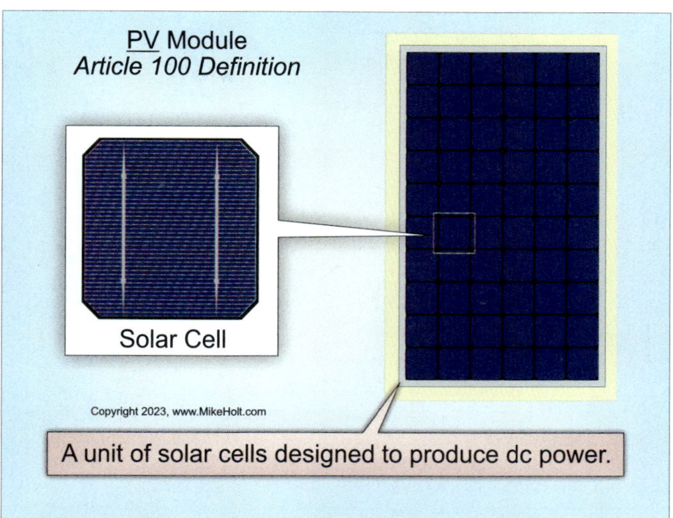

▶Figure 690–9

(C) Qualified Persons. The installation of PV systems must be performed by a qualified person. ▶Figure 690–10

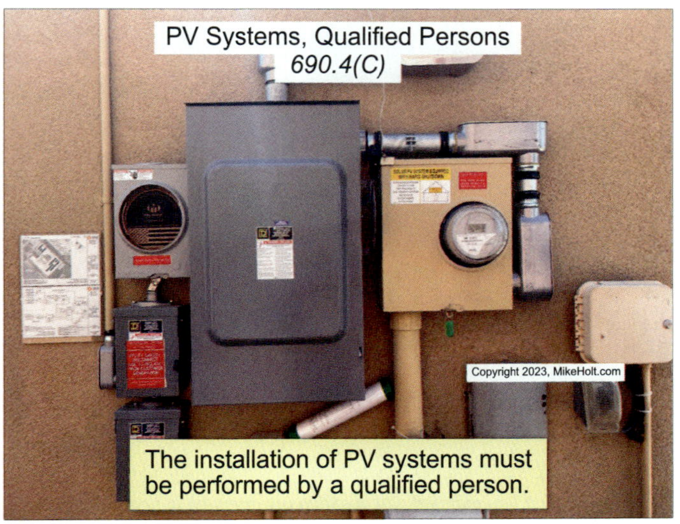

▶Figure 690–10

According to Article 100, a "Qualified Person" has the skills and knowledge related to the construction and operation of electrical equipment and installations. This person must have received safety training to recognize and avoid the hazards involved with electrical systems. ▶Figure 690–11

(D) Multiple PV Systems. Multiple PV systems are permitted on or in a building. ▶Figure 690–12

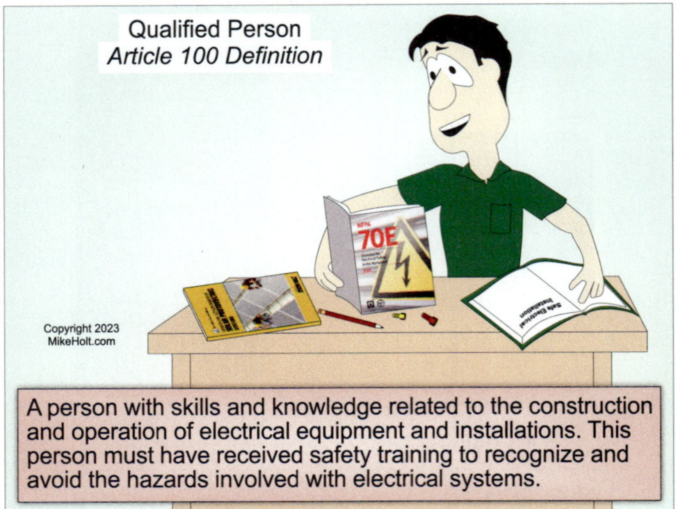

A person with skills and knowledge related to the construction and operation of electrical equipment and installations. This person must have received safety training to recognize and avoid the hazards involved with electrical systems.

▶Figure 690–11

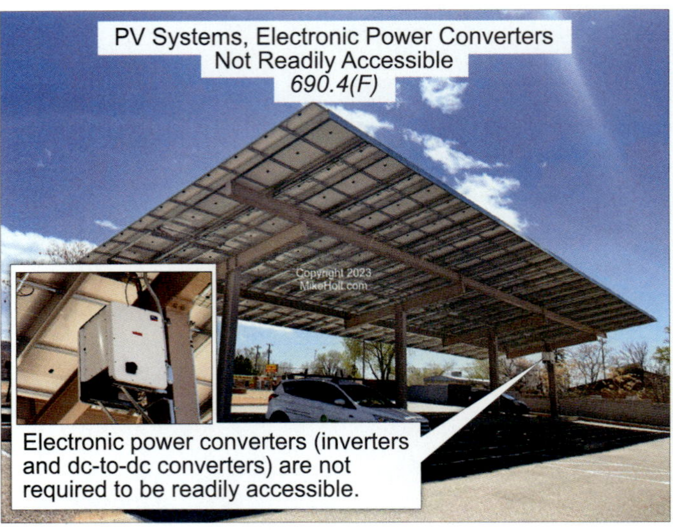

Electronic power converters (inverters and dc-to-dc converters) are not required to be readily accessible.

▶Figure 690–13

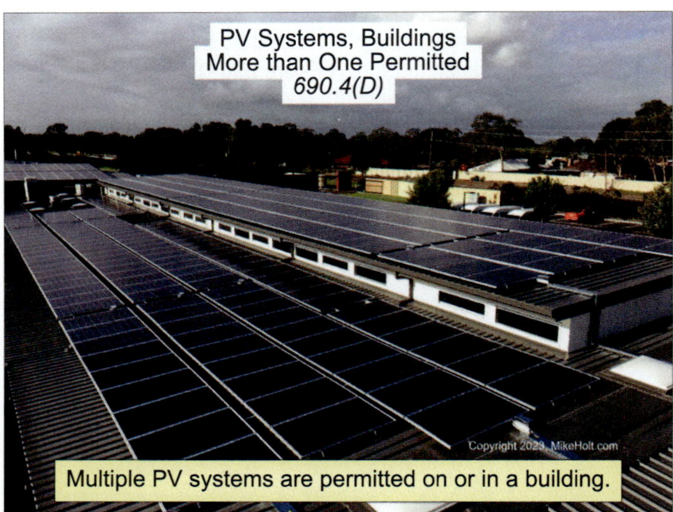

Multiple PV systems are permitted on or in a building.

▶Figure 690–12

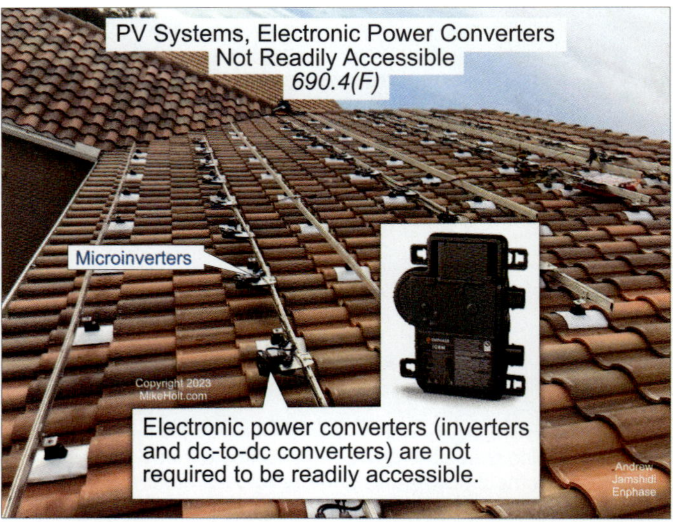

Electronic power converters (inverters and dc-to-dc converters) are not required to be readily accessible.

▶Figure 690–14

(E) Where Not Permitted. PV system equipment is not permitted to be installed within a bathroom.

(F) Not Readily Accessible. Electronic power converters (inverters and dc-to-dc converters) are not required to be readily accessible and can be mounded on roofs or other areas that are not readily accessible. ▶Figure 690–13 and ▶Figure 690–14

(G) PV Equipment Floating on Bodies of Water. PV equipment floating on or attached to structures floating on bodies of water must be identified as being suitable for the purpose and have wiring methods that allow for expected movement of the equipment. ▶Figure 690–15

Note: PV equipment on bodies of water are subject to increased levels of humidity, corrosion, and mechanical and structural stresses.

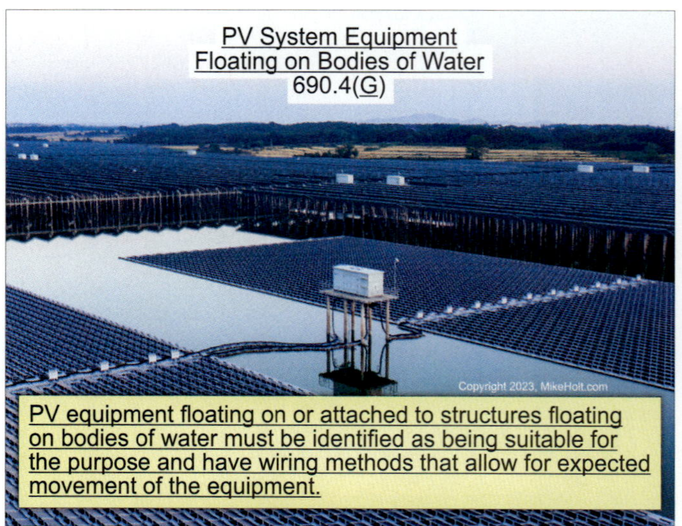

PV equipment floating on or attached to structures floating on bodies of water must be identified as being suitable for the purpose and have wiring methods that allow for expected movement of the equipment.

▶Figure 690–15

690.6 Alternating-Current Modules

According to Article 100, an "AC Module" consists of solar cells, inverters, and other components designed to produce alternating-current power (Article 690). ▶Figure 690–16

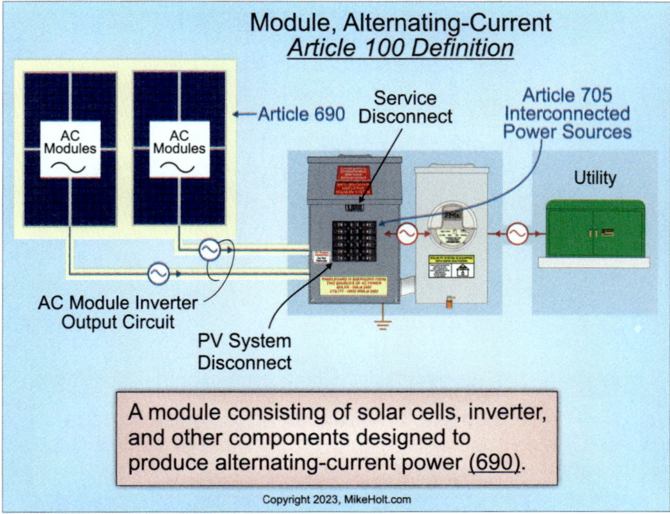

▶Figure 690–16

(A) Source (dc) Circuit. The requirements of Article 690 do not apply to the source circuit conductors of an ac module. ▶Figure 690–17

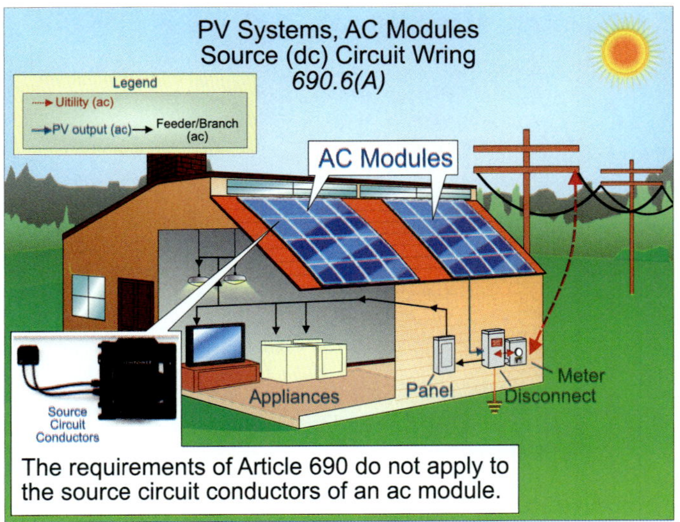

▶Figure 690–17

(B) Output (ac) Circuit. The ac output circuit conductors for an ac module are considered the inverter ac output circuit. ▶Figure 690–18

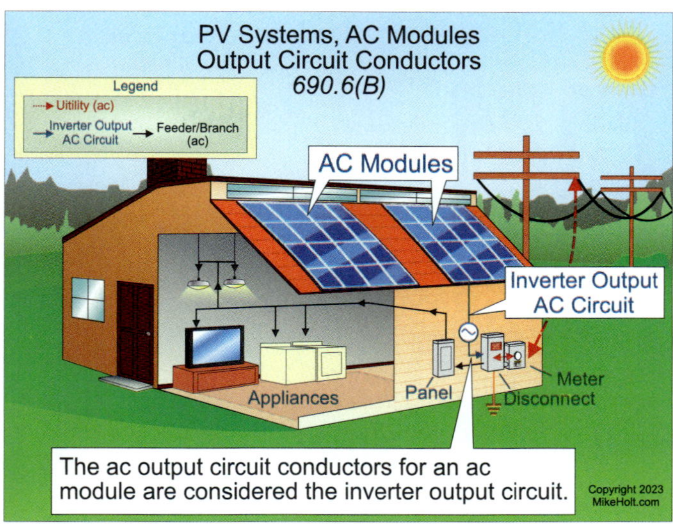

▶Figure 690–18

According to Article 100, an "Inverter Output Circuit" includes the conductors connected to the alternating-current output of an inverter. ▶Figure 690–19 and ▶Figure 690–20

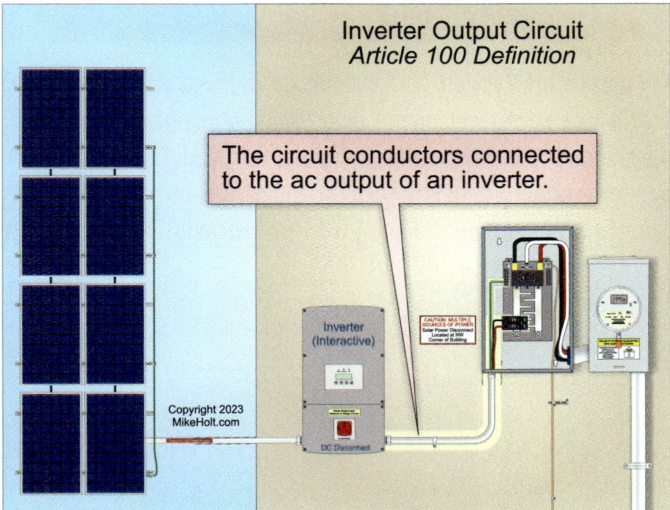

▶Figure 690–19

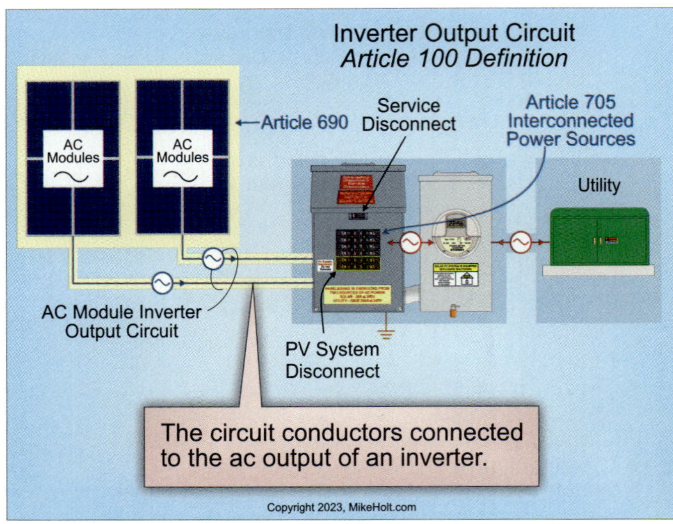

▶Figure 690–20

Part II. Circuit Requirements

690.7 Maximum PV System Direct-Current Circuit Voltage

The maximum PV system dc circuit voltage value is used when selecting conductors, cables, equipment, determining working space, and other applications where circuit voltage ratings are used. The maximum PV system dc circuit voltage is the highest voltage between any two conductors of a circuit and must comply with the following: ▶Figure 690–21

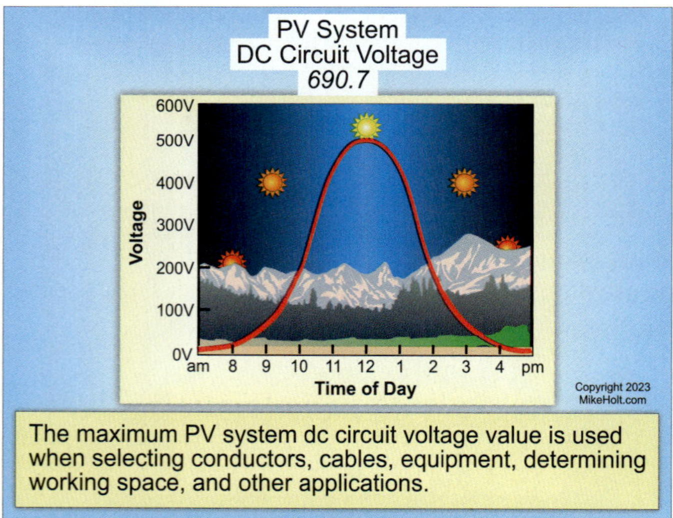

▶Figure 690–21

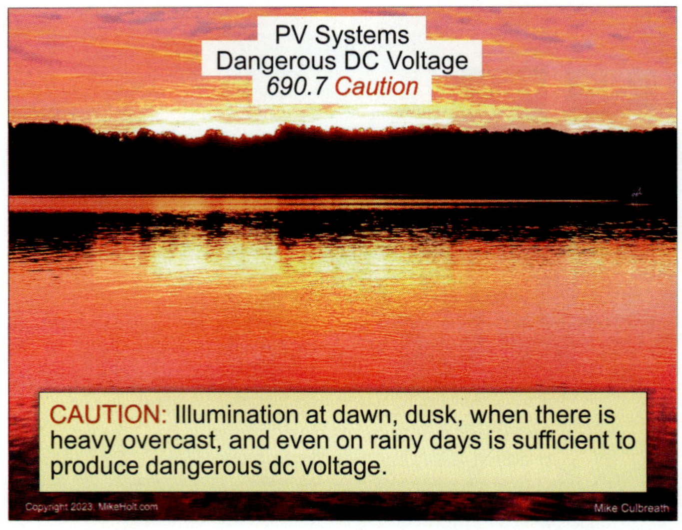

▶Figure 690–22

According to Article 100, a "PV System DC Circuit" consists of any dc conductor in PV source circuits, PV string circuits, and PV dc-to-dc converter circuits. ▶Figure 690–23

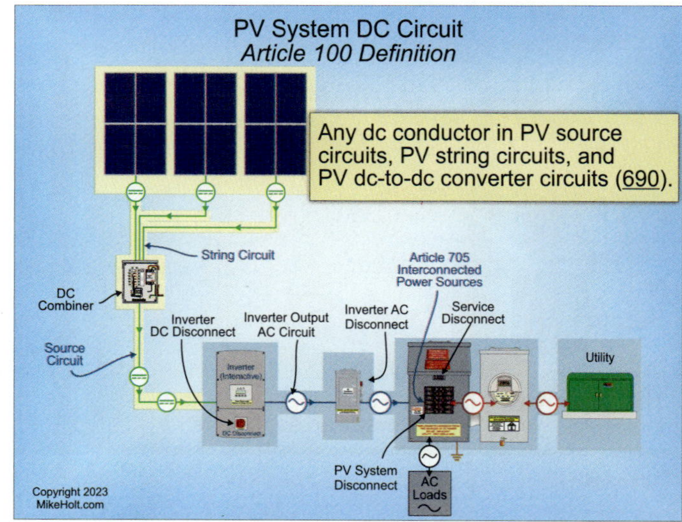

▶Figure 690–23

(1) Commercial and Industrial Buildings. The maximum dc circuit voltage for PV system arrays on commercial and industrial buildings cannot exceed 1000V. ▶Figure 690–24

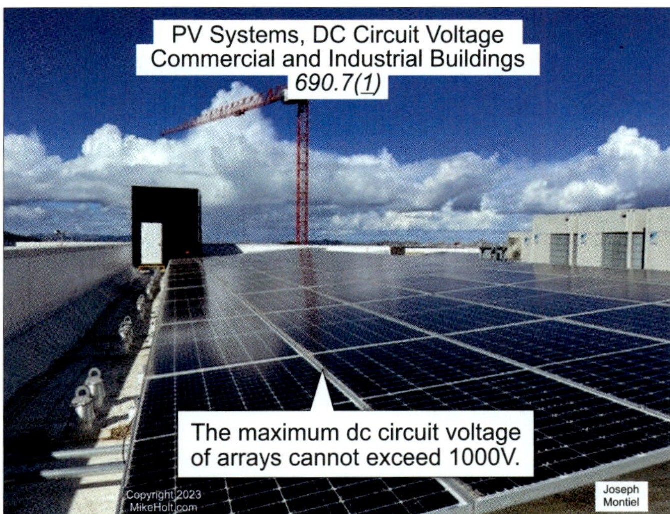

▶Figure 690–24

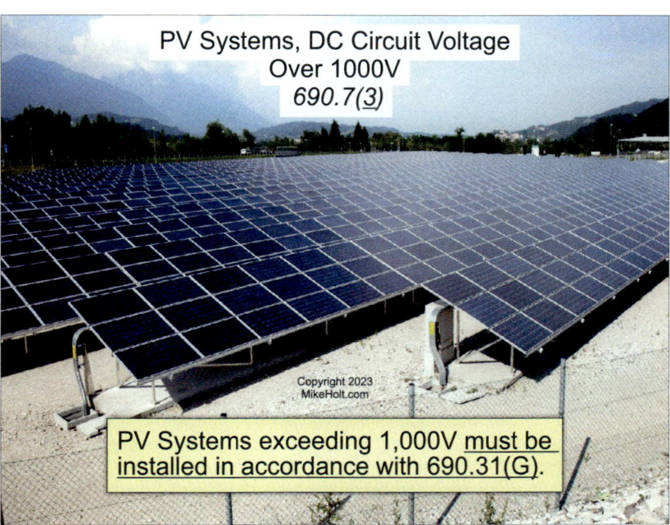

▶Figure 690–26

(2) One- and Two-Family Dwellings. The maximum dc circuit voltage for PV systems on one- and two-family dwellings cannot exceed 600V. ▶Figure 690–25

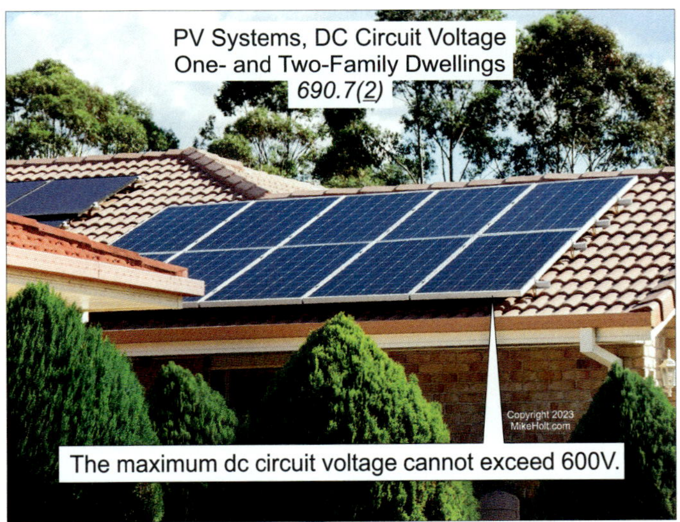

▶Figure 690–25

(3) Over 1000V. PV Systems exceeding 1000V <u>must be installed in accordance with 690.31(G)</u>. ▶Figure 690–26

(A) Calculating PV System Source Circuit Voltage. The maximum calculated PV system <u>dc source circuit</u> voltage is determined by one of the following:

According to Article 100, the "PV Source Circuit" consists of the dc circuit conductors between modules in a PV string and from PV string circuits to dc combiners, electronic power converters, or the PV system dc disconnect (Article 690). ▶Figure 690–27

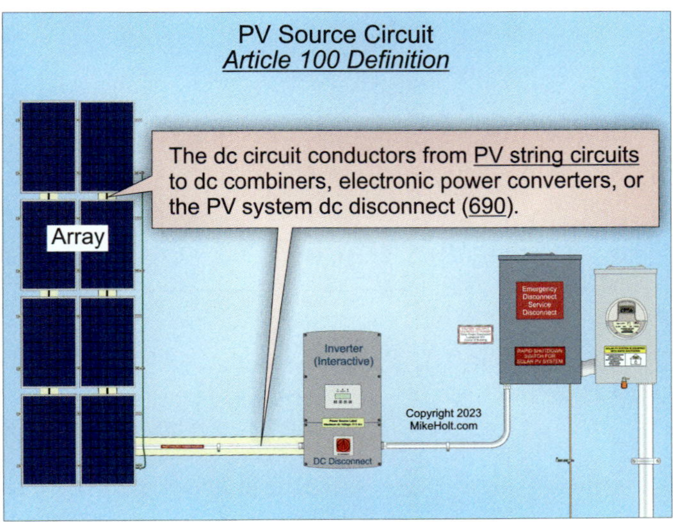

▶Figure 690–27

(1) Manufacturer's Instructions. The PV system dc source circuit voltage is equal to the sum of the series-connected dc modules open-circuit voltage (Voc) <u>in a PV string circuit</u> as corrected for the lowest expected ambient temperature using the manufacturer's voltage temperature coefficient correction. ▶Figure 690–28

According to Article 100, a "PV String" circuit consists of the PV source circuit conductors of one or more series-connected PV modules. ▶Figure 690–29

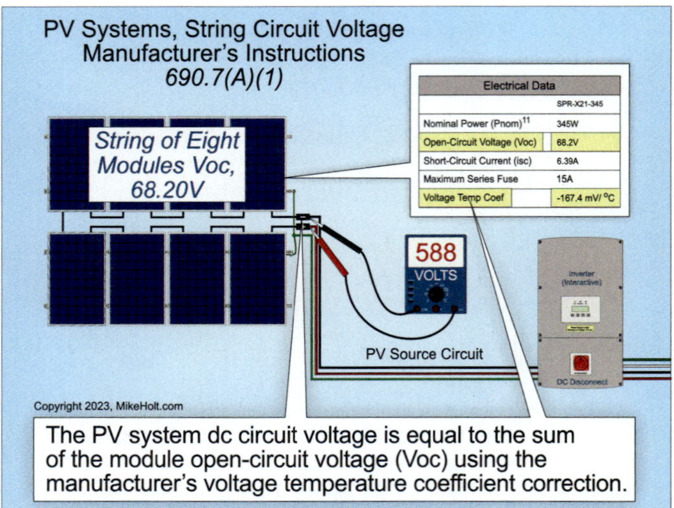

▶Figure 690–28

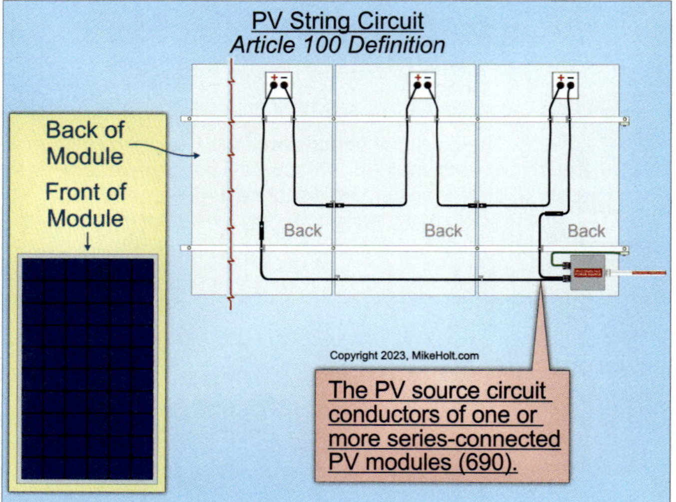

▶Figure 690–29

Author's Comment:

▶ A PV module's dc voltage has an inverse relationship with temperature, which means that at lower ambient temperatures, the module's dc output voltage increases, and at higher ambient temperatures, the modules' dc voltage output decreases.

▶ Maximum PV System DC Voltage, Based on Manufacturer's Temperature Coefficient, V/°C Example 1

Question: *Using the manufacturer's voltage temperature coefficient of –0.167mV/°C, what is the PV source/string circuit dc voltage for eight modules each rated 68.20 Voc at a temperature of –7°C?* ▶Figure 690–30

(a) 539 Vdc   (b) 588 Vdc   (c) 624 Vdc   (d) 641 Vdc

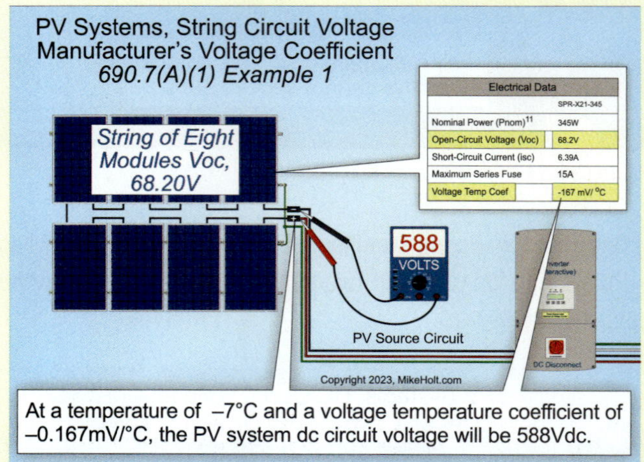

▶Figure 690–30

Solution:

PV Voc (V/°C) = Rated Voc + [(Temp.°C–25°C) × Module Coefficient V/°C] × # Modules

PV Circuit Voltage = {68.20 Vdc + [(–7°C–25°C) × –0.167 Vdc/°C]} × 8 modules

PV Circuit Voltage = [68.20 Vdc + (-32°C × –0.167 Vdc/°C)] × 8 modules

PV Circuit Voltage = (68.20 Vdc + 5.344 Vdc) × 8 modules

PV Circuit Voltage = 73.544 Vdc × 8 modules

PV Circuit Voltage = 588 Vdc

Answer: *(b) 588 Vdc*

▶ Maximum PV System DC Voltage, Based on Manufacturer's Temperature Coefficient, V/°C Example 2

Question: Using the manufacturer's voltage temperature coefficient of –0.167mV/°C, what is the PV source circuit dc voltage for thirteen modules each rated 68.20 Voc at a temperature of –7°C? ▶**Figure 690–31**

(a) 839 Vdc   *(b) 888 Vdc*   *(c) 924 Vdc*   *(d) 956 Vdc*

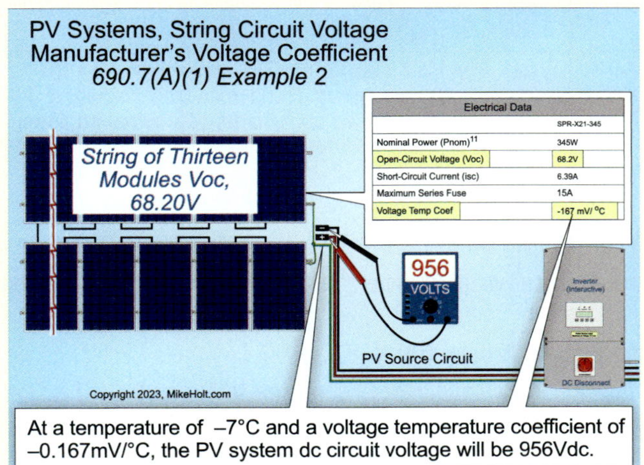

▶Figure 690–31

Solution:

PV Voc (V/°C) = Rated Voc + [(Temp.°C–25°C) × Module Coefficient V/°C] × # Modules

PV Circuit Voltage = {68.20 Vdc + [(–7°C–25°C) × –0.167 Vdc/°C]} × 13 modules

PV Circuit Voltage = [68.20 Vdc + (-32°C × -0.167 Vdc/°C)] × 13 modules

PV Circuit Voltage = (68.20 Vdc + 5.344 Vdc) × 13 modules

PV Circuit Voltage = 73.544 Vdc × 13 modules

PV Circuit Voltage = 956 Vdc

Answer: *(d) 956 Vdc*

Author's Comment:

▶ See www.SolarABCs.org website to find the low temperature data for a specific location for maximum voltage calculations.

(2) Table of Crystalline and Multicrystalline Modules. The PV system dc source circuit voltage is equal to the sum of the series-connected dc modules' rated open-circuit voltage (Voc) in a PV string circuit as corrected for the lowest expected ambient temperature in accordance with Table 690.7(A).

Table 690.7(A) Voltage Correction Factors for Crystalline and Multicrystalline Silicon Modules

Correction Factors for Ambient Temperatures Below 25°C (77°F)

(Multiply the rated open-circuit voltage by the appropriate correction factor shown below.)

Ambient Temperature (°C)	Factor	Ambient Temperature (°F)
24 to 20	1.02	76 to 68
19 to 15	1.04	67 to 59
14 to 10	1.06	58 to 50
9 to 5	1.08	49 to 41
4 to 0	1.10	40 to 32
–1 to -5	1.12	31 to 23
–6 to –10	1.14	22 to 14
–11 to –15	1.16	13 to 5
–16 to –20	1.18	4 to -4
–21 to –25	1.20	–5 to –13
–26 to -30	1.21	–14 to –22
–31 to –35	1.23	–23 to –31
–36 to –40	1.25	–32 to –40

▶ Maximum PV System DC Voltage, Based on Table 690.7(A) Temperature Correction [690.7(A)(2)] Example

Question: Using Table 690.7(A), what is the maximum PV system source circuit dc voltage for twelve crystalline modules each rated 38.30 Voc at a temperature of -7°C? ▶**Figure 690–32**

(a) 493 Vdc   (b) 513 Vdc   (c) 524 Vdc   (d) 541 Vdc

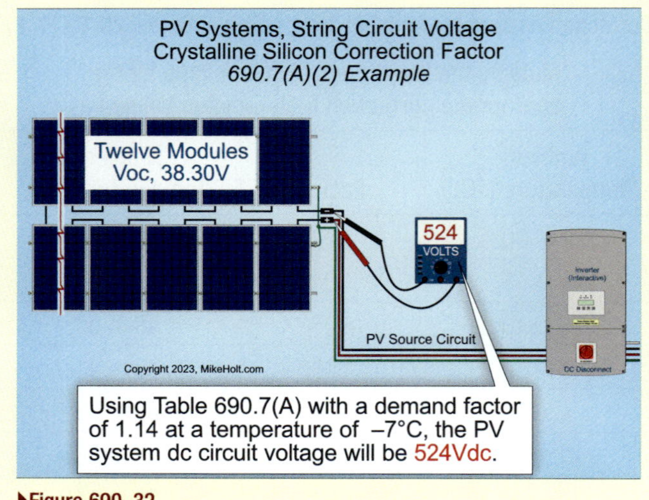

▶Figure 690–32

Solution:

PV Voc = Module Voc × Table 690.7 Correction Factor × # Modules
PV Circuit Voltage = 38.30 Voc × 1.14 × 12 modules
PV Circuit Voltage = 524 Vdc

Answer: (c) 524 Vdc

(3) Engineered Industry Standard Method. For PV systems with an inverter generating capacity of 100 kW or greater, the PV system dc circuit voltage is permitted to be determined by a licensed professional electrical engineer who provides a documented and stamped PV system design using an industry standard method for maximum dc voltage calculation. ▶**Figure 690–33**

Note 1: One source of lowest-expected ambient temperature design data for various locations is the chapter titled "Extreme Annual Mean Minimum Design Dry Bulb Temperature" found in the *ASHRAE Handbook–Fundamentals*. This temperature data can be used to calculate the maximum voltage.

Note 2: One industry standard method for calculating the PV source and output circuit dc voltage is published by Sandia National Laboratories, reference SAND 2004-3535, *Photovoltaic Array Performance Model*.

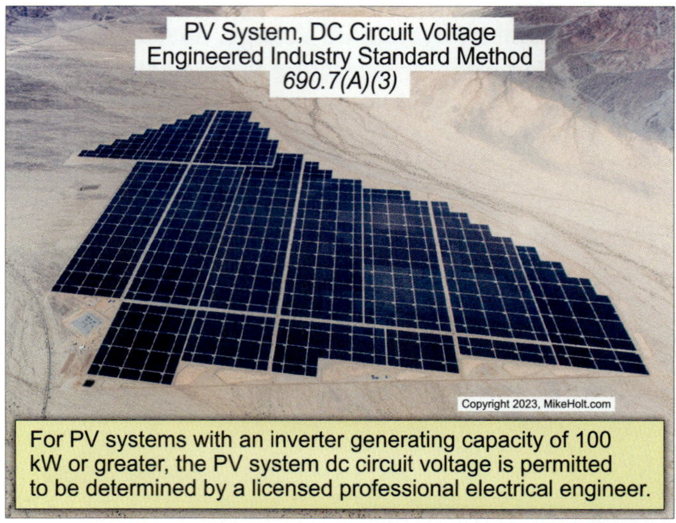

▶Figure 690–33

(B) Calculating DC-to-DC Converter Circuit Voltage. The dc-to-dc converter circuit voltage is determined by one of the following methods:

According to Article 100, a "DC-to-DC Converter Circuit" consists of the dc circuit conductors connected to the output of dc-to-dc converters. ▶**Figure 690–34**

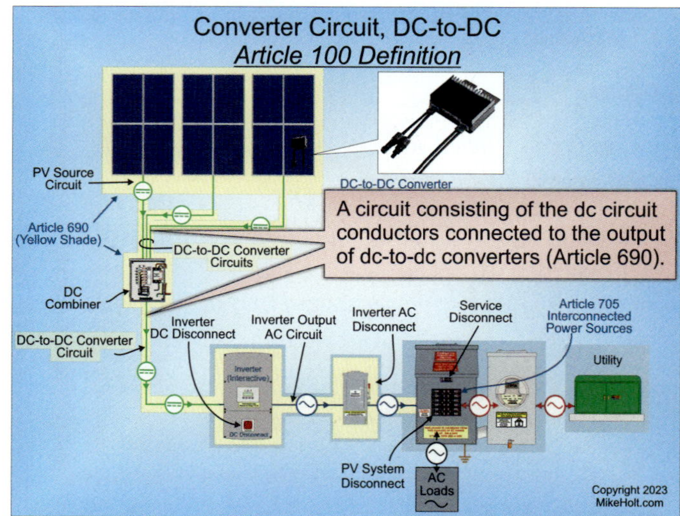

▶Figure 690–34

Author's Comment:

▶ A dc-to-dc converter (optimizer) enables the output circuit voltage to stay within the window that is maximized for direct-current and/or alternating-current power production by the inverter regardless of voltage fluctuations caused by individual module performance or variance in light exposure between modules.

(1) Single DC-to-DC Converter. The output dc voltage for a single dc-to-dc converter (optimizer) is based on the manufactures instructions or equal to the rated output dc voltage of the converter (optimizer). ▶Figure 690–35

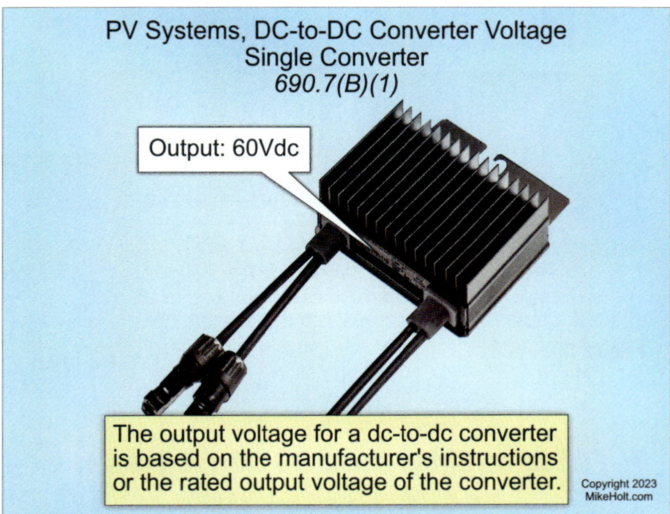

▶Figure 690–35

(2) Series-Connected DC-to-DC Converters. The output dc voltage for multiple dc-to-dc converters connected in series is based on the manufactures instructions or equal to the sum of the rated output voltage of the converters. ▶Figure 690–36

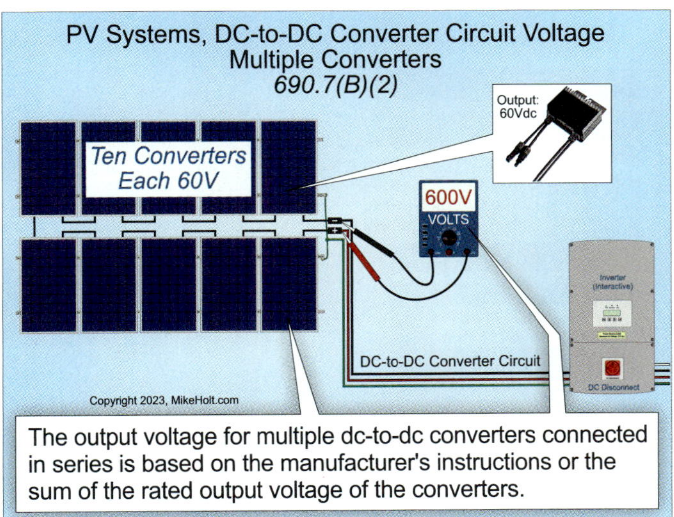

▶Figure 690–36

(D) Marking PV dc Circuit Voltage. A permanent readily visible label indicating the maximum PV system dc circuit voltage, as calculated in accordance with 690.7, must be installed at one of the following locations: ▶Figure 690–37

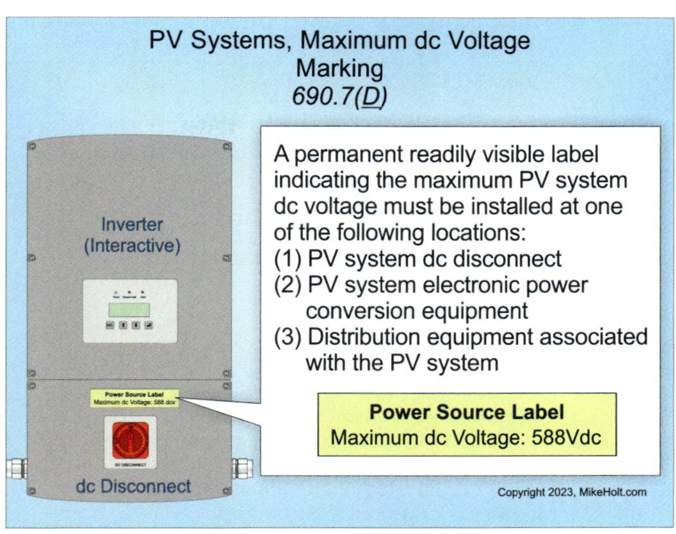

▶Figure 690–37

(1) PV system dc disconnect

(2) PV system electronic power converters

(3) Distribution equipment associated with the PV system

690.8 Circuit Current and Conductor Sizing

(A) Calculation of Maximum PV Circuit Current. The maximum PV system current is calculated in accordance with 690.8(A)(1) or (2):

(1) PV System Circuit Current. The maximum PV system circuit current is calculated in accordance with 690.8(A)(1)(a) through (c).

(a) PV System dc Source/String Circuit Current.

(1) PV Systems of Any kW Rating. The maximum PV source/string circuit dc current is equal to the short-circuit current ratings marked on the modules (Isc) multiplied by 125 percent. ▶Figure 690–38

Author's Comment:

▶ A module can produce more than the rated current when the intensity of the sunlight is greater than the standard used to determine the module's short-circuit rating. This happens when sunlight intensity is affected by altitude, reflection due to snow, refraction through clouds, or low humidity. For this reason, the PV system maximum circuit current is calculated at 125 percent of the module's short-circuit current rating marked on the module's nameplate. This is commonly referred to as an "irradiance factor." ▶Figure 690–39

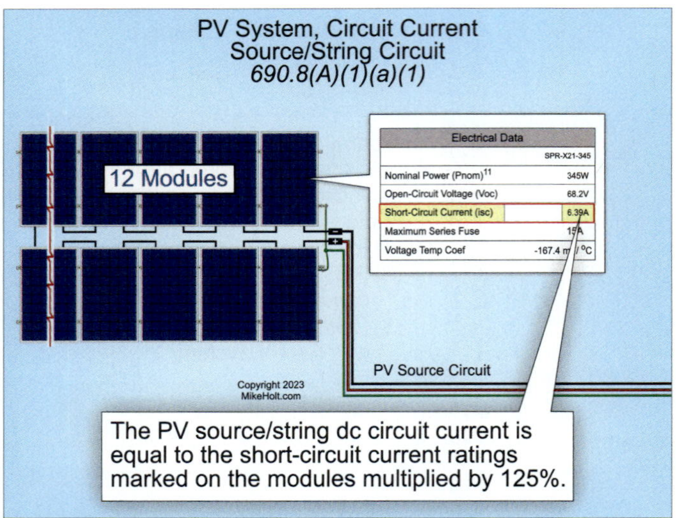

▶Figure 690–38

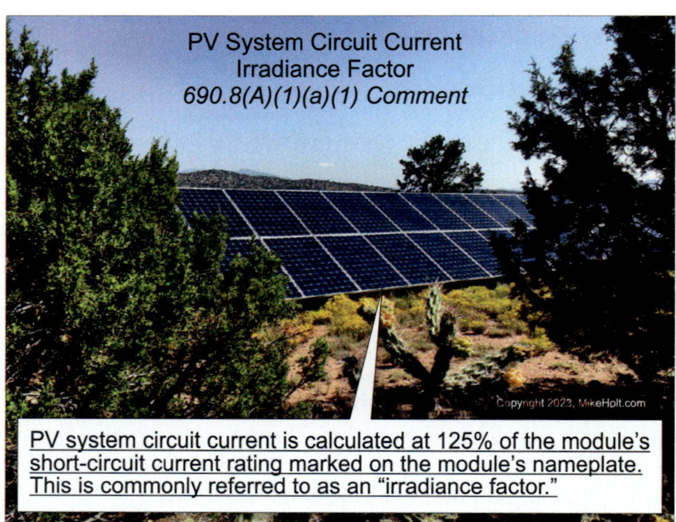

▶Figure 690–39

▶ PV Source/String Circuit DC Current Example 1

Question: *What is the maximum PV string circuit current for 8 series-connected modules having a nameplate short-circuit current (Isc) of 6.39A?* ▶**Figure 690–40**

(a) 8A (b) 9A (c) 10A (d) 11A

Solution:

String Circuit Current = Module Isc × 125%

String Circuit Current = 6.39A × 125%

String Circuit Current = 7.99A

Answer: *(a) 8A*

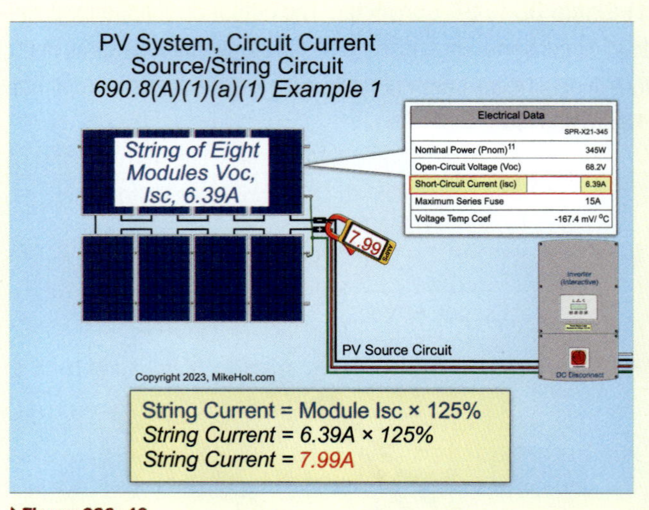

▶Figure 690–40

▶ PV Source/String Circuit DC Current Example 2

Question: *What is the maximum circuit current for four PV string circuits of 8 series-connected modules each having a nameplate short-circuit current (Isc) of 6.39A?* ▶**Figure 690–41**

(a) 22A (b) 32A (c) 42A (d) 52A

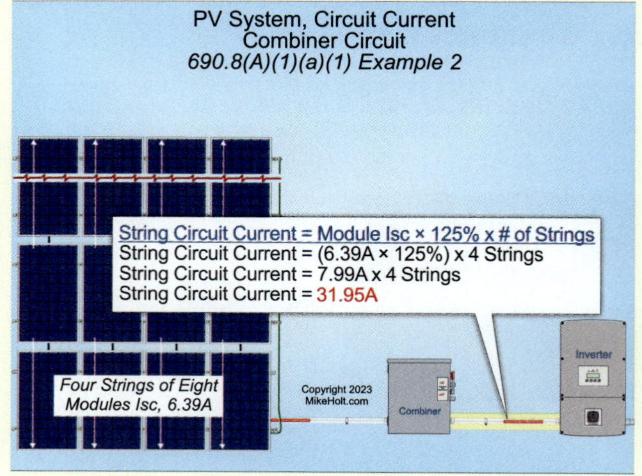

▶Figure 690–41

Solution:

String Circuit Current = Module Isc × 125% × Number of Strings

String Circuit Current = (6.39A × 125%) × 4 Strings

String Circuit Current = 7.99A × 4 Strings

String Circuit Current = 31.95A

Answer: *(b) 32A*

(2) PV Systems Rated 100 kW or Greater. The maximum PV dc source circuit current calculations for PV systems with an inverter generating capacity of 100 kW or greater can be determined by a licensed professional electrical engineer that provides a documented and stamped PV system design using an industry standard method.

The PV source circuit dc current value is based on the highest three-hour current average resulting from the simulated local irradiance on the array accounting for elevation and orientation. In no case is the PV source circuit dc current permitted to be less than 70 percent of the PV source circuit dc current as calculated in 690.8(A)(1)(a)(1).

Note: One industry standard method for calculating the PV source current is available from Sandia National Laboratories, reference SAND 2004-3535, *Photovoltaic Array Performance Model.* This model is used by the System Advisor Model simulation program provided by the National Renewable Energy Laboratory.

(b) PV DC-to-DC Converter Circuit Current. The dc-to-dc circuit current is equal to the <u>sum of the parallel-connected</u> dc-to-dc converter's continuous output current <u>ratings</u>. ▶Figure 690–42

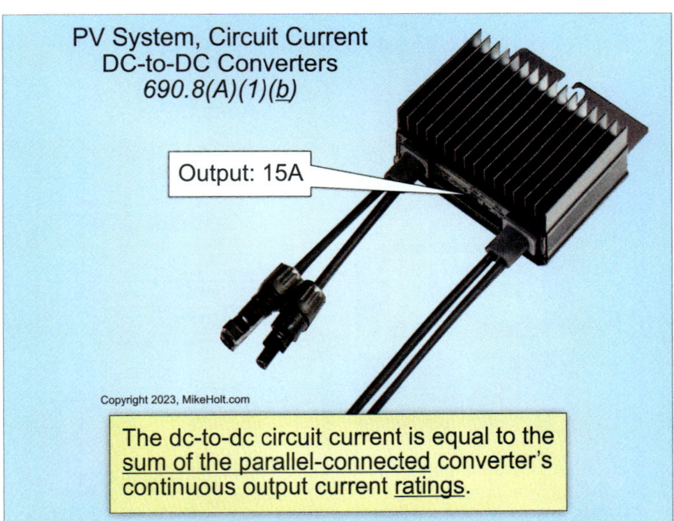

▶Figure 690–42

▶ DC-to-DC Converter Circuit Current Example

Question: What is the PV dc-to-dc converter output circuit current for a single string, where the nameplate output current rating is 15A? ▶Figure 690–43

(a) 15A   (b) 30A   (c) 45A   (d) 60A

Answer: (a) 15A

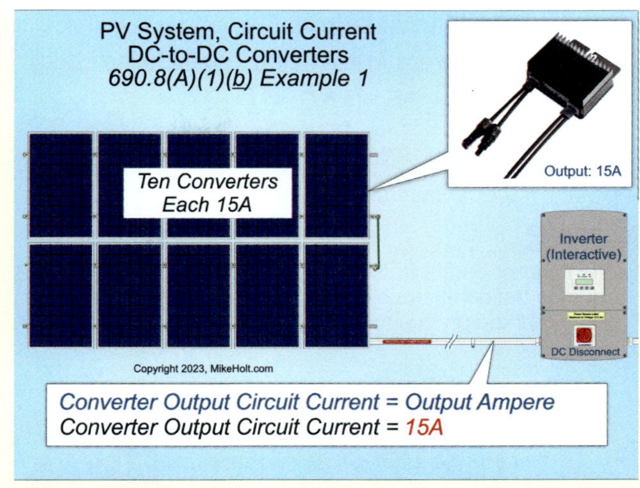

▶Figure 690–43

▶ DC-to-DC Converter Combiner Circuit Current Example

Question: What is the PV dc-to-dc converter output combiner circuit current for four string circuits connected in parallel, each having a nameplate output current rating of 15A? ▶Figure 690–44

(a) 15A   (b) 30A   (c) 45A   (d) 60A

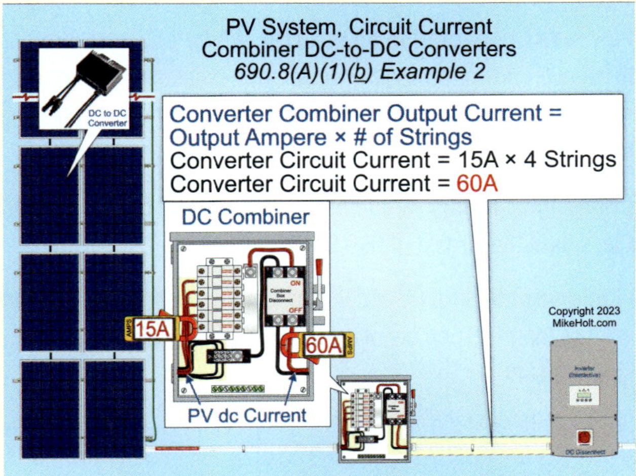

▶Figure 690–44

Solution:

Converter Output Combiner Circuit Current = Output Ampere Rating × Number of Parallel Circuits
Converter Output Combiner Circuit Current = 15A × 4
Converter Output Combiner Circuit Current = 60A

Answer: (d) 60A

(c) Inverter Output Circuit Current. The inverter output ac circuit current is equal to the continuous output current rating marked on the inverter nameplate. ▶Figure 690–45

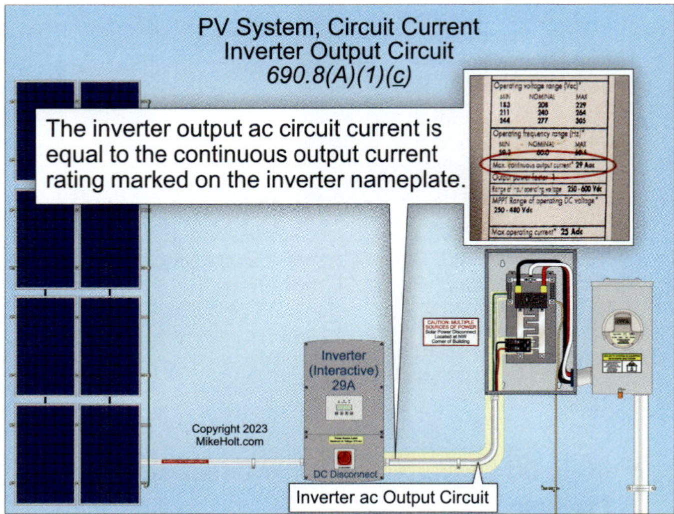

▶Figure 690–45

Note: Modules that can produce electricity when exposed to light on multiple surfaces are labeled with applicable short-circuit currents. Additional guidance is provided in the instructions included with the listing.

(2) Circuits Connected to an Inverter. Where a circuit is protected with an overcurrent protective device not exceeding the conductor ampacity, the maximum current is permitted to be the rated input current of the inverter to which it is connected.

(B) Conductor Sizing. PV circuit conductors must have an ampacity not less than the largest of 690.8(B)(1) or (B)(2).

(1) Conductor Sizing. PV circuit conductors must have an ampacity of not less than 125 percent of the current as determined by 690.8(A). ▶Figure 690–46

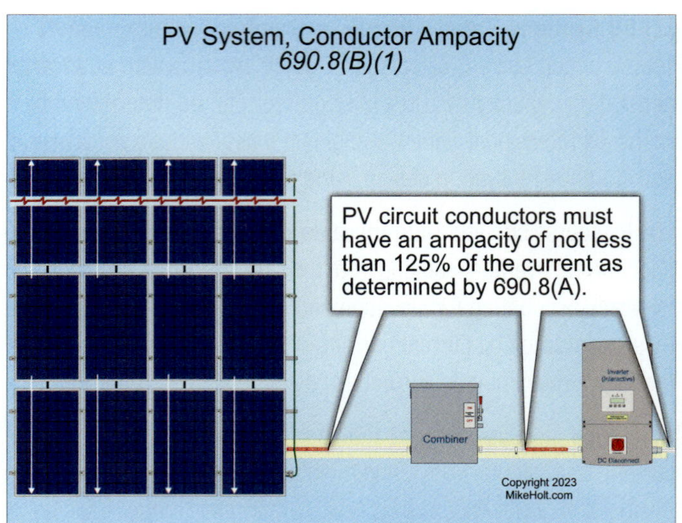

▶Figure 690–46

▶ **Source/String Circuit Conductor Ampacity One-String Example**

Question: What is the minimum circuit conductor ampacity for a single string of 8 series-connected modules having a short-circuit current rating (Isc) of 6.39A? ▶Figure 690–47

(a) 9A   *(b) 10A*   *(c) 11A*   *(d) 12A*

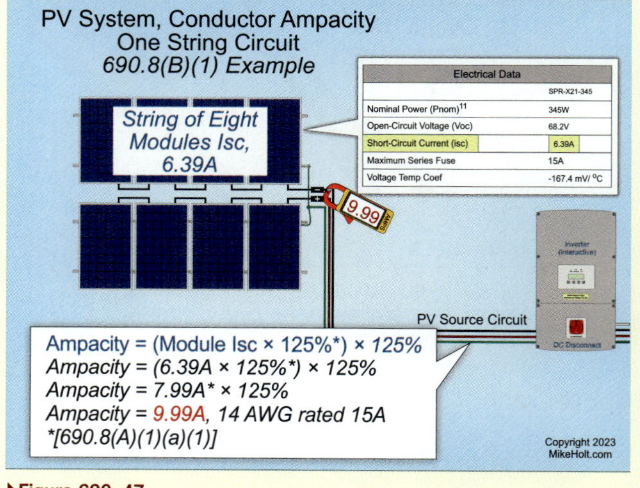

▶Figure 690–47

Solution:

Conductor Ampacity = (Module Isc × 125%) × 125%*
Conductor Ampacity = (6.39A × 125%) × 125%*
Conductor Ampacity = 7.99A × 125%
Conductor Ampacity = 9.99A, 14 AWG rated 15A at 60°C [Table 310.16]
**[690.8(A)(1)(a)]*

Answer: (b) 10A

▶ Source/String Circuit Conductor Ampacity Combiner Example

Question: *What is the minimum circuit conductor ampacity required to supply four strings of 8 series-connected modules having a nameplate short-circuit current (Isc) of 6.39A, terminals rated at 75°C?* ▶Figure 690–48

(a) 25A   (b) 30A   (c) 35A   (d) 40A

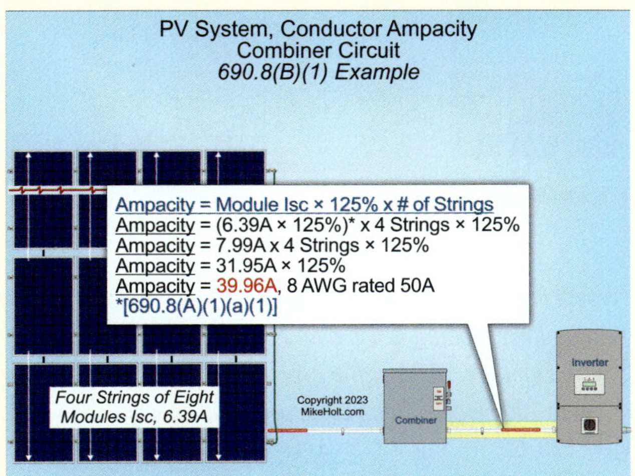

▶Figure 690–48

Solution:

Conductor Ampacity = (Module Isc × 125% × 125%) × Number of Strings

Conductor Ampacity = (6.39A × 125% × 125%) × 4 Strings*

Conductor Ampacity = (7.99A × 125%) × 4 Strings

Conductor Ampacity = 9.99A × 4 Strings

Conductor Ampacity = 39.96A, 8 AWG rated 50A at 75°C [Table 310.16]

**[690.8(A)(1)(a)]*

Answer: *(d) 40A*

▶ DC-to-DC Converter Circuit Conductor Ampacity Example

Question: *What is the PV dc-to-dc converter circuit conductor ampacity for each of the two string circuits connected in parallel, each having a nameplate output current rating of 15A?* ▶Figure 690–49

(a) 18.75A   (b) 19.75A   (c) 21.50A   (d) 23.25A

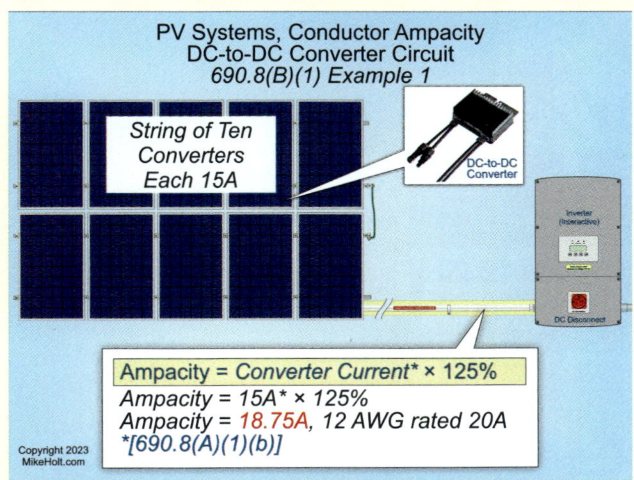

▶Figure 690–49

Solution:

Conductor Ampacity = DC-to-DC Converter Current* × 125%

*Conductor Ampacity = 15A × 125%**

Conductor Ampacity = 18.75A, 12 AWG rated 20A at 60°C [Table 310.16]

**[690.8(A)(1)(b)]*

Answer: *(a) 18.75A*

▶ DC-to-DC Converter Combiner Circuit Conductor Ampacity Example

Question: *What is the PV dc-to-dc converter circuit current for four string circuits connected in parallel, each having a nameplate output current rating of 15A?* ▶**Figure 690–50**

(a) 45A   (b) 55A   (c) 65A   (d) 75A

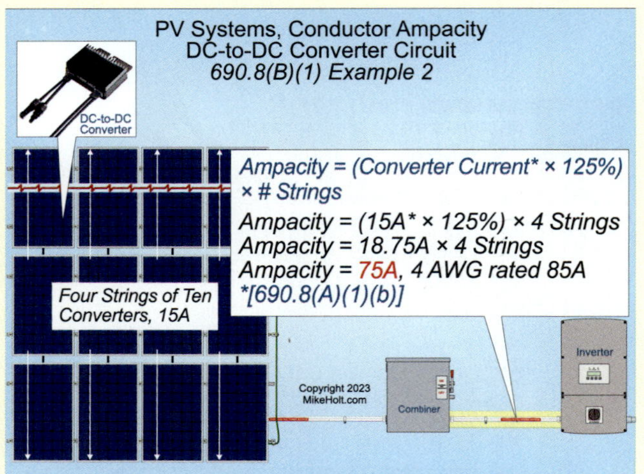

▶Figure 690–50

Solution:

Conductor Ampacity = (DC-to-DC Converter Current* × 125%) × # of Strings

Conductor Ampacity = 15A × 125% × 4 Strings*

Conductor Ampacity = 18.75A × 4 Strings*

Conductor Ampacity = 75A, 4 AWG rated 85A [Table 310.16]

**[690.8(A)(1)(b)]*

Answer: *(d) 75A*

▶ Inverter Output Circuit Ampacity Example

Question: *What is the minimum inverter ac output circuit conductor ampacity required for inverter rated 24A?* ▶**Figure 690–51**

(a) 20A   (b) 25A   (c) 30A   (d) 35A

Solution:

Conductor Ampacity = Inverter Nameplate Rating [690.8(A)(1)(c)] × 125%

Conductor Ampacity = 24A × 125%

Conductor Ampacity = 30A

Answer: *(c) 30A*

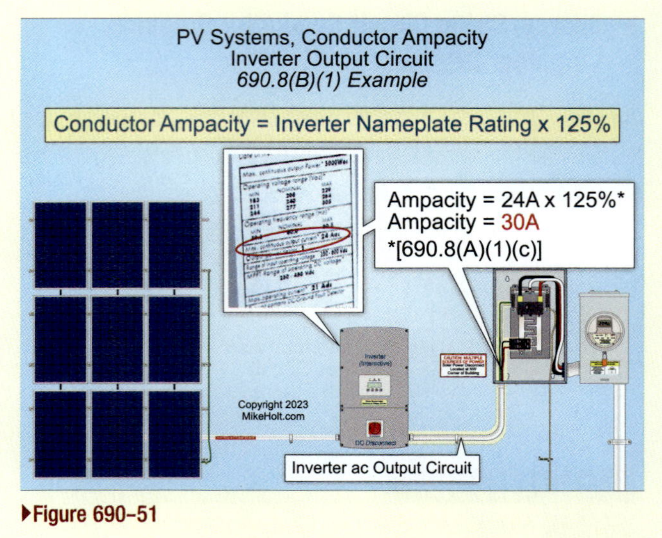

▶Figure 690–51

Ex: Where the assembly, including the overcurrent protective devices protecting the circuit(s), is listed for operation at 100 percent of its rating, the ampere rating of the overcurrent protective device can be sized to 100 percent of the continuous and noncontinuous loads. ▶**Figure 690–52**

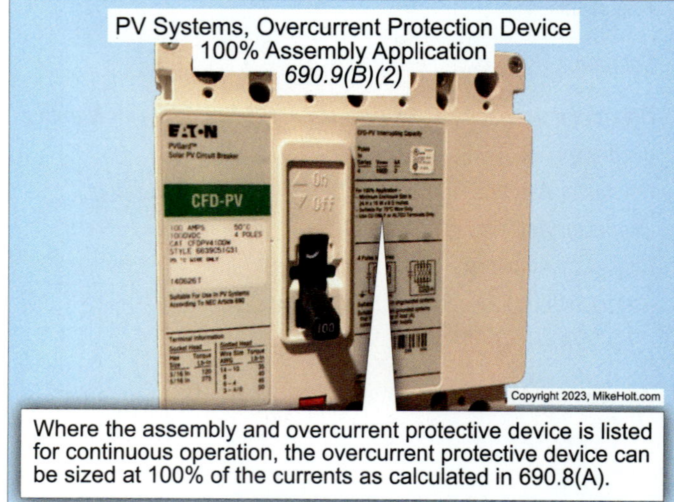

▶Figure 690–52

(2) Conductor Sizing, With Ampacity Correction and/or Adjustment. PV circuit conductors must have an ampacity of not less than 100 percent of the current as determined by 690.8(A) after conductor ampacity correction [Table 310.15(B)(1)(1)] and adjustment [Table 310.15(C)(1)]. ▶**Figure 690–53**

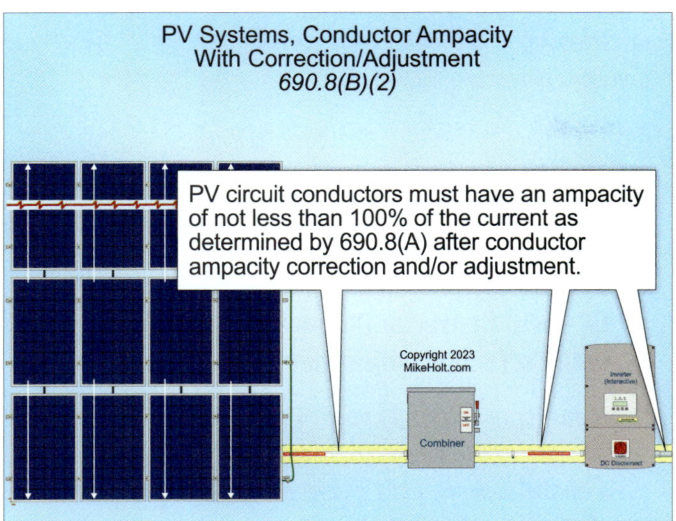

▶Figure 690–53

Author's Comment:

▶ The Table 310.16 ampacity must be corrected when the ambient temperature is greater than 86°F and adjusted when more than three current-carrying conductors are bundled together. The temperature correction [Table 310.15(B)(1)(1)] and conductor bundling adjustment [Table 310.15(C)(1)] are applied to the conductor ampacity based on the temperature rating of the conductor insulation as contained in Table 310.16, typically in the 90°C column [310.15].

▶ Ampacity with Correction One String Example

Question: What is the conductor ampacity for a single string of 8 series-connected modules (Isc 6.39) using 14 AWG, USE-2 rated 90°C conductors within a raceway 1 in. above a roof where the ambient temperature is 94°F in accordance with 310.15(B)(1)? ▶Figure 690–54

(a) 22A   (b) 24A   (c) 26A   (d) 28A

Solution:

Corrected Ampacity = Table 310.16 Ampacity at 90°C Column × Temperature Correction

14 AWG is rated 25A at 90°C [Table 310.16]

Temperature Correction = 0.96 based on a 94°F ambient temperature [Table 310.15(B)(1)(1)]

Corrected Ampacity = 25A × 96%
Corrected Ampacity = 24A

Note: 14 AWG rated 24A is suitable to supply the 7.99A string load (6.99A × 125%) [690.8(A)(1)(a)(1)]

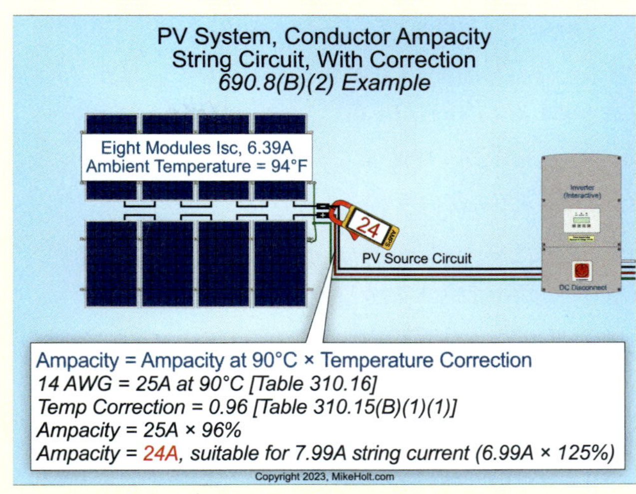

▶Figure 690–54

Answer: (b) 24A

▶ Ampacity with Correction/Adjustment Multistring Example

Question: What is the conductor ampacity for each of four strings of 8 series-connected modules (Isc 6.39) using 14 AWG rated 90°C conductors within a raceway 1 in. above a roof where the ambient temperature is 94°F in accordance with 310.15(B)(1)? ▶Figure 690–55

(a) 14.80A   (b) 15.80A   (c) 16.80A   (d) 17.80A

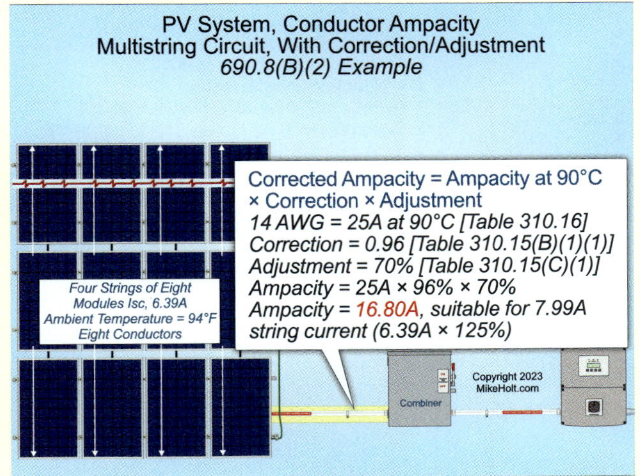

▶Figure 690–55

Solution:

Conductor Ampacity = Table 310.16 Ampacity at 90°C Column × Correction × Adjustment

• • •

14 AWG is rated 25A at 90°C [Table 310.16].

Temperature Correction = 0.96 based on a 94°F ambient temperature [Table 310.15(B)(1)(1)]

Bundle Adjustment = 70% based on eight current-carrying conductors [Table 310.15(C)(1)]

Conductor Corrected/Adjusted Ampacity = 25A × 96% × 70%
Conductor Corrected/Adjusted Ampacity = 16.80A

Note: 14 AWG, rated 16.80A is suitable to supply the 7.99A string load (6.39A × 125%) [690.8(A)(1)(a)(1)].

***Answer:** (c) 16.80A*

▶ Ampacity with Correction Multistring Combiner Output Example

Question: *What is the combiner output conductor ampacity for four input strings of 8 series-connected modules (Isc 6.39) using 8 AWG rated 90°C conductors within a raceway 1 in. above a roof where the ambient temperature is 94°F in accordance with 310.15(B)(1)?* ▶Figure 690–56

(a) 48.80A   (b) 49.80A   (c) 51.80A   (d) 52.80A

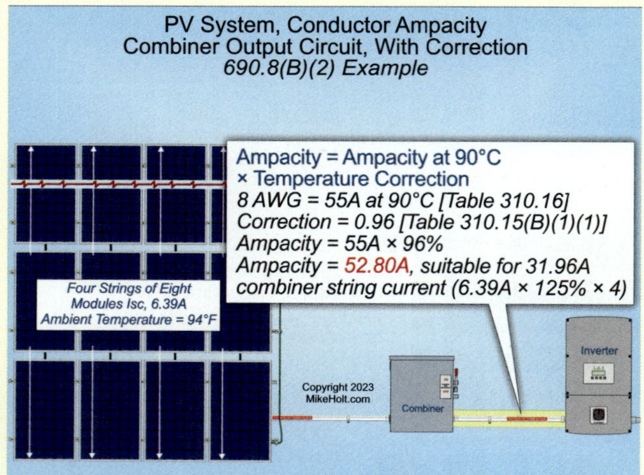

▶Figure 690–56

Solution:

Conductor Ampacity = Table 310.16 Ampacity at 90°C Column × Correction × Adjustment

8 AWG is rated 55A at 90°C [Table 310.16].

Temperature Correction = 0.96 based on a 94°F ambient temperature [Table 310.15(B)(1)(1)]

Corrected Ampacity = 55A × 96%
Corrected Ampacity = 52.80A

Note: 8 AWG, rated 52.80A is suitable to supply the 31.96A combiner string load (6.39A × 125% × 4) [690.8(A)(1)(a)(1)].

***Answer:** (d) 52.80A*

▶ DC-to-DC Converter Circuit Conductor Ampacity with Correction/Adjustment Example

Question: *For an array with dc-to-dc converters having an output current rating of 15A for each dc-to-dc converter circuit, what is the conductor ampacity for eight current-carrying 12 AWG rated 90°C conductors within a raceway 1 in. above a roof where the ambient temperature is 94°F?* ▶Figure 690–57

(a) 20.20A   (b) 21.20A   (c) 22.20A   (d) 23.20A

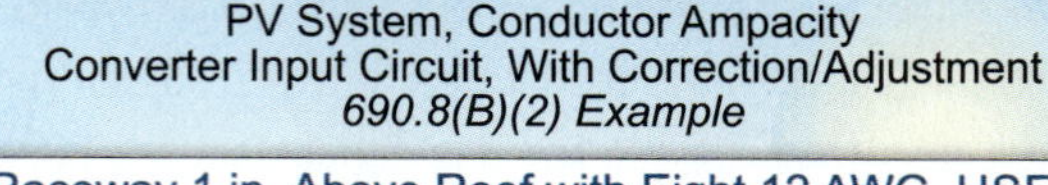
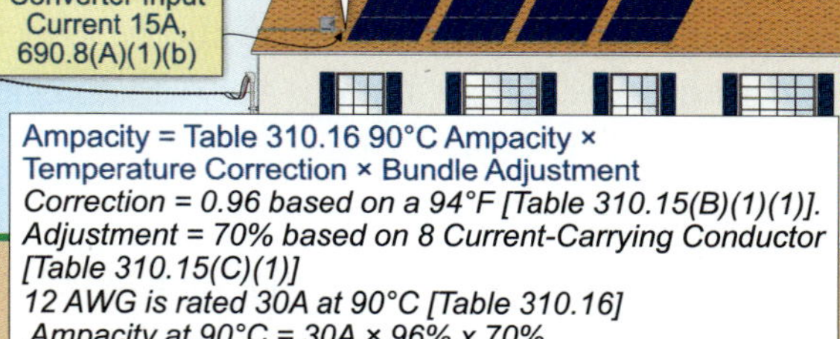

▶Figure 690–57

Solution:

Conductor Ampacity = Table 310.16 Ampacity at 90°C Column × Temperature Correction × Bundle Adjustment

Temperature Correction = 0.96 based on a 94°F ambient temperature [Table 310.15(B)(1)(1)]

Bundle Adjustment = 70% based on eight current-carrying conductors [Table 310.15(C)(1)]

12 AWG is rated 30A at 90°C [Table 310.16].

Conductor Corrected/Adjusted Ampacity = 30A × 96% × 70%
Conductor Corrected/Adjusted Ampacity = 20.16A

***Answer:** (a) 20.20A*

▶ DC-to-DC Converter Combiner Circuit Conductor Ampacity with Correction Example

Question: What is the dc-to-dc converter combiner circuit conductor ampacity for two current-carrying 4 AWG rated 90°C conductors within a raceway 1 in. above a roof where the dc-to-dc converter circuit dc current is 45A and the ambient temperature is 94°F? ▶**Figure 690–58**

(a) 80.20A   (b) 90.20A   (c) 91.20A   (d) 92.20A

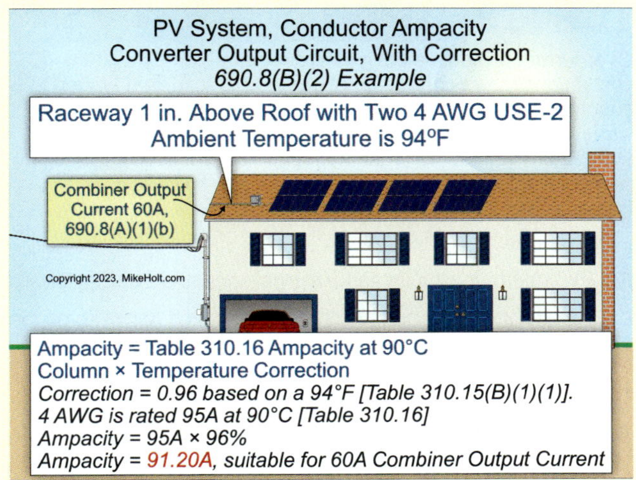

▶Figure 690–58

Solution:

Conductor Ampacity = Table 310.16 Ampacity at 90°C Column × Temperature Correction

Temperature Correction = 0.96 based on 94°F ambient temperature [Table 310.15(B)(1)(1)]

4 AWG is rated 95A at 90°C [Table 310.16].

Conductor Corrected Ampacity = 95A × 96%
Conductor Corrected Ampacity = 91.20A

Answer: (c) 91.20A

▶ Inverter Output Circuit Conductor Ampacity with Correction Example

Question: What is the conductor ampacity for two current-carrying 10 AWG conductors rated 90°C supplying a 24A inverter output circuit installed in a location where the ambient temperature is 94°F? ▶Figure 690–59

(a) 18.40A   (b) 29.40A   (c) 38.40A   (d) 49.40A

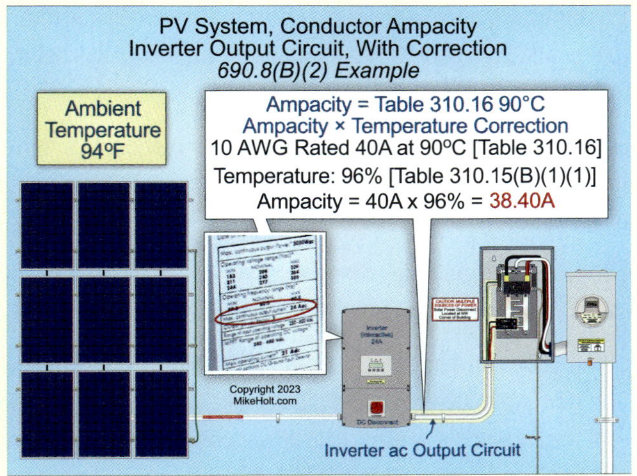

▶Figure 690–59

Solution:

Conductor Ampacity = Ampacity at 90°C Column [Table 310.16] × Temperature Correction

Temperature Correction = 0.96 based on a 94°F ambient temperature [Table 310.15(B)(1)(1)]

10 AWG is rated 40A at 90°C [Table 310.16].

Conductor Ampacity at 90°C = 40A × 96%
Conductor Ampacity at 90°C = 38.40A

Answer: (c) 38.40A

(D) Parallel-Connected PV String Circuits. Where overcurrent is provided for parallel-connected PV string circuits, the conductor ampacity must not be less than:

(1) The rating of the overcurrent device

(2) The sum of the currents as calculated in 690.8(A)(1)(a) for the other parallel-connected PV string circuits protected by overcurrent device

Author's Comment:

▶ Parallel-connected PV string circuits typically occur in large-scale PV electric supply stations (solar farms) within the scope of Article 691.

690.9 Overcurrent Protection

(A) Conductors and Equipment. PV system dc circuit and inverter output conductors and equipment must be protected against overcurrent.

(1) Circuits Without Overcurrent Protective Device. Overcurrent protective devices are not required where both the following conditions are met:

(1) The PV system dc circuit conductors must have an ampacity equal to or greater than the dc current in accordance with 690.8(B).

(2) Where the currents from all PV sources do not exceed the overcurrent protective device rating specified by the manufacturer for the PV module or electronic power converters (inverters and dc-to-dc converters). ▶Figure 690–60

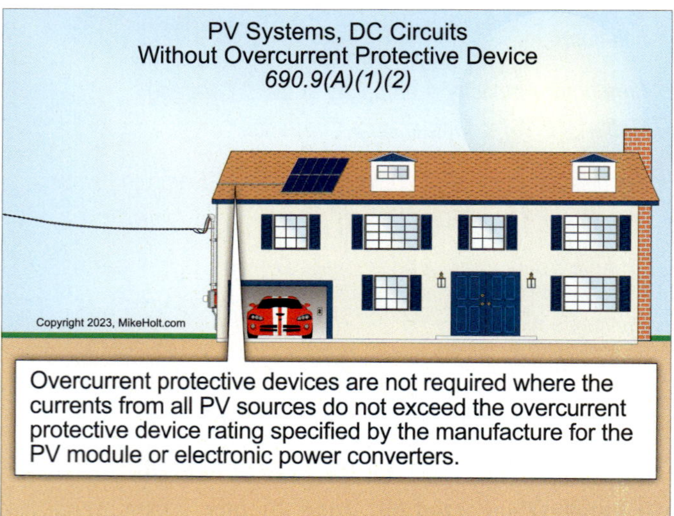

▶Figure 690–60

(2) Overcurrent Protective Device Required. Overcurrent protective devices are required for PV system circuit conductors connected at one end to a current-limited supply and also connected to sources having an available circuit current greater than the ampacity of the conductor at the point of connection to the higher current source. ▶Figure 690–61

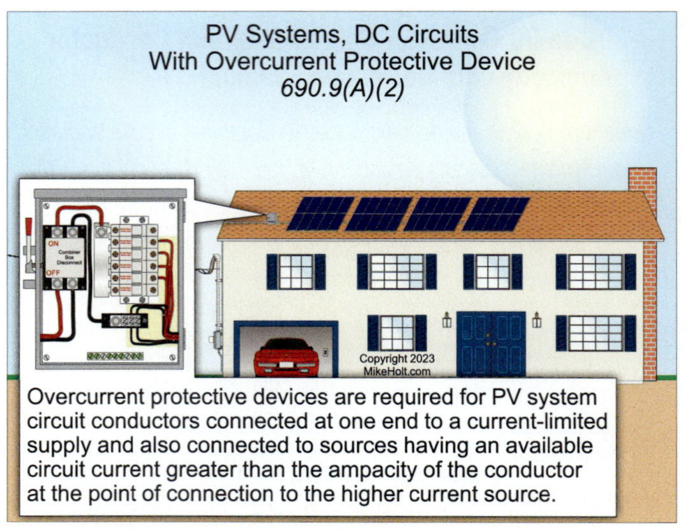

▶Figure 690–61

Note: PV system dc circuits and electronic power converter (inverters and dc-to-dc converters) outputs are current-limited and in some cases do not need overcurrent protection. When these circuits are connected to higher current sources such as parallel-connected PV systems, dc circuits, or energy storage systems the overcurrent protective device is often installed at the higher current source end of the circuit conductor.

(3) Other Circuits. PV circuit conductors that do not comply with 690.9(A)(1) or (A)(2) must have overcurrent protection by one of the following methods:

(1) On Buildings. PV circuit conductors not in a building not longer than 10 ft with overcurrent protection at one end of the circuit.

(2) Within Buildings. PV circuit conductors within a building not longer than 10 ft within a raceway or metal-clad cable with overcurrent protection on one end of the circuit.

(3) Both Ends. PV circuit conductors protected from overcurrent on both ends.

(4) Not On or Within Building. PV circuit conductors not installed on or within buildings are permitted to have overcurrent protection at one end of the circuit if they comply with all the following conditions:

a. The PV system circuit conductors are in metal raceways, metal-clad cables, enclosed metal cable trays, underground, or in pad-mounted enclosures.

b. The PV system circuit conductors terminate to a single circuit breaker or a single set of fuses that limit the current to the ampacity of the conductors.

c. The overcurrent protective device for the conductors is integral with the disconnect or within 10 ft (conductor length) of the disconnect.

d. The disconnect is outside the building or at a readily accessible location nearest the point of entrance of the conductors inside the building. PV circuit conductors are considered outside a building where they are encased or installed under not less than 2 in. of concrete or brick in accordance with 230.6.

(B) Overcurrent Device Ratings. Overcurrent protective devices for PV source (dc) circuits must be listed for PV systems. ▶Figure 690–62

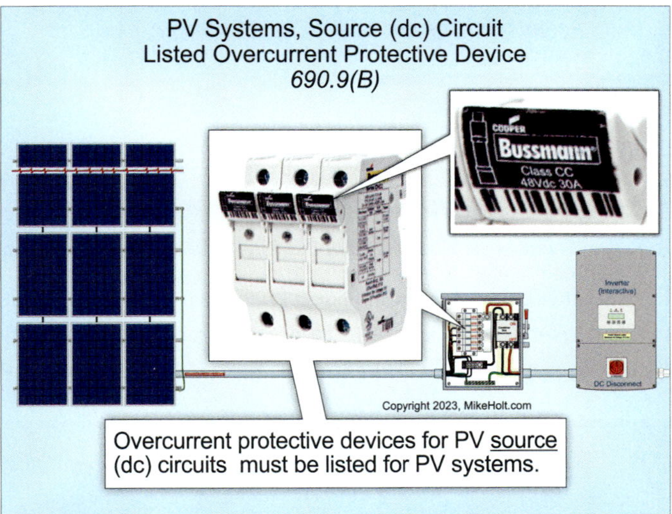

▶Figure 690–62

Electronic devices that are listed to prevent backfeed in PV dc circuits are permitted to prevent overcurrent of conductors on the PV array side of the electronic device.

Overcurrent protective devices required by 690.9(A)(2) must comply with one of the following. The next higher standard size overcurrent protective device in accordance with 240.4(B) is permitted.

(1) Overcurrent protective devices for PV circuits must have an ampere rating of not less than 125 percent of the currents as calculated in 690.8(A). ▶Figure 690–63

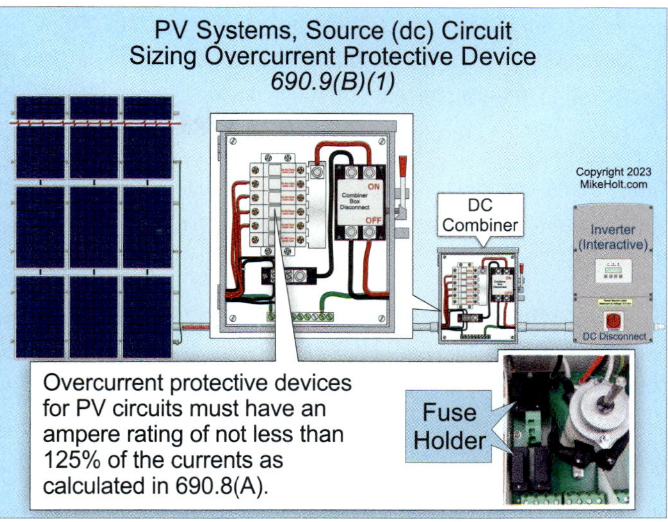

▶Figure 690–63

▶ PV System String Overcurrent Protection Device Sizing Example

Question: *What is the minimum size overcurrent protective device current rating required for one string of 8 series-connected modules having a nameplate short-circuit current (Isc) of 6.39A?* ▶Figure 690–64

(a) 8A　　　　*(b) 9A*　　　　*(c) 10A*　　　　*(d) 111A*

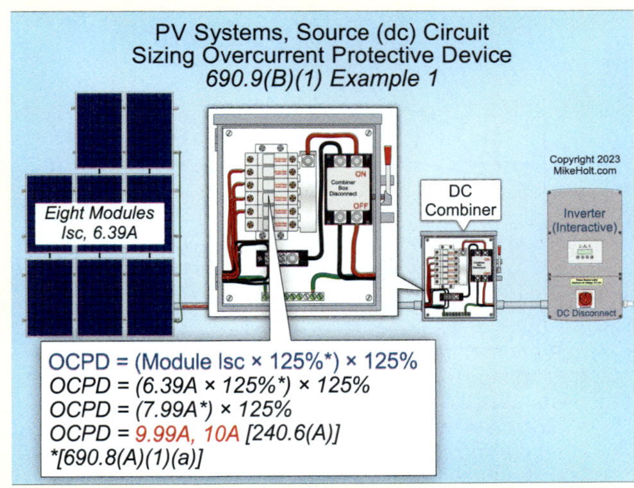

▶Figure 690–64

Solution:

OCPD = (Module Isc × 125%) × 125%*

OCPD = (6.39A × 125%) × 125%*

OCPD = (7.99A) × 125%*

OCPD = 9.99A, 10A [240.6(A)]

**[690.8(A)(1)(a)]*

Answer: *(c) 10A*

(2) Where the assembly, together with its overcurrent protective device(s), is listed for continuous operation at 100 percent of its rating, the overcurrent protective device can be sized at 100 percent of the currents as calculated in 690.8(A).

Note: Some electronic devices prevent backfeed current, which in some cases is the only source of overcurrent protection in PV system dc circuits.

(C) PV System Direct-Current Circuits. A single overcurrent protective device on one of the two circuit conductors can be used to protect PV modules and dc-to-dc converter circuit conductors. Where a single overcurrent protective device is used, it must be placed in the same polarity for all circuits within the PV system.

Note: A single overcurrent protective device in either the positive or negative conductors of a functionally grounded PV system provides adequate overcurrent protection.

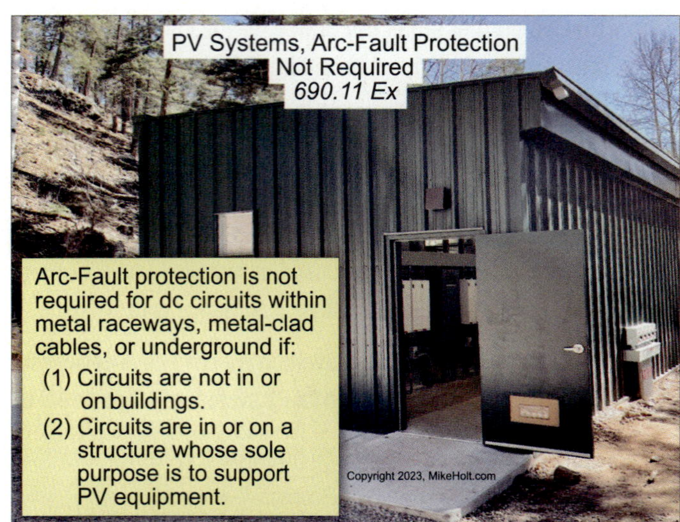

▶Figure 690-66

690.11 Arc-Fault Circuit Protection

PV system dc circuits, on or in a building, operating at 80 Vdc or greater must be protected by a listed PV arc-fault circuit interrupter or other component listed to provide equivalent protection. ▶Figure 690-65

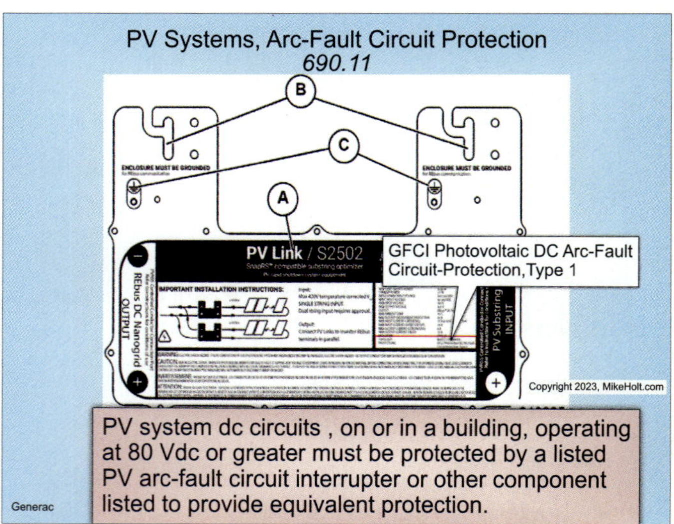

▶Figure 690-65

Ex: Arc fault protection is not required for PV system dc circuits in metal raceways, metal-clad cables, enclosed metal cable trays, or underground if: ▶Figure 690-66

(1) The PV system dc circuits are not installed in or on building or

(2) The PV system dc circuits in or on detached structures whose sole purpose is to support or contain PV system equipment

690.12 Rapid Shutdown—PV Circuits on Building

PV system circuits on or in a building must have a rapid shutdown function to reduce shock hazards for firefighters in accordance with 690.12(A) through (D). ▶Figure 690-67 and ▶Figure 690-68

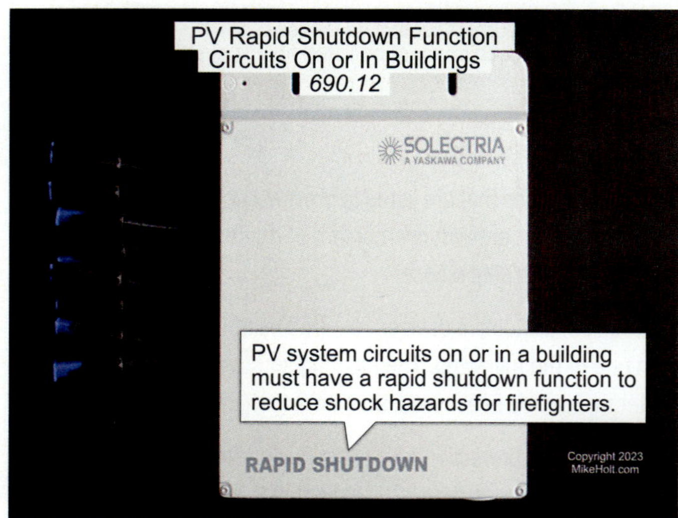

▶Figure 690-67

Ex 1: A rapid shutdown function is not required for ground-mounted PV system conductors that enter buildings whose sole purpose is to house PV system equipment. ▶Figure 690-69

Ex 2: PV equipment and circuits installed on nonenclosed detached structures including, but not limited to, parking shade structures, carports, solar trellises, and similar structures are not required to comply with the rapid shutdown requirements of 690.12. ▶Figure 690-70

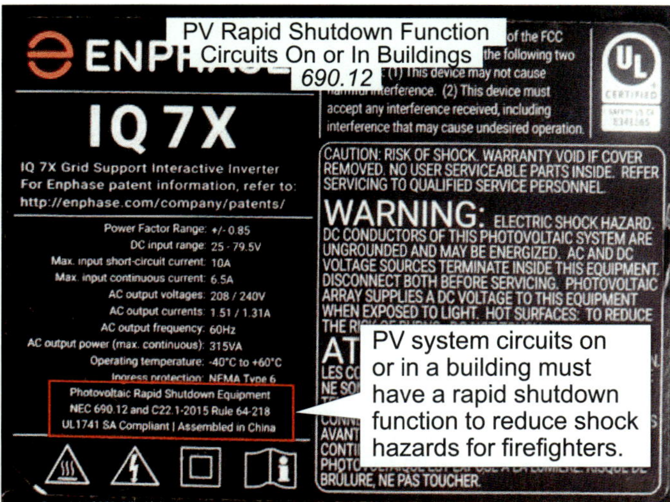

▶Figure 690–68

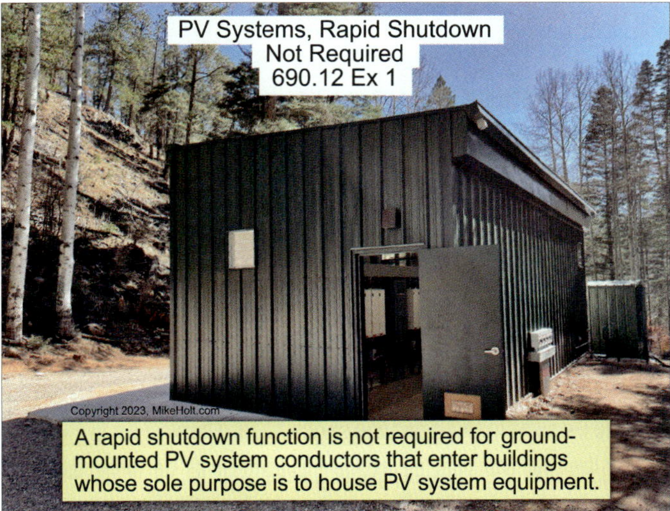

▶Figure 690–69

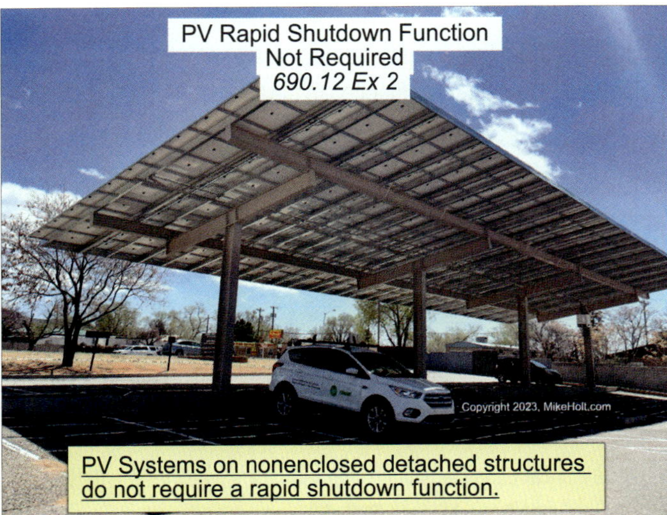

▶Figure 690–70

(A) Controlled Conductors. The following PV conductors on or in a building located outside of the array boundary as defined in 690.12(B) must be controlled by a rapid shutdown function:

(1) PV system dc circuit conductors ▶Figure 690–71

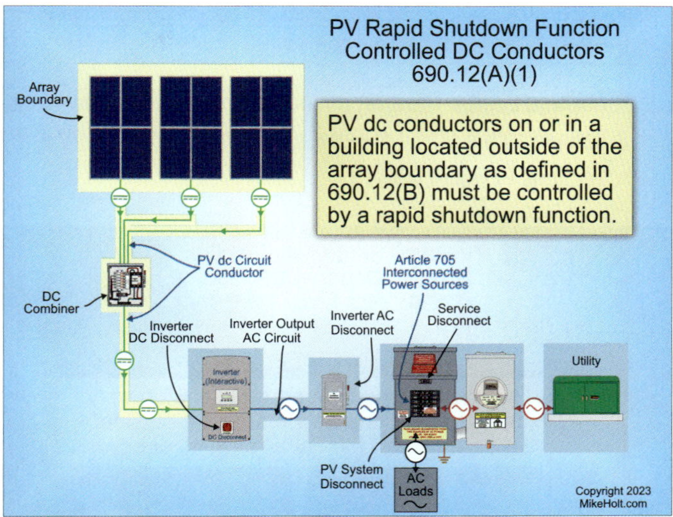

▶Figure 690–71

(2) Inverter output ac circuits originating from inverters within the array boundary ▶Figure 690–72

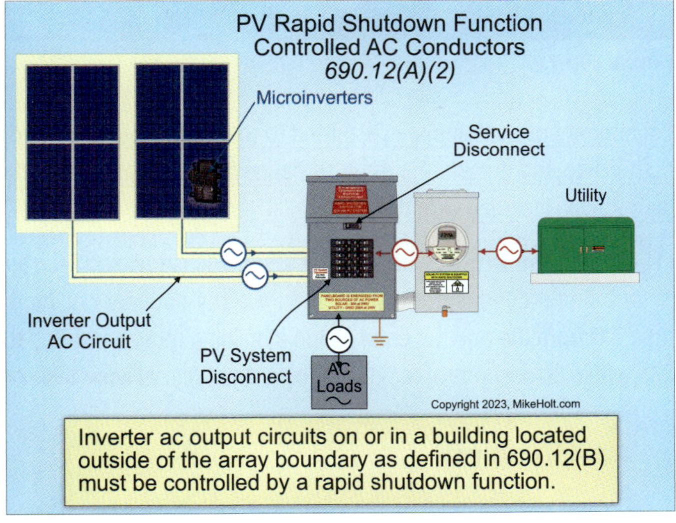

▶Figure 690–72

Note: The rapid shutdown function reduces the risk of electrical shock that dc circuits in a PV system could pose for firefighters. The ac output conductors from PV systems will be either de-energized after shutdown initiation or remain energized if supplied by other sources of power. To prevent PV systems with ac output conductors from remaining energized, they must be controlled by the rapid shutdown function after shutdown initiation.

According to Article 100, "Energize"' means electrically connected to a source of voltage.

Ex: PV system circuits originating within or from arrays not attached to buildings that terminate on the exterior of buildings, and PV system circuits installed in accordance with 230.6, are not considered controlled conductors for rapid shutdown [690.12].

(B) Controlled Limits. The array boundary for a rapid shutdown function is defined as the area 1 ft outside the perimeter of the PV array in all directions. ▶**Figure 690–73**

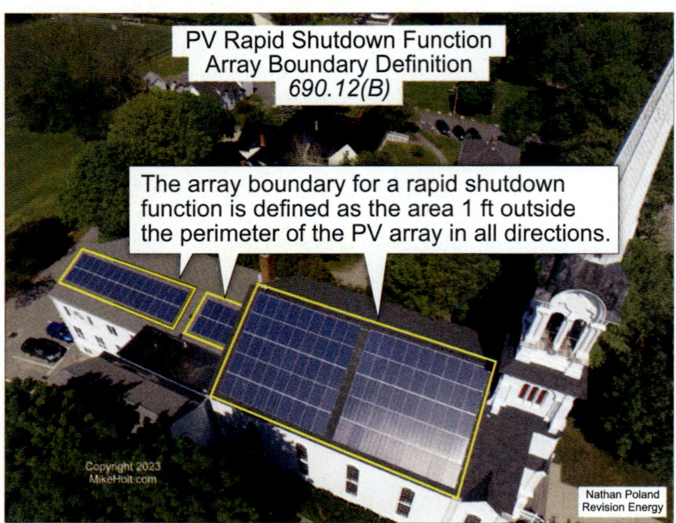

▶Figure 690–73

Equipment and systems are permitted to meet the requirements of both inside and outside the array as defined by the manufacturer's instructions included with the listing.

(1) Outside the Array Boundary. PV system dc circuit and inverter output circuit conductors outside the PV array boundary or more than 3 ft from the point of entry inside a building must be limited to 30V within 30 seconds of rapid shutdown initiation. ▶**Figure 690–74**

> **Author's Comment:**
>
> ▶ Thirty seconds provides sufficient time for the dc capacitors of the inverter to discharge to a value of not more than 30V.

(2) Inside the Array Boundary. The PV system rapid shutdown function must comply with one of the following:

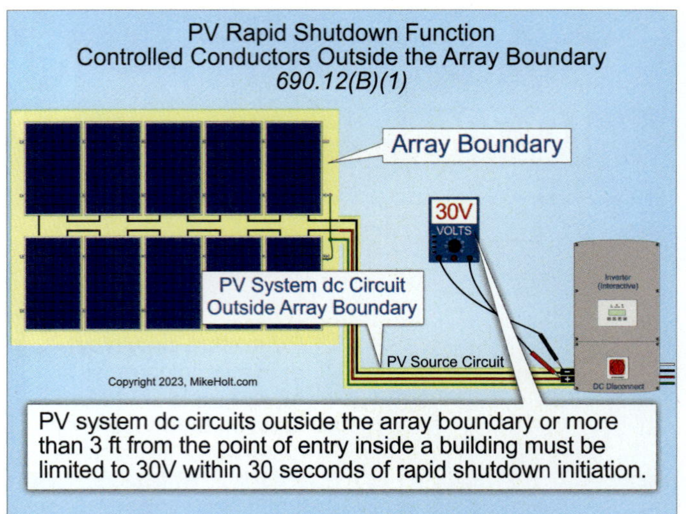

▶Figure 690–74

(1) The PV system must provide shock hazard control for firefighters by using a PV hazard control system installed in accordance with the manufacturer's instructions. Where a PV hazard control system requires initiation to transition to a controlled state, the rapid shutdown initiation device [690.12(C)] must perform this initiation.

Note 1: A listed or field-labeled PV hazard control system is comprised of either an individual piece of equipment that fulfills the necessary functions, or multiple pieces of equipment coordinated to perform the functions as described in the manufacturer's instructions to reduce the risk of electric shock hazard for firefighters.

(2) The PV system must provide shock hazard control for firefighters by limiting the voltage inside equipment or between any two conductors of a circuit, or any conductor and ground inside the array boundary to not more than 80V within 30 seconds of rapid shutdown initiation. ▶**Figure 690–75**

(C) Initiation Device. A rapid shutdown initiation device is required to initiate the rapid shutdown function of the PV system. ▶**Figure 690–76**

One- and Two- Family Dwellings. The rapid shutdown function initiation device must be located outside the building at a readily accessible location. ▶**Figure 690–77**

Single PV System. The rapid shutdown initiation must occur by the operation of :

(1) The service disconnect ▶**Figure 690–78**

(2) The PV system disconnect ▶**Figure 690–79**

(3) A readily accessible switch that indicates whether it is in the "off" or "on" position ▶**Figure 690–80**

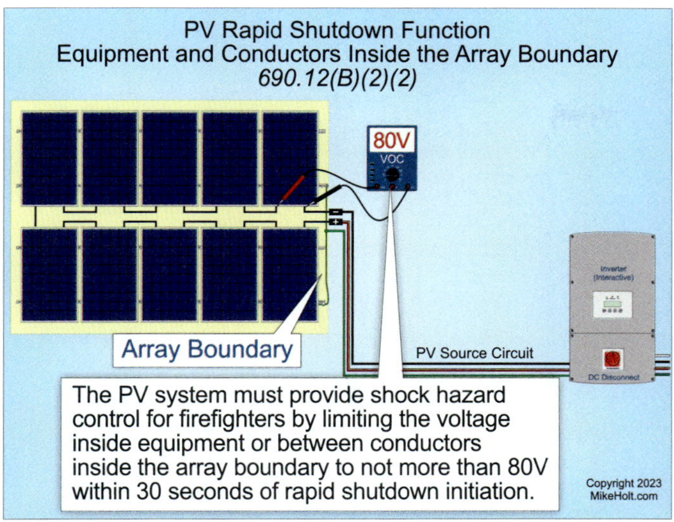

▶Figure 690–75

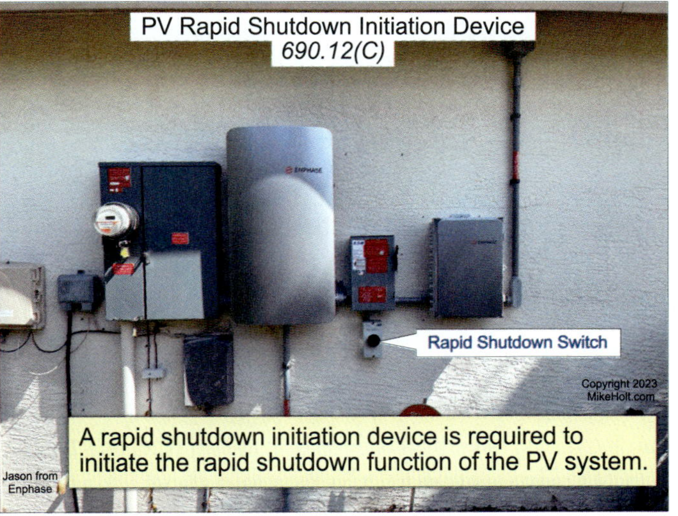

▶Figure 690–76

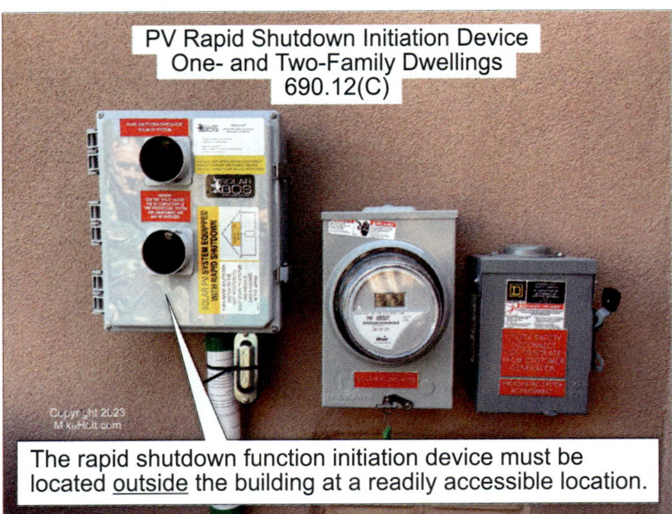

▶Figure 690–77

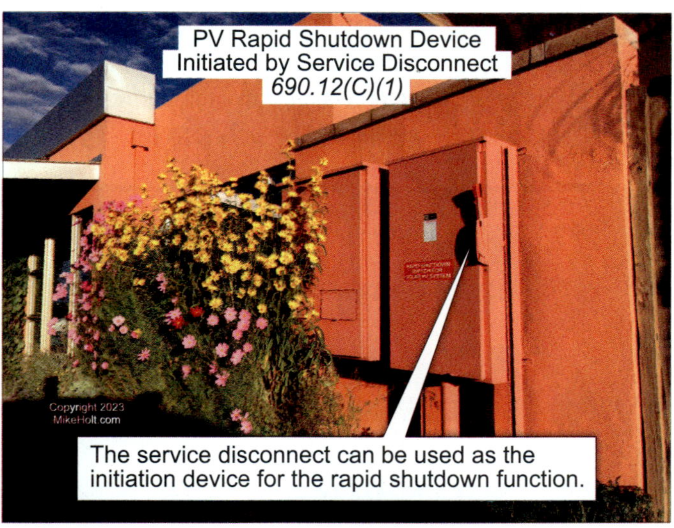

▶Figure 690–78

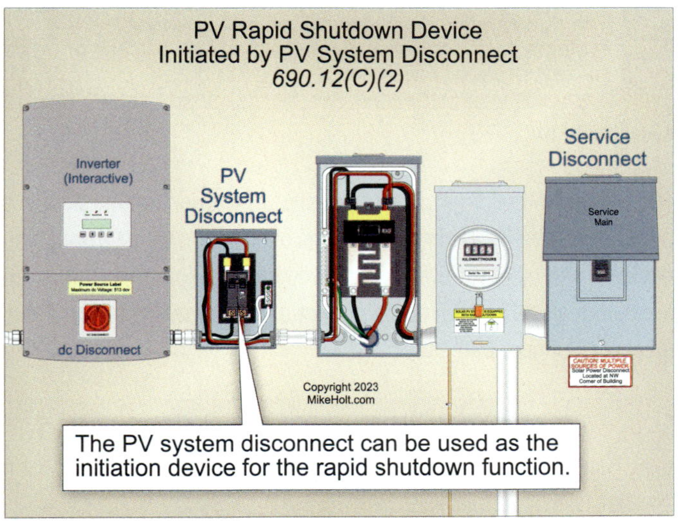

▶Figure 690–79

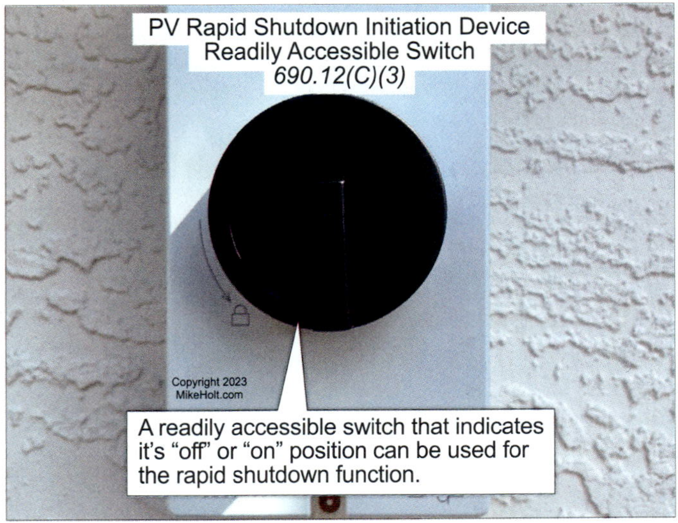

▶Figure 690–80

Multiple PV Systems. The rapid shutdown initiation device(s) for multiple PV systems must consist of not more than six switches or six sets of circuit breakers, or a combination of not more than six switches and sets of circuit breakers. ▶Figure 690–81

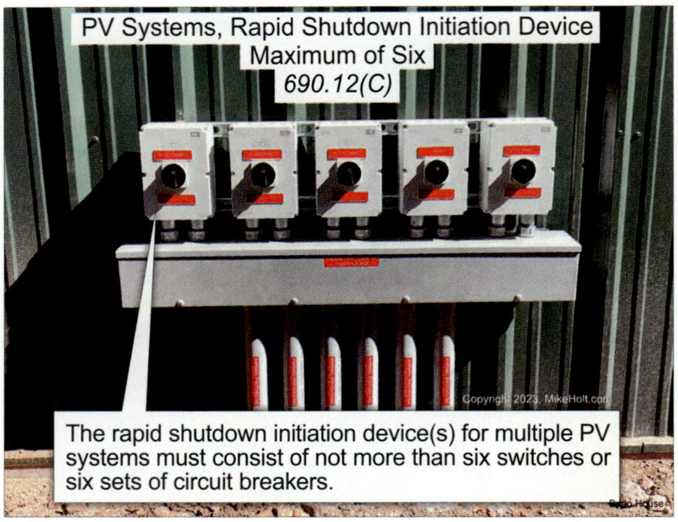

▶Figure 690–81

(D) Labels. A building with a rapid shutdown function must have a permanent label indicating the location of all rapid shutdown initiation devices. The label for the rapid shutdown initiation device must be located near the service equipment or at an approved readily visible location. ▶Figure 690–82

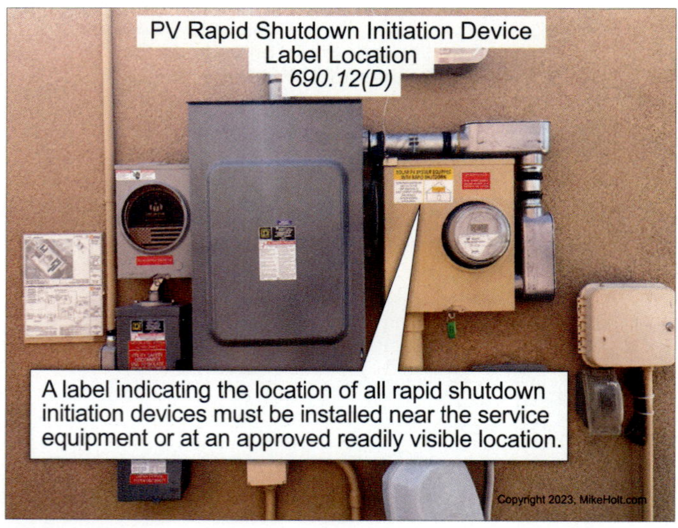

▶Figure 690–82

The rapid shutdown initiation device label must include a diagram of the building with a roof and the following words: ▶Figure 690–83

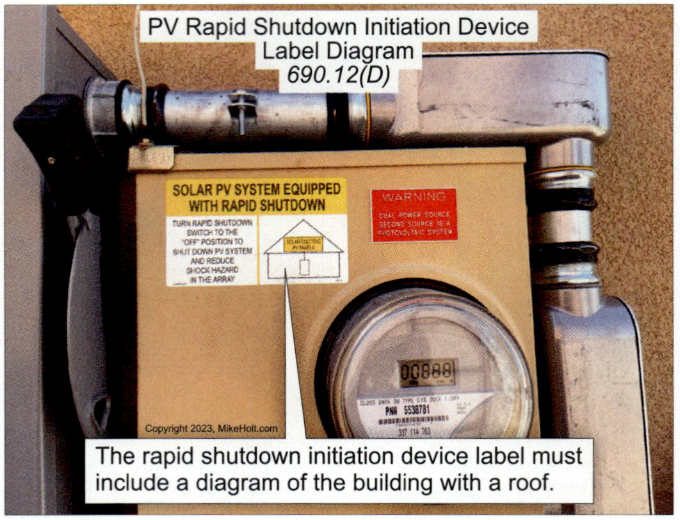

▶Figure 690–83

SOLAR PV SYSTEM IS EQUIPPED WITH RAPID SHUTDOWN. TURN RAPID SHUTDOWN SWITCH TO THE "OFF" POSITION TO SHUT DOWN PV SYSTEM AND REDUCE SHOCK HAZARD IN THE ARRAY.

The title "SOLAR PV SYSTEM IS EQUIPPED WITH RAPID SHUTDOWN" must have capitalized characters with a minimum height of ⅜ in. All text must be legible and contrast with the background.

Note: See 690.12(D) in the *NEC* for an example.

(1) Buildings with More Than One Rapid Shutdown Type. A building having more than one rapid shutdown type, or a building without a rapid shutdown function, must have a label with a detailed plan view diagram of the roof showing each PV system with a dotted line around areas that remain energized after the rapid shutdown has been initiated.

(2) Rapid Shutdown Switch Label. A rapid shutdown switch must have a label including the following wording with all letters capitalized with a minimum height of ⅜ in. in white on a red background located within 3 ft from the rapid shutdown switch. ▶Figure 690–84

"RAPID SHUTDOWN SWITCH FOR SOLAR PV SYSTEM"

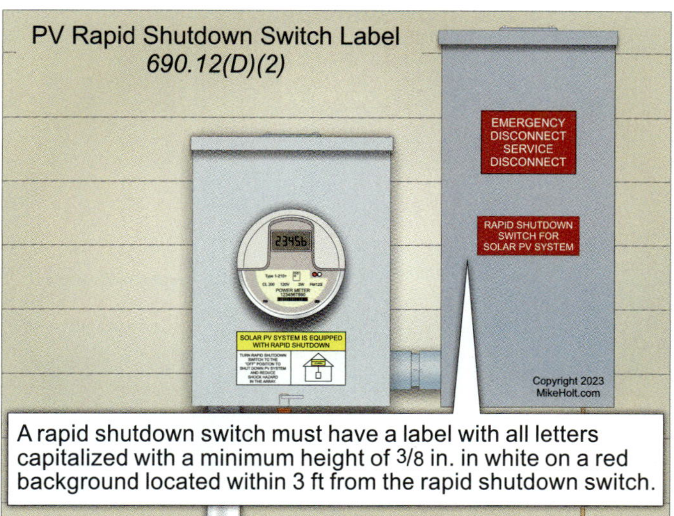

A rapid shutdown switch must have a label with all letters capitalized with a minimum height of 3/8 in. in white on a red background located within 3 ft from the rapid shutdown switch.

▶Figure 690–84

Part III. Disconnect

690.13 PV System Disconnect

A readily accessible disconnecting means is required to disconnect power from each PV system permitted by 690.4.

(A) Location.

(1) Readily Accessible. The PV system disconnect must be readily accessible. ▶Figure 690–85

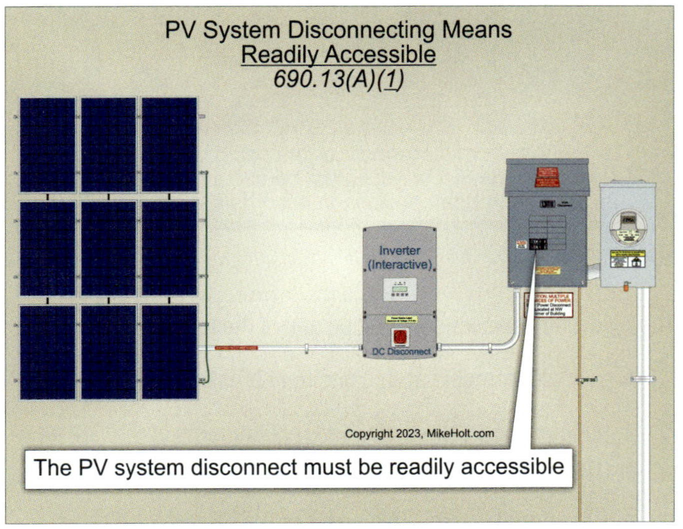

The PV system disconnect must be readily accessible

▶Figure 690–85

(2) Enclosure Door or Cover. The door or hinged cover for the PV system disconnect must be locked or require a tool to open.

(B) Marking. The PV system disconnect must indicate if it is in the open (off) or closed (on) position and be marked "PV SYSTEM DISCONNECT" or equivalent. ▶Figure 690–86

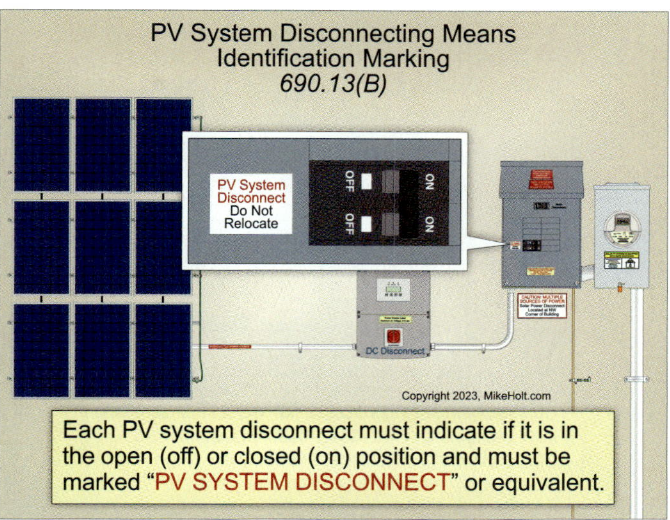

Each PV system disconnect must indicate if it is in the open (off) or closed (on) position and must be marked "PV SYSTEM DISCONNECT" or equivalent.

▶Figure 690–86

Where the line and load terminals of the PV system disconnect may be energized when the disconnect is in the open (off) position, the disconnect must be marked with the following or equivalent: ▶Figure 690–87

WARNING—ELECTRIC SHOCK HAZARD TERMINALS ON THE LINE AND LOAD SIDES MAY BE ENERGIZED IN THE OPEN POSITION

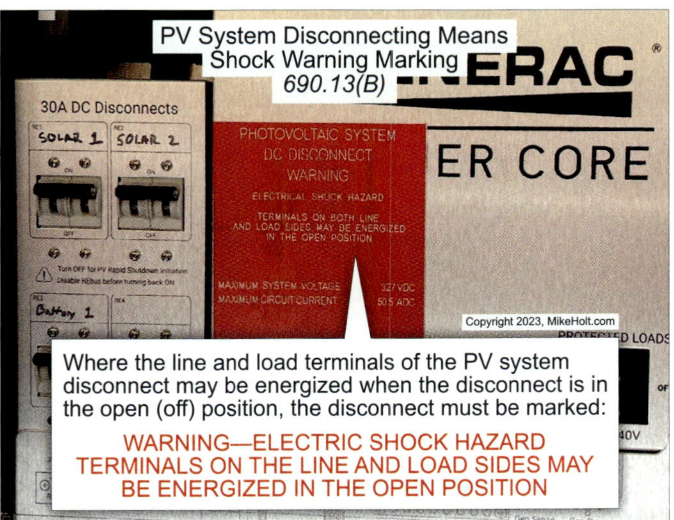

Where the line and load terminals of the PV system disconnect may be energized when the disconnect is in the open (off) position, the disconnect must be marked:

WARNING—ELECTRIC SHOCK HAZARD TERMINALS ON THE LINE AND LOAD SIDES MAY BE ENERGIZED IN THE OPEN POSITION

▶Figure 690–87

The warning markings on the disconnect must be permanently affixed and have sufficient durability to withstand the environment involved [110.21(B)].

(C) Maximum Number of Disconnects. The disconnecting means for each PV system must consist of not more than six switches and/or six sets of circuit breakers. ▶**Figure 690-88**

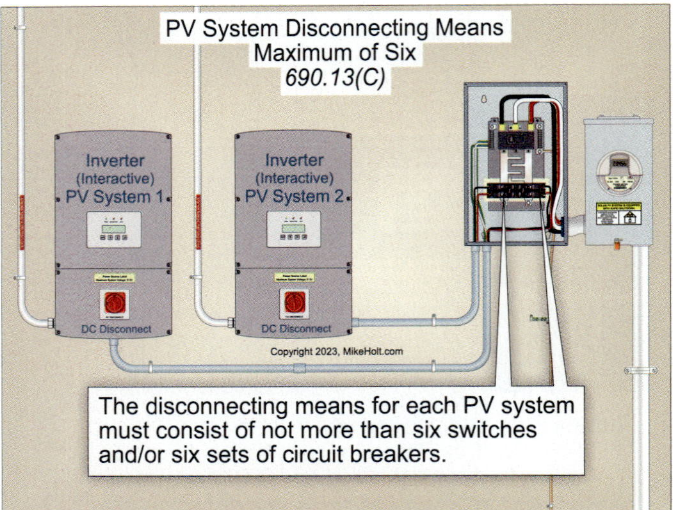

▶**Figure 690-88**

A single PV system disconnect is permitted for the combined ac output of one or more microinverters or ac modules. ▶**Figure 690-89**

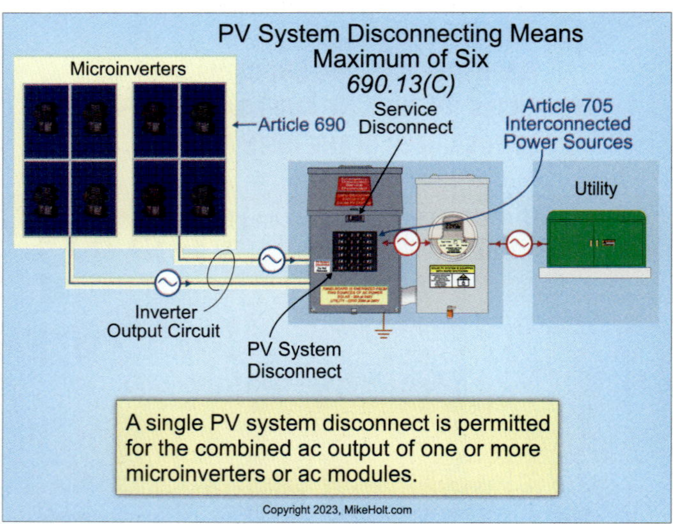

▶**Figure 690-89**

Note: This requirement of a maximum of six PV system disconnects does not limit the number of PV systems on a premises [690.4(D)].

(D) Ratings. The PV system disconnect must be rated for the circuit current, the available fault current, and voltage. ▶**Figure 690-90**

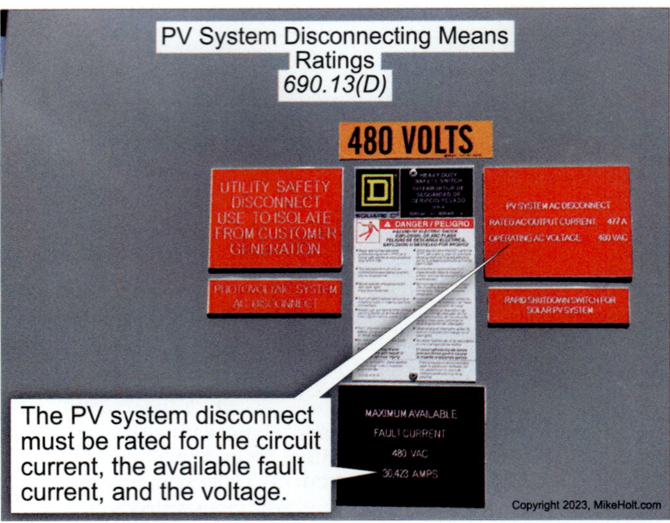

▶**Figure 690-90**

(E) Type of Disconnect. The PV system disconnect or the enclosure providing access to the disconnect must be capable of being locked in the open position in accordance with 110.25. ▶**Figure 690-91**

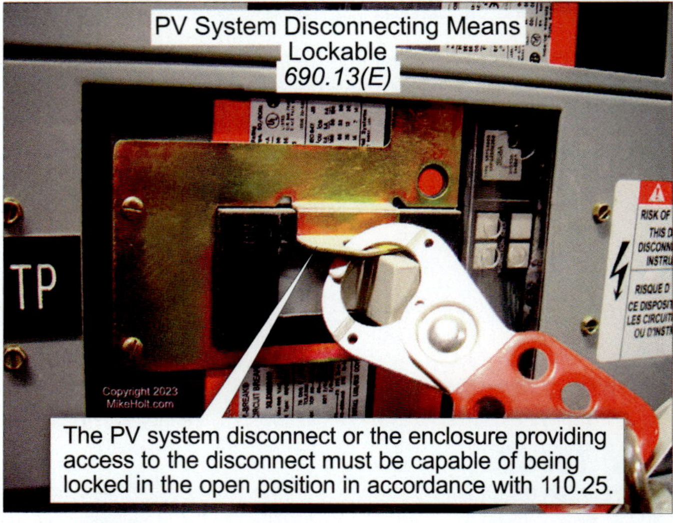

▶**Figure 690-91**

The PV system disconnect must be one of the following types:

(1) A manually operable switch or circuit breaker

(2) A mating connector meeting the requirements of 690.33(D)(1) or (D)(3)

(3) A pull-out switch with sufficient interrupting rating

(4) A remote-controlled switch or circuit breaker that is operable manually and is opened automatically when control power is interrupted

(5) A device listed or approved for the intended application

Note: Circuit breakers marked "line" and "load" may not be suitable for backfeed or reverse current applications. ▶**Figure 690–92**

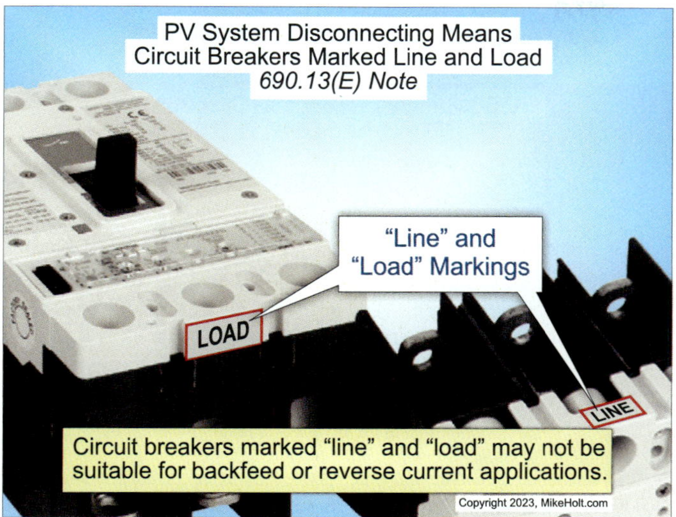

▶Figure 690–92

690.15 PV Equipment Disconnect/Isolating Device

An equipment disconnect or isolating device must be provided for ac PV modules, fuses, dc-to-dc converters, and inverters in accordance with the following: ▶**Figure 690–93**

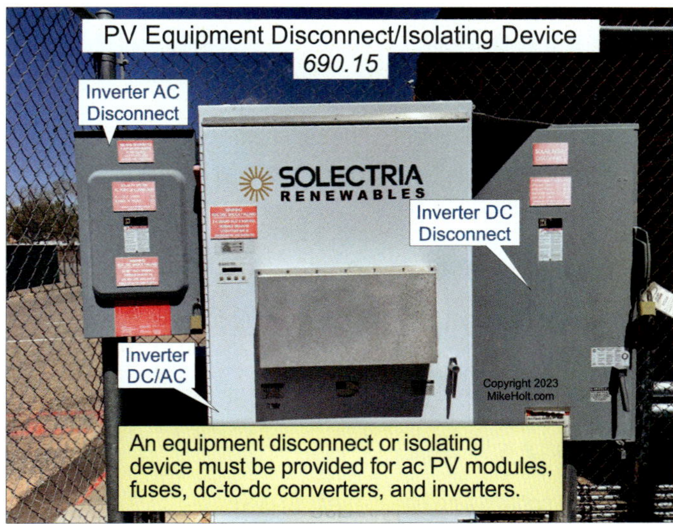

▶Figure 690–93

(A) PV Equipment Disconnecting Means. Where disconnects are required to isolate equipment, the disconnect must be one of the following types:

(1) Over 30A Circuits (load-break). A disconnect in accordance with 690.15(C).

(2) Isolating Device (not load-break). An isolating device that is part of listed equipment.

(3) Not over 30A Circuits (not load-break). An isolating device in accordance with 690.15(B).

(B) PV Equipment Isolating Device (not load-break). An isolating device not rated for interrupting the circuit current must be marked "Do Not Disconnect Under Load" or "Not for Current Interrupting."

Isolating devices must be one of the following types:

(1) A mating connector meeting the requirements of 690.33 if listed and identified for use with specific equipment ▶**Figure 690–94**

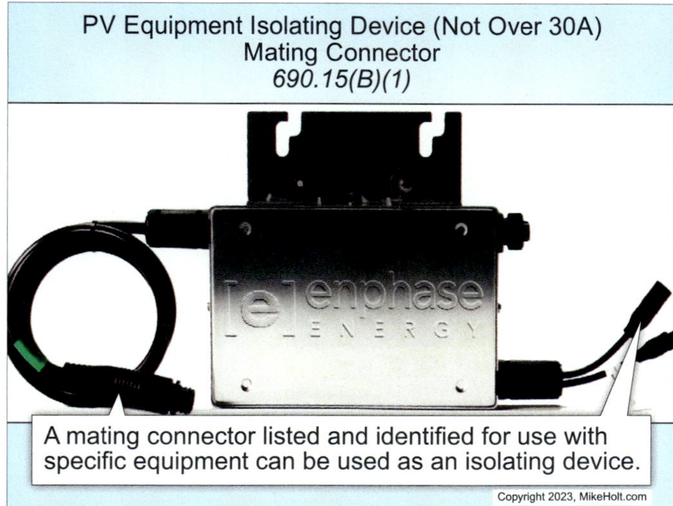

▶Figure 690–94

(2) A finger-safe fuse holder ▶**Figure 690–95**

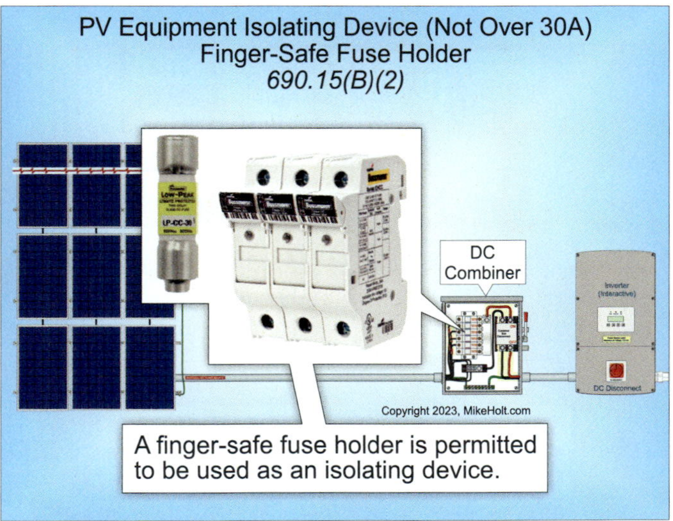

▶Figure 690–95

(3) A device that requires a tool to place it in the open (off) position

(4) A device listed for the intended application

(C) PV Equipment Disconnecting Means (load-break). A PV equipment disconnect must comply with all the following:

(1) The PV equipment disconnect must be rated for the circuit current, the available fault current, and voltage. ▶Figure 690–96

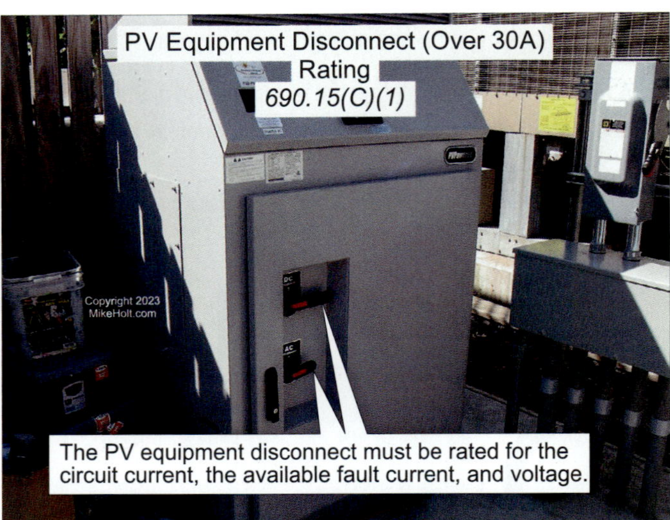

▶Figure 690–96

(2) The PV equipment disconnect must simultaneously disconnect all current-carrying circuit conductors to which it is connected.

(3) The PV equipment disconnect must be externally operable without exposing the operator to contact with energized parts and indicate whether it is in the open (off) or closed (on) position. ▶Figure 690–97

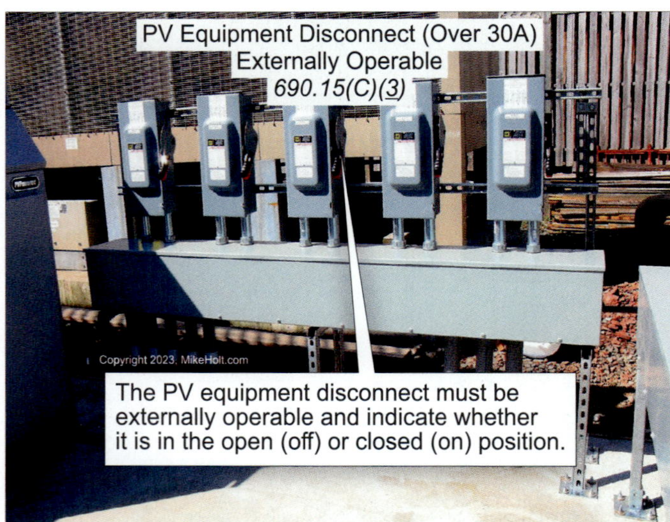

▶Figure 690–97

(4) The PV equipment disconnect must be of the same type as required in 690.13(E). An equipment disconnect must have a warning label in accordance with 690.13(B) if the line and load terminals can be energized in the open position. ▶Figure 690–98

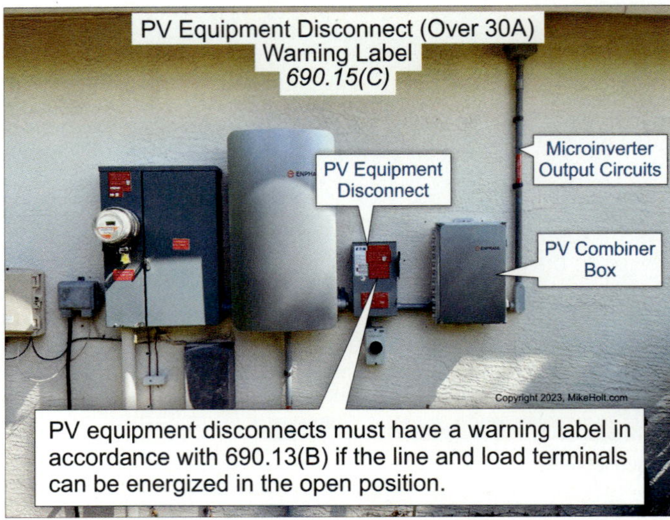

▶Figure 690–98

The warning markings on the disconnect must be permanently affixed and have sufficient durability to withstand the environment involved [110.21(B)].

Note: A common installation practice is to terminate the dc circuit conductors on the line side of a disconnect which will de-energize load-side terminals, blades, and fuses when the disconnect is in the open position.

(D) Location and Control. PV equipment isolating devices and equipment disconnects for PV equipment must comply with any one of the following:

(1) Located within the PV equipment

(2) Located within sight and readily accessible from the PV equipment

(3) Not located within sight and readily accessible from the PV equipment and capable of being locked in the open position in accordance with 110.25

(4) Remote-control with one of the following:

    a. The disconnect and their controls are within the same equipment.

    b. The disconnect must be capable of being locked in the open position in accordance with 110.25 and the location of the controls are marked on the disconnect.

Part IV. Wiring Methods

690.31 Wiring Methods and Materials

(A) Wiring Systems.

(1) Serviceability. Where wiring devices with integral enclosures are used, a sufficient length of cable must be provided to facilitate replacement.

(2) Where Readily Accessible. PV system dc circuit conductors operating at over 30V that are readily accessible to unqualified persons must be guarded, or installed within a raceway, in multiconductor jacketed cable, or Type MC cable. ▶Figure 690–99 and ▶Figure 690–100

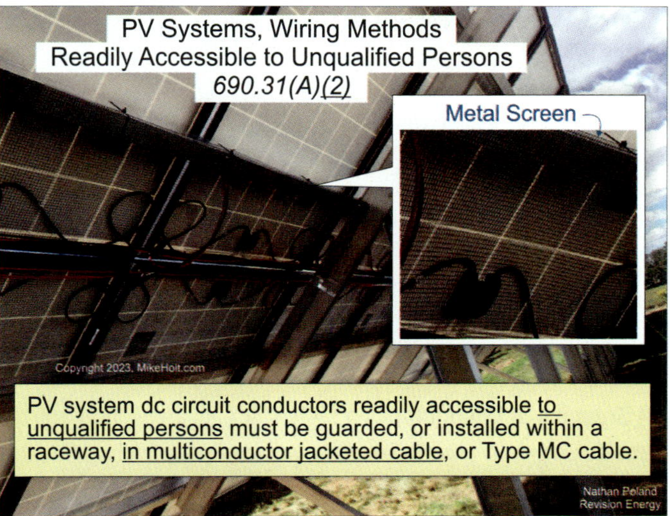

▶Figure 690–99

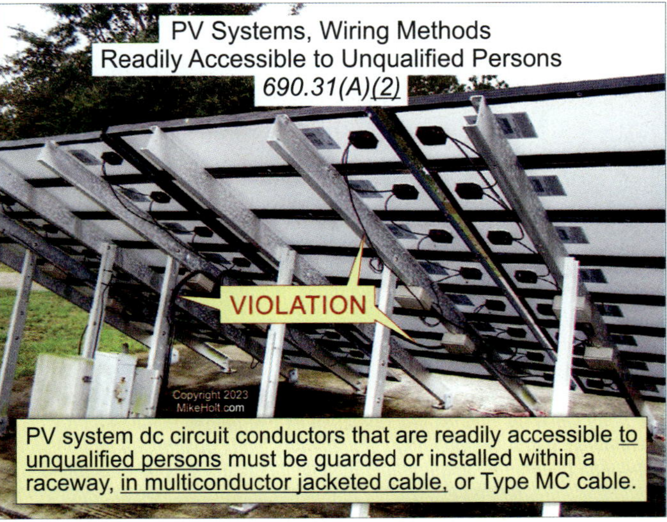

▶Figure 690–100

(3) Conductor Ampacity. PV circuit conductors with insulation rated at 105°C and 125°C can have their ampacities determined by Table 690.31(A)(3)(1) and corrected by Table 690.31(A)(3)(2).

Table 690.31(A)(3)(1) Conductor Ampacity, Not More Than Three Current-Carrying Conductors in Raceway, Cable, or Earth, with Ambient Temperature of 30°C (86°F)

Wire Size AWG	PVC, CPE, XLPE 105°C	XLPE, EPDM 125°C
14	29	31
12	36	39
10	46	50
8	64	69
6	81	87
4	109	118
3	129	139
2	143	154
1	168	181
1/0	193	208
2/0	229	247
3/0	263	284
4/0	301	325

Table 690.31(A)(3)(2) Correction Factors

Ambient Temperature (°C)	Temperature Rating of Conductor		Ambient Temperature (°F)
	105°C (221°F)	125°C (257°F)	
31–35	0.97	0.97	87–95
36–40	0.93	0.95	96–104
41–45	0.89	0.92	105–113
46–50	0.86	0.89	114–122
51–55	0.82	0.86	123–131

(4) Special Equipment. Wiring systems specifically listed for PV systems are permitted.

See 110.14(C) for conductor temperature limitations due to termination provisions.

(B) Identification and Grouping.

(1) Mixing Conductors of Different Systems.

PV System Direct-Current Circuit Conductors. PV system dc circuit conductors are permitted to be installed in the same enclosure, cable, or raceway with other PV system dc circuit conductors, unless prohibited by equipment listing.

PV System Alternating-Current Circuit Conductors. PV system dc circuit conductors are not permitted to be installed in the same enclosure, cable, or raceway with inverter ac output circuit conductors or other conductors unless separated by a barrier or partition.

Ex. Where all conductors or cables have an insulation rating equal to at least the maximum circuit voltage applied to any conductor:

(1) Multiconductor jacketed ac cables can in the same enclosure with dc circuits where all circuits serve the PV system.

(2) Inverter output ac circuits can be in the same enclosure or wireway with PV system dc circuits that are identified and grouped in accordance with 690.31(B)(2) and (B)(3). ▶Figure 690–101

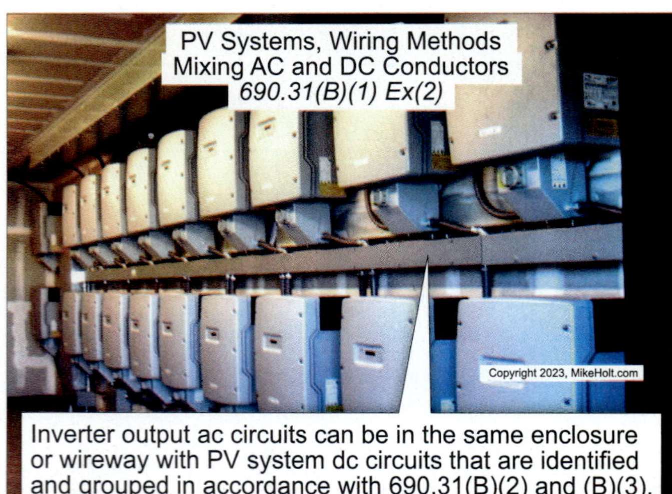

▶Figure 690–101

(3) Multiconductor jacketed cable, Type MC cable, or listed wiring harnesses identified for the application can be in the same enclosure or raceway with non-PV system circuits.

(2) Polarity Identification of Direct-Current Conductors. PV system dc circuit conductors must have all termination, connection, and splice points permanently identified for polarity by color coding, marking tape, tagging, or in accordance with 690.31(B)(2)(a) and (B)(2)(b). ▶Figure 690–102

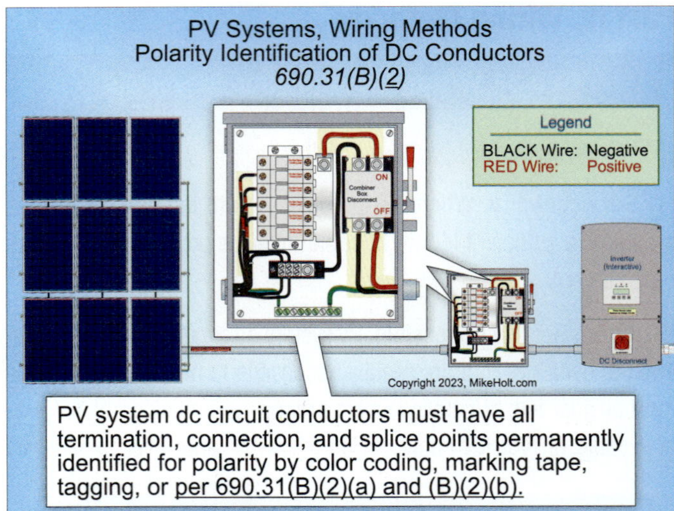

▶Figure 690–102

(a) Conductors must be identified by an approved permanent marking means such as labeling, sleeving, or shrink-tubing that is suitable for the conductor size.

(b) The positive sign (+) or the word "POSITIVE" or "POS" for the positive conductor and the negative sign (−) or the word "NEGATIVE" or "NEG" for the negative conductor. Polarity marking must be durable and be of a color other than green, white, gray, or red.

(3) Grouping of Conductors. PV system dc and ac conductors in the same enclosure or wireway must be grouped separately with cable ties or similar means at least once and at intervals not to exceed 6 ft. ▶Figure 690–103

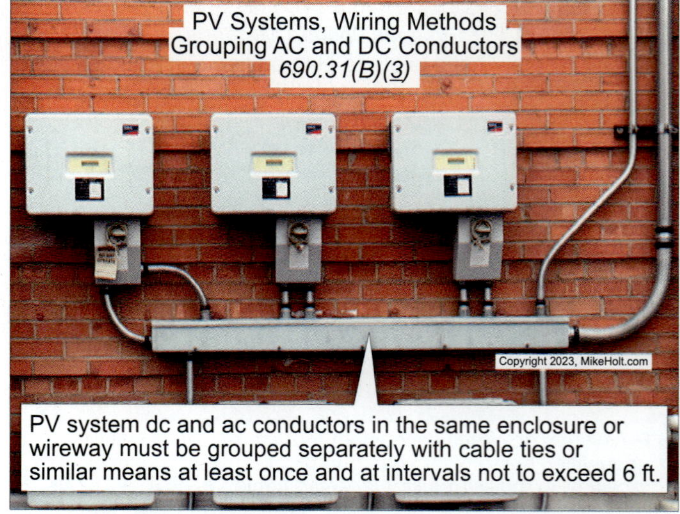

▶Figure 690–103

Ex: Grouping is not required if the dc circuit enters from a cable or raceway unique to the circuit that makes the grouping obvious.

(C) Cables. Type PV wire, Type PV cable, and Type DG cable must be listed.

(1) Single Conductor Cable, Exposed. Single conductor cables for PV systems must comply with 690.31(C)(1)(a) through (C)(1)(c).

(a) Cable Types. Single conductor cables within the PV array that are exposed outdoors must be one of the following types: ▶Figure 690–104

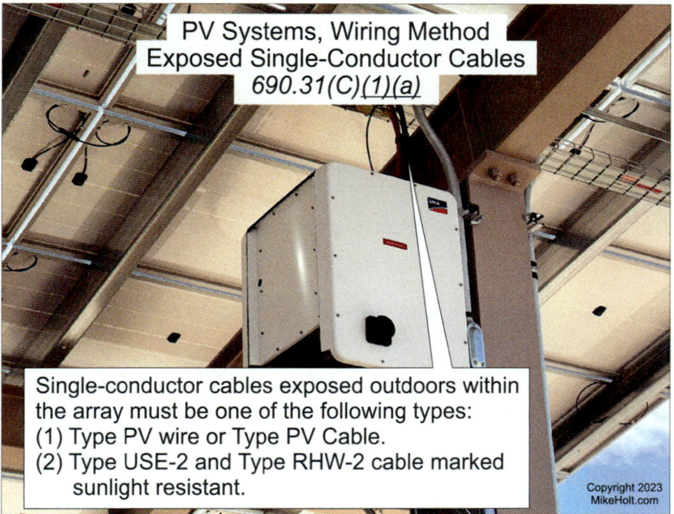

▶Figure 690–104

(1) Type PV wire or Type PV cable

(2) Type USE-2 and Type RHW-2 cable marked sunlight resistant

(b) Support, Cables 8 AWG and Smaller. Exposed cables 8 AWG or smaller must be supported and secured at intervals not to exceed 24 in. by cable ties, straps, hangers, or similar fittings listed and identified for securement and support in outdoor locations.

(c) Support, Cables Larger than 8 AWG. Exposed cables larger than 8 AWG must be supported and secured at intervals not to exceed 54 in. by cable ties, straps, hangers, or similar fittings listed and identified for securement and support in outdoor locations.

(2) Cable Tray. Single-conductor Type PV wire, Type PV cable, or Type DG cable can be installed in cable trays in outdoor locations.

Where installed in uncovered cable trays, the ampacity of single-conductor PV wire smaller than 1/0 AWG and the adjustment factors for 1/0 AWG single-conductor cables in 392.80(A)(2) can be used.

Where single-conductor PV wire smaller than 1/0 AWG is installed in ladder ventilated trough cable trays, the following apply:

(1) All single conductors must be installed in a single layer.

(2) Conductors that are bound together to comprise each circuit pair can be installed in other than a single layer.

(3) The sum of the diameters of all single-conductor cables must not exceed the cable tray width.

(3) Multiconductor Jacketed Cable. Where a multiconductor jacketed cable is part of a listed PV assembly, the cable must be installed in accordance with the manufacturer's instructions. ▶Figure 690–105

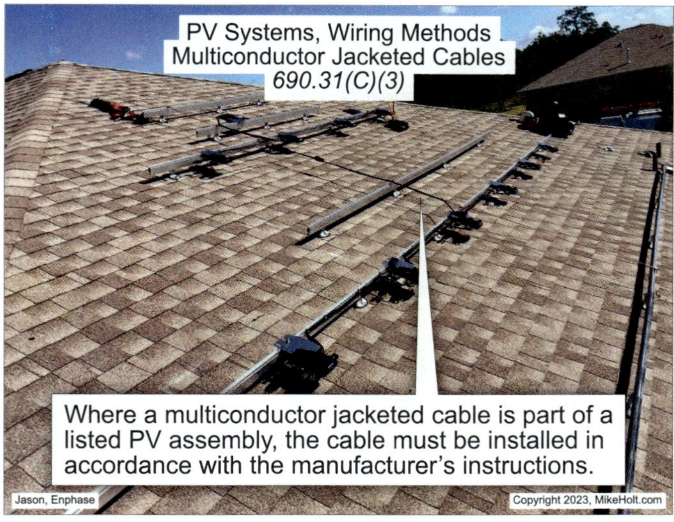

▶Figure 690–105

(4) Flexible Cords and Cables for Tracking PV Arrays. Flexible cords connected to moving parts of tracking PV arrays must be installed in accordance with Article 400, be identified as hard-service cord or portable power cable, be suitable for extra-hard usage, and be listed for outdoor use, water resistant, and sunlight resistant. ▶Figure 690–106

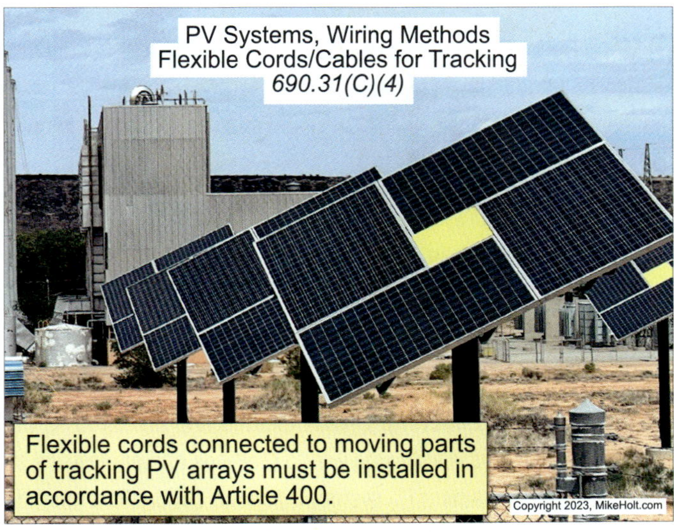

▶Figure 690–106

(5) Flexible, Fine-Stranded Cables. Flexible, finely-stranded cables must terminate on terminals, lugs, devices, or connectors identified for the use of finely stranded conductors in accordance with 110.14. ▶Figure 690–107

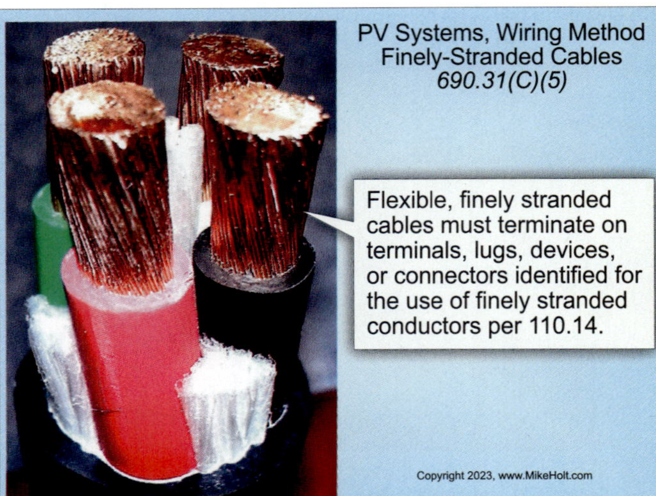

▶Figure 690–107

(6) Small-Conductor Cables. Single conductor cables listed for outdoor use that are sunlight resistant and moisture resistant in sizes 16 AWG and 18 AWG are permitted for module interconnections where the cables have an ampacity for the load.

(D) PV System Direct-Current Circuits On or In Buildings. Wiring methods for PV system dc circuits on or in buildings must comply with the following additional requirements:

(1) Metal Raceways and Enclosures. PV system dc circuit conductors inside a building must be installed in a metal raceway, Type MC cable that complies with 250.118(A)(10)(b) and metal enclosures. ▶Figure 690–108 and ▶Figure 690–109

Ex: PV hazard control system conductors that are installed for a rapid shutdown application in accordance with 690.12(B)(2)(1) can be provided with (or listed for use with) nonmetallic enclosures, nonmetallic raceways, and nonmetallic cables at the point of penetration of the building.

(2) Marking and Labeling. Unless located and arranged so the purpose is evident, the following wiring methods and enclosures on or in buildings containing PV system dc circuit conductors must be marked with a permanent label containing the words "PHOTOVOLTAIC POWER SOURCE" or "SOLAR PV DC CIRCUIT." ▶Figure 690–110

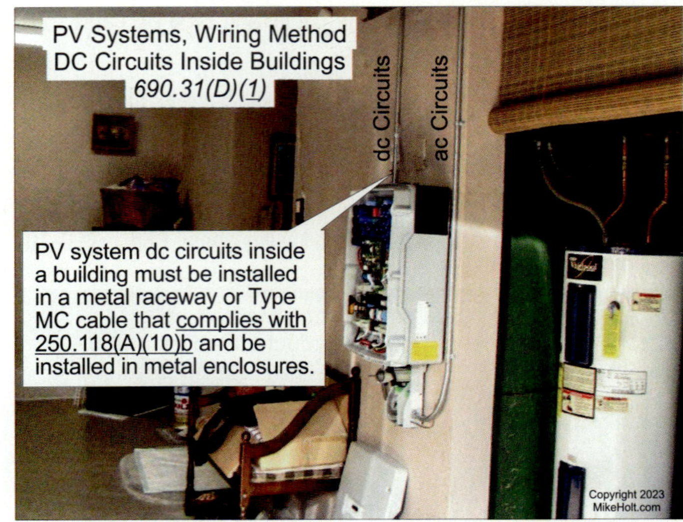

▶Figure 690–108

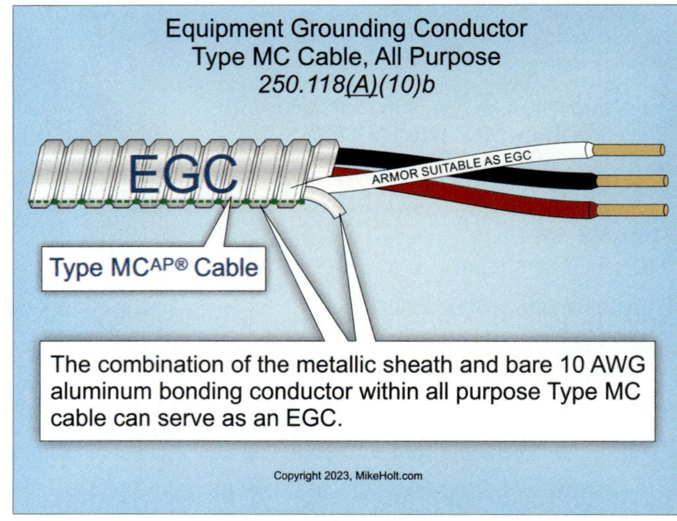

▶Figure 690–109

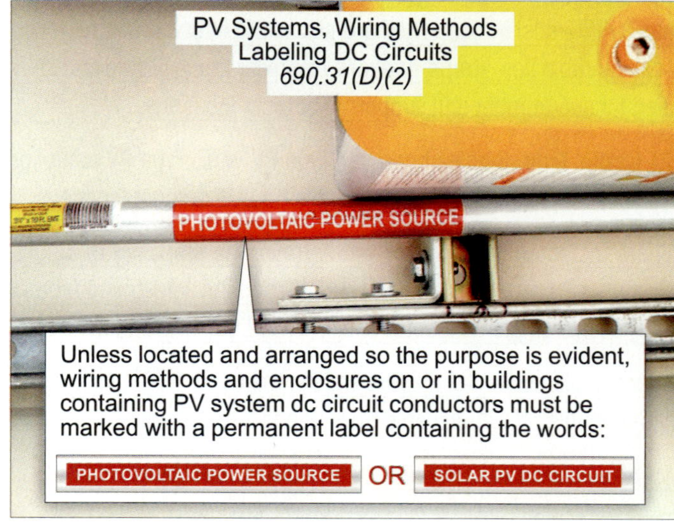

▶Figure 690–110

(1) Exposed raceways, cable trays, and other wiring methods

(2) Covers or enclosures of pull boxes and junction boxes

(3) Conduit bodies having unused openings

The label must be visible after installation. The letters must be capitalized and be a minimum height of ⅜ in. in white on a red background. ▶**Figure 690–111**

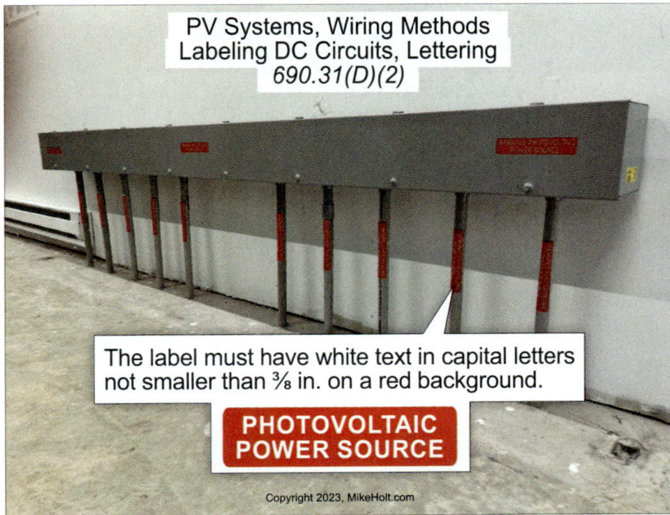

▶**Figure 690–111**

Labels must appear on every section of the wiring system that is separated by enclosures, walls, partitions, ceilings, or floors. Spacing between labels is not permitted to be more than 10 ft, and the label must be suitable for the environment. ▶**Figure 690–112**

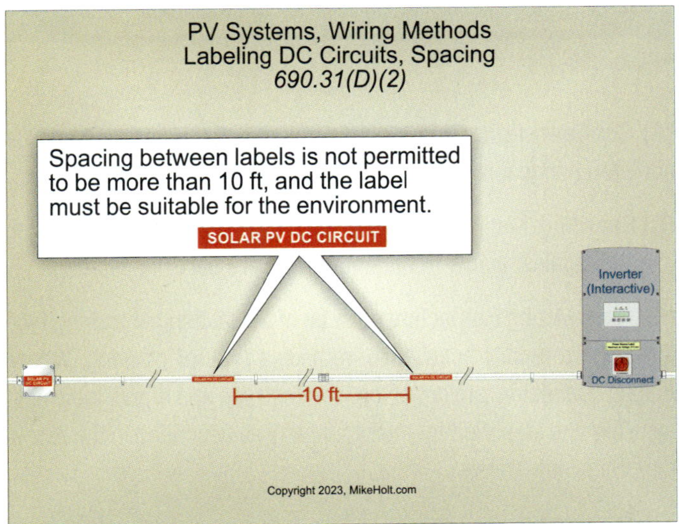

▶**Figure 690–112**

(F) Wiring Methods and Mounting Systems. Roof-mounted PV array mounting systems are permitted to be held in place with an approved means other than those required by 110.13 and must utilize wiring methods that allow for any expected movement of the array.

Note: Expected movement of unattached PV arrays is often included in structural calculations.

(G) Over 1000V Direct Current. PV system dc circuits greater than 1000V: ▶**Figure 690–113**

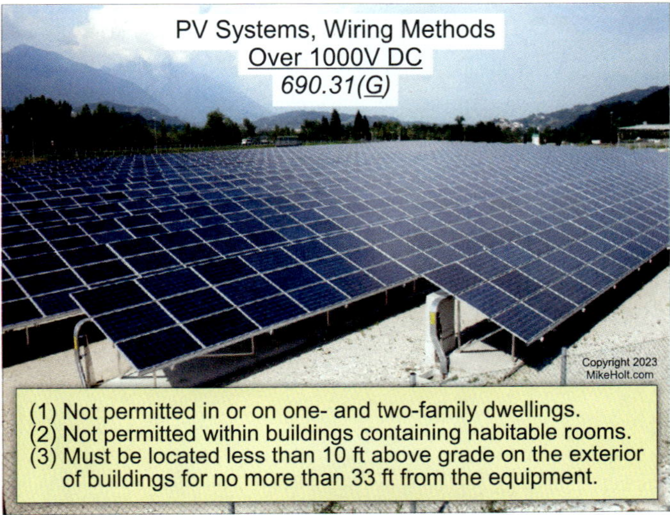

▶**Figure 690–113**

(1) Are not permitted on or in one- and two-family dwellings.

(2) Are not permitted within buildings containing habitable rooms.

(3) Must be located less than 10 ft above grade on the exterior of buildings and cannot be attached to the building surface for more than 33 ft from the equipment.

According to Article 100, "Habitable Room" is defined as a room for living, sleeping, eating, or cooking, excluding bathrooms, toilet rooms, closets, hallways, storage or utility spaces, and similar areas. ▶**Figure 690–114**

690.32 Component Interconnections

Fittings and connectors for PV systems with concealed wiring methods must be listed for the on-site interconnection of modules or other array components. ▶**Figure 690–115**

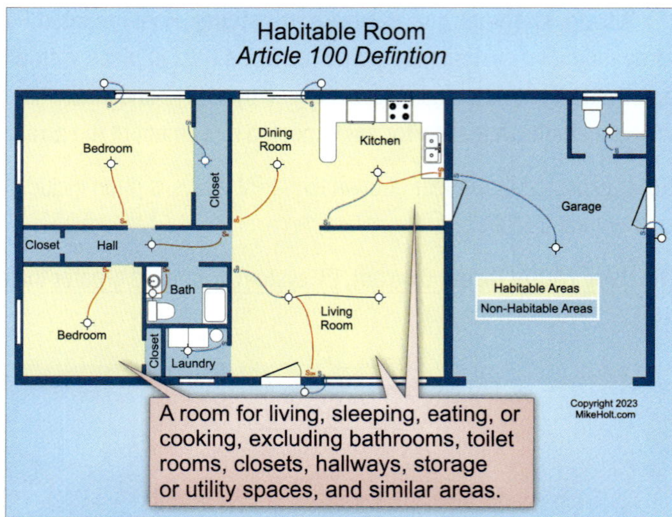

▶Figure 690–114

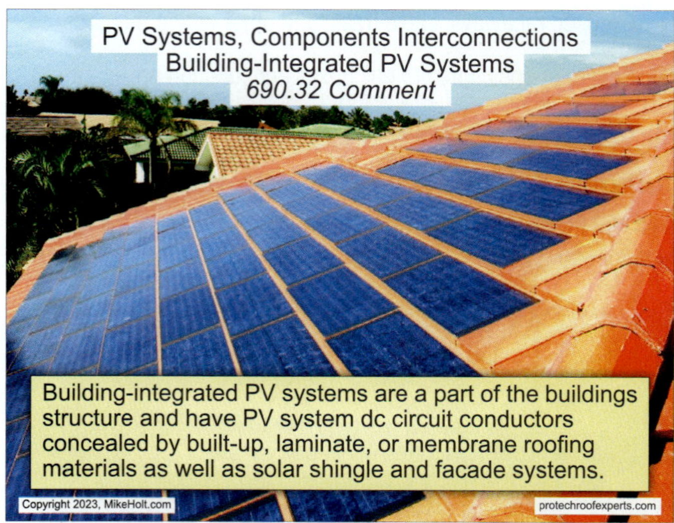

▶Figure 690–116

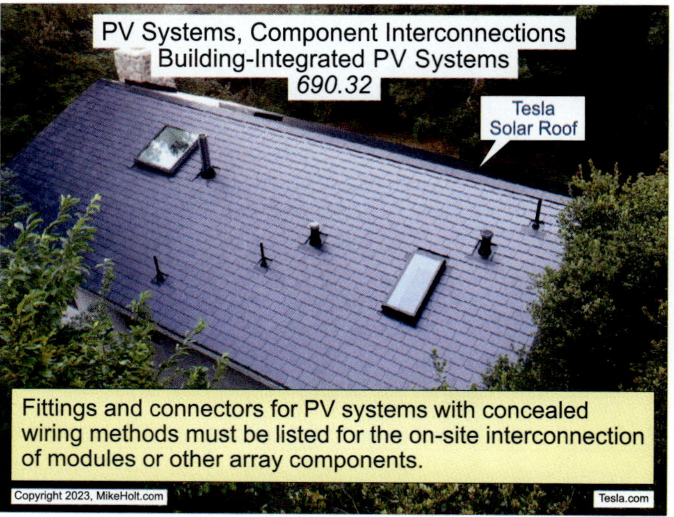

▶Figure 690–115

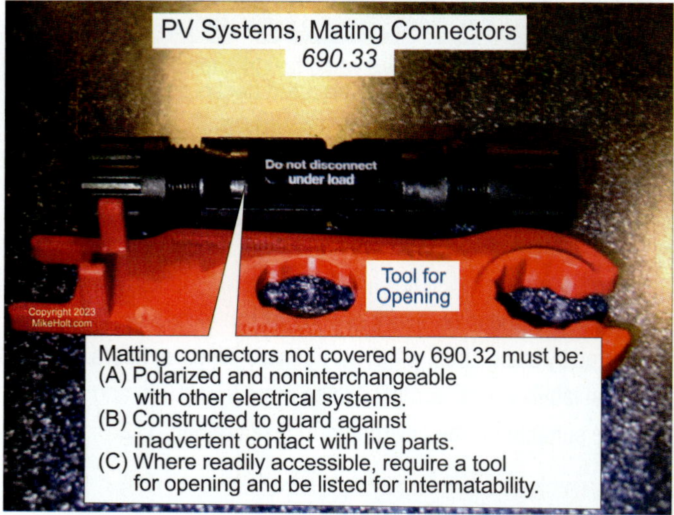

▶Figure 690–117

Author's Comment:

▶ Building-integrated PV systems are a part of the buildings structure and have PV system dc circuit conductors concealed by built-up, laminate, or membrane roofing materials as well as solar shingle and facade systems. ▶Figure 690–116

690.33 Connectors (Mating)

Mating connectors, other than listed connectors for building-integrated PV systems as covered in 690.32, must comply with the following: ▶Figure 690–117

(A) Configuration. Mating connectors must be polarized and be noninterchangeable with other electrical systems on the premises.

(B) Guarding. Mating connectors must be constructed and installed to guard against inadvertent contact with live parts by persons.

(C) Type. Mating connectors must be of the latching or locking type and, where readily accessible, require a tool for opening. Where mating connectors are not of the identical type and brand, they must be listed and identified for intermatability as described in the manufacturer's instructions.

(D) Interruption of Circuit. Mating connectors must comply with one of the following requirements. ▶Figure 690–118

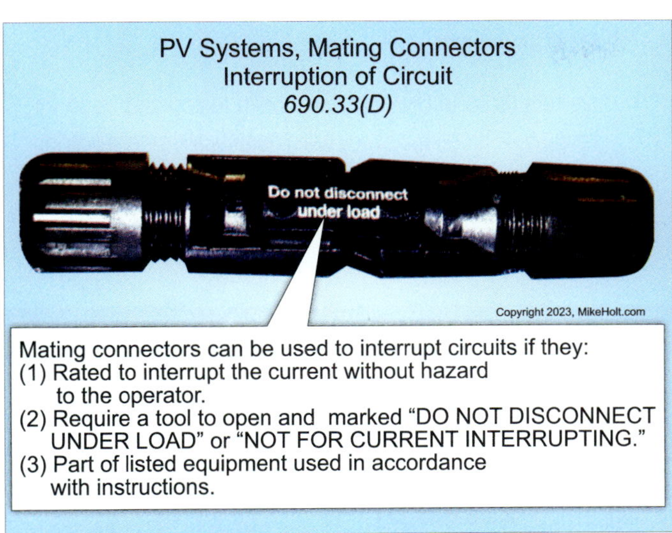

▶Figure 690–118

(1) Mating connectors must be rated to interrupt the current without hazard to the operator.

(2) A tool must be required to open the mating connector, and the mating connectors must be marked "DO NOT DISCONNECT UNDER LOAD" OR "NOT FOR CURRENT INTERRUPTING."

(3) Mating connectors supplied as part of listed equipment must be used in accordance with instructions provided with the listed connected equipment.

Note: Some listed equipment, such as micro-inverters, are evaluated to make use of mating connectors as disconnect devices even though the mating connectors are marked as "DO NOT DISCONNECT UNDER LOAD" OR "NOT FOR CURRENT INTERRUPTING." ▶Figure 690–119

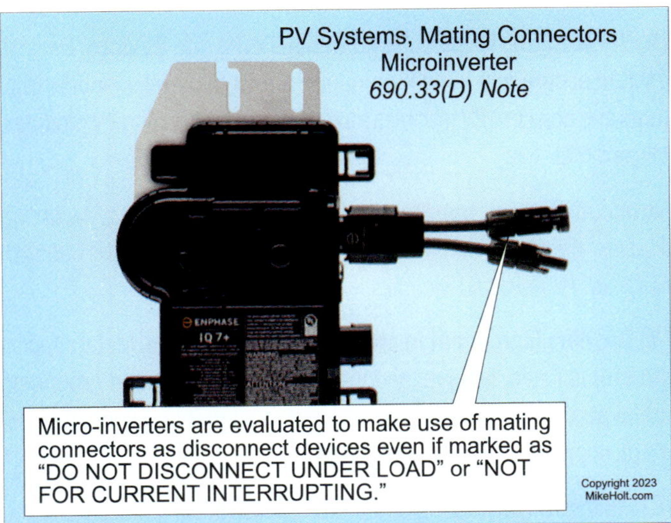

▶Figure 690–119

690.34 Access to Boxes

Junction, pull, and outlet boxes are permitted to be behind PV modules. ▶Figure 690–120

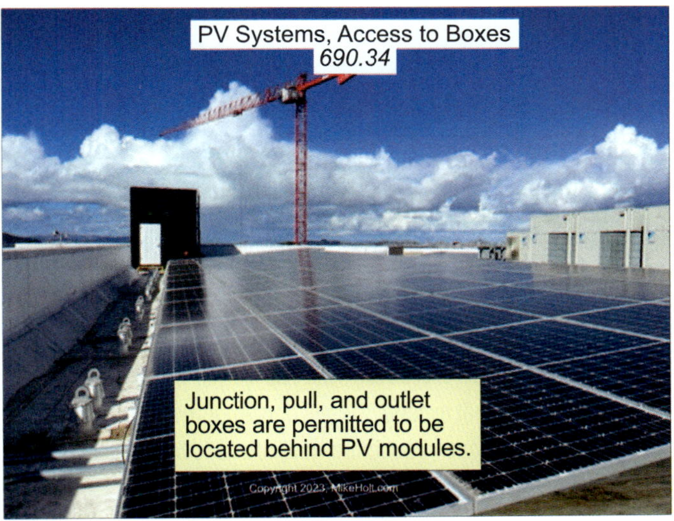

▶Figure 690–120

Part V. Grounding and Bonding

690.41 PV System DC Circuit Grounding and Protection

(A) PV System DC Circuit Grounding Configurations. One or more of the following system configurations are required for PV system dc circuits:

(1) 2-wire circuits with one functionally grounded conductor

(2) Bipolar circuits according to 690.7(C) with a functional ground reference (center tap)

(3) Circuits not isolated from the grounded inverter output circuit (functionally grounded inverter)

(4) Ungrounded circuits

(5) Solidly grounded circuits as permitted in 690.41(B)

(6) Circuits protected by equipment listed and identified for the use

Author's Comment:

▸ Typically, inverters installed today are of the "not isolated from the grounded inverter output circuit" type [690.41(A)(3)]. These PV systems are known as a "functionally grounded inverters."

According to Article 100, a "Functionally Grounded" is a PV system that has an electrical ground reference for operational purposes that is not solidly grounded.

Note: A functionally grounded PV system is often connected to ground through an electronic means that is internal to an inverter or charge controller which provides ground-fault protection.

(B) DC Ground-Fault Detector-Interrupter (GFDI) Protection. PV system dc circuits that exceed 30 volts or 8 amperes must be provided with GFDI protection to reduce fire hazards as follows:

Note: If GFDI is not included in the dc-to-dc converter, then the installation manual must provide a warning statement that indicates GFDI is not included.

According to Article 100, a "Ground-Fault Detector-Interrupter, dc (GFDI)" is a device that provides protection for PV system dc circuits by detecting a ground fault and could interrupt the fault path in the dc circuit.

(1) Ground-Fault Detection. The GFDI device or system must be detect ground fault(s) in the PV system dc circuits, and be listed for providing GFDI protection. For dc-to-dc converters not listed as providing GFDI protection, where required, listed GFDI protection equipment identified for the combination of the dc-to- dc converter and the GFDI device must be installed to protect the circuit.

Note: Some dc-to-dc converters without integral GFDI protection on their input (source) side can prevent other GFDI protection equipment from properly functioning on portions of PV system dc circuits.

(2) Faulted Circuits. The faulted circuits must be controlled by one of the following methods:

(1) The current-carrying conductors of the faulted circuit must be automatically disconnected.

(2) The device providing GFDI protection fed by the faulted circuit must automatically cease to supply power to output circuits and interrupt the faulted PV system dc circuits from the ground reference in a functionally grounded system.

Author's Comment:

▸ Inverters listed to UL 1741 have been tested and listed for ground-fault protection. They will automatically stop supplying power to output circuits and will interrupt the PV system dc circuits from ground reference.

690.43 Equipment Grounding Conductor

Metal parts of PV module frames, PV equipment, and enclosures containing PV system ac and dc conductors must be connected to the circuit equipment grounding conductor in accordance with 690.43(A) through (D). ▸**Figure 690–121**

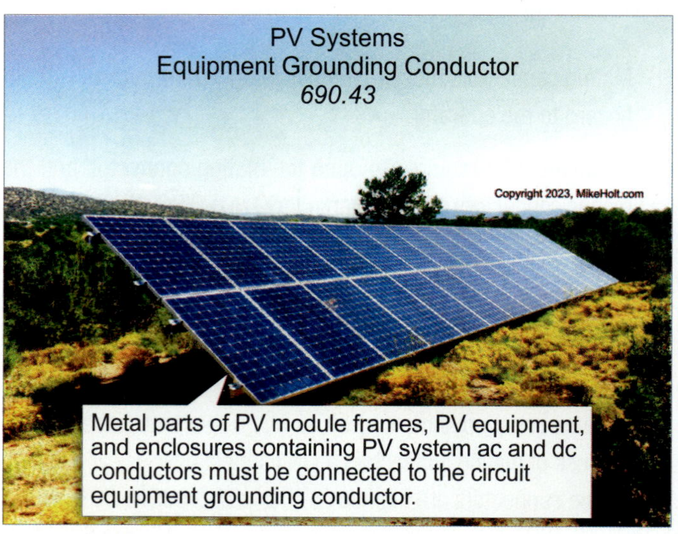

▸Figure 690–121

(A) Photovoltaic Module Mounting Systems and Devices. Devices used to secure and bond PV module frames to metal support structures and adjacent PV modules must be listed for bonding PV modules. ▸Figure 690–122

Note: UL 2703 is the *Standard for Mounting Systems, Mounting Devices, Clamping/Retention Devices, and Ground Lugs for Use with Flat-Plate Photovoltaic Modules.*

(B) Bonding Equipment to Metal Support Structure. Metal support structures listed, labeled, and identified for bonding and grounding metal parts of PV systems can be used to bond PV equipment to the metal support structure. ▸Figure 690–123

(C) Equipment Grounding Conductor Location. Equipment grounding conductors are permitted to be run separately from the PV circuit conductor within the PV array. ▸Figure 690–124

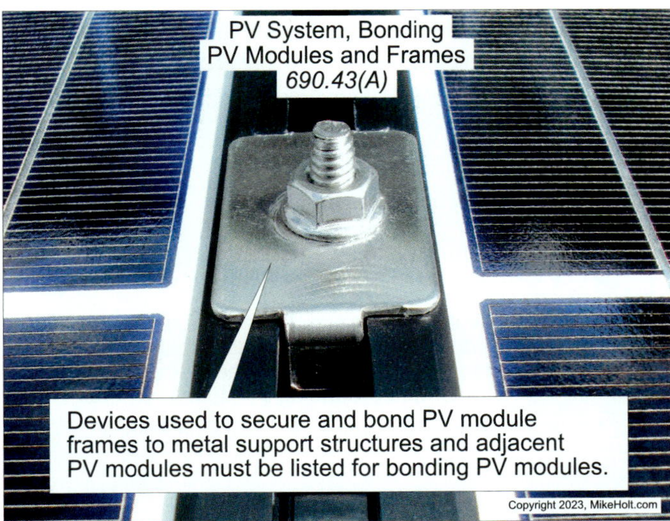

▶Figure 690–122

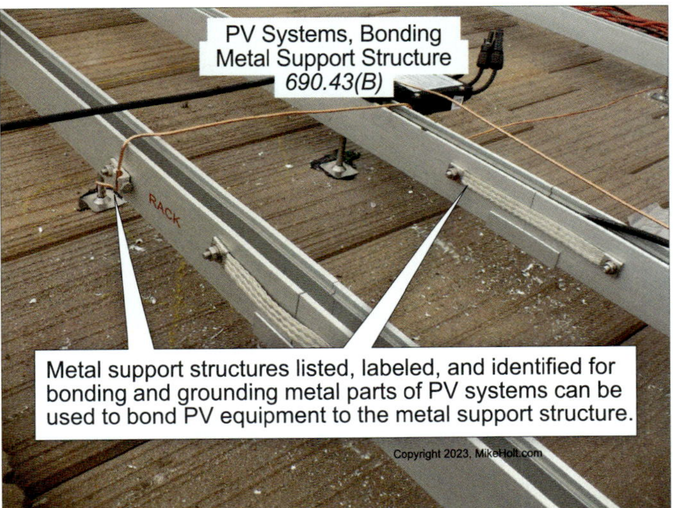

▶Figure 690–123

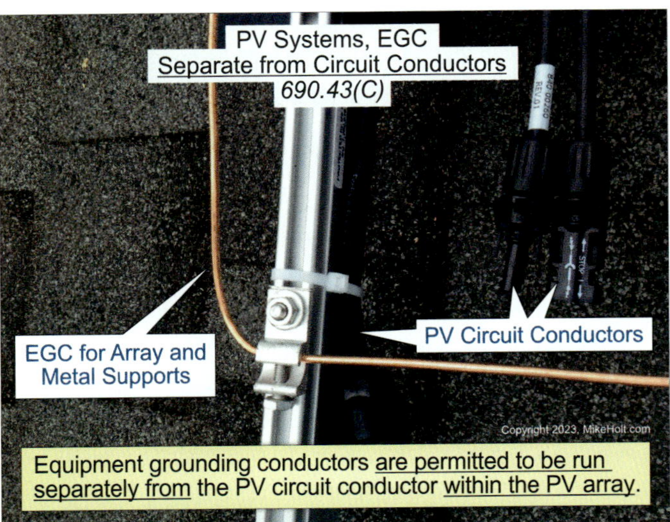

▶Figure 690–124

Where PV system circuit conductors leave the vicinity of the PV array, equipment grounding conductors must comply with 250.134.

(D) Bonding Over 250V. The bonding bushing and bonding jumper requirements contained in 250.97 for circuits over 250V to ground do not apply to metal raceways and metal cables containing PV system dc circuit conductors. ▶Figure 690–125

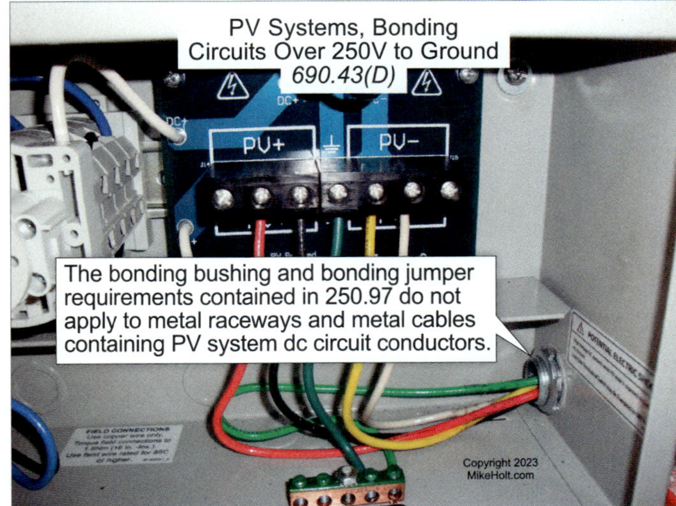

▶Figure 690–125

690.45 Size of Equipment Grounding Conductors

Equipment grounding conductors for PV system circuits must be sized in accordance with 250.122 based on the rating of the circuit overcurrent protective device. ▶Figure 690–126

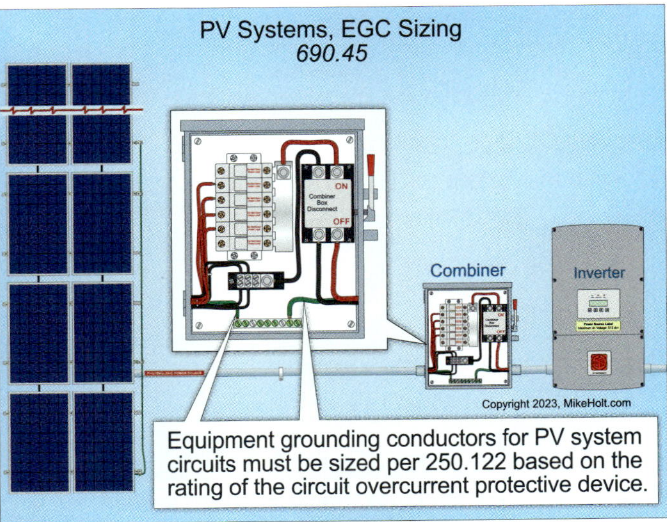

▶Figure 690–126

Where no overcurrent protective device is required [690.9(A)(1)], the equipment grounding conductor for the PV system dc circuit must be sized in accordance with Table 250.122 based on an assumed overcurrent protective device for the circuit sized in accordance with 690.9(B).

Equipment grounding conductors for PV system dc and ac circuits are not required to be increased in size to address voltage-drop considerations. ▶Figure 690–127

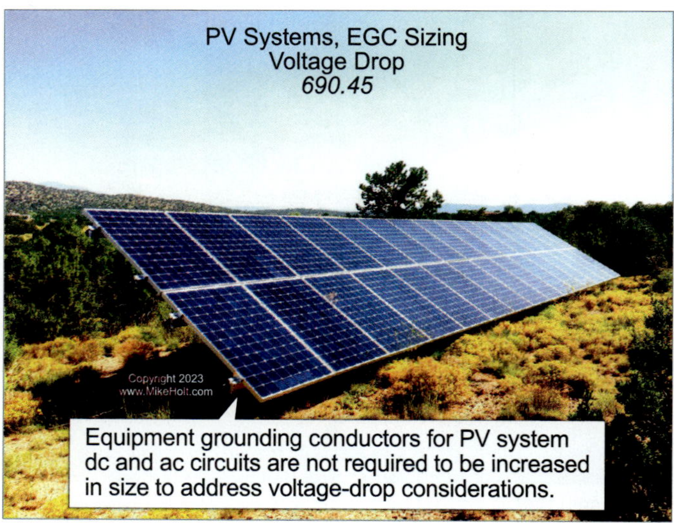

▶Figure 690–127

690.47 Grounding Electrode System

(A) Required Grounding Electrode System. A building or structure supporting a PV system must have a grounding electrode system installed. ▶Figure 690–128

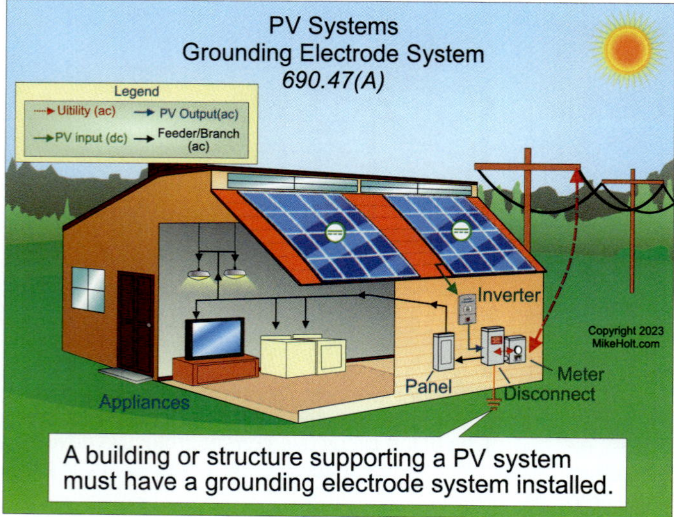

▶Figure 690–128

(1) Grounding PV Systems. PV systems are grounded when the PV inverter output ac circuit equipment grounding conductor terminates to the distribution equipment grounding conductor terminal. ▶Figure 690–129

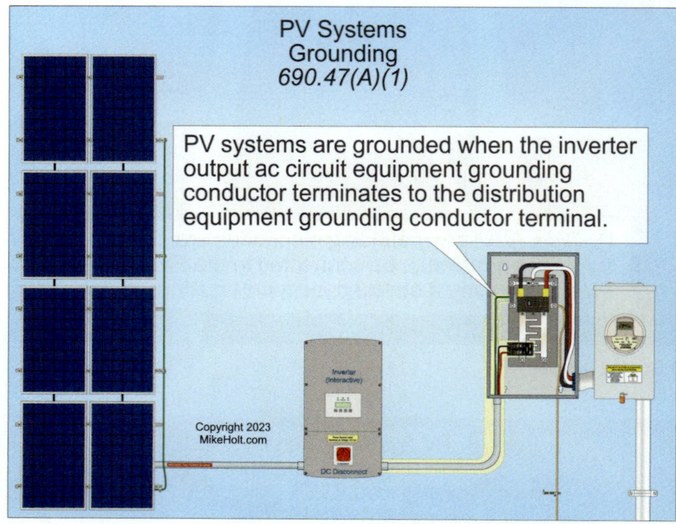

▶Figure 690–129

Note: Most PV systems are functionally grounded rather than solidly grounded.

Author's Comment:

▸ A functionally grounded system is one that has an electrical ground reference for operational purposes that is not solidly grounded. It is often connected to ground through an electronic means that is internal to an inverter or charge controller that provides ground-fault protection.

(B) Auxiliary Grounding Electrode. Auxiliary grounding electrodes, in accordance with 250.54 are permitted to be connected to the PV module frame(s) or support structure. ▶Figure 690–130

Author's Comment:

▸ According to 250.54, if an auxiliary electrode is installed, it is not required to be bonded to the building grounding electrode system, to have the grounding conductor sized to 250.66, nor must it comply with the 25Ω single ground rod requirement of 250.53(A)(2) Ex.

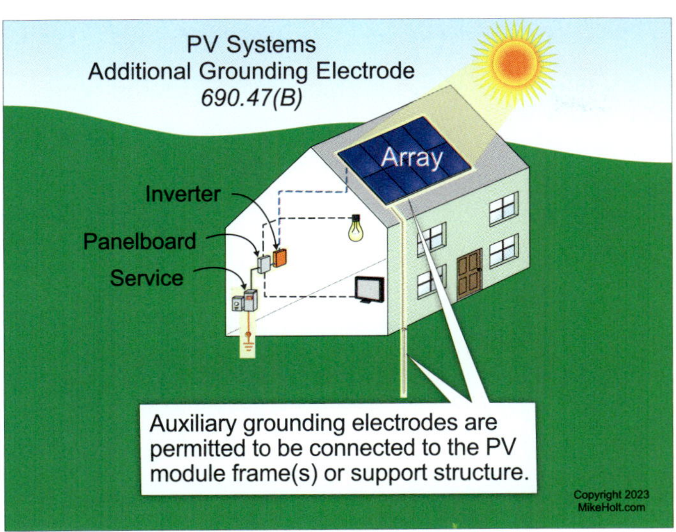

▶Figure 690–130

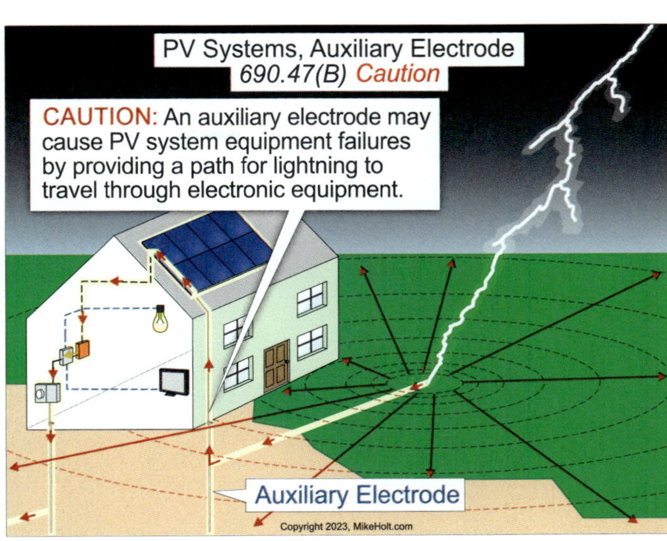

▶Figure 690–131

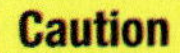
Caution

CAUTION: An auxiliary electrode may cause PV system equipment failures by providing a path for lightning to travel through electronic equipment. ▶Figure 690–131

690.59 Connection to Other Power Sources

PV systems connected in parallel with the electric utility must have the interconnection made in accordance with Article 705.

Part VI. Source Connections

690.56 Identification of Power Sources

Where a PV System operates in parallel with the electric utility as permitted by Article 705, a permanent plaque, label, or directory must be installed at the service disconnect location in accordance with 705.10.

LARGE-SCALE PHOTOVOLTAIC (PV) ELECTRIC SUPPLY STATIONS

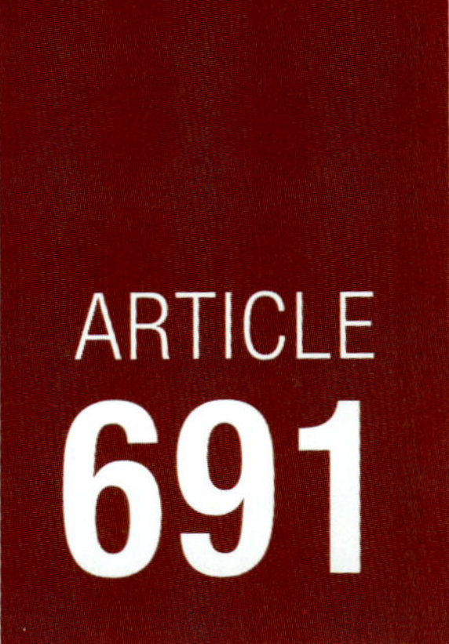

Introduction to Article 691—Large-Scale Photovoltaic (PV) Electric Supply Stations

The general requirements for solar photovoltaic (PV) systems are covered by Article 690. This article defines what a large-scale photovoltaic system is and the additional requirements that must be met to take advantage of the alternative design and safety features unique to large systems. Large-scale PV systems are privately owned PV systems operated solely to provide electricity to a regulated electric utility as compared to the Article 690 systems that may be operated to provide power to the end user, electric utility, or a combination of both. Large-scale photovoltaic (PV) electric supply stations require a careful documented review of the design by an engineer to ensure safe operation and compliance with the applicable electrical standards and industry practices.

691.1 Scope

Article 691 covers the installation of large-scale PV electric supply stations not under control of an electric utility. ▶Figure 691–1

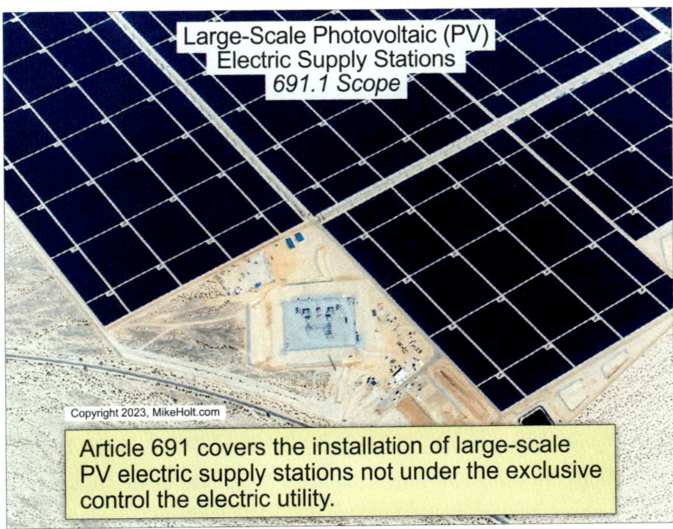

▶Figure 691–1

Note 1: Facilities covered by this article have specific design and safety features unique to large-scale PV facilities outlined 691.4 and are operated for the sole purpose of providing electric supply to a system operated by a regulated electric utility for the transfer of electric energy.

691.4 Special Requirements for Large-Scale PV Electric Supply Stations

Large-scale PV electric supply stations are only permitted to be accessible to authorized personnel and must comply with the following requirements:

(1) Electrical circuits and equipment must be maintained and operated by qualified person.

(2) PV electric supply stations must be restricted in accordance with 110.31 and have field-applied hazard markings that are permanently affixed and have sufficient durability to withstand the environment involved [110.21(B)].

(3) The connection between the PV electric supply and the electric utility system must be through medium- or high-voltage switch gear, substations, switchyards, or similar methods whose sole purpose is to interconnect the two systems.

(4) Loads within the PV electric supply station must only be used to power auxiliary equipment for the generation of the PV power.

(5) Large-scale PV electric supply stations are not permitted to be installed on buildings.

(6) The station is monitored from a central command center.

(7) The station has an inverter generating capacity of not less than 5000 kW.

Some individual sites with capacities less than 5000 kW are operated as part of a group of facilities with a total generating capacity of much greater than 5000 kW.

691.5 Equipment

All electrical equipment must be approved for installation by one of the following:

(1) Listing and labeling

(2) Be evaluated for the application and have a field label applied

(3) Where products complying with 691.5(1) or (2) are not available, by engineering review validating that the electrical equipment is evaluated and tested to relevant standards or industry practice

691.6 Engineered Design

Documentation of the electric supply station must be stamped by a licensed professional electrical engineer and provided upon request of the authority having jurisdiction. Additional stamped independent engineering reports by a licensed professional electrical engineer detailing compliance of the design with applicable electrical standards and industry practice must be provided upon request of the authority having jurisdiction. ▶Figure 691–2

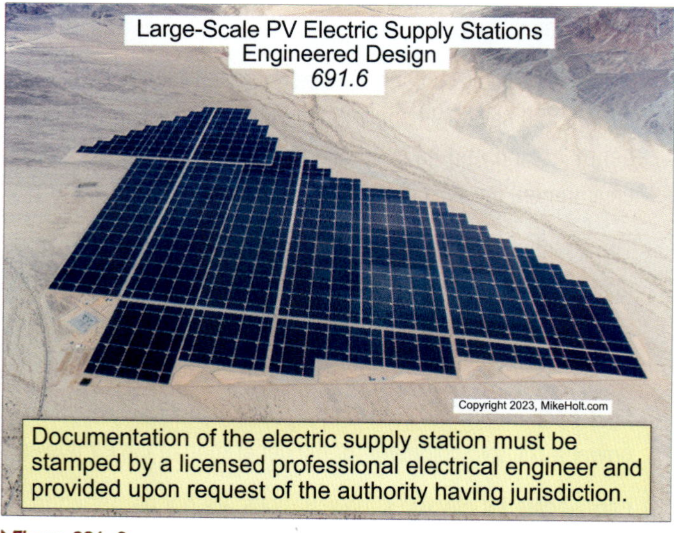

Documentation of the electric supply station must be stamped by a licensed professional electrical engineer and provided upon request of the authority having jurisdiction.

▶Figure 691–2

This documentation must include details of the conformance of the design with Article 690 and any alternative methods to Article 690, or other articles of the *NEC*.

691.7 Conformance of Construction to Engineered Design

Documentation by a licensed professional electrical engineer that the construction of the electric supply station conforms to the electrical engineered design must be provided upon request of the authority having jurisdiction. Additional stamped independent engineering reports by a licensed professional electrical engineer detailing that the construction conforms with this *Code*, applicable standards, and industry practice must be provided upon request of the authority having jurisdiction. This independent engineer must be retained by the system owner or installer.

691.8 Direct-Current Operating Voltage

Large-scale PV electric supply station calculations must be included in the documentation required in 691.6.

691.9 Disconnect for Isolating Photovoltaic Equipment

Equipment disconnects are not required to be within sight of equipment and may be remote from the equipment.

The engineered design required by 691.6 must document disconnection procedures and means of isolating equipment.

For information on electrical system maintenance, see NFPA 70B, *Recommended Practice for Electrical Equipment Maintenance.* For information on written procedures and conditions of maintenance, including lockout/tagout procedures, see NFPA 70E, *Standard for Electrical Safety in the Workplace.*

Buildings whose sole purpose is to house and protect supply station equipment are not required to include a rapid shutdown function to reduce shock hazard for firefighters [690.12]. Written standard operating procedures must be available at the site detailing necessary shutdown procedures in the event of an emergency.

691.10 <u>Fire</u> Mitigation

PV systems that do not provide arc-fault protection as required by 690.11 must include details of fire mitigation plans to address dc arc faults in the documentation required in 691.6.

<u>Fire mitigation plans are typically reviewed by the local fire agency and include topics such as access roads within the facility.</u>

691.11 Fence Bonding and Grounding

Fence grounding requirements and details must be included in the documentation required in 691.6.

Note: See 250.194 for fence bonding and grounding requirements for PV systems that operate at more than 1000V between conductors. Grounding requirements for other portions of electric supply station fencing are assessed based on the presence of overhead conductors, proximity to generation and distribution equipment, and associated step and touch potential.

SPECIAL CONDITIONS

Introduction to Chapter 7—Special Conditions

Chapter 7, which covers special conditions, is the third of the *NEC* chapters that deal with special topics. Chapters 5 and 6 cover special occupancies, and special equipment, respectively. Remember, the first four chapters of the *Code* are sequential and form a foundation for each of the subsequent three. Chapter 8 covers communications systems (twisted pair and coaxial cable) and is not subject to the requirements of Chapters 1 through 7 except where the requirements are specifically referenced there.

What exactly is a "Special Condition"? It is a situation that does not fall under the category of special occupancies or special equipment but creates a need for additional measures to ensure the "safeguarding of people and property" mission of the *NEC* as stated in 90.1(A).

▶ **Article 702—Optional Standby Systems.** Optional standby systems are intended to protect public or private facilities or property where life safety does not depend on the performance of the system. These systems are typically installed to provide an alternate source of electrical power for such facilities as industrial and commercial buildings, farms, and residences, and to serve loads that, when stopped during any power outage, can cause discomfort, serious interruption of a process, or damage to a product or process. Optional standby systems are intended to supply on-site generated power, either automatically or manually, to loads selected by the customer.

▶ **Article 705—Interconnected Electric Power Production Sources.** It used to be that a premises having more than one electric power source was a unique situation, but as more and more facilities supplement their utility electric supply with alternate sources of energy it's become more commonplace. Alternate power sources such as solar or wind turbine that run in parallel with a primary utility source require particular consideration and requirements. Article 705 provides the guidance necessary to ensure a safe installation.

▶ **Article 706—Energy Storage Systems.** Energy storage systems can be (and usually are) connected to other energy sources, such as the local utility distribution system. There can be more than one source of power connected to an ESS and the connection to other energy sources is required to comply with the requirements of Article 705 which covers installation of one or more electric power production sources operating in parallel with a utility source of electricity. It might also be a good idea to be mindful of how this article correlates with other articles in the *Code* such as Articles 480, 690, 692, and 694.

▶ **Article 710—Stand Alone Systems.** A "stand alone system" is an electrical system that is self-sufficient and a completely "off the grid" source of electrical energy such as solar or wind. However, it still may be connected to a utility supply as part of an interconnected system but the fact that it can be self-sustaining is why Article 710 specifically addresses these systems.

▶ **Article 750—Energy Management Systems.** This article applies to the installation and operation of energy management systems. Energy management systems have become very popular and are used in electric vehicle supply equipment to adjust ampere settings, power monitoring devices for panelboards, lighting controls for building automation, load-shedding systems for an alternate power source, and so on. Energy management ensures that the electrical system does not overload a branch circuit, feeder, or service and allows the electrical system to be sized based on the controlled/monitored current settings.

OPTIONAL STANDBY SYSTEMS

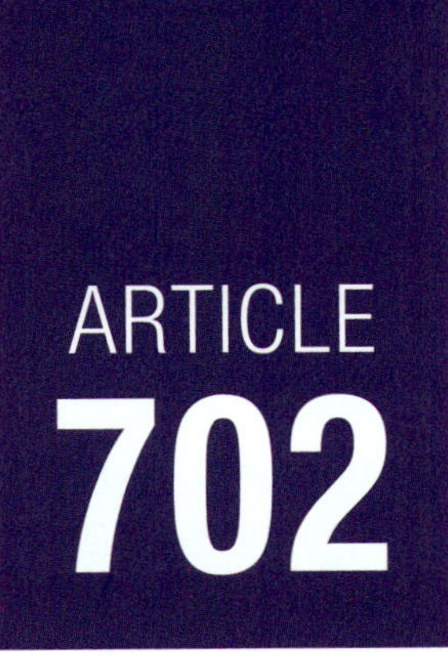

Introduction to Article 702—Optional Standby Systems

Taking third priority after emergency and legally required systems, optional standby systems protect public or private facilities or property where life safety does not depend on the performance of the system. These systems are not required for rescue operations.

Suppose a glass plant loses power. Once glass hardens in the equipment (which it will do when process heat is lost) the plant is going to suffer a great deal of downtime and expense before it can resume operations. An optional standby system can prevent this loss.

You will see these systems in facilities where loss of power can cause economic loss or business interruptions. Data centers can lose millions of dollars from a single minute of lost power. A chemical or pharmaceutical plant can lose an entire batch from a single momentary power glitch. In many cases, the lost revenue cannot be recouped.

This article also applies to the installation of optional standby generators in homes, farms, small businesses, and many other applications where standby power is not legally required.

Part I. General

702.1 Scope

Article 702 covers permanently installed and portable optional standby power systems. ▶Figure 702–1

According to Article 100, "Optional Standby System" is a system intended to supply power where life safety does not depend on the performance of the system. ▶Figure 702–2 and ▶Figure 702–3

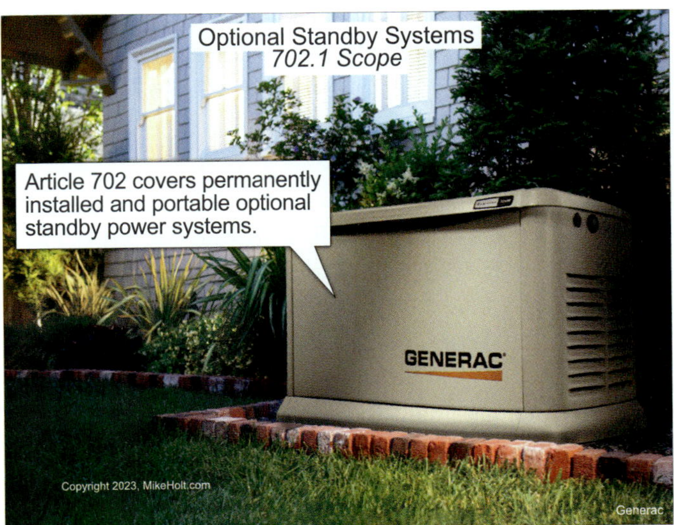

▶Figure 702–1

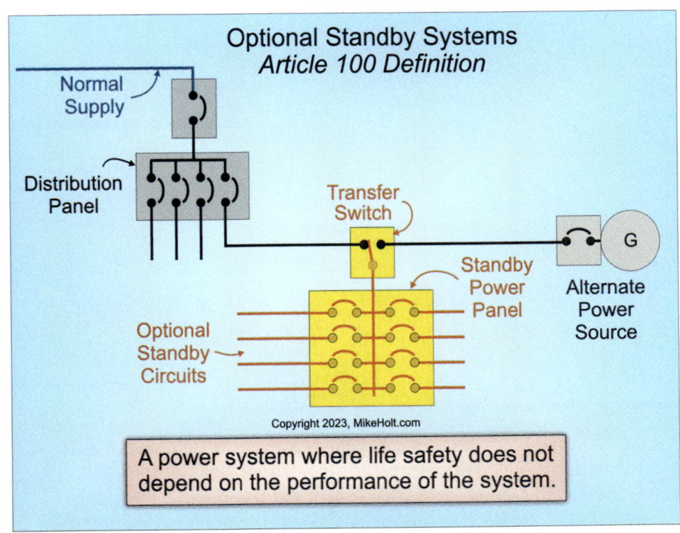

▶Figure 702–2

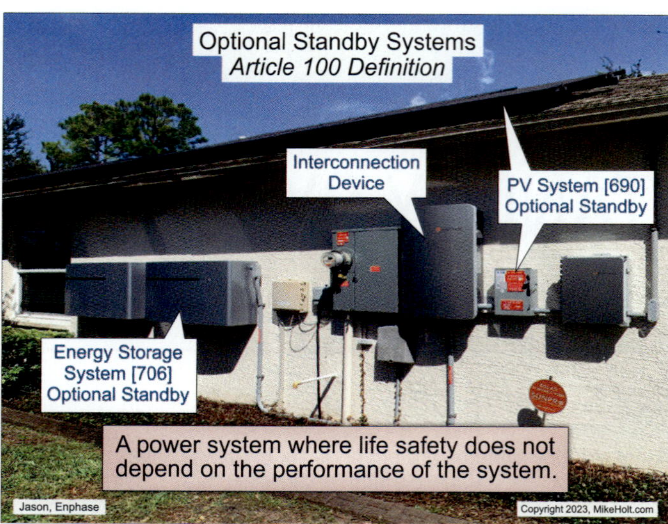

▶Figure 702–3

Author's Comment:

▸ Optional standby systems are typically installed to provide an alternate source of electric power for industrial and commercial buildings, farms, and residences to serve loads such as heating and refrigeration systems, data processing, and industrial processes that when stopped during any power outage can cause discomfort, economic loss, serious interruption of the process, damage to product or the like.

▸ Article 702 also covers portable and trailer- or vehicle-mounted generators that might be used for a dwelling. ▶Figure 702–4

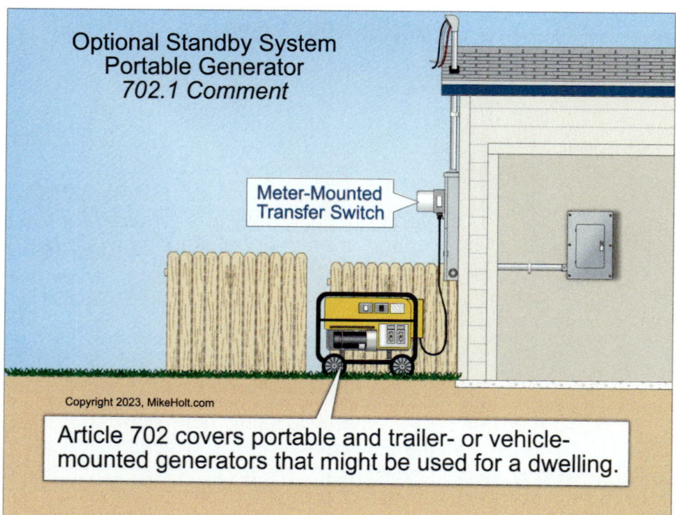

▶Figure 702–4

702.4 Capacity and Rating

(A) System Capacity.

(1) Manual and Nonautomatic Load Connection. If the connection of the loads to the optional standby system is manual or nonautomatic, the optional standby system must be sized to supply all the loads selected by the user intended to be operated at one time. ▶Figure 702–5

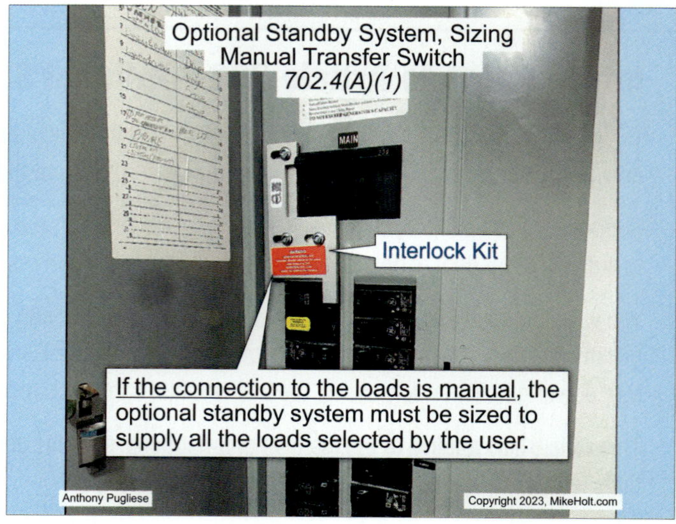

▶Figure 702–5

Note: Manual and nonautomatic transfer switches require human intervention.

(2) Automatic Load Connection. If the connection for a load to the optional standby system is automatic, the optional standby system must be sized as follows:

(a) Full Load. The optional standby source must be capable of supplying the full load that is automatically connected as determined by Article 220 or another approved method. ▶Figure 702–6

Author's Comment:

▸ For existing facilities, the demand data for one year or the average power demand for a 15-minute period over a minimum of 30 days can be used to size the electric power source [220.87]. ▶Figure 702–7

(b) Energy Management System (EMS). Where a system is employed in accordance with 750.30 that will automatically manage the connected load, the standby source must have a capacity sufficient to supply the maximum load that will be connected by the EMS. ▶Figure 702–8

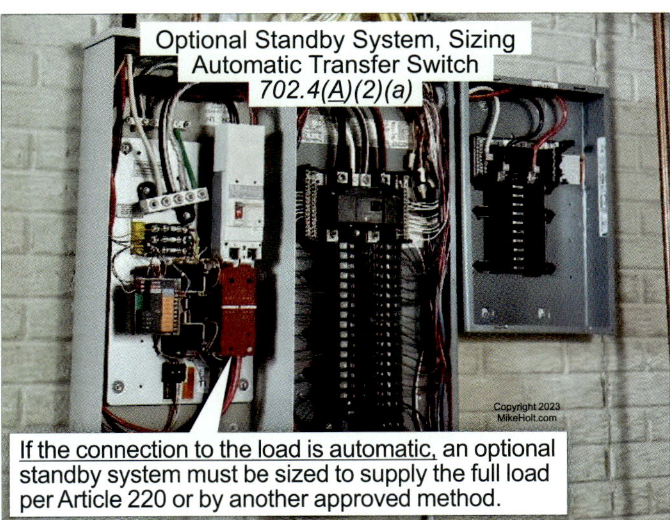

▶Figure 702–6

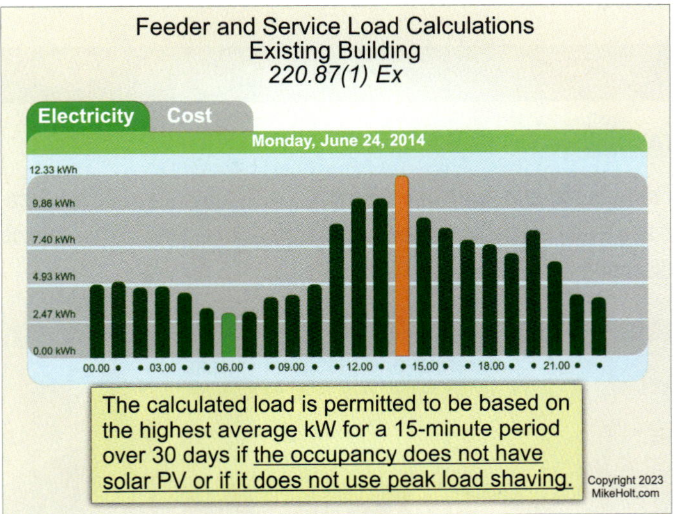

▶Figure 702–7

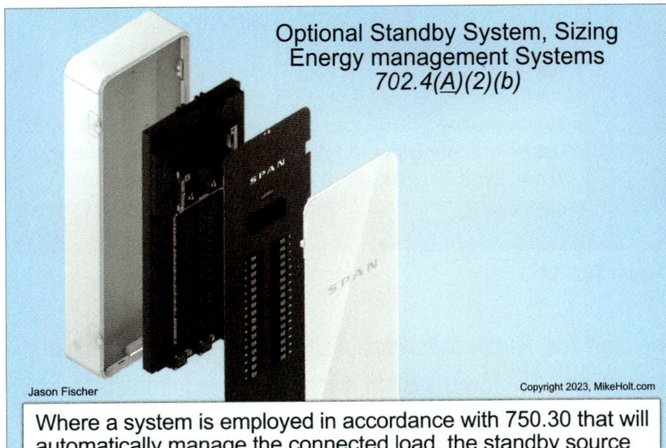

▶Figure 702–8

702.5 Interconnection Equipment or Transfer Equipment

(A) General. Interconnection equipment or a transfer equipment is required for the connection of an optional standby system to premises wiring. ▶Figure 702–9 and ▶Figure 702–10

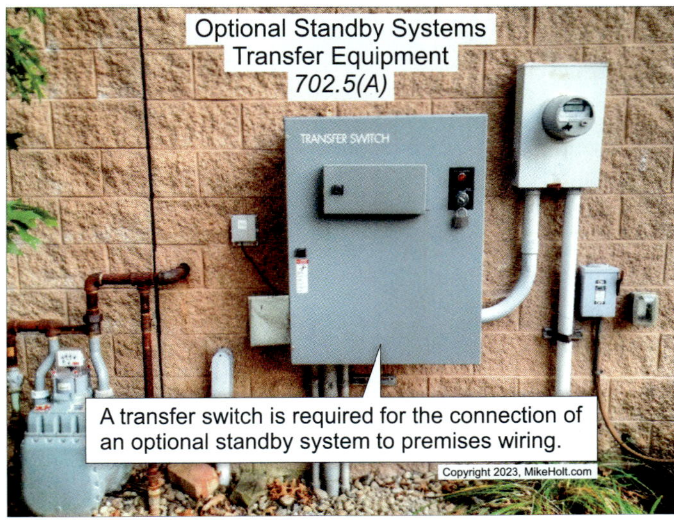

▶Figure 702–9

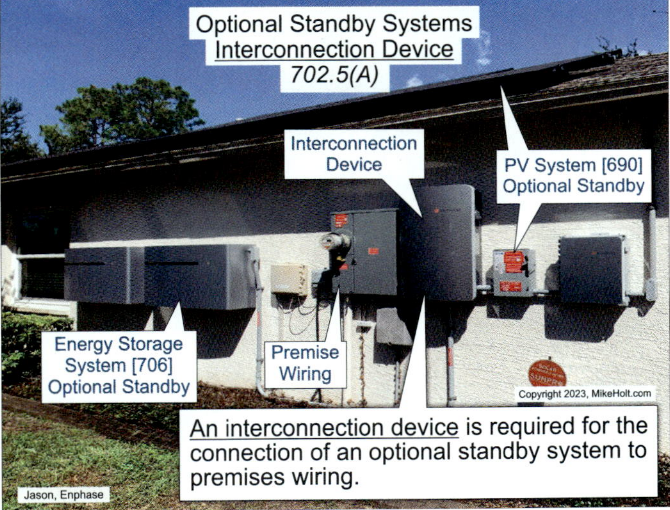

▶Figure 702–10

According to Article 100, a "Transfer Switch" is an automatic or nonautomatic device used to transfer loads from one power source to another. ▶Figure 702–11

Interconnection equipment and transfer switch must be listed and installed to prevent the inadvertent interconnection of all sources of supply.

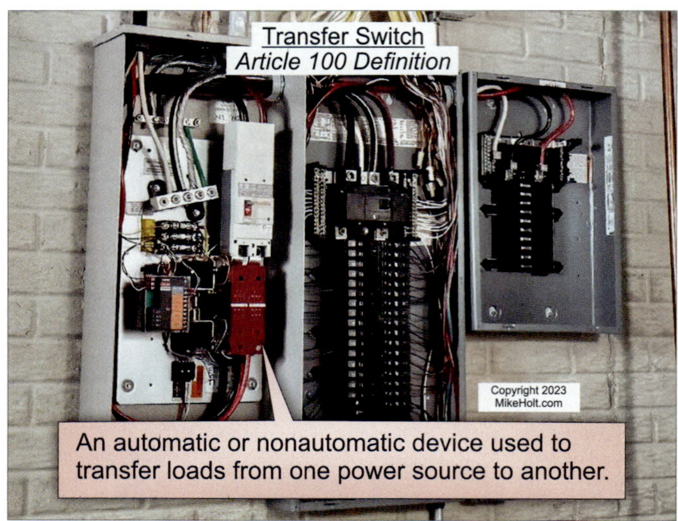

▶Figure 702–11

(B) Meter-Mounted Transfer Switches. A listed meter-mounted transfer switch installed between the electric utility meter and the meter enclosure in accordance with 230.82(11) must be listed. ▶Figure 702–12

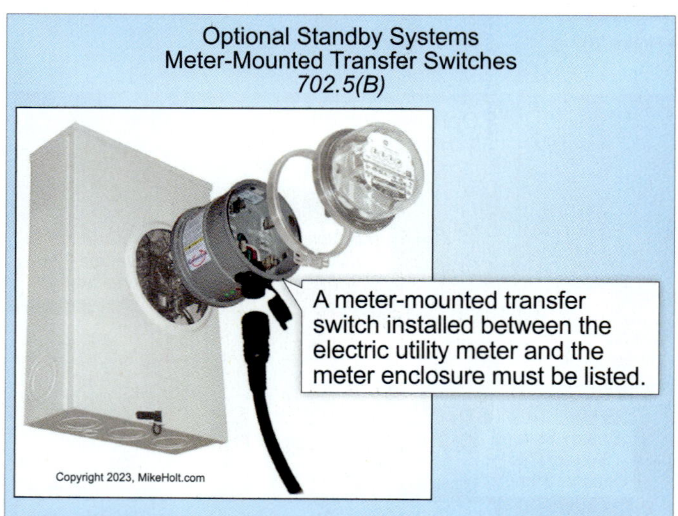

▶Figure 702–12

(C) Documentation. In other than dwelling units, the short-circuit current rating of the transfer equipment, based on the specific overcurrent protective device type and settings protecting the transfer equipment, must be field marked on the exterior of the transfer equipment.

(D) Parallel Installation. Optional standby systems installed in parallel with other power production sources must comply with Parts I or II of Article 705. ▶Figure 702–13

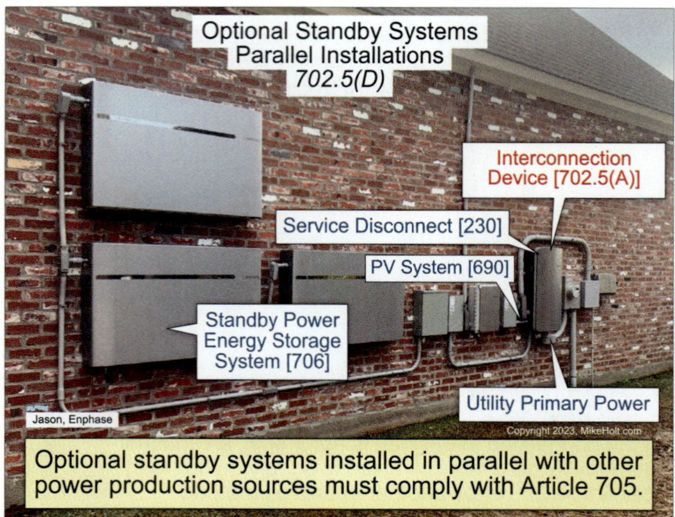

▶Figure 702–13

702.7 Signs

(A) Optional Power Sources.

Commercial and Industrial Installations. A sign indicating the location of each optional standby power system is required at the service disconnect. ▶Figure 702–14

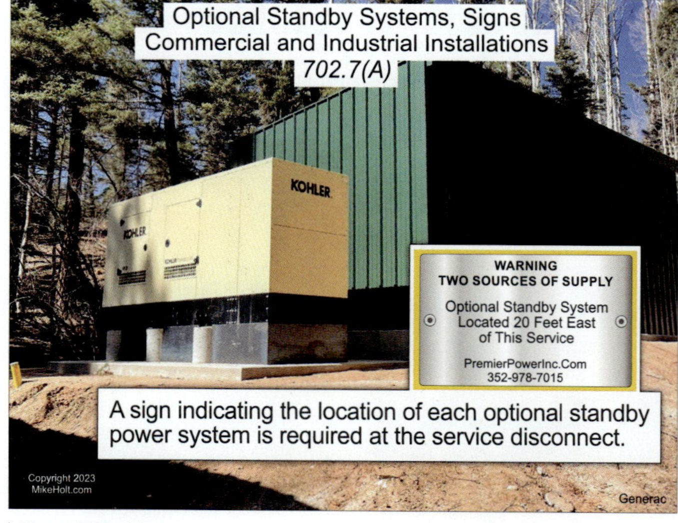

▶Figure 702–14

One- and Two-Family Dwellings. A sign indicating the location of the optional standby power system disconnect is required at the emergency shutoff disconnect [230.85]. ▶Figure 702–15

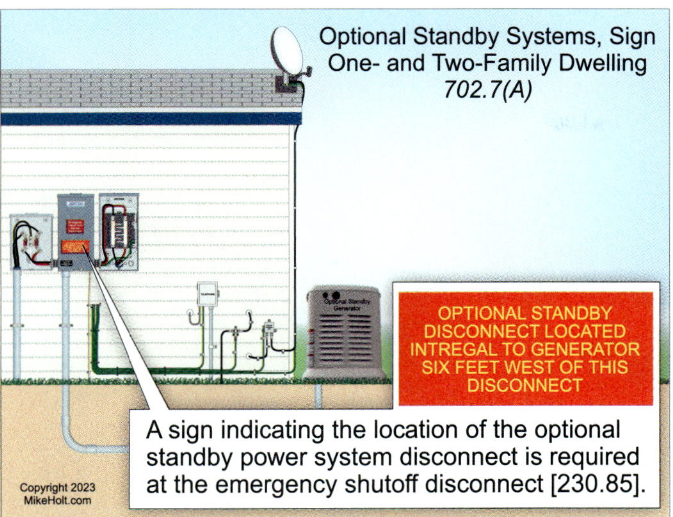

▶Figure 702–15

(C) Power Inlet. Where a power inlet is used for the connection of a portable generator, a warning sign must be placed near the power inlet to indicate the type of generator permitted to be connected to the inlet. The warning sign must state: ▶Figure 702–16

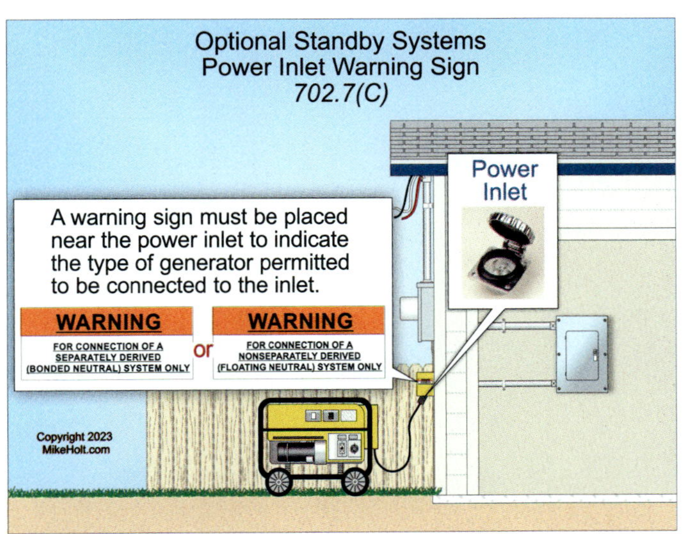

▶Figure 702–16

WARNING—FOR CONNECTION OF A SEPARATELY DERIVED (BONDED NEUTRAL) SYSTEM ONLY

or

WARNING—FOR CONNECTION OF A NONSEPARATELY DERIVED (FLOATING NEUTRAL) SYSTEM ONLY

Part II. Circuit Wiring

702.10 Wiring

Optional standby system wiring can occupy the same raceways, cables, enclosures, and cabinets with other wiring.

702.12 Outdoor Generators

(B) Flanged Inlet. The flanged inlet for a portable generator must be located outside a building or structure. ▶Figure 702–17

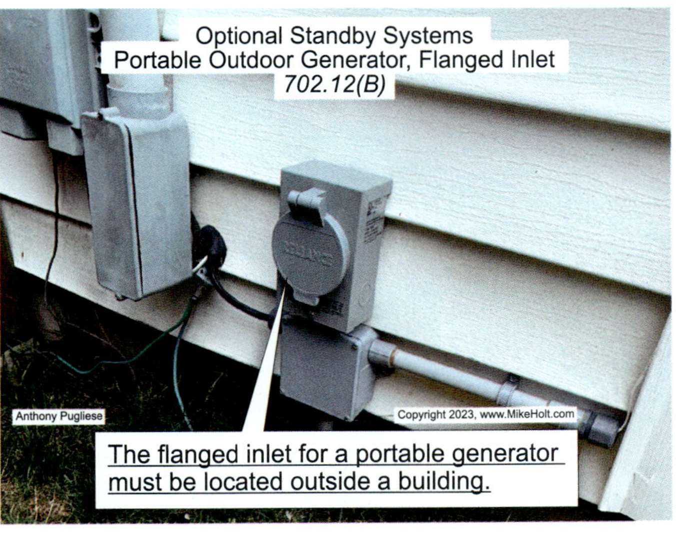

▶Figure 702–17

ARTICLE 705

INTERCONNECTED ELECTRIC POWER PRODUCTION SOURCES

Introduction to Article 705—Interconnected Electric Power Production Sources

Article 705 covers the requirements for the interconnection of PV systems [690], electric vehicles [625] energy storage systems ESS [706], and optional standby system generators [445 and 702] in parallel with the electric utility.

Part I. General

705.1 Scope

This article covers the installation of electric power production sources (PV, ESS, generator) operating in parallel with the primary source of power (electric utility). ▶Figure 705–1 and ▶Figure 705–2

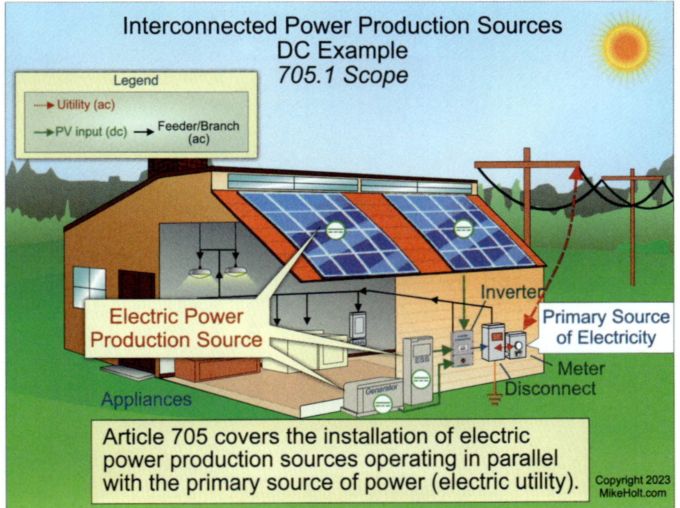

▶Figure 705–2

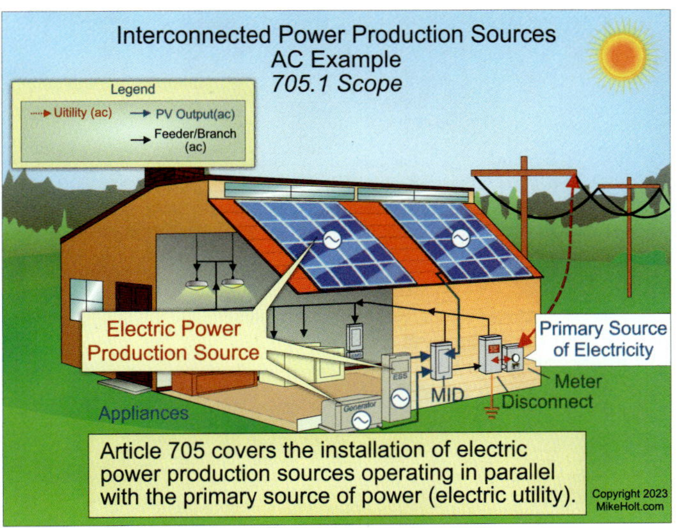

▶Figure 705–1

Note 1: The primary source of power typically includes the electric utility or it can be an on-site power source.

According to Article 100, "Power Production Equipment" is electrical generating equipment up to the system disconnect supplied by any source of electrical power (PV, ESS, generator) other than the electric utility. Examples of power production equipment include such items as generators, PV Systems, and energy storage systems. ▶Figure 705–3 and ▶Figure 705–4

A "Primary Source" is the main source of power in an electric power system.

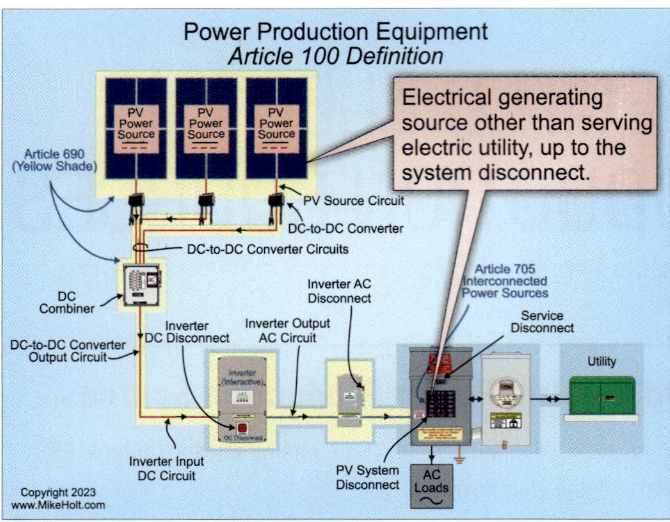

▶Figure 705–3

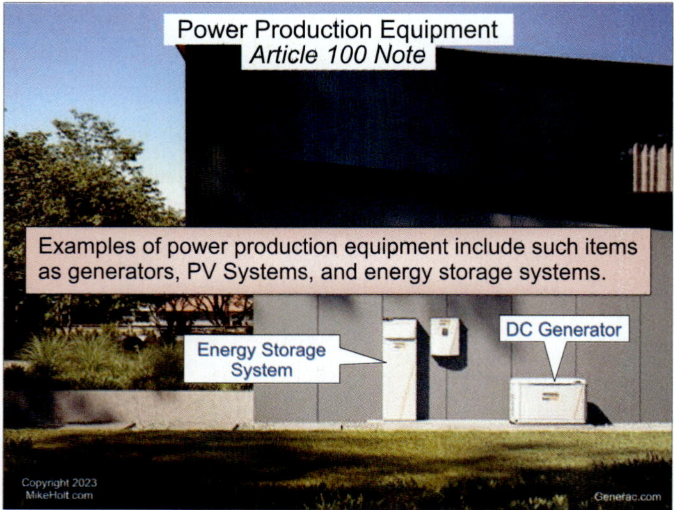

▶Figure 705–4

705.6 Equipment Approval

Interconnection devices and interactive (grid tied) equipment operating in parallel with power production sources (PV, ESS, generator) must be listed for the required interactive (grid tied) function. ▶Figure 705–5, ▶Figure 705–6, ▶Figure 705–7, and ▶Figure 705–8

Note 2: An interactive (grid tied) function is common in microgrid interconnect devices (MID), power control systems, interactive (grid tied) inverters, and ac energy storage systems. ▶Figure 705–9

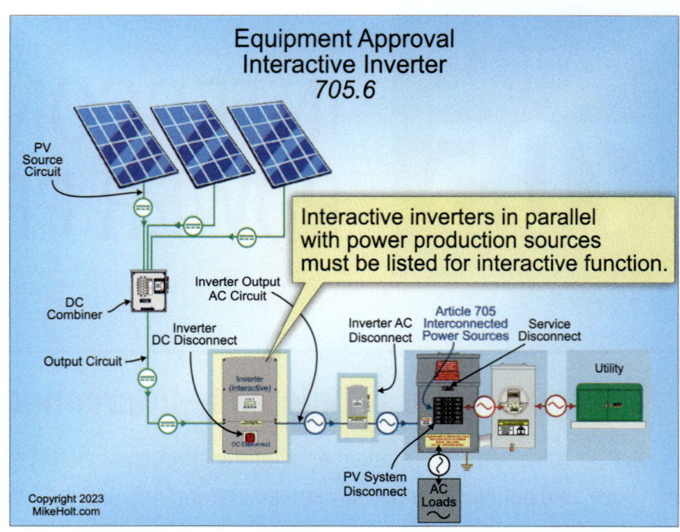

▶Figure 705–5

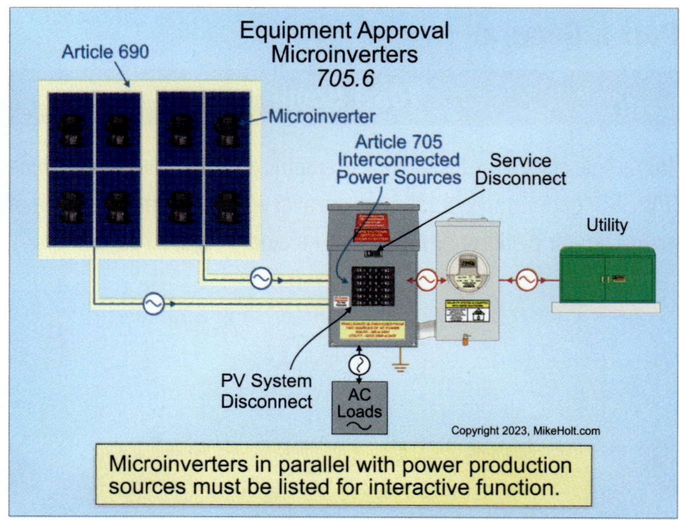

▶Figure 705–6

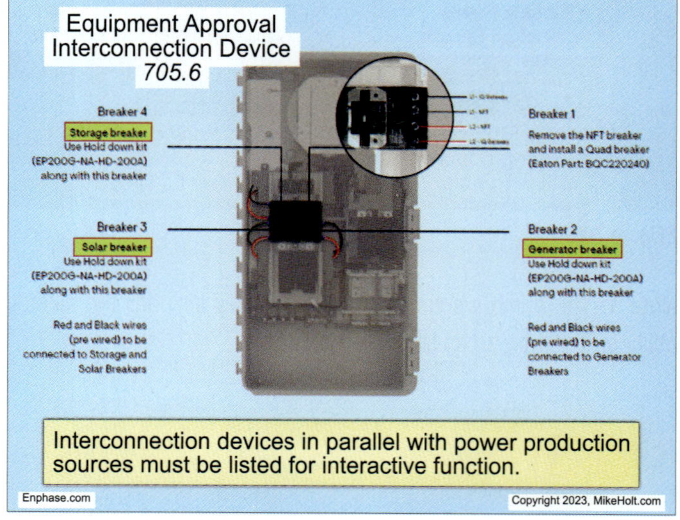

▶Figure 705–7

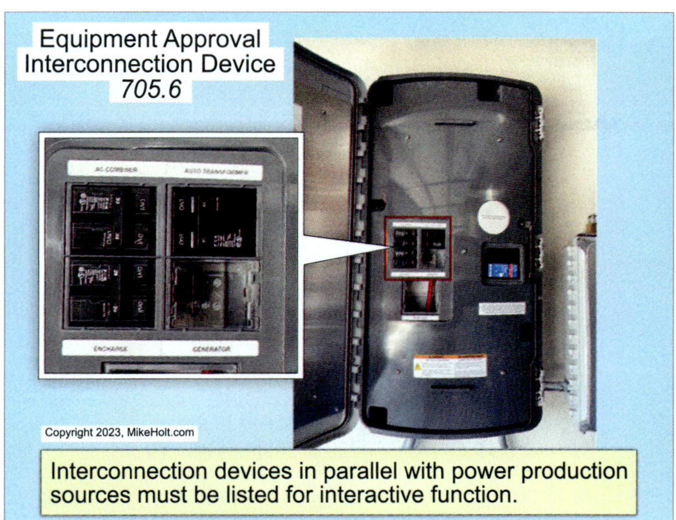

Interconnection devices in parallel with power production sources must be listed for interactive function.

▶Figure 705–8

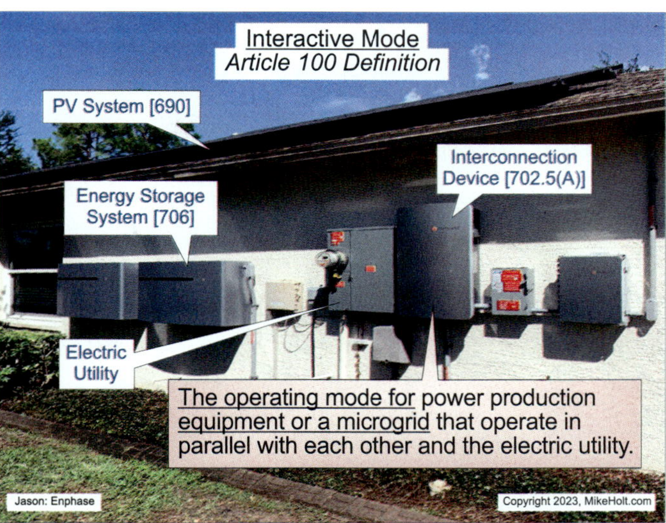

▶Figure 705–10

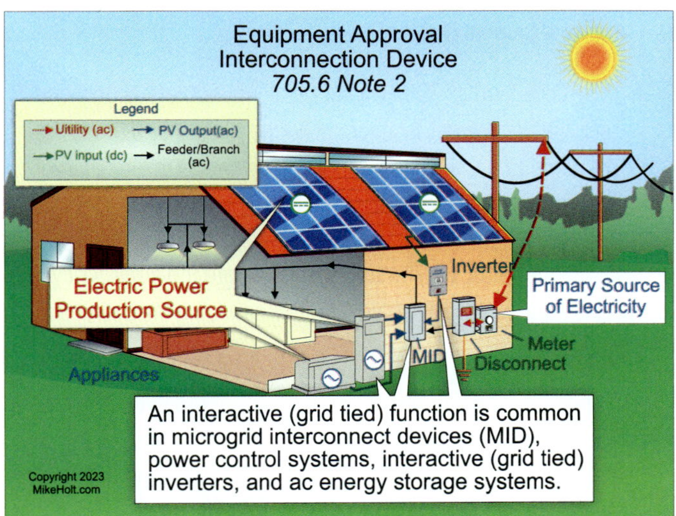

▶Figure 705–9

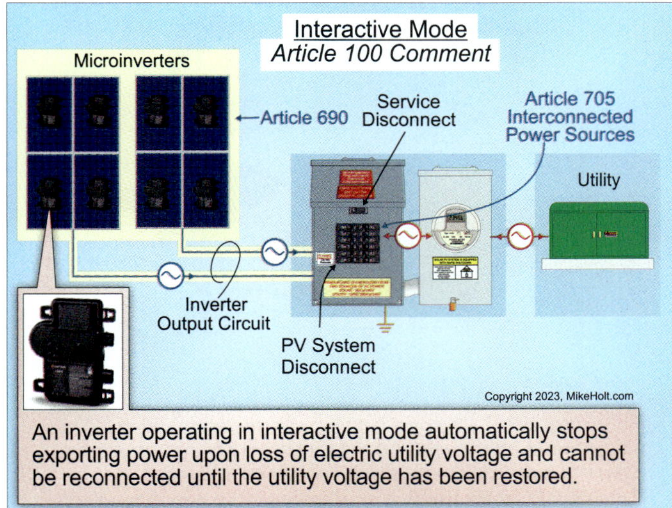

▶Figure 705–11

According to Article 100, "Interactive Mode" means the operating mode where power production equipment or a microgrid are in parallel with each other and the electric utility. ▶**Figure 705–10**

Author's Comment:

▶ A listed interactive (grid tied) power production source automatically stops exporting power upon loss of electric utility voltage and cannot be reconnected until the voltage has been restored. Interactive (grid tied) inverters can automatically or manually resume exporting power to the electric utility once the electric utility source is restored [705.40]. ▶**Figure 705–11**

705.8 System Installation

The installation of power production sources (PV, ESS, generator) in parallel with the electric utility must be performed by a qualified person. ▶**Figure 705–12**

According to Article 100, a "Qualified Person" has the skills and knowledge related to the construction and operation of electrical equipment and installations. This person must have received safety training to recognize and avoid the hazards involved with electrical systems [Article 100]. ▶**Figure 705–13**

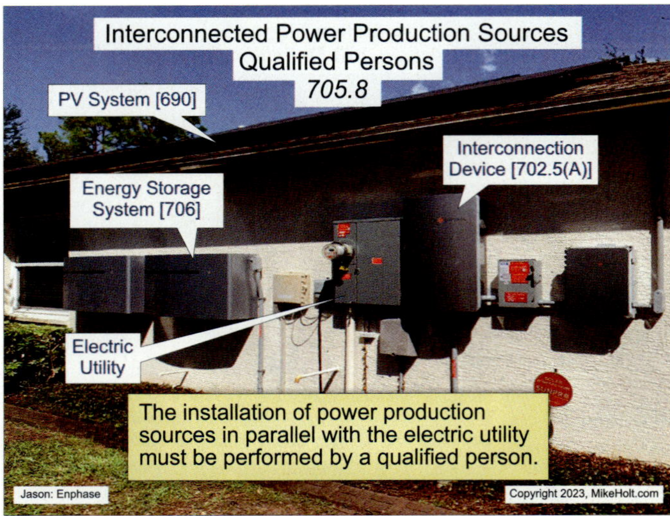

▶Figure 705–12

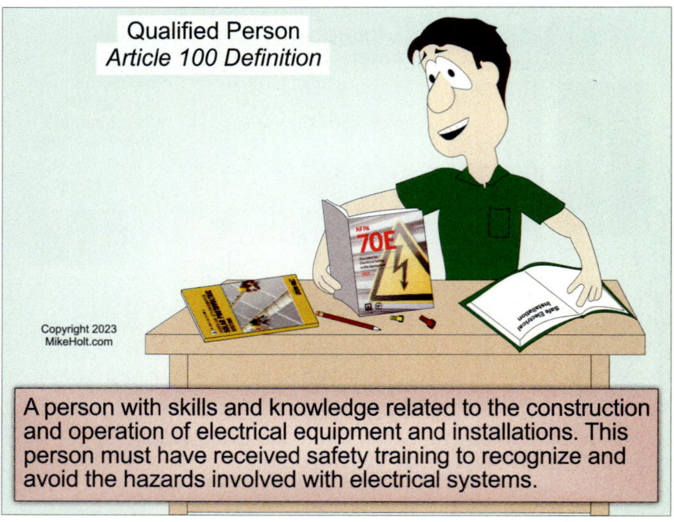

▶Figure 705–13

705.10 Identification of Parallel Power Production Sources

Where power production sources (PV, ESS, generator) operate in parallel with the electric utility, a permanent plaque, label, or directory must be installed at each service disconnect location, or at an approved readily visible location as follows:

(1) The plaque, label, or directory must identify the location of all power production source disconnects. ▶Figure 705–14

Ex: Plaques, labels, or directories for installations having multiple co-located power production sources can be identified as a group(s). A plaque or directory is not required for each power source.

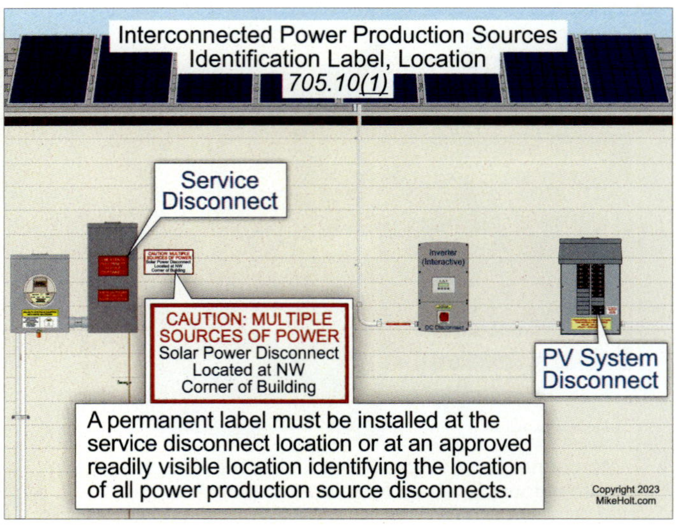

▶Figure 705–14

Author's Comment:

▶ The exception to 705.10 infers that where there is only one service disconnect location, only one plaque or directory is required at the service disconnect indicating the location of the other power production sources.

(2) The plaque, label, or directory must indicate the emergency telephone numbers of any off-site entities servicing the power source systems.

(3) The plaque, label, or directory must be marked with the wording "CAUTION: MULTIPLE SOURCES OF POWER." The marking must be affixed and have sufficient durability to withstand the environment involved [110.21(B)]. ▶Figure 705–15

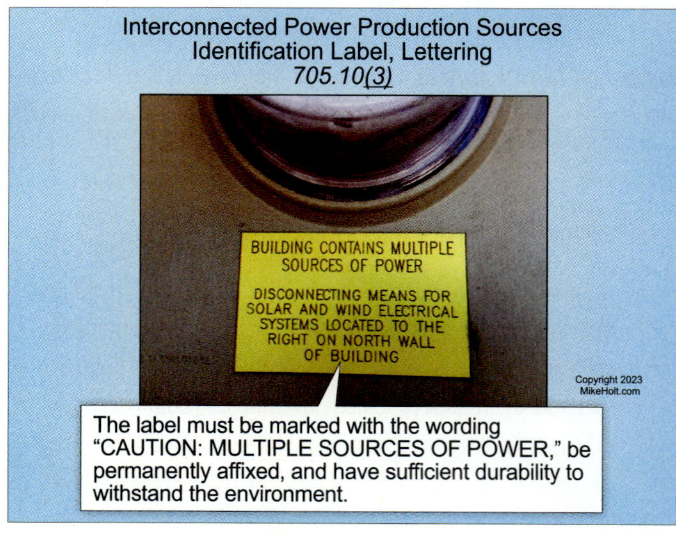

▶Figure 705–15

705.11 Service Connection

(A) Utility Connections. Power production sources can be connected to the electric utility as follows:

(1) Power production sources, such as PV and energy storage systems can be directly connected to the electric utility by a separate service.

(2) Power production sources, such as PV systems can be connected to the supply-side of the service disconnect. ▶Figure 705–16 and ▶Figure 705–17

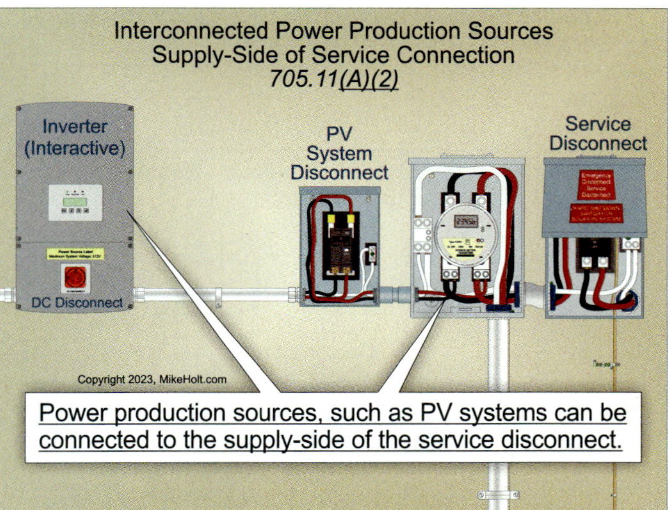

▶Figure 705–16

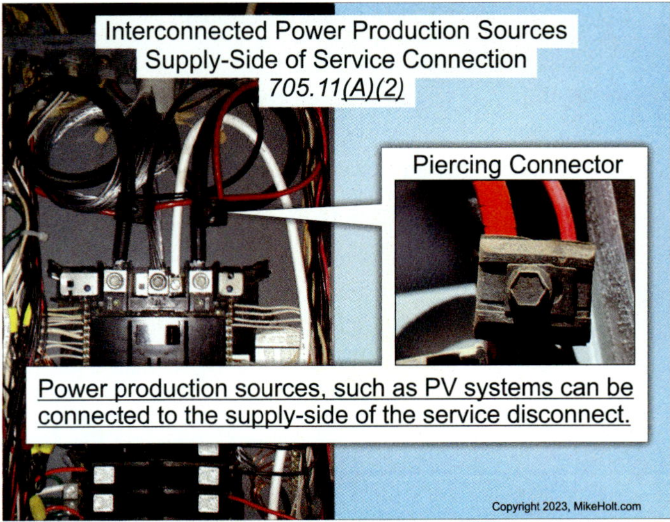

▶Figure 705–17

(3) To an additional set of service entrance conductors in accordance with 230.40 Ex 5.

(B) Conductor Sizing. Power production source supply-side conductors must comply with all the following: ▶Figure 705–18 and ▶Figure 705–19

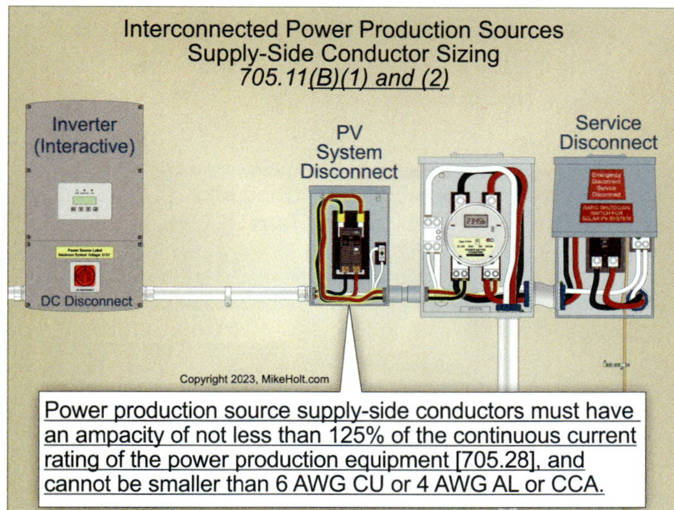

▶Figure 705–18

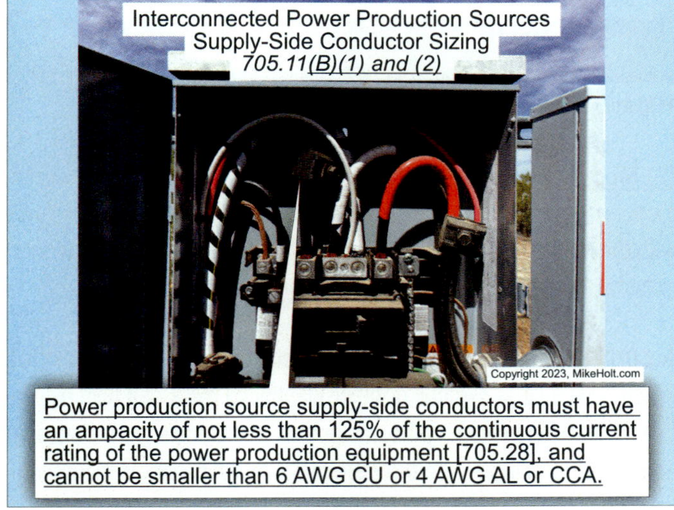

▶Figure 705–19

(1) Power production source supply-side conductors must have an ampacity of not less than 125 percent of the continuous current rating of the power production equipment, see 705.28.

(2) Power production source supply-side conductors must not be smaller than 6 AWG copper or 4 AWG aluminum or copper-clad aluminum.

(C) Supply-Side Connections. Connection to service conductors must comply with the following:

(1) Conductor Splices or Taps. Splices and taps to service conductors must be in accordance with 230.46.

Author's Comment:

▸ According to 230.46, pressure connectors, devices for splices and tap connections, and power distribution blocks installed on service conductors must be listed and marked "suitable for use on the line side of the service equipment" or equivalent. ▸**Figure 705–20**

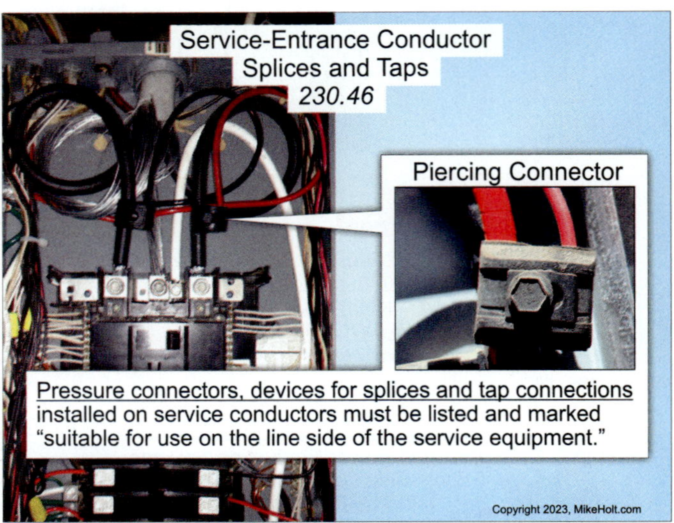

▸Figure 705–20

(2) Modifications to Existing Equipment. Modifications to equipment to accommodate supply-side connections must be in accordance with the manufacturer's instructions or the equipment modification(s) must be <u>field</u> evaluated and <u>be</u> field <u>labeled</u>.

According to Article 100, "Field Labeled" is equipment or materials which have a label, symbol, or other identifying mark of a field evaluation body (FEB) indicating the equipment or materials were evaluated and found to comply with the requirements described in the accompanying field evaluation report.

(3) Utility Meter Enclosure. Supply-side connections within meter socket enclosures under the exclusive control of the electric utility are only permitted where approved by the electric utility. ▸**Figure 705–21**

(D) Power Production Source Disconnect. A disconnecting means in accordance with Article 230, Parts VI through VIII must be provided to disconnect the power production source supply conductor. ▸**Figure 705–22**

(E) Bonding and Grounding. Metal enclosures, metal raceways, and cable methods containing supply-side conductors must be bonded in accordance with Article 250, Parts II through V and VIII. ▸**Figure 705–23**

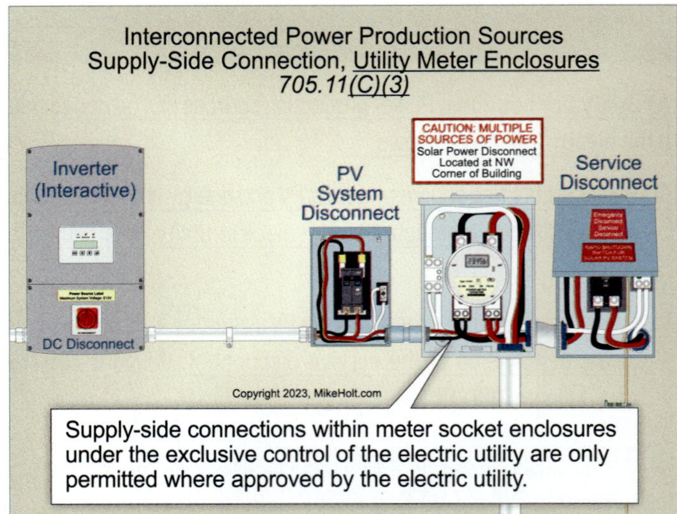

▸Figure 705–21

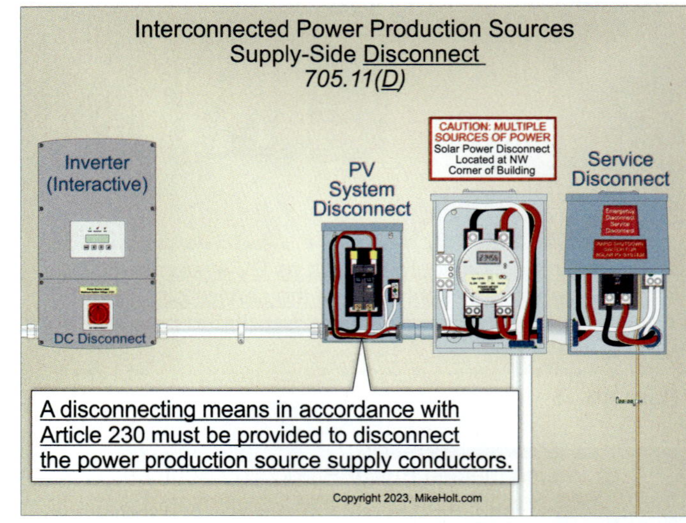

▸Figure 705–22

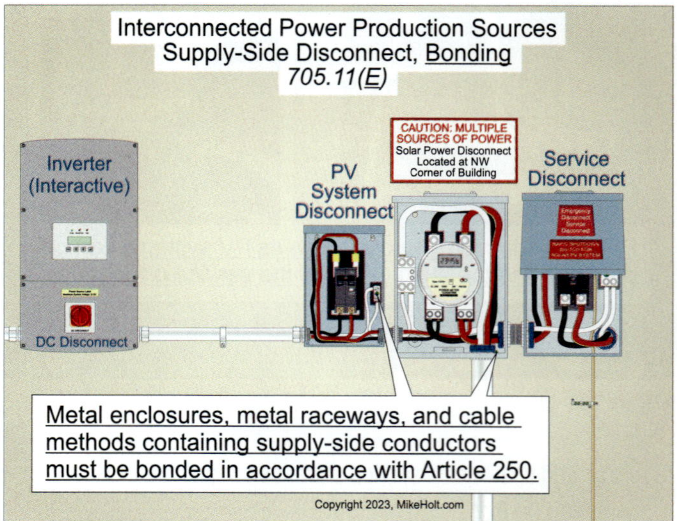

▸Figure 705–23

(F) Overcurrent Protection. Supply-side conductors terminating to the power production disconnect must have overcurrent protection in accordance with Article 230, Part VII. ▶Figure 705–24

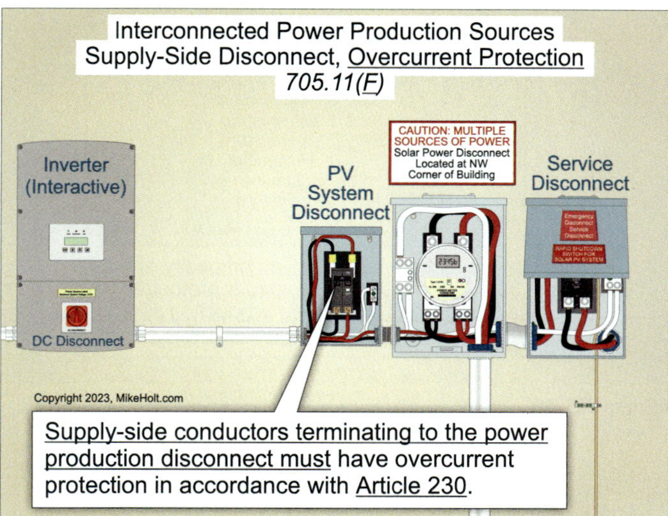

▶Figure 705–24

705.12 Load-Side Source Connection

Electric power production source (PV, ESS, generator) output conductors can be connected to the feeder or feeder equipment (load-side of service disconnect). ▶Figure 705–25

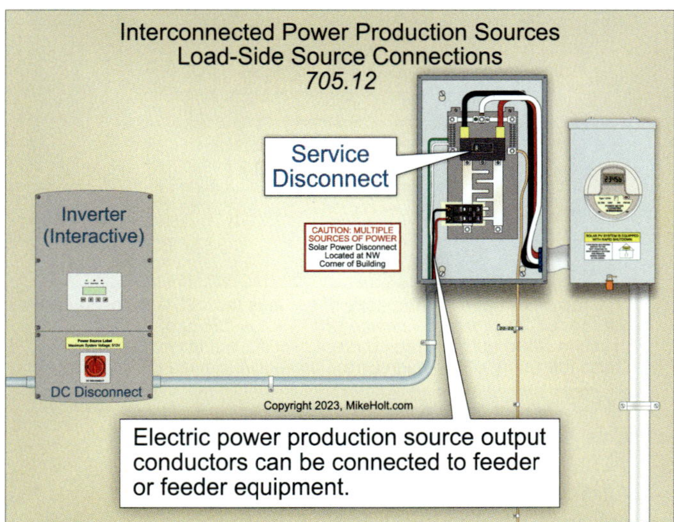

▶Figure 705–25

According to Article 100, "Power Production Source Output Conductors" are the conductors from the power production equipment to premises wiring or service equipment. ▶Figure 705–26 and ▶Figure 705–27

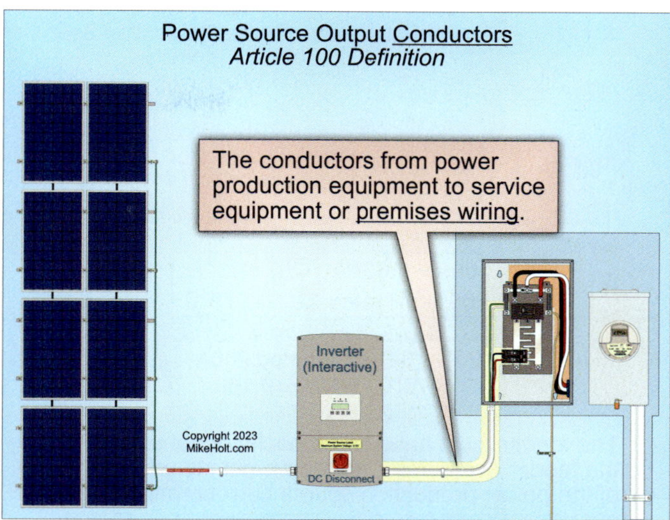

▶Figure 705–26

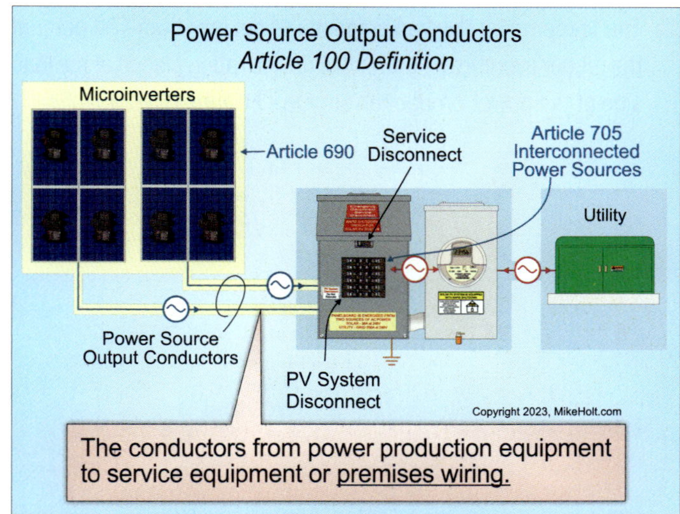

▶Figure 705–27

(A) Feeder and Feeder Taps. Where the power production source (PV, ESS, generator) connection is made to a feeder, the following applies:

(1) The feeder must have an ampacity of not less than 125 percent of the power production source nameplate current in accordance with 705.28(A).

(2) Where a power production source connection is made to a feeder at a location that is not at the opposite end of the feeder overcurrent protective device, that portion of the feeder on the load side of the power source connection must have an ampacity as follows:

(a) The feeder must have an ampacity of not less than the feeder overcurrent protective device, plus 125 percent of the power production source current rating. ▶Figure 705–28

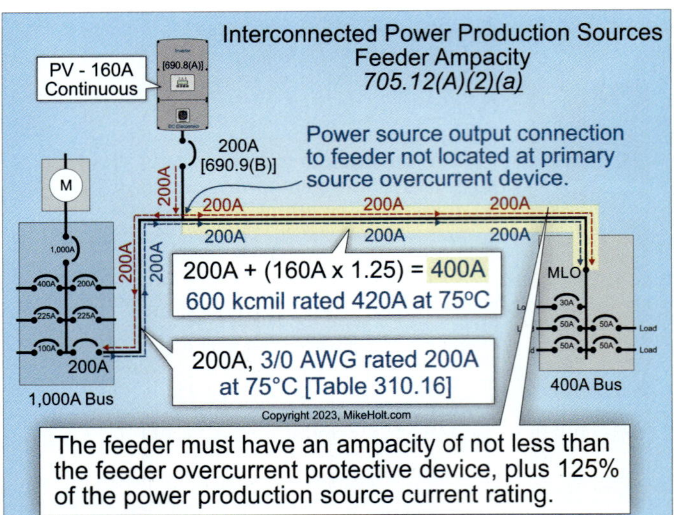

▶Figure 705–28

(b) The feeder must have an ampacity of not less than 100 percent the feeder overcurrent protective device rating placed at the load side of the power production source. ▶Figure 705–29

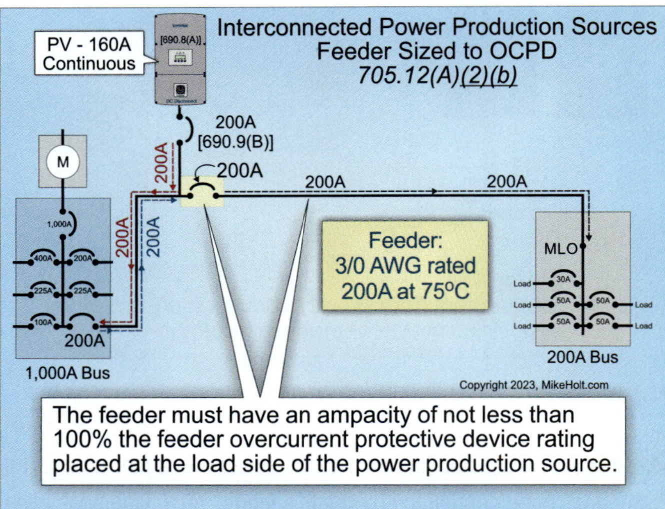

▶Figure 705–29

(3) Where a tap connection is made to a feeder, the tap conductors must have an ampacity of <u>not less than one-third of</u> the rating of the feeder protective device, plus <u>the rating of any power production source overcurrent protective device connected to the feeder.</u> ▶Figure 705–30

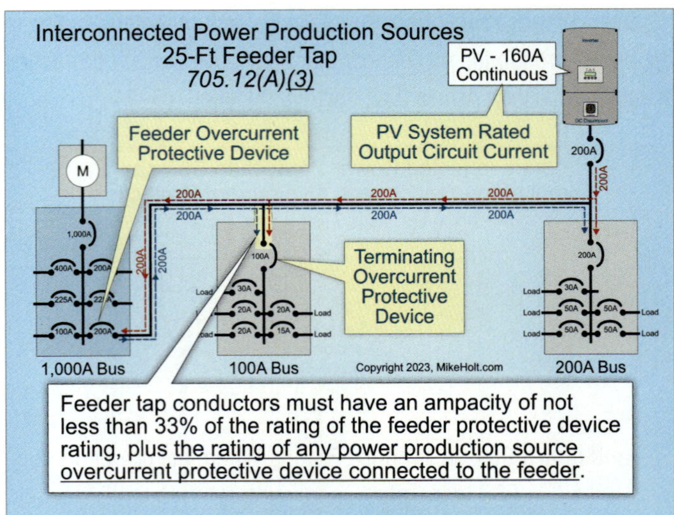

▶Figure 705–30

▶ Feeder Tap—25-Foot Example

Question: *What size tap conductor, not more than 25 ft long made from a 200A-protected feeder supplied with an inverter having an ac current rating of 160A is required to a 100A overcurrent protective device?* ▶Figure 705–31

(a) 3 AWG   (b) 2 AWG   (c) 1 AWG   (d) 1/0 AWG

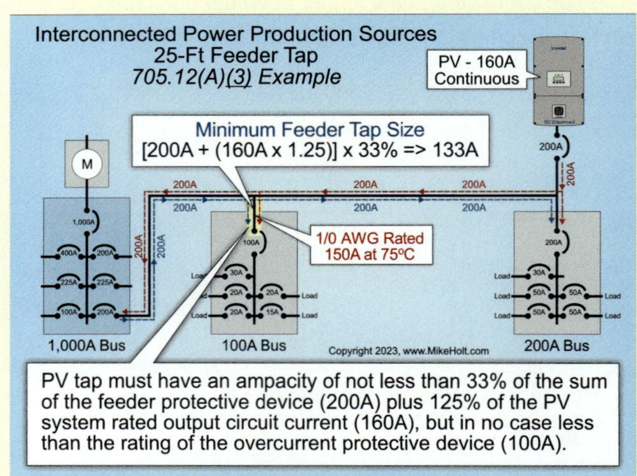

▶Figure 705–31

Solution:

PV system taps not longer than 25 ft must have an ampacity of not less than 33 percent of the feeder overcurrent protective device rating (200A) plus 125 percent of the PV system rated current (160A), but in no case less than the rating of the terminating overcurrent protective device (100A) [240.21(B)(2)].

Feeder Tap Conductor Ampacity = > [200A + (160A × 125%)] × 33%, but not less than 100A

Feeder Tap Conductor Ampacity = > (200A + 200A) × 33%, but not less than 100A

Feeder Tap Conductor Ampacity = > 400A × 33%, but not less than 100A

Feeder Tap Conductor Ampacity = > 133A, but no less than 100A

Feeder Conductor Size = 1/0 AWG rated 150A at 75°C [Table 310.16]

Answer: *(d) 1/0 AWG*

(B) Panelboard Busbar Ampere Rating. Where the power production source (PV, ESS, generator) connection is made to distribution equipment with no specific listing and instructions for combining multiple sources, one of the following methods (B)(1) through (B)(6) must be used:

(1) Overcurrent Protection Device, Anywhere. Where the power production source (PV, ESS, generator) connection is made to a circuit breaker in a panelboard, the panelboard busbar must have an ampere rating of not less than the rating of the panelboard overcurrent protective device, plus 125 percent of the power production source current rating in accordance with 705.28. ▶**Figure 705–32**

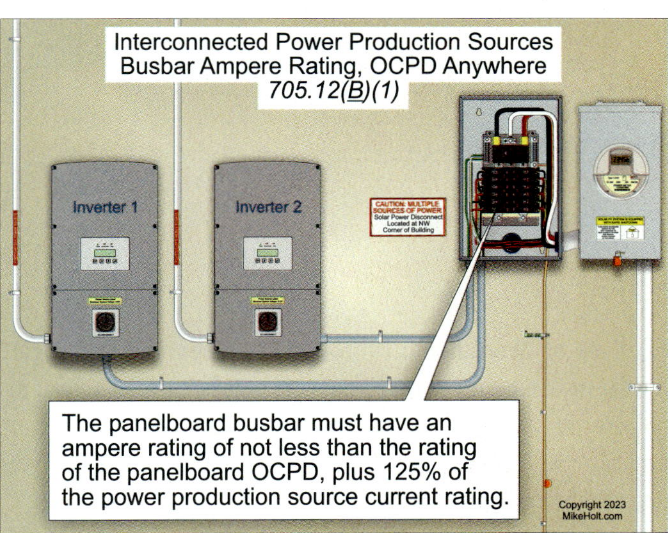

▶Figure 705–32

▶ **Panelboard Busbar Ampere Rating Example**

Question: *What is the minimum busbar ampere rating for a panelboard protected by a 150A overcurrent protective device if it is supplied by two interactive inverters each having an output current rating of 20A?* ▶**Figure 705–33**

(a) 200A   (b) 250A   (c) 260A   (d) 300A

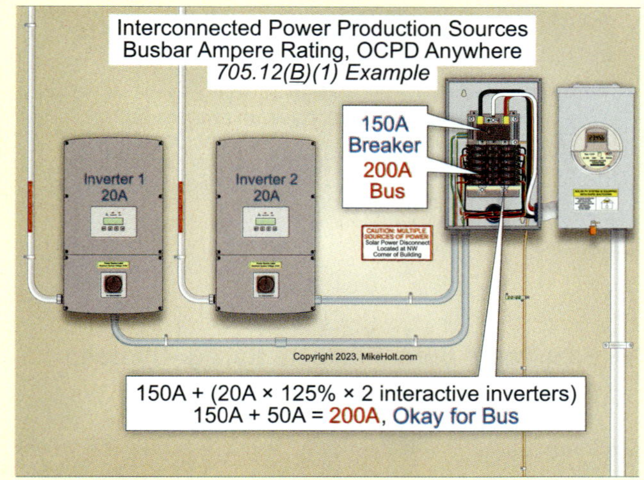

▶Figure 705–33

Solution:

Minimum Busbar Ampere Rating = >150A + (20A × 125% × 2 interactive inverters)

Minimum Busbar Ampere Rating = >150A + 50A

Minimum Busbar Ampere Rating = >200A

Answer: *(a) 200A*

(2) Overcurrent Protection Device, Opposite End of Feeder. Where the power production source terminates in a circuit breaker at not the opposite end of the feeder termination in a panelboard, the panelboard busbar must have an ampere rating of not less than 120 percent of the sum of the panelboard overcurrent protective device, plus 125 percent of the power production source current rating in accordance with 705.28. ▶**Figure 705–34**

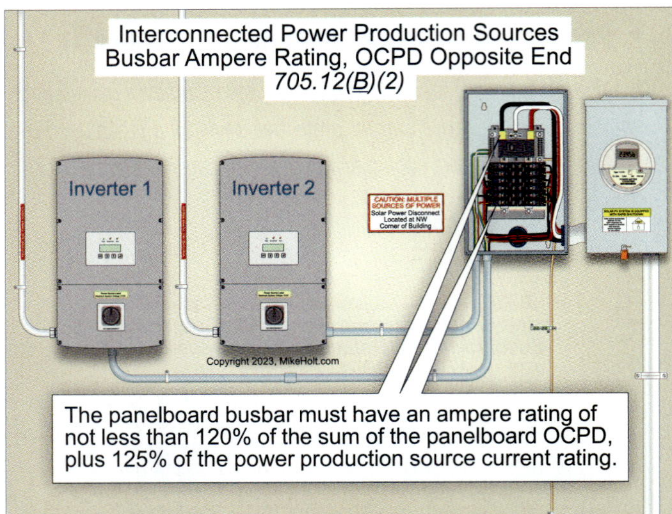

The panelboard busbar must have an ampere rating of not less than 120% of the sum of the panelboard OCPD, plus 125% of the power production source current rating.

▶Figure 705–34

▶ Panelboard Busbar Ampere Rating—Opposite Feeder Termination Example

Question: Can a 200A rated panelboard protected by a 175A overcurrent protective device be supplied by two interactive inverters where each has an output current rating of 24A and are opposite the feeder termination? ▶**Figure 705–35**

(a) Yes   (b) No

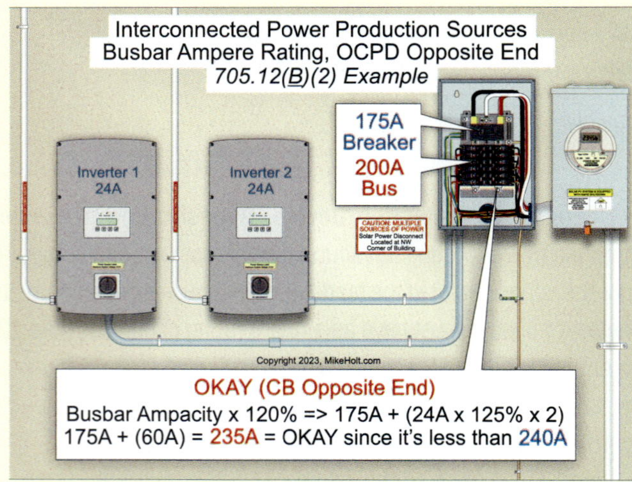

▶Figure 705–35

Solution:

The panelboard busbar ampacity must have an ampacity of not less than 120 percent of the panelboard overcurrent protective device rating, plus 125 percent of the power source(s) current rating in accordance with 705.28.

Panelboard Busbar × 120% => 175A + (24A × 125% ×
 2 interactive inverters)
200A × 120% = >175A + 60A
240A = >235A

Answer: *(a) Yes*

Where the power production source terminates in a circuit breaker at the opposite end of the feeder termination in a panelboard, a warning label with sufficient durability to withstand the environment involved [110.21(B)] must be applied to the distribution equipment next to the power production source backfed breaker and read: ▶**Figure 705–36**

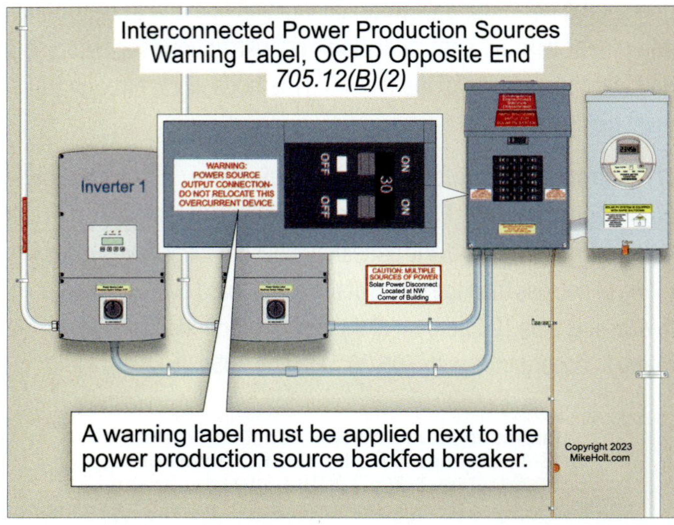

▶Figure 705–36

WARNING—POWER SOURCE OUTPUT DO NOT RELOCATE THIS OVERCURRENT DEVICE

(3) Sum of Overcurrent Protection Devices. The panelboard busbar must have an ampere rating of not less than the sum of the ampere ratings of all overcurrent protective devices in the panelboard, exclusive of the feeder overcurrent protective device protecting the panelboard. ▶**Figure 705–37**

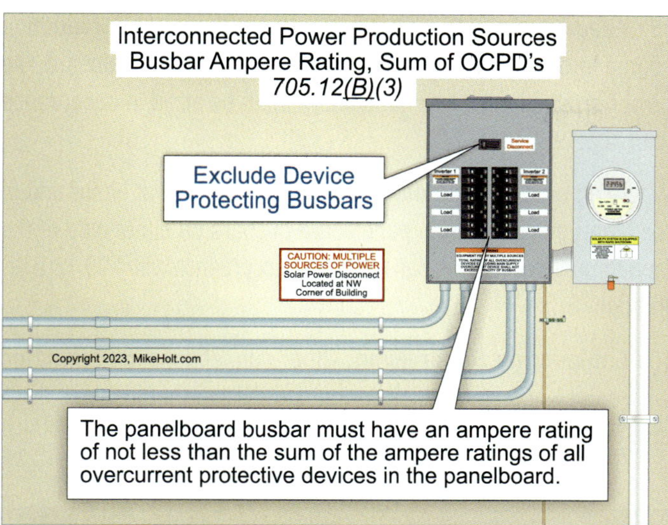

▶Figure 705–37

▶ Panelboard Busbar Ampere Rating—Sum of Breakers Not to Exceed Busbar Ampere Rating Example 1

Question: *What is the minimum busbar ampere rating for a panelboard containing two 30A, two-pole circuit breakers and six 20A, two-pole circuit breakers?* ▶**Figure 705–38**

(a) 12A   (b) 140A   (c) 180A   (d) 210A

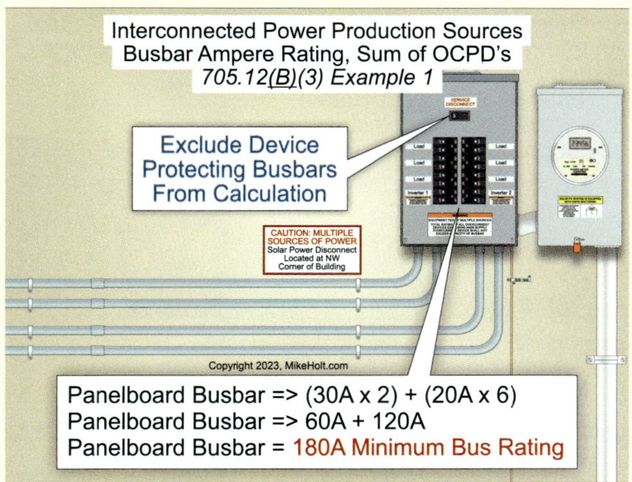

▶Figure 705–38

Solution:

The panelboard busbar ampacity must have an ampere rating of not less than the sum of the ampere ratings of all the overcurrent protective devices, exclusive of the overcurrent protective device protecting the panelboard busbar.

Panelboard Busbar = >(30A × 2) + (20A × 6)
Panelboard Busbar = >60A + 120A
Panelboard Busbar = 180A

Answer: *(c) 180A*

▶ Panelboard Busbar Ampere Rating—Sum of Breakers Not to Exceed Busbar Ampere Rating Example 2

Question: *What is the minimum busbar ampere rating for a panelboard containing six 30A, two-pole circuit breakers and one 20A, one-pole circuit breaker?* ▶**Figure 705–39**

(a) 125A   (b) 150A   (c) 175A   (d) 200A

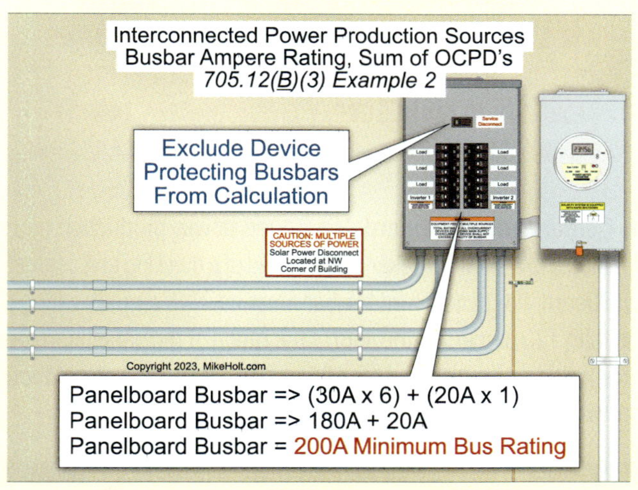

▶Figure 705–39

Solution:

The panelboard busbar ampere rating must be equal to or greater than the sum of the ampere ratings of all the overcurrent protective devices on the panelboard busbar.

Panelboard Busbar = >(30A × 6) + (20A × 1)
Panelboard Busbar = >180A + 20A
Panelboard Busbar = 200A

Answer: *(d) 200A*

Where the panelboard busbar is sized to the sum of the ampere ratings of all overcurrent protective devices in the panelboard, a warning label with sufficient durability to withstand the environment involved [110.21(B)] must be applied to the distribution equipment and read: ▶**Figure 705–40**

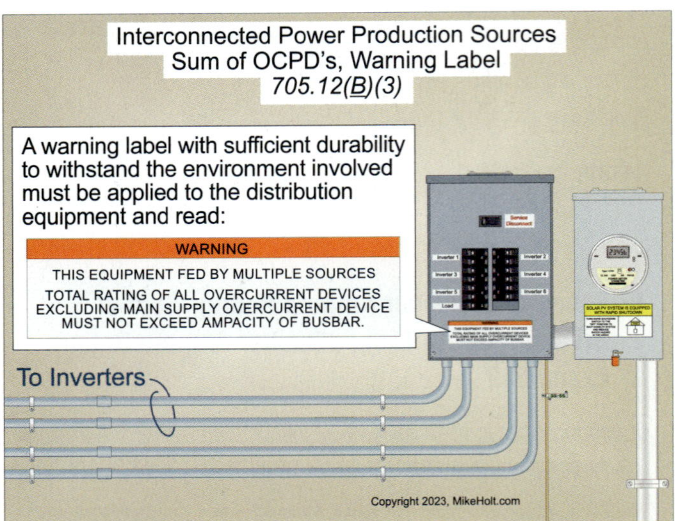

▶Figure 705–40

WARNING—EQUIPMENT FED BY MULTIPLE SOURCES. TOTAL RATING OF ALL OVERCURRENT DEVICES EXCLUDING MAIN SUPPLY OVERCURRENT DEVICE MUST NOT EXCEED AMPACITY OF BUSBAR.

(4) Center-Fed Panelboard. Where the power production source terminates to a circuit breaker at either end of a dwelling unit center-fed panelboard, the panelboard busbar must have an ampere rating not less than 120 percent of the sum of the rating of the panelboard overcurrent protective device, plus 125 percent of the power production source current. ▶Figure 705–41

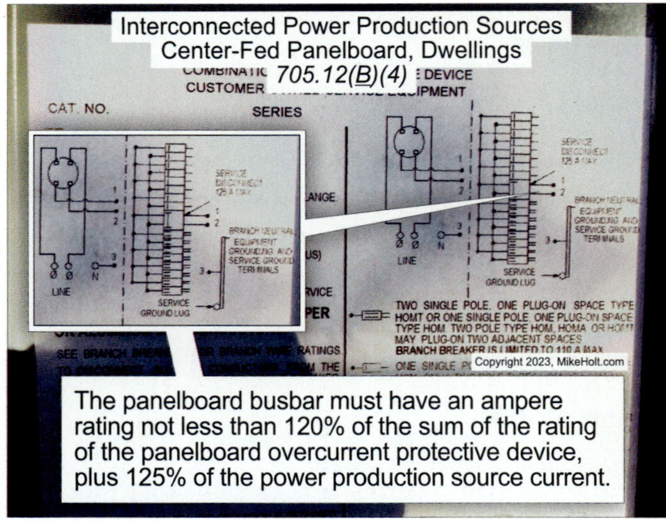

▶Figure 705–41

(5) Feed-Through Connections. Where the power production source terminates to feed-through connections in a panelboard, the power production source conductors must be sized in accordance with 705.12(A).

Where an overcurrent protective device is installed at either end of feed-through conductors, panelboard busbars on either side of the feed-through conductors can be sized in accordance with 705.12(B)(1) through (3).

(6) Engineering Supervision. Other connections are permitted where designed under engineering supervision that includes available fault-current and busbar load calculations.

705.13 Energy Management Systems

An energy management system [750.30] is permitted to limit current on the busbars and conductors that are supplied by power production sources (PV, ESS, generator). ▶Figure 705–42

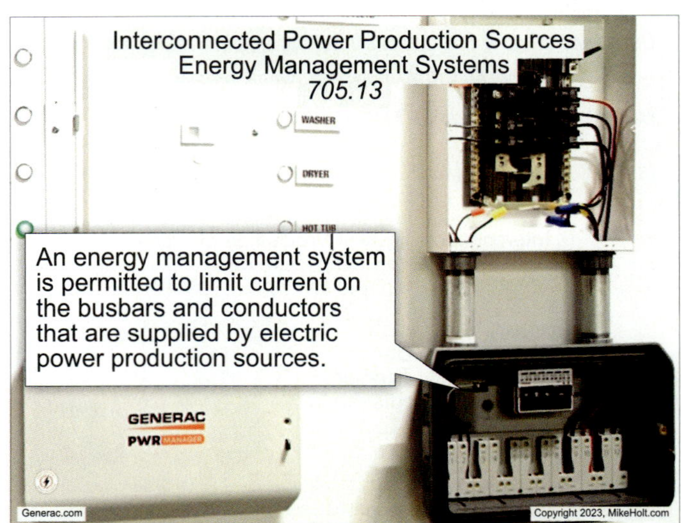

▶Figure 705–42

According to Article 100, an "Energy Management System" consisting of monitor(s), communications equipment, controller(s), timer(s), or other device(s) that monitors and/or controls an electrical load or a power production or storage source. ▶Figure 705–43 and ▶Figure 705–44

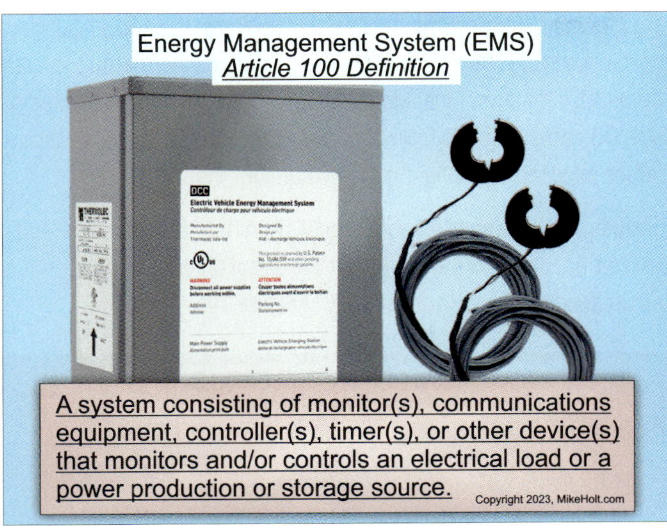

▶Figure 705–43

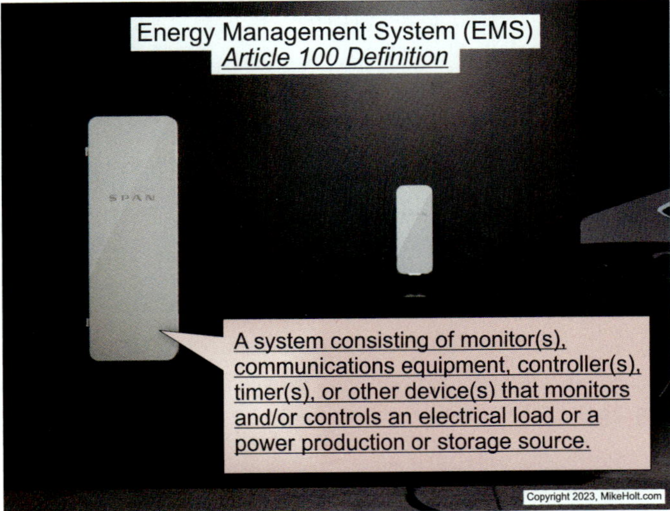

▶Figure 705–44

705.20 Power Production Source Disconnect

A disconnecting means must be provided to disconnect the power production source output conductors (PV, ESS, generator) and comply with the following: ▶Figure 705–45

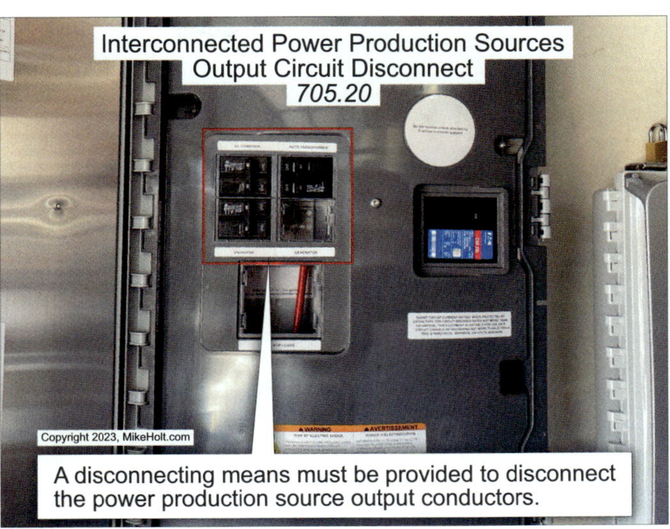

▶Figure 705–45

(1) The disconnect must be one of the following types:

    a. A manually operable switch or circuit breaker

    b. A load-break-rated pull-out switch

    c. A remote-controlled switch or circuit breaker capable of being operated manually and opened automatically when control power is interrupted

    d. A device listed for the intended application

(2) Simultaneously open all ungrounded conductors of the circuit.

(3) Be readily accessible.

(4) Be externally operable.

(5) Indicate if it is in the open (off) or closed (on) position.

(6) Have ratings sufficient for the circuit current, available fault current, and voltage at the terminals.

(7) Where line and load terminals are capable of being energized in the open position, the disconnect must be marked. ▶Figure 705–46

**WARNING: ELECTRIC SHOCK HAZARD
TERMINALS ON THE LINE AND LOAD SIDES MAY
BE ENERGIZED IN THE OPEN POSITION.**

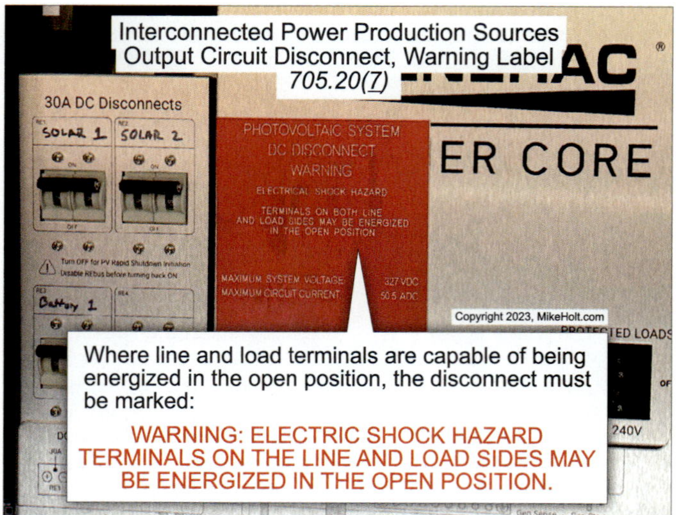

▶Figure 705–46

Note: With interconnected power sources, some switches and fuses are capable of being energized from both directions.

705.25 Wiring Methods

Power source output conductors must comply with 705.25(A) through (C).

(A) General. In addition to Chapter 3 raceways and cables, wiring methods and fittings listed for use with power production equipment are permitted. ▶Figure 705–47

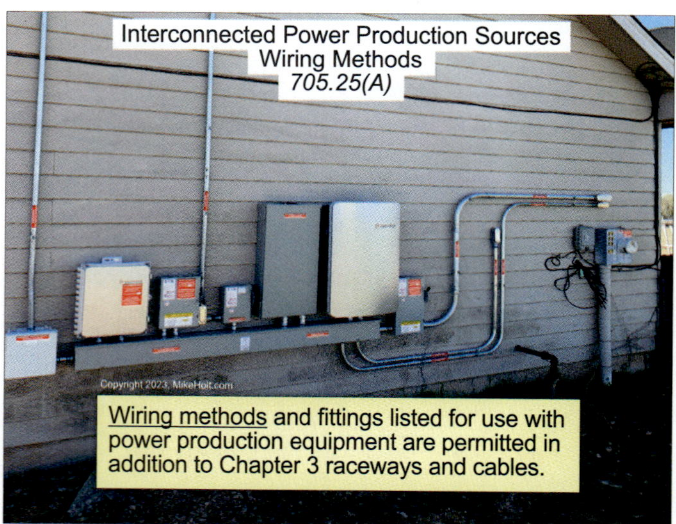

▶Figure 705–47

(B) Flexible Cords and Cables. Flexible cords used to connect moving parts of power production equipment, or where used for ready removal for maintenance and repair, must be listed and identified as Type DG cable, suitable for extra-hard usage, and be water resistant. Cables exposed to sunlight must be sunlight resistant.

Flexible, finely-stranded cables must terminate on terminals, lugs, devices, or connectors identified for the use of finely stranded conductors in accordance with 110.14(A). ▶Figure 705–48

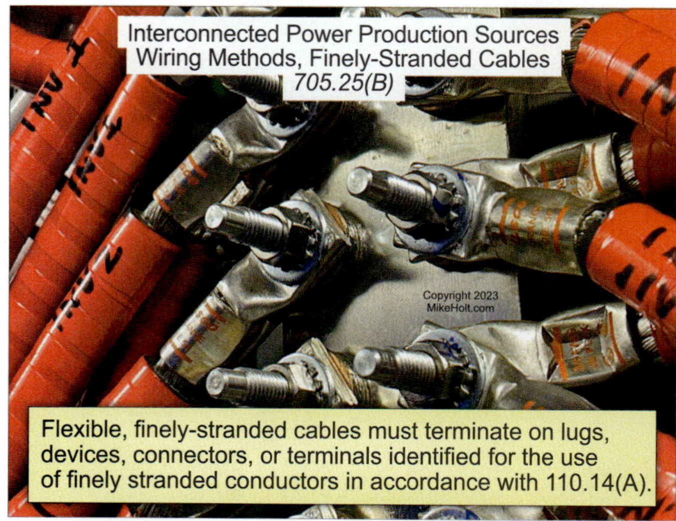

▶Figure 705–48

(C) Multiconductor Cable Assemblies. Multiconductor cable assemblies used in accordance with their listings are permitted. ▶Figure 705–49

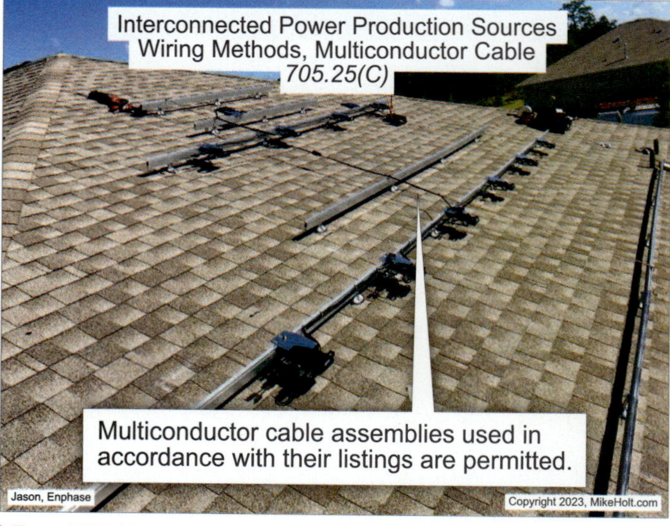

▶Figure 705–49

Note: An ac module harness is one example of a multiconductor cable assembly.

705.28 Output Current and Circuit Sizing

(A) Power Source Output Current.

(1) Equipment Nameplate. The power source output current of power production equipment (PV, ESS, generator) is equal to the sum of the output current of the power production equipment nameplate current rating. ▶Figure 705–50

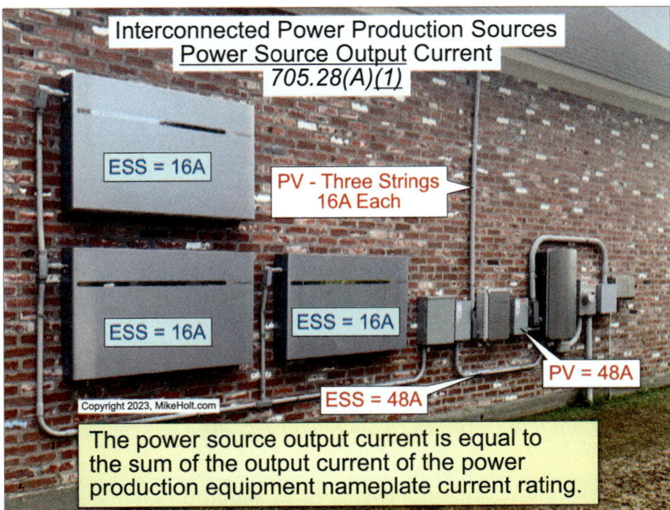

▶Figure 705–50

(2) Energy Management System. The power source output current of all interconnected power production equipment is equal to the current setting of the energy management system [750.30]. ▶Figure 705–51

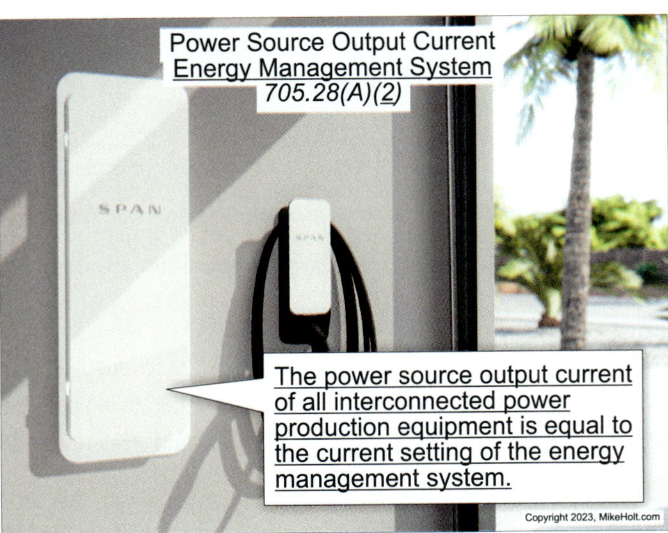

▶Figure 705–51

(B) Power Source Conductor Ampacity. Power production source

(PV, ESS, generator) conductors must have an ampacity as follows:
▶Figure 705–52

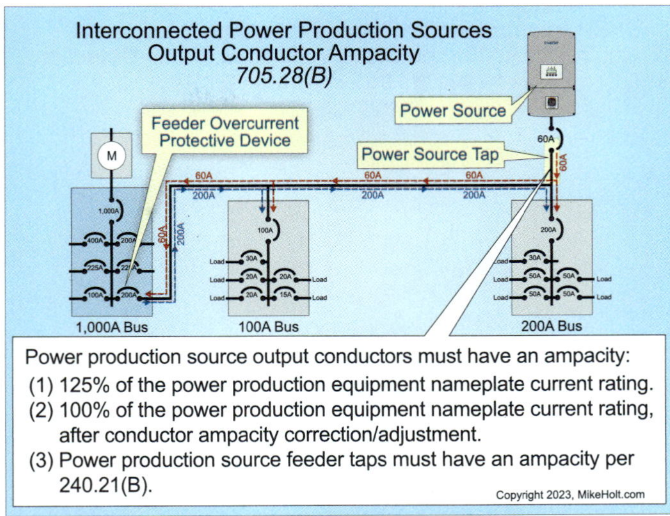

Power production source output conductors must have an ampacity:
(1) 125% of the power production equipment nameplate current rating.
(2) 100% of the power production equipment nameplate current rating, after conductor ampacity correction/adjustment.
(3) Power production source feeder taps must have an ampacity per 240.21(B).
Copyright 2023, MikeHolt.com

▶Figure 705–52

(1) One hundred twenty-five percent of the power production equipment nameplate current rating [705.28(A)]

Ex 1: If the assembly, including the overcurrent protective devices protecting the circuit, is listed for operation at 100 percent, the conductors can be sized at not less than the calculated current of 705.28(A).

Ex 2: Where a circuit is connected at both its supply and load ends to separately installed pressure connections as covered in 110.14(C)(2), the ampacity of the conductors can be sized at not less than the calculated current of 705.28(A). No portion of the circuit can extend into an enclosure.

(2) One hundred percent of the power production equipment nameplate current rating, after conductor ampacity correction and/or adjustment [310.15 and 705.28(A)]

(3) Power production source feeder taps [705.12(A)(3)] must have an ampacity in accordance with 240.21(B)

(C) Neutral Conductors. Neutral conductors must be sized as follows:

(1) Line-to-Neutral Power Sources. The neutral conductor to a single-phase line-to-neutral power production source must have an ampacity of not less than the current calculated in 705.28(A).

(2) Instrumentation, Voltage or Phase Detection. A neutral conductor used solely for instrumentation, voltage detection, or phase detection can be sized in accordance with Table 250.102(C)(1). ▶Figure 705–53

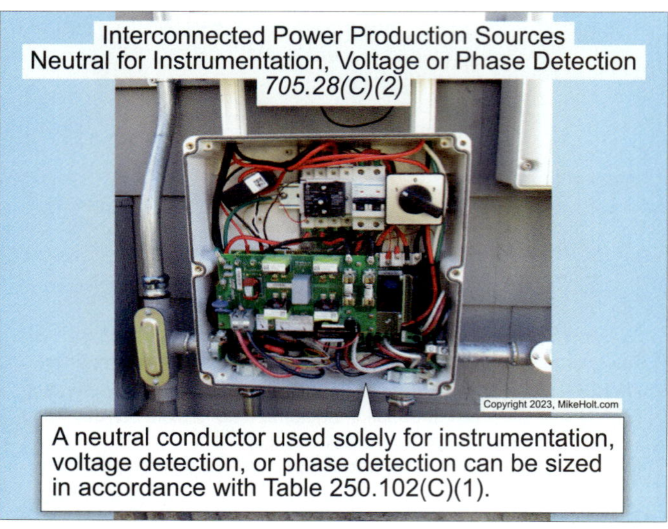

A neutral conductor used solely for instrumentation, voltage detection, or phase detection can be sized in accordance with Table 250.102(C)(1).

▶Figure 705–53

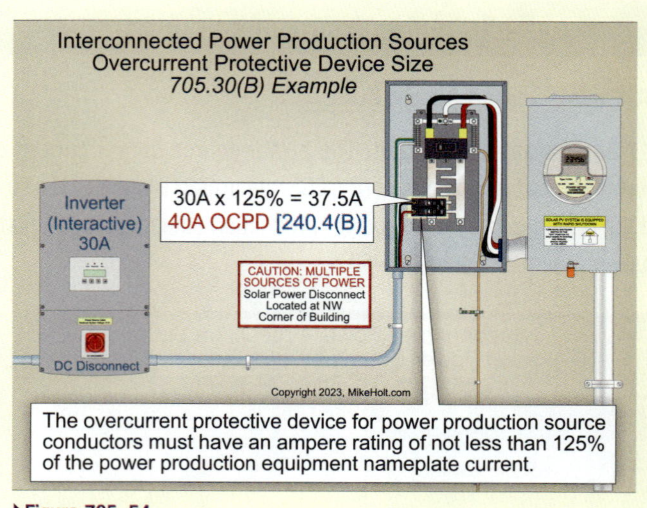

The overcurrent protective device for power production source conductors must have an ampere rating of not less than 125% of the power production equipment nameplate current.

▶Figure 705–54

705.30 Overcurrent Protection

(A) Circuit and Equipment. Power source output conductors and equipment must have overcurrent protection. Circuits connected to more than one electrical source must have overcurrent protection from all sources.

(B) Overcurrent Device Ratings. The overcurrent protective device for power production source (PV, ESS, or generator) conductors must have an ampere rating of not less than 125 percent of the power production equipment nameplate current [705.28(A)].

▶ **Example**

Question: What size overcurrent protective device is required for the power source output circuit conductors installed to an inverter with a nameplate ampere rating of 30A? ▶**Figure 705–54**

(a) 20A   (b) 30A   (c) 40A   (d) 50A

Solution:

OCPD = 30A × 125% [705.30(B)]
OCPD = 37.5A
OCPD = 40A [240.4(B) and 240.6]

Answer: (c) 40A

Ex: Where the assembly, together with its overcurrent protective device(s) is listed for continuous operation at 100 percent of its rating, the overcurrent protective device is permitted to be sized at 100 percent of the current calculated in 705.28(A). ▶**Figure 705–55**

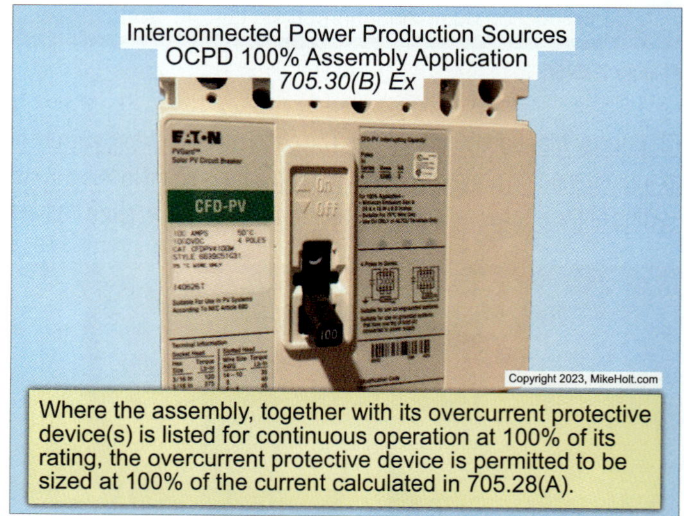

Where the assembly, together with its overcurrent protective device(s) is listed for continuous operation at 100% of its rating, the overcurrent protective device is permitted to be sized at 100% of the current calculated in 705.28(A).

▶Figure 705–55

(C) Marking. Equipment containing overcurrent devices supplied from multiple power production sources must be marked to indicate the presence of all sources of power. ▶**Figure 705–56** and ▶**Figure 705–57**

(D) Suitable for Backfeed. Circuit breakers not marked "line" and "load" are suitable for backfeed or reverse current. ▶**Figure 705–58**

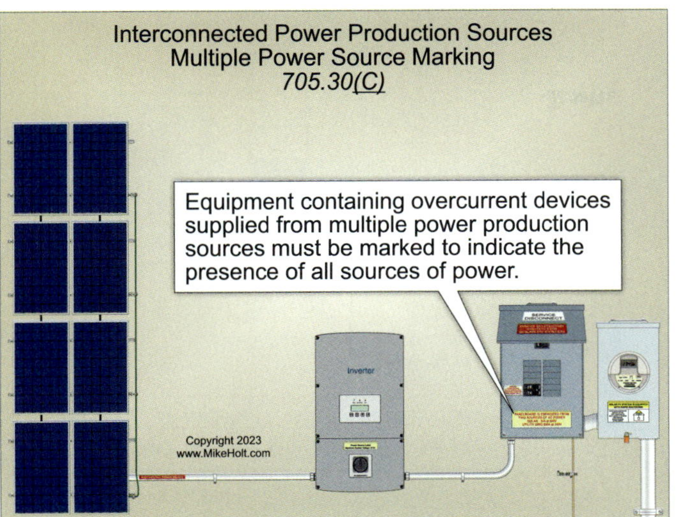

▶Figure 705–56

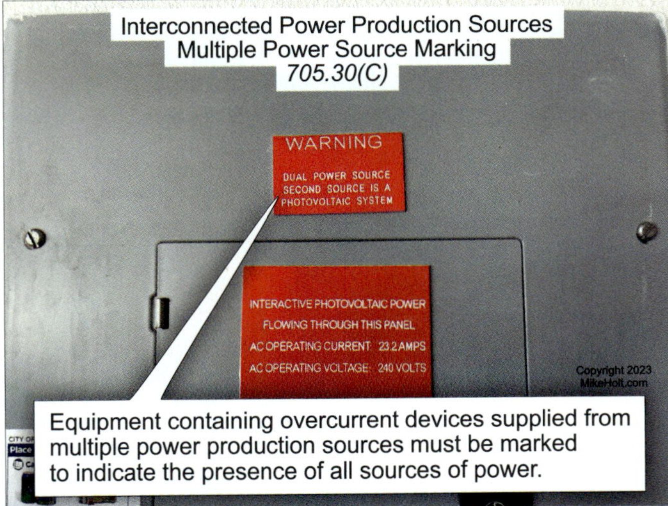

▶Figure 705–57

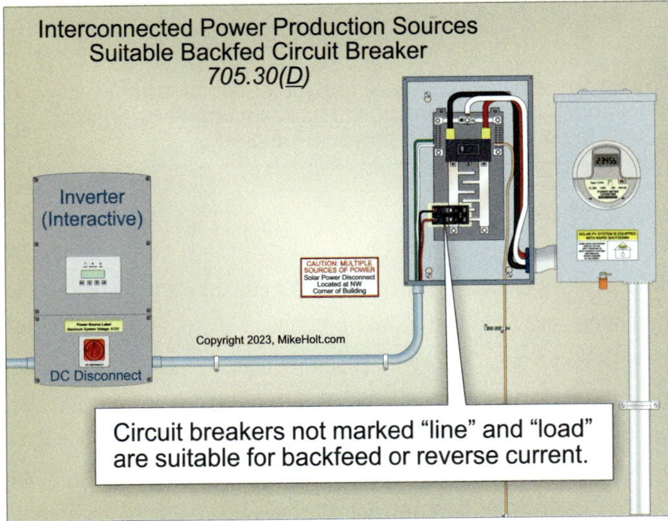

▶Figure 705–58

Circuit breakers marked "line" and "load" are not suitable for back-feed or reverse current. ▶Figure 705–59

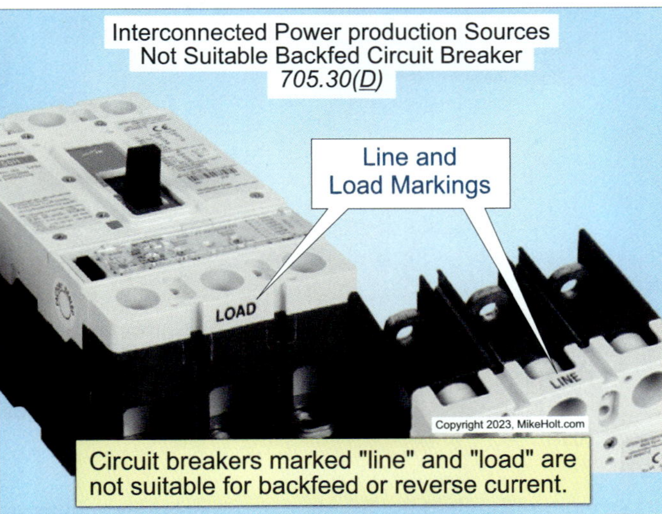

▶Figure 705–59

(E) Fastening. Backfed circuit breakers used for interconnected power production sources (PV, ESS, generator) that are listed as interactive are not required to be secured in place in the panelboard by an additional fastener as required by 408.36(D). ▶Figure 705–60

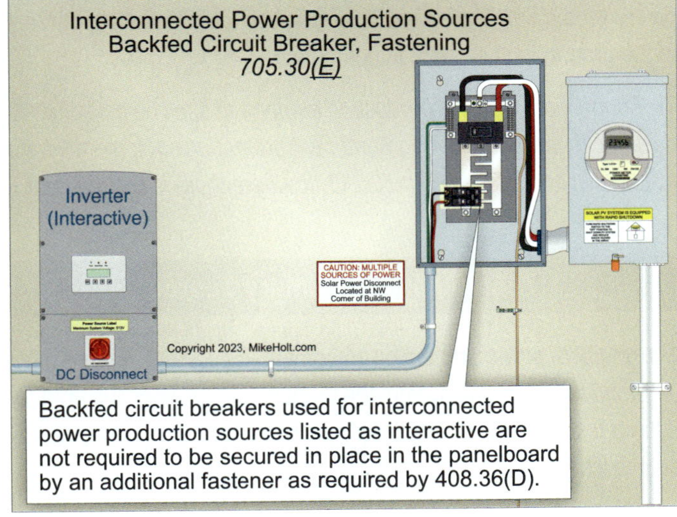

▶Figure 705–60

(F) Transformers.

(1) Overcurrent Protection. The side of a transformer with a source of power on each side that has the highest available fault current is considered the primary side. ▶Figure 705–61

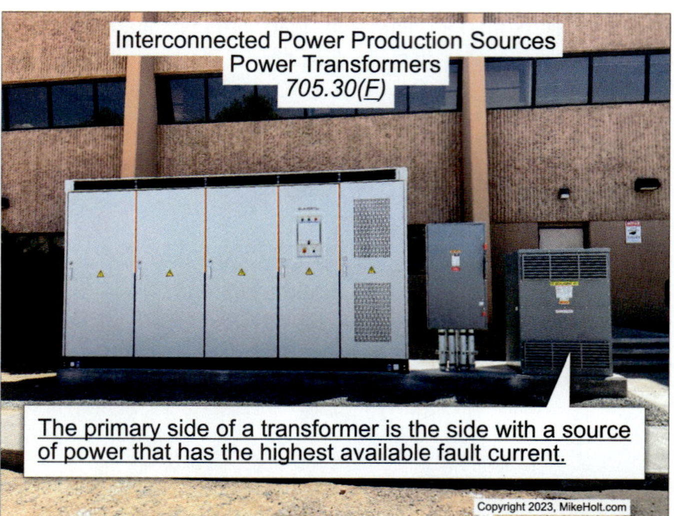

▶Figure 705–61

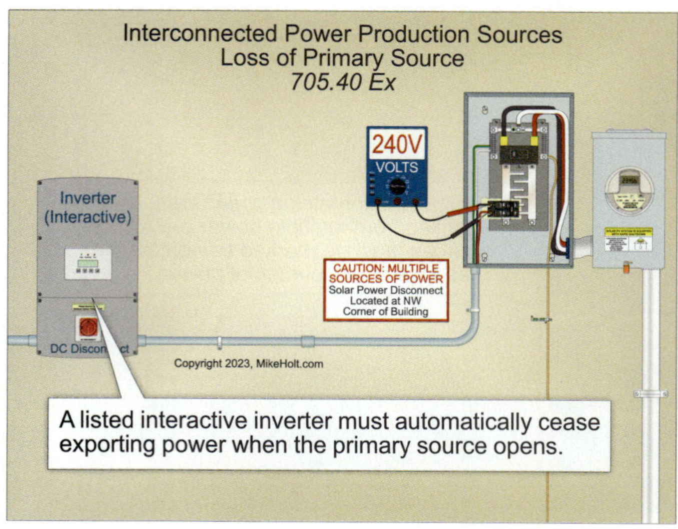

▶Figure 705–62

(2) Secondary Conductors. Transformer secondary conductors are to be sized in accordance with 240.21(C).

705.32 Ground-Fault Protection

Where ground-fault protection of equipment is installed in ac circuits as required else where in this *Code*, the output of interconnected power production equipment must be connected to the supply side of the ground-fault protection equipment.

Ex: Connection of power production equipment shall be permitted to be made to the load side of ground-fault protection equipment where installed in accordance with 705.11 or where there is ground-fault.

705.40 Loss of Primary Source

The output of power production equipment (PV, ESS, generator) must automatically disconnect from the primary source when the primary source loses a phase conductor and reconnect when the primary source is restored.

Ex: A listed interactive inverter must automatically cease exporting power when one or more of the phases of the primary source opens and is not required to automatically disconnect all phase conductors from the primary source. ▶Figure 705–62

▶ If the primary source phase conductor opens, an interactive (grid tied) inverter stops exporting power and remains de-energized until the primary source power is restored. ▶Figure 705–63

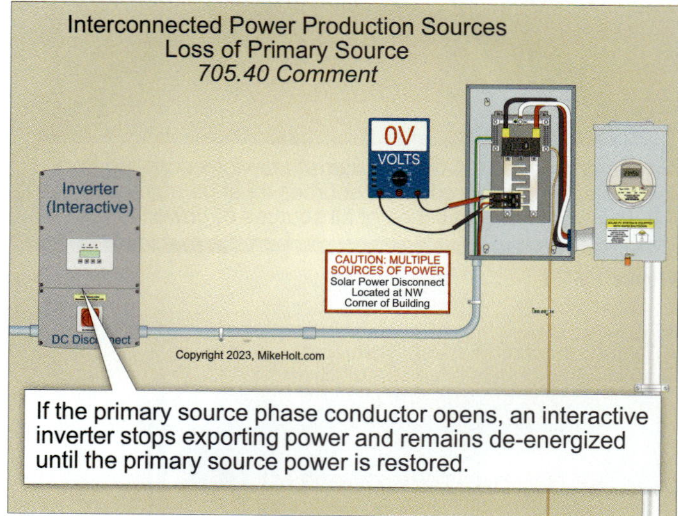

▶Figure 705–63

Note 1: Risks to electric utility personnel and equipment could occur if an interactive (grid tied) power production source is set to operate in the island mode. Special detection methods are required to determine if an electric utility supply system outage has occurred and whether there should be automatic disconnection. When the electric utility supply system is restored, special detection methods are typically required to limit exposure of power production sources to out-of-phase reconnection.

Multimode power production equipment is permitted to operate in island mode to supply loads that have been disconnected from the electric utility. ▶Figure 705–64

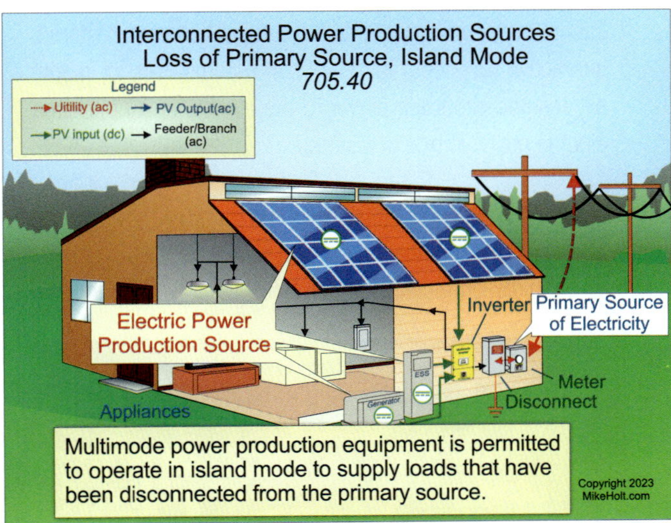

▶Figure 705–64

According to Article 100, "Island Mode" is the operating mode for power production equipment or a microgrid that is disconnected from an electric utility. ▶Figure 705–65

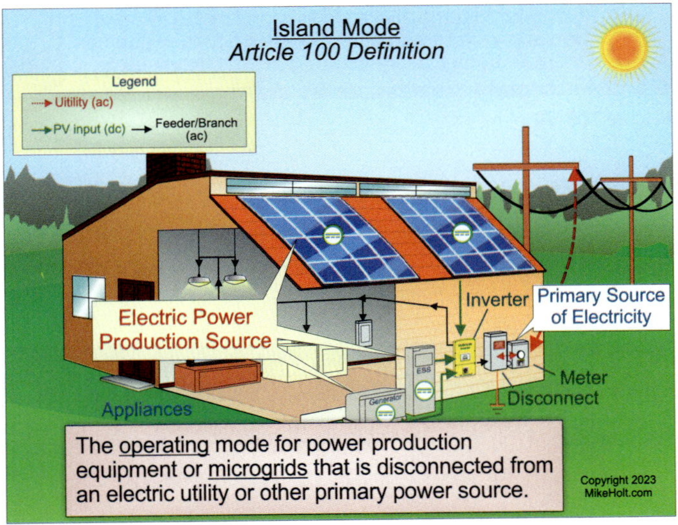

▶Figure 705–65

According to Article 100, "Multimode Inverter's" are listed to operate in both interactive (grid tied) and island mode. ▶Figure 705–66

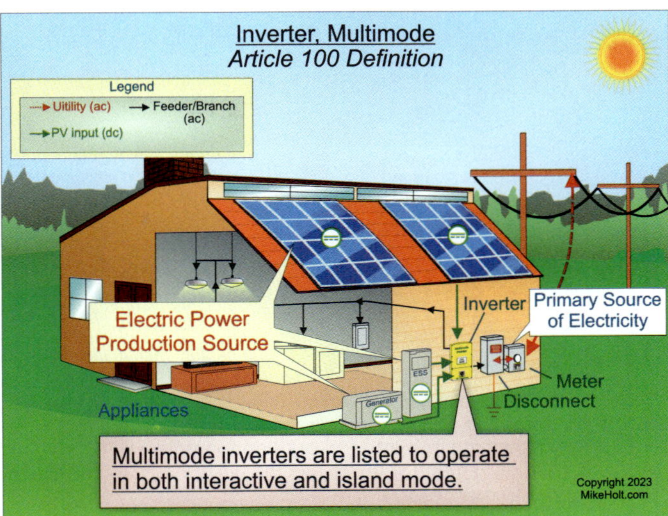

▶Figure 705–66

705.45 Unbalanced Interconnections

(A) Single-Phase. Single-phase inverters must be placed on the electrical system so that unbalanced system voltage at the electric utility service disconnect is not more than three percent.

(B) Three-Phase. Three-phase inverters must have all phases automatically de-energized upon loss of, or unbalanced voltage in one or more phases unless the inverter is designed so significant unbalanced voltages will not result.

Part II. Microgrid Systems

According to Article 100, a "Microgrid" is a collection of power production sources that are capable of operating in island (off-grid) or interactive (grid-tied) mode with the electric utility. Examples of microgrid power sources include photovoltaic systems, energy storage systems, generators, electric vehicles that are used as a source of supply. ▶Figure 100–67

705.50 Microgrid System Operation

Interactive Mode. Microgrid systems operating in interactive (grid tied) mode can supply loads with the electric utility and other power production sources (PV, ESS, generator). ▶Figure 705–68

According to Article 100, "Interactive Mode" is the operating mode for power production equipment or a microgrid that operates in parallel with and can deliver power to the electric utility. ▶Figure 705–69

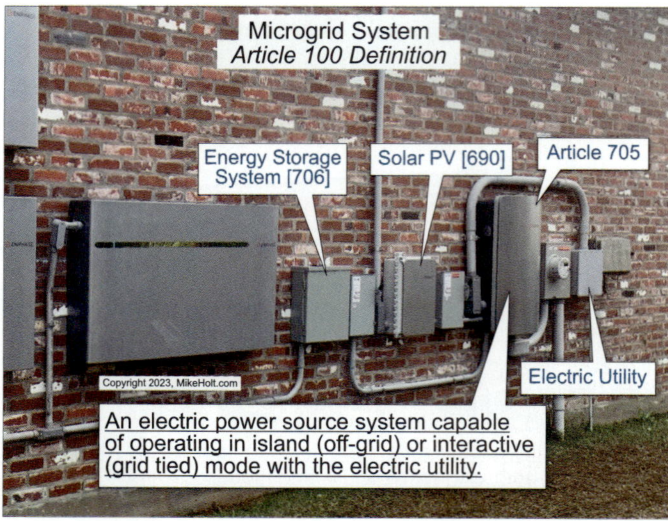

▶Figure 705–67

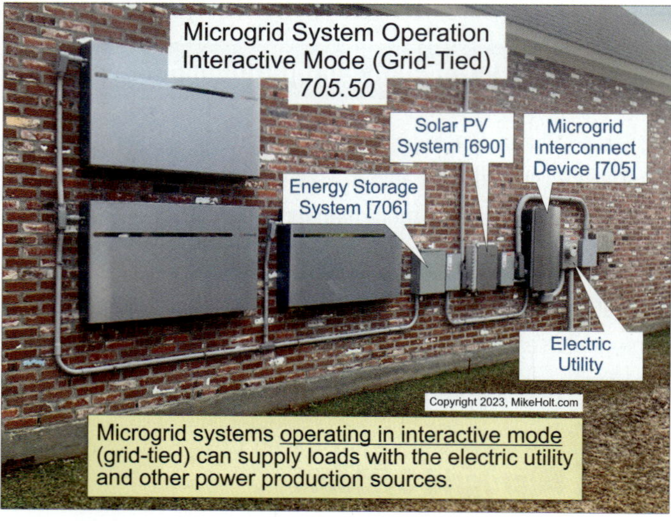

▶Figure 705–68

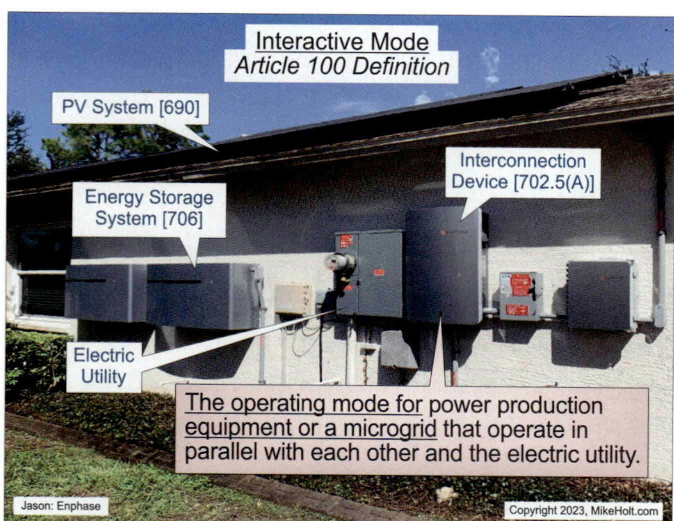

▶Figure 705–69

Author's Comment:

▸ A listed interactive (grid tied) inverter automatically stops exporting power upon loss of electric utility voltage and cannot be reconnected until the voltage has been restored. Interactive (grid tied) inverters can automatically or manually resume exporting power to the electric utility once the electric utility source is restored.

Island Mode. Microgrid systems operating in island (off-grid) mode can supply loads with other power production sources (PV, ESS, generator) that have been disconnected from the electric utility. ▶**Figure 705–70**

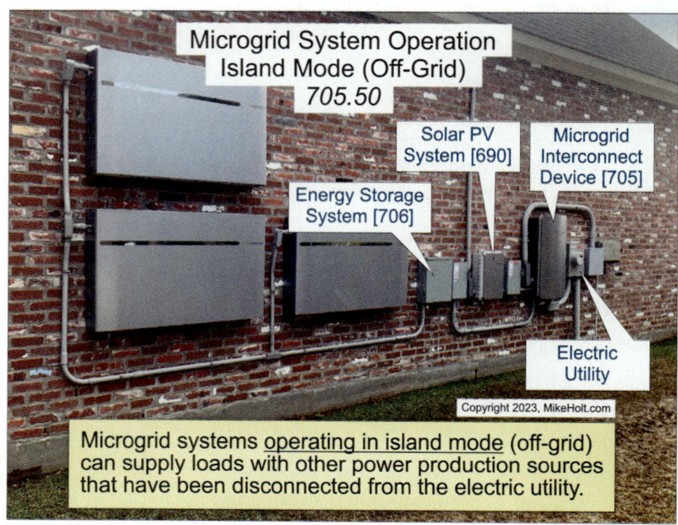

▶Figure 705–70

According to Article 100, "Island Mode" is the operating mode for power production equipment or a microgrid that is disconnected from an electric utility or other primary power source. ▶**Figure 705–71**

705.60 Connections to the Primary Source

Connections of the microgrid to the primary source must be in accordance with 705.11, 705.12, or 705.13. ▶**Figure 705–72**

705.70 Microgrid Interconnect Devices (MID)

According to Article 100, a "Microgrid Interconnect Device (MID)" is a device that enables a microgrid system to disconnect from and reconnect to an interconnected primary power source. ▶**Figure 705–73**

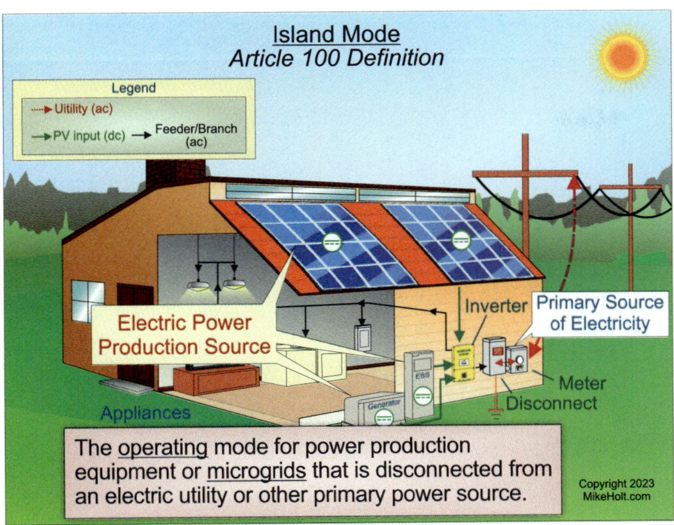

▶Figure 705–71

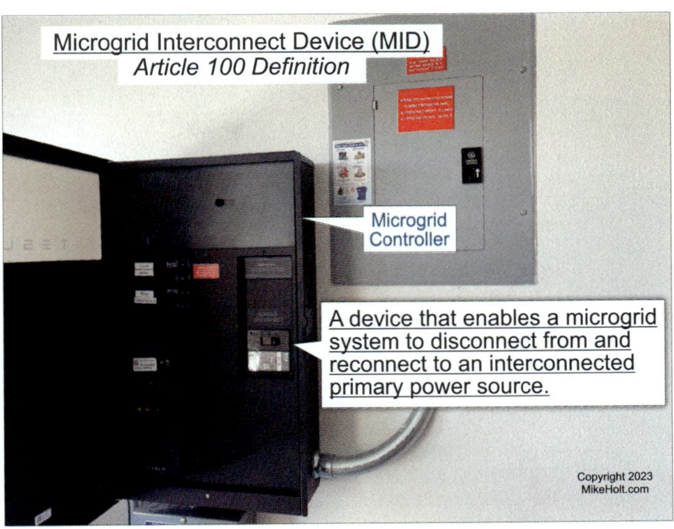

▶Figure 705–73

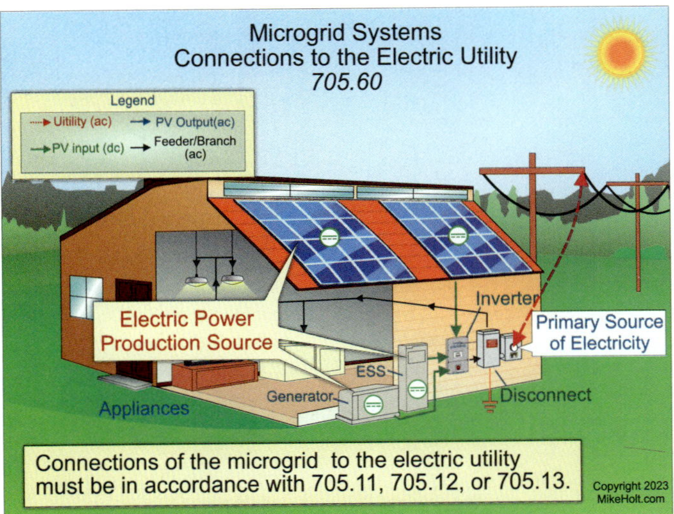

▶Figure 705–72

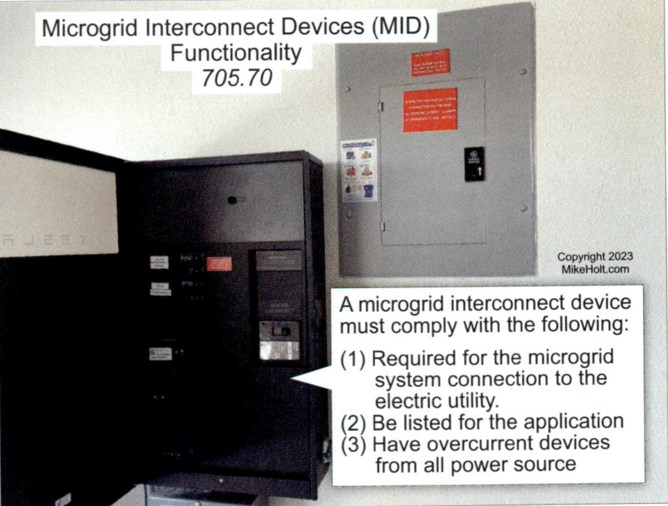

▶Figure 705–74

A microgrid interconnect device must comply with the following:

▶Figure 705–74

(1) Required for the connection between a microgrid system and the electric utility

(2) Be listed for the application

(3) Have overcurrent devices for all power source

Note: MID functionality is often incorporated in an interactive (grid tied) or multimode inverter, energy storage system, or similar device identified for interactive (grid tied) operation.

705.76 Microgrid Control System (MCS)

Microgrid control systems must comply with the following:

(1) Coordinate interaction between multiple power sources

(2) Be evaluated for the application and have a field label applied, or be listed, or be designed under engineering supervision

(3) Monitor and control microgrid power production

(4) Monitor and control transitions with the electric utility

Note: MID functionality is often incorporated in an interactive (grid tied) or multimode inverter, energy storage system, or similar device identified for interactive (grid tied) operation.

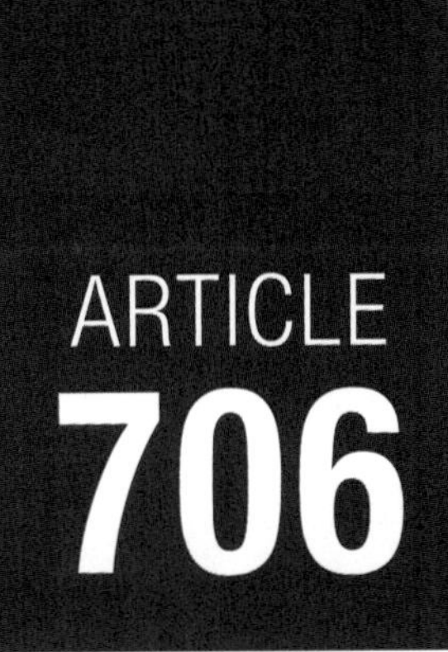

ARTICLE 706

ENERGY STORAGE SYSTEMS

Introduction to Article 706—Energy Storage Systems

It is important to understand what Article 706 does and does not apply to. The scope says it applies to all permanently installed energy storage systems "having a capacity greater than 1 kWh." They may be stand-alone (off-grid) or interactive (grid tied) with other power production sources. Although much of the original language used to create Article 706 came from deleted sections of Article 690 Solar Photovoltaic (PV) Systems, an energy storage system can store energy from any power source, there are no restrictions.

Energy storage systems can include batteries, capacitors, and kinetic energy devices such as flywheels and compressed air. Energy storage systems can include inverters or converters to change voltage levels or to make a change between an alternating-current or a direct-current system.

They may also include inverters and converters to change stored energy into electrical energy. An energy storage system might directly power loads such as in a stand-alone (off-grid) system, or it might provide another energy management function like buffering energy produced by an intermittent source such as a PV system.

Energy storage systems can be (and usually are) connected to other energy sources, such as the local electric utility distribution system. There can be more than one source of power connected to these systems, and their connection to other energy sources must comply with the requirements of Article 705 which provides the rules for installations of one or more power production source operating in parallel with the electric utility.

Part I. General

706.1 Scope

This article applies to energy storage systems that have a capacity greater than 1 kWh that can operate in stand-alone (off-grid) or interactive (grid tied) mode with other electric power production sources. ▶Figure 706–1

According to Article 100, an "Energy Storage Systems" (ESS) has one or more devices installed as a system capable of storing energy and providing electrical energy to the premises wiring system. ▶Figure 706–2

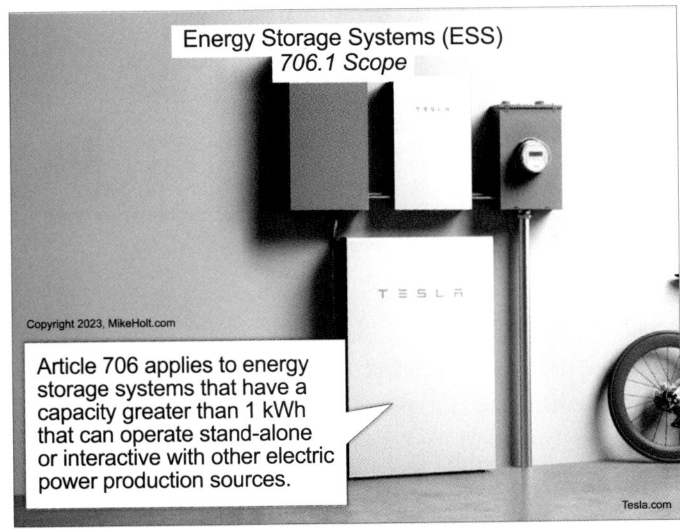

▶Figure 706–1

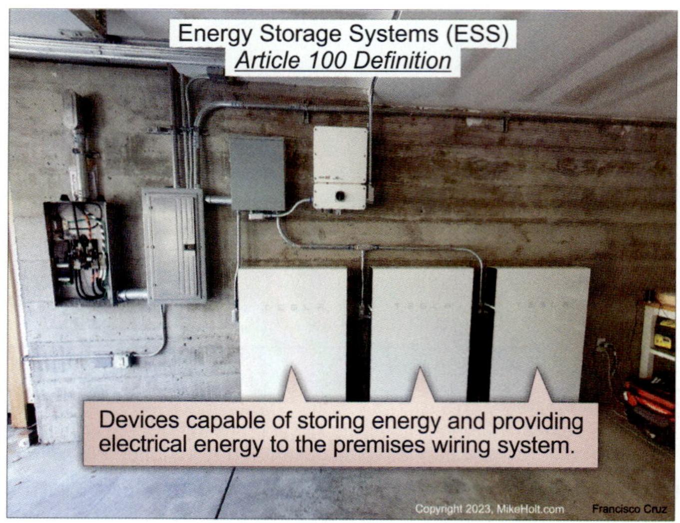

▶Figure 706–2

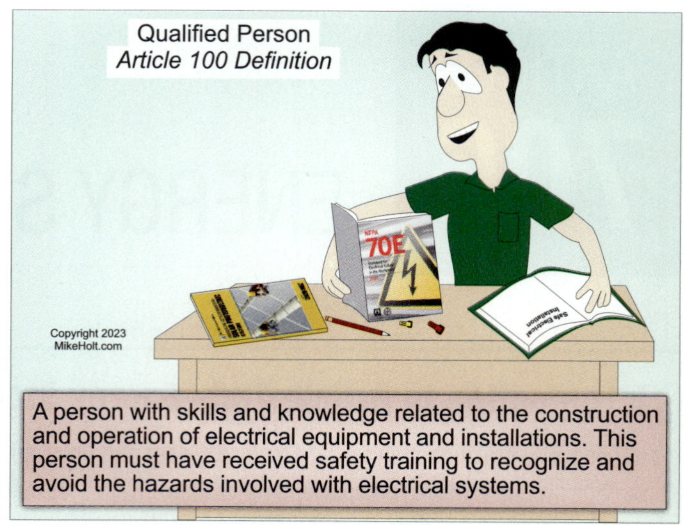

▶Figure 706–4

706.3 Qualified Personnel

The installation and maintenance of energy storage system must be performed by a qualified person. ▶Figure 706–3

706.4 System Nameplate Requirements

Energy storage systems must have the following marked on a nameplate. ▶Figure 706–5 and ▶Figure 706–6

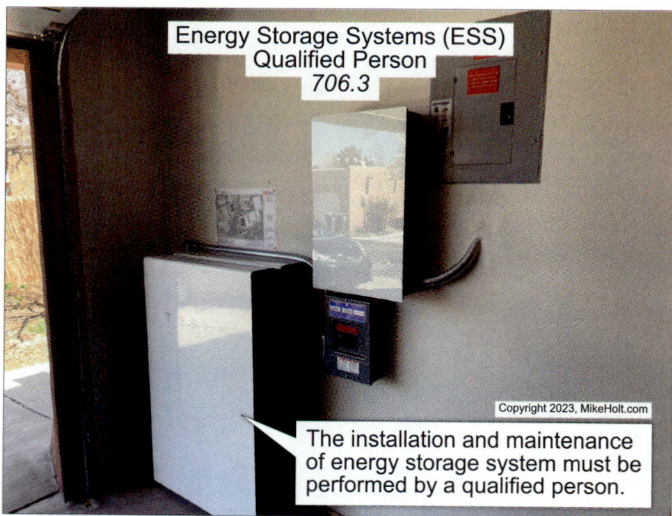

▶Figure 706–3

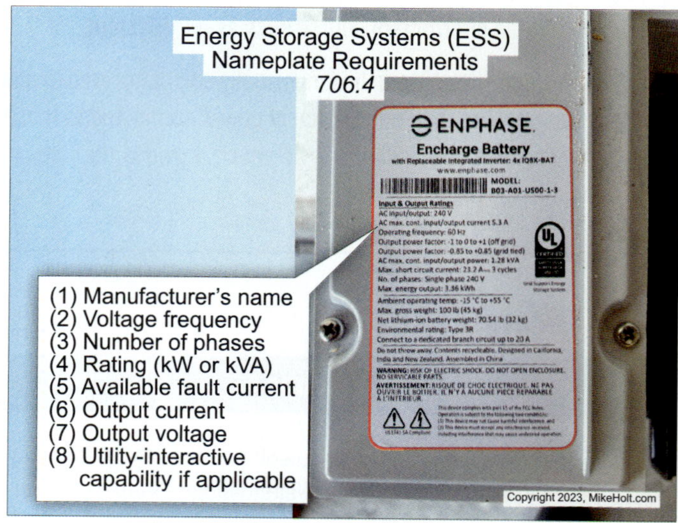

▶Figure 706–5

According to Article 100, a "Qualified Person" has the skills and knowledge related to the construction and operation of electrical equipment and installations. This person must have received safety training to recognize and avoid the hazards involved with electrical systems. ▶Figure 706–4

(1) Manufacturer's name

(2) Rated frequency

(3) Number of phases

(4) Rating (kW or kVA)

(5) Available fault current of ESS

(6) Input and output current

(7) Input and output voltage

(8) Utility-interactive capability if applicable

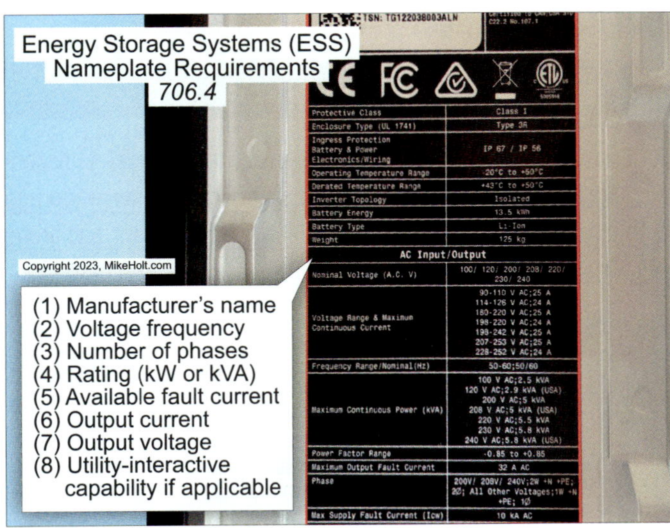

▶Figure 706–6

706.5 Listing

Energy storage systems must be listed. ▶Figure 706–7

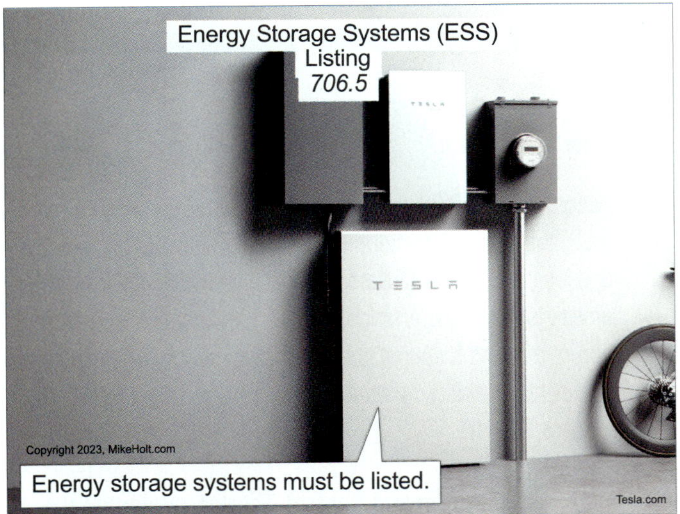

▶Figure 706–7

Author's Comment:

▸ Although the *Code* does not identify the specific standard used to list energy storage systems, updated building and fire codes are more specific and now increasingly require a UL 9540, *Standard for Energy Storage Systems and Equipment*, listing for these systems. Annex A of the *NEC* provides references to product safety standards that the Code-Making Panels believe are generally relevant to each article.

706.6 Multiple Systems

Multiple energy storage systems are permitted on the same premises.

Author's Comment:

▸ As with PV systems, energy storage systems may be composed of multiple pieces of equipment assembled into a single system, or each piece of equipment may be considered an energy storage system on its own. The best way to identify an energy storage system is to look for a nameplate and review the instructions, both of which are part of the equipment's listing.

706.7 Commissioning and Maintenance

(A) Commissioning. For other than one- and two-family dwellings, energy storage systems must be commissioned upon installation. ▶Figure 706–8

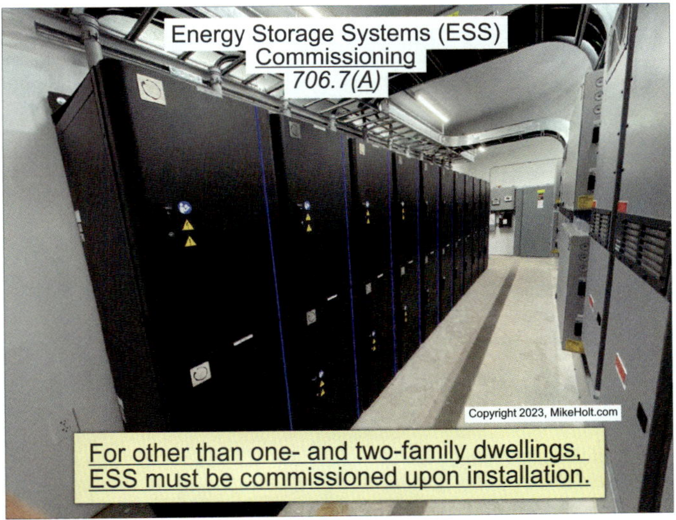

▶Figure 706–8

Note: For information related to the commissioning of ESS, see NFPA 855, *Standard for the Installation of Stationary Energy Storage Systems.*

According to Article 100, "Commissioning" is the process, procedures, and testing used to set up and verify the initial performance, operational controls, safety systems, and sequence of operation of electrical devices and equipment prior to them being placed into active service.

(B) Maintenance. For other than one- and two-family dwellings, energy storage systems must be maintained in proper and safe operating condition in accordance with manufacturer and industry standards. A written record of repairs and replacements must be kept. ▶Figure 706–9

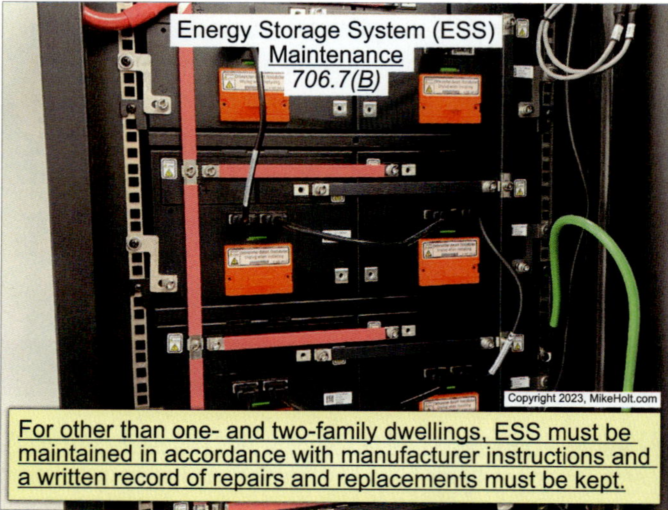

▶Figure 706–9

Note: For information related to general electrical equipment maintenance and developing an effective electrical preventive maintenance program, see NFPA 70B, *Recommended Practice for Electrical Equipment Maintenance*, or ANSI/NETA ATS-2017, *Standard for Acceptance Testing Specifications for Electrical Power Equipment and Systems*. ▶Figure 706–10

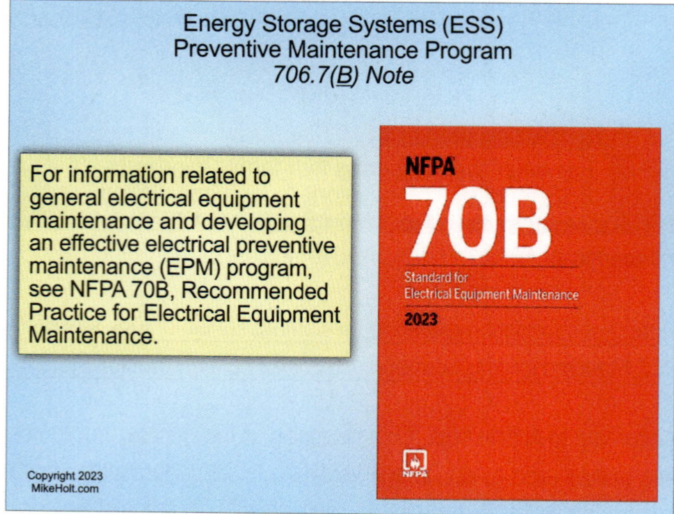

▶Figure 706–10

Part II. Disconnect

706.15 Disconnect

(A) Energy Storage System Disconnecting Means. A disconnecting means must be provided to disconnect the energy storage system from other sources of power, utilization equipment, and premises wiring. ▶Figure 706–11

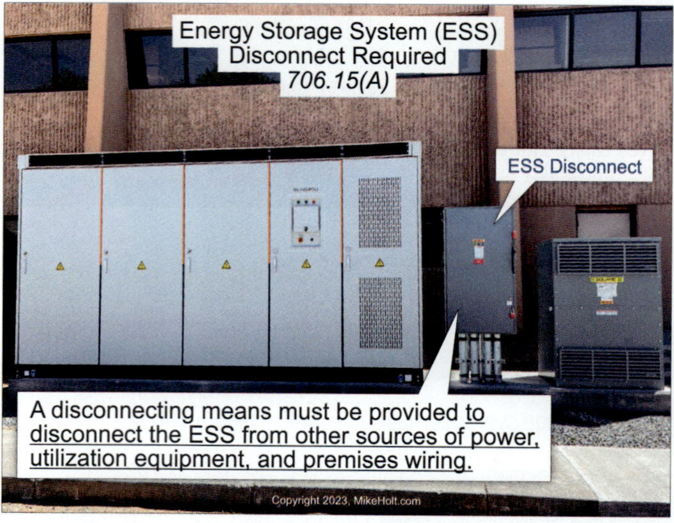

▶Figure 706–11

Author's Comment:

▸ According to 110.22, in other than one- or two-family dwelling units, the disconnect marking must include the identification and location of the circuit source that supplies the disconnect unless located and arranged so the identification and location of the circuit source is evident. The marking must be of sufficient durability to withstand the environment involved. ▶Figure 706–12

(B) Disconnect Location and Control. The energy storage system disconnect must be readily accessible and comply with one of the following: ▶Figure 706–13

(1) The disconnect is located within the energy storage system.

(2) The disconnect is located within sight and not more than 10 ft from the energy storage system.

(3) Where the disconnect is not located within sight of the energy storage system, the disconnect, or the enclosure providing access to the disconnect, must be capable of being locked in the open position in accordance with 110.25.

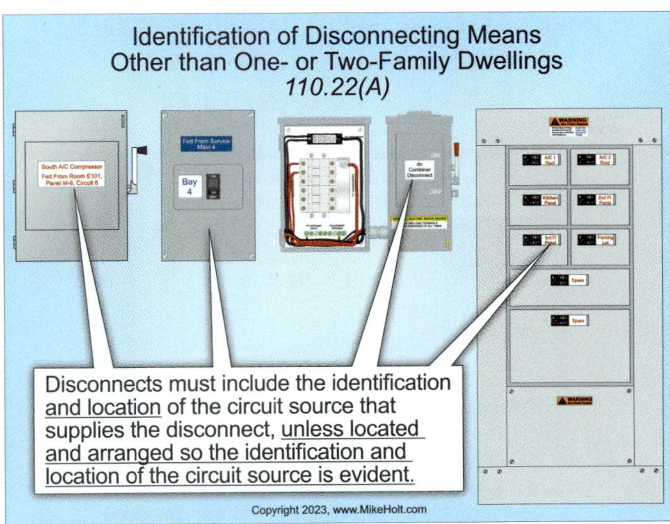

▶Figure 706–12

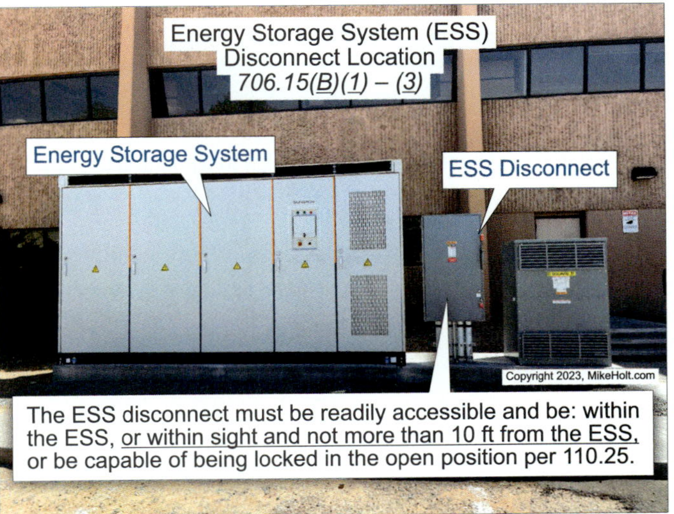

▶Figure 706–13

One- and Two-Family Dwellings. The energy storage system must include an emergency shutdown function to cease the export of power from the energy storage system to premises wiring. The initiation device for the energy storage system emergency shutdown function must be located at a readily accessible location outside the building. ▶Figure 706–14

The energy storage system emergency shutdown initiation device must plainly indicate whether if it is in the "off" or "on" position.

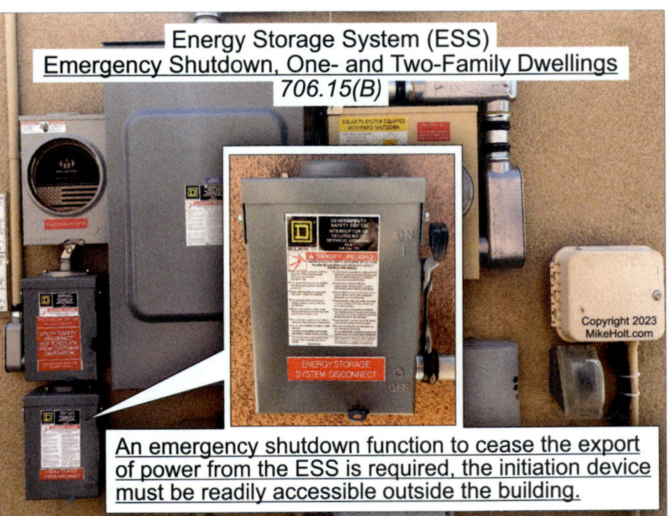

▶Figure 706–14

Author's Comment:

▶ It is important to note that the requirements in 706.15(A) can be met with disconnects that are integral to the listed energy storage system equipment. Since an energy storage system application may have multiple individual energy storage system units, each may require a disconnect, but this does not necessarily mean each will require a separate disconnect switch adjacent to the units. Many energy storage system manufacturers will choose to incorporate a means of disconnect into their energy storage system units. These disconnects will be evaluated during the system's listing.

(C) Disconnect Marking. The energy storage system disconnect must plainly indicate whether it is in the open (off) or closed (on) position and be marked: ▶Figure 706–15

"ENERGY STORAGE SYSTEM DISCONNECT"

For other than one- and two-family dwellings, the energy storage system disconnect must be legibly marked to indicate the following: ▶Figure 706–16

(1) The nominal system voltage

(2) The available fault current of the ESS

(3) An arc-flash label applied in accordance with acceptable industry practice

(4) The date the calculation was performed

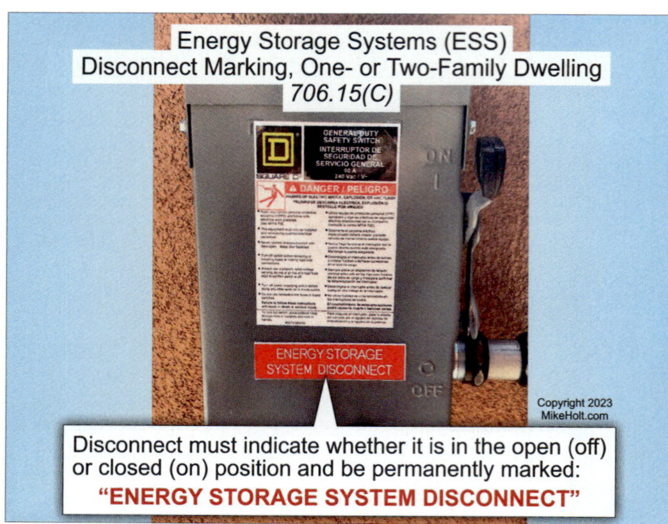

▶Figure 706–15

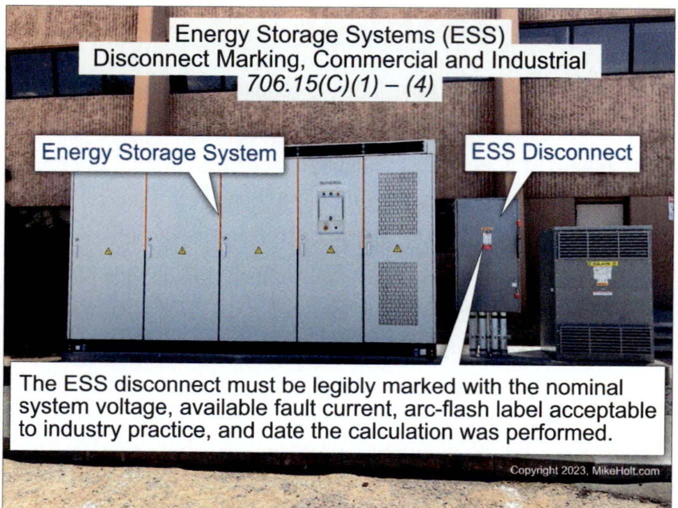

▶Figure 706–16

Note 1: Industry practices for equipment labeling are described in NFPA 70E, *Standard for Electrical Safety in the Workplace.* This standard provides specific criteria for developing arc-flash labels for equipment that provides nominal system voltage, incident energy levels, arc-flash boundaries, minimum required levels of personal protective equipment, and so forth.

Note 2: ESS electronics could include inverters or other types of power conversion equipment.

If line and load terminals within the energy storage system disconnect could be energized in the open position, the disconnect must be marked: ▶Figure 706–17

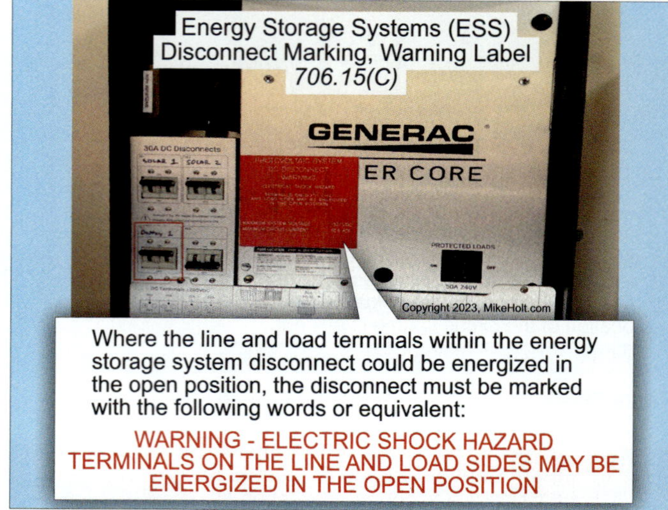

▶Figure 706–17

The marking must have sufficient durability to withstand the environment involved [110.21(B)].

(D) Partitions Between Components. Where energy storage system circuits pass through a wall, floor, or ceiling, a readily accessible disconnect within sight of the energy storage system is required.

Author's Comment:

▶ It is important to note that 706.15(D) will not apply to every energy storage system application where circuit conductors travel through walls, floors, or ceilings. This section is for those applications (typically large ones) where the battery is in one room and other equipment that is part of the energy storage system is in another. In those cases, a disconnect must be in the room containing the battery. This does not apply to situations where the entire energy storage system is in one room and the output circuit from the energy storage system connects to other systems in other rooms. In those cases, the disconnect location requirements in 706.15(A) are all that apply.

(E) Disconnecting Means for Batteries. Where the battery of the energy storage system is separate from the electronics and subject to field servicing, the following applies:

Note: Batteries could include an enclosure, battery monitoring and controls, or other related battery components.

(1) Disconnecting Means. A readily accessible disconnect is required within sight of the battery.

Note: See 240.21(H) for information on the location of the overcurrent protective device for battery conductors.

(3) Remote Activation. Where the battery disconnect is provided with remote controls and the controls are not within sight of the battery, the battery disconnect must be capable of being locked in the open position in accordance with 110.25, and the location of the controls must be field marked on the battery disconnect.

(4) Notification. The battery disconnect must be legibly marked to withstand the environment involved and include:

(1) Nominal battery voltage

(2) Available fault current

Note 1: Battery equipment suppliers can provide information about available fault current on any battery model.

(3) An arc-flash label in accordance with acceptable industry practice

Note 2: See NFPA 70E -2021, *Standard for Electrical Safety in the Workplace*, for assistance in determining the severity of potential exposure, planning safe work practices, determining arc-flash labeling, and selecting personal protective equipment.

(4) Date the calculation was performed

706.16 ESS in Parallel with Other Sources of Power

ESS in parallel with other sources of power must comply with the following: ▶Figure 706–18

(A) Disconnect. All sources of power must have a disconnecting means.

(B) Interactive Inverter. All sources of power must utilize interactive (grid tied) inverters.

(C) Loss of Interactive System Power. Upon loss of the electric utility power, the interactive (grid tied) inverter must automatically disconnect from the electric utility in accordance with 705.40.

(D) Unbalanced Interconnections. Unbalanced ac connections must comply with 705.45 .

(E) Parallel with Other Sources of Power. The parallel connection of the energy storage system to other sources of power must be in accordance with 705.12.

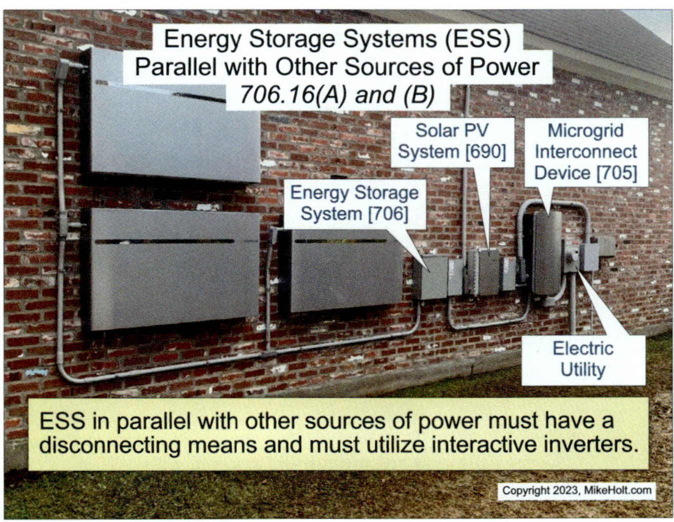

▶Figure 706–18

(F) Stand-Alone Operation. Where the ESS is operating in stand-alone (off-grid) mode, the requirements of 710.15 apply.

Part III. Installation Requirements

706.20 General Installation Requirements

(C) Spaces About Energy Storage Systems.

(1) The working space for energy storage systems must comply with 110.26. ▶Figure 706–19 and ▶Figure 706–20

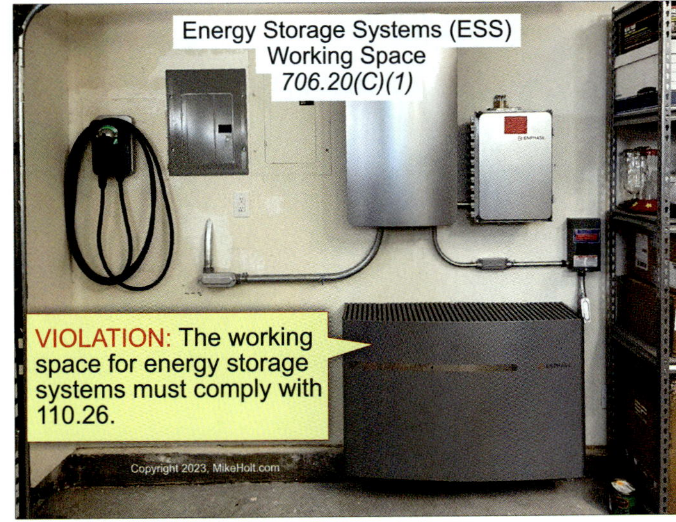

▶Figure 706–19

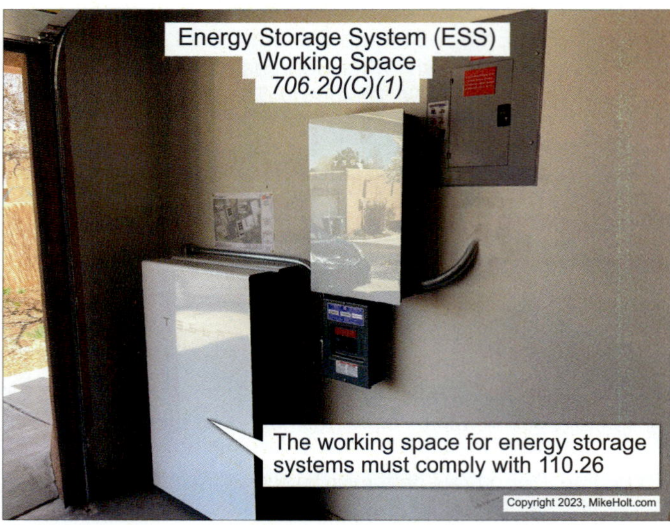

▶Figure 706–20

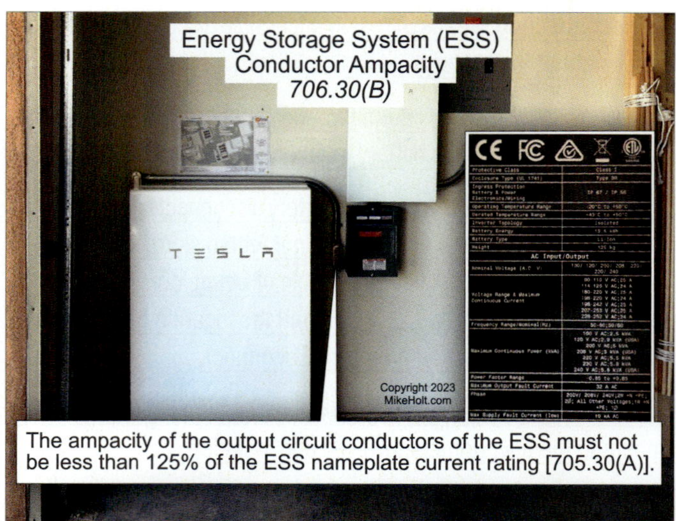

▶Figure 706–21

(2) Energy storage systems must be spaced apart in accordance with the manufacturer's instructions.

Note: Additional space may be needed to accommodate energy storage system hoisting equipment, tray removal, or spill containment.

Part IV. Energy Storage System Circuit Requirements

706.30 Circuit Current Rating

(A) Circuit Current Rating. The maximum current for an energy storage system is as follows:

(1) Nameplate-Rated Circuit Current. The rated current indicated on the energy storage system nameplate.

(2) Inverter Output Current. The continuous inverter output ac current rating.

(3) Inverter Input Current. The continuous inverter input dc current at the lowest input voltage.

(4) Inverter Utilization Output Circuit Current. The continuous inverter output ac current rating.

(5) DC-to-DC Converter Output Current. The continuous dc-to-dc converter's nameplate current rating.

(B) Conductor Ampacity. The ampacity of the output circuit conductors of the energy storage system(s) to the wiring system supplying the load must not be less than 125 percent of the current rating of the energy storage system in accordance with 705.30(A) or the rating of the overcurrent protective device [706.31]. ▶Figure 706–21

▶ Example

Question: *What is the minimum size ampacity conductor required for an energy storage system with a nameplate current rating of 25A?* ▶Figure 705–22

(a) 12 AWG   (b) 10 AWG   (c) 8 AWG   (d) 6 AWG

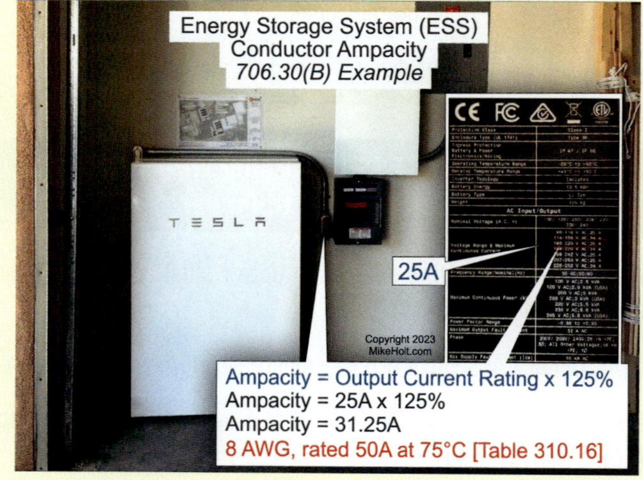

▶Figure 706–22

Solution:

Conductor Ampacity = Output Current Rating × 125%
Conductor Ampacity = 25A × 125%
Conductor Ampacity = 31.25A, 8 AWG rated 50A [Table 310.16]

Answer: *(c) 8 AWG*

706.31 Overcurrent Protection

(A) Circuits and Equipment. Overcurrent protective devices must be in accordance with 706.31(B) through (F).

(B) Overcurrent Device Ratings. Overcurrent protective devices must have an ampere rating of not less than 125 percent of the current marked on the energy storage system nameplate [706.30(A)] ▶Figure 706–23

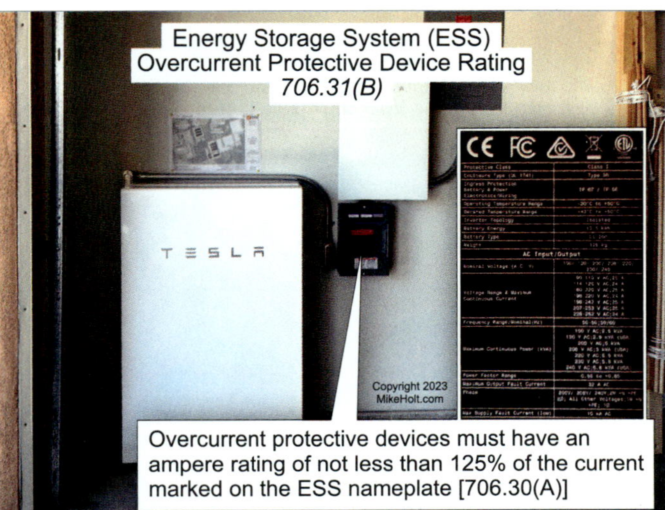

▶Figure 706–23

▶ Example

Question: *What size overcurrent protective device ampere rating is required for an energy storage system with a nameplate current of 25A marked on the equipment?* ▶Figure 705–24

(a) 25A   (b) 30A   (c) 35A   (d) 40A

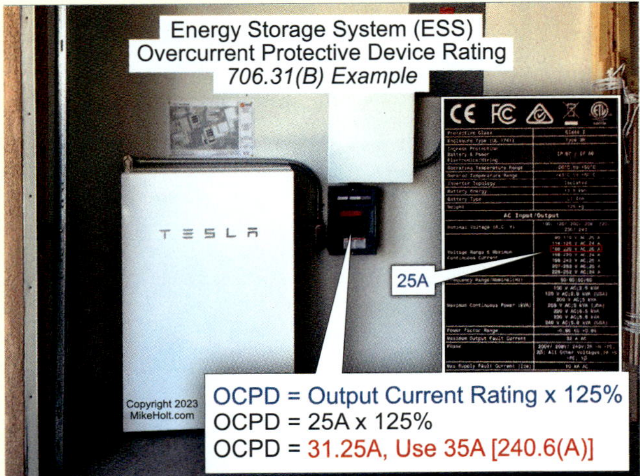

▶Figure 706–24

Solution:

OCPD = Nameplate Current Rating × 125%
OCPD = 25A × 125%
OCPD = 31.25A, use 35A breaker or fuse [240.6]

Answer: *(c) 35A*

Ex: Where the assembly (including the overcurrent protective devices) is listed for operation at 100 percent of its rating, the ampere rating of the overcurrent protective devices is permitted to be not less than the currents calculated in 706.30(B).

(C) Listing. Overcurrent protective devices used for dc circuits must be listed for direct current application.

(D) Current Limiting. Current-limiting overcurrent protective devices must be installed for each energy storage system dc output circuit. ▶Figure 706–25

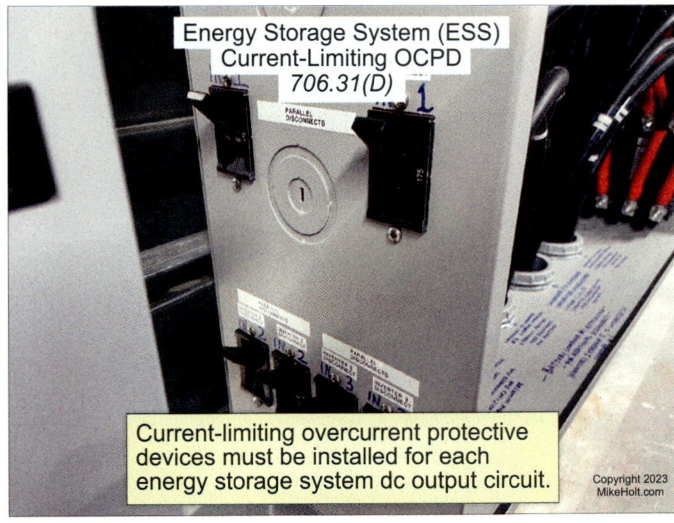

▶Figure 706–25

Ex: Where current-limiting overcurrent protection is provided for the dc output circuits, additional current-limiting overcurrent protective devices are not required.

(E) Disconnect for Fuses. A switch, pullouts, or similar device must be provided to disconnect power to fuses associated with energy storage system when the fuse is energized from both directions and is accessible to other than qualified persons.

(F) Location. Where circuits from the energy storage systems pass through a wall, floor, or ceiling; overcurrent protection must be provided at the energy storage component.

Author's Comment:

▸ As with 706.15(D), this one will not apply to every energy storage system application where circuit conductors travel through walls, floors, or ceilings. This section is for those applications (typically large ones) where the battery is in one room and other equipment that is part of that energy storage system is in another room.

Introduction to Article 710—Stand-Alone Systems

This article covers electric power production systems operating in island (off-grid) mode not connected to an electric utility.

710.1 Scope

This article covers electric power production systems, such as Solar PV, energy storage systems (ESS), and/or generator not connected to an electric utility. ▶Figure 710–1

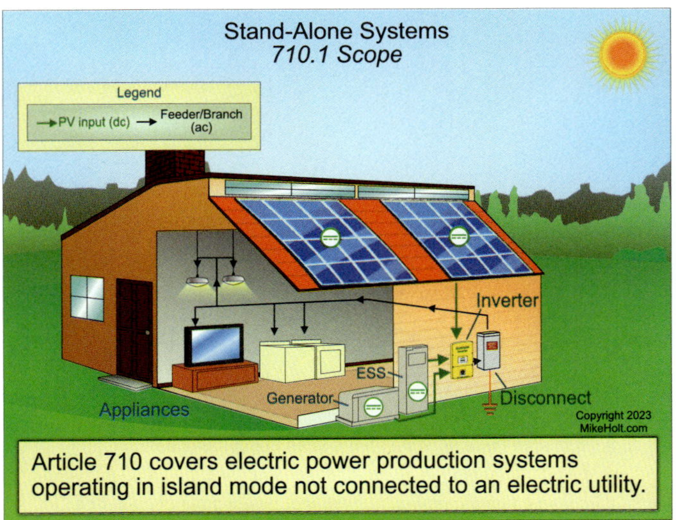

▶Figure 710–1

According to Article 100, a "Stand-Alone System" is an electrical power system that is not interconnected to the electric utility power system.

"Island Mode" is the operating mode for power production equipment or a microgrid that is disconnected from an electric utility or other primary power source. ▶Figure 710-2

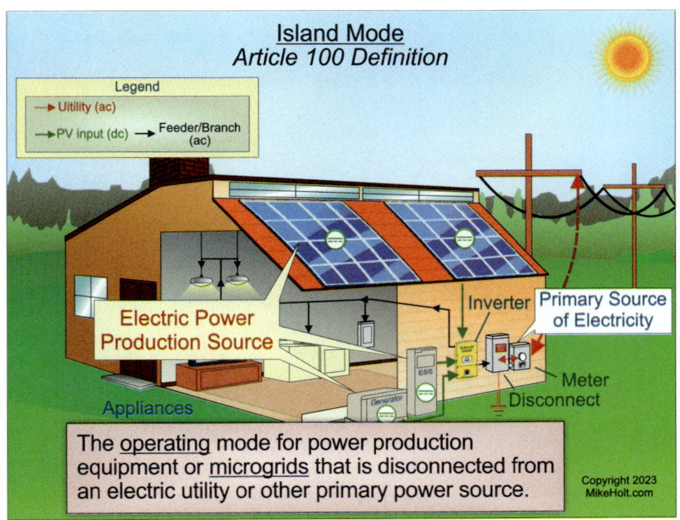

▶Figure 710–2

Note: Stand-alone systems can include any combination of PV, ESS, and/or a generator.

710.6 Equipment Approval

Stand-alone (off-grid) power production equipment must be listed for use in island (off-grid) mode. ▶Figure 710–3

710.10 Identification of Power Sources

A sign is required at the power source disconnect or other approved readily visible location that identifies the location of all power source disconnects installed in accordance with 705.10. ▶Figure 710–4

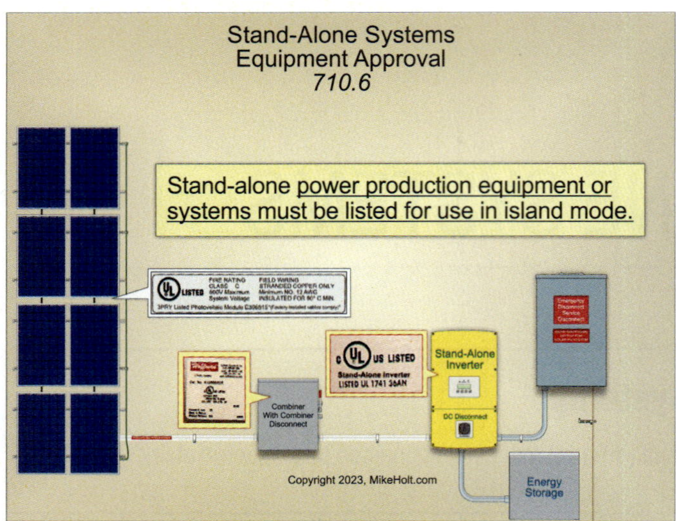

▶Figure 710–3

710.12 Stand-Alone Inverter Input Circuit Current

The maximum stand-alone (off-grid) inverter input circuit current occurs when the inverter is producing rated power at the lowest input voltage.

710.15 Wiring

(A) Power Supply Capacity. The power supply of a stand-alone (off-grid) system must have a capacity of not less than the largest single load.

(B) Conductor Ampacity. The conductors from the power source(s) to the building disconnect must have an ampacity not less than the total output nameplate ampere ratings of all the stand-alone power source(s).

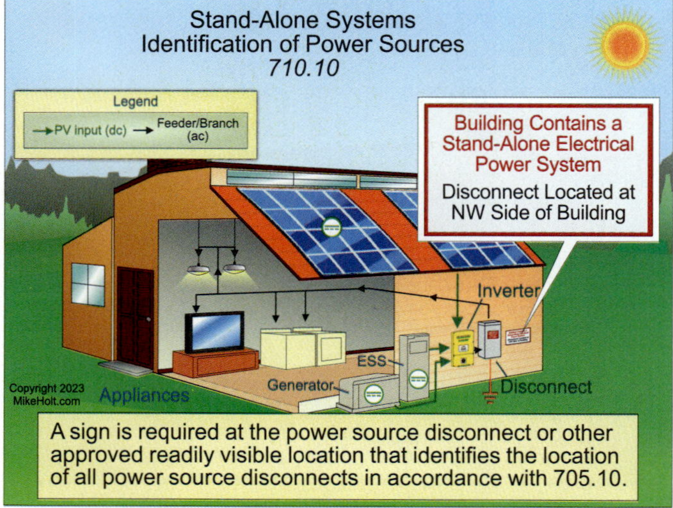

▶Figure 710–4

Introduction to Article 750—Energy Management Systems

This article applies to the installation and operation of energy management systems. Energy management systems have become very popular and are used in electric vehicle supply equipment to adjust ampere settings, power monitoring devices for panelboards, lighting controls for building automation, load-shedding systems for an alternate power source, and so on. Energy management ensures that the electrical system does not overload a branch circuit, feeder, or service and allows the electrical system to be sized based on the controlled/monitored current settings.

750.1 Scope

This article applies to the installation and operation of energy management systems. ▶Figure 750–1

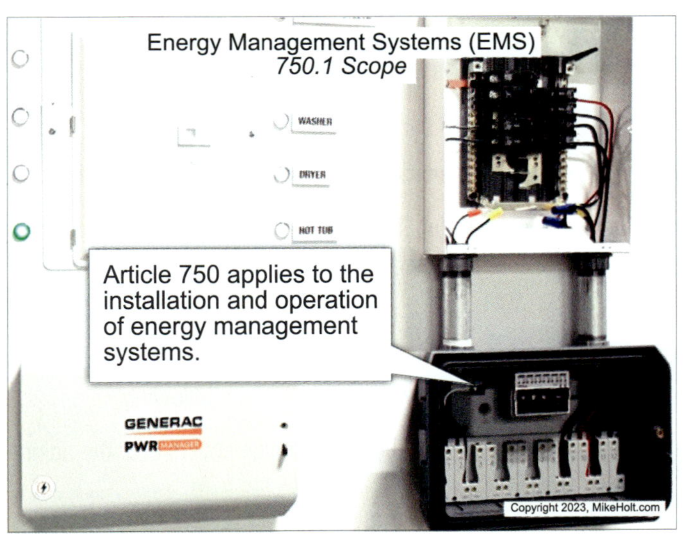

▶Figure 750–1

According to Article 100, an "Energy Management System" is a system consisting of monitor(s), communications equipment, controller(s), timer(s), or other device(s) that monitors and/or controls an electrical load or a power production or storage source. ▶**Figure 750–2** and ▶**Figure 750–3**

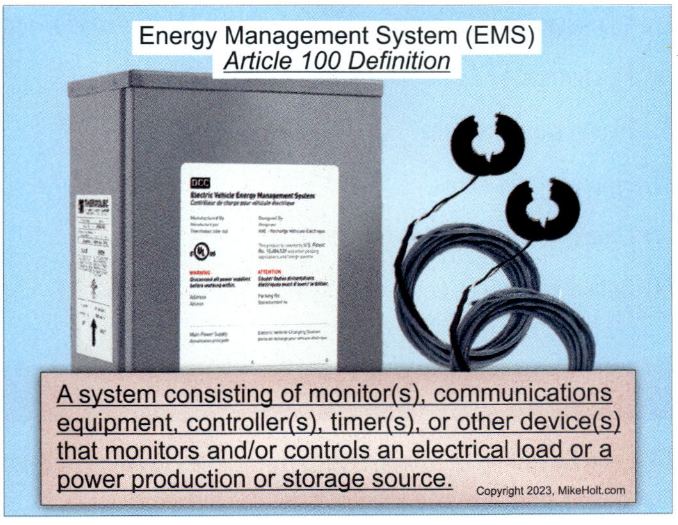

▶Figure 750–2

750.6 Listing

Energy management systems must be one of the following:

(1) Listed as a complete energy management system

(2) Listed as a kit for field installation in switch or overcurrent device enclosures

(3) Listed individual components assembled as a system

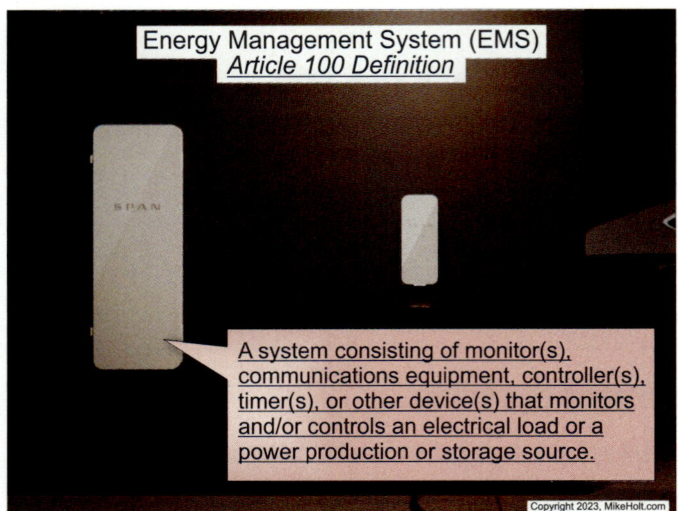

▶Figure 750–3

750.20 Alternate Power Sources

Energy management systems are not permitted to override controls for:

(1) Fire pumps

(2) Health care facilities

(3) Emergency systems

(4) Legally required standby systems

(5) Critical operations power systems

750.30 Load Management

(A) Load Shedding Controls. Energy management systems are not permitted to override load shedding controls put in place to ensure the minimum electrical capacity for:

(1) Fire pumps

(2) Emergency systems

(3) Legally required standby systems

(4) Critical operations power systems

(B) Disconnection of Power. Energy management systems are not permitted to disconnect power for:

(1) Elevators, escalators, moving walks, or stairway lift chairs

(2) Positive mechanical ventilation for hazardous (classified) locations

(3) Ventilation used to exhaust hazardous gas or reclassify an area

(4) Circuits supplying emergency lighting

(5) Essential electrical systems in health care facilities

(C) Limit Current Capacity. An energy management system cannot cause a branch circuit, feeder, or service conductor to be overloaded.

The energy management system can limit the current on the conductor as follows:

(1) Current Setpoint. The setpoint current can be used to:

(1) Calculate the maximum feeder/service continuous load in accordance with 220.70 ▶Figure 750–4

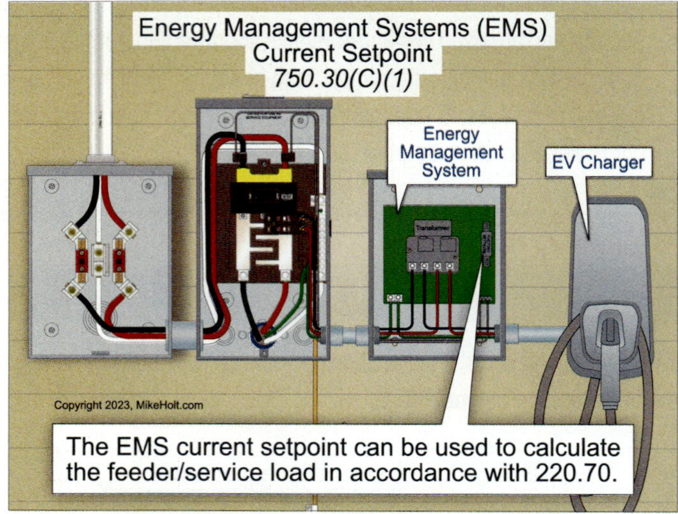

▶Figure 750–4

(2) For the maximum source current permitted by EMS control

(2) System Malfunction. The EMS must have use monitoring and controls to automatically cease current flow upon malfunction of the EMS.

(3) Settings. Adjustable settings must be permitted if access to the settings is accomplished by at least one of the following:

(1) Located behind removable and sealable covers over the adjustment means

(2) Located behind a cover or door that requires the use of a tool to open

(3) Located behind locked doors accessible only to qualified personnel

(4) Password protected with password accessible only to qualified personnel

(5) Software that has password protected access to the adjusting means accessible to qualified personnel only

(4) Marking. The EMS controlled equipment must be field marked with the following: ▶Figure 750–5

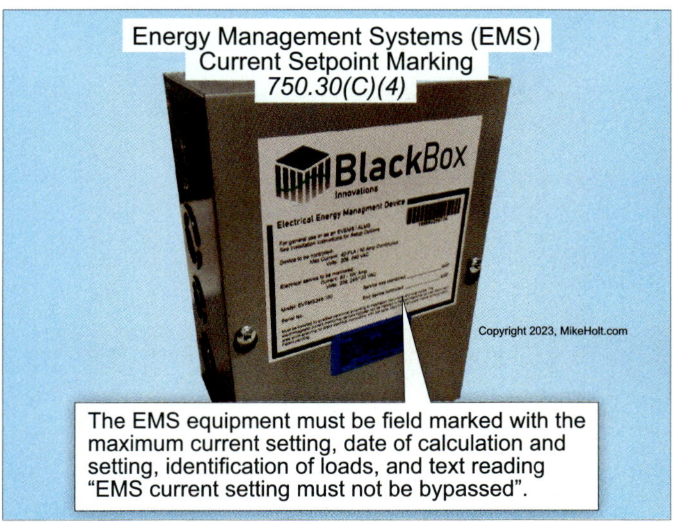

The EMS equipment must be field marked with the maximum current setting, date of calculation and setting, identification of loads, and text reading "EMS current setting must not be bypassed".

▶Figure 750–5

(1) Maximum current setting

(2) Date of calculation and setting

(3) Identification of loads with the current-limiting feature

(4) The wording: "The setting for the EMS current-limiting feature must not be bypassed"

The markings must meet the requirements in 110.21(B) and be such that they are clearly visible to qualified persons before examination, adjustment, servicing, or maintenance of the equipment.

750.50 Directory

Where an energy management system controls a circuit, that circuit must have a label on the enclosure to identify that the circuit is controlled by the energy management system.

EXAM B
STRAIGHT ORDER—
ARTICLES 625–750

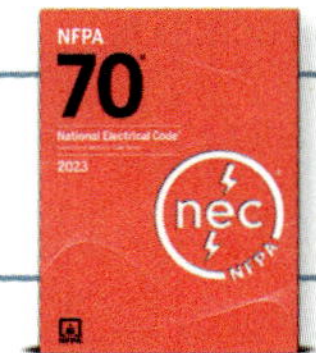

Please use the 2023 *Code* book to answer the following questions.

1. Article 625 covers the electrical conductors and equipment connecting an electric vehicle to premises wiring for the purposes of ______.

   (a) charging
   (b) power export
   (c) bidirectional current flow
   (d) any of these

2. Each outlet installed for the purpose of supplying EVSE (electric vehicle supply equipment) greater than ______ or 120V charging electric vehicles shall be supplied by an individual branch circuit.

   (a) 12A
   (b) 16A
   (c) 18A
   (d) 20A

3. Overcurrent protection for circuits supplying electric vehicle supply (EVSE) and wireless power transfer (WPTE) equipment shall have a current rating of not less than ______ of the maximum load of the electric vehicle supply equipment.

   (a) 100 percent
   (b) 110 percent
   (c) 125 percent
   (d) 150 percent

4. Electric vehicle charging loads shall be considered to be a(an) ______ load.

   (a) noncontinuous
   (b) hard
   (c) extended
   (d) continuous

5. For electric vehicle supply and wireless power transfer equipment (EVSE and WPTE) more than ______ or more than 150V to ground, the disconnecting means shall be provided and installed in a readily accessible location.

   (a) 20A
   (b) 30A
   (c) 50A
   (d) 60A

6. Where a disconnecting means for EVSE and WPTE is required and installed remote from the equipment, a plaque shall be installed ______ denoting the location of the disconnecting means.

   (a) adjacent to the equipment
   (b) on the equipment
   (c) within 3 ft of the equipment
   (d) within sight of the equipment

7. Electric vehicle supply equipment _______ as suitable for charging electric vehicles indoors without ventilation is permitted indoors.

   (a) listed
   (b) labeled
   (c) identified
   (d) all of these

8. All receptacles installed for the connection of electric vehicle charging shall have _______.

   (a) arc-fault circuit-interrupter protection
   (b) ground-fault circuit-interrupter protection
   (c) current-limiting protection
   (d) ground-fault protection for equipment

9. Electronic power converters and their associated devices installed on PV systems can be mounted on roofs or other areas where they are not _______ accessible.

   (a) readily
   (b) easily
   (c) relatively
   (d) any of these

10. The requirements of Article _______ pertaining to PV source circuits shall not apply to ac modules or ac module systems. The PV source circuit, conductors, and inverters shall be considered as internal components of an ac module or ac module system.

    (a) 660
    (b) 670
    (c) 680
    (d) 690

11. In PV systems, the output of an ac module or an ac module system is considered a(an) _______ output circuit.

    (a) inverter
    (b) module
    (c) PV
    (d) subarray

12. For calculating maximum PV source circuit voltage, one source for lowest-expected _______ temperature design data for various locations is the chapter titled Extreme Annual Mean Minimum Design Dry Bulb Temperature found in the *ASHRAE Handbook—Fundamentals*.

    (a) ambient
    (b) average
    (c) medium
    (d) any of these

13. For crystalline and multicrystalline silicon modules, the PV system voltage ambient temperature correction is _______ if the ambient temperature is 20°C.

    (a) 1.02
    (b) 1.04
    (c) 1.06
    (d) 1.08

14. For crystalline and multicrystalline silicon modules, the maximum dc source circuit voltage is equal to the sum of the PV module rated open-circuit voltage of the _______-connected modules in the PV string circuit corrected for the lowest expected ambient temperature using the correction factors provided in Table 690.7(A).

    (a) parallel
    (b) series
    (c) series-parallel
    (d) multiwire

15. For a PV system source circuit with an inverter generating capacity of _______ or greater, the maximum dc voltage is permitted to be a documented and stamped PV system design, using an industry standard method maximum voltage calculation provided by a licensed professional electrical engineer.

    (a) 25 kW
    (b) 50 kW
    (c) 75 kW
    (d) 100 kW

16. A permanent readily visible label indicating the highest maximum dc voltage in a PV system, calculated in accordance with 690.7, shall be provided by the installer at the _______.

    (a) dc PV system disconnecting means
    (b) PV system electronic power conversion equipment
    (c) distribution equipment associated with the PV system
    (d) any of these

17. For circuit sizing and current calculation of PV systems, the maximum PV source current is equal to the sum of the short-circuit current ratings of the PV modules connected in ______ multiplied by 125 percent.

    (a) series
    (b) parallel
    (c) series-parallel
    (d) multiwire

18. For circuit sizing and current calculation of PV systems, the maximum PV inverter output circuit current is equal to the inverter ______ output current rating.

    (a) average
    (b) peak
    (c) continuous
    (d) intermittent

19. For circuit sizing calculations of PV systems without adjustment and/or correction factors, the minimum conductor size must have an ampacity not less than the maximum currents calculated in 690.8(A) multiplied by ______.

    (a) 75 percent
    (b) 100 percent
    (c) 125 percent
    (d) 150 percent

20. Overcurrent protection for PV system dc circuit conductors and equipment shall not be required where the ______.

    (a) conductors have sufficient ampacity for the maximum circuit current
    (b) currents from all sources do not exceed the maximum overcurrent protective device rating specified for the PV module or electronic power converter
    (c) conductors have a short-circuit rating above the available fault current
    (d) conductors have sufficient ampacity for the maximum circuit current and the currents from all sources do not exceed the maximum overcurrent protective device rating specified for the PV module or electronic power converter

21. For PV systems where overcurrent protection is required on one end and the circuit conductor is also connected to a source having an available maximum current greater than the ampacity of the circuit conductor, the circuit conductors shall be protected from overcurrent at the point of connection to ______ current source(s).

    (a) the lower
    (b) the higher
    (c) either
    (d) both

22. Overcurrent devices used in PV source circuits shall be ______ for use in PV systems.

    (a) identified
    (b) approved
    (c) recognized
    (d) listed

23. Overcurrent devices for PV system dc circuits shall be readily accessible.

    (a) True
    (b) False

24. Photovoltaic systems with PV system dc circuits operating at ______ dc or greater between any two conductors shall be protected by a listed PV arc-fault circuit interrupter, or other system components listed to provide equivalent protection.

    (a) 30V
    (b) 50V
    (c) 80V
    (d) 120V

25. PV system dc circuits that utilize metal-clad cables installed ______ shall be permitted without AFCI protection where the circuits are located in or on detached structures whose sole purpose is to support or contain PV system equipment.

    (a) in metal raceways
    (b) in enclosed metal cable trays
    (c) underground
    (d) any of these

26. Ground-mounted PV system circuits that _______ buildings, of which the sole purpose is to house PV system equipment, shall not be required to comply with the 690.12 requirements for rapid shutdown.

    (a) enter
    (b) pass through
    (c) enter or pass through
    (d) none of these

27. PV equipment and circuits installed on nonenclosed _______ structures including but not limited to parking shade structures, carports, solar trellises, and similar structures shall not be required to comply with the 690.12 requirements for rapid shutdown.

    (a) detached
    (b) attached
    (c) fixed
    (d) separate

28. The rapid shutdown function reduces the risk of electrical shock that dc circuits in a PV system could pose for _______.

    (a) personnel
    (b) employees
    (c) firefighters
    (d) installers

29. For the purpose of a PV system rapid shutdown system, the term array boundary as used in 690.12(B) is defined as _______ from the array in all directions.

    (a) 1 ft
    (b) 3 ft
    (c) 5 ft
    (d) 50 ft

30. For PV system rapid shutdown systems, controlled conductors located outside the array boundary or more than 3 ft from the point of entry inside a building shall be limited to not more than _______ within 30 seconds of rapid shutdown initiation.

    (a) 80V
    (b) 50V
    (c) 30V
    (d) 15V

31. For PV system rapid shutdown systems, the rapid shutdown initiation device off position shall indicate that the rapid shutdown function has been _______ for all PV systems connected to that device.

    (a) initiated
    (b) locked out
    (c) disconnected
    (d) activated

32. For one-family and two-family dwellings, the rapid shutdown initiation device(s) where required, shall be located at a(an) _______ location outside the building.

    (a) accessible
    (b) secured
    (c) public
    (d) readily accessible

33. The required label for buildings with PV systems having rapid shutdown shall be titled SOLAR PV SYSTEM IS EQUIPPED WITH RAPID SHUTDOWN in capitalized letters at least _______ high.

    (a) ¼ in.
    (b) ⁵⁄₁₆ in.
    (c) ⅜ in.
    (d) ½ in.

34. A means is required to disconnect the PV system from all wiring systems including power systems, energy storage systems, and utilization equipment and its associated premises wiring.

    (a) True
    (b) False

35. The PV system disconnecting means shall be installed at a(an) _______ location.

    (a) guarded
    (b) accessible
    (c) protected
    (d) readily accessible

36. The PV system disconnecting means shall have ratings sufficient for the _______ that is available at the terminals of the PV system disconnect.

    (a) maximum circuit current
    (b) available fault current
    (c) voltage
    (d) all of these

37. For PV systems, means shall be provided to ______ ac PV modules, fuses, dc-to-dc converters, inverters, and charge controllers from all conductors that are not solidly grounded.

    (a) disconnect
    (b) open
    (c) close
    (d) turn off

38. Where a disconnect is required to isolate PV system equipment, the disconnecting means shall be permitted to be an isolating device as part of listed equipment where an interlock or similar means ______ the opening of the isolating device under load.

    (a) prevents
    (b) prohibits
    (c) facilitates
    (d) any of these

39. Where a disconnect is required to isolate PV system equipment with a maximum circuit current of ______ or less, an isolating device shall be installed in accordance with 690.15(B).

    (a) 15A
    (b) 20A
    (c) 30A
    (d) 50A

40. An isolating device for PV system equipment shall which of the following?

    (a) A mating connector meeting the requirements of 690.33 and listed and identified for use with specific equipment.
    (b) A finger-safe fuse holder or an isolating switch that requires a tool to place the device in the open (off) position.
    (c) An isolating device listed for the intended application.
    (d) any of these

41. The PV system equipment disconnecting means shall have ratings sufficient for the ______ that is available at the terminals of the PV system disconnect.

    (a) maximum circuit current
    (b) available fault current
    (c) voltage
    (d) all of these

42. Where not otherwise allowed in an equipment's listing, PV system dc circuits shall not occupy the same equipment wiring enclosure, cable, or raceway as other non-PV systems, or inverter output circuits, unless separated from other circuits by a ______.

    (a) barrier
    (b) partition
    (c) barrier or partition
    (d) none of these

43. PV system dc circuits shall not occupy the same equipment wiring enclosure, cable, or raceway as other non-PV systems, or inverter output circuits, unless the PV system dc circuits are separated from other circuits by a barrier or ______.

    (a) partition
    (b) sleeve
    (c) double insulation
    (d) shield

44. PV system dc circuit conductors shall have polarity identification at all termination, connection, and splice points by ______.

    (a) color coding
    (b) marking tape
    (c) tagging or other approved means
    (d) all of these

45. PV system dc circuit conductor marking means for nonsolidly grounded positive conductors shall include imprinted plus signs (+) or the word POSITIVE or POS durably marked on insulation of a color other than ______.

    (a) green
    (b) white
    (c) gray
    (d) all of these

46. The requirement for grouping PV system conductors is not required if the circuit enters from a cable or raceway unique to the circuit that makes the grouping obvious.

    (a) True
    (b) False

47. Single-conductor PV system cables with ______ insulation marked sunlight resistant can be used to connect photovoltaic modules in outdoor locations within the PV array.

    (a) THHN
    (b) USE-2
    (c) RHW-2
    (d) USE-2 and RHW-2

48. Single-conductor PV wire or cable of all sizes shall be permitted in cable trays installed in outdoor locations, provided that the cables are supported at intervals not to exceed ______ and secured at intervals not to exceed 54 in.

    (a) 12 in.
    (b) 24 in.
    (c) 36 in.
    (d) 48 in.

49. Flexible cords and flexible cables, where connected to moving parts of tracking PV ______, shall comply with Article 400.

    (a) systems
    (b) arrays
    (c) cells
    (d) modules

50. Where inside buildings, PV system dc circuits that exceed 30V or 8A shall be contained in ______.

    (a) metal raceways
    (b) Type MC cable that complies with 250.118(10)
    (c) metal enclosures
    (d) any of these

51. Equipment and wiring methods containing PV system dc circuits with a maximum voltage greater than 1000V shall not be permitted ______.

    (a) on or in single-family dwellings
    (b) on or in two-family dwellings
    (c) within buildings containing habitable rooms
    (d) all of these

52. Equipment and wiring methods containing PV system dc circuits with a maximum voltage greater than 1000V, where installed on the exterior of buildings, shall be located not less than ______ above grade.

    (a) 8 ft
    (b) 10 ft
    (c) 12 ft
    (d) 15 ft

53. Mating connectors that are readily accessible and that are used in PV source circuits operating at over 30V dc or 15V ac shall require a ______ for opening.

    (a) special access code
    (b) lock combination
    (c) password
    (d) tool

54. Devices and systems used for mounting PV modules that are also used for bonding module frames shall be ______ for bonding PV modules.

    (a) listed
    (b) labeled
    (c) identified
    (d) all of these

55. The bonding requirements contained in 250.97 shall apply only to solidly grounded PV system circuits operating over ______ to ground.

    (a) 30V
    (b) 60V
    (c) 120V
    (d) 250V

56. Equipment grounding conductors for PV system circuits shall be sized in accordance with ______.

    (a) 250.4
    (b) 250.66
    (c) 250.102
    (d) 250.122

57. Large-scale PV systems that do not provide arc-fault protection shall include details of fire mitigation plans to address ______ in the documentation required in 691.6.

    (a) dc arc faults
    (b) dc and ac arc faults
    (c) dc ground faults
    (d) dc and ac ground faults

58. According to 691.1, facilities covered by Article 691 have specific design and safety features unique to large-scale ______ facilities outlined in 691.4 and are operated for the sole purpose of providing electric supply to a system operated by a regulated utility for the transfer of electric energy.

    (a) industrial
    (b) electrical
    (c) distribution
    (d) PV

59. Access to large-scale PV electric supply stations shall be ______ in accordance with 110.31.

    (a) allowed
    (b) restricted
    (c) permitted
    (d) none of these

60. The electrical loads within a large-scale PV electric supply station shall only be used to power auxiliary equipment for the ______ of the PV power.

    (a) distribution
    (b) storage
    (c) generation
    (d) regulation

61. ______ PV electric supply stations are permitted to be installed on buildings.

    (a) Isolated
    (b) Large-scale
    (c) Island mode
    (d) Interconnected

62. Electrical equipment for large-scale PV electric supply stations shall only be approved for installation by ______.

    (a) listing and labeling
    (b) being evaluated for the application and having a field label applied
    (c) qualified personnel
    (d) listing and labeling or by being evaluated for the application and having a field label applied

63. Engineering documentation of large-scale electric supply stations shall include details of conformance of the design with ______.

    (a) Article 250
    (b) Article 690
    (c) Article 702
    (d) Article 710

64. Documentation by a licensed professional ______ that the construction of the large-scale PV electric supply station conforms to the electrical engineered design shall be provided upon request of the authority having jurisdiction

    (a) PV installer
    (b) electrician
    (c) electrical engineer
    (d) electrical inspector

65. Fire mitigation plans, where required for large-scale PV systems, are typically reviewed by the ______ and include topics such as access roads within the facility.

    (a) electrical inspector
    (b) civil engineer
    (c) local fire agency
    (d) forestry service

66. Article 702 applies to ______ optional standby systems.

    (a) temporarily installed
    (b) portable
    (c) readily accessible
    (d) the installation and operation of

67. If the connection of load is manual or nonautomatic, an optional standby system shall have adequate ______ for the supply of all equipment intended to be operated at one time.

    (a) ventilation
    (b) supervision
    (c) fuel supply
    (d) capacity and rating

68. Where automatic transfer equipment is used, an optional standby system shall be capable of supplying ______.

    (a) the full load that is automatically connected
    (b) all equipment where life safety is dependent
    (c) all emergency and egress lighting
    (d) all fire and security systems

69. Optional standby system interconnection or transfer equipment shall be designed and installed so as to prevent the inadvertent interconnection of ______ of supply in any operation of the equipment.

    (a) the normal source
    (b) the standby source
    (c) all sources
    (d) none of these

70. For optional standby purposes, a portable generator rated 15 kW or less is installed using a flanged inlet or other cord-and-plug-type connection, the flanged inlet or other cord-and-plug-type connection shall be located ______ of a building or structure.

    (a) outside
    (b) inside
    (c) outside or inside
    (d) none of these

71. Article 705 covers the installation of one or more electric power production sources operating in parallel with a(an) ______ source(s) of electricity.

    (a) secondary
    (b) alternate
    (c) primary
    (d) stand-alone

72. The output of interactive electric power production sources equipment shall be _______ disconnected from all ungrounded conductors of the primary source when one or more of the phases of the primary source to which it is connected opens.

    (a) manually
    (b) automatically
    (c) manually or automatically
    (d) manually and automatically

73. Interconnection and interactive equipment intended to connect to or operate in parallel with power production sources shall be listed for the required interactive function or be _______ for the interactive function and have a field label applied, or both.

    (a) tested
    (b) evaluated
    (c) approved
    (d) licensed

74. Installations of one or more interconnected electrical power production sources operating in parallel with a primary source(s) of electricity shall be performed only by _______.

    (a) qualified persons
    (b) utility company persons
    (c) the authority having jurisdiction
    (d) utility company persons or the authority having jurisdiction

75. For interconnected electric power production source(s), a permanent _______, denoting the location of each power source disconnecting means for the building or structure, shall be installed at each service equipment location or at an approved readily visible location.

    (a) label
    (b) plaque
    (c) directory
    (d) any of these

76. Interconnected power production installations with multiple co-located power production sources shall be permitted to be _______ as a group(s).

    (a) identified
    (b) labeled
    (c) marked
    (d) all of these

77. Interconnected electric power production source(s) are permitted to be connected to the _______ side of the service disconnecting means in accordance with 230.82(6).

    (a) line
    (b) supply
    (c) source
    (d) any of these

78. For interconnected electric power production source(s) connected to a service, the service conductors connected to the power production source service disconnecting means shall be sized in accordance with 705.28 and not be smaller than _______ copper.

    (a) 8 AWG
    (b) 6 AWG
    (c) 4 AWG
    (d) 3 AWG

79. Interconnected electric power production source metal enclosures, metal wiring methods, and metal parts associated with the service connected to a power production source shall be _______ in accordance with Parts II through V and VIII of Article 250.

    (a) installed
    (b) grounded
    (c) bonded
    (d) protected

80. The rating of the overcurrent protective device of the interconnected electric power production source service disconnecting means shall be used to determine if _______ is required in accordance with 230.95.

    (a) ground-fault protection of equipment
    (b) arc-fault protection
    (c) surge protection
    (d) lightning protection

81. The output of an interconnected electric power source shall be permitted to be connected to the _______ side of the service disconnecting means of the other source(s) at any distribution equipment on the premises.

    (a) load
    (b) bottom
    (c) top
    (d) line

82. Where the interconnected electric power production source output connection is made to a feeder at a location other than the opposite end of the feeder from the primary source overcurrent device, that portion of the feeder on the load side of the power source output connection shall be protected by a(an) ______.

    (a) feeder ampacity not less than the sum of the primary source overcurrent device and 125 percent of the power source output circuit current
    (b) overcurrent device at the load side of the power source connection point rated not greater than the ampacity of the feeder
    (c) feeder ampacity not less than the sum of the primary source overcurrent device and 125 percent of the power source output circuit current, or an overcurrent device at the load side of the power source connection point rated not greater than the ampacity of the feeder
    (d) none of these

83. Where interconnected electric power production source output connections are made at busbars, the sum of ______ of the power source(s) output circuit current and the rating of the overcurrent device protecting the busbar shall not exceed the busbar ampere rating.

    (a) 100 percent
    (b) 110 percent
    (c) 115 percent
    (d) 125 percent

84. Where interconnected electric power production source output connections are made at either end of a ______ panelboard in dwellings, it shall be permitted where the sum of 125 percent of the power-source(s) output circuit current and the rating of the overcurrent device protecting the busbar does not exceed 120 percent of the busbar ampere rating.

    (a) front-fed
    (b) back-fed
    (c) center-fed
    (d) none of these

85. Interconnected electric power production source connections shall be permitted on busbars of panelboards that supply ______ connected to feed-through conductors.

    (a) power distribution blocks
    (b) terminals
    (c) lugs
    (d) none of these

86. An emergency management system (EMS), in accordance with 705.30, shall be permitted to limit current and loading on the busbars and conductors supplied by the output of one or more interconnected electric power production sources or ______ sources.

    (a) utility power
    (b) energy storage
    (c) stand-alone power
    (d) all of these

87. Listed plug-in-type circuit breakers backfed from interconnected electric power production sources that are listed and identified as ______ shall not require a fastener as required by 408.36(D).

    (a) interactive
    (b) active
    (c) reactive
    (d) interactive or active

88. In accordance with Article 705, for the purpose of overcurrent protection, the primary side of transformers with sources on each side shall be the side connected to the largest source of ______ current.

    (a) available fault
    (b) short-circuit
    (c) output power source
    (d) available fault current or short-circuit

89. The installation and maintenance of energy storage system (ESS) equipment and all associated wiring and interconnections shall be performed only by ______.

    (a) qualified persons
    (b) ESS specialists
    (c) licensed electricians
    (d) maintenance personnel

90. Where controls to activate the energy storage system (ESS) battery disconnecting means are used and are not located within sight of the battery, the location of the controls shall be marked ______.

    (a) on the batteries
    (b) adjacent to the batteries
    (c) on the disconnecting means
    (d) in a secure location

91. The energy storage system (ESS) inverter output circuit maximum current shall be ______.

    (a) the inverter continuous output current rating
    (b) the inverter continuous input current rating
    (c) 110 percent of the inverter continuous output current rating
    (d) 125 percent of the inverter continuous input current rating

92. Overcurrent protective devices, where required, shall be rated in accordance with Article 240 and the rating provided on systems serving the energy storage system (ESS) shall be not less than ______ of the maximum currents calculated in 706.30(A).

    (a) 110 percent
    (b) 115 percent
    (c) 125 percent
    (d) 167 percent

93. Article 710 covers electric power production systems that operate in ______ and not connected to an electric utility supply.

    (a) island mode
    (b) standby mode
    (c) tandem mode
    (d) generating mode

94. According to the scope of 710.1, stand-alone systems often include a single or a compatible interconnection of sources such as ______.

    (a) engine generators
    (b) solar PV or wind
    (c) ESS or batteries
    (d) all of these

95. All stand-alone power production equipment or systems shall be approved for use ______.

    (a) as legally required standby power
    (b) as optional standby power
    (c) in island mode
    (d) as supplemental power on demand

96. A permanent ______ shall be installed at a building supplied by a stand-alone system at each service equipment location or at an approved readily visible location and shall denote the location of each power source disconnect for the building or be grouped with other plaques or directories for other on-site sources.

    (a) plaque
    (b) label
    (c) directory
    (d) any of these

97. Power supply to premises wiring systems fed by stand-alone or isolated microgrid power sources is permitted to have ______ than the calculated load.

    (a) less capacity
    (b) greater capacity
    (c) 120 percent greater capacity
    (d) 125 percent greater capacity

98. The circuit conductors between a stand-alone source and a ______ shall be sized based on the sum of the output ratings of the stand-alone source(s).

    (a) distribution panel
    (b) building or structure disconnect
    (c) calculated load
    (d) demand load

99. Article ______ applies to the installation and operation of energy management systems.

    (a) 690
    (b) 724
    (c) 750
    (d) 760

100. Energy management systems shall be listed ______.

    (a) as a complete energy management system
    (b) as a kit for field installation in switch or overcurrent device enclosures
    (c) individual components assembled as a system
    (d) any of these

FINAL EXAM
RANDOM ORDER—
ARTICLES 90–750

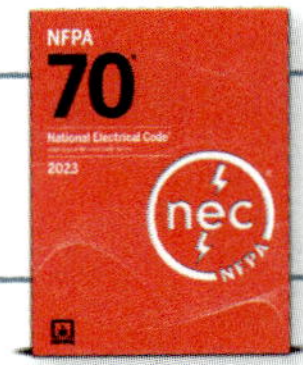

Please use the 2023 *Code* book to answer the following questions.

1. LFMC shall not be required to be secured or supported where fished between access points through _______ spaces in finished buildings or structures and supporting is impractical.

   (a) concealed
   (b) exposed
   (c) hazardous (classified)
   (d) completed

2. In dwelling units and guest rooms or guest suites, voltage shall not exceed 120V for cord and plug equipment connected to loads rated _______.

   (a) 1,440 VA
   (b) 1,500 VA
   (c) 1,800 VA
   (d) 2,400 VA

3. Buildings whose sole purpose is to house and protect large-scale PV supply station equipment shall not be required to comply with 690.12. Written standard _______ shall be available at the site detailing necessary shutdown procedures in the event of an emergency.

   (a) guidelines
   (b) operating procedures
   (c) documentation
   (d) any of these

4. Conductors installed in nonmetallic raceways run underground shall be permitted to be arranged as isolated _______ installations. The raceways shall be installed in close proximity, and the conductors shall comply with 300.20(B).

   (a) neutral
   (b) grounded conductor
   (c) phase
   (d) all of these

5. A cable tray system is a unit or assembly of units or sections and associated fittings forming a _______ system used to securely fasten or support cables and raceways.

   (a) structural
   (b) flexible
   (c) movable
   (d) secure

6. A(An) _______ is a conductive path(s) that is part of an effective ground-fault current path and connects normally noncurrent-carrying metal parts of equipment together and to the system grounded conductor or to the grounding electrode conductor, or both.

   (a) grounding electrode conductor
   (b) main bonding jumper
   (c) system bonding jumper
   (d) equipment grounding conductor

7. The requirements for the controlled conductors that are part of the rapid shutdown of a PV system shall apply to ______.

    (a) PV system dc circuits
    (b) inverter output circuits originating from inverters located within the array boundary
    (c) PV system ac circuits
    (d) PV system dc circuits and inverter output circuits originating from inverters located within the array boundary

8. Mating connectors used for PV circuits shall ______.

    (a) be rated for the interrupting current with no risk of injury or hazard
    (b) require a tool to open and be marked
    (c) be supplied as part of the listed equipment
    (d) any of these

9. One- and two-family dwelling emergency disconnecting means are permitted to be a listed disconnect switch or circuit breaker that is marked ______ for use as service equipment, but not marked as suitable only for use as service equipment, installed on the supply side of each service disconnect.

    (a) suitable
    (b) appropriate
    (c) ready
    (d) none of these

10. In accordance with Article 225—Outside Branch Circuits and Feeders, for installations consisting of not more than two 2-wire branch circuits, the building disconnecting means shall have a rating of not less than ______.

    (a) 15A
    (b) 20A
    (c) 25A
    (d) 30A

11. A generator is a machine that converts mechanical energy into electrical energy by means of a ______ and alternator and/or inverter.

    (a) converter
    (b) rectifier
    (c) prime mover
    (d) turbine

12. Where PV system disconnecting means of systems above ______ are readily accessible to unqualified persons, any enclosure door or hinged cover that exposes live parts when open shall be locked or require a tool to open.

    (a) 30V
    (b) 120V
    (c) 240V
    (d) 600V

13. An ESS(s) (energy storage system) can include but are not limited to ______.

    (a) batteries
    (b) capacitors
    (c) inverters or converters
    (d) any of these

14. Type 2 surge-protective device(s) shall be connected on the load side of the ______ in a separately derived system.

    (a) first overcurrent device
    (b) metering device
    (c) service disconnect
    (d) service entrance

15. If the grounding electrode conductor to a ground rod does not extend on to other types of electrodes, the grounding electrode conductor shall not be required to be larger than ______ copper wire.

    (a) 10 AWG
    (b) 8 AWG
    (c) 6 AWG
    (d) 4 AWG

16. Junction, pull, and outlet boxes located behind modules or panels shall be so installed that the wiring contained in them can be rendered accessible directly or by displacement of a module(s) or panel(s) secured by removable fasteners and connected ______.

    (a) in a raceway
    (b) by a flexible wiring system
    (c) in PVC
    (d) in RMC

17. The smallest size fixture wire permitted by the *NEC* is ______.

    (a) 18 AWG
    (b) 16 AWG
    (c) 14 AWG
    (d) 12 AWG

18. A(An) ______ circuit breaker is a qualifying term indicating that there is a delay purposely introduced in the tripping action of the circuit breaker, and the delay decreases as the magnitude of the current increases.

    (a) adverse time
    (b) inverse time
    (c) time delay
    (d) timed unit

19. The minimum clearance for overhead service conductors that pass over public streets, alleys, roads, parking areas subject to truck traffic is ______.

    (a) 10 ft
    (b) 12 ft
    (c) 15 ft
    (d) 18 ft

20. Product testing, evaluation, and listing (product certification) shall be performed by ______.

    (a) recognized qualified electrical testing laboratories
    (b) the manufacturer
    (c) a qualified person
    (d) an electrical engineer

21. Where a disconnect is required to ______ PV system equipment, the equipment disconnecting means shall be installed in accordance with 690.15(C).

    (a) open
    (b) isolate
    (c) close
    (d) open or close

22. Noncombustible surfaces that are broken or incomplete around boxes employing a flush-type cover shall be repaired so there will be no gaps or open spaces larger than ______ at the edge of the box.

    (a) ¹⁄₁₆ in.
    (b) ⅛ in.
    (c) ¼ in.
    (d) ½ in.

23. Article 706 applies to all energy storage systems (ESS) having a capacity greater than ______ that may be stand-alone or interactive with other electric power production sources.

    (a) 1 kWh
    (b) 2 kWh
    (c) 5 kWh
    (d) 10 kWh

24. The maximum dc voltage for a PV source circuit is permitted to be calculated in accordance with the sum of the PV module-rated open-circuit voltage of the series-connected modules in the PV string circuit ______ for the lowest expected ambient temperature using the open-circuit voltage temperature coefficients in accordance with the instructions included in the listing or labeling of the module.

    (a) corrected
    (b) adjusted
    (c) demanded
    (d) none of these

25. Type ______ is a service-entrance cable, identified for underground use, having a moisture-resistant covering, but not required to have a flame-retardant covering.

    (a) SE
    (b) NM
    (c) UF
    (d) USE

26. Overhead service conductors shall have a horizontal clearance of not less than ______ from a pool.

    (a) 8 ft
    (b) 10 ft
    (c) 12 ft
    (d) 14 ft

27. Every panelboard circuit and circuit modification shall be provided with a legible and permanent description that is described with a degree of detail and clarity that is unlikely to result in confusion between circuits and is clear in explaining ______.

    (a) abbreviations and symbols
    (b) trademarks
    (c) listings
    (d) installer information and dates

28. In cases where the battery is separate from the energy storage system (ESS) electronics and is subject to field servicing, a disconnecting means shall be readily accessible and located _______ the battery.

    (a) adjacent to
    (b) within 3 ft of
    (c) within sight of
    (d) within 25 ft of

29. For buildings that have PV systems with more than one rapid shutdown type or PV systems with no rapid shutdown, a detailed plan view diagram of the roof shall be provided showing each different PV system with a dotted line around areas that remain _______ after rapid shutdown is initiated.

    (a) energized
    (b) de-energized
    (c) grounded
    (d) none of these

30. A disconnecting means in accordance with Parts VI through VIII of Article 230 shall be provided to _______ all ungrounded conductors of an interconnected electric power production source from the conductors of other systems.

    (a) coordinate
    (b) disconnect
    (c) protect
    (d) all of these

31. Overcurrent devices for PV source circuits shall be sized not less than _______ of the maximum currents calculated in 690.8(A).

    (a) 80 percent
    (b) 100 percent
    (c) 125 percent
    (d) 250 percent

32. Examples of approved means of achieving the indicated _______ values include torque tools or devices such as shear bolts or breakaway-style devices with visual indicators that demonstrate that the proper torque has been applied.

    (a) pressure
    (b) torque
    (c) tightening
    (d) tension

33. For PV systems that are not solidly grounded, the _______ for the output of the PV system, where connected to associated distribution equipment connected to a grounding electrode system, shall be permitted to be the only connection to ground for the system.

    (a) equipment grounding conductor
    (b) grounding conductor
    (c) grounded conductor
    (d) any of these

34. Where an EMS is employed to control electrical power through the use of a remote means, a directory identifying the controlled device(s) and circuit(s) shall be posted on the _______.

    (a) enclosure of the controller
    (b) disconnect
    (c) branch-circuit overcurrent device
    (d) any of these

35. PV system circuits originating within or from arrays not attached to buildings that terminate on the _______ of buildings shall not be considered controlled conductors for the purposes of requiring a rapid shutdown function.

    (a) exterior
    (b) interior
    (c) inside
    (d) none of these

36. PV system equipment and disconnecting means shall not be installed in bathrooms, unless listed for the application.

    (a) True
    (b) False

37. If _______, a grounding electrode conductor or its enclosure shall be securely fastened to the surface on which it is carried.

    (a) concealed
    (b) exposed
    (c) accessible
    (d) none of these

38. PV equipment floating on or attached to structures floating on bodies of water shall be _______ and shall utilize wiring methods that allow for any expected movement of the equipment.

    (a) designed for the purpose
    (b) listed for the purpose
    (c) identified as being suitable for the purpose
    (d) approved by marine authorities

39. Overhead service conductors shall have a minimum vertical clearance of _______ from final grade over residential property and driveways, as well as over commercial areas not subject to truck traffic where the voltage does not exceed 300V to ground.

    (a) 10 ft
    (b) 12 ft
    (c) 15 ft
    (d) 18 ft

40. All equipment intended for use in PV systems shall be listed or be _______ for the application and have a field label applied.

    (a) identified
    (b) marked
    (c) approved
    (d) evaluated

41. In cases where the battery is separate from the energy storage system (ESS) electronics, the batteries could include an enclosure, battery monitoring and controls, or other related battery components.

    (a) True
    (b) False

42. The engineered design required for large-scale PV electric supply stations, shall document _______ procedures and means of isolating equipment.

    (a) disconnection
    (b) maintenance
    (c) inspection
    (d) installation

43. For _______ dwelling units, a sign shall be placed at the disconnecting means required in 230.85 that indicates the location of each permanently installed on-site optional standby power source disconnect or means to shut down the prime mover as required in 445.19(C).

    (a) apartment
    (b) guest suite
    (c) multi-family
    (d) one- and two-family

44. In accordance with 250.94(A), the intersystem bonding termination device shall _______.

    (a) be securely mounted and electrically connected to service equipment, the meter enclosure, or exposed nonflexible metallic service raceway, or be mounted at one of these enclosures and be connected to the enclosure or grounding electrode conductor with a minimum 6 AWG copper conductor
    (b) be securely mounted to the building/structure disconnecting means, or be mounted at the disconnecting means and be connected to the metallic enclosure or grounding electrode conductor with a minimum 6 AWG copper conductor
    (c) have terminals that are listed as grounding and bonding equipment
    (d) all of these

45. Cable tray systems shall not be used _______.

    (a) in hoistways
    (b) where subject to severe physical damage
    (c) in hazardous (classified) locations
    (d) in hoistways or where subject to severe physical damage

46. Where used to securely fasten LFMC, cable ties shall be _______ for securement and support.

    (a) identified
    (b) labeled
    (c) marked
    (d) listed and identified

47. SPD's required by 225.42(A), shall be installed _______ the distribution equipment that is connected to the load side of the feeder and contains branch circuit overcurrent protective device(s).

    (a) in or adjacent to
    (b) within 3 ft of
    (c) within 10 ft of
    (d) within sight of

48. Raceways shall be _______ between outlet, junction, or splicing points prior to the installation of conductors.

    (a) installed complete
    (b) tested for ground faults
    (c) a minimum of 80 percent complete
    (d) torqued

49. A(An) ______ or larger grounding electrode conductor exposed to physical damage shall be protected in rigid metal conduit, IMC, Schedule 80 PVC conduit, reinforced thermosetting resin conduit Type XW (RTRC-XW), EMT, or cable armor.

    (a) 10 AWG
    (b) 8 AWG
    (c) 6 AWG
    (d) 4 AWG

50. For PV dc-to-dc converter circuits connected to the output of a single dc-to-dc converter, the ______ shall be determined in accordance with the instructions included in the listing or labeling of the dc-to-dc converter.

    (a) minimum voltage
    (b) minimum current
    (c) maximum voltage
    (d) maximum current

51. Connected (connecting) to ground or to a conductive body that extends the ground connection is called ______.

    (a) equipment grounding
    (b) bonded
    (c) grounded
    (d) all of these

52. Energy storage system (ESS) battery disconnecting means shall be legibly marked in the field and shall include the ______.

    (a) nominal battery voltage
    (b) available fault current and arc-flash label
    (c) date the calculation was performed
    (d) all of these

53. When determining the ampere rating of busbars associated with load-side source connections of interconnected electric power production sources, one can use the sum of the ampere ratings of all overcurrent devices on ______, both load and supply devices, excluding the rating of the overcurrent device protecting the busbar, but shall not exceed the ampacity of the busbar.

    (a) metering equipment
    (b) panelboards
    (c) switchgear
    (d) all of these

54. There shall be no more than ______ service disconnects installed for each service or for each set of service-entrance conductors as permitted in 230.2 and 230.40.

    (a) two
    (b) four
    (c) six
    (d) eight

55. An ac module is a complete, environmentally protected unit consisting of ______, designed to produce ac power.

    (a) solar cells
    (b) inverters
    (c) other components
    (d) all of these

56. Where RMC enters a box, fitting, or other enclosure, ______ shall be provided to protect the wire from abrasion, unless the design of the box, fitting, or enclosure affords equivalent protection.

    (a) a bushing
    (b) duct seal
    (c) electrical tape
    (d) seal fittings

57. Electric vehicle power transfer system equipment for the purposes of charging, power export, or bidirectional current flow shall be ______.

    (a) listed
    (b) labeled
    (c) identified
    (d) all of these

58. Services and feeders for EVSE shall be sized in accordance with the product ratings unless the overall rating of the installation can be limited through ______.

    (a) an energy management system (EMS) that provides load management of the EVSE
    (b) EVSE that has an ampere adjustment means with restricted access
    (c) ampere adjustments that are in accordance with the manufacturer's instructions
    (d) all of these

59. By special permission, the authority having jurisdiction may waive *NEC* requirements or approve alternative methods where equivalent ______ can be achieved and maintained.

    (a) safety
    (b) workmanship
    (c) installations
    (d) job progress

60. Where the disconnecting means for energy storage systems cannot be located within sight of the ESS, the disconnecting means, or the enclosure providing access to the disconnecting means, shall be capable of being ______ in accordance with 110.25.

    (a) locked
    (b) labeled
    (c) installed remotely
    (d) identified

61. Conductors carrying alternating current installed in ferrous metal raceways or enclosures shall be arranged so as to avoid heating the surrounding ferrous metal by induction. To accomplish this, the ______ conductor(s) shall be grouped together.

    (a) phase
    (b) grounded
    (c) equipment grounding
    (d) all of these

62. PV system circuits installed on or in buildings shall include ______ to reduce shock hazard for firefighters.

    (a) ground-fault circuit protection
    (b) arc-fault circuit protection
    (c) a rapid shutdown function
    (d) automated power transfer

63. Metal wireways shall not be permitted for ______.

    (a) exposed work
    (b) hazardous (classified) locations
    (c) wet locations
    (d) severe corrosive environments

64. Article 690 applies to solar ______ systems, including the array circuit(s), inverter(s), and controller(s) for such systems.

    (a) photoconductive
    (b) PV
    (c) photogenic
    (d) photosynthesis

65. Mating connectors used in PV source circuits shall be polarized and shall have a configuration that are ______ with receptacles in other electrical systems on the premises.

    (a) noninterchangeable
    (b) interchangeable
    (c) compatible
    (d) none of these

66. For required notification and marking purposes for energy storage systems (ESS) for available fault current derived from the stationary battery system, ______ can provide information about available fault current on any particular battery model.

    (a) UL listings
    (b) battery equipment suppliers
    (c) equipment labeling
    (d) the design engineer

67. Bonding jumpers from grounding electrodes are permitted to be connected to a busbar not less than ______.

    (a) ⅛ in. thick × 1 in. wide
    (b) ⅛ in. thick × 2 in. wide
    (c) ¼ in. thick × 1 in. wide
    (d) ¼ in. thick × 2 in. wide

68. In walls constructed of wood or other ______ material, electrical cabinets shall be flush with the finished surface or project therefrom.

    (a) nonconductive
    (b) porous
    (c) fibrous
    (d) combustible

69. Where PV source and output circuits operating at over 30V are installed in readily accessible locations, circuit conductors shall be guarded or installed in ______.

    (a) Type MC cable
    (b) multiconductor jacketed cable
    (c) a raceway
    (d) any of these

70. For interconnected electric power production sources connected to a service, the ampacity of the _______ connected to the power production source service disconnecting means shall not be less than the sum of the power production source maximum circuit current in 705.28(A).

    (a) service conductors
    (b) power production source output current
    (c) service disconnect rating
    (d) sum of all overcurrent protective devices

71. The number and size of conductors and cables in any raceway shall not be more than will _______.

    (a) permit dissipation of heat
    (b) prevent damage to insulation during installation
    (c) prevent damage to insulation during removal of conductors
    (d) all of these

72. Where a power inlet is used for an optional standby system's temporary connection to a portable generator, a warning sign shall be placed near the inlet to indicate the _______ that the system is capable of, based on the wiring of the transfer equipment.

    (a) type of fuel supply
    (b) type of derived system
    (c) type of GFCI protection
    (d) temporary power supply time

73. Optional standby system wiring is permitted to occupy the same _______ with other general wiring.

    (a) raceways
    (b) cables
    (c) boxes and cabinets
    (d) all of these

74. Each energy storage system (ESS) shall be provided with a nameplate plainly visible after installation and marked with the _______.

    (a) rated frequency
    (b) number of phases (if ac)
    (c) rating in kW or kVA
    (d) all of these

75. A means external to enclosures for connecting intersystem _______ conductors shall be provided at the service equipment or metering equipment enclosure and disconnecting means of buildings or structures supplied by a feeder or branch circuit.

    (a) bonding
    (b) ungrounded
    (c) secondary
    (d) bonding and ungrounded

76. PV system dc circuit conductors that rely on other than color coding for polarity identification shall be identified by an approved permanent marking means such as _______.

    (a) labeling
    (b) sleeving
    (c) shrink-tubing
    (d) any of these

77. For the purpose of a PV system rapid shutdown system, equipment and systems shall be permitted to meet the requirements of both inside and outside the array as defined by the _______.

    (a) manufacturer's instructions included with the listing
    (b) installer
    (c) inspector
    (d) local utility

78. The maximum allowable ampacity for each of 6 THW conductors in a raceway is _______.

    (a) 55A
    (b) 65A
    (c) 70A
    (d) 80A

79. For the purposes of determining box fill, each device or utilization equipment in the box which is wider than a single device box counts as two volume allowances for each _______ required for the mounting.

    (a) in.
    (b) ft
    (c) gang
    (d) box

80. A dc combiner is an enclosure that includes devices used to connect two or more PV system dc circuits in _______.

    (a) series
    (b) series-parallel
    (c) parallel
    (d) parallel-series

81. The white conductor within a cable assembly can be used for a(an) ______ conductor where permanently reidentified to indicate its use as an ungrounded conductor at each location where the conductor is visible and accessible.

    (a) grounded
    (b) ungrounded
    (c) equipment grounding
    (d) grounding electrode

82. ENT shall not be used where exposed to the direct rays of the sun, unless identified as ______.

    (a) high-temperature rated
    (b) sunlight resistant
    (c) Schedule 80
    (d) suitable for the application

83. Splices and taps are permitted within metal wireways provided they are accessible and shall not fill the wireway to more than ______ of its area at that point.

    (a) 35 percent
    (b) 40 percent
    (c) 55 percent
    (d) 75 percent

84. Interconnected electric power production sources microgrid systems shall be capable of operating in interactive mode with a primary source of power, or electric utility, or other electric power production and distribution network and shall be permitted to disconnect from other sources and operate in ______ mode.

    (a) automated
    (b) emergency
    (c) isolated
    (d) island

85. Labels or markings of PV system raceways and enclosures shall be suitable for the environment and be placed with a maximum of ______ of spacing.

    (a) 5 ft
    (b) 10 ft
    (c) 20 ft
    (d) 25 ft

86. Tap connections to a common grounding electrode conductor for multiple separately derived systems may be made to a copper or aluminum busbar that is ______ and of sufficient length to accommodate the number of terminations necessary for the installation.

    (a) smaller than ¼ in. thick × 4 in. wide
    (b) not smaller than ¼ in. thick × 2 in. wide
    (c) not smaller than ½ in. thick × 2 in. wide
    (d) not smaller than ¼ in. thick × 2½ in. wide

87. A connection used for no other purpose shall be made between the metal box and the equipment grounding conductor(s). The equipment bonding jumper or equipment grounding conductor shall be sized from Table 250.122 based on the largest ______ conductors in the box.

    (a) overcurrent device protecting circuit
    (b) ungrounded
    (c) grounded
    (d) neutral

88. Meter-mounted optional standby system transfer switches installed between the ______ and the meter enclosure shall be listed meter-mounted transfer switches.

    (a) service connection point
    (b) utility meter
    (c) utility transformer
    (d) cold sequence disconnect

89. Each feeder disconnect rated 1,000A or more and installed on solidly grounded wye electrical systems of more than 150V to ground, but not exceeding ______ phase-to-phase, shall be provided with ground-fault protection of equipment in accordance with 230.95.

    (a) 50V
    (b) 150V
    (c) 600V
    (d) 1,000V

90. Screws or other fasteners installed in the field that enter wiring spaces penetrating a wall of a pull or junction box exceeding 100 cu in. shall extend no more than ¼ in., or more than 7/16 in. if located within ______ of cabinets and cutout boxes of an adjacent box wall.

    (a) ⅛ in.
    (b) ¼ in.
    (c) ⅜ in.
    (d) ½ in.

91. Fused disconnects at interconnected electric power production source output connections are considered suitable for ______ unless otherwise marked.

    (a) backfeed
    (b) current limiting
    (c) current adjustment
    (d) slash rating

92. Where ac and dc conductors of PV systems occupy the same junction box, pull box, or wireway, the ac and dc conductors shall be grouped separately by cable ties or similar means at least once and at intervals not to exceed ______.

    (a) 1 ft
    (b) 3 ft
    (c) 6 ft
    (d) 10 ft

93. PV system dc circuits that utilize metal-clad cables installed ______ shall be permitted without AFCI protection where the circuits are not installed in or on buildings.

    (a) in metal raceways
    (b) in enclosed metal cable trays
    (c) underground
    (d) any of these

94. A structure is that which is ______, other than equipment.

    (a) built
    (b) constructed
    (c) built or constructed
    (d) none of these

95. Where two interconnected electric power production sources are located at opposite ends of a busbar that contains loads, the sum of 125 percent of the power-source(s) output circuit current and the rating of the overcurrent device protecting the busbar shall not exceed ______ of the busbar ampere rating.

    (a) 100 percent
    (b) 115 percent
    (c) 120 percent
    (d) 125 percent

96. Flexible metal conduit shall be supported at intervals not exceeding ______.

    (a) 1 ft
    (b) 3 ft
    (c) 4½ ft
    (d) 6 ft

97. A sign shall be placed at the service-entrance equipment for other than one- and two-family dwellings that indicates the ______ of each on-site optional standby power source.

    (a) installer
    (b) date of installation
    (c) date of last testing
    (d) type and location

98. For interconnected electric power production source system(s), single-phase power sources in interactive systems shall be connected to three-phase power systems in order to limit unbalanced voltages at the point of interconnection to not more than ______.

    (a) 2 percent
    (b) 3 percent
    (c) 5 percent
    (d) 10 percent

99. Type UF cable used with a 24V landscape lighting system can have a minimum cover of ______.

    (a) 6 in.
    (b) 12 in.
    (c) 18 in.
    (d) 24 in.

100. Manual and nonautomatic transfer equipment for optional standby systems require ______ intervention.

    (a) human
    (b) animal
    (c) electrician
    (d) inspector

Understanding 2023 NEC Requirements for Solar PV and Energy Storage Systems | MikeHolt.com | **637**

INDEX

G

ABOUT THE AUTHOR

Mike Holt—Author

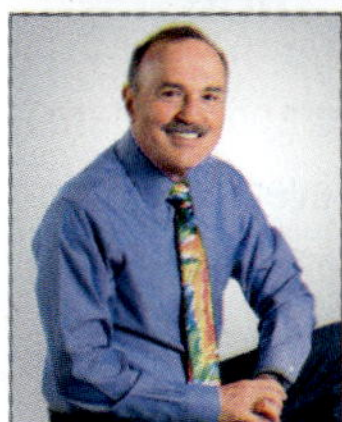

Mike Holt
Founder and President
Mike Holt Enterprises
Groveland, Florida

Mike Holt is an author, businessman, educator, speaker, publisher and *National Electrical Code* expert. He has written hundreds of electrical training books and articles, founded three successful businesses, and has taught thousands of electrical *Code* seminars across the U.S. and internationally. His dynamic presentation style, deep understanding of the trade, and ability to connect with students are some of the reasons that he is one of the most sought-after speakers in the industry.

His company, Mike Holt Enterprises, has been serving the electrical industry for almost 50 years, with a commitment to creating and publishing books, videos, online training, and curriculum support for electrical trainers, students, organizations, and electrical professionals. His devotion to the trade, coupled with the lessons he learned at the University of Miami's MBA program, have helped him build one of the largest electrical training and publishing companies in the United States.

Mike is committed to changing lives and helping people take their careers to the next level. He has always felt a responsibility to provide education beyond the scope of just passing an exam. He draws on his previous experience as an electrician, inspector, contractor and instructor, to guide him in developing powerful training solutions that electricians understand and enjoy. He is always mindful of how hard learning can be for students who are intimidated by school, by their feelings towards learning, or by the complexity of the *NEC*. He's mastered the art of simplifying and clarifying complicated technical concepts and his extensive use of illustrations helps students apply the content and relate the material to their work in the field. His ability to take the intimidation out of learning is reflected in the successful careers of his students.

Mike's commitment to pushing boundaries and setting high standards extends into his personal life as well. He's an eight-time Overall National Barefoot Waterski Champion. Mike has more than 20 gold medals, many national records, and has competed in three World Barefoot Tournaments. In 2015, at the tender age of 64, he started a new adventure—competitive mountain bike racing and at 65 began downhill mountain biking. Every day he continues to find ways to motivate himself, both mentally and physically.

Mike and his wife, Linda, reside in New Mexico and Florida, and are the parents of seven children and seven grandchildren. As his life has changed over the years, a few things have remained constant: his commitment to God, his love for his family, and doing what he can to change the lives of others through his products and seminars.

Special Acknowledgments

My Family. First, I want to thank God for my godly wife who's always by my side and for my children.

My Staff. A personal thank you goes to my team at Mike Holt Enterprises for all the work they do to help me with my mission of changing peoples' lives through education. They work tirelessly to ensure that, in addition to our products meeting and exceeding the educational needs of our customers, we stay committed to building life-long relationships throughout their electrical careers.

The National Fire Protection Association. A special thank you must be given to the staff at the National Fire Protection Association (NFPA), publishers of the *NEC*—in particular, Jeff Sargent for his assistance in answering my many *Code* questions over the years. Jeff, you're a "first class" guy, and I admire your dedication and commitment to helping others understand the *NEC*.

ABOUT THE ILLUSTRATOR

Mike Culbreath—Illustrator

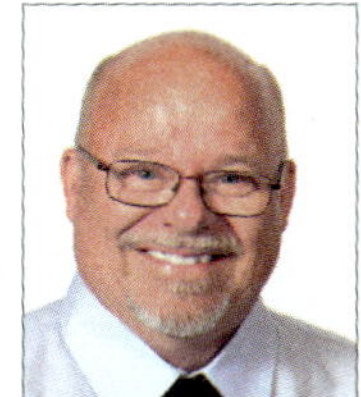

Mike Culbreath
Graphic Illustrator
Alden, Michigan

Mike Culbreath has devoted his career to the electrical industry and worked his way up from apprentice electrician to master electrician. He started working in the electrical field doing residential and light commercial construction, and later did service work and custom electrical installations. While working as a journeyman electrician, he suffered a serious on-the-job knee injury. As part of his rehabilitation, Mike completed courses at Mike Holt Enterprises, and then passed the exam to receive his Master Electrician's license. In 1986, with a keen interest in continuing education for electricians, he joined the staff to update material and began illustrating Mike Holt's textbooks and magazine articles.

Mike started with simple hand-drawn diagrams and cut-and-paste graphics. Frustrated by the limitations of that style of illustrating, he took a company computer home to learn how to operate some basic computer graphics software. Realizing that computer graphics offered a lot of flexibility for creating illustrations, Mike took every computer graphics class and seminar he could to help develop his skills. He's worked as an illustrator and editor with the company for over 30 years and, as Mike Holt has proudly acknowledged, has helped to transform his words and visions into lifelike graphics.

Originally from South Florida, Mike now lives in northern lower Michigan where he enjoys hiking, kayaking, photography, gardening, and cooking; but his real passion is his horses. He also loves spending time with his children Dawn and Mac and his grandchildren Jonah, Kieley, and Scarlet.

ABOUT THE MIKE HOLT TEAM

There are many people who played a role in the production of this textbook. Their efforts are reflected in the quality and organization of the information contained in this textbook, and in its technical accuracy, completeness, and usability.

Technical Writing

Mario Valdes is the Technical Content Editor and works directly with Mike to ensure that content is technically accurate, relatable, and valuable to all electrical professionals. He plays an important role in gathering research, analyzing data, and assisting Mike in the writing of the textbooks. He reworks content into different formats to improve the flow of information and to ensure expectations are being met in terms of message, tone, and quality. He edits illustrations and proofreads content to "fact-check" each sentence, title, and image structure. Mario enjoys working in collaboration with Mike and Brian to enhance the company's brand image, training products, and technical publications.

Editorial and Production

Brian House is part of the content team that reviews our material to make sure it's ready for our customers. He also coordinates the team that constructs and reviews this textbook and its supporting resources to ensure its accuracy, clarity, and quality.

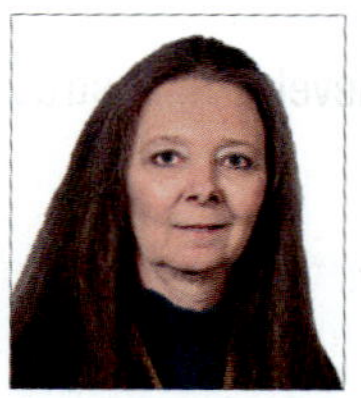

Toni Culbreath worked tirelessly to proofread and edit this publication. Her attention to detail and her dedication is irreplaceable. A very special thank you goes out to Toni (Mary Poppins) Culbreath for her many years of dedicated service.

Cathleen Kwas handled the design, layout, and typesetting of this book. Her desire to create the best possible product for our customers is greatly appreciated, and she constantly pushes the design envelope to make the product experience just a little bit better.

Vinny Perez and **Eddie Anacleto** have been a dynamic team. They have taken the best instructional graphics in the industry to the next level. Both Eddie and Vinny bring years of graphic art experience to the pages of this book and have been a huge help updating and improving the content, look, and style our graphics.

Dan Haruch is an integral part of the video recording process and spends much of his time making sure that the instructor resources created from this product are the best in the business. His dedication to the instructor and student experience is much appreciated.

Video Team

Special thank you to **Peter Furrow**, owner of Earth Electric Inc. of Cape Canaveral, Florida, for attending this video recording as a guest and contributing his time and energy to help us.

The following special people provided technical advice in the development of this textbook as they served on the video team along with author **Mike Holt**.

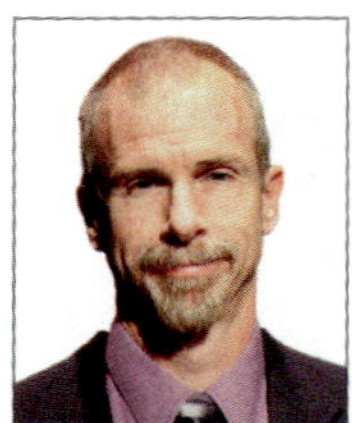

Bill Brooks
Principal Engineer
Vacaville, California
www.BrookSolar.com

Bill Brooks has over 30 years of experience designing, installing, and evaluating grid-connected PV systems. He holds B.S. and M.S. degrees in Mechanical Engineering from North Carolina State University and is a registered Professional Mechanical and Electrical Engineer. More than 15,000 installers and inspectors have attended his courses and he's written several important technical manuals for the industry throughout the U.S. and the world. His field troubleshooting skills have been valuable in determining where problems occur, and to focus training on those issues of greatest need. His recent publications include the *Expedited Permit Process for PV Systems*, the *Field Inspection Guidelines for PV Systems*, and *Understanding the CalFire Solar PV Installation Guidelines*, as well as articles in *IAEI* and *SolarPro* magazines.

Bill is actively involved in the development of PV codes and standards including IEEE-929 and IEEE1547 (PV Utility Interconnection), the *National Electrical Code* Article 690 (Solar Photovoltaic Systems), and IEC TC82 (International PV Standards). He's an active participant on many codes and standards panels including Code-Making Panel 4 of the *NEC*, and UL1703 and UL1741 Standards Technical Panels.

He was a member of the California Office of the State Fire Marshal's (Cal Fire) PV Task force that developed the Solar Photovoltaic Installation Guideline, which became the model for national fire regulation. In addition, he chaired the NFPA Large-Scale PV Electric Supply Station task group, the NFPA Firefighter Safety and PV systems task group, and two of the Article 690 task groups for Code-Making Panel 4 for the 2020 *NEC*.

Bill enjoys helping people make progress toward reaching their God-given potential. His interests include sailing, motorcycle riding, performance automobiles, home theater, and all types of music.

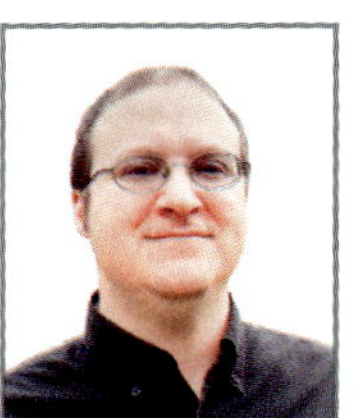

Jason Fisher

Founder, Solar Technical Consulting
Charlottesville, Virginia
www.solartechconsulting.com

Jason Fisher has earned his living in the renewable energy industry for over 25 years. He is a licensed Master Electrician and founded the first fully licensed PV contracting firm in Maryland in 1996. There he designed and installed many of the District of Columbia region's earliest utility-interconnected PV systems, including systems for the Pentagon, Department of State, and White House.

He has broad experience in the development and application of codes and standards and currently serves as the principal representative for the Solar Energy Industries Association (SEIA) on the NEC Code-Making Panel 4, as well as being an alternate representative for Solar Energy International (SEI) on the NEC Code-Making Panel 13. He is also a member of several Standards Technical Panels applicable to renewable energy technologies including UL1741, UL 3741, UL9540, UL9741, and UL916. During the NEC 2023 revision cycle, Jason chaired the NEC Correlating Committee task group on Microgrids and was a member of the NEC Correlating Committee Energy Management Systems task group.

Jason obtained his NABCEP™ PV Installation Professional certification in 2003 and is a UL Certified PV System Installer. He has over 15 years of experience training thousands of engineers, installers, and inspectors in PV applications and the NEC. He's also the author of several technical articles and textbooks on PV applications.

As an independent consultant, Jason provides technical services to organizations including product certification, compliance support, inspections and commissioning, technical training, design review, system optimization, and owner's agent services.

Jason lives in Charlottesville Virginia with his wife and two children.

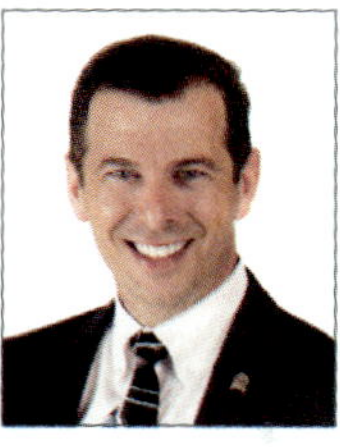

Daniel Brian House

Vice President of Digital and Technical Training
Mike Holt Enterprises, Instructor, Master
Electrician
Brian@MikeHolt.com
Ocala, Florida

Brian House is Vice President of Digital and Technical Training at Mike Holt Enterprises, and a Certified Mike Holt Instructor. He is a permanent member of the video teams, on which he has served since the 2011 *Code* cycle. Brian has worked in the trade since the 1990s in residential, commercial and industrial settings. He opened a contracting firm in 2003 that designed energy-efficient lighting retrofits, explored "green" biomass generators, and partnered with residential PV companies in addition to traditional electrical installation and service.

In 2007, Brian was personally selected by Mike for development and began teaching seminars for Mike Holt Enterprises after being named a "Top Gun Presenter" in Mike's Train the Trainer boot camp. Brian travels around the country teaching electricians, instructors, military personnel, and engineers. His experience in the trenches as an electrical contractor, along with Mike Holt's instructor training, gives him a teaching style that is practical, straightforward, and refreshing.

Today, as Vice President of Digital and Technical Training at Mike Holt Enterprises, Brian leads the apprenticeship and digital product teams. They create cutting-edge training tools, and partner with in-house and apprenticeship training programs nationwide to help them reach the next level. He is also part of the content team that helps Mike bring his products to market, assisting in the editing of the textbooks, coordinating the content and illustrations, and assuring the technical accuracy and flow of the information.

Brian is high energy, with a passion for doing business the right way. He expresses his commitment to the industry and his love for its people in his teaching, working on books, and developing instructional programs and software tools.

Brian and his wife Carissa have shared the joy of their four children and many foster children during 25 years of marriage. When not mentoring youth at work or church, he can be found racing mountain bikes or SCUBA diving with his kids. He's passionate about helping others and regularly engages with the youth of his community to motivate them into exploring their future.

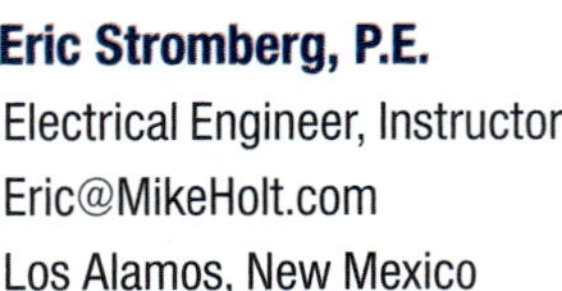

Eric Stromberg, P.E.
Electrical Engineer, Instructor
Eric@MikeHolt.com
Los Alamos, New Mexico

Eric Stromberg has a bachelor's degree in Electrical Engineering and is a professional engineer. He started in the electrical industry when he was a teenager helping the neighborhood electrician. After high school, and a year of college, Eric worked for a couple of different audio companies, installing sound systems in a variety of locations from small buildings to baseball stadiums. After returning to college, he worked as a journeyman wireman for an electrical contractor.

After graduating from the University of Houston, Eric took a job as an electronic technician and installed and serviced life safety systems in high-rise buildings. After seven years he went to work for Dow Chemical as a power distribution engineer. His work with audio systems had made him very sensitive to grounding issues and he took this experience with him into power distribution. Because of this expertise, Eric became one of Dow's grounding subject matter experts. This is also how Eric met Mike Holt, as Mike was looking for grounding experts for his 2002 Grounding vs. Bonding video.

Eric taught the *National Electrical Code* for professional engineering exam preparation for over 20 years, and has held continuing education teacher certificates for the states of Texas and New Mexico. He was on the electrical licensing and advisory board for the State of Texas, as well as on their electrician licensing exam board. Eric now consults for a Department of Energy research laboratory in New Mexico, where he's responsible for the electrical standards as well as assisting the laboratory's AHJ.

Eric's oldest daughter lives with her husband in Zurich, Switzerland, where she teaches for an international school. His son served in the Air Force, has a degree in Aviation logistics, and is a pilot and owner of an aerial photography business. His youngest daughter is a singer/songwriter in Los Angeles.

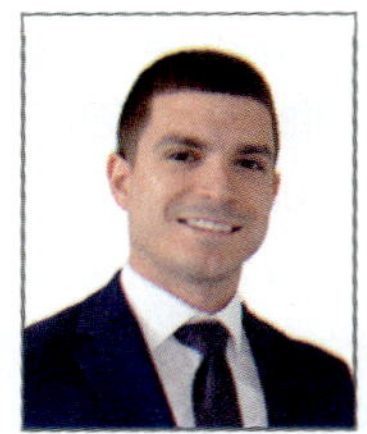

Mario Valdes, Jr.
Technical Content Editor Mike Holt Enterprises,
 Electrical Inspector, Electrical Plans Examiner,
 Master Electrician
Mario@MikeHolt.com
Ocala, Florida

Mario Valdes, Jr. is a member of the technical team at Mike Holt Enterprises, working directly with Mike Holt in researching, re-writing, and coordinating content, to assure the technical accuracy of the information in the products. He is a permanent member of the video teams, on which he has served since the 2017 *Code* cycle.

Mario is licensed as an Electrical Contractor, most recently having worked as an electrical inspector and plans examiner for an engineering firm in South Florida. Additionally, he was an Electrical Instructor for a technical college, teaching students pursuing an associate degree in electricity. He taught subjects such as ac/dc fundamentals, residential and commercial wiring, blueprint reading, and electrical estimating. He brings to the Mike Holt team a wealth of knowledge and devotion for the *NEC*.

He started his career at 16 years old in his father's electrical contracting company. Once he got his Florida State contractor's license, he ran the company as project manager and estimator. Mario's passion for the *NEC* prompted him to get his inspector and plans review certifications and embark on a new journey in electrical *Code* compliance. He's worked on complex projects such as hospitals, casinos, hotels and multi-family high rise buildings. Mario is very passionate about educating electrical professionals about electrical safety and the *National Electrical Code*.

Mario's a member of the IAEI, NFPA, and ICC, and enjoys participating in the meetings; he believes that by staying active in these organizations he'll be ahead of the game, with cutting-edge knowledge pertaining to safety codes.

When not immersed in the electrical world Mario enjoys fitness training. He resides in Pembroke Pines, Florida with his beautiful family, which includes his wife and his two sons. They enjoy family trip getaways to Disney World and other amusement parks.

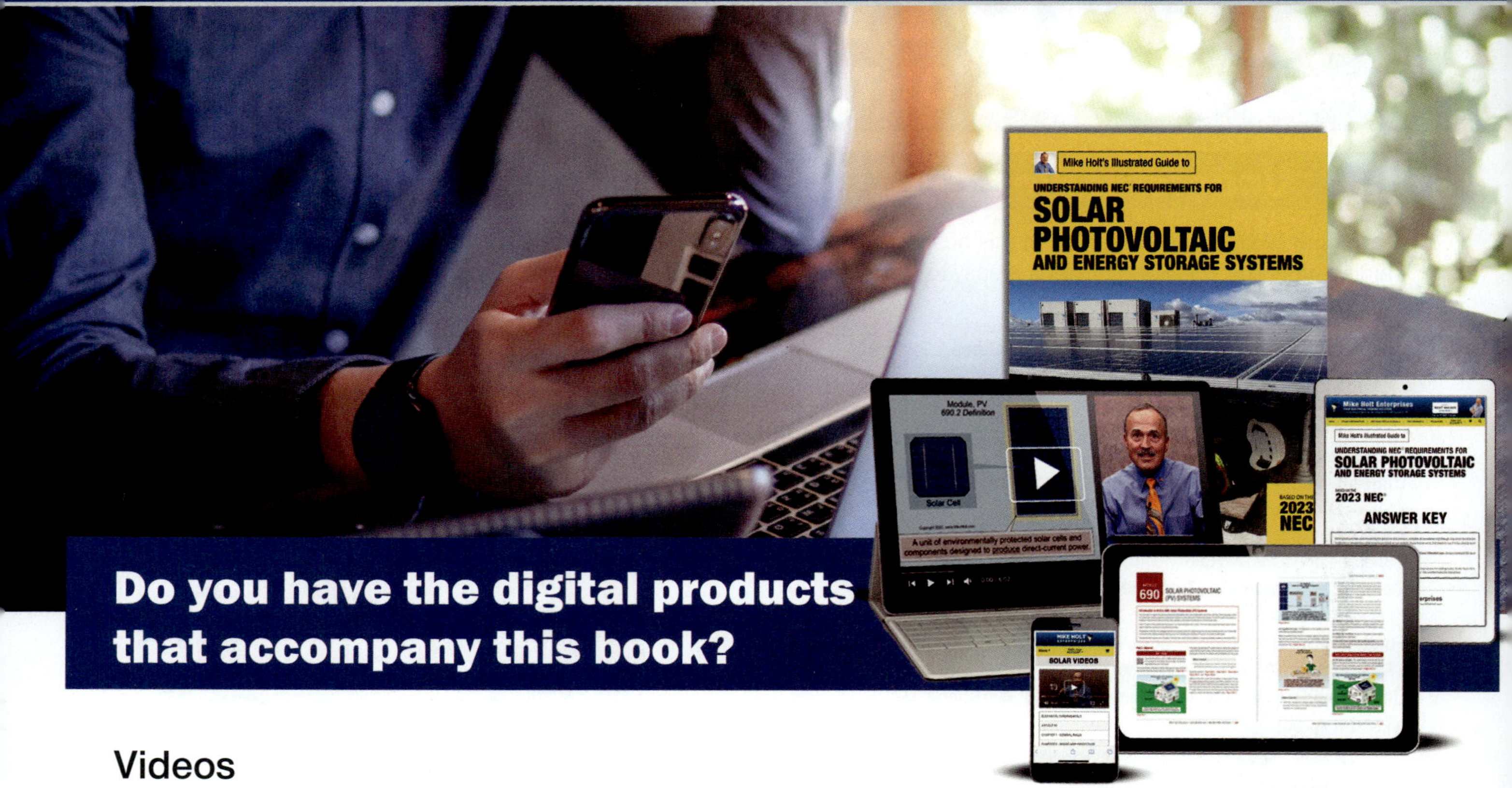